The SAGE Handbook of

Prejudice, Stereotyping and Discrimination

The SAGE Handbook of
Prejudice, Stereotyping and Discrimination

Edited by
John F. Dovidio, Miles Hewstone,
Peter Glick and Victoria M. Esses

Los Angeles • London • New Delhi • Singapore • Washington DC

SAGE Publications Ltd
1 Oliver's Yard
55 City Road
London EC1Y 1SP

SAGE Publications Inc.
2455 Teller Road
Thousand Oaks, California 91320

SAGE Publications India Pvt Ltd
B 1/I 1 Mohan Cooperative Industrial Area
Mathura Road
New Delhi 110 044

SAGE Publications Asia-Pacific Pte Ltd
33 Pekin Street #02-01
Far East Square
Singapore 048763

Library of Congress Control Number: 2009937768

British Library Cataloguing in Publication data

A catalogue record for this book is available from the British Library

ISBN 978-1-4129-3453-4

Typeset by Glyph International Ltd. Bangalore, India
Printed in India at Replika Press Pvt Ltd
Printed on paper from sustainable resources

For Linda, who has been patient and supportive throughout – JFD
For Howie Giles, an inspirational first teacher – MH
For Kathy, who inspires … everything – PG
For Isaac and Alex, who have heard me preach many of the lessons of this volume – VME

Contents

Notes on Contributors

Dominic Abrams received his PhD from the University of Kent, UK. After holding positions at Bristol and Dundee Universities he returned to Kent where he is Professor of Social Psychology and director of the Centre for the Study of Group Processes. He is a Fellow of SPSSI, SPSP, and the UK Academy of Social Sciences. He has been closely associated with social identity theory, particularly working on the relationship between social inclusion and social identity. His research in both social and developmental psychology spans basic intergroup processes from childhood to old age, and he is also working with government and national organizations to bring social psychological research and theory on prejudice into their policy frameworks.

Terrance L. Albrecht is the Interim Associate Director for Population Sciences and Leader of the Communication and Behavioral Oncology Program at the Karmanos Cancer Institute and Professor of Family Medicine and Public Health Sciences at Wayne State University. She received her PhD in Communication from Michigan State University in 1978. Her primary research interests are communication theory, health disparities, and physician-patient-family communication in oncology interactions. She is an author or co-author of over 125 articles and four books on these and related topics. She was the lead author on articles on physician-patient communication in *Cancer* (2007), *Journal of Clinical Oncology* (2008) and a chapter in the volume, *The Handbook of Communication in Cancer and Palliative Care.*

Steven A. Arthur received his MSc from the University of Kentucky in 2003. He is currently a doctoral candidate at Purdue University. His research interests include stereotyping and prejudice, self-regulation of prejudicial responding, and factors that influence interracial interactions.

Caroline Bennett-AbuAyyash is a PhD student in Social Psychology at The University of Western Ontario, Canada. She holds a BA in Public Administration and Political Science from the American University of Beirut, and a MSc. in Psychology from The University of Western Ontario. She is interested in a variety of issues within the context of intergroup relations, including the role of prejudice in the discounting of immigrants' skills, the functions of group membership, and individual differences in the perception of difference as threat.

Arthur Paul Brief is the David S. Eccles Chair in Business Ethics and Presidential Professor at the University of Utah. His research focuses on the moral dimensions of organizational life (e.g., ethical decision-making, race relations, and worker well-being). In addition to numerous journal articles, Art is author of several books. Art is a past editor of the *Academy of Management Review*, and now co-edits *Research in Organizational Behavior* and the *Academy of Management Annals*. He is a Fellow of the Academy of Management, American Psychological Society, and the American Psychological Association.

Oliver Christ is a Senior Lecturer in Psychological Methods at the Department of Psychology at Philipps-University Marburg, Germany. He received his PhD in Social Psychology from Philipps-University Marburg in 2005. His research interests are in intergroup relations and social identity processes in organizations.

Adrienne Colella is a Professor and Freeman Chair in the Freeman School of Business at Tulane University. She received her PhD in Industrial/Organizational Psychology from the Ohio State University. She is a Fellow of the Society for Industrial and Organizational Psychology (SIOP) and the American Psychological Association. Professor Colella's research focuses on persons with disabilities and workplace discrimination. Her research appears in management, psychology, and rehabilitation journals. She is co-editor of a SIOP Frontiers Series book on the psychology of workplace discrimination and a co-author on an organizational behavior textbook. Professor Colella serves on the editorial boards of numerous journals.

Donyell Coleman is a Postdoctoral Fellow in the Communication and Behavioral Oncology Program at Karmanos Cancer Institute. She is funded by a diversity award from the National cancer Institute. She received her PhD in Developmental Psychology from Wayne State University in 2006. Her primary research interests are cancer health disparities and barriers to help-seeking and service use by minority cancer patients. She is a co-author of a review of health disparities that appeared in the first issue of *Social Issues and Policy Review* (2008) and a chapter on evolutionary perspectives on human development, which appeared in the volume *Further Thoughts on Adolescence* (2006).

Lucian Gideon Conway, III received his PhD from the University of British Columbia in 2001 and is currently an Associate Professor of Psychology at the University of Montana. His primary research interests lie in political and social psychology; he is the author of over two dozen articles, commentaries, and book chapters in these areas. In particular, his interests revolve around (1) how shared cultural beliefs emerge, persist, and have influence, and (2) the causes of complex (as opposed to simple) thinking and the subsequent consequences on decision-making in political and social arenas.

Joshua Correll joined the faculty of the University of Chicago in 2005. He received his PhD from the University of Colorado at Boulder and his MA from the University of Waterloo. Generally, his work involves intergroup relations, stereotyping, and prejudice. His primary line of research uses a videogame simulation of a police encounter to examine bias in shoot/don't-shoot decisions.

Richard J. Crisp is Professor of Psychology at the University of Kent. He did his undergraduate degree at the University of Oxford and his PhD at Cardiff University. He has published over 70 articles and chapters on prejudice, social categorization, identity and intergroup contact. He has previously edited (with Miles Hewstone) a volume on *Multiple Social Categorization* and authored (with Rhiannon Turner) a textbook, *Essential Social Psychology*. He is an Associate Editor for the *Journal of Experimental Social Psychology*, and past winner of the British Psychological Society's Spearman Medal. In 2009 he was elected an Academician of the Academy of Social Sciences.

Jennifer Crocker is Claude M. Steele Collegiate Professor of Psychology at the University of Michigan, and Research Professor at the Institute for Social Research. She received her PhD from Harvard University in 1979, and previously served on the faculties of Northwestern University and SUNY at Buffalo. Author of over 100 articles and chapters, she received the Gordon Allport

Intergroup Relations Prize. She is currently President of the Society for Personality and Social Psychology, and was President of the International Society for Self and Identity, the Society for the Psychological Study of Social Issues and was Chair of the Executive Committee for the Society for Experimental Social Psychology. In July, 2010 she will become an Ohio Eminent Scholar at the Ohio State University.

Faye Crosby is a scholar, writer, consultant, and social activist. She received her PhD in 1976. Since 1997, Crosby has been Professor of Psychology at University of California, Santa Cruz. Previous faculty appointments included Rhode Island College, Yale University, The Kellogg School of Management, and Smith College. Crosby has authored or co-authored five books and has edited or co-edited another 10 volumes. Her articles and chapters number over 150. Most of her work concerns sex and race discrimination and focuses on remedies. She is the recipient of numerous awards. She is the founder of Nag's Heart, an organization whose mission is the replenishment of the feminist spirit.

Rafaela Dancygier is Assistant Professor of Politics and Public and International Affairs at Princeton University. She has been on the faculty at Princeton since 2007 and received her PhD from Yale University in the same year. Dr. Dancygier's research and publications have focused on the domestic consequences of international immigration, the political incorporation of immigrants, and the determinants of ethnic conflict.

Stéphanie Demoulin is currently Professor at the Catholic University of Louvain where she received her PhD in 2002. Dr. Demoulin's research interests are on infra-humanization, intergroup relations, intergroup emotions, intergroup misunderstandings, and negotiations. Recently, she has developed a new line of research in which she looks at intergroup negotiations and the processes that impact negotiations when negotiator partners do not share the same social categorization. She is a member of a number of different psychological associations including the European Association of Social Psychology, and she is a faculty member of the International Graduate College on 'Conflict and Cooperation between Social Groups'. Recently, she has co-edited a book on *Intergroup Misunderstandings*.

Amanda Diekman is Associate Professor of Psychology at Miami University. She joined the faculty after serving as a Visiting Assistant Professor at Purdue University and completing her doctoral work at Northwestern University. Her research interests include stereotyping and prejudice, gender, and social change. She is currently serving as an Associate Editor for *Basic and Applied Social Psychology*.

Julie Dimmitt completed her Honors BA in Psychology at University of California, Santa Cruz and is currently a Pre-Doctoral scholar at Pacific Graduate School of Psychology, Palo Alto University. Her major area of interest includes the prevention and treatment of Posttraumatic Stress Disorder (PTSD) and underlying resilience and vulnerability factors associated with PTSD symptomatology. Her professional background includes writing, teaching, and social advocacy for minority youth. She is the recipient of the UC Santa Cruz Undergraduate Research Award in Psychology, UC Santa Cruz Campus Merit and Sage Scholarships, and USA Funds Scholarship.

John F. Dovidio is currently Professor of Psychology at Yale University. Before that, he was a professor at the University of Connecticut and at Colgate University, where he also was Provost and Dean of the Faculty. Dr. Dovidio has served as Editor of the *Journal of Personality and Social Psychology – Interpersonal Relations and Group Processes* and *Personality and Social Psychology Bulletin*. He is currently Co-Editor of *Social Issues and*

Policy Review. Dr. Dovidio has been President of the Society for the Psychological Study of Social Issues (SPSSI), President of the Society for Personality and Social Psychology (SPSP), and Chair of the Executive Committee of the Society for Experimental Social Psychology (SESP). His research interests are in stereotyping, prejudice, and discrimination; social power and nonverbal communication; and altruism and helping.

John Duckitt is Professor of Psychology at the University of Auckland in New Zealand, where he has been on the faculty since 1995. He received his PhD from the University of the Witwatersrand in South Africa in 1990. His major area of interest is the study of prejudice and intergroup hostility and he has contributed many articles on this topic. Other research interests include the study of group identification and political ideology. He is author of *The Social Psychology of Prejudice* (Praeger, 1992/1994) and co-editor (with Stanley Renshon) of *Political Psychology: Cultural and Cross-Cultural Foundations* (New York University Press/Macmillan, 2000).

Alice Eagly is Professor of Psychology, James Padilla Chair of Arts and Sciences, and Faculty Fellow in the Institute for Policy Research, all at Northwestern University. She has served as the Chair of the Department of Psychology at Northwestern University. Dr. Eagly has also held faculty positions at Michigan State University, University of Massachusetts in Amherst, and Purdue University. Her research and writing pertain to the study of gender, attitudes, prejudice, cultural stereotypes, and leadership. She is the author of numerous journal articles and three books, *Sex Differences in Social Behavior: A Social Role Interpretation* (1987), (with Shelly Chaiken) *The Psychology of Attitudes* (1993), (with Linda Carli), *Through the Labyrinth: The Truth About How Women Become Leaders* (2007).

Naomi Ellemers is Professor of Social and Organizational Psychology at Leiden University. After completing her studies at the University of California at Berkeley and the University of Groningen, where she obtained her PhD, she was Assistant Professor and Associate Professor at the Free University of Amsterdam. Her research addresses a range of topics in group processes and intergroup relations, and includes experimental studies as well as more applied research in organizations. She has co-edited several books, for instance on stereotyping, on social identity theory, and on social identity processes in organizations. In 2008 she received the Kurt Lewin Award for her research contribution to social psychology, from the European Association of Social Psychology.

Victoria M. Esses received her PhD from the University of Toronto and is Professor of Psychology and Director of the Centre for Research on Migration and Ethnic Relations at The University of Western Ontario, Canada. Her research examines prejudice, discrimination, and intergroup relations, with a particular interest in issues surrounding immigration and cultural diversity. Her work has covered such topics as the role of perceived competition and threat in determining attitudes toward immigrants and immigration; the dehumanization of refugees; the framing of national identity and public attitudes toward immigration and cultural diversity; and the role of ethnic and religious prejudice in immigrant skills discounting. She is co-editor of *Social Issues and Policy Review*, a new journal of the Society for the Psychological Study of Social Issues.

Susan T. Fiske is Eugene Higgins Professor of Psychology, Princeton University (PhD, Harvard University; honorary doctorates, Université Catholique de Louvain-la-Neuve, Belgium; Universiteit Leiden, Netherlands). She investigates cognitive stereotypes and emotional prejudices at cultural, interpersonal, and neural levels, with Russell Sage Foundation support. The Supreme Court cited her gender-bias testimony, and she testified for President Clinton's

Race Initiative. Editor of *Annual Review of Psychology* and *Handbook of Social Psychology*, she wrote *Social Beings: Core Motives in Social Psychology* and *Social Cognition; From Brains to Culture*. She recently won the Association for Psychological Science's William James Award and a Fellowship in the American Academy of Arts and Sciences.

Sarah McQueary Flynn is currently a fourth year graduate student at the University of Kentucky working toward her PhD in Experimental Social Psychology. She completed her MSc under the direction of Dr. Suzanne Segerstrom, and she currently works as a research assistant in the University of Kentucky College of Medicine Department of Behavioral Sciences. Her primary research interests include social emotions and their link to physiological outcomes.

Samuel L. Gaertner (BA, 1964, Brooklyn College, PhD, 1970; The City University of New York: Graduate Center) is Professor of Psychology at the University of Delaware. His research interests involve intergroup relations with a focus on understanding and reducing prejudice, discrimination and racism. He has served on the editorial boards of the *Journal of Personality and Social Psychology, Personality and Social Psychology Bulletin*, and *Group Processes and Intergroup Relations*. Professor Gaertner's research has been supported by grants from the Office of Naval Research, the National Institutes of Mental Health and currently, the National Science Foundation. Together with John Dovidio, he has shared the Gordon Allport Intergroup Relations Prize in 1985 and 1998, and in 2004, the Kurt Lewin Memorial Award (a career award) from the Society for the Psychological Study of Social Issues, Division 9 of the American Psychological Association.

Julie A. Garcia is Assistant Professor in the Psychology and Child Development Department at California Polytechnic State University, San Luis Obispo. She began her faculty position in the Fall of 2007 after completing her PhD in Social Psychology from The University of Michigan in 2005 and a National Science Foundation Postdoctoral Fellowship at Stanford University in 2007. Her research interests include: stigma, identity negotiation, intergroup relationships, and self-esteem.

Peter Glick (PhD in Psychology from the University of Minnesota) is the Henry Merritt Wriston Professor in the Social Sciences and Professor of Psychology at Lawrence University in Appleton, Wisconsin. His research focuses on ambivalent prejudices toward women and minority groups. Dr. Glick is a fellow of (among others) the American Psychological Association and the Association for Psychological Science. He serves on the editorial boards of four professional journals and the governing councils for the Society for the Psychological Study of Social Issues and the Society for Experimental Social Psychology.

Seth K. Goldman is a PhD candidate at the Annenberg School for Communication at the University of Pennsylvania. His research interests include media effects, public opinion, and political communication, especially as they relate to stereotyping and prejudice.

Donald P. Green is Professor of Political Science and Psychology at Yale University, where he has taught since receiving his PhD from the University of California, Berkeley in 1988. His books and articles span a wide array of topics: prejudice, rationality, political campaigns, social identities, voting behavior, experimental design, and multi-method measurement. Dr. Green recently co-authored with Elizabeth Levy Paluck an article titled 'Prejudice reduction: What works? A Review and Assessment of Research and Practice,' which appeared in the 2009 *Annual Review of Psychology*.

Geoffrey Haddock is Reader in Social Psychology at Cardiff University, where he has been a faculty member since 2001. He received his PhD from the University of Waterloo in 1995. His major area of interest is the study of attitudes and attitude change, and he has contributed over 50 articles and chapters on this topic. He is co-author of *The Psychology of Attitudes and Attitude Change*, with Greg Maio.

Michelle R. (Mikki) Hebl is an Associate Professor of Psychology at Rice University. She has been on the Rice faculty since 1998, after receiving her PhD and teaching for one year at Dartmouth College. Her major area of interest is the study of diversity and discrimination. She has contributed over 70 articles and chapters on this topic, many of which pertain to sexual orientation.

Wilhelm Heitmeyer is professor for socialization and director of the Institute for Interdisciplinary Research on Conflict and Violence at the University of Bielefeld, Germany. His major areas of interest are violence, right-wing extremism, group-focused enmity, and social disintegration. He is editor or managing editor of several book series and editor (in chief) of the *International Journal of Conflict and Violence*.

P. J. Henry is Associate Professor of Psychology at New York University – Abu Dhabi, where he has been on the faculty since 2009. He received his PhD from UCLA in 2001. His major area of interest is the study of prejudice and stigma, including most recently his theory of low-status compensation. He has held research and teaching appointments nationally and internationally, including at the American University of Beirut (Lebanon), Yale University, UCSB, DePaul University, and the University of Bielefeld (Germany) where he was awarded an Alexander von Humboldt Research Fellowship.

Miles Hewstone completed his BSc at the University of Bristol, followed by his D Phil at Oxford University, his *Habilitation*, at the Univesity of Tuebingen, and his DSc at the University of Oxford. He is currently Professor of Social Psychology at the University of Oxford and a Fellow of New College, and his main research interests are in intergroup contact and the reduction of intergroup conflict. He is a recipient of the British Psychological Society's Spearman Medal, and Presidents' Award for Distinguished Research Contributions, the European Association of Experimental Social Psychology's Kurt Lewin Award, and the Gordon Allport Prize for Intergroup Relations from the Society for the Psychological Study of Social Issues. He is a Fellow and outgoing Vice-President (Social Sciences) of the British Academy.

Michael Hogg received his PhD from Bristol University. He is currently Professor of Social Psychology at Claremont Graduate University, and retains Honorary Professorships at the Universities of Kent and Queensland. He is a Fellow of SPSSI, SPSP, WPA and the Academy of the Social Sciences in Australia. His work is closely associated with the development of social identity theory, on which he has published 260 books, chapters and articles. An associate editor of the *Journal of Experimental Social Psychology*, he is founding co-editor with Dominic Abrams of the journal *Group Processes and Intergroup Relations*, and senior consultant editor for the Sage Social Psychology Program. Current research foci include leadership, deviance, uncertainty reduction, extremism, and subgroup relations.

Melissa A. Houlette (BA, 1996, Miami University; PhD, 2003, University of Delaware) is an Assistant Professor of Psychology and Organizational Leadership at the College of Mount St. Joseph in Cincinnati, Ohio, holding a joint appointment in Behavioral Sciences and the Department of Business Administration. Her research interests include the causes and consequences of intergroup bias, the development of means to improve relations between groups, and decision making and information sharing in groups that are functionally and demographically diverse.

Lynne Jackson (PhD University of Western Ontario) is Associate Professor at King's University College at The University of Western Ontario, Canada. She conducts research related to prejudice, discrimination, and intergroup relations. Particular areas of focus include prejudice between religious groups and connections between prejudice and environmental decision making. She also has a research interest in human-animal relations.

Amanda Johnston is an advanced doctoral student of psychology at Miami University. Her research interests include gender, goal pursuit, social change, and social justice. Her teaching interests include Social Psychology, Statistics, and Psychology of Women.

Charles M. Judd is College Professor of Distinction at the University of Colorado. He received his PhD from Columbia University. His research interests include social cognition, attitudes, and research methods and data analysis. He is the editor of the *Journal of Personality and Social Psychology: Attitudes and Social Cognition.*

Rachel W. Kallen is currently an Assistant Professor in the Psychology department at University of Cincinnati. She received her PhD in Social Psychology from the University of Connecticut in 2005, and her overall research centers around understanding consequences of prejudice and intergroup relations primarily from the target's perspective.

Kerry Kawakami (MA, 1989, University of Amsterdam, PhD, 1995, University of Toronto) is an Associate Professor of Psychology at York University. Her research examines strategies to reduce implicit prejudice, stereotyping, and discrimination using social cognitive methodologies. She is currently on the editorial boards of the European Journal of Social Psychology and Social Psychological and Personality Science. Professor Kawakami's research has been supported by grants from the Social Sciences and Humanities Research Council of Canada (SSHRC), the Canadian Foundation for Innovation Fund (CFI), and the Netherlands Organization for Scientific Research (NWO). She has received the Premiers Research Excellence Award and, together with John Dovidio, the Gordon Allport Intergroup Relations Prize in 2000 from Division 9 of the American Psychological Association.

Megan Clark Kelly is a doctoral student at the University of Maryland. Her major areas of interest are social development and contextual factors related to intergroup bias. Other research interests include gender stereotyping, and social exclusion.

Melanie Killen is Professor of Human Development and Affiliate Professor of Psychology at the University of Maryland, College Park. She received her PhD from the University of California at Berkeley in Developmental Psychology in 1985. Her major areas of interest include social cognitive development, developmental intergroup attitudes, social reasoning about exclusion, and moral judgments. She was the Editor of the *Handbook of Moral Development* (2006) with Judith Smetana, and the Co-Editor of *Intergroup Attitudes and Relations from Childhood to Adulthood* (2008) with Sheri Levy (Editor), along with four other edited volumes. She is Associate Editor of *Child Development*, and she serves on the Society for Research in Child Development Governing Council. She is the Director of the National Institute of Child Health and Human Development Training Program in Social Development at the University of Maryland, and the Associate Director for the Center for Children, Relationships, and Culture.

Her research is funded by the National Science Foundation and the National Institutes of Health (NICHD).

Eden King is an Assistant Professor of Psychology at George Mason University. She has been on the George Mason faculty since 2006, after receiving her PhD from Rice University. She is interested in issues pertaining to discrimination and its remediation. In her short time in academia, she has already amassed more than 35 publications.

Charlie Law is an Assistant Professor of Psychology at Penn State - Schuylkill. He has been on the faculty since 2008, after receiving his PhD from Rice University. He is interested in studying discrimination on the basis of sexual orientation but is also more generally interested in diversity issues. He is currently co-chair of SIOP's LGBT ad hoc committee and faculty sponsor of the Penn State – Schuylkill Psychology Club.

Jacques-Philippe Leyens is Professor emeritus of the Catholic University of Louvain (UCL) at Louvain-la-Neuve. He got his PhD in 1969 at UCL before spending two years as Research Associate at the University of Wisconsin-Madison. He has been successively interested in media violence, implicit theories of personality, person perception, stereotyping, racism and he is continuing research on infra-humanization. He has been president of the European Association of Experimental Social Psychology, and received its greatest award: the Tajfel Award. He has collaborated on articles and books in different languages, most recently co-editing *Intergroup Misunderstandings* with Stéphanie Demoulin and John Dovidio.

Diane M. Mackie became Professor of Psychology and Communication at the University of California, Santa Barbara, after receiving a BA from the University of Auckland, New Zealand, and a MA and PhD in Social Psychology from Princeton University. Her research interests span evaluation, emotion, social influence, and intergroup relations. In addition to publishing articles, chapters, and two edited volumes on these topics, she is the co-author (with Eliot Smith) of *Social Psychology*, an introductory textbook.

C. Neil Macrae completed his BSc, PhD and DSc at the University of Aberdeen, Scotland. Having moved around a bit, he returned to Scotland in 2005 and is Professor of Social Cognition at the University of Aberdeen. He has been fortunate to receive several career awards (BPS Spearman Medal, APA Early Career Award, EAESP Jaspars Award, SESP Career Trajectory Award, EAESP Kurt Lewin Award, Royal Society-Wolfson Fellowship) and is a Fellow of the Royal Society of Edinburgh (FRSE). His interests lie in social cognition and social cognitive neuroscience.

Gregory R. Maio is a Professor of Social Psychology at Cardiff University, where he has been a faculty member since 1997. He received his PhD from the University of Western Ontario in 1997 and has published widely on the topics of values, attitudes, and social cognition. He is co-author (with Geoff Haddock) of *The Psychology of Attitudes and Attitude Change*.

Brenda Major is Professor of Psychology at the University of California, Santa Barbara. She received her PhD in Social Psychology from Purdue University in 1978 and taught at the State University of New York at Buffalo from 1978 to 1995 before joining the faculty at UCSB. She has published more than 100 articles in refereed journals and edited books, and co-edited the book *The Psychology of Legitimacy*. She was awarded the Gordon Allport Intergroup Relations Prize from the Society for the Psychological Study of Social Issues in 1986, in 1988, and received Honorable Mention in 2002. She has been an Associate Editor of

Personality and Social Psychology Bulletin and *Group Processes and Intergroup Relations*. Her research centers on psychological resilience – how people cope with, adapt to, and overcome adverse life circumstances. Current research interests include the psychology of stigma and prejudice, self and social identity, and legitimacy. Her work has been supported by grants from the National Science Foundation and the National Institute of Mental Health.

Antony S. R. Manstead is Professor of Psychology at Cardiff University, where he has been a faculty member since 2004. He received his DPhil. from the University of Sussex in 1978. His research focuses on emotion, attitudes, and social identity. He is co-author (with Brian Parkinson and Agneta Fischer) of *Emotion in Social Relations: Cultural, Group, and Interpersonal Processes*.

Malia Mason is an Assistant Professor of Management at Columbia University. She received her PhD from Dartmouth University in 2005 and then did a Post Doctoral Fellow for two years before joining the faculty in 2007. Her major area of interest is the study of social cognition. Other research interests include social perception, perspective taking and attention.

Margo J. Monteith is a Professor in the Department of Psychological Sciences at Purdue University. She received her PhD in 1991 from the University of Wisconsin, and she was a faculty member at Texas Tech University (two years) and the University of Kentucky (12 years) prior to joining the Purdue faculty in 2006. Her major area of interest is the study of stereotyping and prejudice, particularly mechanisms and processes involved in bias reduction. She has contributed several dozen articles and book chapters on this topic, and her research has been funded primarily by the National Institute of Mental Health.

Diana C. Mutz is the Samuel A. Stouffer Professor of Political Science and Communication at the University of Pennsylvania. She received her PhD from Stanford University in 1988. Her major areas of interest are political psychology and the study of communication's effects on public opinion. She has contributed many journal articles on this topic as well as two award-winning books, *Hearing the Other Side: Deliberative versus Participatory Democracy* (Cambridge University Press, 2006) and *Impersonal Influence* (Cambridge University Press, 1998). Mutz served as co-PI of Time-sharing Experiments for the Social Sciences (TESS) and is a fellow of the American Academy of Arts and Sciences.

Heather Orom is an Assistant Professor in the Department of Health Behavior at the University of Buffalo. Prior to this appointment she was a Postdoctoral Fellow at Wayne State University's Institute of Gerontology and Karmanos Cancer Institute. She received her PhD in Social and Personality Psychology at University of Illinois Chicago in 2006. Her primary research interests are improving prevention and screening among families at increased risk for certain diseases. She is the lead author of a 2009 article in Psycho-Oncology on personality correlates of prostate cancer treatment decisions and a 2008 article in Cancer on health risks in immigrant populations.

Bernadette Park is Professor of Psychology at the University of Colorado. She has been on the faculty at Colorado since receiving her PhD from Northwestern University in 1985. Her major area of interest is the study of stereotyping and prejudice, including work on race bias and gender stereotypes. She also has interests in the study of person perception and has published extensively in these areas.

K. Michelle Peavy received her doctorate in clinical psychology at The University of Montana. Her primary interests are in substance abuse, attitudes of professionals in the field of substance abuse, and stigmatized groups within the substance abusing population. Her research includes examination of substance abuse treatment providers' explicit and implicit attitudes regarding sexual minorities, and she is currently examining motivation to enter treatment in a group of incarcerated substance abusers. She is currently a postdoctoral fellow at the VA Puget Sound Health Care System in Seattle, Washington.

Louis A. Penner is a Senior Scientist in Communication and Behavioral Oncology program at Karmanos Cancer Institute and Professor Family Medicine and Public Health Sciences at Wayne State University. He also is a Research Associate in the Research Center for Group Dynamics at the Institute for Social Research, University of Michigan. He received his PhD in Social Psychology from Michigan State University in 1969. His major research interests are prosocial behavior and health disparities. He is the author or co-author of over 100 articles and chapters, and 8 books on these and related topics. He was the lead author on a 2005 article in the *Annual Review of Psychology* on prosocial behavior and a 2008 article in *Social Issues and Policy Review* on causes of health disparities.

Thomas F. Pettigrew is Research Professor of Social Psychology at the University of California, Santa Cruz. A Harvard PhD, he also taught at Harvard (1957–1980), and Amsterdam (1986–1991). He was a Fellow at the Center for Advanced Study in the Behavioral Sciences and the Netherlands Institute for Advanced Study and has conducted intergroup research throughout the world. He was president of the Society for the Psychological Study of Social Issues and has received the Society's Kurt Lewin Award, twice its Gordon Allport Intergroup Research Award, the American Sociological Association's Spivack Award, the Society for Experimental Social Psychology's Distinguished Scientist Award, the International Academy for Intercultural Research's Lifetime Achievement Award, the University of California's Panunzio Award and the Society for the Study of Peace, Conflict and Violence's Ralph White Lifetime Achievement Award.

Susanne Quadflieg completed her PhD at the University of Aberdeen (Scotland) in 2009. She studied psychology at Dartmouth College (USA) and at the University of Jena (Germany). Her major area of interest is the study of person perception and construal, as reflected in several articles on the topic. Other research interests include the role of embodiment in social cognition and self-referential processing.

Diane M. Quinn is an Associate Professor of Psychology at the University of Connecticut. She has been on the faculty since receiving her PhD from the University of Michigan in 1999. Her major area of research includes examining how living with visible and concealable stigmatized identities affect behavioral, psychological, and health outcomes.

Ana Rasquiza graduated from the University of California, Santa Cruz in 2008 with a BA in legal studies. In her studies, Ana focused on the policy implications of race, gender and sexuality. She currently works at Preschool California, a nonprofit advocacy organization working to increase access to high-quality preschool for all of California's children, starting with those who need it most. She lives in Oakland, CA.

Cameron B. Richardson is a doctoral student at the University of Maryland. His major area of interest is in the field of moral psychology, in particular, the study of the contextual and situational factors that to contribute to social and moral reasoning. Other research interests include the study of intergroup relations, stereotyping, and social exclusion.

Jennifer A. Richeson is an Associate Professor of Psychology and African American Studies and Faculty Fellow at the Institute for Policy Research at Northwestern University. She earned a PhD in Social Psychology from Harvard University in 2000 then spent five years on the faculty in the Department of Psychological and Brain Sciences at Dartmouth College prior to moving to Northwestern in 2005. She is currently involved in several areas of research that aim to contribute to a better understanding of intergroup relations, as well as to elucidate pitfalls in current approaches to prejudice reduction and 'managing' diversity. Her work has been published in various scholarly journals, including *Psychological Science*, the *Journal of Personality and Social Psychology, Nature Neuroscience*, and the *Journal of Experimental Social Psychology*.

Laurie A. Rudman (PhD in Psychology from the University of Minnesota) is a Professor of Psychology at Rutgers University in New Brunswick, New Jersey. Her research interests focus on stereotypes, prejudice, and discrimination, especially with respect to how they deter gender and racial equality. The author of over 50 peer-reviewed publications, Dr. Rudman is a fellow of the American Psychological Association, the Association for Psychological Science, and the Society for Experimental Social Psychology. She serves on the Advisory Council for the National Science Foundation and is a council member of the Federation of Behavioral, Psychological, and Cognitive Sciences.

Ann Marie Russell, a PhD candidate in Princeton's Social Psychology and Social Policy program, investigates social psychological reactions to stigmatized social classes. Her primary research concerns the role of perceived threat to symbolic values in people's extreme and ambivalent reactions to economically disadvantaged individuals. Another research program investigates differences in welfare policy preferences as a function of the perceived deservingness of the beneficiary group. A final line of research explores how social class memberships shape psychological orientations, particularly goals and decision-making. Russell's research is supported by a National Science Foundation graduate research fellowship, the Russell Sage Foundation, and a Society for Personality and Social Psychology Diversity Fund award.

Mark Schaller is Professor of Psychology at the University of British Columbia. His research focuses on social cognition in general, and the psychology of stereotypes and prejudices in particular. In pursuing these research topics, he also explores broader questions about the influence of human evolutionary history on psychological processes, and about the impact of psychological processes on human culture. Among his publications are edited books on the *Social Psychology of Prejudice, Evolution and Social Psychology*, and *The Psychological Foundations of Culture*.

Kristina R. Schmukler is currently a PhD candidate in Social Psychology at the University of California, Santa Cruz. She is a scholar, teacher, researcher, and advocate interested in many social-justice issues including, economic justice, and the advancement of women and people of color in the sciences. Kristina graduated with her bachelors degree from Humboldt State University with an award for excellence in the natural sciences as well as a Sally Casanova Pre-Doctoral Scholar. Her latest publication may be read in *Critical Race Realism: Intersections of Psychology, Race and Law,* edited by Gregory S. Parks, Shayne Jones, and W. Jonathan Cardi, Chapter 4 'Affirmative Action: Images and Realities'.

J. Nicole Shelton is an Associate Professor of Psychology at Princeton University. She earned a PhD in Psychology in 1998 from the University of Virginia and after a two-year post-doctoral fellowship at the University of Michigan, joined the Princeton faculty in 2000. Her primary research focuses on how Whites and ethnic minorities navigate issues of prejudice in interracial interactions. Specifically, she is interested in how Whites' concerns with appearing prejudiced and ethnic minorities' concerns with being the target of prejudice influence affective, cognitive, and behavioral outcomes during interracial interactions. Her work has been published in various scholarly journals, including *Psychological Science*, the *Journal of Personality and Social Psychology, Personality and Social Psychology Bulletin*, and the *Journal of Experimental Social Psychology*.

Alexis Nicole Smith received her PhD in Organizational Behavior from Tulane University's Freeman School of Business and received her BA in Psychology from Rice University. Lex's focal areas of research are status, power and bias in and around organizations. She also does research on the quality and utility of workplace health and safety interventions. Her work appears in journals and edited books in the fields of management, psychology, and workplace safety. In addition, Lex is a member of and has presented research at the Academy of Management, the Southern Management Association, and the Society for Industrial and Organizational Psychology.

Eliot R. Smith is Chancellor's Professor of Psychological and Brain Sciences at Indiana University, Bloomington, where he moved in 2003 after serving on the faculty at Purdue University. He holds A.B. and PhD degrees from Harvard University. Major research interests include socially situated cognition and the role of emotion in prejudice and intergroup behavior. With Diane Mackie he co-edited *From Prejudice to Intergroup Emotions* (2002, Psychology Press).

Leanne Son Hing is a Professor of Psychology Department at the University of Guelph. She has been at Guelph since she received her PhD from the University of Waterloo in 2000. She is interested in the disparities or inequalities that exist between individuals and groups in terms of status, power, and outcomes. Her lines of research converge on this issue (e.g., prejudice, discrimination, meritocracy, incompetence stereotypes, and inequality in the workplace). She is a Fellow of the Canadian Institute for Advanced Research.

Russell Spears is Professor of Psychology at Cardiff University, where he has been a faculty member since 2003. He received a PhD from Exeter in 1985. His research interests are in social identity and intergroup relations (and the role of group-based emotions in these phenomena). He co-authored/co-edited *The Social Psychology of Stereotyping and Group Life*, and *Social Identity: Context, Commitment, Content* (both Blackwell).

Steven J. Spencer is Professor of Psychology at the University of Waterloo. He has been on the faculty since 1997. He received his PhD from the University of Michigan in 1993. His major area of interest is the study of stereotyping and prejudice, and he has contributed several dozen articles on this topic. Other research interests include the self and consciousness. He is the co-editor of three books and an author of a social psychology text book.

Nicole Tausch obtained her D.Phil at the University of Oxford in 2006. She is currently a British Academy Postdoctoral Fellow at Cardiff University where she is working on a project examining predictors of support for terrorism. Her research interests lie broadly in the areas of social identity, intergroup relations, prejudice, and collective action. She has published work on intergroup contact, group-based threat, and trait attribution in journals such as *Journal of Personality and Social Psychology, British Journal of Social Psychology*, and *Political Psychology*.

Sarah S. M. Townsend is a doctoral student in social psychology at the University of California Santa Barbara. Her research interests primarily relate to intergroup relations, with a focus on prejudice and discrimination. Her current work examines the moderating role that both ideological beliefs and chronic perceptions of discrimination play in psychological and physiological reactions to prejudice. Other research interests include the cultural patterning of psychological processes and the experience of mixed race individuals in the United States.

Willie Underwood III is an Assistant Professor of Urologic Oncology at the Roswell Park Cancer Institute in Buffalo New York. Previously, he was on the faculty at the University of Michigan and Wayne Sate University Medical Schools. He received his MD from the Syracuse, Upstate Medical University in 1994 and completed his residency at the University of Connecticut Health Center. His primary research interest is health disparities in the treatment of genito-urinary cancers. He has published over 30 articles on this topic, including a recent review article on treatment in the *Canadian Journal of Urology* (2009) and a 2006 article on disparities in the treatment of bladder cancer in the *Journal of Urology*.

Colette van Laar is on the faculty in social and organizational psychology at Leiden University. She attended the University of California, Los Angeles as a Fulbright Scholar to obtain a PhD in Social Psychology. She was a Visiting Scholar at the Russell Sage Foundation and a member of the governing council of the Society for the Psychological Study of Social Issues. Her research focuses on intergroup relations, contact and the consequences of stigma for cognition, affect, and motivation in members of low status or disadvantaged groups.

Ulrich Wagner is Professor of Social Psychology at the Department of Psychology and the Center for Conflict Studies at Philipps-University Marburg, Germany. He has received his PhD from The University of Bochum in 1982. His major areas of interest are the studies of intergroup relations and intergroup conflict, and he has contributed several dozen articles on this topic. Other research interests include the prevention of prejudice and intergroup violence as well as the evaluation of intervention programs. He is co-editor of the recent issue of *The Journal of Social Issues* on Ethnic Prejudice and Discrimination in Europe (2008).

Bernd Wittenbrink is Professor of Behavioral Science at the University of Chicago in the Booth School of Business. He received his PhD from the University of Michigan. His research concerns the role stereotypes and group attitudes play in social judgment and behavior. His work has been published in, among others, the *Journal of Personality and Social Psychology*, the *Journal of Experimental Social Psychology*, and the *Personality and Social Psychology Bulletin*.

Stephen C. Wright is Professor and Canada Research Chair in Social Psychology at Simon Fraser University. He received his PhD from McGill University, and was a faculty member in the Psychology Department at University of California, Santa Cruz from 1991 to 2003. His research focuses broadly on intergroup relations, with specific interests in: the consequences of membership in stigmatized groups, antecedent and barriers to collective action, prejudice and its reduction, and issues of minority languages and cultures. His work has been published widely in scholarly volumes and major social, educational, and cross-cultural psychology journals.

Vincent Yzerbyt took his PhD from the Université Catholique de Louvain where he is now Professor of Psychology. His major area of interest is the study of stereotyping and intergroup relations, especially issues of stereotype formation and change, group-based emotions, and group perception. Other interests include methods and statistics. A former president of the European Association of Social Psychology, he is the founding editor of *Social Psychological and*

Personality Science, co-author of *Stereotypes and Social Cognition* (with Leyens and Schadron) and co-editor of *Stereotypes as Explanations* (with McGarty and Spears) and *The Psychology of Group Perception* (with Judd and Corneille). He is the recipient of the 2007 Career Trajectory Award from the Society of Experimental Social Psychology and received the 2008 Kurt Lewin Award from the European Association of Social Psychology.

Mark Zanna is a University Professor and Chair at the University of Waterloo. He received his PhD from Yale University. His area of research is the psychology of attitudes. Currently, he is studying prejudice at both the explicit and implicit levels. A former President of the Society of Experimental Social Psychology and the Society of Personality and Social Psychology, he edits *Advances in Experimental Social Psychology* and the *Ontario Symposium on Personality and Social Psychology*. A Fellow of the Royal Society of Canada, he is the recipient of the Distinguished Scientist Awards from the Canadian Psychological Association, SPSP, SESP, and SPSSI.

Preface

This is a sizable volume. It contains 36 chapters representing the contributions of 83 different authors and co-authors, who have made significant contributions to the study of prejudice, stereotyping, and discrimination.

This volume is truly a handbook, in the sense of a volume that sets down a marker in the literature. The goals of each chapter and of the chapters collectively are to provide a comprehensive summary and critical analysis of the state of theory and research on prejudice, stereotyping, and discrimination. This is not the typical edited volume in which each contributor presents his or her own theory and latest research. Rather, the authors present succinct, consistently-edited, comprehensive and impartial reviews of specific topics, describing the current state of knowledge and identifying the most productive new directions for future research. The volume has five main sections, with chapters that (a) provide a historical and methodological overview; (b) examine basic processes and causes of prejudice, stereotyping, and discrimination; (c) consider specific types of biases (e.g., sexism, racism, anti-immigration attitudes) and how they are expressed; (d) discuss the social impact of prejudice, stereotyping, and discrimination; and (e) recommend ways to combat intergroup bias. A concluding chapter by the senior academic in the field offers a broad, integrative perspective on the topics of prejudice, stereotyping, and discrimination.

This volume is designed with several audiences in mind. It is accessible to a general lay audience, and policy makers will find a rich array of the multiple contributions of social psychology to the challenges posed to contemporary societies by issues concerning intergroup relations. It is also a crucial resource for advanced undergraduates, graduate students, and professionals who are interested in the areas of prejudice, stereotyping, and discrimination. It generally represents a social psychological orientation, but the volume should also appeal to students and scholars in sociology, political science, and education, as well as academics and practitioners interested in anti-bias education and prejudice reduction techniques and strategies.

This volume is large because it has to be: it tackles complex issues with broad applications and implications. Social biases present difficult theoretical and practical challenges for theory and research. The problems addressed here are not new and remain fundamental to the human experience. Centuries before psychology existed as a separate field, the prevalence of prejudice, stereotyping, discrimination, and intergroup conflict led philosophers to ponder the inherent nature of humans and the role of society in shaping good and evil. These topics have been at the core of work in both psychology and sociology from the inception of these disciplines. The theorists and researchers who made landmark early contributions to the study of prejudice – including Gordon Allport, Muzafer Sherif, and Henri Tajfel – are among the most prominent social psychologists in the field; their names remain readily recognizable to any student of psychology. These pioneers were followed by thousands of researchers who created a substantial empirical database upon which this volume rests. There are almost 2,500 references cited across the chapters in this book. The field not only 'stands on the shoulders of giants' but also on mountains of data, which are reviewed and systematized here.

This book not only reviews the current state of knowledge about prejudice, stereotyping, and discrimination, but also identifies what remains to be discovered. Each chapter looks forward as well as backward. The recurrence of genocide across history reminds us all of the evil of intergroup bias. However, the daily micro events of intergroup aggression and other forms of subtle discrimination that people suffer also take a significant human toll and violate, in less blatant ways, fundamental principles of fairness, justice, and human dignity. Thus, this volume attempts to guide the field toward new insights and research. It is our hope that it will not only result in conceptual advancements but also effective interventions with the potential to foster more positive and productive intergroup relations, to the benefit of all.

We acknowledge the substantial amount of encouragement, assistance, and support that made this book possible. We are very grateful to Sage Publications; we particularly appreciate the patience, wisdom, and guidance of Michael Carmichael and Sophie Hine. We also acknowledge the various forms of support that each of us has received to assist us in our efforts for the volume: For Jack Dovidio, the support provided by the National Science Foundation (Grant # 0613218) and the Spencer Foundation (Grant # 200900193), as well as by the University of Connecticut and Yale University; for Miles Hewstone, a programme grant from the Leverhulme Trust; for Peter Glick, sabbatical support from Lawrence University; and for Victoria Esses, the support provided by the Social Sciences and Humanities Research Council of Canada, as well as the University of Western Ontario.

PART I

Overview of the Topic

Prejudice, Stereotyping and Discrimination: Theoretical and Empirical Overview

John F. Dovidio, Miles Hewstone,
Peter Glick, and Victoria M. Esses

ABSTRACT

This chapter has two main objectives: to review influential ideas and findings in the literature and to outline the organization and content of the volume. The first part of the chapter lays a conceptual and empirical foundation for other chapters in the volume. Specifically, the chapter defines and distinguishes the key concepts of prejudice, stereotypes, and discrimination, highlighting how bias can occur at individual, institutional, and cultural levels. We also review different theoretical perspectives on these phenomena, including individual differences, social cognition, functional relations between groups, and identity concerns. We offer a broad overview of the field, charting how this area has developed over previous decades and identify emerging trends and future directions. The second part of the chapter focuses specifically on the coverage of the area in the present volume. It explains the organization of the book and presents a brief synopsis of the chapters in the volume.

Throughout psychology's history, researchers have evinced strong interest in understanding prejudice, stereotyping, and discrimination (Brewer & Brown, 1998; Dovidio, 2001; Duckitt, 1992; Fiske, 1998), as well as the phenomenon of intergroup bias more generally (Hewstone, Rubin, & Willis, 2002). Intergroup bias generally refers to the systematic tendency to evaluate one's own membership group (the ingroup) or its members more favorably than a non-membership group (the outgroup) or its members. These topics have a long history in the disciplines of anthropology and sociology (e.g., Sumner, 1906). However, social psychologists, building on the solid foundations of Gordon Allport's (1954) masterly volume, *The Nature of Prejudice*, have developed a systematic and more nuanced analysis of bias and its associated phenomena. Interest in prejudice, stereotyping, and discrimination is currently shared by allied disciplines such as sociology and political science, and emerging disciplines such as neuroscience. The practical implications of this large body of research are widely recognized in the law (Baldus, Woodworth, & Pulaski, 1990; Vidmar, 2003), medicine (Institute of Medicine, 2003), business (e.g., Brief, Dietz, Cohen, et al., 2000), the media, and education (e.g., Ben-Ari & Rich, 1997; Hagendoorn & Nekuee, 1999).

In recent years, research on prejudice and stereotyping has rapidly expanded in both quantity and perspective. With respect to quantity, even when the term 'discrimination' is omitted because of its alternative meaning in perception and learning, a PsychInfo search for entries with prejudice, stereotypes, or stereotyping in the title reveals a geometric progression, roughly doubling or tripling from each decade to the next, from only 29 works in the 1930s to 1,829 from 2000 through 2008. Of course, scientific information has accelerated generally. Thus, we examined the percentage of articles in which prejudice, stereotypes, or stereotyping appeared in the abstract, relative to the total number of articles published, in four leading general-interest journals in social psychology: *Journal of Personality and Social Psychology*, *Personality and Social Psychology Bulletin*, *Journal of Experimental Social Psychology*, and *European Journal of Social Psychology*. Figure 1.1 presents the overall trend from 1965 to the present. From 1965 through 1984, 1–2 percent of the articles in these journals examined prejudice or stereotypes. Beginning in 1985, interest jumped; in recent years,

almost 10 percent of the articles published in these mainstream journals study these phenomena. Moreover, as Figure 1.2 shows, the trend was similar across journals.

Approaches to understanding prejudice, stereotyping, and discrimination have also significantly broadened. Early theorists focused on individual differences, and associated prejudice with psychopathology (e.g., Adorno, Frenkel-Brunswik, Levinson, et al., 1950). In the 1970s and 1980s, the cognitive revolution in psychology generated interest in how cognitive processes lead to stereotyping and prejudice (e.g., Fiske & Taylor, 1984); simultaneously European researchers focused on how group processes and social identities affect bias (e.g., Tajfel & Turner, 1979). Both perspectives emphasized how normal psychological and social processes foster and maintain prejudice and stereotyping. The expansion has continued in recent years, with new perspectives on how specific emotions, nonconscious processes, and fundamental neural processes contribute to biases. In addition to 'drilling down' into the nonconscious mind and brain processes, the field has expanded upwards to consider how social structure creates and justifies biases, which permeate social institutions, such as the legal and health-care systems. In sum, the study of prejudice, stereotyping, and discrimination represents a well-established area incorporating traditional and emerging

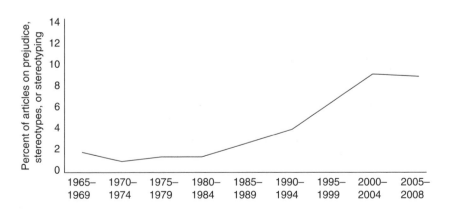

Figure 1.1   Percent of articles in four leading social psychology journals that use the term prejudice, stereotypes, or stereotyping in the abstract (data aggregated across journals).

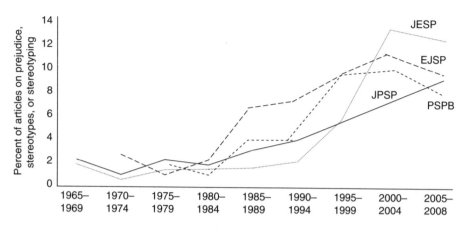

Figure 1.2 Percent of articles in four leading social psychology journals (*Journal of Personality and Social Psychology* – JPSP, *Personality and Social Psychology Bulletin* – PSPB, *Journal of Experimental Social Psychology* – JESP, and *European Journal of Social Psychology* – EJSP) that use the term prejudice, stereotypes, or stereotyping in the abstract.

(often multi-disciplinary) perspectives that have consistently attracted significant empirical and theoretical attention.

This volume provides a comprehensive summary of the state of research on prejudice, stereotyping, and discrimination. Each chapter reviews the history of a specific topic, critically analyses what the field understands and does not yet know, and identifies promising avenues for further study. As a whole, the volume considers the causes and consequences of bias toward a range of social groups, theoretical perspectives, and applications, summarizing current knowledge within a single volume that can serve as a key resource for students and scholars.

This introductory chapter lays the foundations for the volume by defining and distinguishing key concepts, identifying basic underlying processes, outlining past research, and anticipating future directions, while explaining the general organization and content of the book.

KEY CONCEPTS

The current volume focuses on three forms of social bias toward a group and its members: (a) prejudice, an attitude reflecting an overall evaluation of a group; (b) stereotypes, associations, and attributions of specific characteristics to a group; and (c) discrimination, biased behavior toward, and treatment of, a group or its members. Conceptualizations of each of these aspects of bias have evolved over time. For example, recent research distinguishing between implicit and explicit cognition has greatly affected how theorists define prejudice and stereotypes. Likewise, concepts of discrimination have gone from a tight focus on individuals engaging in biased treatment to how institutional policies and cultural processes perpetuate disparities between groups. We briefly review the development of each of these central concepts below.

Prejudice

Prejudice is typically conceptualized as an attitude that, like other attitudes, has a cognitive component (e.g., beliefs about a target group), an affective component (e.g., dislike), and a conative component (e.g., a behavioral predisposition to behave negatively toward the target group). In his seminal volume, *The Nature of Prejudice*, Allport (1954) defined prejudice as 'an antipathy based on faulty and inflexible generalization. It may be felt or expressed. It may be directed toward a group as a whole, or toward an individual because he

[sic] is a member of that group' (p. 9). Most researchers have continued to define prejudice as a negative attitude (i.e., an antipathy).

Psychologists have assumed that, like other attitudes, prejudice subjectively organizes people's environment and orients them to objects and people within it. Prejudice also serves other psychological functions, such as enhancing self-esteem (Fein & Spencer, 1997) and providing material advantages (Sherif & Sherif, 1969). However, whereas psychologists have focused on prejudice as an intrapsychic process (an attitude held by an individual), sociologists have emphasized its group-based functions. Sociological theories emphasize large-scale social and structural dynamics in intergroup relations, especially race relations (Blauner, 1972; Bonacich, 1972). Sociological theories consider the dynamics of group relations in economic- and class-based terms – often to the exclusion of individual influences (see Bobo, 1999).

Despite divergent views, both psychological and sociological approaches have converged to recognize the importance of how groups and collective identities affect intergroup relations (see Bobo, 1999; Bobo & Tuan, 2006). Blumer (1958a, 1958b, 1965a, 1965b), for instance, offered a sociologically based approach focusing on defense of group position, in which group competition is central to the development and maintenance of social biases. With respect to race relations, Blumer (1958a) wrote, 'Race prejudice is a defensive reaction to such challenging of the sense of group position ... As such, race prejudice is a protective device. It functions, however shortsightedly, to preserve the integrity and position of the dominant group' (p. 5). From a psychological orientation, in their classic Robbers Cave study, Sherif, Harvey, White, et al. (1961) similarly proposed that the functional relations between groups are critical in determining intergroup attitudes. Specifically, they argued that competition between groups produces prejudice and discrimination, whereas intergroup interdependence and cooperative interaction that leads to successful outcomes reduces intergroup bias (see also Bobo, 1988; Bobo &

Hutchings, 1996; Campbell, 1965; Sherif, 1966).

Recent definitions of prejudice bridge the individual-level emphasis of psychology and the group-level focus of sociology by concentrating on the dynamic nature of prejudice. Eagly and Diekman (2005), for example, view prejudice as a mechanism that maintains status and role differences between groups. But, they also emphasize how individuals' reactions contribute to this process. People who deviate from their group's traditional role arouse negative reactions; others who exhibit behaviors that reinforce the *status quo* elicit positive responses. Consistent with this view, prejudice toward women has both 'hostile' and 'benevolent' components (Glick & Fiske, 1996). Hostile sexism punishes women who deviate from a traditional subordinate role ('Most women fail to appreciate fully all that men do for them'), whereas benevolent sexism celebrates women's supportive, but still subordinate, position ('Women should be cherished and protected by men'). This perspective reveals that current prejudices do not always include only an easily identifiable negative view about the target group, but may also include more subtle, but patronizing and also pernicious 'positive' views.

Because prejudice represents an individual-level psychological bias, members of traditionally disadvantaged groups can also hold prejudices toward advantaged groups and their members. Although some research shows that minority-group members sometimes accept cultural ideologies that justify differences in group position based on the positive qualities of the advantaged group (Jost, Banaji, & Nosek, 2004; Sidanius & Pratto, 1999), there is considerable evidence that minority-group members also harbor prejudice toward majority group members. However, much of this prejudice is reactive, reflecting an anticipation of being discriminated *against* by majority group members (Johnson & Lecci, 2003; Monteith & Spicer, 2000).

These complexities, and others considered throughout the current volume, make it difficult to formulate a single, overarching definition of prejudice. Nevertheless, we suggest the following definition, based on extensive social-psychological research of the sort reviewed in this volume: Prejudice is an individual-level attitude (whether subjectively positive or negative) toward groups and their members that creates or maintains hierarchical status relations between groups.

Stereotypes

By most historical accounts, Lippmann (1922) introduced the term 'stereotype' to refer to the typical picture that comes to mind when thinking about a particular social group. Whereas early research conceptualized stereotyping as a rather inflexible and faulty thought process, more recent research emphasizes the functional and dynamic aspects of stereotypes as simplifying a complex environment. Stereotypes are cognitive schemas used by social perceivers to process information about others (Hilton & von Hippel, 1996). Stereotypes not only reflect beliefs about the traits characterizing typical group members but also contain information about other qualities such as social roles, the degree to which members of the group share specific qualities (i.e., within-group homogeneity or variability), and influence emotional reactions to group members. Stereotypes imply a substantial amount of information about people beyond their immediately apparent surface qualities and generate expectations about group members' anticipated behavior in new situations (to this extent they can, ironically, be seen as 'enriching'; Oakes & Turner, 1990). Yet, of course, stereotypes also constrain. In general, stereotypes produce a readiness to perceive behaviors or characteristics that are consistent with the stereotype. At the earliest stages of perceptual processing, stereotype-consistent characteristics are attended to most quickly. For instance, because cultural stereotypes associate Black people with violent crime in the United States, White people are quicker to recognize objects associated with crime (e.g., a gun) when primed with a

Black person than a White person (e.g., Payne, 2001).

Recent work also explores how social structure affects the specific content of stereotypes. Stereotypes can not only promote discrimination by systematically influencing perceptions, interpretations, and judgments, but they also arise from and are reinforced by discrimination, justifying disparities between groups. In particular, people infer the characteristics of groups based on the social roles they occupy (Hoffman & Hurst, 1990; Eagly & Diekman, 2005; Jost & Banaji, 1994). As a consequence, people view members of groups with lower socioeconomic status (even if caused by discrimination) as less competent and/or less motivated than high-status group members. Moreover, minority group members are also socialized to adopt 'system-justifying ideologies,' including stereotypic beliefs about their own group, that rationalize the group's social position (Jost, Banaji, Nosek, et al., 2004).

Although some components of group stereotypes relate to unique aspects of intergroup history (e.g., enslavement of Black people in the United States, middle-man roles performed by Jews who were excluded from other forms of employment since the Middle Ages in Europe), systematic principles shape the broader content of stereotypes. The Stereotype Content Model (Fiske, Cuddy, Glick, et al. 2002) proposes two fundamental dimensions of stereotypes: warmth (associated with 'cooperative' groups and denied to 'competitive' groups) and competence (associated with high-status groups and denied to low-status groups). Groups with stereotypes that are similarly high or low on each of the two dimensions of warmth and competence arouse similar emotions. Stereotypically warm and competent groups (e.g., the ingroup, close allies) elicit pride and admiration; stereotypically warm but incompetent groups (e.g., housewives, the elderly) produce pity and sympathy; stereotypically cold but competent groups (e.g., Asians, Jews) elicit envy and jealousy; and stereotypically cold and incompetent groups (e.g., welfare recipients, poor people) generate disgust, anger, and resentment. This powerful approach helps to explain why two quite distinct ethno-religious groups (e.g., the Chinese in Southeast Asian countries such as Malaysia and Indonesia, and Jews in Europe) are stereotyped in very similar ways (see Bonacich, 1973; Hewstone & Ward, 1985).

Cultural stereotypes tend to persevere for both cognitive and social reasons. Cognitively, people often discount stereotype-discrepant behaviors, attributing them to situational factors, while making dispositional (and stereotype-reinforcing) attributions for stereotype-consistent behaviors (Hewstone, 1990; Pettigrew, 1979). Socially, people behave in ways that elicit stereotype-confirming reactions, creating self-fulfilling prophecies. Biased expectancies influence how perceivers behave, causing targets, often without full awareness, to conform to perceivers' expectations (e.g., von Baeyer, Sherk, & Zanna, 1981). In addition, language plays an important role in the transmission of stereotypes. When communicating, people focus on the traits viewed as the most informative. Because stereotypical traits are distinctive to a group, people are more likely to use them in social discourse than traits perceived as unrelated to group membership. Stereotypical traits are generally high on communicability (viewed as interesting and informative), contributing to persistent use (Schaller, Conway, & Tanchuk, 2002). A further insight of social-psychological research on stereotypes is that the traits that tend to form their core are characterized not only by high central tendency (e.g., the British are very *cold*), but also by low variability (e.g., most British occupy the 'cold' end of a warm–cold continuum; see Ford & Stangor, 1992; Judd & Park, 1993).

Whereas psychological research on stereotypes has traditionally focused on the perceiver, work in sociology, stimulated by Goffman's (1963) classic book, *Stigma: Notes on the Management of Spoiled Identity*, has emphasized the experience of targets of stereotypes. As psychology has increasingly turned to understanding the effects on targets, two influential directions have emerged: tokenism and stereotype threat. Kanter (1977a, 1977b) provided a pioneering

sociological analysis of the consequences of group proportions such as skewed sex ratios which, at the extremes, involve very small numbers of the minority group, even a sole individual. When people are tokens, one of relatively few members of their group in a social context, they feel particularly vulnerable to being stereotyped by others. This occurs especially when the individual is the only member of their group (solo status) in the situation. Tokens or solos experience high levels of self-consciousness and threat, which reduces their ability to think and act effectively (Lord & Saenz, 1985; Sekaquaptewa & Thompson, 2003).

More recent research has identified the phenomenon of stereotype threat that occurs when members of a stereotyped group become aware of negative stereotypes about them, even when (a) a person holding the stereotype is not present and (b) they personally do not endorse the stereotype. Thus, making group membership salient can impair performance by producing anxiety and cognitive preoccupation with a negative stereotype (Steele, 1997).

In sum, stereotypes represent a set of qualities perceived to reflect the essence of a group. Stereotypes systematically affect how people perceive, process information about, and respond to, group members. They are transmitted through socialization, the media, and language and discourse. For the present volume, we define stereotypes as associations and beliefs about the characteristics and attributes of a group and its members that shape how people think about and respond to the group.

Discrimination

In the context of intergroup relations, discrimination has a pejorative meaning. It implies more than simply distinguishing among social objects, but refers also to inappropriate and potentially unfair treatment of individuals due to group membership. Discrimination may involve actively negative behavior toward a member of a group or, more subtly, less positive responses than those toward an ingroup member in comparable circumstances. According to Allport (1954), discrimination involves denying 'individuals or groups of people equality of treatment which they may wish' (p. 51). Jones (1972) defined discrimination as 'those actions designed to maintain own-group characteristics and favored position at the expense of the comparison group' (p. 4).

Discrimination is generally understood as biased behavior, which includes not only actions that directly harm or disadvantage another group, but those that unfairly favor one's own group (creating a relative disadvantage for other groups). Allport (1954) argued that ingroup favoritism plays a fundamental role in intergroup relations, taking psychological precedence over outgroup antipathy. He noted that 'in-groups are psychologically primary. We live in them, and sometimes, for them' (p. 42), and proposed that 'there is good reason to believe that this love-prejudice is far more basic to human life than is … hate-prejudice. When a person is defending a categorical value of his own, he may do so at the expense of other people's interests or safety. Hate prejudice springs from a reciprocal love prejudice underneath' (p. 25).

In the 50 years since Allport's observation, a substantial body of research has confirmed that intergroup bias in evaluations (attitudes) and resource allocations (discrimination) often involves ingroup favoritism in the absence of overtly negative responses to outgroups (Brewer, 1979, 1999; Otten & Mummendey, 2000).

Even though much of the traditional research on bias has not made the distinction between ingroup favoritism and outgroup derogation a central focus, the distinction is crucial, and each of them requires methodological concision and has distinct practical consequences. Methodologically, to separate the two components of ingroup favoritism and outgroup derogation we need to include an independent assessment of ingroup and outgroup evaluations, and a control condition. Practically, the bias uncovered in much social-psychological research predominantly takes the mild form of ingroup favoritism,

rather than outgroup derogation (see Brewer, 1999, 2001). This raises the question of when ingroup favoritism gives way to derogation, hostility, and antagonism against outgroups (e.g., Brewer, 2001, Mummendey & Otten, 2001).

A number of analyses argue that the constraints normally in place that limit intergroup bias to ingroup favoritism are lifted when outgroups are associated with stronger emotions (Brewer, 2001, Doosje, Branscombe, Spears, et al., 1998; Mackie & Smith, 1998; Mummendey & Otten, 2001). There is ample scope for these emotions in the arousal that often characterizes intergroup encounters, which can be translated into emotions such as fear, hatred, or disgust (Smith, 1993; Stephan & Stephan, 2000), and emotions experienced in specific encounters with groups can be an important cause of people's overall reactions to groups (e.g., Esses, Haddock, & Zanna, 1993). As part of a shift from exclusive concern with cognition in intergroup bias, Smith (1993) differentiated milder emotions (e.g., disgust) from stronger emotions (e.g., contempt, anger) most likely to be aroused in an intergroup context, and linked specific emotions, perceptions of the outgroup, and action tendencies (see Mackie, Devos, & Smith, 2000). Thus an outgroup that violates ingroup norms may elicit disgust and avoidance; an outgroup seen as benefiting unjustly (e.g., from government programs) may elicit resentment and actions aimed at reducing benefits; and an outgroup seen as threatening may elicit fear and hostile actions. Thus, weaker emotions imply only mild forms of discrimination, such as avoidance, but stronger emotions imply stronger forms, such as movement against the outgroup, and these latter emotions could be used to justify outgroup harm that extends beyond ingroup benefit (Brewer, 2001). This is not, however, to imply that pro-ingroup biases need not concern us. They can perpetuate unfair discrimination by advantaging dominant ingroups, often with less personal awareness and recognition by others, making them as pernicious as discrimination based on anti-outgroup orientations (Gaertner, Dovidio, Banker, et al., 1997).

For the present volume, we define discrimination by an individual as behavior that creates, maintains, or reinforces advantage for some groups and their members over other groups and their members.

Explicit and implicit bias

Whereas discrimination can occur toward a specific member of a group or the group as a whole, stereotypes and prejudice are intrapsychic phenomena. That is, they occur within an individual and may vary not only in their transparency to others but also in the level of awareness of the person who harbors stereotypes and prejudice. Traditionally, stereotypes and prejudice have been conceived as explicit responses – beliefs and attitudes people know they hold, subject to deliberate (often strategic) control in their expression (Fazio, Jackson, Dunton, et al., 1995). In contrast to these explicit, conscious, and deliberative processes, implicit prejudices and stereotypes involve a lack of awareness and unintentional activation. The mere presence of the attitude object may activate the associated stereotype and attitude automatically and without the perceiver noticing.

Although implicit attitudes and stereotype measures are now commonly used (Fazio & Olson, 2003), researchers continue to debate their psychological meaning. Some contend that implicit measures of bias primarily represent overlearned and 'habitual' cultural associations rather than attitudes (Karpinski & Hilton, 2001). Others argue that implicit and explicit measures assess a single attitude measured at different points in the process of expression, with social desirability concerns more strongly shaping overt expressions (Fazio, Jackson, Dunton, et al., 1995). And still others consider implicit and explicit measures to reflect different components of a system of dual attitudes, with implicit responses often representing 'older' attitudes and stereotypes that have been 'overwritten' by newer, explicit forms of bias or incompletely replaced by individuals who strive for egalitarian beliefs (Wilson, Lindsey, &

Schooler, 2000), or reflecting different aspects of attitudes, such as affective and cognitive components (Rudman, 2004). Nevertheless, there is consensus that implicit manifestations of attitudes and stereotypes exist and reliably predict some behaviors, often independently from explicit attitudes and stereotypes. We purposefully avoided reference to intentionality or personal endorsement in our working definitions of prejudice and stereotypes to accommodate implicit biases.

Institutional and cultural discrimination

Although psychologists have historically focused on the individual-level processes in intergroup relations, newer research informed by approaches from sociology, Black psychology, and cultural psychology illuminate how, independent of individual efforts or orientation, institutional and cultural forces maintain and promote intergroup bias and disparities. Institutional discrimination, which may originally stem from individuals' prejudices and stereotypes, refers to the existence of institutional policies (e.g., poll taxes, immigration policies) that unfairly restrict the opportunities of particular groups of people. These laws and policies foster ideologies that justify current practices. Historically, for example, White Americans developed racial ideologies to justify laws that enabled two forms of economic exploitation: slavery of Black people and the seizure of lands from native peoples. Similarly, until relatively recently, immigration policies in many parts of the world favored White immigrants over immigrants of racial minorities.

Although individual prejudice and stereotypes may produce actions, such as political support for laws and policies that lead to institutional discrimination, institutional discrimination can operate independently from individual discrimination. Institutional discrimination does not require the active support of individuals, their intention to discriminate, or awareness that institutional practices have discriminatory effects. Indeed, people often do not recognize the existence of institutional discrimination because laws (typically assumed to be right and moral) and long-standing or ritualized practices seem 'normal.' Furthermore, ideologies – whether explicitly prejudicial or obscuring prejudice (e.g., by suggesting that if discriminatory effects are unintended, there is no 'problem') – justify the 'way things are done.' The media and public discourse also often direct attention away from potential institutional biases.

Because institutional discrimination is not necessarily intentional or dependent on the overt efforts of individuals, it often must be inferred from disparate outcomes between groups traced back to differential policies, even those that might appear to be unrelated to group membership. These effects may appear economically (e.g., in loan policies after controlling for differences in qualifying conditions), educationally (e.g., in admission and financial aid policies), in employment (e.g., height requirement for employment as a police officer), in the media (e.g., exaggerating the association of minority groups with violence or poverty), in the criminal justice system (e.g., group differences in incarceration rates for similar crimes), and in mental and physical health (e.g., social stress or lesser care) (see Feagin, 2006; Institute of Medicine, 2003; Sidanius & Pratto, 1999).

Whereas institutional discrimination is associated with formal laws and policies, cultural discrimination is deeply embedded in the fiber of a culture's history, standards, and normative ways of behaving. Cultural discrimination occurs when one group exerts the power to define values for a society. It involves not only privileging the culture, heritage, and values of the dominant group, but also imposing this culture on other less dominant groups. As a consequence, everyday activities implicitly communicate group-based bias, passing it to new generations. We thus define cultural discrimination as beliefs about the superiority of a dominant group's cultural heritage over those of other groups, and the expression of such beliefs in individual actions or institutional policies.

Under some circumstances, members of a minority group may adopt system-justifying ideologies propagated by the dominant cultural group that distract attention from group-based disparities and inequities. Thus, members of a disadvantaged group may develop a 'false consciousness' in which they not only comply with but also endorse cultural values that systematically disadvantage them. For example, an exclusive emphasis on individually oriented meritocracy may obscure cultural and institutional discrimination and lead to an over-reliance on individual rather than collective action to address discrimination. Thus, the unique power of cultural discrimination resides in its power to shape how members of different groups interpret and react to group disparities, fostering compliance to the status quo without explicit intentions, awareness, or active support for these group-based disparities.

Each form of bias – prejudice, stereotypes, and discrimination – can occur at the individual, institutional, and cultural levels. Furthermore, these biases are often perpetuated by habitual practices and even formal laws, and justified by ideologies (some of which may obscure the existence of discrimination). In the next section, we consider the social-psychological assumption that, despite all of the various forms bias may take, some basic and fundamental processes generally foster and reinforce stereotypes, prejudice, and discrimination.

BASIC PROCESSES IN PREJUDICE, STEREOTYPING, AND DISCRIMINATION

Summarizing the extensive research on social biases with a limited number of themes, Haslam and Dovidio (2010) identified basic factors that foster and maintain bias: (a) personality and individual differences, (b) group conflict, (c) social categorization, and (d) social identity. We review each below.

Personality and individual differences

Responding to the Nazi's rise to power in Germany and the subsequent horrors of the Holocaust, psychologists initially focused on understanding 'What type of person would harbor the kinds of prejudices and stereotypes that would lead to genocide?' Given its prominence in psychological thought at the time, many of the answers relied on Freudian psychodynamic theory (see Allport, 1954). These approaches proposed that (a) the accumulation of psychic energy, due to frustration and guilt inevitably produced by society's restrictions on instinctual drives for sex and aggression, power intergroup bias and hostility; and (b) an individual's expression of prejudice has an important cathartic function in releasing pent-up energy and restoring the individual to a state of equilibrium.

Other approaches adopted elements of psychodynamic theory with critical variations. In their Frustration–Aggression Hypothesis, Dollard, Doob, Miller, et al. (1939) presented a drive-reduction model that included Freud's proposition that drives sought discharge in behavior, but characterized aggression as a response to circumstances that interfered with goal-directed activity, not as an innate drive. Dollard et al. in their account of scapegoating, further hypothesized that aggression is often displaced onto an innocent target if the true source of frustration is powerful and potentially threatening (see Glick, 2005). Hovland and Sears (1940) argued that historically the relationship between economic downturns (a source of frustration) and the lynchings of Black people (1882–1930) in southern states in the United States provided support for this account of scapegoating (see also Green, Glaser, & Rich, 1998).

Both of these accounts of scapegoating have been challenged recently. Using the Stereotype Content Model perspective, Glick (2005) argued that successful minorities, stereotyped as competent but cold competitors (not as weak and vulnerable) are most likely to be scapegoated. Only envied minorities are viewed as having both the ability (competence) and intent (coldness) to have deliberately caused widespread misfortunes (e.g., the Nazis blamed the 'worldwide Jewish conspiracy' for causing Germany's collapse, citing the Jews' relative success in banking, industry, the media, and government). This

model, then, focuses on collective attributions rather than Freudian psychodynamics.

The most influential work within the psychoanalytic tradition was Adorno, Frenkel-Brunswik, E., Levinson, et al.'s (1950) research, represented in their classic volume, *The Authoritarian Personality*. These researchers conducted extensive qualitative and quantitative work on the psychological substrates of anti-Semitism and susceptibility to fascistic propaganda. Adorno et al. identified patterns of cognition differentiating prejudiced (authoritarian) individuals from others who were more tolerant or open-minded. Specifically, prejudiced individuals exhibited intolerance of ambiguity, rigidity, concreteness (poor abstract reasoning), and over-generalization. Such individuals were thus portrayed as seeing the social world in black-and-white terms – evincing strong and disdainful rejection of others perceived as inferior to themselves and their ingroup.

The origins of the authoritarian personality were also traced to individuals' childhood experiences, specifically to hierarchical relations with punitive parents. In contrast, liberals (non-authoritarians) were believed to be the product of a more egalitarian upbringing that fostered more cognitive flexibility and rejection of stereotypic representations of others (see Jost, Glaser, Kruglanski, et al., 2003). In response to subsequent methodological and conceptual challenges, ideas about authoritarianism evolved to emphasize the role of social norms and standards, rather than Freudian dynamics. The most current conceptualization, Right-Wing Authoritarianism (Altemeyer, 1996, 1998), focuses on worldviews, and predicts negative attitudes toward a variety of groups, particularly those socially rejected by society (e.g., Altemeyer, 1996; Esses, Haddock, Zanna, et al., 1993).

Social Dominance Theory (Sidanius & Pratto, 1999) represents another recent approach to social biases, containing a focus on individual differences, which has similarly eschewed psychodynamic theory. This theory focuses on individual differences in whether people view intergroup relations as a competition in which it is appropriate for some groups to dominate others. People who score high in Social Dominance Orientation endorsing items such as, 'Some groups of people are simply inferior to other groups' and 'Sometimes other groups must be kept in their place,' show more prejudice and discrimination toward a range of outgroups.

Social Dominance Theory, while including an individual differences approach, focuses on an enduring theme in the study of social biases – the degree of competition between groups. This concern has been an abiding theme in understanding intergroup bias.

Group conflict

The early representation of prejudice as reflecting a dysfunctional personality was highly influential, not least because it fit with lay theories that viewed social biases as abnormal, a form of social pathology. However, a number of researchers argued instead that social biases are not restricted to a small group of people and represent a *group-level* phenomenon, and thus developed theories focusing on the functional relations between groups.

Theories based on functional relations often point to competition and consequent perceived threat as fundamental causes of intergroup prejudice and conflict. Realistic Group Conflict Theory (Campbell, 1965; Sherif, 1966) posits that perceived group competition for resources leads to efforts to reduce the access of other groups to resources. Classic field work by Muzafer Sherif and his colleagues (Sherif, Harvey, White, et al., 1961) examined intergroup conflict at a boys' camp adjacent to Robbers Cave State Park in Oklahoma (United States). In this study, twenty-two 12-year-old boys attending summer camp were randomly assigned to two groups (who subsequently named themselves Eagles and Rattlers). When the groups engaged in a series of competitive activities (a tug-of-war and baseball, and touch football games), intergroup bias and conflict quickly developed. Group members regularly exchanged verbal insults (e.g., 'sissies,' 'stinkers,' and 'cheaters'), and each

group conducted raids on the other's cabin, resulting in property destruction and theft. The investigators then altered the functional relations between the groups by introducing a set of superordinate goals (goals that could not successfully be achieved without the full cooperation of both groups). Achieving these goals together led to more harmonious relations and large reductions in intergroup bias.

Sherif, Harvey, White, et al. (1961) proposed that functional relations between groups strongly influence intergroup attitudes. When groups are competitively interdependent, the success of one group is contingent on the failure of the other. Thus, each group's attempt to obtain favorable outcomes for itself is also realistically perceived to frustrate the goals of the other group. Such a win-lose, zero-sum competitive relation between groups initiates mutually negative feelings and stereotypes toward the members of the other group. In contrast, cooperatively interdependent relations between groups (i.e., needing each other to achieve common goals) reduce bias (e.g., Blanchard, Adelman, & Cook, 1975).

Functional relations do not have to involve explicit competition to generate biases. In the absence of any direct evidence, people typically presume that members of other groups will act competitively and hinder the attainment of one's goals (Fiske & Ruscher, 1993; Insko, Schopler, Gaertner, et al., 2001). In addition, individual differences in intergroup perceptions (e.g., Social Dominance Orientation) can moderate responses regardless of the actual functional relations between groups (Esses, Dovidio, Jackson, et al., 2001a). It was also recognized that social biases can serve less tangible or symbolic collective functions such as garnering prestige or social status, in addition to instrumental objectives such as obtaining economic advantage (Allport 1954; Blumer, 1958a). Indeed, it has been suggested that symbolic, psychological factors are typically more important sources of intergroup bias than is competition for tangible resources (Esses, Jackson, Dovidio, et al., 2005). Thus, additional themes in the study of social bias have focused on the psychological consequences of seeing others and oneself in terms of group membership.

Social categorization

A further critical step toward recognition of prejudice as an aspect of normal rather than diseased minds was taken by Allport (1954). Allport's answer to the question, 'Why do human beings slip so easily into ethnic prejudice?' was that 'They do so because [its] two essential ingredients – erroneous generalization and hostility – are natural and common capacities of the human mind' (p. 17). Central to the first point, Allport recognized that prejudice relies on people's propensity to categorize, reacting to other people based on their group membership, rather than as individuals. He observed that the 'human mind must think with the aid of categories,' and 'Once formed categories are the basis for normal prejudgment. We cannot possibly avoid this process. Orderly living depends upon it' (p. 20).

Tajfel (1969), in his highly influential paper on the 'Cognitive Aspects of Prejudice,' elaborated on the role social categorization plays in intergroup biases. Like Allport, Tajfel rejected the idea that prejudice and stereotyping must be irrational and pathological. Instead, he argued that these social biases reflect the importance of people's group memberships and their attempts to understand features of the social world (in particular, the actions of other groups) that impinge upon their groups. This analysis opened the door to a 'cognitive revolution' that informed the greater part of social psychological research into prejudice and stereotyping during the 1970s and 1980s. This approach paved the way for viewing prejudice as an aspect of general *social cognition*.

Since then, a large body of research has demonstrated that social categorization profoundly influences social perception, affect, cognition, and behavior. Perceptually, when perceivers categorize people or objects into groups, they gloss over differences between members of the same category (Tajfel, 1969), treating members of the same group as 'all alike,' while between-group differences become exaggerated (Abrams, 1985; Turner, 1985). Emotionally, people spontaneously experience more positive affect toward members of their ingroup than toward members of outgroups (Otten & Moskowitz, 2000), particularly toward ingroup members who are most prototypical of their group (Hogg & Hains, 1996). Cognitively, people retain more and more detailed information for ingroup than for outgroup members (Park & Rothbart, 1982), better remember ways in which ingroup members are similar to and outgroup members are dissimilar to the self (Wilder, 1981), and remember less positive information about outgroup members (Howard & Rothbart, 1980).

In terms of behavioral outcomes, people help ingroup members more than outgroup members (Dovidio, Gaertner, Validzic, et al., 1997), and work harder for groups identified as ingroups than outgroups (Worchel, Rothgerber, Day, et al., 1998). When ingroup–outgroup social categorizations, rather than personal identities, are salient, people behave in a greedier and less trustworthy way toward members of other groups than when they respond to others as individuals (Insko, Schopler, Gaertner, et al., 2001). Thus, although functional relations between groups can further influence the degree to which discrimination is manifested (Campbell, 1965; Sherif, 1966), the process of social categorization itself provides the basis for social biases to develop and persist.

Social identity

While Tajfel's ideas spawned social cognitive approaches to stereotyping and prejudice, his own work developed in a somewhat different direction based on the results of his minimal group studies. In the early 1970s, Tajfel showed that artificial groups created in the lab, devoid of naturalistic meaning and a history of functional relations, nevertheless showed at least mild forms of prejudice and discrimination. This work inspired Social Identity Theory (Tajfel & Turner, 1979), which characterizes social bias as a context-specific response to the position of one's group within a particular system of intergroup relations.

Both Social Identity Theory (Tajfel & Turner, 1979) and the related Self-Categorization Theory (Turner, 1985; see also Onorato & Turner, 2001) emphasize the distinction between personal and social identities (see Spears, 2001). When personal identity (the self perceived as an individual) is salient, a person's individual needs, standards, beliefs, and motives primarily determine behavior. In contrast, when social identity (the self perceived as a member of a group) is salient, 'people come to perceive themselves as more interchangeable exemplars of a social category than as unique personalities defined by their individual differences from others' (Turner, Hogg, Oakes, et al., 1987: 50). Under these conditions, collective needs, goals, and standards are primary.

This perspective also proposes that a person defines or categorizes the self along a continuum that ranges from seeing the self as a separate individual with personal motives, goals, and achievements to viewing the self as an embodiment of a social collective or group. At the individual level, one's personal welfare and goals are most salient and important. At the group level, the goals and achievements of the group are merged with one's own (see Brown & Turner, 1981), and the group's welfare is paramount. At one extreme, self interest is fully represented by the first-person pronoun 'I' and, at the other extreme, group interest is fully represented by the collective pronoun 'We.' Intergroup relations begin when people think about themselves, and others, as group members rather than as distinct individuals.

Illustrating the dynamics of this distinction, Verkuyten and Hagendoorn (1998) found that when individual identity was primed, individual differences in authoritarianism strongly predicted Dutch students' prejudice toward Turkish migrants. In contrast, when social identity (i.e., national identity) was made salient, ingroup stereotypes and standards primarily predicted prejudiced attitudes. Thus, whether personal or collective identity is more salient critically shapes how a person perceives, interprets, evaluates, and responds to situations and to others.

In summary, whereas the section on Key Concepts emphasized distinctions between various forms of social biases, this section considered common elements that produce prejudice, stereotypes, and discrimination. Prejudice, stereotypes, and discrimination are complex, multi-determined processes. Therefore, basic factors related to individual differences, group conflict, social categorization, and social identity should not be viewed as competing but rather as complementary explanations, which can combine and operate in different ways under different conditions.

In discussing key concepts and underlying processes, we have illustrated how approaches to understanding prejudice, stereotypes, and discrimination have evolved such that different facets of social bias and different influences have been emphasized at different times. The history of research on bias is explored in more detail in Duckitt's chapter in this volume (Chapter 2). In the next section, however, we offer our own historical perspective, looking forward as much as back.

THE PAST AND THE FUTURE

Building on Duckitt's (1992) insightful historical analysis, Dovidio (2001) identified three general 'waves' of scholarship, reflecting different assumptions and paradigms, in the social psychological study of social biases. The first wave, from the 1920s through the 1950s, portrayed social biases as psychopathology, with prejudice conceived as a kind of social cancer. Research during this wave focused first on measuring and describing the problem and monitoring any changes (e.g., Gilbert, 1951; Katz & Braly, 1933), and then on understanding the source of the problem (e.g., in family relations, feelings of personal inadequacies, and psychodynamic processes; Adorno, Frenkel-Brunswik, E., Levinson, et al., 1950). If the problem was confined to certain 'diseased' individuals (much as a cancer begins with diseased cells), prejudice might be localized and removed or treated, containing the problem and preserving the health of society as a whole. Thus, researchers concentrated on identifying, through personality and attitude tests such as the authoritarian personality scale, prejudiced individuals so that remedial efforts could be focused on this subset of the population. This approach also directed attention toward a traditional, conservative, and not highly educated segment of the population – a group comfortably (for the researchers themselves) unlike the academics studying prejudice.

The second wave of theorizing and research began with an opposite assumption: prejudice is rooted in normal rather than abnormal processes. Thus, the focus turned to how normal processes, such as socialization into prevailing norms, supports and transmits prejudice. This approach revealed that changing general social norms, not simply targeting interventions toward a subset of 'abnormal' individuals, is necessary for combating prejudice. The typical focus of social psychology in North America on the individual in a social context was complemented by two other approaches in the 1970s. On the one hand, at a more macro level, Tajfel's work (Tajfel & Turner, 1979) persuasively demonstrated the important role of social identity, as well as individual identity, in producing prejudice. Evidence that assigning people to temporary groups based on arbitrary criteria was sufficient to produce ingroup-favoring prejudices (Brewer, 1979; Tajfel, 1970), and, when other factors (e.g., competition) were added, outgroup hostility reinforced the emerging conception of prejudice as a normal mechanism.

On the other hand, at a more micro level, the development of new theories and instrumentation for investigating social cognition further emphasized the normality and, some argued, the inevitability of prejudice. Prejudice, stereotyping, and discrimination were conceived as outcomes of normal cognitive processes associated with simplifying and storing the overwhelming quantity and complexity of information people encounter daily (see Hamilton, 1981). To the extent that social categorization was hypothesized to be a critical element in this process (Hamilton & Trolier, 1986), this cognitive, intra-individual perspective complemented Tajfel's motivational, group-level approach in reinforcing the normality of prejudice.

Together, these orientations helped to divert the focus away from the question, 'Who is prejudiced?' – the answer seemed to be 'everyone.' If prejudice reflects normal cognitive processes and group life, not just personal needs and motivations, bias should be the norm. Researchers therefore turned to examining bias among the 'well-intentioned' and to the apparent inconsistencies between self-reported attitudes, which suggested that the vast majority of Westerners were non-prejudiced, and the continued evidence of disparities and discrimination (e.g., Gaertner & Dovidio, 1986). The key question therefore became, 'Is anyone truly *not* prejudiced?' Theories of racial ambivalence (Katz, 1981; Katz, Wackenhut, & Hass, 1986) and of subtle and unintentional types of biases, such as symbolic racism (Sears, 1988; Sears, Henry, & Kosterman, 2000), modern racism (McConahay, 1986), and aversive racism (Gaertner & Dovidio, 1986; Kovel, 1970) emerged during this period. These theories all proposed that changing social norms in the United States (after the Civil Rights era) had driven racism 'underground,' either because of people's genuine desire to be egalitarian or a simple realization that overt racism would elicit social disapproval. While the theories disagree on whether racism has merely become covert or individuals are truly conflicted about their attitudes, all agree that a lifetime of exposure to negative stereotypes fuels the persistence of prejudiced attitudes that are not readily apparent.

The third wave of research on prejudice, beginning in the mid-1990s and characterizing much current research, emphasizes the multidimensional aspect of prejudice and takes advantage of new technologies to study processes that earlier theorists hypothesized but had no way to measure. For example, aversive racism, modern racism, and symbolic racism – distinctly different theories about contemporary racial prejudice – all assumed widespread unconscious negative feelings and beliefs by White people toward Black people. However, it was not until the 1990s that new conceptual perspectives (e.g., Greenwald & Banaji, 1995) and technologies (e.g., response latency procedures; Dovidio & Fazio, 1992; Greenwald, McGhee, & Schwartz, 1998) emerged, allowing researchers to measure implicit (i.e., automatic and unconscious) attitudes and beliefs. These new technologies permit the assessment of individual differences in implicit, as well as explicit, racial attitudes and may thus help distinguish traditional racists, aversive or modern racists, and the truly non-prejudiced White people. These methods also open doors for developing ways to combat subtle forms of prejudice. The adaptation of fMRI procedures to study brain processes involved in social phenomena promises further links to cognitive neuropsychological processes and a more comprehensive, interdisciplinary, and multidimensional understanding of prejudice (Phelps, O' Connor, Cunningham, et al., 2000).

Besides addressing the multidimensional intrapersonal processes associated with prejudice and racism, the current wave of research more explicitly considers the interpersonal and intergroup context. That is, whereas previous research focused largely on perceivers' attitudes and how these attitudes biased their evaluations, decisions, and behavior, third-wave work considers how targets respond and adapt, and how prejudice unfolds in interactions between perceivers and targets. Targets are no longer viewed as passive victims of bias, an assumption implicit in Allport's (1954) question, 'What would happen to your personality if you heard it said over and over again that you are lazy and had inferior blood?' (p. 42) and explicit in his answer: 'Group oppression may destroy the integrity of the ego entirely, and reverse its normal pride, and create a groveling self-image' (p. 152). Current work demonstrates that minorities to some extent internalize social biases and implicit stereotypes (Johnson, Trawalter, & Dovidio, 2000), which can become activated

(even in the absence of interaction with Whites), with detrimental consequences (e.g., on academic tests) (Steele, 1997). However, the consequences of stigmatization are now understood to be more dynamic and complex than Allport and his contemporaries assumed (see Crocker & Major, 1989; Miller & Myers, 1998).

What, then, lies ahead? Each chapter in this volume specifically addresses this question. Here, we consider the broad picture and suggest eight general trends, ranging from the intra-individual (in fact, the intra-cranial) to the societal. The first trend is a more elaborated conception of the neuroscience of bias, which can help distinguish the underpinnings of different types of bias. Whereas social psychology operationalizes ingroup-outgroup relations in a variety of different ways (e.g., sex, race, age, weight), neuroscience points to fundamental differences in various forms of categorization. Racial categorization relates to structures that have evolved for sensitivity to novelty or threat (amygdala) and neural systems that track coalitions and alliances (Cosmides, Tooby, & Kurzban, 2003), but sex and age are encoded in other regions of the brain (frontocentral regions). Thus, although racism and sexism may share some similar behavioral dynamics and social consequences, social neuroscience data suggest fundamental differences in perception and encoding. Such different neural underpinnings may have critical implications for cognitive, affective, and behavioral reactions (Amodio & Devine, 2006; Amodio, Devine, & Harmon-Jones, 2007).

A second emerging trend is closer attention to understanding how interpersonal interactions relate to larger-scale social biases. As Shelton and Richeson (2006; see also Shelton, Dovidio, Hebl, et al., 2009) have argued, interpersonal interactions between members of different groups represent critical encounters. Such encounters not only reflect contemporary group relations but also produce impressions and outcomes that can reinforce or diminish further bias. Interpersonal interactions between members of different groups are highly susceptible to communication problems and misunderstandings. They are fraught with anxiety over how one is being perceived, making them highly cognitively demanding both for majority group members, who often strive to behave in an unbiased manner (Dovidio & Gaertner, 2004; Shelton & Richeson, 2005), and for minority group members, who are vigilant for cues of bias (Shelton, Richeson, Salvatore, et al., 2005). These demands can arouse intergroup anxiety and its behavioral manifestations (Stephan & Stephan, 1985). Because many signals of anxiety are also cues for dislike, expectations of rejection by members of another group (Shelton & Richeson, 2005) can lead to misattributions to unfriendliness that exacerbate interpersonal and, ultimately, intergroup tensions (Pearson, West, Dovidio, et al., 2008). Thus, understanding how and why intergroup misunderstandings develop during interpersonal interactions can complement structural and intergroup approaches aimed at alleviating intergroup conflict and achieving stable harmonious intergroup relations.

A third recent trend that is likely to broaden future research is the internationalization of psychology and the resultant focus on groups other than Whites and Blacks in the United States. As a result of these broadening horizons, research is increasingly examining such relations as those between immigrants and members of host nations (e.g., Esses, Dovidio, & Dion, 2001b), between Catholics and Protestants in Northern Ireland (e.g., Paolini, Hewstone, Cairns, et al., 2004), between groups identified on the basis of religious affiliation (e.g., Hunsberger & Jackson, 2005), between homosexuals and heterosexuals (Gabriel, Banse, & Hug, 2007), and between ethnic groups other than Whites and Blacks (e.g., Zick, Pettigrew, & Wagner, 2008). In addition to examining the applicability of theories developed to explain relations between Whites and Blacks (e.g., Bell & Esses, 1997), these expansions provide new understandings of the basis of prejudice, and point to new foci for intervention (e.g., Nickerson & Louis, 2008). The continent of Europe, for example, is replete with examples of interactions between members of different ethnic and religious groups coming together in differing circumstances with different norms, and against the backdrop of different legal and political systems.

A fourth focus likely to generate considerable future research is a variation on an older theme. Since Allport's pioneering work, social psychology has focused on how to reduce bias in the most effective, generalizable, and enduring way. For over 50 years, intergroup contact theory (Allport, 1954; Williams, 1947; see also Dovidio, Gaertner, & Kawakami, 2003; Pettigrew, 1998) has represented one of psychology's most effective strategies for reducing bias and improving intergroup relations. This framework proposes the conditions under which intergroup contact can ameliorate intergroup prejudice and conflict. Much of the research on this topic has been devoted to establishing that intergroup contact does indeed reduce bias and to evaluating the relative importance of the conditions specified in Contact Theory (see Pettigrew & Tropp, 2006). In recent years, however, work has moved beyond specifying the conditions that reduce bias to understanding the underlying processes (e.g., changes in social categorization) by which they work (see Pettigrew, 1998). A number of empirically-supported category-based alternatives have been proposed that involve de-emphasizing group membership and establishing personalized relations (Brewer & Miller, 1984; Miller, 2002; Wilder, 1986), recategorizing groups within a common group identity (Gaertner & Dovidio, 2000), or maintaining distinct group identities but within the context of positive interdependence between groups (Brown & Hewstone, 2005). Future research will likely examine more closely the implications of various mediating processes for better understanding the conditions under which contact is more effective (e.g., for mild intergroup tensions versus open hostility) and how various types of contact and their resulting cognitive representations may operate sequentially, in a complementary fashion, to reduce bias.

More generally, future research is likely to investigate the effectiveness of other strategies for reducing bias. For example, because of world events, recent attention has turned to considering whether multiculturalism is effective for promoting intergroup harmony within a nation (e.g., Correll, Park, & Smith, 2008). Similarly, social cognitive associative training has been harnessed for reducing the application of stereotypes (e.g., Kawakami, Dovidio, & van Kamp, 2007). These strategies take advantage of knowledge of the sources of prejudice to develop strategies for counteracting such effects. Thus, as knowledge and understanding of the neurological and other bases of prejudice accrues, so too should new strategies be developed and evaluated that target such processes.

Two key aspects of this future work on bias reduction constitute independent themes in their own right; they can be illustrated with reference to intergroup contact, but are by no means exclusive to it. A fifth recent trend is shift from a static to a dynamic approach. At one level this is seen in the relational approach taken to intergroup interactions by Richeson, Shelton and their colleagues (see Shelton & Richeson, 2006). How one person perceives and interprets an interaction partner has a direct impact on how that partner interprets and responds. Thus how behavior unfolds over time becomes a critical focus. At another level, static, cross-sectional analyses of intergroup relations are no longer seen as sufficient to understand what are, essentially, dynamic phenomena. To give one example, more than 70 percent of the research on intergroup contact reported in a meta-analysis by Pettigrew and Tropp (2006) involved respondents retrospectively reporting prior or current levels of contact. This reliance on cross-sectional, correlational studies needs to be gradually replaced with more complex longitudinal studies (e.g., Binder, Zagefka, Brown, et al., 2009; Levin, van Laar, & Sidanius, 2003).

A sixth, also methodological, focus, barely in its infancy, is for social psychology to complement its long-held expertise in laboratory research with adventurous excursions outside the lab, where members of different groups live, work, cooperate and sometimes fight with each other. In one example, Pettigrew (2008) recently called for a greater focus on the multi-level nature of intergroup contact where, for example, members of different groups may inhabit different neighborhoods, but come together in common classrooms, in different schools. Pettigrew and Tropp's (2006) meta-analysis of intergroup contact included no multi-level studies, yet these are crucial for practical applications (see Pettigrew, 2006).

Integrating the traditional social psychological emphasis on intra-individual and interpersonal processes with macro institutional and societal factors that have been the province of sociology and political science represents a seventh fertile area for future research. Recent social phenomena, such as unprecedented rates of international immigration and the purported clash of eastern and western cultures, highlight the importance of multi-disciplinary approaches to social problems. The complexity of these issues speaks to the need to adopt truly multidisciplinary approaches that incorporate the different perspectives and methods of fields such as economics, political science, sociology, psychology, and anthropology (Esses, Semenya, Stelzl, et al., 2006). Initiatives in this area will likely require greater investment in field research, studying actual groups in extended conflict, than has been the case in recent years in psychology.

A final future direction we would like to see unfold is a greater input from social psychological research on prejudice, stereotyping, and discrimination to relevant policy. The findings reviewed in the chapters in this volume have important and multiple implications for government policy, ranging from increasing the educational aspirations of minority youth, to providing equal access to health care irrespective of ethnic group, to promoting effective interventions to improve social harmony. A case in point is the burning question of whether residential diversity is associated with reduced levels of trust, as claimed by political scientist Robert Putnam (2007), and what to do about it. Ensuing debate, drawn from multiple disciplines, has failed to reach agreement on the reliability of the findings (see, for example, Briggs, 2008; Dawkins, 2008; Lancee & Dronkers, 2008). One reason why Putnam's main pessimistic finding should be considered premature is that it largely neglects to measure actual face-to-face contacts between members of different groups, as opposed to merely living in the same neighbourhood. This is a conflation of *opportunity for contact* and *actual contact*. Social psychologists have long appreciated that living in a street or neighbourhood peopled by members of different ethnic groups does not constitute contact until and unless there is actual face-to-face interaction between them (see Hewstone, Tausch, Voci, et al., 2008; see also Hooghe, Reeskens, Stolle, et al., 2009; Stolle, Soroka, & Johnston, 2008). Yet perhaps it was easy to overlook social psychology's contribution because so little of it dealt with the complexities of diversity and intergroup interaction outside the laboratory, or at least the campus, and in the community, and because social psychologists have sometimes been rather reluctant to press home the policy impact of their research. We hope that our discipline will be more effective in the future, and that a volume such as this one will help, as will the recent founding of social psychological journal outlets with an explicit focus on policy (e.g., *Social Issues and Policy Review*).

The purpose of the current volume is to provide a comprehensive summary of theory and research on prejudice, stereotyping, and discrimination that establishes a solid foundation for identifying and pursuing new work on intergroup bias. The scope of the volume is broad, and it adopts a multi-level perspective. Still, we acknowledge the coverage is far from exhaustive. Nevertheless, the chapters in this volume illustrate the landscape of social psychological work on intergroup bias, drawing on the expertise of international scholars who have made significant contributions to this area.

ORGANIZATION AND OVERVIEW OF THE VOLUME

The current volume is organized into six discrete sections. The first section, which contains the present chapter, represents an overview of the topic. The present chapter introduced basic concepts that will be referred to across the chapters, summarized the major conceptual approaches in this area, and identified promising directions for further study. The next chapter, Historical Overview by John Duckitt, describes historical developments, conceptual and empirical, in the study of prejudice, stereotyping, and discrimination. Duckitt emphasizes the interplay between society and science. He proposes that these paradigmatic transitions did not simply represent a systematic evolution of knowledge, but rather reflected responses to specific social and historical circumstances. Then Correll, Judd, Park, and Wittenbrink in their chapter, Measuring Stereotypes, Prejudice, and Discrimination, review the methodological challenges and tools associated with research in this area. Beyond describing different techniques for studying bias, the authors argue that measurement itself has fundamentally affected theories of the nature and origins of prejudice, stereotypes, and discrimination. These three chapters combined thus not only review basic issues for studying prejudice, stereotyping, and discrimination, but also they illustrate the importance of social context for theory and research in this area.

The second main section of this volume is Basic Processes and Causes of Prejudice, Stereotyping, and Discrimination. This is the largest section of the volume and includes 12 chapters that explore the origins of different forms of bias. The section begins with a chapter on processes at the most micro level, neural processes, and ends with macro processes, the influence of mass media.

In the first chapter of the second section, Social Cognitive Neural Processes, Quadflieg, Mason, and Macrae describe the latest findings from studies on intergroup bias in social cognitive neuroscience, considered in light of current theoretical models of person perception, social cognition, and social categorization. Next, Schaller, Conway, and Peavy, in their chapter Evolutionary Processes, identify two kinds of evolutionary processes contributing to bias, one genetic and the other social that relate to how knowledge is selectively transmitted between individuals. Killen, Richardson, and Kelly then discuss, in Developmental Perspectives, how intergroup attitudes emerge, change, and are manifested throughout development.

The next three chapters in the section examine cognitive, affective, and motivational processes in prejudice, stereotyping, and discrimination. In their chapter, Cognitive Processes, Fiske and Russell review social cognitive perspectives on prejudice, stereotyping, and discrimination, focusing on underlying thought processes that create and maintain bias. Smith and Mackie follow with a chapter on Affective Processes. The authors explore ways that incidental affect, affect arising from an interaction, and affect experienced when they think of themselves as a member of a social group influences cognitive processes and behavioral reactions. Yzerbyt attempts to integrate research on cognitive and affective processes in bias in his chapter; he analyses bias from the perspective of fundamental integrity concerns to know and to control, to be connected with others, and to have value.

The volume then moves from intrapersonal processes to a focus on the individual. The chapter, Individual Differences, by Son Hing and Zanna, identifies ideological and dispositional influences that shape the degree to which different people harbor intergroup biases. Abrams and Hogg consider the roles of identity, personal and collective, in their chapter, Social Identity and Self-Categorization. From the perspective of social identity theory, the authors explain how prejudice, stereotypes, and discrimination arise and are maintained. The next two chapters, Group Realities by Leyens and Demoulin and Intergroup Competition by Esses, Jackson, and Bennet-AbuAyyash, demonstrate how groups influence the way individuals perceive

each other and develop social relations that both create and justify intergroup bias. The chapter, Social Structure, by Diekman, Eagly, and Johnston examines prejudice as resulting from social cognitive elements, such as attitudes and stereotypes, and social structural elements, such as roles and contexts, and they offer an integrative perspective, the role congruity model of prejudice. In the final chapter of the section, Mass Media, Mutz and Goldman consider how the ways different groups are portrayed in the media can influence intergroup attitudes and beliefs. They outline the contributions and limitations of past work on this topic, and point to the most promising theoretical frameworks for studying media influence on outgroup attitudes. Thus, this section spans different levels of analysis for understanding prejudice, stereotyping, and discrimination.

The third section of the volume is Expression of Prejudice, Stereotyping, and Discrimination. This section explores how bias is expressed sometimes subtly but other times blatantly in attitudes, interpersonal interactions, and intergroup relations. The chapter, Attitudes and Intergroup Relations by Maio, Haddock, Manstead, and Spears, which begins this section, reviews research on the content, structure, and function of attitudes in general and their relationship to intergroup biases. Richeson and Shelton focus on the role of prejudice in interpersonal interaction. They consider how the reciprocal ways stigmatized and non-stigmatized individuals influence each other in interactions shape intergroup perceptions and outcomes. Dancygier and Green focus on one extreme outcome, Hate Crime. They explore motivational influences and contextual factors (including political, historical-cultural, sociological, and economic circumstances) that elicit hate crimes. The next four chapters in the section discuss four different forms of intergroup bias. The first three explore well-known '-isms'; Glick and Rudman focus on sexism; Dovidio, Gaertner, and Kawakami discuss racism; Hebl, Law, and King consider heterosexism. In the following chapter Wagner, Christ, and Heitmeyer examine anti-immigration bias.

Although far from exhaustive, these four chapters provide 'case studies' illustrating both common elements and unique aspects of discrimination toward different groups.

The fourth section of the volume is Social Impact of Prejudice, Stereotyping, and Discrimination. Quinn, Kallen, and Spencer, in their chapter, Stereotype Threat, review the general evidence on stereotype threat, discuss potential underlying processes, and consider the role of varying group identities in stereotype threat outcomes. The chapter, Internalized Devaluation and Situational Threat by Crocker and Garcia examines research and theory on the idea that prejudice and discrimination lower the self-esteem of people with stigmatized identities and these authors identify moderating factors. They view the stigmatized as caught between protecting self-esteem at the cost of learning, relationships, and/or motivation versus sustaining learning, motivation, and relationships at the cost of self-esteem. Major and Townsend's chapter, Coping with Bias, attempts to strike a balance between acknowledging the negative impact of prejudice, stereotyping, and discrimination on the lives of the stigmatized and recognizing the multiple strengths and resilience that stigmatized individuals and groups also display.

The next five chapters in the section consider the impact of prejudice, stereotyping, and discrimination institutionally, organizationally, and socially. Henry describes the dynamics of Institutional Bias generally. Smith, Brief, and Collela study the operation of intergroup bias in organizations, whereas Schmukler, Rasquiza, Dimmit, and Crosby examine bias in public policy. The impact of intergroup bias on a key area of society, health care, and outcomes, is reviewed by Penner, Albrecht, Orom, Coleman, and Underwood.

The fifth section of the volume is Combating Bias. It contains seven chapters that present a range of perspectives, conceptual and practical, for controlling and eliminating prejudice, stereotyping, and discrimination. Monteith, Arthur, and Flynn, in their chapter on Self-Regulation, discuss motivational factors influencing regulatory inclinations and explain how suppression of prejudicial biases often backfires. In the chapter, Multiple Identities, Crisp provides a review and integration of research into how the recognition and use of multiple identities in person perception can encourage reductions in intergroup biases. Gaertner, Dovidio, and Houlette explore how social categorization, which often produces intergroup bias, can be redirected through recategorization to reduce bias. Tausch and Hewstone present an overview of the vast literature on intergroup contact, highlighting recent developments in the field, and identifying moderating factors and mediating mechanisms.

Ellemers and van Laar consider individual mobility, while Wright discusses collective action. Specifically, Ellemers and van Laar argue that individual mobility beliefs and behaviors tend to reinforce rather than challenge group-based inequality. Wright, in his chapter, Collective Action and Social Change, describes four psychological processes that underpin collective action: collective identity, perceived boundary permeability, feelings of legitimacy/injustice, and collective control (instability/agency). He concludes the chapter by contrasting the psychology of collective action with that of prejudice reduction.

The final 'Commentary' section of this volume features a capstone chapter, written by the senior scholar in this field who brings over five decades of experience to this task. This chapter, Looking to the Future, by Thomas Pettigrew identifies conceptual threads that run through the chapters of this volume and discusses a series of pressing concerns for future work, including the need for more integrative, multi-level, and contextually sensitive analysis.

Taken together, the chapters in this volume provide a broad overview of classic and current research and theory on prejudice, stereotyping, and discrimination. Each of the chapters is integrative and reflective. Moreover, and most importantly, they are collectively generative. The chapters offer critical analysis and insights that reveal gaps in what we know about intergroup bias and they highlight promising directions for future work. They map the extensive knowledge base on this important issue and provide a blueprint for researchers to pursue individually and collectively, not only to better understand the phenomena of prejudice, stereotyping, and discrimination but also to develop new techniques for eliminating intergroup bias.

REFERENCES

Abrams, D. (1985). Focus of attention in minimal intergroup discrimination. *British Journal of Social Psychology*, 24, 65–74.

Adorno, T. W., Frenkel-Brunswik, E., Levinson, D. J., & Sanford, R. N. (1950). *The Authoritarian Personality.* New York: Harper.

Allport, G. W. (1954). *The Nature of Prejudice.* Cambridge, MA: Addison-Wesley.

Altemeyer, B. (1996). *The Authoritarian Specter.* Cambridge, MA: Harvard University Press.

Altemeyer, B. (1998). The other authoritarian personality. In M. P. Zanna (Ed.), *Advances in Experimental Social Psychology* (Vol. 30, pp. 47–92). San Diego: Academic Press.

Amodio, D. M., & Devine, P. G. (2006). Stereotyping and evaluation in implicit race prejudice: Evidence for independent constructs and unique effects on behavior. *Journal of Personality and Social Psychology*, 91, 652–661.

Amodio, D.M., Devine, P.G., & Harmon-Jones, E. (2007). A dynamic model of guilt: Implications for motivation and self-regulation in the context of prejudice. *Psychological Science*, 18, 524–530.

Baldus, D., Woodworth, G., & Pulaski, C. (1990). *Equal Justice and the Death Penalty: A Legal and Empirical Analysis.* Boston, MA: Northeastern University Press.

Bell, D. W., & Esses, V. M. (1997). Ambivalence and response amplification toward native peoples. *Journal of Applied Social Psychology*, 27, 1063–1084.

Ben-Ari, R., & Rich, Y. (Eds) (1997). *Enhancing Education in Heterogeneous Schools: Theory and Application.* Ramat-Gun, Israel: Bar-Illan University Press.

Binder, J., Zagefka, H., Brown, R., Funke, F., Kessler, T., Mummendey, A., et al. (2009). Does contact reduce prejudice or does prejudice reduce contact? A longitudinal test of the contact hypothesis among majority and minority groups in three European countries. *Journal of Personality and Social Psychology*, 96, 843–856.

Blanchard, F. A., Adelman, L., & Cook, S. W. (1975). Effect of group success upon interpersonal attraction in cooperating interracial groups. *Journal of Personality and Social Psychology*, 31, 1021–1030.

Blauner, R. (1972). *Race Oppression in America.* New York: Harper & Row.

Blumer, H. (1958a). Race prejudice as a sense of group position. *Pacific Sociological Review*, 1, 3–7.

Blumer, H. (1958b). Recent research on race relations in the United States of America. *International Social Science Bulletin*, 10, 403–477.

Blumer, H. (1965a). Industrialization and race relations. In G. Hunter (Ed.), *Industrialization and Race Relations: A Symposium* (pp. 228–229). New York: Oxford University Press.

Blumer, H. (1965b). The future of the Color Line. In J. C. McKinney & E. T. Thompson (Eds), *The South in Continuity and Change* (pp. 322–336). Durham, NC: Seeman.

Bobo, L. (1988). Group conflict, prejudice, and the paradox of contemporary racial attitudes. In P. A. Katz & D. A. Taylor (Eds), *Eliminating Racism: Profiles in Controversy* (pp. 85–114). New York: Plenum.

Bobo, L. D. (1999). Prejudice as group position: Microfoundations of a sociological approach to racism and race relations. *Journal of Social Issues*, 55, 445–472.

Bobo, L., & Huchings, V. L. (1996). Perceptions of racial group competition: Extending Blumer's theory of group position to a multiracial context. *American Sociological Review*, 61, 951–972.

Bobo, L., & Tuan, M. (2006). *Prejudice in Politics: Group Position, Public Opinion and the Wisconsin Treaty Rights Dispute.* Cambridge, MA: Harvard University Press.

Bonacich, E. (1972). A theory of ethnic antagonism. *American Sociological Review*, 77, 547–559.

Bonacich, E. (1973). A theory of middleman minorities. *American Sociological Review*, 38, 583–594.

Brewer, M. B. (1979). Ingroup bias in the minimal intergroup situation: A cognitive motivational analysis. *Psychological Bulletin*, 86, 307–324.

Brewer, M. B. (1999). The psychology of prejudice: Ingroup love or outgroup hate? *Journal of Social Issues*, 55, 429–444.

Brewer, M. B. (2001). Ingroup identification and intergroup conflict: When does ingroup love become outgroup hate? In R.E. Ashmore & L. Jussim (Eds), *Social Identity, Intergroup Conflict, and Conflict Reduction. Rutgers Series on Self and Social Identity*, (Vol. 3., pp. 17–41). London, England: Oxford University Press.

Brewer, M. B., & Brown, R. J. (1998). Intergroup relations. In D. T. Gilbert, S. T. Fiske & G. Lindzey (Eds), *Handbook of Social Psychology* (4th ed., Vol. 2, pp. 554–594). New York: McGraw Hill.

Brewer, M. B., & Miller, N. (1984). Beyond the contact hypothesis: Theoretical perspectives on desegregation. In N. Miller & M. B. Brewer (Eds), *Groups in Contact: The Psychology of Desegregation* (pp. 281–302). Orlando FL: Academic Press.

Brief, A. P., Dietz, J., Cohen, R. R., Pugh, S. D., & Vaslow, J. B. (2000). Just doing business: Modern racism and obedience to authority as explanations for employment discrimination. *Organizational Behavior and Human Decision Processes.* 81, 72–97.

Briggs, X. de S. (2008). On half-blind men and elephants: Understanding greater ethnic diversity and responding to good-enough evidence. *Housing Policy Debate*, 19, 218–229.

Brown, R., & Hewstone, M. (2005). An integrative theory of intergroup contact. In M. P. Zanna (Ed.), *Advances in Experimental Social Psychology* (Vol. 37, pp. 255–343). San Diego, CA: Academic Press.

Brown, R. J., & Turner, J. C. (1981). Interpersonal and intergroup behavior. In J. C. Turner & H. Giles (Eds.), *Intergroup Behavior* (pp. 33–64). Chicago, IL: University of Chicago Press.

Campbell, D. T. (1965). Ethnocentric and other altruistic motives. In D. Levine (Ed.), *Nebraska Symposium on Motivation* (Vol. 13, pp. 283–311). Lincoln: University of Nebraska Press.

Correll, J., Park, B., & Smith, J. A. (2008). Colorblind and multicultural prejudice reduction strategies in high-conflict situations. *Group Processes and Intergroup Relations*, 11, 471–491.

Cosmides, L., Tooby, J., & Kurzban, R. (2003). Perceptions of race. *Trends in Cognitive Science*, 7, 173–179.

Crocker, J., & Major, B. (1989). Social stigma and self-esteem: The self-protective properties of stigma. *Psychological Review.* 96, 608–630.

Dawkins, C. (2008). Reflections on diversity and social capital: A critique of Robert Putnam's. 'E Pluribus Unum: Diversity and community in the twenty-first century the 2006 Johan Skytte prize lecture'. *Housing Policy Debate*, 19, 208–217.

Dollard, J., Doob, L. W., Miller, N. Mowrer, O. H., & Sears, R. R. (1939). *Frustration and Aggression.* New Haven, CT: Yale University Press.

Doosje, B., Branscombe, N. R., Spears, R., & Manstead, A. S. R. (1998). Guilty by association: When one's group has a negative history. *Journal of Personality and Social Psychology*, 75, 872–886.

Dovidio, J. F. (2001). On the nature of contemporary prejudice: The third wave. *Journal of Social Issues*, 57, 829–849.

Dovidio, J. F., & Fazio, R. H. (1992). New technologies for the direct and indirect assessment of attitudes. In J. Tanur (Ed.), *Questions About Survey Questions: Meaning, Memory, Attitudes, and Social Interaction* (pp. 204–237). New York: Russell Sage Foundation.

Dovidio, J. F., & Gaertner, S. L. (2004). Aversive racism. In M. P. Zanna (Ed.), *Advances in Experimental Social Psychology* (Vol. 36, pp. 1–51). San Diego, CA: Academic Press.

Dovidio, J. F., Gaertner, S. L., & Kawakami, K. (2003). The Contact Hypothesis: The past, present, and the future. *Group Processes and Intergroup Relations*, 6, 5–21.

Dovidio, J. F., Gaertner, S. L., Validzic, A., Matoka, K., Johnson, B., & Frazier, S. (1997). Extending the benefits of re-categorization: Evaluations, self-disclosure and helping. *Journal of Experimental Social Psychology*, 33, 401–420.

Duckitt, J. (1992). Psychology and prejudice: A historical analysis and integrative framework. *American Psychologist*, 47, 1182–1193.

Eagly, A. H., & Diekman, A. B. (2005). What is the problem? Prejudice as an attitude-in-context. In J. F. Dovidio, P. Glick, & L. A. Rudman (Eds), *On the Nature of Prejudice: Fifty Years After Allport* (pp. 19–35). Malden, MA: Blackwell.

Esses, V. M., Dovidio, J. F., & Dion, K. L. (Eds) (2001b). Immigrants and immigration. *Journal of Social Issues*, 57.

Esses, V. M., Dovidio, J. F., Jackson, L. M., & Armstrong, T. M. (2001a). The immigration dilemma: The role of perceived group competition, ethnic prejudice, and national identity. *Journal of Social Issue*, 57, 389–412.

Esses, V. M, Haddock, G., & Zanna, M. (1993). Values, stereotypes, and emotions as determinants of intergroup attitudes. In D. M. Mackie, & D. L. Hamilton (Eds), *Affect, Cognition and Stereotyping: Interactive Processes in Group Perception* (pp. 137–166). San Diego, CA: Academic Press.

Esses, V. M., Jackson, L. M., Dovidio, J. F., & Hodson, G. (2005). Instrumental relations among groups: Group competition, conflict, and prejudice. In J. F. Dovidio, P. Glick, & L. A. Rudman (Eds), *On the Nature of Prejudice: Fifty Years After Allport* (pp. 227–243). Malden, MA: Blackwell.

Esses, V. M., Semenya, A. H., Stelzl, M., Dovidio, J. F., & Hodson, G. (2006). Maximizing social psychological contributions to addressing social issues: The benefits of interdisciplinary perspectives. In P. A. M. van Lange (Ed.), *Bridging Social Psychology: Benefits of Transdisciplinary Approaches* (pp. 403–408). Mahwah, NJ: Erlbaum.

Fazio, R. H., Jackson, J. R., Dunton, B. C., & Williams, C. J. (1995). Variability in automatic activation as an unobtrusive measure of racial attitudes: A *bona fide* pipeline? *Journal of Personality and Social Psychology*, 69, 1013–1027.

Fazio, R. H., & Olson, M. A. (2003). Implicit measures in social cognition research: Their meaning and uses. *Annual Review of Psychology*, 54, 297–327.

Feagin, J. R. (2006). *Systemic Racism: A Theory of Oppression*. New York: Routledge.

Fein, S., & Spencer, S. J. (1997). Prejudice as self-image maintenance: Affirming the self through derogating others. *Journal of Personality and Social Psychology*, 73, 31–44.

Fiske, S. T. (1998). Stereotyping, prejudice, and discrimination. In D. T. Gilbert, S. T. Fiske, & G. Lindzey (Eds), *The Handbook of Social Psychology* (4th ed., Vol. 2, pp. 357–411). New York: McGraw-Hill.

Fiske, S. T., Cuddy, A. J. C., Glick, P., & Xu, J. (2002). A model of (often mixed) stereotype content: Competence and warmth respectively follow from perceived status and competition. *Journal of Personality and Social Psychology*, 82, 878–902.

Fiske, S. T., & Ruscher, J. B. (1993). Negative interdependence and prejudice: Whence the affect?, In D. M. Mackie, & D. L. Hamilton (Eds), *Affect, Cognition, and Stereotyping: Interactive Processes in Group Perception* (pp. 239–268). New York: Academic Press.

Fiske, S. T. & Taylor, S. E. (1984). *Social Cognition*. New York: Random House.

Ford, T. E., & Stangor, C. (1992). The role of diagnosticity in stereotype formation: Perceiving group means and variances. *Journal of Personality and Social Psychology*, 63, 356–367.

Gabriel, U., Banse, R., & Hug, T. (2007). Predicting public and private helping behaviour by implicit attitudes and motivation to control prejudiced reactions. *British Journal of Social Psychology*, 46, 365–382.

Gaertner, S. L., & Dovidio, J. F. (1986). The aversive form of racism. In J. F. Dovidio, & S. L. Gaertner (Eds), *Prejudice, Discrimination, and Racism* (pp. 61–89). Orlando, FL: Academic Press.

Gaertner, S. L. & Dovidio, J. F. (2000). *Reducing Intergroup Bias: The Common Ingroup Identity Model*. Philadelphia, PA: Psychology Press.

Gaertner, S. L., Dovidio, J. F., Banker, B. S., Rust, M. C., Nier, J. A., & Ward, C. M. (1997). Does pro-whiteness necessarily mean anti-blackness? In M. Fine, L. Powell, L. Weis, & M. Wong (Eds), *Off White* (pp.167–178). New York: Routledge.

Gilbert, G. M. (1951). Stereotype persistence and change among college students. *Journal of Abnormal and Social Psychology*, 46, 245–254.

Glick, P. (2005). Choice of scapegoats. In J. F. Dovidio, P. Glick, & L. A. Rudman (Eds), *On the Nature of Prejudice: Fifty Years After Allport* (pp. 244–261). Malden, MA: Blackwell.

Glick, P., & Fiske, S. T. (1996). The Ambivalent Sexism Inventory: Differentiating hostile and benevolent sexism. *Journal of Personality and Social Psychology*, 70, 491–512.

Goffman, E. (1963). *Stigma: Notes on the Management of Spoiled Identity*. Englewood Cliffs, NJ: Prentice-Hall.

Green, D. P., Glaser, J., & Rich, A. (1998). From lynching to gay bashing: The elusive connection between economic conditions and hate crime. *Journal of Personality and Social Psychology*, 75, 82–92.

Greenwald, A. G., & Banaji, M. (1995). Implicit social cognition: Attitudes, self-esteem, and stereotypes. *Psychological Review*, 102, 4–27.

Greenwald, A. G., McGhee, D., & Schwartz, J. (1998). Measuring individual differences in implicit cognition: The Implicit Association Test. *Journal of Personality and Social Psychology*, 74, 1464–1480.

Hagendoorn, L., & Nekuee, S. (Eds) (1999). *Education and Racism: A Cross-National Inventory of Positive Effects of Education on Ethnic Tolerance*. Aldershot, UK: Ashgate.

Hamilton, D. L. (1981). Stereotyping and intergroup behavior: Some thoughts on the cognitive approach. In D. L. Hamilton (Ed.), *Cognitive Processes in Stereotyping and Intergroup Behavior* (pp. 333–353). Hillsdale, NJ: Erlbaum.

Hamilton, D. L, & Trolier, T. K. (1986). Stereotypes and stereotyping: An overview of the cognitive approach. In J. F. Dovidio, & S.L. Gaertner (Eds), *Prejudice, Discrimination, and Racism* (pp. 127–163). New York: Academic Press.

Haslam, S. A., & Dovidio, J. F. (2010). Prejudice. In J. M. Levine, & M. A. Hogg, (Eds), *Encyclopedia of Group Processes and Intergroup Relations* (Vol. 2, pp. 655–660). Thousand Oaks, CA: Sage.

Hewstone, M. (1990). The "ultimate attribution error"? A review of the literature on intergroup attributions. *European Journal of Social Psychology*, 20, 311–335.

Hewstone, M., Rubin, M., & Willis, H. (2002). Intergroup bias, *Annual Review of Psychology*, 53, 575–604.

Hewstone, M., Tausch, N., Voci, A., Kenworthy, J., Hughes, J., & Cairns, E. (2008). Why neighbors kill: Prior intergroup contact and killing of ethnic outgroup neighbors. In V. M. Esses, & R. A. Vernon (Eds), *Explaining the Breakdown of Ethnic Relations: Why Neighbors Kill* (pp. 61–91). Malden, MA: Blackwell.

Hewstone, M., & Ward, C. (1985). Ethnocentrism and causal attribution in Southeast Asia. *Journal of Personality and Social Psychology*, 48, 614–623.

Hilton, J. L., & von Hippel, W. (1996). Stereotypes. *Annual Review of Psychology*, 47, 237–271.

Hoffman, C., & Hurst, N. (1990). Gender stereotypes: Perception or rationalization? *Journal of Personality and Social Psychology*, 58, 197–208.

Hogg, M. A., & Hains, S. C. (1996). Intergroup relations and group solidarity: Effects of group identification and social beliefs on depersonalized attraction. *Journal of Personality and Social Psychology*, 70, 295–309.

Hooghe, M., Reeskens, T., Stolle, D. & Trappers, A. (2009). Ethnic diversity and generalized trust in Europe: A cross-national multilevel study. *Comparative Political Studies*, 42, 198–223.

Hovland C. I., & Sears, R. R. (1940). Minor studies of aggression: VI. Correlation of lynchings with economic indices. *Journal of Psychology*, 9, 301–310.

Howard, J. M., Rothbart, M. (1980). Social categorization for in-group and out-group behavior. *Journal of Personality and Social Psychology*, 38, 301–310.

Hunsberger, B. & Jackson, L. M. (2005). Religion, meaning, and prejudice. *Journal of Social Issues*, 61, 807–826.

Insko, C. A., Schopler, J., Gaertner, L., Wildschut, T., Kozar, R., Pinter, B., et al. (2001). Interindividual-intergroup discontinuity reduction through the anticipation of future interaction. *Journal of Personality and Social Psychology*, 80, 95–111.

Institute of Medicine (2003). *Unequal treatment: Confronting racial and ethnic disparities in health care*. (B.D. Smedley, A.Y. Stith, & A.R. Nelson, Eds). Washington, DC: National Academies Press.

Johnson, J. D., & Lecci, L. (2003). Assessing anti-White attitudes and predicting perceived racism: The Johnson-Lecci scale. *Personality and Social Psychology Bulletin*, 29, 299–312.

Johnson, J. D., Trawalter, S., & Dovidio, J. F. (2000). Converging interracial consequences of violent rap music on stereotypical attributions of Blacks. *Journal of Experimental Social Psychology*, 36, 233–251.

Jones, J. M. (1972). *Prejudice and Racism*. Reading, MA: Addison-Wesley

Jost, J. T. & Banaji, M. R. (1994). The role of stereotyping in system-justification and the production of false consciousness. *British Journal of Social Psychology*, 33, 1–27.

Jost, J. T., Banaji, M., & Nosek, B. A. (2004). A decade of System Justification Theory: Accumulated evidence of conscious and unconscious bolstering of the *status quo*. *Political Psychology*, 25, 881–919.

Jost, J. T., Glaser, J., Kruglanski, A. W., & Sulloway, F. (2003). Political conservatism as motivated social cognition. *Psychological Bulletin*, 129, 339–375.

Judd, C. M., & Park, B. (1993). Definition and assessment of accuracy in social stereotypes. *Psychological Review*, 100, 109–128.

Kanter, R. M. (1977a). Some effects of proportions on group life: Skewed sex ratios and responses to token women. *American Journal of Sociology*, 82, 965–990.

Kanter, R. M. (1977b). *Men and Women of the Corporation*. New York: Basic Books.

Karpinski, A., & Hilton, J. L. (2001). Attitudes and the Implicit Association Test. *Journal of Personality and Social Psychology*, 81, 774–788.

Katz, D., & Braly, K. W. (1933). Racial stereotypes of 100 college students. *Journal of Abnormal and Social Psychology*, 28, 280–290.

Katz, I. (1981). *Stigma: A Social-Psychological Perspective*. Hillsdale, NJ: Erlbaum.

Katz, I., Wackenhut, J., & Hass, R. G. (1986). Racial ambivalence, value duality, and behavior. In J. F. Dovidio, S. L. Gaertner (Eds), *Prejudice, Discrimination, and Racism* (pp. 35–59). Orlando, FL: Academic Press.

Kawakami, K., Dovidio, J. F., & van Kamp, S. (2007). The impact of counterstereotypic training and related correction processes on the application of stereotypes. *Group Processes and Intergroup Relations*, 10, 141–158.

Kovel, J. (1970). *White Racism: A Psychohistory*. New York: Pantheon.

Lancee, B., & Dronkers, J. (2008, May). *Ethnic diversity in neighbourhoods and individual trust of immigrants and natives: A replication of Putnam (2007) in a West European country*. Paper presented at the International conference on theoretical perspectives on social cohesion and social capital, Royal Flemish Academy of Belgium for Science and the Arts. Brussels, Belgium.

Levin, S., van Laar, C., & Sidanius, J. (2003). The effects of ingroup and outgroup friendships on ethnic attitudes in college: A longitudinal study. *Group Processes and Intergroup Relations*, 6, 76–92.

Lippmann, W. (1922). *Public Opinion*. New York: Harcourt, Brace.

Lord, C. G., & Saenz, D. S. (1985). Memory deficits and memory surfeits: Differential cognitive consequences of tokenism for tokens and observers. *Journal of Personality and Social Psychology*, 49, 918–926.

Mackie, D. M., Devos, T., & Smith, E. R. (2000). Intergroup emotions: Explaining offensive action tendencies in an intergroup context. *Journal of Personality and Social Psychology*, 79, 602–616.

Mackie, D. M., & Smith, E. R. (1998). Intergroup relations: Insights from a theoretically integrative approach. *Psychological Review*, 105, 499–529.

McConahay, J. B. (1986). Modern racism, ambivalence, and the modern racism scale. In J. F. Dovidio, & S. L. Gaertner (Eds), *Prejudice, Discrimination, and Racism* (pp. 91–125). Orlando, FL: Academic Press.

Miller, C. T., & Myers, A. M. (1998). Compensating for prejudice: How heavyweight people (and others) control outcomes despite prejudice. In J. K. Swim, & C. Stangor (Eds), *Prejudice: The Target's Perspective*. San Diego, CA: Academic Press.

Miller, N. (2002). Personalization and the promise of Contact Theory. *Journal of Social Issues*, 58, 387–410.

Monteith, M. J., & Spicer, C. V. (2000). Contents and correlates of Whites' and Blacks' racial attitudes. *Journal of Experimental Social Psychology*, 36, 125–154.

Mummendey, A., & Otten, S. (2001). Aversive discrimination. In R Brown, & S. L. Gaertner (Eds), *Blackwell Handbook of Social Psychology: Intergroup Processes* (pp. 112–132). Malden, MA: Blackwell.

Nickerson, A. M., & Louis, W. R. (2008). Nationality versus humanity? Personality, identity, and norms in relation to attitudes toward asylum seekers. *Journal of Applied Social Psychology*, 38, 796–817.

Oakes, P. J., & Turner, J. C. (1990). Is limited information processing the cause of social stereotyping? In W. Stroebe, & M. Hewstone (Eds). *European Review of Social Psychology* (Vol. 1, pp. 111–125). Chichester, UK: Wiley.

Onorato, R. S., & Turner, J. C. (2001). The "I," "me," and the "us": The psychological group and self-concept maintenance and change. In C. Sedikides, & M. B. Brewer (Eds). *Individual Self, Relational Self, Collective Self* (pp. 147–170). Philadelphia, PA: Psychology Press.

Otten, S., & Moskowitz, G. B. (2000). Evidence for implicit evaluative in-group bias: Affect-based spontaneous trait inference in a minimal group paradigm. *Journal of Experimental Social Psychology*, 36, 77–89.

Otten, S., & Mummendey, A. (2000). Valence-dependent probability of ingroup-favoritism between minimal groups: An integrative view on the positive-negative asymmetry in social discrimination. In D. Capozza, & R. Brown (Eds). *Social Identity Processes* (pp. 33–48). London: Sage.

Paolini, S., Hewstone, M., Cairns, E., & Voci, A. (2004). Effects of direct and indirect cross-group friendships on judgments of Catholics and Protestants in Northern Ireland: The mediating role of an anxiety-reduction mechanism. *Personality and Social Psychology Bulletin*, 30, 770–786.

Park, B., & Rothbart, M. (1982). Perception of out-group homogeneity and levels of social categorization:

Memory for the subordinate attributes of in-group and out-group members. *Journal of Personality and Social Psychology*, 42, 1051–1068.

Payne, B. K. (2001). Prejudice and perception: The role of automatic and controlled processes in misperceiving a weapon. *Journal of Personality and Social Psychology*, 81, 181–192.

Pearson, A. R., West, T. V., Dovidio, J. F., Powers, S. R., Buck, R., & Henning, R. (2008). The fragility of intergroup relations. *Psychological Science*, 19, 1272–1279.

Pettigrew, T. F. (1979). The ultimate attribution error: Extending Allport's cognitive analysis of prejudice. *Personality and Social Psychology Bulletin*, 5, 461–476.

Pettigrew, T. F. (1998). Intergroup Contact Theory. *Annual Review of Psychology*, 49, 65–85.

Pettigrew, T. F. (2006). The advantages of multi-level approaches. *Journal of Social Issues*, 62, 615–620.

Pettigrew, T. F. (2008). Future directions for intergroup contact theory and research. *International Journal of Intercultural Relations*, 32, 187–199.

Pettigrew, T. F., Tropp, L. (2006). A meta-analytic test of intergroup contact theory. *Journal of Personality and Social Psychology*, 90, 751–783.

Phelps, E. A., O'Connor, K. J., Cunningham, W. A., Funayama, E. S., Gatenby, J. C., Gore, J. C., et al. (2000). Performance on indirect measures of race evaluation predicts amygdala activation. *Journal of Cognitive Neuroscience*, 12, 729–738.

Putnam, R. D. (2007). *E Pluribus Unum*: Diversity and community in the twenty-first century: The 2006 Johan Skytte Prize Lecture. *Scandanavian Political Studies*, 30, 137–174.

Rudman, L. A. (2004). Sources of implicit attitudes. *Current Directions in Psychological Science*, 13, 80–83.

Schaller, M., Conway, L. G., III, & Tanchuk, T. (2002). Selective pressures on the once and future contents of ethnic stereotypes: Effects of the communicability of traits., *Journal of Personality and Social Psychology*, 82, 861–877.

Sears, D. O. (1988). Symbolic racism. In P. A. Katz, & D. A. Taylor (Eds), *Eliminating Racism: Profiles in Controversy* (pp. 53–84). New York: Plenum Press.

Sears, D. O., Henry, P. J., Kosterman, R. (2000). Egalitarian values and contemporary racial politics. In D. O. Sears, J. Sidanius, & L. Bobo (Eds), *Racialized Politics: The Debate about Racism in America* (pp. 75–117). Chicago, IL: University of Chicago Press.

Sekaquaptewa, D., & Thompson, M. (2003). Solo status, stereotype threat, and performance expectancies: Their effects on women's performance.

Journal of Experimental Social Psychology, 39, 68–74.

Shelton, J. N., Dovidio, J. F., Hebl, M., & Richeson, J. A. (2009). Prejudice and intergroup interaction. In S. Demoulin, J-P Leyens, & J. F. Dovidio (Eds). *Intergroup Misunderstandings: Impact of Divergent Social Realities* (pp. 21–38). New York: Psychology Press.

Shelton, J. N., & Richeson, J. A. (2005). Intergroup contact and pluralistic ignorance. *Journal of Personality and Social Psychology*, 88, 91–107.

Shelton, J. N., & Richeson, J. A. (2006). Interracial interactions: A relational approach. In M. P. Zanna (Ed.), *Advances in Experimental Social Psychology* (Vol. 38, pp. 121–181). New York: Academic Press.

Shelton, J. N., Richeson, J. A., Salvatore, J., & Trawalter, S. (2005). Ironic effects of racial bias during interracial interactions. *Psychological Science*, 16, 397–402.

Sherif, M. (1966). *Group Conflict and Cooperation: Their Social Psychology*. London: Routledge and Kegan Paul.

Sherif, M., Harvey, O. J., White, B. J., Hood, W. R., & Sherif, C. W. (1961). *Intergroup Conflict and Cooperation. The Robbers Cave Experiment*. Norman, OK: University of Oklahoma Book Exchange.

Sherif, M., & Sherif, C. W. (1969). *Social Psychology*. New York: Harper & Row.

Sidanius, J., & Pratto, F. (1999). *Social Dominance: An Intergroup Theory of Social Hierarchy and Oppression*. New York: Cambridge University Press.

Smith, E. R. (1993). Social identity and social emotions: Toward new conceptualizations of prejudice. In D. M. Mackie, & D. L. Hamilton (Eds), *Affect, Cognition, and Stereotyping: Interactive Processes in Group Perception* (pp. 297–315). San Diego: Academic Press.

Spears, R. (2001). The interaction between the individual and the collective self: Self-categorization in context. In C. Sedikides, & M. B. Brewer (Eds), *Individual Self, Relational Self, Collective Self* (pp. 171–198). Philadelphia, PA: Psychology Press.

Steele, C. M. (1997). A threat in the air: How stereotypes shape intellectual identity and performance. *American Psychologist*, 52, 613–629.

Stephan, W., & Stephan, C. W. (1985). Intergroup anxiety. *Journal of Social Issues*, 41, 157–175.

Stephan, W. G., & Stephan C. W. (2000). An integrated threat theory of prejudice. In S. Oskamp (Ed.), *Reducing Prejudice and Discrimination* (pp. 23–45). Hillsdale, NJ: Erlbaum.

Stolle, D., Soroka, S., & Johnston, R. (2008). When does diversity erode trust? *Political Studies*, 56, 57–75.

Sumner, W. G. (1906). *Folkways*. Boston, MA: Ginn.

Tajfel, H. (1969). Cognitive aspects of prejudice. *Journal of Social Issues*, 25 (4), 79–97.

Tajfel, H. (1970). Experiments in intergroup discrimination. *Scientific American*, 223, 96–102.

Tajfel, H., & Turner, J. C. (1979). An integrative theory of intergroup conflict. In W. G. Austin, & S. Worchel (Eds), *The Social Psychology of Intergroup Relations* (pp. 33–48). Monterey, CA: Brooks/Cole.

Turner, J. C. (1985). Social categorization and the self-concept: A social cognitive theory of group behavior. In E. J. Lawler (Ed.), *Advances in Group Processes* (Vol. 2, pp. 77–122). Greenwich, CT: JAI Press.

Turner, J. C., Hogg, M. A., Oakes, P. J., Reicher, S. D., & Wetherell, M. S. (1987). *Rediscovering the Social Group: A Self-Categorization Theory*. Oxford, U.K.: Basil Blackwell.

Verkuyten, M., & Hagendoorn, L. (1998). Prejudice and self-categorization: The variable role of authoritarianism and in-group stereotypes. *Personality and Social Psychology Bulletin*, 24, 99–110.

Vidmar, N. (2003). When all of us are victims: Juror prejudice and "terrorist" trials. *Chicago-Kent Law Review*, 78, 1143.

von Baeyer, C. L., Sherk, D.L., & Zanna, M. P. (1981). Impression management in the job interview: When the female applicant meets the male (chauvinist) interviewer, *Personality and Social Psychology Bulletin*, 7, 45–51.

Wagner, U., & Zick, A. (1995). Formal education and ethnic prejudice, *European Journal of Social Psychology*, 25, 41–56.

Wilder, D. A. (1981). Perceiving persons as a group: Categorization and intergroup relations. In D. L. Hamilton (Ed.), *Cognitive Processes in Stereotyping and Intergroup Behavior* (pp. 213–257). Hillsdale, NJ: Erlbaum.

Wilder, D. A. (1986). Social categorization: Implications for creation and reduction of intergroup bias. In L. Berkowitz (Ed.), *Advances in Experimental Social Psychology* (Vol. 19, pp. 291–355). Orlando, FL: Academic Press.

Williams, R. M., Jr. (1947). *The Reduction of Intergroup Tensions*. New York: Social Science Research Council.

Wilson, T. D., Lindsey, S., & Schooler, T. Y. (2000). A model of dual attitudes. *Psychological Review*, 107, 101–126.

Worchel, S., Rothgerber, H., Day, E. A., Hart, D., & Butemeyer, J. (1998). Social identity and individual productivity within groups. *British Journal of Social Psychology*, 37, 389–413.

Zick, A., Pettigrew, T. F., & Wagner, U. (2008). Ethnic prejudice and discrimination in Europe. *Journal of Social Issues*, 64, 233–251.

2

Historical Overview

John Duckitt

ABSTRACT

The concepts of prejudice, stereotyping, and discrimination emerged early in the twentieth century and soon became central social issues of the times. Over the next century the way in which these concepts were explained theoretically, the dominant research approaches, and their implications for social policy, underwent systematic historical changes. These can be seen as successive paradigms organizing understanding and inquiry. It is suggested that these paradigmatic transitions did not just represent a systematic evolution of knowledge, but were responses to specific social and historical circumstances. These circumstances made particular questions about the nature and causation of prejudice salient for social scientists, and the paradigms that emerged in response constituted their attempts to answer these questions. These salient questions therefore determined the kinds of theories formulated, issues researched, and the social policies proposed to reduce prejudice. This analysis illustrates how changes in the zeitgeist may constrain and determine social-scientific knowledge.

HISTORICAL OVERVIEW

In historical terms, the social scientific study of prejudice and discrimination began only recently. Both prejudice and discrimination can be seen as uniquely twentieth-century concepts, becoming prominent in the social sciences only in the 1920s. Prior to this, prejudice was typically viewed not as a social problem or a scientific construct; instead negative intergroup attitudes were generally seen as natural and inevitable responses to group differences. After prejudice was 'discovered,' the way in which it was conceptualized seemed to undergo marked changes during the twentieth century. It is suggested that each conceptualization of prejudice derived logically from a particular way of explaining prejudice, which in turn implied particular social policies, forming distinct paradigms of prejudice that dominated different historical periods (Duckitt, 1992).

Why did these shifts occur? One possibility is that they reflected the development of knowledge – the progressive replacement of approaches shown to be inadequate by better theories. Sometimes this does seem to have been the case, but only partially so. For example, the theory of the authoritarian personality, which dominated the 1950s, did have important methodological problems (Altemeyer, 1981), and could not easily explain prejudice at the group or societal level, while the socio-cultural approach, which succeeded it in the 1960s and 1970s could explain group differences in prejudice.

The cognitive perspective, which followed, could account for intergroup bias, stereotyping, and competition in minimal group situations where socio-cultural or personality factors did not appear to be operating.

These shifts in emphasis, however, do not seem to be fully explained in terms of the evolution of knowledge. Typically older perspectives and theories were not refuted, or even shown to be seriously inadequate. Although displaced from the mainstream of psychological interest, they were not discarded, but often remain relevant in accounting for prejudice. It is suggested that instead of new perspectives and approaches replacing their predecessors, they seem to illuminate quite different issues and problems. What appears to happen, therefore, is fundamental shifts of interest away from certain issues concerning the causes of prejudice to new or different ones, which require different theories and perspectives.

Fairchild and Gurin (1978) have suggested that the topics psychologists chose for study reflected events that were of local or national importance at the time, but this seems too limited. Historical events and circumstances can have more profound effects on thinking about prejudice than merely shifting interest to new research topics. Important historical circumstances may make fundamentally new and different questions about the nature of prejudice salient, while obscuring others. This could generate a shift in the way prejudice is conceptualized and explained. New conceptual and explanatory paradigms would then powerfully influence the research issues investigated, and the kind of social policy interventions favored.

It is suggested that at least eight distinct periods in the way in which prejudice has been understood by psychologists may be identified. Each of these periods will be briefly discussed. It will be suggested that social circumstances and historical events, interacting with the evolution of knowledge, seem to have focused attention on different issues and questions in each period. Each question then tended to be associated with a particular image of prejudice, and so

generated a distinctive theoretical orientation and social policy emphasis that was widely held during that period (see Table 2.1).

UP TO THE 1920S: RACE PSYCHOLOGY

During the nineteenth century virtually all scientific thought in both America and Europe accepted the idea of race inferiority, and the concept of White racial prejudice was not an issue (Haller, 1971). White attitudes of superiority or antipathy to Blacks were accepted as inevitable and natural responses to the seemingly obvious 'inferiority' and 'backwardness' of Blacks and other colonial peoples.

There was an obvious connection between these attitudes and European colonialism and American slavery or segregation. As Fairchild and Gurin (1978) pointed out, the idea of the superiority of the White race was useful in justifying the subjugation of people of color. These historical circumstances generated an interest among scientists in delineating and explaining the inferiorities of 'backward' races. As a result 'race theories' dominated social scientific thinking about racial differences, and explained Black 'inferiority' in terms of evolutionary backwardness, limited intellectual capacity, and even excess sexual drive (Haller, 1971). With the development of intelligence testing early in the twentieth century, psychologists contributed prominently to research supporting these race theories. In 1925 an influential paper by Thomas Garth in the *Psychological Bulletin* reviewed 73 studies on the issue of race and intelligence, which he concluded seemed to indicate the mental superiority of the White race. These attitudes had their logical social policy expressions in segregation, exclusion, and institutionalized discrimination against these 'backward' peoples.

THE 1920S: RACE PREJUDICE

Samelson (1978) has pointed out that during the 1920s the manner in which psychology defined the 'race problem' changed

Table 2.1 Historical shifts in dominant theoretical and social policy approaches to prejudice

Social and historical context and issues	Concept of prejudice and dominant theoretical approach	Dominant social policy orientation to prejudice and discrimination
Up to the 1920s: White domination and colonial rule of "backward peoples"	Prejudice as a natural response to the deficiencies of "backward" peoples: Race theories	Domination, discrimination, and segregation are natural and justified social policies
The 1920s: The legitimacy of White domination challenged	Prejudice as irrational and unjustified: Measuring and describing prejudice	Prejudice will fade as the social sciences clarify how wrong and unjustified it is
The 1930s and 1940s: The ubiquity and tenacity of White racism	Prejudice as an unconscious defence: Psychoanalytic and frustration theories	Gradual acceptance as minorities and colonial peoples become assimilated
The 1950s: Nazi racial ideology and the holocaust	Prejudice rooted in anti-democratic ideology and authoritarian personalities	Democracy and liberal values will erode intolerance and prejudice
The 1960s: The problem of institutionalised racism in the American South	Sociocultural explanations: Racism rooted in social norms of discriminatory social structures	Desegregation and anti-discriminatory laws will erode and eliminate racism and prejudice
The 1970s: The problem of informal racism and discrimination in the North	Prejudice as an expression of dominant group interests in maintaining intergroup inequality	Reducing intergroup inequality through affirmative action and minority empowerment
The 1980s and 1990s: The stubborn persistence of stereotyping, prejudice, and discrimination	Prejudice as an expression of universal cognitive processes: Social categorization and identity	Multicultural policies to provide minorities with esteem, positive identities, and foster tolerance
Post 2000: Confronting a complex world of multiple based and often irrationally intense intergroup hostilities	Prejudice as complex, affective, and motivationally driven?	Broader approaches with strategies flexibly adapted to varying patterns of prejudice and situational dynamics?

completely: 'In 1920 most psychologists believed in the existence of mental differences between races; by 1940 they were searching for the sources of "irrational prejudice". In a few decades, a dramatic reversal of the dominant paradigm for the study of groups and group relations had occurred' (p. 265). It is tempting to see this as an example of the progress of empirical science: the triumph of objective data over prejudices, misconceptions, and speculation. However, this seems to be a myth. Writing many decades later in 1978, Samelson noted the then current controversy over the heritability of intelligence between respected psychologists at Harvard, Berkeley, and Princeton, a debate even more recently reignited by the book, *The Bell Curve* (Hernstein & Murray, 1994).

This change in the 1920s seems more feasibly interpreted as a response to two important historical developments after the First World War (Milner, 1975). These were the emergence of a Black civil rights movement in the United States and movements challenging White European domination of colonial peoples, both of which gained sympathy among intellectuals and social scientists. Samelson (1978) mentions several other possible factors in the United States. The restriction of immigration in the early 1920s may have shifted attention from justifying the exclusion of certain peoples to conflict resolution within the country. The period was also characterized by an influx of 'ethnics', particularly Jewish people, into the profession of psychology, a leftward shift among psychologists during the Depression, and finally, a desire to unite the country against an enemy proclaiming racial superiority.

Overall, these historical developments influenced a rapid shift among social scientists away from beliefs of White racial superiority and the inferiority of other races. This, however, raised a crucial question. If other races were not inferior, how could their deprivations and stigmatization be explained? According to Milner (1975), Floyd Allport in 1924 was the first social psychologist to explicitly pose this issue with the statement: 'The discrepancy in mental ability is not great enough to account for the problem, which centers around the American Negro or to explain fully *the ostracism* to which he is subjected' (p. 21; italics in the original).

In order to answer this question, psychologists shifted their attention to White racial attitudes. With the belief in racial equality came the idea that negative White racial attitudes were unjustified and unfair. This resulted in the emergence of the concept of prejudice as a basically unjustified, irrational, or, in some way faulty, negative intergroup attitude.

Initially research focused on measuring racial prejudice and delineating its extent. Bogardus published his research on the social distance scale in 1925, and in the next decade literally hundreds of studies were reported describing social distance patterns. Katz and Braly's (1933) stereotype checklist had a similar impact, followed by the use of Thurstone and later Likert scaling to measure interracial attitudes. The major social policy implication of the 'discovery' of prejudice as a profoundly irrational, and unjust group attitude held by Whites seems to have been the optimistic assumption that as social scientists identified and documented the problem, knowledge and rationality would gradually banish the injustice of prejudice.

The identification, measurement, and description of the extent of racial prejudice, however, raised a new question – that of how prejudice was to be explained. During the 1930s social scientists began to turn their attention to this issue.

THE 1930S AND 1940S: PSYCHODYNAMIC PROCESSES

Research soon revealed that White racism was both widespread and highly resistant to change, and that merely identifying the problem would not banish it. This raised an important question. If racism was a fundamentally irrational and unjustified response, how could its pervasiveness and tenacity be explained? Psychodynamic theory seemed to answer this question neatly in terms of the operation of universal psychological processes such as defense mechanisms. These processes operated unconsciously, channeling tensions arising either within the personality or from environmental frustrations and threats into prejudice against minorities. The universality of these processes accounted for the ubiquity of prejudice, and their unconscious defensive function for its irrationality and rigidity.

A variety of psychodynamic processes were implicated, such as projection, scapegoating, repressed frustration, and displaced hostility. These processes were elegantly integrated into a coherent explanation of prejudice in terms of displaced aggression, originating from chronic social frustrations, which was directed against minorities as scapegoats (Dollard, Doob, Miller, et al., 1939). This seemed able to explain the ubiquity of White racism in the United States, as well as the rise of Nazism and virulent anti-Semitism in Germany at the time.

These explanations had important social policy implications. Because psychodynamic processes such as displacement and scapegoating were inherently human, they could not be changed easily. However, they would only be directed against outgroups seen as different – culturally, ethnically, and socioeconomically. Thus, as culturally different and disadvantaged minorities became more similar to the majority, prejudice and discrimination against them would gradually disappear. The dominant social policy approach of this era was therefore that of assimilation or the 'melting pot'.

This paradigm stimulated research using a variety of strategies. A number of experimental studies during the late 1940s and early 1950s (e.g., Miller & Bugelski, 1948) did seem to support the idea that frustrations could be displaced in the form of prejudice. However, around 1950 attention shifted to a new and different approach to explaining prejudice.

THE 1950S: THE PREJUDICED PERSONALITY

The new paradigm for explaining prejudice that arose after the Second World War and towards the end of the 1940s was initially still psychodynamically based. However, there was a crucial difference. Instead of explaining prejudice in terms of universal intrapsychic processes, the new paradigm viewed prejudice in terms of particular personality structures that conditioned the adoption of right-wing political ideologies and prejudiced attitudes. The shock and revulsion inspired by the holocaust played a major role in precipitating this shift. As Milner (1981) points out: 'the very obscenity of the holocaust connoted a kind of mass pathology, a collective madness. Explanations were therefore sought in the disturbed personality, for it was hardly conceivable that these could be the actions of normal men' (p. 106).

Prejudice was therefore seen as the expression of an inner need that was characteristic of a particular kind of disturbed personality. This meshed with the well-established finding that prejudice was a generalized characteristic of individuals (Allport, 1954). Thus, persons who were anti-Semitic would be more likely to be anti-Black or, for that matter, less favorable towards any minority or outgroup. Consequently, the crucial social scientific question became that of identifying and describing the personality structures and characteristics making individuals likely to adopt authoritarian ideologies and prone to prejudice and ethnocentrism.

The most influential answer to this question was the theory of the authoritarian personality (Adorno, Frenkel-Brunswick, Levinson, et al., 1950). This described a personality dimension determining the degree to which individuals would be prone to adopt right-wing ideologies and prejudiced attitudes. Such personalities were formed by harsh, punitive parenting within authoritarian families, which were in turn reinforced by repressive, authoritarian socio-political milieus and ideologies. This theory was partly formulated in psychodynamic terms, but other approaches to the same issue were not, such as Rokeach's dogmatism (Rokeach, Smith, & Evans, 1960).

The dominant paradigm during this period was therefore not psychodynamic *per se*, but an individual differences orientation to the explanation of prejudice. Fairchild and Gurin (1978) have argued that this individual difference perspective was well suited to the spirit of postwar America. The war had been won. The national mood was one of optimism, commitment to superordinate goals, and faith in democracy. Consequently, they suggested, there tended to be little inclination to question the social system or look to institutional explanations of prejudice and discrimination.

The social policy implications of the approach were optimistic. If authoritarian personalities were produced by punitive, repressive authoritarian families and societies, then the spread of political democracy and liberal values would gradually but systematically eliminate the social and familial structures producing such personalities. Thus, social progress would result in the defeat of authoritarianism in all its forms and its replacement by liberal and democratic values and government. This would be associated with the progressive growth of political and racial tolerance. During the 1960s, however, the critical question about prejudice confronting social scientists in America changed, and produced a very different approach to prejudice.

THE 1960S AND 1970S: CULTURE AND SOCIETY

At the end of the 1950s the emphasis in explaining prejudice moved away from individual psychological factors to social and cultural influences (Ashmore & DelBoca, 1981). This socio-cultural perspective seems to have been dominant during the 1960s and 1970s and, in the latter decade particularly, tended to be associated with a decline of interest in specifically psychological explanations of prejudice in favor of more sociological ones. It has been suggested that two distinct phases can be distinguished within this period (e.g., Ashmore & DelBoca, 1981). These seem to represent different responses to the distinctive historical contexts and explanatory problems of American race relations, first in the 1960s, when the emphasis was on normative influence, and then in the 1970s, when the emphasis shifted to intergroup conflicts of interest. Ashmore and DelBoca (1981) have described these as consensus and conflict versions of the socio-cultural perspective on prejudice.

The shift away from an individual differences paradigm could be attributed to the inability of this approach to account for the high levels of prejudice in social settings such as the American South or South Africa, as Pettigrew's (1958, 1959) research so clearly demonstrated. However, prior research had also revealed these limitations, if not quite as clearly, before this shift in perspective occurred (e.g., Minard, 1952; Prothro, 1952). The historical circumstance that may have been instrumental in precipitating the shift in perspective seems likely to have been that the civil rights campaign in the American South, which exploded into public awareness in the late 1950s making salient the social problem of institutionalized racism and segregation there (Blackwell, 1982).

Prejudice in the American South could not be plausibly explained as an expression of underlying pathology or in terms of individual difference constructs. Pettigrew's (1958) classic research confirmed this by showing that the high levels of racial prejudice in South Africa and the American South were not due to persons from these societies being higher in authoritarianism. It seemed that in such settings an entire society was racist, and so was the 'good citizen' (Ashmore & DelBoca, 1981: 23). This focused attention on the normative character of prejudice in highly prejudiced societies specifically, and also by extension, in all settings where prejudice was socially widespread.

The dominant image of prejudice was therefore that of a norm embedded in the social environment, which suggested that prejudice might be substantially explained in terms of socialization in, and conformity to, traditional norms and institutionalized patterns of interracial behavior and segregation (e.g., Proshansky, 1966; Westie, 1964). This normative approach to prejudice tended to suggest a basically optimistic view of the future of race relations. There tended to be a widespread assumption that the 'problem' South could become like the 'liberal' North by legally abolishing segregation, discrimination, and institutionalized barriers to contact, and desegregating schools and workplaces and that these measures in themselves would be sufficient to erode and ultimately eliminate racism. Fairchild and Gurin (1978) have characterized this point of view as a 'consensus model' of race relations, which took racial integration as its primary goal and largely ignored issues of conflict, power, inequality and dominance relations.

They suggest that this perspective was widely held until the mid-1960s. At that time these optimistic assumptions became increasingly untenable with the urban revolts of the mid-to-late 1960s and the hardening of resistance to the civil rights movement as its targets changed from integration in public accommodations to voting rights, jobs, and income inequalities (Fairchild & Gurin, 1978). Bowser (1985) argues also that it then became increasingly evident that the problem of race relations in the United States was not just one of Southern prejudice and institutionally entrenched segregation. The informal and more covert pattern of racial segregation and dominance of the industrial and urban North was left virtually untouched by the civil rights movement and the 1964 Civil Rights Bill and began to gradually replace the overt and internationally embarrassing caste system in the South.

Racism and discrimination, it seemed, were far more deeply rooted in American society. Socially shared and normative patterns of prejudice and discrimination could no longer be viewed as just cultural and institutional traditions characteristic of the South. As the institutionalized segregation and old-fashioned racism of the South disappeared, it seemed to be replaced by informal discrimination and segregation, and the subtle 'modern' racism of the North. The paradigm that emerged saw racism and discrimination as being rooted in the power relations between Whites and Blacks in American society as a whole. The question that therefore became particularly salient during the 1970s – the second phase of this period of socio-cultural emphasis – was that of identifying and explaining the intergroup conflicts of interest and structural power relations that maintained racism and discrimination in America.

Answers to this question were proposed in terms of factors such as internal colonialism (Blauner, 1972), a split labor market (Bonacich, 1972), institutionalized racism (Carmichael & Hamilton, 1967), and the socio-economic advantages for Whites of maintaining a stable Black underclass (Thurow, 1969). The new paradigm of the 1970s therefore viewed racial prejudice as expressing the interests of the dominant White group, which were served by the maintenance of racial inequality and keeping Blacks as a disadvantaged, powerless, and impoverished underclass. White American racism was seen as a direct expression of elite group self-interest and the desire to maintain historic privilege (Bowser, 1985).

With this shift in the dominant understanding of racial prejudice in America came a shift in the social policies favored to reduce prejudice. To eliminate racism, the social, economic, and political inequalities between Blacks and Whites would have to be changed, most notably through affirmative action and the political empowerment of Blacks in American society (Crosby, 2004). For a time affirmative action policies were implemented, and although they led to undeniable advances in Black empowerment and the growth of a Black middle class, they were largely abandoned by the conservative administrations of the 1990s. By this time, however, a new shift had occurred in the way in which prejudice was conceptualised and explained that led to an emphasis on new and somewhat different policies to reduce prejudice.

THE 1980S AND 1990S: THE COGNITIVE APPROACH

During the 1970s and 1980s important research findings suggested that the persistence and pervasiveness of prejudice might not just be due to group interests, power relations, and social structure, but involved other, perhaps more fundamental psychological processes. Research in the United States suggested that racism had not declined, but merely changed its form. These findings indicated that despite survey evidence of sharp declines in Whites' racial prejudice from about 1960, discriminatory behavior and racial inequality had not decreased correspondingly (Crosby, Bromley, & Saxe, 1980), and many ostensibly nonprejudiced Whites opposed policies to reduce these inequalities (Huddy & Sears, 1995). Research also indicated that Whites' overtly friendly behavior to Blacks or apparently nonprejudiced questionnaire responses could be accompanied by covert negative affect revealed by subtle indicators such as voice tone and seating distance, or detected using the bogus pipeline technique (Fazio & Olson, 2003). Overall, these findings suggested that the traditional or old-fashioned American racism characterized by beliefs in Black biological inferiority, White supremacy, and support for segregationist and discriminatory practices had merely been supplanted by a new, more subtle, and socially acceptable form of racism.

There have been several different conceptualizations of this new racism, such as symbolic or modern racism (McConahay & Hough, 1976), racial resentment (Kinder & Sanders, 1996), and subtle prejudice (Pettigrew & Meertens, 1995). Similar perspectives have emphasized ambivalence in White American racial attitudes (Katz & Hass, 1988), and the concept of aversive racism, which suggests that most Whites hold superficially egalitarian beliefs and a nonprejudiced self-image at a conscious level together with underlying covert negative feelings to Blacks (Dovidio & Gaertner, 2004; Gaertner & Dovidio, 1986).

These findings have also led to research distinguishing explicit and implicit stereotyping and prejudice (Greenwald & Banaji, 1995). Explicit measures of prejudice and stereotyping, such as measures of modern or symbolic racism, operate at a conscious level, while implicit measures are assumed to operate in an unconscious and automatic fashion. A variety of implicit measures have been used with the most common being measures of response latency for the activation of positive or negative stereotypes following category priming and variations of that procedure, such as the Implicit Association Test (Greenwald, McGhee, & Schwartz, 1998).

While these implicit measures have tended to be only weakly associated with measures of explicit racism, there is evidence that they are more strongly related to people's spontaneous and automatic responses to Blacks than are explicit prejudice measures Blacks (Dovidio, Brigham, Johnson, et al., 1996). Whites have also shown markedly greater negativity to Blacks on implicit measures than they do on explicit measures (Fazio & Olson, 2003). In general, therefore, findings using measures of implicit racism supported the conclusion from research using subtle measures of explicit prejudice that White American racism remained a major social problem.

At the same time that research was establishing that racism, albeit in newer and more subtle forms, was still pervasive in American society, important findings also emerged from research in Europe using minimal groups. In this research, individuals were divided into groups on an essentially arbitrary basis with no contact or interaction between groups and no conflict of interest or realistic basis for antagonism. Yet the members of these minimal groups still showed bias, discrimination, and a competitive orientation in favor of the ingroup against the outgroup. These findings seemed to have fundamental implications, suggesting that the mere perception of belonging to two distinct groups, that is, social categorization *per se*,

seemed to be sufficient to trigger intergroup discrimination favoring the ingroup (Tajfel & Turner, 1979).

Intergroup bias and discrimination were therefore seen as inevitable outcomes of a normal, natural, and universal cognitive process that functioned to simplify the complexity of the social world (Hamilton, 1981a). This seemed to explain why prejudice and discrimination were such ubiquitous, intractable, and almost universal social phenomena. It provided a new, powerful, and distinctively psychological perspective for understanding important social problems, such as the persistence of racism in America and an upsurge of neo-fascism, anti-Semitism, and anti-immigrant sentiment in Western Europe in the 1970s.

Two broad approaches to the issue of how basic cognitive processes, such as categorization, influence prejudice and discrimination could be distinguished: a pure cognitive approach, and a cognitive-motivational approach. The pure cognitive approach focused on the concept of stereotype as a cognitive structure directly determined by categorization that organizes and represents information about social categories. This social-cognitive perspective generated a great deal of experimental research, much of which has investigated the role of cognitive structures, such as stereotypes, in biasing information processing and social behavior, particularly discriminatory behavior (e.g., Hamilton, 1981a). It was widely accepted that much of prejudice and discrimination can be accounted for in such terms.

The second cognitive-motivational approach also assumed that cognitive factors were primary, but viewed social categorization as triggering a basic motivational process to evaluate one's ingroup positively relative to outgroups (Tajfel & Turner, 1979). The research emerging from this cognitive-motivational approach has also been predominantly experimental, and has mostly focused on testing predictions from social identity theory (SIT) concerning effects on ingroup bias, favoritism, and discrimination in either minimal or real intergroup situations

(Brown, 2000; Hewstone, Rubin, & Willis, 2002). The social-cognitive and cognitive-motivational perspectives were the dominant psychological approaches to explaining and understanding prejudice and intergroup relations during the last two decades of the twentieth century.

This new paradigm seemed to have important implications for reducing prejudice. Previously, policies to reduce prejudice had often been interpreted or implemented in ways consistent with the assimilationist assumptions that reducing the salience of group and racial differences and making society colorblind would reduce and ultimately eliminate racism and prejudice. The new cognitive paradigm helped to show that assimilationist and colorblind policies would disadvantage minorities by reinforcing an intolerant attitude to cultural and group differences and so maintain covert prejudice and discrimination against them (e.g., Schofield, 1986). It also emphasized the inevitability of group differentiation and the importance, particularly for minorities, of maintaining positively valued and differentiated group identities (Brown & Hewstone, 2005; Hewstone & Brown, 1986). During the 1980s and 1990s multiculturalism, therefore, became the dominant approach to prejudice reduction espoused by social scientists.

During the past decade, however, significant limitations of the social-cognitive and cognitive-motivational approaches to understanding prejudice have become apparent, suggesting that a new paradigm shift may be underway. Most of these limitations have not emerged recently but had been apparent right from the very beginning of the cognitive paradigm, supporting the view that these paradigm shifts have been driven primarily by changes in social zeitgeist rather than by theoretical or empirical considerations. For example, a major limitation of the cognitive perspective has been its neglect of motivational and affective factors, or in the case of the cognitive-motivational perspective, its relegation of affective and motivational factors to a secondary role (Mackie & Hamilton, 1993; Smith & Mackie,

2005). Yet, this concern was not new. Two and a half decades ago, Hamilton (1981b) had concluded an influential edited volume on the cognitive approach by acknowledging that 'if there is any domain of human interaction that history tells us is laden with strong, even passionate, feelings, it is in the area of intergroup relations' (p. 347). He, therefore, concluded that the cognitive approach, despite the advances that it had made, was by itself incomplete.

A second limitation of the cognitive perspective, and in particular of the cognitive-motivational approach, is that it was never clear that the kind of bias and favoritism observed in minimal intergroup situations was the same as the intergroup prejudice and hostility observed in natural social contexts. Most research evidence indicates that the bias in minimal intergroup situations reflects ingroup favoritism rather than outgroup derogation (Brewer, 1999; Brown, 2000). These findings suggest that this ingroup bias may be only a precursor that is elaborated into prejudice under particular social conditions. Again, this limitation was not recent; it was cogently noted by Brewer (1979) in her early and influential review of minimal intergroup research and the social identity approach.

The cognitive approach has also not fared well in empirical research on prejudice. Park and Judd (2005) reviewed 40 years of research and concluded that social categorization has little influence on intergroup animosity. Research on cognitive-motivational approaches, such as SIT, has also not fared well. The core propositions of this approach concerning the role of self-esteem maintenance and enhancement as the underlying motivation generating intergroup bias, or that group identification should be a powerful predictor of intergroup prejudice, have not been supported (Aberson, Healy, & Romero, 2000; Brown, 2000; Rubin & Hewstone, 1998). Findings relating group identification to prejudice have at best suggested that only specific kinds of group identification might interact with more fundamental causal variables, such as intergroup threat, to cause prejudice under certain conditions (see Brown, 2000;

Duckitt, Callaghan, & Wagner, 2005; Gibson, 2006; Mummendey, Klink, & Brown, 2001). Research testing the core prediction from SIT that low intergroup distinctiveness would be a primary driver of the degree to which a group would differentiate itself from relevant comparison groups has found no such effect overall, and only a very weak, effectively trivial effect ($r = 0.04$) for highly identified members of such groups (Jetten, Spears, & Postmes, 2004).

Finally, and most tellingly, when research on prejudice in naturalistic social conditions has compared the predictive power of predictions from SIT against predictions from Realistic Conflict Theory (RCT), the latter have invariably shown greater explanatory power than the former (e.g., Brown, 2000; Gibson, 2006; Shamir & Sagiv-Schiffer, 2006). Once again, this was not a new finding. Research reported as early as 1978 by van Knippenberg had demonstrated this, so that Tajfel and Turner (1979), in one of their first systematic expositions of SIT, were compelled to acknowledge that SIT was not intended to replace RCT, but only to supplement it.

While inconclusive, weak, and inconsistent research findings were accumulating about the link between cognitive and cognitive-motivational processes and prejudice, concerns were also beginning to be voiced about the effectiveness of multiculturalism as a social policy to reduce prejudice. It has been noted that the way in which multicultural policies have been implemented might create or reinforce barriers to contact that would impede the development of more positive intergroup attitudes (e.g., Brewer, 1999). These concerns have been strengthened by new research showing how potent interpersonal contact and friendship across group boundaries under decategorized conditions can be in reducing prejudice (Pettigrew & Tropp, 2006; see also, Gaertner & Dovidio, 2000).

To sum up, it became apparent during the 1970s that despite dramatic social changes and new norms against prejudice, racism persisted, though in a more subtle, symbolic, or even implicit forms. It seemed that the intractability and persistence of racism in America might involve more fundamental factors than social structure and group interests. Thus, explanations for prejudice were formulated in terms of basic, universal, and essentially normal cognitive processes, such as social categorization and group identification. After several decades, however, serious doubts have emerged about the capacity of this paradigm to provide clear and empirically supported explanations for prejudice, together with this a growing awareness of the pitfalls of simplistically applying the multicultural social policies associated with it.

POST 2000 – A NEW PARADIGM? AFFECT, MOTIVATION, AND THE COMPLEXITY OF PREJUDICE

The cognitive approach focusing on universally pervasive, though generally mild, intergroup biases and stereotyping had seemed to answer the questions that were most salient for social scientists during the last few decades of the twentieth century, that is, explaining the persistence and pervasiveness of racial stereotyping and subtle or implicit racial biases and discrimination. With the new millennium, however, important changes in the historical context have begun to make different questions about prejudice, and different kinds of prejudice, salient for social scientists. These new questions were ones the cognitive approach could not answer adequately.

Thus, the cognitive approach has shown little relevance for explaining the intense, passionate, ideologically grounded ethnocentric group loyalties, and extreme intergroup animosities that have risen to the fore internationally following the collapse of the relatively stable bipolar world order that existed up to the 1990s. Events such as the 9/11 terrorist attacks and the ensuing 'wars on terror' have shifted attention to different questions about prejudice. The emphasis, which for so long was on White racism in the United States as the prototypal prejudice, has now begun to broaden and encompass the affectively intense, ideologically and motivationally driven intergroup hatreds and hostilities underlying broader intergroup conflicts that threaten global security.

These new issues seem to signal the emergence of a new paradigm for understanding prejudice. Although the shape of this new paradigm is not yet entirely clear, a number of theories of prejudice have become prominent that respond to these new issues, and share important themes. In particular, they tend to see prejudice as complex and multifaceted, as primarily affective, as motivationally driven and rooted in ideological beliefs, and as powerfully influenced by both individual differences and by intergroup social and power relations, particularly involving threat, competition, and inequality.

The complexity of prejudice became increasingly apparent as it became evident that the new and implicit racisms had not simply replaced older, traditional, and explicit prejudices, but that both new and old, implicit and explicit, were different and equally important manifestations of prejudice and discrimination that all required explanation (Dovidio, Kawakami, & Gaertner, 2002; Pettigrew & Meertens, 1995; Wilson, Lindsey, & Schooler, 2000). Evidence from the emerging area of the social cognitive neuroscience of prejudice confirms this by showing neural differences between Whites' automatic or implicit responses to Black faces and their more controlled responses, with the latter more controlled responses able to modulate the more automatic neural responses (Cunningham, Johnson, Raye, et al., 2004).

Further developments have also shown that explicit prejudice itself may have different expressions. For example, Glick and Fiske (2001) have shown how three distinct kinds of explicit prejudice (paternalistic, contemptuous, and envious) with different affective expressions (pity, envy, and contempt, respectively) are generated by different combinations of the two stereotype dimensions of warmth and competence.

Further research deriving from threat-based theories of intergroup attitudes has shown that different kinds of outgroup threat or relations between groups will produce qualitatively different patterns of prejudice (Cottrell & Neuberg, 2005; Esses & Dovidio, 2002; Kurzban & Leary, 2001; Mackie, Devos, & Smith, 2000; Stephan & Stephan, 2000).

During the same period, researchers also began to rediscover a view of prejudice as intrinsically affective in nature. In 1993, Mackie and Hamilton edited an important volume on the role of affect in intergroup relations. In the following decade new theories have emerged focusing explicitly on prejudice as affective, such as intergroup emotions theory (Mackie, Devos, & Smith, 2000), the stereotype content model (Fiske, Cuddy, Glick, et al., 2002), and Cottrell and Neuberg's (2005) socio-functional approach. Empirical findings have indicated that affective responses to outgroups were markedly better predictors of overall outgroup evaluation or discrimination than were stereotypes (e.g., Dovidio, Brigham, Johnson, et al., 1996). In addition, an important new meta-analysis by Pettigrew and Tropp (2006) showed that intergroup contact does seem to play a vital role in reducing prejudice, and suggested that contact involving positive affect (such as close friendships) might be particularly significant in this respect.

The new emphasis on prejudice as complex and primarily affective also involved a view of prejudice as motivationally based. Thus, theories focusing on intergroup relations of threat, competition, or inequality have viewed prejudice as a motivated affective response. Intergroup threat theories presuppose that perceived threat from outgroups causes reactive hostility to those groups by activating motives to manage, control, or reduce threat, uncertainty or insecurity. The specific kind of outgroup threat can vary. Terror Management theory emphasizes outgroup threat to worldview beliefs (Greenberg, Solomon, & Pyszczynski, 1997), evolutionary theories have emphasized how prejudiced attitudes constitute adaptive responses, to various kinds of outgroup threats, that have survival value for groups (Cottrell & Neuberg, 2005; Kurzban & Leary, 2001), and Integrated Threat Theory (Stephan & Stephan, 2000) provides a taxonomy of the different kinds of outgroup threat that elicit prejudice.

A second basic human motive that has been central to intergroup theories of prejudice is that of power, dominance, or more generally, enhancement motivation. Social dominance theory, for example, sees the motive for group-based dominance as fundamental to the establishment of social hierarchies, and discrimination and prejudice aimed at maintaining social inequality (Sidanius & Pratto, 1999). System justification theory proposes that prejudiced attitudes and negative stereotypes of low-status groups derive from the motive to justify and legitimize unequal social systems, even among those disadvantaged by the inequality (Jost & Banaji, 1994).

Intergroup theories focusing on competition between groups have involved both threat and dominance as motives for prejudice. Intergroup competition would activate the desire to win, and therefore motives for dominance and superiority as well as a fear of losing, and therefore threats of loss or harm. Sherif's (1967) Realistic Conflict Theory, for example, was originally seen as arousing intergroup hostility through activating motivated desires to win a sporting competition and establish superiority over a competing group, but later also seen as causing prejudice through competitively generated threats of harm or loss (LeVine & Campbell, 1972). Intergroup competition involving both threat and dominance motives also seems central to the Instrumental Model of Group Conflict (Esses, Jackson, Dovidio, et al., 2005) and the Stereotype Content Model (Fiske, Cuddy, Glick, et al., 2002). Social Identity Theory sees competitive desires to establish and maintain the evaluative superiority of one's ingroup as an important motive for intergroup bias and discrimination (Tajfel & Turner, 1979). Finally, Group Position Theory also involves both motives for dominance and response to perceived threat in seeing

prejudice as the response of a dominant social group to outgroups seen as encroaching on or challenging its dominant position (Bobo, 1999).

Individual difference explanations of prejudice have also been interpreted in similar motivational terms. Research has shown that two individual difference dimensions, Right Wing Authoritarianism (RWA) and Social Dominance Orientation (SDO), powerfully predict the prejudiced attitudes of individuals (Altemeyer, 1981; Sidanius & Pratto, 1999). While these dimensions, and particularly RWA, were originally seen as personality dimensions, they have more recently been interpreted as ideological social attitude dimensions that express basic motivational goals or values. RWA expresses the need for societal or group security, order, or harmony, and SDO the desire for group power or dominance (Duckitt, 2001; Stangor and Leary, 2006). Research has supported this motivational approach by showing that the effects of RWA and SDO on prejudiced attitudes were indeed mediated by perceived outgroup threat and by competitiveness over relative dominance, respectively (Duckitt, 2006).

SUMMARY AND CONCLUSIONS

Overall, therefore, important changes seem to have been occurring in the way social scientists have understood and studied prejudice during the first decade of the twenty-first century. While these changes have been influenced by research, they may, perhaps more fundamentally, reflect important social developments during the past decade. As a result, the emphasis now seems to be shifting away from seeing prejudice in fundamentally cognitive terms, generated almost automatically by the basic cognitive process of categorization. Instead prejudice seems to be increasingly viewed as a much more complex and multidimensional construct, affective in nature, and expressing basic human motives activated by particular social and intergroup conditions. It may well be these social and motivational processes that elaborate relatively mild stereotypes and biases that are automatically elicited by salient social categorizations and identities into the more virulent manifestations of prejudice and discrimination. This new paradigm would thus retain a role for cognitive processes such as categorization and identification, but in an essentially secondary role – as necessary conditions for prejudice, or precursors of it.

At present these new emphases characterize a number of theories, which have different foci, but also important complementarities. The most important task for theory and research in this new era may be to elucidate these complementarities in order to develop the kind of integrative theoretical frameworks that may be needed to provide a more complete and comprehensive understanding of a complex and multifaceted phenomenon. Together with this development may come more sophisticated approaches to interventions to reduce prejudice and discrimination. Recognition of the complexity of prejudice should bring the development of broader and more flexible intervention programs that will incorporate those particular prejudice-reduction strategies that are specifically targeted at particular kinds of prejudice and their different social and motivational bases.

REFERENCES

Aberson, C. L., Healy, M., & Romero, V. (2000) Ingroup bias and self-esteem: A meta-analysis, *Personality and Social Psychology Review*, 4, 157–173.

Adorno, T., Frenkel-Brunswik, E., Levinson, D., & Sanford, R. (1950) *The Authoritarian Personality*. New York: Harper.

Allport, G. (1954) *The Nature of Prejudice*. Reading, MA: Addison-Wesley.

Altemeyer, B. (1981) *Right-Wing Authoritarianism*. Winnipeg, Manitoba, Canada: University of Manitoba Press.

Ashmore, R., & DelBoca, F. (1981). Conceptual approaches to stereotypes and stereotyping. In D. Hamilton (Ed.), *Cognitive Processes in Stereotyping and Intergroup Behavior* (pp. 1–36). Hillsdale, NJ: Erlbaum.

Blackwell, J. (1982). Persistence and change in intergroup relations: The crisis upon us. *Social Problems*, 2, 325–346.

Blauner, R. (1972) *Racial Oppression in America*. New York: Harper & Row.

Bobo, L. (1999). Prejudice as group position: Micro-foundations of a sociological approach to racism and race relations. *Journal of Social Issues*, 55, 445–472.

Bogardus, E. (1925). Measuring social distance. *Journal of Applied Sociology*, 9, 299–308.

Bonacich, E. (1972). A theory of ethnic antagonism: The split labor market. *American Sociological Review*, 37, 447–559.

Bowser, B. (1985). Race relations in the 1980s: The case of the United States. *Journal of Black Studies*, 15, 307–324.

Brewer, M. B. (1979). In-group bias in the minimal inter-group situation: A cognitive-motivational analysis. *Psychological Bulletin*, 86, 307–324.

Brewer, M. B. (1999). The psychology of prejudice: Ingroup love or outgroup hate. *Journal of Social Issues*, 55, 429–444.

Brown, R. (2000). Social identity theory: Past achievements, current problems and future challenges. *European Journal of Social Psychology*, 30, 745–778.

Brown, R., & Hewstone, M. (2005). An integrative theory of intergroup contact. In M. P. Zanna (Ed.), *Advances in Experimental Social Psychology* (Vol. 37, pp. 255–343). San Diego, CA: Academic Press.

Carmichael, S., & Hamilton, C. (1967). *Black Power*. New York: Random House.

Cottrell, C. A., & Neuberg, S. L. (2005). Different emotional reactions to different groups: A sociofunctional threat-based approach to "prejudice". *Journal of Personality and Social Psychology*, 88, 770–789.

Crosby, F. J. (2004). *Affirmative Action is Dead; Long Live Affirmative Action*. New Haven, CT: Yale University Press.

Crosby, F. J. Bromley, S., & Saxe, L. (1980). Recent unobtrusive studies of Black and White discrimination and prejudice: A literature review. *Psychological Bulletin*, 87, 546–563.

Cunningham, W. A, Johnson, M. K., Raye, C. L., Gatenby, J. C., Gore, J. C., & Banaji, M. R. (2004). Separable neural components in the processing of Black and White faces. *Psychological Science*, 15, 806–813.

Dollard, J., Doob, L., Miller, N. E., Mowrer, O., & Sears, R. (1939). *Frustration and Aggression*. New Haven, CT: Yale University Press.

Dovidio, J. F., Brigham, J. C, Johnson, B. T., & Gaertner, S. L. (1996). Stereotyping, prejudice, and discrimination: Another look. In C. N. Macrae,

C. Stangor, & M. Hewstone (Eds), *Stereotypes and Stereotyping* (pp. 276–319). New York: Guilford.

Dovidio, J. F., Gaertner, S. L. (2004). Aversive racism. In M. P. Zanna (Ed.), *Advances in Experimental Social Psychology* (Vol. 36, pp. 1–52). San Diego, CA: Academic Press.

Dovidio, J. F., Kawakami, K., & Gaertner, S. L. (2002). Implicit and explicit prejudice and interracial interaction. *Journal of Personality and Social Psychology*, 82 (1), 62–68.

Duckitt, J. (1992). *The Social Psychology of Prejudice.* New York: Praeger.

Duckitt, J. (2001). A dual process cognitive-motivational theory of ideology and prejudice. In M. P. Zanna (Ed.), *Advances in Experimental Social Psychology* (Vol. 33, pp. 41–113). San Diego, CA: Academic Press.

Duckitt, J., Callaghan, J., & Wagner, C. (2005). Group identity and intergroup attitudes in South Africa: A multidimensional approach. *Personality and Social Psychology Bulletin*, 31, 633–646.

Duckitt, J. (2006). Differential effects of Right Wing Authoritarianism and Social Dominance Orientation on outgroup attitudes and their mediation by threat from competitiveness to outgroups. *Personality and Social Psychology Bulletin*, 32, 684–696.

Esses, V. M., & Dovidio, J. F. (2002). The role of emotions in determining willingness to engage in intergroup contact. *Personality and Social Psychology Bulletin*, 28, 1202–1214.

Esses, V. M., Jackson, L. M., Dovidio, J. F., & Hodson, G. (2005). Instrumental relations among groups: Group competition, conflict, and prejudice. In J. Dovidio, P. Glick, & L. Rudmin (Eds), *On the Nature of Prejudice: Fifty Years after Allport* (pp. 227–223). Malden, MA: Blackwell.

Fairchild, H., & Gurin, P. (1978). Traditions in the social psychological analysis of race relations. *American Behavioral Scientist*, 21, 757–778.

Fazio, R. H., & Olson, M. A. (2003). Implicit measures in social cognition research: Their meaning and use. *Annual Review of Psychology*, 54, 297–327.

Fiske, S. T., Cuddy, A. J. C., Glick, P., & Xu, J. (2002). A model of (often mixed) stereotype content: Competence and warmth respectively follow from perceived status and competition. *Journal of Personality and Social Psychology*, 82, 878–902.

Gaertner, S. L., & Dovidio, J. F. (1986). The aversive form of racism. In J. Dovidio & S. Gaertner (Eds), *Prejudice, Discrimination, and Racism* (pp. 61–89). Orlando, FL: Academic Press.

Gaertner, S. L., & Dovidio, J. F. (2000). *Reducing Intergroup Bias: The Common Ingroup Identity Model.* New York: Psychology Press.

Gibson, J. (2006). Do strong identities fuel intolerance? Evidence from the South African case. *Political Psychology*, 27, 665–705.

Glick, P., & Fiske, S. T. (2001). Ambivalent sexism. In M. P. Zanna (Ed.), *Advances in Experimental Social Psychology* (Vol. 33, pp. 115–188). San Diego, CA: Academic Press.

Greenberg, J., Solomon, S., & Pyszczynski, T. (1997). Terror management theory of self-esteem and cultural worldviews. Empirical assessments and cultural refinements. In M. P. Zanna (Ed.), *Advances in Experimental Social Psychology* (Vol. 29, pp. 61–139). Orlando, FL: Academic Press.

Greenwald, A. G., & Banaji, M. R. (1995). Implicit social cognition: Attitudes, self-esteem, and stereotypes. *Psychological Review*, 102, 4–27.

Greenwald, A. G., McGhee, D. E., & Schwartz, J. L. K. (1998). Measuring individual differences in implicit cognition: The Implicit Association Test. *Journal of Personality and Social Psychology*, 74, 1464–1480.

Haller, J. (1971). *Outcasts From Evolution: Scientific Attitudes of Racial Inferiority: 1859–1900.* Urbana: University of Illinois Press.

Hamilton, D. L. (Ed.). (1981a). *Cognitive Processes in Stereotyping and Intergroup Behavior.* Hillsdale, NJ: Erlbaum.

Hamilton, D. L. (1981b). Stereotyping and intergroup behavior: Some thoughts on the cognitive approach. In D. L. Hamilton (Ed.), *Cognitive Processes in Stereotyping and Intergroup Behavior* (pp. 333–353). Hillsdale, NJ: Erlbaum.

Hernstein, R., & Murray, C. (1994). *The Bell Curve.* New York: The Free Press.

Hewstone, M., & Brown, R. (1986). Contact is not enough: An intergroup perspective on the "Contact Hypothesis". In M. Hewstone & R. Brown (Eds), *Contact and Conflict in Intergroup Encounters* (pp. 1–44). Oxford: Blackwell.

Hewstone, M., Rubin, M., & Willis, H. (2002). Intergroup bias. *Annual Review of Psychology*, 53, 575–604.

Huddy, L., & Sears, D. O. (1995). Opposition to bilingual education: Prejudice or the defense of realistic interests. *Social Psychology Quarterly*, 58, 133–143.

Jetten, J., Spears, R., & Postmes, T. (2004). Ingroup distinctiveness and differentiation: A meta-analytic integration. *Personality and Social Psychology Review*, 86, 862–879.

Jost, J. T., & Banaji, M. R. (1994). The role of stereotyping in system justification and the production of false consciousness. *British Journal of Social Psychology*, 33, 1–27.

Katz, D., & Braly, K. (1933). Racial stereotypes in one hundred college students. *Journal of Abnormal and Social Psychology*, 28, 280–290.

Katz, I., & Hass, R. (1988). Racial ambivalence and American value conflict: Correlational and priming studies of dual cognitive structures. *Journal of Personality and Social Psychology*, 59, 692–704.

Kinder, D. R., & Sanders, L. (1996). *Divided by Color: Racial Politics and Democratic Ideals*. Chicago: University of Chicago Press.

Kurzban, R., & Leary, M. (2001). Evolutionary origins of stigmatization: The functions of social exclusion. *Psychological Bulletin*, 127, 167–208.

LeVine, R. A., & Campbell, D. (1972) *Ethnocentrism: Theories of Conflict, Ethnic Attitudes and Group Behavior*. New York: Wiley.

Mackie, D. M., Hamilton, D. L. (Eds) (1993). *Affect, Cognition and Stereotyping: Interactive Processes in Group Perception*. San Diego, CA: Academic Press.

Mackie, D. M., Devos, T., & Smith, E. R. (2000). Intergroup emotions: Explaining offensive action tendencies in an intergroup context. *Journal of Personality and Social Psychology*, 79, 602–616.

McConahay, J. B., & Hough, J. C. (1976). Symbolic racism. *Journal of Social Issues*, 32, 23–45.

Miller, N., & Bugelski, R. (1948). Minor studies of aggression: II. The influence of frustration imposed by the in-group on attitudes expressed toward out-groups. *Journal of Psychology*, 25, 437–442.

Milner, D. (1975) *Children and Race*. Harmondsworth, England: Penguin.

Milner, D. (1981). Racial prejudice. In J. Turner & H. Giles (Eds), *Intergroup Behavior* (pp. 102–143). Oxford, England: Blackwell.

Minard, R. (1952). Race relationships in the Pocahontas coal field. *Journal of Social Issues*, 8, 29–44.

Mummendey, A., Klink, A., & Brown, R. (2001). Nationalism and patriotism: National identification and out-group rejection. *British Journal of Social Psychology*, 40, 159–172.

Park, B., & Judd, C. M. (2005). Rethinking the link between categorization and prejudice within the social cognition perspective. *Personality and Social Psychology Review*, 9, 108–130.

Pettigrew, T. F. (1958). Personality and socio-cultural factors in intergroup attitudes: A cross-national comparison. *Journal of Conflict Resolution*, 2, 29–42.

Pettigrew, T. F. (1959). Regional differences in anti-Negro prejudice. *Journal of Abnormal and Social Psychology*, 59, 28–36.

Pettigrew, T. F., & Meertens, R. W. (1995). Subtle and blatant prejudice in Western Europe. *European Journal of Social Psychology*, 25, 57–75.

Pettigrew, T. F., & Tropp, L. A. (2006). A meta-analytic test of intergroup contact theory. *Journal of Personality and Social Psychology*, 90, 751–783.

Proshansky, H. M. (1966). The development of intergroup attitudes. In L. W. Hoffman & M. L. Hoffman (Eds), *Review of Child Development Research* (pp. 311–371). New York: Russell Sage Foundation.

Prothro, E. T. (1952). Ethnocentrism and anti-Negro attitudes in the deep South. *Journal of Abnormal and Social Psychology*, 47, 105–108.

Rokeach, M., Smith, P., & Evans, R. (1960). Two kinds of prejudice or one? In M. Rokeach (Ed.), *The Open and the Closed Mind* (pp. 132–168). New York: Basic Books.

Rubin, M., & Hewstone, M. (1998). Social identity theory's self-esteem hypothesis: and review and some suggestions for clarification. *Personality and Social Psychology Review*, 2, 40–62.

Samelson, F. (1978). From "race psychology" to "studies in prejudice": Some observations on the thematic reversal in social psychology. *Journal of the History of the Behavioral Sciences*, 14, 265–278.

Schofield, J. W. (1986). Causes and consequences of the colorblind perspective. In J. F. Dovidio & S. L. Gaertner (Eds), *Prejudice, Discrimination, and Racism* (pp. 231–254). Orlando, FL: Academic Press.

Shamir, M., & Sagiv-Schiffer, T. (2006). Conflict, identity, and tolerance: Israel in the Al-Aqsa intifada. *Political Psychology*, 27, 569–595.

Sherif, M. (1967). *Group Conflict and Cooperation*. London: Routledge & Kegan Paul.

Sidanius, J., & Pratto, F. (1999). *Social Dominance: An Intergroup Theory of Social Hierarchy and Oppression*. Cambridge, England: Cambridge University Press.

Smith, E. R., & Mackie, D. M. (2005). Aggression, hatred, and other emotions. In J. Dovidio, P. Glick, & L. Rudman (Eds), *On the Nature of Prejudice: Fifty Years after Allport* (pp. 361–376). Malden, MA: Blackwell.

Stangor, C., & Leary, S. P. (2006). Intergroup beliefs: Investigations from the social side. In M. P. Zanna (Ed.), *Advances in Experimental Social Psychology* (Vol. 38, pp. 243–281). New York: Academic Press.

Stephan, W. G., & Stephan, C. W. (2000). An integrated threat theory of prejudice. In S. Oskamp (Ed.), *Reducing Prejudice and Discrimination: Claremont Symposium on Applied Social Psychology* (pp. 23–46). Hillsdale, N.J.: Erlbaum.

Tajfel, H., & Turner, J. C. (1979). An integrative theory of intergroup conflict. In W. Austin & S. Worchel (Eds), *The Social Psychology of Intergroup Relations* (pp. 33–47). Monterey, California: Brooks/Cole.

Thurow, L. (1969). *Poverty and Discrimination.* Washington, DC: Brookings Institute.

van Knippenberg, A. (1978). Status differences, comparative relevance and intergroup differentiation. In H. Tajfel (Ed.), *Differentiation Between Social Groups* (pp. 171–200). San Diego, CA: Academic Press.

Westie, F. R. (1964). Race and ethnic relations. In R. E. L. Faris (Ed.), *Handbook of Modern Sociology* (pp. 576–618). Chicago: Rand McNally.

Wilson, T. D., Lindsey, S., & Schooler, T. Y. (2000). A model of dual attitudes. *Psychological Review,* 107, 101–126.

3

Measuring Prejudice, Stereotypes and Discrimination

Joshua Correll, Charles M. Judd,
Bernadette Park, and Bernd Wittenbrink

ABSTRACT

This chapter focuses on historical and current approaches to measuring prejudice, stereotypes, and discrimination. A central distinction that motivates much of the chapter is between implicit and explicit measures, with the latter implying awareness and control over responses. In addition to reviewing a myriad of measurement approaches, we argue that measurement itself has fundamentally affected theories of the nature and origins of prejudice, stereotypes, and discrimination. Ultimately we suggest that there is no single best approach to measuring the multifaceted constructs that are central to this handbook.

INTRODUCTION

A chapter on the measurement of prejudice, stereotypes, and discrimination necessarily starts by defining the constructs. The normative assumption is that measurement develops in response to theoretical needs. Although we start with theoretical definitions of the constructs and proceed to the measures that assess them, one theme of this chapter will be that theory in social psychology evolves as measurement procedures are developed and refined. The issues we consider in this chapter: How we measure prejudice, stereotypes, and discrimination, turn out to be fundamentally important for our theoretical understanding of these constructs.

DEFINING THE CONSTRUCTS

Prejudice

The study of prejudice has a long history in social psychology throughout which its definition has evolved (Allport, 1954; Fiske, 1998). Probably the most widely shared definition considers prejudice to be a negative attitude toward a particular social group and its members. As such, and consistent with the literature on attitudes more broadly, prejudice is seen to have three components: cognitive, affective, and behavioral. The first of these is equivalent to what we will define as a stereotype. The second is a purer affective or evaluative response to the group, void of any particular semantic content. And the third consists of behaviors and behavioral tendencies that discriminate against, or in favor of, a group. Because this broad definition encompasses stereotypes and discrimination (as we will define them), it is useful to define prejudice more narrowly. Accordingly, we define prejudice as a valenced affective or evaluative response (positive or negative) to a social category and its members. The utility of this narrower definition is that it permits us to distinguish between measures that focus on prejudice, stereotypes, and discrimination. While prejudice defined in this way is purely affective and evaluative, it is typically accompanied by stereotypic beliefs that serve either as the foundation for prejudice or as its justification. Additionally, prejudice may give rise to discriminatory behavior.

Stereotypes

We define stereotypes as category-based generalizations that link category members to typical attributes. For example, one might consider the stereotype that physicists are intelligent but socially awkward or that accountants are organized but boring. Each stereotype connects typical members of a social category with distinctive traits. There is nothing in this definition that specifies the evaluative nature of the attributes associated with category members. It may typically be the case that stereotypes about certain groups, for instance disliked outgroups, have a strongly valenced character, but we do not assume this generally to be the case.

Discrimination

We define discrimination as behavior directed toward category members that is consequential for their outcomes, and that

is directed toward them not because of any particular deservingness or reciprocity, but simply because they happen to be members of that category. This leaves open the possibility that behaviors, which some judge to be discriminatory, will not be seen in that way by others. Targets of the discrimination may define some behaviors as having negative consequences while the perpetrators of those behaviors may not. Additionally, perpetrators may see their behaviors as justified by the deservingness of the targets, while the targets themselves may disagree. Thus, particularly for discrimination, definitions may depend on the attributions that a perceiver makes for a given behavior.

HISTORICAL BACKGROUND

Since Katz and Braly's (1933) early study on stereotypes, the most common approach to measuring prejudice, stereotyping, and discrimination has been to ask respondents directly about their attitudes. However, self-reporting measures have the obvious limitation that they yield accurate estimates only if the respondents are both willing and able to report their sentiments. In the case of intergroup attitudes, there are reasons to doubt that these preconditions are always met. Changes in societal norms have made overt expression of bias unacceptable (Schuman, Steeh, Bobo, et al., 1997), and simple explicit measures may be problematic because participants are not always fully aware of their own attitudes (Gaertner & Dovidio, 1986; Nosek, Greenwald, & Banaji, 2007).

To address these problems, researchers have developed less obtrusive measures, using a variety of methodologies. One strategy relies on explicit self-reports but alleviates respondents' concerns with social desirability by offering response alternatives that frame bias in socially-accepted terms or by ensuring anonymity. Another strategy aims to conceal the purpose of the assessment and/or minimize participants' ability to control their responses. Measures of this kind have a long history in social psychology (e.g., Rankin &

Campbell, 1955), but in the 1990s, with social psychology's discovery of priming procedures that had been developed by cognitive psychology, a whole new approach to unobtrusive assessment became possible. The majority of these measures use computers to present stimuli very briefly and require participants to make relatively quick responses, minimizing both awareness of the experimental goals and the ability to respond strategically. Moreover, because these implicit measures do not rely on respondents' introspection, they may capture hidden attitudes – sentiments of which respondents may not themselves be aware. Although there are several perspectives on what makes a measure implicit or explicit, we define explicit measures as those involving (a) awareness that prejudice, stereotypes, or discrimination are being assessed, and (b) responses that can be controlled or modified by the respondent. Implicit measures do not share one or both of these characteristics.

The distinction between explicit and implicit measures is not identical to the distinction between controlled and automatic processes (e.g., Bargh, 1994; Fazio & Olson, 2003). Social psychology has examined several characteristics that differentiate relatively automatic processes (which proceed efficiently without intention, awareness, or control) from controlled processes (which do not). Although implicit measures may yield insights into automatic processes and explicit measures largely tap controlled processes, we consider a *measure* to be either implicit or explicit, whereas *cognitive processes* are either automatic or controlled.

MEASURING PREJUDICE

Research has investigated prejudice toward a variety of groups, but in the United States prejudice of Whites toward Blacks has received the most attention. Accordingly, we will often refer to racial prejudice measures as illustrative examples, but our review is meant to capture principled issues relevant to the assessment of prejudice more generally.

Explicit measures of prejudice

Measures of global evaluation

Several measures aim to capture general evaluations of a group, without any specific semantic content. Probably, the most widely used measures of this kind are the Feeling Thermometer and the Social Distance Scale.

Feeling thermometer   Respondents indicate their attitudes on a 0–100 point scale. As suggested by its name, the thermometer involves a metaphor, conceptualizing feelings toward a given group as temperature readings, ranging from 'very cold, unfavorable feelings' to 'very warm, favorable feelings.' Although the thermometer typically requires a lengthy introduction, respondents understand the measure easily (see Converse & Presser, 1986). Also, as a continuous 100-point scale, thermometers offer a large number of response alternatives and accordingly show relatively high reliability (Alwin, 1992).

Social distance measures   Another global measure, Bogardus's (1933) Social Distance Scale, presents seven statements, describing forms of contact with the target group that increase in social intimacy. Respondents indicate their willingness to tolerate each form of contact. The measure was originally conceived as a cumulative Guttman scale: the score was based on the most proximate contact endorsed by the respondent. In practice, Social Distance Scale responses are not always consistent with the assumptions underlying such a scale. Researchers have scored the total number of 'Yes' responses (e.g., Brewer, 1968), or have used Likert scales for each statement (Byrnes & Kiger, 1988).

Content measures

In contrast to global measures of prejudice, content measures focus on respondents' beliefs concerning a particular group and its role in society, and thus reflect the cognitive underpinnings of a person's group evaluation. Most content measures are specific to a single group. That is, they measure agreement with beliefs associated with attitudes toward a given group. Item content therefore varies from measure to measure.

To assess prejudice toward Blacks, for example, many content-based measures exist (Biernat & Crandall, 1999), which differ considerably in their theoretical assumptions. Some target beliefs are thought to stem from general values. For example, the Pro- and Anti-Black Attitude Scales developed by Katz and Hass (1988) assume that attitudes toward Blacks reflect beliefs about the protestant work ethic and egalitarian values. Others, like the Modern Racism Scale (McConahay, Hardee, & Batts, 1981), assess beliefs that are seen as contemporary, socially sanctioned expressions of anti-Black sentiment.

Modern racism scale (MRS)   McConahay's scale originated from research on symbolic racism (Kinder & Sears, 1981). Symbolic racists, though committed to equal rights, might portray Blacks as violating traditional American values of individualism, work ethic, and discipline. Prejudice, theoretically, stems from the violation of those values rather than from a belief that Blacks are inherently inferior. The MRS attempts to capture this more contemporary form of prejudice. Respondents indicate agreement with several belief statements, using a Likert scale response format, which are collapsed to yield an overall index.

Like other content measures, MRS items refer to specific policies, leading to criticism that the scale measures political preferences rather than prejudice (Sniderman, Piazza, Tetlock, et al., 1991), thus questioning its conceptualization as 'racism' (Bobo, 1983; Sniderman & Tetlock, 1986). However, much of the research that has employed the MRS has used the scale not to test the theory of symbolic racism, but simply as a less reactive self-report measure of racial prejudice (e.g., Devine, 1989). Indeed, the MRS seems less sensitive to social desirability concerns than traditional racial prejudice measures (McConahay, Hardee, & Batts, 1981). Various studies have found the MRS to show construct validity (Pratto, Sidanius, Stallworth, et al., 1994; Wittenbrink, Judd, & Park, 1997) and

to predict relevant criteria (McConahay & Hough, 1976; Wittenbrink & Henly, 1996).

Social dominance orientation (SDO)   The SDO Scale by Sidanius and Pratto (Pratto, Sidanius, Stallworth 1994) is not a measure of prejudice in a strict sense. It measures the predisposition to favor group-based hierarchies. According to the theory, this orientation should predict prejudice toward outgroups in general (at least on the part of members of the dominant group). The idea that prejudice toward outgroups in general shares a common denominator has a long tradition (Adorno, Frenkel-Brunswick, Levinson, et al., 1950), and there is support for the contention that SDO coincides with prejudiced evaluations of many groups (e.g., Arabs, Blacks, gays and lesbians; Sidanius & Pratto, 1999). The SDO scale asks respondents to indicate their agreement with several statements, using a seven-point Likert response format. Several versions of the scale exist; a recent review by Pratto, Sidanius, and Levin (2006) appears to favor a 16-item version. A related scale, again assessing a common tendency in support of the status quo along with prejudiced evaluations of many outgroups, is the Right-Wing Authoritarian Scale (Altemeyer, 1981, 1988).

Strategic responding

One concern with explicit measures is that respondents might misrepresent their true attitudes so as to appear unprejudiced. Aside from the steps implemented in some of the measures described above, researchers have used two strategies to limit misrepresentation. The first involves minimizing incentives for socially desirable self-presentation by assuring anonymity and confidentiality. It is sometimes feasible to use self-administered questionnaires and have participants drop them off anonymously. For interviewer-administered settings, more complex, randomized response techniques may be used (Bradburn, Sudman, & Wansink, 2004). A second strategy is to create a disincentive for socially desirable responding. Sigall and Page's (1971) 'bogus pipeline' aims to limit misrepresentation by convincing respondents that the researcher can discern their true attitudes by means of an elaborate (but fake) physiological measurement apparatus. Under bogus-pipeline conditions, White participants report more negative assessments of Blacks (Allen, 1975; Sigall & Page, 1971).

Implicit measures of prejudice

All of the approaches described above presume that respondents actually know their attitudes, whether or not they are willing to report them. Implicit measures aim to assess prejudice even if people are otherwise unwilling and/or unable to report it.

Response latency measures

Implicit measures based on response latencies infer attitudes from the impact that a group-related stimulus has on the speed with which a person can make judgments. To date, the two most frequently used measures using this approach are priming measures and the Implicit Association Test (IAT).

Evaluative priming (EP)

The most common priming procedure used for prejudice measurement was introduced by Fazio, Jackson, Dunton, et al. (1995). They refer to it as 'evaluative priming' while others refer to it as 'affective priming' (Klauer & Musch, 2003). It is based on a paradigm in which two stimuli are presented in short succession on a computer screen, a prime followed by a target. The participant's task is to classify the target as quickly as possible based on its evaluative connotation. In this paradigm, valenced primes tend to facilitate classification of evaluatively congruent targets. As a measure of prejudice, the procedure pairs group primes (e.g., a Black or a White face) with target words of polarized valence (e.g., pleasant, awful), and assesses whether the prime facilitates responses to positive targets and/or negative targets. The magnitude of the priming effect serves as an index of a person's underlying group evaluation. Depending on the design, the procedure can assess attitudes toward multiple target groups

and, if a neutral prime condition is included, it can offer separate attitude estimates for each. Moreover, indices can separate positive and negative aspects of the overall sentiment (see Wittenbrink, 2007).

One critical difference between EP and the measures we have reviewed thus far is that EP attempts to capture the automatic activation of group attitudes, a reaction that is triggered relatively passively, requiring neither the intent to evaluate the primes nor awareness of the stimulus or of the evaluative process. Related assumptions underlie many of the implicit measures in this chapter. In principal, then, EP should not be compromised by strategic self-presentation, but Teige-Mocigemba and Klauer (2008) observed that responses in EP can be faked. To address this issue, 'subliminal' presentation may conceal the nature of the prime (Wittenbrink, Judd, & Park, 1997), and shortened response windows can preclude strategic influences by enforcing rapid responses (Degner, in press).

Only a few studies have investigated the validity of prejudice estimates from EP. In some, the measure predicted relevant behavior (Fazio, Jackson, Dunton, 1995; Towles-Schwen & Fazio, 2006), but others have produced less promising results (e.g., Banse, 2001). This ambiguity may reflect the relatively low reliability of EP (Banse, 2001; Cameron, Alvarez, & Bargh, 2000), which itself may result from the use of exemplars as primes (e.g., photos of group members). Unlike generic group labels (e.g., 'Blacks,' 'Women'), exemplars may be categorized in unpredictable ways. (De Houwer, Teige-Mocigemba, Spruyt, et al., in press). Olson and Fazio (2003) suggest that EP becomes more sensitive to group-level attitudes when participants categorize the primes according to the relevant group (e.g., 'keep a mental tally of the number of Black faces and White faces that you see').

The fact that EP is sensitive to task instructions highlights an important characteristic of these measures that is sometimes misunderstood: implicit measures do not, by their nature, produce more stable attitude estimates than other measures. Though EP aims to capture products of automatic processes, these processes may well be sensitive to variations in the experimental context (Wittenbrink, Judd, & Park, 2001).

Implicit association test (IAT) The IAT (Greenwald, McGhee, & Schwartz, 1998) has become the most widely used implicit prejudice measure. It involves a computer-based response-conflict paradigm in which two alternative categorization stimuli are pitted against one another. Participants classify two sets of targets along two different dimensions. One set consists of exemplars of two target groups (e.g., Black and White faces), which participants classify by group using two response keys. A second set of targets includes positive and negative items (e.g., poison, love), which are classified by valence, again using two response keys. During critical trials, targets from the two sets appear in random order, and both judgment tasks are performed using the same two response keys (each key is associated with two response options: Black/positive and White/negative). Two assessment blocks manipulate the response combinations so that each group is paired once with the positive key and once with the negative key (e.g., Black/positive and White/negative versus Black/negative and White/positive). Presumably, classification speed reflects the association between the target groups and the evaluative concepts. The IAT index assesses which of the two judgment combinations produces faster responses on average. For example, faster responses for the Black/negative and White/positive combination compared to the Black/positive and White/negative combination are thought to indicate prejudice toward Blacks (see Greenwald, Nosek, & Banaji, 2003).

The IAT is one of the more thoroughly investigated prejudice measures. Its test–retest reliability is adequate (Nosek, Greenwald, Banaji, 2007), and a recent meta-analysis identified 184 studies on the IAT's predictive validity (Greenwald, Poehlman, Uhlmann, et al., in press). Across a range of domains and criterion variables, the IAT showed moderate predictive validity (average

$r = 0.27$), with slightly lower results for the intergroup domains relevant to the current review than in the case of implicit attitudes toward other kinds of objects (e.g., an IAT that measures attitudes toward spiders). Interestingly, self-report measures of intergroup attitudes in these studies fared somewhat worse than the IAT.

Though the IAT is thought to tap automatic responses, the task may be fairly transparent to participants. De Houwer and Moors (reported in De Houwer, Teige-Mocigemba, Spruyt, in press) found that 80 percent of participants correctly identified the purpose of a race IAT. The IAT is also not impervious to strategic responding. Participants can fake their attitudes when instructed to do so (Fiedler & Bluemke, 2005; Steffens, 2004). We mention these findings not to suggest that attitudes can be readily misrepresented on the IAT (they cannot – faking requires practice), but because they suggest that IAT responses are subject to controlled, nonautomatic processes.

IAT variants One of the primary difficulties with the IAT is that the measure confounds two sources of input. A high score on a race IAT may reflect *either* negative sentiments toward Blacks *or* positive attitudes toward Whites. Several variations of the procedure have been proposed, in part to address this concern by providing an attitude estimate for individual targets: the Go/No-Go Association Task (GNAT; Nosek & Banaji, 2001), the Extrinsic Affective Simon Task (EAST; De Houwer, 2003a), and two almost identical procedures, the Single-Category IAT and the Single-Target IAT (SC-IAT; Karpinski & Steinman, 2006; Wigboldus, Holland, & van Knippenberg, 2004). Another issue is that the IAT may measure implicit associations that that are widely shared in a culture rather than personal implicit associations. Olson and Fazio (2004) have developed a 'personalized' IAT approach in an attempt to avoid this difficulty.

Physiological measures
Physiological attitude measures capture the physiological correlates of evaluative

responses. Early examples related to prejudice involved autonomic responses such as skin conductance. Rankin and Campbell (1955) observed an elevated galvanic skin response (GSR) among White participants during interactions with a Black, compared to a White, experimenter. However, GSR is sensitive to arousal in general rather than the evaluative valence of a stimulus (Cacioppo & Sandman, 1981).

Electromyography (EMG) Facial EMG assesses electrical activity in facial muscles, even in the absence of visible movement. Vanman, Saltz, Nathan, et al. (2004) assessed EMG activity in brow and cheek areas (corresponding to the muscles used when frowning and smiling, respectively) in response to photos of Black and White students. Cheek-based activity reliably predicted bias in an impression formation task. A related approach measures the activity of muscles involved in eyeblinks. In this procedure, a probe (e.g., a short blast of acoustic noise) elicits a reflexive blink roughly 500 ms after the onset of a stimulus (e.g., a group member's photograph). Positive stimuli tend to inhibit eyeblink reflexes, whereas negative stimuli amplify reflexes (Lang, Bradley, & Cuthbert, 1990). Thus, blink amplitude serves as an indicator of evaluative responses toward the target group (Amodio, Harmon-Jones, & Devine, 2003). However, eyeblink modulation may occur only for highly arousing stimuli, limiting its usefulness as an individual difference measure (Cuthbert, Bradley, Lang, 1996).

Measures of brain activity A final set of physiological attitude measures is based on the assessment of brain activity, including event-related brain potentials, and functional magnetic resonance imagery. These techniques have provided insight into the processes underlying, and the specific brain areas involved in, evaluative responses to social groups (for a review, see Ito, Willadsen-Jensen, & Correll, 2007, and Quadflieg, Mason, & Macrae, this volume).

Other implicit measures
Affect misattribution procedure (AMP)
The AMP (Payne, Cheng, Govorum, et al., 2004) is derived from a priming task used by Murphy and Zajonc (1993). Similar to EP, the AMP captures evaluative effects of a group prime on responses to a subsequent target. The AMP is not based on latencies but on liking judgments of the target (an unfamiliar stimulus, e.g., a Chinese ideograph). As in EP, positive primes yield relatively higher liking judgments. The AMP has some practical advantages: it produces relatively large effect sizes and may be useful in contexts that preclude speeded response tasks.

Paper-and-pencil measures Some implicit measures can be completed merely with paper, pencil, and stopwatch. Lowery, Hardin, and Sinclair (2001) employed the basic IAT rationale, presenting stereotypic first names and valenced target items in random order down the center of a page. Participants performed two types of classification, based on group membership and valence (indicating their responses with a checkmark on either the left-hand or right-hand side of the column). Like the IAT, different combinations of response labels were used, but the manipulation was implemented with different sheets of paper. The number of correctly completed items per condition served as the critical measure. For other examples of creative low-tech measures, see Vargas, Sekaquaptewa, and von Hippel (2007).

MEASURING STEREOTYPES

Next, we examine the measurement of stereotypes: beliefs or other cognitive associations relating a social category or its members to particular characteristics. Again, this section is organized around the distinction between explicit and implicit measures, which often involve dramatically different methodologies and also imply somewhat different definitions of stereotypes. Though we consider all stereotypes to be generalizations about the attributes of a group, explicit measures typically ask about consciously held *beliefs*, whereas implicit measures assess associations between the group and its attributes, whether or not these associations constitute beliefs that the respondent endorses.

Explicit stereotype measures

Park and Judd (1990; Judd & Park, 1993) critically distinguished between measures that assess the degree to which stereotypic attributes characterize a typical group member (stereotypicality) and measures that assess variability within the group (dispersion). Their studies tested an array of measures, many of which are summarized below.

Explicit measures of stereotypicality

The primary question in explicit stereotyping concerns the degree to which the individual believes that members of a social category are characterized by a given attribute. High stereotypicality suggests a belief that most group members demonstrate the attribute in question. For example, the idea that *most* cab drivers are rude seems to capture the essence of a stereotype. This is, in essence, a question of the perceived prevalence of a trait. A related, but distinct, question concerns extremity. Even if all cab drivers are seen as rude, a researcher may ask whether cabbies are seen as somewhat rude or extremely rude. Prevalence and extremity characterize the most commonly used measures of stereotypicality.

Adjective checklists   The first psychological investigation of stereotypes was Katz and Braly's (1933) study in which participants indicated the traits they viewed as most typical (presumably due to both prevalence and extremity) of various groups. The checklists allowed Katz and Braly to aggregate across individuals to describe the stereotypes held by this particular population. Though potentially valuable in describing shared group stereotypes, checklists are insensitive at the individual level.

Trait ratings   Trait ratings are one of the most face-valid stereotype measures. Participants are presented with target groups and a set of traits, and simply indicate the extent to which each attribute (e.g., *rude*) characterizes each group. Participants may respond via unipolar scales with anchors such as 'not at all' and 'very much,' or bipolar scales with anchors such as 'rude' and 'polite.' A trait that characterizes most group members should be seen as more characteristic of the group as a whole, and participants who view a group as extreme on a trait may also rate that trait as more characteristic. Most individual-difference measures of stereotypicality include both stereotypic (e.g., *rude*) and counterstereotypic items (e.g., *polite*), allowing researchers to compute a difference score (cabbies are rude but not polite), minimizing the effects of individual differences in scale usage.

Percentage estimates   Percentage estimates (Park & Rothbart, 1982) are a common measure of prevalence. These measures present one or more social categories (e.g., men and women) and one or more stereotype-relevant attributes, such as traits, behaviors or statements (e.g., *ambitious* or *likely to help others*). Participants indicate, for each attribute, the percentage of the group they believe to be characterized by that attribute or likely to engage in that behavior. Park and Judd (1990) concluded that Percentage Estimates were both easy for participants to complete and reliable measures of stereotypicality.

Distribution measures   A variety of stereotype measures instruct the participant to specify the distribution of members of a group along some dimension of interest. A *histogram* task presents participants with a target group and a particular trait dimension (e.g., stingy–generous) and asks the participants to draw a histogram indicating the proportion of the group at each point along the dimension. From this distribution, the mean can be computed providing an estimate of the group's extremity. A similar task involves asking the respondent to simply indicate the location of the typical group member on the dimension as well as the highest and lowest group members (*range* task). One advantageous property of these measures is that they also assess dispersion (see below).

Explicit measures of dispersion

In addition to stereotypicality, explicit measures can be used to assess perceptions about the degree to which group members vary on a given characteristic (Park & Judd, 1990). Two participants may both rate cab drivers as moderately rude on average, with trait ratings of 8 on an 11-point scale. But measures of stereotypicality provide no information about the degree to which the participants perceive variability in the group. One participant may believe that cab drivers are uniform in their moderately rude natures. The other participant, while agreeing about the group's general rating, may see dramatic variability among group members. Although the question of dispersion or variability has received less attention than that of stereotypicality in the literature, it represents a crucial component because high variability should diminish one's ability to make inferences about individuals based on stereotypes (e.g., Lambert, Payne, Ramsey, et al., 2005; Park & Rothbart, 1982; Park & Judd, 1990; Ryan, Judd, & Park, 1996).

Distribution measures   One nice feature of the histogram and range tasks (described above) is that they simultaneously measure both stereotypicality (extremity of the mean) and dispersion (the variance of the distribution in the histogram task, the range of the most extreme group members in the range task). Though the histogram task is relatively labor intensive for participants, the range task is an easy measure that provides reliable estimates of both stereotypicality and dispersion (Park & Judd, 1990).

Similarity or homogeneity ratings   One straightforward assessment of dispersion simply involves asking participants how similar members are to one another. Similarity measures may focus on the group as a whole, asking participants to rate cabbies

on a 10-point scale from *all alike* to *large differences* (Park & Rothbart, 1982). An alternative measure involves paired-similarity ratings of individual group members. In this task, participants consider a subset of people, two at a time, and rate the similarity of each pair of individuals. By including pairs of individuals from the same group, researchers can assess *within*-group similarity. By including individuals from two different groups, researchers can assess *between*-group similarity. By calculating the ratio of within-group similarity to between-group similarity (a metacontrast ratio, Turner, Oakes, Haslam, et al., 1994), the researcher can assess differentiation within and between groups.

Implicit stereotype measures

Implicit stereotype measures usually assess stereotypicality (rather than dispersion) and generally rely on computer presentation of stimuli and response recording. These methods constitute the bulk of the discussion that follows, but we conclude by describing implicit measures that gauge both stereotypicality and dispersion without the use of computers.

Implicit measures of stereotypicality
Lexical decision task (LDT)   Early work on semantic priming in cognitive psychology (e.g., Meyer & Schvaneveldt, 1971) showed that participants could recognize letter strings as words more quickly when those strings were preceded by semantically related words. The judgment task in these early studies involved a lexical decision – participants decided whether the string was (or was not) a word. Several studies build directly on this approach for the purpose of measuring stereotypes (e.g., Dovidio, Evans, & Tyler, 1986; Gaertner & McLaughlin, 1983; Wittenbrink, Judd, & Park, 1997). For example, Wittenbrink, Judd, & Park (1997) briefly presented participants with either social category labels (BLACK or WHITE) or a meaningless string of letters (XXXXX). Subsequently, a target letter string appeared,

including nonwords and words that were stereotypic of either Blacks (athletic, poor) or Whites (ambitious, stuffy). In keeping with work on semantic priming, racial labels facilitated judgments of stereotype-congruent words.

Response-compatibility tasks

Because a LDT requires word–nonword judgments, responses to the words require the same response, whether they are stereotypic of Whites or Blacks. Effects in this paradigm are therefore presumably due to compatibility between the prime and target stimuli, rather than between the primes and the response options (De Houwer, 2003b). This characteristic differentiates the LDT from a number of other priming tasks in which participants classify a target according to some category-relevant dimension. For example, Banaji and Hardin (1996) presented 200-ms primes related to stereotypically gendered occupations (e.g., nurse, mechanic), followed by target words consisting of male and female pronouns (e.g., he, she). Participants classified these targets as either male or female by pressing one of two buttons. The results suggest that female-stereotypic primes facilitate classification of female pronouns and male-stereotypic primes facilitate classification of male pronouns. But note that, in these studies, it is unclear whether the primes affect the accessibility of the target representation (i.e., the prime 'nurse' makes it easier to recognize the pronoun 'she') or whether they predispose participants to make the congruent response (e.g., the prime 'nurse' promotes a response using the button associated with female). Similar tasks involving images, rather than words, have used Black and White faces as primes and shown that guns, for instance, are classified as such more readily following Black faces than White faces (Payne, 2001).

Implicit association test

The IAT (Greenwald et al., 1998) is discussed thoroughly in the section titled "Measuring Prejudice". We mention it here because the task can easily be adapted for measurement of stereotypes by replacing the positive/negative stimuli with items related to the semantic dimension of interest (Greenwald, Banaji, Rudman, et al., 2002).

Linguistic intergroup bias

Several clever, noncomputer-based tasks can be used to implicitly measure stereotypes. Drawing on Fiedler, Semin, and Bolten's (1989) linguistic category model, Maass (1999) suggested that participants use more abstract terminology to describe behavior on the part of a group member that was stereotypic of the group as a whole. Because such behavior presumably reflects more stable characteristics, it should be described in a general, abstract fashion ('Robert is smart'). By contrast, atypical behavior should be described in a concrete, situation-specific fashion ('Robert answered the question correctly'). Accordingly, a chess master's intelligent behavior may be described in more abstract terms than the same behavior when it is attributed to a hairdresser, but a hairdresser's sociable behavior may be described more abstractly than such behavior when it is attributed to a chess master (e.g., Wenneker, Wigboldus, & Spears, 2005).

Behavioral priming

Bargh, Chen, and Burrows (1996) offer another measure of implicit stereotyping. These researchers asked participants to perform a task in which they had embedded a number of words related to the stereotype of elderly people. The manipulation prompted participants to behave in a manner consistent with the stereotype of the primed social category, walking more slowly. The authors argue that consideration of the group activates thoughts about group-typical behavior, which in turn increases the likelihood of engaging in that behavior (cf. Cesario, Plaks, & Higgins, 2006).

Implicit measures of dispersion

Who-said-what paradigm

Confronted with two groups of people, an observer may attend to relevant category information rather than individuating information. Taylor, Fiske, Etcoff, et al. (1978) simulated a group discussion of male and female teachers and asked participants to keep track of who said what. Participants were more likely to confuse the comments of one woman for those of another woman or to confuse the comments of one man for another man than they were to confuse the comments of a woman for those of a man or vice versa. That is, the participants made more within-category confusions than between-category confusions. This paradigm provides, in essence, an implicit measure of within-group dispersion and metacontrast. The original paradigm was methodologically complicated, but subsequent work has streamlined the procedure (e.g., Kurzban, Tooby, & Cosmides, 2001).

DISCRIMINATION

Discrimination involves behavior directed toward members of a social category that is consequential for their outcomes and that is directed toward them simply because of their category membership. *Behavior* is defined broadly to include both actions directed toward group members, as well as judgments/decisions regarding these individuals, such as hiring decisions.

Discriminatory behavior presumably derives in part from stereotypes and prejudices, and assessment of discrimination therefore has much in common with measurement of these constructs. However, measurement of discrimination is uniquely difficult. First, behavior is multiply determined. In a classic field paradigm (West, Whitney, & Schnedler, 1975), confederates posed as stranded motorists and frequency of helping was observed. If the motorist is wearing a traditional Muslim Hijab, stereotypes and prejudices may come to mind and affect the rate of helping. However, helping depends not only on the headdress and what it brings to mind, but on how busy the traveler is, whether the traveler feels capable of offering assistance, and whether screaming children are in the traveler's car. Though differences in helping can be observed, the data are often very noisy. Second, strong norms exist regarding acceptable behavior.

In general, people may feel entitled to their own preferences and beliefs, but behavior is somewhat different, as indicated by the laws that dictate acceptable behavior (but not feelings or beliefs) toward various social groups (e.g., the US Civil Rights Act). Third, unlike stereotypes and prejudices that can be measured relatively efficiently, behaviors must occur in a context with some degree of realism to be ecologically valid. The importance of both normative constraints and ecological validity constitute serious challenges for measurement. Normative pressure increases the importance of implicit measures of discrimination, which limit either control or awareness. But, it is very hard to construct ecologically meaningful paradigms that are so demanding or fast that they are no longer controllable. Implicit measures of discrimination therefore focus primarily on masking the true nature of the study. Working within these constraints, three types of paradigms dominate discrimination research: Laboratory experiments that disguise the nature of the research, field experiments, and outcome studies.

Laboratory studies

Many laboratory studies examine concrete behavior. For example, in the classic seating task developed by Weitz (1972), participants are asked to arrange chairs in a room for an upcoming discussion with another participant who belongs to a social group of interest (e.g., Blacks). A more elaborate task measures nonverbal behavior in an interaction between, for example, a White subject acting as interviewer, and a Black 'interviewee' (Word, Zanna, & Cooper, 1974). In both cases, discrimination is reflected in behaviors that distance the participant from the interaction partner. Many studies examine differential helping or punishment. Gaertner and Dovidio (1977) utilized the Lady-in-Distress paradigm to feign an emergency in which the (White) participant's willingness to help was examined as a function of the victim's race. Donnerstein and

Donnerstein (1972) employed the teacher–learner paradigm, measuring aggression toward Black versus White learners via the intensity and duration of shocks administered. Discrimination can also be assessed via participants' decisions about how to distribute resources among members of various groups (e.g., Tajfel, Billig, Bundy, et al., 1971).

Other laboratory studies examine more abstract judgments (as opposed to concrete behavior), assuming that they have consequences for downstream behavior. Heilman, Martell, and Simon (1988) asked students in a laboratory setting to judge job candidates, examining bias as a function of applicant gender. Bodenhausen and Lichtenstein (1987) examined the effect of ethnicity on judgments of a defendant's guilt in a court case. Ryan, Judd, and Park (1996) examined the perceived math ability of members of a work team as a function of target ethnicity (Asian versus other) where the group stereotype might be relevant to success.

These paradigms require great care to conceal the nature of the investigation. The critically independent variable (e.g., the ethnicity of the suspect on trial) should be varied between participants, in an effort to minimize the participants' awareness. Thus, a participant might read about *either* a Latino *or* a White suspect in a court case (never both). Even with such precautions, factors that call attention to group membership may invoke norms and eliminate evidence of discrimination (Sommers & Ellsworth, 2000). When the participant is unaware, then these can be seen as implicit discrimination measures.

Field studies

Because field experiments occur in a more natural setting, there is less concern over arousing suspicion. These methods, however, tend to be time intensive and expensive. A number of field experiments have examined helping behavior. In the Lost Letter Technique (Milgram, Mann, & Harter, 1965), stamped letters addressed to various organizations are left in public places. The number of letters

that passers-by ultimately mail is assessed as a function of the addressee. Bushman and Bonacci (2004) present a modern version of this paradigm, the lost email technique, in which participants mistakenly receive an email intended for another student (who is Arab or not) with time-sensitive news. Of interest is whether the student alerts the sender to the mistake. Other paradigms gauge willingness to help a caller who has just spent his/her last dime mistakenly calling you (though in the age of cell phones, the utility of this paradigm is questionable), someone who drops papers or books, or knocks over a cup of pencils (Crosby, Bromley, & Saxe, 1980). Saucier, Miller, and Doucet (2005) provide a meta-analysis of these studies, noting that the most interesting effects involved moderating factors, such as whether participants could rationalize a failure to help (e.g., it takes too long), in which case Blacks were less likely to be helped than Whites.

A second group of field experiments focuses on discriminatory (rather than helping) behavior. La Piere (1934) and Schuman (1983) examined real world instances of discrimination at restaurants and/or hotels toward ethnic minority groups. Glick, Zion, and Nelson (1988) examined gender discrimination in hiring by asking professionals to evaluate bogus resumes of men and women for jobs that were either masculine or feminine in nature. One of the strongest methodologies used in field research involves paired tests in which carefully matched testers that vary only on the critical dimension (e.g., race) are meticulously trained and then sent into the field to buy a car or rent an apartment. Typically tests are conducted across a wide geographic area (e.g., Ross & Turner, 2005). As is clear in these examples of field experiments, external and internal validity are high, but the studies are labor intensive and therefore quite costly to conduct.

Outcome studies

Finally, outcomes studies document disparities in important domains as a function of group membership. Based on a huge number of such studies, there is little question as to whether or not these disparities exist (see the chapters that make up Part V of this volume). Ethnic minorities consistently experience worse health outcomes (e.g., Barnett & Halverson, 2001), worse school performance (e.g., Cohen, Garcia, Apfel, et al., 2006), and harsher treatment in the justice system (Geller, 1982). In both business and academic domains, women are paid less and hold positions of lower status than men, controlling for occupation and qualifications (see Goldman, Gutek, Stein, et al., 2006; Handelsman, Cantor, Carnes, 2005).

Conceptual difficulties

The field does not lack for sheer quantity of research examining discrimination. Still, numerous difficulties surround this research. We focus on two. One of the most profound questions involves the interpretation of research findings. It seems clear that differences exist, but what causes them and what do they mean? Does discrimination, itself, contribute to racial differences in health outcomes over and above, for example, biology, education, and culture? In outcome studies this problem is obvious. But even in laboratory studies where control is maximal, we are left with the question of how best to interpret the effects. For example, Word, Zanna, & Cooper (1974) found that Black (relative to White) interviewees experienced shorter interviews, more speech errors, less eye contact, and greater physical distance from the interviewer. Do these differences derive from prejudice, or do they indicate merely that the interviewers are anxious when interviewing Blacks? Goff, Steele, and Davies (2008) argue that distancing behavior might reflect Whites' concern over appearing racist even without interracial animosity. Indeed, Shelton, Richeson, Salvatore, et al. (2005) found that Blacks actually preferred an interaction with more (versus less) prejudiced Whites, presumably because high-prejudice Whites worked harder to manage impressions (see Chapter 17 by Richeson & Shelton, this volume). Though it may appear

simple, the interpretation of behavior is rarely straightforward.

A related issue concerns the very definition of discrimination. The legal world has defined discrimination as involving motivation and a conscious awareness that one is discriminating (Krieger, 1995, 2004). This raises two questions. First, does variation in the strength of prejudiced feelings or stereotypic beliefs predict discrimination? Second, is it possible for discrimination to occur without the actor's awareness? Dovidio, Kawakami, and Gaertner (2002) examined explicit and implicit measures of prejudice as well as actual and perceived bias in verbal and nonverbal interactions with Blacks. Explicit attitudes predicted bias in verbal behavior and participants' self-perceptions of friendliness. But implicit attitudes predicted friendliness in nonverbal behavior, as well as confederates' and observers' perceptions of friendliness. Discrimination may depend partly on explicitly articulated attitudes, but implicit attitudes also seem to have consequences for the target, presumably without the actor's awareness. As discussed in the introduction, the separable effects of implicit and explicit attitudes suggest that interactions, which seem innocuous to one person, may seem like clear-cut evidence of discrimination to another.

CONCLUDING COMMENTS AND FUTURE DIRECTIONS

This necessarily concise review of measurement approaches to prejudice, stereotyping, and discrimination leads us to a number of conclusions. The complexity of these constructs has given rise to a profusion of measurement techniques, making it clear that there is no 'best' or preferred measurement approach. Multiple approaches exist because the constructs, themselves, are multifaceted. As measures have been elaborated, they have helped students of this area identify important distinctions. For example, the construct of stereotypicality differs from that of dispersion; modern racism, with its emphasis on the violation of values, cannot be equated with simple racial hatred; and probably most dramatically, implicit measures assess very different kinds of attitudes than do explicit measures. As we noted in the introduction, new approaches to measurement have powerfully shaped the development of theory about prejudice, stereotyping, and discrimination.

A second and related point is that the plethora of approaches and the complexity of the constructs that are measured, suggest that the issue of convergent validity among the different measures is a complex one. Most recently, a great deal of attention has been focused on the extent to which implicit and explicit measures of prejudice and stereotyping are related to each other (e.g., Nosek, 2005). What is clear is that such relationships depend on a variety of factors, such as the target group toward which attitudes are assessed and the situational contexts and demands under which the attitudes are measured. While we might expect that different measures of the same or related constructs covary, the variable pattern of relationships between explicit and implicit measures of prejudice and stereotyping strongly suggest that these constructs operate at many different levels and deserve a multifaceted approach.

In a related vein, the issue of how measures of prejudice and stereotyping, on the one hand, relate to behavioral discrimination, on the other hand, is also a complex subject that we have only just touched on. One of the interesting emerging suggestions (Fazio, Jackson, J. R., Dunton, 1995; McConnell & Leibold, 2001) is that such relationships also depend on whether prejudice and stereotyping are measured with implicit or explicit procedures. Different sorts of behaviors may be predicted by different approaches to the measurement of prejudice.

A final, related point is that, just as there is no best approach to measurement, we would suggest that there is no single construct to be measured. There is no 'true' intergroup attitude that might be measured once and for all if only we had the proper approach. Views fluctuate as a function of the situation, the groups involved, the kind of response that is demanded of participants (to name only a few). Initially there was great excitement as implicit measures were developed that they might permit a final and conclusive view of prejudice levels. In retrospect, it is clear that, while they provide powerful insight, implicit assessments are far from definitive. Just as theoretical perspectives on prejudice, stereotyping and discrimination will continue to mature in the coming years, we have no doubt that new approaches to measurement will develop. We view the reciprocal effects of these refinements, as theory shapes measurement and measurement guides theory, as one hallmark of a vibrant field of study.

REFERENCES

Adorno, T. W., Frenkel-Brunswick, E., Levinson, D. J., & Sanford, R. N. (1950). *The Authoritarian Personality.* New York: Harper and Row.

Allen, B. P. (1975). Social distance and admiration reactions of "unprejudiced" Whites. *Journal of Personality*, 43, 709–726.

Allport, G. W. (1954). *The Nature of Prejudice.* Reading, MA: Addison-Wesley.

Altemeyer, B. (1981). *Right-Wing Authoritarianism.* Winnipeg, Canada: University of Manitoba Press.

Altemeyer, B. (1988). *Enemies of Freedom: Understanding Right-Wing Authoritarianism.* San Francisco: Jossey-Bass.

Alwin, D. F. (1992). Information transmission in the survey interview: Number of response categories and the reliability of attitude measurement. *Sociological Methodology*, 22, 83–118.

Amodio, D. M., Harmon-Jones, E., & Devine, P. G. (2003). Individual differences in the activation and control of affective race bias as assessed by startle eyeblink response and self-report. *Journal of Personality and Social Psychology*, 84, 738–753.

Banaji, M. R., & Hardin, C. D. (1996). Automatic stereotyping. *Psychological Science*, 7, 136–141.

Banse, R. (2001). Affective priming with liked and disliked persons: Prime visibility determines congruency and incongruency effects. *Cognition and Emotion*, 15, 501–520.

Bargh, J. A. (1994). The four horsemen of automaticity: Awareness, intention, efficiency, and control in social cognition. In R. S. Wyer, & T. K. Srull (Eds), *Handbook of Social Cognition* (2nd edition, pp. 1–40). Hillsdale, NJ: Erlbaum.

Bargh, J.A., Chen, M., & Burrows, L. (1996). Automaticity of social behavior: Direct effects of trait construct and stereotype activation on action. *Journal of Personality and Social Psychology*, 71, 230–244.

Barnett, E., & Halverson, J. A. (2001). Local increases in coronary heart disease mortality among blacks and whites in the United States, 1985 to 1995. *American Journal of Public Health*, 21, 1499–1506.

Biernat, M., & Crandall, C.S. (1999). Racial attitudes. In J. P. Robinson, P. R. Shaver, & L. S. Wrightsman (Eds), *Measures of Political Attitudes* (pp. 297–411). Academic Press: San Diego.

Bobo, L. (1983). 'Whites' opposition to busing: Symbolic racism or realistic group conflict? *Journal of Personality and Social Psychology*, 45, 1196–1210.

Bodenhausen, G. V., & Lichtenstein, M. (1987). Social stereotypes and information processing strategies: The impact of task complexity. *Journal of Personality and Social Psychology*, 52, 871–880.

Bogardus, E. S. (1933). A social distance scale. *Sociology and Social Research*, 17, 265–271.

Bradburn, N., Sudman, S., & Wansink, B. (2004). *Asking Questions: The Definitive Guide to Questionnaire Design – For Market Research, Political Polls, and Social and Health Questionnaires* (Revised edition). San Francisco: Jossey-Bass.

Brewer, M. B. (1968). Determinants of social distance among East African tribal groups. *Journal of Personality and Social Psychology*, 10, 279–289.

Bushman, B. J., & Bonacci, A. M. (2004). You've got mail: Using e-mail to examine the effect of prejudiced attitudes on discrimination against Arabs. *Journal of Experimental Social Psychology*, 40, 753–759.

Byrnes, D. A., & Kiger, G. (1988). Contemporary measures of attitudes toward Blacks. *Educational and Psychological Measurement*, 48, 107–118.

Cacioppo, J. T., & Sandman, C. A. (1981). Psychophysiological functioning, cognitive responding, and attitudes. In R. E. Petty, T. M. Ostrom, & T. C. Brock (Eds), *Cognitive Responses in Persuasion* (pp. 81–103). Hillsdale, NJ: Lawrence Erlbaum Associates.

Cameron, J. A., Alvarez, J. M., & Bargh, J. A. (2000). *Examining the Validity of Implicit Measures of Prejudice.* Paper presented at the First meeting of the Society for Personality and Social Psychology, Nashville, TN.

Cesario, J., Plaks, J. E., & Higgins, E. T. (2006). Automatic social behavior as motivated preparation to interact. *Journal of Personality and Social Psychology*, 90, 893–910.

Cohen, G. L., Garcia, J., Apfel, N., & Master, A. (2006). Reducing the racial achievement gap: A social-psychological intervention. *Science*, 313, 1307–1310.

Converse, J. M., & Presser, S. (1986). *Survey Questions: Handcrafting the Standardized Questionnaire.* Belmont, CA: Sage Publications.

Crosby, F., Bromley, S., & Saxe, L. (1980). Recent unobtrusive studies of Black and White discrimination and prejudice: A literature review. *Psychological Bulletin*, 87, 546–563.

Cuthbert, B. N., Bradley, M. M., & Lang, P. J. (1996). Probing picture perception: Activation and emotion. *Psychophysiology*, 33, 103–111.

De Houwer, J. (2003a). The extrinsic affective Simon task. *Experimental Psychology*, 50, 77–85.

De Houwer, J. (2003b). A structural analysis of indirect measures of attitudes. In J. Musch, & K. C. Klauer (Eds). *The Psychology of Evaluation: Affective Processes in Cognition and Emotion* (pp. 219–244). Mahwah, NJ: Erlbaum.

De Houwer, J., Teige-Mocigemba, S., Spruyt, A., & Moors, A. (in press). Implicit measures: A normative analysis and review. *Psychological Bulletin.*

Degner, J. (in press). On the (un)controllability of affective priming: Strategic manipulation is feasible but can possibly be prevented. *Cognition and Emotion.*

Devine, P.G. (1989). Stereotypes and prejudice: Their automatic and controlled components. *Journal of Personality and Social Psychology*, 56, 5–18.

Donnerstein, E., & Donnerstein, M. (1972). White rewarding behavior as a function of the potential for black retaliation. *Journal of Personality and Social Psychology*, 24, 327–333.

Dovidio, J. F., Evans, N., & Tyler, R. (1986). Racial stereotypes: The contents of their cognitive representations. *Journal of Experimental Social Psychology*, 22, 22–37.

Dovidio, J. F., Kawakami, K., & Gaertner, S. L. (2002). Implicit and explicit prejudice and interracial interaction. *Journal of Personality and Social Psychology*, 82, 62–68.

Fazio, R. H., Jackson, J. R., Dunton, B.C., & Williams, C.J. (1995). Variability in automatic activation as an unobtrusive measure of racial attitudes: A bona fide pipeline? *Journal of Personality and Social Psychology*, 69, 1013–1027.

Fazio, R. H., & Olson, M. A. (2003). Implicit measures in social cognition research: Their meaning and use. *Annual Review of Psychology*, 54, 297–327.

Fiedler, K., & Bluemke, M. (2005). Faking the IAT: Aided and unaided response control on the implicit association tests. *Basic and Applied Social Psychology*, 27, 307–316.

Fiedler, K., Semin, G. R., & Bolten, S. (1989). Language use and reification of social information: Top-down and bottom-up processing in person cognition. *European Journal of Social Psychology*, 19, 271–295.

Fiske, S. T. (1998). Stereotyping, prejudice, and discrimination. In D. T. Gilbert, S. T. Fiske, & G. Lindzey (Eds), *The Handbook of Social Psychology* (4th edition, Vol. 2, pp. 357–414). Boston: McGraw-Hill.

Gaertner, S. L., & Dovidio, J. F. (1977). The subtlety of White racism, arousal, and helping behavior. *Journal of Personality and Social Psychology*, 35, 691–707.

Gaertner, S. L., & Dovidio, J. F. (1986). The aversive form of racism. In J. F. Dovidio, & S. L. Gaertner (Eds), *Prejudice, Discrimination, and Racism* (pp. 61–89). Orlando, FL: Academic Press.

Gaertner, S. L., & McLaughlin, J. P. (1983). Racial stereotypes: Associations and ascriptions of positive and negative characteristics. *Social Psychology Quarterly*, 46, 23–30.

Geller, W. A. (1982). Deadly force: What we know. *Journal of Police Science and Administration*, 10, 151–177.

Glick, P., Zion, C., & Nelson, C. (1988). What mediates sex discrimination in hiring decisions? *Journal of Personality and Social Psychology*, 55, 178–186.

Goff, P. A., Steele, C. M., & Davies, P. G. (2008). The space between us: Stereotype threat and distance in interracial contexts. *Journal of Personality and Social Psychology*, 94, 91–107.

Goldman, B. M., Gutek, B. A., Stein, J. H., & Lewis, K. (2006). Employment discrimination in organizations: Antecedents and consequences. *Journal of Management*, 32, 786–830.

Greenwald, A. G., Banaji, M. R., Rudman, L. A., Farnham, S. D., Nosek, B. A., & Mellott, D. S. (2002). A unified theory of implicit attitudes, stereotypes, self-esteem, and self-concept. *Psychological Review*, 109, 3–25.

Greenwald, A. G., McGhee, D. E., & Schwartz, J. L. K. (1998). Measuring individual differences in implicit cognition: The implicit association test. *Journal of Personality and Social Psychology*, 74, 1464–1480.

Greenwald, A. G., Nosek, B. A., & Banaji, M. R. (2003). Understanding and using the Implicit Association Test: I. An improved scoring algorithm. *Journal of Personality and Social Psychology*, 85, 197–216.

Greenwald, A. G., Poehlman, T. A., Uhlmann, E. L., & Banaji, M. R. (in press). Understanding and using the Implicit Association Test: III. Meta-analysis of predictive validity. *Journal of Personality and Social Psychology*.

Handelsman, J., Cantor, N., Carnes, N., Denton, D., Fine, E., Grosz, B., et al. (2005). More women in science. *Science*, 309, 1190–1191.

Heilman, M. E., Martell, R. F., & Simon, M. C. (1988). The vagaries of sex bias: Conditions regulating the undervaluation, equivaluation, and overvaluation of female job applicants. *Organizational Behavior and Human Decision Processes*, 41, 98–110.

Ito, T. A., Willadsen-Jensen, E., & Correll, J. (2007). Social neuroscience and social perception: New perspectives on categorization, prejudice, and stereotyping. In E. Harmon-Jones, & P. Winkielman (Eds), *Social Neuroscience: Integrating Biological and Psychological Explanations of Social Behavior* (pp. 401–421). Guilford Press: New York.

Judd, C. M., & Park, B. (1993). Definition and assessment of accuracy in social stereotypes. *Psychological Review*, 100, 109–128.

Karpinski, A., & Steinman, R. B. (2006). The single category implicit association test as a measure of implicit social cognition. *Journal of Personality and Social Psychology*, 91, 16–32.

Katz, D., & Braly, K. (1933). Racial stereotypes of one hundred college students. *Journal of Abnormal and Social Psychology*, 28, 280–290.

Katz, I., & Hass, R. G. (1988). Racial ambivalence and American value conflict: Correlational and priming studies of dual cognitive structures. *Journal of Personality and Social Psychology*, 55, 893–905.

Kinder, D. R., & Sears, D. O. (1981). Prejudice and politics: Symbolic racism versus racial threats to the good life. *Journal of Personality and Social Psychology*, 40, 414–431.

Klauer, K. C., & Musch, J. (2003). Affective priming: Findings and theories. In J. Musch, & K. C. Klauer (Eds), *The Psychology of Evaluation: Affective Processes in Cognition and Emotion* (pp. 7–50). Mahwah, NJ: Lawrence Erlbaum Associates.

Krieger, L. H. (1995). The content of our categories: A cognitive bias approach to discrimination and equal employment opportunity. *Stanford Law Review*, 47, 1161–1248.

Krieger, L. H. (2004). The intuitive psychologist behind the bench: Models of gender bias in social psychology and employment discrimination law. *Journal of Social Issues*, 60, 835–848.

Kurzban, R., Tooby, J., & Cosmides, L. (2001). Can race be erased? Coalitional computation and social categorization. *Proceedings of the National Academy of Sciences*, 98, 15387–15392.

La Piere, R. T. (1934). Attitudes vs. action. *Social Forces*, 13, 230–237.

Lambert, A. J., Payne, B. K., Ramsey, S., & Shaffer, L. M. (2005). On the predictive validity of implicit attitude measures: The moderating effect of perceived group variability. *Journal of Experimental Social Psychology*, 41, 114–128.

Lang, P. J., Bradley, M. M., & Cuthbert, B. N. (1990). Emotion, attention, and the startle reflex. *Psychological Review*, 97, 377–395.

Lowery, B. S., Hardin, C. D., & Sinclair, S. (2001). Social influence effects on automatic racial prejudice. *Journal of Personality and Social Psychology*, 81, 842–855.

Maass, A. (1999). Linguistic intergroup bias: Stereotype perpetuation through language. In M. P. Zanna (Ed.), *Advances in Experimental Social Psychology* (Vol. 31, pp. 79–121). San Diego, CA: Academic Press.

McConahay, J. B., & Hough, J. C. (1976). Symbolic racism. *Journal of Social Issues*, 32, 23–45.

McConahay, J. B., Hardee, B. B., & Batts, V. (1981). Has racism declined in America? It depends on who is asking and what is asked. *Journal of Conflict Resolution*, 25, 563–579.

McConnell, A. R., & Leibold, J. M. (2001). Relations among the Implicit Association Test, discriminatory behavior, and explicit measures of racial attitudes. *Journal of Experimental Social Psychology*, 37, 435–442.

Meyer, D. E., & Schvaneveldt, R. W. (1971). Facilitation in recognizing pairs of words: Evidence of a dependence between retrieval operations. *Journal of Experimental Psychology*, 90, 227–234.

Milgram, S., Mann, L., & Harter, S. (1965). The lost-letter technique: A tool of social research. *Public Opinion Quarterly*, 29, 437–438.

Murphy, S. T., & Zajonc, R. B. (1993). Affect, cognition, and awareness: Affective priming with optimal and suboptimal stimulus exposures. *Journal of Personality and Social Psychology*, 64, 723–739.

Nosek, B. A. (2005). Moderators of the relationship between implicit and explicit evaluation. *Journal of Experimental Psychology: General*, 134, 565–584.

Nosek, B. A., & Banaji, M. R. (2001). The go/no-go association task. *Social Cognition,* 19, 625–666.

Nosek, B. A., Greenwald, A. G., & Banaji, M. R. (2007). The implicit association test at age 7: A methodological and conceptual review. In J. A. Bargh (Ed.), *Social Psychology and the Unconscious: The Automaticity of Higher Mental Processes* (pp. 265–292). Psychology Press: New York.

Olson, M. A., & Fazio, R. H. (2003). Relations between implicit measures of prejudice: What are we measuring? *Psychological Science*, 14, 636–639.

Olson, M. A., & Fazio, R. H. (2004). Reducing the influences of extrapersonal associations on the Implicit Association Test: Personalizing the IAT.

Journal of Personality and Social Psychology, 86, 653–667.

Park, B., & Judd, C. M. (1990). Measures and models of perceived group variability. *Journal of Personality and Social Psychology, 59*, 173–191.

Park, B., & Rothbart, M. (1982). Perception of out-group homogeneity and levels of social categorization: Memory for the subordinate attributes of in-group and out-group members. *Journal of Personality and Social Psychology*, 42, 1051–1068.

Payne, B. K. (2001). Prejudice and perception: The role of automatic and controlled processes in misperceiving a weapon. *Journal of Personality and Social Psychology*, 81, 181–192.

Payne, B. K., Cheng, C. M., Govorum, O., & Stewart, B. D. (2004). *An Inkblot for Attitudes: Affect Misattribution as Implicit Measurement.* Unpublished manuscript, Ohio State University.

Pratto, F., Sidanius, J., & Levin, S. (2006). Social dominance theory and the dynamics of intergroup relations: Taking stock and looking forward. *European Review of Social Psychology*, 17, 271–320.

Pratto, F., Sidanius, J., Stallworth, L. M., & Malle, B. F. (1994). Social dominance orientation: A personality variable predicting social and political attitudes. *Journal of Personality and Social Psychology*, 67, 741–763.

Rankin, R. E., & Campbell, D. T. (1955). Galvanic skin response to Negro and White experimenters. *Journal of Abnormal and Social Psychology*, 51, 30–33.

Ross, S. L., & Turner, M. A. (2005). Housing discrimination in metropolitan America: Explaining changes between 1989 and 2000. *Social Problems*, 52, 152–180.

Ryan, C. S., Judd, C. M., & Park, B. (1996). Effects of racial stereotypes on judgments of individuals: The moderating role of perceived group variability. *Journal of Experimental Social Psychology*, 32, 71–103.

Saucier, D. A., Miller, C. T., & Doucet, N. (2005). Differences in helping Whites and Blacks: A meta-analysis. *Personality and Social Psychology Review*, 9, 2–16.

Schuman, H. (1983). Discriminatory behavior in New York restaurants: 1950 and 1981. *Social Indicators Research*, 13, 69–83.

Schuman, H., Steeh, C., Bobo, L., & Krysan, M. (1997). *Racial Attitudes in America: Trends and Interpretations* (Revised edition). Cambridge: Harvard University Press.

Shelton, J. N., Richeson, J. A., Salvatore, J., & Trawalter, S. (2005). Ironic effects of racial bias during interracial interactions. *Psychological Science*, 16, 397–402.

Sidanius, J., & Pratto, F. (1999). *Social Dominance: An Intergroup Theory of Social Hierarchy and Oppression.* New York: Cambridge University Press.

Sigall, H., & Page, R. (1971). Current stereotypes: A little fading, a little faking. *Journal of Personality and Social Psychology*, 18, 247–255.

Sniderman, P. M., & Tetlock, P. E. (1986). Symbolic racism: Problems of motive attribution in political analysis. *Journal of Social Issues*, 42, 129–150.

Sniderman, P. M., Piazza, T., Tetlock, P. E., & Kendrick, A. (1991). The new racism. *American Journal of Political Science*, 35, 423–447.

Steffens, M. C. (2004). Is the Implicit Association Test immune to faking? *Experimental Psychology*, 51, 165–179.

Sommers, S. R., & Ellsworth, P. C. (2000). Race in the courtroom: Perceptions of guilt and dispositional attributions. *Personality and Social Psychology Bulletin*, 26, 1367–1379.

Taylor, S. E., Fiske, S. T., Etcoff, N. L., & Ruderman, A. J. (1978). Categorical and contextual bases of person memory and stereotyping. *Journal of Personality and Social Psychology*, 36, 778–793.

Tajfel, H., Billig, M. G., Bundy, R. P., & Flament, C. (1971). Social categorization and intergroup behaviour. *European Journal of Social Psychology*, 1, 149–178.

Teige-Mocigemba, S., & Klauer, K.C. (2008). "Automatic" evaluation? Strategic effects on affective priming. *Journal of Experimental Social Psychology*, 44, 1414–1417.

Towles-Schwen, T., & Fazio, R. H. (2006). Automatically activated racial attitudes as predictors of the success of interracial roommate relationships. *Journal of Experimental Social Psychology*, 42, 698–705.

Turner, J. C., Oakes, P. J., Haslam, S. A., & McGarty, C. (1994), Self and collective: Cognition and social context. *Personality and Social Psychology Bulletin*, 20, 454–463.

Vanman, E. J., Saltz, J. L., Nathan, L. R., & Warren, J. A. (2004). Racial discrimination by low-prejudiced Whites facial movements as implicit measures of attitudes related to behavior. *Psychological Science*, 15, 711–714.

Vargas, P. T., Sekaquaptewa, D., & von Hippel, W. (2007). Armed only with paper and pencil: "Low-tech" measures of implicit attitudes. In B. Wittenbrink, & N. Schwarz (Eds), *Implicit measures of attitudes* (pp. 103–124). New York, NY: Guilford Press.

Weitz, S. (1972). Attitude, voice, and behavior: A repressed affect model of interracial interaction. *Journal of Personality and Social Psychology*, 24, 14–21.

Wenneker, C. P. J., Wigboldus, D. H. J., & Spears, R. (2005). Biased language use in stereotype maintenance: The role of encoding and goals. *Journal of Personality and Social Psychology*, 89, 504–516.

West, S. G., Whitney, G., & Schnedler, R. (1975). Helping a motorist in distress: The effects of sex, race, and neighborhood. *Journal of Personality and Social Psychology*, 31, 691–698.

Wigboldus, D. H. J., Holland, R. W., & van Knippenberg, A. (2004). Single target implicit associations. *Unpublished mansucript.*

Wittenbrink, B. (2007). Measuring attitudes through priming. In B. Wittenbrink, & N. Schwarz (Eds), *Implicit Measures of Attitudes* (pp. 17–58). New York, NY: Guilford Press.

Wittenbrink, B., & Henly, J.R. (1996). Creating social reality: Informational social influence and the content of stereotypic beliefs. *Personality and Social Psychology Bulletin*, 22, 598–610.

Wittenbrink, B., Judd, C. M., & Park, B. (1997). Evidence for racial prejudice at the implicit level and its relationship with questionnaire measures. *Journal of Personality and Social Psychology*, 72, 262–274.

Wittenbrink, B., Judd, C. M., & Park, B. (2001). Spontaneous prejudice in context: Variability in automatically activated attitudes. *Journal of Personality and Social Psychology*, 81, 815–827.

Word, C. O., Zanna, M. P., & Cooper, J. (1974). The nonverbal mediation of self-fulfilling prophecies in interracial interaction. *Journal of Experimental Social Psychology*, 10, 109–120.

PART II

Basic Processes and Causes of Prejudice, Stereotyping and Discrimination

Social Cognitive Neural Processes

Susanne Quadflieg, Malia F. Mason,
and C. Neil Macrae

ABSTRACT

To simplify the complexities of everyday interaction, perceivers often use information-processing strategies that result in the stereotype-based construal and treatment of others. Recently, researchers have incorporated neuroscientific tools into the repertoire of techniques they use to elucidate exactly how this process unfolds in the brain. The current chapter reviews some of the latest findings from studies that employ social cognitive neuroscience approaches and considers their significance in light of existing theoretical models of person understanding.

SOCIAL COGNITIVE NEUROSCIENCE: A BRIEF HISTORY

Social psychologists have spent the last 50 years striving to elucidate the strategies that individuals employ when encountering others. But only since the early 1990s has the related interdisciplinary field of social cognitive neuroscience explored core social psychological topics. By combining evidence from classic social-psychological studies with data acquired from neuroimaging, event-related brain potentials, and lesion studies, social cognitive neuroscience strives to explore the social mind from a multilevel perspective. While some of the dominant methods such as neuroimaging have only become available and popular during the last decades, the exploration of the intimate relationship between the human brain and the human mind has a long and impressive scientific history.

Although Galen attributed faculties of the human mind to the brain as early as the second century AD, it was not until the nineteenth century that particular attention was called to the role of the brain for social interaction. By that time, a few well-publicized clinical cases suggested that the frontal lobes might play a pivotal role in the maintenance of social behavior in humans. Most prominently, in 1848, at the age of 25, Phineas Gage, a railroad construction foreman known to be responsible, intelligent, and socially well-adapted, became the victim of an accident. During an explosion a 'tamping iron was hurled, rocket-like, through his face, skull, brain, and then into the sky'

(Damasio, Grabowski, & Frank, et al., 1994, p. 1102), destroying sections of his frontal lobe. Despite surviving the injury without any severe impairments of movement, speech, learning, memory, or intelligence, Gage suffered major changes to his personality leaving him irreverent, irresponsible, and ignorant to social conventions and the needs of others.

The term social neuroscience, however, was not coined until 1992 when Cacioppo and Berntson (1992) called for an interdisciplinary approach to develop and refine our understanding of human social behavior based on biological concepts and methods. During this past quarter century, advances in imaging technology have helped to illuminate how faculties and processes in the human brain differ depending on whether humans encounter and think about conspecifics rather than inanimate objects or nonhuman creatures. As a result of this dramatic growth in neuroscientific data on the 'social brain' (Brothers, 1990) it now seems uncontroversial that 'the human brain has evolved to deal with complex social coordination that supports higher social cognitive functions such as imitation, communication, empathy, theory of mind, interactions, relationships, and collective enterprises' (Cacioppo, Amaral, & Blanchard, et al., 2007, p. 99–100).

Most recently, social-cognitive neuroscientists have also begun to study the neural correlates of stereotyping, prejudice, and discrimination. In attempting to do so it has been noted, however, that these aspects of social cognition cannot be fully elucidated before more fundamental processes of person perception and construal are understood. Although a mere glance at others can be sufficient to construe them quickly as members of generic social categories (i.e., person categorization), this glance also allows the extraction of a wide range of additional person-related information. For instance, facial and bodily cues can be used to infer personality traits or to consider others as unique entities with specific identities (i.e., person individuation). As a result, the attempt to understand how person perception and construal can be tainted by stereotypes and prejudice critically depends on a better understanding of how more primitive aspects of person perception are accomplished in the brain.

THE NEURAL SUBSTRATES OF PERSON PERCEPTION

The ability of the human mind to transform complex 3D visual stimuli that are constantly moving and encountered under varying conditions (i.e., across changes in lighting, distances, and viewpoints) into meaningful percepts of human beings is nothing short of astonishing. Intriguingly, human faces and bodies are reliably discriminated from other object categories early in the visual processing cascade. Recordings of event-related brain potentials (ERPs) indicate that faces, relative to a variety of other objects, elicit an enhanced negative potential at around 170 ms after the onset of a stimulus. This so-called N170 response has reliably been detected using diverse facial stimuli such as schematic, sketched, painted, drawn, and photographed faces, prompting researchers to conclude that the signal is associated with detecting common structural properties of facial stimuli rather than a response to low-level visual properties of faces (see Rossion & Jacques, 2008). In a similar vein, photographs and point-light animations depicting human bodies, silhouettes and stick figures all seem to elicit a body-specific negative component peaking at 190 ms after stimulus onset compared to pictures displaying faces or objects (Hirai, Fukushima, & Hiraki, 2003; Jokisch, Daum, & Suchan, et al., 2005; Pourtois, Peelen, & Spinelli, et al., 2007; Thierry, Pegna, & Dodds, et al., 2006). Taken together, these findings suggest that the brain discriminates the unique properties of human faces and bodies rapidly from other kinds of visual input.

Daily experience attests that from minimal facial and bodily cues, one can quickly decode whether a person is male or female, old or young, happy, distracted, trustworthy, and so on. The human mind is so adroit at reading readily available person cues such as facial features and expression, eye and body orientation, body shape and posture, and/or way of movement that drawing person-based inferences seems to be an inescapable facet of everyday social interaction. Over the last two decades, accumulating neuroscientific evidence has demonstrated that perceiving and construing others is accomplished by an extensive and widely distributed neural system of brain regions. A model by Haxby and colleagues (originally restricted to face perception but applicable to person perception more generally) suggests that brain regions involved in the person-perception process can be divided into two distinct subsystems (Haxby, Hoffman, & Gobbini, 2000; Gobbini & Haxby, 2007): A core neural system that accomplishes the structural and motion-related visual analysis of human faces and bodies based on input from early visual brain regions; and an extended system of brain regions subserving the construal of person inferences using information obtained from the visual analysis accomplished in the core neural system.

Prior to considering recent insights into these subsystems, however, a brief neuro-anatomical orientation may be useful. At a global level, the brain is subdivided into four structures: the *frontal, parietal, temporal,* and *occipital* lobes (see Figure 4.1). *Anterior* refers to the front of the brain, while *posterior* refers to the rear. *Dorsal* regions reside towards the top of the brain, while *ventral* regions are located towards the bottom.

Structures situated close to the midline of the brain (i.e., where the two hemispheres meet) are termed *medial* structures; those located towards the side of the brain are termed *lateral* structures. The terms *superior* and *inferior* mean above and below, respectively. Finally, a *gyrus* refers to a ridge on the surface of the brain, whereas a *sulcus* denotes a depression.

The person perception process consists of a cascade of events that begins when visual light stimulates photoreceptor cells located in the back of the human eye. From the eyes, visual information is sent via fibers in the optic nerve to the brain, with the majority of those fibers terminating in the lateral geniculate nucleus (LGN). From there the information is projected to the primary visual cortex and then distributed via visual association cortices onto two visual pathways, often referred to as the *dorsal* and the *ventral* visual streams (Goodale & Milner, 1992). While the dorsal processing stream is known for its dominant role in stimulus localization, or identifying 'where' in space an object is located, the ventral processing stream determines the identity of a stimulus, or 'what' the object may be (see Figure 4.2). Of particular interest to researchers studying person perception is evidence that four brain regions in the ventral processing stream appear to be specialized for extracting person-related visual information from the environment. Two face-specific areas, the occipital face area (OFA) in the posterior inferior temporal sulcus as well as the fusiform face area (FFA) in the posterior

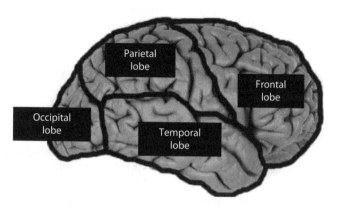

Figure 4.1   The four lobes of human brain.

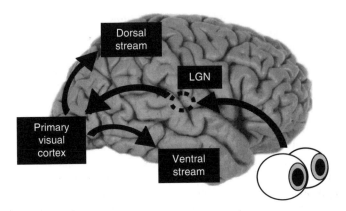

Figure 4.2   Visual pathways in the human brain.

fusiform gyrus, show increased activity when participants view human faces compared to other common objects and nonsense stimuli (Haxby, Hoffman, & Gobbini, 2000; Yovel & Kanwisher, 2005). Similarly, two body-specific areas, the extrastriate body area (EBA) in close proximity but slightly superior to the OFA and the fusiform body area (FBA) situated adjacent to and overlapping with the FFA, display selectively enhanced activity to human bodies (Peelen & Downing, 2007). Interestingly, while the OFA and the EBA seem to encode featural information by processing faces and bodies on the basis of their parts, the FFA and the FBA appear to dominantly support holistic processing by analysing the configuration of these parts (Kanwisher & Yovel, 2006; Pitcher, Walsh, & Yovel, et al., 2007; Rossion, 2008; Taylor, Wiggett, & Downing, 2007; Yovel & Kanwisher, 2005). Hence, it is only through the combined effort of these four cortical regions that a specific structural representation of an individual's facial and bodily appearance can be achieved.

Of considerable debate has been the putative status of person perception in the brain. In brief, the dispute centers around two competing positions. According to the *domain-specific* account, the computations performed by person perception areas evolved specifically for the detection and registration of conspecifics. In contrast, the *domain-general* account contends that the mental

processes engaged during person perception are not specific to people but are flexible and can potentially contribute to the perception of a variety of stimuli. According to this account, processing in person perception areas reflects the encoding of exemplars from classes of homogenous stimuli (e.g., faces, cars). Stimuli of this type can only be differentiated if people attend to diverse stimulus features and their configuration, a task which requires substantial expertise (see Gauthier, Skudlarski, & Gore, et al., 2000). There is evidence, however, that patients who have lost the ability to discriminate faces still retain the capacity to discriminate exemplars within a nonface object category (Duchaine, Yovel, & Butterworth, et al., 2006). Several findings also suggest that the response in core person-perception areas such as the FFA is highly stimulus-specific (for a review see Kanwisher & Yovel, 2006). For example, while car and bird experts exhibit increased FFA responses to these items relative to items for which they do not possess visual expertise, the observed effects are usually small and significantly less strong than the FFA response to faces (see Kanwisher & Yovel, 2006). In addition, even when forced to process houses with the same attention to configural information as is usually paid to faces, activity in the FFA is still only a third as strong relative to when these individuals process faces (Yovel & Kanwisher, 2004). Finally, it can most certainly be assumed that although faces and bodies are visually different, most people have developed substantial expertise to reliably distinguish between different individuals based on both facial and body cues. Nevertheless the FFA and FBA have tuning properties that are strongly selective towards whether they receive body-related or face-related visual input, a finding which also speaks in favor of the domain-specific view.

While the four brain regions in the ventral processing stream contribute to the encoding of static facial and bodily features and their structural configuration (i.e., person snapshots), the posterior superior temporal sulcus (pSTS) which is situated where the dorsal and ventral visual stream converge, integrates static and dynamic person-related information (Blake & Shiffrar, 2007). Robust and selective pSTS activity has been reported when people watch facial movements (e.g., from the eye or mouth region; Puce, Allison, & Bentin, et al., 1998) as well as whole-body or body-part motion relative to when they watch the motion of non-social stimuli (Grèzes, Fonlupt, & Bertenthal, et al., 2001; Pelphrey, Mitchell, & McKeown, et al., 2003). Taken together, the interplay and outputs of the OFA, FFA, EBA, FBA, and pSTS seem to enable the generation of a dynamic person percept.

FROM PERSON PERCEPTION TO INTEGRATIVE PERSON CONSTRUAL

Driven by the goal of making sense of others rapidly and efficiently, perceivers regularly rely on categorical knowledge structures to simplify the person perception process. As a result, impressions and evaluations of others are influenced by the social categories to which they belong (Macrae & Bodenhausen, 2000). With regard to category-based person perception, social psychologists have long distinguished between social categorization (the classification of others according to salient categorical markers), stereotyping (the activation and application of consensual beliefs, i.e., semantic knowledge towards others based on their category memberships),

and prejudice (the evaluation of others based on their group memberships). Given that the indiscriminate application of stereotypes and prejudice can promote judgmental inaccuracy, societal inequality, and intergroup conflict, considerable research efforts have centred on investigating the mental and neural mechanisms that support these processes.

Interestingly, while social psychologists have made noticeable progress at elucidating how social categorization, stereotyping, and prejudice shape person perception and construal, neuroscientific studies have focused almost exclusively on exploring the social categorization of conspecifics. Naturally, a perceiver's propensity to classify others according to meaningful social groups depends on the ease with which this information can be extracted from available visual cues. Critically, the 'big three' categories in person perception – sex, race, and age – can easily be gleaned from facial and bodily cues and therefore dominate people's perceptions of others across a range of social situations. ERP data on race perception have demonstrated that the extraction of categorical markers from faces occurs as quickly as 170–200 ms after face onset (Dickter & Bartholow, 2007; Ito, Thompson, & Cacioppo, 2004; Stahl, Wiese, & Schweinberger, 2008; Walker, Silvert, & Hewstone, et al., 2008). In addition, fMRI data suggest that the fusiform cortex contributes particularly strongly to the extraction of facial gender or race cues (Cloutier, Turk, & Macrae, 2007; Golby, Gabrieli, & Chiao, et al., 2001; Kim, Yoon, & Kim, et al., 2006; Ng, Ciaramitaro, & Anstis, et al., 2006). Most notably, it has been shown that fusiform activation which is thought to reflect the in-depth structural analysis of faces is diminished during the perception of outgroup relative to ingroup faces (i.e., faces that mismatch or match the perceiver on an important social category such as race; Golby, Gabrieli, & Chiao, 2001; Van Bavel, Packer, & Cunningham, 2008). This observation supports previous behavioral research which suggests that categorical face processing reduces the search for unique, individuating characteristics in outgroup faces (Bernstein, Young, &

Hugenberg, 2007). In further support of this idea, it has been found that the difference in fusiform activation towards ingroup and outgroup faces disappears when outgroup faces depict highly familiar others whose unique individuating characteristics are perceptually salient (Kim, Yoon, & Kim, et al., 2006).

Importantly, in contrast to the view that social categorization is an automatic and unavoidable aspect of person perception, recent behavioral evidence suggests that passively viewing a face or making a superficial perceptual judgment (e.g., dot detection) is insufficient to reliably trigger social categorization according to a person's race, age, or sex (Macrae, Quinn, & Mason, et al., 2005; Quinn & Macrae, 2005). To extract such categorical markers, it seems necessary to process the face for social meaning (Macrae, Bodenhausen, & Milne, et al., 1997). These behavioural findings have been mirrored by a pattern of activity observed in the amygdala when people are asked to judge faces under varying processing demands. The amygdala is an almond-shaped mass of nuclei located deep within the medial temporal lobes. Whereas activity in this brain structure tracks with racial status (i.e., the amygdala exhibits increased responses for faces that do not match the perceiver's own race) when participants are making socially meaningful judgments of the targets such as judging their age or sex (e.g., Hart, Whalen, & Shin, et al., 2000; Ronquillo, Denson, & Lickel, et al., 2007; Wheeler & Fiske, 2005), the activity in this region is insensitive to target race when faces are processed at a superficial visual level (i.e., during a dot detection task or a perceptual matching task; Cunningham, Johnson, & Raye, et al., 2004; Phelps, O'Connor, & K. J., Cunningham, et al., 2000; Wheeler & Fiske, 2005). Intriguingly though, the more individuals associate their racial ingroup with positivity and the outgroup with negativity as measured by the implicit association test (IAT), the stronger amygdala activity differentiates between different race faces even under mere perceptual processing conditions (Cunningham, Johnson, & Raye, et al., 2004;

Phelps, O'Connor, & Cunningham, et al., 2000). These findings may suggest that if perceivers consider certain social categories (i.e. race) as particularly important dimensions for construing others, the amygdala's threshold to detect associated categorical markers becomes more sensitive.

Despite the recent advances in understanding the neural underpinnings of social categorization, the exact functional contribution of the amygdala to race-based person perception remains unclear. The activation is unlikely to reflect processes of stereotyping given that it is well known that faces with more Afrocentric features elicit stronger activation of the African-American stereotype than faces with less prototypical features (Blair, Judd, & Sadler, et al., 2002; Eberhardt, Davies, & Purdie-Vaughns, et al., 2006; Maddox, 2004), but a recent neuroimaging study failed to find differences in amygdala activation towards light- and dark-skinned Black faces (Ronquillo, Denson, & Lickel, et al., 2007). Unless differences in racial stereotype activation are not driven by colour cues alone but require the consistent detection of other facial features (i.e., wide nose and full lips) these findings suggest that the extent of elicited stereotype activation upon face perception is not reflected by the magnitude of activity in the amygdala. Furthermore, spontaneous amygdala activation towards outgroup faces is unlikely to reflect processes of explicit prejudice, given that none of the studies required participants to respond in a prejudiced manner while perceiving the faces, nor were the studies able to demonstrate that a relationship exists between participants' explicit prejudice (as tapped into by the Modern Racism Scale) and the magnitude of amygdala response to outgroup members (Cunningham, Johnson, & Raye, et al., 2004; Phelps, O'Connor, & Cunningham, et al., 2000; Wheeler & Fiske, 2005). It has also been argued that the amygdala may be involved in rapid negative evaluations of outgroup members (i.e., implicit prejudice, Amodio, 2008). This claim has been challenged by data demonstrating that amygdala activity is increased during rapid positive associations with ingroup members rather than during negative associations with outgroup members (Beer, Stallen, & Lombardo, et al., 2008). Furthermore, patient data have demonstrated that rapid evaluative associations for ingroup and outgroup members remain normal even when recruitment of the amygdala is impossible due to brain damage (Phelps, Cannistraci, & Cunningham, 2003). Alternatively, it has been proposed that the amygdala may signal higher vigilance towards outgroup members per se, an assumption that was contradicted by findings showing that sometimes the perception of ingroup compared to outgroup faces elicits increased amygdala activation (Van Bavel, Packer, & Cunningham, 2008; Wright, Negreira, & Gold, et al., 2008). Thus, the precise contribution of the amygdala to social categorization requires further empirical attention.

In addition to implicating the amygdala, several neuroimaging studies measuring differences in the incidental processing of unfamiliar own-race versus other-race faces have reported differential activity in the dorsolateral prefrontal cortex and the anterior cingulate cortex (Cunningham, Johnson, & Raye, et al., 2004; Richeson, Baird, & Gordon, et al., 2003). In light of evidence that these cortical areas are involved in cognitive control, these findings have been interpreted as indication that the mere detection of outgroup members can elicit attempts to control automatically elicited race-based evaluations (Stanley, Phelps, & Banaji, 2008). In line with this argument, activity in both these regions was found to be increased in an associative judgment task that required participants to overcome automatic race-based evaluations (Beer, Stallen, & Lombardo, et al., 2008). Further converging evidence has been provided by the so-called weapon identification task, which requires participants to categorize pictures of either guns or tools following the presentation of black and white faces (Payne, 2001). Using this sequential priming paradigm, it could be demonstrated that the error-related negativity (ERN) wave, an ERP-component generated by the anterior cingulate indexing the need for control, was larger

when tools were erroneously classified as guns following Black relative to White faces (Amodio, Harmon-Jones, & Devine, et al., 2004). Put differently, responses which tended to be race-biased elicited a stronger ERN (i.e., stronger activity in the anterior cingulate) most likely due to an increased need for bias control. A follow-up study using the same paradigm revealed that when the need to control race bias was driven mainly by a perceiver's internal motivation, response regulation was associated with activity in the dorsal anterior cingulate, whereas motivation to control race bias based on external pressure particularly engaged the rostral anterior cingulate (Amodio, Kubota, & Harmon-Jones, et al., 2006). Based on such findings, it has been argued that the observed activity in the anterior cingulate towards unfamiliar outgroup faces may also signal the need to control race bias. Although this might be a valid interpretation, several crucial questions remain. What exactly is it that White participants try to suppress or inhibit when they see a Black face and why would they feel motivated to do so in a mere perceptual task (see also Amodio, 2008)?

Going beyond previous studies which have focused on social categorization, several recent investigations have tried to specifically target mental processes underlying prejudice and stereotyping. For instance, data suggest that strongly negative explicit evaluations towards members of social groups that are seen as hostile and incompetent (such as homeless people and drug addicts) can evoke disgust-like neural responses in the amygdala and the insula, and result in the absence of medial prefrontal activation (Harris & Fiske, 2006). Given that medial prefrontal activation is usually reliably elicited when perceivers encounter other human beings, it has been suggested that the lack of such activation when evaluating others may reflect processes of dehumanization. Further neuroimaging data indicates that stereotype activation elicits enhanced responses in brain regions associated with the representation of semantic knowledge (e.g., middle temporal gyrus and supramarginal gyrus) and evaluative processing (e.g., ventral medial prefrontal cortex and amygdala, see Quadflieg, Turk, & Waiter, et al., 2009). In line with social-psychological findings, such data indicate that thinking stereotypically may be an inherently evaluative rather than mere cognitive process (Wilson, Lindsey, & Schooler, 2000). Additionally, refraining from applying stereotypes to facilitate person understanding has been associated with decreased activity in an extensive region of the right frontal cortex (Mitchell, Ames, & Jenkins, et al., 2009). While further research is necessary to fully understand the neural signature of stereotype activation and application, notably both of the above studies have found evidence that the activity in the neural circuitry supporting stereotypic responses reflects the strength with which individuals endorse stereotypic beliefs in everyday life (Mitchell, Ames, & Jenkins, et al., 2009; Quadflieg, Turk, & Waiter, et al., 2009). Hence, in accordance with data from previous research, these findings indicate that even though most people can retrieve culturally shared stereotypic beliefs when asked to do so, the actual occurrence and extent of stereotype activation and application when perceiving others is modulated by personal convictions (Devine, 1989).

Importantly, when encountering others the diversity of available person cues allows perceivers not only to construe targets as members of generic social categories but also in terms of their personalities. Numerous lines of research (Albright, Kenny, & Malloy, 1988; Ambady & Rosenthal, 1992; Borkenau & Liebler, 1992; Willis & Todorov, 2006) have provided compelling evidence that trait judgments are readily made from a person's physiognomy (facial features), outer appearance (clothing), or demeanour (posture, walking style). An outer appearance that signals the possession of a certain characteristic or trait can have far-reaching consequences in many domains of everyday life. The extent of competence signaled by the mere facial appearance of political candidates has been demonstrated to be predictive of peoples' political voting decisions (Todorov, Mandisodza, & Goren, et al.,

2005). Wearing revealing clothes, a signal of immodesty and apparent promiscuity, was found to cause lay people, judges, police officers, and prosecutors alike to hold victims of rape to be more responsible for their assault (Lennon, Johnson, & Schulz, 1999). Surprisingly though, the neural networks contributing towards appearance-based trait inferences have rarely attracted empirical attention. This empirical lacuna is particularly unfortunate given that personality inferences are known to profoundly modulate a person's categorization. Facial maturity as an indicator of an individual's dominance, for instance, influences gender stereotyping: Only mature-faced males and babyfaced females are judged in accordance with sex stereotypes (e.g., women are warmer and less powerful than men); whereas for males and females equivalent in facial maturity or mature-faced women and babyfaced men stereotypic judgments are typically weakened or even reversed (Friedman & Zebrowitz, 1992). How such interactions are accomplished in the human brain remains uncertain at this time. Thus far, initial work targeting face-based trait inferences has mainly focused on the perception of trustworthiness. It has been demonstrated that faces which are perceived as untrustworthy elicit an enhanced amygdala response compared to more trustworthy looking persons (Engell, Haxby, & Todorov, 2007; Winston, Strange, & O'Doherty, et al., 2002). Beyond face-based trait inferences, studies using point-light displays of human movement have revealed that drawing inferences about a person's disposition (e.g., extraversion, warmth, and trustworthiness) from motion cues involves the left premotor cortex and the left inferior parietal cortex (Heberlein, Adolphs, & Tranel, et al., 2004; Heberlein & Saxe, 2005). Interestingly, both regions are believed to play a central role in inferring meaning from human movement through 'simulation' (Grèzes & Decety, 2001) suggesting that movement-based trait inferences may involve a simulation component.

Decades of social-psychological research further indicates that the ascription of personality traits is influenced by a person's attractiveness. Attractive people are perceived as possessing more positive traits and are treated more positively than their less attractive counterparts – a phenomenon that has been labeled the *beauty-is-good stereotype* (Dion, Berscheid, & Walster, 1972). Coupled with beautiful people attracting bundles of positivity, unattractive people are commonly viewed and evaluated in an unfavorable manner. For example, they are deemed to be less sociable, altruistic, and intelligent than their attractive counterparts (Griffin & Langlois, 2006). The force of these stereotypes can be clearly quantified across the life span. Attractive children elicit more attention and affection and are punished less severely than unattractive children (Dion, 1972; Langlois, Ritter, & Casey, et al., 1995). In adulthood, heightened attractiveness is related to increased mating opportunities (Epstein, Klinkenberg, & Scandell, et al., 2007), better employment prospects (Dubois & Pansu, 2004), advantageous work evaluations (Hamermesh & Parker, 2005), and increased earning potential (Frieze, Olson, & Russell, 1991). First neuroscientific investigations suggest that the orbitofrontal cortex (OFC) plays a major role in the perception of facial attractiveness. Several investigations have reported that the magnitude of activity detected in the OFC increases with the attractiveness of a target face, even when the information is irrelevant to the task at hand, such as when perceivers categorize faces according to sex or age (O'Doherty, Winston, & Critchley, et al., 2003; Winston, O'Doherty, & Kilner, et al., 2007). It is well known that the OFC plays a crucial role in the evaluation of sensory signals and their reward value to guide a perceiver's responses to his or her environment (for a review see Rolls, 2000). Thus, the OFC may provide the signal that biases people to view attractive people more favourably, regardless of the relevance of attractiveness to the judgment or inference in question.

Just as important as drawing inferences about strangers is identifying and making sense of individuals for whom we have a wealth of previous experience (e.g., friends, colleagues, family members). Despite the ease with which perceivers recognize familiar individuals, construing person identity is no small feat (Gobbini & Haxby, 2007). Findings from ERP studies generally converge on the conclusion that information about person familiarity is available about 250 ms after a face has been perceived (the 'N250'; e.g., Tanaka, Curran, & Porterfield, et al., 2006). Recent neuropsychological work involving patients suggests that visual familiarity and the affective response to familiarity are dissociable. Patients suffering from prosopagnosia – a disorder characterized by an inability to recognize familiar faces – display increased skin conductance to familiar but not unfamiliar faces, thereby demonstrating intact affective recognition of known others (De Haan, Bauer, & Greve, 1992; Tranel & Damasio, 1985). In direct contrast, patients suffering from Capgras' syndrome – a disorder in which individuals continue to recognize familiar others but deny their authenticity, claiming that relatives or friends have been replaced by a duplicate (Capgras & Reboul-Lachaux, 1923) – do not show any skin conductance differences in response to familiar or unfamiliar faces (Ellis, Young, & Quayle, et al., 1997). One potential explanation underlying this effect is a lack of felt familiarity (e.g., emotional recognition) when known targets are encountered. This observed double dissociation between visual and affective familiarity suggests that both processes contribute to person identification in an important way. In line with this idea, neuroimaging studies have revealed that perceiving familiar others induces a weaker amygdala response and an increased response in the anterior temporal lobe (aTL) than perceiving strangers (Chan, Peelen, & Downing, 2004; Gobbini & Haxby, 2007; Kriegeskorte, Formisano, & Sorger, et al., 2007). It has been speculated that the reduced activity in the amygdala may reflect a lower level of vigilance when encountering someone we know, whereas the increased aTL activity may signal the spontaneous activation of person-specific semantic and biographical knowledge (Gobbini & Haxby, 2007). Of course, sometimes targets are encountered on numerous occasions yet no specific target-related knowledge is acquired (i.e., the man one sees in the bakery every morning). What then happens when these familiar yet unknown others are perceived? Recent work suggests that perceptually familiar individuals tend to be construed in an even stronger categorical manner than unfamiliar others (Smith, Miller, & Maitner, et al., 2006), perhaps reflecting perceivers' need to make sense of frequently encountered targets.

IMPLICATIONS FOR MODELS OF PERSON PERCEPTION AND PROMISING DIRECTIONS

To gain a comprehensive understanding of the process and products of person perception, integrative theorizing and experimentation is required. In this respect, neuroscience research provides valuable information about the neuroanatomy and temporal characteristics of person perception that challenges previous models of person understanding. For instance, an influential early cognitive model of face perception and recognition proposed that the structural encoding of a person's appearance precedes the access to further person-related knowledge (Bruce & Young, 1986). Recent neuroscientific investigations into person perception provide accumulating evidence that many aspects of person construal seem to be organized in a parallel rather than a sequential fashion. Following brain damage, for example, patients with a deficiency in recognizing faces and yet a spared ability to read facial expressions of emotion (as well as the reverse pattern of effects) have been reported, indicating that the detection and analysis of facial affect and the structural encoding of facial features are subserved by partly unique neural networks (Posamentier & Abdi, 2003). In a similar vein, it has been demonstrated that the emotional response to a familiar face can be independent from its visual recognition (Gobbini & Haxby, 2007). Furthermore,

prosopagnosic patients who are unable to perceive the identity of a face were found to show normal perception of trustworthy and untrustworthy faces (Todorov & Duchaine, 2008), suggesting that the extraction of facial identity and the extraction of trait knowledge from facial cues can also be dissociated. Most interestingly with regard to the topic of this book, lesion, imaging, and behavioral data have demonstrated that person individuation (i.e., the discrimination of a particular person) and person categorization (i.e., the assignment of person to sex, age, or race groups) rely on separable neural components (Mason & Macrae, 2004; Sanders, McClure, & Zárate, 2004; Zárate, Stoever, & MacLin, et al., 2008). Taken together, these neuroscientific data suggest that the various aspects of person construal are not simply divergent products of a common processing architecture. Rather, perceiving social targets on multiple dimensions (i.e., human, middle-aged black men, politician, Barack Obama) seems to make different demands on parts of the distributed cortical network that subserve person perception, demands that can become partially impaired by brain damage without interrupting the person perception process as a whole.

Nevertheless, one of the major challenges for future behavioral and neuroscientific research is to understand how the human mind forms a unified impression of others based on the diversity of person cues available and neural systems involved. The question that poses itself is how the products of different processing streams become integrated. Although distinguishing between person categorization and other kinds of person perception may be useful to theorize about person construal, it needs to be acknowledged that when encountering others in everyday life a wide variety of person cues are extracted simultaneously and collectively influence the person perception process. For instance, it has recently been demonstrated that the increased amygdala activity towards outgroup faces is modulated by gaze direction. Black targets seem to only elicit greater amygdala activity than White targets in a White perceiver when displaying direct rather than averted gaze (Richeson, Todd, & Trawalter, et al., 2008). Detecting the presence of eyes and determining where they are looking has long been suggested to be one of the primary objectives of the social brain (Brothers, 1990). Direct gaze is known to capture the attention of perceivers (e.g., Senju & Hasegawa, 2005), presumably because there is considerable adaptive value in being able to rapidly determine that one has suddenly become the target of another person's interest. Consistent with this possibility, direct relative to averted gaze increases activity in core face-processing areas such as the FFA (George, Driver, & Dolan, 2001) and enhances the efficiency of basic social-cognitive operations, such as person categorization, person evaluation and person memory (Macrae, Hood, & Milne, et al., 2002; Mason, Hood, & Macrae, 2004, 2005).

What such data demonstrates is that social neuroscientists face the challenge to be more precise in their scientific questions when trying to advance our understanding of social categorization, stereotyping, and prejudice. Decades of research in person perception and social psychology have demonstrated that person construal in terms of social categories is a highly flexible process. Not only does eye gaze modulate stereotyping and prejudice (Blair, Judd, & Sadler, et al., 2002; Eberhardt, Davies, & Purdie-Vaughns, et al., 2006; Maddox, 2004), so too can the circumstances or context under which individuals are encountered. For example, viewing an Asian woman performing a typical female activity (e.g., applying cosmetics) or a typical Asian activity (e.g., eating with chopsticks) is sufficient to prompt either the sex or the race of the target respectively to dominate the categorization process (Macrae, Bodenhausen, & Milne, 1995). Similarly, stereotype activation is amplified when an African American target is encountered in an expected rather than unexpected setting (e.g., street corner versus outside a church, see Wittenbrink, Judd, & Park, 2001) or in expected rather than unexpected clothing (e.g., dressed as a criminal or a lawyer in prison, see

Barden, Maddux, & Petty, et al., 2004). Collectively, these findings indicate that although category-based perception of others is often done unintentionally (Macrae & Bodenhausen, 2000), the activation and application of stereotypes and prejudice based on social categories is moderated by a variety of factors. Social-cognitive neuroscience has yet to investigate how brain activity towards in- and outgroup members is modulated by these factors in order to understand the mechanisms underlying person construal.

Importantly, whereas many previous investigations have explored how person perception triggers person construal, social-cognitive neuroscience also enables us to study extensively how the human mind employs pre-existing beliefs to interpret incoming sensory information. First data suggest that expectations regarding a person's group membership can elicit top-down modulations of how others are perceived. When, for example, racially ambiguous faces are labeled as Black, participants judge skin tone to be darker than when the identical faces are labeled as White (Levin & Banaji, 2006). Similarly, when the group membership of faces is made obvious through the addition of stereotypical African American rather than Hispanic hairstyles, identical faces are perceived to be darker and to contain deeper eyes and a wider mouth (MacLin & Malpass, 2003). Whether such top-down modulations really modify early perceptual processes or merely alter the outcomes of such processes is an interesting question for further neuroscientific studies that can be answered increasingly better, the better we understand how the person perception processing cascade spreads in the brain.

Last but not least, researchers have recently begun to investigate how hormones may influence person construal. First evidence indicates that a perceiver's hormonal status can modulate both the speed with which targets are categorized according to their social group memberships and the ease with which stereotypic beliefs are activated. For instance, it has been shown that women categorize men more rapidly and access stereotypic beliefs about them more easily during the phase of high conception risk in their menstrual cycle (Macrae, Alnwick, & Milne, et al., 2002). Additionally, it has been found that increased cortisol reactivity during an interaction with a racial outgroup member may reduce the ability to control unwanted race bias (Amodio, 2009). Such preliminary data suggest that including endocrinology into the toolbox of social neuroscientists promises to become another exiting avenue to advance our understanding of the human social mind.

SUMMARY AND CONCLUSIONS

When encountering conspecifics, the visual perception of bodily and facial cues allows humans to quickly judge their opponents' social category memberships, personality, attractiveness, and familiarity. About two decades ago, social-cognitive neuroscience began to elucidate how the brain enables the human mind to be so adroit at inferring person knowledge from available cues. Converging evidence from ERP, neuroimaging and lesions studies now indicate that perceiving and construing others recruits an extensive and widely distributed neural system of brain regions.

A core neural system consisting of the OFA, FFA, EBA, FBA, and the pSTS has been identified to accomplish the early visual analysis and transformation of complex 3D visual stimuli that are constantly moving into dynamic percepts of human faces and bodies. In addition, the generation of person inferences based on these percepts depends on the recruitment of further brain regions that become part of the person perception system by acting in concert with the core regions. One of the neural substrates found to be most diversely involved in such person inferences appears to be the amygdala. Although still poorly understood with regard to its functional contribution, the amygdala is involved in processes of social categorization, stereotyping, trustworthiness perception, eye gaze detection, and the recognition of familiar others . The OFC, in contrast, seems to have a highly specific role during person construal. As a brain region dedicated towards detecting attractiveness, it potentially contributes towards the widely spread *beauty-is-good-stereotype*. Similarly, the aTL seems to be uniquely dedicated towards the processing of familiar others by providing person-specific semantic and biographical knowledge. Furthermore, initial investigations have reported the anterior cingulate to play a major role in people's attempt to control biases in person perception.

In combination with research in cognitive and social psychology, social-cognitive neuroscience is likely to grow further into a useful tool to advance our understanding of which person-related cues people use to construe others, how the process of personal construal is modulated by processing goals and individual differences, and to what extent early perceptual operations guide the generation of people's post-perceptual products, such as their impressions, evaluations, and memories. Thus, using a range of complementary techniques and approaches will enable us to unlock the beguiling mysteries of the person perception process and its common biases.

REFERENCES

Albright, L., Kenny, D. A., & Malloy, T. E. (1988). Consensus in personality judgments at zero acquaintance. *Journal of Personality and Social Psychology*, 55, 387–395.

Ambady, N., & Rosenthal, R. (1992). Thin slices of expressive behavior as predictors of interpersonal consequences: A meta-analysis. *Psychological Bulletin*, 111, 256–274.

Amodio, D. M. (2008). The social neuroscience of intergroup relations', *European Review of Social Psychology*, 19, 1–54.

Amodio, D. M. (2009). Intergroup anxiety effects on the control of racial stereotypes: A psychoneuroendocrine analysis. *Journal of Experimental Social Psychology*, 45, 60–67.

Amodio, D. M., Harmon-Jones, E., Devine, P., Curtin, J. J., Hartley, S. L., & Covert, A. E. (2004). Neural signals for the detection of unintentional race bias. *Psychological Science*, 15, 88–93.

Amodio, D. M., Kubota, J. T., Harmon-Jones, E., & Devine, P. G. (2006). Alternative mechanisms for regulating racial responses according to internal vs. external cues. *Social Cognitive and Affective Neuroscience*, 1, 26–36.

Barden, J., Maddux, W. W., Petty, R. E., & Brewer, M. B. (2004). Contextual moderation of racial bias: The impact of social roles on controlled and automatically activated attitudes. *Journal of Personality and Social Psychology*, 87, 5–22.

Beer, J. S., Stallen, M., Lombardo, M. V., Gonsalkorale, K., Cunningham, W. A., & Sherman, J. W. (2008). The quadruple process model approach to examining the neural underpinnings of prejudice. *NeuroImage*, 43, 775–783.

Bernstein, M. J., Young, S. G., & Hugenberg, K. (2007). The cross category effect: Mere social categorization is sufficient to elicit an own-group bias in face recognition. *Psychological Science*, 18, 706–712.

Blake, R., & Shiffrar, M. (2007). Perception of human motion. *Annual Review of Psychology*, 58, 47–73.

Blair, I. V., Judd, C. M., Sadler, M. S., & Jenkins, C. (2002). The role of afrocentric features in person perception: Judging by features and categories. *Journal of Personality and Social Psychology*, 83, 5–25.

Borkenau, P., & Liebler, A. (1992). Trait inferences: Sources of validity at zero acquaintance. *Journal of Personality and Social Psychology*, 62, 645–657.

Brothers, L. (1990). The social brain: A project for integrating primate behaviour and neurophysiology in a new domain. *Concepts in Neuroscience*, 1, 27–51.

Bruce, V., & Young, A. (1986). Understanding face recognition. *British Journal of Psychology*, 77, 305–327.

Cacioppo, J. T., Amaral, D. G., Blanchard, J. J., Cameron, J. L., Carter, S., Crews, D. et al. (2007). Social neuroscience: Progress and implications for mental health. *Perspectives on Psychological Science*, 2, 99–123.

Cacioppo, J. T., & Berntson, G. G. (1992). Social psychological contributions to the decade of the brain: Doctrine of multilevel analysis. *American Psychologist*, 47, 1019–1028.

Capgras, J. M. J., & Reboul-Lachaux, J. (1923). L'illusion des "sosies" dans un délire systématisé chronique. *Bulletin in Society and Clinical Medicine Mental*, 11, 6–16.

Chan, A. W-Y., Peelen, M., & Downing, P. (2004). The effect of viewpoint on body representation in the extrastriate body area. *NeuroReport*, 15, 2407–2410.

Cloutier, J., Turk, D. J., & Macrae, C. N. (2007). Extracting variant and invariant information from faces: The neural substrates of gaze detection and sex categorization. *Social Neuroscience*, 3, 69–78.

Cunningham, W. A., Johnson, M. K., Raye, C. L., Gatenby, J. C., Gore, J. C., & Banaji, M. R. (2004). Separable neural components in the processing of black and white faces. *Psychological Science*, 15, 806–813.

Damasio, H., Grabowski, T., Frank, R., Galaburda, A. M., & Damasio, A. R. (1994). The return of Phineas Gage: Clues about the brain from the skull of a famous patient. *Science*, 264, 1102–1105.

De Haan, E. H. F., Bauer, R. M., & Greve, K. W. (1992). Behavioural and physiological evidence for covert face recognition in a prosopagnosic patient. *Cortex*, 28, 77–95.

Devine, P. G. (1989). Stereotypes and prejudice: Their automatic and controlled components. *Journal of Personality and Social Psychology*, 56, 5–18.

Dickter, C. L., & Bartholow, B. D. (2007). Racial ingroup and outgroup attention biases revealed by event-related potentials. *Social, Cognitive, and Affective Neuroscience*, 2, 189–198.

Dion, K. (1972). Physical attractiveness and evaluation of children's transgressions. *Journal of Personality and Social Psychology*, 24, 207–213.

Dion, K., Berscheid, E., & Walster, E. (1972). What is beautiful is good. *Journal of Personality and Social Psychology*, 24, 285–290.

Dubois, M., & Pansu, P. (2004). Facial attractiveness, applicants' qualifications, and judges' expertise about decisions in preselective recruitment. *Psychological Reports*, 95, 1120–1134.

Duchaine, B., Yovel, G., Butterworth, E., & Nakayama, K. (2006). Elimination of alldomain-general hypotheses of prosopagnosia in a single individual with developmental prosopagnosia. *Cognitive Neuropsychology*, 23, 714–747.

Eberhardt, J. L., Davies, P. G., Purdie-Vaughns, V. J., & Johnson, S. L. (2006). Looking deathworthy: Perceived stereotypicality of Black defendants predicts capital-sentencing outcomes. *Psychological Science*, 17, 382–386.

Ellis, H. D., Young, A. W., Quayle, A. H., & De Pauw, K. W. (1997). Reduced autonomic responses to faces in Capgras delusion. *Proceedings of the Royal Society of London. Series B. Biological Sciences*, 264, 1085–1092.

Engell, A. D., Haxby, J. V., & Todorov, A. (2007). Implicit trustworthiness decisions: Automatic coding of face properties in the human amygdala. *Journal of Cognitive Neuroscience*, 19, 1508–1519.

Epstein, J., Klinkenberg, W. D., Scandell, D. J., Faulkner, K., & Claus, R. E. (2007). Perceived physical attractiveness, sexual history, and sexual intentions: An internet study. *Sex Roles*, 56, 23–31.

Friedman, H., & Zebrowitz, L. A. (1992). The contribution of typical sex differences in facial maturity to sex role stereotypes. *Personality and Social Psychology Bulletin*, 18, 430–438.

Frieze, I. H., Olson, J. E., & Russell, J. (1991). Attractiveness and income for men and women in management. *Journal of Applied Social Psychology*, 21, 1039–1057.

Gauthier, I., Skudlarski, P., Gore, J. C., & Anderson, A. W. (2000). Expertise for cars and birds recruits brain areas involved in face recognition. *Nature Neuroscience*, 3, 191–197.

George, N., Driver, J., & Dolan, R. J. (2001). Seen gaze-direction modulates fusiform activity and its coupling with other brain areas during face processing. *NeuroImage*, 13, 1102–1112.

Gobbini, M. I., & Haxby, J. V. (2007). Neural systems for recognition of familiar faces. *Neuropsychologia*, 45, 32–41.

Golby, A. J., Gabrieli, J. D. E., Chiao, J. Y., & Eberhardt, J. L. (2001). Differential responses in the fusiform region to same-race and other-race faces. *Nature Neuroscience*, 4, 845–850

Goodale, M. A., & Milner, A. D. (1992). Separate pathways for perception and action. *Trends in Neurosciences*, 15, 20–25.

Grèzes, J., & Decety, J. (2001). Functional anatomy of execution, mental simulation, observation, and verb generation of actions: A meta-analysis. *Human Brain Mapping*, 12, 1–19.

Grèzes, J., Fonlupt, P., Bertenthal, B., Delon-Martin, C., Segebarth, C., & Decety, J. (2001). Does perception of biological motion rely on specific brain regions? *NeuroImage*, 13, 775–785.

Griffin, A. M., & Langlois, J. H. (2006). Stereotype directionality and attractiveness stereotyping: Is beauty good or is ugly bad? *Social Cognition*, 24, 187–206.

Hamermesh, D. S., & Parker, A. (2005). Beauty in the classroom: Instructors' pulchritude and putative pedagogical productivity. *Economics of Education Review*, 24, 369–376.

Hart, A. J., Whalen, P. J., Shin, L. M., McInerney, S. C., Fischer, H., & Rauch, S. L. (2000). Differential response in the human amygdala to racial outgroup vs ingroup face stimuli. *NeuroReport*, 11, 2351–2355.

Haxby, J. V., Hoffman, E. A., & Gobbini, M. A. (2000). The distributed human neural system for face perception. *Trends in Cognitive Sciences*, 4, 223–233.

Heberlein, A. S., Adolphs, R., Tranel, D., & Damasio, H. (2004). Cortical regions for judgments of emotions

and personality traits from point-light walkers. *Journal of Cognitive Neuroscience*, 16, 1143–1158.

Heberlein, A. S., & Saxe, R. R. (2005). Dissociation between emotional and personality judgments: Convergent evidence from functional neuroimaging. *NeuroImage*, 28, 770–777.

Hirai, M., Fukushima, H., & Hiraki, K. (2003). An event-related potentials study of biological motion perception in humans. *Neuroscience Letters*, 344, 41–44.

Ito, T. A., Thompson, E., & Cacioppo, J. T. (2004). Tracking the timecourse of social perception: The effects of racial cues on event-related brain potentials. *Personality and Social Psychology Bulletin*, 30, 1267–1280.

Jokisch, D., Daum, I., Suchan, B., & Troje, N. F. (2005). Structural encoding and recognition of biological motion: Evidence from event-related potentials and source analysis. *Behavioural Brain Research*, 157, 195–204.

Kanwisher, N., & Yovel, G. (2006). The fusiform face area: A cortical region specialized for the perception of faces. *Philosophical Transactions of the Royal Society B*, 361, 2109–2128.

Kim, J. S., Yoon, H. W., Kim, B. S., Jeun, S. S., Jung, S. L., & Choe, B. Y. (2006). Racial distinction of the unknown facial identity recognition mechanism by event-related fMRI. *Neuroscience Letters*, 397, 279–284.

Kriegeskorte, N., Formisano, E., Sorger, B., & Goebel, R. (2007). Individual faces elicit distinct patterns in human anterior temporal cortex. *Proceedings of the National Academy of Sciences*, 104, 20600–20605.

Langlois, J. H., Ritter, J. M., Casey, R. J., & Sawin, D. B. (1995). Infant attractiveness predicts maternal behaviors and attitudes. *Developmental Psychology*, 31, 464–472.

Lennon, S. J., Johnson, K. K. P., & Schulz, T. L. (1999). Forging linkages between dress and law in the U.S., part I: Rape and sexual harassment. *Clothing and Textiles Research Journal*, 17, 144–156.

Levin, D. T., & Banaji, R. (2006). Distortions in the perceived lightness of faces: The role of race categories. *Journal of Experimental Psychology: General*, 135, 501–512.

MacLin, O. H., & Malpass, S. (2003). The ambiguous-race face illusion. *Perception*, 32, 249–252.

Macrae, C. N., Alnwick, K. A., Milne, A.B., & Schloerscheidt, A. M. (2002). Person perception across the menstrual cycle: Hormonal influences on social-cognitive functioning. *Psychological Science*, 13, 532–536.

Macrae, C. N., & Bodenhausen, G. V. (2000). Social cognition: Thinking categorically about others. *Annual Review of Psychology*, 51, 93–120.

Macrae, C. N., Bodenhausen, G. V., & Milne, A. B. (1995). The dissection of selection in person perception: Inhibitory processes in social stereotyping. *Journal of Personality and Social Psychology*, 69, 397–407.

Macrae, C. N., Bodenhausen, G. V., Milne, A. B., Thorn, T. M. J., & Castelli, L. (1997). On the activation of social stereotypes: The moderating role of processing objectives. *Journal of Experimental Social Psychology*, 33, 471–489.

Macrae, C. N., Hood, B. M., Milne, A. B., Rowe, A. C., & Mason, M. F. (2002). Are you looking at me? Eye gaze and person perception. *Psychological Science*, 13, 460–464.

Macrae, C. N., Quinn, K. A., Mason, M. F., & Quadflieg, S. (2005). Understanding others: The face and person construal. *Journal of Personality and Social Psychology*, 89, 686–695.

Maddox, K. B. (2004). Perspectives on racial phenotypicality bias. *Personality and Social Psychology Review*, 8, 383–401.

Mason, M. F., Hood, B. M., & Macrae, C. N. (2004). Look into my eyes: Gaze direction and person memory. *Memory*, 12, 637–643.

Mason, M. F., & Macrae, C. N. (2004). Categorizing and individuating others: The neural substrates of person perception. *Journal of Cognitive Neuroscience*, 16, 1785–1795.

Mason, M. F., Tatkow, E. P., & Macrae, C. N. (2005). The look of love: Gaze shifts and person perception. *Psychological Science*, 16, 236–239.

Mitchell, J. P., Ames, D. L., Jenkins, A. C., & Banaji, M. R. (2009). Neural correlates of stereotype application. *Journal of Cognitive Neuroscience, 21*, 594–604.

Ng, M., Ciaramitaro, V. M., Anstis, S., Boynton, G. M., & Fine, I. (2006). Selectivity for the configural cues that identify the gender, ethnicity, and identity of faces in human cortex. *Proceedings of the National Academy of Sciences*, 103, 19552–19557.

O'Doherty, J., Winston, J., Critchley, H., Perrett, D., Burt, D. M., & Dolan, R. J. (2003). Beauty in a smile: The role of medial orbitofrontal cortex in facial attractiveness. *Neuropsychologia*, 41, 147–155.

Payne, B.K. (2001). Prejudice and perception: The role of automatic and controlled processes in misperceiving a weapon. *Journal of Personality and Social Psychology*, 81, 181–192.

Peelen, M. V., & Downing, P. E. (2007). The neural basis of visual body perception. *Nature Reviews Neuroscience*, 8, 636–648.

Pelphrey, K. A., Mitchell, T. V., McKeown, M. J., Goldstein, J., Allison, T., & McCarthy, G. (2003). Brain activity evoked by the perception of human walking: Controlling for meaningful coherent motion. *The Journal of Neuroscience*, 23, 6819–6825.

Phelps, E., Cannistraci, C., & Cunningham, W. (2003). Intact performance on an indirect measure of race bias following amygdala damage. *Neuropsychologia*, 41, 203–208.

Phelps, E. A., O'Connor, K. J., Cunningham, W. A., Funayama, E. S., Gatenby, J C., & Gore, J. C., et al. (2000). Performance on indirect measures of race evaluation predicts amygdala activation. *Journal of Cognitive Neuroscience*, 12, 72–738.

Pitcher, D., Walsh, V., Yovel, G., & Duchaine, B. (2007). TMS evidence for the involvement of the right occipital face area in early face processing. *Current Biology*, 17, 1568–1573.

Posamentier, M. T., & Abdi, H. (2003). Processing faces and facial expressions. *Neuropsychology Review*, 13, 113–143.

Pourtois, G., Peelen, M., Spinelli, L., Seeck, M., & Vuilleumier, P. (2007). Direct intracranial recording of body-selective responses in human extrastriate visual cortex. *Neuropsychologia*, 45, 2621–2625.

Puce, A., Allison, T., Bentin, S., Gore, J. C., & McCarthy, G. (1998). Temporal cortex activation of humans viewing eye and mouth movements. *The Journal of Neuroscience*, 18, 2188–2199.

Quadflieg, S., Turk, D. J., Waiter, G. D., Mitchell, J. P., Jenkins, A. C., & Macrae, C. N. (2009). Exploring the neural correlates of social stereotyping. *Journal of Cognitive Neuroscience, 21*, 1560–1570.

Quinn, K. A., & Macrae, C. N. (2005). Categorizing others: The dynamics of person construal. *Journal of Personality and Social Psychology*, 88, 467–479.

Richeson, J. A., Baird, A. A., Gordon, H. L., Heatherton, T. F., Wyland, C. L., & Trawalter, S., et al. (2003). An fMRI investigation of the impact of interracial contact on executive function. *Nature Neuroscience*, 6, 1323–1328.

Richeson, J. A., Todd, A. R., Trawalter, S., & Baird, A. A. (2008). Eye-gaze direction modulates race-related amygdala activity. *Group Processes and Intergroup Relations*, 11, 233–246.

Rolls, E. T. (2000). The orbitofrontal cortex and reward. *Cerebral Cortex*, 10, 284–294.

Ronquillo, J., Denson, D. F., Lickel, B., Lu, Z.-L., Nandy, A., & Maddox, K. B. (2007). The effects of skin tone on race-related amygdala activity: An fMRI investigation. *Social Cognitive and Affective Neuroscience*, 2, 39–44.

Rossion, B. (2008). Constraining the cortical face network by neuroimaging studies of acquired prosopagnosia. *NeuroImage*, 40, 423–426.

Rossion, B., & Jacques, C. (2008). Does physical interstimulus variance account for early electrophysiological face sensitive responses in the human brain? Ten lessons on the N170. *NeuroImage*, 39, 1959–1979.

Sanders, J. D., McClure, K. A., & Zárate, M. A. (2004). Cerebral hemispheric asymmetries in social perception: Perceiving and responding to the individual and the group. *Social Cognition*, 22, 279–291.

Senju, A., & Hasegawa, T. (2005). Direct gaze captures visuospatial attention. *Visual Cognition*, 12, 127–144.

Smith, E. R., Miller, D. A., Maitner, A. T., Crump, S. A., Garcia-Marques, T., & Mackie, D. M. (2006). Familiarity can increase stereotyping. *Journal of Experimental Social Psychology*, 42, 471–478.

Stahl, J., Wiese, H., & Schweinberger, S. R. (2008). Expertise and own-race bias in face processing: An event-related potential study. *NeuroReport*, 19, 583–587.

Stanley, D., Phelps, E., & Banaji, M. (2008). The neural basis of implicit attitudes. *Current Directions in Psychological Science*, 17, 164–170.

Tanaka, J. W., Curran, T., Porterfield, A. L., & Collins, D. (2006). Activation of preexisting and acquired face representations: The N250 event-related potential as an index of face familiarity. *Journal of Cognitive Neuroscience*, 18, 1488–1497.

Taylor, J. C., Wiggett, A. J., & Downing, P. E. (2007). fMRI analysis of body and body part representations in the extrastriate and fusiform body areas. *Journal of Neurophysiology*, 98, 1626–1633.

Thierry, G., Pegna, A. J., Dodds, C., Roberts, M., Basan, S., & Downing, P. (2006). An event-related potential component sensitive to images of the human body. *NeuroImage*, 32, 871–879.

Tranel, D., & Damasio, A. R. (1985). Knowledge without awareness: An autonomic index of facial recognition by prosopagnosics. *Science*, 228, 1453–1454.

Todorov, A., & Duchaine, B. (2008). Reading trustworthiness in faces without recognizing faces. *Cognitive Neuropsychology*, 25, 395–410.

Todorov, A., Mandisodza, A. N., Goren, A., & Hall, C. C. (2005). Inferences of competence from faces predict election outcomes. *Science*, 308, 1623–1626.

Van Bavel, J. J., Packer, D. J., & Cunningham, W. A. (2008). The neural substrates of in-group bias: A functional magnetic resonance imaging investigation. *Psychological Science*, *19*, 1131–1139.

Walker, P. M., Silvert, L., Hewstone, M., & Nobre, A. C. (2008). Social contact and other–race face processing in the human brain. *Social, Cognitive and Affective Neuroscience*, 3, 16–25.

Wheeler, M. E., & Fiske, S. T. (2005). Controlling racial prejudice. *Psychological Science*, 16, 56–62.

Willis, J., & Todorov, A. (2006). First impressions. Making up your mind after a 100-ms exposure to a face. *Psychological Science*, 17, 592–598.

Wilson, T. D., Lindsey, S., & Schooler, T. Y. (2000). A model of dual attitudes. *Psychological Review*, 107, 101–126.

Winston, J. S., O'Doherty, J., Kilner, J. M., Perrett, D. I., & Dolan, R. J. (2007). Brain systems for assessing facial attractiveness. *Neuropyschologia*, 45, 195–206.

Winston, J. S., Strange, B. A., O'Doherty, J., & Dolan, R. J. (2002). Automatic and intentional brain responses during evaluation of trustworthiness of faces. *Nature Neuroscience*, 5, 277–283.

Wittenbrink, B., Judd, C. M., & Park, B. (2001). Spontaneous prejudice in context: Variability in automatically activated attitudes. *Journal of Personality and Social Psychology*, 81, 815–827.

Wright, C. I., Negreira, A., Gold, A. L., Britton, J. C., Williams, D., & Feldman Barrett, L. (2008). Neural correlates of novelty and face–age effects in young and elderly adults. *NeuroImage*, 42, 956–968.

Yovel, G., & Kanwisher, N. (2004). Face perception: Domain specific, not process specific. *Neuron*, 44, 747–748.

Yovel, G., & Kanwisher, N. (2005). The neural basis of the behavioral face-inversion effect. *Current Biology*, 15, 2256–2262.

Zárate, M.A., Stoever, C. J., MacLin, M. K., & Arms-Chavez, C. J. (2008). Neurocognitive underpinnings of face perception: Further evidence of distinct person and group perception processes. *Journal of Personality and Social Psychology*, 94, 118–115.

5

Evolutionary Processes

Mark Schaller, Lucian Gideon Conway III, and
K. Michelle Peavy

ABSTRACT

Two kinds of evolutionary processes inform psychological research on stereotypes and prejudices. One is a process through which genetic variants are selectively transmitted from individuals to their offspring through sexual reproduction; this process has shaped psychological mechanisms that characterize contemporary human populations. The other is a process through which knowledge structures are selectively transmitted between individuals through interpersonal communication; this process shapes the belief systems that characterize human cultures. Inquiry into the first kind of process (genetic evolution) produces novel discoveries about contemporary human prejudices and the cues that trigger them. Inquiry into the second kind of process (cultural evolution) produces novel discoveries about the contents of popular stereotypes. This chapter reviews these bodies of research, and their implications.

EVOLUTIONARY PROCESSES

Two distinct types of evolutionary process are relevant to the psychology of stereotypes and prejudices. One is articulated within the vast scientific literature on human evolutionary biology. This is a process through which some genetic variants, rather than others, are selectively transmitted from individuals to their offspring through sexual reproduction, with resulting consequences for the phenotypic characteristics of human populations. The human brain is a product of this evolutionary process. Consequently, understanding how the brain evolved in response to selection pressures in ancestral environments leads to novel discoveries about psychological phenomena in contemporary environments.

The other kind of evolutionary process focuses not on genes, but on *memes* – a word coined by the biologist Richard Dawkins (1976) to refer to the vast array of cognitive structures (such as stereotypes) and behavioral tendencies that may, or may not, become widespread within a population. Some memes, rather than others, are especially likely to be transmitted from one individual to another (through ordinary interpersonal communication processes), and this selective interpersonal transmission has implications for the shared belief systems that define human cultures. This process – conceptually distinct from but analogous to genetic evolution (Mesoudi, Whiten, & Laland, 2006) – has been referred to variously as 'social evolution,' 'socio-cultural evolution,' and 'cultural evolution.' For the remainder of this chapter we use the latter term.

Both processes are 'evolutionary' in the sense that, over a period of time, some variants of information (either genes or memes) are more likely than others to be selectively transmitted and selectively retained within a population. But the mechanistic details of each process are very different, and they have very different kinds of implications when applied to the psychology of prejudices and stereotypes. Genetic evolutionary processes operate across vast time scales, and are not themselves the subject of direct empirical inquiry within the psychological sciences. Rather, rigorous theorizing about the consequences of human genetic evolution provides a logical framework within which it is possible to deduce novel hypotheses about the contemporary human prejudices and the variables that influence these prejudices (e.g., the hypothesis, and consequent empirical discovery, that women are especially xenophobic and ethnocentric during the few weeks of pregnancy; Navarrete, Fessler, & Eng, 2007). In contrast, cultural evolutionary processes often occur within relatively short periods of time, and so can be empirically observed with psychological research methods. Among these empirical observations are novel findings pertaining to variables that influence the emergence, persistence, and change of widespread stereotypes (e.g., the finding that interpersonal communication norms predict changes in the specific contents of African-American stereotypes over the course of the twentieth century; Schaller, Conway, & Tanchuck, 2002). Conceptually distinct bodies of psychological research reveal the implications of each kind of evolutionary process. This chapter reviews these bodies of research.

We begin with a brief historical overview. Then, in the second section we review many different ways in which conceptual speculations about human genetic evolution have led to novel discoveries about contemporary human prejudices. In the third section, we review research on cultural evolutionary

processes and their consequences on the contents of popular stereotypes. In the fourth and final section, we discuss integrative themes and directions for future research.

HISTORICAL BACKGROUND

Evolutionary approaches to human behavior have scholarly roots that are both long and deep. Darwin's (1859) original treatise on evolution by natural selection focused on non-human species, but several of his subsequent books attended more explicitly to human evolution and implications for specific kinds of psychological phenomena, such as emotions (Darwin, 1871, 1872). Since then, enormous bodies of research have articulated the evolutionary origins of human cognition and behavior. Inquiries into evolutionary origins focus mainly on processes that operated on ancestral populations over long periods of time. In contrast, psychological inquiries typically focus on processes operating at an individual level of analysis, usually within very short periods of time. Given these different levels of analysis, insights about the evolutionary origins of human behavior do not translate easily into sophisticated hypotheses about contemporary psychological processes. Only in the last few decades have psychological scientists begun to employ evolutionary principles to develop and test such hypotheses (for reviews, see Buss, 2005; Crawford & Krebs, 2008; Dunbar & Barrett, 2007; Gangestad & Simpson, 2007; Schaller, Simpson, & Kenrick, 2006).

Donald Campbell was among the first psychological scientists to seriously consider the implications of human genetic evolution for the psychology of prejudice. In a chapter titled 'Ethnocentric and Other Altruistic Motives,' Campbell (1965a) discussed the psychological connections between two superficially distinct phenomena – altruism and ethnocentrism – suggesting that the evolutionary bases of altruism may have additional implications for intergroup prejudices as well. The influence of Campbell's work on this topic is apparent in many contemporary programs of prejudice research (e.g., Brewer, 1999; Brewer & Caporael, 2006), and is discussed more extensively below.

Campbell was also instrumental in introducing the study of *cultural* evolutionary processes to the psychological sciences. Inquiry into cultural evolution has an even longer history than theories of genetic evolutionary processes (Hull, 1988). But, again, because the consequences of cultural evolution manifest at the level of whole populations, and not just individuals, these processes are easily viewed as lying largely outside the domain of psychological inquiry. Campbell (1965b, 1974, 1975) published a series of important articles in which he articulated the implications of cultural evolutionary processes for exactly the kinds of things – knowledge structures and social behaviors – that psychologists care about.

Stereotypes are, of course, also among the things that psychologists care about. There is a venerable tradition of psychological research devoted to assessing and documenting changes in widespread stereotypes (e.g., Katz & Braly, 1933; Madon, Guyll, & Aboufadel, et al., 2001), as well as on how stereotypes are communicated from one person to another (e.g., Clark & Kashima, 2007; Lyons & Kashima, 2003; Ruscher, 1998, 2001). The logic of cultural evolution provides a set of conceptual tools through which these two research traditions can be connected, such that stereotype communication affects the contents of widely shared stereotypes. Thus, just as cultural evolutionary processes influence the myths, legends, and other narratives that define popular culture (e.g., Heath, Bell, & Sternberg, 2001; Norenzayan, Atran, Faulkner, et al., 2006), these processes also influence the extent to which some stereotypes, rather than others, have enduring social consequences.

We elaborate below on the implications of cultural evolution for the study of stereotypes. But first, we review the more substantial body of research that focuses on human genetic evolution and its implications for the study of human prejudices.

GENETIC EVOLUTION AND THE PSYCHOLOGY OF PREJUDICE(S)

Evolutionary inquiry into human psychology assumes that if (a) some specific psychological tendency has some genetic basis, and (b) that psychological tendency, relative to alternative tendencies, promotes reproductive fitness (i.e., the perpetuation of genes into subsequent generations), then (c) that specific psychological tendency (along with its genetic basis) will become increasingly widespread within a population. Within that meta-theoretical framework, specific hypotheses can be deduced by identifying ecological circumstances that, over long stretches of human evolutionary history, were likely to have imposed enduring selection pressures on psychological tendencies that conferred higher levels of reproductive fitness. In the absence of any countervailing selection pressure, these adaptive psychological tendencies are presumed to have become widespread within the population, influencing human affect, cognition, and behavior in contemporary environments.

These psychological adaptations may take many forms, including attentional biases (Maner, Gailliot, Rouby, et al., 2007), cognitive shortcuts in information processing (Gigerenzer, Todd, & the ABC Research Group, 1999), competencies in logical reasoning (Cosmides & Tooby, 2005), and means of learning and knowledge acquisition (Öhman & Mineka, 2001). When applied to the psychology of prejudice, this adaptationist logic typically focuses on specific stimulus–response associations, such as the tendency for a specific superficial characteristic (e.g., facial scar, for example) to trigger a particular set of affective, cognitive, and/or behavioral responses. Many lines of research have identified prejudices (i.e., specific stimulus–response associations) that are likely to have been adaptive over the course of human history. Importantly, this body of work does much more than merely speculate about the evolutionary origins of these prejudices; it also has produced many novel hypotheses specifying particular circumstances under which these prejudices are either more, or less, likely to emerge.

Obligatory interdependence and ingroup favoritism

One line of research emerges from the fact that, compared to many other species, *Homo sapiens* is an unimposing physical specimen. Humans are relatively weak, and lack the physical weaponry (sharp fangs, claws, or talons) and protective armor (thick hides, hard shells) that characterize many other species. Human offspring also mature slowly. These limitations are likely to have imposed severe fitness costs on individuals who lived solitary lifestyles. These limitations are ameliorated, however, for individuals who live within the protective milieu of a coalitional group. Humans also are characterized by extraordinary psychological proficiencies – including capacities for language, planning, and perspective-taking. These psychological assets would be valuable under any circumstance, but are especially powerful aids to reproductive fitness when employed within a group context where knowledge (e.g., where to find food, how to construct a weapon) can be passed on to others. Thus, compared to those who pursued solitary lifestyles, significant fitness benefits accrued to our ancestors who lived in highly interdependent, cooperative groups. Thus, it has been speculated that there evolved psychological mechanisms disposing humans toward a lifestyle characterized by *obligatory interdependence* with other people (Brewer, 1997; Brewer & Caporael, 2006).

Interdependence is not without its perils. In any population characterized by obligations to others, there is the risk of exploitation by individuals who reap benefits from others' largesse while neglecting to contribute to the common good. Many psychological adaptations have been identified that may help resolve this dilemma (e.g., Cosmides & Tooby, 2005). One set of adaptations is specifically relevant to intergroup prejudice: Psychological mechanisms that allow individuals to identify the boundaries of a coalitional ingroup so as to behave altruistically toward individuals within the ingroup, but not to individuals outside this boundary (Brewer, 1999; Brewer & Caporael, 2006; Campbell, 1965a).

An important implication of this analysis is that the resulting prejudice (favoring members of coalitional ingroups, relative to others) represents ingroup favoritism (preference for the ingroup) rather than outgroup derogation (dislike of outgroups). Thus, ingroup favoritism need not be associated with any aversive response toward outgroups (Brewer, 2007). This implication is consistent with the results of experiments conducted within the 'minimal groups paradigm' (which assesses evaluations of, and rewards allocated to, ad-hoc groups created in laboratory environments) that show greater evidence of ingroup favoritism than outgroup derogation (Brewer, 1999). Indeed, ingroup favoritism can be shown even in the absence of an outgroup (Brewer, 1979; Gaertner, Iuzzini, Witt, et al., 2006).

The evolution of coalitional psychology and its implications

Theoretical inquiry into the evolutionary importance of coalitional groups has yielded additional implications. One is that many contemporary social categorizations (e.g., categorizations based on race or ethnicity) – and the prejudices associated with them – are context-specific manifestations of deeper, universal psychological mechanisms that evolved to distinguish between coalitional ingroups and outgroups. Although individuals may be hyper-vigilant to markers of race or ethnicity in some contemporary cultural contexts, this tendency exists not because there is anything evolutionarily fundamental about race or ethnicity, but because race and ethnicity happen to be superficial markers for the evolutionarily fundamental distinction between coalitional groups. As a consequence, the perceptual and mnemonic potency of racial cues (e.g., skin color) may disappear under circumstances in which other, even more powerful indicators of coalitional group membership exist. One set of studies found that any tendency to categorize individuals according to race entirely disappeared when those individuals wore clothing (sports team uniforms) that served as more meaningful signal of coalitional group membership (Kurzban, Tooby, & Cosmides, 2001).

The emphasis on coalitional groups stems from the assumption that strong fitness benefits accrue to individuals who live within coalitional groups. These benefits are greatest when within-group interaction is efficient, cooperative, and coordinated by normative rules. Any breakdown in social coordination imposes fitness costs. Thus, prejudices against individuals who threatened social coordination may have evolved (Neuberg, Smith, & Asher, 2000; Schaller & Neuberg, 2008). Coalitional outgroup members may represent one such threat, because they likely adhere to rules and norms that deviate from those observed within an ingroup. This implies one evolutionary basis for xenophobia. But ingroup members may also undermine social coordination if they exhibit attitudes or behaviors that deviate from important group norms, implying an evolutionary basis for prejudices directed against ingroup members who violate group norms. Such deviant ingroup members are especially likely to be targets of prejudice under conditions in which their counter-normative attitudes appear especially likely to undermine effective group coordination, such as when those individuals are in positions of influence over others. Consistent with this implication, employment discrimination against homosexuals is especially strong when they are being considered for positions that connote considerable social influence (e.g., schoolteachers), compared to positions (e.g., jobs in the retail industry) that provide less opportunity for far-reaching social influence (Neuberg, Smith, & Asher, 2000).

Different fitness-relevant threats and different prejudice syndromes

A deficit in social coordination is just one kind of fitness-relevant cost that may result from the actions (or mere presence) of other people. Fitness costs may also be implied by specific attitudes, actions, or characteristics. People who fail to reciprocate acts of generosity can impose fitness costs. So can people who threaten one's physical safety (e.g., through acts of aggression) or health (e.g., because they have an infectious disease). Kurzban and Leary (2001) argued that specific psychological mechanisms evolved to stigmatize, discriminate against, and socially exclude individuals who represent these threats.

Importantly, this line of reasoning has implications that extend far beyond the mere observation that people do not much like folks who pose threats to their fitness. Neuberg and his colleagues (Cottrell & Neuberg, 2005; Neuberg & Cottrell, 2006; Schaller & Neuberg, 2008) have suggested that qualitatively different kinds of fitness threats are associated with psychologically distinct prejudices. Thus, just as different nonsocial threats (predators, poisons) inspire very different emotional responses (fear, disgust), different social threats inspire very different *prejudice syndromes* – defined by distinct affective experiences, cognitive associations, and behavioral consequences (Neuberg & Cottrell, 2006). Each prejudice syndrome represents a functionally adaptive response to a particular form of threat. Consistent with this evolutionary analysis, empirical evidence reveals that different social groups are associated with functionally distinct kinds of threat and, correspondingly, distinct emotional responses (Cottrell & Neuberg, 2005). This evolutionary analysis implies that the psychology of prejudice is more accurately characterized as the psychology of prejudices (plural).

An additional implication (with important practical applications) is that each distinct prejudice syndrome may vary across contexts, depending on the extent to which perceivers feel vulnerable to different types of threats. According to Neuberg and Cottrell (2006, p. 174), 'if prejudice syndromes are indeed responses to specific threats … they ought to be triggered more easily, and experienced more intensely, in some (specific) situations (i.e., those that suggest a vulnerability to the target-relevant threat)' and for some (specific) individuals (i.e., those who have a low threshold for perceiving – accurately or not – the target-relevant threat).

Supporting evidence emerges mainly from two distinct research programs, one of which focuses on the threat of interpersonal aggression, and the other on the threat of disease. We briefly review each.

Implied threat of interpersonal aggression and its implications

Throughout much of human evolutionary history, intergroup contact was often associated with an increased likelihood of interpersonal aggression and physical injury (Schaller & Neuberg, 2008). As a consequence, psychological mechanisms (and their underlying genetic bases) may have evolved to dispose individuals to implicitly associate outgroup members with traits connoting aggression, violence, and danger. But, while there may be fitness benefits associated with such prejudicial beliefs (e.g., hypervigilant avoidance of potentially-dangerous intergroup encounters), there may be costs as well (e.g., caloric costs associated with the fearful avoidance behaviors). Therefore, these prejudice processes are expected to be sensitive to additional information indicating the extent to which their benefits outweigh their costs. The upshot is that prejudicial responses are especially likely to be triggered under conditions in which perceivers sense that they may be especially vulnerable to danger, but may be muted when perceivers feel relatively invulnerable.

This line of reasoning has resulted in novel discoveries about when specific prejudicial beliefs (but not others) emerge. For instance, people typically feel more vulnerable to danger when they are in the dark (Grillon, Pellowski, Merikangas, et al., 1997). Consequently, ambient darkness disposes people to perceive ethnic outgroups to be more aggressive and hostile – and this effect is especially pronounced among individuals who are chronically concerned with interpersonal threat (Schaller, Park, & Faulkner, 2003; Schaller, Park, & Mueller, 2003). Importantly, this effect is specific to

prejudicial beliefs along danger-connoting traits (e.g., hostility); no such effect is observed on equally negative but danger-irrelevant traits (e.g., ignorance).

In fact, while increased vulnerability promotes evaluatively negative stereotypic beliefs on traits connoting aggression and untrustworthiness, it can actually promote ostensibly positive stereotypic beliefs along other trait dimensions (such as competence or agency). For example, in an experiment conducted within the context of the ongoing ethnic conflict in Sri Lanka, a temporarily increased sense of vulnerability caused Sinhalese Sri Lankans to perceive an ethnic outgroup (Sri Lankan Tamils) as especially aggressive, but also as especially skillful and competent (Schaller & Abeysinghe, 2006) – presumably because, in the context of malevolent intentions, a high level of competence connotes a especially high level of danger.

This perspective implies gender differences as well. Historically, violent intergroup contact was especially likely to occur between males. This implies that men (compared to women) are especially likely to perceive outgroup members as stereotypically dangerous, and are especially prone to have these prejudicial perceptions triggered by contextual cues (such as darkness) connoting vulnerability to harm. Several studies show such gender differences (see Schaller & Neuberg, 2008). In addition, given their greater physical strength and aggressiveness, men have typically posed a greater fitness-relevant threat to others. This implies that (compared to female outgroup members) male outgroup members are especially likely to trigger danger-connoting cognitive and affective associations and this has been shown to be so (Maner, Kenrick, Becker, et al., 2005; Navarrete, Olsson, Ho, et al., 2009).

Finally, this line of theorizing has important implications in the domain of person memory. There is a well-documented cross-race face recognition bias, such that perceivers are very accurate at distinguishing between individual ingroup members, but not so accurate at distinguishing between outgroup members (Anthony, Copper, & Mullen, 1992).

The bias is commonly presumed to result from constraints on perceivers' perceptual processing capacities and from perceivers' tendency to pragmatically allocate perceptual resources (e.g., Sporer, 2001). The evolutionary framework yields new explanatory and predictive insights. Limited cognitive resources (necessary for the encoding and memory for individuating facial features) are likely to be selectively allocated to those individuals who are presumed to have the most immediate implications for reproductive fitness: members of coalitional ingroups. However, any potentially aggressive individual (as indicated by an obviously angry facial expression) is highly fitness-relevant, whether a member of an ingroup or outgroup. It follows that recognition memory for angry faces is likely to be highly accurate even for outgroup members and this has been shown to be the case (Ackerman, Shapiro, Neuberg, et al., 2006). In fact, historically, angry outgroup members may have posed especially profound threats to reproductive fitness (compared to angry ingroup members, whose actual aggression may be muted by norms prescribing within-group cooperation). Thus, perceivers may actually be especially accurate in recognizing angry outgroup faces – a reversal of the face-recognition bias. Exactly such a reversal does emerge in studies assessing recognition memory for angry faces (Ackerman, Shapiro, & Neuberg, et al., 2006).

Implied threat of disease transmission and its implications

Even well-meaning individuals pose a threat to reproductive fitness if they carry infectious pathogens. Given the powerful fitness costs associated with pathogenic diseases, there likely evolved a suite of psychological mechanisms that sensitize perceivers to others who appear to pose an infection risk, and that facilitate aversive responses to those individuals. Moreover, consistent with the evolutionary cost–benefit logic discussed above, these prejudicial responses are especially likely to be triggered under conditions in which perceivers feel especially vulnerable to the

transmission of disease, but may be muted when perceivers feel relatively invulnerable to disease transmission (Schaller & Duncan, 2007).

Because pathogenic diseases are associated with a wide range of morphological and behavioral anomalies, anomalous appearance of just about any kind may trigger prejudicial responses – even if these anomalies are not actually symptomatic of disease (Kurzban & Leary, 2001; Schaller & Duncan, 2007). Indeed, under circumstances in which individuals feel especially vulnerable to infectious diseases, they show especially strong implicit prejudices against people characterized by many different kinds of non-normative physical characteristics, including people who are physically disabled, obese, or elderly (Duncan & Schaller, 2009; Park, Faulkner, & Schaller, 2003; Park, Schaller, & Crandall, 2007). In fact, physical unattractiveness of any kind might serve as a sort of crude heuristic cue for ill-health, and may thus lead to aversive trait inferences (Zebrowitz, Fellous, Mignault, et al., 2003).

This particular prejudice syndrome may also contribute to xenophobia and ethnocentrism. Historically, intergroup contact led to increased exposure to pathogenic diseases. Also, given that many cultural norms (e.g., pertaining to hygiene practices and food preparation) serve as buffers against infection, contact with subjectively foreign peoples (those who ascribe to different cultural norms) may have posed a especially high risk of disease transmission. Consequently, people are likely to heuristically associate subjectively foreign outgroups with the threat of disease. This analysis suggests a disease-avoidance basis for xenophobia and ethnocentrism, with the additional implication that xenophobia and ethnocentrism may be exaggerated when perceivers feel especially vulnerable to infection. This appears to be the case (Faulkner, Schaller, Park, et al., 2004) when Canadians perceive themselves to be especially vulnerable to disease, they show especially strong prejudices against subjectively foreign immigrant groups (e.g., immigrants from Peru and Mongolia), but no such increase in prejudice against immigrants from subjectively familiar countries (such as Poland or Taiwan). Furthermore, ethnocentrism and xenophobia are also exaggerated among individuals who are temporarily immunosuppressed (women in the first trimester of pregnancy), and so actually are more vulnerable to infection (Navarrete, Fessler & Eng, 2007).

Other cue-based interpersonal prejudices

Two important evolutionary psychological principles are exemplified by the preceding line of research. First, people are perceptually sensitive to specific sets of physical characteristics that serve as heuristic cues connoting specific kinds of fitness-relevant categories (e.g., morphological anomalies are heuristic cues connoting potential infection risk). And second, given the signal-detection problem inherent in any such cue-based inference process, people often respond to an over-general set of cues (*any* morphological anomaly may serve as a cue connoting potential infection risk).

These principles also underlie a line of research documenting prejudicial perceptions of adults who happen to have childlike features. Because newborn infants are helpless and dependent on adults for survival, and because an adult's own reproductive fitness depends on the survival of one's infant offspring, the perception of babyish features in others may heuristically trigger functionally correspondent inferences (e.g., helplessness). This may happen even when rational analysis reveals that the target person is not at all infantile. The implication is a set of predictable stereotypes and prejudices: Compared to other adults, baby-faced adults are pre-judged to be relatively more ignorant, incapable, and guileless (e.g., Zebrowitz & Montepare, 1992, 2006; Zebrowitz & McDonald, 1991).

Other kinds of superficial physical features may trigger other kinds of prejudicial responses. For example, drawing on evolutionary biological research on kin selection and kin recognition, an extensive body of psychological research shows that perceived self-other similarity inclines people to implicitly judge others – even total strangers – to be more kin-like (Park & Schaller, 2005; Park, Schaller, & Van Vugt, 2008). This sets the stage for many predictable prejudices in a variety of behavioral domains including sexual behavior, altruistic behavior, and even political outcomes (Bailenson, Iyengar, Yee, et al., 2008; DeBruine, 2005; Krupp, DeBruine, & Barclay, 2008)

Social dominance and its implications

Finally, there is an important line of research (associated with *social dominance theory*; Sidanius & Pratto, 1999) informed by the observation that fitness benefits are likely to have been associated with hierarchical group structures, and that most contemporary human societies are organized as group-based social hierarchies – with some groups of people exercising a disproportionate amount of power. Social dominance theory is not deduced strictly from evolutionary principles. Rather, it is a hybrid conceptual framework that integrates conceptual insights from different levels of analysis (e.g., evolutionary, psychological, sociological). The integrative framework produces hypotheses bearing on individuals' motivations to maintain existing group-based hierarchies and the social inequities implied by these hierarchies (Pratto, Sidanius, & Levin, 2006; Sidanius & Kurzban, 2003).

One implication is that many different prejudices may result, in part, from the tendency to justify and maintain the inequitable outcomes associated with dominant versus subordinate social categories. Consistent with this implication, individuals who score high on measures of social dominance orientation (i.e., people who are especially favorable toward the maintenance of dominance hierarchies) are especially prejudiced against a variety of different groups, and these prejudices are especially likely to emerge when intergroup context and other dominance-relevant considerations are temporarily paramount

(Pratto & Shih, 2000; Pratto, Sidanius, & Levin, 2006; Pratto, Sidanius, & Stallworth 1994).

Social dominance theory also has important implications for understanding 'modern racism' – the phenomenon in which overtly non-prejudiced attitudes mask more subtle expressions of racism. One set of studies found that overtly race-neutral objections to American-affirmative action policies were predicted by dominance-related concerns, and that this relationship was especially strong among well-educated White people – who, presumably, stood to benefit the most from existing employment inequities (Frederico & Sidanius, 2002). Thus, 'principled' objections to affirmative action are not quite as principled as they appear, but may instead be based on latent desires to maintain the existing social hierarchy.

Social dominance theory, however, pertains not just to racial prejudice. The theory implies that the specific targets of dominance-based prejudices are likely to vary predictably, depending on the specific sociological context of inequality (Sidanius & Pratto, 1999). For instance, in societies described by salient race-based inequalities (e.g., North America, South Africa), social dominance orientation is especially like to predict racial prejudice. But, in societies in which social stratification is defined more saliently by social class or caste or religion (as in much of southern Asia), social dominance orientation is more likely to predict prejudices based on those particular categorical distinctions instead.

The theory also makes many unique predictions pertaining to sexism and gender stereotypes. In most human societies, men have historically exercised a disproportionate amount of societal power relative to women. It follows that men (compared to women) are especially disposed toward the maintenance of dominance hierarchies, and to show especially strong prejudices toward those who threaten their status in an existing dominance hierarchy (Pratto, Sidanius, Stallworth, 1994; Sidanius & Kurzban, 2003; Sidanius, Pratto, & Brief, 1995). In addition, social dominance orientation predicts gender-stereotypical attitudes. Among men, higher levels of social dominance orientation are associated with lower levels of commitment to marriage and to offspring care; among women, higher levels of social dominance orientation are associated with a greater desire to marry a wealthy, high-status man (Pratto & Hegarty, 2000).

CULTURAL EVOLUTION AND POPULAR STEREOTYPES

To this point, we have discussed how ancient evolutionary pressures, by operating on genes over many generations, may have shaped the psychology of prejudice. In addition, many scholars have observed that variation-and-selective-retention processes – which underlie genetic evolution – operate on other kinds of information too (e.g., Campbell, 1965b; Dawkins, 1976; Hull, 1988; Mesoudi, Whiten, & Laland, 2006). Specifically, selection mechanisms guide the evolution of cultural memes. Stereotypes are one such meme.

Many meaningful consequences of stereotypes exist only because those stereotypes are popular. Consider the phenomenon whereby African-Americans perform poorly on academic tests under conditions that make salient others' stereotypic beliefs about their ethnic group (Steele, 1997). This effect emerges only because the academic underachievement stereotype is widely shared across the American population, and has been for some time. The implication is hardly limited to this particular phenomenon. Stereotypes that are more popular are more likely to be activated in working memory, and these stereotypes in turn have more powerful consequences on individual behavior (Sechrist & Stangor, 2001; Stangor, Sechrist, & Jost, 2001). To the extent that stereotypes matter at all, they matter more whenever they are more popular (Schaller & Conway, 2001).

Why are some stereotypes popular, while others are not? Why do some stereotypes remain popular, while others disappear from the cultural landscape? Cultural evolutionary processes provide an answer to those questions.

Four key elements underlie a cultural evolutionary approach to stereotypes. First, there is a dualistic nature to the representation of stereotypes. At one level of analysis, stereotypes are individual-level cognitive representations; but at a second level of analysis, stereotypes are cultural representations shared by many members of a population (Stangor & Schaller, 1996). Second, the cultural representation of a stereotype – the extent to which it is popular – is driven largely by interpersonal communication processes. Third, interpersonal communication is a selective process: People are more likely to communicate about some things rather than others. The consequence is that certain kinds of stereotypes become, and remain, popular across the social landscape, but others do not. Fourth, the selective pressures imposed by communication are far from random. Individual-level psychological processes (motives, goals, etc.) predictably influence the extent to which people communicate about specific stereotypes. Consequently, these psychological processes influence the extent to which some stereotypes, rather than others, become enduring features of the popular landscape.

Trait communicability predicts stereotype popularity

A fundamental implication of this conceptual analysis is that, to the extent that an idiosyncratic bit of stereotypic knowledge is more likely to be talked about, it is not likely to remain idiosyncratic. If it is communicable, it is likely to become popular.

In one test of this hypothesis, Schaller, Conway, and Tanchuk (2002) obtained ratings for dozens of stereotypic traits indicating the extent to which information bearing on these traits is likely to be talked about. A separate sample of participants indicated the extent to which each trait was stereotypical of particular ethnic groups within the local geographical region. For prominent ethnic groups – those that people actually do talk about – more

highly communicable traits were more likely to be central to the popular stereotype. An additional study examined the effects of a trait's communicability on its persistence in the popular stereotype of American ethnic groups across 60 years. The communicability of a trait predicted the extent to which it remained central to the cultural stereotype of the most populous and prominent ethnic groups (e.g., Jews, African-Americans). Traits that people are especially likely to talk about (e.g., lazy) persisted in the popular stereotype, decade after decade, while less communicable traits (e.g., superstitious) did not.

It is notable that the predictive effect of trait communicability occurred only for conversationally prominent groups. This further implicates the importance of actual interpersonal communication. It is through acts of communication – individuals' choices about what to talk about and what not to talk about – that selection occurs, and this selection process predicts the evolving contents of popular stereotypes.

Influences on communicability and their implications

Why are some stereotypic traits more communicable than others? An answer lies in the analogy between genes and memes. The communicability of a gene (the extent to which it is transmitted to future generations) depends fundamentally on the ecological context. The communicability of a meme (such as a stereotypic trait) depends fundamentally on the *psychological* context – on the psychological state of the people who might, or might not, introduce that information into their conversations with others.

People generally communicate information they judge to be useful to their conversational partners. Information bearing on physical health and safety represents one of the most useful types to know about others. For example, people judge news stories to be more important, and to be more worthy of broadcast, if they arouse more fear (Young, 2003). Urban legends are more communicable to the extent that they arouse disgust (Heath, Bell,

& Sternberg, 2001). And in the context of impression formation, people prioritize trait information bearing on interpersonal trust or distrust (Cottrell, Neuberg, & Li, 2007). Similarly, the communicability of a stereotypic trait positively correlates with the extent to which it connotes interpersonal danger or safety, and these same traits have been more persistent in the cultural stereotype of African-Americans (Schaller, Faulkner, Park, et al., 2004).

In addition to selectively crafting their communications to serve the needs of others, people also selectively craft their communications to serve self-interested goals, such as the desire to make a positive impression on others. Among other things, this accounts for individuals' reluctance to be the bearer of bad news (Rosen & Tesser, 1972). Impression management goals also influence the communicability of specific stereotypic traits. For example, if people believe that others will think more highly of them if they talk about positive traits, then they selectively talk about the positive characteristics of a group (e.g., intelligence); but if they believe that others will think more highly of them if they talk about negative traits, then they selectively talk about the negative characteristics of a group (e.g., aggressiveness). This direct impact of impression management goals on trait communicability has a consequent indirect effect – entirely unintended – on the emerging contents of socially shared stereotypes (Schaller & Conway, 1999).

Impression management goals may influence the communication of stereotypes in more subtle ways as well – favoring certain variations of the same trait over other, slightly different variations. In terms of functional implications, the blatantly sexist belief that 'women are not capable of taking care of themselves' is not very different from the more benevolent belief that 'women are sensitive and need protection.' But among people who worry about being perceived as prejudiced, these two beliefs may vary considerably in their communicability. The same is true of stereotypic information describing many ethnic minority groups. This may help to explain why, in the wake of the civil rights movements, blatant forms of racism are replaced in the population by more discreet variations of the same essential prejudice (Gaertner & Dovidio, 1986; Swim, Aikin, Hall, et al., 1995).

INTEGRATIVE THEMES, BROADER IMPLICATIONS, AND FUTURE DIRECTIONS

We have reviewed many different lines of theory and research, each focusing on a specific set of phenomena relevant to the psychology of stereotypes and prejudices. While conceptually distinct, these lines of research are united by their emphasis on the variation-and-selective-retention mechanisms that define both genetic and cultural evolutionary processes.

Additional commonalities underlie the different lines of research that consider human evolutionary origins of contemporary prejudices. Whether the primary focus is on some specific kind of fitness-relevant danger (the threat of aggression, disease, etc.) or opportunity (the benefits of coalitional groups, hierarchical structures, etc.), these research programs all imply that contemporary prejudices emerge from psychological mechanisms that were adaptive in ancestral social ecologies, and that these mechanisms evolved because they help to solve fitness-relevant 'problems' (prospects to be attained, perils to be avoided) inherent to those ecologies.

Importantly, however, this does not mean that these prejudices are functionally adaptive in contemporary environments. Nor does it mean that these prejudices are inevitable or unchangeable. Quite the contrary. Evolutionary cost–benefit analyses imply the evolution of psychological mechanisms that are flexible and sensitive to contextual cues (Schaller, Park, & Kenrick, 2007). Evolutionary models that employ cost–benefit analyses often produce novel hypotheses about the specific contexts that are likely to either amplify or inhibit prejudicial responses. This not only yields novel scientific discoveries (e.g., the effects of immunosuppression on xenophobia and ethnocentrism; Navarrete, Fessler, & Eng, 2007), it also provides a basis for the development of interventions that might help to moderate prejudices in contemporary environments (Neuberg & Cottrell, 2006; Schaller & Neuberg, 2008). Xenophobic responses to immigrant populations, for example, might be diminished by progressive public health policies and other interventions that reduce individuals' perceived vulnerability to infectious disease.

The psychological products of genetic evolution can influence cultural evolutionary processes too. Fitness-relevant information (e.g., traits connoting malevolence) may be especially communicable, especially within contexts (e.g., warfare, threat of terrorism) that enhance the salience of specific fitness-relevant prospects or perils. This has consequences on the evolving contents of popular stereotypes. Thus, just as evolutionarily informed interventions may inhibit the activation of pernicious prejudices (at an individual level of analysis), these interventions may also have additional consequences on the spread of stereotypes across a cultural landscape. Currently there is very little research that rigorously addresses this intersection of the two levels (individual and cultural) at which evolutionary processes operate. This remains an important topic for future research, which will not only contribute to the psychological understanding of stereotypes and prejudices, but also to a growing body of interdisciplinary attempts to integrate processes operating at evolutionary, cognitive, and cultural levels of analysis (Mesoudi, Whiten, & Laland, 2006).

Evolutionary insights can be useful not only in predicting stereotypes and prejudicial beliefs within a culture, but also in explaining the differences *between* cultures. There are substantial cross-cultural differences in the expression of specific kinds of prejudices (Inglehart, Basenez, & Moreno, 1998), but the origins of these cross-cultural differences remain largely unexplained. Recent research has employed evolutionary cost–benefit analyses to predict and explain relations between specific ecological variables (e.g., pathogen prevalence) and specific cross-cultural differences (e.g., individualistic versus collectivistic value systems; Fincher, Thornhill, Murray, et al., 2008). Similar analyses may help explain cross-cultural differences in specific kinds of prejudices as well.

Of course, to fully articulate the relations between evolution processes and contemporary prejudices, it will be necessary not merely to predict prejudices at a psychological level. Researchers will need to show how selection pressures influenced the frequencies of specific genetic variants within human (and pre-human) populations, and to identify relations between specific genes and prejudices. It will be useful to show how and why and under what circumstances those genes are (or are not) expressed during development. Additionally, research should attempt to trace the expression of those genes to the social and psychological processes through which individuals acquire prejudicial beliefs in the first place (e.g., associative learning mechanisms; e.g., Navarrete, Olsson, & Ho, et al., 2009). And it will be useful to link the expression of those genes to the specific physiological mechanisms (neurotransmitter systems, neuroendocrine systems) that actually govern the experience, expression, and communication of prejudice at any particular moment in time.

SUMMARY AND CONCLUSIONS

We have reviewed two distinct ways in which inquiry into evolutionary processes informs the psychological study of stereotypes and prejudices.

One approach draws upon foundational research in genetics and evolutionary biology, and applies these insights toward conceptual speculations about psychological adaptations that contribute to prejudices in contemporary social environments. Many of these deductions yield novel hypotheses, and novel empirical discoveries, about specific circumstances under which specific prejudices are likely to be either exaggerated or inhibited.

The second approach focuses not on genetic evolutionary processes, but instead on cultural evolutionary processes – the selective means through which some knowledge structures (rather than others) become, and remain, popular within any human society. Focused inquiry into cultural evolutionary processes yields novel hypotheses, and novel empirical discoveries, about specific circumstances under which specific stereotypes are likely to be social problems.

Both bodies of psychological research are informed by inquiries in other domains of biological and social science. The challenge associated with any evolutionary approach to human stereotypes and prejudices is that scientists must forge connections between phenomena operating at different levels of analysis. The benefit, ultimately, is a more complete understanding of human stereotypes and prejudices and what can be done to eliminate them.

REFERENCES

Ackerman, J. M., Shapiro, J. R., Neuberg, S. L., Kenrick, D. T., Becker, D. V., Griskevicius, V., et al. (2006). They all look the same to me (unless they're angry): From out-group homogeneity to out-group heterogeneity. *Psychological Science*, 17, 836–840.

Anthony, T., Copper, C., & Mullen, B. (1992). Cross-racial facial identification: A social cognitive integration. *Personality and Social Psychology Bulletin*, 18, 296–301.

Bailenson, J. N., Iyengar, S. Yee, N., & Collins, N. (2008). Facial similarity between voters and candidates causes influence *Public Opinion Quarterly*, 72, 935–961.

Brewer, M. B. (1979). Ingroup bias in the minimal intergroup situation: A cognitive motivational analysis. *Psychological Bulletin*, 17, 475–482.

Brewer, M. B. (1997) On the social origins of human nature. In C. McGarty, & S. A. Haslam (Eds), *The Message of Social Psychology* (pp. 54–62). Oxford, UK: Blackwell.

Brewer, M. B. (1999). The psychology of prejudice: Ingroup love and outgroup hate? *Journal of Social Issues*, 55, 429–444.

Brewer, M. B. (2007). The importance of being we: Human nature and intergroup relations. *American Psychologist*, 62, 728–738.

Brewer, M. B., & Caporael, L. (2006). An evolutionary perspective on social identity: Revisiting groups. In M. Schaller, J. A. Simpson, & D. T. Kenrick (Eds), *Evolution and Social Psychology* (pp. 143–161). New York: Psychology Press.

Buss, D. M. (Ed.) (2005). *The Handbook of Evolutionary Psychology*. New York: Wiley.

Campbell, D. T. (1965a). Ethnocentric and other altruistic motives. In D. Levine (Ed.), *Nebraska Symposium on Motivation* (pp. 283–311). Lincoln: University of Nebraska Press.

Campbell, D. T. (1965b). Variation and selective retention in socio-cultural evolution. In H. R. Barringer, G. I. Blanksten, & R. W. Mack (Eds), *Social Change in Developing Areas* (pp. 19–49). Cambridge MA: Schenkman.

Campbell, D. T. (1974). Evolutionary epistemology. In P. A. Schilpp (Ed.), *The Philosophy of Karl Popper* (pp. 413–463). La Salle IL: Open Court.

Campbell, D. T. (1975). On the conflicts between biological and social evolution and between psychology and moral tradition. *American Psychologist*, 30, 1103–1126.

Clark, A. E., & Kashima, Y. (2007). Stereotypes help people connect with others in the community: A situated functional analysis of the stereotype consistency bias in communication. *Journal of Personality and Social Psychology*, 93, 1028–1039.

Cosmides, L., & Tooby, J. (2005). Neurocognitive adaptations designed for social exchange. In D. M. Buss (Ed.), *The Handbook of Evolutionary Psychology* (pp. 584–627). New York: Wiley.

Cottrell, C. A., & Neuberg, S. L. (2005). Different emotional reactions to different groups: A sociofunctional threat-based approach to "prejudice". *Journal of Personality and Social Psychology*, 88, 770–789.

Cottrell, C. A., Neuberg, S. L., & Li, N. P. (2007). What do people desire in others? A sociofunctional perspective on the importance of different valued characteristics. *Journal of Personality and Social Psychology*, 92, 208–231.

Crawford, C., & Krebs, D. L. (Eds) (2008). *Foundations of Evolutionary Psychology*. Mahwah NJ: Lawrence Erlbaum Associates.

Darwin, C. (1859). *On the Origin of Species by Means of Natural Selection*. London: John Murray.

Darwin, C. (1871). *The Descent of Man, and Selection in Relation to Sex*. London: John Murray.

Darwin, C. (1872). *The Expression of the Emotions in Man and Animals*. London: John Murray.

Dawkins, R. (1976). *The Selfish Gene*. Oxford UK: Oxford University Press.

DeBruine L. M. (2005). Trustworthy but not lust-worthy: Context-specific effects of facial resemblance. *Proceedings of the Royal Society of London B*, 272, 919–922.

Dunbar, R. I. M., & Barrett L. (Eds) (2007). *Oxford Handbook of Evolutionary Psychology*. Oxford UK: Oxford University Press.

Duncan, L. A., & Schaller, M. (2009). Prejudicial attitudes toward older adults may be exaggerated when people feel vulnerable to infectious disease: Evidence and implications. *Analyses of Social Issues and Public Policy*, 9, 97–115.

Faulkner, J., Schaller, M., Park, J. H., & Duncan, L. A. (2004). Evolved disease-avoidance mechanisms and contemporary xenophobic attitudes. *Group Processes and Intergroup Relations*, 7, 333–353.

Fincher, C. L., Thornhill, R., Murray, D. R., & Schaller, M. (2008). Pathogen prevalence predicts human cross-cultural variability in individualism/collectivism. *Proceedings of the Royal Society B*, 275, 1279–1285.

Frederico, C. M., & Sidanius, J. (2002). Racism, ideology, and affirmative action revisited: The antecedents and consequences of "principled objections" to affirmative action. *Journal of Personality and Social Psychology*, 82, 488–502.

Gaertner, L., Iuzzini, J., Witt, M. G., & Orina, M. M. (2006). Us without them: Evidence for an intragroup origin of positive in-group regard. *Journal of Personality and Social Psychology*, 90, 426–439.

Gaertner, S. L., & Dovidio, J. F. (1986). An aversive form of racism. In J. F. Dovidio, & S. L. Gaertner (Eds), *Prejudice, Discrimination, and Racism* (pp. 61–89). New York: Academic Press.

Gangestad, S. W., & Simpson, J. A. (Eds) (2007). *The Evolution of Mind: Fundamental Questions and Controversies*. New York: Guilford Press.

Gigerenzer, G., Todd, P. M., & the ABC Research Group (1999). *Simple Heuristics That Make Us Smart*. New York: Oxford University Press.

Grillon, C., Pellowski, M., Merikangas, K. R., & Davis, M. (1997). Darkness facilitates acoustic startle reflex in humans. *Biological Psychiatry*, 42, 453–460.

Heath, C., Bell, C., & Sternberg, E. (2001). Emotional selection in memes: The case of urban legends. *Journal of Personality and Social Psychology*, 81, 1028–1041.

Hull, D. L. (1988). *Science as a Process*. Chicago: University of Chicago Press.

Inglehart, R., Basenez, M., & Moreno, A. (1998). *Human Values and Beliefs*. Ann Arbor: University of Michigan Press.

Katz, D., & Braly, K. (1933). Racial stereotypes in one hundred college students. *Journal of Abnormal and Social Psychology*, 28, 280–290.

Krupp, D. B., DeBruine, L. M, & Barclay, P. (2008). A cue of kinship promotes cooperation for the public good. *Evolution and Human Behavior*, 29, 49–55.

Kurzban, R, & Leary, M. R. (2001). Evolutionary origins of stigmatization: The functions of social exclusion. *Psychological Bulletin*, 127, 187–208.

Kurzban, R., Tooby, J., & Cosmides, L. (2001). Can race be erased? Coalitional computation and social categorization. *Proceedings of the National Academy of Sciences*, 98, 15387–15392.

Lyons, A., & Kashima, Y. (2003). How are stereotypes maintained through communication? The influence of stereotype sharedness. *Journal of Personality and Social Psychology*, 85, 989–1005.

Madon, S., Guyll, M., Aboufadel, K., Montiel, E., Smith, A., Palumbo, P., et al. (2001). Ethnic and national stereotypes: The Princeton Trilogy revisited and revised. *Personality and Social Psychology Bulletin*, 27, 996–1010.

Maner, J. K., Gailliot, M. T., Rouby, D. A., & Miller, S. L. (2007). Can't take my eyes off you: Attentional adhesion to mates and rivals. *Journal of Personality and Social Psychology*, 93, 389–401.

Maner, J. K., Kenrick, D. T., Becker, D. V., Robertson, T., Hofer, B., Neuberg, S. L., et al. (2005). Functional projection: How fundamental social motives can bias interpersonal perception. *Journal of Personality and Social Psychology*, 88, 63–78.

Mesoudi, A., Whiten, A., & Laland, K. N. (2006). Towards a unified science of cultural evolution. *Behavioral and Brain Sciences*, 29, 329–383.

Navarrete, C. D., Fessler, D. M. T., & Eng, S. J. (2007). Elevated ethnocentrism in the first trimester of pregnancy. *Evolution and Human Behavior*, 28, 60–65.

Navarrete C. D., Olsson, A., Ho, A. K., Mendes, W. B., Thomsen, L., & Sidanius, J. (2009). Fear extinction to an outgroup face: The role of target gender. *Psychological Science*, 20, 155–158.

Neuberg, S.L., & Cottrell, C.A. (2006). Evolutionary bases of prejudices. In M. Schaller, J.A. Simpson, & D.T. Kenrick (Eds). *Evolution and Social Psychology* (pp. 163–187). New York: Psychology Press.

Neuberg, S. L., Smith, D. M., & Asher, T. (2000). Why people stigmatize: Toward a biocultural framework. In T. Heatherton, R. Kleck, J. G. Hull, & M. Hebl (Eds), *The Social Psychology of Stigma* (pp. 31–61). New York: Guilford.

Norenzayan, A., Atran, S., Faulkner, J., & Schaller, M. (2006). Memory and mystery: The cultural selection of minimally counterintuitive narratives. *Cognitive Science*, 30, 531–553.

Öhman, A., & Mineka, S. (2001). Fears, phobias, and preparedness: Toward an evolved module of fear and fear learning. *Psychological Review*, 108, 483–522.

Park, J. H., Faulkner, J, & Schaller, M. (2003). Evolved disease-avoidance processes and contemporary anti-social behavior: Prejudicial attitudes and avoidance of people with physical disabilities. *Journal of Nonverbal Behavior*, 27, 65–87.

Park, J. H., & Schaller, M. (2005). Does attitude similarity serve as a heuristic cue for kinship? Evidence of an implicit cognitive association. *Evolution and Human Behavior*, 26, 158–170.

Park, J. H., Schaller, M., & Crandall, C. S. (2007). Pathogen-avoidance mechanisms and the stigmatization of obese people. *Evolution and Human Behavior*, 28, 410–414.

Park, J., Schaller, M., & Van Vugt, M. (2008). The psychology of human kin recognition: Heuristic cues, erroneous inferences, and their implications. *Review of General Psychology*, 12, 215–235.

Pratto, F., & Hegarty, P. (2003). The political psychology of reproductive strategies. *Psychological Science*, 11, 57–62.

Pratto, F., & Shih, M. (2000). Social dominance orientation and group context in implicit group prejudice. *Psychological Science*, 11, 521–524.

Pratto, F., Sidanius, J., & Levin, S. (2006). Social dominance theory and the dynamics of intergroup relations: Taking stock and looking forward. *European Review of Social Psychology*, 17, 271–320.

Pratto, F., Sidanius, J., Stallworth, L. M., & Malle, B. F. (1994). Social dominance orientation: A personality variable relevant to social roles and intergroup relations. *Journal of Personality and Social Psychology*, 67, 741–763.

Rosen, S., & Tesser, A. (1972). Fear of negative evaluation and the reluctance to transmit bad news. *Journal of Communication*, 22, 124–141.

Ruscher, J. B. (1998). Prejudice and stereotyping in everyday communication. In M. P. Zanna (Ed.), *Advances in Experimental Social Psychology* (Vol. 30, pp. 241–307). San Diego, CA: Academic Press.

Ruscher, J. B. (2001). *Prejudiced Communication*. New York: Guilford.

Schaller, M., & Abeysinghe, A. M. N. D. (2006). Geographical frame of reference and dangerous intergroup attitudes: A double-minority study in Sri Lanka. *Political Psychology*, 27, 615–631.

Schaller, M., & Conway, L. G., III (1999). Influence of impression-management goals on the emerging contents of group stereotypes: Support for a social-evolutionary process. *Personality and Social Psychology Bulletin*, 25, 819–833.

Schaller, M., & Conway, L. G., III (2001). From cognition to culture: The origins of stereotypes that really matter. In G. B. Moscowitz (Ed.), *Cognitive Social Psychology: The Princeton Symposium on the Legacy and Future of Social Cognition* (pp. 163–176). Mahwah, NJ: Erlbaum.

Schaller, M., Conway, L. G., III, & Tanchuk, T. (2002). Selective pressures on the once and future contents of ethnic stereotypes: Effects of the communicability of traits. *Journal of Personality and Social Psychology*, 82, 861–877.

Schaller, M., & Duncan, L. A. (2007). The behavioral immune system: Its evolution and social psychological implications. In J. P. Forgas, M. G. Haselton, & W. von Hippel (Eds), *Evolution and the Social Mind: Evolutionary Psychology and Social Cognition* (pp. 293–307). New York: Psychology Press.

Schaller, M., Faulkner, J., Park, J. H., Neuberg, S. L., & Kenrick, D. (2004). Impressions of danger influence impressions of people: An evolutionary perspective on individual and collective cognition. *Journal of Cultural and Evolutionary Psychology*, 2, 231–247.

Schaller, M., & Neuberg, S. L. (2008). Intergroup prejudices and intergroup conflicts. In C. Crawford, & D. L. Krebs (Eds), *Foundations of Evolutionary Psychology* (pp. 399–412). Mahwah NJ: Lawrence Erlbaum Associates.

Schaller, M., Park, J. H., & Faulkner, J. (2003). Prehistoric dangers and contemporary prejudices. In W. Stroebe, & M. Hewstone (Eds), *European Review of Social Psychology* (Vol. 14, pp. 105–137). Hove, UK: Psychology Press.

Schaller, M., Park, J. H, & Kenrick, D. T. (2007). Human evolution and social cognition. In R. I. M. Dunbar, & L. Barrett (Eds), *Oxford Handbook of Evolutionary Psychology*. Oxford, UK: Oxford University Press.

Schaller, M., Park, J. H., & Mueller, A. (2003). Fear of the dark: Interactive effects of beliefs about danger and ambient darkness on ethnic stereotypes. *Personality and Social Psychology Bulletin*, 29, 637–649.

Schaller, M., Simpson, J. A, & Kenrick, D. T. (Eds) (2006). *Evolution and Social Psychology*. New York: Psychology Press.

Sechrist, G. B., & Stangor, C. (2001). Perceived consensus influences intergroup behavior and stereotype accessibility. *Journal of Personality and Social Psychology*, 80, 645–654.

Sidanius, J. & Kurzban, R. (2003). Evolutionary approaches to political psychology. In D. O. Sears, L. Huddy, & R. Jervis (Eds). *Oxford Handbook of Political Psychology* (pp. 146–181). New York: Oxford University Press.

Sidanius, J., & Pratto, F. (1999). *Social Dominance: An Intergroup Theory of Social Hierarchy and Oppression*. New York: Cambridge University Press.

Sidanius, J., Pratto, F., & Brief, D. (1995). Group dominance and the political psychology of gender: A cross-cultural comparison. *Political Psychology*, 16, 381–396.

Sporer, S. L. (2001). Recognizing faces of other ethnic groups: An integration of theories. *Psychology, Public Policy, and Law*, 7, 36–97.

Stangor, C., & Schaller, M. (1996). Stereotypes as individual and collective representations. In C. N. Macrae, C. Stangor, & M. Hewstone (Eds), *Stereotypes and Stereotyping* (pp. 3–37.). New York: Guilford.

Stangor, C., Sechrist, G. B., & Jost, J. T. (2001). Social influence and intergroup beliefs: The role of perceived social consensus. In J. P. Forgas, & K. D. Williams (Eds), *Social Influence: Direct and Indirect Processes* (pp. 235–252). Philadelphia: Psychology Press.

Steele, C. M. (1997). A threat in the air: How stereotypes shape intellectual identity and performance. *American Psychologist*, 52, 613–629.

Swim, J. K., Aikin, K. J., Hall, W. S., & Hunter, B. A. (1995). Sexism and racism: Old-fashioned and modern prejudices. *Journal of Personality and Social Psychology*, 68, 199–214.

Young, J. R. (2003). The role of fear in agenda setting by television news. *American Behavioral Scientist*, 46, 1673–1695.

Zebrowitz, L. A., Fellous, J. M., Mignault, A., & Andreoletti, C. (2003). Trait impressions as over-generalized responses to adaptively significant facial qualities: Evidence from connectionist modeling. *Personality and Social Psychology Review*, 7, 194–215.

Zebrowitz, L. A., & McDonald, S. M. (1992). The impact of litigants. Baby-facedness and attractiveness on adjudications in small claims courts. *Law and Human Behavior*, 15, 603–623.

Zebrowitz, L. A., & Montepare, J. M. (1992). Impressions of babyfaced males and females across the lifespan. *Developmental Psychology*, 28, 1143–1152.

Zebrowitz, L. A., and Montepare, J. (2006). The ecological approach to person perception: Evolutionary roots and contemporary offshoots. In M. Schaller, J. A. Simpson, & D. T. Kenrick (Eds), *Evolution and Social Psychology* (pp. 81–113). New York: Psychology Press.

6

Developmental Perspectives

Melanie Killen, Cameron B. Richardson,
and Megan Clark Kelly

ABSTRACT

This chapter reviews developmental approaches to intergroup attitudes re-garding prejudice, stereotyping, and discrimination. How intergroup attitudes emerge, change, and are revealed throughout development is described, particularly regarding every day, familiar peer and parent-child exchanges. Social developmental psychology has drawn on social psychological constructs to understand children's and adolescents' judgments about individuals from different group memberships (particularly gender, race, ethnicity, and culture), and has provided new insights into the emergence of intergroup attitudes. An integrative approach for investigating the development of intergroup attitudes serves to advance the field, and provide a multi-level approach for addressing pervasive problems of exclusion and prejudice from childhood to adulthood.

INTERGROUP ATTITUDES IN CHILDHOOD AND ADOLESCENCE

Humans have the propensity to prejudge, stereotype, and discriminate as well as the capacity for upholding principles of equality, justice, and fairness. Investigating how and when children and adolescents reveal these propensities is an essential part of understanding the origins, formation, and developmental trajectory of prejudice, stereotyping, and discrimination. Social psychological research has demonstrated that there are contexts and conditions under which individuals are motivated to inhibit prejudicial attitudes (Devine, Plant, Amodio, et al., 2002). In developmental psychology, the task is somewhat different because both prejudice and moral motivations are newly emerging orientations.

In fact, the question may be reversed given that extensive research indicates that moral judgments and inclusive orientations (cooperation, prosociality) emerge early in childhood, prior to stereotyping and inter-group bias (Killen, Margie, & Sinno, 2006; Warneken & Tomasello, 2007). The question becomes, then, what bearing do stereotypes, prejudice, and bias have on early morality, and what are the contexts and conditions (explicit and implicit) that prompt children to subordinate their moral orientations? For these reasons then, it is important both to investigate and understand the origins of intergroup attitudes as well as to study the emergence of conceptions of equality, justice, and fairness, as these concepts are often intertwined with prejudicial attitudes in complex ways throughout development.

In this chapter, we present an overview of how developmental psychological research has contributed to the study of prejudice and discrimination by providing an account of the emergence, nature of change, and sources of influence on prejudice and discrimination. In so doing, we also identify what a developmental account entails, and how current research has provided new insights into the nature of prejudice in human social interaction, attitudes, and relationships. We begin by describing the theoretical history of the field of developmental intergroup research, then review current findings on developmental intergroup attitudes, and conclude by providing an integrative approach for investigating explicit and implicit attitudes and judgments in children, adolescents, and adults.

Definitions of constructs

Prejudice, stereotyping, discrimination

While the definitions of the constructs associated with prejudice in the developmental literature are closely related to those in the social psychological field, the way the constructs are measured, assessed, and analyzed is quite different (Aboud & Amato, 2001; Killen, McGlothlin, & Henning, 2008; Levy & Killen, 2008)). The display of discriminatory behavior, or the holding of derogatory attitudes, takes different meaning in childhood than adulthood because cognitive, social, and emotional concepts are qualitatively and fundamentally different in early development than they are in later development. For example, prejudice generally refers to negative attitudes about an individual based on group membership (Augoustinos & Rosewarne, 2001; Nesdale, 2004; Powlishta, Serbin, Doyle, et al., 1994). Does this mean that the holding of a prejudicial attitude implies an awareness of the 'outgroup' and, if so, what does this entail in terms of social-cognitive categorization and awareness of the category referred to as the 'outgroup'? What are the features of an 'outgroup' member

that are recognized or salient, and what are the criteria to determine that an attitude is 'negative'? Understanding the origins of intergroup attitudes requires a conceptual analysis of the component parts of intergroup attitudes.

Thus, one aspect of developmental intergroup research that differs from adult intergroup research is the necessity of determining the ways in which children's social cognition and cognitive abilities constrain their responses, judgments, and intentions towards others, and particularly regarding the relationship between the ingroup and the outgroup. To do this, developmental psychology researchers analyze children's interpretations of a number of dimensions, including the social context (where does prejudice or bias occur?), types of relationship (who is involved? peer, adult, family), forms of identification with the ingroup (am I a member of this group and what is the nature of my affiliation, and how much do I value it?), social experiences (what is the nature of my history of intergroup contact and experiences with discrimination?), social categorization (who is a member of the ingroup or the outgroup?) and the social construal (what meaning do I give to the situation?).

Fairness, equality, and morality

Defining morality as well as identifying how individuals formulate this construct is necessary to achieve a fuller understanding of how intergroup attitudes, and, more specifically, how prejudice emerges. Theoretically, prejudice and morality are diametrically opposed: prejudging violates principles of equal treatment, discrimination violates fairness principles, and stereotyping violates the integrity of individuals by discounting intragroup variation and associating traits solely on the basis of group membership.

What this means is that if concepts of equality emerge prior to the onset of prejudice and bias in childhood then it is important to analyze how it is that children become prejudiced given that this construct violates norms already understood by the child. There are several ways to investigate this issue.

It could be that children's concepts of equality at an early age apply only to the ingroup, for example, and what is left out has to do with applying equality concepts to members of outgroups. Further, it could be that what counts as prejudice is multidimensional, and that while prejudice is not revealed until middle childhood, early precursors are evident in early childhood and these precursors need to be better understood. While conceptualizations of morality reflect extensive philosophical and psychological debates, the general definition of morality in the literature is that morality refers to principles about how individuals ought to treat one another with respect to justice, fairness, equality, rights, and others' welfare, that is, the prevention of harm to others (Appiah, 2005; Nussbaum, 1999; Turiel, 1998). Just as notions of prejudice are emerging in childhood, so too are concepts of morality and fairness, which begin in early development and evolve from childhood to adulthood. As will be discussed below, new research from domain-specific models of social cognition have provided a means for understanding the seemingly contradictory findings that young children are both 'moral' and, at the same time, display 'prejudicial' attitudes.

History of research on children's prejudice and social judgments

Developmental approaches to children's social attitudes have been guided by Piagetian theory, which explains the origins and emergence of knowledge, and provides, to a large degree, the foundations for the field of developmental psychology. While Piaget (1932, 1952) did not directly study children's prejudice or stereotyping, he conducted a set of sociological studies in which he examined children's notions of other cultures by interviewing them about where they lived and how their own culture fitted into the larger category of the world's cultures (e.g., 'Can someone be both Genevan and Swiss?') (Piaget, 1977/1995). Piaget's research on this topic was rooted in the logical categorization of cultural identity, and not with the dynamic

relationship between ingroup and outgroup attitudes. Yet, his theory provided the basis for several key lines of research on children's intergroup attitudes and beliefs, not surprisingly, given that his theory of the emergence of knowledge provided the foundation for the field of developmental psychology (Piaget, 1932, 1952, 1970).

Clark and Clark (1939), who conducted the classic doll studies that provided evidence about low self-esteem in Black children enrolled in segregated schools in the United States (and was instrumental in the US Supreme Court decision outlawing segregation in the schools), cited Piaget's theory (1932) on children's self concept for the basis for their research. Piaget (1932) had proposed that children's self-consciousness emerged as a result of social comparisons with others, and Clark and Clark (1939) conducted a study on children's consciousness of self and racial identification to provide evidence that African-American children's development followed a path similar to that of European-American children (this being distinct from measures of self-esteem, which were tested in the doll studies).

In general, Piaget's theory made several claims that are relevant for intergroup theory and that have been validated in current research. First, Piaget's methodology involved the analyses of children's judgments and reasoning as well as peer relationships to demonstrate that social cognition undergoes qualitative changes from early development (childhood) to later development (adulthood). From his viewpoint, a fundamental mistake in research on children's intelligence was the assumption that children were 'little adults' (Piaget, 1952). Children do not just have 'less' intelligence than adults. Instead, children's thinking reflects laws and principles that evolve and undergo fundamental transformations from early- to middle childhood and adolescence. Thus, understanding prejudice requires determining how prejudice manifests in children's social cognition. As with the example of 'intelligence' above, children do not just have 'less' (or 'more') prejudice than adults. Instead, prejudice is qualitatively different in childhood than adulthood. Developmental intergroup research examines how children understand and evaluate prejudicial behavior as it occurs in their social interactions, peer groups, and daily experiences, using developmentally relevant assessment techniques to discover experimentally the underlying social cognition about ingroups and outgroups in children's lives.

Second, Piaget's theory of acquisition was rooted in children's abstraction of their experiences, evaluations, and judgments rather than as a result of a direct transmission from adults. This was contrary to other prevailing theories about child development at the time of Piaget's writings, and particularly in contrast to Behaviorism, which dominated American psychology in the 1950s (when Piaget's book were being translated into English). Piaget's unique viewpoint was social-cognitive because he investigated children's understanding of the social world. Interestingly, Allport's (1954), writing about the nature of prejudice was sympathetic to Piaget's theory. Allport (1954) made a distinction between adopting *prejudice* and *developing* prejudice, where the latter reflected notions similar to Piaget's theory of acquisition (Allport, 1954).

Piaget's findings demonstrated that children do not learn through imitation or direct copying but interpret the world through their own lens. Piaget's theory was similar to Asch's (1952) notion of construal, but applied to a developmental framework, charting how construals in meaning evolve overtime. Supporting this view, Aboud's own research, as well as her review of the developmental literature, led to a rejection of the view that prejudice is a result of imitation of adult attitudes, instead demonstrating that children construct their own theories that lead to prejudicial attitudes (Aboud & Amato, 2001). This conclusion was based on the fact that age-related changes regarding prejudicial attitudes are not reflective of the individual variability that exists in adult (parental) levels of bias. Children's prejudice is more consistently related to their social-cognitive and cognitive developmental change rather than to parental

beliefs, which are quite variable and often contradictory.

An exhaustive review of the literature reveals mixed findings regarding correlations between child and adult 'levels' of prejudice. In one study by Sinclair and colleagues (2005), researchers found a significant relationship between parental attitudes about race and implicit preference in children, when children were highly identified with their parents; the response rate was only 14 percent, however, indicating a potential sampling bias (Sinclair, Dunn, & Lowery, 2005). In another study, adolescents' willingness to have cross-race friendships was related to their perception of their parents' messages about cross-race relationships (friendship and dating) but intergroup contact was a more significant variable because adolescents with high intergroup contact were more willing to have cross-race relationships, despite negative parental messages (Edmonds & Killen, 2009).

Together these findings indicate that more research is needed to fully understand the relation between parental attitudes and children's racial bias. Moreover, prejudicial attitudes reflect age-related changes in social-cognition as well as reactions to implicit and indirect messages, as will be described below.

DEVELOPMENTAL THEORIES REGARDING INTERGROUP ATTITUDES

Social domain theory

Domain-specific models identify the contextual parameters, criteria, and categorization abilities that reflect how children understand the world (Keil, 2006; Kuhn & Siegler, 2006). In the area of social judgments, attitudes, and beliefs, the Social Domain Model has identified how children interpret and evaluate social acts, events, interactions, and relationships (Killen, Margie, & Sinno, 2006; Rutland, Killen, & Abrams, in press; Smetana, 2006; Turiel, 2008). This model has provided a framework for determining when individuals view ingroup/outgroup relationships from a moral (fairness), conventional (traditions, group functioning) and/or psychological (autonomy) perspective (Abrams & Rutland, 2008; Abrams, Rutland, Ferrell, et al., (2009); Crystal, Killen, & Ruck, 2008; Killen, 2007; Killen, Henning, Kelly, et al., 2007; Sinno & Killen, 2009; Verkuyten & Steenhuis, 2005). These studies have revealed significant age-related changes regarding W. Damon & R. M. Lerner coordination of different constructs, understanding of social concepts, and identification with groups, when evaluating straightforward and complex social issues, such as those created by intergroup encounters.

In contrast to social learning theories, children construct knowledge through their interactions in the world and their knowledge is not solely a product of parental attitudes. Developmental experience and social cognitive change, rather than direct transmission from adults, account for how children make judgments about others. Further, current research from cognitive developmental and social-cognitive developmental models for examining developmental intergroup attitudes points to age-related changes, and developmental trajectories.

Social identity theory

Tajfel's Social Identity Theory is another foundational theoretical framework for current developmental intergroup research (Tajfel & Turner, 1979). Tajfel proposed that social identity is a natural outcome of social categorization and that this propensity to categorize leads to ingroup and outgroup distinctions which, in turn, lead to bias and prejudice (see Abrams and Hogg, Chapter 11 this volume). As an example, Abrams and Rutland (2008) propose that how one functions in a group, the status and dynamics of the ingroup, and the concept of social groups more generally, contribute to self-identity, social categorization, and prejudice (Bennett & Sani, 2008; Nesdale, 2004; Rutland, Abrams, & Levy, 2007). While Tajfel's theory was not developmental, several basic assumptions are shared with

Piagetian theory such as the focus on social cognition, beliefs, judgments, and social experience (in the form of intergroup contact) as contributing to the development of stereotypes and prejudice, as discussed below under current research (Abrams, Hogg, & Marques, 2005; Bennett & Sani, 2008; Bennett & Sani, 2004; Nesdale, 2008; Rutland, 2004).

As will be demonstrated in the next section, a child's prejudice does not appear to emerge in broad, global stages (often referred to as 'domain general'), but rather is varied as a function of the context, the target, and the child's social cognition in terms of the ability to make moral judgments (i.e., to reject prejudicial decisions and discriminatory behavior) and to critically evaluate stereotypic labels (often referred to as 'domain specific'). The ability to reject stereotypes and prejudicial attitudes is a function, in part, of the nature of the issue, prior experience, social-cognitive evaluation, interpretation of competing considerations, and the source of influence (parental or peer) on the nature of the decision.

CURRENT DEVELOPMENTAL INTERGROUP RESEARCH: AN OVERVIEW

During the first decade of the twenty-first century, developmental intergroup research has expanded greatly to focus on a number of topics that reflect the same breadth of issues that have been investigated by social psychologists, including children's prejudice, social identity, stereotypes and stereotype threat, discrimination, intergroup bias, ethnic identity intergroup contact, and exclusion, as reflected in recent volumes devoted to developmental intergroup attitude (Killen & McKown, 2005; Levy & Killen, 2008; Quintana & McKown, 2007). It is essential to note that developmental intergroup work greatly differs from most social developmental research currently conducted in the area of developmental psychology. To date, most social developmental research, particularly in the areas of children's rejection and deviance has focused on individual differences. This research typically examines how psychological deviance stems from individual social deficits, such as a child's temperament (wariness, fearfulness, behavioral withdrawal), lack of social skills, and aggressiveness, with an aim to understand and identify predictors of at-risk behaviors for unhealthy development or psychopathology (Rubin, Bukowski, & Parker, 2006).

In contrast, developmental intergroup research shares the social psychological focus on the group (Asch, 1952), and on social attitudes (Dovidio & Gaertner, 2004). In the case of deviance, for example, individuals may be rejected from the group for reasons that have to do with group membership (such as gender, race, ethnicity), and not solely as a function of behavioral traits and individual differences regarding social deficits (although these two reasons for rejection often co-occur). Moreover, understanding normative age-related changes in social cognition has shed light on the underlying factors that contribute to bullying, shyness, and deviance, concluding that children's motives reveal their social behavior (Arsenio & Lemerise, 2004). Social psychology research on intergroup attitudes has also undergone its own change in focus from one that explained intergroup attitudes in terms of psychopathology (Adorno, Frenkel-Brunswick, Levinson, et al., 1950; Duckitt, 1992) to one that examines attitudes as a result of basic, and normal, categorization (Dovidio & Gaertner, 2004)

Developmental intergroup research has demonstrated how negative biases about others are often maintained by attitudes from the 'majority' group, that is, the dominant social, ethnic, or gender group, in a given social context. As articulated by political and social theorists, hierarchical relationships within and between cultures are often maintained by conventions and stereotypic expectations, which too often perpetuate power and status relationships (Nussbaum, 1999; Turiel, 2002). These types of status relationships begin in childhood, and evolve throughout childhood and adolescence, and into adulthood (for reviews, see Abrams & Rutland, 2008; Bigler & Liben, 2006; Killen, Sinno, & Margie, 2007; Levy & Killen, 2008).

As found by social identity theorists, the process of social categorization begins early in childhood. If I identify with girls and I categorize myself as a girl then I am also not a member of the boy's group (Bennett & Sani, 2008; Nesdale, 2004; Ruble, Martin, & Berenbaum, 2006). To the extent that traits and attributes become associated with gender, as an example, then judgments that reflect group membership and social identity can potentially reflect stereotypes. Holding a stereotype, while not a moral transgression alone, often leads to prejudicial and discriminatory attitudes and behavior, such as unfair treatment of others. In contrast, becoming a member of a group has potentially adaptive dimensions in terms of nurturing an individual and forming a society that takes care of others as well. Yet, determining which aspects of group identity result in positive dimensions and which aspects contribute to stereotyping and prejudice is complex, and developmental research has been designed to understand this relationship. In either case, the foundational processes of group formation and identity are not solely rooted in individual deviance or extreme psychopathology.

Parents and peers

Most developmental intergroup research points to two fundamental sources of influence on children's prejudice: parents and family as well as peers and school. Both sources contribute to children's developing notions of ingroups and outgroups, and neither source is solely deterministic. Children interpret, reflect, and reject or accept messages from adults and peers. The rejection or acceptance of stereotypic and prejudicial messages changes with age, as well as with the target in question. In one study, for example, with increasing age, children rejected *parental* messages about racial exclusion but accepted *peer* expectations to exclude others based on race, as in a friendship context (Killen, Lee-Kim, McGlothlin, et al., 2002). Levy and colleagues (2005) have studied the types of teaching strategies that reduce prejudice and have found that adult messages that combine the uniqueness of individuals as well as the commonalities are most effective (Levy, West, Bigler, et al., 2005), rather than just one or the other. In another study, adolescents who reported that their parents discouraged cross-race dating were less likely to expect that they would date someone of another race (Edmonds & Killen, 2009). These studies indicate that children pay close attention to the nature of the messages from adults. Further, the school climate and environment have a significant impact on stereotyping and prejudice in the context of children's social experience and intergroup contact (Tropp & Prenovost, 2008).

Stereotyping, prejudice, and discrimination in childhood

While there has been extensive research in the area of gender stereotypes in childhood (Ruble & Martin, 1998), there has been less research on racial and ethnic stereotypes (Fisher, Jackson, & Villarruel, 1998; Quintana, 1998; Rowley, Kurtz-Costes, Mistry, et al., 2007). In general, research has shown that children have better memory, recognition, and recall for stereotype-consistent than stereotype-inconsistent information (Liben & Bigler, 2002). This is particularly the case for gender stereotypes, in which information about gender roles remains explicit and concrete. For example, when presented with picture cards of a male teacher, a female teacher, a male doctor, and a female doctor, children remember the female teacher and the male doctor (Ruble & Martin, 1998). Research in child development has shown that parents encourage gender stereotypes very early on by buying gender-specific clothes and toys and by creating same-gender peer groups and using normative statements about being a girl or a boy (Pomerleau, Malcuit, & Sabatier, 1991). This is demonstrated by the early onset of the acquisition of gender stereotypes by young children (Ruble & Martin, 1998).

In contrast, racial stereotypes are perpetuated in more subtle ways in early childhood and become more explicit by adolescence.

McKown and Weinstein (2003) conducted a study with children aged 6–10 years on stereotype consciousness and found that, with age, children became better at inferring individuals' stereotypes (using an imaginary world of the Green and the Blue children who had different talents). While only a small percentage of 6-year olds made judgments reflecting stereotypes (18 percent), the percentage of 10-year olds doing the same was 93 percent. (McKown & Weinstein, 2003).

In a recent study, Rowley and her colleagues (Rowley, Kurtz-Costes, Mistry, et al., 2007) measured social status as a predictor of gender- and race-based stereotypes about academics (science, reading, math), music, and sports in 4th-, 6th-, and 8th- grade students. The findings indicated that children in low-status groups (girls and African-American children) did not endorse stereotypes that reflected negatively on their own group, but did report stereotypes that reflected positively. High-status groups (boys and European-American children) endorsed most traditional stereotypes, whether positive or negative for their own group. Significantly, status effects were more pronounced with age. What was not measured was whether participants would include or exclude others on the basis of these stereotypic traits, which would provide another dimension for determining how these stereotypes bear on their moral judgments.

Further, Bigler and her colleagues (Bigler & Liben, 1993) have documented how racial stereotyping is applied to children's knowledge about occupations and other work-related contexts. As mentioned above, stereotyping alone is not the same as discrimination, which involves acting on prejudiced thoughts. However, stereotypes and the associated cognitive processes (which are necessarily tied to one's social experiences) have the potential to be related to later prejudice and discriminatory behaviors in childhood and adolescence.

Recently, Sinno and Killen (2009) drew from Biernat's social psychological theory, referred to as Shifting Standards, to examine young children's social reasoning about gender roles, specifically career and domestic decisions made by parent (Biernat, Manis,

& Nelson, 1991). Shifting standards research has shown that individuals use a different 'ruler' to measure competence revealing underlying stereotypes (e.g., a woman who jogs three times a week is viewed as 'very athletic' in contrast to a man who jogs three times a week who would be viewed only as 'moderately athletic'). Does the shifting standard 'ruler' apply to children's evaluations of parental roles in the family? Children's evaluations of parental roles based on societal norms were assessed in 7- and 10-year-old children using the Social Reasoning about Gender Roles task (Sinno & Killen, 2009), and the Shifting Standards task (Biernat & Manis, 1994). The results revealed that children viewed it as acceptable for both their mother and father to work full-time, but found it less acceptable for fathers to choose to stay at home than for mothers to choose to go to work, using stereotypes to explain who should take care of children. Further, children viewed it as unfair for a father to deny a mother the chance to go to work, but did not apply this type of moral reasoning for a mother's denial of a father to stay at home to take care of the children.

In the Shifting Standards task, children evaluated a father's competence at a stereotypic-male job (auto mechanic) using reasoning based on personal effort ('He's good because he works hard.') but were more likely to use gender stereotypes ('It's what moms do.') when evaluating the mother's competence at a stereotypic-female job (making dinner). Thus, children's interpretation of competence and ability in the caretaker role was highly dependent on gender of the parent, providing support for the Shifting Standards phenomenon with children. Children assessed situations with moral, conventional, and psychological reasoning as well as stereotypic expectations, and the priority given to these judgments, again, depended on the gender of the parent.

Beginning at 3, 4, and 5 years of age, children evaluate situations involving stereotypes using fairness reasoning (Killen, Pisacane, Lee-Kim, Pisacane, Lee-Kim, et al., 2001). Based on a child's gender stereotyped or nonstereotyped choices for whom to include in four different types of play activities (e.g., dolls, trucks, firefighter, teacher), experimenters offered children one of two 'counterprobes,' equal opportunity reasoning (e.g., 'Boys don't get a chance.') *or* stereotypic reasoning (e.g., 'Dolls are for girls.'). The results revealed that children who initially relied on stereotypic expectations to make a decision about whom to include in a play group (picking a boy for trucks or a girl for dolls, etc.) were more likely to switch their judgment after hearing a 'moral' counterprobe than children who initially relied on moral judgments (equal opportunity) to make their decision; children who initially used moral judgments did not change their decision after hearing a 'stereotypic' counterprobe.

These findings indicate that moral judgments are less malleable than social-conventional and stereotypic judgments. Moral principles are generalizable and thus would be expected to apply across contexts, as children demonstrated in their judgments when using a counterprobe technique (but would not necessarily be revealed without this type of probing). Moreover, very few children who made nonstereotypic choices changed their decisions after hearing a stereotypic counterprobe, in contrast to the many children who changed their decisions after hearing the moral counterprobe.

Rather than expecting children's judgments about intergroup exclusion to reflect broad stage-like schemes in which one form of reasoning is used across contexts, such as punishment-oriented, in the case of Kohlberg's theory, or preoperational thought in the case of Piaget's scientific reasoning (Kohlberg, 1984; Piaget, 1932), reasoning, empathy, and perspective-taking serve as a basis to reject unfair exclusion and prejudice in different contexts (Abrams, Rutland, Cameron, et al., 2007; Killen, et al., 2001) Intergroup bias results when moral judgments fail to emerge (or the moral relevance of an act or thought is not recognized), and stereotypic considerations overwhelm children's decisions about how individuals should be treated.

Many factors make it difficult for children to reject stereotypes: cultural conventions, adult messages, peer influences, the ease with which such information is processed (cognitively and neurophysiologically), and identity with groups. For example, research by Bar-Haim, Shulman, Lamy, et al. (2006) revealed that infants' racial preferences for faces are related to the degree of exposure to different race faces in the home and the community (Bar-Haim, Shulman, Lamy, et al., 2006). Regarding social identity, Abrams and Rutland (2008) assert that children are motivated to sustain a positive social identity and this identity leads to the desire to affirm a positive association with the ingroup. In some contexts, this identity with the ingroup results in a negative association with the outgroup (although not automatically), and often this outgroup negativity is a function of the salience of direct comparisons.

Understanding social identification in childhood requires assessments that capture the subjective nature of identification, as put forth by Bennett and Sani (2008). They state that little is actually known about whether, and when, children subjectively identify with groups because most assessments are static, that is, most self-identification tasks rely solely on self-labeling (I am a girl) without a measure of the child's views about the group's norms, actions, and intentions, which are reflective of whether and how a child identifies with a group. Other recent studies have provided more in-depth information on how children categorize themselves with respect to group norms and expectations (Patterson & Bigler, 2005). Findings from developmental intergroup approaches to identification provide the basis for asserting that stereotyping, and its negative outcomes, such as prejudice and discrimination, often stem from basic categorization processes rather than personality deficits.

Social cognitive developmental research on intergroup attitudes

A complicated social cognitive task for an individual is to determine when to give priority to considerations of fairness and justice in contrast to group identity (Abrams & Rutland, 2008), conventions and traditions (Turiel, 1998) or group norms (Killen, Pisacane, Lee-Kim, et al., 2001). Conventions, for example, which are often established to promote the smooth functioning of social groups (Turiel, 1983) may result in certain individuals being excluded from a peer club or a social clique in the child's world, or excluded from social organizations and work-related activities in the adult world due to characteristics that are perceived to hinder the ability of the social group to function smoothly (constraints regarding group identity will be discussed below). As children's understanding of morality, groups, conventions, and autonomy changes, so do their exclusion evaluations given multiple domains that have to be weighed and coordinated. Social conventional traditions are multifaceted, and the dimensions that create inequalities are often not well understood or recognized by children.

Social experience and social reasoning

Social-conventional reasons for exclusion appear to increase with age, and vary by the context and target of exclusion as well as social experience (Killen, 2007). Gender exclusion is more readily condoned than racial exclusion due to social-conventional roles that remain accepted by society. As an example of age-related changes in the use of social reasoning to evaluate peer group exclusion based on gender, 9-year olds use more social-conventional reasoning to justify gender exclusion from stereotypic groups (e.g., boys from ballet or girls from baseball) than do 6-year olds (Killen & Stangor, 2001).

As with extensive research in social psychology (Hewstone, Rubin, & Willis, 2002; Mendoza-Denton & Page-Gould, 2008; Pettigrew & Tropp, 2005), it has also been demonstrated that positive intergroup contact with others, as well as being a member of a group that has been historically excluded (e.g., being a girl, or a member of an ethnic minority group), are related to children and adolescents' intergroup attitudes (Tropp &

Prenovost, 2008). In developmental psychology, intergroup contact has been shown to be related to prejudice reduction using different outcome variables than have been used with adults. In one study, researchers modified an existing assessment developed by the Harvard Civil Rights Project to record outcomes of school desegregation policies (Kurlaender & Yun, 2001; Orfield & Kurlaender, 2001) to create an intergroup contact measure (Crystal, Killen, & Ruck, 2008). Children were asked to fill out a 12-item survey in which they were asked how many friends they had from different ethnic backgrounds in classrooms, schools, and neighborhoods, and to rate the classroom environment in terms of whether the teacher promoted intergroup interactions.

The goal of the study was to examine how social experience was related to social reasoning about exclusion. Children and adolescents reporting higher levels of positive intergroup contact (mostly cross-race friendships) gave higher ratings of the wrongfulness of racial exclusion in a range of peer settings, and used more moral reasons to explain their judgments, than participants reporting lower levels of such contact. Positive intergroup contact also predicted students' attributions of race-based motives for exclusion, with higher intergroup contact being related to viewing parental approval of racial exclusion as deriving from racial (rather than non racial) motives (Crystal, Killen, & Ruck, 2008). Thus, beyond the choice of friendship, children's social reasoning about racial exclusion varied as a function of intergroup contact. This study provided an example of developmental research that has extended social psychological research to natural environments, which reflects an ecologically valid measure for studying intergroup contact in childhood, as suggested by social psychologists (Dixon, Durrheim, & Tredoux, 2005; Hewstone, Rubin, & Willis, 2002; Pettigrew & Tropp, 2005).

In a recently completed study, and as shown in Figure 6.1, European-American children reporting low intergroup contact were more likely to use *stereotypes* to explain racial discomfort (such as 'Black and White kids don't have much in common because Black kids like different music') than European-American students reporting high intergroup contact (Killen, Kelly, Richardson, Crystal, et al., in press). Further, European-American children reporting low intergroup contact were less likely to *recognize* that someone might use a stereotype to justify exclusion than were European-American

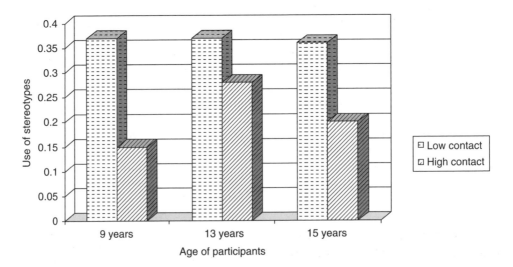

Figure 6.1 **Proportion of European-American children who explicitly used stereotypes to explain why peers would be exclude on the basis of race (Killen et al., in press).**

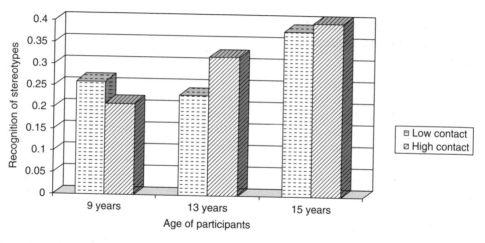

Figure 6.2   Proportion of European-American students who recognize that peers use stereotypes to exclude in interracial peer dyads (Killen et al., in press).

children reporting high intergroup contact (see Figure 6.2), such as 'Some people think that Black kids like different music but that's not a reason to exclude someone.' These findings indicated that social experiences are significantly related to the use of social reasoning and explicit judgments about intergroup exclusion.

Other developmental research has shown how the school context is related to social experience for ethnic minority adolescents. For example, minority children who attended heterogeneous schools experienced less victimization than minority children who attend mostly majority homogeneous schools (Juvonen, Nishina, & Graham, 2006). Diverse schools were defined as schools that had at least 30 percent ethnic minority students, including African-, Asian-, and Latino Americans. For ethnic minority students, there was a perception of greater safety in ethnically heterogeneous schools than ethnically homogeneous schools. In another study by Bellmore and colleagues (Bellmore, Nishina, Witkow, et al., 2007), the classroom's ethnic composition was related to children's same- and other-ethnicity peer 'liking' nominations (who they like to hang around with). They found that all students made more nominations to same-ethnicity peers when there were large numbers of same-ethnicity peers in the students' classrooms; this pattern

differed for students in classrooms with few same-ethnicity peers. These findings provide caution for interpreting the implications of same-ethnicity preference when the numeric balance of diverse ethnic groups in a classroom or school context is not known.

Developmental psychologists have additionally examined social experience in terms of extended contact, as documented by social psychologist Wright and colleagues (Wright, Aron, McLaughlin-Volpe, et al., 1997). Extended contact pertains to knowing or learning about someone in one's own group who has friendships with others from different backgrounds, and can include exposure to curriculum and reading materials that positively depict interactions between individuals from different ethnic and racial backgrounds (Cameron, Rutland, Brown, et al., 2006). Cameron and her colleagues found that White British children who were exposed to curriculum materials that depicted positive images of minority children were less racially prejudiced than were children who were not presented with such materials, suggesting that direct contact in combination with inclusive, tolerant, respectful curricula helps reduce outgroup animosity. Overall, social experience influences the emergence of stereotypes and prejudice, and positive experiences enable children to challenge (and reject) existing stereotypes in the culture.

Developmental approaches to intergroup bias and implicit attitudes

Dovidio and Gaertner's (Dovidio & Gaertner, 2004) Aversive Racism theory has demonstrated that while explicit prejudice has decreased dramatically over the past 50 years, implicit bias remains pervasive. Thus, many social psychology researchers investigating prejudice in adulthood have turned to implicit measures for documenting the prevalence and emergence of intergroup bias (Dovidio, Kawakami, & Gaertner, 2002). This is based on a number of factors, including the general conclusion from researchers that social desirability masks individuals' 'true' racial attitudes as measured by survey instruments and 'feeling thermometers' (McConnell & Leibold, 2001). Studies using implicit measures have revealed racial bias in individuals who would otherwise not display explicit negative racial attitudes on survey instruments such as the 'feeling thermometer.'

Findings using the Implicit Association Test (IAT) with young children (Baron & Banaji, 2006; Rutland, Cameron, Milne, et al., 2005) indicate that implicit associations exist, similar to what has been shown with adults. Differences have been found between the IAT and more explicit paradigms regarding contextual demands such as self-presentational expectations, which affect the explicit bias of older children more than that of younger children (Rutland, Cameron, Milne, et al., 2005). Rutland and colleagues found that children below 10 years of age only inhibited their explicit bias under high public self-focus (e.g., being videotaped). Older children showed an implicit but not explicit bias indicating that they were motivated to suppress their explicit bias.

One caution about interpreting these findings, however, is the uni-dimensional nature of the explicit judgment measures, which consisted of a trait assignment task in which the participant has to determine which of two picture cards (ingroup or outgroup) is associated with positive and negative adjectives (e.g., dirty, nice, clean). Trait assignment tasks have potential confounds, including being unable to disentangle ingroup preference from outgroup derogation (Nesdale, 2004). Moreover, explicit judgments reflect a wide range of reasoning, including the use of norms, customs, traditions, as well as principles to justify or reject exclusion. Further research on the relationship between implicit associations and explicit judgments is warranted.

Other research in developmental psychology has examined children's intergroup bias using indirect methods (rather than automatic, uncontrolled responses as elicited on the IAT). In one set of studies, modified from Sagar and Schofield (1980), children were asked to make attributions of intentions in ambiguous interracial situations, and to determine whether children use race, unbeknownst to them, to evaluate interracial interactions in which one child could potentially be a transgressor, referred to as an indirect measure of bias (Margie, Killen, Sinno, et al., 2005; McGlothlin & Killen, 2005, 2006; McGlothlin, Killen, & Edmonds, 2005a; Sagar & Schofield, 1980).

In these studies, McGlothlin and colleagues asked 6- to 9-year old children to evaluate potential ambiguous moral transgressions such as pushing, stealing money, cheating, and not sharing toys. In one version of the ambiguous situation, for example, a White child is picking up money and a Black child is looking in his/her pocket. In a second version, a Black child is picking up money and a White child is looking in his/her pocket (McGlothlin & Killen, 2006). The results over several studies have shown that while children in heterogeneous schools (European-American, African-American, Asian-American, and Latino) did not display racial bias, European-American children in homogeneous schools displayed an ingroup racial bias (Margie, Killen, M., Sinno, et al., 2005; McGlothlin & Killen, 2006, in press; McGlothlin, Killen, & Edmonds, 2005b). These findings indicate that not all young children display racial bias; it depends on their social experience and the context. Even for the children in European-American homogeneous schools, for example, bias emerged for pushing and stealing but it was absent for cheating and not sharing toys. This approach differs from the standard IAT measure in that it assesses children's use of racial bias regarding a familiar, everyday encounter on the playground among peers. In addition, in the studies described, the participant is asked to make a judgment ('What is happening in the picture?'). Although space constraints limit a discussion of the relative merits of different types of indirect methods of intergroup bias, we contend that many forms of assessment provide important information.

The effects of social experience and social influences persist through adolescence. In a study using ambiguous interracial peer encounters, we found that majority of European-American adolescents were more likely to attribute negative intentions overall when evaluating interracial interactions than were ethnic minority adolescents; this negativity decreased with age (decreasing from 13 to 16 years) and was more prominent for males than for females (Killen, Kelly, Richardson, et al., in press). Thus, there may be contexts in which bias is not connected to the intentions of the target, but the interracial context itself invokes negative attributions from ethnic majority adolescents.

FUTURE DIRECTIONS

Prejudice, stereotyping, and discrimination emerge in childhood in peer groups, cliques, and social networks. At the same time, children have strong views about fairness, justice, and equality. Children struggle with when and how to give priority to morality (fairness and equality) and the strength with which morality is given priority varies as a function of many factors, including the social context, the target of prejudice, personal experience, indirect messages, and school environments. These factors require systematic scrutiny from a multi-method approach, as well as from domain-specific analyses of social cognitive development. Children's acquisition of social conventions, traditions, and customs that emerge during the

preschool period complicates their inclusion and exclusion decisions as stereotypes are often justified by society as a way to preserve groups and maintain hierarchies (Turiel, 2002). Domain-specific knowledge about morality, on the one hand, and conventions and group identity, on the other hand, emerge early in development; determining when children give priority to these different concepts and values remains both a key to understanding prejudice, stereotyping, and discrimination, as well as a serving as a research agenda for future directions.

In general, we propose that emerging notions of prejudice as well as existing levels of implicit bias in childhood are fluid, changing as a function of social experience, social cognitive development, and evidence challenging stereotypic assumptions. Thus, whereas prejudice and bias may be deeply entrenched and somewhat difficult to change by adulthood (Stangor & Schaller, 1996), these constructs are newly emerging and subject to change in childhood. As a result, interventions will be highly effective in early development.

There are several directions for future research that would be fruitful. First, integrative studies using both direct and indirect measures of explicit judgments and intergroup bias would be beneficial. Moreover, we recommend that how explicit judgments are measured, particularly in childhood, but in adulthood as well, be expanded. Social reasoning regarding situations involving exclusion, prejudice, and bias reveals much about individuals' motivations and intentions. How adults evaluate exclusion situations could be similarly revealing about intergroup attitudes. Second, what are the contexts and conditions that enable individuals to give priority to moral, rather than social-conventional or personal reasons, when making decisions about inclusion and exclusion? With age, children focus on group functioning to justify exclusion; yet, with age, children use more complex moral reasons (such as the wrongfulness of historical and societal discrimination) to reject exclusion. What factors are given priority when a child is evaluating exclusion? Further, what types of individual differences exist regarding these orientations? Motivations to inhibit prejudice have been documented with adults (Devine, Plant, Amodio, et al., 2002) and understanding the range of factors that bear on motivation to inhibit prejudice in childhood would be helpful.

Third, how do social experience and prior experiences with exclusion impact children's as well as adults' explicit judgments and intergroup bias? Experiences with exclusion may provide a basis for empathy and perspective-taking but little empirical research has systematically analyzed the role of empathy. Too much exclusion, however, leads to social rejection and withdrawal which is related to a lack of empathy. Thus, experience alone is not enough to contribute to an individual's judgment that exclusion is wrong. What other factors enable experiences with exclusion to lead to an empathetic or moral perspective on the wrongfulness of prejudicial attitudes and the use of stereotypic expectations to deny others access to opportunities based on group membership? This line of research would provide a basis for developing effective intervention programs and curricula.

Developmental intergroup research provides a wealth of findings that bear on social psychological theories about prejudice, stereotyping, and discrimination in adulthood. The methodologies are often quite different, and yet, a convergence of shared techniques could be quite fruitful for systematically understanding the origins, change, and evolution of intergroup attitudes. Children's judgments about others provide a unique window into the emergence of prejudice. The contradictions and inconsistencies revealed in child data provide important areas for further empirical pursuit with adults. This involves understanding how traditions, customs, and norms serve as a proxy for stereotyping or discriminatory practices in adulthood.

At the same time, evidence of young children's morality demonstrates that fairness and equality principles are deeply rooted as well, and that determining how best to nurture and realize these emerging principles can go a long way towards preventing intergroup tensions and conflicts in adults. Addressing the research questions surrounding prejudice, stereotyping, and discrimination from an integrative perspective, and one that focuses on moral judgments as well as prejudicial ones, will help mobilize a multi-level approach for combating and addressing the pervasive and systemic problems associated with prejudice and exclusion in adulthood.

ACKNOWLEDGEMENTS

We would like to thank the editors and Kelly Lynn Mulvey for helpful feedback on the manuscript. The research described in this chapter was supported, in part, by grants from the National Science Foundation (#BCS0346717) and the National Institute of Child Health and Human Development (#1R01HD04121-01). Correspondence should be directed to: Melanie Killen, Department of Human Development, 3304 Benjamin Building, University of Maryland, College Park, MD, 20742-1131, USA. E-mail: mkillen@umd.edu.

REFERENCES

Aboud, F. E., & Amato, M. (2001). Developmental and socialization influences on intergroup bias. In R. Brown & S. L. Gaertner (Eds.), *Blackwell Handbook of Social Psychology: Intergroup Relations* (pp. 65–85). Oxford, England: Blackwell Publishers.

Abrams, D., Hogg, M. A., & Marques, J. M. (2005). A social psychological framework for understanding social inclusion and exclusion. In D. Abrams, M. A. Hogg & J. M. Marques (Eds.), *The Social Psychology of Inclusion and Exclusion*. New York: Psychology Press.

Abrams, D., & Rutland, A. (2008). The development of subjective group dynamics. In S. R. Levy, & M. Killen (Eds.), *Intergroup Relations and Attitudes in Childhood through Adulthood* (pp. 47–65). Oxford, UK: Oxford University Press.

Abrams, D., Rutland, A., Ferrell, J. M., & Pelletier, J. (2008). Children's judgments of disloyal and immoral peer behavior: Subjective group dynamics in minimal intergroup contexts. *Child Development*, 79, 444–461.

Abrams, D., Rutland, A., Cameron, L., & Ferrell, J. (2007). Older but wilier: In-group accountability and the development of subjective group dynamics. *Developmental Psychology, 43*, 134–148.

Adorno, T. W., Frenkel-Brunswick, E., Levinson, D. J., & Sanford, R. N. (1950). *The Authoritarian Personality*. New York: Harper Press.

Allport, G. W. (1954). *The Nature of Prejudice*. Reading, MA: Addison Wesley.

Appiah, K. A. (2005). *The Ethics of Identity*. Princeton: Princeton University Press.

Arsenio, W. F., & Lemerise, E. A. (2004). Aggression and moral development: Integrating social information processing and moral domain models. *Child Development, 75*, 987–1002.

Asch, S. (1952). *Social Psychology*. Englewood Cliffs, NJ: Prentice-Hall.

Augoustinos, M., & Rosewarne, D. L. (2001). Stereotype knowledge and prejudice in children. *British Journal of Developmental Psychology, 19*, 143–156.

Bar-Haim, Y., Shulman, C., Lamy, D., & Reuveni, A. (2006). Nature and nurture in own-race face processing. *Psychological Science, 17*, 159–163.

Baron, A. S., & Banaji, M. R. (2006). The development of implicit attitudes: Evidence of race evaluations from ages 6 and 10 and adulthood. *Psychological Science, 17*, 53–58.

Bellmore, A., Nishina, A., Witkow, M., Graham, S., & Juvonen, J. (2007). The influence of classroom ethnic composition on same- and other-ethnicity peer nominations in middle school. *Social Development, 16*, 721–740.

Bennett, M., & Sani, F. (2008). Children's subjective identification with social groups. In S. Levy, & M. Killen (Eds.), *Intergroup Attitudes and Relationships from Childhood through Adulthood* (pp. 19–31). Oxford, U.K.: Oxford University Press.

Bennett, M., & Sani, F. (Eds.) (2004). *The Development of the Social Self*. New York: Psychology Press.

Biernat, M., & Manis, M. (1994). Shifting standards and stereotype-based judgments. *Journal of Personality and Social Psychology, 66*, 5–20.

Biernat, M., Manis, M., & Nelson, T. E. (1991). Stereotypes and standards of judgment. *Journal of Personality and Social Psychology, 60*, 485–499.

Bigler, R. S., & Liben, L. S. (1993). A cognitive-developmental approach to racial stereotyping and reconstructive memory in Euro-American children. *Child Development, 64*, 1507–1518.

Bigler, R. S., & Liben, L. (2006). A developmental intergroup theory of social stereotypes and prejudice. In R. Kail (Ed.), *Advances in Child Psychology* (pp. 39–90). New York: Elsevier.

Cameron, L., Rutland, A., Brown, R., & Douch, R. (2006). Changing children's intergroup attitudes towards refugees: Testing different models of extended contact. *Child Development, 77*, 1208–1219.

Clark, K. B., & Clark, M. P. (1939). The development of consciousness of self and the emergence of racial identification in negro preschool children. *The Journal of Social Psychology, 10*, 591–599.

Crystal, D. S., Killen, M., & Ruck, M. D. (2008). It's who you know that counts: Intergroup contact and judgments about race-based exclusion. *British Journal of Developmental Psychology, 26*, 51–70.

Devine, P. G., Plant, E. A., Amodio, D. M., Harmon-Jones, E., & Vance, S. L. (2002). The regulation of explicit and implicit race bias: The role of motivations to respond without prejudice. *Journal of Personality & Social Psychology, 82*, 835–848.

Dixon, J., Durrheim, K., & Tredoux, C. (2005). Beyond the optimal contact strategy. *American Psychologist, 60*, 697–711.

Dovidio, J. F., & Gaertner, S. L. (2004). Aversive racism. In M. P. Zanna (Ed.), *Advances in Experimental Social Psychology* (pp. 1–52). San Diego, CA: Academic Press.

Dovidio, J. F., Kawakami, K., & Gaertner, S. L. (2002). Implicit and explicit prejudice and interracial interaction. *Journal of Personality and Social Psychology, 82*, 62–68.

Duckitt, J. H. (1992). Psychology and prejudice: A historical analysis and integrative framework. *American Psychologist, 47*, 1182–1193.

Edmonds, C., & Killen, M. (2009). Do adolescents' perceptions of parental racial attitudes relate to their intergroup contact and cross-race relationships? *Group Processes and Intergroup Relations, 12*, 5–21.

Fisher, C. B., Jackson, J. F., & Villarruel, F. A. (1998). The study of African-American and Latin-American children and youth. In W. Damon & R. Lerner (Eds.), *Handbook of Child Psychology* (5th ed., Vol. 1: Theoretical Models of Human Development, pp. 1145–1207). New York: Wiley.

Hewstone, M., Rubin, M., & Willis, H. (2002). Intergroup bias. *Annual Review of Psychology, 53*, 575–604.

Juvonen, J., Nishina, A., & Graham, S. (2006). Ethnic diversity and perceptions of safety in urban middle schools. *Psychological Science, 17*, 394–401.

Keil, F. (2006). Cognitive science and cognitive development. In W. Damon & R. M. Lerner (Eds.), *Handbook of Child Psychology* (pp. 609–635). Hoboken, NJ: Wiley.

Killen, M. (2007). Children's social and moral reasoning about exclusion. *Current Directions in Psychological Science, 16*, 32–36.

Killen, M., Henning, A., Kelly, M. C., Crystal, D. S., & Ruck, M. D. (2007). Evaluations of interracial peer encounters by majority and minority U.S. children and adolescents. *International Journal of Behavioral Development, 31*, 491–500.

Killen, M., Kelly, M. C., Richardson, C. B., Crystal, D. S., & Ruck, M. D. (in press). European-American children's and adolescents' evaluations of interracial exclusion. *Group Processes and Intergroup Relations*.

Killen, M., Kelly, M. C., Richardson, C. B., & Jampol, N. S. (in press). Adolescents' attributions of bias in interracial peer exchanges. *Developmental Psychology*.

Killen, M., Lee-Kim, J., McGlothlin, H., & Stangor, C. (2002). How children and adolescents evaluate gender and racial exclusion, *Monographs of the Society for Research in Child Development* (Serial No. 271, Vol. 67, No. 4). Oxford, England: Blackwell Publishers.

Killen, M., Margie, N. G., & Sinno, S. (2006). Morality in the context of intergroup relationships. In M. Killen & J. G. Smetana (Eds.), *Handbook of Moral Development* (pp. 155–183). Mahwah, NJ: Lawrence Erlbaum Associates.

Killen, M., McGlothlin, H., & Henning, A. (2008). Implicit biases and explicit judgments: A developmental perspective. In S. R. Levy & M. Killen (Eds.), *Intergroup Attitudes and Relations in Childhood through Adulthood.* (pp. 126–145). Oxford, U.K.: Oxford University Press.

Killen, M., & McKown, C. (2005). How integrative approaches to intergroup attitudes advance the field. *Journal of Applied Developmental Psychology, 26*, 616–622.

Killen, M., Pisacane, K., Lee-Kim, J., & Ardila-Rey, A. (2001). Fairness or stereotypes? Young children's priorities when evaluating group exclusion and inclusion. *Developmental Psychology, 37*, 587–596.

Killen, M., & Stangor, C. (2001). Children's social reasoning about inclusion and exclusion in gender and race peer group contexts. *Child Development, 72*, 174–186.

Kohlberg, L. (1984). *Essays on Moral Development: The Psychology of Moral Development – The Nature and Validity of Moral Stages.* (Vol. 2) San Francisco: Harper & Row.

Kuhn, D., & Siegler, R. S. (2006). Cognition, perception, and language. In W. Damon & R. M. Lerner (Eds.), *Handbook of Child Psychology* (6th ed.). Hoboken, NJ: Wiley.

Kurlaender, M., & Yun, J. T. (2001). Is diversity a compelling educational interest? In G. Orfield (Ed.), *Diversity Challenged: Evidence on the Impact of Affirmative Action* (pp. 111–141). Cambridge, MA: Harvard Education Publishing Group.

Levy, S. R., & Killen, M. (2008). *Intergroup Attitudes and Relations in Childhood through Adulthood.* Oxford, U.K.: Oxford University Press.

Levy, S. R., West, T., Bigler, R. S., Karafantis, D., Ramirez, L., & Velilla, E. (2005). Messages about the uniqueness and similarities of people: Impact on U.S. Black and Latino youth. *Journal of Applied Developmental Psychology, 26*, 714–733.

Liben, L. S., & Bigler, R. S. (2002). The developmental course of gender differentiation: Conceptualizing, measuring and evaluating constructs and pathways. *Monographs of the Society for Research in Child Development* (Serial No. 269, Vol. 67, No. 2). Oxford, England: Blackwell Publishers.

Margie, N. G., Killen, M., Sinno, S., & McGlothlin, H. (2005). Minority children's intergroup attitudes about peer relationships. *British Journal of Developmental Psychology, 23*, 251–259.

McConnell, A. R., & Leibold, J. M. (2001). Relations among the implicit association test, discriminatory behavior, and explicit measures of racial attitudes. *Journal of Experimental Social Psychology, 37*, 435–442.

McGlothlin, H., & Killen, M. (2005). Children's perceptions of intergroup and intragroup similarity and the role of social experience. *Journal of Applied Developmental Psychology, 26*, 680–698.

McGlothlin, H., & Killen, M. (2006). Intergroup attitudes of European American children attending ethnically homogeneous schools. *Child Development, 77*, 1375–1386.

McGlothlin, H., & Killen, M. (in press). How social experience is related to children's intergroup attitudes. *European Journal of Social Psychology: Special Issue: Children's Intergroup Attitudes*.

McGlothlin, H., Killen, M., & Edmonds, C. (2005). European-American children's intergroup attitudes about peer relationships. *British Journal of Developmental Psychology, 23*, 227–249.

McKown, C., & Weinstein, R. S. (2003). The development and consequences of stereotype consciousness in middle childhood. *Child Development, 74*, 489–515.

Mendoza-Denton, R., & Page-Gould, E. (2008). Can cross-group friendships influence minority students' well-being at historically white universities? *Psychological Science, 19*, 933–939.

Nesdale, D. (2004). Social identity processes and children's ethnic prejudice. In M. Bennett & F. Sani (Eds.), *The development of the social self* (pp. 219–245). New York: Psychology Press.

Nesdale, D. (2008). Peer group rejection and children's intergroup prejudice. In S. R. Levy & M. Killen (Eds.), *Intergroup Attitudes and Relations in Childhood through Adulthood* (pp. 32–46). Oxford, U.K.: Oxford University Press.

Nussbaum, M. C. (1999). *Sex and Social Justice.* Oxford, England: University of Oxford Press.

Orfield, G., & Kurlaender, M. (2001). *Diversity Challenged: Evidence on the Impact of Affirmative Action.* Cambridge, MA: Harvard Education Publishing Group.

Patterson, M. M., & Bigler, R. S. (2005). Preschool children's attention to environmental messages about groups: Social categorization and the origins of intergroup bias. *Child Development, 77,* 847–860.

Pettigrew, T. F., & Tropp, L. R. (2005). Allport's intergroup contact hypothesis: Its history and influence. In J. F. Dovidio, P. Glick & L. Rudman (Eds.), *Reflecting on the Nature of Prejudice: Fifty Years after Allport* (pp. 262–277). Malden, MA: Blackwell.

Piaget, J. (1932). *The Moral Judgment of the Child.* New York: Free Press.

Piaget, J. (1952). *The Origins of Intelligence in Children.* New York: International Universities Press.

Piaget, J. (1970). *The Principles of Genetic Epistemology* (W. Mays, Trans.). London: Routledge & Kegan Paul.

Piaget, J. (1977/1995). *Sociological Studies* (L. Smith, Trans.). London: Routledge.

Pomerleau, A., Malcuit, G., & Sabatier, C. (1991). Child-rearing practices and parental beliefs in three cultural groups of Montréal: Québécois, Vietnamese, Haitian. In M. H. Bornstein (Ed.), *Cultural Approaches to Parenting* (pp. 45–68). Hillsdale, NJ: Lawrence Erlbaum Associates, Inc.

Powlishta, K. K., Serbin, L. A., Doyle, A., & White, D. R. (1994). Gender, ethnic, and body type biases: The generality of prejudice in childhood. *Developmental Psychology, 30,* 526–536.

Quintana, S. M., & McKown, C. (2007). *The Handbook of Race, Racism, and the Developing Child.* New York: Wiley & Sons.

Quintana, S. M. (1998). Children's developmental understanding of ethnicity and race. *Applied and Preventative Psychology, 7,* 27–45.

Rowley, S., Kurtz-Costes, B., Mistry, R., & Leagans, L. (2007). Social status as a predictor of race and gender stereotypes in childhood and early adolescence. *Social Development, 16,* 151–168.

Rubin, K., Bukowski, W., & Parker, J. (2006). Peers, relationships, and interactions. In W. Damon & R. M. Lerner (Eds.), *Handbook of Child Psychology* (pp. 571–645). NY: Wiley Publishers.

Ruble, D. N., & Martin, C. L. (1998). Gender development. In W. Damon (Ed.), *Handbook of Child Psychology* (5th ed., Vol. 3, pp. 933–1016). New York: Wiley.

Ruble, D. N., Martin, C. L., & Berenbaum, S. (2006). Gender development. In W. Damon & R. M. Lerner (Ed.), *Handbook of Child Psychology: Personality and Social Development* (6th ed., Vol. 3). New York: Wiley Publishers.

Rutland, A. (2004). The development and self-regulation of intergroup attitudes in children. In M. Bennett & F. Sani (Eds.), *The Development of the Social Self* (pp. 247–265). New York: Psychology Press.

Rutland, A., Abrams, D., & Levy, S. R. (2007). Social identity and intergroup attitudes in children and adolescents: Special Issue. *International Journal of Behavioral Development, 31,* 417–418.

Rutland, A., Cameron, L., Milne, A., & McGeorge, P. (2005). Social norms and self-presentation: Children's implicit and explicit intergroup attitudes. *Child Development, 76,* 451–466.

Sagar, H. A., & Schofield, J. W. (1980). Racial and behavioral cues in Black and White children's perceptions of ambiguously aggressive acts. *Journal of Personality and Social Psychology, 39,* 590–598.

Sinclair, S., Dunn, E., & Lowery, B. S. (2005). The relationship between parental racial attitudes and children's implicit prejudice. *Journal of Experimental Social Psychology, 41*(3), 283–289.

Sinno, S., & Killen, M. (2009). Moms at work and dads at home: Children's evaluations of parental roles. *Applied Developmental Science, 13,* 16–29.

Smetana, J. G. (2006). Social domain theory: Consistencies and variations in children's moral and social judgments. In M. Killen & J. G. Smetana (Eds.), *Handbook of Moral Development* (pp. 119–154). Mahwah, NJ: Lawrence Erlbaum Associates.

Stangor, C., & Schaller, M. (1996). Stereotypes as individual and collective representations. In C. N. Macrae, M. Hewstone & C. Stangor (Eds.), *Foundations of Stereotypes and Stereotyping* (pp. 3–37). New York: Guilford Press.

Tajfel, H., & Turner, J. C. (1979). An integrative theory of intergroup conflict. In W. G. Austin & S. Worchel (Eds.), *The Social Psychology of Intergroup Relations* (pp. 33–47). Monterey, CA: Brooks-Cole.

Tropp, L. R., & Prenovost, M. A. (2008). The role of intergroup contact in predicting children's interethnic attitudes: Evidence from meta-analytic and field studies. In S. R. Levy & M. Killen (Eds.), *Intergroup attitudes and relations in childhood through adulthood* (pp. 236–248). Oxford, U.K.: Oxford University Press.

Turiel, E. (1983). *The Development of Social Knowledge: Morality and Convention*. Cambridge, England: Cambridge University Press.

Turiel, E. (1998). The development of morality. In W. Damon (Ed.), *Handbook of Child Psychology*: (Social, Emotional, and Personality Development (5th ed., Vol. 3 pp. 863–932). New York: Wiley.

Turiel, E. (2002). *The Culture of Morality*. Cambridge, England: Cambridge University Press.

Turiel, E. (2008). Thought about actions in social domains: Morality, social conventions, and social interactions. *Cognitive Development, 23*,136–154.

Verkuyten, M., & Steenhuis, A. (2005). Preadolescents' understanding and reasoning about asylum seeker peers and friendships. *Journal of Applied Developmental Psychology, 26*, 660–679.

Warneken, F., & Tomasello, M. (2007). Helping and cooperation at 14 months of age. *Infancy, 11*, 271–294.

Wright, S. C., Aron, A., McLaughlin-Volpe, T., & Ross, S. A. (1997). The extended contact effect: Knowledge of cross-group friendships and prejudice. *Journal of Personality and Social Psychology, 73*, 73–90.

7

Cognitive Processes

Susan T. Fiske and Ann Marie Russell

ABSTRACT

This chapter describes the history, contemporary context, and future of research on cognitive bias, which focuses on stereotypes as beliefs about groups. After early studies measured stereotype contents, Allport (1954) proposed that ordinary cognitive processes, such as categorization, underlie stereotyping. Subsequently, the cognitive miser approach examined how stereotypes provide mental shortcuts, while social identity and self-categorization approaches investigated the relative judgments of ingroup and outgroup categories. Motivated tactician approaches emphasized how goals shift responses between automaticity and control. Current research focuses on subtle biases: automatic (rapid, unconscious, unintentional), ambiguous (based on interpretation, attribution), and ambivalent (mixed valence on perceived warmth and competence dimensions). Threat to self and ingroup exaggerates cognitive biases. Cures rely on information and various motivations (belonging, understanding, controlling, self-enhancing, trusting). Future directions will link cognition to emotion, thence to behavior, and all three to neural systems.

COGNITIVE PROCESSES

With the whole world watching, at least the world of social psychology, a new theoretical and empirical approach to prejudice took hold during the late 1970s and early 1980s. Cognitive explanations belied the common-sense view that bigots are a rare and sick type of person (though of course, some are). Instead, researchers now understand that prejudice is the all-too-universal result of everyday habits of mind. Prejudice is more ordinary and therefore more insidious than people thought. What's more, the cognitive approach does provide solutions.

This chapter reviews social cognitive approaches to the study of prejudice, stereotyping, and discrimination, focusing on the underlying thought processes that create and maintain bias. The chapter first examines the intellectual history that shaped the field's emphases and set its modern research agenda. Then, contemporary research showcases current understandings of cognitive bias in its varied forms. Finally, observing the current empirical and intellectual tides forecasts the likely future of such study.

We give particular attention to cognition, that is, the contents and processes in people's minds that contribute to bias. Cognition inevitably implicates affect, motivation, behavior, and neural processes within perceivers, plus social structure and intergroup relations outside the perceiver (see relevant chapters).

COGNITION IN BIAS: CLASSIC RESEARCH

Psychology's interest in bias surfaced early in the field's history. The first published investigations of bias appeared in a 1920s article exploring race and social distance (Bogardus, 1928). Soon, in the pre-theoretical 1920s and 1930s, research emphasized measuring racial attitudes, stereotyping, and prejudice in undergraduates, focusing on stereotypes' contents (Bogardus, 1933; Katz & Braly, 1933, 1935).

During the 1950's, Gordon Allport's ground-breaking text *Nature of Prejudice* (1954; see Dovidio, Glick, & Rudman, 2005, for an update) revolutionized the field's perspective on prejudice by suggesting that prejudiced thinking is normal, not deviant, as was popularly believed. Allport argued that bias is a natural byproduct of ordinary human cognition and, in particular, of categorization.

Allport viewed categorization as not only normal, but necessary and useful for navigating a complex world. Human beings need to sort diverse stimuli to identify and react properly. Categorizing objects (furniture into tables and chairs) enables appropriate behavior, putting a drink on one and sitting on the other. Similarly categorizing individuals as 'waiter' and 'chef,' ordering food from one and complimenting the other, informs differential interaction with each person. This natural inclination toward categorizing objects and people also leads people to group themselves and others into categories, creating *us* and *them*. Group categories produce generalizations about ingroups (us) and outgroups (them) that *minimize* within-group differences and *exaggerate* between-group differences. Intergroup generalizations enable stereotyping and prejudice.

Although Allport's analysis was ground-breaking, active empirical follow-up awaited the 1970s, during the 'cognitive revolution.' Cognition research, previously eschewed in favor of an anti-mentalist behaviorism, now resurged, figuring prominently in psychology. Although *social* psychology had always remained cognitive, studying cognitive attitudes, stereotypes, and mechanisms, the cognitive revolution shifted social psychological perspectives. Cognitive methods and theories affected various traditional topics, including bias research (Fiske & Taylor, 1984, 2008; Hamilton, 1981a). Tajfel's (1978) social identity theory and Turner's related self-categorization theory (Turner, Hogg, Oakes, et al., 1987) exemplified European approaches (see chapter by Abrams & Hogg, this volume).

In the 1980s, cognitive approaches continued focusing on categorization, and developed the 'cognitive miser' perspective (Taylor, 1981): People's limited mental resources compel cognitive shortcuts, such as categorization, to most efficiently use such scarce cognitive capital. As a cognitive shortcut, social categorization easily leads to stereotyping and prejudice. Categorization (a) tags information by physical and social distinctions such as race and gender, (b) minimizes within-group differences and exaggerates between-group differences, and (c) causes group members' behavior to be interpreted stereotypically. Increased familiarity with an outgroup, however, can (d) encourage perceiving within-group distinctions and (e) subtyping, to accommodate stereotype-defying group members as exceptions, without changing overall stereotypes. As an empirical example, people confuse people within social categories such as race and gender, more than between such categories (Taylor, Fiske, Etcoff, et al., 1978). Category confusion receives more attention later in this chapter.

Further research in the cognitive-miser vein showed how cognitive shortcuts increase the perceived homogeneity of group members, encourage misperceived correlations between minority categories and negative behaviors, and bias memory for stereotype-consistency, all falsely confirming expectancies (Hamilton, 1981b; Rothbart, 1981;

Wilder, 1981). The cognitive shortcuts viewpoint continues in current thought on bias.

In the 1990s, the cognitive-miser metaphor shifted to appearing as merely one cognitive option among others. Discoveries revealed the decisive role of motivation in selecting cognitive shortcuts, inventing the 'motivated tactician' metaphor: the naïve perceiver as a strategist managing cognitive resources. People engage cognitive shortcuts as a default, unless motivated to go beyond these shortcuts and use more effort. Various models explained when people engage effortful versus effortless cognitive strategies.

Motivated opening and closing of the mind (Kruglanski, 1989; Kruglanski & Webster, 1996) reflects individual differences in motivation and situational pressures that influence the *need for cognitive closure* (i.e., closing of the mind). People high in need-for-closure urgently seek definitive answers and thus rely on stereotypes. By contrast, people higher in tolerance for ambiguity (low in need for closure) recruit more deliberative cognitive strategies.

Impression formation ranges along a spectrum from *stereotypic, category-based* through *individuated, attribute-based* impressions (Fiske & Neuberg, 1990). This continuum model explains that perceivers automatically rely on category-based judgments unless the target does not match the stereotype or unless motivated to individuate. If perceivers need more detail, they use more cognitive effort to attend to the target's actual behaviors and to judge based on individual attributes.

Stereotypes develop via differentiated *expectancy-confirming* (automatic) versus *accuracy-oriented* (deliberative) processing goals (Stangor & Ford, 1992). Two modes of impression formation may include *pictoliteral representations,* derived from category-based prototypes, and *personalized representations,* based on networks of attributes linked to a single person (Brewer, 1988). All these approaches view perceivers' current situational goals or individual differences in motivation as determining the use of one cognitive strategy over another.

REVIEW OF THE CURRENT LITERATURE: STEALTH STEREOTYPING AS BIAS IN THE NEW MILLENNIUM

Shifting cultural norms, prompted by civil rights and women's movements, scorn overt old-fashioned bias, rendered taboo in modern society. Today's multi-racial, global culture has driven out intentional public expressions of bias, as witnessed by a 75 percent drop in Americans' reported prejudice (Bobo, 2001). Incidences of overt bias now meet public contempt and condemnation. Despite appearances, bias has certainly not vanished from the American psyche. Current research demonstrates that intergroup bias persists, but its face has changed, adopting subtle manifestations. Thus, the field must use more sophisticated methods to investigate hidden biases. The next sections highlight major contemporary research.

Automatic, ambiguous, and ambivalent forms of bias

Whereas traditional research emphasized explicitly reportable bias, current research shows some biases operating unconsciously and therefore not reportable by the perceiver. Biases are *automatic* when outside conscious intention, awareness, effort, or control. Automatic biases result from over-learned group categories and their negative or positive associations. People categorize others by race, sex, and age within milliseconds (see Fiske, 1998, for a review). Rapid categorization simultaneously activates associated stereotypes, which are then applied to the individual. Following are various relatively automatic biases, then ambiguous and ambivalent ones.

Automatic category confusions

As previously noted, category confusions occur when people perceive and identify others primarily by their race, gender, and age rather than as individuals, mixing-up people in the same category. The earlier-described manifestation of category confusions is the who-said-what phenomenon (Taylor, Fiske, Etcoff, et al., 1978), in which people have trouble distinguishing which category member (e.g., Asian, woman, or teenager) said what in a group discussion. These confusions encompass categories including gender, race, age, sexual orientation, attitudes, attractiveness, skin tone, and type of relationship (Maddox & Chase, 2004; Maddox & Gray, 2002). Category confusions are relatively automatic because they appear unintentional, effortless, and uncontrollable.

Automatic, indirect racial attitudes

Indirect priming also measures automatic racial bias, using people's immediate associations between a race-related prime (e.g., the word 'black') and negative stimuli. Most commonly, race-related words appear subliminally (too quick for conscious perception), facilitating responses to subsequently presented stimuli. For example, Dovidio, Evans, and Tyler (1986) subliminally presented either the word 'black' or 'white' to white participants during a computer task and demonstrated subsequently faster recognition of negative or positive attributes, respectively. This technique reveals automatic, category-based evaluative content and indirectly measures racial attitudes. Indirect priming predicts nonverbal behavior toward outgroup members, ratings of an essay written by an outgroup member, affective responses to outgroup members, and various negative outgroup attitudes (for review, see Fazio & Olson, 2003).

Automatic, implicit associations

Due partly to its internet presence, implicit associations enjoy considerable attention from popular culture and news media. The implicit association test (IAT; Greenwald, McGhee, & Schwartz, 1998) assesses automatic biases by measuring the strength of positive and negative associations with attitude objects, such as social categories. In a computer task, participants pair positive and negative words with category-relevant cues, such as black or white faces. The test compares speed of responses, to detect faster pairing of positive or negative words with one group or the other. Usually, biased responses favor cultural default groups and disfavor cultural outgroups, showing that societal-ingroup/positive-word pairings prompt more rapid responses, compared with outgroups, more rapidly associated with negative words.

The biases are implicit because relatively unconscious associations are often inaccessible to the perceiver. Many people find their biases distressing because they would otherwise characterize themselves as egalitarian. That people who are at least consciously well-intentioned may possess unconscious biases leads to the important question: How do conscious and unconscious beliefs affect actual behavior? Implicit beliefs especially affect *nonverbal* behavior, whereas explicit beliefs predict *verbal* behavior, such as policy preferences (Dovidio, Kawakami, & Gaertner, 2002).

Automatic stereotyping under cognitive load

Category activation and application are closely related, yet remain distinct. Although each is relatively automatic, they depend on perceivers' current cognitive load (placing demand on limited on-line mental resources). A person under high load, engaged in a task requiring significant cognitive effort (i.e., solving a *New York Times* crossword), reduces the attentional resources available for other cognitive processes. Competing cognitive processes require the mind to prioritize, so some processes win over others. This has direct implications for the activation and application of social categories.

Category activation happens so rapidly that we encode others by category before fully recognizing their individual identity. However, exposure to a target does not necessarily always trigger automatic categorization (Macrae, Bodenhausen, Milne, et al., 1997). Under cognitive load, people can perceive cues to multiple social categories, but activate only the category most currently relevant

(Quinn & Macrae, 2005). Also, people tend to activate only the most accessible categories (Castelli, Macrae, Zogmaister, et al., 2004).

After activating a category, people can easily process stereotype-consistent information (i.e., stereotypical appearance or behavior). Because stereotype-consistent information requires minimal effort, people under cognitive load tend to devote most attention to stereotype-inconsistent information (i.e., counter-stereotypic behavior). Prejudiced people especially attend to expectancy-inconsistent information because they seek an explanation that leaves intact their general stereotype (Sherman, Conrey, & Groom, 2004, 1998).

During early stereotype application, people must work to assimilate stereotype-inconsistent information into a coherent impression. Their attention aids their memory for stereotype-inconsistent information (see Fiske & Taylor, 2008, for review). However because they usually find a way to assimilate or explain away counter-stereotypic information, it rarely changes their overall stereotypic bias toward the group. During later stereotype application, people under cognitive load use stereotypes more for judgments (e.g., Bodenhausen & Wyer, 1985; van Knippenberg, Dijksterhuis, & Vermeulin, 1999) than do people not under cognitive load. Besides these processes of relatively automatic stereotyping, next comes ambiguous and ambivalent stereotyping.

Ambiguous stereotyping

As aversive racism shows (see Chapter 19 by Dovidio, Gaertner, & Kawakami, this volume) bias is not always obvious; sometimes it depends on interpretation. Ambiguous situations allow people to behave in biased ways that they can justify with non-biased explanations. Sometimes people interpret ambiguous stimuli as confirming their stereotypes. For example, police and probation officers subliminally primed with black-stereotypic words then read a race-ambiguous vignette about a shoplifting and assault crime (Graham & Lowery, 2004). The race prime influenced the offender's rated hostility, culpability, recidivism likelihood, and deserved punishment. Here, racial biases unconsciously skewed interpretation of an ambiguous event, but stereotypic construals are not only preconscious. Other participants, judging the negative facial expression of a doll, interpreted the same expression as sad if the doll was dressed as female and angry if male (Plant, Kling, & Smith, 2004). Ambiguous situations also allow people to hide biases from themselves. White participants, rating white and black job applicants, weighted the credentials of their ingroup candidate more favorably. These participants could justify their ingroup favoritism by viewing those particular qualifications as more valuable than those of the different-but-equally talented black contender (Norton, Vandello, & Darley, 2004.). People use shifting standards depending on the group being judged (Biernat & Vescio, 2002).

Stereotyping can be ambiguous in other ways. For example, people favor the ingroup more than they disfavor the outgroup (Brewer & Brown, 1998). In zero-sum games, ingroup favoritism *is* outgroup disadvantage (e.g., one hires the ingroup candidate instead of the outgroup candidate). However, the ingroup member experiences mainly comfort with similar others, not active derogation of unfamiliar others.

Ambiguity also pertains to attributions for group outcomes. People often attribute ingroup successes and outgroup failures to each group's fixed features (dispositions), but dismiss ingroup failures and outgroup successes as temporary and circumstantial (Pettigrew, 1979). This bias is well-disguised because its subtle attributions perpetuate stereotypic dispositions.

Beyond dispositional inferences about individuals, groups may seem variably entitative (i.e., a definite unit, with clear boundaries). An entitative group seems more agentic, coherent, cohesive, and appealing to its members (Castano, Yzerbyt, Paladino, et al., 2002). But group entitativity polarizes intergroup relations (Castano, Sacchi, & Gries, 2003). Entitativity supports essentialism, that is, viewing group differences as emerging from fixed biology (Rothbart & Taylor, 1992). Essentialism encourages stereotypes (Bastian & Haslam, 2006; Yzerbyt, Rocher, & Schadron, 1997).

Ambivalent stereotyping

As described, some stereotyping reflects solely negative biases against outgroups. More often, outgroup stereotypes are ambivalent, mixing positive and negative stereotypes. For example, Asian or Jewish people are stereotyped as competent (positive), but interpersonally cold (negative), while disabled or elderly people are perceived as personally warm, but incompetent. In the Stereotype Content Model (SCM; Fiske, Cuddy, Glick, et al., 2002; Fiske, Cuddy, & Glick, 2007), warmth and competence constitute core trait dimensions of group stereotypes. Judged outgroup warmth reflects perceived competitive *intentions* against societal ingroups' interests: Competitive groups are allegedly cold, but cooperative (non-competitive) groups are allegedly warm. Perceived outgroup competence reflects their perceived *ability* to enact their warm or cold intentions. Assessed outgroup competence reflects its perceived social status, or relative position. The high status seem more competent than the low (Russell & Fiske, 2008).

SCM competence-by-warmth space comprises two ambivalent clusters and two univalent clusters. The high-warmth, low-competence cluster includes elderly, disabled, and mentally challenged people. These groups elicit pity, active helping, but simultaneous neglect (Cuddy, Fiske, & Glick, 2007). Groups perceived as high-competence but low-warmth include rich people, Asians, Jews, minority professionals, and female professionals. They elicit envy, passive accommodation, but potential active attack (Cuddy, Fiske, & Glick, 2007).

The rare univalent negative stereotypes target homeless people, drug addicts, and welfare recipients. These stereotypes elicit disgust, an emotion usually directed toward objects, not human beings. And indeed, neuroimaging suggests that people dehumanize these groups, failing to activate social-cognition areas that normally activate when perceiving people (Harris & Fiske, 2006). These groups elicit both passive neglect and active attack.

Finally, purely positive stereotypes are exclusively reserved for the cultural ingroups: middle-class, Americans, and Christians, evaluated as both competent and warm. They elicit pride and admiration, plus passive accommodation and active help.

While stereotype contents change across time and place, ambivalence toward outgroups appears universal, occurring in a dozen cultures and all demographics (Cuddy, Fiske, & Glick, 2007; Cuddy, Fiske, Kwan, et al., 2009). Indeed SCM's warmth-by-competence space reflects 80–90 percent of the variance in ordinary person's perception (Wojciszke, 1994; Wojciszke, Bazinska, & Jaworski, 1998), supporting the principles of warmth, competence, and ambivalence.

Ambivalent racism and sexism

Ambivalent racism describes white Americans' mixed evaluations of black Americans. On one hand, whites possess 'positive' pro-black attitudes, that is, paternalistic pity for blacks' disadvantaged circumstances due to historical and continuing discrimination. However, whites simultaneously endorse anti-black beliefs, for example, blacks' alleged laziness, and thus responsibility for their disadvantage (Katz & Hass, 1986). These beliefs polarize (exaggerated positive or negative) reactions within individuals, depending on salient beliefs. In SCM terms, these beliefs most likely target poor blacks, rather than black professionals, as social class begins to trump race.

Ambivalent sexism (Glick & Fiske, 1996, 2001) describes benevolent and hostile sexism toward women. 'Benevolent' sexism appears positive, but belittles women. Benevolent sexism targets women in traditional gender roles, granting male protection at the expense of respect. These women locate in SCM's high-warmth/low-competence cluster.

Better-known, hostile sexism targets women who violate traditional gender roles, affording men's respect, but not the affection. These women locate in SCM's high-competence/low-warmth cluster. Hostile sexists tolerate sexual harassment (Begany & Milburn, 2002; Wiener, Hurt, Russell, et al., 1997) and spousal abuse (Glick, Diebold, Bailey-Werner, et al., 1997).

Threat exaggerates bias

Accordingly, bias thrives in automaticity, ambiguity, and ambivalence. Ambiguity allows people under threat to recruit biased beliefs that create certainty. In one study (Fein & Spencer, 1997), after people suffered self-esteem threat due to task failure, they then derogated an ethnically ambiguous outgroup member, presumably to resolve damaged self-perception. Intergroup threat causes uncertainty that provokes defenses against outgroups.

Biased beliefs deter threat in two ways. First, stereotyping demarcates an unambiguous line between friend and foe. Second, bias explains groups in simple terms, and threatened people seek certainty's solace. This section discusses theories that link intergroup bias and perceived threats, both tangible and symbolic. This prejudice is more overt than the just-discussed subtle manifestations. Nevertheless, blatant prejudices reflect some subtle cognitive processes involved in belief systems, ideologies, and legitimating views of society's status quo.

Right-wing authoritarianism

Right-wing authoritarianism (RWA) views the world as dangerous, requiring ingroup unity behind traditional values, to fight threat. Three themes compose RWA: *conventionalism*, adherence to traditional values; *authoritarian submission*, compliance with established leaders; and *authoritarian aggression*, hostility targeted at deviants from societal conventions (Altemeyer, 1981, 1988). High RWA predicts biased beliefs against various outgroups perceived as morally threatening, including feminists and homosexuals

(Duckitt, 1993; Haddock & Zanna, 1994; Haddock, Zanna, & Esses, 1993; Meloen, Van der Linden, & De Witte, 1996).

Social dominance orientation

According to social dominance theory (SDT), groups have a natural, adaptive inclination to establish category-based hierarchies that ultimately provide stability by regulating further group conflict. Societies, groups, and individuals vary in their support for group hierarchy (Sidanius & Pratto, 1999). SDT describes individual, situational, and societal variations in status-system beliefs. Individuals high in social dominance orientation (SDO) endorse legitimizing myths and ideologies that maintain the status-quo inequalities.

People high in SDO possess tough-minded views of the world as competitive (Duckitt, 2001). Motivated to maintain status systems, high-SDO individuals select and excel in work that enhances hierarchy, such as law enforcement, business, and public prosecution. Low-SDO individuals pursue careers that attenuate hierarchy, such as social work, teaching, and public defense (Kemmelmeier, Danielson, & Basten, 2005; Pratto, Stallworth, Sidanius, et al., 1997).

High SDO predicts outgroup bias (Amiot & Bourhis, 2005; Pratto, Sidanius, Stallworth, et al., 1994), opposition to policies reducing inequality (e.g., affirmative action; Sidanius, Pratto, & Bobo, 1996), ingroup favoritism among high-status groups, as well as favoring the powerful among low-status groups who view the current hierarchy as legitimate (Levin, Federico, Sidanius, et al., 2002). Perhaps to maintain the system, SDO strengthens the already-robust relationship between perceived status and perceived merit (Cuddy, Fiske, Kwan, et al., 2009; Oldmeadow & Fiske, 2007).

Although SDO and RWA both involve perceived threat to the ingroup, they differ in their strategies for dealing with it. SDO promotes ingroup advantage, especially economic and political, whereas RWA strives to prevent ingroup disadvantage, especially in values and norms. People high on both SDO and

RWA are among society's most prejudiced (Altemeyer, 2004).

Terror management theory

People's ultimate threat is their own mortality. Terror management theory concerns people dealing with their fears about death. Humans desire to continue living and resist the uncertainty surrounding their death's inevitable timing and circumstances. Confronting this threat, people seek reassurance in cultural belief systems that represent order, stability, and permanence. Clinging to cultural world views allows them to feel part of something more enduring than themselves. This enables them to experience a vicarious immortality (Greenberg, Solomon, & Pyszczynski, 1997).

Mortality salience has various implications for intergroup biases. Under mortality threat, people react negatively toward outgroups and deviants from cultural values (Greenberg, Pyszczynski, & Solomon et al., 1990; McGregor, Zanna, Holmes, et al., 2001; Schimel, Simon, Greenberg, et al., 1999). Mortality salience also increases ingroup favoritism and intensifies allegiance to political ideologies, with liberals becoming more tolerant and conservatives less so.

System justification theory

System justification theory (SJT) posits that people are motivated to preserve, legitimatize, and justify the societal status quo (Jost & Banaji, 1994). For high-status groups, justifying the system has obvious ingroup benefits. Counter to self-protective motives implicit in other theories, SJT argues that even the disadvantaged support the system, at their own expense, because they seek system stability (Jost, Banaji, & Nosek, 2004).

When subordinate groups cannot change their situation, they may be especially motivated to view powerful groups as deserving their status, which justifies their situation (Dépret & Fiske, 1999; Pepitone, 1950; Stevens & Fiske, 2000). Chronic oppression can further cause disadvantaged groups to internalize their inferior status (Ellemers, Spears, & Doosje, 2002).

ANALYSIS OF WHERE WE STAND: BIASES CAN BE CONTROLLED

People can control their biases through information and motivation (Fiske, Lin, & Neuberg, 1999; Fiske & Neuberg, 1990). Although cognitive tendencies toward stereotyping make it seem inevitable, people can overcome their mental habits.

Information as a cure

People do respond to diagnostic, counter-stereotypic information. If unambiguous, plentiful, and relevant, information can change people's stereotypes (e.g., Pratto & Bargh, 1991; Seta & Seta, 1993), particularly if stereotypes are weak (e.g., De Dreu, Yzerbyt, & Leyens, 1995), and disconfirming information is associated with typical group members (Hewstone & Hamberger, 2000). On the other hand, if stereotypes are strong and information is mixed, then people reinterpret the information to maintain their stereotypes (see Fiske, 1998, for a review). Ambiguous information can be assimilated to the stereotype (e.g., Hilton & von Hippel, 1990).

Motivation as a cure

Motivation cuts both ways. As seen earlier, threat can motivate stereotyping, in the service of self-protection. But self-protection also can motivate the avoidance of stereotyping (overt, at least) in aversive racists protecting their egalitarian self-image (see Chapter 19 by Dovidio, Gaertner, & Kawakami, this volume). Several motivations can undercut the cognitive processes underlying stereotypes. After all, motivations do motivate. We will parse the most common social motivations according to a typology developed by Fiske (1998, 2010); they all relate to people's quest for social survival (Stevens & Fiske, 1995).

Belonging

People are motivated to get along with others, especially those on whom they depend, usually their ingroups. Ingroups entail social identity and shared attitudes

(Hogg, 2001), including stereotypes. Hence, people will often go along with group norms about stereotyping and expressing bias, in either a prejudiced or unprejudiced direction (e.g., Blanchard, Crandall, & Brigham, 1994). Sexual harassment depends entirely on group norms combined with individual differences (Pryor, Geidd, & Williams, 1995). Socially skilled people follow the prevalent norms, in either a biased or unbiased direction (Fiske & Von Hendy, 1992). Within a specific interaction, people motivated to get along will go along with their partners' attitudes (Chen, Schechter, & Chaiken, 1996) and even their partners' stereotypes about them (Sinclair, Lowery, Hardin, et al., 2005; Snyder & Haugen, 1995).

Besides being motivated to maintain one's identity and get along with ingroup others, belonging also means depending on others for valued outcomes. When people depend on someone, they go beyond their stereotypes, attending to expectancy-inconsistent information, making personal dispositional inferences, and forming more idiosyncratic impressions (see Fiske, 2000, for a review). They do this to increase their sense of understanding and control, covered next.

Understanding

To interact effectively, people develop shared social cognitions, and stereotypes are one efficient shortcut. For example, when two people must reach consensus about a third party, they often focus on stereotypes of the third-party target (Ruscher, Hammer, & Hammer, 1996).

In contrast, when people are motivated to be especially accurate, they turn away from stereotypes toward more individuating processes (Neuberg, 1989; Neuberg & Fiske, 1987) and systematic processing (Chen, Schechter, & Chaiken, 1996). Accuracy motivation interferes with stereotypic impressions and automatic behavior (Dijksterhuis, Spears, & Lépinasse, 2001). Fear of invalidity also reduces stereotyping (Kruglanski & Mayseless, 1988), as do accuracy goals (Weary, Jacobson, Edwards, et al., 2001). Thus, the need for understanding can promote

or reduce biased processing, depending on the apparent best route to prediction.

Controlling

Beyond understanding and predicting others, people try to influence their own outcomes in interdependent interactions. When people's control needs increase, they seek detailed social information (Pittman, 1998). As noted, interdependence, which entails a loss of control, also increases social information seeking (Fiske, 2000). But people have to feel that they have a chance at exerting control; when they feel that the potentially individuating information cannot help them influence the other, they resort to stereotypes (Dépret & Fiske, 1999).

Generally, high needs for control promote stereotypes. As noted, need for closure, need for structure, and time pressure all focus people on finding well-defined answers (Jamieson & Zanna, 1989; Kruglanski & Webster, 1996; Neuberg, Judice, & West, 1997). Stereotypes are nothing if not well-defined explanations for the social world, and their use increases under these pressured conditions. Pressure to implement a decision has similar effects (Gollwitzer & Kinney, 1989). High need for dominance also promotes stereotyping (Goodwin, Operario, & Fiske, 1998). When people do control others' outcomes, they also are more prone to stereotyping (Fiske & Dépret, 1996; Goodwin, Gubin, Fiske, et al., 2000).

Enhancing self

Threats to self generally increase outgroup derogation, as described earlier, especially regarding right-wing authoritarianism and social dominance orientation, which respectively react against perceived value threats and resource threats. On an individual level, being insecure or anxious increases prejudice and stereotyping (Stephan & Stephan, 2000). Under threat, the beneficial effects of interdependence diminish (Fiske, 2000). As noted, specific threats to the self can increase stereotyping (Fein & Spencer, 1997). Stereotypes guide the self-defensive projection of one's own negative traits onto outgroup others

(Govorun, Fuegen, & Payne, 2006). Besides threats to the individual, threats to collective self-esteem also increase bias (Crocker & Luhtanen, 1990).

Trusting

People trust ingroup others more than outgroup others, expecting the worst from the latter. They are motivated to see the best in close others, such as team members (Darley & Berscheid, 1967; Klein & Kunda, 1992), evaluators (Pepitone, 1950; Stevens & Fiske, 2000), and potential romantic partners (Berscheid, Graziano, Monson, et al., 1976; Goodwin, Fiske, Rosen, et al., 2002; Murray, Holmes, & Griffin, 1996). Because outgroup members are typically excluded from these trusting relationships, negative stereotypes more easily persist.

However, the structured interdependence of constructive intergroup contact can overcome distrust, under the right conditions, which are conducive to building friendship (Pettigrew & Tropp, 2006). Trust specifically builds when outgroup members do not gratuitously dwell on group membership, because that conveys potential prejudice, reducing acceptance (Tropp, Stout, Boatswain, et al., 2006) (see Chapter 33 by Tausch & Hewstone, this volume).

Despite the best intentions

People cannot always think what they want. Deliberate attempts to suppress stereotypes create an ironic rebound (Wegner, 1994). People may be temporarily successful in suppressing a stereotype, but when they cease, the stereotype can come back, with redoubled expression (Bodenhausen & Macrae, 1996; Macrae, Stangor, & Milne, 1994). Suppression attempts self-control and taxes self-regulation resources (Richeson & Shelton, 2003), but all this just contributes to the hyper-accessibility of the stereotype, especially for people with a low internal motivation to suppress (Gordijn, Hindriks, Koomen, et al., 2004). Efforts to control stereotypes depend on available resources (Blair & Banaji, 1996), level of prejudice, and current goals

(Monteith, Sherman, & Devine, 1998), so all is not lost.

FUTURE DIRECTIONS

The chapter began by noting the first precedents for cognitive approaches to stereotyping, starting with Allport's foundational book, followed by social categorization approaches, resulting in dual-process models that contrast more automatic and controlled systems. Subtle, unexamined stereotyping is more automatic, ambiguous, and ambivalent than common sense would assume. Stereotyping increases under threat to the self and its ingroups. Stereotyping gives way, sometimes, to information and motivation.

These rich insights leave many questions begging for research attention. Increasingly, cognitive researchers have linked social categories to complex intergroup emotions (see Chapter 8 by Smith & Mackie, this volume) and to deliberate and automatic behaviors (Dovidio, Kawakami, & Gaertner, 2002). Increasingly, evidence suggests that cognitive stereotypes influence emotions, which more directly influence behavior (Cuddy, Fiske, & Glick, 2007; Dovidio, Brigham, Johnson, et al., 1996; Pettigrew & Tropp, 2006; Talaska, Fiske, & Chaiken, 2008). Research linking cognition to emotion and behavior still demands attention.

Alongside appreciating the role of distinct emotions, cognitive approaches increasingly spill over to neural analyses of prejudice (see Chapter 4 by Quadflieg, Mason, & Macrae, this volume). Researchers are thus realizing that the brain does not divide along departmental boundaries; social, affective, cognitive, and behavioral processes all mingle. The challenge for next-generation research will be to incorporate these complexities while still addressing general principles.

REFERENCES

Allport, G. W. (1954). *The Nature of Prejudice.* Reading, MA: Addison-Wesley.

Altemeyer, B. (1981). *Right-Wing Authoritarianism*. Winnipeg: University of Manitoba Press.

Altemeyer, B. (1988). *Enemies of Freedom*. San Francisco: Jossey-Bass.

Altemeyer, B. (2004). Highly dominating, highly authoritarian personalities. *Journal of Social Psychology*. 144, 421–447.

Amiot, C. E,. & Bourhis, R. Y. (2005). Ideological beliefs as determinants of discrimination in positive and negative outcome distributions. *European Journal of Social Psychology*, 35, 581–598.

Begany, J. J,. & Milburn, M. A. (2002). Psychological predictors of sexual harassment: Authoritarianism, hostile sexism, and rape myths. *Psychology of Men and Masculinity*, 3, 119–126.

Bastian, B., & Haslam, N. (2006). Psychological essentialism and stereotype endorsement. *Journal of Personality and Social Psychology*, 42, 228–235.

Berscheid, E., Graziano, W., Monson, T., & Dermer, M. (1976). Outcome dependency: Attention, attribution, and attraction. *Journal of Personality and Social Psychology*, 34, 978–989.

Biernat, M., & Vescio, T. K. (2002). She swings, she hits, she's great, she's benched: Implications of gender-based shifting standards for judgment and behavior. *Personality and Social Psychology Bulletin*, 28, 66–77.

Blair, I. V., & Banaji, M. R. (1996). Automatic and controlled processes in stereotype priming. *Journal of Personality and Social Psychology*, 70, 1126–1141.

Blanchard, F. A., Crandall, C. S., Brigham, J. C., & Vaughn, L. A. (1994). Condemning and condoning racism: A social context approach to interracial settings. *Journal of Applied Social Psychology*, 79, 993–997.

Bobo, L. D. (2001). Racial attitudes and relations at the close of the twentieth century. In N. J. Smelser, W. J. Wilson, & F. Mitchel (Eds) *American Becoming* (pp. 264–301). Washington, DC: National Academy Press.

Bodenhausen, G. V., & Macrae, C. N. (1996). The self-regulation of intergroup perception: Mechanisms and consequences of stereotype suppression. In C. N. Macrae, C. Stangor, & M. Hewstone (Eds), *Stereotypes and Stereotyping* (pp. 227–253). New York: Guilford.

Bodenhausen, G. V., & Wyer, R. S. (1985). Effects of stereotypes on decision making and information processing strategies. *Journal of Personality and Social Psychology*, 48, 267–282.

Bogardus, E. S. (1928). Occupational distance. *Sociology and Social Research*, 13, 73–81.

Bogardus, E. S. (1933). A social distance scale. *Sociology and Social Research*, 17, 265–271.

Brewer, M. B. (1988). A dual process model of impression formation. In T. K. Srull, & R. S. Wyer, Jr. (Eds), *Advances in Social Cognition* (Vol. 1, pp. 1–36). Hillsdale, NJ: Erlbaum.

Brewer, M. B., & Brown, R. J. (1998). Intergroup relations. In D. T. Gilbert, S. T. Fiske, & G. Lindzey (Eds), Handbook of Social Psychology. (4th edition, Vol. 2, pp. 554–594). New York: McGraw Hill.

Castano, E., Sacchi, S., & Gries, P. H. (2003). The perception of the other in international relations: Evidence for the polarizing effect on entitativity. *Political Psychology*, 24, 449–468.

Castano, E., Yzerbyt, V., Paladino, M., & Sacchi, S. (2002). I belong, therefore, I exist: Ingroup identification, ingroup entitativity, and ingroup bias. *Personality and Social Psychology Bulletin*, 28, 135–143.

Castelli, L., Macrae, C. N., Zogmaister, C., & Arcuri, L. (2004). A tale of two primes: Contextual limits on stereotype activation. *Social Cognition*, 22, 233–247.

Chen, S., Schechter, D., & Chaiken, S. (1996). Getting the truth or getting along: Accuracy- vs. impression-motivated heuristic and systematic processing. *Journal of Personality and Social Psychology*, 71, 262–275.

Crocker, J., & Luhtanen, R. (1990). Collective self-esteem and ingroup bias. *Journal of Personality and Social Psychology*, 58, 60–67.

Cuddy, A. J. C., Fiske, S. T., & Glick, P. (2007). The BIAS map: Behaviors from intergroup affect and stereotypes. *Journal of Personality and Social Psychology*, 92, 631–648.

Cuddy, A. J. C., Fiske, S. T., Kwan, V. S. Y., Glick, P., Demoulin, S., Leyens, J-Ph. et al. (2009). Is the stereotype content model culture-bound? A cross-cultural comparison reveals systematic similarities and differences. *British Journal of Social Psychology*, 48, 1–33.

Darley, J. M., & Berscheid, E. (1967). Increased liking as a result of the anticipation of personal contact'. *Human Relations*, 20, 29–40.

De Dreu, C. K. W., Yzerbyt, V. Y., & Leyens, J.-Ph. (1995). Dilution of stereotype-based cooperation in mixed-motive interdependence. *Journal of Experimental Social Psychology*, 31, 575–593.

Dépret, E. F., & Fiske, S. T. (1999). Perceiving the powerful: Intriguing individuals versus threatening groups. *Journal of Experimental Social Psychology*, 35, 461–480.

Dijksterhuis, A., Spears, R., & Lepinasse, V. (2001). Reflecting and deflecting stereotypes: Assimilation and contrast in impression formation and automatic behavior. *Journal of Experimental Social Psychology*, 37, 286–299.

Dovidio, J. F., Brigham, J. C., Johnson, B. T., & Gaertner, S. L. (1996). Stereotyping, prejudice, & discrimination: Another look. In N. Macrae, C. Stangor, & M. Hewstone (Eds), *Stereotypes and Stereotyping* (pp. 276–319). New York: Guilford.

Dovidio, J. F., Evans, N., & Tyler, R. B. (1986). Racial stereotypes: The contents of their cognitive representations. *Journal of Experimental Social Psychology*, 22, 22–37.

Dovidio, J. F., Glick, P., & Rudman, L. A. (Eds) (2005). *Reflecting on 'The Nature of Prejudice.'* Malden, MA: Blackwell.

Dovidio, J. F., Kawakami, K., & Gaertner, S. L. (2002). Implicit and explicit prejudice and interracial interaction. *Journal of Personality and Social Psychology*, 82, 62–68.

Duckitt, J. (1993). Right-wing authoritarianism among white South American students: Its measurement and correlates. *Journal of Social Psychology*, 133, 553–563.

Duckitt, J. (2001). A dual-process cognitive-motivational theory of ideology and prejudice. In M. P. Zanna (Ed.), *Advances in Experimental Social Psychology* (Vol. 33, pp. 41–113). New York: Academic Press.

Ellemers, N., Spears, R., & Doosje, B. (2002). Self and social identity. *Annual Review of Psychology*, 53: 161–186.

Fazio, R. H., & Olson, M. A. (2003). Implicit measures in social cognition research: Their meaning and use. *Annual Review of Psychology*, 54, 297–327.

Fein, S., & Spencer, S. J. (1997). Prejudice as self-image maintenance: Affirming the self through derogating others. *Journal of Personality and Social Psychology*, 73, 31–44.

Fiske, S. T. (1998). Stereotyping, prejudice, and discrimination. In D. T. Gilbert, S. T. Fiske, & G. Lindzey (Eds), *Handbook of Social Psychology*. (4th edition, Vol. 2, pp. 357–411). New York: McGraw-Hill.

Fiske, S. T. (2000). Interdependence and the reduction of prejudice. In S. Oskamp (Ed.) *Reducing Prejudice and Discrimination* (pp. 115–135). Mahwah, NJ: Erlbaum.

Fiske, S. T. (2010). *Social Beings: Core Motives in Social Psychology*. New York: Wiley.

Fiske, S. T., Cuddy, A. J. C., & Glick, P. (2007). Universal dimensions of social perception: Warmth and competence. *Trends in Cognitive Science*, 11, 77–83.

Fiske, S. T., Cuddy, A. J. C., Glick, P., & Xu, J. (2002). A model of (often mixed) stereotype content: Competence and warmth respectively follow from perceived status and competition. *Journal of Personality and Social Psychology*, 82, 878–902

Fiske, S. T., & Dépret, E. (1996). Control, interdependence, and power: Understanding social cognition in its social context. In W. Stroebe & M. Hewstone (Eds), *European Review of Social Psychology* (Vol. 7, pp. 31–61). Chichester, UK: Wiley.

Fiske, S. T., Lin, M. H., & Neuberg, S. L. (1999). The Continuum Model: Ten years later. In S. Chaiken, & Y. Trope (Eds.), *Dual Process Theories in Social Psychology* (pp. 231–254). New York: Guilford.

Fiske, S. T., & Neuberg, S. L. (1990). A continuum of impression formation, from category-based to individuating processes: Influences of information and motivation on attention and interpretation. In M. P. Zanna (Ed.), *Advances in Experimental Social Psychology* (Vol. 23, pp 1–74). New York: Academic Press.

Fiske, S. T., & Taylor, S. E. (1984). *Social Cognition*. New York: Random House.

Fiske, S. T., & Taylor, S. E. (2008). *Social Cognition: From Brains to Culture*. New York: McGraw-Hill.

Fiske, S. T., & Von Hendy, H. M. (1992). Personality feedback and situational norms can control stereotyping processes. *Journal of Personality and Social Psychology*, 62, 577–596.

Glick, P., Diebold, J., Bailey-Werner, B., & Zhu, L. (1997). The two faces of Adam: Ambivalent sexism and polarized attitudes toward women. *Personality and Social Psychology Bulletin*, 23, 1323–1334.

Glick, P., & Fiske, S. T. (1996). The Ambivalent Sexism Inventory: Differentiating hostile and benevolent sexism. *Journal of Personality and Social Psychology*, 70, 491–512.

Glick, P., & Fiske, S. T. (2001). Ambivalent sexism. In M. P. Zanna (Ed.), *Advances in Experimental Social Psychology* (Vol. 33, pp. 115–188). Thousand Oaks, CA: Academic Press.

Gollwitzer, P. M., & Kinney, R. F. (1989). Effects of deliberative and implemental mind-sets on illusion of control. *Journal of Personality and Social Psychology*, 56, 531–542.

Goodwin, S. A., Fiske, S. T., Rosen, L. D., & Rosenthal, A. M. (2002). The eye of the beholder: Romantic goals and impression biases. *Journal of Experimental Social Psychology*, 38, 232–241.

Goodwin, S. A., Gubin, A., Fiske, S. T., & Yzerbyt, V. (2000). Power can bias impression formation: Stereotyping subordinates by default and by design. *Group Processes and Intergroup Relations*, 3, 227–256.

Goodwin, S. A., Operario, D., & Fiske, S. T. (1998). Situational power and interpersonal dominance facilitate bias and inequality. *Journal of Social Issues*, 54, 677–698.

Gordijn, E. H., Hindriks, I., Koomen, W., Dijksterhuis, A., & van Knippenberg, A. D. (2004). Consequences of stereotype suppression and internal suppression motivation: A self-regulation approach. *Personality and Social Psychology Bulletin*, 30, 212–224.

Govorun, O., Fuegen, K., & Payne, B. K. (2006). Stereotypes focus defensive projection. *Personality and Social Psychology Bulletin*, 32, 781–793.

Graham, S., & Lowery, B. S. (2004). Priming unconscious racial stereotypes about adolescent offenders. *Law and Human Behavior*, 28, 483–504.

Greenberg, J., Solomon, S. and Pyszczynski, T. (1997). Terror management theory of self-esteem and cultural worldviews: Empirical assessments and conceptual refinements. In M. P. Zanna (Ed.), *Advances in Experimental Social Psychology* (Vol. 29, pp. 61–139). San Diego, CA: Academic Press.

Greenberg, J., Pyszczynski, T., Solomon, S., Rosenblatt, A., Veeder, M., Kirkland, S., et al. (1990). Evidence for terror management theory II: The effects of mortality salience on reactions to those who threaten or bolster the cultural worldview. *Journal of Personality and Social Psychology*, 58, 308–318.

Greenwald, A. G., McGhee, D. E., & Schwartz, J. L. K. (1998). Measuring individual differences in implicit cognition: The Implicit Association Test. *Journal of Personality and Social Psychology*, 74, 1464–1480.

Haddock, G., & Zanna, M. P. (1994). Preferring "housewives" to "feminists". *Psychology of Women Quarterly*, 18, 25–52.

Haddock, G., Zanna, M. P., & Esses, V. M. (1993). Assessing the structure of prejudicial attitudes: The case of attitudes toward homosexuals. *Journal of Personality and Social Psychology*, 65, 1105–1118.

Hamilton, D. L. (Ed.) (1981a). *Cognitive Processes in Stereotyping and Intergroup Behavior*. Hillsdale, NJ: Erlbaum.

Hamilton, D. L. (1981b). Organizational processes in impression formation. In E. T. Higgins, C. P. Herman, & M. P. Zanna (Eds), *Social Cognition: The Ontario Symposium* (Vol. 1, pp. 135–160). Hillsdale, NJ: Erlbaum.

Harris, L. T., & Fiske, S. T. (2006). Dehumanizing the lowest of the low: Neuro-imaging responses to extreme outgroups. *Psychological Science*, 17, 847–853.

Harris, L. T., & Fiske, S. T. (2006). Social groups that elicit disgust are differentially processed in mPFC. *Social Cognitive and Affective Neuroscience*, 2, 45–51.

Hewstone, M., & Hamberger, J. (2000). Perceived variability and stereotype change. *Journal of Experimental Social Psychology*, 36, 103–124.

Hilton, J. L., & von Hippel, W. (1990). The role of consistency in the judgment of stereotype-relevant behaviors. *Personality and Social Psychology Bulletin*, 16, 430–448.

Hogg, M. A. (2001). Social identity and the sovereignty of the group: A psychology of belonging. In C. Sedikides, & M. B. Brewer (Eds). *Individual Self, Relational Self, Collective Self* (pp. 123–143). New York, NY: Psychology Press.

Jamieson, D. W., & Zanna, M. P. (1989). Need for structure in attitude formation and expression. In A. R. Pratkanis, S. J. Breckler, & A. G. Greenwald (Eds). *Attitude Structure and Function* (pp. 383–406). Hillsdale, NJ: Erlbaum.

Jost, J. T., & Banaji, M. R. (1994). The role of stereotyping in system justification and the production of false consciousness. *British Journal of Social Psychology*, 33, 1–27.

Jost, J. T., Banaji, M. R., & Nosek, B. A. (2004). A decade of system justification theory: Accumulated evidence of conscious and unconscious bolstering of the status quo. *Political Psychology*, 25, 881–920.

Katz, D., & Braly, K. (1933). Racial stereotypes of one hundred students. *Journal of Aboral and Social Psychology*, 28, 280–290.

Katz, D., & Braly, K. (1935). Racial prejudice and racial stereotypes. *Journal of Abnormal and Social Psychology*, 30, 175–193.

Katz, I., & Hass, R. G. (1986). Racial ambivalence, value duality, and behavior. In J. F. Dovidio, & S. L. Gaertner (Eds), *Prejudice, Discrimination, and Racism* (pp. 35–59). Thousand Oaks, CA: Academic Press.

Kemmelmeier, M., Danielson, C., & Basten, J. (2005). What's in a grade? Academic success and political orientation. *Personality and Social Psychology Bulletin*, 31, 1386–1399.

Klein, W. M., & Kunda, Z. (1992). Motivated person perception: Constructing justifications for desired beliefs. *Journal of Experimental Social Psychology*, 28, 145–168.

Kruglanski, A. W. (1989). The psychology of being "right": On the problem of accuracy in social perception and cognition. *Psychological Bulletin*, 106, 395–409.

Kruglanski, A. W., & Mayseless, O. (1988). Contextual effects in hypothesis testing: The role of competing alternatives and epistemic motivations. *Social Cognition*, 6, 1–20.

Kruglanski, A. W., & Webster, D. M. (1996). Motivated closing of the mind: "Seizing" and "freezing". *Psychological Review*, 103, 263–283.

Levin, S., Federico, C. M., Sidanius, J., & Rabinowitz, J. L. (2002). Social dominance orientation and intergroup bias: The legitimation of favoritism for high-status groups. *Personality and Social Psychology Bulletin*, 28, 144–157.

Macrae, C. N., Stangor, C., & Milne, A. B. (1994). Activating social stereotypes: A functional analysis. *Journal of Experimental Social Psychology*, 30, 370–389.

Macrae, C. N., Bodenhausen, G. V., Milne, A. B., Thorn, T. M. J., & Castelli, L. (1997). On the activation of social stereotypes: The moderating role of processing objectives. *Journal of Experimental Social Psychology*, 33, 471–489.

Maddox, K. B., & Chase, S. G. (2004). Manipulating subcategory salience: Exploring the link between skin tone and social perception of Blacks. *European Journal of Social Psychology*, 34, 533–546.

Maddox, K. B., & Gray, S. A. (2002). Cognitive representations of Black Americans: Reexploring the role of skin tone. *Personality and Social Psychology Bulletin*, 28, 250–259.

McGregor, I., Zanna, M. P., Holmes, J. G., & Spencer, S. J. (2001). Compensatory conviction in the face of personal uncertainty: Going to extremes and being oneself. *Journal of Personality and Social Psychology*, 80, 472–488.

Meloen, J. D., Van der Linden, G., & De Witte, H. (1996). A test of the approaches of Adorno et al., Lederer, and Altemeyer of authoritarianism in Belgian Flanders: A research note. *Political Psychology*, 17, 643–656.

Monteith, M. J., Sherman, J. W., & Devine, P. G. (1998). Suppression as a stereotype control strategy. *Personality and Social Psychology Review*, 2, 63–82.

Mullen, B., Dovidio, J. F., Johnson, C., & Copper, C. (1992). In-group and out-group differences in social projection. *Journal of Experimental Social Psychology*, 28, 422–440.

Murray, S. L., Holmes, J. G., & Griffin, D. W. (1996). The benefits of positive illusions: Idealization and the construction of satisfaction in close relationships. *Journal of Personality and Social Psychology*, 70, 79–98.

Neuberg, S. L. (1989). The goal of forming accurate impressions during social interactions: Attenuating the impact of negative expectancies. *Journal of Personality and Social Psychology*, 56, 374–386.

Neuberg, S. L., & Fiske, S. T. (1987). Motivational influences on impression formation: Outcome dependency, accuracy-driven attention, and individuating processes. *Journal of Personality and Social Psychology*, 53, 431–444.

Neuberg, S. L., Judice, T. N., & West, S. G. (1997). What the Need for Closure Scale measures and what it does not: Toward differentiating among related epistemic motives. *Journal of Personality and Social Psychology*, 72, 1396–1412.

Norton, M. I., Vandello, J. A., & Darley, J. M. (2004). Casuistry and social category bias. *textitJournal of Personality and Social Psychology*, 87, 817–831.

Oldmeadow, J., & Fiske, S. T. (2007). Ideology moderates status = competence stereotypes: Roles for belief in a just world and social dominance orientation. *European Journal of Social Psychology*, 37, 1135–1148.

Pepitone, A. (1950). Motivational effects in social perception. *Human Relations*, 3, 57–76.

Pettigrew, T. F. (1979). The ultimate attribution error: Extending Allport's cognitive analysis of prejudice. *Personality and Social Psychology Bulletin*, 5, 461–476.

Pettigrew, T. F., & Tropp, L. R. (2006). A meta-analytic test of intergroup contact theory. *Journal of Personality and Social Psychology*, 90, 751–783.

Pittman, T. S. (1998). Motivation. In D. T. Gilbert, S. T. Fiske, & G. Lindzey (Eds), *The Handbook of Social Psychology* (4th edition, Vol. 1, pp. 549–590). New York: McGraw-Hill.

Plant, E. A., Kling, K. C., & Smith, G. L. (2004). The influence of gender and social role on the interpretation of facial expressions. *Sex Roles*, 51, 187–196.

Pratto, F., & Bargh, J. A. (1991). Stereotyping based on apparently individuating information: Trait and global components of sex stereotypes under attention overload. *Journal of Experimental Social Psychology*, 27, 26–47.

Pratto, F., Sidanius, J., Stallworth, L. M., & Malle, B. F. (1994). Social dominance orientation: A personality variable predicting social and political attitudes. *Journal of Personality and Social Psychology*, 67, 741–763.

Pratto, F., Stallworth, L. M., Sidanius, J., & Siers, B. (1997). The gender gap in occupational attainment: A social dominance approach. *Journal of Personality and Social Psychology*, 72, 37–53.

Pryor, J. B., Giedd, J. L., & Williams, K. B. (1995). A social psychological model for predicting sexual harassment. *Journal of Social Issues*, 51, 69–84.

Quinn, K. A., & Macrae, C. N. (2005). Categorizing others: The dynamics of person construal. *Journal of Personality and Social Psychology*, 88, 467–479.

Richeson, J. A., & Shelton, J. N. (2003). When prejudice does not pay: Effects of interracial contact on executive function. *Psychological Science*, 14, 287–290.

Rothbart, M. (1981). Memory processes and social beliefs. In D. Hamilton (Ed.), *Cognitive Processes in Stereotyping and Intergroup Behavior* (pp. 145–182). Hillsdale, NJ: Erlbaum.

Rothbart, M., & Taylor, M. (1992). Category labels and social reality: Do we view social categories as natural kinds? In G. Semin, & K. Fiedler (Eds), *Language, Interaction and Social Cognition* (pp. 11–36). London: Sage.

Ruscher, J. B., Hammer, E. Y., & Hammer, E. D. (1996). Forming shared impressions through conversation: An adaptation of the continuum model. *Personality and Social Psychology Bulletin*, 22, 705–720.

Russell, A. M., & Fiske, S. T. (2008). It's all relative: Competition and status drive interpersonal perception. *European Journal of Social Psychology*, 38, 1193–1201.

Seta, J. J., & Seta, C. E. (1993). Stereotypes and the generation of compensatory and noncompensatory expectancies of group members. *Personality and Social Psychology Bulletin*, 19, 722–731.

Schimel, J., Simon, L., Greenberg, J., Pyszczynski, T., Solomon, S., Waxmonsky, J., et al. (1999). Stereotypes and terror management: Evidence that mortality salience enhances stereotypic thinking and preferences. *Journal of Personality and Social Psychology*, 77, 905–926.

Sherman, J. W., Conrey, F. R., & Groom, C. J. (2004). Encoding flexibility revisited: Evidence for enhanced encoding of stereotype-inconsistent information under cognitive load. *Social Cognition*, 22, 214–232.

Sherman, J. W., Lee, A.Y., Bessenoff, G.R., & Frost, L.A. (1998). Stereotype efficiency reconsidered: Encoding flexibility under cognitive load. *Journal of Personality and Social Psychology*, 75, 589–606.

Sidanius, J., & Pratto, F. (1999). *Social Dominance: An Intergroup Theory of Social Hierarchy and Oppression*. New York: Cambridge University Press.

Sidanius, J., Pratto, F., & Bobo, L. (1996). Racism, conservatism, affirmative action, and intellectual sophistication: A matter of principled conservatism or group dominance? *Journal of Personality and Social Psychology*, 70, 476–490.

Sinclair, S., Lowery, B. S., Hardin, C. D., & Colangelo, A. (2005). Social tuning of automatic racial attitudes: The role of affiliative motivation. *Journal of Personality and Social Psychology*, 89, 583–592.

Snyder, M., & Haugen, J. A. (1995). Why does behavioral confirmation occur? A functional perspective on the role of the target. *Personality and Social Psychology Bulletin*, 21, 963–974.

Stangor, C., & Ford, T. E. (1992). Accuracy and expectancy-confirming processing orientations and the development of stereotypes and prejudice. In W. Stroebe, & M. Hewstone (Eds) *European Review of Social Psychology* (Vol. 3, pp. 57–89). Chichester, UK: Wiley.

Stephan, W. G., & Stephan, C. W. (2000). An integrated threat theory of prejudice. In S. Oskamp (Ed.), *Reducing Prejudice and Discrimination* (pp. 23–45). Mahwah, NJ: Lawrence Erlbaum Associates Publishers.

Stevens, L. E., & Fiske, S. T. (1995). Motivation and cognition in social life: A social survival perspective. *Social Cognition*, 13, 189–214.

Stevens, L. E., & Fiske, S. T. (2000). Motivated impressions of a powerholder: Accuracy under task dependency and misperception under evaluative dependency. *Personality and Social Psychology Bulletin*, 26, 907–922.

Tajfel, H. (Ed.) (1978). *Differentiation Between Social Groups: Studies in the Social Psychology of Intergroup Relations*. London: Academic Press.

Talaska, C. A., Fiske, S. T., & Chaiken, S. (2008). Legitimating racial discrimination: A meta-analysis of the racial attitude-behavior literature shows that emotions, not beliefs, best predict discrimination. *Social Justice Research*, 21, 263–296.

Taylor, S. E. (1981). A categorization approach to stereotyping. In D. L. Hamilton (Ed.), *Cognitive Processes in Stereotyping and Intergroup Behavior* (pp. 83–114). Mahwah, NJ: Erlbaum.

Taylor, S. E., Fiske, S. T., Etcoff, N. L., & Ruderman, A. J. (1978). Categorical and contextual bases of person memory and stereotyping. *Journal of Personality and Social Psychology*, 36, 778–793.

Tropp, L. R., Stout, A. M., Boatswain, C., Wright, S., & Pettigrew, T. F. (2006). Trust and acceptance in response to references to group membership: Minority and majority perspectives on cross-group interactions. *Journal of Applied Social Psychology*, 36, 769–794.

Turner, J. C., Hogg, M.A., Oakes, P. J., Reicher, S. D., & Wetherell, M. S. (1987). *Rediscovering the Social Group: A Self-Categorization Theory*. Cambridge, MA: Basil Blackwell.

van Knippenberg, A., Dijksterhuis, A., & Vermueulen, D. (1999). Judgment and memory of a criminal act: The effects of stereotypes and cognitive load. *European Journal of Social Psychology*, 29, 191–201.

Weary, G., Jacobson, J. A., Edwards, J. A., & Tobin, S. J. (2001). Chronic and temporarily activated causal uncertainty beliefs and stereotype usage. *Journal of Personality and Social Psychology*, 81, 206–219.

Wegner, D. M. (1994). Ironic processes of mental control. *Psychological Review*, 101, 34–52.

Wiener, R. L., Hurt, L., Russell, B., Mannen, K., & Gasper, C. (1997). Perceptions of sexual harassment: The effects of gender, legal standard, and ambivalent sexism. *Law and Human Behavior*, 21, 71–93.

Wilder, D. A. (1981). Perceiving persons as a group: Categorization and intergroup relations. In D. L. Hamilton (Ed.), *Cognitive Processes in Stereotyping and Intergroup Behavior* (pp. 213–258). Hillsdale, NJ: Erlbaum.

Wojciszke, B. (1994). Multiple meanings of behavior: Construing actions in terms of competence or morality. *Journal of Personality and Social Psychology*, 67, 222–232.

Wojciszke, B., Bazinska, R., & Jaworski, M. (1998). On the dominance of moral categories in impression formation. *Personality and Social Psychology Bulletin*, 24, 1251–1263.

Yzerbyt, V., Rocher, S., & Schadron, G. (1997). Stereotypes as explanations: A subjective essentialistic view of group perception. In R. Spears, P. J. Oakes, N. Ellemers, & S. A. Haslam (Eds). *The Social Psychology of Stereotyping and Group Life* (pp. 20–50). Malden, MA: Blackwell.

8

Affective Processes

Eliot R. Smith and Diane M. Mackie

ABSTRACT

Emotional or affective reactions are frequently part of people's reactions to disliked groups, contributing to discrimination. This chapter reviews research on three main topics. First, affect, even if it occurs for irrelevant reasons, can influence cognitive processes that are relevant to prejudice and discrimination, such as people's tendency to use stereotypes. Second, emotions (such as anxiety) frequently arise when individuals encounter outgroup members, and contribute to discomfort and unpleasantness in the interaction. Third, people can experience emotions when they think of themselves as members of social groups, for example, when political party members feel joy or disappointment at their party's electoral outcomes. These group-based emotions also have implications for feelings and behaviors toward outgroups.

AFFECTIVE PROCESSES

Prejudice and discrimination very often involve strong feelings and emotions. This is not always the case; sometimes discrimination can involve cool, unemotional assumptions that members of a negatively regarded group simply do not have what it takes when they are being evaluated for jobs, home loans, or educational opportunities. But more often emotions are part of the picture. People feel irritated or disgusted when they encounter homeless folk on the street, resentful when they read news stories about political demands by an ethnic minority group, or enraged when they think about 'welfare queens' or gay marriages. And the very names of places like Northern Ireland, Iraq, Rwanda, or Darfur (let alone Auschwitz) remind us of the terrible power of extreme intergroup fear and hatred to produce suffering, destruction, and death.

In this chapter we describe several aspects of the emotional or affective side of prejudice and discrimination. Following a section clarifying definitions and a brief overview of the history of research on this topic, we review current research on three main topics: effects of affect (arising from any source) on cognitive processes relevant to prejudice and discrimination; emotions arising in individual encounters with outgroup members; and emotions that people experience when they think of themselves as members of social groups. Finally, we summarize the major implications of the research and suggest avenues for future investigation.

First, we need to define key terms. *Affect* or what is termed core affect (Russell & Barrett, 1999; Russell, 2003) involves the two dimensions of valence (pleasant/unpleasant) and arousal (energized/passive), which are fundamental to all moods as well as emotions.

Affect fluctuates in response to positive or negative external events as well as physiological states (daily cycles, ingestion of caffeine, etc.; Russell, 2003), and people can perceive their current affective state as the sense of feeling good or bad, tired or energized. More formally, affect is a 'neurophysiological state that is consciously accessible as a simple, nonreflective feeling that is an integral blend of hedonic (pleasure-displeasure) and arousal (sleepy-activated) values' (Russell, 2003, p. 147; see also Barrett, 2006b; Watson & Tellegen, 1985). *Mood* is an affective state that is relatively long-lasting and not necessarily attributed to any specific cause. Moods conceptually have the same two-dimensional structure as affect, although only positive versus negative moods are distinguished in most research.

Finally, an *emotional episode* is a subjectively experienced and time-bounded state that combines an affective state with relevant cognitions (beliefs, interpretations, appraisals) and behaviors (instrumental behaviors, such as fleeing in fear, and facial behaviors, such as smiling in happiness). Different theories take different viewpoints on the exact nature of this combination. Appraisal theories of emotion (e.g., Frijda, 1986; Roseman, 1984) hold that emotions are generated by *appraisals* of objects or events that impinge on the self. Appraisals, which may be conscious or nonconscious, are subjective interpretations of objects or events. A specific configuration of appraisals (e.g., the perception that a threatening object has just appeared) generates the emotional episode, including the subjective experience of having an emotion, affective changes (e.g., the onset of negative arousal), as well as changes in expressive and instrumental behavior. Because appraisals are subjective interpretations, two different people (or one person at different times) may appraise an identical event differently – say, as a dangerous threat versus an energizing challenge – resulting in different emotional reactions.

While appraisal theories of emotion have been most influential within social psychology, they are by no means the only class of theories. Basic emotion theories (e.g., Ekman, 1972; LeDoux, 1996) hold that there are perhaps a half-dozen 'basic' emotions dictated by biological pathways, and that more complex emotions are blends of the basic ones. Another approach, the core affect model (Barrett, 2006b; Russell & Barrett, 1999; Russell, 2003) holds that external events first produce an affective response, with the subjective experience of an emotion arising later as the result of a categorization process. The person categorizes the episode as an instance of fear (or anger, or joy, etc.) based on the experienced affect, salient objects or event in the environment that are interpreted as causing the affect, and cultural or personal knowledge about emotion. These perception and categorization processes may involve mistakes about the cause of an emotion (e.g., misattributions). Overall, although there are several distinctly different and competing theoretical approaches to emotion in general, current investigations of the role of emotion in prejudice have not required delving into these relatively subtle differences (see Smith & Mackie, 2008).

HISTORY

In view of the obvious presence of emotion in most manifestations of prejudice and discrimination, it is odd that the research literature until fairly recently devoted very little attention to affective processes. A summary of historical trends offers at least a partial explanation for this pattern.

Immediate post-World-War-II era

Modern research on prejudice and related issues began in the aftermath of World War II, as social scientists sought to understand the roots of Nazism and American researchers began to come to grips with racial injustice in the United States (Myrdal, 1944). Prominent among the early contributors were the *Authoritarian Personality* research group (Adorno, Frenkel-Brunswik, Levinson, et al., 1950). They took a psychodynamic approach, using

Freudian theory to understand the roots of Nazism in people's deep subconscious psychological conflicts. To deal with unconscious anxiety resulting from particular patterns of child-rearing, authoritarians were said to long to follow strong authority figures and to take a highly punitive orientation toward outsiders or norm-violators. Of course, this psychological configuration would account readily for German authoritarians' willingness to follow Hitler and to blame the Jews for economic troubles. In the same era, Gordon Allport (1954) published his seminal work on *The Nature of Prejudice*. Among many other factors ranging from the cultural to the cognitive, he discussed an affective pattern termed 'character-conditioned hatred' arising from a lifetime of disappointments and frustration. The hatred may be targeted on a group that has no real relationship to the source of the individual's frustration. Rather, the individual 'thinks up some convenient victim and some good reason. The Jews are conspiring against him, or the politicians are set on making things worse' (Allport, 1954, p. 342). As these examples illustrate, the target will often be some socially defined outgroup or scapegoat.

These two early conceptual frameworks share major similarities. They emphasize affective processes, extreme negative emotions toward outgroups. They regard these emotions as irrational, seeing them as generated by more or less unconscious sources of motivation and targeted at outgroups without logical justification. Finally, both Adorno et al. and Allport sought to explain the psychology and behavior of the extreme bigot: the Nazi or Ku Klux Klan member, for example. Indeed, in thinking about such unsympathetic people, explanations that invoke irrational, deep-seated unconscious motives seem intuitively appealing and compelling.

The 1960s through the 1980s

Beginning around 1960, several factors led to a decline in the popularity of the earlier, more affectively based theories of prejudice. First, the Authoritarian Personality research attracted significant criticism, both conceptual and methodological (e.g., Christie & Jahoda, 1954). Second, a revolution in psychological science began to get underway, promising to explain the mind using the concepts of information processing (e.g., Miller, Galanter, & Pribram, 1960; Neisser, 1967). The cognitive revolution along with other factors contributed to Freudian psychodynamic theory's fall from favor within scientific psychology.

Finally, and perhaps most important, researchers began increasingly to realize that prejudice could be identified not only in fanatically bigoted, psychologically disturbed Nazis, but in ordinary people – in fact, people uncomfortably like ourselves. An important early push in this direction came from Pettigrew's (1958) landmark work suggesting that anti-Black prejudice in the American South was driven mostly by conformity to social norms rather than by inner psychodynamic conflicts. And research in social psychology began applying cognitive principles to understanding social judgment and person perception (e.g., Higgins, Rholes, & Jones, 1977; Srull & Wyer, 1979). This approach soon established that people's thinking about (and therefore their treatment of) other people was pervasively influenced by their general beliefs – including their stereotypes of social groups. Importantly, both conformity to social norms and application of stereotype knowledge structures are ordinary, everyday processes that influence all of us, not only extreme bigots. Some of Allport's (1954) analysis of prejudice anticipated this more modern cognitive emphasis.

Complementing the ideas that prejudice stems partly from conformity and partly from the automatic application of well-learned knowledge structures, a third theoretical perspective was formulated around the same time. Working in Europe, Henri Tajfel (1978) and his colleagues developed Social Identity Theory and its later offshoot Self-Categorization Theory (Turner, Hogg, Oakes, et al., 1987). These theories attributed people's biases favoring their own group over outgroups to a psychological motive to view their ingroups (and hence themselves) in a positive light, by seeking to positively differentiate their groups from others. This line of thinking offered a third explanation for some forms of prejudice and negative intergroup behavior in terms of 'normal' psychological processes – processes that might affect any of us, not only a few deranged swastika-wavers or cross-burners.

All three of these explanations are reviewed elsewhere in this handbook. For our purposes, the key point is that all three lines tended to de-emphasize affect in favor of 'cold' psychological processes involving people's desires to conform to the standards of their groups, to understand the world by applying their existing knowledge, and to see themselves and others connected to them in a positive light. The social identity approach, however, by emphasizing motivation and the involvement of the self in intergroup relations, did lay the groundwork for bringing emotions back into the picture.

The 1980s through the present

Beginning in the middle of the 1980s, researchers began to study the role of emotions in immediate, face-to-face intergroup interactions. As we will describe below, Stephan and Stephan (1985), Gaertner and Dovidio (1986), and Dijker (1987) pioneered explorations of how people might experience negative emotions such as anxiety, unease, or irritation in encounters with members of outgroups. These emotions in turn were found to have powerful consequences, including the avoidance of outgroup members.

In the 1990s, while research continued to examine the negative feelings arising from intergroup interaction, two additional approaches to affect and its contribution to intergroup behavior came into focus. First, extending earlier work on the impact of affect on cognition in general (e.g., Isen & Daubman, 1984), researchers began to investigate how emotional states might affect cognitive processes (such as stereotyping) that are relevant to prejudice and intergroup behavior. For example, Stroessner and Mackie (1992) found that positive affect increased people's tendency to use stereotypes, consistent with other findings that positive affect reduced thoughtful cognitive processing. Much work on this theme was collected in an edited volume published in 1993 (Mackie & Hamilton, 1993). At the same time, Smith (1993) coupled the social identity perspective to emotion theory, arguing that if people treat a social group membership as part of the self then they might respond emotionally to events that affect the group.

All three of these lines have remained important to the present day, and are reviewed in the next section of this chapter. In a way, these streams of research can be seen as rediscovering the earlier emphasis from the 1950s on affective processes and their contribution to prejudice, which tended to be lost or obscured during the intervening decades. However, one crucial difference should be noted: the new thinking takes as a starting point the idea that emotions are 'normal' and can affect anyone reacting to members of an outgroup, rather than being the hallmark only of a few extreme and irrationally driven bigots. Indeed, basic theories of emotion itself have matured, and now tend to emphasize its generally functional, adaptive qualities rather than its irrationality and destructiveness.

REVIEW AND CONCEPTUAL FRAMEWORK

As just discussed, three major lines of research and theory target affective processes in the domain of prejudice and intergroup behavior. One represents an application of the more general idea that affect can moderate and regulate cognitive processes, applied to understand how emotions that may arise in intergroup situations might exacerbate stereotyping or other cognitive processes. A second line investigates the often negative emotions that people feel during actual (or, sometimes, imagined) face-to-face intergroup encounters. And the third line takes up the insight of the social identity approach, that group identification makes an ingroup part of the psychological self, and examines how events that impinge on a group can excite emotional responses in an individual group member – even one who is not *personally* affected by the event.

Incidental affect: Affect moderates cognitive processes

Affective states influence cognitive processes; this can be testified by anyone who has ever been 'so mad I can't think straight.' Because cognitive processes such as the application of stereotypes are key contributors to prejudice and related phenomena, it became natural to investigate whether affect might influence processes relevant to intergroup behavior. This line of work focuses on the *general* processing effects of an affective state, which itself may stem from some completely irrelevant source (i.e., not necessarily from the intergroup situation itself). For this reason, it is often termed 'incidental affect.' Thus, a typical study in this line of research induces an affective state in experimental participants by having them watch a film clip, recall an autobiographical emotional episode, or the like, and then measures their judgments or behavior in an intergroup situation.

Such studies have found that incidental affect influences many types of cognitive processes relevant to stereotyping. One type of influence is that affective states, for cognitive or motivational reasons, often degrade people's ability to perform complex cognitive tasks. As mentioned earlier, Stroessner and Mackie (1992) found that positive affect increased people's reliance on stereotypes of groups (see also Mackie, Queller, Stroessner, et al., 1996), and reduced the variability they perceived among group members. Another study (reported in Bodenhausen, 1993) examined effects of happiness, sadness, or anger (induced by recalling past emotional events) on stereotyping. Results showed that happy and angry participants were more likely to stereotype, compared to sad ones. The researchers concluded that although sadness increases detailed information processing (reducing stereotyping), both happiness and

anger produce less detailed 'heuristic' processing including the use of readily available social stereotypes.

Until recent years, hypotheses about effects of incidental affect were largely based on two straightforward theoretical ideas, which reflected the general conceptual focus of the time on cognitive processes. One is that affective states (whether positive or negative), if they are intense enough, can influence people's general *ability to process* – by distracting them or draining cognitive capacity. The second is the idea that affective states influence people's *motivation to process*, which could occur in several possible ways. One proposal is that positive moods signal that 'things are OK' and let people coast along without doing much deep processing, while negative moods signal 'better look out' and motivate detailed processing of information about the environment (Schwarz & Clore, 1983). Another possibility (Isen & Levin, 1972) is that processing itself can be used as a mood maintenance or repair strategy; for example, happy people may refuse to process information in depth because it might bore them and wreck the enjoyable positive mood, or sad people might process intensively as a potential distraction from their aversive mood state. Combined with the widely accepted idea that stereotyping represents a cognitively simple strategy that does not involve deep processing, these theoretical notions generate predictions about the effects of affective states on stereotyping. However, all of these ideas suggest that all positive states should have similar effects on processing (assuming intensity is constant), and also that all negative states should have similar processing effects. But we have already seen in Bodenhausen's (1993) results that sadness and anger, both negative states, produced opposite effects on people's tendency to stereotype.

More recently, a new perspective has been advanced that can make sense of such effects of discrete emotions. Building on appraisal theories of emotions (Frijda, 1986; Frijda, Kuipers, & ter Schure, 1989; Roseman, 1984), researchers have found that incidental emotions such as anger, fear, or sadness influence people's judgments about objects that are unrelated to the emotion, in ways that depend on the emotion's associated appraisals (Lerner & Keltner, 2000). For example, fear involves an appraisal that a negative event may possibly happen – that is, it involves an appraisal of uncertainty. Hence, research shows that people in a fearful state judge many types of events to be relatively uncertain (Tiedens & Linton, 2001). Interestingly, these feelings of uncertainty may in turn lead people to engage in more extensive cognitive processing, but unlike the processing effects described above, this effect would be specific to the emotion of fear but would not result from other negative emotions. As another example, because anger involves an appraisal that someone else is responsible for a negative event, people feeling anger (for whatever reason) tend to judge other people as responsible. Recently, researchers have applied this theoretical principle to judgments related to social groups. DeSteno, Dasgupta, Bartlett, et al. (2004) hypothesized that anger would involve appraisals related to intergroup conflict and competition, so incidental anger should make people display more bias against an outgroup. Consistent with the hypothesis, their studies found that induced anger (but not sadness) increased prejudice against an outgroup in a minimal intergroup situation, assessed by an implicit measure. As this study illustrates, the line of research pioneered by Lerner and Keltner (2000) on emotion effects on appraisal-relevant judgments permits predictions about differentiated effects of specific emotions on specific judgments – not just general predictions about effects of positive versus negative affective states on the nature or amount of cognitive processing.

Emotions in intergroup encounters

Negative emotions in intergroup interaction

While research on the effects of incidental affect grew out of the broader study of affective influences on cognition, another major line of work on affective influences stems from a close examination of concrete processes of intergroup interaction, with the insight that emotions often arise from the interaction itself (rather than from irrelevant, external sources). Stephan and Stephan (1985) conceptualized this emotion as 'intergroup anxiety,' negative feelings arising from a lack of knowledge or experience interacting with members of the particular outgroup. This anxiety imposes a cognitive load (worry, intrusive thoughts) during the interaction, which may disrupt smooth social behavior – and in this way harm the interaction in a self-fulfilling manner. Intergroup anxiety can also lead to avoidance of interaction with outgroup members. One noteworthy aspect of this model is that intergroup anxiety is not motivated by sheer prejudice or antipathy against the outgroup, nor by negative stereotypes of the group; instead, it is fueled by relatively innocuous sources like the desire for an interaction to go smoothly, uncertainty about how to interact, and the desire not to give offense or to appear prejudiced.

Gaertner and Dovidio (1986) similarly argued that good-hearted, well-intentioned people who explicitly endorse nondiscriminatory or egalitarian views might nevertheless experience negative affect in cross-group interaction. They analysed this 'aversive racism' as stemming from long-socialized negative images of outgroups (e.g., African Americans) that are not consciously acknowledged because they conflict with the individual's more explicit egalitarian attitudes. This suppressed conflict can lead to outcomes similar to intergroup anxiety, such as disrupted thoughts and feelings, and strong but possibly ineffectual efforts to control behavior in the interaction. One provocative aspect of Gaertner and Dovidio's thinking is the prediction that the underlying negative feelings may lead to avoidance or discriminatory treatment of outgroup members, but only when these behaviors can be rationalized as due to some nonracial cause. Several studies have supported this prediction (summarized in Gaertner & Dovidio, 1986).

Along similar lines, Dijker (1987), in studies conducted in the Netherlands, found that native Dutch people often reported experiencing negative emotions such as anxiety or irritation in encounters with members of minority ethnic groups, especially those groups that were most culturally dissimilar to the Dutch. Of course, people often feel strong attachment to their ingroup's cultural symbols and preferences, and so encounters with outgroup members who are culturally different will often cause negative feelings. However, some of Dijker's (1987) respondents also reported feeling positive emotions during intergroup contact, especially with members of more culturally similar outgroups. Finally, other negative emotions besides anxiety and irritation can arise in intergroup interaction, including emotions that are more self-directed, such as guilt. Devine and Monteith (1993) and others have examined how recognition of one's own stereotypic or prejudiced thoughts may produce guilt in some people who wish to be nonprejudiced, motivating them to try to act correctly in the situation or even to work toward changing their stereotypes.

Positive emotions from friendly intergroup contact

Although the research just discussed found that emotions occurring in intergroup contact are often negative, positive emotions may also be present, and their effects have been explored in research on how prejudice can be reduced. One of the earliest hypotheses in this area, introduced by Allport (1954), is that friendly, personal contact across group lines should generally reduce prejudice. A recent meta-analysis (Pettigrew & Tropp, 2006) of the voluminous literature over the last half-century strongly confirms the hypothesis. But what specific processes mediate between contact and prejudice reduction? Although it has often been assumed that the disconfirmation of inaccurate negative stereotypes about the outgroup is the main story, affective mediators seem more important (Brown & Hewstone, 2005; Tropp & Pettigrew, 2005). Other studies (Miller, Smith, & Mackie, 2004;

Voci & Hewstone, 2003; Wolsko, Park, & Judd, 2003) make the same point: intergroup contact typically has its effects by increasing positive emotions and decreasing negative emotions regarding the outgroup, rather than by changing stereotypic beliefs or other cognitions about them. In other words, the right kind of contact can make people feel friendly toward an outgroup member in a way that generalizes to a more positive regard for the outgroup as a whole, even while leaving previous stereotypes about the outgroup essentially unchanged. Findings such as these underline the pragmatic as well as theoretical importance of affective processes in prejudice and intergroup relations.

Emotions stemming from group identification

A third general approach to the role of emotions in intergroup behavior is based on the idea (drawn from the social identity perspective) that group identification makes an ingroup part of the self. As such, any event or object that is relevant to the group becomes self-relevant, and therefore can generate emotional responses, which can be conceptualized as group-level emotions (Smith, Seger, & Mackie, 2007). The distinction between group and individual emotion parallels that between 'fraternal' (group-level) and individual or 'egoistic' relative deprivation (Runciman, 1966). The former is based on comparing one's group's outcomes to those of other groups, while the latter is based on comparing oneself as an individual to other individuals. In short, the core idea is that emotion can arise because of group belonging, and thus emotions can be group-level as well as individual-level phenomena.

This idea has been developed in intergroup emotions theory (IET) (Mackie, Devos, & Smith, 2000; Smith, 1993, 1999). To the fundamental postulate of the socially extended self, IET couples appraisal theories of emotions. In these theories, as described above, emotions are generated by appraisals of objects or events that impinge on the individual self (Frijda, 1986; Roseman, 1984).

IET holds that like all emotions, group emotions are generated by appraisal processes. The difference is simply that when a group membership is salient, people appraise the effects that events, objects, and groups have on the ingroup (not just the individual self). For example, if someone who thinks of himself or herself as a group member perceives that the ingroup is threatened by an outgroup's goals or actions and believes that the ingroup is strong, he or she may experience group anger (Mackie, Devos, & Smith, 2000). Like all emotions, group emotions are coupled to action tendencies (desires to take specific types of action). In the example, the individual may desire to attack or confront the outgroup.

As this example illustrates, IET postulates that there may be multiple types of 'prejudice:' distinct psychological and behavioral reactions to social groups are determined by the differentiated emotional reactions to those groups. So one outgroup may be perceived to be a dangerous threat, while another is viewed as violating ingroup norms, and yet another as making unfair demands on the ingroup. These three outgroups might be regarded with distinct group-level feelings of fear, disgust, and anger, respectively, and the perceiver's behavioral responses might be quite distinct (e.g., avoidance for fear or disgust, confrontation or attack for anger). All outgroups are not treated in an undifferentiated negative manner (Mackie & Smith, 2002). Elaborating on this principle, Cottrell and Neuberg (2005) have demonstrated that White Americans regard specific outgroups as posing distinct types of threat (e.g., threats of disrupting ingroup norms, of contamination or disease, of violating territorial integrity) and correspondingly feel distinct patterns of emotional response toward those outgroups.

Group emotions need not be directed only at outgroups, but may include emotions directed at the ingroup as well. For example, people may feel collective pride if they see their group as winning a competition, or they may experience collective guilt if they appraise their group as having violated important moral principles (Doosje, Branscombe, Spears, et al., 1998).

As a result of all these processes, groups may in time become associated with specific profiles of emotional feelings that group members tend to experience when they are thinking about that particular social identity: pride when thinking about a national identity, for example, or anger whenever they think about an outgroup with which their ingroup is in intense conflict. In a conceptual parallel, research has found that individuals tend to have specific emotional profiles (Watson & Clark, 1992), differing in the extent to which they *generally* feel a number of emotions (rather than just in their emotional responses to a particular stimulus object or event). Similarly, particular groups have relatively stable emotion profiles (Smith, Seger, & Mackie, 2007). This means that when people think of themselves as members of one group they might tend to feel high levels of anxiety or low levels of satisfaction, compared to the same people when they are responding as individuals, or as members of a different group.

In summary, IET postulates that when people identify with a group, they will appraise social objects or events in terms of their implications for the group. These appraisals generate group emotions and, in turn, relevant action tendencies. However, one might wonder whether these emotions truly are rooted in people's group memberships as the theory holds. Are they meaningfully distinct from individual-level emotions? Do they function (like other emotions) to adaptively regulate behavior – in this case, behaviors toward ingroups and outgroups? Research of several types supports the conclusions that group-level emotions are meaningful and distinct from individual-level emotions (see Mackie, Silver, & Smith, 2004; Smith, Seger, & Mackie, 2007).

Group emotions distinct from individual-level emotions

In a direct examination of relations between group and individual-level emotions, Smith, Seger, & Mackie, (2007) obtained people's reports of 12 specific emotions experienced as individuals and as members of several different ingroups (university, national, and political party groups). Emotions at the individual and group level were moderately correlated, but profiles of group emotions and individual emotions were meaningfully and qualitatively distinct. The relative independence between group and individual emotions implies that people can experience emotions on behalf of a group or fellow group members even when the perceivers are not personally affected (e.g., Mackie, Silver, & Smith, 2004; Yzerbyt, Dumont, Wigboldus, et al., 2003). For example, one study (Yzerbyt, Dumont, Gordijn, et al., 2002) showed that when a particular group membership is salient, people react emotionally to events that affect other ingroup members – even though the events have no implications for the perceiver personally.

Group emotions depend on group identification

Theoretically, group identification is what incorporates the ingroup as part of the self, and enables the experience of group emotions. In addition, positive group emotions such as pride and satisfaction are likely to encourage identification with a particular group. Consistent with these ideas, Smith, Seger, & Mackie, (2007) found a strong relation between positive group emotions and identification with the ingroups they studied. Anger at the outgroup was also positively related to group identification, consistent with some other research (Kessler & Hollbach, 2005). In contrast, other negative group emotions such as guilt, anxiety, and irritation were generally negatively related to identification. This finding may reflect strong group identifiers' tendency to reinterpret events and situations to avoid painful negative feelings, as demonstrated in work by Doosje, Branscombe, Spears, et al. (1998).

Group emotions are socially shared within an ingroup

Smith, Seger, & Mackie (2007) found that people's group emotions are socially shared,

and shared more strongly by people who identify more with the group. That is, each social group seems to have a characteristic profile of group emotions (such as high irritation, low satisfaction, moderate guilt), and when members think of themselves as belonging to that particular group, their emotions tend to converge toward the group profile.

Group emotions regulate intergroup and intragroup attitudes and behavioral tendencies

A wide range of research confirms that group emotions influence people's attitudes and behaviors relevant to the group. Smith, Seger, & Mackie, (2007) investigated action tendencies involving ingroup support and solidarity, outgroup confrontation, and outgroup avoidance, and found that group emotions rather than individual-level emotions predicted these action tendencies. Other studies in a number of different settings provide further evidence that group emotions are important causes and mediators of intergroup behavior. Anger and fear experienced in response to the September 11, 2001 attacks on the United States had distinct effects on people's political tolerance for outgroups several months later (Skitka, Bauman, & Mullen, 2004). Guilt regarding an ingroup's historically exploitative actions, as well as ingroup-directed anger, explain support for political actions aimed at making reparations for those actions (Leach & Iyer, 2006). Emotions toward an outgroup mediate willingness to engage in contact with group members (Esses & Dovidio, 2002) and desires to attack that group (Mackie, Devos, & Smith, 2000). Finally, feelings of satisfaction or guilt regarding an ingroup's aggression influence people's willingness to support similar aggressive actions in the future (Maitner, Mackie, & Smith, 2007).

Fluid boundaries between individual and group emotions

The line between individual and group emotions depends on the way the individual is thinking of him- or herself at the moment – as an individual or as a group member – and as a result the situation can be ambiguous. Consider the negative emotions that people often experience during intergroup contact, as demonstrated by research discussed above (e.g., Stephan & Stephan, 1985). These emotions may sometimes remain at the individual level, if feelings of irritation or unease have to do with perceptions that the other person has *individual* characteristics that are annoying, or with perceptions that one *personally* lacks the knowledge and skills to make the cross-group interaction flow smoothly. But in contrast, someone in such a situation might think of him- or herself primarily as a group member rather than a unique individual. A White person's concern about personally appearing prejudiced in a cross-group interaction would be an individual emotion, but thinking of the self as a representative of the entire White group may bring to the fore anxiety about confirming the stereotype that Whites are generally racist, which would be a group emotion. A woman may be angered as an individual at being made to look stupid by a man's snide comment. But if the same woman interprets the comment as intended to make her look stupid *because* she was a woman, the resulting anger might be group-level. Because people can switch fluently between individual and collective identities (and between different groups that constitute alternative collective identities), an experienced emotion may be either individual or group level, making the distinction at times difficult to draw. Still, the existence of difficult borderline cases does not diminish the conceptual importance of distinguishing individual from group emotions, any more than the existence of warm water means that hot is the same as cold.

Other approaches linking emotions to group membership

Several theoretical models build on the idea that emotions can be grounded in people's group memberships and directed at specific groups. Cottrell and Neuberg (2005) take a sociofunctional approach that emphasizes the variety of potential intergroup threats that may elicit distinct emotional reactions. For example, an outgroup may threaten an ingroup by invading its territory, appropriating its property, infecting it with diseases, etc. Cottrell and Neuberg hypothesize that humans are predisposed by their evolutionary history to respond to such group-level threats (as well as individual-level threats) with distinct emotional reactions. This approach complements a group-based emotional approach with an evolutionary analysis of the functionality of such emotions.

The stereotype content model (SCM) of Fiske, Cuddy, Glick, and Xu (2002) postulates that people can experience four emotions directed at different groups, depending on the two key dimensions of the group's stereotypical warmth and competence. Warmth in turn is linked to the perception of common or competitive goals between the perceiver's own group and the target group, whereas competence is strongly related to the target group's overall status in society. Warm and competent groups such as middle-class Americans elicit emotions of pride. Groups seen as competent but not warm, such as Jews, elicit envy. Warm and incompetent groups such as the elderly may elicit feelings of pity, while cold and incompetent groups (such as welfare recipients) elicit contempt. Unlike many models of group-based emotions, the SCM has typically been tested in studies that ask people to describe how 'society as a whole' reacts to different groups, rather than how they *themselves* feel about the groups. In addition, the SCM focuses on just two appraisal dimensions (warmth and competence) which combine to yield four discrete emotions. This makes it more limited in scope compared to Cottrell and Neuberg's sociofunctional approach (which allows for a large number of distinct group emotions driven by different types of threats) or to IET (which postulates that any configuration of appraisals could in principle be applied to an intergroup situation, resulting in group-based forms of any and all emotions).

Finally, image theory (IT) has been advanced by Alexander, Brewer, and Hermann (1999). This model assumes that negative emotional reactions and desires to act against threatening outgroups often come first, then can be rationalized after the fact by adopting corresponding beliefs. For example, disgust felt at an outgroup may be rationalized by a 'barbarian' image, the idea that the outgroup is strong but uncultured, interested only in destruction. Anger at an outgroup may be associated with an 'enemy' image, which portrays the outgroup as more or less a mirror image of the ingroup itself: holding opposing goals, but matching the ingroup in strength, intelligence, and sophistication. This model reminds us that emotions can be not only a consequence, but also a cause of corresponding beliefs or appraisals about groups.

Perception of emotions across group boundaries

In an intergroup situation, it can be important for members of each group to understand the emotional reactions of the other group – to know, for example, whether the outgroup feels afraid, angry, or simply disappointed regarding the actions of the ingroup. Leyens and his colleagues (Leyens, Paladino, Rodriguez-Torres, et al., 2000) have described a bias that can affect perceptions of emotions across group lines: an unwillingness to attribute what they term 'uniquely human' emotions to outgroup members as strongly as to ingroup members. In their model, some emotions (such as anger, fear, or happiness) are assumed to be more basic and non-uniquely human – that is, they are shared even by higher nonhuman animals. In contrast, some emotions, such as remorse or shame, are 'uniquely human,' and several studies have found that perceivers are relatively unwilling to attribute them to outgroup members, in a sense denying those people the full essence of humanity.

Although this perceptual bias can obviously influence the accuracy with which people perceive others' emotions across group boundaries, it remains important to know how others are feeling, to predict their behavior, and hence to plan one's own actions. Hence, adaptive social perceivers should display considerable accuracy in predicting the group-level emotions of members of an outgroup. Seger, Smith, Kinias, and Mackie (2009) tested this hypothesis using several complementary groups (such as Democrats and Republicans or men and women) and found, as hypothesized, considerable although imperfect accuracy in outgroup predictions.

PROMISING FUTURE DIRECTIONS

The ongoing rediscovery of the role of affective processes in prejudice and intergroup behavior leads to several potential lines of theoretical and empirical development.

First, one important area will be increased linkages between the areas of prejudice and intergroup behavior and fundamental research on emotion in general. To date, most of those involved in studying prejudice have backgrounds in the social cognition or social identity research traditions, so collaborations with expert emotion researchers might be valuable. In-depth understanding of emotions should contribute to the precision and specificity of predictions regarding prejudice, obviously. But in addition, studies in this area may enrich and even fundamentally reshape theoretical conceptions of emotion. For example, one insight from work on group-level emotions (Smith & Mackie, 2006) is that emotions are part of a specific *identity* (e.g., a personal identity or one or another important group membership) rather than of a biological *individual*. Shifting identities leads to shifts in emotions, even though the same person is involved in both cases.

Second, and following on the above theme, prejudice researchers should follow the best practices recommended by emotion researchers and advance beyond self-report measures of emotions. This suggestion is not made because self-report measures specifically are flawed, but because any single measurement approach is overly narrow. In the area of prejudice there are a few studies that apply physiological or brain-imaging measures (e.g., Blascovich, Mendes,

Hunter, et al., 2001; Phelps, O'Connor, & Cunningham, 2000) but as yet few that engage in a full multimethod measurement approach. Measurement at all levels (core affect, physiological responses, facial expressions, overt behavior as well as self-reports of subjective experience) will prove extremely helpful in clarifying the respective roles of the multiple processes that contribute to a full-blown emotional episode (Barrett, 2006a).

Third, the fact that emotions pertain to a particular individual or social identity suggests that people can use identity change as an emotion regulation strategy (Smith & Mackie, 2006; Ray, Mackie, & Smith, 2008), different from those that have typically been studied (Gross, 1998). There is already evidence, for example, that positive or negative group emotions may lead people to increase or decrease identification with a particular ingroup (Kessler & Hollbach, 2005), and we know that group identification has important potential consequences downstream.

Fourth, one of the more salient differences between emotions and cognitions, such as stereotypes, is that emotions change rapidly over time (with a course of seconds to hours) while stereotypes are generally regarded as highly stable and resistant to change. This observation suggests the importance of studying the interactions between stable and more transitory states, whether affective or cognitive, that could influence prejudiced judgments and discriminatory actions. For example, research has already found that when people are specifically in an angry state, they display more implicitly measured prejudice against an outgroup (DeSteno, Dasgupta, Bartlett, et al., 2004).

Finally, the new recognition of the importance of affect suggests a new portfolio of strategies for reducing prejudice. Existing strategies tend to emphasize changing stereotypes (e.g., through learning about counterstereotypic group members) or altering social group boundaries (e.g., through recategorization strategies). Supplementing these, we can now begin to draw on ideas from the literatures on emotion regulation, misattribution, and so on. For example, Rydell, Mackie, & Maitner, (2008) found that an emotion misattribution manipulation reduced the anger felt at an outgroup. No one strategy is likely to prove a 'magic bullet' that can profoundly reduce the individual and social effects of prejudice and discrimination, but an increased range of possible approaches should over time add to the ultimate practical value of our research efforts.

ACKNOWLEDGEMENTS

Preparation of this chapter was supported by NIMH Grant R01 MH63762 and NSF Grant BCS-0719876. We are grateful to our collaborators and those who have assisted us with comments on this chapter, particularly Angela Maitner and Charles Seger. Correspondence should be directed to: Eliot Smith, Department of Psychological and Brain Sciences, 1101 E. Tenth St., Indiana University, Bloomington, IN 47405-7007. E-mail: esmith4@indiana.edu

REFERENCES

Adorno, T. W., Frenkel-Brunswik, E., Levinson, D. J., & Sanford, R. N. (1950). *The Authoritarian Personality.* New York: Harper.

Alexander, M. G., Brewer, M. B., & Hermann, R. K. (1999). Images and affect: A functional analysis of out-group stereotypes. *Journal of Personality and Social Psychology*, 77, 78–93.

Allport, G. W. (1954). *The Nature of Prejudice.* MA: Addison-Wesley.

Barrett, L. F. (2006a). Emotions as natural kinds? *Perspectives on Psychological Science*, 1, 28–58.

Barrett, L. F. (2006b). Solving the emotion paradox: Categorization and the experience of emotion. *Personality and Social Psychology Review*, 10, 20–46.

Blascovich, J., Mendes, W. B., Hunter, S. B., Lickel, B., & Kowai-Bell, N. (2001). Perceiver threat in social interactions with stigmatized others. *Journal of Personality and Social Psychology*, 80, 253–267.

Bodenhausen, G. V. (1993). Emotions, arousal and stereotyping judgments: A heuristic model of affect and stereotyping. In D. M. Mackie, & D. L. Hamilton

(Eds), *Affect, Cognition, and Stereotyping: Inter-active Processes in Group Perception* (pp. 13–37). San Diego: Academic Press.

Brown, R., & Hewstone, M. (2005). An integrative theory of intergroup contact. In M. P. Zanna (Ed.), *Advances in Experimental Social Psychology* (Vol. 37, pp. 255–343). San Diego, CA: Elsevier Academic Press.

Christie, R., & Jahoda, M. (1954). *Studies in the Scope and Method of 'The Authoritarian Personality.'* Glencoe, IL: Free Press.

Cottrell, C. A., & Neuberg, S. L. (2005). Different emotional reactions to different groups: A socio-functional threat-based approach to "prejudice". *Journal of Personality and Social Psychology*, 88, 770–789.

DeSteno, D., Dasgupta, N., Bartlett, M. Y., & Cajdric, A. (2004). Prejudice from thin air: The effect of emotion on automatic intergroup attitudes. *Psychological Science*, 15, 319–324.

Devine, P. G., & Monteith, M. J. (1993). The role of discrepancy-associated affect in prejudice reduction. In D. M. Mackie, & D. L. Hamilton (Eds.), *Affect, Cognition, and Stereotyping* (pp. 317–344). San Diego: Academic Press.

Dijker, A. J. (1987). Emotional reactions to ethnic minorities. *European Journal of Social Psychology*, 17, 305–325.

Doosje, B., Branscombe, N. R., Spears, R., & Manstead, A. S. R. (1998). Guilty by association: When one's group has a negative history. *Journal of Personality and Social Psychology*, 75, 872–886.

Ekman, P. (1972). Universal and cultural differences in facial expression of emotion. In J. R. Cole (Ed.), *Nebraska Symposium on Motivation 1971* (pp. 207–208). Lincoln: University of Nebraska Press.

Esses, V. M., & Dovidio, J. F. (2002). The role of emotions in determining willingness to engage in intergroup contact. *Personality and Social Psychology Bulletin*, 28, 1202–1214.

Fiske, S. T., Cuddy, A. J. C., Glick, P., & Xu, J. (2002). A model of (often mixed) stereotype content: Competence and warmth respectively follow from perceived status and competition. *Journal of Personality and Social Psychology*, 82, 878–902.

Frijda, N. H. (1986). *The Emotions.* Cambridge, UK: Cambridge University Press.

Frijda, N. H., Kuipers, P., & ter Schure, E. (1989). Relations among emotion, appraisal, and emotional action readiness. *Journal of Personality and Social Psychology*, 57, 212–228.

Gaertner, S. L., & Dovidio, J. F. (1986). The aversive form of racism. In J. F. Dovidio, & S. L. Gaertner (Eds),

Prejudice, Discrimination, and Racism (pp. 61–90). Orlando, FL: Academic Press.

Gross, J. J. (1998). Antecedent- and response-focused emotion regulation: Divergent consequences for experience, expression, and physiology. *Journal of Personality and Social Psychology*, 74, 224–237.

Higgins, E. T., Rholes, W. S., & Jones, C. R. (1977). Category accessibility and impression formation. *Journal of Experimental Social Psychology*, 13, 141–154.

Isen, A. M., & Daubman, K. A. (1984). The influence of affect on categorization. *Journal of Personality and Social Psychology*, 47, 1206–1217.

Isen, A. M., & Levin, P. F. (1972). The effect of feeling good on helping: Cookies and kindness. *Journal of Personality and Social Psychology*, 21, 384–388.

Kessler, T., & Hollbach, S. (2005). Group-based emotions as determinants of ingroup identification. *Journal of Experimental Social Psychology*, 41, 677–685.

Leach, C. W., & Iyer, A. (2006). Anger and guilt about in-group advantage explain the willingness for political action. *Personality and Social Psychology Bulletin*, 32, 1232–1245.

LeDoux, J. E. (1996). *The Emotional Brain: The Mys-terious Underpinnings of Emotional Life.* New York: Simon & Schuster.

Lerner, J. S., & Keltner, D. (2000). Beyond valence: Toward a model of emotion–specific influences on judgement and choice. *Cognition and Emotion*, 14, 473–493.

Leyens, J.-P., Paladino, P. M., Rodriguez-Torres, R., Vaes, J., Demoulin, S., Rodriguez-Perez, A., et al. (2000). The emotional side of prejudice: The attribution of secondary emotions to ingroups and outgroups. *Personality and Social Psychology Review*, 4, 186–197.

Mackie, D. M., & Hamilton, D.L. (Eds) (1993). *Affect, Cognition, and Stereotyping: Interactive Processes in Group Perception.* San Diego: Academic Press.

Mackie, D. M., & Smith, E. R. (Eds) (2002). *From Prejudice to Intergroup Emotions: Differentiated Reactions to Social Groups.* Philadelphia: Psychology Press.

Mackie, D. M., Devos, T., & Smith, E. R. (2000). Intergroup emotions: Explaining offensive action tendencies in an intergroup context. *Journal of Personality and Social Psychology*, 79, 602–616.

Mackie, D. M., Queller, S., Stroessner, S. J., & Hamilton, D. L. (1996). Making stereotypes better or worse: Multiple roles of positive affect in group impressions. In R. M. Sorrentino, & E. T. Higgins (Eds), *Handbook of Motivation and Cognition* (Vol. 3, pp. 371–396). New York: Guilford Press.

Mackie, D. M., Silver, L. A., & Smith, E. R. (2004). Intergroup emotions: Emotion as an intergroup phenomenon. In L. Z. Tiedens, & C. W. Leach (Eds), *The Social Life of Emotions* (pp. 227–245). Cambridge, UK: Cambridge University Press.

Maitner, A. T., Mackie, D. M., & Smith, E. R. (2007). Antecedents and consequences of satisfaction and guilt following ingroup aggression. *Group Processes and Intergroup Relations*, 10, 223–238.

Miller, D. A., Smith, E. R., & Mackie, D. M. (2004). Effects of intergroup contact and political predispositions on prejudice: Role of intergroup emotions. *Group Processes and Intergroup Relations*, 7, 221–237.

Miller, G. A., Galanter, E., & Pribram, K. H. (1960). *Plans and the Structure of Behavior*. Oxford, UK: Holt.

Myrdal, G. (1944). *An American Dilemma: The Negro Problem and American Democracy*. New York: Harper & Row.

Neisser, U. (1967). *Cognitive Psychology*. New York: Appleton-Century-Crofts.

Pettigrew, T. F. (1958). Personality and sociocultural factors in intergroup attitudes: A cross-national comparison. *Journal of Conflict Resolution*, 2, 29–42.

Pettigrew, T. F., & Tropp, L. R. (2006). A meta-analytic test of intergroup contact theory. *Journal of Personality and Social Psychology*, 90, 751–783.

Phelps, E. A., O'Connor, K. J., Cunningham, W. A., Funayama, E. S., Gatenby, J. C., Gore, J. C., et al. (2000). Performance on indirect measures of race evaluation predicts amygdala activation. *Journal of Cognitive Neuroscience*, 12, 729–738.

Ray, D. G., Mackie, D. M., Rydell, R. J., & Smith, E. R. (2008). Changing categorization of self can change emotions about outgroups. *Journal of Experimental Social Psychology*, 44, 1210–1213.

Roseman, I. J. (1984). Cognitive determinants of emotion: A structural theory. *Review of Personality and Social Psychology*, 5, 11–36.

Runciman, W. G. (1966). *Relative Deprivation and Social Justice*. Berkeley, CA: University of California Press.

Russell, J. A. (2003). Core affect and the psychological construction of emotion. *Psychological Review*, 110, 145–172.

Russell, J. A., & Barrett, L. F. (1999). Core affect, prototypical emotional episodes, and other things called emotion: Dissecting the elephant. *Journal of Personality and Social Psychology*, 76, 805–819.

Rydell, R. J., Mackie, D. M., Maitner, A. T., Claypool, H. M., Ryan, M. J., & Smith, E. R. (2008). Arousal, processing, and risk taking: Consequences of intergroup anger. *Personality and Social Psychology Bulletin*, 34, 1141–1152.

Schwarz, N., & Clore, G. L. (1983). Mood, misattribution, and judgments of well-being: Informative and directive functions of affective states. *Journal of Personality and Social Psychology*, 45, 513–523.

Seger, C. R., Smith, E. R., Kinias, Z., & Mackie, D. M. (2009). Knowing how they feel: Predicting emotions felt by outgroups. *Journal of Experimental Social Psychology*, 45, 80–89.

Skitka, L. J., Bauman, C. W., & Mullen, E. (2004). Political tolerance and coming to psychological closure following the September 11, 2001 terrorist attacks: An integrative approach. *Personality and Social Psychology Bulletin*, 30, 743–756.

Smith, E. R. (1993). Social identity and social emotions: Toward new conceptualizations of prejudice. In D. M. Mackie, & D. L. Hamilton (Eds), *Affect, Cognition, and Stereotyping: Interactive Processes in Group Perception* (pp. 297–315). San Diego: Academic Press.

Smith, E. R. (1999). Affective and cognitive implications of a group becoming part of the self: New models of prejudice and of the self-concept. In D. Abrams, & M. A. Hogg (Eds), *Social Identity and Social Cognition* (pp. 183–196). Oxford: Blackwell.

Smith, E. R., & Mackie, D. M. (2008). Intergroup emotions. In M. Lewis, J. Haviland-Jones, and L. F. Barrett (Eds), *Handbook of Emotions* (3rd edition, pp. 428–439). New York: Guilford Publications.

Smith, E. R., & Mackie, D. M. (2006). It's about time: Intergroup emotions as time-dependent phenomena. In R. Brown, & D. Capozza (Eds), *Social Identities: Motivational, Emotional, and Cultural Influences* (pp. 173–187). New York: Psychology Press.

Smith, E. R., Seger, C. R., & Mackie, D. M. (2007). Can emotions be truly group-level? Evidence regarding four conceptual criteria. *Journal of Personality and Social Psychology*, 93, 431–446.

Srull, T. K., & Wyer, R. S. (1979). The role of category accessibility in the interpretation of information about persons: Some determinants and implications. *Journal of Personality and Social Psychology*, 37, 1660–1672.

Stephan, W. G., & Stephan, C. W. (1985). Intergroup anxiety. *Journal of Social Issues*, 41, 157–175.

Stroessner, S. J., & Mackie, D.M. (1992). The impact of induced affect on the perception of variability in social groups. *Personality and Social Psychology Bulletin*, 18, 546–554.

Tajfel, H. (Ed.) (1978), *Differentiation Between Social Groups: Studies in the Social Psychology of Intergroup Relations*. London: Academic Press.

Tiedens, L. Z., & Linton, S. (2001). Judgment under emotional certainty and uncertainty: The effects of specific emotions on information processing. *Journal of Personality and Social Psychology*, 81, 973–988.

Tropp, L. R., & Pettigrew, T. F. (2005). Differential relationships between intergroup contact and affective and cognitive dimensions of prejudice. *Personality and Social Psychology Bulletin*, 31, 1145–1158.

Turner, J. C., Hogg, M. A., Oakes, P. J., Reicher, S. D., & Wetherell, M. S. (1987). *Rediscovering the Social Group: A Self-Categorization Theory*. Oxford: Blackwell.

Voci, A., & Hewstone, M. (2003). Intergroup contact and prejudice toward immigrants in Italy: The mediational role of anxiety and the moderational role of group salience. *Group Processes and Intergroup Relations*, 6, 37–52.

Watson, D., & Clark, L. A. (1992). On traits and temperament: General and specific factors of emotional experience and their relation to the five-factor model. *Journal of Personality*, 60, 441–476.

Watson, D., & Tellegen, A. (1985). Toward a consensual structure of mood. *Psychological Bulletin*, 98, 219–235.

Wolsko, C., Park, B., Judd, C. M., & Bachelor, J. (2003). Intergroup contact: Effects on group evaluations and perceived variability. *Group Processes and Intergroup Relations*, 6, 93–110.

Yzerbyt, V. Y., Dumont, M., Gordijn, E., & Wigboldus, D. (2002). Intergroup emotions and self-categorization: The impact of perspective-taking on reactions to victims of harmful behavior. In D. M. Mackie, & E. R. Smith (Eds), *From Prejudice to Intergroup Emotions* (pp. 67–88). New York: Psychology Press.

Yzerbyt, V. Y., Dumont, M., Wigboldus, D., & Gordijn, E. (2003). I feel for us: The impact of categorization and identification on emotions and action tendencies. *British Journal of Social Psychology*, 42, 533–549.

9

Motivational Processes

Vincent Y. Yzerbyt

ABSTRACT

Motivation and cognition have often been seen in opposition when it comes to explaining prejudice. Similarly, more social versus more cognitive approaches often tend to be disconnected from each other. This has led to the adoption of a dominant framework that obliterates the strong connection between these aspects. To overcome this limitation, we analyse prejudice from the perspective of the basic human needs, that is, to know and to control, to be connected with others, and to have value. These integrity concerns provide a rich analytic tool allowing us to appraise a vast array of theoretical and empirical contributions. Although these integrity concerns constitute powerful factors leading to the emergence of prejudice, we suggest that the same concerns must be used if one wishes to fight prejudice.

SHOULD WE BE CONCERNED ABOUT INTEGRITY CONCERNS?

This chapter is about motivation in stereotyping, prejudice, and discrimination. The construct of motivation encompasses a large array of phenomena ranging from transient and specific goals of an individual to chronic and global needs characterizing all humans. Motivation also concerns explicit and controlled objectives, or unconscious and diffuse preoccupations. Finally, motivation may stem from the person's own initiative or from the operation of external forces. This chapter considers all of these cases and refers to motivation in a general way. However, because motivational forces underlying prejudice are more than goals, especially conscious and internally-driven ones, we speak of integrity

concerns. This term does justice to the breadth of the concept both in process and content. Importantly, we do not refer here to the state of tension directly associated with the experience of prejudice. Although prejudice is an affective state that fuels people's chauvinistic behaviors down the line, we concentrate on integrity concerns insofar as they constitute efficient or final causes of stereotyping, prejudice, and discrimination.

Motivation and cognition have always been viewed as an odd couple and are often suspected of leading independent lives, a perspective embraced by contemporary dual system models (Strack & Deutsch, 2004). However, motivation and cognition have also been envisioned as intertwined and working hand in hand so as to best serve individuals. Within research on intergroup relations, motivation has traditionally been viewed as the main cause of bias and prejudice and, indeed, motivational accounts are at the heart of an impressive number of efforts (Spencer, Fein, Zanna, et al., 2002). After a long period characterized by the cognitive revolution, needs, goals, and other vested interests have gained new respectability in the eyes of scholars interested in issues of intergroup relations (Dovidio & Gaertner, 2010; Fiske & Taylor, 2008; Yzerbyt & Demoulin, 2010). In short, cognitive processes have ceased to be viewed in opposition to motivations. While acknowledging perceivers' *partial* appraisal of their social environment, current research also aims at better understanding the motivational factors underlying people's *partisan* view of the social world. This convergence is palpable both in matters of theoretical positions and of methods. The outcome is the emergence of a rich picture of social perceivers, one in which appraisal of the world is affected as much by reality constraints, which Allport (1954) called 'the light without', as by what Allport labeled 'the light within', which we referred to earlier as integrity concerns (Yzerbyt & Corneille, 2005).

The first section of the chapter assesses the early contributions on the role of motivation in stereotyping, prejudice, and discrimination. A classic two-dimensional view is used to organize the research traditions: Whereas the first dimension opposes those views for which prejudice originates inside or outside perceivers, the second distinguishes whether or not conflict underlies the emergence of intolerance and bias (Stroebe & Insko, 1989). The second section reviews several empirical efforts suggesting that this two-dimensional view fails to provide an accurate picture of the complexities of phenomena. The third section presents an alternative framework that integrates contemporary theory and research by building on the basic human needs. Although these needs can individually, and also sometimes in combination, foster prejudice, these 'integrity concerns' can also be used to fight bigotry and intolerance. A final section provides suggestions for future work.

HISTORICAL BACKGROUND

In the early days of research on prejudice, motivation was a key theme (Brewer & Brown, 1998). Disliking members of other groups was seen as a deeply engrained response, a gut reaction, in most social perceivers. Using modern terminology, bigotry and chauvinism were means to self-regulate in response to deficiencies of the self. In their classic motivational approach, Adorno, Frenkel-Brunswick, Levinson, et al. (1950) singled out the intra-psychic conflict experienced by individuals in response to beloved parents who, at the same time, were exceedingly punitive because they were over-vigilant with respect to the dominant norms and rules. This clash between love and admiration on the one hand and frustration and hatred on the other was thought to lead to prejudice against those considered to be out of line. In short, a tormented ego resulting from dysfunctional child-raising practices could find salvation in derogating different and fragile others (but see Glick, 2002). Theoretical difficulties and empirical limitations led to questioning of this work on the so-called 'authoritarian personality' but this approach inspired generations of researchers and has recently been revisited with such constructs as right-wing authoritarianism (Altemeyer, 1998).

Allport (1954) was among the first to suggest that prejudice is not only a course adopted by twisted minds relying on unwarranted generalizations but that stereotyping is grounded in a basic, unavoidable, categorization process. Categorization is a prerequisite for human thinking for it gives meaning to new experiences. It facilitates learning and guides people's adjustments to the social world. By abstracting sensory inputs, categorization allows individuals to quickly interpret, and react to, their environment. The problem is that categorization prevents people from perceiving some aspects of the world: idiosyncrasies are overlooked. Categorization impoverishes experiences, leading to a host of perceptual, judgmental, and memory biases.

By emphasizing the normality of people's faulty perceptions, Allport claimed the study of prejudice and stereotyping as part of mainstream social psychology. Researchers thus oriented their efforts toward clarifying the role of cognitive processes in the formation, use, and modification of stereotypes. Within one generation, cognitive processes became the guilty party and, indeed, almost the sole focus of interest (Fiske & Taylor, 1984; Hamilton, 1981). Inspired by the growing popularity of views linking cognition to affect and mood but perhaps even more by the challenge posed by social identity researchers (Tafjel & Turner, 1979), students of social perception soon realized that cognitive processes were not the end of the story. Motivation and, more generally, affective processes could simply not be ignored in order to account for the prevalence of prejudice (Fiske & Neuberg, 1990; Mackie & Hamilton, 1993).

Replacing the 'cognitive miser' perspective, the 'motivated tactician' view gave motivation a new role that was the exact opposite of its mission in the psychodynamic tradition (Fiske, 1998). Motivation was now seen as an asset, fostering defiance toward quick and stereotyped responses and closer scrutiny of the specificities of the information (Fiske & Neuberg, 1990). Several versions of this view still populate the research market, namely the work on the impact of egalitarian goals (Crandall & Eshleman, 2003; Monteith, Sherman, & Devine, 1998; Moskowitz, Gollwitzer, Wasel, et al., 1999) and motivation to avoid stereotyping (Amodio, Harmon-Jones, & Devine, 2003; Devine, Plant, Amodio, et al., 2002; Dunton & Fazio, 1997; Plant & Devine, 1998, 2001).

Two other lines of work posited instead the social origin of prejudice. One, decidedly conflict-based, promoted the view that stereotypes, prejudice, and discrimination occur because individuals belong to groups that compete for limited resources. Only when groups need to cooperate to achieve common goals do intergroup relations improve. For these advocates of the realistic conflict approach (Levine & Campbell, 1972) or simply opponents of individualistic approaches (Sherif, 1967), interdependence combined with status differences between groups predicts intergroup responses. To the extent that hostility toward members of other groups depends on the way people appraise the structural features that regulate intergroup relations, these efforts are a legacy of Lewin's phenomenological approach.

Social identity theory (Tajfel & Turner, 1979), self-categorization theory (Turner, Hogg, Oakes, et al., 1987), and their heirs also see the social dimension as central to the emergence of bias (for a recent review, see Yzerbyt & Demoulin, 2010). Individuals see themselves, and are seen by others, as belonging to certain groups. As a consequence, aspects of who they are, along with their worth, derive from group membership. The focus here is on the group in the individual rather than the individual in the group. As such, this approach to prejudice represents an ingenious blend between the three perspectives presented above. Categorization in groups, along with the cognitive simplification it creates, joins with individuals' concern for a positive self-esteem. On top of these factors, the structural features of the social system shape people's perceptions of the intergroup situation, determining reactions toward members of other groups. Whereas social cognition and social identity approaches initially agreed on the pivotal role of categorization processes, they diverged on the impact of motivation. Whereas motivation is a springboard to redemption in social cognition, it fuels stereotyping, prejudice, and discrimination in the eyes of social identity theorists.

Clearly, the role of motivation is most explicit in the psychodynamic individualistic approach and the social identity theories. In their more recent typology of prejudiced motivations, Jost and Banaji (1994) refer to these two views as addressing ego- and group-threat, respectively. At the same time, motivation also assumes a clear role in some of the other views, be it the motivated tactician approach (Fiske, 1998) or the conflict theories (Brown & Hewstone, 2005).

Recent years have witnessed the emergence of new ways of conceptualizing prejudice and the role of motivation. It is now widely assumed that stereotypes and prejudice are largely disseminated and characterized by a high level of inertia. At the same time, only a limited amount of research has been directed at uncovering processes responsible for deep-grained intolerance. In line with Crandall and Eshleman's (2003) distinction between what they call 'genuine prejudice' on the one hand and the expression of bias on the other, the bulk of contemporary work is on factors that moderate the release or suppression of prejudice (Shelton & Richeson, 2006). The next section reviews a series of empirical efforts that point to the factors contributing to stereotyping and prejudice and also reveals the limits of the classic typology presented earlier. In the following section, we then provide an alternative integrative framework, proposing that integrity concerns often foster prejudice but can also, at times, prevent the emergence of prejudice.

THE RELEVANT LITERATURE: EMPIRICAL ILLUSTRATIONS OF THE ROLE OF MOTIVATION IN STEREOTYPING AND PREJUDICE

Contemporary researchers clearly abandoned the sharp distinction between individualistic and social approaches on the one hand or between conflict and nonconflict approaches on the other. For instance, even when studying so-called deep individual differences, the tone has decidedly changed from a 'trait' approach to an 'attitude' approach, with some room given for the impact of situational determinants and more transient factors that lead people to fall back on, or avoid, their chauvinistic beliefs. Similarly, the social cognitive approach has examined the consequences of attacks on the image of the self on the emergence of prejudiced reactions. Finally, factors such as conflict and power have become even more explicit in social identity approaches. In this section, we

illustrate the richness of current efforts by dwelling on a series of illustrative studies. The section focuses on the three most prolific lines of work among the four quadrants, namely the individual/conflict approach, the individual/nonconflict approach, and, finally, the social/nonconflict approach.

Turning to the individual conflict approach first, Duckitt (2001; see Chapter 2 by Duckitt, this volume) proposed a model that combines the early work on the authoritarian personality (Adorno, Frenkel-Brunswick, & Levinson, 1950) and more recent efforts on the role of personality factors in the emergence of prejudice (Altemeyer, 1998; Sidanius & Pratto, 1999). Perceptions of threat to the social order, a notion reminiscent of the idea of symbolic threat (Sears & Henry, 2003), or to the privileged position of the ingroup, a notion related to the idea of realistic threat (Esses, Jackson, & Armstrong, 1998) in intergroup threat theory (Stephan & Stephan, 2000), stimulate the adoption of various beliefs and attitudes (embodied in such scales as right-wing authoritarianism (RWA), and social dominance orientation (SDO) respectively). These beliefs and attitudes then trigger feelings of prejudice. Eventually, these emotional reactions materialize into manifestations of ingroup favoritism and outgroup discrimination. Duckitt's (2001) model sits comfortably within current conceptions of prejudice in which appraisals impact behavior through the emotional experience they trigger. It also provides room for both large-scale and slow determinants, such as life-long socialization practices, and for specific and short-term causes, such as rapid changes in the information regarding the social environment or modification in the particular power position that people occupy. By enriching the traditional approach encountered in differential psychology with the situationist perspective characterizing social psychology, Duckitt's (2001) model bridges the gap between the individualist (personality) and social (realistic conflict) motivations underlying prejudice.

A remarkable illustration of the power of social factors in orienting people's perceptions of their world, with direct consequences for the adoption of certain attitudinal beliefs and the expression of prejudice, can be found in the work by Guimond and colleagues (Guimond, Dambrun, Michinov, et al., 2003). These authors showed that SDO, that is, the belief that certain groups ought to dominate other groups in society and that equality is to be avoided, is affected by the specific major that people select in college (Guimond, Dambrun, Michinov, et al., 2003: Experiments 1 and 2). Not only did Law school students manifest higher levels of SDO than psychology students at the outset of their university trajectory, confirming the idea that people high in SDO are attracted to powerful professions, but SDO scores of law students increased over the years of study whereas those of psychology students decreased. Even more strikingly, Guimond and colleagues (2003: Experiment 4) showed that a simple manipulation assigning participants to a high-power as opposed to low-power role influenced SDO levels. In all of these studies, SDO mediated the impact between power and prejudice. Such findings (Danso & Esses, 2001; Schmitt, Branscombe, & Kappen, 2003) suggest that SDO is best seen as a set of beliefs that proves sensitive to strategic interests emerging in a dynamic context of intergroup relations (Turner & Reynolds, 2003). In a similar vein, researchers have examined other ideological orientations thought to generate prejudice. In particular, conservatism has long been linked to prejudice because it entails a strong faith in personal responsibility for one's negative outcomes whereas the propensity to blame the victim appears less strongly engrained among liberals (Skitka, Mullen, Griffin, et al., 2002). Jost, Glaser, Kruglanski, et al. (2003) recently argued that political conservatism is best seen as motivated social cognition, serving a range of ideological (e.g., group-based dominance), existential (e.g., terror management), and epistemic (e.g., intolerance of ambiguity) motives.

The social cognition tradition also evolved to include factors that were initially neglected. People may sometimes feel that their self-worth is being questioned and such situations may promote bias and intolerance in how information is processed. In one illustrative example, Kunda and colleagues (Kunda, Davies, Adams, et al., 2002) conjectured that, when confronted with an individual who fits multiple categories (e.g., an Asian doctor), people may choose to appraise this target using one of several categorical bases (e.g., doctor or Asian). The selection of a particular category depends upon the way the interaction unfolds. If the target somehow 'frustrates' the well-being of the perceiver or counters self-enhancement goals, the more derogatory category (e.g., ethnicity) will impose itself whereas the more flattering category will be inhibited. Of importance too, stereotype activation effects may be brief (Kunda & Spencer, 2003) and stereotypes may not be applied as the interaction proceeds unless some event (e.g., a disagreement) triggers a need for people to fall back on their a priori views. That social perceivers may go back and forth to stereotypes as a function of their relevance is consistent with the view that stereotypes are used when they prove useful in guiding perceivers' behavior.

Personal threats or frustrations may influence judgments even when only incidentally related to the interaction. Fein and Spencer (1997) showed that people who learn that they failed rather than succeeded at a test express more disparaging judgments when the feedback provider is member of a stigmatized category. Moreover, the more negatively the threatened individuals rate the target, the better they feel. Clearly, an individual whose self-integrity is being questioned, whether or not in the context of the interaction, turns to stereotypes as a means of recovering from the frustrating episode.

The above work makes it tempting to conclude that low self-esteem people are more likely than high self-esteem people to stereotype, to be prejudiced, and to discriminate. The picture is more complex. Chronic low self-esteem people are reluctant to express prejudice whereas high self-esteem people are often more expressive in their dislikes for other groups (Aberson, Healy, & Romero, 2000). In line with a variety of self-projection conceptions of group identity (Gramzow & Gaertner, 2005; Krueger, 2007; Otten & Wentura, 2001), individuals high in self-esteem may also be expected to favor their ingroup more easily because they project their own characteristics, and thus their sense of self-worth, on other ingroup members. This issue is reminiscent of the debate among social identity theorists about the causal relation between self-esteem and ingroup bias. The proposition that successful discrimination enhances self-esteem has received substantial empirical support (Verkuyten, 2007; for reviews, see Aberson, Healy, & Romero, 2000; Rubin & Hewstone, 1998), but there is not much evidence for a direct impact of low self-esteem on bias and prejudice.

Although stereotyping and prejudice may be instrumental in attaining some desired states, upholding a simplified, partisan, and often derogatory view of other people and groups often constitutes a motivation in its own right. Perceivers sometimes devote considerable cognitive resources in order to *save* their current views. Similarly, research on stereotype change has emphasized the active role that perceivers play in keeping their preconceptions intact (Kunda & Oleson, 1995; Yzerbyt, Coull, & Rocher, 1999). All in all, social cognition research confirms that perceivers are motivated to maintain their stereotyped beliefs, creating considerable mental inertia. In fact, stereotypes are likely to be even more resistant if they survive a stage of thorough examination during which perceivers actively reaffirm them. This means that stereotypes can emerge in two rather different contexts. Besides being handy interpretations of the evidence, susceptible to being abandoned or modified whenever more attention is devoted to the stimulus information (Fiske & Neuberg, 1990), they may also result from a thorough rationalization process, thereby becoming deeply rooted beliefs likely to resist most contradictory facts (Yzerbyt & Corneille, 2005). These conflicting views that motivation can either decrease stereotyping or fuel the preservation of prejudiced conceptions permeate contemporary views (Crandall & Eshleman, 2003).

One remarkable evolution in modern work though is the role afforded to automatic and unconscious processes, which we examine in the next section.

The social identity tradition also suggests the complex nature of phenomena by stressing the role of motivation in the emergence of prejudice. Not surprisingly, numerous studies examining the impact of identity threat (for a collection, see Ellemers, Spears, & Doosje, 1999) and of relative deprivation (for a recent review, Walker & Smith, 2002) show that prejudice emerges when people feel that their group's status or identity is threatened. Relative deprivation theory stipulates that people feel deprived and dissatisfied when they experience unfavorable comparisons between their current situation and, for example, their past situation or the current situation of others. Group-relative deprivation refers to the perception that a group that one identifies highly with is deprived relative to an outgroup. Group, but not personal, relative deprivation is thought to be related to intergroup variables. Recently, Pettigrew, Christ, Wagner, et al. (2008) tested this proposition using three large-scale European surveys. Both personal and group-relative deprivations were stronger among low-status individuals and correlated with a sense of political inefficacy. But only group-relative deprivation was a proximal correlate of prejudice and fully mediated any relationship between personal deprivation and prejudice (Tougas & Beaton, 2001).

Unexpectedly, recent studies also reveal that prejudice may result from success, economic prosperity, or relative gratification, the opposite of relative deprivation (Dambrun, Taylor, McDonald, et al., 2006). In this context, prejudice functions to justify the economic and social superiority of those who are dominant. In other words, when people occupy a dominant position, they translate this advantage into flattering stereotypes for themselves and derogatory stereotypes of less successful groups, mobilizing beliefs to justify their superior social position (Kay, Jost, Mandisodza, et al., 2007; Yzerbyt, Rocher, & Schadron, 1997; see also, Morton, Hornsey, & Postmes, 2009).

As the work reviewed in this section suggests, the typology opposing individual and group interests on a first dimension and social conflict versus more cognitive perspectives on a second dimension fails to capture the complex role of motivation in the emergence of stereotyping, prejudice, and discrimination. In the next section, we offer an alternative view of the motivational antecedents of prejudice along with empirical evidence that supports it.

INTEGRATIVE FRAMEWORK: THE ROLE OF INTEGRITY CONCERNS

Considering the basic needs or 'core motives' that typically govern social behavior provides a fruitful way to look at the role of motivation in stereotyping and prejudice (Fiske, 2004; Yzerbyt & Demoulin, 2010). In line with the idea that core motives influence people's beliefs, feelings, and behaviors in a wide variety of social settings, we propose that people's 'integrity concerns' – which engage a variety of core motives – fundamentally shape stereotyping, prejudice, and discrimination.

First, people have a basic need to understand and control their world. That is, they want to believe that what they 'know' about the world is firm and sound, motivating them to see the world as congruent with their expectations. Much early social cognition work, that is, attribution theories and balance theories, are rooted in the notion that people construct social knowledge to feel that they can understand, predict, and control their environment. Once people have secured a comprehension that seems functional, they will stick to it. To the extent that knowledge is socially validated, bias (or the lack thereof) will likely be affected by people's assumptions about what others around them profess.

Of course, the informational value of others hangs on who they are, which brings us to another integrity concern driving people's prejudice: Perceivers are likely to be biased against others in response to the need to belong, also sometimes called the need to

feel connected (Baumeister & Leary, 1995; Fiske, 2004). This concern is linked to the unmistakable reality that humans, as social animals, depend on others and are finely tuned to the reactions of others. In this respect, people's attachment to significant others represents a powerful force in leading people to adopt particular beliefs. Over and over, normative preoccupations promote dominant, often derogatory, views about outgroups. When people fear the vicissitudes of social exclusion (Williams, 2007) or contemplate their own mortality (Greenberg, Koole, & Pyszczynski, 2004), they are quick to conform and boost the values that they see as distinguishing their group from other groups.

A third and final integrity concern, long linked to prejudice, is people's desire to have a positive view of themselves and their peers (Crocker & Knight, 2005; Swann, 1987). This need to have value is at the heart of an enormous amount of theoretical and empirical work. Obviously, research examining the impact of individual characteristics such as self-esteem as well as the efforts aimed at uncovering the role of group membership and social identity in prejudice falls under this umbrella.

We now outline empirical findings that illustrate the role of these three integrity concerns in the emergence of prejudice. The three main classes of concerns – to know and to control, to belong and to connect, and to have positive value – all clearly play a role in the emergence of prejudice. At the same time, stereotyping, prejudice, and discrimination are often, if not always, over-determined. Does this all mean that prejudice is an unavoidable consequence of the existence of integrity concerns? We do not think so. In a final subsection, we outline the various ways by which these concerns can also be exploited to fight bigotry.

Integrity concerns and prejudice: The need to know and to control

Being in a state of uncertainty is unpleasant and people are therefore quick to rely on, or stick to, information that clarifies their course of action. This concern for knowledge and mastery represents the main (but not only) concern responsible for people's tendency to see individuals as simple instantiations of the stereotype of their group and the related propensity to see groups as homogeneous entities. That is, social categorization represents a prime tool for satisfying the need for mastery because it buys perceivers an enormous amount of information about others at a very low cost. One obvious explanation for people's reluctance to abandon their stereotypic beliefs is thus that they are not willing to question their *a priori* views that have generally served them well in the past. As a consequence, confirmation of hypotheses and even Pygmalion effects (i.e., self-fulfilling prophecies) are commonplace when it comes to stereotypic beliefs (Klein & Snyder, 2003).

One admittedly subtle way by which people perpetuate their *a priori* conception of groups is selective use of language. For instance, the linguistic category model (LCM, Semin & Fiedler, 1988), distinguishes four levels of language abstraction. Descriptive action verbs (DAV) are descriptions of an action with reference to a specific object and situation; they are context dependent (e.g., John kisses Angela). Interpretative action verbs (IAV) are interpretations of an action. IAV refers to a specific object and situation but goes beyond a mere description (e.g., John is comforting Angela). State verbs (SV) refer to a mental or emotional state, with reference to a specific object but not to a specific situation. They are independent of context (e.g., John loves Angela). Adjectives (ADJ) are highly abstract person dispositions. ADJ make no reference to specific objects, situations, or context (e.g., John is romantic). The LCM thus offers an ideal and indeed unobtrusive instrument to tap dispositional inferences. Building upon the LCM, Wigboldus, Semin, and Spears (2000) predicted and found that people rely on more (versus less) abstract language to describe and communicate information that was consistent (versus inconsistent) with their stereotypic expectations (Wigboldus & Douglas, 2007).

Tajfel (1981) suggested that stereotypes enable differentiation between groups, supply an explanation for the existing state of affairs, and provide people with a justification for their behaviors toward outgroup and outgroup members (Yzerbyt, Rocher, & Schadron, 1997). Similar positions can be found in current approaches that examine factors shaping the content of intergroup stereotypes (Cuddy, Fiske, & Glick, 2007; Fiske, Xu, Cuddy, 1999). For instance, according to the stereotype content model (Fiske, Xu, Cuddy, 1999), the characteristics that are typically selected in order to portray groups and group members are best considered as cognitive appraisals that feed into emotional reactions and behavior tendencies (Cuddy, Fiske, & Glick, 2007). Fiske and her colleagues (1999) provided impressive empirical evidence for the fact that stereotypic depictions are organized around two dimensions. The first, warmth, is responsive to the nature of the interdependence and level of cooperation between the groups and thus refers to people's expectations regarding others' intentions toward them. The second, competence, is sensitive to the differential hierarchical positions of the groups in the social system and has to do with the extent to which people think that others can act upon their intentions. This research on the fundamental dimensions of social perception (Abele & Wojciszke, 2007; Fiske, Cuddy, & Glick, 2007; Judd, James-Hawkins, Yzerbyt, et al., 2005) confirms but also specifies how social perceivers capitalize on stereotypes in order for group members to simultaneously secure the social system and provide value to their own group (Kay, Jost, & Mandisodza, 2007).

Integrity concerns and prejudice: The need to feel connected

The need to feel connected also promotes stereotyping and prejudice. It has long been suggested that social norms exert a huge impact on the way people embrace and propagate derogatory beliefs (Minard, 1952; Pettigrew, 1958). More recent work suggests that people support the views allegedly shared within their group as a means of coordinating their social behavior and securing group membership (Haslam, Oakes, McGarty, et al., 1996; Sechrist & Stangor, 2001).

For instance, Stangor, Sechrist, and Jost (2001) told participants about the beliefs held by other individuals (i.e., ingroup members) regarding African Americans. This information was either systematically more favorable or more unfavorable than the stereotype participants thought was shared within their ingroup. Participants showed a more positive (negative) stereotype when they learned that relevant others held a more favorable (unfavorable) stereotype. Focusing on stereotype change, Carnaghi and Yzerbyt (2007) investigated the effect of stereotypes held by a prospective audience on participants' reactions to a stereotype-disconfirming group member. Belgian participants learned about a stereotype allegedly held by an ingroup or an outgroup audience about Belgians and then received information about a Belgian who disconfirmed the stereotype. As predicted, the deviant was seen as less typical when he violated the stereotype held by an ingroup than by an outgroup audience. Also, participants' stereotype about Belgians was more similar to the one held by the ingroup audience. A mediational analysis confirmed that participants subtyped the disconfirming member in order to embrace the stereotype advocated by the ingroup audience. These findings emphasize the role of people's concern for the way their beliefs match those of a beloved group.

Integrity concerns and prejudice: The need to have value

Last but not least, the need to have value is a powerful force leading to the emergence of bias in favor of the ingroup and against the outgroup. Although ethnocentrism, a notion initially proposed by Sumner (1906), has always been the focus of much research, ingroup bias became a dominant topic of research among social psychologists after Tajfel and colleagues (Tajfel, Billig, Bundy, et al., 1971) reported their minimal group paradigm findings. Despite the fact that all factors known to trigger group favoritism, such as knowledge of group members, common fate, competition, etc., had been stripped from the experimental setting, their participants countered the norm of fairness and expressed bias in favor of their ingroup. This unexpected pattern proved extremely robust and constitutes the cornerstone of one of the most fruitful lines of research on intergroup relations (Brewer & Brown, 1998; Tajfel & Turner, 1979; for a recent review, Yzerbyt & Demoulin, 2010).

Other findings emphasize the combined impact of the need to have value and the need to know on information processing. The so-called ultimate attribution error constitutes a good illustration (Pettigrew, 1979). Researchers have proposed that the need to control their social environment leads perceivers to prefer dispositional over situational explanations to account for other people's actions (for a review, see Gilbert, 1998). For example, perceivers tend to assume that a person who lashes out must have an 'aggressive personality' rather than have been provoked. This is known as 'correspondence bias' or the 'fundamental attribution error.' But in intergroup situations, the need to have value intrudes, such that people preferentially use dispositional explanations for positive behaviors of ingroup members and negative behaviors of outgroup members, but prefer situational explanations of negative behaviors of ingroup members and positive behaviors of outgroup members. As further evidence of the subtle role played by language, Maass (1999) found that people select more (versus less) abstract linguistic forms to communicate about positive (versus negative) ingroup behaviors and negative (versus positive) outgroup behaviors.

Another example of the combined impact of the need to see one's group in a positive light and the need to know comes from the recent work on the ingroup projection model (IPM; Mummendey & Wenzel, 1999). According to the IPM, group members tend to perceive their own group as more prototypical of the inclusive category than the outgroup, at least if both the ingroup and the superordinate category are psychologically relevant for the self (i.e., high identification) and positively evaluated. Hence, the IPM claims that people who belong to a group tend to generalize typical ingroup characteristics to the superordinate category, that is, they project ingroup features (the prototype) onto the inclusive category. Not surprisingly, the more group members perceive their ingroup as relatively prototypical of the superordinate category, the more negative are their attitudes toward an outgroup.

The motivation not to be prejudiced

As much as integrity concerns may fuel bias, they may also be mobilized to minimize the impact of prejudice. There are several versions of this idea in contemporary research. For example, several researchers noted that the global decline of explicit, blatant, or so-called 'Jim Crow' racism can be attributed to the fact that new norms have been established and that people are keen to think of themselves as being in line with the current zeitgeist. As a result, social perceivers may not agree with stereotypic views as readily and definitely not discriminate against members of stigmatized groups as easily as when dominant norms promoted bigotry and derogatory opinions toward outgroups. Unfortunately, this does not mean that racism, sexism, ageism, and other 'isms' have disappeared (see Chapters in this volume by Dovidio et al.; Glick et al.). For some, the old ways have been truly abandoned in favor of genuine open-mindedness. For others, however, tolerance is less authentic because of lingering feelings of discomfort and dislike. In such cases, bias takes on more subtle forms and people embrace various routes to rationalization of prejudice.

The theory of modern racism (McConahay, 1986) and the related approach of symbolic racism (Sears & Henry, 2003) hold that people resolve the conflict between their egalitarian goals and their negative feelings about minorities by claiming that discrimination no longer exists (Swim, Aiken, Hall, et al., 1995). While endorsing equality (of opportunity) as an abstract principle, modern racists see their hostility to anti-discrimination policies as being based on rational grounds such as issues of fairness and justice. Modern racists think that they are treated unfairly and feel deprived. Closely linked to modern racism, the construct of subtle prejudice was developed to study prejudice against ethnic groups in Europe (Pettigrew & Meertens, 1995). Compared to modern racism, one belief that is also associated with subtle prejudice is the exaggeration of cultural differences. Although modern or subtle racism scales correlate with old-fashioned and blatant racism scales, respectively, these scales tend to uncover useful variability among individuals and this variability can then be linked to discrimination.

According to the work on aversive racism (Dovidio & Gaertner, 2004), the dissociation between supporting an egalitarian value system while at the same time experiencing negative feelings toward minorities as a result of socialization encourages people to deny the existence of any unflattering emotional reactions and pretend that members of minority groups only evoke positive feelings. The desire to appear unprejudiced, combined with the experience of discomfort and fear, leads aversive racists to avoidance and disengagement. When contact cannot be prevented, they opt for ambiguous behaviors or overcompensation. Negative feelings toward minorities can also leak out in subtle and rationalizable ways. The resulting behavior is not so much 'anti-minority' but subtly biased in favor of the dominant group. Ambiguity sometimes serves the purpose of avoidance. In a classic study, Snyder, Kleck, Strenta, et al. (1979) had nondisabled participants chose whether they wanted to watch a movie alongside a disabled individual or next to a nondisabled individual (both were confederates). When participants thought that the exact same (versus a different) movie was being played, they chose to watch the movie slightly more often (versus almost never) in the company of the disabled individual.

In the absence of good reasons to discriminate, people exercise scrupulous censorship over their discriminatory responses and try their best to suppress their derogatory beliefs (Monteith, Sherman, & Devine, 1998). Suppression may be practiced to such an extent among some low-prejudiced people (Monteith, Spicer, & Tooman, 1998) or people with chronic egalitarian goals (Moskowitz, Gollwitzer, Wasel, et al., 1999) that it becomes efficient and even automatized. Still, for other people, attempts at suppression are not always successful, meaning that suppression may have paradoxical rebound effects and even increase prejudice (Macrae, Bodenhausen, Milne, et al., 1994).

Several individual difference measures gauge the motivation to control and suppress prejudice. Plant and Devine (1998, 2001) suggest that the desire to respond without prejudice stems from two sources: because prejudice conflicts with a personal belief system or as a result of social pressure. For Crandall and Eshleman (2003), the role of normative responses should not be downplayed. Provided the environment is arranged so as to minimize or even proscribe stigmatizing reactions, people develop an internal motivation to control prejudice. The more an individual has come to internalize the egalitarian norm, the lower the expressed prejudice will be, even on implicit measures (Amodio, Harmon-Jones, & Devine, 2003). The interest of Plant and Devine's (2001) distinction is that violations against internal motivation should produce feelings of guilt. In contrast, failure in the case of external motivation should result in reactions of anger as well as threat regarding other people's reactions. Additionally, it has been shown that people high in internal motivation but low in external motivation respond in more positive ways, in some respects, than those high on both.

Dunton and Fazio (1997) combine internal and external motivation to control prejudice into a general concern with acting prejudiced that finds its roots in a pro-egalitarian upbringing and positive experiences with stigmatized people. Dunton and Fazio (1997) also point to

people's restraint to avoid disputes that stem from a prejudiced background and negative experiences with stigmatized members, which involves staying away from trouble and arguments with targets of the prejudice. Using a basic psychological distinction in regulatory focus (Higgins, 1997) and in light of their specific antecedents, the concern with acting prejudiced could be reformulated in terms of a promotion focus whereas the restraint to avoid dispute can best be reframed in terms of a prevention focus.

Even when prejudiced people would seem to be in control and act in a nonprejudiced manner, a sizeable share of their responses to the situation is less controllable and allows prejudice to 'leak out.' Dovidio and colleagues (Dovidio, Kawakami, & Gaertner, 2002) found evidence for such dissociation, and thus a mix of cues disconfirming and confirming prejudice, when they asked their White participants to meet with Black confederates. Whereas participants' explicit prejudice was correlated with the friendliness of what they said (a controlled behavior), their implicit prejudice was linked to the friendliness of their nonverbal actions (an automatic behavior). In general, situations in which behavioral control is more difficult, such as when norms remain unclear or when the measures are unobtrusive may facilitate the materialization of prejudice. Recent research also confirms that the suppression of prejudice requires cognitive resources and factors that undermine people's mental energy allow prejudice to be expressed in behavior (Richeson & Shelton, 2007).

PROMISING AVENUES

Our review suggests that the role of motivation in prejudice is best understood as reflecting the same core motives (to know, to belong, and to have positive value) that underlie other human behavior. The need to belong and the need to have value are perhaps the two most widely recognized concerns that are likely to foster distrust and derogation. In contrast, the motive to know and to control has long been overlooked as a concern in its own right. Because people have a basic need to feel that they master their environment and know what they are confronted with, they are not tempted to question their *a priori* beliefs. This means that substantial energy may be invested in trying to bring the information coming from the environment in line with stereotypic beliefs. That this concern should drive unwanted affective reactions and discriminatory behaviors should thus come as no surprise. As we hope to have shown, stereotyping, prejudice, and discrimination thus occur because biases often fulfill one or more of these three concerns.

But while such integrity concerns certainly bias perception, people still have to deal with situational constraints and the actual characteristics of the stimulus (i.e., reality also constrains perceptions). We are inclined to think, however, that reality constraints enjoy limited power in modifying people's conceptions. Clearly, stereotypic expectations can only be questioned to the extent that members of the stereotyped group provide a sufficient amount of evidence of disconfirming behaviors. However, the ability for social perceivers to confirm their beliefs, both through biased perception and through shaping their environment so that it matches or at least fails to question their expectations, cannot be underestimated. For instance, in a series of studies examining why people often do not want to have contact with outgroup members, Shelton and Richeson (2005) found that individuals explained their own inaction in terms of their fear of being rejected because of their race but attributed the out-group members' inaction to their lack of interest. Evidently, if people avoid contact in the first place, little can be done to correct misconceptions, the first of which is the very reason underlying the absence of contact. If people manage to overcome their reluctance to meet and interact with members of a stigmatized minority and if accumulated information contradicts the validity of whatever *a priori* beliefs are brought into the situation, people may eventually modify their views and abandon

erroneous stereotypes. However, although factual information is important, no amount of information will suffice to counter old habits if individuals experience that their integrity concerns are being hurt.

Just as integrity concerns trigger bias, it is most important to rely on people's core motives in order to combat prejudice. Perhaps the most striking examples of the efficiency of such a strategy come from the rich line of work devoted to intergroup contact (for reviews, see Brown & Hewstone, 2005; see Chapter 33 by Tausch & Hewstone, in this volume). In light of the fact that people will be motivated to have value for their group, intergroup settings that stress the existence of a common ingroup at the same time that they emphasize the unique features of the different subgroups are the ones that are most likely to be conducive to successful intergroup contact experiences. In our opinion, this position dovetails nicely with the growing understanding that groups and categories are not to be banned by definition and that a multicultural approach is often more profitable than a color-blind approach (Park & Judd, 2005). Multicultural settings would seem to provide both the need to know and the need to have value while at the same time allowing for prejudice to recede. Obviously, research on these issues offer much promise and should be intensified. Along similar lines, the work on (extended) intergroup friendship and perspective taking that capitalizes on people's tendency to see some overlap between themselves and outgroup members demonstrates how the value attached to the self can go hand in hand to promote understanding and combat prejudice (Brown & Hewstone, 2005). More research on this front is definitely in order.

As the above reference to multiculturalism suggests, the need to belong could also be used as a lever with which new normative beliefs can be promoted. In other words, people's sensitivity for inclusion constitutes an enormously powerful factor leading to opinion change and approval of new ways of approaching other groups, in particular stigmatized groups (Yzerbyt & Carnaghi, 2007). As Lewin (1948) illustrated in his classic research on people's food preferences: Change is best promoted by capitalizing on motivational forces, and in particular those factors that allow people to define together what reality ought to be.

CONCLUSION

At the end of this journey on the role of motivational processes in stereotyping, prejudice, and discrimination, it is possible to draw three lessons. The first is that cognition and motivation are definitely not to be considered in opposition when it comes to their impact on prejudice. The second is that the social and psychological forces that impinge on perceivers also work hand in hand to produce stereotypes, prejudice, and discrimination. Together, these two messages allow one to question a typology that has long worked as an implicit framework. The third, and most important, lesson is that it would be scientifically wrong and plain foolish to equate motivation with prejudice. In the battle against intolerance, motivation is as much the enemy as it is an ally.

REFERENCES

Abele, A. E., & Wojciszke, B. (2007). Agency and communion from the perspective of self versus others. *Journal of Personality and Social Psychology*, 93, 751–763.

Aberson, C. L., Healy, M., & Romero, V. (2000). Ingroup bias and self-esteem: A meta-analysis. *Personality and Social Psychology Review*, 4, 157–173.

Adorno, T. W., Frenkel-Brunswick, E., Levinson, D. J., & Sanford, R. N. (1950). *The Authoritarian Personality*. New York: Harper & Row.

Allport, G. W. (1954). *The Nature of Prejudice*. Cambridge, MA: Addison-Wesley.

Altemeyer, B. (1998). The other "authoritarian personality". In L. Berkowitz (Ed.), *Advances in Experimental Social Psychology* (Vol. 30, pp. 47–92). San Diego, CA: Academic Press.

Amodio, D. M., Harmon-Jones, E., & Devine, P. G. (2003). Individual difference in the activation and control of affective race bias as assessed by startle eye blink response and self-report. *Journal of Personality and Social Psychology*, 84, 738–753.

Baumeister, R. F., & Leary, M. R. (1995). The need to belong: Desire for interpersonal attachment as a fundamental human motivation. *Psychological Bulletin*, 117, 497–529.

Brewer, M. B., & Brown, R. J. (1998). Intergroup relations. In D. T. Gilbert, S. T. Fiske, & G. Lindzey (Eds), *The Handbook of Social Psychology*. (4th edition, Vol. 2, pp. 554–594). Boston, MA: McGraw-Hill.

Brown, R. J., & Hewstone, M. (2005). An integrative theory of intergroup contact. In M. P. Zanna (Ed.), *Advances in Experimental Social Psychology* (Vol. 37, pp. 255–343). San Diego, CA: Academic Press.

Carnaghi, A., & Yzerbyt, V. Y. (2007). Social consensus and stereotypes: The role of the audience in the maintenance of stereotypic beliefs. *European Journal of Social Psychology*, 37, 902–922.

Crandall, C. S., & Eshleman, A. (2003). A justification-suppression model of the expression and experience of prejudice. *Psychological Bulletin*, 129, 414–446.

Crocker, J. and Knight, K. M. (2005). Contingencies of self-worth. *Current Directions in Psychological Science*, 14, 200–203.

Cuddy, A. J. C., Fiske, S. T., & Glick, P. (2007). The BIAS Map: Behaviors from intergroup affect and stereotypes. *Journal of Personality and Social Psychology*, 92, 631–648.

Dambrun, M., Taylor, D. M., McDonald, D. A., Crush, J., & Méot, A. (2006). The relative deprivation-gratification continuum and the attitudes of South African toward immigrants: A test of the V-curve hypothesis. *Journal of Personality and Social Psychology*, 91, 1032–1044.

Danso, H. A., & Esses, V. M. (2001). Black experimenters and the intellectual test performance of White participants: The tables are turned. *Journal of Experimental Social Psychology*, 37, 158–165.

Devine, P. G., Plant, E. A., Amodio, D. M., Harmon-Jones, E., & Vance, S. L. (2002). The regulation of explicit and implicit race bias: The role of motivations to respond without prejudice. *Journal of Personality and Social Psychology*, 82, 835–848.

Dovidio, J. F., & Gaertner, S. L. (2004). Aversive racism. In M. P. Zanna (Ed.), *Advances in Experimental Social Psychology* (Vol. 36, pp. 1–52). Thousand Oaks, CA: Sage.

Dovidio, J. F., and Gaertner, S. L. (2010). Intergroup bias, In S. T. Fiske, D. T. Gilbert, and G. Lindzey (Eds), *The Handbook of Social Psychology*. (5th edition, Vol. 2, pp. 1084–1121). Hoboken, NJ: Wiley.

Dovidio, J. F., Kawakami, K., & Gaertner, S. L. (2002). Implicit and explicit prejudice and interracial interaction. *Journal of Personality and Social Psychology*, 82, 62–68.

Duckitt, J. (2001). A dual-process cognitive-motivational theory of ideology and prejudice. In M. P. Zanna (Ed.), *Advances in Experimental Social Psychology* (Vol. 33, pp. 41–112). San Diego, CA: Academic Press.

Dunton, B. C., & Fazio, R.H. (1997). An individual difference measure of motivation to control prejudiced reactions. *Personality and Social Psychology Bulletin*, 23, 316–326.

Ellemers, N., Spears, R., & Doosje, B. (1999). *Social Identity: Context, Commitment, Content*. Oxford, UK: Blackwell.

Esses, V. M., Jackson, L. M., & Armstrong, T. L. (1998). Intergroup competition and attitudes toward immigrants and immigration: An instrumental model of group conflict. *Journal of Social Issues*, 54, 699–724.

Fein, S., & Spencer, S. J. (1997). Prejudice as self-image maintenance: Affirming the self through derogating others. *Journal of Personality and Social Psychology*, 73, 31–44.

Fiske, S. T. (1998). Stereotyping, prejudice, and discrimination. In D. T. Gilbert, S. T. Fiske, & G. Lindzey (Eds), *The Handbook of Social Psychology*. (4th edition, Vol. 2, pp. 357–411). New York: McGraw-Hill.

Fiske, S. T. (2004). *Social Beings: A Core Motives Approach to Social Psychology*. New York: Wiley.

Fiske, S. T., Xu, J., Cuddy, A. C., & Glick, P. (1999). (Dis)respecting versus (dis)liking: Status and interdependence predict ambivalent stereotypes of competence and warmth. *Journal of Social Issues*, 55, 473–489.

Fiske, S. T., Cuddy, A. J. C., & Glick, P. (2007). First judge warmth, then competence: Fundamental social dimensions. *Trends in Cognitive Sciences*, 11, 77–83.

Fiske, S. T., & Neuberg, S. L. (1990). A continuum model of impression formation from category-based to individuating processes: Influences of information and motivation on attention and interpretation. In L. Berkowitz (Ed.), *Advances in Experimental and Social Psychology* (Vol. 23, pp. 1–74). San Diego, CA: Academic Press.

Fiske, S. T., & Taylor, S. E. (1984). *Social Cognition*. Reading, MA: Addison-Wesley.

Fiske, S. T., & Taylor, S. E. (2008). *Social Cognition: From Brains to Culture*. (1st edition). New York: McGraw-Hill.

Gilbert, D. T. (1998). Ordinary personology. In D. T. Gilbert, S. T. Fiske, & G. Lindzey (Eds), *The Handbook of Social Psychology*. (4th edition, Vol. 2, pp. 89–150). New York: McGraw-Hill.

Glick, P. (2002). Sacrificial lambs dressed in wolves' clothing: Envious prejudice, ideology, and the scapegoating of Jews. In L. S. Newman, & R. Erber (Eds), *Understanding Genocide: The Social Psychology of the Holocaust* (pp. 113–142). Oxford University Press.

Gramzow, R. H., & Gaertner, L. (2005). Self-esteem and favoritism toward novel in-groups: The self as an evaluative base. *Journal of Personality and Social Psychology*, 88, 801–815.

Greenberg, J., Koole, S. L., & Pyszczynski, T. (2004) (Eds), *Handbook of Experimental Existential Psychology*. New York: Guilford.

Guimond, S., Dambrun, M., Michinov, N., & Duarte, S. (2003). Does social dominance generate prejudice? Integrating individual and contextual determinants of intergroup cognition. *Journal of Personality and Social Psychology*, 84, 697–721.

Hamilton, D. L. (1981). *Cognitive Processes in Stereotyping and Intergroup Behavior*. Hillsdale, NJ: Lawrence Erlbaum Associates.

Haslam, S. A., Oakes, P. J., McGarty, C., Turner, J. C., Reynolds, K., & Eggins, R. (1996). Stereotyping and social influence: The mediation of stereotype applicability and sharedness by the views of in-group and out-group members. *British Journal of Social Psychology*, 35, 369–397.

Higgins, E. T. (1997). Beyond pleasure and pain. *American Psychologist*, 52, 1280–1300.

Hogg, M. A., & Abrams, D. (1988). *Social Identification: A Social Psychology of Intergroup Relations and Group Processes*. London: Routledge.

Jost, J. T., & Banaji, M. R. (1994). The role of stereotyping in system justification and the production of false consciousness. *British Journal of Social Psychology*, 33, 1–27.

Jost, J. T., Glaser, J., Kruglanski, A. W., & Sulloway, F. J. (2003). Political conservatism as motivated social cognition. *Psychological Bulletin*, 129, 339–375.

Judd, C. M., James-Hawkins, L., Yzerbyt, V. Y., & Kashima, Y. (2005). Fundamental dimensions of social judgment: Understanding the relations between competence and warmth. *Journal of Personality and Social Psychology*, 89, 899–913.

Kay, A. C., Jost, J. T., Mandisodza, A. N., Sherman, S. J., Petrocelli, J. V., & Johnson, A. L. (2007). Panglossian ideology in the service of system justification: How complementary stereotypes help us to rationalize inequality. *Advances in Experimental Social Psychology*, 38, 305–358.

Klein, O., & Snyder, M. (2003). Stereotypes and behavioral confirmation: From interpersonal to intergroup perspectives. *Advances in Experimental Social Psychology*, 35, 153–234.

Krueger, J. I. (2007). From social projection to social behaviour. *European Review of Social Psychology*, 18, 1–35.

Kunda, Z., & Oleson, K.C. (1995). Maintaining stereotypes in the face of disconfirmation: Constructing grounds for subtyping deviants. *Journal of Personality and Social Psychology*, 68, 565–79.

Kunda, Z., & Spencer, S. J. (2003). When do stereotypes come to mind and when do they color judgment? A goal-based theoretical framework for stereotype activation and application. *Psychological Bulletin*, 129, 522–544.

Kunda, Z., Davies, P. G., Adams, B. D., & Spencer, SJ. (2002). The dynamic time course of stereotype activation: Activation, dissipation, and resurrection. *Journal of Personality and Social Psychology*, 82, 283–299.

Levine, R. A., & Campbell, D. T. (1972). *Ethnocentrism: Theories of Conflict, Attitudes and Group Behavior.* New York: Willey.

Lewin, K. (1948). *Resolving Social Conflicts.* New York: Harper & Ross.

Maass, A. (1999). Linguistic intergroup bias: Stereotype perpetuation through language. *Advances in Experimental Social Psychology*, 31, 79–121.

Mackie, D. M., & Hamilton, D. L. (1993). *Affect, Cognition, and Stereotyping: Interactive Processes in Group Perception.* San Diego, CA: Academic Press.

Macrae, C. N., Bodenhausen, G. V., Milne, A. B., & Jetten, J. (1994). Out of mind but back in sight: Stereotypes on the rebound. *Journal of Personality and Social Psychology*, 67, 808–817.

McConahay, J. B. (1986). Modern racism, ambivalence, and the Modern Racism Scale. In J. F. Dovidio, & S. L. Gaertner (Eds), *Prejudice, Discrimination, and Racism* (pp. 91–125). Orlando, USA: Academic Press.

Minard, R. (1952). Race relation in Pocahontas coal field. *Journal of Social Issues*, 8, 29–44.

Monteith, M. J., Sherman, J. W., & Devine, P. G. (1998). Suppression as a stereotype control strategy. *Personality and Social Psychology Review*, 2, 63–82.

Monteith. M. J., Spicer, C. V., & Tooman, J. D. (1998). Consequences of stereotype suppression: Stereotypes on and not on the rebound. *Journal of Experimental Social Psychology*, 34, 355–377.

Morton T. A., Postmes, T., Haslam, S. A., and Hornsey, M. J. (2009). Theorizing gender in the face of social change: Is there anything essential about essentialism? *Journal of Personality and Social Psychology*, 96, 653–664.

Moskowitz, G. B., Gollwitzer, P. M., Wasel, W., & Schaal, B. (1999). Preconscious control of stereotype activation through chronic egalitarian goals. *Journal of Personality and Social Psychology*, 77, 167–184.

Mummendey, A., & Wenzel, M. (1999). Social discrimination and tolerance in intergroup relations: Reactions to intergroup difference. *Personality and Social Psychology Review*, 3, 158–174.

Otten, S., & Wentura, D. (2001). Self-anchoring and in-group favoritism: An individual profile analysis. *Journal of Experimental Social Psychology*, 37, 525–532.

Park, B., & Judd, C. M. (2005). Rethinking the link between categorization and prejudice within the social cognition perspective. *Personality and Social Psychology Review*, 9, 108–130.

Pettigrew, T. F. (1958). Personality and socio-cultural factors in intergroup attitudes: A cross-national comparison. *Journal of Conflict Resolution*, 2, 29–42.

Pettigrew, T. F. (1979). The ultimate attribution error: Extending Allport's cognitive analysis of prejudice. *Personality and Social Psychology Bulletin*, 5, 461–476.

Pettigrew, T. F., & Meertens, R. W. (1995). Subtle and blatant prejudice in Western Europe. *European Journal of Social Psychology*, 25, 57–75.

Pettigrew, T. F., Christ, O., Wagner, U., Meertens, R. W., van Dick, R., & Zick, A. (2008). Relative deprivation and intergroup prejudice. *Journal of Social Issues*, 64, 385–401.

Plant, E. A., & Devine, P. G. (1998). Internal and external motivation to respond without prejudice. *Journal of Personality and Social Psychology*, 75, 811–832.

Plant, E. A., & Devine, P. G. (2001). Responses to other-imposed pro-Black pressure: Acceptance or backlash? *Journal of Experimental Social Psychology*, 37, 486–501.

Richeson, J. A., & Shelton, J. N. (2007). Negotiating interracial interactions: Costs, consequences, and possibilities. *Current Directions in Psychological Science*, 16, 316–320.

Rubin, M., & Hewstone, M. (1998). Social identity theory's self-esteem hypothesis: A review and some suggestions for clarification. *Personality and Social Psychology Review*, 2, 40–62.

Schmitt, M. T., Branscombe, N. R., & Kappen, D. M. (2003). Attitudes toward group-based inequality: Social dominance or social identity? *British Journal of Social Psychology*, 42, 161–186.

Sears, D. O., & Henry, P. J. (2003). The origins of symbolic racism. *Journal of Personality and Social Psychology*, 85, 259–275.

Sechrist, G. B., & Stangor, C. (2001). Perceived consensus influences intergroup behavior and stereotype accessibility. *Journal of Personality and Social Psychology*, 2, 645–654.

Semin, G. R., & Fiedler, K. (1988). The cognitive functions of linguistic categories in describing persons: Social cognition and language. *Journal of Personality and Social Psychology*, 54, 558–567.

Shelton, J. N., & Richeson, J. A. (2005). Intergroup contact and pluralistic ignorance. *Journal of Personality and Social Psychology*, 88, 91–107.

Shelton, J. N., & Richeson, J. A. (2006). Interracial interactions: A relational approach. *Advances in Experimental Social Psychology*. 38, 121–181.

Sherif, M. (1967). *Group Conflict and Co-operation: Their Social Psychology*. London: Routledge and Kegan Paul.

Sidanius, J., & Pratto, F. (1999). *Social Dominance: An Intergroup Theory of Social Hierarchy and Oppression*. New York: Cambridge University Press.

Skitka, L. J., Mullen, E., Griffin, T., Hutchinson, S., & Chamberlin, B. (2002). Dispositions, scripts, or motivated correction? Understanding ideological differences in explanations for social problems. *Journal of Personality and Social Psychology*, 83, 470–487.

Snyder, M. L., Kleck, R. E., Strenta, A., & Mentzer, S. J. (1979). Avoidance of the handicapped: An attributional ambiguity analysis. *Journal of Personality and Social Psychology*, 37, 2297–2306.

Spencer, S. J., Fein, S., Zanna, M., & Olson, J. M. (2002). *Motivated Social Perception: The Ontario Symposium* (Vol. 9). Mahwah, NJ: Erlbaum.

Stangor, C., Sechrist, G. B., & Jost, J. T. (2001). Changing racial beliefs by providing consensus information. *Personality and Social Psychology Bulletin*, 27, 486–496.

Stephan, W. G., & Stephan, C. W. (2000). An integrated threat theory of prejudice. In S. Oskamp (Ed.), *Reducing Prejudice and Discrimination: The Claremont Symposium on Applied Psychology* (pp. 23–45). Mahwah, NJ: Erlbaum.

Strack, F., & Deutsch, R. (2004). Reflective and impulsive determinants of social behavior. *Personality and Social Psychology Review*, 8, 220–247.

Stroebe, W., & Insko, C. A. (1989). Stereotypes, prejudice, and discrimination. Changing conceptions in theory and research. In D. Bar-Tal, C. F. Grauman, A. W. Kruglanski, & W. Stroebe (Eds), *Stereotypes and Prejudice: Changing Conceptions* (pp. 3–34). New York: Springer-Verlag.

Sumner, W. G. (1906). *Folkways*. New York: Ginn.

Swann, W. B. (1987). Identity negotiation: Where two roads meet. *Journal of Personality and Social Psychology*, 53, 1038–1051.

Swim, J. K., Aiken, K. J., Hall, W. S., & Hunter, B. A. (1995). Sexism and racism: Old-fashioned and modern prejudices. *Journal of Personality and Social Psychology*, 68, 199–214.

Tajfel, H. (1981). *Human Groups and Social Categories*. Cambridge: Cambridge University Press.

Tajfel, H., & Turner, J. C. (1979). An integrative theory of intergroup relations. In W. G. Austin, & S. Worchel (Eds), *The Psychology of Intergroup Relations*. Monterey, CA: Brooks-Cole.

Tajfel, H., Billig, M. G., Bundy, R. P., & Flament, C. (1971). Social categorization and intergroup behaviour. *European Journal of Social Psychology*, 1, 149–178.

Tougas, F., & Beaton, A. M. (2001). Personal and group relative deprivations: Connecting the "I" to the "we". In I. Walker, & H. Smith (Eds), *Relative Deprivation: Specification, Development, and Integration* (pp. 119–135). New York: Cambridge University Press.

Turner, J. C., & Reynolds, K. J. (2003). Why social dominance theory has been falsified. *British Journal of Social Psychology*, 42, 199–206.

Turner, J. C., Hogg, M. A., Oakes, P. J., Reicher, S. D., & Wheterel, MS. (1987). *Rediscovering the Social Group. A Self-Categorization Theory*. Oxford, UK: Blackwell.

Verkuyten, M. (2007). Ethnic in-group favoritism among minority and majority groups: Testing the self-esteem hypothesis among preadolescents. *Journal of Applied Social Psychology*, 37, 486–500.

Walker, I., & Smith, H. J. (2002). *Relative Deprivation Theory: Specification, Development, and Integration*. New York: Cambridge University Press.

Wigboldus, D. H. J., Semin, G. R., & Spears, R. (2000). How do we communicate stereotypes? Linguistic biases and inferential consequences. *Journal of Personality and Social Psychology*, 78, 5–18.

Wigboldus, D. H. J., & Douglas, K. M. (2007). Language, expectancies and intergroup relations. In K. Fiedler (Ed.), *Social Communication* (pp. 79–106). New York: Psychology Press.

Williams, K. D. (2007). Ostracism. *Annual Review of Psychology*, 58, 425–452.

Yzerbyt, V. Y., & Carnaghi, A. (2007). Stereotype change in the social context. In Y. Kashima, K. Fiedler, & P. Freytag (Eds), *Stereotype Dynamics: Language-based Approaches to Stereotype Formation, Maintenance, and Transformation*. Mahwah, NJ: Laurence Erlbaum. Associates.

Yzerbyt, V.Y., & Corneille, O. (2005). Cognitive process: Reality constraints and integrity concerns in social perception. In J. F. Dovidio, P. Glick, & L. Rudman (Eds), *On the Nature of Prejudice: 50 Years After Allport* (pp. 175–191). London, UK: Blackwell.

Yzerbyt, V. Y., & Demoulin, S. (2010). Intergroup relations. In S. T. Fiske, D. T. Gilbert, & G. Lindzey

(Eds), *The Handbook of Social Psychology* (5th edition, Vol. 2, pp. 1023–1083). Hoboken, NJ: Wiley.

Yzerbyt, V. Y., Rocher, S. J., & Schadron, G. (1997). Stereotypes as explanations: A subjective essentialistic view of group perception. In R. Spears, P. Oakes, N. Ellemers, & A. Haslam (Eds), *The Psychology of Stereotyping and Group Life* (pp. 20–50). Oxford: Basil Blackwell.

Yzerbyt, V. Y., Coull, A., & Rocher, S. J. (1999). Fencing off the deviant: The role of cognitive resources in the maintenance of stereotypes. *Journal of Personality and Social Psychology*, 77, 449–62.

10

Individual Differences

Leanne S. Son Hing and Mark P. Zanna

ABSTRACT

People have generalized prejudice levels: those who are more prejudiced toward one outgroup tend to be more prejudiced toward others. We review how individual differences in prejudice have been assessed (explicitly and implicitly) and the predictors of generalized prejudice. Social dominance orientation (SDO) and right-wing authoritarianism (RWA) are the best predictors of explicit prejudice. Why? One account suggests that they are dispositional sources, and a second proposes that they are ideological sources, of explicit prejudice. A third account suggests that they are both aspects of conservatism, which predicts prejudice. Finally, a fourth account suggests that they are aspects of higher order constructs that are the sources of both explicit and implicit prejudice. We close with suggested research directions and conclusions.

INDIVIDUAL DIFFERENCES

Although definitions vary, prejudice can be defined as a negative attitude toward outgroups marked by cognitions (e.g., stereotypes), affects (e.g., antipathy), and behaviors (e.g., discrimination; Zanna & Rempel, 1988). Just as individuals differ in the extent to which they endorse any attitude, they differ in the extent to which they endorse prejudiced attitudes, such as racism or sexism. How stable are individual differences in prejudice across target groups? On the one hand, it is possible that prejudice toward a specific group is an attitude formed on the basis of particular, unique experiences with that group. On the other hand, it is possible that prejudice toward one group reflects a general tendency to form negative evaluations toward a variety of outgroups. By and large, the evidence supports the latter: prejudice toward various groups tends to covary. Put differently, people differ in how dispositionally prejudiced they are (Allport, 1954). Dispositional roots of prejudice include personality traits, such as authoritarianism; cognitive biases, such as inflexible thinking; and socio-political ideologies, such as conservatism or a desire for group hierarchy.

In this chapter, we present a brief history of the measurement and sources of individual differences in prejudice. There are different ways in which these diverse literatures can be integrated, and evidence is presented for and against these perspectives. Given the current integration and analyses, suggestions are made for future research that would best advance our understanding of individual differences in prejudice. A summary conclusion is provided.

BRIEF HISTORY

Before discussing the bases of individual differences in prejudice, it is important to consider how to measure such potentially sensitive attitudes. Approaches to this problem have changed over time. Individual differences in self-reported prejudice are typically assessed with questionnaire measures. Historically, scales tapped people's endorsement of traditional or old-fashioned prejudice (e.g., opposition to racial integration); however, as social tolerance for prejudice has decreased, so has the endorsement of (Firebaugh & Davis, 1988; Schuman, Steeh, & Bobo, 1985) and the predictive validity of (McConahay, 1983; Pettigrew & Meertens, 1995) old-fashioned prejudice measures. Consequently, scales were designed to tap more subtle and contemporary forms of prejudice, such as modern racism (McConahay, 1986). In time, measures of contemporary prejudice were demonstrated to have face validity. Knowing that their outgroup attitudes are being assessed, participants can choose to appear less prejudiced on self-report measures (Fazio, Jackson, Dunton, et al., 1995). For instance, the stronger people's internal motivation to respond without prejudice, the lower their scores on the Modern Racism Scale (Plant & Devine, 1998). Still, measures of contemporary prejudice predict attitudes toward social issues, such as voting preferences (Swim, Aikin, Hall, et al., 1995) or affirmative action attitudes (Bobocel, Son Hing, et al., 1998).

Given concerns regarding the transparency of explicit measures of prejudice, more indirect means of measurement were developed, namely implicit ones. Whereas explicit measures of prejudice assess participants' consciously accessed, self-reported attitudes toward outgroups, implicit measures typically assess participants' split second, positive or negative associations with outgroups – often in comparison with in-groups (e.g., The Implicit Association Test or IAT; Greenwald, McGhee, & Schwartz, 1998). Some contend that people hold only one attitude, which can be assessed with implicit measures and that any disconnect between people's implicit prejudice and their self-reported explicit prejudice can be explained by their motivation to control prejudice (Dunton & Fazio, 1997; Fazio & Olson, 2003) and by their perceptions of the prevalence of discrimination (Gawronski & Bodenhausen, 2006). However, others suggest that people hold both implicit and explicit prejudiced attitudes, and that each reflects an important and potentially independent component of one's attitude toward outgroups (Wilson, Lindsey, & Schooler, 2000). Indeed, explicit and implicit prejudice load on separate factors (Cunningham, Nezlek, & Banaji, 2004), tend to be only weakly related (Hofmann, Gawronski, Gschwendner, et al., 2005) and they account for different (Dovidio, Kawakami, Johnson, et al., 1997; McConnell & Leibold, 2001) and unique effects in people's discriminatory behavior (Lambert, Payne, Ramsey, et al., 2005). Therefore, when exploring the bases of prejudice, both explicit and implicit prejudice should be considered.

Turning now to the issue of what predicts individual differences in prejudice, it is essential to note that people who score high on an explicit measure of prejudice toward one group, such as visible minorities (or people of color), also tend to score higher in prejudice toward other groups such as gays, women, and the poor (Altemeyer, 1998; Aosved & Long, 2006; Bäckström & Björklund, 2007). The same is true for implicit measures of prejudice (Cunningham, Nezlek, & Banaji,, 2004). Why are some people higher in generalized prejudice than others?

Early theory, which stemmed from a psychoanalytic approach, focused on the authoritarian personality (Adorno, Frenkel-Brunswik, Levinson, et al., 1950). Authoritarians are thought to have overly strict parents and to hold rigid regard for conventions. Authoritarians' prejudice was thought to result from a projection of unacceptable impulses (e.g., fear, sex) onto powerless outgroup members. The focus was on individual differences that made people susceptible to prejudice due to pathological personalities

(Duckitt, 1992; see Chapter 2 by Duckitt, this volume). Expanding on these ideas, Allport (1954) wrote of the 'prejudiced personality,' which is characterized by a threat orientation, moralistic values, punitive attitudes, bifurcated thinking, need for definiteness and social order, and a preference for authority and hierarchy. In addition, Allport focused on the cognitive components of prejudice (i.e., stereotypes) that stem from normal processes (Pettigrew, 2005).

Research on authoritarianism waned due to theoretical ambiguities, unsupportive findings, a move away from psychoanalytic approaches, and flaws with the measures (e.g., acquiescence bias) used to assess authoritarianism (Christie, 1991; Nelson, 2006). In the 1960s and 1970s, researchers departed from an individual difference approach for understanding the roots of prejudice and instead focused on socio-cultural factors, such as group interests (Duckitt, 1992). Then, with the cognitive revolution in psychology and investigations of the minimal group paradigm (Tajfel, 1970), investigations of stereotypes and categorizations dominated those of prejudice (Pettigrew, 2005).

An exception to this trend, in the 1980s, was the aforementioned work on contemporary forms of prejudice, such as symbolic racism (Kinder & Sears, 1981), aversive racism (Gaertner & Dovidio, 1986), and ambivalent racism (Katz & Hass, 1988). These models all share the assumption that people's expression of prejudice depends on the strength of suppression factors, such as egalitarianism (Crandall & Eshleman, 2005). Measures of contemporary prejudice were shown to predict opposition toward racial policies, such as busing and affirmative action (Sears & Henry, 2005; McConahay, 1986). Thus, individual differences in prejudice were still a significant social issue (Duckitt, 1992). However, this research did not test the bases of individual differences in contemporary prejudice.

Work on cognitive processes and stereotyping led to investigations of prejudice and how it is related to individual differences in styles of thinking. The higher people are in their need for cognitive closure, rigidity

(Webster & Kruglanski, 1994), need for simple structure, personal need for structure (Neuberg & Newsom, 1993), preference for consistency (Cialdini, Trost, & Newsom, 1995), and intolerance of ambiguity (Budner, 1962); or the lower their need for cognition (Cacioppo & Petty, 1982), or cognitive complexity (Webster & Kruglanski, 1994), the more they tend to express explicit prejudice and tend to stereotype outgroup members (Rokeach, 1948; Schaller, Boyd, Yohannes, et al., 1995; Stangor & Thompson, 2002). This style of thinking, marked by rigidity and a desire for simplicity and certainty, can be described as cognitive conservatism. Interestingly, cognitive conservatism is not only related to participants' explicit prejudice, but it is also related to prejudice levels assessed with implicit measures (Cunningham, Nezlek, & Banaji, 2004).

Starting in the 1980s, research on the bases of individual differences in prejudice was revived by work on right-wing authoritarianism (RWA) (Altemeyer, 1981, 1998). RWA is a refined conceptualization and measurement of authoritarianism that involves: authoritarian submission or a tendency to defer to those considered to be legitimate authority figures, authoritarian aggression (i.e., holding punitive attitudes toward those labeled wrongdoers by authorities), and conventionalism or adherence to the norms that authorities establish (Altemeyer, 1981). RWA predicts explicit prejudice toward ethnic minorities, women, disabled people, deviants, and in particular gays (Duckitt, 2006; Lippa & Arad, 1999; Peterson, Doty, & Winter, 1993; Whitely, 1999). Alone RWA significantly predicts *implicit* prejudice toward Blacks (Rowatt & Franklin, 2004) but not gays (Rowatt, Tsang, Kelly, et al., 2006) or Muslims (Rowatt, Franklin, & Cotton, 2005). When aggregated with other measures of ideology, RWA predicts implicit prejudice toward gays, Jews, and the poor (Cunningham, Nezlek, & Banaji, 2004). Hence, the evidence for RWA to predict implicit prejudice is mixed.

In the 1990s, work on individual differences received further attention due to the introduction of social dominance theory

(Sidanius and Pratto, 1999). Social dominance orientation (SDO) is the degree to which people oppose equality and believe that society should be hierarchically structured, with some groups having higher status than others (Pratto, Sidanius, Stallworth, et al., 1994). There is a great deal of evidence that people higher in SDO are more sexist, racist (e.g., toward Blacks, Aboriginals, Indians, Arabs, Asians), and prejudiced toward immigrants, lesbians, gay men, feminists, housewives, and physically disabled people (e.g., Altemeyer, 1998; Duckitt, 2001, 2006; Duckitt, Wagner, du Plessis, et al., 2002; Lippa & Arad, 1999; Pratto, Sidnius, Stallworth, et al., 1994; Van Hiel & Mervielde, 2002; Whitley, 1999). To date, there is no evidence that, under normal conditions, SDO predicts implicit prejudice toward outgroups (Pratto & Shih, 2000; Rowatt, Franklin, & Cotton, 2005). SDO might predict explicit, but not implicit, prejudice if SDO guides people's attitudes in a deliberative manner based on propositional reasoning (i.e., consistency with other beliefs; Gawronski & Bodenhausen, 2006).

Remarkably, it has recently been discovered that SDO and RWA together account for up to 50 per cent of the variance in people's level of explicit prejudice toward a variety of outgroups (Altemeyer, 1998; McFarland & Adelson, 1996). McFarland and Adelson (1996) found that SDO and RWA accounted for the bulk of individual differences in people's generalized prejudice (i.e., prejudice toward a variety of groups). The only predictors to account for additional variance in generalized prejudice were participants' gender and levels of empathy. In general, the relation between SDO and RWA is positive but weak, particularly in North American samples (Duckitt, 2001). Together, SDO and RWA are powerful predictors because they each uniquely account for prejudice (e.g., Altemeyer, 1998; Duckitt, Wagner, du Plessis, et al., 2002). Altemeyer (2004) examined those cases where individuals scored high (i.e., in the top quartile) in both SDO and RWA. These 'double highs' were significantly more prejudiced toward a variety

of ethnic groups, compared with other study participants.

In the last couple of decades, due to theoretical and methodological advances in studying personality (i.e., the Big Five), research on the link between personality and the susceptibility of being prejudiced has re-emerged. People who are lower in the big five-personality factor of agreeableness (Ekehammar, Akrami, Gylje, et al., 2004; Graziano, Bruce, Tobin, et al., 2007), and its facet tender-mindedness (Duckitt, 2001; Ekehammar & Akrami, 2007), tend to be more prejudiced; as do people lower in empathy for others (Bäckström and Björklund, 2007; Stephan & Finlay, 1999) and in warmth (Ekehammar & Akrami, 2007).[1] In addition, people who are lower in the big five personality factor of openness to experience; and its facets, openness to re-examining values and openness to one's feelings, tend to be more prejudiced (Ekehammar & Akrami, 2003).

Finally, people have studied religiosity as a basis of prejudice. The more people hold fundamentalist religious beliefs, the more they tend to be explicitly prejudiced (Altemeyer, 1996; Altemeyer & Hunsberger, 1992), and implicitly prejudiced (Rowatt & Franklin, 2004). However, those who hold merely orthodox (as distinct from fundamentalist) beliefs are not necessarily more prejudiced (Laythe, Finkel, Bringle, et al., 2002). In the contexts where religion is positively related to prejudice, it is due primarily to the rigid thinking (fundamentalism, authoritarianism) that often accompanies religious belief. However, when examining people who are equal in such rigidity, greater religiosity is actually associated with less prejudice (Hansen & Norenzayan, 2006).

ANALYSES AND INTEGRATIVE FRAMEWORKS

The individual differences that predict generalized prejudice can appear to be a laundry list. In addition, it is unclear why SDO and RWA play such a central role in predicting prejudice. There are four related, yet separate, perspectives in the literature that can be drawn on to address this issue. One theoretical perspective depicts SDO and RWA as dispositional sources of prejudice. A second portrays SDO and RWA as ideological sources of prejudice. A third perspective, which frames SDO and RWA as conservatism, can be drawn on to help account for their relations with prejudice. Finally, a fourth perspective considers SDO and RWA as indicators of broader socio-political ideologies, which are the source of prejudice. This final perspective considers both dimensions of prejudice: explicit and implicit.

One perspective is that SDO and RWA are personality types prone to prejudice. SDO could be the dispositional basis for a form of prejudice driven by self-enhancement and competition with other groups (Altemeyer, 1998; Whitely, 1999), as people higher in SDO are more likely to value power (Duriez & Van Hiel, 2002), strive for dominance (Son Hing, Bobocel, Zanna, et al., 2007), and see the world as a competitive place (Duckitt, 2001). RWA could be the dispositional basis for a form of prejudice driven by a fear of deviant or dangerous groups, who threaten traditional values (Altemeyer, 1998; Whitely, 1999), as people higher in RWA will submit more to authority (Heaven & Bucci, 2001; Son Hing, Bobocel, Zanna, et al., 2007) and to conventions (Altemeyer, 1996), and see the world as a dangerous place (Duckitt, 2001).

To explore whether high SDOs authoritarian dominance and high RWAs authoritarian submission are, in fact, *dispositional* sources of prejudice, it is important to consider how SDO and RWA relate to personality traits that predict prejudice. People higher in SDO score lower on the big five factor agreeableness, are less warm, sympathetic, expressive, agreeable, nurturing, concerned with others, and tender-minded than people lower in SDO (Heaven & Bucci, 2001; Pratto, Sidnius, Stallworth, et al., 1994). As discussed earlier, this cluster of personality traits predicts prejudice. Similarly, people higher in RWA score lower on the big five factor openness to experience (Ekehammar, Akrami, Gylje, et al., 2004; Heaven & Bucci,

2001), and are judged to be less creative and more narrow in interests (Lippa & Arad, 1999). As stated earlier, these traits predict prejudice. It has been found that the path from agreeableness (or tender-mindedness) to prejudice is mediated by SDO (Sibley & Duckitt, 2008). Similarly, the relation between openness to experience and prejudice is partially mediated by RWA (Sibley & Duckitt, 2008). Thus, it appears that SDO and RWA are related to personality traits that predict prejudice.

A second perspective (Duckitt, 2001) discounts the notion that SDO and RWA are personality constructs because both measures require participants to indicate their social attitudes – not their dispositions (Duckitt, Wagner, du Plessis, et al., 2002). In addition, the effects of SDO and RWA on behavior depend on situational primes, which could suggest that SDO and RWA are not dispositional (Reynolds, Turner, Haslam, et al., 2001; Schmitt, Branscombe, & Kappen, 2003). Rather, it is proposed that SDO and RWA represent two socio-political and socio-cultural attitude-value-belief dimensions (Duckitt, 2001). Repeatedly, investigations of socio-political attitudes and values reveal two independent dimensions. One reflects social conservatism,[2] authoritarianism, and traditionalism versus liberalism, openness, and personal freedom; and the second reflects power, hierarchy, and selfishness versus egalitarianism, humanism, and altruism (Eysenck, 1954; Kerlinger, 1984; Saucier, 2000; Stangor & Leary, 2006). SDO is significantly related to the second dimension but not the first; RWA is significantly related to the first dimension but not the second (Altemeyer, 1998; Duriez & Van Hiel, 2002; Saucier, 2000).

Duckitt (2001) has found convincing support for his model that SDO and RWA are socio-political ideologies that independently stem from different worldviews. People higher (versus lower) in SDO are more likely to view the world as a competitive jungle, whereas people higher (vs. lower) in RWA are more likely to view the world as a dangerous place. These worldviews are shaped by different personalities (i.e., low tender-mindedness, and high social conformity, respectively). This model suggests that SDO should lead to a competitive/dominance driven prejudice, whereas RWA should lead to a threat/control driven prejudice (Duckitt, Wagner, du Plessis, et al., 2002). Duckitt (2006) has found that the relation between SDO and prejudice is mediated by perceptions that one must compete with outgroups for outcomes and resources. Similarly, the relation between RWA and prejudice is mediated by perceptions that outgroups threaten one's traditions and stability. Furthermore, SDO – more than RWA – predicts prejudice toward powerless groups, and RWA – more than SDO – predicts prejudice toward unconventional groups (Altemeyer, 1998).

A third perspective is that SDO and RWA reflect two basic components of political conservatism (Jost, Glaser, Kruglanski, et al., 2003). An implication of this perspective is that conservatism could be considered the root of people's prejudice. According to Jost et al., political conservatism has two components. First, conservatism purportedly involves acceptance of inequality, as captured by the SDO scale. In support of this notion, SDO and political conservatism are related (Federico & Sidanius, 2002; Sidanius & Pratto, 1993; Sidanius, Pratto, & Bobo, 1996). Second, conservatism involves resistance to change, as captured by the RWA Scale. In support of this notion, RWA and political conservatism are related (Altemeyer, 1998; Feldman, 2003; Van Hiel, Pandalaere, & Duriez, 2004). The ideological belief systems of acceptance of inequality and resistance to change ostensibly are adopted to help combat the psychological bases of political conservatism: threat and uncertainty (Jost, Napier, Thorisdottir, et al., 2007).

Not only can Jost, Glaser, Kruglanski, et al.'s (2003) model explain why prejudice and political conservatism are related (Meertens & Pettigrew, 1997; Tarman & Sears, 2005; Van Hiel et al., 2004; cf. Sidanius, Pratto, & Bobo et al., 1996) but, following the causal chain backward, it could account for why prejudice is related

to cognitive conservatism: both reflect an intolerance of uncertainty. Similarly, this model could account for why prejudice is related to holding rigid beliefs, such as religious fundamentalism. In support of this model, cognitive conservatism, RWA, (anti)egalitarianism, explicit prejudice, and implicit prejudice have all been found to interrelate (Cunningham , Nezlek, & Banaji, et al., 2004).

If conservatism is the root of prejudice, then prejudice should generally be higher among those on the political right than those on the political left. Yet, the evidence is mixed. This inconsistency could derive from a variety of issues. First, conservatism might not always predict prejudice because the construct is operationally defined in too many, potentially discrepant ways. In other words, it might be inappropriate to treat conservatism as a unitary construct (Crowson, Thoma, & Hestevold, 2005). There is evidence that political, economic, and social conservatism are separate and only weakly related (Duckitt, 2001; Fleishman, 1988), with differential relations with other constructs (Van Hiel & Mervielde, 2004). For instance, social conservatism – but not economic conservatism – is uniquely predicted by RWA (controlling for SDO), whereas economic conservatism – but not social conservatism – is uniquely predicted by SDO (controlling for RWA; Duriez & Van Hiel, 2002; Van Hiel, Pandelaere, & Duriez, 2004). Of greater relevance for the current purpose, social conservatism and political conservatism are more strongly related to racism, compared with economic conservatism (Cornelis & Van Hiel, 2006).

Second, conservatism might not strongly predict prejudice if a number of people on the right are not prejudiced. Some argue that it is possible to be conservative without being prejudiced, that is, it is possible to be a principled conservative (Sniderman & Carmines, 1997; Sniderman & Tetlock, 1986). Principled conservatives are those with right-wing policy preferences that have negative consequences for group equality; yet these preferences are driven by nonracial principles.

For instance, conservatives might oppose redistributive social policies like affirmative action, not because they are prejudiced, but because they believe such programs violate cherished values, such as meritocracy and individualism. Moreover, employing a Modern Racism Scale to assess prejudice might exaggerate the relation with conservatism because such measures are purposefully confounded with political conservatism (Sniderman & Tetlock, 1986). This is because Modern Racism as a construct involves the blending of racial antipathy with symbolic (i.e., abstract) values, such as justice, order, and in particular, conservatism (Kinder, 1986; Sears & Henry, 2003).

Similarly, conservatism might not strongly predict prejudice if many people on the left are prejudiced. The theory of aversive racism is specifically about the form of prejudice that liberals hold (Gaertner & Dovidio, 1986). According to Dovidio and Gaertner (2005), most liberal North Americans who value fairness and espouse egalitarian values are actually aversive racists. Theoretically, aversive racists differ from modern racists in that they are more liberal and they have internalized nonprejudiced values to a greater degree (Nail, Harton, & Decker, 2003). However, aversive racists are theorized to unconsciously hold negative feelings toward outgroup members. There is evidence of racial bias among those on the left (Sniderman & Piazza, 1993), although it has not been demonstrated that these people are aversive racists because measures of aversive racism were not available.

Finally, a fourth perspective by Son Hing, Chung-Yan, Hamilton, et al. (2008) follows closely from Duckitt (2001) and Duriez and Van Hiel (2002) by proposing that, at the root of people's prejudice, there are two basic and relatively independent dimensions of socio-political ideology: egalitarianism/humanism and social conservatism (cf., Christopher & Mull, 2006). Egalitarianism/humanism is marked by supporting equality for, recognizing the worth of, and feeling a connection with, all individuals and groups. Social conservatism involves conventionalism, traditionalism, authoritarianism, and a desire for social control (Saucier, 2000; Stangor & Leary, 2006). Others have investigated the ideological bases of only explicit prejudice (e.g., Duckitt) or they have treated explicit prejudice as a mediator of the relation between ideology and implicit prejudice (Cunningham , Nezlek, & Banaji, 2004). In contrast, Son Hing, Chung-Yan, Hamilton, et al. (2008) tested the ideological roots of prejudice for people with different prejudice profiles, characterized by their level of explicit and implicit prejudice, which creates a two-dimensional model of prejudice. In other words, people can be low explicit/low implicit, or low explicit/high implicit, or high explicit/low implicit, or high explicit/high implicit prejudiced.

The construct egalitarianism/humanism extends previous work on egalitarianism (e.g., assessed with the SDO Scale reverse keyed) as a predictor of prejudice toward groups of lower status or groups with which one must compete (Duckitt, 2006; Duckitt, Wagner, du Plessis, et al., 2002). Son Hing, Chung-Yan, Hamilton, et al. (2008) proposed that wanting group equality might not be enough to be truly low in prejudice. Rather, people must also adopt a humanist ideology; that is, they must feel a sense of identification with, and relatedness to, and similarity to, outgroup members (Son Hing, Chung-Yan, Hamilton, et al., 2008). People higher in humanism should be higher in empathy, which is related to prejudice (McFarland & Mathews, 2005; Pedersen, Beven, Walker, et al., 2004), even when controlling for SDO (Backström & Björklund, 2007; McFarland & Adelson, 1996). Humanism differs from empathy in that the former primarily involves recognizing all people as intrinsically similar; whereas the latter involves an ability to understand other's emotions. People higher in humanism should be less likely to dehumanize outgroup members, which may be a key component of prejudice (Hodson & Costello, 2007; Vaes, Paladino, Castelli, et al., 2003), even at the implicit level (Goff, Eberhardt, Williams, et al., 2008). Finally, people higher in humanism should be more likely to recognize that they share a superordinate identity (i.e., humanity) with outgroups, and sharing a common in-group identity should reduce prejudice (Gaertner & Dovidio, 2000).

Egalitarianism/humanism is different from Katz and Hass' (1988) Humanitarianism-Egalitarianism Scale, which focuses on the degree to which people strive for social responsibility for the less fortunate. Humanism also differs from human identity salience (Nickerson & Louis, 2008), which is the extent to which people get a sense of their identity from being a human. Consequently, people with a stronger human identity should maximize differences between humans and outgroups (e.g., nonhuman animals; Nickerson & Louis, 2008). However, people who are higher in egalitarianism/humanism should feel a stronger relatedness to nonhuman animals, compared with people lower in egalitarianism/humanism. The concept of humanism is most similar to Universal Orientation (Phillips & Ziller, 1997), which involves seeing similarities between oneself and others. For instance, people higher in Universal Orientation perceive greater similarity between humans and nonhuman animals (Costello & Hodson, 2008).

Social conservatism (i.e., a desire for order, tradition, stability) is closely related to right-wing authoritarianism (conventionalism, obedience, aggression). Indeed, although they are conceptually distinguishable, the evidence suggests that they go hand in hand (Duckitt, 2001; Van Hiel, Cornelis, Roets, et al., 2007). RWA is an excellent predictor of generalized prejudice (Duckitt, Wagner, du Plessis, et al., 2002), and it appears to have greater predictive power than other measures of social conservatism (Cornelis, & Van Hiel, 2006). Indeed, social conservatism is not always found to predict outgroup prejudice (Stangor & Leary, 2006). This is likely because social conservatism should not predict prejudice toward all groups. Rather, people who are more socially conservative should be more prejudiced only toward outgroups that are seen as unconventional and as threatening the moral order (see also Duckitt, 2006; Feldman, 2003; Haddock, Zanna, & Esses, 1993). For instance, Lambert and Chasteen (1997) found that social conservatism predicted negative attitudes toward Blacks, but positive attitudes toward the elderly. Importantly, participants rated Blacks as less conventional than the elderly; however, such perceptions did not mediate the relation between conservatism and prejudice.

A major advantage of using the two-dimensional model of prejudice, which simultaneously considers explicit and implicit attitudes, to study individual differences in prejudice is that it allows for understanding the roots of prejudice among those who are politically conservative as well as those who are liberal. According to Son Hing, Chung-Yan, Hamilton, et al. (2008), people who are modern racists should score relatively high on an explicit measure of modern racism because they experience racial resentment and they should score high on an implicit measure of prejudice because they have well-practiced, early acquired, automatic negative reactions toward outgroup members (McConahay, 1986; Rudman, 2004). Principled conservatives should score relatively high on an explicit measure of modern racism because they cherish conservative values confounded with the scale content. However, if they are not prejudiced (in any way), then they should score low in implicit prejudice. This model also sheds light on prejudice on the left. Aversive racists should score low in explicit modern racism because they value egalitarianism and believe themselves to be nonprejudiced; however, because they have negative automatic associations or feelings toward outgroup members, they should score high in implicit prejudice (Son Hing, Li, & Zanna, 2002a, 2008; see also Dovidio & Gaertner, 2005). In contrast, someone who is truly low in prejudice should score low on both types of prejudice, explicit and implicit (Moskowitz, Gollwitzer, Wasel, et al., 1999).[3]

Therefore it is possible to examine how participants with varying prejudice profiles (low vs. high explicit x low vs. high implicit) vary in their socio-political ideologies. Son Hing, Chung-Yan, Hamilton, et al. (2008) investigated prejudice toward East and

Southeast Asians in Canada (e.g., Chinese, Japanese, Korean, Filipino) and found that truly low prejudiced participants (i.e., those low in both explicit and implicit prejudice) were the highest in egalitarianism/humanism; whereas, modern racists were the lowest. Egalitarianism/humanism might predict explicit and implicit prejudice against Asians because (a) some might find them hard to identify with as they might be seen as different and perhaps less human, and (b) they might provoke dominance motives because of their supposed competence (Fiske, Xu, Cuddy, et al., 1999). That egalitarianism/humanism predicts implicit prejudice, whereas previously SDO did not, supports the assertion that to be truly low prejudiced, one must not only desire equality between all groups but also feel sense of connection and identification with outgroup members.

In addition, truly low prejudiced participants scored lower than all others in social conservatism; whereas modern racists scored higher than all others, followed by principled conservatives. Social conservatism might predict both explicit and implicit prejudice toward Asians because they are seen as cold (Fiske, Xu, Cuddy, et al., 1999) or cliquish, as failing to adapt to the dominant group's social norms (Lin, Kwan, Cheung, et al., 2005) or as 'unCanadian,' provoking threat concerns.

In contrast, those higher in implicit prejudice (modern racists and aversive racists) tended to be lower in economic/political conservatism than those lower in implicit prejudice (principled conservatives and truly low prejudiced people). In addition economic/political conservatism was positively related to explicit prejudice, perhaps because Modern Racism Scales are confounded with political conservatism. The negative relation between economic/political conservatism and implicit prejudice supports the notion that some conservatives are principled rather than racist (at least in terms of implicit prejudice).

For the current chapter, we re-analysed the Son Hing, Chung-Yan, Hamilton, et al. (2008) data by running a discriminant function analysis to test how the three socio-political ideologies predict participants' membership in each of these prejudice groups. Two orthogonal functions significantly distinguished the four groups (see Table 10.1). Individuals high in both forms of prejudice (i.e., modern racists) and those low in both forms of prejudice (i.e., individuals truly low in prejudice) were well differentiated by a function that reflects high social conservatism and low egalitarianism/humanism. Modern racists are high on this dimension, whereas individuals truly low in prejudice are low on this dimension. In addition, individuals who scored moderately on this first function (i.e., principled conservatives and aversive racists) were distinguished by a second, independent function that reflects their level of economic/political conservatism. Principled conservatives are, not surprisingly, high on this dimension, whereas aversive racists are low on this dimension. Thus, economic/political conservatism successfully distinguished between aversive racists who are theorized to be liberal and principled conservatives who are theorized to be conservative, but it did not distinguish between the most and least prejudiced of the groups (i.e., low/low and high/high subgroups), when investigating prejudice toward East and Southeast Asians in Canada.

Table 10.1 Group averages on each function

Group	Function	
	1	2
	High social conservatism and low egalitarianism/humanism	High economic/political conservatism
Truly low prejudiced	−.99	.12
Aversive racists	−.38	−.47
Principled Conservatives	.25	.44
Modern racists	.89	−.15

SUGGESTIONS FOR FUTURE RESEARCH

In future research, a better measure of humanism should be developed and validated. For instance, humanism should be related to and yet empirically distinct from constructs such as empathy, collectivism, human identity, and humanitarianism-egalitarianism. It is also imperative to better understand how egalitarianism and humanism might be related. It might be possible for people to hold strong egalitarian beliefs while being low in humanism; however, the reverse might be less likely. Can people feel a strong sense of connection with others as sharing a basic humanity and also believe that some groups should have higher status than others?

RWA plays such a critical role because it reflects the socio-political ideology of social conservatism that predicts prejudice toward outgroups that are seen as unconventional. Social conservatism (i.e., a desire for order, tradition, stability) and right-wing authoritarianism (conventionalism, obedience, aggression) are highly related multi-faceted constructs (Van Hiel, Cornelis, Roets, et al., 2007). In future research, the relations between the facets of these constructs and their independent roles in prejudice should be more closely examined (Cornelis & Van Hiel, 2006).

Economic and political conservatism appear to play a complicated role in individual differences in prejudice. First, economic/political conservatism has been found to be positively related to explicit prejudice, perhaps because a modern racism scale, which is confounded with political conservatism, was used. In future work, the relations between political/economic conservatism and a more 'pure' measure of prejudice (e.g., a semantic differential) should be investigated. Second, economic/political conservatism was inversely related to implicit prejudice. In other words, people who were more economically/politically conservative had more positive associations with Asians at the implicit level. Perhaps those who more

strongly endorse free-market capitalism and individualism have more positive automatic associations with Asians because of their stereotype as competitive and competent (Fiske, Xu, Cuddy, et al., 1999).

Future research, using better measures, should investigate how economic conservatism and political conservatism independently relate to explicit and implicit prejudice toward outgroups other than Asians. In particular, prejudice toward outgroups who are stereotyped as less competent and competitive, such as traditional women or Blacks should be investigated. In fact, one could investigate whether the ideological bases of prejudice differ depending how the outgroups are perceived employing the two dimensions suggested by Fiske, Xu, Cuddy, et al. (1999): low versus high competence, and low versus high warmth.

More research should be devoted to understanding how economic and political conservatism relates to egalitarianism/humanism and social conservatism. It has been argued that because economic conservatism inherently involves inequality, it should inversely predict egalitarianism (Sidanius, Pratto, & Bobo, 1996). This is because on the face of it, a system like capitalism treats people on the basis of their individual merit, yet in reality, such systems affect groups differently because they have different opportunities and challenges (Son Hing, Bobocel, et al., 2002b). Economic conservatism might also inversely predict humanism because it is likely harder for people who identify and connect more with others to believe that poverty is a deserved consequence for those who are less competitive. Finally, people who are more economically and politically conservative are likely to be more socially conservative as well.

Knowing that the socio-political ideologies of egalitarianism/humanism and social conservatism serve as the basis for individual differences in explicit and implicit prejudice, it is important to study the social contexts in which these ideologies are developed. Existing research suggests that parenting styles influence the development of RWA and SDO. Parents who are more harsh or strict raise offspring higher in RWA, and those who are less affectionate raise offspring higher in SDO (Duckitt, 2001). There is also evidence that parents who emphasize extrinsic over intrinsic goal pursuits raise children higher in SDO, and parents who emphasize conformity raise children higher in RWA (Duriez, Soenens, & Vansteenkiste, 2007). In future research, the processes through which parents' styles and goals influence their children's socio-political ideologies and subsequent prejudice should be clarified.

Other socialization experiences, such as peer influence and the role of institutions (e.g., university) likely influence socio-political ideology and subsequent prejudice (see Chapter 6 by Killen, this volume). For instance, college students in a hierarchy-enhancing program (i.e., law) were found to be higher in their levels of SDO in later (vs. earlier) years of training whereas students in a hierarchy-attenuating program (i.e., psychology) were lower in SDO in later (versus earlier) years of the program (Guimond, Dambrun, Michinov, et al., 2003). Furthermore, higher SDO was related to greater prejudice. It is possible that the effect of program is driven by differences in perceived norms. Similarly, time spent at a military college is related to increases in SDO but not in RWA (Nicol, Charbonneau, & Boies, 2007). Unfortunately, neither set of studies clearly outlines what socialization experiences lead to increases in SDO. In future research, the socialization experiences that occur in school and at work that differentially influence people's levels of egalitarianism/humanism and their social conservatism should be investigated. Within organizational contexts, issues such as peers' beliefs, group norms, leader's behavior, organizational mission and culture, as well as structural factors like formal and informal reward and punishment systems likely play a critical role.

SUMMARY AND CONCLUSION

People differ in their levels of generalized prejudice and this is true for both explicit and implicit prejudice. The bases of explicit prejudice are well researched: Together SDO and RWA are the best predictors of people's self-reported prejudice (Altemeyer, 1998). Less is known about the bases of implicit prejudice. There is only mixed evidence that RWA predicts generalized implicit prejudice and there is no evidence that SDO predicts implicit prejudice. Thus, these relations need to be further investigated.

Three theoretical perspectives were presented that aim to explain the important roles that SDO and RWA play in predicting individual differences in *explicit* prejudice. The first proposes that SDO and RWA are personality types prone to prejudice (Altemeyer, 1998). Indeed, SDO and RWA are related to personality traits (agreeableness and openness to experience) that predict prejudice (Sibley & Duckitt, 2008). The second proposes that SDO and RWA represent two socio-political/socio-cultural attitude-value-belief dimensions that predict prejudice (Duckitt, 2001). There is compelling evidence for this model. The third model suggests that SDO and RWA reflect two basic components of political conservatism (Jost, Glaser, Kruglanski, et al., 2003); thus, conservatism predicts prejudice. In support of this perspective, conservatism, RWA, SDO, cognitive conservatism, and explicit prejudice have all been found to interrelate (Cunningham, Nezlek, & Banaji, et al., 2004).

A fourth perspective proposes that SDO and RWA play important roles in predicting individual differences in prejudice – both explicit and implicit – because they constitute critical elements of the ideological bases of prejudice: egalitarianism/humanism and social conservatism (Son Hing, Chung-Yan, Hamilton, et al., 2008). SDO (when reverse coded) is a core component of egalitarianism/humanism and RWA is a core component of social conservatism. Together, being low in egalitarianism/humanism and being high in social conservatism function as the ideological basis of prejudice toward Asians in Canada. Conversely, those who are low in prejudice – explicitly and implicitly – are more likely to believe in-group equality, identify with all humanity, and be open to social change and to challenge of conventions. In addition, economic/political conservatism distinguishes those who are prejudiced on the left and prejudiced on the right but it does not distinguish those who are most versus least prejudiced. Consequently, economic/political conservatism should not be aggregated with the other ideologies as a basis of prejudice.

The effects of egalitarianism/humanism and of social conservatism might extend beyond individual differences in prejudice. Just as a strong endorsement of egalitarianism, a strong sense of connection to humanity, and a weak valuing of tradition and conformity are necessary to be truly low prejudiced, this combination of beliefs is also likely needed for people to advocate for social change that would create greater equality and inclusion for all people in our societies.

ACKNOWLEDGEMENTS

We would like to thank Dustin Burt, Emily Clark, David Clarke, Ian Hansen, Donna Garcia, Jessica Hershfield, and Suzanne Kiani for their comments on the manuscript and Numrah Irfan for helping to prepare it. Correspondence should be directed to Leanne S. Son Hing, Department of Psychology, University of Guelph, Guelph, ON, Canada N1G 2W1. E-mail: sonhing@uoguelph.ca

Mark P. Zanna, Department of Psychology, University of Waterloo, Waterloo, ON, Canada N2L 3G1. E-mail: mzanna@watarts.uwaterloo.ca

NOTES

1 Low tender-mindedness and high tough-mindedness are two different measures but they reflect very similar constructs so the term tender-minded is used to refer to both.

2 We use the term social conservatism to also refer to cultural conservatism because the labels appear to be used interchangeably in the literature.

3 Son Hing et al. (2008) demonstrated that aversive racists and modern racists discriminated more against an outgroup member under a condition of attributional ambiguity, compared with a control condition. In contrast, truly low prejudiced participants and principled conservatives did not discriminate regardless of condition.

REFERENCES

Adorno, T. W., Frenkel-Brunswik, E., Levinson, D. J., & Sanford, R. N. (1950). *The Authoritarian Personality.* Oxford: Harpers.

Allport, G. W. (1954). *The Nature of Prejudice.* Oxford: Addison-Wesley.

Altemeyer, B. (1981). *Right-Wing Authoritarianism.* Winnipeg, MB: University of Manitoba Press.

Altemeyer, B. (1996). *The Authoritarian Apecter.* Cambridge, MA: Harvard University Press.

Altemeyer, B. (1998). The other "authoritarian personality". In M. P. Zanna (Ed.), *Advances in Experimental Social Psychology* (Vol. 30, pp. 47–92). San Diego, CA: Academic Press.

Altemeyer, B. (2004). Highly dominating, highly authoritarian personalities. *The Journal of Social Psychology*, 144, 421–447.

Altemeyer, B., & Hunsberger, B. E. (1992). Authoritarianism, religious fundamentalism, quest, and prejudice. *International Journal for the Psychology of Religion*, 2, 113–133.

Aosved, A. C., & Long, P. J. (2006). Co-occurrence of rape myth acceptance, sexism, racism, homophobia, ageism, classism, and religious intolerance. *Sex Roles*, 55, 481–492.

Bäckström, M., & Björklund, F. (2007). Structural modeling of generalized prejudice: The role of social dominance, authoritarianism, and empathy. *Journal of Individual Differences*, 28, 10–17.

Bobocel, D. R., Son Hing, L. S., Davey, L. M., Stanley, D. J., & Zanna, M. P. (1998). Justice-based opposition to social policies: Is it genuine? *Journal of Personality and Social Psychology*, 75, 653–669.

Budner, S. (1962). Intolerance of ambiguity as a personality variable. *Journal of Personality*, 30, 29–50.

Cacioppo, J. T., & Petty, R. E. (1982). The need for cognition. *Journal of Personality and Social Psychology*, 42, 116–131.

Christie, R. (1991). *Authoritarianism and Related Constructs.* San Diego, CA: Academic Press.

Christopher, A. N., & Mull, M. S. (2006). Conservative ideology and ambivalent sexism. *Psychology of Women Quarterly*, 30, 223–230.

Cialdini, R. B., Trost, M. R., & Newsom, J. T. (1995). Preference for consistency: The development of a valid measure and the discovery of surprising behavioral implications. *Journal of Personality and Social Psychology*, 69, 318–328.

Cornelis, I., & Van Hiel, A. (2006). The impact of cognitive styles on authoritarianism based conservatism and racism. *Basic and Applied Social Psychology*, 28, 37–50.

Costello, K., & Hodson, G. (2008). Re-humanization: The role of human-animal similarity I reducing prejudice towards immigrants and non-human animals. Unpublished Master's thesis. Brock University.

Crandall, C. S. & Eshleman, A. (2005). The justification-suppression model of prejudice: An approach to the history of prejudice research. In C. S. Crandall, & M. Shaller (Eds). *Social Psychology of Prejudice: Historical and Contemporary Issues* (pp. 233–263). Lawrence, KS: Lewinian Press.

Crowson, H. M., Thoma, S. J., & Hestevold, N. (2005). Is political conservatism synonymous with authoritarianism? *Journal of Social Psychology*, 145, 571–592.

Cunningham, W. A., Nezlek, J. B., & Banaji, M. R. (2004). Implicit and explicit ethnocentrism: Revisiting the ideologies of prejudice. *Personality and Social Psychology Bulletin*, 30, 1332–1346.

Dovidio, J. F., & Gaertner, S. L. (2005). Aversive racism. In M. P. Zanna (Ed.), *Advances in Experimental Social Psychology* (Vol. 36, pp. 1–52). San Diego, CA: Academic Press.

Dovidio, J. F., Kawakami, K., Johnson, C., Johnson, B., & Howard, A. (1997). On the nature of prejudice: Automatic and controlled processes. *Journal of Experimental Social Psychology*, 33, 510–540.

Duckitt, J. (1992). Psychology and prejudice: A historical analysis and integrative framework. *American Psychologist*, 47, 1182–1193.

Duckitt, J. (2001). A dual process cognitive–motivational theory of ideology and prejudice. In M. P. Zanna (Ed.), *Advances in Experimental Social Psychology* (Vol. 33, pp. 41–113). San Diego, CA: Academic Press.

Duckitt, J. (2006). Differential effects of right wing authoritarianism and social dominance orientation on outgroup attitudes and their mediation by threat from and competitiveness to outgroups. *Personality and Social Psychology Bulletin*, 32, 684–696.

Duckitt, J., Wagner, C., du Plessis, I., & Birum, I. (2002). The psychological bases of ideology and prejudice: Testing a dual process model. *Journal of Personality and Social Psychology*, 83, 75–93.

Dunton, B. C., & Fazio, R. H. (1997). An individual difference measure of motivation to control prejudiced reactions. *Personality and Social Psychology Bulletin*, 23, 316–326.

Duriez, B., Soenens, B., & Vansteenkiste, M. (2007). In search of the antecedents of adolescent authoritarianism: The relative contribution of parental goal promotion and parenting style dimensions. *European Journal of Personality*, 21, 507–527.

Duriez, B., & Van Hiel, A. (2002). The march of modern fascism: A comparison of social dominance orientation and authoritarianism. *Personality and Individual Differences*, 32, 1199–1213.

Ekehammar, B., & Akrami, N. (2007). Personality and prejudice: From big five personality factors to facets. *Journal of Personality*, 75, 899–925.

Ekehammar, B., Akrami, N., Gylje, M., & Zakrisson, I. (2004). What matters most to prejudice: Big five personality, social dominance orientation, or right-wing authoritarianism? *European Journal of Personality*, 18, 463–482.

Ekehammar, B., & Akrami, N. (2003). The relation between personality and prejudice: A variable- and a person-centred approach. *European Journal of Personality*, 17, 449–464.

Eysenck, H. J. (1954). *The Psychology of Politics*. London: Routledge and Keegan Paul.

Fazio, R. H., Jackson, J. R., Dunton, B. C., & Williams, C. J. (1995). Variability in automatic activation as an unobtrusive measure of racial attitudes. A bona fide pipeline? *Journal of Personality and Social Psychology*, 69, 1013–1027.

Fazio, R. H., & Olson, M. A. (2003). Implicit measures in social cognition research: Their meaning and use. *Annual Review of Psychology*, 54, 297–327.

Federico, C. M., & Sidanius, J. (2002). Racism, ideology, and affirmative action revisited: The antecedents and consequences of "principled objections" to affirmative action. *Journal of Personality and Social Psychology*, 82, 488–502.

Feldman, S. (2003). Enforcing social conformity: A theory of authoritarianism. *Political Psychology*, 24, 41–74.

Firebaugh, G., & Davis, K. E. (1988). Trends in antiblack prejudice, 1972–1984: Region and cohort effects. *American Journal of Sociology*, 94 (2), 251–72.

Fiske, S. T., Xu, J., Cuddy, A. C., & Glick, P. (1999). (Dis)respecting versus (dis)liking: Status and interdependence predict ambivalent stereotypes of competence and warmth. *Journal of Social Issues*, 55, 473–489.

Fleishman, J. A. (1988). Attitude organization in the general public: Evidence for a bidimensional structure. *Social Forces*, 67, 159–184.

Gaertner, S. L., & Dovidio, J. F. (1986). The aversive form of racism. In J. F. Dovidio, & S. L. Gaertner (Eds), *Prejudice, Discrimination, and Racism* (pp. 61–86). Orlando, FL: Academic Press.

Gaertner, S. L., & Dovidio, J. F. (2000). *The Aversive Form of Racism*. New York, NY, US: Psychology Press.

Gawronski, B., & Bodenhausen, G. V. (2006). Associative and propositional processes in evaluation: An integrative review of implicit and explicit attitude change. *Psychological Bulletin*, 132, 692–731.

Goff, P. A., Eberhardt, J. L., Williams, M. J., & Jackson, M. C. (2008). Not yet human: Implicit knowledge, historical dehumanization, and contemporary consequences. *Journal of Personality and Social Psychology*, 94, 292–306.

Graziano, W. G., Bruce, J., Sheese, B. E., & Tobin, R. M. (2007). Attractions, personality, and prejudice: Liking none of the people most of the time. *Journal of Personality and Social Psychology*, 93, 565–582.

Greenwald, A. G., McGhee, D. E., & Schwartz, J. L. K. (1998). Measuring individual differences in implicit cognition. *Journal of Personality and Social Psychology*, 74, 1464–1480.

Guimond, S., Dambrun, M., Michinov, N., & Duarte, S. (2003). Does social dominance generate prejudice? Integrating individual and contextual determinants of intergroup cognitions. *Journal of Personality and Social Psychology*, 84, 697–721.

Haddock, G., Zanna, M. P., & Esses, V. (1993). Assessing the structure of prejudiced attitudes: The case of attitudes toward homosexuals. *Journal of Personality and Social Psychology*, 65, 1105–1118.

Hansen, I., & Norenzayan, A. (2006). Between yang and yin and heaven and hell: Untangling the complex relationship between religion and intolerance. In P. McNamara (Ed.). *Where God and Science Meet [Three Volumes]: How Brain and Evolutionary Studies Alter our Understanding of Religion* (pp. 187–211). Westport, CT: Praeger.

Heaven, P. C. L., & Bucci, S. (2001). Right-wing authoritarianism, social dominance orientation and personality: An analysis using the IPIP measure. *European Journal of Personality*, 15, 49–56.

Hodson, G., & Costello, K. (2007). Interpersonal disgust, ideological orientations, and dehumanization as predictors of intergroup attitudes. *Psychological Science*, 18, 691–698.

Hofmann, W., Gawronski, B., Gschwendner, T., Le, H., & Schmitt, M. (2005). A meta-analysis on the correlation between the Implicit Association Test and explicit self-report measures. *Personality and Social Psychology Bulletin*, 31, 1369–1385.

Jost, J. T., Glaser, J., Kruglanski, A. W., & Sulloway, F. (2003). Political conservatism as motivated social cognition. *Psychological Bulletin*, 129, 339–375.

Jost, J. T., Napier, J. L., Thorisdottir, H., Gosling, S. D., Palfai, T. P., & Ostafin, B. (2007). Are needs to manage uncertainty and threat associated with political conservatism or ideological extremity? *Personality and Social Psychology Bulletin*, 33, 989–1007.

Katz, I., & Hass, G. R. (1988). Racial ambivalence and American value conflict: Correlational and priming studies of dual cognitive structures. *Journal of Personality and Social Psychology*, 55, 893–905.

Kerlinger, F. N. (1984). *Liberalism and Conservatism: The Nature and Structure of Social Attitudes*. Hillsdale, NJ: Lawrence Erlbaum.

Kinder, D. R. (1986). The continuing American dilemma: White resistance to racial change 40 years after Myrdal. *Journal of Social Issues*, 42, 151–171.

Kinder, D. R., & Sears, D. O. (1981). Prejudice and politics: Symbolic racism versus racial threats to the good life. *Journal of Personality and Social Psychology*, 40, 414–431.

Lambert, A. J., & Chasteen, A. L. (1997). Perceptions of disadvantage versus conventionality: Political values and attitudes toward the elderly versus Blacks. *Personality and Social Psychology Bulletin*, 23, 469–481.

Lambert, A. J., Payne, B. K., Ramsey, S., & Shaffer, L. M. (2005). On the predictive validity of implicit attitude measures: The moderating effect of perceived group variability. *Journal of Experimental Social Psychology*, 41, 114–128.

Laythe, B., Finkel, D., Bringle, R., & Kirkpatrick, L. A. (2002). Religious fundamentalism as a predictor of prejudice: A two-component model. *Journal for the Scientific Study of Religion*, 41, 623–635.

Lin, M. H., Kwan, V. S. Y., Cheung, A., & Fiske, S. T. (2005). Stereotype content model explains prejudice for an envied outgroup: Scale of Anti-Asian American stereotypes. *Personality and Social Psychology Bulletin*, 31, 34–47.

Lippa, R., & Arad, S. (1999). Gender, personality, and prejudice: The display of authoritarianism and social dominance in interviews with college men and women. *Journal of Research in Personality*, 33, 463–493.

McConahay, J. B. (1983). Modern racism and modern discrimination: The effects of race, racial attitudes, and context on simulated hiring decisions. *Personality and Social Psychology Bulletin*, 9, 551–558.

McConahay, J. B. (1986). Modern racism, ambivalence, and the Modern Racism Scale. In J. F. Dovidio, & S. L. Gaertner (Eds), *Prejudice, Discrimination, and Racism* (pp. 91–125). San Diego, CA: Academic Press.

McConnell, A. R., & Leibold, J. M. (2001). Relations among the Implicit Association Test, discriminatory behavior, and explicit measures of racial attitudes. *Journal of Experimental Social Psychology*, 37, 435–442.

McFarland, S. G., & Adelson, S. (1996). An omnibus study of personality, values, and prejudice. Paper presented at the annual convention of the International Society for Political Psychology, Vancouver, British Columbia, July 1996.

McFarland, S., & Mathews, M. (2005). Who cares about human rights? *Political Psychology*, 26, 365–385.

Meertens, R. W., & Pettigrew, T. F. (1997). Is subtle prejudice really prejudice? *Public Opinion Quarterly*, 61, 54–71.

Moskowitz, G. B., Gollwitzer, P. M., Wasel, W. S., & Schaal, B. (1999). Preconscious control of stereotype activation through chronic egalitarian goals. *Journal of Personality and Social Psychology*, 77, 167–184.

Nail, P. R., Harton, H. C., & Decker, B. P. (2003). Political orientation and modern versus aversive racism: Tests of Dovidio and Gaertner's (1998) Integrated Model. *Journal of Personality and Social Psychology*, 84, 754–770.

Nelson, T. D. (2006). *The Psychology of Prejudice*. Needham Heights, MA, US: Allyn & Bacon.

Neuberg, S. L., & Newsom, J. T. (1993). Personal need for structure: Individual differences in the desire for simpler structure. *Journal of Personality and Social Psychology*, 65, 113–131.

Nickerson, A. M., & Louis, W. R. (2008). Nationality versus humanity? Personality, identity, and norms in relation to attitudes toward asylum seekers. *Journal of Applied Psychology*, 38, 796–817.

Nicol, A. A. M., Charbonneau, D., & Boies, K. (2007). Right-wing authoritarianism and social dominance orientation in a Canadian military sample. *Military Psychology*, 19, 239–257.

Pedersen, A., Beven, J., Walker, I., & Griffiths, B. (2004). Attitudes toward indigenous Australians: The role of empathy and guilt. *Journal of Community and Applied Social Psychology*, 14, 233–249.

Peterson, B. E., Doty, R. M., & Winter, D. G. (1993). Authoritarianism and attitudes toward contemporary social issues. *Personality and Social Psychology Bulletin*, 19, 174–184.

Pettigrew, T. F. (2005). The social science study of American race relations in the 20th century. In C. S. Crandall, & M. Shaller (Eds). *Social Psychology of Prejudice: Historical and Contemporary Issues* (pp. 233–263). Lawrence, KS: Lewinian Press.

Pettigrew, T. F., & Meertens, R. W. (1995). Subtle and blatant prejudice in Western Europe. *European Journal of Social Psychology*, 25, 57–75.

Phillips, S. T., & Ziller, R. C. (1997). Toward a theory and measure of the nature of nonprejudice. *Journal of Personality and Social Psychology*, 72, 420–434.

Plant, E. A., & Devine, P. G. (1998). Internal and external motivation to respond without prejudice. *Journal of Personality and Social Psychology*, 75, 811–832.

Pratto, F., & Shih, M. (2000). Social dominance orientation and group context in implicit group prejudice. *Psychological Science*, 11, 515–518.

Pratto, F., Sidanius, J., Stallworth, L. M., & Malle, B. F. (1994). Social dominance orientation: A personality variable predicting social and political attitudes. *Journal of Personality and Social Psychology*, 67, 741–763.

Reynolds, K. J., Turner, J. C., Haslam, S. A., & Ryan, M. K. (2001). The role of personality and group factors in explaining prejudice. *Journal of Experimental Social Psychology*, 37, 427–434.

Rokeach, M. (1948). Generalized mental rigidity as a factor in ethnocentrism. *The Journal of Abnormal and Social Psychology*, 43, 259–278.

Rowatt, W. C., & Franklin, L. M. (2004). Christian orthodoxy, religious fundamentalism, and right-wing authoritarianism as predictors of implicit racial prejudice. *International Journal for the Psychology of Religion*, 14, 125–138.

Rowatt, W. C., Franklin, L. M., & Cotton, M. (2005). Patterns and personality correlates of implicit and explicit attitudes toward Christians and Muslims. *Journal for the Scientific Study of Religion*, 44, 29–43.

Rowatt, W. C., Tsang, J., Kelly, J., LaMartina, B., Mccullers, M., & McKinley, A. (2006). Associations between religious personality dimensions and implicit homosexual prejudice. *Journal for the Scientific Study of Religion*, 45, 397–406.

Rudman, L. A. (2004). Social justice in our minds, homes, and society: The nature, causes, and consequences of implicit bias. *Journal of Social Issues*, 17, 129–142.

Saucier, G. (2000). Isms and the Structure of Social Attitudes. *Journal of Personality and Social Psychology*, 78, 366–385.

Schaller, M., Boyd, C., Yohannes, J., & O'Brien, M. (1995). The prejudiced personality revisited: Personal need for structure and formation of erroneous group stereotypes. *Journal of Personality and Social Psychology*, 68, 544–555.

Schmitt, M. T., Branscombe, N. R., & Kappen, D. M. (2003). Attitudes toward group-based inequality: Social dominance or social identity? *British Journal of Social Psychology*, 42, 161–186.

Schuman, H., Steeh, C., & Bobo, L. (1985). *Racial Attitudes in America: Trends and Interpretations*. Cambridge, MA, US: Harvard University Press.

Sears, D. O., & Henry, P. J. (2003). The origins of symbolic racism. *Journal of Personality and Social Psychology*, 85, 259–275.

Sears, D. O., & Henry, P. J. (2005). Over thirty years later: A contemporary look at symbolic racism. In M. P. Zanna (Ed.), *Advances in Experimental Social*

Psychology (Vol. 37, pp. 95–150). San Diego: Elsevier Academic Press.

Sibley, C. G., & Duckitt, J. (2008). Personality and prejudice: A meta-analysis and theoretical review. *Personality and Social Psychology Review*, 12, 248–279.

Sidanius, J., & Pratto, F. (1993). Racism and support of free–market capitalism: A cross-cultural analysis. *Political Psychology*, 14, 381–401.

Sidanius, J., & Pratto, F. (1999). *Social Dominance: An Intergroup Theory of Social Hierarchy and Oppression.* New York: Cambridge University Press.

Sidanius, J., Pratto, F., & Bobo, L. (1996). Racism, conservatism, affirmative action, and intellectual sophistication: A matter of principled conservatism or group dominance? *Journal of Personality and Social Psychology*, 70, 476–490.

Sniderman, P. M., & Carmines, E. G. (1997). *Reaching Beyond Race.* Cambridge, MA: Harvard University Press.

Sniderman, P. M., & Piazza, T. (1993). *The Scar of Race.* Cambridge, MA: Harvard University Press.

Sniderman, P. M., & Tetlock, P. (1986). Symbolic racism: Problems of motive attribution in political debate. *Journal of Social Issues*, 42, 129–150.

Son Hing, L. S., Bobocel, D. R., & Zanna, M. P. (2002b). Meritocracy and opposition to affirmative action: Making concessions in the face of discrimination. *Journal of Personality and Social Psychology*, 83, 493–509.

Son Hing, L. S., Bobocel, D. R., Zanna, M. P., & McBride, M. V. (2007). Authoritarian dynamics and unethical decision making: High social dominance orientation leaders and high right–wing authoritarianism followers. *Journal of Personality and Social Psychology*, 92, 67–81.

Son Hing, L. S., Chung-Yan, G. A., Hamilton, L. K., & Zanna, M. P. (2008). A two-dimensional model that employs explicit and implicit attitudes to characterize prejudice. *Journal of Personality and Social Psychology*, 94, 971–987.

Son Hing, L. S., Li, W., & Zanna, M. P. (2002a). Inducing hypocrisy to reduce prejudicial responses among aversive racists. *Journal of Experimental Social Psychology*, 38, 71–78.

Stangor, C., & Leary, S. (2006). Intergroup beliefs: Investigations from the social side. In M. P. Zanna (Ed.), *Advances in Experimental Social Psychology* (Vol. 38, pp. 243–281). San Diego: Academic Press.

Stangor, C., & Thompson, E. P. (2002). Needs for cognitive economy and self-enhancement as unique predictors of intergroup attitudes. *European Journal of Social Psychology*, 32, 563–575.

Stephan, W. G., & Finlay, K. (1999). The role of empathy in improving intergroup relations. *Journal of Social Issues*, 55, 729–743.

Swim, J. K., Aikin, K. J., Hall, W. S., & Hunter, B. A. (1995). Sexism and racism: Old-fashioned and modern prejudices. *Journal of Personality and Social Psychology*, 68, 199–214.

Tajfel, H. (1970). Experiments in intergroup discrimination. *Scientific American*, 223, 96–102.

Tarman, C., & Sears, D. O. (2005). The conceptualization and measurement of symbolic racism. *Journal of Politics*, 67, 731–761.

Vaes, J., Paladino, M. P., Castelli, L., Leyens, J., & Giovanazzi, A. (2003). On the behavioral consequences of infrahumanization: The implicit role of uniquely human emotions in intergroup relations. *Journal of Personality and Social Psychology*, 85, 1016–1034.

Van Hiel, A., Cornelis, I., Roets, A., & De Clercq, B. (2007). A comparison of various authoritarianism scales in Belgian Flanders. *European Journal of Personality*, 21, 149–168.

Van Hiel, A., & Mervielde, I. (2002). Explaining conservative beliefs and political preferences: A comparison of social dominance orientation and authoritarianism. *Journal of Applied Social Psychology*, 32, 965–976.

Van Hiel, A., & Mervielde, I. (2004). Openness to experience and boundaries in the mind: Relationships with cultural and economic conservative beliefs. *Journal of Personality*, 72, 659–686.

Van Hiel, A., Pandelaere, M., & Duriez, B. (2004). The impact of need for closure on conservative beliefs and racism: Differential mediation by authoritarian submission and authoritarian dominance. *Personality and Social Psychology Bulletin*, 30, 824–837.

Webster, D. M., & Kruglanski, A. W. (1994). Individual differences in need for cognitive closure. *Journal of Personality and Social Psychology*, 67, 1049–1062.

Whitely, B. E., Jr. (1999). Right-wing authoritarianism, social dominance orientation, and prejudice. *Journal of Personality and Social Psychology*, 77, 126–134.

Wilson, T. D., Lindsey, S., & Schooler, T. Y. (2000). A model of dual attitudes. *Psychological Review*, 107, 101–126.

Zanna, M. P., & Rempel, J. K. (1988). Attitudes: A new look at an old concept. In D. Bar-Tal, & A. W. Kruglanski (Eds), *The Social Psychology of Knowledge* (pp. 315–334). New York: Cambridge University Press.

11

Social Identity and Self-Categorization

Dominic Abrams and Michael A. Hogg

ABSTRACT

Social identity theory is one of the most influential and far reaching theories of intergroup relations and group processes. The theory addresses both group and intergroup processes and behavior, embodied in a variety of specific sub-theories, including self-categorization theory. These share a common meta-theoretical framework that links social structure and context with categorization and identity processes. The core process is transformation from categorizing and viewing the self and others as individuals to seeing the self and others in terms of their representativeness of contrasting social groups and categories. We first outline the theoretical background and history of social identity theory. We then describe (a) the nature of the transformation from individual to collective representations; (b) how social identity has been conceptualized more recently, in terms of its motivational implications; and (c) the consequences for biases in intragroup and intergroup behavior.

SOCIAL IDENTITY AND SELF-CATEGORIZATION

This chapter describes the main features of social identity theory (SIT) – the nature and function of social identity, and the process and effects of categorizing oneself and other people. SIT has become one of social psychology's most influential theories, providing wide-ranging explanations of group behavior and intergroup relations, and thus of prejudice and discrimination. For example, a Google search (March 12, 2009) on the term 'social identity theory' produced 71,100 hits, compared with 36,300 for 'cognitive dissonance theory,' and 25,500 for 'terror

management theory'. Between 1997 and 2007, of publications on intergroup relations in social psychology's top eight journals 36.1 per cent invoked social identity as a key concept (Randsley de Moura, Leader, Pelletier, et al., 2008).

SIT, and the approach or perspective it entails, encompasses a number of different sub-theories of the social-cognitive, motivational, social interactive and macro-social facets of group life. The two fundamental components are Tajfel and Turner's (1979) 'social identity theory of intergroup relations' and Turner's (1985) 'social identity theory of the group', subsequently developed into self-categorization theory (SCT) (Turner, Hogg,

Oakes, et al., 1987). SIT focuses on the role of identity in intergroup conflict and harmony, while SCT focuses on the social-cognitive architecture of social identity processes. These form the groundwork for social identity theories and explanations of stereotyping, collective action, group cohesion, leadership, group decision-making, social influence, deviance, motivation, and the self. The overarching meta-theory prioritizes the reciprocal relationship between intergroup relations and self-conception, and the development and articulation of theoretical constructs at the social cognitive, social interactive, intergroup, and societal level (Abrams & Hogg, 2004).

This chapter provides a brief history of the development of SIT, then its key concepts and sub-theories, recent developments, and applications. We conclude by identifying potentially important controversies and avenues for future research.

SOCIAL IDENTITY THEORY

The most basic conceptual components of SIT were developed by Henri Tajfel and John Turner with their students, the 'Bristol School' during the 1970s and early 1980s. Tajfel's experiences as a Polish Jew in France during, and immediately after, the Second World War fired him with a passion to understand prejudice, discrimination, and intergroup conflict. This first surfaced conceptually in Tajfel's work on the accentuation principle (Tajfel, 1959). Framed by Bruner's (1957) 'new look' in perception, Tajfel proposed and demonstrated that when people categorize objects and other people they perceptually accentuate similarities within and differences between categories on dimensions they believe are correlated with the categorization, particularly if the categorization or correlated dimension are important or valued. In a classic paper on the cognitive aspects of prejudice, Tajfel (1969) argued that he had discovered a fundamental cognitive bias that helped explain stereotyping – when people categorize others they see them as stereotypically similar to fellow group members and different from members of other groups.

But Tajfel's research team hypothesized that, just as categorization automatically produces perceptual accentuation, perhaps it also produces behavioral discrimination. To test this idea they added a new twist. The categorization explicitly involved the self – participants were randomly categorized into minimally defined groups. Tajfel showed that, to ensure their own group gained more than the outgroup, individuals sacrificed personal self-interest as well as larger total for their group. Ingroup bias occurred even when the gain was symbolic rather than material. The minimal group paradigm has subsequently been adopted widely as a baseline condition for intergroup relations research (Bourhis, Sachdev, & Gagnon, 1994).

The evidence from minimal group studies led Tajfel to distinguish between social identity and personal identity, which maps on to group/intergroup processes and individual/interpersonal processes respectively. Social identity is 'the individual's knowledge that he belongs to certain social groups together with some emotional and value significance to him of this group membership' (Tajfel, 1972: 292).

Tajfel's early findings in this area led him to first define social identity and explain how a social-identity related motive to make one's ingroup distinct in evaluatively positive ways from relevant outgroups underpinned ethnocentric perception, behavioral ingroup favoritism, and the existence of status hierarchies in society. This theory of intergroup relations holds that prejudice and bias often reflect the way people protect and promote their positive distinctiveness, and their views of outgroups are framed by their beliefs about the nature of relations among groups in society (Tajfel, 1974; Tajfel & Turner, 1979). People's beliefs about relative group statuses, whether these are legitimate and stable, whether boundaries between groups are permeable (i.e., individuals can successfully move between groups through hard work and ability), and the reality of alternative social relations (i.e., the stability of the relationship) determine how groups and their members protect and promote their social identity.

When people perceive that status differences are stable and legitimate, and that boundaries between groups are permeable, low-status group members may adopt a *social mobility* strategy. They dis-identify with their low-status group and try to attain membership of the higher status group. Members of lower status groups who hold social mobility beliefs, such as the Protestant work ethic, are less likely to work for the advancement of their group as a whole and more likely to pursue individual mobility, despite the fact that upward mobility is difficult to achieve. The presence of objective and informal barriers to social mobility may leave those who try to 'pass' into the dominant group with a marginal identity (Breakwell, 1986); they are regarded as a traitor by their original group and a nonmember by the dominant group.

Many intergroup boundaries, such as those based on gender or skin color, are acknowledged to be impermeable. Then, low-status group members may adopt a collective strategy of *social creativity* that could involve downwards comparisons with even lower status groups, positively redefining ingroup attributes, or finding new dimensions of comparison on which to establish positive distinctiveness from the higher status group. For example, low status groups may emphasize their 'solidarity' and cohesiveness, depicting higher status groups as relatively cold and unfriendly (e.g., Fiske, Cuddy, Glick, et al., 2002). It is when status differences are insecure (illegitimate and/or unstable) and alternatives to the status quo can be envisaged that lower status groups adopt a *social competition* strategy – challenging the higher status group directly on dimensions that define its superiority (see also Taylor & Moghaddam, 1984).

The various outcomes of belonging to groups of different status combined with different social belief structures (see Hogg & Abrams 1988) have subsequently been expanded and developed by social identity researchers (e.g., Ellemers, Spears & Doosje, 1999a) and theories of system justification

(Jost & Hunyadi, 2002), just world beliefs (Furnham & Proctor, 1989), and social dominance (Sidanius & Pratto, 1999). Other extensions include theories of leadership (Hogg & van Knippenberg, 2003), de-individuation and collective behavior (Reicher, Spears, & Postmes, 1995), subjective group dynamics and deviance (Marques & Páez 1994), and accounts of identity processes that include optimal distinctiveness (Brewer, 1991), identity complexity (Roccas & Brewer, 2002), and self-conceptual uncertainty (Hogg, 2007). The focus of these theories is *how* people find a meaningful and acceptable self-concept through comparisons between the groups they belong to and the groups they do not. It is not simply the objective situation (such as relative wealth or power) that matters. The theories emphasize that social identity is most strongly associated with people's perception and interpretation of the intergroup differences (such as whether an outgroup's wealth was bestowed or acquired, and whether the means by which power is held were fair or not).

SELF-CATEGORIZATION THEORY

The self-categorization part of SIT yielded further important developments. A significant avenue was the explanation of social influence, referent informational influence theory. This initially focused on influence in groups (Turner, 1982) and was later articulated more closely with the self-categorization process (Abrams & Hogg, 1990). Another significant conceptual sub-theory focused on group cohesion and solidarity (Hogg, 1993). A third strand of theory focused on the cognitive salience of social identity (Oakes, Haslam, & Turner, 1994).

To explain *which* group memberships become salient, and thereby influence behavior, it is necessary to explain how and why group memberships become salient. Oakes (1987) proposed that social identity salience is based on an interaction of *accessibility* and *fit*. Categorizations are cognitively more accessible because they are used frequently (chronic accessibility) or are obviously relevant in a situation (situational accessibility). They are likely to fit better if they account for relevant similarities and differences among people (what they say, what they do, how they look) in a particular context (*comparative fit*), and make sense of people's behavior (*normative fit*). For example, an American–Canadian categorization would fit only if Americans and Canadians behaved differently and their behavior was consistent with one's stereotypes (prototypes) of the two national groups.

To explain the specific attributes that people associate with ingroups and outgroups, self-categorization theory holds that social comparisons determine the prototypical attributes of groups. These *prototypes* are derived by psychologically by maximizing the *metacontrast* – intergroup differences relative to intragroup differences. Clearer and more distinct group prototypes maximize group entitativity – the properties of a category that make it appear to be a cohesive and clearly structured entity that is distinct from other entities (Hamilton & Sherman, 1996). Prototypes of a particular group will vary, depending on the other groups with which it is compared, and which dimensions or attributes are most important. Ingroup prototypes are polarized away from focal outgroups, so ingroup prototypes tend to capture ideal rather than actual attributes, often resulting in intergroup biases.

Because category members are viewed as sharing the same social identity and associated group prototypical attributes, they are perceptually *depersonalized*. Perceptual depersonalization of outgroup members is usually termed stereotyping. A key insight of self-categorization theory is that, when group memberships are salient, categorization-based depersonalization also results in *self*-stereotyping in terms of in-group attributes. Perceived similarity within the in-group promotes greater liking, trust, and solidarity with in-group members. Note that depersonalization is different from dehumanization, which is a degraded perception of others as not worthy of being treated as human beings, and different from deindividuation, which

happens when anonymity and low accountability reduce self-regulation and increase disinhibition (Diener, 1980). The concept of depersonalization is fundamentally important for explaining why it is that people act and react in the name of groups to which they belong, and hence why groups are capable of concerted and coordinated actions that bring about social change. The nature and implications of this process are developed further in the next section.

THEORETICAL THEMES AND DEVELOPMENTS

Social identity salience transforms self-perception, thereby introducing biases and prejudices to intergroup relations that are rooted in the structure and processes of the self-concept. This section describes how SIT has been developed to include theories of the self-concept and motivation, processes within groups, complex intergroup situations, and reactions to collective disadvantage.

Many qualities may objectively define a group, such as common fate, interdependence, interaction, shared goals, group structure and other attributes of entitativity (Hamilton & Sherman, 1996). Groups vary in size, function, and history (Deaux, Reid, Mizrahi, et al., 1995). Some are similarity-based/categorical, common identity groups, and others are interaction-based/dynamic, common bond groups (Prentice, Miller & Lightdale, 1994). For SIT, a group is defined simply as two or more people who share the same social self-definition – the same social identity. People's commitment to a group, and adherence to its norms, depend on shared self-categorization and depersonalization. Consistent with the idea that the group and the self can be psychologically the same, people readily assume in-groups share their own attributes (Cadinu & Rothbart, 1996; Otten, 2002). Conversely, people can internalize the properties of other people, and of the ingroup as a whole, as part of the self (e.g., Wright, Aron & Tropp, 2002).

Self-structure and process

Although Tajfel defined social identity as including cognitive, emotional, and connotative components (see also, Jackson & Smith, 1999), there have been many efforts to refine and subdivide this definition. For example, Cameron (2004) describes three separate but related aspects: centrality (cognitive accessibility); ingroup affect (self-evaluative identity-based feelings); and ingroup ties (attachment and belonging to the group). It has also been proposed that social identity can be characterized by varying degrees of complexity involving structural overlap among self-categorizations, as well as varying numbers of different self-categorizations (Roccas & Brewer, 2002). Social identity complexity is greater when a person has a larger number of nonoverlapping identities because there are more non-compatible prototypes to contend with.

Brewer (2001) suggested that there could be four types of social identity: (a) *person-based social identities* involve internalization of properties of groups as part of the self-concept of individual members; (b) *relational social identities* are based on specific relationships within the context of the a group (see Markus & Kitayama's (1991) 'interdependent self'); (c) *group-based social identities* are self-categorized social identities as traditionally defined; and (d) *collective identities* involve engagement in social action to define the image of the group to others. These distinctions highlight that, even if a particular interaction is between two individuals (e.g., a dyadic discussion), they involve social identity if interactants view one another in terms of shared category or group characteristics. This may depend on the task at hand and the wider socio-cultural context. For example, Marques, Abrams and Seriodio (2001: Experiment 2) showed that participants more strongly derogated a person whose opinion (on an ethical issue) differed from those of the majority if they viewed the person and majority as part of their ingroup rather than purely as individuals.

In a further elaboration, Roccas, Sagiv, Schwartz, et al. (2008) proposed that, for national identity, there are four distinct modes of group identification – the *importance* of identity, *commitment* to benefit the group, *superiority* (desire for positive distinctiveness), and *deference* (embracing norms and leadership goals as one's own). These modes may differ in terms of situational and dispositional variability. Identification in different modes might have contradictory implications for behavior (e.g., if *commitment* suggests one course of action but *deference* another).

A related debate surrounds the connection between social identity and other aspects of the self. Individual, relational, and collective selves may be connected in complex ways (Brewer & Gardner, 1996). For example, social identity may develop through personal acceptance/adoption of group memberships, relational social identities that are specific to particular group contexts (Brewer, 2001), and through sustained interpersonal attraction and interdependence among group members (Henry, Arrow, & Carini, 1999).

SIT holds that personal and social identity are at opposite ends of a single continuum, and SCT describes them as being different levels of a hierarchy of self-categorizations. Both SIT and SCT view personal and social identity not as structures but as self-conceptualizations that can emerge from the same process involving different social comparative contexts and content (Abrams & Hogg, 2001). For example, consistent with the idea that social identity salience yields distinct phenomena, research on intergroup emotions shows that threats to social identity can evoke distinct group-level emotions of anger and fear that are associated with distinct, fight or flight, intergroup action tendencies (Mackie, Devos, & Smith, 2000).

Some have argued that there are structurally separate private, public, and collective aspects of the self (Greenwald & Pratkanis, 1984). Intuitively, personal identity seems likely to be more stable, enduring, and cognitively accessible than social identity, thus giving primacy to the individual self

(Sedikides & Gaertner, 2001). For example, Gaertner, Sedikides and Graetz (1999) found that positive and negative feedback had more impact when it was aimed at the individual rather than at the group, suggesting that people may be more sensitive to threats to personal identity. However, Spears, Doosje, et al. (1997) found that when an ingroup was under threat, low identifiers distanced themselves from the group (psychologically protecting the individual self), whereas high identifiers 'closed ranks,' emphasizing their collective self. This finding suggests that the question of *whether* the individual or collective self is primary may be the wrong question. The more critical questions, and the ones that are central to SIT, are when and why one or the other level of self takes primacy (Simon, 2004).

One possibility is that individual or collective self-primacy may be culturally determined. It seems possible that social identity is more important in collectivist cultures, such as those of Japan and China, where people appear to display more conformity to group norms (Bond & Smith, 1996). Dyadic relational identities in individualistic cultures may separate people from group memberships; whereas in collectivist cultures a person's network of relationships may locate him or her firmly within particular groups (Oyserman, Coon, & Kemmelmeier, 2002), suggesting that social identity is likely to be manifested in relational terms. However, it seems likely that, rather than involving different levels of primacy for individual and collective identities, different cultures differ in the way such identities are experienced and manifested. Although collectivist cultures foster greater commitment to specific types of group and interdependencies, individualistic cultures may offer people greater latitude to choose their groups rather than being chosen by groups. Indeed, individualism within Western culture may be a type of group norm (Jetten, Postmes & McAuliffe, 2002a), because people who identify with an individualistic group behave more individualistically (McAuliffe, Jetten, Hornsey, et al., 2003). Therefore, even if social identity is manifested

differently cross-culturally, the extent and underlying processes of social identification seem to be the same. For example, group identity motivates commitment to organizations to a similar degree in both types of culture (Randsley de Moura, Abrams, Retter, et al., 2009).

Motivation

Once social identity is salient, what motivates group and intergroup behavior, particularly ethnocentrism? Three connected themes emerge from social identity research: esteem, distinctiveness and meaning (Abrams & Hogg, 1988). SIT drew on basic human motives for self-enhancement and self-esteem (Sedikides & Strube, 1997), proposing that people are motivated to attain positive distinctiveness of their ingroup vis-à-vis outgroups. Abrams and Hogg (1988) unpacked this 'self-esteem hypothesis' into the distinct propositions that ingroup favoritism should enhance self-esteem, and that low self-esteem should enhance a striving for positive ingroup distinctiveness. Evidence is more consistent with the idea that high self-esteem and ingroup bias are positively related than with the idea that ingroup bias is a compensation strategy for low self-esteem. One of the few methodologically complete tests of the self-esteem hypothesis (Houston & Andreopoulou, 2003) supports the conclusion that group identification is more likely to influence self-esteem than vice versa. Moreover, the relationship between self-esteem and intergroup bias is affected by other variables such as the extremity of self-esteem, how strongly people identify with the group and whether members feel under threat (see, Aberson, Healy, & Romero, 2000; Rubin & Hewstone, 1998). Also, even though a devalued or stigmatized social identity is potentially depressing (Branscombe, Schmitt, & Harvey, 1999), people have a variety of ways to buffer the self-evaluative consequences of stigma (Major, Quinton, & McCoy, 2002; see also Chapter 24 by Crocker & Garcia and Chapter 25 by Major & Townsend in this volume).

Regardless of the status of one's group, uncertainty-identity theory (Hogg, 2007) proposes that uncertainty reduction is an epistemic motive associated with social categorization. Social categorization reduces uncertainty by establishing group prototypes that describe how people (including the self) will, and ought to, behave and interact with one another. These prototypes represent a subjective sense of consensus which validates both the situational definition of the self and the norms and world view of the ingroup. Therefore, facing self-conceptual uncertainty, people are motivated to self-categorize, preferably as a member of a group that is distinctive, highly entitative, and has a clear prototype.

Uncertainty reduction is likely to motivate the maintenance of intergroup boundaries and greater intragroup uniformity, and may help to explain the functions served by extremist groups that have tightly controlled belief systems, often with authoritarian structures. Just as terror management theory holds that mortality salience promotes world view defense (Pyszczynski, Greenberg, & Solomon, 1997), the wider argument can be made that espousing belief systems such as belief in a just world (Furnham & Procter, 1989) or right wing authoritarianism (Altemeyer, 1998), are liable to be more prevalent under conditions of social uncertainty and instability. Moreover, system justifying beliefs may be adopted by subordinate groups in part because a predictable status quo is preferable to high levels of self-conceptual uncertainty (see also Jost & Hunyadi, 2002).

Group membership *per se* may not always satisfy certainty needs because these are connected to group distinctiveness. According to Brewer (1991), in order to achieve optimal distinctiveness, people seek a balance between two conflicting motives, for inclusion/sameness and distinctiveness/uniqueness. Thus, minority group membership can sometimes satisfy the need for optimal distinctiveness and self-definition, although extreme or very low minority status may prove uncomfortable and thus reduce the likelihood of identification with the group.

Laboratory studies manipulating transitory perceptions of their (minimal or student) group's numerical distinctiveness show that when distinctiveness is either too high or too low people will compensate by elevating evaluations and changing the stereotypes of their ingroups (e.g., Pickett & Brewer, 2005). People also show commitment to social identity through their consumer preferences (Berger & Heath, 2008). For example, the music preferences and investments of a national sample of 2624 people aged 18 to 21 years showed higher levels of interest and investment in music styles that had objectively intermediate rather than high or low levels of distinctiveness (Abrams, 2009).

Social identity within groups

When group membership becomes salient, the basis of evaluations of and feelings for other people (i.e., liking) is transformed from personal identity based *personal attraction* (traditional interpersonal attraction) to prototype based depersonalized *social attraction* (Hogg, 1993). Consequently, social identity is a potent basis for intragroup cooperation because it decreases the perceived difference between individual welfare and the welfare of the group and increases trust and confidence that fellow group members will make an equal contribution. (De Cremer & van Vugt, 1999). However, just as one may like or dislike another individual for their personal traits, when social identity is salient people are judged as group members, based on their closeness to ingroup and outgroup prototypes. This has implications for the way groups deal with dissent and deviance.

Less prototypical members, particularly those who are prototypically marginal, are not liked (social attraction) or trusted much by the group, and are therefore relatively un-influential and are cast as deviants who are especially vulnerable to social exclusion. Deviants attract attention because they potentially affect the subjective validity of ingroup norms. People are generally more intolerant of ingroup deviants than of outgroup deviants, a so called 'black sheep effect'

(Marques, & Páez, 1994). For example derogation of ingroup deviants results in more positive ingroup stereotypes (Hutchison, Abrams, Guitierrez, et al., 2008) and more positive social identity (Marques, Abrams, Taboada, et al., 1998). Overall, the evidence shows very consistently that group members' reactions to deviants reflect a strategic goal of sustaining positive ingroup identity. Indeed, from as young as 7-years old children seem to understand that group members have these goals and use them to exclude relevant group members (Abrams, Rutland, Pelletier, et al., 2009).

In line with this theme that people are especially inclusive of protoptypical, and exclusive of deviant, ingroup members, the SIT of leadership holds that group members who embody group norms better than others are more prototypical, disproportionately influential and likely to be viewed as leaders (Hogg & van Knippenberg, 2003), Such leaders are figural against the background of the rest of the group so their behavior is internally attributed, constructing a leadership persona that further facilitates effective leadership, and conformity by other members. This can create a virtuous circle whereby a valued leader sees him or herself as highly prototypical member, identifies more strongly with the group and behaves in a group-serving manner which builds further trust for them among fellow members (Tyler, 1997).

If groups are prone to chastising or even evicting their deviant members, how are they able to develop and change, and does social identity inevitably result in the kind of highly polarized group norms often associated with political or religious extremism? Although marginal members are generally treated negatively by the group, they may also fulfill important social change functions for the group so that normative dissent is likely to be accepted by the group (Packer, 2008). Moreover, leaders who are trusted to be acting in the best interest of the group are given greater latitude than other group members to be innovative and non-conformist (Abrams, Randsely de Moura, Hutchison, et al., 2008). Groups

also accept criticism more readily from loyal ingroup members than from outgroup members (Hornsey, Grice, Jetten, et al., 2007).

Intergroup structure and organization

Cohesion and conformity within groups are also connected strongly to the intergroup context. Whereas SIT mostly considered situations only involving comparisons between two groups, many groups find themselves embedded in more complex structures. Ashforth and Mael's (1989) application of SIT to organizational settings stimulated a significant upsurge in research in this area (e.g., Haslam, 2004; Hogg & Terry, 2000). For example, research on organizational commitment and turnover (e.g., Ellemers, Kortekaas, & Ouwerkerk, 1999a; Randsley de Moura, Abrams, Retter, et al., 2009) shows that identification with the organization is consistently related to other forms of commitment such as team and organizational citizenship, loyalty, turnover and related constructs. Tyler and Blader's (2003) Group Engagement Model highlights the importance of procedural justice for the valuing of social identity within organizations, and the way people then engage with others. In particular, people identify more with an organization if they perceive it is has high status which is reflected by it being affected by fair procedures. A heightened sense of group status means that they engage psychologically with the organization, expressed via their attitudes, adoption of shared values, and voluntarily engaging in behavior that supports the organization.

Organizations often contain departments or teams that allow identification with subordinate categories vis à vis the organization as a whole. Thus, people may be biased against other work groups while sustaining positive identification with the overarching organization (Hennessy & West, 1999). Mergers also present special challenges to social identity (e.g., Terry, Carey, & Callan, 2001), which may only result in stronger superordinate identity among groups that experience continuity of identity in the merged organization (van Leeuwen, van Knippenberg, et al., 2003). Increasing the relative salience of a common ingroup identity is potentially beneficial for social harmony between subgroups (Gaertner & Dovidio, 2000; see also Gaertner, Dovidio, & Houlette's Chapter 32 in this volume) – for example Barak Obama's emphasis on national unity and identity during his 2008 presidential election campaign to bridge the gulf between Republicans and Democrats. However, Hornsey and Hogg (2000) have suggested that dual identification with both the subgroup and superordinate levels might prove most effective (see also Crisp, Ensari, Hewstone, et al., 2003). Similarly, Brown and Hewstone (2005) have shown that successful intergroup contact may depend on the sustained salience of distinctive identities even while cross-group friendships are being established.

An additional complexity is that subgroups are likely to differ in their power and status, so that the superordinate level offers different opportunities for each. The ingroup projection model (Wenzel, Mummendey, & Waldzus, 2007) suggests that one nested group almost invariably occupies a dominant position in the superordinate category, creating identity threat for other subgroups. Moreover, such situations are a seed bed for schisms (Sani & Reicher, 2000). For example, Waldzus and Mummendey (2004) observed that the more strongly German participants viewed Germany as prototypical of Europe the less positively they evaluated Poland (another part of Europe).

Collective action and protest

One of Tajfel's original concerns was how and when minority groups would mobilize to contest inequality, prejudice and discrimination and situations of relative deprivation (see also Wright's Chapter 35). Runciman's (1966) distinction between egoistic (or personal) and fraternalistic (group) deprivation has been fundamental in research showing that indeed deprivation at these two levels is not experienced as the same thing or in the same way

(Walker & Mann, 1987). Understanding the intergroup context and group identification helps to account for the nature and target of collective action (Kawakami & Dion, 1995). The social identity-deindividuation interpretation of collective aggression and violence is that these arise because depersonalization transforms the self from being a unique individual to being a representative of a social category or group for which such conduct is prototypical. This reasoning has been used to explain why riots (e.g. in Bristol during the 1980s, or the Rodney King riots) often have a clearly delimited target. These may be the police, authorities, or selected neighborhoods or particular shops, or categories of people, which are focal points at which particular intergroup conflicts find their expression (Reicher, Spears, & Postmes, 1995). It is rarely the case that rioters vent their anger on one another, and it is instead the case that violence targeted at an out-group, such as lynchings, may become more extreme when factors such as relative group size increase the salience of ingroup/ outgroup differences (Leader, Mullen, & Abrams, 2008).

Neither deprivation or identification alone will necessarily provoke reaction to unfair inequality. Research suggests that social identity and rational-choice can have additive and independent effects (Simon, Loewy, Sturmer, et al., 1998), and Simon and Klandermans' (2001) model of politicized collective identity holds that political mobilization involves a sequence from construing shared grievances, to blaming political opponents and then seeking to make connections between one's own group's cause and the values of society as a whole. Recently, van Zomeron, Postmes and Spears (2008) marshaled meta-analytic evidence to argue that social identity provides the binding medium through which the sense of efficacy and injustice may influence collective action. However, the connection between deprivation and disadvantage and social identification seems to be complex and dynamic. For example, ability to leave a disadvantaged group does not necessarily result in disidentification or personal mobility out of that group (Abrams & Randsley de Moura,

2002; Kelly & Breinlinger, 1996) and the mere possibility of social mobility may be enough to quell potential protest (Wright, Taylor & Moggadham, 1990).

OTHER DEVELOPMENTS AND FUTURE DIRECTIONS

SIT is an unusually far-reaching and generative theoretical framework, and it has been applied to a range of other research directions beyond those covered in previous sections. Among these are Tajfel's (1981) powerful analysis of stereotyping which emphasized the shared nature of stereotypes, and their social functions. These functions include social differentiation between groups, attribution or explanation for differences between groups, and justification for differential status or treatment of groups. These functions are rooted not just in individual motivation, but in social structural relationships between groups and the shared reality in which these are embedded. Extrapolating from past research it is inevitable that social identity theory still has a great deal to offer the analysis of prejudice and discrimination. In particular, because it focuses on intergroup differences, the theory highlights that there are always at least two perspectives in any intergroup situation (the ingroup's and the outgroup's), as well as the third (those of noninvolved groups and observers or analysts). Most research has focused on participant's perspectives as ingroup members. There remains a great deal of scope for developing work that considers multiple perspectives in the same situation.

Previous research has focused on how people regulate social identity strategically (Abrams, 1994; Emler & Reicher, 2005; Jetten, Branscombe & Spears, 2002b). This also represents an important avenue for future research, both in terms of whether people structure their plans for action differently when social rather than personal identifications are involved (Sassenberg & Woltin, 2008), and in terms of the external realities and relationships that may constrain or direct behavior as a group member. We should not forget the links to sociology, economics and politics, namely that there are social structural forces that change the contingencies affecting groups. There is much to be gained by developing social identity theory and research with ideas from these related disciplines.

Another important avenue for future research is how social identity processes operate and develop from early childhood. There is already clear evidence that young children show both category-based ingroup bias and a sophisticated understanding of contrasting social norms in intergroup situations (Levy & Killen, 2008). However, it remains unclear quite how children make sense of their experiences of being treated *variably*, sometimes as a group member (e.g. as 'a boy', 'white') and sometimes as an individual. To what extent are they able to use these experiences strategically to forge a positive identity, or to create coalitions and alliances with other children? To what extent does childhood experience of social identification have implications for identity and group behavior as an adult?

There is a large volume of work that has dwelled on the nature of perceiving groups (e.g., McGarty, Yzerbyt & Spears, 2002), and related work on entitativity (Yzerbyt, Judd & Corneille, 2004). Now, however, it is necessary for research to investigate whether there is anything especially unique about the identity of 'human'. This is a neglected aspect of self-categorization research but is specified as the relevant superordinate category in many intergroup situations. It is becoming increasingly important as non-human metaphors abound for the social world (e.g. the person as part of an information system, as a molecule, as an evolutionary organism, or as a product of neuropsychological processes), and as our collective common fate becomes increasingly relevant (via global warming, global economic crises, pandemics and collective threats such as terrorism). Does our use of these metaphors, or alternatively our focus on shared humanity, strip away people's multiple social identifications? Will it reduce people's sense of collective engagement and efficacy?

More broadly, there is a role for applying social identity research to significant and important relationships of many kinds, whether it be in understanding how intergroup contact may be most beneficial in reducing intergroup bias (Brown & Hewstone, 2005; Wagner, Tropp, Finchilescu, et al., 2008), or the role of multiple social identities in social exclusion and community cohesion (Abrams & Christian, 2007). Finally, communication is a crucial vehicle for social identity dynamics, and language, with its strong cultural and historical roots, is one of the most potent symbols of identity (Reid & Giles, 2005). There is ample scope for development of research and theory that integrates self-categorization and social identity to improve the analysis and interpretation of both person-to-person and mass communications.

SUMMARY AND CONCLUSIONS

This chapter has outlined the key points of social identity and self-categorization theories. By conceptualizing group and intergroup behavior as emanating from a transformation of self-categorization these theories provide a coherent framework within which to explain a wide range of phenomena, and in particular the biases and prejudices that appear to result from people's memberships of different groups.

We showed how the theory explains the function of the self-concept as a continuous process that responds to and reflects salient social categories. We also considered how the theory incorporates the motivational themes of esteem, distinctiveness and meaning. We showed why social identity has powerful implications for the social inclusion and exclusion of members within groups, and how it explains collective action and reactions to disadvantage. Along the way we also considered the links between social identity and stereotypes, multiple identities and more complex sets of social relationships.

One may pessimistically conclude that social identity is at the root of all prejudice and bias against outgroups. As other chapters in this volume attest, conditions of conflict and inequality can greatly strengthen the salience of social identity and are likely to provoke more extreme instances of intergroup hatred and rivalry, or intragroup intolerance and pressures to conform (see Chapter 14 by Esses, Jackson, & Bennett-AbuAyyash). However, social identity can also promote constructive, group-supporting behavior as well as social competition against out-groups. It is also clear that social identity provides important sources of meaning, continuity, and direction in people's lives.

REFERENCES

Aberson, C. L., Healy, M. R., & Romero, V. L. (2000). Ingroup bias and self-esteem: A meta-analysis. *Personality and Social Psychology Review*, 4, 157–173.

Abrams, D. (1994). Social self-regulation. *Personality and Social Psychology Bulletin*, 20, 473–483.

Abrams, D. (2009). Social identity on a national scale: Optimal distinctiveness and young people's self-expression through musical preference. *Group Processes and Intergroup Relations*, 12, 303–317.

Abrams, D., & Christian, J. N. (2007). A relational analysis of social exclusion. In D. Abrams, J. N. Christian, & D. Gordon (Eds), *Multidisciplinary Handbook of Social Exclusion Research* (pp. 211–232). Oxford: Wiley-Blackwell.

Abrams, D., & Hogg, M. A. (1988). Comments on the motivational status of self-esteem in social identity and intergroup discrimination. *European Journal of Social Psychology*, 18, 317–334.

Abrams, D., & Hogg, M. A. (1990). Social identification, self-categorization and social influence. In W. Stroebe, & M. Hewstone (Eds), *European Review of Social Psychology* (Vol 1, pp. 195–228). Chichester, UK: John Wiley.

Abrams, D., & Hogg, M. A. (2001). Collective identity: Group membership and self-conception. In M. A. Hogg, & R. S. Tindale, (Eds), *Blackwell Handbook of Social Psychology: Group Processes* (pp. 425–460). Oxford, UK: Blackwell.

Abrams, D., & Hogg, M. A. (2004). Metatheory: Lessons from social identity research. *Personality and Social Psychology Review*, 8, 98–106.

Abrams, D., & Randsley de Moura, G. (2002). The psychology of collective political protest. In V. C. Ottati, R. S. Tindale, J. Edwards, D. O'Connell, E. Posavac, E. Suarez-Balcazar, L. Heath, & F. Bryant

(Eds). *The Social Psychology of Politics: Social Psychological Application to Social Issues* (Vol. 5, pp. 193–214). New York: Plenum Press.

Abrams, D., Randsley de Moura, G., Hutchison, P., & Marques, J. M. (2008). Innovation credit: When can leaders oppose their groups? *Journal of Personality and Social Psychology*, 95, 662–678.

Abrams, D., Rutland, A., Pelletier, J., & Ferrell J. (2009). Group nous and social exclusion: The role of theory of social mind, multiple classification skill and social experience of peer relations within groups. *Child Development*, 80, 224–243.

Altemeyer, B. (1998). The other "authoritarian personality". In M. Zanna (ed.), *Advances in Experimental Social Psychology* (Vol. 30, pp. 47–92). Orlando, FL: Academic Press.

Ashforth, B. E., & Mael, F. A. (1989). Social identity theory and the organization. *Academy of Management Review*, 14, 20–39.

Berger, J., & Heath, C. (2008). Who drives divergence? Identity-signaling, out-group dissimilarity, and the abandonment of cultural tastes. *Journal of Personality and Social Psychology*, 95, 593–607.

Bond, R., & Smith, P. B. (1996). Culture and conformity: A meta-analysis of studies using Asch's (1952b, 1956) line judgment task. *Psychological Bulletin*, 119, 111–137.

Bourhis, R. Y., Sachdev, I., & Gagnon, A. (1994). Intergroup research with the Tajfel matrices: Methodological notes. In M. Zanna, & J. Olson (Eds), *The Psychology of Prejudice: The Ontario Symposium* (Vol. 7, pp. 209–22). Hillsdale, NJ: Erlbaum.

Branscombe, N. R., Schmitt, M. T., & Harvey, R. D.(1999). Perceiving pervasive discrimination among African Americans: Implications for group identification and well-being. *Journal of Personality and Social Psychology*, 77, 135–149.

Breakwell, G. (1986). *Coping With Threatened Identities.* London: Methuen.

Brewer, M. B. (1991). The social self: On being the same and different at the same time. *Personality and Social Psychology Bulletin*, 17, 475–482.

Brewer, M. B. (2001). The many faces of social identity: Implications for political psychology. *Political Psychology*, 22, 115–125.

Brewer, M. B., & Gardner, W. (1996). Who is this "we"? Levels of collective identity and self representations. *Journal of Personality and Social Psychology*, 71, 83–93.

Brown, R. J., & Hewstone, M. (2005). An integrative theory of intergroup contact. In M. P. Zanna (Ed.), *Advances in Experimental Social Psychology* (Vol. 37, pp. 255–343). Orlando, FL: Academic Press.

Bruner, J. S. (1957). On perceptual readiness. *Psychological Review*, 64, 123–152.

Cadinu, M. R., & Rothbart, M. (1996). Self-anchoring and differentiation processes in the minimal group setting. *Journal of Personality and Social Psychology*, 70, 661–677.

Cameron, J. E. (2004). A three-factor model of social identity. *Self and Identity*, 3, 239–262.

Crisp, R., Ensari, N., Hewstone, M., & Miller, N. (2003). A dual-route model of crossed categorization effects. In W. Stroebe, & M. Hewstone (Eds), *Euorpean Review of Social Psychology* (Vol 13, pp. 35–74). New York: Psychology Press.

Deaux, K., Reid, A., Mizrahi, K., & Ethier, K. A. (1995). Parameters of social identity. *Journal of Personality and Social Psychology*, 68, 280–291.

de Cremer, D., & van Vugt, M. (1999). Social identification effects in social dilemmas: A transformation of motives. *European Journal of Social Psychology*, 29, 871–893.

Diener, E. (1980). Deindividuation: The absence of self-awareness and self-regulation in group members. In P. B. Paulus (Ed.), *Psychology of Group Influence* (pp. 209–242). Hillsdale, NJ: Erlbaum.

Ellemers, N., Spears, R., & Doojse, B. (Eds) (1999a). *Social Identity.* Oxford, UK: Blackwell.

Ellemers, N., Kortekaas, P., & Ouwerkerk, J. W. (1999b). Self-categorization, commitment to the group and group self-esteem as related but distinct aspects of social identity. *European Journal of Social Psychology*, 29, 371–389.

Emler, N., & Reicher, S.D. (2005). Delinquency: Causes or consequences of social exclusion? In D. Abrams, M. A. Hogg, & J. M. Marques (Eds). *The Social Psychology of Inclusion and Exclusion* (pp. 211–242). New York: Psychology Press.

Fiske, S. T., Cuddy, A. J. C., Glick, P., & Xu, J. (2002). A model of (often mixed) stereotype content: Competence and warmth respectively follow from perceived status and competition. *Journal of Personality and Social Psychology*, 82, 878–902.

Furnham, A., & Procter, E. (1989). Belief in a just world: Review and critique of the individual difference literature. *British Journal of Social Psychology*, 28, 365–384.

Gaertner, L., Sedikides, C., & Graetz, K. (1999). In search of self-definition: Motivational primacy of the individual self, motivational primacy of the collective self, or contextual primacy? *Journal of Personality and Social Psychology*, 76, 5–18.

Gaertner, S. L., & Dovidio, J. F. (2000). *Reducing Intergroup Bias: The Common In-group Identity Model.* New York: Psychology Press.

Greenwald, A. G., & Pratkanis, A. R. (1984). The self. In R. S. Wyer, & T. K. Srull (Eds), *Handbook of*

Social Cognition (Vol. 3, pp. 129–178). Hillsdale, NJ: Erlbaum.

Hamilton, D. L., & Sherman, S. J. (1996). Perceiving persons and groups. *Psychological Review*, 103, 336–355.

Haslam, S. A. (2004). *Psychology in Organisations: The Social Identity Approach* (2nd edition). London: Sage.

Hennessy, J., & West, M. A. (1999). Intergroup behavior in organizations. *Small Group Research*, 30, 361–382.

Henry, K. B., Arrow, H., & Carini, B. (1999). A tripartite model of group identification: theory and measurement. *Small Group Research*, 30, 558–581.

Hogg, M. A. (1993). Group cohesiveness: A critical review and some new directions. In W. Stroebe, & M. Hewstone (Eds), *European Review of Social Psychology* (Vol. 4, pp. 85–111). Chichester, UK: John Wiley.

Hogg, M. A. (2007). Uncertainty-identity theory. In M. P. Zanna (Ed.), *Advances in Experimental Social Psychology* (Vol. 39, pp. 69–126). San Diego, CA: Academic Press.

Hogg, M. A., & Abrams, D. (1988). *Social Identifications: A Social Psychology of Intergroup Relations and Group Processes*. London and New York: Routledge.

Hogg, M. A., & Terry, D. J. (2000). Social identity and self-categorization processes in organizational contexts. *Academy of Management Review*, 25, 121–140.

Hogg, M. A., & van Knippenberg, D. (2003). Social identity and leadership processes in groups. In M. P. Zanna (Ed.), *Advances in Experimental Social Psychology* (Vol. 35, pp. 1–52). San Diego, CA: Academic Press.

Hornsey, M. J., & Hogg, M. A. (2000). Assimilation and diversity: An integrative model of subgroup relations. *Personality and Social Psychology Review*, 4, 143–156.

Hornsey, M. J., Grice, T., Jetten, J., Paulsen, N., & Callan, V. (2007). Group directed criticisms and recommendations for change: Why newcomers arouse more resistance than old-timers. *Personality and Social Psychology Bulletin*, 33, 1036–1048.

Houston, D. M., & Andreopoulou, A. (2003). Tests of both corollaries of social identity theory's self-esteem hypothesis in a real group setting. *British Journal of Social Psychology*, 42, 357–370.

Hutchison, P., Abrams, D., Gutierrez, R., & Viki, T. (2008). Getting rid of the bad ones: The relationship between group identification, deviant derogation and identity maintenance. *Journal of Experimental Social Psychology*, 44, 874–881.

Jackson, J. W., & Smith, E. R. (1999). Conceptualizing social identity: A new framework and evidence for the impact of different dimensions. *Personality and Social Psychology Bulletin*, 25, 120–135.

Jetten, J., Branscombe, N., & Spears, R. (2002b). On being peripheral: effects of identity insecurity on personal and collective self esteem. *European Journal of Social Psychology*, 32, 105–123.

Jetten, J., Postmes, T., & McAuliffe, B. J. (2002a). "We're all individuals": Group norms of individualism and collectivism, levels of identification, and identity threat. *European Journal of Social Psychology*, 32, 189–207.

Jost, J. T., & Hunyadi, O. (2002). The psychology of system justification and the palliative function of ideology. In W. Stroebe, & M. Hewstone (Eds), *European Review of Social Psychology* (Vol. 13, pp. 111–153). Hove, UK: Psychology Press.

Kawakami, K., & Dion, K. L. (1995). Social identity and affect as determinants of collective action: towards an integration of relative deprivation and social identity theories. *Theory and Psychology*, 5, 551–577.

Kelly, C., & Breinlinger, S. (1996). *The Social Psychology of Collective Action: Identity, Injustice and Gender*. London: Taylor & Francis.

Klandermans, B. (1997). *The Social Psychology of Protest*. Oxford, UK: Blackwell.

Leader, T., Mullen, B., & Abrams, D. (2008). Without mercy: The immediate impact of group size on lynch mob atrocity. *Personality and Social Psychology Bulletin*, 33, 1340–1352.

Levy, S. R., & Killen, M. (Eds) (2008). *Intergroup Attitudes and Relations in Childhood Through Adulthood*. Oxford, England: Oxford University Press.

Mackie, D. M., Devos, T., & Smith, E. R. (2000). Intergroup emotions: Explaining offensive action tendencies in an intergroup context. *Journal of Personality and Social Psychology*, 79, 602–616.

Major, B., Quinton, W. J., & McCoy, S. K. (2002). Antecedents and consequences of attributions to discrimination: Theoretical and empirical advances. In M. P. Zanna (Ed.), *Advances in Experimental Social Psychology* (Vol. 34, pp. 251–330). San Diego, CA: Academic Press.

Markus, H., & Kitayama, S. (1991). Culture and the self: Implications for cognition, emotion and motivation. *Psychological Review*, 98, 224–253.

Marques, J., Abrams, D., Páez, D., & Martinez-Taboada, C. (1998). The role of categorization and in-group norms in judgments of groups and their members. *Journal of Personality and Social Psychology*, 75, 976–988.

Marques, J. M, Abrams, D., & Serodio, R. (2001). Being better by being right: Subjective group dynamics and derogation of in-group deviants when generic norms are undermined. *Journal of Personality and Social Psychology*, 81, 436–447.

Marques, J. M., & Páez, D. (1994). The black sheep effect: Social categorization, rejection of in-group deviates, and perception of group variability. In W. Stroebe, & M. Hewstone (Eds), *European Review of Social Psychology* (Vol. 5, pp. 37–68). Chichester, UK: John Wiley.

McAuliffe, B. J., Jetten, J., Hornsey, M. J., & Hogg, M. A. (2003). Individualist and collectivist group norms: When it's OK to go your own way. *European Journal of Social Psychology*, 33: 57–70.

McGarty, C., Yzerbyt, V.Y., & Spears, R., (Eds) (2002). *Stereotypes as Explanations. The Formation of Meaningful Beliefs About Social Groups.* Cambridge: Cambridge University Press.

Oakes, P. J. (1987). The salience of social categories. In J. C. Turner, M. A. Hogg, P. J. Oakes, S. D. Reicher, & M. S. Wetherell (Eds). *Rediscovering the Social Group: A Self-Categorization Theory* (pp. 117–141). Oxford: Blackwell.

Oakes, P. J., Haslam, S. A., & Turner, J. C. (1994). *Stereotyping and Social Reality.* Oxford, UK: Blackwell.

Otten, S. (2002). "Me" and "us" or "us" and "them"? The self as heuristic for defining novel ingroups. In W. Stroebe, & M. Hewstone (Eds), *European Review of Social Psychology* (Vol. 13, pp. 1–33). Hove, UK: Psychology Press.

Oyserman, D., Coon, H. M., & Kemmelmeier, M. (2002). Rethinking individualism and collectivism: Evaluation of theoretical assumptions and meta-analyses. *Psychological Bulletin*, 128, 3–72.

Packer, D. J. (2008). On being with us and against us: A normative conflict model of dissent in social groups. *Personality and Social Psychology Review*, 12, 50–72.

Pickett, C. L., & Brewer, M. B. (2005). The role of exclusion in maintaining in-group inclusion. In D. Abrams, M. A. Hogg, & J. M. Marques (Eds), *The Social Psychology of Inclusion and Exclusion* (pp. 89–112). New York: Psychology Press.

Prentice, D. A., Miller, D., & Lightdale, J. R. (1994). Asymmetries in attachment to groups and to their members: Distinguishing between common-identity and common-bond groups. *Personality and Social Psychology Bulletin*, 20, 484–493.

Pyszczynski, T., Greenberg, J., & Solomon, S. (1997). Why do we need what we need? A terror management perspective on the roots of human social motivation. *Psychological Inquiry*, 8, 1–20.

Randsley de Moura, G., Abrams, D., Retter, C., Gunnarsdottir, S., & Ando, K. (2009). Identification as an organizational anchor: How identification and job satisfaction combine to predict turnover intention. *European Journal of Social Psychology*, 39, 540–557.

Randsley de Moura, G.R., Leader, T.I., Pelletier, J.P., & Abrams, D. (2008). Prospects for group processes and intergroup relations research: A review of 70 years' progress. *Group Processes and Intergroup Relations*, 11, 575–596.

Reicher, S. D., Spears, R., & Postmes, T. (1995). A social identity model of deindividuation phenomena. In W. Stroebe, & M. Hewstone (Eds), *European Review of Social Psychology* (Vol. 6, pp 161–198). Chichester, UK: John Wiley.

Reid, S. A., & Giles, H. (2005). Intergroup relations: Its linguistic and communicative parameters. *Group Processes and Intergroup Relations*, 8, 211.

Roccas, S., & Brewer, M. B. (2002). Social identity complexity. *Personality and Social Psychology Review*, 6, 88–109.

Roccas, S., Sagiv, L., Schwartz, S., Halevy, N., & Eidelson, R. (2008). Toward a unifying model of identification with groups: Integrating theoretical perspectives. *Personality and Social Psychology Review*, 12, 280–306.

Rubin, M., & Hewstone, M. (1998). Social identity theory's self-esteem hypothesis: A review and some suggestions for clarification. *Personality and Social Psychology Review*, 2, 40–62.

Runciman, W.G. (1966). *Relative Deprivation and Social Justice.* London: Routledge.

Sani, F., & Reicher, S.D. (2000). Contested identities and schisms in groups: Opposing the ordianation of women as priests in the Church of England. *British Journal of Social Psychology*, 39, 95–112.

Sassenberg, K., & Woltin, K. (2008). Group-based self-regulation: The effects of regulatory focus. In W. Stroebe, & M. Hewstone (Eds), *European Review of Social Psychology* (Vol. 19, pp. 126–164). New York: Psychology Press.

Sedikides, C., & Gaertner, L. (2001). A homecoming to the individual self. Emotional and motivational primacy. In C. Sedikides, & M. B. Brewer (Eds), *Individual Self, Relational Self, Collective Self* (pp. 7–25). Philadelphia: Psychology Press.

Sedikides, C., & Strube, M. J. (1997). Self-evaluation: To thine own self be good, to thine own self be sure, to thine own self be true, and to thine own self be better. In M. P. Zanna (Ed.), *Advances in Experimental Social Psychology* (Vol. 29, pp. 209–296). New York: Academic Press.

Sidanius, J., & Pratto, F. (1999). *Social Dominance: An Intergroup Theory of Social Hierarchy and Oppression.* Cambridge: Cambridge University Press.

Simmel, G. (1955). *Conflict and the Web of Group Affiliations.* New York: Free Press.

Simon, B. (2004). *Identity in a Modern Society: A Social Psychological Perspective.* Oxford: Blackwell.

Simon, B., & Klandermans, B. (2001). Politicized collective identity: A social psychological analysis. *American Psychologist*, 56, 319–331.

Simon, B., Loewy, M., Sturmer, S., Weber, U., Freytang, P., Habig, C., et al., (1998). Collective identification and social movement participation. *Journal of Personality and Social Psychology*, 74, 646–658.

Spears, R., Doosje, B., & Ellemers, N. (1997). Self-stereotyping in the face of threats to group status and distinctiveness: The role of group identification. *Personality and Social Psychology Bulletin*, 23, 538–553.

Tajfel, H. (1959). Quantitative judgement in social perception. *British Journal of Psychology*, 50, 16–29.

Tajfel, H. (1969). Cognitive aspects of prejudice. *Journal of Social Issues*, 25, 79–97.

Tajfel, H. (1972). Social categorization. English manuscript of "La catégorisation sociale". In S. Moscovici (Ed.), *Introduction à la Psychologie Sociale* (Vol. 1, pp. 272–302). Paris: Larousse.

Tajfel, H. (1974). *Intergroup Behaviour, Social Comparison and Social Change*. Unpublished Katz-Newcomb lectures, University of Michigan, Ann Arbor.

Tajfel, H. (1981). Social stereotypes and social groups. In J. C. Turner, & H. Giles (Eds), *Intergroup Behaviour* (pp. 144–167). Oxford: Blackwell.

Tajfel, H., & Turner, J. C. (1979). An integrative theory of intergroup conflict. In W. G. Austin, & S. Worchel (Eds), *The Social Psychology of Intergroup Relations* (pp. 33–47). Monterey, CA: Brooks/Cole. (reprinted in M. A. Hogg, & D. Abrams (2001) *Intergroup Relations*). New York: Psychology Press.

Taylor, D. M., & Moghaddam, F. M. (1984). *Theories of Intergroup Relations: International Social Psychological Perspectives*. Westport Conn.: Praeger.

Terry, D. J., Carey, C. J., & Callan, V. J. (2001). Employee adjustment to an organizational merger: An intergroup perspective. *Personality and Social Psychology Bulletin*, 27, 267–280.

Turner, J. C. (1982). Towards a cognitive redefinition of the social group. In H. Tajfel (Ed.), *Social Identity and Intergroup Relations* (pp. 15–40). Cambridge, UK: Cambridge University Press.

Turner, J. C. (1985). Social categorization and the self-concept: A social cognitive theory of group behavior. In E. J. Lawler (Ed.), *Advances in Group Processes: Theory and Research* (Vol. 2, pp. 77–122). Greenwich, CT: JAI Press.

Turner, J. C., Hogg, M. A., Oakes, P. J., Reicher, S. D., & Wetherell, M. S. (1987). *Rediscovering the Social Group: A Self-Categorization Theory*. Oxford, UK: Blackwell.

Tyler, T. R. (1997). The psychology of legitimacy: A relational perspective on voluntary deference to authorities. *Personality and Social Psychology Review*, 1, 323–345.

Tyler, T. R., & Blader, S. L. (2003). The Group Engagement Model: Procedural justice social identity and cooperative behavior. *Personality and Social Psychology Review*, 7, 349–361.

van Leeuwen, E., van Knippenberg, D., & Ellemers, N. (2003). Continuing and changing group identities: The effects of merging on social identification and ingroup bias. *Personality and Social Psychology Bulletin*, 29, 697–690.

Van Zomeren, M., Postmes, T., & Spears, R. (2008). Towards an integrative social identity model of collective action. A quantitative research synthesis of three socio-psychological perspectives. *Psychological Bulletin*, 134, 504–535.

Wagner, U., Tripp, L.R., Finchilescu, G., & Tredoux, C. (Eds) (2008). *Improving Intergroup Relations: Building on the Legacy of Thomas F. Pettigrew*. Oxford: Blackwell.

Waldzus, S., & Mummendey, A. (2004). Inclusion in a superordinate category, in-group prototypicality, and attitudes towards out-groups. *Journal of Experimental Social Psychology*, 40, 466–477.

Walker, I., & Mann, L. (1987). Unemployment, relative deprivation and social protest. *Personality and Social Psychology Bulletin*, 13, 275–283.

Wenzel, M., Mummendey, A., & Waldzus, S. (2007). Superordinate identities and intergroup conflict: The ingroup projection model. In W. Stroebe, & M. Hewstone (Eds), *European Review of Social Psychology* (Vol. 18, pp. 331–372). Hove, UK: Psychology Press.

Wright, S. C., Aron, A., & Tropp, L. R. (2002). Including others (and groups) in the self: Self-expansion and intergroup relations. In J. P. Forgas, & K. D. Williams (Eds), *The Social Self: Cognitive, Interpersonal, and Intergroup Perspectives* (pp. 343–363). New York: Psychology Press.

Wright, S. C., Taylor, D. M., & Moghaddam, F. M. (1990), Responding to membership in a disadvantaged group: From acceptance to collective protest. *Journal of Personality and Social Psychology*, 58, 994–1003.

Yzerbyt, V., Judd, C., & Corneille, O. (Eds) (2004). *The Psychology of Group Perception: Perceived Variability, Entitativity, and Essentialism*. New York: Psychology Press.

12

Ethnocentrism and Group Realities

Jacques-Philippe Leyens and Stéphanie Demoulin

ABSTRACT

Group members construct consensual beliefs – group realities – the function of which reflects more an ethnocentric than objective reality. Ingroup favoritism and outgroup derogation are key concepts in this perspective. Maintenance and reinforcement of these group realities are helped by a series of micro-processes such as expectations, selective attention, vigilance, and confirmatory bias. While advantageous, the juxtaposition of these processes does not help to create an overarching theory(ies). The Stereotype Content Model and infra-humanization are offered as attempts at formalization. Finally, it is suggested that reduction of conflicts between groups might be obtained by respecting their ethnocentric group realities rather than suppressing the group reality of the weaker side, and letting them use different strategies rather than imposing a unique standard.

GROUP REALITIES

Groups develop specific social constructions – group realities – that may be based on the surrounding reality but diverge considerably from objective facts. For example, when Sumner (1906) introduced the term 'ethnocentrism,' he literally meant that each ethnic group considered itself the center of the world, with other groups being gauged with respect to it along a continuum ranging from best to worse, with 'best' corresponding to the ingroup. Ethnocentrism therefore represents ingroup members' belief in their group's superiority to outgroups even when objective measures might contradict or fail to support this belief.

Group realities remain fundamentally shaped by intergroup processes that give rise to intergroup beliefs or 'social products' such as ingroup favoritism, outgroup derogation and infra-humanization. These shared products correspond to group, more than strictly objective, realities. That is, each group defines its own reality and means of testing its beliefs. For example, when the Catholic Spanish first encountered Indians in the Americas they debated the humanity of the Indians given that the latter did not believe in God – imposing their group reality of what it means to be 'human.' Indians similarly questioned the humanity of the Spaniards, but answered the question by observing whether dead Spanish putrefied, to see whether the process was similar to what happened to their own dead (Lévi-Strauss, 1952/1987).

This chapter explains how group realities are subjectively constructed and then socially validated as 'facts.' We begin with historical background using ethnographic data and show how psychologists subsequently approached the phenomenon from an individual point of view. We end this brief historical overview by reviewing past debates over motivational and cognitive explanations of the formation and maintenance of group realities. Subsequently, we argue that motivation and cognition must be simultaneously considered and attempt to integrate different approaches to understanding group realities, leading to suggestions for future research.

BRIEF HISTORY OF GROUP REALITIES

Despite the fact that ethnocentric group realities are a human universal and may be grounded in evolution (Jahoda, 1999), they were not an early concern for social psychologists. The phenomenon was, however, vividly illustrated in reactions of early explorers to the appearances and customs of newly discovered societies. Members of these societies were described as completely different from typical human beings, often as bestial, evil, and lust-ridden (Jahoda, 1999). Similar constructions of group realities continued when scientific anthropologists replaced explorers. For instance, French anthropologist Levy-Bruhl (1922) considered members of indigenous tribes to be 'primitives' lacking individuality. Marcel Mauss (1925) restored balance by explaining how seemingly strange customs possessed significant meaning in 'primitive' societies, portraying them as neither senseless nor stupid. Cultural relativists such as Ruth Benedict (1934) took a similar stance, seeing richness in each specific, and different, culture.

Lévi-Strauss (1952) went even further, arguing that ethnocentrism confuses difference in inequality or equality with difference in terms of identity. One could say that the founder of structuralism saw in ethnocentrism

both racism by exclusion and racism by inclusion. Racism by exclusion is obtained because some societies are too unequal in material resources or customs compared with dominant ones, and therefore too different from the standard, to be accepted (Jost & Banaji, 1994; Sidanius & Pratto, 1999; Tajfel, 1981). Racism by inclusion means that dominated societies have to lose their identity and are obliged to assimilate to dominant groups (Maquil, Demoulin, & Leyens, 2009). Either dominant societies reject dominated people or they absorb and assimilate them to the extent that dominated people conform to the powerful model.

Interestingly, despite its centrality to biasing group realities, the term 'ethnocentrism' is absent from the glossary and the index of two classic textbooks of social psychology: *Foundations of Social Psychology* (Jones & Gerard, 1967) and *Social Psychology* (Secord & Backman, 1964). It is widely present, however, in the chapter on 'Prejudice and ethnic relations' of the second edition of the *Handbook of Social Psychology* (Harding, Kutner, Proshansky, et al., 1954). This latter publication is representative of the focus privileged by social psychologists at the time. For them, ethnocentrism was principally an individual characteristic, nourished by socialization (and thus distally by culture). The 'authoritarian personality' (Adorno, Frenkel-Brunswik, Levinson, et al., 1950) represents the most famous example of this individual-difference approach. Ethnocentrism, along with anti-Semitism, fascism, and politico-economic conservatism, formed a central component of this personality syndrome. Later work by Pettigrew (1958) in South Africa and the Southern United States, however, revealed that ethnocentric attitudes had less to do with individuals' underlying personalities than with the widespread and accepted beliefs of the group to which the individual belongs. In other words, the problem is not mainly a matter of personality but of constructed group realities.

These findings led to explorations of the 'social dimension' of intergroup attitudes (Tajfel, 1984), which superseded individual difference accounts (though see Altemeyer, 1998; Sidanius & Pratto, 1999). But even though they largely abandoned the individual difference perspective, social psychologists devoted only limited attention to ethnocentric biases in group realities (see Gilbert, Fiske, & Lindzey, 1998). Two main schools developed, however, that pointed at the subjectivity of the perceptions of one's own group and of the outgroup – a critical aspect of group reality. These frameworks became known as the New Look and Naïve Realism.

In the 1950s, under the inspiration of Bruner (Bruner & Goodman, 1947), psychologists of the New Look perspective considered the influence of selective motivation on perception. A classic study by Hastorf and Cantril (1954) illustrates the essence of this approach. Astonished by the controversy following a rough football match between Princeton University and Dartmouth College, Hastorf and Cantril showed a film of the game to students of both universities and asked them to indicate the number of penalties committed by each team as well as their severity. Princeton students saw twice as many penalties committed by the Dartmouth team than by their own, and the Dartmouth students evaluated the fouls of Princeton's players as particularly severe. The authors concluded ironically that the students from the two universities had seen two different films. In both cases, participants had constructed a positive, pleasant reality for their ingroup, and a much somber one for the outgroup.

In contrast to the motivational focus of the New Look, in the 1980s psychologists came to be interested in different models of cognition. One such approach, Naïve Realism, postulated that people assume that they directly perceive events as objectively real (Ross & Ward, 1996), that is, beliefs about reality are immediately taken for reality. The classic experiment that illustrates Naïve Realism is quite different in its staging than that of Hastorf and Cantril (1954). Vallone and colleagues (1985) showed an 'objectively neutral' videotape of the Israelis' involvement in Lebanon (massive killings in the Palestinian camps of Sabra and Chatilla) to three types of participants: students who held neutral, pro-Israel, or pro-Palestine views about the conflict. They asked about the fairness of the video-program and the percentage of favorable, neutral, and unfavorable references to Israel. The 'balanced' video was viewed as such by the neutral participants. In contrast, involved participants saw the news as biased against their side, even when controlling for the alleged number of references to Israel. According to the authors, involved participants had prior construals (Ross & Nisbett, 1991) of the conflict and, because the video did not reflect their 'objective' vision of reality, they concluded that the report was biased. Vallone, Ross, & Lepper (1985) thus favored a cognitive explanation for the development of different social realities in their research.

Although some phenomena may be essentially or purely explainable in motivational or cognitive terms, we believe that such unilateral explanations are unlikely to be efficient with respect to divergent group realities. As noted earlier, group realities tend toward ethnocentrism, a concept that is inherently motivational. At the same time, cognition plays a central role as well because ethnocentric motivations push people to adopt a certain point of view. In Hastorf and Cantril's (1954) football experiment, participants value their group but can only do so through cognitive processes that select and interpret other's behaviors and not theirs as aggressive. In Vallone, Ross, & Lepper's (1985) Chabra and Shatila study, participants' preference for their ingroup was evidenced in spite of their accurate memory for the report they viewed. In the remaining part of this chapter, we will thus adopt a social cognition view of group realities that integrates both motivational and cognitive processes.

The two studies reviewed above also inform us about two complementary aspects of group realities. The football study exemplifies ingroup favoritism, whereas the Sabra and Chatila investigation illustrates outgroup derogation. In the football case, one's team transgressions are overlooked whereas, in the Middle East case, perceivers view the other group as presented too favorably. Both phenomena were already noted in LeVine and Campbell's (1972 famous book: *Ethnocentrism: Theories of Conflict, Ethnic Attitudes, and Group Behavior.* Reviewing her cross-cultural work with Campbell (Brewer & Campbell, 1976), Brewer (1999) also distinguishes between ingroup love and outgroup hate.

Below, we theoretically distinguish these two components. Pragmatically, however, the two usually co-occur. Each is implicitly constructed to give special importance to the reality and standing of one's group.

Ingroup favoritism

The distinction between ingroup favoritism and outgroup derogation is a critical one for understanding intergroup bias. Enhancement of the ingroup is a classic observation. Its most vivid illustration was probably due to Tajfel's minimal group paradigm (Tajfel, Billig, Bundy, et al., 1971). Tajfel, who wanted to go beyond the theory of realistic conflict (LeVine & Campbell, 1972 Sherif, 1966), found discrimination in what he anticipated to be a control condition with no occurrence of discrimination. In his classic experiment, participants were categorized into groups on the basis of an irrelevant criterion, did not know which individuals were assigned to their own versus another group, did not interact with others, and allocated symbolic, rather than real, resources to members of these artificial, 'minimal' groups. Nevertheless, participants gave relatively more points to their ingroup than to the outgroup even when they could have earned more in absolute terms by allocating more points to the outgroup. At the time of the initial experiment, this bias was interpreted as showing both a predilection for the ingroup *and* derogation of the outgroup, as if comparisons occurred in a zero-sum game (Leyens, Paladino, Rodriguez, et al., 2003). However, the measure of discrimination used in these minimal group experiments did not allow the researchers to separate ingroup

favoritism from outgroup derogation (but see Brewer & Silver, 1978).

Outgroup derogation

Although ingroup bias is often naturally confounded with outgroup derogation, it is important to distinguish between the two. One striking example that makes the distinction evident concerns patriotism versus nationalism, or attachment versus glorification (Roccas, Klar, & Liviatan, 2004). Patriotism represents pride in one's country while nationalism reflects not just pride in one's country but also contempt for other countries. Roccas and her colleagues speak of attachment to one's country versus glorification. In both cases, one's country remains at the center but the attitude towards other national groups differs. Attachment is the sense of oneness with the ingroup, while glorification of the ingroup expresses the tendency to view the ingroup in the best possible light. Roccas, Klar, & Leviatan, (2004) report an interesting study about old dramatic incidents committed by Jews and judged by Jewish students. It appeared clearly that responsibilities for the massacres depended on the group realities to which the judges adhered. Israeli students who were attached to their country accepted much more easily responsibility for the massacres committed by their forebears than did those who glorified their Israeli group.

Under the title of 'Value of life,' Pratto and Glasford (2008: Experiment 2) have attempted to answer what might be seen as an 'offensive' question. Using sophisticated analyses, they showed that for Americans, saving versus losing American or Afghan lives during the current conflict in Afghanistan, had different values and led to very different strategies. Participants were presented with non-military strategies, with economic costs that would risk or help to save the lives of the different protagonists (from 20 to 20000 in Experiment 2). While the risk of 20 lives for both sides did not lead to much difference in preferred actions, this was no longer the case for higher numbers: 'The number of lives at stake mattered less for enemy civilians than it did for conational combattants' (Pratto & Glasford: 1411). These results remind us of Stalin's view (quoted by Nisbett and Ross, 1980) that that the death of a million soldiers was a statistic, while the death of a single Russian soldier was a tragedy. Stalin's view touched upon a psychological truth about how people perceive the value of human life of individualized ingroup members versus 'faceless' others.

Pratto and Glasford (2008, p. 1425) conclude: 'We suggest that how individuals value the life of another can be described by how people implicitly answer two questions in turn. The first question is, "Is the life in question included in my scope of moral concern?" ... The second question is, "Does the life in question compete with the interests of others in my scope of concern? That is, does the life compete against the interest of those I care for?"'

Pratto and Glasford's (2008) study considers simultaneously both ingroup favoritism and outgroup derogation. Saving more lives of the ingroup than of the outgroup is ingroup favoritism while being willing to lose many more lives of the outgroup than of one's own group is outgroup derogation. In spite of the importance of the theoretical distinction between the two biases, it is not necessarily easy to find pure examples of the two kinds. Moreover, and more importantly maybe, it is remarkable how people confound the two to their advantage. The different examples provided in this section testify that groups or subgroups elaborate their group reality and this group reality becomes 'The Reality.'

PROCESSES THAT REINFORCE GROUP REALITIES

The construction of ethnocentric group realities needs to be fed, or reinforced, in order for these realities to be functional, constantly available, and to maintain, if not increase, their strength. We now turn to specific (micro) processes that contribute to, and reinforce, the construction of group realities. For concision, we focus on a few key processes: expectancies, selective attention, vigilance, and confirmatory bias.

Expectancies

Because of direct and indirect experience with others, people form category-based expectancies about others' traits and likely behaviors. Rightly or wrongly, women may portray men as brutal machos or paternalistic hypocrites (Glick & Fiske, 1996; see Glick & Rudman's Chapter 20 in this volume) and they have at their disposal panoply of stereotypes corresponding to these two types of men. In a study by Dardenne, Dumont, and Bollier (2007), men supervised the work of non-university women. Women's performance was worse when they expected benevolent sexism, and their impaired performance was fully mediated by intrusive thoughts about others' perceptions of their competence. Expectations, thus, do not only concern the images held by other people but affect the targets of these perceptions who are concerned about how they are perceived. Thus, not only do people have stereotypes about outgroups (and ingroups) but they also have ideas about the stereotypes held by these outgroups towards them. These specific beliefs are called meta-stereotypes, and are used less to reflect on oneself and one's group than to guide actions towards outgroup members (Vorauer, Main, & O'Connel, 1998).

Affect constitutes another source of expectancy. When entering a cross-race interaction, Whites fear being seen as racists and Blacks worry about being discriminated against. In other words, members of both groups fear rejection and believe that the outgroup members are not genuinely interested in the interaction (Shelton & Richeson, 2005; see Chapter 17 by Richeson & Shelton, this volume). This ethnocentric view leads to intergroup avoidance and reinforces widespread *clichés* about each group.

Yet another specific and sophisticated expectancy is the belief in a conspiracy against one's group. Bogart and Thorburn (2005) reviewed a considerable amount of evidence that Blacks, more than Whites, believe that

HIV is a man-made virus aimed at affecting Black people and that birth control is meant to limit the Black population in the United States. Crocker, Luhtanen, Broadnax, et al., (1999) have extended this evidence of perceived conspiracies to other domains (e.g., the death penalty). Goertzel (1994) reviewed a wide range of types of conspiracy and reached the same conclusions as Bogart and Thorburn (2005). The point is that conspiracy theories explain bad group outcomes by blaming another group. Things happen as if people thought: 'it is not our weakness but your viciousness.'

These different types of expectations explain how people as a group construct the surrounding reality. The example of erroneous beliefs concerning interracial interactions is a prime illustration of the way group members come to a consensual, group belief about who they are, what they can do, and how they might be treated. The same is true of hetero-, auto-, and meta-stereotypes. People cannot live without pre-judgment, but they are quick at transforming the pre-judgments into true realities.

Selective attention

Selective attention is a motivated cognitive tool by which people construct a good story about their own and other groups. Recall the Princeton and Dartmouth (Hastorf & Cantril, 1954) students who seemed to see different games, each favoring the moral superiority of the ingroup over the outgroup. In the same vein, and because stereotypes are not often flattering, people pay special attention to information that contradicts negative stereotypes of their own group, but focus on information that reinforces negative stereotypes of the outgroup (Koomen & Dijker, 1997).

Recent studies of reaction times in decisions about whether to shoot a target who might have a gun versus a harmless object in his hand show differences in behavior towards Blacks and Whites (see Unkelbach, Forgas, & Denson, 2008). Although not all of these studies show identical results, White participants tend to shoot a Black target more readily than a White one. When Blacks are replaced by Muslims (indicated by a turban) and mood is taken into account, participants shot more frequently at Muslims than at non-Muslims, but accuracy concerning the decision to shoot or not when the target did or did not have a gun, was above chance level. These studies controlled for darkness of targets' skin pigmentation (without making targets appear to be Black or Asian). There were as many male as female targets and all participants were females. Accuracy, that is, shooting armed targets and not shooting unarmed ones, was also better for female and non-Muslim targets. As the authors concluded, the bias to shoot was stronger against Muslims, and non-Caucasian males, and weakest against non-Muslim and Caucasian females (Unkelbach, Forgas, & Denson, 2008, p. 1411). What is especially interesting is the impact of mood. Not surprisingly, anger led to a greater likelihood of shooting, but a happy mood provoked selective shooting against Muslims. The authors explain this result by their affect-cognitive theory that predicts a reaction based on beliefs. Not just any violent cue leads to aggression; rather, acquired negative stereotypes against Muslims seemed to trigger the finger. This conclusion is congruent with the point that people attend to elements in their environment that reinforce their own group's consensual beliefs. In other words, they select material so that perceived reality matches their beliefs.

Vigilance

When making decisions (e.g., forming impressions, sentencing criminals), people need all kinds of resources, such as time, information, and motivation. The degree to which people need such resources (e.g., sufficient time) varies as a function of the group membership of targets of the decisions. If people want to protect their group reality they have to be vigilant against so-called errors.

For example, because anti-Semites define Jews as 'enemies,' researchers hypothesized that anti-Semitic individuals would be more attuned to classifying others as having 'Jewish' faces. Participants, some prejudiced against Jews and others not, viewed a series of pictures, half of which were of Jewish individuals and the other half not (e.g., Allport & Kramer, 1946). Prejudiced people were better at recognizing Jews reflecting greater vigilance – defensively classifying anyone who might look Jewish as such in order to defend against the 'enemy.' Leyens and Yzerbyt (1992) showed that these earlier results represented vigilance, not 'against' the outgroup (against the enemy), but 'for' the ingroup (in an attempt to avoid 'contamination'). French- or Dutch-speaking Belgians received positive or negative stereotypical information about an individual. Each piece of information was delivered one at a time about each target, and French-speaking participants were free to decide when they were sure that the target was Walloon (French-speaking) or Flemish (Dutch-speaking). Less negative information was needed for participants to feel certain that the target was an outgroup member (i.e., Flemish), and participants required the most positive information to classify the target as an ingroup member (i.e., a fellow Walloon). In other words, ingroup members showed vigilance to make sure that someone was not mistakenly classified as part of their ingroup, keeping intact their view of the ingroup as good and pure by making sure it could not be contaminated by including outside elements.

Vigilance is especially likely to play a role when people are suspicious about each other's attitudes. Dovidio, Kawakami, and Gaertner (2002) have shown that, in cross-race interactions, Whites attend to their verbal but not to their non-verbal behaviors. Blacks, in contrast, attend to Whites' non-verbal behavior while disregarding the more controllable verbal behavior. Whites, who are concerned about appearing racist, try to offer a positive representation of themselves, while their Black interaction partners, who fear being discriminated against, pay special attention to non-controllable cues that may signal negative orientations. This study shows a failure of vigilance on the part of Whites that

may have important consequences. Imagine an aversive racist (Dovidio & Gaertner, 2004) who does not want to appear racist but is unconsciously ambivalent towards Blacks. This person's verbal behavior, of which he/she is strongly aware, will be perfectly pleasant, but his/her non-verbal behavior will reflect the negative side of ambivalence. As the Black person notices the gap between the two types of behavior and, interpret it as hypocrisy, he/she might become rude in the interaction. The White person will then be shocked by the non-receptive reaction and a vicious circle will start and reinforce the conscious and unconscious beliefs underlying the group realities of each person.

Confirmation bias

It is well-known that people who are convinced of the reality of a given idea unconsciously behave in a biased way. Because people treat assumptions as facts, they display biased behaviors that transform the idea into reality (Nickerson, 1998; Snyder, 1984). Even when they have almost no experience with exemplars of specific outgroups, people readily attribute outgroup members the stereotypes shared by their ingroup. These stereotypical attributions are nicely illustrated in a study by Darley and Gross (1983). These authors presented their participants with a video of Hannah in her home and school surroundings. Depending on the condition, Hannah obviously came from a privileged or poor background. When asked about her intelligence, people who merely viewed background information did not discriminate between the rich and poor Hannah. Unfortunately, when people subsequently saw Hannah perform inconsistently on a non-diagnostic intelligence test, participants believed that the rich Hannah had done better on the test and was more advanced in school than the poor Hannah. The ambiguous intelligence test had allowed people to confirm their group realities: Poor people do not do well in school whereas upper middle-class children do.

Subsequently, Yzerbyt, Schadron, Leyens, et al., (1994) demonstrated that the depiction of the intelligence test was not necessary to obtain the same results. For people to confirm the truth of group realities, it is sufficient that they believe they possess information about the targets, even if they actually do not. In other words, to feel entitled to judge according to group realities, it suffices that cues make the judgment seem applicable (Leyens, Yzerbyt, & Corneille, 1996; Leyens, Yzerbyt, & Schadron, 1992). People resist making a judgment about a person on the basis of mere categorization, but the false impression of having individuating information reduces this resistance and psychologically legitimates the imposition of stereotypical interpretations. Since there is no real information, the judgment can only be stereotypical.

Similarly, in classic research by Word, Zanna, and Cooper (1974), White participants playing the role of recruiters behaved in ways that led White candidates to perform better in a job interview than Black candidates. The authors showed that the difference was due to the behavioral posture adopted by the recruiters toward Black candidates. When interviewers were subsequently trained to display this posture toward White candidates, the latter also performed poorly.

One aim of this section was to sample a few cognitive-motivational processes related to the construction or maintenance of group realities. Other processes such as attributions or stereotype threat are similarly relevant. Another aim was to show how these processes both nourish, and are nourished by ethnocentrism. For instance, people are vigilant so that their group appears in its best light; thus vigilance feeds ethnocentrism. People are also vigilant because, being convinced of the excellence of their group, they do not want this group reality to be spoiled by the inclusion of 'intruders' or outgroup members.

INTEGRATING CURRENT RESEARCH AND THEORY

So far, we have suggested that ethnocentrism leads to group realities represented by ingroup bias and outgroup derogation through a series of processes. However, we have focused more on research findings and micro-processes rather than overarching theories. Below we summarize two theoretical attempts at systematizing group realities. Their premises are very different but complementary. After briefly reviewing the main tenets of each perspective, we consider how they can enrich each other.

The stereotype content model

Interpersonal perception appears to be organized along two dimensions: social goodness and competence (Rosenberg & Sedlack, 1972). Fiske and colleagues (Cuddy, Fiske & Glick, 2008; Fiske, Cuddy, Glick, et al., 2002) presumed and found that these two dimensions – labeled as competence and warmth – also organize representations of groups. Their Stereotype Content Model (SCM) provides four quadrants in which most groups can be arranged: high competence and warmth (e.g., the ingroup), high competence and low warmth (e.g., bankers), high warmth and low competence (e.g., housewives), and low competence and warmth (e.g., drug addicts). This model has been supported in research using various samples from different continents (Cuddy, Fiske, Kwan, et al., 2009). Although some groups (e.g., welfare recipients or disabled) may change quadrants in different cultures or over time, the general structure of the warmth–competence space remains intact. For instance, group stereotypes may change due to group alliances being formed or dissolved (e.g., the Allies may have viewed Russians as 'warm' during WWII, but this perception reversed as they became enemies in the subsequent Cold War). These changes, however, are systematic and relate to perceptions of groups as cooperatively versus competitively interdependent (determining perceptions of warmth versus coldness) and as high versus low status (with perceived competence being directly related to status).

In addition to determining the types of stereotypes that are associated with each group, the four quadrants also evoke different affective reactions toward targets. People admire the groups stereotyped as high competence and high warmth but experience disgust toward groups stereotyped in the low competence and low warmth quadrant. Envy is directed at stereotypically high-competent and low-warm groups, and pity is experienced for groups placed in the low competence and high warmth quadrant.

According to Cuddy, Fiske, & Glick, (2008), diverse behaviors – linked to different kinds of prejudice – are also elicited by the clustering of groups. Warmth stereotypes predict active behavioral tendencies (helping warm groups, attacking cold groups), and competence stereotypes predict passive behavioral tendencies (associating with competent groups and neglecting incompetent groups). Low-competence and high-warmth groups receive help because they are liked, but they tend also to be ignored because they are not respected; this represents paternalistic prejudice. Groups high in competence but low in warmth are disliked and tend to elicit harm when competition is fierce; but they are also respected and might be useful when competition dissipates so that they simultaneously engage association; this represents envious prejudice. Because low-competence and low-warmth groups are neither respected nor liked, they are both attacked and avoided, suffering contemptuous prejudice. Finally, admired high-competence and high-warmth groups benefit from both passive and active help. Because one feels pride for them, one will be ready to help them and wish to be associated with them (see also Fiske, Harris, Russell, et al., 2009).

What is remarkable with the SCM is that it is based only on the two main dimensions of impression formation but has a number of consequences. It takes into account objective reality (the structure of society), stereotyping (to place the groups in the quadrants), affective reactions, behaviors, and prejudice. The real cement of the model is constituted by the stereotypes induced by competence and warmth. The next theory has a very different foundation.

Infra-humanization

According to Leyens and colleagues (2000) groups may appear so fundamentally dissimilar that people attribute different 'essences' to them (seeing them as biologically distinct, for example). The most general essence is the human one, which is ethnocentrically assigned to the ingroup. In other words, some groups, especially the ingroup, are considered human or even supra-human, whereas other groups, usually outgroups, are infra-humanized (viewed as less fully human) or even 'bestialized' (viewed as mere animals, such as apes). For instance, Blacks are often bestialized. US newspapers use about four times more animal words (e.g., beast, predator, savage) for Black than White criminals, and the more these criminals are bestialized, the more likely they are to be sentenced to the death penalty (Goff, Eberhardt, Williams, et al., 2008). In extreme cases, devaluation may lead to outgroup members being dehumanized (see Haslam, 2006; Haslam, Loughnan, Kashima, et al., 2008). Dehumanization is common in times of war or armed conflicts (Haslam, 2006). In those cases, the enemy is reduced, for example, to vermin (e.g., rats) with the implication that they should simply be exterminated.

To measure infra-humanization (a milder form of dehumanization), Leyens and colleagues (for reviews, see Demoulin, Cortes, Viki, et al., 2004; Leyens, Demoulin, Vaes, et al., 2007) looked at the differential attributions to ingroup and outgroups of uniquely human sentiments (e.g., love, contempt), relative to emotions that are not uniquely human (e.g., happiness, anger – basic emotions that animals may also experience). The choice of emotions as an index of humanization stemmed from findings that Belgian and Spanish people rated 'sentiments,' along with language, immediately after intelligence as uniquely human traits. The word 'emotions' was almost never used; as even animals are perceived as experiencing 'emotions.' Because the distinction between 'sentiments' and 'emotions' is crucial in Roman languages but not in others, we conducted a cross cultural study to validate their cross-cultural applicability in five languages. Participants received a list of emotional terms and were asked to rate them on a series of dimensions. Uniquely human emotions, relatively to non-uniquely human emotions, were rated as less intense and visible, lasting longer, and appearing later in age. Given the characteristics of the non-uniquely emotions, already labeled as 'primary' (Ekman, 1992), Niedenthal (personal communication) suggested the term 'secondary emotions' to indicate these more elaborated, uniquely human emotions.

The basic hypothesis was that secondary emotions would be attributed to ingroups more than outgroups, and that associations of secondary emotions with ingroup members would be made more rapidly than associations with outgroup members. This prediction was verified for many samples, in different countries, different languages, and a variety of emotional terms. In the vast majority of studies, no ingroup–outgroup differences emerged for attributions of, or associations with, primary emotions. Importantly, these results occur independent of the valence of the secondary emotions, that is, infra-humanization of outgroups is not directly synonymous with ingroup favoritism (Demoulin, Cortes, Viki, et al., 2008). Instead, there is evidence that infra-humanization combines both ingroup love and outgroup hate. Humanity is given to the ingroup at the same time that it is refused to outgroups (Leyens, Cortes, Demoulin, et al., 2003). Not only do people attribute few secondary emotions to outgroup members, but they are reluctant to accept that outgroup members can have such emotions (Gaunt, Leyens, & Demoulin, 2002), and show various kinds of avoidance behaviors towards strangers who claim the same humanity as their own (Vaes, Paladino, Castelli, et al., 2003).

Importantly, and unlike the SCM, infra-humanization is independent of the status of the groups and does not require conflict. In other words, dominated groups infra-humanize dominant groups, and vice-versa, and this reaction may occur in the absence

of any conflict between the groups, although conflict, such as competition for jobs, may exacerbate this bias (Cortes, 2005).

Attempts at integration

The SCM and infra-humanization theory seek to explain intergroup relations in very different ways. What is encouraging is that theorists from both perspectives have made efforts to integrate the two approaches. Harris and Fiske (2006) successfully related the SCM to variations in the perceived humanity of outgroups using neural measures (fMRI). When participants view pictures of people, activation of the medial prefrontal cortex (mPFC), the region of the brain involved in social judgments, typically occurs. This activation occurred in response to members of a variety of groups, except for those in the low-competence–low-warmth quadrant. With respect to the mPFC, the brain did not react differently for drug addicts or homeless people than it did to objects, such as chairs. Moreover, presentation of people in this quadrant (i.e., drug addicts, homeless people) elicited exaggerated amygdala and insula reactions consistent with disgust. Thus, using the SCM, Harris and Fiske showed neural evidence that people in some groups are particularly dehumanized. Although reactions to outgroups in the other quadrants probably also differ from reactions to ingroup members, the measures used in this study may not be suited to showing these subtle differences, that is, they were unable to capture infra-humanization as compared to dehumanization.

In contrast to Harris and Fiske (2006), Vaes and Paladino (2007) did the reverse, examining infra-humanization through stereotypes, and using the quadrants of the SCM. Their Italian participants had to rate the humanity, typicality, and valence of stereotypes of the ingroup and of a group belonging to one of the three other quadrants of the SCM. In line with Leyens, Paladino, Rodriguez, et al.'s (2000) reasoning, there was overall infra-humanization of ambivalently stereotyped outgroups (i.e., high competence but low warmth, and low competence but high warmth). Consistent with results obtained by Harris and Fiske (2006), the uniformly 'bad' groups, low in competence and warmth, were dehumanized in the sense that the more stereotypes lacked humanity the more they were perceived as typical of these groups.

These first steps toward integration further illustrate the centrality of ethnocentrism to group realities. 'We' are the divine group; other groups, while they may possess strengths as well as weaknesses, are not fully human.

PROMISING AVENUES FOR FUTURE RESEARCH

Readers may have noticed that the words 'dominant and dominated groups,' 'minority and majority' did not often appear in the preceding sections of this chapter. This may seem strange, notably because dominant groups, or majorities, are often considered to define social realities. According to Jost and Banaji (1994), dominant groups maintain or even increase their higher status by controlling social reality, dominating how the world is viewed, while dominated groups respect the ideology of the dominants. It is true that dominated groups often remain passive for a variety of reasons alien to ideology: lack of material resources, helplessness, lack of education, etc. Nevertheless, dominated groups, like dominant ones, construct their own group realities. It is for this reason that infra-humanization does not relate to the status of the group being evaluated, but rather is a function of whether that group represents an ingroup or an outgroup.

The issues addressed here require further empirical research. We speculate that the different behaviors of minorities (dominated) and majorities (dominant), which are often interpreted as resulting from differences in power, may reflect different strategies for managing conflict. Dominant and dominated groups face different challenges in their attempts to preserve their own group reality.

Broad-minded, dominant majorities are keen to show minorities that they are making efforts toward solidarity, while minorities are more interested in preserving their differences in the face of majority pressures (Gaunt, 2007; Judd, Park, Ryan, et al., 1995; Saguy, Pratto, Dovidio, et al., 2009; Saguy, Dovidio, & Pratto, 2008).

In acculturation terms (see Chapter 22 by Wagner, Christ, and Heitmeyer, this volume), one could say that people who want to minimize conflict typically favor integration because dominants will accept the dominated provided that the latter integrate as part of a common group. Dominated people, also, are more likely to get along with majorities if they can preserve their own cultures. Everything is a trade-off between what is common and different. If the conflict worsens rather than diminishes, majorities may force assimilation, that is, allow only what is common to them, whereas minorities may move towards segregation where only their specificity matters. This reasoning contrasts with Jost and Banaji's (1994) contention that dominated minorities accept the majority's view of reality, because if their argument about dominated groups were right, everyone would favor assimilation, and research has established that this not the case (Maquil, Demoulin, & Leyens, 2009).

This common-difference trade-off seems essential for understanding intergroup relations. Integrating this dimension into the theories reviewed earlier would considerably enrich each perspective in two ways, practical and theoretical. Insisting on emphasizing difference in verbal interactions is a kind of reproach on the part of minorities that want to strengthen their weaker position. Focus on commonalities among open-minded majorities may be a sign of sincere tolerance. In both cases, the two types of groups do not renounce their deep group reality, but one may hope for improvement in intergroup relations. This improvement is the practical interest of the common-difference trade-off.

The different strategies by which dominants and minorities maintain their group realities are not only a fascinating topic but also may provide ways to address intergroup conflict. Improving intergroup relations may not require the exclusion of ethnocentric group realities, which is almost impossible, but an 'integration' of a pair of transformed ethnocentrisms in which each group preserves its identity and does not perceive intergroup relations as a zero-sum situation. In this way, ethnocentrism of both groups will no longer be composed of ingroup bias and outgroup derogation; ingroup bias remains and outgroup derogation vanishes as much as possible.

SUMMARY AND CONCLUSIONS

Group members consensually construe 'group realities.' These construals are subjective rather than objective. They are shared beliefs that determine the view of the world, influence behaviors, and impact intergroup relations. Given almost universal ethnocentrism (Jahoda, 2002), these group realities have the function to provide a positive image of the group to its members. For researchers in social psychology, this goal or function has usually led us to investigate ingroup favoritism and outgroup derogation. There are indeed several ways to attain a positive image. One can promote the ingroup, denigrate the outgoup, or adopt both strategies at the same time. The last alternative is probably the most current one (Brewer, 1999). To perpetuate ingroup favoritism and outgroup derogation, members have at their disposal a series of micro processes such as expectancies, selective attention, vigilance, and confirmatory bias.

What the area of 'groups realities' lacks is an overarching theory. In this chapter, we suggest that the SCM and the work on infra-humanization could serve as first attempts, especially when we seek convergence between the two lines of research. Both show very clearly the result of ethnocentrism in the perception of groups. In all cases, the ingroup is considered superior while other groups are infra-humanized, and even dehumanized. Relations between dominant and dominated groups were discussed towards the end of this chapter. Both types of

groups are ethnocentric but their strategies are different. We suggested that, in the case of conflict, respective ethnocentrisms are to be respected, and that special attention should be paid to different, but not incompatible, strategies.

What can be concluded from this examination of group realities? For a long time, social psychologists have been concerned, for example, with accuracy in social perception, in hypothesis-testing, and in decision-making. The cognitive revolution even came up with the magnificent metaphor of 'cognitive misers' to describe the performance of experimental participants. With group realities, one emphasizes subjectivity and biases, and how the latter are seen as useful tools, rather than limitations.

Social reality is, most of the time, the result of a social construction, and if the strength of this construction is important and consensual enough, reality is said to be 'objective'. Group realities, also, may be so powerfully accepted by members that they are capable of transforming subjective reality into an objective one (Neuberg, 1989), or, at least, of persuading group members that they are indeed 'the' real reality. If groups have relational problems, and if members of each group are convinced that their existence and points of view represent the 'truth', the 'true, objective reality', one may understand that these problems are almost impossible to resolve; their solution would be an extinction of ethnocentrism, something hardly believable. Take the examples of racism or of the war between Palestinians and Israelis. Despite all the efforts, from within and outside, progress is superficial when it exists at all. A possible reason for these enduring problems is that the proposed solutions attack group realities, and most likely, one group's reality more than the other. It is the case when the French government, for instance, asks Maghrebi (North-African) people to forget their origins and assimilate completely to the French culture. Recent research (Maquil, Demoulin, & Leyens, 2009; Saguy, Pratto, Dovidio, et al., 2009) suggests that one should not attempt to confront group realities directly, but rather to use their privileged tools, or strategies, instead. Some groups like to show their strength in acting, others in discussing. For some groups merit is individual while for others it is collective. Solutions to conflicts are possible if they do not aim to erase group subjective or objective group-realities.

REFERENCES

Adorno, T. W., Frenkel-Brunswik, E, Levinson, D. J., & Sanford, R. N. (1950). *The Authoritarian Personality*. New York: Harper & Row.

Allport, G. W., & Kramer, B. M. (1946). The roots of prejudice. *Journal of Psychology: Interdisciplinary and Applied*, 22, 9–39.

Altemeyer, B. (1998). The other "authoritarian personality. In M. P. Zanna (Ed.), *Advances in Experimental Social Psychology* (Vol. 30, pp. 47–92). New York: Academic Press.

Benedict, R. (1934). *Patterns of Culture*. New York: Mariner Books.

Bogart, L. M., & Thorburn, S. (2005). Are HIV/AIDS conspiracy beliefs a barrier to HIV prevention among African Americans? *Journal of Acquired Immune Deficiency Syndromes*, 38, 213–218.

Brewer, M. B. (1999). The psychology of prejudice: Ingroup love or outgroup hate? *Journal of Social Issues*, 55, 429–444.

Brewer, M. B., & Campbell, D. T. (1976). *Ethnocentrism and Intergroup Attitudes: East African Evidence*. Thousand Oaks, CA: Sage.

Brewer, M. B., & Silver, M. (1978). Ingroup bias as a function of task characteristics. *European Journal of Social Psychology*, 8, 393–400.

Bruner, J. S., & Goodman, C. C. (1947). Value and need as organizing factors in perception. *Journal of Abnormal and Social Psychology*, 18, 14–31.

Cortes, B. P. (2005). *Looking for Conditions Leading to Infra-Humanization*. Doctoral dissertation. Université catholique de Louvain, Louvain–la–Neuve, Belgium.

Crocker, J., Luthanen, R., Broadnax, S., & Blaine, B. E. (1999). Belief in U.S. government conspiracies against Blacks among Black and White college students: Powerlessness or system blame? *Personality and Social Psychology Bulletin*, 25, 941–953.

Cuddy, A. J. C., Fiske, S. T,. & Glick, P. (2008). Warmth and competence as universal dimensions of social perception: The Stereotype Content Model and the BIAS Map. In M. P. Zanna (Ed.), *Advances in Experimental Social Psychology* (Vol. 40, pp. 61–149). New York: Academic Press.

Cuddy, A. J. C., Fiske, S. T., Kwan, V. S. Y., Glick, P., Demoulin, S. p., Leyens, J.-P., et al. (2009). Stereotype content model across cultures: Towards universal similarities and some differences. *British Journal of Social Psychology*, 48, 1–33.

Dardenne, B., Dumont, M., & Bollier, T. (2007). Insidious dangers of benevolent sexism: Consequences for women's performance', *Journal of Personality and Social Psychology*, 93, 764–779.

Darley, J. M., & Gross, P. H. (1983). A hypothesis-confirmation bias in labeling effects. *Journal of Personality and Social Psychology*, 44, 20–33.

Demoulin, S., Rodriguez, R. T., Rodriguez, A. P., Vaes, J., Paladino, M. P., Gaunt, R. et al. (2004). Emotional prejudice can lead to infra-humanization. *European Review of Social Psychology*, 15, 259–296.

Demoulin, S., Cortes, B. P., Viki, T. G., Rodriguez, A. P., Rodriguez, R. T., & Paladino, M. P. (2008). The role of ingroup identification in infra-humanization. *International Journal of Psychology*, 44, 4–11.

Dovidio, J.F., Kawakami, K., & Gaertner, S.L. (2002). Implicit and explicit prejudice and interracial interaction. *Journal of Personality and Social Psychology*, 82, 62–68.

Dovidio, J. F., & Gaertner, S. L. (2004). Aversive racism. In M. P. Zanna (Ed.), *Advances in Experimental Social Psychology* (Vol. 36, pp. 1–51). San Diego, CA: Academic Press.

Ekman, P. (1992). Facial expressions of emotion: New findings, new questions. *Psychological Science*, 3, 2.

Fiske, S. T., Cuddy, A. J. C., Glick, P., & Xu, J. (2002). A model of (often mixed) stereotype content: Competence and warmth respectively follow from perceived status and competition. *Journal of Personality and Social Psychology*, 82, 878–902.

Fiske, S. T., Harris, T., Russell, A. M., & Shelton, J. N. (2009). Divergent social realities, depending on where you sit: Perspectives from the Stereotype Content Model. In S. Demoulin, J. Ph. Leyens, & J. F. Dovidio (Eds), *Intergroup Misunderstandings: Impact of Divergent Social Realities* (pp. 173–189). New York: Psychology Press.

Gaertner, S. L., & Dovidio, J. F. (1986). The aversive form of racism. In J. F. Dovidio, & S. L. Gaertner (Eds), *Prejudice, Discrimination, and Racism*. Orlando, FL: Academic Press.

Gaunt, R (2007). *Infra-Humanization and Super–Ordinate Categorization of Groups*. Unpublished data. Bar-Ilan University, Israel.

Gaunt, R., Leyens, J. Ph., & Demoulin, S. (2002). Intergroup relations and the attribution of emotions: Control over memory for secondary emotions associated with ingroup or outgroup. *Journal of Experimental Social Psychology*, 38, 508–514.

Gilbert, D., Fiske, S. T., & Lindzey, G. (1998). *The Handbook of Social Psychology*. New York: McGraw-Hill.

Glick, P., & Fiske, S. T. (1996). The Ambivalent Sexism Inventory: Differentiating hostile and benevolent sexism: *Journal of Personality and Social Psychology*, 70, 491–512.

Goertzel, T. (1994). Belief in conspiracy theories', *Political Psychology*, 15, 733–744.

Goff, P. A., Eberhardt, J. L., Williams, M. J., & Jackson, M. C. (2008). Not yet human: Implicit knowledge, historical dehumanization, and contemporary consequences. *Journal of Personality and Social Psychology*, 94, 292–306.

Harding, J., Kutner, I., Proshansky, H., & Chein, G. (1954). Prejudice and ethnic relations. In G.Lindzey, & E. Aronson (Eds). *Handbook of Social Psychology* (Vol. 2. pp. 1021–1061). Cambridge, MA: Addison-Wesley.

Harris, L. T., & Fiske, S. T. (2006). Dehumanizing the lowest of the low: Neuroimaging responses to extreme out-groups. *Psychological Science*, 17, 847–853.

Haslam, N. (2006). Dehumanization: An integrative review. *Personality and Social Psychology Review*, 10, 252–264.

Haslam, N., Loughnan, S., Kashima, Y., & Bain, P. (2008). Attributing and denying humanness to others. European Review of Social Psychology, 19, 55–85.

Hastorf, A. H., & Cantril, H. (1954). They saw a game: A case study. *Journal of Abnormal and Social Psychology*, 49, 129–134.

Jahoda, G. (1999). *Images of Savages: Ancient Roots of Modern Prejudice in Western Culture*. London: Routledge.

Jahoda, G. (2002). On the origins of antagonism towards The Others. *Zeitschrift für Ethnologie*, 127, 1–16.

Jones, E. E., & Gerard, H. B. (1967). *Foundations of Social Psychology*. New York: Wiley.

Jost, J. T., & Banaji, M. R. (1994). The role of stereotyping in system-justification and the production of false consciousness. *British Journal of Social Psychology*, 33, 1–27.

Judd, C. M., Park, B., Ryan, C. S., Brauer, M., & Kraus, S. (1995). Stereotypes and ethnocentrism: Diverging interethnic perceptions of African American and White American youth. *Journal of Personality and Social Psychology*, 69, 460–481.

Koomen, W., & Dijker, A. J. (1997). Ingroup and outgroup stereotypes and selective processing. *European Journal of Social Psychology*, 27, 589–601.

LeVine, R. A., & Campbell, D. T. (1972). *Ethnocentrism: Theories of Conflict, Ethnic Attitudes, and Group Behavior*. New York: Wiley.

Lévy-Bruhl, L. (1922). *La Mentalité Primitive*. Paris Alcan.

Lévi-Strauss, C. (1952/1987). *Race et Histoire*. Paris: Denoel.

Leyens, J. Ph., Paladino, M. P., Rodriguez, R. T., Vaes, J., Demoulin, S., Rodriguez, A. P. et al. (2000). The emotional side of prejudice: The attribution of secondary emotions to ingroups and outgroups. *Personality and Social Psychology Review*, 4, 186–197.

Leyens, J. Ph., Cortes, B. P., Demoulin, S., Dovidio, J., Fiske, S. T., Gaunt, R. et al. (2003). Emotional prejudice, essentialism, and nationalism. *European Journal of Social Psychology*, 33, 703–717.

Leyens, J. Ph., & Yzerbyt, V. Y. (1992). The ingroup overexclusion effect: Impact of valence and confirmation on stereotypical information search. *European Journal of Social Psychology*, 22, 549–569.

Leyens, J. Ph., Demoulin, S., Vaes, J., Gaunt, R., & Paladino, M. P. (2007). Infra-humanization: The wall of group differences. *Social Issues and Policy Review*, 1, 139–172.

Leyens, J. Ph., Yzerbyt, V. Y., & Corneille, O. (1996). The role of concept applicability in the overattribution bias. *Journal of Personality and Social Psychology*, 70, 219–229.

Leyens, J. Ph., Yzerbyt, V. Y., & Schadron, G. (1992). *Stereotypes and Social Cognition*. London: Sage.

Maquil, A., & Demoulin, S. Leyens, J. Ph. (2009). Strategies for Prejudice reduction. The Norms of nondiscrimination. In S. Demoulin, J. Ph.. Leyens, & J. F. Dovidio (Eds), *Intergroup Misunderstandings: Impact of Divergent Social Realities* (pp. 251–271). New York: Psychology Press.

Mauss, M. (1925/2007). *Essai sur le don. Forme et Raison de l'Echange dans les Sociétés Archaïques*. Paris: Presses Universitaires de France.

Neuberg, S. L. (1989). The goal of forming accurate impressions during social interactions: Attenuating the impact of negative expectancies. *Journal of Personality and Social Psychology*, 56, 374–386.

Nickerson, R. S. (1998). Confirmation bias: A ubiquitous phenomenon in many guises. *Review of General Psychology*, 2, 175–200.

Nisbett, R., & Ross, L. (1980). *Human Inference: Strategies and Shortcomings of Social Judgment*. New York: Prentice Hall.

Pettigrew, T. (1958). Personality and sociocultural factors in intergroup attitudes: A cross-national comparison. *Journal of Conflict Resolution*, 2, 29–42.

Pratto, F., & Glasford, D. E. (2008). Ethnocentrism and the value of a human life. *Journal of Personality and Social Psychology*, 95, 1411–1428.

Roccas, S., Klar, Y., & Leviatan, I. (2004). Exonerating cognitions, group identification, and personal values as predictors of collective guilt among Jewish-Israelis. In N. R. Branscombe, & B. Doosje (Eds), *Collective Guilt* (pp 130–147). Cambridge, England: Cambridge University Press.

Rosenberg, S., & Sedlack, A. (1972). Structural representations of implicit personality theory. In L. Berkowitz (Ed.), *Advances in Experimental Social Psychology* (Vol. 6, 235–297). New York: Academic Press.

Ross, L., & Nisbett, R. E. (1991). *The Person and the Situation.* New York: McGraw-Hill.

Ross, L., & Ward, A. (1996). Naive realism in everyday life: Implications for social conflict. In S. R. De Reed, E. Turiel, & T. Brown (Eds), *Values and Knowledge* (pp. 103–136). Mahwah, NJ: Erlbaum.

Saguy, T., Dovidio, J. F., & Pratto, F. (2008). Beyond contact: Intergroup contact in the context of power relations. *Personality and Social Psychology Bulletin*, 34, 419–445.

Saguy, T., Pratto, F., Dovidio, J. F., & Nadler, A. (2009). Talking about power: Group power and the desired content of intergroup interactions. In S. Demoulin, J. Ph. Leyens, & J. F. Dovidio (Eds), *Intergroup Misunderstandings* (pp. 213–232). London: Psychology Press.

Secord, P. F., & Backman, C. W. (1964). *Social Psychology.* New York: McGraw-Hill.

Shelton, J. N., & Richeson, J. A. (2005). Intergroup contact and pluralistic ignorance. *Journal of Personality and Social Psychology*, 88, 91–107.

Sherif, M. (1966). *In Common Predicament: Social Psychology of Intergroup Conflict and Cooperation.* Boston, MA: Houghton Mifflin.

Sidanius, J., & Pratto, F. (1999). *Social Dominance: An Intergroup Theory of Social Hierarchy and Oppression.* New York: Cambridge University Press.

Snyder, M. (1984). When beliefs create reality. In L. Berkowitz (Ed.), *Advances in Experimental Social Psychology* (Vol. 18, pp. 248–306). New York: Academic Press.

Sumner, W. G. (1906) *Folkways.* New York: Ginn.

Tajfel, H. (1981). *Human Groups and Social Categories.* Cambridge, England: Cambridge University Press.

Tajfel, H. (1984). *The Social Dimension.* Cambridge, England: Cambridge University Press.

Tajfel, H., Billig, M., Bundy, R., & Flament, C. (1971). Social categorization and intergroup behaviour. *European Journal of Social Psychology*, 1, 149–178.

Unkelbach, C., Forgas, J. P., & Denson, T. F. (2008). The turban effect: The influence of Muslim headgear and induced affect on aggressive responses in the shooter bias paradigm. *Journal of Experimental Social Psychology*, 44, 1409–1413.

Vaes, J., Paladino, M. P., Castelli, L., Leyens, J. Ph., & Giovanazzi, A. (2003). On the behavioral consequences of infra-humanization: The role of uniquely human emotions on intergroup relations. *Journal of Personality and Social Psychology*, 85, 1016–1034.

Vaes, J., & Paladino, M. P. (2007). The human content of stereotypes: Subtle infra–humanization versus dehumanization. Manuscript submitted for publication, University of Padova, Italy.

Vallone, R. P., Ross, L., & Lepper, M. R. (1985). The hostile media phenomenon: Biased perceptions of media bias in coverage of the Beirut massacre. *Journal of Personality and Social Psychology*, 49, 577–585.

Vorauer, J. D., Main, K. J., & O'Connell, G. B. (1998). How do individuals expect to be viewed by members of lower status groups? Content and implications of meta-stereotypes. *Journal of Personality and Social Psychology*, 4, 917–937.

Word, C. O., Zanna, M. P., & Cooper, J. (1974). The nonverbal mediation of self-fulfilling prophecies in interracial interaction. *Journal of Experimental Social Psychology*, 10, 109–120.

Yzerbyt, V. Y., Schadron, G., Leyens, J. Ph., & Rocher, S. (1994). Social judgeability: The impact of meta-informational rules on the use of stereotypes. *Journal of Personality and Social Psychology*, 66, 48–55.

13

Social Structure

Amanda B. Diekman, Alice H. Eagly,
and Amanda M. Johnston

ABSTRACT

In this chapter, we examine prejudice as resulting from social cognitive elements, such as attitudes and stereotypes, and social structural elements, such as roles and contexts. After reviewing classic treatments of social-structural influences on prejudice, we examine challenges to traditional explanations of prejudice. We then propose a new framework in which prejudice stems from incongruity between individuals' roles and the stereotypes associated with their group memberships (e.g., gender, age, ethnicity). In this role congruity model of prejudice, the fundamental principle is that prejudice results from individuals' stereotype-based misalignment with the social roles that they occupy or are vying to occupy. Finally, this integrative perspective has numerous benefits for research and theory on prejudice.

SOCIAL STRUCTURE

The decades since Allport (1954/1979) published his classic analysis of prejudice have witnessed major changes in social scientists' understanding of this multifaceted phenomenon. As social groups have encountered new challenges arising from prejudice, researchers have refined their approaches to studying its origins and consequences. Given the insights that have emerged, we contend that prejudice is best analysed in light of both social cognitive elements (i.e., attitudes, stereotypes) and social structural elements (i.e., roles, contexts). In this analysis, prejudice lies at the intersection of psychological and social processes, stemming from groups' position in the social structure while helping to maintain this social position.

Classically, prejudice was defined as a negative attitude toward a group, which affected judgments of individuals and produced inequitable treatment. Social psychologists often invoked stereotypes, defined as the beliefs that underlie the attitude (Eagly & Chaiken, 1993), to explain this negativity. This view was inherent in Allport's well-known definition of prejudice as 'an antipathy based upon a faulty and inflexible generalization' (1954/1979: 9). Despite the intuitive appeal of the ideas that prejudice is typically negative and that stereotypes are inaccurate, the accumulated evidence challenges these assumptions. In a revisionist spirit, we propose dialectical principles whereby prejudice can flow from positive or negative attitudes, and the stereotypes that underlie prejudice may typically be moderately accurate at the group level, but typically inaccurate for the individuals who are the targets of prejudice.

Our goal in this chapter is to synthesize topics extensively studied by social psychologists – in particular, beliefs and attitudes about groups – with knowledge about groups' social roles and positioning in society. Each of these traditions provides a distinct perspective on the causes of group disadvantage and prejudice. Social psychologists have generally focused on prejudice as the principal reason why certain groups are disadvantaged, but a fuller understanding of prejudice can result from attending to its broader societal context. Shifts in economic or political contexts can lead directly to changes in group members' social roles, and changes in attitudes toward these groups eventually follow. For example, in the twentieth century, industrialization fostered women's engagement in the paid labor force, their decreased fertility rate, and their increased education and political participation (Goldin, 2006; Inglehart & Norris, 2003; Jackson, 1998). Analyses of such modernization processes show that the fundamental causes of intergroup relations of equality and inequality have less to do with people's attitudes and more to do with the role arrangements fostered by societal institutions. For the most part, people's attitudes accommodate to the position of groups in the social structure. Although such attitudes can impede social change, they can also facilitate social change (Inglehart & Norris, 2003). The integration of social cognitive and social structural perspectives may thus yield important insight into the causes and the consequences of prejudice.

We begin with a brief historical overview of the social structural principles classically regarded as relevant to the formation and maintenance of prejudice. We then summarize contemporary insights about attitudes and prejudice that raise questions about the adequacy of these earlier approaches. We argue instead that groups' typical social roles are the critical aspect of social structure that illuminates the conditions that elicit prejudice. Finally, we analyse how changes in groups' social roles can erode their structural disadvantage and reduce prejudice.

CLASSIC VIEWS OF SOCIAL STRUCTURAL INFLUENCES ON PREJUDICE

Initial discussions of the contribution of social structure to prejudice emphasized cooperative and competitive intergroup relations. Within societies, groups may be situated so that they have mainly cooperative or competitive relations with one another. The usual claim was that competitive relations between groups create prejudice and cooperative relations reduce prejudice. Hints that intergroup relations might be responsible for the negativity of many stereotypes emerged in the studies known as the *Princeton trilogy* (see Gilbert, 1951; Karlins, Coffman, & Walters, 1969; Katz & Braly, 1933). These studies showed that much of the content of stereotypes about ethnic, racial, and nationality stereotypes waxed and waned with shifts in intergroup relations and international politics, presumably reflecting changes in cooperative and competitive relationships.

The focus on competitive and cooperative relations was furthered by Allport (1954/1979), who argued that prejudice stems from 'many economic, international, and ideological conflicts that represent a genuine clash of interests' (p. 233). Intergroup conflict could be realistic (e.g., economic competition) or symbolic (e.g., ideological). In Allport's view, hostile attitudes toward other groups are a common outcome of intergroup competition. Sherif's (1966) subsequent studies of the Robbers Cave boys' summer camp showed that competitive relations between groups of boys fostered intergroup hostility, even though friendships had previously existed across group lines. Moreover, reduction of this hostility was not achieved by the simple removal of competitive relations, but instead by requiring that the groups work together to attain a series of superordinate goals.

Allport's (1954/1979) influential statement of the conditions under which intergroup contact reduces prejudice inspired work on the *contact hypothesis* (see Chapter 33 by Tausch & Hewstone, this volume). Building on earlier research (e.g., Williams, 1947), Allport maintained that intergroup contact reduces prejudice only when four conditions are present: cooperative relations between the groups; equal status relations between the groups; common goals; and support from authorities, laws, or customs (for a meta-analysis confirming the contact hypothesis, see Pettigrew & Tropp, 2006).

Other researchers sought to uncover the minimal conditions needed to elicit prejudice. Tajfel's minimal group paradigm (see Tajfel, Billig, Bundy, et al., 1971) demonstrated that the mere belonging to a group, even when groups were formed in experiments on trivial dimensions, led to bias in favor of the ingroup over the outgroup. This provocative work suggested that social structures that merely group or categorize individuals on an arbitrary basis can foster prejudice that is fueled by group members' tendencies to ground their identities in their own groups.

Two main principles emerged from this classic work on the relation between social structure and prejudice: First, the mere grouping of individuals can engender a degree of prejudice, and second, the competitive intergroup relations intensify negativity while cooperative intergroup relations foster positivity.

CHALLENGES TO TRADITIONAL CONCEPTIONS OF PREJUDICE

The foundational ideas about prejudice, however useful as initial insights, were subsequently challenged and revised to account for the more complex phenomena that surfaced in the expanding field of prejudice research. In particular, the ambivalent nature of prejudice led to the reconsideration of its causes and consequences.

Prejudice following from ambivalent and positive attitudes

As research on attitudes toward disadvantaged groups developed in the late twentieth century, researchers found that prejudices were not necessarily uniformly hostile. This decrease in overall negativity appeared in research on so-called 'modern' intergroup attitudes based on ethnic subgroups in the United States (e.g., Madon, Guyll, Aboufadel, et al., 2001) and nationality groups in Europe (Meertens & Pettigrew, 1997). Similarly, in research on intergroup relations, Brewer (1999) argued that outgroups do not typically elicit strongly negative evaluation but merely fail to elicit positive evaluation. Despite some apparent erosion of negativity, it appeared that racism had hardly disappeared (e.g., Swim, Hyers, Cohen, et al., 2003). On the basis of the data accumulating near the end of the twentieth century, psychologists thus began to evaluate whether prejudice is necessarily founded on hostile attitudes.

More radically, others argued that prejudice can be associated with attitudes that are positive, a claim that emerged in research on sexism. Although social scientists recognized that women were often targets of prejudice and discrimination, research found that women as a social group are evaluated on the whole quite favorably – even more favorably than men. This 'women-are-wonderful' effect (Eagly & Mladinic, 1989) provided the strongest challenge to the traditional understanding of prejudice as a negative attitude toward a target group.

Developments in attitude theory and research further influenced the study of prejudice. Specifically, attitude theorists questioned the classic notion of an attitude as a point along a bipolar evaluative continuum and proposed a more complex treatment that allowed for individuals to hold both positive and negative attitudes toward the same attitude object (Eagly & Chaiken, 1998; Fabrigar, MacDonald, & Wegener, 2005). Coexisting positive and negative evaluations defined the attitudinal state of *ambivalence*, which provided a suitable frame for thinking about modern prejudices that lack blatant negativity (e.g., McConahay, 1986; see also Chapter 19 by Dovidio & Gaertner in this volume). Researchers argued that these modern attitudes may appear to be relatively positive but generally have a dark side. For example, widely endorsed beliefs denying that minorities' social and economic problems can be ascribed to external factors such as job discrimination implicitly ascribe disadvantage to internal factors such as lack of motivation.

The idea that prejudice consists of coexisting positive and negative attitudes was prominently displayed in ambivalent sexism theory (Glick & Fiske, 1996, 2001), which posits that sexism includes both *hostile sexism*, an 'old-fashioned' component that devalues women in nontraditional roles, and *benevolent sexism*, which values women's traditional roles as wives and mothers. Positive and negative beliefs are thus interwoven in people's attitudes toward women.

Social psychologists also recognized that the content of many societal stereotypes is ambivalent. In research by Fiske, Cuddy, Glick, et al., (2002) that placed group stereotypes on dimensions of warmth and competence, many stereotypes consisted of mixed combinations of high warmth and low competence (e.g., elderly people, disabled people) or low warmth and high competence (e.g., rich people, professionals). Thus, stereotypes – and presumably the attitudes that are linked to these stereotypes – can be ambivalent.

The understanding of prejudice as often ambivalent has also benefited from research that distinguished between explicit and implicit attitudes. Explicit attitudes are evaluations that are reported by the person who holds the attitude, and implicit attitudes are those that people do not consciously recognize (Greenwald & Banaji, 1995). These implicit attitudes need not have the same valence as the attitudes that are expressed or consciously experienced. For example, aversive racism theory highlighted the inconsistency that often exists between people's explicit egalitarian attitudes and their implicit negative attitudes that derive from well-learned cultural associations (Dovidio & Gaertner, 2004).

In conclusion, the realization that attitudes, including attitudes toward disadvantaged groups, are not necessarily uniformly negative but are often more complexly ambivalent emerged on more than one front in social psychology. Although this insight has gradually gained favor compared with the traditional concept of prejudice as mere negativity or antipathy toward a target group, it has challenged social scientists to understand the causes of ambivalence.

The roots of ambivalent prejudice in complex intergroup relations

An examination of the positioning of groups in the social structure can help to illuminate why people would often hold ambivalent attitudes toward societal groups. However, answering this question requires recognition of the complexity of relationships among groups. After all, the classic emphasis on competitive and cooperative intergroup relations does not lead to predictions of ambivalent prejudice. A rationale for the prevalence of ambivalence emerged from insights concerning the relationships of domination and subordination that exist in the context of largely cooperative intergroup relations. Dominant groups generally rely on the cooperation of subordinate groups, and this cooperation is most easily ensured, not by instilling hostile attitudes toward subordinates, but by promoting more positive attitudes that are nonetheless founded on maintaining relationships of inequality. As Jackman (1994, 2005), the leading proponent of this viewpoint, wrote, 'Dominants prefer to befriend, love, or reason with the subordinates on whose cooperation they depend' (Jackman, 2005, p. 97). Therefore, members of dominant groups generally admire members of subordinate groups for the qualities that fit them to their subordinate roles. Simultaneously, dominants generally believe that members of subordinate groups are not as competent or worthy as their own group when it comes to occupying roles held by dominants.

Subordinates, in turn, may admire dominants' power and competence yet resent their exploitation and control.

Gender relations are amenable to this analysis because attitudes toward gender groups do not easily fit the mold of hostility following from competitive intergroup relations. Instead, the sexes have existed within a paternalistic system that promotes ambivalence in attitudes and stereotypes. The positive and negative stereotypes commonly held about women fit them perfectly into their subordinate roles as caretakers of children and cheerful denizens of the domestic space where family needs take precedence over individual achievement. Women's stereotypical qualities of kindness, gentleness, and helpfulness incite admiration and the love of men. Simultaneously, these qualities can disqualify women from the employment roles that offer authority and high wages.

Race relations also offer similar complexities. The historic interdependence of Blacks and Whites in the United States, for example, was founded on Whites' need for a reliable supply of relatively inexpensive agricultural and household labor. The attitudes that Whites held toward Blacks as slaves and servants were not uniformly negative but instead paternalistically ambivalent (Jackman, 1994). The continued interdependence of Blacks and White within a system that maintains considerable inequality along with substantial physical segregation usually prevents widespread expressions of interracial hostility. Instead, ambivalence continues to hold sway. These insights about the complexities of intergroup relations thus coordinate with social psychologists' discoveries that gender and racial attitudes are best analyzed as an ambivalent mix of positive and negative elements.

NEW FRAMEWORK: PREJUDICE AS INCONGRUITY BETWEEN ROLES AND STEREOTYPES

The research reviewed here clearly demonstrates that the positioning of groups in the social structure elicits certain beliefs and attitudes. We now analyse how social contexts and individual-level processes intersect to produce prejudice. We argue that social context, especially as defined by social roles, is essential to understanding prejudice because prejudice and discrimination can arise when perceivers consider an individual in a particular role context.

The key aspect of groups' social position is the social roles that they commonly occupy; these roles frame evaluations of group members (Eagly & Diekman, 2005; Eagly & Karau, 2002). Individuals' mere occupancy of roles leads observers to infer that they have traits consistent with the role (Ross, Amabile, & Steinmetz, 1977). This psychological process of inferring traits from observations extends readily to perceptions of entire groups of people. Based on observations of groups' common role occupancies, group stereotypes emerge. These stereotypes consist of the characteristics – both positive and negative – that observers think facilitate performance in group members' typical roles. Stereotypes in turn produce prejudice toward individuals because evaluations of individuals become less positive when they seek new roles that misalign with the attributes considered inherent in their group membership. Men, for example, may be viewed with suspicion if they seek roles as child care providers or secretaries – roles that are thought to require qualities not ordinarily ascribed to men (Davison & Burke, 2000). It is this decrease in positivity – often paired with an increase in negativity – based on group membership that we identify as prejudicial.

If prejudice derives from the roles that group members typically occupy, it is helpful to distinguish groups from roles. Roles differ from groups in the specificity of the settings within which they are influential. A *role* is a set of expectations associated with a particular social position in a specific setting (e.g., Biddle, 1979). A school teacher, for example, has obligations in relation to role partners (pupils, parents, school principal) within a school setting but minimal obligations when sitting in a cafe or visiting a distant city. In contrast, membership in a social *group* based on demographic variables such as age, race, gender, and socioeconomic status and on physical appearance variables such as attractiveness has trans-situational influence. A man, for example, has obligations based on being male in all settings in which his gender is identified – that is, at his workplace, in his home, on the street, or in a distant city. Beautiful people have advantages that transcend specific situations. The prejudices that become salient in societies are generally based on social groups.

The influence of groups' social roles on the content of their stereotypes has been extensively studied in research on gender stereotypes (Eagly & Steffen, 1984; Eagly, Wood, & Diekman, 2000). According to social role theory, the gendered division of labor fosters beliefs that each sex is equipped to fulfill these roles. For example, men tend to occupy roles that emphasize leadership and economic provision; men are thus assumed to have *agentic* qualities, such as being assertive, competitive, and self-promoting. In parallel, women tend to occupy roles that emphasize caregiving for others; women are thus assumed to have *communal* qualities, such as being sensitive, kind, and oriented toward others (see Chapter 20 by Glick & Rudman, this volume). Consistent with the principle of correspondence bias (Gilbert & Malone, 1995), perceivers tend to assume that people *are* what they do. Role occupancy thus contributes to perceived group differences because role occupants are perceived as carrying out certain tasks, and perceivers fail to correct for the role constraints that would elicit such role-consistent behaviors (Hoffman & Hurst, 1990).

In general, role behavior in local contexts constitutes the elementary observations that produce group stereotypes (Ridgeway, 2006). The traits that perceivers infer from group members' role behavior generalize from roles to groups because group membership is confounded with roles. Perceivers also observe the structural relations between occupants of different roles, which yield inferences about groups' status and interdependence. For example, inter-role relationships can encompass status hierarchies (e.g., between bosses and subordinates) and interdependence relations, which may take the form of cooperation (e.g., between teachers and pupils) or competition (e.g., between business owners and labor union representatives). Consistent with the stereotype content model (Fiske, Cuddy, Glick, et al., 2002), status and interdependence then influence trait inferences, along with information directly derived from social roles.

In this elaborated version of the social role theory of stereotype content (Koenig & Eagly, 2008), observations of groups' roles and their associated intergroup relations contribute to stereotypes by determining beliefs about the competence, agency, and communion of group members. These beliefs in turn can contribute to prejudice when the particular pattern of beliefs fails to match the demands inherent in the current situation. The fundamental role congruity principle is that evaluations of individuals are lowered when they are perceived as misaligning with the requirements of the social roles that they occupy or are vying to occupy. The individual's characteristics are considered along with the requirements of the current role to produce role congruity or incongruity, which then leads to a relatively more positive or more negative evaluation. In the next section, we review evidence that role-incongruent traits are devalued, examine how stereotypes influence judgments of an individual's attributes, and discuss the implications of considering prejudice as an attitude that emerges from a particular context.

Devaluation under conditions of role incongruity

Consistent with the role congruity perspective is empirical evidence, across both field and laboratory contexts, documenting greater negativity or lesser positivity toward individuals whose stereotypical attributes misalign with their social roles. Prejudice may be thought of as 'potential prejudice' in much the way that physicists think of potential energy: Group members may elicit positive or ambivalent evaluations generally but be devalued when they attempt to enter roles that are not consistent with their group's stereotype.

A wide range of evidence suggests that negativity emerges when individuals fail to fit the requirements of their roles. This effect has been demonstrated repeatedly within the framework of Heilman's (1983) Lack of Fit Model, which posits that decreased performance expectations derive from perceived inconsistencies between workplace roles and female-stereotypical attributes. Eagly and Karau (2002) focused on female leaders as often experiencing incongruity between their leadership role and gender role, creating prejudice toward them. In this model, prejudice against female leaders results from beliefs that women's characteristics disqualify them from leader roles, as well as from relatively negative evaluations of female leaders' behavior once they occupy leader roles.

Despite the general tendency for men to be regarded more positively than women in leader roles, specific role requirements can moderate or reverse this tendency. For example, in an analysis of archival performance evaluations, Lyness and Heilman (2006) found that the type of managerial role affected evaluations of female and male role occupants. Specifically, in line-managerial positions, which entail direct responsibility for decisions and organizational outcomes, women received lower performance evaluations than men; in staff managerial positions, which provide support for line managers, women received higher performance evaluations than men. Further suggesting that evaluations of leaders depend on the social context is evidence that women's chances of emerging as a leader are increased by tasks that are socially complex (Eagly & Karau, 1991) or female-stereotypical (Ritter & Yoder, 2004).

In experimental research, bias is often demonstrated by comparing evaluations of resumes or task performances that are matched except for the male or female name

of the candidate. A meta-analysis of such experiments evaluating leadership behavior showed that women are devalued, compared with equivalent men, when occupying male-dominated leader roles (Eagly, Makhijani, & Klonsky, 1992). Naturalistic *audit studies* in which job applications or actual applicants differing only in applicant sex are presented to real employers, demonstrated a high incidence of sex discrimination against women in the more senior jobs that yield higher status and wages and against both sexes when they applied for jobs dominated by the other sex (Riach & Rich, 2002). Also, a meta-analysis of experiments in simulated employment contexts that typically presented resumes differing only in applicant sex found that in male-sex-typed jobs (e.g., auto salesperson), men were preferred over women, whereas in female-sex-typed jobs (e.g., secretary), women were preferred over men (Davison & Burke, 2000; see also Swim, Borgida, Maruyama, et al., 1989). Across both field and laboratory evidence, role-congruent traits and behaviors meet with greater positivity than role-incongruent traits and behaviors. We next turn to the question of how these judgments of role congruity are formed.

Group stereotypes that lower individuals' fit to roles

The principle underlying role-incongruity prejudice is that group stereotypes affect judgments of fit to roles. In the analysis of female leaders (Eagly & Karau, 2002), for example, societal gender stereotypes facilitate the selection and positive evaluation of men as leaders. Research on ageism in hiring preferences (Diekman & Hirnisey, 2007) provided evidence for the hypothesized process that observed group membership elicits stereotypic trait inferences, which then affect hiring evaluations. In three studies, participants evaluated job candidates for companies that were described either as quickly changing or stable (with perceived success of companies held consistent across conditions). For quickly-changing companies, participants preferred the younger candidate. For stable companies, however, this preference was smaller or even reversed. Moreover, the preference for younger workers in quickly changing contexts was mediated by the stereotypical perception that younger workers are more adaptable. In essence, ageist bias in this simulated hiring context was explained by the stereotypic ascription of age-congruent traits to job candidates.

Judgments of an individual's traits or abilities generally reflect individuating information as well as group stereotypes. Diagnostic behavioral information or enhanced perceiver motivation can lead to the individuation of group members (Fiske, Lin, & Neuberg, 1999; Kunda & Spencer, 2003). However, a target's characteristics can be construed differently depending on his or her social categorization, so that social category membership and target features combine to produce an evaluation of the target. For example, applicants who most closely matched the gender-typing of an occupational role, through both their sex categorization and their individual personality, are most preferred (e.g., for male-stereotypical jobs, masculine men are the most positively evaluated; Glick, 1991; Judd & Oswald, 1997). Social category information can thus influence evaluations of targets even in the presence of individuating information.

ADVANTAGES OF AN INTEGRATED VIEW OF PREJUDICE

Our analysis of how social cognitive elements (i.e., attitudes, beliefs) intersect with social structures (i.e., social roles, context) can resolve some of the complexities that have challenged prejudice researchers, especially in two areas of recent debate. First we consider the situational malleability of prejudicial attitudes. Then we evaluate evidence that stereotypes are often accurate at the group level, despite their inaccuracy when generalizations about groups are misapplied to individuals.

Situational malleability of prejudicial attitudes

If role incongruity is the key to understanding prejudice toward individuals, attitudes toward members of social groups must be quite malleable, depending on the role context in which they are observed. Although traditional views of attitudes rested on the assumption that attitudes are fairly stable (Allport, 1935), it is obvious that not all attitudes are enduring. Some attitude theorists have even argued that all attitudes are constructed in the moment, rather than stored as stable representations (Schwarz & Bohner, 2001). Contrary to this radical view, instability in expressions of attitudes does not necessarily indicate instability in the evaluative tendency that constitutes attitude itself (Eagly & Chaiken, 2007). It is more plausible to regard evaluative judgments as constructed on each occasion of encountering an instance of an attitude object. For example, the presence of an audience with polarized views on an issue can cause a person to render relatively superficial evaluative judgments that have the goal of pleasing audience members (Prislin & Wood, 2005). Such judgments would reflect the demands of the current situation as much as or even more than the influence of the person's preexisting attitude.

Evidence has mounted that expressions of attitudes show considerable contextual malleability, regardless of whether attitudes are assessed with implicit or explicit measures (e.g., Blair, 2002). For example, implicit evaluations of a Black target varied depending on the target's physical context (e.g., in a church or on a street corner; Wittenbrink, Judd, & Park, 2001). In addition, explicit and implicit evaluations were responsive to the target's occupational role (Barden, Maddux, Petty, et al., 2004). White participants' implicit and explicit responses reflected ingroup bias when viewing Black and White targets in prison roles but showed outgroup bias when viewing targets in lawyer roles. It thus appears that changes in targets' physical setting and occupational roles can lead to changes in both implicit and explicit evaluations.

Recent advances in attitude theory have delineated how different sources of information may combine to produce evaluative responses, and how the accessibility of these different types of information depends on the situation. Connectionist models of mental representation (Smith, 1998) and attitudes (Bassili & Brown, 2005) represent attitudes by a collection of elements that are coordinated to memories and feelings associated with the attitude object. In any particular situation, a pattern of activation develops among these elements. Context affects the associations that are activated, with the result that the pattern of associations for a target differs in different contexts.

Given such developments, it is not at all implausible that attitudes toward members of disadvantaged groups are highly contextual. Much of this malleability can be understood in terms of explicit or implicit portrayal of role contexts. When individuals violate the bounds of valued social roles that are typical of their group, attitudes toward them become more negative or less positive. The study of social structure (e.g., context, roles) along with stereotypes and attitudes reveals some of the mechanisms underlying this malleability of prejudice.

Accuracy of group stereotypes

A perennial challenge for prejudice research concerns how to change prejudices. Such efforts typically aim at altering inaccurate beliefs; however, the assumption of stereotypes' inaccuracy may itself be inaccurate. If stereotypes follow from correspondent inferences from role behavior to personal attributes, they invariably have a degree of accuracy at the group level. If women care for young children, they engage in nurturing behavior. Are women 'really' nurturing at the level of personality or merely fulfilling a child caretaker role? Research on stereotypes generally does not address this question but merely asks for generalizations about group members being warm, caring, socially sensitive, and the like. Of course, individuals are socialized into roles and thereby internalize

role requirements, which become personal motives and ideals. Moreover, as illustrated by research on the *self-fulfilling prophecy*, the expectation that a group member will possess certain traits leads to differential behavior toward that group member, eliciting responses that confirm the initial expectations (e.g., Skrypnek & Snyder, 1982).

These insights coordinate with discoveries that beliefs about groups are not necessarily inaccurate (e.g., Lee, Jussim, & McCauley, 1995). However appealing it might seem that mere education about the real attributes of disadvantaged groups would reduce prejudice, accuracy has proven much more impressive than implied by Allport's acknowledgement that stereotypes often have a 'kernel of truth' (p. 190, 1954/1979). Although group stereotypes can be inaccurate (Judd & Park, 1993), many stereotypes appear to be moderately accurate when evaluated in relation to objective criteria, such as group attitudes assessed in nationally representative samples (Diekman, Eagly, & Kulesa, 2002) or meta-analytic summaries of group attributes (Hall & Carter, 1999; see also review by Ryan, 2002).

Accuracy related to groups and accuracy related to individuals, however, are entirely different matters. Beliefs about groups, which represent generalizations based on group averages (e.g., Americans are materialistic), are generally inaccurate to some degree when applied to individuals within groups (e.g., Richard is an American and therefore is materialistic). Viewing prejudice as stemming from role incongruity suggests that much of the inaccuracy in stereotyping stems from the misapplication of group stereotypes to individuals who do not conform to their traditional group stereotype. Individuals who strive to occupy roles not traditionally occupied by their group are often exceedingly well prepared for the new roles, but have to prove themselves by meeting standards that are set higher than those applied to the traditional occupants of the roles (Eagly & Diekman, 2005; Eagly & Karau, 2002). Such individuals are inaccurately perceived.

In summary, regarding prejudice as evaluations of individuals that are elicited in particular social contexts reveals the conditions under which prejudice occurs. Individual members of groups that are regarded positively or ambivalently may be devalued relative to members of other groups if their stereotypical traits fail to align with the role at hand. Under such circumstances, the group stereotype may be accurate for the group as a whole but mischaracterize many individual group members. These insights derive from examining prejudiced responses as emerging at the intersection of the target's qualities, the perceivers' ascription of stereotypes, and the role context.

FUTURE DIRECTIONS: UNDERSTANDING POSSIBILITIES FOR CHANGE IN THE SOCIAL STRUCTURE

The study of prejudice often stems from a desire to improve the status of disadvantaged groups. Despite this motivation, scant research has explored the broad process of social change, particularly in ways that integrate across levels of analysis or cross disciplinary boundaries. In this section, we examine challenges to social change, and we note particular opportunities for the systematic investigation of processes underlying social change and stability.

From a social structural perspective, as a group changes its social roles, so too will beliefs and attitudes about the group change. Yet, social change that affects role occupancies elicits many of the complexities that we identified as hallmarks of many contemporary prejudices. Beliefs about a group that were accurate at one point may become less accurate and quite inaccurate in relation to individuals striving to enter new roles. Indeed, it may be unclear to perceivers whether group members should be held to the standards of their 'old' or 'new' roles. In addition, ambivalence may be enhanced because some group members continue to occupy traditional roles, and thus are viewed positively by many, while others break from

these roles, and thus are viewed negatively by many. These propositions, as well as others detailed below, await research investigating the processes involved in social change and stability.

A group's changing role context generally brings prejudice to public consciousness. Because people are perceived as fitting their established roles, role-congruity prejudice is latent until a group desires new roles within society. The characteristics stereotypically ascribed to a group may not be problematic— and thus not labeled as 'prejudice' – until those characteristics are perceived as disqualifying the group members from pursuing new roles. Such role incongruity phenomena fueled twentieth century social movements of civil and women's rights. In the twenty-first century, the gay/lesbian rights movement encounters strong rejections of gay and lesbian individuals as occupants of roles such as marital partner and teacher of children.

Role change: Congruity to traditional or new roles?

Social change is restricted by the disapproval often accorded to those who deviate from their group's normative roles. Change in the social structure, by definition, necessitates that some people will cross the boundaries of their traditional roles – and most likely elicit negative consequences. For instance, work on the *backlash effect* (e.g., Rudman & Fairchild, 2004) demonstrates that women experience negative social and economic consequences for violating their gender role expectations. Indeed, the mere fear of backlash can produce motivation to conform. Even simply imagining performing behaviors stereotypical of devalued groups (e.g., homosexuals, nerds) leads to psychological discomfort, in part stemming from fear of being misclassified as belonging to these devalued groups (Bosson, Prewitt-Freilino, & Taylor, 2005). These conformity processes perpetuate the traditional social structure because people continue to uphold traditional roles and fail to demonstrate their ability or desire to fulfill nontraditional roles.

Despite the motivation to adhere to established roles, adaptability to emerging norms is also apparent. Evidence that role changes, lead to a change in how traits are valued comes from research on beliefs and attitudes about men and women of the past, present, and future. Our research on *dynamic stereotypes* (e.g., Diekman & Eagly, 2000) has shown that people project women to possess increasing levels of male-stereotypic characteristics from the past to the future, and that this projected increase stems from the perception of greater nontraditionalism of female and male roles. Additional studies (Diekman & Goodfriend, 2006) documented that participants projected more favorability for women's agentic characteristics over time, and that this positivity was correlated with women's perceived entry into male-dominated roles. Moreover, research with experimentally-created social groups revealed that the perceived utility of traits mediated the relationship between social roles and traits' positivity (Diekman & Goodfriend, 2006: Experiment 3). Positivity toward traits thus corresponds to anticipated change in social roles. Indeed, when individuals perceive society as changing in a nontraditional manner, they project a higher likelihood of success for themselves in nontraditional careers (Diekman, Johnston, & Truax, 2008). In general, the belief that the system is changing can elicit supportive attitudinal changes.

The malleability of a social system, however, is constrained to some extent by motivations to preserve the system itself. System justification theory (Jost, Banaji, & Nosek, 2004) posits that individuals are motivated to preserve the status quo, even if the system does not benefit them personally. In any hierarchically-organized society, people often endorse legitimizing myths that provide a rationale for the hierarchical arrangement of groups. One such legitimizing myth is the endorsement of complementary stereotypes; for example, people who endorse the 'poor but happy' or 'poor but moral' stereotypes tend to be more satisfied with the status quo (Kay & Jost, 2003). Consistent with our earlier point, these stereotypes can include

positive valence but nonetheless contribute to maintaining social equality. Similarly, social dominance theory (Sidanius & Pratto, 1999) posits that those who hold roles with greater power are most likely to endorse hierarchical relations among groups and to resist the rise of subordinate groups.

Motivations to legitimize the system may be reduced when people view the system as no longer inevitable but rather as malleable (Jost & Banaji, 1994). Beliefs that the social system can change can themselves contribute to social change. For example, providing sociocultural explanations rather than biological explanations for group differences leads to a reduction in the perceived inevitability of group differences and reduced stereotype endorsement (Brescoll & LaFrance, 2004).

One challenge to social change is that motivation to adhere to normative roles also follows from individuals' internalization of group-stereotypical activities, traits, or abilities as part of the self (Diekman & Eagly, 2008). Such internalization stems from groups' social position because their members are socialized to have the skills that help them to carry out their social roles. For example, parents encourage boys and girls to pursue different chores and leisure activities (Lytton & Romney, 1991). Men and women report, on average, gender-stereotypical self-attributes (e.g., Costa, Terracciano, & McCrae, 2001), and individuals who hold gender norms as important tend to experience positive affect after witnessing or remembering a gender-stereotypical interaction, relative to a counter-stereotypical interaction (Wood, Christensen, Hebl, et al., 1997). However, consistent with adaptability to new contexts, even apparently internalized traits fluctuate with the contextual salience of group membership: For example, individuals for whom gender is salient tend to give more gender-stereotypic assessments of their abilities than individuals for whom ethnicity is salient (Sinclair, Hardin, & Lowery, 2006).

These internalized and culturally shared beliefs can elicit group differences, and in so doing maintain traditional social arrangements. This process coheres with

Ridgeway's (2006) consideration of the connection between interpersonal relations and social structure: According to this perspective, people enter interactions with social ordering schemas (i.e., beliefs about the status of groups) that tend to be socially shared and that influence their interactions. Behaviors influenced by such beliefs reproduce societal structure. Status beliefs perpetuate the traditional social structure by providing rationales for status distinctions between groups. This theoretical stance illuminates how group status differences emerge from the interplay of individual, interpersonal, and societal forces.

The slow pace of social change

Change in prejudice typically occurs slowly and incrementally. Social change can elicit conflict because motivations both for and against change exist: Change might be regarded as progress by some but a massive setback by others, or some individuals might see both the positive and the negative aspects of change. Indeed, experimental data show that even minor social change in pursuit of a positively-regarded goal can elicit ambivalence (Diekman & Goodfriend, 2007).

A further barrier to social change is that members of disadvantaged groups may be unwilling to participate in collective action. When a high status group appears open to low status group members, individual action is preferred; collective action is favored only when a high status group appears closed to low status group members (Wright, Taylor, & Moghaddam, 1990). Therefore, the presence of a small number of individuals from low status groups who achieve higher status can reduce willingness to engage in collective action on behalf of disadvantaged groups, thus maintaining the social structure (Wright & Taylor, 1998). Of course, if these rare individuals inspire members of their own groups to undertake the individual actions that yield access to higher-status roles, change can transpire through individual mobility. For example, those few women who appear in highly visible leadership roles – such as Condoleezza Rice and Nancy Pelosi – may

inspire girls and young women to strive for achievement as individuals even if they do not inspire collective action on behalf of women as a group.

Even after group members enter into new roles, societal beliefs and attitudes may be slower to change than social structures, consistent with the concept of *cultural lag* (Brinkman & Brinkman, 1997; Ogburn, 1964). Groups that succeed in entering new roles may still be identified in the culture at least partially in terms of their traditional roles and associated characteristics, as is the case when communal attributes continue to be especially important in evaluations of female job candidates, despite the agentic requirements of the role (Rudman & Glick, 1999). Such continuation of traditional standards can occur nonconsciously because people's associations with social category memberships may change only with accumulated experience. Understanding the complexities of evaluations of transitional social actors is a worthwhile direction for future research, because the continuing perception of these actors in terms of their traditional roles undermines the changes that the group is seeking, thus maintaining the social structure. Consistent with cultural lag, even when certain traditional beliefs are labeled as 'prejudice,' it might be acceptable in the short term to continue subscribing to these beliefs. However, over time the social acceptability of the prejudice should decrease (e.g., Crandall, Eshleman, & O'Brien, 2002; Inglehart & Norris, 2003; Jackson, 1998). A critical goal for future research, and one that we hope to facilitate by our integration of social structural and social cognitive theory and research, is to understand both accommodation and resistance to social change.

CONCLUSIONS AND IMPLICATIONS

The systematic study of how the social structure influences reactions to individuals is fundamental to understanding prejudice. Although sociostructural perspectives have a long and distinguished history in prejudice research, the approach has featured disparate themes that have not been integrated into an overall understanding of the social conditions that elicit prejudice. Our effort to integrate sociostructural perspectives with social psychological insights about stereotyping and prejudice can provide enhanced ability to reduce prejudice and discrimination. As Allport (1954/1979) noted long ago, the social structure can facilitate social change just as effectively as it can inhibit such change. Despite encountering negativity, the entry of group members to new roles can initiate a series of processes that eventually result in less prejudicial beliefs and behaviors. Our task, therefore, is to understand more about the fundamental ways in which the social structure, along with interpersonal and intrapersonal processes, can elicit prejudiced – or nonprejudiced – responses.

REFERENCES

Allport, G. W. (1935). Attitudes. In C. Murchison (Ed.), *Handbook of Social Psychology* (pp. 798–844). Worcester, MA: Clark University Press.

Allport, G. W. (1954/1979). *The Nature of Prejudice*. Cambridge, MA: Perseus Books.

Barden, J., Maddux, W. W., Petty, R. E., & Brewer, M. B. (2004). Contextual moderation of racial bias: The impact of social roles on controlled and automatically activated attitudes. *Journal of Personality and Social Psychology*, 87, 5–22.

Bassili, J. N., & Brown, R. D. (2005). Implicit and explicit attitudes: Research, challenges, and theory. In D. Albarracin, B. T. Johnson, & M. P. Zanna (Eds), *The Handbook of Attitudes* (pp. 543–574). Mahwah, NJ: Erlbaum.

Biddle, B. J. (1979). *Role Theory: Expectances, Identities, and Behaviors*. New York: Academic Press.

Blair, I. V. (2002). The malleability of automatic stereotypes and prejudice. *Personality and Social Psychology Review*, 6, 242–261.

Bosson, J. K., Prewitt-Freilino, J. L., & Taylor, J. N. (2005). Role rigidity: A problem of identity misclassification? *Journal of Personality and Social Psychology*, 89, 552–565.

Brescoll, V., & LaFrance, M. (2004). The correlates and consequences of newspaper reports of research on sex differences. *Psychological Science*, 15, 515–520.

Brewer, M. B. (1999). The psychology of prejudice: Ingroup love or outgroup hate? *Journal of Social Issues*, 55, 429–444.

Brinkman, R. L., & Brinkman, J. E. (1997). Cultural lag: Conception and theory. *International Journal of Social Economics*, 24, 609–631.

Costa, P. T., Jr., Terracciano, A., & McCrae, R. R. (2001). Gender differences in personality traits across cultures: Robust and surprising findings. *Journal of Personality and Social Psychology*, 81, 322–331.

Crandall, C. S., Eshleman, A., & O'Brien, L. (2002). Social norms and the expression and suppression of prejudice: The struggle for internalization', *Journal of Personality and Social Psychology*, 82, 359–378.

Davison, H. K., & Burke, M. J. (2000). Sex discrimination in simulated employment contexts: A meta-analytic investigation. *Journal of Vocational Behavior*, 56, 225–248.

Diekman, A. B., & Eagly, A. H. (2000). Stereotypes as dynamic constructs: Women and men of the past, present, and future. *Personality and Social Psychology Bulletin*, 26, 1171–1188.

Diekman, A. B., & Eagly, A. H. (2008). Of men, women, and motivation: A role congruity account. In J. Shah, & W. L. Gardner (Eds), *Handbook of Motivational Science* (pp. 434–447). New York: Guilford.

Diekman, A. B., Eagly, A. H., & Kulesa, P. (2002). Accuracy and bias in stereotypes about the social and political attitudes of women and men. *Journal of Experimental Social Psychology*, 38, 268–282.

Diekman, A. B., & Goodfriend, W. (2006). Rolling with the changes: A role congruity perspective on gender norms. *Psychology of Women Quarterly*, 30, 369–383.

Diekman, A. B., & Goodfriend, W. (2007). The good and bad of social change: Ambivalence toward activist groups. *Social Justice Research*, 20, 401–417.

Diekman, A. B., & Hirnisey, L. (2007). The effect of context on the silver ceiling: A role congruity perspective on prejudiced responses. *Personality and Social Psychology Bulletin*, 33, 1353–1366.

Diekman, A. B., Johnston, A. M., & Truax, A. (2008). When social roles shift: Effects of perceived social change on the self. Unpublished manuscript, Miami University.

Dovidio, J. F., & Gaertner, S. L. (2004). Aversive racism. In M. P. Zanna (Ed.), *Advances in Experimental Social Psychology* (Vol. 36, pp. 1–52). San Diego, CA: Elsevier.

Eagly, A. H., & Chaiken, S. (1993). *The Psychology of Attitudes*. Fort Worth, TX: Harcourt Brace Jovanovich.

Eagly, A. H., & Chaiken, S. (1998). Attitude structure and function. In D. T. Gilbert, S. T. Fiske, & G. Lindzey (Eds),

The Handbook of Social Psychology (4th edition, Vol. 1, pp. 269–322). New York: McGraw-Hill.

Eagly, A. H., & Chaiken, S. (2007). The advantages of an inclusive definition of attitude. *Social Cognition*, 25, 582–602.

Eagly, A. H., & Diekman, A. B. (2005). What is the problem? Prejudice as an attitude-in-context. In J. F. Dovidio, P. Glick, & L. A. Rudman (Eds), *On the Nature of Prejudice: Fifty Years after Allport* (pp. 19–35). Malden, MA: Blackwell.

Eagly, A. H., & Karau, S. J. (1991). Gender and the emergence of leaders: A meta-analysis. *Journal of Personality and Social Psychology*, 60, 685–710.

Eagly, A. H., & Karau, S. J. (2002). Role congruity theory of prejudice toward female leaders. *Psychological Review*, 109, 573–598.

Eagly, A. H., Makhijani, M. G., & Klonsky, B. G. (1992). Gender and the evaluation of leaders: A meta-analysis. *Psychological Bulletin*, 111, 3–22.

Eagly, A. H., & Mladinic, A. (1989). Gender stereotypes and attitudes toward women and men. *Personality and Social Psychology Bulletin*, 15, 543–558.

Eagly, A. H., & Steffen, V. J. (1984). Gender stereotypes stem from the distribution of women and men into social roles. *Journal of Personality and Social Psychology*, 46, 735–754.

Eagly, A. H., Wood, W., & Diekman, A. B. (2000). Social role theory of sex differences and similarities: A current appraisal. In T. Eckes, & H. M. Trautner (Eds), *The Developmental Social Psychology of Gender* (pp. 123–174). Mahwah, NJ: Erlbaum.

Fabrigar, L. R., MacDonald, T. K., & Wegener, D. T. (2005). The structure of attitudes. In D. Albarracin, B. T. Johnson, & M. P. Zanna (Eds), *The Handbook of Attitudes* (pp. 79–125). Mahwah, NJ: Erlbaum.

Fiske, S. T., Cuddy, A. J. C., Glick, P., & Xu, J. (2002). A model of (often mixed) stereotype content: Competence and warmth respectively follow from perceived status and competition. *Journal of Personality and Social Psychology*, 82, 878–902.

Fiske, S. T., Lin, M., & Neuberg, S. L. (1999). The continuum model: Ten years later. In S. Chaiken, & Y. Trope (Eds), *Dual-process Theories in Social Psychology* (pp. 231–254). New York: Guilford.

Gilbert, G. M. (1951). Stereotype persistence and change among college students. *Journal of Abnormal and Social Psychology*, 46, 245–254.

Gilbert, D. T., & Malone, P. S. (1995). The correspondence bias. *Psychological Bulletin*, 117, 21–38.

Glick, P. (1991). Trait-based and sex-based discrimination in occupational prestige, occupational salary, and hiring. *Sex Roles*, 25, 351–378.

Glick, P., & Fiske, S. T. (1996). The Ambivalent Sexism Inventory: Differentiating hostile and benevolent sexism. *Journal of Personality and Social Psychology*, 70, 491–512.

Glick, P., & Fiske, S. T. (2001). An ambivalent alliance: Hostile and benevolent sexism as complementary justifications for gender inequality. *American Psychologist*, 56, 109–118.

Goldin, C. (2006). The rising (and then declining) significance of gender. In F. D. Blau, M. C. Brinton, & D. B. Grusky (Eds), *The Declining Significance of Gender* (pp. 67–101)? New York: Russell Sage Foundation.

Greenwald, A. G., & Banaji, M. R. (1995). Implicit social cognition: Attitudes, self-esteem, and stereotypes. *Psychological Review*, 102, 4–27.

Hall, J. A., & Carter, J. D. (1999). Gender-stereotype accuracy as an individual difference. *Journal of Personality and Social Psychology*, 77, 350–359.

Heilman, M. E. (1983). Sex bias in work settings: The Lack of Fit model. *Research in Organizational Behavior*, 5, 269–298.

Hoffman, C., & Hurst, N. (1990). Gender stereotypes: Perception or rationalization? *Journal of Personality and Social Psychology*, 58, 197–208.

Inglehart, R., & Norris, P. (2003). *Rising Tide: Gender Equality and Cultural Change Around the World*. New York: Cambridge University Press.

Jackman, M. R. (1994). *The Velvet Glove: Paternalism and Conflict in Gender, Class, and Race Relations*. Berkeley: University of California Press.

Jackman, M. R. (2005). Rejection or inclusion of outgroups? In J. F. Dovidio, P. Glick, & L. A. Rudman (Eds), *Reflections on the Nature of Prejudice: Fifty Years after Allport* (pp. 89–105). Malden, MA: Blackwell.

Jackson, R. M. (1998). *Destined for Equality: The Inevitable Rise of Women's Status*. Cambridge, MA: Harvard University Press.

Jost, J. T., & Banaji, M. R. (1994). The role of stereotyping in system-justification and the production of false consciousness. *British Journal of Social Psychology*, 33, 1–27.

Jost, J. T., Banaji, M. R., & Nosek, B. A. (2004). A decade of system justification theory: Accumulated evidence of conscious and unconscious bolstering of the status quo. *Political Psychology*, 25, 881–920.

Judd, C. M., & Park, B. (1993). Definition and assessment of accuracy in social stereotypes. *Psychological Review*, 100, 109–128.

Judd, P. C., & Oswald, P. A. (1997). Employment desirability: The interactive effects of gender-typed profile, stimulus sex, and gender-typed occupation. *Sex Roles*, 37, 467–476.

Karlins, M., Coffman, T. L., & Walters, G. (1969). On the fading of social stereotypes: Studies in three generations of college students. *Journal of Personality and Social Psychology*, 13, 1–16.

Katz, D., & Braly, K. (1933). Racial stereotypes of one hundred college students. *Journal of Abnormal and Social Psychology*, 28, 280–290.

Kay, A. C., & Jost, J. T. (2003). Complementary justice: Effects of "poor but happy" and "poor but honest" stereotype exemplars on system justification and implicit activation of the justice motive. *Journal of Personality and Social Psychology*, 85, 823–837.

Koenig, A. M., & Eagly, A. H. (2008). The sources of stereotypes: How observations of groups' social roles shape stereotype content. Unpublished manuscript, University of San Diego.

Kunda, Z., & Spencer, S. J. (2003). When do stereotypes come to mind and when do they color judgment? A goal-based theoretical framework for stereotype activation and application. *Psychological Bulletin*, 129, 522–544.

Lee, Y.-T., Jussim, L. J., & McCauley, C. R. (Eds) (1995), *Stereotype Accuracy: Toward Appreciating Group Differences.* Washington, DC: American Psychological Association.

Lyness, K. S., & Heilman, M. E. (2006). When fit is fundamental: Performance evaluations and promotions of upper-level female and male managers. *Journal of Applied Psychology*, 91, 777–785.

Lytton, H., & Romney, D. M. (1991). 'Parents' differential socialization of boys and girls: A meta-analysis. *Psychological Bulletin*, 109, 267–296.

Madon, S., Guyll, M., Aboufadel, K., Montiel, E., Smith, A., Palumbo, P. et al. (2001). Ethnic and national stereotypes: The Princeton trilogy revisited and revised. *Personality and Social Psychology Bulletin*, 27, 996–1010.

McConahay, J. B. (1986). Modern racism, ambivalence, and the Modern Racism Scale. In J. F. Dovidio, & S. L. Gaertner (Eds), *Prejudice, Discrimination, and Racism* (pp. 91–125). San Diego, CA: Academic Press.

Meertens, R. W., & Pettigrew, T. F. (1997). Is subtle prejudice really prejudice? *Public Opinion Quarterly*, 61, 54–71.

Ogburn, W. F. (1964). *Social Change With Respect to Culture and Original Nature.* Gloucester, MA: Peter Smith (Original work published 1922).

Pettigrew, T. F., & Tropp, L. R. (2006). A meta-analytic test of intergroup contact theory. *Journal of Personality and Social Psychology*, 90, 751–783.

Prislin, R., & Wood, W. (2005). Social influence in attitudes and attitude change. In D. Albarracin, B. T. Johnson, & M. P. Zanna (Eds), *The Handbook of Attitudes* (pp. 671–705). Mahwah, NJ: Erlbaum.

Riach, P. A., & Rich, J. (2002). Field experiments of discrimination in the market place. *Economic Journal*, 112, F480–F518.

Ridgeway, C. L. (2006). Linking social structure and interpersonal behavior: A theoretical perspective on cultural schemas and social relations', *Social Psychology Quarterly*, 69, 5–16.

Ritter, B. A., & Yoder, J. D. (2004). Gender differences in leader emergence persist even for dominant women: An updated confirmation of role congruity theory. *Psychology of Women Quarterly*, 28, 187–193.

Ross, L. D., Amabile, T. M., & Steinmetz, J. L. (1977). Social roles, social control, and biases in social-perception processes. *Journal of Personality and Social Psychology*, 35, 485–494.

Rudman, L. A., & Fairchild, K. (2004). Reactions to counterstereotypic behavior: The role of backlash in cultural stereotype maintenance. *Journal of Personality and Social Psychology*, 87, 157–176.

Rudman, L. A., & Glick, P. (1999). Feminized management and backlash toward agentic women: The hidden costs to women of a kinder, gentler image of middle managers. *Journal of Personality and Social Psychology*, 77, 1004–1010.

Ryan, C. S. (2002). Stereotype accuracy. In W. Stroebe, & M. Hewstone (Eds), *European Review of Social Psychology* (Vol. 13, pp. 75–109). Hove, England: Psychology Press/Taylor & Francis.

Schwarz, N., & Bohner, G. (2001). The construction of attitudes. In A. Tesser, & N. Schwarz (Eds), *Blackwell Handbook of Social Psychology: Intraindividual Processes* (Vol. 1, pp. 436–457). Oxford, UK: Blackwell.

Sherif, M. (1966). *In Common Predicament: Social Psychology of Intergroup Conflict and Cooperation.* New York: Houghton Mifflin.

Sidanius, J., & Pratto, F. (1999). *Social Dominance: An Intergroup Theory of Social Hierarchy and Oppression.* New York: Cambridge University Press.

Sinclair, S., Hardin, C. D., & Lowery, B. S. (2006). Self-stereotyping in the context of multiple social identities. *Journal of Personality and Social Psychology*, 90, 529–542.

Skrypnek, B. J., & Snyder, M. (1982). On the self-perpetuating nature of stereotypes about women and men. *Journal of Experimental Social Psychology*, 18, 277–291.

Smith, E. R. (1998). Mental representation and memory. In D. T. Gilbert, S. T. Fiske, & G. Lindzey (Eds), *The Handbook of Social Psychology.* (4th edition, Vol. 1, pp. 391–445) New York: Oxford University Press.

Swim, J., Borgida, E., Maruyama, G., & Myers, D. G. (1989). Joan McKay versus John McKay: Do gender stereotypes bias evaluations? *Psychological Bulletin*, 105, 409–429.

Swim, J. K., Hyers, L. L., Cohen, L. L., Fitzgerald, D. C., & Bylsma, W. H. (2003). African American college students' experiences with everyday racism: Characteristics of and responses to these incidents. *Journal of Black Psychology*, 29, 38–67.

Tajfel, H., Billig, M. G., Bundy, R. P., & Flament, C. (1971). Social categorization and intergroup behaviour. *European Journal of Social Psychology*, 1, 149–178.

Williams, R. M., Jr. (1947). *The Reduction of Intergroup Tensions: A Survey of Research on Problems of Ethnic, Racial, and Religious Group Relations.* New York: Social Science Research Council.

Wittenbrink, B., Judd, C. M., & Park, B. (2001). Spontaneous prejudice in context: Variability in automatically activated attitudes. *Journal of Personality and Social Psychology*, 81, 815–827.

Wood, W., Christensen, P. N., Hebl, M. R., & Rothgerber, H. (1997). Conformity to sex-typed norms, affect, and the self-concept. *Journal of Personality and Social Psychology*, 73, 523–535.

Wright, S. C., & Taylor, D. M. (1998). Responding to Tokenism: Individual action in the face of collective injustice. *European Journal of Social Psychology*, 28, 647–667.

Wright, S. C., Taylor, D. M., & Moghaddam, F. M. (1990). Responding to membership in a disadvantaged group: From acceptance to collective protest. *Journal of Personality and Social Psychology*, 58, 994–1003.

14

Intergroup Competition

Victoria M. Esses, Lynne M. Jackson,
and Caroline Bennett-AbuAyyash

ABSTRACT

Competition between groups for resources, be they tangible or symbolic in nature, is a fundamental trigger of prejudice and discrimination. Research in this area has shifted from a focus on trying to understand true conflicts of interest between groups to an acknowledgement that *perceptions* of conflicts of interest are of utmost importance. Recent theory and research in this area can be classified as focusing on more distal, ideological factors versus proximal, situational, an target-relevant factors leading to group conflict. After briefly reviewing the history of research in this area and providing an overview of recent theory and research, we describe the Unified Instrumental Model of Group Conflict that incorporates the variety of factors that have been examined in this context. We then discuss potential fruitful directions for future research, and provide a summary of the state of knowledge in this area.

INTERGROUP COMPETITION

Group conflict and competition seem to be inevitable features of human social behavior. Though we consider twenty-first century humans to be highly civilized, we have not escaped the tendency to form groups and then compete with other groups over tangible resources, such as land, fossil fuel reserves, and employment opportunities, or over intangible, more symbolic resources, such as status, prestige, and religious dominance. Within social psychology, group competition has historically been considered of key importance in understanding prejudice and discrimination, though its presumed role has shifted over time. In this chapter, we provide a brief history of theory and research on the role of group competition in prejudice and discrimination, survey the research in this area, and present our Unified Instrumental Model of Group Conflict that integrates and builds on this literature. We then suggest important directions for future research that will not only allow us to gain a deeper understanding of the role of competition in prejudice and discrimination, but will also hopefully suggest points of intervention to promote more harmonious group relations.

HISTORY AND BACKGROUND

Theory and research on intergroup competition can be traced back to the 1950s with the development of Realistic Group Conflict Theory. In a series of studies beginning in 1949, including the classic Robbers Cave experiment, Sherif and his colleagues (e.g., Sherif, Harvey, White, et al., 1961) demonstrated that functional relations among groups are critical in determining intergroup attitudes. Sherif (1966, p. 81) proposed, 'when members of two groups come into contact with one another in a series of activities that embody goals which each urgently desires, but which can be attained by one group only at the expense of the other, competitive activity toward the goal changes, over time, into hostility between the groups and their members.'

In the now famous field study conducted at a boy's summer camp in Robbers Cave State Park, Oklahoma, Sherif and his colleagues studied a group of 11-year-old boys with no prior history of attachments. The boys were first divided into two groups and engaged in pleasant activities in their separate groups to develop some group cohesion. The two groups became known as the Eagles and Rattlers. To test the hypothesis about the development of group competition and conflict, competition between the groups was then induced through competitive sports, including baseball, football, and tug of war. Sherif and his colleagues observed that as competition between the groups developed over time, negative attitudes and behavior toward members of the outgroup became prevalent, including both verbal and physical aggression. Sherif, Harvey, White, et al. (1961: 99) wrote, 'The build-up of negative attitudes was cumulative with rapid spurts at times, as determined by the nature of the encounter.'

At the same time as these studies were being conducted, Allport (1954) was theorizing about the causes and consequences of prejudice. In Chapter 14 of *The Nature of Prejudice* (1954), Allport explored when and how conflicts of interest between groups create, sustain, and magnify prejudice (the focus of the current chapter), as well as how cooperative interdependence between groups can be used to reduce prejudice

(see Chapter 33 by Tausch & Hewstone in this volume). Allport suggested that in heterogeneous societies in which group distinctions are noticeable, there is a tendency for people to link their individual material and identity needs to the interests of their group. As a result, when collective social mobility is possible, people are especially attuned to actual or potential changes in the status of their own and other groups. These concerns for group status produce competition between groups for material resources and for value dominance. According to Allport, this competition promotes prejudice between groups. Allport observed that it is often difficult to disentangle genuine conflicts of interest between groups from prejudice, in part because they often operate in concert; additionally, once initiated, genuine conflicts of interest tend to take on 'excess baggage' in the form of prejudice, so that the conflict is magnified. Nevertheless, Allport argued that it is important, both conceptually and practically, to distinguish between 'the inherently competitive elements in the situation' (p. 231) and prejudice.

Allport (1954) noted that group relations may be realistically competitive in two respects. First, he suggested that because demands for material resources often exceed their supply, individuals may see others as rivals for obtaining these resources. Of importance, although such competition may actually exist at the individual level, individuals may nonetheless perceive the competition to be at the group level. Thus, Allport described realistic group conflict as reflecting the common perception that competition for tangible resources involves group identities and has collective consequences. Second, Allport considered competitive relations between groups to be realistic when the competition involves less tangible resources, such as religious or political belief systems. In particular, belief systems may be seen as in direct competition by those who endorse the relevant beliefs and wish their beliefs to dominate. Allport also suggested that in social contexts in which equality of opportunity is prized and social mobility is encouraged, perceived competition is especially likely. He noted that allowance or encouragement of upward social mobility makes evident the possibility of downward social mobility, which, in the presence of a salient outgroup, generates competition and hostility.

In contrast to Allport's focus on the importance of distinguishing between genuine conflicts of interest between groups versus prejudice, theorizing by Campbell (1965; see also LeVine & Campbell, 1972) was concerned with how *perceptions* of group conflict and competition are central to understanding prejudice. On the basis of a review of the literature in a variety of disciplines, Campbell (1965) put forward a number of propositions about group conflict, competition, and intergroup relations, forming the basis of much research to follow. Some of Campbell's important propositions are as follows. At a basic level, Campbell suggested that intergroup conflict and threat increase as perceived competition for resources between groups increases, and as the conflicting groups have more to gain by succeeding. Campbell also proposed that the greater the intergroup threat and conflict, the more hostility is expressed toward the source of the threat. This hostility helps to justify the conflict and the unfavorable treatment of outgroup members. In addition, Campbell asserted that when competition over resources is present, proximity and contact increase intergroup hostility, rather than decreasing it.

In discussing the effects of group competition on ingroup relations and solidarity, Campbell (1965, p. 289) pointed out that group competition leads to not only a 'magnification of outgroup vices,' but an 'exaggeration of ingroup virtues,' while also promoting a tightening of group boundaries. Campbell emphasized that the competition need not be genuine for these effects to occur, but need only be perceived in the minds of group members. Thus, for example, Campbell (1965, p. 291) suggested that the identification of a (fictitious) competitor outgroup, whether a foreign power or a local minority group, is a strategy often used by manipulative national leaders in order to increase ingroup unity and

solidarity: 'This is certainly one of the most ubiquitous observations on the exploitative opportunism of nationalistic politics.' We might add that this exploitation of purported group competition is not only practiced at the national level, but is also utilized by individuals and groups at all levels of society. Overall, Realistic Group Conflict Theory has received considerable empirical support through subsequent research in psychology and a variety of other disciplines (e.g., sociology, see Bobo, 1999; Bobo & Tuan, 2006).

In response to what they saw as an excessive focus in prejudice research on the role of competition for tangible resources, Tajfel and Turner (1979) developed Social Identity Theory to highlight the importance of competition over positive group identity and self-esteem in promoting intergroup bias (see also Chapter 10 by Abrams & Hogg in this volume). The basic premise of Social Identity Theory (SIT; see also Self-Categorization Theory: Turner, Hogg, Oakes, et al., 1987) is that people obtain a sense of self worth from the groups to which they belong, so that self and group identity are linked. As a result, individuals seek to belong to groups that are evaluated positively in comparison to other groups, and will denigrate other groups and limit their opportunities in order to obtain this outcome. Thus, what is at stake in this drive for positive group distinctiveness is positive identity and esteem, and it is perceived in a relative or comparative sense versus other groups, so that groups are seen as competing for these symbolic resources. Early support for SIT was obtained from research on discrimination in the minimal group paradigm, in which participants discriminated between ingroups and outgroups, despite a lack of history with the groups in question and the fact that no benefits to the self could be obtained from this discrimination (Tajfel, Billig, Bundy, et al., 1971; Turner, 1975).

As we will discuss shortly, recent conceptualizations of intergroup conflict have attempted to integrate competition over both tangible and intangible resources, and to consider the conditions under which each is most likely to operate. Though Realistic Group

Conflict versus Social Identity explanations of intergroup hostility and discrimination have at times been seen as competing perspectives, more recent conceptualizations have attempted to consider the complementarity of these perspectives. We turn next to a review of contemporary research in this area, which has focused on both distal and proximal factors leading to prejudice and discrimination.

REVIEW OF CONTEMPORARY RESEARCH ON INTERGROUP COMPETITION

Following the development of Realistic Group Conflict Theory and early research conducted to test its major propositions, a hiatus occurred in theorizing and research in this area. Although the basic foundations of the theory were empirically confirmed, through the 1980s and much of the 1990s attention was drawn to more cognitive elements of stereotyping, prejudice and discrimination, and few researchers focused on motivations and goals likely to underlie negative intergroup relations. One exception was the work of Bobo (e.g., Bobo, 1983, 1988, 1999; Bobo & Hutchings, 1996; Bobo & Tuan, 2006), who conducted research on applications of Realistic Group Conflict Theory to a variety of intergroup domains, including racialized politics in the United States, relations among a variety of ethnic groups in Los Angeles County (White, Black, Asian, Latino), and responses to Chippewa Indian fishing and hunting rights in Wisconsin. In addition to its focus on predictions derived from Realistic Group Conflict Theory, this research also addressed several of the propositions of Blumer's (1958) Theory of Group Position, which dealt primarily with the origins of group competition and conflict: 'Feelings of competition and hostility emerge from historically and collectively developed judgments about the positions in the social order that in-group members should rightfully occupy relative to members of an out-group' (Bobo & Hutchings, 1996, p. 955).

The Theory of Group Position (Blumer, 1958) proposes that when members of the ingroup have assumptions about their entitlement to certain resources, rights, and privileges, but outgroup members are perceived to be making claims to a share of these resources, rights, and privileges, intergroup competition and hostility are likely to result. Of particular importance, Bobo (e.g., Bobo & Hutchings, 1996) developed several items for assessing zero-sum beliefs (beliefs that the more another group obtains, the less is available for one's own group) as a critical tool for testing these assumptions.

Based on this foundation, much recent theorizing and research on intergroup relations has included the perception of group competition as a central facet of prejudice and discrimination. This work can be broadly divided into that focusing on more distal factors, particularly ideologies, and work focusing on more proximal factors, including situational and target-relevant triggers of intergroup hostility.

Ideological factors

Distal-level theories such as Social Dominance Theory (Pratto, 1999; Sidanius & Pratto, 1999), System Justification Theory (e.g., Jost & Banaji, 1994; Jost, Burgess, & Mosso, 2001), and Terror Management Theory (Greenberg, Pyszczynski, Solomon, et al., 1990; Greenberg, Solomon, & Pyszczynski, 1997) have sought to explain how ideologies that serve to promote group conflict and competition in society are maintained, and the functions they may serve. Social Dominance Theory suggests that in almost all societies, socially constructed groups are hierarchically organized so that certain groups receive a disproportionate share of positive outcomes (e.g., money, power). Supporting ideologies are then developed to ensure that these hierarchies are maintained in a stable system. Of particular relevance in the current context, for those receiving disproportionate positive outcomes these ideologies include beliefs about the legitimacy of their position in society and beliefs about inherent zero-sum competition among groups. That is, those in positions of power are especially likely to believe that allocations of resources and social value are zero-sum so that in order for them to prosper, others must suffer; if other groups were to begin to prosper, this would necessarily be at the expense of the dominant group. According to Social Dominance Theory, then, a belief in group conflict and competition serves to maintain group dominance and inequality in society.

There is considerable support for these propositions, most notably in the context of research on individual differences in Social Dominance Orientation (Pratto, Sidanius, Stallworth, et al., 1994; see Chapter 10 by Son Hing & Zanna's chapter in this volume). Individuals who are higher in social dominance orientation tend to believe in group inequality and support hierarchies in society; they also tend to belong to groups that are higher in status and power in society (e.g., men, ethnic majority groups; see Sidanius & Pratto, 1999). A number of studies have demonstrated that individuals who are higher in social dominance orientation are especially likely to see the world in zero-sum terms and as a competitive jungle in which only the strong succeed; in turn, these beliefs about group competition lead to prejudice and intergroup hostility (e.g., Dru, 2007; Duckitt, 2006; Duckitt, Wagner, du Plessis, et al., 2002; Esses, Hodson, & Dovidio, 2003; Esses, Jackson, & Armstrong, 1998; Sidanius & Pratto, 1999). Of interest, in the context of relations with immigrants, high social dominance oriented individuals not only perceive zero-sum competition for resources such as jobs and political power; they also perceive zero-sum competition for value dominance (Esses, Hodson, & Dovidio, et al., 2003). That is, they see different sets of values as being inherently incompatible and in opposition, and view immigrants as competing with members of the host society for determining whose values will dominate in society. Thus, it seems that group dominance is not only a matter of having wealth and power, but of having moral hegemony.

Relatedly, System Justification Theory (Jost & Banaji, 1994; Jost, Burgess, & Mosso, et al., 2001) discusses the processes that ensure that people generally believe that the hierarchically structured society in which they live is legitimate and fair. In particular, the theory proposes that stereotypes of dominant and subordinate groups serve the function of legitimizing the system in which these groups exist. These stereotypes justify the positive outcomes of dominant groups, the negative outcomes of subordinate groups, and the exploitation of subordinate groups by dominant groups.

Research supports the assertion that in order to support the system, dominant group members tend to be stereotyped as relatively high in agentic traits – intelligent and hardworking – whereas subordinate group members tend to be stereotyped as unintelligent and lazy. Nonetheless, there is evidence that complementary stereotypes also exist in which subordinate group members are stereotyped as especially high in communal traits – friendly and emotional (Jost, Kivetz, Rubini, et al., 2005). For example, Jost et al. examined the consensual stereotypes of Southerners (higher status) and Northerners (lower status) held by Southerners and Northerners in England. In support of the system-justifying function of complementary stereotypes, both groups rated Southerners as higher on agentic traits, and Northerners as higher on communal traits. In addition, participants who perceived a larger status difference between the two groups were especially likely to show this complementary stereotype effect, and in turn this pattern of stereotyping was associated with greater perceptions of the legitimacy and stability of the social system. Related research has also shown that threats to the status quo heighten endorsement of these stereotypes in an attempt to defend and strengthen the system (Jost & Hunyady, 2005; Kay, Jost, & Young, 2005).

Terror Management Theory takes a different perspective, focusing on less tangible resources and outcomes (e.g., Greenberg, Pyszczynski, Soloman, et al., 1990; Greenberger, Solomon, & Pyszczynski, 1997). The theory proposes that because humans can reflect on their own inevitable deaths, they are subject to the terror of their own ultimate meaninglessness. To counteract this terror, it is argued, people create cultural worldviews that give meaning and significance to their lives. These worldviews provide the possibility of symbolic or true immortality to those who meet standards of value. Because of their often absolute nature, however, these worldviews are not impervious to threat and competition from other worldviews. Group conflict and competition arise, then, because those with different worldviews from us are seen as suggesting that our own worldview is incorrect, threatening the very basic premises on which the meaning and significance of our lives are based.

A large body of research supports the assertion that the salience of mortality and death increases prejudice against dissimilar outgroups, particularly those who threaten the ingroup's religious or political views (e.g., Greenberg, Pyszczynski, Soloman, et al., 1990; McGregor, Lieberman, Greenberg, et al., 1998; Schimel, Simon, Greenberg, et al., 1999). For example, Greenberg, Pyszczynski, & Soloman, et al. asked self-described Christian participants to write about what will happen to them when they physically die (mortality salience condition) or provided them with no writing task (control condition), and then asked them to rate Jewish and Christian targets. In support of Terror Management Theory, in the mortality salience condition participants were especially likely to evaluate the Christian target positively and the Jewish target negatively.

A variety of ideologies may thus lead to perceived group competition and conflict. We turn now to more proximal factors – situational and target-relevant factors – that may also play a role in this process.

Situational and target-relevant factors

At a proximal level, psychologists have examined how situations likely to promote perceived competition and threat can lead to prejudice and discrimination, and how

prejudice can also enhance perceptions of group conflict and competition. The Instrumental Model of Group Conflict (Esses, Dovidio, Jackson, et al., 2001; Esses, Jackson, & Armstong, 1998) and the Integrated Threat Theory of Prejudice (Stephan & Stephan, 2000) have focused on how perceptions of threat and group competition lead to prejudice and discrimination toward specific groups, and the conditions likely to promote or prevent these perceptions. The Instrumental Model of Group Conflict (Esses, Jackson, & Armstrong, et al., 1998; Esses, Dovidio, Jackson, et al., 2001) proposes that resource stress – the perception that there are not enough resources to go around – and the presence of a potentially competitive outgroup lead to perceived competition. A variety of resources may be seen to be at stake, including more tangible resources, such as employment opportunities and other economic resources, and more intangible, symbolic resources, such as values and status. In either case, perceptions of group competition are proposed to lead to prejudice and discrimination that are instrumental in their attempts to remove group competition. Research support for these propositions has been obtained in the context of relations between members of host societies and immigrant groups, using manipulations of portrayals of immigrant groups in media presentations, as well as measures of zero-sum beliefs about immigrants (e.g., Esses, Jackson, & Armstrong, 1998; Esses, Hodson, & Dovidio, 2003). The model has also been applied to the ongoing conflict between Arabs and Africans in Sudan (Esses & Jackson, 2008).

The Integrated Threat Theory of Prejudice (Stephan & Stephan, 2000) stresses intergroup threats and fears as major causes of prejudice and discrimination, and focuses on realistic threats (e.g., economic power), symbolic threats (e.g., different values), intergroup anxiety (e.g., anxious, tense), and negative stereotypes (e.g., lazy, untrustworthy) as sources of threat and fear. Support for one or several of these factors in predicting prejudice has been obtained in a variety of contexts, including relations between Blacks and Whites in the United States, between members of host societies and immigrants in a variety of countries, and between Catholics and Protestants in Northern Ireland (e.g., Stephan, Boniecki, Ybarra, et al., 2002; Stephan, Ybarra, Martinez, Schwarzwald, et al., 1998; Tausch, Hewstone, Kenworthy, et al., 2007).

In terms of target group characteristics, Fiske, Cuddy, and Glick's Stereotype Content Model suggests that the stereotypes of groups are captured by two dimensions, competence and warmth, and that these perceptions have implications for emotional reactions and behavioral tendencies to groups (Cuddy, Fiske, & Glick, 2007; Fiske, Cuddy, Glick, et al., 2002; see also Chapter 7 by Fiske & Russell, in this volume). It is interesting to note that the dimensions of competence and warmth map well onto the agentic and communal traits that form the complementary stereotypes proposed to serve system-justifying functions (as discussed earlier). The Stereotype Content Model further suggests that groups perceived as competing with one's ingroup are likely to be seen as low in warmth, whereas groups seen as low in status are likely to be seen as low in competence. These perceptions then have implications for emotional reactions to outgroups, with low warmth outgroups eliciting envy or contempt, depending on their perceived competence (low warmth and high competence = envy, low warmth and low competence = contempt). In turn, these emotional reactions mediate the relation between stereotypes and behavioral tendencies, with envy leading to passive facilitation of other groups and active harm, and contempt leading to passive and active harm. Considerable support has now accrued for the basic tenets of the model, using a large variety of target groups (e.g., Cuddy, Fiske, & Glick, 2007; Fiske, Cuddy, Glick, et al., 2002; Lee & Fiske, 2006). It is important to note, however, that perceptions of intergroup competition need not originate in the intergroup context in order to have deleterious effects. That is, when a competitive mindset is induced in a context irrelevant to intergroup relations, it may carryover so that groups that have no relevance to the competition may nonetheless be perceived in a competitive light. In turn, increases in prejudice toward these groups may result (Sassenberg, Moskowitz, Jacoby, et al., 2007).

Competition over tangible versus symbolic resources

Recent theorizing on conflicts of interest between groups has tended to subsume these conflicts within two categories: conflict over relatively tangible resources, such as economic resources and group power, and conflict over more symbolic factors, such as values and positive group distinctiveness (e.g., Esses, Hodson, & Dovidio, 2003; Stephan & Stephan, 2000). Although considerable research has been conducted that attempts to pit symbolic or social identity explanations for prejudice against explanations based on more tangible conflicts of interest (e.g., Gagnon & Bourhis, 1996; Rabbie, Schot, & Visser, 1989), recent attempts have been made to reconcile and integrate these perspectives (e.g., Esses, Hodson, & Dovidio, et al., 2003; Scheepers, Spears, Doosje, et al., 2003; Stephan & Stephan, 2000; Zárate, Garcia, Garza, et al., 2004).

For example, Esses, Jackson, Dovidio, et al., (2005) have suggested that symbolic threat might give rise to material threat, and *vice versa*. They propose that in the context of social change in which the dominance of one's value system is seen as being threatened, identity may be protected by targeting out-groups as competitors for more tangible resources. Gaining resources may serve the function of allowing one's group to ensure that its values have representation and status. Alternatively, competition for material resources may generate exaggerated claims of value differences in order to justify the less palatable, material conflict. Scheepers, Spears, & Doosje, et al., (2003) provide compelling evidence that both social identity concerns and concern with material resources drive intergroup differentiation, though under different conditions.

It may also be the case that there are individual differences in the extent to which individuals are sensitive to competition over more tangible resources versus more symbolic factors. Although there is likely to be considerable overlap, it may be the case that individuals high in social dominance orientation are particularly attuned to competition over tangible resources, whereas high right-wing authoritarians and religious fundamentalists are particularly attuned to competition over more symbolic factors (see also Duckitt, 2006; Duckitt, Wagner, du Plessis, et al., 2002). Indeed, research has shown that individuals who are high in social dominance orientation – who believe in group inequality and support group hierarchies in society – tend to see the world in terms of inherent competition among groups for dominance and power, and thus are especially likely to display prejudice and discrimination toward those who are seen as potential competitors for resources (e.g., Duckitt, Wagner, du Plessis, et al., 2002; Esses, Jackson, & Armstrong, 1998; Sidanius & Pratto, 1999).

Research has also shown that individuals who are high in right-wing authoritarianism are especially sensitive to threats to their traditional values, and display negative attitudes and behavior toward those seen to hold values different from their own (e.g., Altemeyer, 1996; Esses, Haddock, & Zanna, 1993, see also Chapter 10 by Son Hing & Zanna in this

volume). Similarly, religious fundamentalists, who tend to see their religious beliefs as absolute truths, tend to hold negative attitudes toward those who hold different values and beliefs (e.g., Hunsberger & Jackson, 2005; Jackson & Esses, 1997). It may thus be the case that right-wing authoritarians and religious fundamentalists see their own and other groups' religious beliefs and values as in direct competition for dominance in society.

These distal and more proximal factors shown to be important triggers of intergroup hostility may operate in concert, increasing the probability that prejudice and discrimination will result. The Unified Instrumental Model of Group Conflict considers the mutual relations among these factors and the consequences for relations among groups.

THE UNIFIED INSTRUMENTAL MODEL OF GROUP CONFLICT

The various perspectives that we have been discussing have been integrated into our Unified Instrumental Model of Group Conflict (see Figure 14.1). In general, we suggest that ideologies and situational factors may be mutually reinforcing in initiating the process of perceiving group competition and conflict. Perceptions of group competition

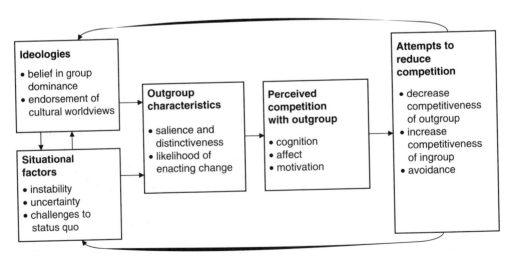

Figure 14.1   Unified Instrumental Model of Group Conflict.
(*Source: Adapted from Esses, Jackson, Dovidio, et al., 2005.*)

are most likely to arise, however, when a relevant outgroup is available, though irrelevant groups may also be targeted. Once perceived intergroup competition is initiated, a variety of cognitive, affective, and motivational reactions may be initiated. As a result, various attempts will be made to reduce this competition, including the expression of prejudice and discrimination. The resulting attitudes and behaviors may then feed back on the ideologies and situational factors, reducing or exacerbating the belief structures and situational factors that initiated the process. This model can be applied to understand a broad range of intergroup relations, including relations between immigrants and members of host countries, relations between religious groups, and relations between a variety of racial and ethnic groups. We now discuss each of these steps in more detail.

Both belief systems that promote group dominance and those that promote particular culture worldviews may lead to chronic perceptions of group competition, though the resources seen to be primarily at stake may differ. Belief systems that promote group dominance may primarily lead to perceived competition over relatively tangible resources, such as money and power. In order for some groups in society to dominate others, they must have disproportionate access to valued resources. It is not sufficient for them to have a great deal in an absolute sense; they must have more than others in a relative sense. As a result, in societies in which group dominance is evident, there is likely to be a perception that there are not enough valued resources to go around. This will lead to the belief that groups are chronically competing for valued and scarce resources. Dominant group members are especially likely to hold a belief in zero-sum competition between groups because it is in their interests to maintain the hierarchy (Sidanius, Levin, & Pratto, 1996; Sidanius & Pratto, 1999). As mentioned earlier, research on Social Dominance Orientation has demonstrated that members of dominant or majority groups in society are especially likely to be high in social dominance orientation, and that social dominance orientation is highly correlated with a belief in zero-sum competition among groups (e.g., Esses, Jackson, Armstrong, et al., 1998; Esses, Dovidio, & Jackson, et al., 2001; Esses, Hodson, & Dovidio, 2003; Sidanius & Pratto, 1999; Sidanius, Pratto, & Bobo, 1994). In turn, these zero-sum beliefs mediate the relation between social dominance orientation and negative attitudes toward outgroups, particularly outgroups seen to be succeeding in society (Esses, Jackson, Armstrong, et al., 1998; Esses, Dovidio, & Jackson, et al., 2001; Esses, Hodson, & Dovidio, 2003).

Cultural worldviews may be at the heart of perceived competition over more symbolic factors such as values. Worldviews often have an absolute nature so that they not only prescribe appropriate modes of thinking and behaving, but proscribe others (Batson & Burris, 1994; Greenberg, Pyszcynski, Solomon, et al., 1990; Greenberg, Solomon, & Pyszcynski, 1997). As a result, cultures may be seen to be competing to obtain 'truth.' The correctness of a cultural worldview may be promoted, then, by proving the incorrectness of opposing views. As discussed above, it is also the case that there are individual differences in the extent to which people endorse and seek to defend their cultural perspectives, as assessed by such measures as right-wing authoritarianism and religious fundamentalism (Altemeyer, 1996; Altemeyer & Hunsberger, 1992).

Ideologies related to group dominance and cultural worldviews may lead to a chronic belief in group competition. However, situational factors may also have an important role to play in terms of making salient and heightening perceived competition among groups. We propose that perceived challenges to the status quo, instability, and uncertainty are likely to have such effects. For example, major events such as economic upheaval, threat of war, and even natural disasters may lead not only to increased protection of tangible resources held by one's group, but protection of more symbolic factors such as values and positive group distinctiveness (Brancati, 2007; Hogg, 2006; Rothgerber, 1997; Worchel & Coutant, 1997).

For example, Brancati analysed the impact of earthquakes on intrastate conflict in 185 countries over a period of 27 years. These analyses provide statistical support for the assertion that the incidence of earthquakes, particularly higher magnitude earthquakes, increases the likelihood of intergroup conflict within nations. More minor situational influences, such as media reports of unemployment rates in different segments of the population or debate over men and women's roles in society, may have similar effects (e.g., Esses, Jackson, & Armstrong, 1998). For example, in a laboratory experiment, Esses et al. asked participants to read an editorial that either emphasized immigrants' success in a tight job market or made no mention of this issue. Results demonstrated that participants who read about immigrants' success in a tight job market were especially likely to perceive new immigrants in a negative light and to support restrictive immigration policies.

In the case of both relevant ideologies and situational influences, the increased motivation to protect group interests is likely to increase perceived competition with other groups. In addition, ideologies and situational factors that promote perceived group competition may be mutually reinforcing so that the ideologies may heighten sensitivity to situational factors, and the situational factors may reinforce and strengthen the ideologies. For example, high right-wing authoritarians are particularly sensitive to perceived threats to their values (Esses, Haddock, & Zanna, 1994) and conversely, national threat and uncertainty have been shown to lead to increased expressions of authoritarianism (Altemeyer, 1988; Doty, Peterson, & Winter, 1991; Sales, 1973).

Although ideologies and situational factors may promote the likelihood of perceiving zero-sum competition among groups, some groups are more likely to be perceived as competitors than are others. Groups that are salient and distinct from the ingroup are especially likely to stand out as potential competitors. For example, groups that are large or are increasing in size, and are distinctive in terms of appearance or behavior

are especially likely to be viewed as potential competitors (e.g., Brewer, 1979; Masgoret, Esses, & Ward, 2004). In addition, outgroups seen as capable of enacting changes in the status quo are also especially likely to be perceived as potential competitors. Thus, for example, as Blacks have made gains in the United States, they are more likely to be seen as a competitive threat to Whites (e.g., Bobo, 1988; Sidanius, Pratto, & Bobo, 1996).

Perceptions of group competition have cognitive, affective, and motivational components. The cognitive component may involve not only beliefs about the nature of the competition with this group (e.g., zero-sum beliefs relevant to the nature of the resources seen to be at stake; Esses, Hodson, & Dovidio, 2003) but, as suggested by Fiske and her colleagues (Fiske, Cuddy, Glick, et al., 2002), stereotypes associated with perceived competition, including lack of warmth. The cognitive component may also include an increase in mental rigidity and black and white thinking (Carnevale & Probst, 1998). The affective component may involve anxiety and fear (Fiske & Ruscher, 1993; Stephan & Stephan, 2000), as well as more specific emotions directed toward the group, such as envy or contempt (Fiske, Cuddy, Glick, et al., 2002). Finally, the perceived competition is likely to elicit a motivation to reduce the sense of group competition and the emotions that may accompany it.

Attempts to reduce group competition may take a variety of forms, reflecting various manifestations of prejudice and discrimination toward outgroups. We discuss three general strategies here, though we certainly acknowledge that others may exist. The first two strategies correspond to the distinction between outgroup derogation and discrimination versus ingroup enhancement and preferential treatment (Brewer, 1999, 2001). It has been suggested that outgroup derogation and ingroup favoritism are not merely two sides of the same coin or reciprocally related, but are conceptually and empirically distinguishable (see Chapter 12 by Leyens & Demoulin in this volume). For example, Brewer (1999, 2001) has discussed the importance of distinguishing between ingroup love and outgroup hatred, and has suggested that intergroup discrimination is at times a function of preferential treatment of the ingroup, rather than direct hostility toward outgroups. In addition, research on discrimination in the minimal group paradigm used to test the premises of SIT has distinguished between providing more rewards or positive outcomes to the ingroup than to outgroups versus providing more costs or negative outcomes to outgroups than to the ingroup (e.g., Blanz, Mummendey & Otten, 1997; Buhl, 1999; Mummendey, Simon, Dietze, et al., 1992). Thus, attempts to reduce an outgroup's competitiveness may occur through enhancement of the ingroup or derogration of the outgroup.

A group may attempt to reduce the outgroup's perceived competitiveness by expressing negative attitudes and attributions about members of the other group in an attempt to convince one's own group and other groups of the competitor's lack of worth. This may include heightened endorsement of stereotypes about the outgroup, used to justify the system as it currently exists (Jost & Banaji, 1994; Jost, Burgess, & Mosso, 2001). Attempts to reduce the outgroup's competitiveness may also entail overt discrimination and opposition to programs and policies that may change the status quo (Bobo, 1999; Jackson & Esses, 2000; Pratto & Lemieux, 2001). At an extreme level, the attempt to reduce an outgroup's competitiveness may lead to dehumanization – denying a group its basic humanity (e.g., Esses & Jackson, 2008) – and devaluation of the very lives of outgroup members (Pratto & Glasford, 2008).

Alternatively, or in addition, a group may attempt to increase the ingroup's competitiveness through the expression of ingroup-enhancing attitudes aimed at convincing one's own group and other groups of the ingroup's entitlement to the resources at stake, be they tangible resources or more symbolic moral certainty and social value (Jost & Banaji, 1994; Jost, Burgess, & Mosso, 2001). Attempts to increase the ingroup's competitiveness may also entail

preferential treatment in the allocation of positive outcomes (Mullen, Brown, & Smith, 1992; Sidanius & Pratto, 1999).

The third strategy that may be used to reduce group competition is avoidance. The competitor outgroup may be denied access to the ingroup's territory or kept at a distance (e.g., Bobo, 1988; Esses, Jackson, & Armstrong, 1998). In addition, the outgroup may be denied voice so that its challenges to the status quo are silenced (Esses & Jackson, 2008; McFarland & Warren, 1992). As a result, the competition, or the salience of the competition, may be reduced. For example, Esses and her colleagues (e.g., Esses, Jackson, & Armstrong, 1998; Esses, Hodson, & Dovidio, 2003; see also Chapter 22 by Wagner, Christ, & Heitmeyer in this volume) have demonstrated that perceptions of competition with immigrants for both tangible and more symbolic resources leads to increased support for restrictive immigration policies that deny immigrants access to the ingroup's territory.

The process does not necessarily end here. Instead, attempts to reduce group competition may feed back to the ideologies and situational factors that elicited the competition. For example, outgroup derogation, ingroup enhancement, and avoidance may reinforce the ideologies of group dominance and strengthen the perceived 'correctness' of one's worldview, increasing the likelihood of further perceptions of competition. In terms of situational factors, however, if the attempts to reduce competition are successful, they may increase the stability of the system and reduce challenges to the status quo and uncertainty, so that situational factors promoting group competition are no longer operating. As a result of mutual effects of group ideologies and situational factors, further group competition may be perpetuated or attenuated.

Thus, the Unified Instrumental Model of Group Conflict subsumes both ideological and situational influences, and considers resultant perceptions of group competition over both tangible and more symbolic resources. It also takes into account those groups that are most likely to be perceived as competitors, and the affective, cognitive, and behavioral components of group competition. Finally, the theory considers prejudice and discrimination that result as instrumental in their goal of ultimately attempting to reduce group competition or the salience of this competition. Feedback systems are also incorporated into the model, as an acknowledgement of potentially bidirectional effects.

FUTURE DIRECTIONS

Our analysis suggests a number of fruitful directions for future research. As discussed previously, the relation between competition over more tangible resources and competition over symbolic resources has yet to be fleshed out, and research examining the extent and nature of reciprocity between these two forms of competition would provide a significant contribution to this literature. We have proposed that competition over tangible resources may at times be justified by appealing to value competition, and that competition over values may at times spill over into competition over tangible resources to ensure that one's values have representation and status. There are a number of contexts in which such hypotheses might be tested, including for example, international relations (e.g., competition over oil and natural resources justified by appealing to purported value competition) and competition among political parties and their supporters (e.g., competition for value dominance leading to competition for economic resources to promote one's party).

In terms of tangible resources, a problem of increasing concern worldwide is environmental degradation and resultant scarcity of natural resources. Thus, an issue that is likely to be of growing importance in the near future is competition over environmental resources, such as arable land, potable water, and perhaps even clean air (see also Bobo & Tuan, 2006; Janes, Jackson, Esses, et al., 2009). Such competition may be particularly virulent given that basic environmental resources are essential for our very existence. As a result, research on competition for environmental resources may make a particularly important practical contribution.

It is also the case that research on group competition has not yet examined in detail its cognitive, affective, and motivational underpinnings, nor the specific role that they play individually and in concert in leading to bias and discrimination. Such research would not only provide a strong theoretical contribution, but would provide insight into potential targets for intervention. Longitudinal research might prove particularly useful in this regard, allowing a full investigation of the process from initial ideologies and situational triggers to eventual outcomes. Analyses of media presentations of group-relevant issues may also prove insightful, focusing on the potential progression from ideologies and situational triggers to portrayals of group competition to conflictual outcomes, including derogation of competitor outgroups and support for exclusionary policies and practices.

Finally, an increased examination of strategies for preventing or reducing group competition and fostering social inclusion is warranted. Though our review has made clear that we now know a great deal about group competition and its consequences, its deleterious effects continue to plague modern society both within and between nations. Progress has indeed been made at both a theoretical and practical level in developing techniques for promoting intergroup harmony. Yet work on such techniques has not fully examined how group competition potentially moderates their effects, and is particularly needed to develop strategies for overcoming unintended negative consequences. For example, theory and research on the contact hypothesis has emphasized that an important condition for contact to lead to positive intergroup attitudes is contact under conditions of cooperation rather than competition (e.g., Pettigrew & Tropp, 2006). Real world strategies for reducing competition under conditions in which crucial resources are considered to be at stake would make a significant contribution in this regard.

SUMMARY AND CONCLUSION

An understanding of the role of group competition in promoting intergroup hostility and conflict is as important today as it was when Sherif began to conduct research on boys at summer camp close to 60 years ago. Psychologists and researchers in other disciplines now know a great deal about factors that may promote group competition – both ideological and situational triggers – and some of its major consequences for intergroup relations. Group competition has been investigated in a wide variety of domains, including relations between immigrants and members of host societies, between religious groups, between ethnic majority and minority groups, and between Native and non-Native Americans. Future research would do well both to investigate mediators of these effects in more detail and to apply current knowledge to new sources of group competition and to strategies for promoting intergroup harmony. In this way, our work will prove useful in grappling with some of the major challenges that confront us in the twenty-first century.

ACKNOWLEDGEMENT

Preparation of this chapter was facilitated by a grant from the Social Sciences and Humanities Research Council of Canada to Victoria Esses. Correspondence should be directed to Victoria Esses, Department of Psychology, University of Western Ontario, London, Ontario, Canada N6A 5C2. E-mail: vesses@uwo.ca

REFERENCES

Allport, G. W. (1954). *The Nature of Prejudice*. Reading, MA: Addison-Wesley.

Altemeyer, B. (1988). *Enemies of Freedom: Understanding Right-Wing Authoritarianism*. San Francisco, CA, US: Jossey-Bass.

Altemeyer, B. (1996). *The Authoritarian Specter*. Cambridge, MA, US: Harvard University Press.

Altemeyer, B., & Hunsberger, B. E. (1992). Authoritarianism, religious fundamentalism, quest, and prejudice. *International Journal for the Psychology of Religion*, 2, 113–133.

Batson, C. D., & Burris, C. T. (1994). Personal religion: Depressant or stimulant of prejudice and discrimination?. In M. P. Zanna, & J. M. Olson (Eds), *The Psychology of Prejudice: The Ontario Symposium* (Vol. 7, pp. 149–169). Hillsdale, NJ: Lawrence Erlbaum.

Blanz, M., Mummendey, A., & Otten, S. (1997). Normative evaluations and frequency expectations regarding positive versus negative outcome allocations between groups. *European Journal of Social Psychology*, 27, 165–176.

Blumer, H. (1958). Race prejudice as a sense of group position. *Pacific Sociological Review*, 1, 3–7.

Bobo, L. D. (1983). 'Whites' opposition to busing: Symbolic racism or realistic group conflict? *Journal of Personality and Social Psychology*, 45, 1196–1210.

Bobo, L. (1988). Group conflict, prejudice, and the paradox of contemporary racial attitudes. In P.A. Katz, & D.A. Taylor (Eds), *Eliminating Racism: Profiles in Controversy* (pp. 85–114). New York: Plenum.

Bobo, L. D. (1999). Prejudice as group position: Microfoundations of a sociological approach to racism and race relations. *Journal of Social Issues*, 55, 445–472.

Bobo, L., & Hutchings, V. L. (1996). Perceptions of racial group competition: Extending Blumer's Theory of Group Position to a multiracial social context. *American Sociological Review*, 61, 951–972.

Bobo, L. D., & Tuan, M. (2006). *Prejudice in Politics: Group Position, Public Opinion, and the Wisconsin Treaty Rights Dispute*. Cambridge, MA: Harvard University Press.

Brancati, D. (2007). Political aftershocks: The impact of earthquakes on intrastate conflict. *Journal of Conflict Resolution*, 51, 715–743.

Brewer, M. B. (1979). In-group bias in the minimal intergroup situation: A cognitive-motivational analysis. *Psychological Bulletin*, 86, 307–324.

Brewer, M. B. (1999). The psychology of prejudice: Ingroup love or outgroup hate?', *Journal of Social Issues*, 55, 429–444.

Brewer, M. B. (2001). Ingroup identification and intergroup conflict: When does ingroup love become outgroup hate? In R. D. Ashmore, L. Jussim, & D. Wilder (Eds), *Social Identity, Intergroup Conflict, and Conflict Reduction* (pp. 17–41). New York, NY: Oxford University Press.

Buhl, T. (1999). Positive–negative asymmetry in social discrimination: Meta-analytical evidence', *Group Processes and Intergroup Relations*, 2, 51–58.

Campbell, D. T. (1965). Ethnocentric and other altruistic motives. In D. Levine (Ed.), *Nebraska Symposium on Motivation* (Vol. 13, pp. 283–311). Lincoln, NE: University of Nebraska Press.

Carnevale, P. J., & Probst, T. M. (1998). Social values and social conflict in creative problem solving and categorization. *Journal of Personality and Social Psychology, 74,* 1300–1309.

Cuddy, A. J. C., Fiske, S. T., & Glick, P. (2007). The BIAS map: Behaviors from intergroup affect and stereotypes. *Journal of Personality and Social Psychology, 92,* 631–648.

Doty, R. E., Peterson, B. E., & Winter, D. G. (1991). Threat and authoritarianism in the United States, 1978–1987. *Journal of Personality and Social Psychology, 61,* 629–640.

Dru, V. (2007). Authoritarianism, social dominance orientation and prejudice: Effects of various self-categorization conditions. *Journal of Experimental Social Psychology, 43,* 877–883.

Duckitt, J. (2006). Differential effects of right wing authoritarianism and social dominance orientation on outgroup attitudes and their mediation by threat from and competitiveness to outgroups. *Personality and Social Psychology Bulletin, 32,* 684–696.

Duckitt, J., Wagner, C., du Plessis, I., & Birum, I. (2002). The psychological bases of ideology and prejudice: Testing a dual process model. *Journal of Personality and Social Psychology, 83,* 75–93.

Esses, V. M., Dovidio, J. F., Jackson, L. M., & Armstrong, T. L. (2001). The immigration dilemma: The role of perceived group competition, ethnic prejudice, and national identity. *Journal of Social Issues, 57,* 389–412.

Esses, V. M., Haddock, G., & Zanna, M. P. (1993). Values, stereotypes, and emotions as determinants of intergroup attitudes. In D. M. Mackie, & D. L. Hamilton (Eds), *Affect, Cognition, and Stereotyping: Interactive Processes in Group Perception* (pp. 137–166). San Diego, CA, US: Academic Press.

Esses, V. M., Haddock, G., & Zanna, M. P. (1994). The role of mood in the expression of intergroup stereotypes. In M. P. Zanna, & J. M. Olson (Eds), *The Psychology of Prejudice: The Ontario Symposium* (Vol. 7, pp. 77–101). Hillsdale, NJ: Lawrence Erlbaum.

Esses, V. M., Hodson, G., & Dovidio, J. F. (2003). Public attitudes toward immigrants and immigration: Determinants and policy implications. In C. M. Beach, A. G. Green, & J. G. Reitz (Eds), *Canadian Immigration Policy for the 21st Century* (pp. 507–535). Montreal, Canada: McGill Queen's Press.

Esses, V. M., & Jackson, L. M. (2008). Applying the unified instrumental model of group conflict to understanding ethnic conflict and violence: The case of Sudan. In V. M. Esses, & R. A. Vernon (Eds), *Explaining the Breakdown of Ethnic Relations: Why Neighbors Kill* (pp. 223–243). Malden: Blackwell Publishing.

Esses, V. M., Jackson, L. M., & Armstrong, T. L. (1998). Intergroup competition and attitudes toward immigrants and immigration: An instrumental model of group conflict. *Journal of Social Issues, 54,* 699–724.

Esses, V. M., Jackson, L. M., Dovidio, J. F., & Hodson, G. (2005). Instrumental relations among groups: Group competition, conflict, and prejudice. In J. F. Dovidio, P. Glick, & L. A. Rudman (Eds), *On the Nature of Prejudice: Fifty Years after Allport* (pp. 227–243). Malden: Blackwell Publishing.

Fiske, S. T., Cuddy, A. J. C., Glick, P., & Xu, J. (2002). A model of (often mixed) stereotype content: Competence and warmth respectively follow from perceived status and competition. *Journal of Personality and Social Psychology, 82,* 878–902.

Fiske, S. T., & Ruscher, J. B. (1993). Negative interdependence and prejudice: Whence the affect? In D. M. Mackie, & D. L. Hamilton (Eds). *Affect, Cognition, and Stereotyping: Interactive Processes in Group Perception* (pp. 239–268). San Diego, CA, US: Academic Press.

Gagnon, A., & Bourhis, R. Y. (1996). Discrimination in the minimal group paradigm: Social identity or self-interest? *Personality and Social Psychology Bulletin, 22,* 1289–1301.

Greenberg, J., Pyszczynski, T., Solomon, S. & Rosenblatt, A. (1990). Evidence for terror management theory II: The effects of mortality salience on reactions to those who threaten or bolster the cultural worldview. *Journal of Personality and Social Psychology, 58,* 308–318.

Greenberg, J., Solomon, S., & Pyszczynski, T. (1997). Terror management theory of self-esteem and cultural worldviews: Empirical assessments and cultural refinements. In M. P. Zanna (Ed.), *Advances in Experimental Social Psychology* (Vol. 29, pp. 61–139). Orlando, FL: Academic Press.

Hogg, M. A. (2006). Self-conceptual uncertainty and the lure of belonging. In R. Brown, & D. Capozza (Eds), *Social Identities: Motivational, Emotional and Cultural Influences* (pp. 33–49). Hove, England: Psychology Press/Taylor & Francis (UK).

Hunsberger, B., & Jackson, L. M. (2005). Religion, meaning, and prejudice. *Journal of Social Issues, 61,* 807–826.

Jackson, L. M., & Esses, V. M. (1997). Of scripture and ascription: The relation between religious fundamentalism and intergroup helping. *Personality and Social Psychology Bulletin*, 23, 893–906.

Jackson, L. M. & Esses, V. M. (2000). Effects of perceived economic competition on people's willingness to help empower immigrants. *Group Processes and Intergroup Relations*, 3, 419–435.

Janes, L., Jackson, L. M., Esses, V. M., & Sibanda, C. (2009). Resource entitlement: Is environmental damage to foreign nations more acceptable if Canada stands to benefit? Paper presented at the annual meeting of the Canadian Psychological Association, Montreal, Canada.

Jost, J. T., & Banaji, M. R. (1994). The role of stereotyping in system-justification and the production of false consciousness. *British Journal of Social Psychology*, 33, 1–27.

Jost, J. T., Burgess, D., & Mosso, C. O. (2001). Conflicts of legitimation among self, group, and system: The integrative potential of system justification theory. In J. T. Jost, & B. Major (Eds), *The Psychology of Legitimacy: Emerging Perspectives on Ideology, Justice, and Intergroup Relations* (pp. 363–388). New York: Cambridge University Press.

Jost, J. T., & Hunyady, O. (2005). Antecedents and consequences of system–justifying ideologies. *Current Directions in Psychological Science*, 14, 260–265.

Jost, J. T., Kivetz, Y., Rubini, M., Guermandi, G., & Mosso, C. (2005). System-justifying functions of complementary regional and ethnic stereotypes: Cross-national evidence. *Social Justice Research*, 18, 305–333.

Kay, A. C., Jost, J. T., & Young, S. (2005). Victim derogation and victim enhancement as alternate routes to system justification. *Psychological Science*, 16, 240–246.

Lee, T. L., & Fiske, S. T. (2006). Not an outgroup, but not yet an ingroup: Immigrants in the stereotype content model. *International Journal of Intercultural Relations*, 30, 751–768.

LeVine, R. A., & Campbell, D. T. (1972). *Ethnocentrism: Theories of Conflict, Ethnic Attitudes, and Group Behavior*. Oxford, England: John Wiley & Sons.

Masgoret, A. M., Esses, V. M., & Ward, C. (2004). Examining the bases of intergroup competition and their role in determining immigration attitudes in New Zealand In K. Deaux (Chair), *Looking at Immigrants: What Influences Attitudes and Evaluations of the Newcomer?* Symposium conducted at the International Congress of Psychology, Beijing, China.

McFarland, S. G., & Warren, J. C. (1992). Religious orientations and selective exposure among fundamentalist Christians. *Journal for the Scientific Study of Religion*, 31, 163–174.

McGregor, H. A., Lieberman, J. D., Greenberg, J., Solomon, S., Arndt, J., Simon, L., et al. (1998). Terror management and aggression: Evidence that mortality salience motivates aggression against worldview-threatening others. *Journal of Personality and Social Psychology*, 74, 590–605.

Mullen, B., Brown, R., & Smith, C. (1992). Ingroup bias as a function of salience, relevance, and status: An integration. *European Journal of Social Psychology*, 22, 103–122.

Mummendey, A., Simon, B., Dietze, C., & Grünert, M. (1992). Categorization is not enough: Intergroup discrimination in negative outcome allocation. *Journal of Experimental Social Psychology*, 28, 125–144.

Pettigrew, T. F., & Tropp, L. R. (2006). A meta-analytic test of intergroup contact theory. *Journal of Personality and Social Psychology*, 90, 751–783.

Pratto, F. (1999). The puzzle of continuing group inequality: Piecing together psychological, social, and cultural forces in social dominance theory. In M. P. Zanna (Ed.), *Advances in Experimental Social Psychology* (Vol. 31, pp. 191–263). San Diego: Academic Press.

Pratto, F., & Glasford, D. E. (2008). Ethnocentrism and the value of a human life. *Journal of Personality and Social Psychology*, 95, 1411–1428.

Pratto, F., & Lemieux, A. F. (2001). The psychological ambiguity of immigration and its implications for promoting immigration policy. *Journal of Social Issues*, 57, 413–430.

Pratto, F., Sidanius, J., Stallworth, L. M., & Malle, B. F. (1994). Social dominance orientation: A personality variable predicting social and political attitudes. *Journal of Personality and Social Psychology*, 67, 741–763.

Rabbie, J. M., Schot, J. C., & Visser, L. (1989). Social identity theory: A conceptual and empirical critique from the perspective of a behavioural interaction model. *European Journal of Social Psychology*, 19, 171–202.

Rothgerber, H. (1997). External intergroup threat as an antecedent to perceptions in in-group and out-group homogeneity. *Journal of Personality and Social Psychology*, 73, 1206–1212.

Sales, S. M. (1973). Threat as a factor in authoritarianism: An analysis of archival data. *Journal of Personality and Social Psychology*, 28, 44–57.

Sassenberg, K., Moskowitz, G. B., Jacoby, J., & Hansen, N. (2007). The carry-over effect of competition: The impact of competition on prejudice towards uninvolved outgroups, *Journal of Experimental Social Psychology*, 43, 529–538.

Scheepers, D., Spears, R., Doosje, B., & Manstead, A. S. R. (2003). Two functions of verbal intergroup discrimination: Identity and instrumental motives as a result of group identification and threat. *Personality and Social Psychology Bulletin*, 29, 568–577.

Schimel, J., Simon, L., Greenberg, J., Pyszczynski, T., Solomon, S., Waxmonsky, J., et al. (1999). Stereotypes and terror management: Evidence that mortality salience enhances stereotypic thinking and preferences. *Journal of Personality and Social Psychology*, 77, 905–926.

Sherif, M. (1966). *Group Conflict and Cooperation: Their Social Psychology*. London: Routledge and Kegan Paul.

Sherif, M., Harvey, O. J., White, B. J., Hood, W. R., & Sherif, C. W. (1961). *Intergroup Conflict and Cooperation. The Robbers Cave Experiment*. Norman, OK: University of Oklahoma Book Exchange.

Sidanius, J., Levin, S., & Pratto, F. (1996). Consensual social dominance orientation and its correlates within the hierarchical structure of American society. *International Journal of Intercultural Relations*, 20, 385–408.

Sidanius, J., & Pratto, F. (1999). *Social Dominance: An Intergroup Theory of Social Hierarchy and Oppression*. New York: Cambridge University Press.

Sidanius, J., Pratto, F., & Bobo, L. (1994). Social dominance orientation and the political psychology of gender: A case of invariance? *Journal of Personality and Social Psychology*, 67, 998–1011.

Sidanius, J., Pratto, F., & Bobo, L. (1996). Racism, conservatism, affirmative action, and intellectual sophistication: A matter of principled conservatism or group dominance? *Journal of Personality and Social Psychology*, 70, 476–490.

Stephan, W. G., Boniecki, K. A., Ybarra, O., Bettencourt, A., Ervin, K. S., Jackson, L. A., et al. (2002). The role of threats in the racial attitudes of blacks and whites. *Personality and Social Psychology Bulletin*, 28, 1242–1254.

Stephan, W. G., & Stephan, C. W. (2000). An integrated threat theory of prejudice. In S. Oskamp (Ed.), *Claremont Symposium on Applied Social Psychology* (pp. 23–46). Hillsdale, NJ: Lawrence Erlbaum.

Stephan, W. G., Ybarra, O., Martínez, C. M., Schwarzwald, J., & Tur-Kaspa, M. (1998). Prejudice toward immigrants to Spain and Israel: An integrated threat theory analysis. *Journal of Cross-Cultural Psychology*, 29, 559–576.

Tajfel, H., Billig, M. G., Bundy, R. P., & Flament, C. (1971). Social categorization and intergroup behaviour. *European Journal of Social Psychology*, 1, 149–178.

Tajfel H., & Turner, J. C. (1979). An integrative theory of intergroup conflict. In W. G. Austin, & S. Worchel (Eds), *The Social Psychology of Intergroup Relation* (pp. 33–47). Monterey, CA: Brooks/Cole Publishing Company.

Tausch, N., Hewstone, M., Kenworthy, J. B., & Cairns, E. (2007). Cross-community contact, perceived status differences and intergroup attitudes in Northern Ireland: The mediating roles of individual-level vs. group-level threats and the moderating role of social identification. *Political Psychology*, 28, 53–68.

Turner, J. C. (1975). Social comparison and social identity: Some prospects for intergroup behaviour. *European Journal of Social Psychology*, 5, 5–34.

Turner, J. C., Hogg, M. A., Oakes, P. J., Reicher, S. D., & Wetherell, M. S. (1987). *Rediscovering the Social Group: A Self-Categorization Theory*. Oxford, U.K.: Basil Blackwell.

Worchel, S., & Coutant, D. (1997). The tangled web of loyalty: Nationalism, patriotism, and ethnocentrism. In D. Bar-Tal, & E. Staub (Eds), *Patriotism in the Life of Individuals and Nations* (pp. 190–210). Chicago, IL: Nelson–Hall Publishers.

Zárate, M. A., Garcia, B., Garza, A. A., & Hitlan, R. T. (2004). Cultural threat and perceived realistic group conflict as dual predictors of prejudice. *Journal of Experimental Social Psychology*, 40, 99–105.

15

Mass Media

Diana C. Mutz and Seth K. Goldman

ABSTRACT

The way outgroup members are portrayed in the media is widely believed to have consequences for levels of prejudice and stereotyping in the mass public. The visual nature of television and its heavy viewership make it a key source of information for impressions that ingroup members may have of other social groups. However, most research to date has focused on documenting the portrayals of various groups in television content, with only a few studies documenting the causal impact of television viewing. To further understanding of this hypothesis, we outline the contributions and limitations of past work, and point to the most promising theoretical frameworks for studying media influence on outgroup attitudes.

MASS MEDIA

Stereotypes, Gordon Allport wrote, 'are socially supported, continually revived and hammered in, by our media of mass communication—by novels, short stories, newspaper items, movies, stage, radio, and television' (1954, p. 200). Yet, Allport provided no direct evidence that media exposure increased stereotyping or prejudice. Today most researchers concur that a systematic agenda examining the nature and consequences of mass media on stereotyping and prejudice is warranted, but lacking – an oversight this chapter hopes to begin to correct. We limit our discussion of mass media to television, the dominant medium in countries with well-developed national media systems. Moreover, the audio-visual nature of the medium best approximates face-to-face intergroup contact, and makes the group identities of people and characters on television salient to viewers, thus facilitating potential effects on outgroup attitudes.

OVERVIEW

Fifty years after Allport's observation about the potential importance of media, scores of studies have examined representations of a broad range of social groups in news, entertainment, and advertising, but empirical evidence of effects from exposure has lagged considerably behind descriptive studies of media content. Content analyses have examined portrayals of African Americans, Latinos, gays and lesbians, women, and older people, as well as a smattering of other social groups. Perhaps because of television's heavy emphasis on the criminal justice system in both fictional and non-fictional programming, the most common subjects have been crime and criminality, and media portrayals that link crime to racial or ethnic outgroups.

Content is only half of the story, but historically it is where the greatest research effort has been focused. Despite the many studies of outgroup portrayals, scholars have been unable to systematically sample from a universe of media content, or sample from the same programs over a long period of time. In the United States, for example, television archives include only a few news programs that are no longer as widely viewed, and contain no entertainment programs at all. In other countries, systematically collected broadcast archives are even more difficult to come by. For this reason, research tends not to characterize the portrayal of outgroups in a given media environment of a given country or time period, but instead characterizes a particular television program or small set of programs at a particular point in time. Little, if any, systematic evidence of change goes beyond impressionistic accounts to document how televised images of social groups have changed over time.

Beyond content analyses, scholars do not even agree about the predicted *direction* of effects from the same media content. For example, will frequent media portrayals of well-to-do African Americans improve Whites' attitudes toward Blacks, or only serve to convince Whites that Blacks who have not 'made it' are not trying hard enough?

This chapter is organized into three parts, progressing from a discussion of research on media content, to a review of evidence of actual effects on stereotyping and prejudice. To date, a relatively small body of evidence bears on the critical issue of impact. Moreover, much of the research is correlational, showing associations between amount of television viewing and prejudice, but leaving causality disappointingly ambiguous. Finally, we review the most promising theoretical frameworks for future examinations of media effects on stereotyping and prejudice. Because of the limited progress that has been made in this area of research, we suggest a reordering of priorities, essentially

reversing the emphases to date. Instead of descriptive analyses of media content, we suggest that scholars first direct their efforts toward a theoretical understanding of what kinds of content will influence prejudice and stereotypes and through what process. Without knowing what kinds of content are most important in shaping viewers' ideas about outgroups, or the process by which media representations exercise influence, scholars studying media content alone are blindly guessing about what is worth analysing. The small number of studies documenting effects is not all that surprising in light of the lack of theoretical frameworks to guide this research. By offering three potentially fruitful theoretical frameworks, we hope to draw related research together in productive ways.

MEDIA PORTRAYALS OF OUTGROUPS

In lieu of an exhaustive list of findings about portrayals of various outgroups in different genres of media content, we focus our discussion on the multiple analytical frameworks used to examine media content, and what they suggest about the need for a greater theoretical understanding of how media exposure affects viewers' perceptions of outgroups. The varying strategies of comparative analysis employed in content-analytic studies suggest different implicit theories as to the kinds of content that are likely to influence audiences. Moreover, although the results of a given content-analytic study tend to be specific to the media of a given country, a particular television program, and a historical point in time, content-analytic strategies are not specific to any national boundaries. We illustrate these analyses with examples drawn primarily, though not exclusively, from studies of American media, where content analysis has been a particularly popular approach. However, the same problematic theoretical issues pertain equally well to other media environments.

Analyses of media content have generally come in one of three forms (see Dixon &

Linz, 2000a, 2000b). One variety, *intragroup comparisons*, considers how common a certain role, behavior, or characteristic is among members of a social group *relative to that same social group in some other role*. On local and national network news, for example, Blacks are more commonly portrayed as perpetrators than victims of crime (Dixon & Linz, 2000b; Dixon, Azocar, & Casas, 2003; Romer, Jamieson, & de Coteau, 1998). Along similar lines, a study of reality-based police programs showed that Blacks and Hispanics were more often depicted as perpetrators than police officers (Oliver, 1994). Yet, in prime-time as a whole, Blacks are more likely to be seen as police officers than as perpetrators, and are rarely shown as victims (Tamborini, Mastro, Chory-Assad, et al., 2000).

As these illustrative studies suggest, intragroup comparisons do not suggest consistently more negative portrayals across genres or roles. The usual implication drawn from such studies is that the more Blacks are depicted in high- versus low-status roles, the more positive white viewers' attitudes should become, and vice versa. But it is unclear how one would expect this information to influence attitudes toward outgroups. The world of prime-time television has an unusually high percentage of lawyers, doctors, and law enforcement personnel, regardless of race. So what is influential could instead be the sheer number of Blacks shown in high-status roles. As Whites become accustomed to seeing Blacks as doctors, lawyers, judges, and police, harmful negative stereotypes may change. Moreover, depictions of Blacks as loving parents on sitcoms might likewise alter White viewers' attitudes.

The second content-analytic approach asks whether certain roles, behaviors, and the like are more commonly portrayed among members of one social group relative to members of another group. These *intergroup comparisons* are most often used to contrast media portrayals of one racial outgroup relative to a majority of ingroup, with the assumption that more positive portrayals of outgroups relative to ingroups will improve attitudes toward outgroups.

Focusing, as in the example earlier, on Whites' attitudes toward Blacks, findings from intergroup comparisons have been inconsistent with respect to whether Blacks or Whites are more commonly shown as the perpetrators of crimes. In studies of local TV news, some have found that most perpetrators were Black (Dixon & Linz, 2000b; Gross, 2006), while others have found that most perpetrators were White (Gilliam & Iyengar, 2000; Klite, Bardwell, & Salzman, 1997). Because these studies differed in many ways – including the time frames, cities, and the number of TV stations analysed within each city – it is impossible to pinpoint the source of variations in the results. On network news, prime-time, and in reality-based shows (e.g., *America's Most Wanted*), Whites were more likely to be shown as perpetrators than Blacks (Dixon, Azocar, & Casas, 2003; Entman, 1994; Oliver, 1994; Tamborini, Mastro, Chory-Assad, et al., 2000).

Still other intergroup comparisons focus on more subtle differences in portrayals of one group relative to another. For example, Black suspects on local TV news were more likely than Whites to be shown poorly dressed (i.e., in jeans and a t-shirt or wearing jail clothing), in mug shots, and without a specified name (Entman, 1992; Entman & Rojecki, 2000). According to the authors of these studies, the implicit message is twofold: that people of color are more likely to be guilty and dangerous than White criminal suspects; and that the 'individual identity [of a Black suspect] does not matter … the accused is part of a single undifferentiated group of violent offenders: just another Black criminal' (Entman & Rojecki, 2000: 82).

Because prejudice is centrally concerned with intergroup relations, still other intergroup comparisons have considered how members of different social groups interact (or fail to) in the mass mediated world, comparing characteristics of interracial relationships to same-race relationships. Interestingly, most interracial interactions in prime-time television in the United States are hierarchical, occurring in the workplace between a higher-ranked employee and a subordinate, whereas most White–White interactions take place between peers (Entman & Rojecki, 2000). Perhaps surprisingly, Black characters are more likely to be in the superior than the subordinate position relative to Whites – what Entman and Rojecki (2000) call a 'utopian reversal' relative to the likely positions of Blacks and Whites in the real world.

Although it is clear that effects on viewers from *intergroup* and *intragroup* comparisons would involve different processes and could lead to substantively different conclusions, it is rare for scholars to consider the two side-by-side. One notable exception comes from Gamson's (1998) analysis of portrayals of gays and lesbians on daytime television talk shows. On the one hand, he found that gays on these programs (e.g., *Jerry Springer* and *Ricki Lake*) were often portrayed stereotypically (e.g., flamboyant, hypersexual, and incapable of maintaining healthy romantic relationships). On the other hand, heterosexual guests were portrayed in similarly unflattering ways. More important than the stereotyping of gays (i.e., the intragroup comparison) was the appearance of similarity between gays and straights (i.e., the intergroup comparison): 'Not only are we everywhere, apparently, we are also just as loud, goofy, dysfunctional, funny, nasty, emotional, and combative as everyone else' (Gamson, 1998: 64).

The third type of content-analytic approach rests on the assumption that media's effects on prejudice and stereotyping will be observable only when mediated representations of outgroups fail to mirror the real world. To identify these inconsistencies, *television-reality comparisons* compare portrayals of social groups in mass media to the real-world frequency of the same characteristic. For instance, compared to government arrest statistics, local TV news over-represents Whites as perpetrators of crime in both portrayals of violent and non-violent crime; Blacks are slightly over-represented as perpetrators of violent crime (Gilliam, Iyengar, Simon, et al., 1996). On network news, both Blacks and Whites are represented as perpetrators of violent and non-violent crime in the same proportions as they are in national government arrest

statistics (Dixon, Azocar, & Casas, 2003). Reality-based police shows also portray both groups accurately as perpetrators of violent crime, although they under-represent Whites and over-represent Blacks in non-violent crime stories (Oliver, 1994).

Television-reality comparisons tend to use national or local statistics to make their central points about over- or under-representation. And yet, upon reflection it seems obvious that few, if any, people are in touch with 'reality' as it exists statistically at a national, or even a local level. Instead, perceived realities tend to be rooted in people's immediate environments and networks; television is probably most influential when it deviates from those realities rather than from official statistics on abstract entities such as cities, counties, or nations. Still, one might expect heavy television viewers' images of their nation to have less variance than those of non-television viewers because heavy viewers' perceptions would drift toward the televised version of reality, whereas non-viewers should instead reflect variations in personal networks and local realities (see Mutz, 1992).

Through content analyses, scholars have provided numerous points of entry for researchers interested in studying potential effects of media exposure on prejudice and stereotyping. But the perspective used in analysing media representations can lead to divergent findings and contradictory predictions.

One particularly illuminating example is the contentious debate over *The Cosby Show*, a hugely popular prime-time hit featuring an upper middle-class black family, in which the mother is a lawyer and the father is a doctor. For Jhally and Lewis (1992), the show fails to represent the true situation of most African-Americans, who are disproportionately likely to be less well-off than Whites. The probable result, they argue, is the impression among Whites that Blacks are no longer economically disadvantaged; rather, the message is that Blacks who try hard can succeed (as the Cosby family does), while those who do not must be lazy. Bogle (2001) argues, alternatively, that the Cosby family is a refreshing example of a counter-stereotypic representation of Blacks in mass media. Examples of middle-class Black families were almost non-existent until the airing of *The Cosby Show*, thus perhaps this content countered Americans' tendency to inaccurately stereotype poor people as overwhelmingly Black (e.g., Gilens, 1996).

The theories used to predict effects from television content are no less ambiguous in that they do not suggest *which aspects* of media content are most important to the outcome. For example, two different analyses of *Will & Grace*, a prime-time show featuring two gay male characters, produced opposing predictions. Schiappa, Gregg, and Hewes (2006) emphasized that the gay characters were likeable, with the resulting hypothesis that exposure to the show would lead viewers to form more positive judgments about gay men. Others predicted more negative attitudes about gay men because of the stereotypically effeminate portrayals of these same characters, and their apparent inability to have healthy, long-lasting romantic relationships (Battles & Hilton-Morrow, 2002; Gross, 2001).

Unfortunately, the absence of empirical data on the validity of these predictions limits the usefulness of this approach. Indeed, the content-analytic approach more generally is plagued by a wealth of interesting descriptive findings that in the end cannot tell us much about the effects of media on prejudice or stereotyping. The ultimate lesson of our review is that content-analytic studies are, despite their illuminating qualities, inherently speculative.

EFFECTS OF OUTGROUP PORTRAYALS

Studies of media impact on prejudicial attitudes date back at least to the 1940s, when results most often suggested limited or no impact due to selective perception; that is, viewers rejected the intended premise of the message because it did not mesh with their pre-existing prejudices. For example, some people who read comic strips designed to ridicule a character named 'Mr. Biggott'

dismissed the cartoon character as so unusual and extreme that they simply ridiculed him without examining the implications of the cartoon for their own prejudices (Cooper & Jahoda, 1947; Kendall & Wolf, 1949). Decades later in the 1970s, a study of the hit prime-time show *All in the Family* produced similarly disappointing findings. Producers of the program claimed that it ridiculed Archie Bunker, the white family's openly-racist father. Yet, a survey of viewers revealed that many people saw 'nothing wrong' with Archie's racial slurs; by the end of a typical episode, these viewers believed that Archie, rather than his anti-racist son-in-law, had 'won' (Vidmar & Rokeach, 1974; see also Brigham & Giesbrecht, 1976).

Concerns about selectivity in exposure and perception of media messages remain today. And like the studies described above, most of the research conducted since the 1970s has been observational rather than experimental. Surveys have demonstrated significant correlations between self-reported media exposure – including overall recalled television exposure, exposure to particular topics and genres, and exposure to specific programs – and prejudice toward a variety of social groups. So, for instance, three meta-analyses reported correlations between self-reported media exposure and stereotypical beliefs about women, though the type of self-report measures employed were not specified (Herrett-Skjellum & Allen, 1995; Mares & Woodard, 2005; Oppliger, 2007). In the case of race, surveys showed positive correlations between both overall recalled TV viewing and watching *All in the Family*, on the one hand, and more prejudice toward Blacks, on the other (Gross, 1984; Vidmar & Rokeach, 1974). On the subject of sexuality, one survey showed a correlation between overall recalled TV viewing and *more* prejudice toward gays (Gross, 1984), while another survey showed a correlation between watching *Will & Grace* and *less* prejudice toward gays (Schiappa, Gregg, & Hewes, 2006). As a final example, one survey demonstrated a correlation between self-reported exposure to TV about the homeless and lower levels of prejudice toward the homeless (Lee, Farrell, & Link, 2004).

Correlational evidence, however, provides a weak basis for causal inference for a multitude of reasons in this particular case. First, because many of the analyses failed to control for factors related to both media exposure and prejudice, the association between these two variables may have been spurious (e.g., Gross, 1984; Oppliger, 2007; Signorielli, 1989). Second, the association between exposure and prejudice could be accounted for by reverse causation; that is, people selectively exposing themselves to media content congruent with their prejudices (e.g., Ball-Rokeach, Grube, & Rokeach, 1981; see also, Morgan, 1982, 1987). Third, in observational studies media exposure to positive or negative portrayals of outgroups is inferred through self-reports. The well-known weaknesses of self-reported exposure measures in terms of both validity and reliability (see, e.g., Bartels, 1993; Price & Zaller, 1993), combined with the lack of evidence that these respondents were exposed to any prejudice-reducing or enhancing messages when watching, means that many of these studies lack a convincing connection between exposure to media portrayals of outgroups and attitudes toward those same outgroups.

For these reasons, we focus our review on studies that are experimental or quasi-experimental in design. Notably, the outcome measures of stereotyping and prejudice used in these studies vary widely – from beliefs about the outgroup as a whole, to judgments about outgroup members in unrelated situations, to behaviors. Nonetheless, collectively these studies make a convincing case that exposure to mass media has the capacity to alter levels of prejudice in both positive and negative directions.

For example, using a longitudinal quasi-experimental design to examine the impact of television viewing on adolescents' sex-role attitudes, greater television viewing produced more sexist attitudes six months to a year later (Morgan, 1982, 1987). An Australian field study evaluating the effects of a campaign designed to reduce the belief that indigenous Australians (Aborigines) were lazy produced similar effects, this time in the direction of reducing prejudice (Donovan & Leivers, 1993). Compared to respondents surveyed before the campaign, the post-campaign sample was more likely to believe that Aborigines remained in their jobs for more than one year.

The strongest evidence to date for a causal link between mass media exposure and prejudice comes from five studies employing fully-randomized experimental designs. Exposure to a sympathetic documentary about one of the first openly-gay elected officials in the United States (*The Times of Harvey Milk*) reduced negative attitudes toward gays (Riggle, Ellis, & Crawford, 1996). Further, a study carried out in Germany exposed adolescents to one talk show episode a day over five days – each including tolerant content about gays. A week after the final exposure, participants in the treatment condition reported stronger pro-gay attitudes (Rossler & Brosius, 2001). In two other experimental studies, watching multiple episodes of programs including gay male characters (*Six Feet Under* and *Queer Eye for the Straight Guy*) or a stand-up comedy act performed by Eddie Izzard (*Dress to Kill*) dressed in women's attire led to more tolerant attitudes toward gay men and transvestites, respectively (Schiappa, Gregg, & Hewes, 2005).

In a fifth study, participants viewed a televised comedy skit portraying Blacks stereotypically (poor, uneducated, and prone to acts of violence and crime) or to a neutral comedy skit featuring Blacks, but not in stereotypical ways (Ford, 1997). They subsequently read a vignette about a student accused of physically assaulting his roommate – with no conclusive evidence, but some circumstantial evidence of guilt. The accused person was named either Tyrone or Todd, to suggest a Black or White suspect. Whereas the perceived guilt of the White student suspect (Todd) did not vary by condition, participants who viewed the stereotypical portrayal of Blacks first were more likely to perceive the Black student (Tyrone) as guilty than were participants who viewed the neutral portrayal.

In addition to these five experiments, two additional studies provide evidence claiming that portrayals of outgroup members 'prime' prejudice and stereotyping. Although these findings are not framed as direct evidence that media increase or decrease prejudice, given that the results are consistent with either interpretation, we include them as support for this general argument. In the first experiment, participants saw newsletters including autobiographical essays by either a stereotypic Black college student, a counter-stereotypic Black student, or a control. Participants in the stereotypic condition were more likely to endorse the anti-Black stereotypes highlighted in the treatment (lazy, aggressive, unintelligent, and socially destructive) than were participants in the counter-stereotypic condition. But most importantly, participants in the stereotypic condition were more likely to generalize these conclusions to seemingly unrelated people, becoming increasingly likely to suggest that African-American Rodney King brought the highly publicized beating by Los Angeles police on himself (relative to the counter-stereotypic condition), while participants in the counter-stereotypic condition were more likely to say that King was innocent (relative to the control and stereotypic conditions) (Power, Murphy, & Coover, 1996).

In a similar experiment, participants who saw newsletters including autobiographical essays by a stereotypic female college student were more likely to endorse negative stereotypes of women (self-centered, weak, overemotional, and unintelligent) than were participants in a counter-stereotypic condition. Participants who read the stereotypic portrayal also generalized these stereotypes to other situations, becoming less likely to believe the sexual harassment allegations Anita Hill made against Clarence Thomas during his US Supreme Court nomination hearings (relative to the control and counter-stereotypic conditions) (Power, Murphy, & Coover, 1996).

Thus, despite preceding decades of disappointingly inconclusive or null findings, experimental studies have demonstrated that media exposure to even a single outgroup member can both produce and reduce prejudice toward a variety of social groups. Yet the issue of selective exposure is still yet to be fully addressed. Selective exposure is of particular concern in generalizing from experimental studies because experiments force people to watch television programs that they might not otherwise have chosen to view. Thus, these findings leave us confident that media can, in fact, alter levels of prejudice, but not that media, as it occurs and is widely viewed by the public, often does so in real world settings.

Concerns about the potential for selective exposure are heightened by the growth of cable television and the enormous increase in the range of program choices now available to the average viewer. On the one hand, greater choice should enable viewers to more easily avoid content that might contradict their views. But on the other hand, only a small proportion of programming wears its outgroup politics on its sleeve. When people watch a crime drama, for example, they seldom select it for the anticipated race of the victims versus perpetrators. And sitcoms are watched because they are funny or clever, not because of the stereotypes they convey.

Moreover, there is an element of voyeurism in television viewing that may attract viewers to precisely the kind of content they find titillating, though repugnant and disagreeable. *Jerry Springer* and related programs are interesting to watch precisely because they feature people who are unlike those most people know in their everyday lives (e.g., a father who marries his child's grandmother, Ku Klux Klan parents, and so forth). Thus the exercise of selectivity in viewing may be incomplete at best.

Overall, our own assessment of the likelihood of positive influence on outgroup attitudes from television is far more optimistic than those of earlier scholars who argued that television merely reflected and reinforced existing prejudices and stereotypes. First, mass media provide a potential source of 'contact' that ingroup members can have with outgroup members. The omnipresence of mass media in contemporary life means that the majority of people are exposed to outgroup members more through mass media than through face-to-face contact (e.g., Bowman & Foster, 2006; Charles, 2003; Dixon & Rosenbaum, 2004; Logan, 2001). Thus media constitute an especially important source of information about minority group members with whom majority group members otherwise have limited or no face-to-face contact.

Second, although some televised exposure to outgroup members undoubtedly reinforces negative outgroup stereotypes, it also exposes viewers to more positively-valenced stereotypes than they are likely to encounter in everyday life, if only because of their relative isolation from outgroup members. Moreover, blatantly stereotypical portrayals of outgroup members often produce a public outcry that focuses attention on the negative stereotype, thus negating its potential impact (see Mendelberg, 2001). Unfortunately, the relative extent of positive to negative portrayals of a given outgroup in a given culture's television programming or in a given individual's chosen content remains largely unknown and probably highly variable across individuals as well as cultures. However, to the extent that some positively-valenced portrayals reach viewers through media, when they generally do not reach people through other avenues, one might expect media's net contribution to be positive – that is, unless positive portrayals produce negative consequences, as has been argued by some. Ultimately, however, this is an empirical question, and one that is unanswerable without a theoretical framework from which to understand media's impact.

THEORETICAL FRAMEWORKS

Three theoretical perspectives seem potentially applicable to understanding the role of media in prejudice and stereotyping. However, as we argue later, evidence to date points to one of these theoretical frameworks as particularly well suited to the expansion of our knowledge of the influence of mass media on prejudicial attitudes. For this reason, we focus first and more briefly on the alternatives, and then turn to a more lengthy discussion of the most promising model. Although the empirical studies discussed earlier generally reference at least one of these theoretical perspectives, the evidence itself typically does not allow the reader to distinguish support for one theoretical model from another.

Parasocial interaction

First coined in 1956 (Horton & Wohl, 1956), the term *parasocial interaction* means that viewers feel and react toward people and characters on television just as they do in face-to-face interactions (Kanazawa, 2002). More recently, Schiappa and his colleagues (2005) proposed the 'parasocial contact hypothesis,' positing that if viewers get to know and like outgroup members on television, then their attitudes toward the outgroup as a whole will improve. As implied by its title, this perspective proposes that mediated contact fits alongside face-to-face intergroup contact (e.g., Pettigrew & Tropp, 2006) as a viable strategy for reducing prejudice. Yet both the conceptualization and measurement of what constitutes 'parasocial interaction' remain highly variable (e.g., Giles, 2002). One study, for instance, included measures of whether viewers felt they knew the characters, found them physically attractive, wanted to be their friend, thought they did their jobs well, or perceived themselves as similar to the characters (Schiappa, Gregg, & Hewes, 2005). Moreover, the impact of parasocial interaction on prejudice reduction has received mixed empirical support, with a preponderance of either unsupportive evidence or evidence that could be interpreted through multiple theoretical frameworks (Schiappa, Gregg, & Hewes, 2005, 2006).

Nonetheless, studies of narrative persuasion and transportation – that is, becoming 'absorbed in the narrative world, leaving the real world, at least momentarily, behind' (Green & Brock, 2002: 317) – further underline the possibility that viewers may become so immersed in a storyline, and so empathic with respect to characters and their interactions, that they experience the same kind of human contact that fuels the positive effects of intergroup contact (Green & Brock, 2000). Although the extent to which people report experiencing transportation has been associated with more positive evaluations of sympathetic characters (Green & Brock, 2000), to date evidence linking transportation with beliefs about social groups is lacking (Green, 2004).

However, to the extent that viewers do form affective bonds with television characters, this perspective opens up the possibility of not only direct parasocial contact effects (i.e., the viewer has a parasocial relationship with an outgroup member), but also *indirect* parasocial contact effects (i.e., the viewer has a parasocial relationship with an ingroup member who has a positive relationship with an outgroup member). Support for this idea comes from research showing prejudice-reducing effects from either having an ingroup member say that he or she had a friendly interaction with an outgroup member, or by witnessing a friendly intergroup interaction (Wright, Aron, McLaughlin, et al., 1997). If merely witnessing a friendly interaction can produce these effects in interpersonal contexts, then witnessing intergroup contact on television may produce similar influence.

Intergroup contact via mass media may be particularly advantageous because it avoids the anxiety that often characterizes face-to-face intergroup interactions (Dovidio, Gaertner, & Kawakami, 2003; Greenland & Brown, 1999; Pettigrew & Tropp, 2006; Stephan & Stephan, 1985). Anxiety and feelings of threat are known barriers to achieving the benefits of intergroup contact (Paolini, Hewstone, Cairns, et al., 2004). To the extent that television, for example, allows people to be exposed to those who are different from themselves, to empathize with their plights, to listen to their stories, without the anxiety associated with in-person contact, then prejudice toward the group may be likely to decline (Dovidio, Gaertner, & Kawakami, 2003; Pettigrew & Tropp, 2006).

Although parasocial relationships provide a plausible route through which media exposure could reduce prejudice, the requirements of this theory create a narrow scope of potential impact. In part, it is limited because beneficial effects would require strong and positive emotional bonds with outgroup characters, the kind resulting from repeated exposures. Many people probably have feelings about television characters, but only with a relatively few television characters do viewers form deep bonds (i.e., parasocial *relationships*). Further, precisely because of pre-existing prejudice, ingroup viewers would be unlikely to perceive an outgroup television character as highly familiar, likeable, and similar to him or herself.

Modeling intergroup interactions

A second theoretical framework, known as modeling theory or social cognitive theory (Bandura, 2002), suggests that viewers emulate the relations between ingroups and outgroups that they observe enacted on television. If, for example, television portrays ingroup and outgroup members resolving their differences through violence, then viewers will follow that example. And if viewers witness peaceful, friendly intergroup interactions, then they will emulate those behaviors instead. In both cases, television provides low-cost opportunities for people to observe ingroup and outgroup members interacting.

Viewing intergroup exchanges on television may also affect viewers' levels of anxiety about future face-to-face interactions. By teaching ingroup members new social skills, or 'rules of behavior,' exposure may increase self-efficacy when engaging in real-world intergroup contact (Bandura, 1986: 47; Green, 2006). According to this model, ingroup members should engage in less prejudicial behaviors only if the intergroup interactions they view on television engender more positive than negative outcomes (Bandura, 1986, 2001).

Viewers will emulate some television characters more than others, depending upon characteristics of the ingroup member (Bandura, 1977). The more a viewer identifies with a televised person, the more he or she is expected to model that character's behaviors (Eyal & Rubin, 2003). Identification occurs because the viewer sees himself or herself as similar to the ingroup member and vicariously participates in their experiences (Hoffner, 1996). Viewers are expected to develop the same emotional reactions to outgroup members as the ingroup member they identify with on television (Bandura, 1999).

The vicarious learning suggested by this model occurs because the viewer is so immersed in the character's perspective that he or she emulates the character's emotional reactions. In this respect, social cognitive theory supports what studies of 'transportation' via mass media also have suggested: that influence occurs when viewers are sufficiently absorbed by a narrative that they take on the perspective of a character and truly feel themselves to be personally involved. However, in the case of social modeling, the person must engage in intergroup interactions as part of the narrative.

Interestingly, although vicarious learning has long been championed as the mechanism linking television violence to aggressive behavior in children, it has not been well studied as a means of either reducing or producing prejudice (see Graves, 1999; and Ortiz & Harwood, 2007, for exceptions). Many children's television programs are premised on the belief that viewers will model the friendly intergroup interactions they witness, but there is a lack of causal evidence to confirm this.

As with the parasocial interaction explanation, social modeling puts limits on potential media influence on outgroup attitudes through its various requirements. Most importantly, influence can occur only when there are intergroup interactions to model. Moreover, the viewer must clearly identify with the ingroup character engaged in the intergroup interaction. Overall, there is probably a limited amount of naturally-occurring television content that meets all of the requirements for the social modeling process. And regardless, it is difficult to differentiate this process

and its predictions from alternative theories.

The media world as real world

As initially suggested, we favor a third, more general information-processing model that both broadens the set of media portrayals with the potential for media influence, and reduces the intensity of affective response required from viewers. In short, this perspective suggests that viewers process televised portrayals of people largely as if they were real-world, first-hand observations. Intergroup attitudes are influenced by salient outgroup exemplars, many of which people observe through mass media.

It is a well-worn truism that people do not experience a large proportion of the world first-hand. Instead, 'the images in our heads' are often formed from the images and information found in the media, particularly on television (Lippmann, 1922). To the extent that people either perceive media as conveying accurate depictions of the world (as in news consumption) or subconsciously process media content as if it were real (as in fictional dramas), media portrayals of both ingroup and outgroup members should be consequential.

We find this theory both plausible and appealing for a number of reasons. First, it predicts that both fictional and non-fictional portrayals of outgroup members have potential for influence. For televised social information to be discounted so that it does not influence social judgments, viewers would need to remember the source of information and then purposefully disregard it – conditions which appear unlikely to co-occur without explicit intervention (Shapiro & Lang, 1991; Shrum, Wyer, & O'Guinn, 1998).

Second, research on human-media interaction bolsters the idea that there are minimal differences between the firsthand experience of others and viewing them on television. Although adults clearly understand that all events seen on television did not actually happen, this is a learned reaction (Worth & Gross, 1974). And regardless of their awareness, people's physiological and psychological reactions to television exposure are fundamentally the same as their reactions to real people and events. So, for instance, exposure to a human being who appears larger and closer due to a larger television screen produces more arousal, better memory for the content, and more liking of the content than exposure to the same content on a smaller screen. When a person comes physically closer in real life, and fills more of the viewer's field of vision, the same reactions occur. 'All of these results are pretty much the same in the real world,' according to Reeves and Nass (1996: 198). Along similar lines, attention (as measured by brain activity) synchronizes with motion on television – that is, within about a second of televised movement, attention increases (Reeves & Nass, 1996). Again, these reactions are the same as those found in face-to-face contact. Physiological reactions notwithstanding, most existing research on media effects implicitly or explicitly assumes that people process media as informative about the real world. To the extent that this claim is supported, media content has obvious relevance for prejudice and perceptions of social norms.

A third argument in favor of this far more encompassing, information-processing approach is that there are fewer necessary conditions required than in other theoretical perspectives. In order for portrayals of outgroups to be influential, exemplars need only be observed by viewers. It is not necessary that viewers identify with the outgroup member, nor that successful intergroup interactions be featured, nor that the viewer feel he/she has a personal relationship with someone on television. Some evidence suggests that merely imagining contact with an outgroup member may reduce intergroup bias (Turner, Crisp & Lambert, 2007). To the extent that intergroup influence is brought about more easily than was once thought, then loosening requirements for media influence also seems reasonable.

How well does evidence support assertions that media supply influential exemplars in social judgment? Correlational studies consistently support the idea that media portrayals affect perceptions of the frequency of events such as crime and, by extension, the prevalence of crime associated with specific outgroup members. However, there is less evidence of influence on personal attitudes and beliefs about social groups (e.g., personal fear of crime) (Gerbner, Gross, Morgan, et al., 1980; Gross, 1984; Hawkins & Pingree, 1981; Signorielli, 1989). Effects have been somewhat stronger when using genre-specific measures of exposure (e.g., crime dramas), rather than global measures of television exposure (e.g., hours of viewing per day), leading many to suggest that perhaps these effects would be clearer if exposure were controlled in a laboratory setting rather than self-reported (Hawkins & Pingree, 1981; Potter, 1993; Shrum, 1996; Shrum, & O'Guinn, 1993; but see Shrum, Wyer, & O'Guinn, 1998). Indeed, some recent quasi-experimental and experimental findings demonstrate that exemplars of outgroup members viewed on television influenced intergroup attitudes, even in the short-term after relatively little exposure (e.g., Morgan, 1982, 1987; Rossler & Brosius, 2001).

If we view media as simply one of many potential sources of exemplars that can shape outgroup attitudes, then it is possible to evaluate the effects of atypical exemplars like the Cosby family, and sort out the contradictory predictions that have been made about its effects. For example, if social judgment of outgroups depends upon exemplars that are readily available in people's minds, and media are major suppliers of salient exemplars, then television's ready supply of middle and upper class Black exemplars is noteworthy. Indeed, Bodenhausen, Schwarz, Bless, et al., (1995) find that atypical Black exemplars who are successful and well-liked positively affect judgments and beliefs about Blacks, and increase perceptions of majority discrimination against the minority. If it is pointed out that these exemplars are atypical, however, the positive effects disappear.

Integration

The three theoretical models that we have discussed suggest quite different kinds of influence processes, and they point to different kinds of content as important to understand the influence of media on prejudice. If one were interested in the potential for media to serve as a source of modeling information, one would want to study content such as the prevalence of interracial marriage on television. If instead one viewed mediated experience as a source of interpersonal contact with outgroups, one would care about the incidence of ingroup members viewing likable outgroup members on television. And if one were studying this hypothesis from the perspective that media simply provide exemplars that prime people's perceptions of the real world, then one would want to know which kinds of exemplars were most relevant to human judgment – portrayals of outgroups, ingroups relative to outgroups, outgroups relative to real world experience, and so forth.

FUTURE DIRECTIONS

Our review has focused on the potential for television to serve as a form of intergroup contact, primarily because television's audio-visual stimuli do such an excellent job of simulating the experience of being near another human being (see Reeves & Nass, 1996). This is not to say that novels, radio, or other media should not have an impact, but television's pervasiveness, sensory simulation of reality, and engrossing storylines make it a natural first place to look.

Notably, our discussion has not differentiated between studies of media influence on the extent of stereotyping, attitudes toward outgroups, and actual behaviors. Nor has it included an exhaustive review of all potentially relevant studies, including those with media content designed explicitly for purposes of public information campaigns to reduce prejudice (see Paluck & Green, 2009, for a review), or prosocial children's television programming designed to reduce stereotyping and prejudice (for meta-analyses, see Mares & Woodward, 2005; Oppliger, 2007). Indeed, our review has largely neglected the body of research known as 'education-entertainment' initiatives, which purposely

embed educational messages within entertainment programs (see Singhal & Rogers, 2002). Studies of this kind are not based on any one theoretical model, but rather tend to use a shotgun approach, using all available suggestions about what would increase chances of success. For example, some education-entertainment projects focus on how development of parasocial relationships with positive role models increases the persuasive impact of the educational message (Papa, Singhal, Law, et al., 2000). Others rely on social-cognitive theory to maximize potential impact. For the most part, entertainment-education has been applied to public health concerns, with only limited evidence regarding social group attitudes, such as gender equality (Slater, 2002). However, in one recent exception, Paluck (2007, 2009) reports the results of a year-long education-entertainment effort in Rwanda, designed purposely to reduce outgroup prejudice. Those who listened to a radio program emphasizing intergroup reconciliation were more likely than those in the control condition to express positive attitudes about intergroup marriage, though social distance measures did not suggest reduced prejudice. Because attempts at education-entertainment tend to be large-scale and expensive, they simultaneously incorporate many characteristics thought to be potentially beneficial, thus making it difficult to ascertain what aspects of the media content are effective, if any (see Paluck, 2009, for a review).

Despite Allport's (1954) admonition about the importance of mass media as a source of intergroup contact, we know surprisingly little about its role in prejudice. Mass media are rich sources of information about outgroup members, and the forms that intergroup interactions may take. Currently, our understanding of these processes is largely limited to speculation, albeit based on thoughtful considerations of media content. The small number of studies that have undertaken empirical verification of the effects of mass media on prejudice demonstrate the potential for mediated contact to influence real-world attitudes and beliefs about social groups, as well as the potential limitations posed by selectivity, both in perception and exposure. In order to improve upon these initial suggestions of impact, however, theoretical frameworks must be advanced and tested.

How might such a research agenda proceed? Although the tremendous emphasis to date on studies of media content may seem self-explanatory to a casual observer, to empirical social scientists it should be recognized as putting the cart before the horse: content does not equal effects. Before more scholarly time and energy are devoted to documenting the most prevalent types of content, it is incumbent upon scholars to figure out which kinds of media content comparisons ultimately matter to intergroup attitudes.

There are several ways that researchers might go about this, but it seems clear upon reflection that more experimental studies of effects are needed, particularly ones that can differentiate between influence that flows from intragroup and intergroup media portrayals, as well as whether it matters if television differs from the real world, at least as it is perceived by viewers. Because experiments must often rely on one-shot exposure to a media stimulus, or at least on a small number of exposures, within-subject designs may be key to obtaining the statistical power that is necessary to isolate the impact of a tiny number of exposures relative to the enormous amount of ongoing television content consumed by the average person in developed countries.

Moreover, because of the sensitive nature of intergroup attitudes, such studies may also require augmenting self-reports with unobtrusive measures, such as the Implicit Association Test (IAT) (see Greenwald & Banaji, 1995). Although the IAT is controversial as a measure of prejudice, it is uncontroversial as a measure of the extent to which people have formed positive or negative associations with members of certain groups (see Arkes & Tetlock, 2004). If media portrayals in an experimental setting consistently link Blacks with crime, for example, these effects may be more easily observed using techniques such as the IAT. If instead (or in addition), what matters is whether a television program associates Blacks with crime more often than it associates Whites with crime, then the presence of ingroup associations will matter as much as outgroup associations.

Finally, and perhaps most importantly, scholarly attention needs to be directed toward theoretical development. Because studies documenting effects remain few and far between at this point, scholars have been satisfied with merely demonstrating effects, and offering convenient theoretical frameworks to explain them. Such emphases are natural given the incipient nature of this research. However, what these studies lack is the ability to differentiate between the various theoretical models in order to determine the underlying process of influence. Without understanding process, scholars' ability to determine the kinds of media content that are beneficial or harmful to intergroup attitudes will remain speculative at best.

SUMMARY AND CONCLUSION

A long history of interest in mass media's impact on intergroup attitudes has, nonetheless, produced limited evidence of effects. On the one hand, studies of media content have flourished, providing many descriptive accounts of how people of various races, ethnicities, sexualities, and genders are portrayed in various television genres. On the other hand, scholars still know relatively little about the kind of content that is most influential in either encouraging or discouraging prejudice. For this reason, we recommend that the emphasis in future work shift in the direction of first seeking to understand the underlying process of influence, so that subsequent analyses of media content can be guided by knowledge of the specific kinds of media portrayals that matter.

To date, only a few experimental studies have established a causal connection between media portrayals of outgroup members and the attitudes that ingroup viewers hold toward them. More such studies are needed, to be sure. Once this causal process is well understood, scholars will need to combine evidence of impact with evidence from the audiences viewing such content in naturalistic settings to eliminate the possibility that selective exposure limits media exposure to content that is congruent with people's prejudices. Only by combining experimental work on the process of influence with observational studies of viewing habits will we ultimately be able to address Allport's hypothesis about the importance of media.

REFERENCES

Allport, G. W. (1954). *The Nature of Prejudice*. Reading, MA: Addison-Wesley.

Arkes, H., & Tetlock, P.E. (2004). Attributions of implicit prejudice, or would Jesse Jackson fail the implicit association test? *Psychological Inquiry*, 15, 257–278.

Ball-Rokeach, S., Grube, J., & Rokeach, M. (1981). "Roots: The Next Generation"—Who watched and with what effect? *Public Opinion Quarterly*, 45, 58–68.

Bandura, A. (2002). Social cognitive theory of mass communication. In J. Bryant, & D. Zillman (Eds), *Media Effects: Advances in Theory and Research*. (2nd edition, pp. 121–153). Hillsdale, NJ: Lawrence Erlbaum Associates.

Bandura, A. (1977). *Social Learning Theory*. Englewood Cliffs, NJ: Prentice Hall.

Bandura, A. (1986). *Social Foundations of Thought and Action: A Social Cognitive Theory*. Englewood Cliffs, NJ: Prentice Hall.

Bandura, A. (1999). Social cognitive theory of personality. In D. Cervone, & Y. Shoda (Eds), *The Coherence of Personality* (pp. 185–241). New York: Guilford Press.

Bandura, A. (2001). Social cognitive theory of mass communication. *Media Psychology*, 3, 265–299.

Bartels, L. M. (1993). Messages received: The political impact of media exposure. *American Political Science Review*, 87, 267–285.

Battles, K., & Hilton-Morrow, W. (2002). Gay characters in conventional spaces: *Will & Grace* and the situation comedy genre. *Critical Studies in Media Communication*, 19, 87–105.

Bodenhausen, G. V., Schwarz, N., Bless, H., & Waenke, M. (1995). Effects of atypical exemplars on racial beliefs: Enlightened racism or generalized appraisals. *Journal of Experimental Social Psychology*, 31, 48–63.

Bogle, D. (2001). *Primetime Blues: African Americans on Network Television*. New York: Farrar, Straus, & Giroux.

Bowman, K., & Foster, A. (2006). *Attitudes about Homosexuality and Gay Marriage*. Washington, DC: American Enterprise Institute.

Brigham, J., & Giesbrecht, L. (1976). "All in the Family": Racial attitudes. *Journal of Communication*, 26, 69–74.

Charles, C. Z. (2003). The dynamics of racial residential segregation. *Annual Review of Sociology*, 29, 167–207.

Cooper, E., & Jahoda, M. (1947). The evasion of propaganda: How prejudiced people respond to anti-prejudice propaganda. *Journal of Psychology*, 23, 15–25.

Dixon, J. C., & Rosenbaum, M. S. (2004). Nice to know you? Testing contact, cultural, and group threat theories of anti-black and anti-hispanic stereotypes. *Social Science Quarterly*, 85, 257–279.

Dixon, T. L., & Linz, D. (2000a). Overrepresentation and underrepresentation of African Americans and Latinos as lawbreakers on television news. *Journal of Communication*, 50, 131–54.

Dixon, T. L., & Linz, D. (2000b). Race and the misrepresentation of victimization on local television news. *Communication Research*, 27, 547–573.

Dixon, T. L., Azocar, C. L., & Casas, M. (2003). The portrayal of race and crime on television network news. *Journal of Broadcasting and Electronic Media*, 47, 498–523.

Donovan, R. J., & Leivers, S. (1993). Using paid advertising to modify racial stereotype beliefs. *Public Opinion Quarterly*, 57, 205–218.

Dovidio, J. F., Gaertner, S. L., & Kawakami, K. (2003). Intergroup contact: The past, present, and the future. *Group Processes and Intergroup Relations*, 6, 5–21.

Entman, R. M. (1992). Blacks in the news: Television, modern racism and cultural change. *Journalism Quarterly*, 69, 341–361.

Entman, R. M. (1994). Representation and reality in the portrayal of blacks on network television news. *Journalism Quarterly*, 71, 509–520.

Entman, R. M., & Rojecki, A. (2000). *The Black Image in the White Mind: Media and Race in America*. Chicago: University of Chicago Press.

Eyal, K., & Rubin, A. M. (2003). Viewer aggression and homophily identification and parasocial relationships with television characters. *Journal of Broadcasting and Electronic Media*, 47, 77–98.

Ford, T. E. (1997). Effects of stereotypical television portrayals of African-Americans on person perception. *Social Psychology Quarterly*, 60, 266–275.

Gamson, J. (1998). *Freaks Talk Back: Tabloid Talk Shows and Sexual Nonconformity*. Chicago: University of Chicago Press.

Gerbner, G., Gross, L., Morgan, M., & Signorielli, N. (1980). Aging with television: Images on television drama and conceptions of social reality. *Journal of Communication*, 30, 37–47.

Gilens, M. (1996). Race and poverty in America. *Public Opinion Quarterly*, 60, 515–541.

Giles, D. C. (2002). Parasocial interaction: A review of the literature and a model for future research. *Media Psychology*, 4, 279–305.

Gilliam, F. D. Jr., Iyengar, S., Simon, A., & Wright, O. (1996). Crime in black and white: The violent, scary world of local news. *Harvard International Journal of Press/Politics*, 1, 6–23.

Gilliam, F. D. Jr., & Iyengar, S. (2000). Prime suspects: The influence of local television news on the viewing public. *American Journal of Political Science*, 44, 560–573.

Graves, S. B. (1999). Television and prejudice reduction: When does television as a vicarious experience make a difference? *Journal of Social Issues*, 55, 707.

Green, M. C. (2004). Transportation into narrative worlds: The role of prior knowledge and perceived realism. *Discourse Processes*, 38, 247–266.

Green, M. C. (2006). Narratives and cancer communication. *Journal of Communication*, 56S, 163–183.

Green, M. C., & Brock, T. C. (2000). The role of transportation in the persuasiveness of public narratives. *Journal of Personality and Social Psychology*, 79, 701–721.

Green, M. C., & Brock, T. C. (2002). In the mind's eye: Transportation-imagery model of narrative persuasion. In M. C. Green, J. J. Strange, & T. C. Brock (Eds), *Narrative Impact: Social and Cognitive Foundations* (pp. 315–342). Mahwah, NJ: Lawrence Erlbaum Associates, Inc.

Greenland, K., & Brown, R. (1999). Categorization and intergroup anxiety in contact between British and Japanese nationals. *European Journal of Social Psychology*, 29, 503–21.

Greenwald, A. G., & Banaji, M. R. (1995). Implicit social cognition: Attitudes, self–esteem, and stereotypes. *Psychological Review*, 102, 4–27.

Gross, K. (2006). Covering crime in Washington D.C.: Examining the nature of local television news coverage of crime and its effect on emotional response. Research paper R–28. Cambridge, MA: The Joan Shorenstein Center on the Press, Politics and Public Policy, Harvard University.

Gross, L. (1984). The cultivation of intolerance: Television, blacks and gays. In G. Melischek, K. E. Rosengren, & J. Stappers (Eds), *Cultural Indicators: An International Symposium* (pp. 345–363). Vienna: Osterreichische Akademie der Wissenschaften.

Gross, L. (2001). *Up from Invisibility: Lesbians, Gay Men, and the Media in America.* New York: Columbia University Press.

Hawkins, R. P., & Pingree, S. (1981). Uniform messages and habitual viewing: Unnecessary assumptions in social reality effects. *Human Communication Research*, 7, 291–301.

Herrett-Skjellum, J., & Allen, M. (1995). Television programming and sex stereotyping: A meta-analysis. In B. R. Burleson (Ed.), *Communication Yearbook 19* (pp. 157–185). Troy: NY: Sage.

Hoffner, C. (1996). Children's wishful identification and parasocial interaction with favorite television characters. *Journal Broadcasting and Electronic Media*, 40, 389–402.

Horton, D., & Wohl, R.R. (1956). Mass communication and para-social interaction: Observations on intimacy at a distance. *Psychiatry*, 19, 215–229.

Jhally, S., & Lewis, J. (1992). *Enlightened Racism: The Cosby Show, Audiences, and the Myth of the American Dream.* Boulder, CO: Westview Press.

Kanazawa, S. (2002). Bowling with our imaginary friends. *Evolution and Human Behavior*, 23, 167–171.

Kendall, P. L., & Wolf, K. M. (1949). The analysis of deviant case studies in communications research. In P. Lazarsfeld, & F. Stanton (Eds), *Communications Research 1948–1949* (pp. 152–179). New York: Harper.

Klite, P., Bardwell, R. A., & Salzman, J. (1997). Local TV news: Getting away with murder. *Harvard International Journal of Press/Politics*, 2, 102–112.

Lee, B. A., Farrell, C. R., & Link, B. G. (2004). Revisiting the contact hypothesis: The case of public exposure to homelessness. *American Sociological Review*, 69, 40–63.

Lippmann, W. (1922). *Public Opinion.* New York: Harcourt, Brace, & Co.

Logan, J. (2001). Ethnic diversity grows, neighborhood integration lags behind. Report by the Lewis Mumford Center. University at Albany, State University of New York.

Mares, M., & Woodard, E. (2005). Positive effects of television on children's social interactions: A meta-analysis. *Media Psychology*, 7, 301–322.

Mendelberg, T. (2001). *The Race Card: Campaign Strategy, Implicit Messages, and the Norm of Equality.* Princeton, NJ: Princeton University Press.

Morgan, M. (1982). Television and adolescents' sex role stereotypes: A longitudinal study. *Journal of Personality and Social Psychology*, 43, 947–955.

Morgan, M. (1987). Television, sex-role attitudes, and sex-role behavior. *Journal of Early Adolescence*, 7, 269–282.

Mutz, D. C. (1992). Mass media and the depoliticization of personal experience. *American Journal of Political Science*, 36, 483–508.

Oliver, M. B. (1994). Portrayals of crime, race, and aggression in "reality-based" police shows: A content analysis. *Journal of Broadcasting and Electronic Media*, 38, 179–93.

Oppliger, P. A. (2007). Effects of gender stereotyping on socialization. In R. W. Preiss, B. M. Gayle, N. Burrell, & M. Allen (Eds), *Mass Media Effects Research: Advances Through Meta-Analysis* (pp. 199–214). Mahwah, NJ: Lawrence Erlbaum Associates.

Ortiz, M., & Harwood, J. (2007). A social cognitive theory approach to the effects of mediated intergroup contact on intergroup attitudes. *Journal of Broadcasting and Electronic Media*, 51, 615–631.

Paluck, E. L. (2007). Reducing intergroup prejudice and conflict with the media: A field experiment in Rwanda. Ph.D. Dissertation. Yale University.

Paluck, E. L. (2009). Reducing intergroup prejudice and conflict using the media: A field experiment in Rwanda. *Journal of Personality and Social Psychology*, 96, 574–587.

Paluck, E. L., & Green, D. P. (2009). Prejudice reduction: What works? A review and assessment of research and practice. *Annual Review of Psychology*, 60, 339–67.

Paolini, S., Hewstone, M., Cairns, E., & Voci, A. (2004). Effects of direct and indirect cross-group friendships on judgments of Catholics and Protestants in Northern Ireland: The mediating role of an anxiety-reducing mechanism. *Personality and Social Psychology Bulletin*, 30, 770–86.

Papa, m. J., Singhal, A., Law, S., Pant, S., Sood, S., & Rogers, E., et al. (2000). Entertainment-education and social change: An analysis of parasocial interaction, social learning, collective efficacy, and paradoxical communication. *Journal of Communication*, 50, 31–55.

Pettigrew, T. F., & Tropp, L. R. (2006). A meta-analytic test of intergroup contact theory. *Journal of Personality and Social Psychology*, 90, 751–783.

Potter, W. J. (1993). Cultivation theory and research: A conceptual critique. *Human Communication Research*, 19, 564–601.

Power, J. G., Murphy, S. T., & Coover, G. (1996). Priming prejudice: How stereotypes and counter-stereotypes influence attribution of responsibility and credibility among ingroups and outgroups. *Human Communication Research*, 23, 36–58.

Price, V., & Zaller, J. (1993). Who gets the news? Alternative measures of news reception and their implications for public opinion research. *Public Opinion Quarterly*, 57, 133–164.

Reeves, B., & Nass, C. (1996). *The Media Equation*. New York: Cambridge University Press.

Riggle, E. D. B., Ellis, A. L., & Crawford, A. M. (1996). The impact of "media content" on attitudes toward gay men. *Journal of Homosexuality*, 31, 55–69.

Romer, D., Jamieson, K. H., & de Coteau, N. J. (1998). The treatment of persons of color in local television: Ethnic blame discourse or realistic group conflict? *Communication Research*, 25, 286–305.

Rossler, P., & Brosius, H. (2001). Do talk shows cultivate adolescents' views of the world? A prolonged-exposure experiment. *Journal of Communication*, 51, 143–163.

Schiappa, E., Gregg, P. B., & Hewes, D. E. (2005). The parasocial contact hypothesis. *Communication Monographs*, 72, 92–115.

Schiappa, E., Gregg, P. B., & Hewes, D. E. (2006). Can one TV show make a difference? Will & Grace and the parasocial contact hypothesis. *Journal of Homosexuality*, 51, 15–37.

Shapiro, M. A., & Lang, A. (1991). Making television reality: Unconscious processes in the construction of social reality. *Communication Research*, 18, 685–705.

Shrum, L. J. (1996). Psychological processes underlying cultivation effects: Further tests of construct accessibility. *Human Communication Research*, 22, 482–509.

Shrum, L. J., & O'Guinn, T. C. (1993). Processes and effects in the construction of social reality. *Communication Research*, 20, 436–471.

Shrum, L. J., Wyer, Jr., R. S., & O'Guinn, T. C. (1998). The effects of television consumption on social perceptions: The use of priming procedures to investigate psychological processes. *Journal of Consumer Research*, 24, 447–458.

Signorielli, N. (1989). Television and conceptions about sex roles: Maintaining conventionality and the status quo. *Sex Roles*, 21, 341–360.

Singhal, A., & Rogers, E. M. (2002). A theoretical agenda for entertainment-education. *Communication Theory*, 12, 117–135.

Slater, M. D. (2002). Entertainment education and the persuasive impact of narratives. In M. C. Green, J. J. Strange, & T. C. Brock (Eds), *Narrative Impact: Social and Cognitive Foundations* (pp. 157–181). Mahwah, NJ: Lawrence Erlbaum Associates, Inc.

Stephan, W. G., & Stephan, C.W. (1985). Intergroup anxiety. *Journal of Social Issues*, 41, 157–75.

Tamborini, R., Mastro, D., Chory-Assad, R., & Huang, R. (2000). The color of crime and the court: A content analysis of minority representation on television. *Journalism and Mass Communication Quarterly*, 77, 639–654.

Turner, R. N., Crisp, R. J., & Lambert, E. (2007). Imagining intergroup contact can improve intergroup attitudes. *Group Processes and Intergroup Relations*, 10, 427–41.

Vidmar, N., & Rokeach, M. (1974). Archie Bunker's bigotry: A study in selective perception and exposure. *Journal of Communication*, 24, 36–47.

Voci, A., & Hewstone, M. (2003). Intergroup contact and prejudice toward immigrants in Italy: The meditational role of anxiety and the moderational role of group salience. *Group Processes and Intergroup Relations*, 6, 37–54.

Worth, S., & Gross, L. (1974). Symbolic strategies. *Journal of Communication*, 24, 27–39.

Wright, S. C., Aron, A., McLaughlin, T., & Ropp, S. A. (1997). The extended contact effect: Knowledge of cross-group friendships and prejudice. *Journal of Personality and Social Psychology*, 73, 73–90.

PART III

Expression of Prejudice, Stereotyping and Discrimination

16

Attitudes and Intergroup Relations

Gregory R. Maio, Geoffrey Haddock,
Antony S. R. Manstead, and Russell Spears

ABSTRACT

Attitudes have played a central role in the study of prejudice, stereotyping, and discrimination since the beginning of research on these topics. Although subsequent research on intergroup relations has developed independently of attitudes theory, there are still many links between the two topics and much that can be learned from integrating this work. This chapter takes a comprehensive look at the current overlap between the fields of attitudes and intergroup relations. Discussion is structured around three key properties of attitudes: content, structure, and function (Maio & Haddock, 2004, 2010). These properties make salient important theoretical and empirical puzzles, novel topics of importance, and promising avenues for future conceptual integration and research.

ATTITUDES AND INTERGROUP RELATIONS

Attitudes are unfavorable or favorable evaluations of objects in our social world. They capture our likes and dislikes. Over 70 years ago, Gordon Allport (1935) asserted that the attitude construct is the most indispensable concept in social psychology. Part of the reason for this assertion was that people hold attitudes toward an incredible variety of *attitude objects*, which include anything that can be the target of a favorable or unfavorable evaluation. Examples include specific behaviors (e.g., going to see a particular film), people (e.g., my boss), and social groups (e.g., Asians). Another reason

for Allport's claim is that attitudes affect the way we perceive the world and how we behave. Both reasons illustrate why attitudes are important for understanding intergroup relations: Attitudes can be held toward particular social groups, and these attitudes should influence how we perceive members of these groups and behave toward them. In theory, then, many of the basic principles that govern the understanding of attitudes should also help to understand intergroup relations. Indeed, it is no coincidence that Gordon Allport had a significant influence in research on intergroup relations, including his influential volume, *The Nature of Prejudice* (Allport, 1954).

Since Allport's contributions, introductory texts on social psychology tend to define prejudice as a negative attitude toward other groups (e.g., Aronson, Wilson, & Akert, 2005; Taylor, Peplau, & Sears, 2006). Viewed in this way, there are at least three ways in which research on attitudes and intergroup relations overlap. These three commonalities pertain to three core properties of attitudes: their *content* (i.e., affective, behavioral, and cognitive information), *structure* (i.e., uni- or bidimensional), and *function* (i.e., motivations). Maio and Haddock (2004, 2007, 2010) labeled these three properties the 'three witches' of attitudes, because, like witches in folklore (and *Macbeth*), it takes all three to make a potent 'brew'. In other words, consideration of each aspect in isolation presents only one portion of the attitude construct, and a more complete picture emerges by considering all three aspects simultaneously. The same argument can be made for understanding intergroup relations. For example, considering nuances of content, structure, and function allows us to conceptualize forms of prejudice that transcend the simple negative affect definition, such as benevolent sexism and paternalistic racism.

It turns out, however, that this complete picture of these nuances has not yet emerged because research on attitudes and intergroup relations has proceeded more independently in recent years. Despite the strong connections between the areas, there is room for a better understanding of the role of the three witches in understanding prejudice. After reviewing basic aspects of attitude measurement and attitudes' prediction of behavior, this chapter will consider the three witches and their relevance to intergroup relations.

REVIEW AND HISTORY

Until the last decade, most measures of attitude and of prejudice relied almost exclusively on self-report scales. For example, researchers often asked participants to rate their attitude toward an object on several seven-point scales anchored at opposite ends by opposing evaluative terms, such as favorable–unfavorable, good–bad, and like–dislike. Although indices derived from these scales can exhibit statistical reliability and meaningful relations with relevant behavior (Glasman & Albarracín, 2006), interpretation of these measures becomes difficult when (a) social norms proscribe specific responses, or (b) people are unaware of their true attitude.

These issues helped spur the development of a new generation of measures that use techniques derived from the study of implicit memory (Fazio & Olson, 2003). Two of the first measures to use this approach, the evaluative priming technique (Fazio, Jackson, Dunton, et al., 1995) and the Implicit Association Test (IAT) (Greenwald, McGhee, & Schwartz, 1998), initially demonstrated their utility by assessing prejudice. For example, Fazio, Jackson, Dunton, et al. (1995) found that, among White participants, the presentation of a Black individual's face caused White participants to identify the unfavorable meaning of subsequent negative adjectives more quickly and identify the favorable meaning of subsequent positive adjectives more slowly (relative to what was found in response to the presentation of White faces). These differences in response times were unrelated to self-report measure of prejudice, and, more importantly, they predicted actual behavior toward a Black experimenter, *over and above* self-reported prejudice. Since this research, implicit measures have shown utility in many studies of prejudice (Maio, Haddock, Watt, et al., 2008) and in many studies examining other topics (Petty, Fazio, & Briñol, 2009).

Nonetheless, it is important to recognize that implicit *and* explicit measures predict attitude-relevant behaviors (see Friese, Hofmann, & Schmitt, 2008). Implicit measures may simply predict *different* types of behavior than explicit measures (see Fazio & Olson, 2003; see also Vargas, Von Hippel, & Petty, 2004). Implicit measures are better predictors of behavior that is relatively spontaneous and automatic, whereas explicit measures tend to be better predictors of behavior that is relatively deliberative and controlled (Czopp, Monteith, Zimmerman, et al., 2004; McConnell & Leibold, 2001). Similar results have been obtained in studies of prejudice: self-reported measures of prejudice are superior predictors of conscious, deliberative behaviors toward minorities (e.g., interview assessments), and implicit measures are superior predictors of nonconscious, spontaneous responding (e.g., Dovidio, Kawakami, & Gaertner, 2002). These results provide convergent support for the notion that each set of measures has implications for different classes of behavior.

There is also a broader problem in identifying 'if,' 'when,' and 'how' attitudes *influence* behavior. For instance, Fishbein and Ajzen's (1975) landmark treatise showed why many studies had failed to reveal correlations between self-report measures of attitude and later measures of 'behavior'. Often, the assessed behaviors were either much more global or much more specific than the behaviors specified in the attitude measure. Echoing the point made by Fishbein and Ajzen, measures of prejudice may focus on behavioral responses that have little relevance to the discriminatory behaviors of interest. Most research on prejudice focuses on links between attitudes toward an abstract category (e.g., a specific ethnicity) and behavior toward a specific individual in a specific setting – the very context in which the ability to detect effects is likely to be lowest.

This issue of fit is further emphasized by Attitude Representation Theory (ART) (Lord & Lepper, 1999). This theory holds that when we indicate attitudes toward an abstract category we have a particular exemplar in mind. If this is not the exemplar that we assess in a later measure of behavior, then we will probably observe low attitude-behavior correspondence. This problem is particularly important when examining behavior toward moderately typical and atypical members of a group (Lord, Lepper, & Mackie, 1984). In such instances, discrimination may be poorly understood if researchers focus exclusively on measures of attitude toward the abstract category.

It is also vital to appreciate the role of other variables in the prediction of behavior. A variety of additional variables are considered in Eagly and Chaiken's (1993, 1998) composite model of attitude-behavior relations. Building on the prior theories of Reasoned Action and

Planned Behavior (Ajzen, 1991; Fishbein & Ajzen, 1975), the composite model proposes a number of factors that affect attitudes toward behaviors: habits (relevant past behavior), attitudes toward targets (the target of the behavior), utilitarian outcomes (rewards and punishments associated with performing the behavior), normative outcomes (approval and disapproval from others that might occur from performing the behavior), and self-identity outcomes (how performing the behavior might influence the self-concept). Eagly and Chaiken suggested that these factors can affect either intentions or behavior directly.

Research assessing norms and attitudes in an intergroup context has found that they can vary in their impact on intentions and behavior. For example, there is evidence that the perceived norms of a reference group influence behavioral intentions among people who identify strongly with the group more than among people who identify less strongly with the group, whereas attitudes predict behavioral intentions more strongly among low identifiers than among high identifiers (Terry & Hogg, 1996). For high identifiers, then, the norms seem more highly distinct from the attitudes. The extent to which norms operate separately from attitudes can also be influenced by the nature of the predicted behavior (Finlay, Trafimow, & Villareal, 2002; Trafimow & Fishbein, 1994), individual differences in the relative importance of norms and attitudes (Trafimow & Finlay, 1996), and the temporary salience of the self-concept from a collective, group perspective (Ybarra & Trafimow, 1998). Overall, it is becoming increasingly clear that (group) norms play a large role in intergroup relations, distinct from the role of intergroup attitudes (Crandall, Eshleman, & O'Brien, 2002; Turner, 1991) .

The inclusion of habits is an important aspect of Eagly and Chaiken's (1993) model, because numerous studies have found that past behaviors predict future behavior *over and above* the roles of attitudes and norms (Ouellette & Wood, 1998). Not all behavior is deliberative and planned and one potential reason is the role of routine or habit.

Quite often we act spontaneously, without consciously thinking of what we intend to do because this is what we have done before. When behavior is spontaneous, attitudes, utilitarian outcomes, normative outcomes, and identity outcomes may not operate through a thoughtful and deliberate contemplation of intentions.

Effects of attitude on spontaneous behavior are explained by Fazio's (1990) MODE model of attitude-behavior relations. MODE refers to Motivation and Opportunity as DEterminants of behavior. Based on abundant evidence examining attitudes in general (Fazio, 1990), the model suggests that individuals base their behavior on a deliberative consideration of available information if they have *both* sufficient motivation and opportunity. However, when either the motivation or the opportunity to make a thoughtful decision is low, accessible attitudes will predict behavior. Similar conclusions may be drawn about the influence of prejudice on discrimination. In this context, accessible attitudes have been assessed using various implicit measures of prejudice, as described earlier in the chapter. Evidence indicates that these implicit measures are stronger predictors of subsequent perceptions and judgments for individuals who have a low motivation to control prejudice than among individuals who are high in this motivation (Olson & Fazio, 2004; Payne, 2001). Of interest, people who are high in motivation to control prejudice can also inhibit negative attitudes toward an outgroup on an implicit measure, although primarily in contexts that cue prejudice (Maddux, Barden, Brewer, et al., 2005) and among people who are driven by internal egalitarian values rather than by an external compunction to seem nonprejudiced (Hausmann & Ryan, 2004).

ANALYSIS AND FRAMEWORK FOR INTEGRATION

The content of prejudice

Intergroup relations are fraught with tensions that arise from three types of information that are considered to be building-blocks of attitudes: feelings, beliefs, and behavioral experiences (Eagly & Chaiken, 1998; Zanna & Rempel, 1988). In this section, we use research to illustrate how each type of information is relevant to understanding prejudice.

Affective content

The affective component of prejudice refers to feelings or emotions associated with other groups. Research on attitudes has indicated that feelings can become associated with attitude objects in several ways. One method involves evaluative priming, which occurs when the affective information precedes the presentation of the attitude object. For example, Krosnick, Betz, Jussim, et al., (1992) found that an unfamiliar person was liked more when photos of the individual were repeatedly presented after subliminal flashes of positive images than after repeated flashes of negative images. There is evidence that a similar mechanism might shape attitudes toward other ethnic, religious, and social groups (Olson & Fazio, 2006).

Another way in which affect guides attitudes comes from research by Zajonc and colleagues (see Zajonc, 2001). This research has examined how mere exposure to unfamiliar stimuli (e.g., various Chinese characters) affects later attitudes toward the stimuli. A large number of studies have revealed that stimuli that have been presented many times are liked more than stimuli that have not been seen before (Bornstein, 1989; Zajonc, 2001). This effect is also obtained when *people* are the stimuli that are seen many or fewer times (Moreland & Beach, 1992). Given that we see people in our own groups more than people from other groups, the mere exposure phenomenon may contribute to any automatic tendencies to experience more positive affect to members of our own group than to members of an outgroup. Mere exposure may also be a useful tool for reducing negative affect against outgroup members (Bornstein, 1993). Consistent with some evidence concerning the effects of intergroup interactions on attitudes

(Amir, 1969), the magnitude of this effect depends on the presence of a positive context during exposure (Bornstein, 1993).

Effects of mood on attitude also show the importance of affective content. In general, people in a positive mood tend to like things more than people in a neutral or negative mood (Bower, 1991; Mayer, Gaschke, Braverman, et al., 1992). Research on intergroup relations has found that people also tend to like members of other groups more when they are in a positive mood than in a neutral mood (Dovidio, Gaertner, Isen, et al., 1995; Forgas & Moylan, 1991), and such effects appear to be more likely when individuals tend to experience their moods intensely (Haddock, Zanna, & Esses, 1994). Positive mood even affects judgments of people who are randomly assigned to arbitrary group categories (Abele, Gendolla, & Petzold, 1998). Nonetheless, it is also evident that such effects depend on the salience of the group label (Abele, Gendolla, & Petzold, et al., 1998), the amount of motivation to correct for bias in judgments (Bodenhausen, Sheppard, & Kramer, 1994), and the valence of the stereotypes that are salient at the time of judgment (Lambert, Khan, Lickel, et al., 1997). These are just some of many moderators of the impact of mood, and theoretical attempts have been made to integrate knowledge of these factors in a way that may help to understand the role of mood for theories of attitude and of intergroup relations (Forgas, 1995).

The importance of affective bases of prejudice has been emphasized by many researchers (Bodenhausen, 1993; Mackie, Devos, & Smith, 2000; Smith, 1993). However, there may be important individual differences in the role of affect within prejudice. For example, people who tend to habitually experience more intense emotions are also more likely to express intergroup attitudes that are influenced by mood (Haddock, Zanna, & Esses, et al., 1994). Extending the conceptualization of prejudice beyond evaluation to emotional reactions to out groups (Smith, 1993) also allows us not only to distinguish different kinds of negative prejudice (e.g., based on anger, fear, disdain

and disgust), but also opens the door to forms of prejudice based on positive reactions (e.g., pity and paternalism). In short, the meaning of affective content in intergroup attitudes is important as well as valence.

Cognitive content

The cognitive component of prejudice refers to beliefs about the attributes of another group. This component can include *stereotypes*, which are beliefs about the personality traits of group members (e.g., lazy, intelligent), and *symbolic beliefs*, which are beliefs about the values (e.g., power, tradition) held by group members (Esses, Haddock, & Zanna, 1993). Many studies have revealed that possessing negative stereotypes and symbolic beliefs about a group of people is associated with having a prejudicial attitude toward the group, although studies have also indicated that affective responses make an important additional contribution to the prediction of prejudice (Haddock, Zanna, & Esses, 1993; Kawakami, Dion, & Dovidio, 1998). Research is providing greater insight into the neurological, cognitive, motivational, and social mechanisms underlying the role of stereotypes, as shown elsewhere in this volume (e.g., Chapters 4, 5, 7, 8, 18). For example, there is interesting evidence that training in the mental negation of stereotypes can reduce subsequent (implicitly measured) prejudice (Kawakami, Dovidio, Moll, et al., 2000).

Here again, the history of research on the cognitive component of attitudes furnishes some important questions for the understanding of prejudice. For instance, probabilogical models (McCauley, Stitt, & Segal, 1980; McGuire, 1960; Wyer, 1970) are founded on the premise that relations between beliefs follow from the laws of probability theory. These models specify how particular beliefs should be related and how beliefs should change in response to the addition of new information. If these models are considered in the intergroup context, it becomes clear that stereotypes and symbolic beliefs can vary in their logical relations. For example, how plausible is it to assume that someone who is lazy is also intelligent? The assessment of such fit has been labeled *descriptive* processing by researchers studying how it affects memory for a person's traits (Srull & Wyer, 1989).

This general importance of such logical/descriptive assessments has been demonstrated in a study of how values are used in forming attitudes toward individuals (Gebauer, Maio, & Pakizeh, 2008; Maio, 2010). This research asked whether people feel more attitudinal conflict or ambivalence when they consider an individual who seems to value ideals that seem to serve conflicting motives. For example, how plausible is it that a person who values power also cherishes the importance of helping others? It turns out that people report much more ambivalence toward people who possess motivationally incongruent values than motivationally congruent values (Gebauer, Maio, & Pakizeh, 2008). Importantly, this effect happens even when the congruent and incongruent values are seen as being equally desirable – so the ambivalence does not stem from conflict between a disliked value and a liked value.

Behavioral content

The behavioral component of prejudice refers to past behavioral actions toward a group. For instance, people's jobs may require that they are pleasant and helpful to customers of a different ethnicity or, conversely, their daily activities might routinely take them away from a part of town that is populated by a new immigrant group. The approach-oriented, pleasant behavior and the avoidance-oriented, distancing behavior should lead to positive and negative attitudes, respectively, even if people initially possess few feelings or beliefs about the group.

There is an important distinction between our conceptualization of behavioral content in intergroup attitudes and abundant research on intergroup contact. Research on intergroup contact has focused on the amount of behavioral experience with outgroups and the positivity of those experiences (Kenworthy, Turner, Hewstone, et al., 2005; see Chapter 33 by Tausch & Hewstone, this volume).

Often, these behavioral experiences are positive or negative because of feelings and beliefs that flow from the interactions. In contrast, we are focusing on effects of the individuals' own behaviors on their own attitudes. That is, what are the effects of initiating a positive behavior or an avoidance behavior toward a group?

The idea that people's attitudes might be shaped by their prior behavior was developed by dissonance theory and self-perception theory. According to Festinger's (1964) dissonance theory, people alter their attitudes in order to make them more consistent with behaviors that they have performed. This attitude change occurs because it helps to reduce any aversive tension that results from awareness of having an attitude that is inconsistent with past behavior, and there are many experiments broadly consistent with this reasoning (Harmon-Jones & Mills, 1999). Bem's (1972) self-perception theory also predicts that behaviors can shape attitudes, but does not claim that this effect is mediated by aversive arousal arising from perceived inconsistency. According to this theory, individuals do not always have direct access to their opinions (see also Nisbett & Wilson, 1977). Bem argued that this is especially true when the person's attitude is weak or ambiguous. In these situations, participants' attitudes can be shaped by the behaviors that are subtly elicited by other factors (e.g., job requirements, daily routines), but seem to have been chosen by the self. The results of several experiments are consistent with this reasoning (Chaiken & Baldwin, 1981; Holland, Verplanken, & van Knippenberg, 2002), and it would be interesting to see applications of this research to understanding prejudice.

In fact, diverse behaviors that are associated with positive or negative consequences can influence the favorability of attitudes and perhaps prejudice in particular. For example, Briñol and Petty (2003) told participants that a headphone manufacturer was interested in determining how headphones performed when listeners were engaged in various movements, such as dancing and jogging. Briñol and Petty asked participants move their heads in either an up-and-down motion (nodding their head) or a side-to-side motion (shaking their head) as they listened to an editorial that was played over the headphones. When the arguments contained in the editorial were strong, it was expected that moving one's head in an up-and-down motion would lead participants to be more positive about the position being advocated in the message, because nodding is a motion that is commonly associated with agreement. The results revealed that participants were more likely to agree with the content of a highly persuasive appeal when they moved their heads up-and-down as compared to side-to-side. Similar effects have been obtained using other behaviors, such as arm flexion and extension (Cacioppo, Priester, & Berntson, 1993) and smiling (Strack, Martin, & Stepper, 1988). These findings show that a direct physical behavior, and the meaning of the content of that behavior, influenced the favorability of participants' attitudes. This fits with much recent research on the power of 'embodiment' (Niedenthal, Barsalou, Winkielman, et al., 2005), reminding us that attitudes are not just mental representations but also have a (more classical) bodily dimension. Such results should extend to the intergroup domain and may have practical applications. For example, interviewers might be trained in postures and movements that help to minimize nonconsciously activated negative bias in the presence of outgroup members.

The structure of prejudice

Interest in the structure of attitudes has mirrored developments in understanding the structure of prejudice. Several theories of prejudice emphasize the importance of understanding conflict between a positive dimension of intergroup attitude and a negative dimension. Over 30 years ago, Kaplan (1972) and Scott (1969) pointed out that people can feel both negatively *and* positively toward an object, rather than simply negatively or positively: Their attitudes can range

from 'not negative' to 'very negative' and from 'not positive' to 'very positive'. In addition, some types of cognitive content may convey the negative evaluation (e.g., hostile symbolic beliefs), while other types of content convey the positive evaluation (e.g., benevolent stereotypes, Glick & Fiske, 2001). The same might be said for different types of affective content (e.g., anger, paternalism) and behavioral content (e.g., aggression, helping).

One interesting development in the study of prejudice was the discovery of response polarization toward people who are targets of ambivalence (Katz & Hass, 1988). That is, people may respond more extremely to members of groups about which they are ambivalent than to members of groups about which they are nonambivalent. For example, Bell and Esses (2002) found that, among participants who were ambivalent toward Native Canadians (i.e., felt positively *and* negatively toward them), and in a positive mood evaluated this group more positively than ambivalent participants in a negative mood. This effect of mood was not evident among the nonambivalent participants (i.e., who felt positively *or* negatively). This pattern is consistent with a view that, if people are ambivalent toward an outgroup, then the strong negative and positive dimension in the attitude toward the outgroup should be activated by negative or positive contexts that activate these dimensions.

Although the evidence for this polarization is provocative, several interesting issues need to be addressed before accepting that polarization is a consequence of ambivalence. First, to our knowledge, no research has shown that a manipulation of ambivalence toward a group yields polarized responses to it – the extant research has either measured ambivalence or has simply assumed differences in ambivalence between target groups. These paradigms do not unequivocally identify a causal role for ambivalence. Second, the evidence for polarization must be reconciled with evidence that people may react more negatively to ingroup members who behave negatively than toward outgroup members who behave in the same way, at least when perceivers identify highly with their ingroup (Marques, Abrams, & Serodio, 2001). This so-called 'black sheep effect' poses a challenge for the polarization view because researchers tend to assume that people are more ambivalent toward outgroups than toward ingroups. If this assumption were true, the response polarization evidence would indicate that people should be more negative toward outgroup individuals who perform negative behaviors than ingroup individuals who perform the same behaviors. Yet, the black sheep effect reveals more negative evaluations of ingroup members.

This complex pattern of results suggests that other inter-personal and inter-group processes must be invoked to fully understand the polarization effect. Consistent with this view, attitude research has found that feelings of ambivalence can stem more from differences between one person's views and the views of close others than from intra-psychic discrepancies in positivity and negativity (Priester & Petty, 2001). In an intergroup context, it may be the case that ambivalence is felt strongly when there are disagreements with ingroup members, with whom one would expect to agree (Turner, 1991), particularly when there is high identification with the ingroup.

Another interesting aspect of ambivalence is its ability to predict scrutiny of incoming persuasive messages. Many researchers have predicted and found that message recipients who are ambivalent toward the topic of a message scrutinize it more carefully than do message recipients who are not ambivalent toward the topic (Briñol, Petty, & Tormala, 2003; Maio, Bell, & Esses, 1996). This scrutiny is presumably aimed at gathering information that can help to reduce an aversive state of tension that is created by ambivalence, by making the attitude positive or negative, rather than ambivalent. This role of aversive tension has been supported by evidence in the intergroup context (Britt, Boniecki, Vescio, et al., 1996; Hass, Katz, Rizzo, et al., 1992).

An important aspect of ambivalent individuals' message scrutiny is that it makes them more sensitive to the quality of message arguments. As a result, messages that promote positive attitudes toward other groups can backfire among individuals who are ambivalent toward the groups when the messages lack cogent arguments (Bell, Esses, & Maio, 1996; Maio, Haddock, Watt, et al., 2008). This evidence raises issues for the effectiveness of social marketing attempts to reduce racism, because most anti-racism advertisements use a simple, easy-to-process print format that does not contain cogent arguments.

The functions of prejudice

Classic research on attitudes and intergroup relations has stressed the role of similar psychological motivations. Several functions have received empirical attention, but two have elicited more direct scrutiny than the others and are examined below.

The role of values and ideologies

The capacity of attitudes to express values is reflected in measures of attitude that specifically include value-relevant beliefs. This capacity is also highlighted by theories describing social values (Rokeach, 1973), the value-expressive function of attitudes (Maio & Olson, 2000b), and the role of values in ideological and inter-attitudinal consistency (Thomsen, Lavine, & Kounios, 1996). Some theories go a step further by describing how attitudes express ideologies, which are clusters of thematically related values and attitudes (Ashton, Danso, Maio, et al., 2005). For example, liberal ideologies encompass attitudes and values that promote universal rights and benevolence, whereas conservative ideologies encompass attitudes and values that promote freedom and self-enhancement (Ashton, Danso, Maio, et al., 2005).

These general views have been mirrored by a strong interest in the role of values and ideology in prejudice. Several theories of Whites' prejudice against Blacks identify roles for the egalitarian values and/or achievement-oriented values, consensually agreeing that increased endorsement of equality in American society has been a factor leading to decreases in blatant prejudice and *increases* in ambivalence in attitudes toward Blacks (Gaertner & Dovidio, 2005; Katz & Hass, 1988). At the same time, researchers have identified many ideologies related to prejudice, including multiculturalism versus color-blindness (Wolsko, Park, Judd, et al., 2000), individualism versus communalism (Katz & Hass, 1988), right-wing authoritarianism (Altemeyer, 1988), and social dominance orientation (Pratto, Sidanius, Stallworth, et al., 1994).

This list reveals one of several glaring 'holes' in our current understanding of the role of values and ideologies in prejudice, which echo the gaps present in research on attitudes. Specifically, it is not clear whether some of these ideologies exert a more dominant influence than others, or whether they interact with each other. For example, there is evidence that conservative ideology tends to be applied more in Whites' policy toward Blacks than toward other groups (Reyna, Henry, Korfmacher, et al., 2006). Work by Duckitt (2006) contrasts prejudice arising from right-wing authoritarianism (Altemeyer, 1988) with that arising from social dominance (Pratto, Sidanius, Stallworth, et al., 1994), and these can be viewed as contrasting ideologies that have independent routes to prejudice and discrimination. Another possibility is that some ideologies pertain to a variety of outgroups. For example, social dominance ideology presumably helps to understand prejudice toward diverse groups, although some have argued that social dominance orientation is an abstraction that derives from more specific attitudes towards groups such as African Americans (Schmitt & Branscombe, 2003; cf. Sidanius & Pratto, 2003). Research is needed to identify more conclusively how diverse ideologies relate to each other and to different groups.

The role of values is also relevant to an important distinction between a value-expressive function of attitudes and a more instrumental function (Maio & Olson, 2000a). This distinction has been usefully carried over to the realm of intergroup relations, in particular helping to shed light on the different functions of discrimination and ingroup bias (Scheepers, Spears, Doosje, et al., 2003, 2006). Sometimes group members will differentiate the ingroup and derogate the outgroup as a means to affirm their group's value (Esses, Haddock, & Zanna, 1993; Haddock, Zanna, & Esses, 1993); other times they will do it to claim resources or some advantage (Bobo, 2004). Once again, we find parallels in the one realm that can be usefully applied to gain insights in the other realm.

The role of object-appraisal

Several contemporary theories of attitude function argue that the most basic function of attitudes is to provide a ready-made, easy-to-retrieve guide for appraising objects. Fazio (2000) has shown that this function is more strongly served by attitudes that are easy to retrieve from memory than by attitudes that are less easy to retrieve from memory. In addition, attitudes that are easy to retrieve from memory have led to quicker attitude-consistent decisions and lower physiological reactivity during the decisions (Blascovich, Ernst, Tomaka, et al., 1993). Thus attitude accessibility is an indicator of the extent to which attitudes fulfill the object appraisal function.

In a similar way, research on prejudice is consistent with the notion that positive or negative intergroup attitudes might serve this object appraisal function. In particular, several experiments have obtained evidence that stereotypes simplify processing of information about outgroup members in a spontaneous manner that helps to conserve mental resources for other tasks (Macrae, Milne, & Bodenhausen, 1994; Wigboldus, Sherman, Franzese, et al., 2004). This research has focused on the energy-saving utility of the cognitive component of prejudice (i.e., stereotypes), whereas the research on attitudes suggests that this utility should extend to judgments formed on affective information and on past behaviors. That is, acquired emotions and habits regarding an outgroup may also function as energy-saving guides, even when relevant stereotypes are controlled. Moreover, stereotypes foster object appraisal because they reflect social reality (raising issues of validity, accuracy and adaptiveness) as well as by simplifying and saving resources (Spears & Haslam, 1997). It is possible that some emotions and habits reflect social reality in the same manner.

Such themes are made more explicit in the attitude literature. The importance of object appraisal is also identified in contemporary models of attitude change (Albarracin, 2002; Chen & Chaiken, 1999; Kruglanski, Fishbach, Erb, et al., 2004; Petty & Wegener, 1999). These models indicate that people are often motivated to form an *accurate* attitude. When this motive is made dominant in a situation, people respond by more closely scrutinizing incoming information relevant to the attitude. As a consequence, the resulting post-message attitudes may be particularly strong and resistant to change (Petty & Wegener, 1999). In a similar way, when stereotypes influence attitudes toward a particular group member, the attitude is especially resistant to change if the influence occurred during effortful, thoughtful processing of information about the individual (Wegener, Clark, & Petty, 2006). It is therefore conceivable that augmentations of the object appraisal motive in outgroup attitudes make these attitudes stronger and more resistant to change.

FUTURE DIRECTIONS

We began this chapter by noting that the overlap between research on attitudes and research on intergroup relations can be explored more fully. Our review and analysis thus far has pointed to several potential avenues of exploration. Two additional directions merit mention before concluding the chapter.

First, there is a lack of theory and evidence describing when values will be justifications for prejudice or non-prejudice, rather than true antecedents of either attitude. This issue is reflected in research on attitudes in general, where there is little evidence documenting

precisely how attitudes express broad values and ideologies. Values may often function as post hoc justifications for attitudes, rather than as their psychological basis (Kristiansen & Zanna, 1988). As yet, there is no research identifying when values lead, rather than follow.

Second, there is a lack of knowledge about the role of ego-defense as a psychological function of prejudice. Adorno and colleagues' seminal theory of prejudice stressed the notion that prejudice protects the self-concept from threat, particularly among individuals raised in authoritarian surroundings (Adorno, Frenkel-Brunswik, Levinson, et al., 1950). However, their tests of the role of ego-defense yielded mixed results. Moreover, research has not yet developed a suitable method for testing whether an attitude serves a defensive function. This function is difficult to assess because people are presumably unaware of the extent to which an attitude exists merely to protect their ego (Katz, 1960). However, current self-report measures rely on such awareness (Herek, 1986). Research on threats to social identity, and defense at the group level, faces similar questions. In our view, the development of a paradigm for assessing this function would be a great leap forward for both attitude research and for research on intergroup relations.

In closing, we would like to note that it is easy to imagine a sequel to this chapter that focuses on intervention. The issues we have described have important ramifications for understanding attempts to reduce prejudice and discrimination. There is a large array of relevant theory and evidence about how people respond to messages that attempt to induce attitude change, and this information is highly relevant to understanding the effects of many interventions to reduce prejudice and discrimination. Our observation about negative effects of weak advertisements is just one example of this relevance. With greater integration of research on attitude change and prejudice reduction, the potential for enhancing basic understanding and for designing more effective interventions should become increasingly apparent.

ACKNOWLEDGEMENTS

We thank Jack Dovidio, Miles Hewstone, Vicki Esses, and Peter Glick for their feedback on this chapter. Correspondence should be directed to Greg Maio, School of Psychology, Cardiff University, 70 Park Place, Cardiff CF10 3AT. E-mail: maio@cardiff.ac.uk

REFERENCES

Abele, A., Gendolla, G., & Petzold, P. (1998). Positive mood and in-group/out-group differentiation in a minimal group setting. *Personality and Social Psychology Bulletin*, 24, 1343–1357.

Adorno, T. W., Frenkel-Brunswik, E., Levinson, D. J., & Sanford, R. N. (1950). *The Authoritarian Personality*. Oxford, England: Harpers.

Ajzen, I. (1991). The theory of planned behavior. *Organizational Behavior and Human Decision Processes*, 50, 179–211.

Albarracin, D. (2002). Cognition in persuasion: An analysis of information processing in response to persuasive communications. In M. Zanna (Ed.), *Advances in Experimental Social Psychology* (Vol. 34, pp. 61–130). San Diego, CA: Academic Press.

Allport, G. W. (1935). Attitudes. In C. Murchison (Ed.), *Handbook of Social Psychology* (pp. 798–844). Worcester, MA: Clark University Press.

Allport, G. W. (1954). *The Nature of Prejudice*. Reading, MA: Addison-Wesley.

Altemeyer, B. (1988). *Right-Wing Authoritarianism*. Winnepeg, Canada: University of Manitoba Press.

Amir, Y. (1969). Contact hypothesis in ethnic relations. *Psychological Bulletin*, 71, 319–342.

Aronson, E., Wilson, T. D., & Akert, R. M. (2005). *Social Psychology*. (5th edition). Upper Saddle River, NJ: Pearson Education.

Ashton, M. E., Danso, H. A., Maio, G. R., Bond, M. H., Esses, V., & Keung, D. K. Y. (2005). Two dimensions of political attitudes and their individual difference correlates: A cross-cultural perspective. In R. M. Sorrentino, D. Cohen, J. M. Olson, & M. P. Zanna (Eds.), *Culture and Social Behavior: The Ontario Symposium* (Vol. 10, pp. 1–29). Mahwah, NJ: Erlbaum.

Bell, D. W., & Esses, V. M. (2002). Ambivalence and response amplification: A motivational perspective. *Personality and Social Psychology Bulletin*, 28, 1143–1152.

Bell, D. W., Esses, V. M., & Maio, G. R. (1996). The utility of open-ended measures to assess intergroup ambivalence. *Canadian Journal of Behavioural Science*, 28, 12–18.

Bem, D. J. (1972). Self-perception theory. In L. Berkowitz (Ed.), *Advances in Experimental Social Psychology* (Vol. 6, pp. 1–62). San Diego, CA: Academic Press.

Blascovich, J., Ernst, J. M., Tomaka, J., Kelsey, R. M., Salomon, K. L., & Fazio, R. H. (1993). Autonomic reactivity as a moderator of autonomic reactivity during decision making. *Journal of Personality and Social Psychology*, 64, 165–176.

Bobo, L. (2004). Group conflict, prejudice and the paradox of contemporary racial attitudes. In J. T. Jost, & J. Sidanius (Eds.), *Political Psychology: Key Readings* (pp. 333–357). New York, NY: Psychology Press.

Bodenhausen, G. V. (1993). Emotions, arousal, and stereotypic judgments: A heuristic model of affect and stereotyping. In D. M. Mackie, & D. L. Hamilton (Eds.), *Affect, Cognition, and Stereotyping: Interactive Processes in Group Perception* (pp. 13–37). San Diego, CA: Academic Press.

Bodenhausen, G. V., Sheppard, L. A., & Kramer, G. P. (1994). Negative affect and social judgment: The differential impact of anger and sadness. *European Journal of Social Psychology*, 24, 445–462.

Bornstein, R. F. (1989). Exposure and affect: Overview and meta-analysis of research, 1968–1987. *Psychological Bulletin*, 106, 265–289.

Bornstein, R. F. (1993). Mere exposure effects with outgroup stimuli. In D. M. Mackie, & D. L. Hamilton (Eds.), *Affect, Cognition, and Stereotyping: Interactive Processes in Group Perception* (pp. 195–211). San Diego, CA: Academic Press.

Bower, G. H. (1991). Mood congruity of social judgments. In J. P. Forgas (Ed.), *Emotion and Social Judgment* (pp. 31–53). Oxford, England: Pergamon.

Briñol, P., & Petty, R. E. (2003). Overt head movements and persuasion: A self-validation analysis. *Journal of Personality and Social Psychology*, 84, 1123–1139.

Briñol, P., Petty, R. E., & Tormala, Z. L. (2003). Ambivalence: (II) Implications for discrepancies between implicit and explicit self-construals. Paper presented at the University of Amsterdam Symposium on Attitudinal Incongruence, Amsterdam, Netherlands.

Britt, T. W., Boniecki, K. A., Vescio, T. K., Biernat, M., & Brown, L. M. (1996). Intergroup anxiety: A person X situation approach. *Personality and Social Psychology Bulletin*, 22, 1177–1188.

Cacioppo, J. T., Priester, J. R., & Berntson, G. G. (1993). Rudimentary determinants of attitudes: II. Arm flexion and extension have differential effects on attitudes. *Journal of Personality and Social Psychology*, 65, 5–17.

Chaiken, S., & Baldwin, M. W. (1981). Affective-cognitive consistency and the effect of salient behavioral information on the self-perception of attitudes. *Journal of Personality and Social Psychology*, 41, 1–12.

Chen, S., & Chaiken, S. (1999). The heuristic-systematic model in its broader context. In S. Chaiken, & Y. Trope (Eds.), *Dual-Process Theories in Social Psychology* (pp. 73–96). New York: Guilford Press.

Crandall, C. S., Eshleman, A., & O'Brien, L. (2002). Social norms and the expression and suppression of prejudice: The struggle for internalization. *Journal of Personality and Social Psychology*, 82, 359–378.

Czopp, A. M., Monteith, M. J., Zimmerman, R. S., & Lynam, D. R. (2004). Implicit attitudes as potential protection from risky sex: Predicting condom use with the IAT. *Basic and Applied Social Psychology*, 26, 227–236.

Dovidio, J. F., Gaertner, S. L., Isen, A. M., & Lowrance, R. (1995). Group representations and intergroup bias: Positive affect, similarity, and group size. *Personality and Social Psychology Bulletin*, 21, 856–865.

Dovidio, J. F., Kawakami, K., & Gaertner, S. L. (2002). Implicit and explicit prejudice and interracial interaction. *Journal of Personality and Social Psychology*, 82, 62–68.

Duckitt, J. (2006). Differential effects of right wing authoritarianism and social dominance orientation on outgroup attitudes and their mediation by threat from and competitiveness to outgroups. *Personality and Social Psychology Bulletin*, 32, 684–696.

Eagly, A. H., & Chaiken, S. (1993). *The Psychology of Attitudes*. Orlando, FL: Harcourt Brace Jovanovich.

Eagly, A. H., & Chaiken, S. (1998). Attitude structure and function. In D. T. Gilbert, S. T. Fiske, & G. Lindzey (Eds.), *Handbook of Social Psychology*. (4th edition, Vol. 1, 269–322). New York, NY: Oxford University Press.

Esses, V. M., Haddock, G., & Zanna, M. P. (1993). Values, stereotypes, and emotions as determinants of intergroup attitudes. In D. M. Mackie, & D. L. Hamilton (Eds.), *Affect, Cognition, and Stereotyping: Interactive Processes in Group Perception* (pp. 137–166). San Diego, CA: Academic Press.

Fazio, R. H. (1990). Multiple processes by which attitudes guide behavior: The MODE model as an integrative framework. In L. Berkowitz (Ed.), *Advances in Experimental Social Psychology* (Vol. 23, pp. 75–109). San Diego, CA: Academic Press.

Fazio, R. H. (2000). Accessible attitudes as tools for object appraisal: Their costs and benefits. In G. R. Maio, & J. M. Olson (Eds.), *Why we Evaluate: Functions of Attitudes* (pp. 1–36). Mahwah, NJ: Erlbaum.

Fazio, R. H., Jackson, J. R., Dunton, B. C., & Williams, C. J. (1995). Variability in automatic activation as an unobtrusive measure of racial attitudes: A bona fide pipeline? *Journal of Personality and Social Psychology*, 69, 1013–1027.

Fazio, R. H., & Olson, M. A. (2003). Implicit measures in social cognition research: Their meaning and use. *Annual Review of Psychology*, 54, 297–327.

Festinger, L. (1964). *Conflict, Decision, and Dissonance*. Stanford, CA: Stanford University Press.

Finlay, K. A., Trafimow, D., & Villareal, A. (2002). Predicting exercise and health behavioral intentions: Attitudes, subjective norms, and other behavioral determinants. *Journal of Applied Social Psychology*, 32, 342–358.

Fishbein, M., & Ajzen, I. (1975). *Belief, Attitude, Intention, and Behavior: An Introduction to Theory and Research*. Reading, MA: Addison-Wesley.

Forgas, J. P. (1995). Mood and judgement: The affect infusion model (AIM). *Psychological Bulletin*, 117, 39–66.

Forgas, J. P., & Moylan, S. J. (1991). Affective influences on stereotype judgments. *Cognition and Emotion*, 5, 379–395.

Friese, M., Hofmann, W., & Schmitt, M. (2008). When and why do implicit measures predict behavior? Empirical evidence for the moderating role of opportunity, motivation, and process reliance. *European Review of Social Psychology*, 19, 285–338.

Gaertner, S. L., & Dovidio, J. F. (2005). Understanding and addressing contemporary racism: From aversive racism to the common ingroup identity model. *Journal of Social Issues*, 61, 615–639.

Gebauer, J., Maio, G. R., & Pakizeh, A. (2008). *Feeling Torn When Everything Seems Right: Structural vs. Evaluative Sources of Felt Ambivalence*. Unpublished manuscript.

Glasman, L. R., & Albarracín, D. (2006). Forming attitudes that predict future behavior: A meta-analysis of the attitude-behavior relation. *Psychological Bulletin*, 132, 778–822.

Glick, P., & Fiske, S. T. (2001). Ambivalent sexism. In M. Zanna (Ed.), *Advances in Experimental Social Psychology* (Vol. 33, pp. 115–188). San Diego, CA: Academic Press.

Greenwald, A. G., McGhee, D. E., & Schwartz, J. K. L. (1998). Measuring individual differences in implicit cognition: The implicit association test. *Journal of Personality and Social Psychology*, 74, 1464–1480.

Haddock, G., Zanna, M. P., & Esses, V. M. (1993). Assessing the structure of prejudicial attitudes: The case of attitudes toward homosexuals. *Journal of Personality and Social Psychology*, 65, 1105–1118.

Haddock, G., Zanna, M. P., & Esses, V. M. (1994). Mood and the expression of intergroup attitudes: The moderating role of affect intensity. *European Journal of Social Psychology*, 24, 189–205.

Harmon-Jones, E., & Mills, J. (1999). An introduction to cognitive dissonance theory and an overview of current perspectives on the theory. In E. Harmon-Jones, & J. Mills (Eds.), *Cognitive Dissonance: Progress on a Pivotal Theory in Social Psychology* (pp. 3–21). Washington, DC: American Psychological Association.

Hass, R. G., Katz, I., Rizzo, N., Bailey, J., & Moore, L. (1992). When racial ambivalence evokes negative affect, using a disguised measure of mood. *Personality and Social Psychology Bulletin*, 18, 786–797.

Hausmann, L. R. M., & Ryan, C. S. (2004). Effects of external and internal motivation to control prejudice on implicit prejudice: The mediating role of efforts to control prejudiced responses. *Basic and Applied Social Psychology*, 26, 215–225.

Herek, G. M. (1986). The instrumentality of attitudes: Toward a neofunctional theory. *Journal of Social Issues*, 42, 99–114.

Holland, R. W., Verplanken, B., & van Knippenberg, A. (2002). On the nature of attitude-behavior relations: The strong guide, the weak follow. *European Journal of Social Psychology*, 32, 869–876.

Kaplan, K. J. (1972). On the ambivalence-indifference problem in attitude theory and measurement: A suggested modification of the semantic differential technique. *Psychological Bulletin*, 77, 361–372.

Katz, D. (1960). The functional approach to the study of attitudes. *Public Opinion Quarterly*, 24, 163–204.

Katz, I., & Hass, R. G. (1988). Racial ambivalence and American value conflict: Correlational and priming studies of dual cognitive structures. *Journal of Personality and Social Psychology*, 55, 893–905.

Kawakami, K., Dion, K. L., & Dovidio, J. F. (1998). Racial prejudice and stereotype activation. *Personality and Social Psychology Bulletin*, 24, 407–416.

Kawakami, K., Dovidio, J. F., Moll, J., Hermsen, S., & Russin, A. (2000). Just say no (to stereotyping): Effects of training in the negation of stereotypic associations on stereotype activation. *Journal of Personality and Social Psychology*, 78, 871–888.

Kenworthy, J. B., Turner, R. N., Hewstone, M., & Voci, A. (2005). Intergroup contact: When does it work, and why? In J. F. Dovidio, P. Glick, & L. A. Rudman (Eds.), *On the Nature of Prejudice: Fifty years after Allport* (pp. 278–292). Malden, MA: Blackwell.

Kristiansen, C. M., & Zanna, M. P. (1988). Justifying attitudes by appealing to values: A functional perspective. *British Journal of Social Psychology*, 27, 247–256.

Krosnick, J. A., Betz, A. L., Jussim, L. J., & Lynn, A. R. (1992). Subliminal conditioning of attitudes. *Personality and Social Psychology Bulletin*, 18, 152–162.

Kruglanski, A. W., Fishbach, A., Erb, H.-P., Pierro, A., & Mannetti, L. (2004). The parametric unimodel as a theory of persuasion. In G. Haddock, & G. R. Maio (Eds.), *Contemporary Perspectives on the Psychology of Attitudes* (pp. 399–422). New York, NY: Psychology Press.

Lambert, A. J., Khan, S. R., Lickel, B. A., & Fricke, K. (1997). Mood and the correction of positive versus negative sterotypes. *Journal of Personality and Social Psychology*, 72, 1002–1016.

Lord, C. G., & Lepper, M. R. (1999). Attitude Representation Theory. In M. P. Zanna (Ed.), *Advances in Experimental Social Psychology* (Vol. 31, pp. 265–343). San Diego, CA: Academic Press.

Lord, C. G., Lepper, M. R., & Mackie, D. M. (1984). Attitude prototypes as determinants of attitude-behavior consistency. *Journal of Personality and Social Psychology*, 46, 1254–1266.

Mackie, D. M., Devos, T., & Smith, E. R. (2000). Intergroup emotions: Explaining offensive action tendencies in an intergroup context. *Journal of Personality and Social Psychology*, 79, 602–616.

Macrae, C. N., Milne, A. B., & Bodenhausen, G. V. (1994). Stereotypes as energy-saving devices: A peek inside the cognitive toolbox. *Journal of Personality and Social Psychology*, 66, 37–47.

Maddux, W. W., Barden, J., Brewer, M. B., & Petty, R. E. (2005). Saying no to negativity: The effects of context and motivation to control prejudice on automatic evaluative responses. *Journal of Experimental Social Psychology*, 41, 19–35.

Maio, G. R. (2010). Mental representations of social values. In M. P. Zanna (Ed.), *Advances in Experimental Social Psychology* (Vol. 42, pp. 1–43). San Diego, CA: Academic Press.

Maio, G. R., Bell, D. W., & Esses, V. M. (1996). Ambivalence and persuasion: The processing of messages about immigrant groups. *Journal of Experimental Social Psychology*, 32, 513–536.

Maio, G. R., & Haddock, G. (2004). Theories of attitude: Creating a witches' brew. In G. Haddock, & G. R. Maio (Eds.), *Contemporary Perspectives on the Psychology of Attitudes* (pp. 425–453). New York, NY: Psychology Press.

Maio, G. R., & Haddock, G. (2007). Attitude change. In A. W. Kruglanski, & E. T. Higgins (Eds.), *Social Psychology: Handbook of Basic Principles* (2nd edition, pp. 565–586). New York, NY: Guilford.

Maio, G. R., & Haddock, G. (2010). The psychology of attitudes and attitude change. London: Sage.

Maio, G. R., Haddock, G. G., Watt, S. E., & Hewstone, M. (2008). Implicit measures in applied contexts: An illustrative examination of antiracism advertising. In R. E. Petty, R. H. Fazio, & P. Brinol (Eds.), *Attitudes: Insights From the New Wave of Implicit Measures* (pp. 327–357). New York, USA: Psychology Press.

Maio, G. R., & Olson, J. M. (2000a). Emergent themes and potential approaches to attitude function: The function-structure model of attitudes. In G. R. Maio, & J. M. Olson (Eds.), *Why we Evaluate: Functions of Attitudes* (pp. 417–442). Mahwah, NJ: Erlbaum.

Maio, G. R., & Olson, J. M. (2000b). What is a "value-expressive" attitude? In G. R. Maio, & J. M. Olson (Eds.), *Why we Evaluate: Functions of Attitudes* (pp. 249–269). Mahwah, NJ: Erlbaum.

Marques, J. M., Abrams, D., & Serodio, R. G. (2001). Being better by being right: Subjective group dynamics and derogation of in-group deviants when generic norms are undermined. *Journal of Personality and Social Psychology*, 81, 436–447.

Mayer, J., Gaschke, Y., Braverman, D., & Evans, T. (1992). Mood-congruent judgment is a general effect. *Journal of Personality and Social Psychology*, 63, 119–132.

McCauley, C., Stitt, C. L., & Segal, M. (1980). Stereotyping: From prejudice to prediction. *Psychological Bulletin*, 87, 195–208.

McConnell, A. R., & Leibold, J. M. (2001). Relations among the Implicit Association Test, discriminatory behavior, and explicit measures of racial attitudes. *Journal of Experimental Social Psychology*, 37, 435–442.

McGuire, W. J. (1960). Direct and indirect persuasive effects of dissonance-producing messages. *Journal of Abnormal and Social Psychology*, 60, 354–358.

Moreland, R. L., & Beach, S. R. (1992). Exposure effects in the classroom: The development of affinity among students. *Journal of Experimental Social Psychology*, 28, 255–276.

Niedenthal, P. M., Barsalou, L. W., Winkielman, P., Krauth-Gruber, S., & Ric, F. (2005). Embodiment in attitudes, social perception, and emotion. *Personality and Social Psychology Review*, 9, 184–211.

Nisbett, R. E., & Wilson, T. D. (1977). Telling more than we can know: Verbal report on mental processes. *Psychological Review*, 84, 231–259.

Olson, M. A., & Fazio, R. H. (2004). Trait inferences as a function of automatically activated racial attitudes and motivation to control prejudiced reactions. *Basic and Applied Social Psychology*, 26, 1–11.

Olson, M. A., & Fazio, R. H. (2006). Reducing automatically activated prejudice through implicit evaluative conditioning. *Personality and Social Psychology Bulletin*, 32, 421–433.

Ouellette, J. A., & Wood, W. (1998). Habit and intention in everyday life: The multiple processes by which past behavior predicts future behavior. *Psychological Bulletin*, 124, 54–74.

Payne, B. K. (2001). Prejudice and perception: The role of automatic and controlled processes in misperceiving a weapon. *Journal of Personality and Social Psychology*, 81, 181–192.

Petty, R. E., Fazio, R. H., & Briñol, P. (2009). The new implicit measures: An overview. In R. E.Petty, R. H. Fazio & P. Briñol (Eds.), *Attitudes: Insights from the New Implicit Measures* (pp.3–18). New York, NY: Psychology Press

Petty, R. E., Fazio, R. H., & Briñol, P. (2008). The new implicit measures: An overview. In R. E. Petty, R. H. Fazio, & P. Briñol (Eds.), *Attitudes: Insights From the New Implicit Measures*. New York, NY: Psychology Press.

Petty, R. E., & Wegener, D. T. (1999). The Elaboration Likelihood Model: Current status and controversies. In S. Chaiken, & Y. Trope (Eds.), *Dual Process Theories in Social Psychology* (pp. 41–72). New York, NY: Guilford.

Pratto, F., Sidanius, J., Stallworth, L. M., & Malle, B. F. (1994). Social dominance orientation: A personality variable predicting social and political attitudes. *Journal of Personality and Social Psychology*, 67, 741–763.

Priester, J. R., & Petty, R. E. (2001). Extending the bases of subjective attitudinal ambivalence: Interpersonal and intrapersonal antecedents of evaluative tension. *Journal of Personality and Social Psychology*, 80, 19–34.

Reyna, C., Henry, P. J., Korfmacher, W., & Tucker, A. (2006). Examining the principles in principled conservatism: The role of responsibility stereotypes as cues for deservingness in racial policy decisions. *Journal of Personality and Social Psychology*, 90, 109–128.

Rokeach, M. (1973). *The Nature of Human Values.* New York, NY: Free Press.

Scheepers, D., Spears, R., Doosje, B., & Manstead, A. S. R. (2003). Two functions of verbal intergroup discrimination: Identity and instrumental motives as a result of group identification and threat. *Personality and Social Psychology Bulletin*, 29, 568–577.

Scheepers, D., Spears, R., Doosje, B., & Manstead, A. S. R. (2006). Diversity in in-group bias: Structural factors, situational features, and social functions.

Journal of Personality and Social Psychology, 90, 944–960.

Schmitt, M. T., & Branscombe, N. R. (2003). Will the real social dominance theory please stand up? *British Journal of Social Psychology*, 42, 215–219.

Scott, W. A. (1969). Structure of natural cognitions. *Journal of Personality and Social Psychology*, 12, 261–278.

Sidanius, J., & Pratto, F. (2003). Social dominance theory and the dynamics of inequality: A reply to Schmitt, Branscombe, & Kappen and Wilson & Liu. *British Journal of Social Psychology*, 42, 207–213.

Smith, E. R. (1993). Social identity and social emotions: Toward new conceptualizations of prejudice. In D. M. Mackie, & D. L. Hamilton (Eds.), *Affect, Cognition, and Stereotyping: Interactive Processes in Group Perception* (pp. 297–315). San Diego, CA: Academic Press.

Spears, R., & Haslam, S. A. (1997). Stereotyping and the burden of cognitive load. In R. Spears, P. J. Oakes, N. Ellemers, & S. A. Haslam (Eds.), *The Social Psychology of Stereotyping and Group Life* (pp. 171–207). Malden, MA: Blackwell Publishing.

Srull, T. K., & Wyer, R. S., Jr. (1989). Person memory and judgment. *Psychological Review*, 96, 58–83.

Strack, F., Martin, L. L., & Stepper, S. (1988). Inhibiting and facilitating conditions of the human smile: A nonobtrusive test of the facial feedback hypothesis. *Journal of Personality and Social Psychology*, 54, 768–777.

Taylor, S. E., Peplau, L. A., & Sears, D. O. (2006). *Social Psychology* (12th edition). Upper Saddle River, NJ: Pearson Education.

Terry, D. J., & Hogg, M. A. (1996). Group norms and the attitude-behavior relationship: A role for group identification. *Personality and Social Psychology Bulletin*, 22, 776–793.

Thomsen, C. J., Lavine, H., & Kounios, J. (1996). Social value and attitude concepts in semantic memory: Relational structure, concept strength, and the fan effect. *Social Cognition*, 14, 191–225.

Trafimow, D., & Finlay, K. A. (1996). The importance of subjective norms for a minority of people: Between-subjects and within-subjects analyses. *Personality and Social Psychology Bulletin*, 22, 820–828.

Trafimow, D., & Fishbein, M. (1994). The moderating effect of behavior type on the subjective norm-behavior relationship. *Journal of Social Psychology*, 134, 755–763.

Turner, J. C. (1991). *Social Influence*. Milton Keynes: Open University Press.

Vargas, P. T., Von Hippel, W., & Petty, R. E. (2004). Using partially structured attitude measures to enhance the attitude-behavior relationship. *Personality and Social Psychology Bulletin*, 30, 197–211.

Wegener, D. T., Clark, J. K., & Petty, R. E. (2006). Not all stereotyping is created equal: Differential consequences of thoughtful versus nonthoughtful stereotyping. *Journal of Personality and Social Psychology*, 90, 42–59.

Wigboldus, D., Sherman, J. W., Franzese, H. L., & van Knippenberg, A. (2004). Capacity and comprehension: Spontaneous stereotyping under cognitive load. *Social Cognition*, 22, 292–309.

Wolsko, C., Park, B., Judd, C. M., & Wittenbrink, B. (2000). Framing interethnic ideology: Effects of multicultural and color-blind perspectives on judgments of groups and individuals. *Journal of Personality and Social Psychology*, 78, 635–654.

Wyer, R. S., Jr. (1970). Quantitative prediction of belief and opinion change: A further test of a subjective probability model. *Journal of Personality and Social Psychology*, 16, 559–570.

Ybarra, O., & Trafimow, D. (1998). How priming the private self or collective self affects the relative weights of attitudes and subjective norms. *Personality and Social Psychology Bulletin*, 24, 362–370.

Zajonc, R. B. (2001). Mere exposure: A gateway to the subliminal. *Current Directions in Psychological Science*, 10, 224–228.

Zanna, M. P., & Rempel, J. K. (1988). Attitudes: A new look at an old concept. In D. Bar-Tal, & A. Kruglanski (Eds.), *The Social Psychology of Knowledge* (pp. 315–334). Cambridge, UK: Cambridge University Press.

17

Intergroup Dyadic Interactions

Jennifer A. Richeson and J. Nicole Shelton

ABSTRACT

This chapter reviews the effects of prejudice on intergroup interactions. We first offer a brief history of research on interactions between members of non-stigmatized groups and members of stigmatized groups. Then, we examine processes that influence the behavior that non-stigmatized individuals display during intergroup interactions. We then consider how stigmatized individuals influence the bias expressed by their non-stigmatized interaction partners during, as well as the behavioral dynamics of, intergroup interactions. After, we explore interaction dynamics beyond bias expression; namely, individuals' cognitive and affective experiences during and after the interaction. Last, we offer some new directions for research that we believe will provide a richer understanding of interaction dynamics for both members of stigmatized and non-stigmatized groups.

PREJUDICE IN INTERGROUP DYADIC INTERACTIONS

Intergroup bias is a pervasive phenomenon found in virtually all cultures (Sidanius & Pratto, 1999). It is supported by, and often grounded in, a number of relatively normal processes. For instance, the ability to sort people into meaningful categories, rapidly and with minimum effort, seems to be a universal and essential facet of human perception (Allport, 1954). Social categorization, furthermore, involves a basic distinction between groups containing the self (the ingroup) and other groups (outgroups) – or between the 'we's' and the 'they's' (Turner, Hogg, Oakes, et al., 1987). This recognition of different group memberships influences perception, cognition, affect, and behavior in ways that systematically produce pervasive intergroup biases (Chapter 7 by Fiske & Russell and

Chapter 4 by Quadflieg, Mason, & Macrae, this volume). Indeed, the very processes of mind that allow us to navigate complex and potentially hostile environments also seem to predispose us to process information in biased ways.

According to conventional wisdom, the expression of these biases during intergroup interactions depends largely, if not solely, upon the attitudes of the interactants. That is, prejudiced people are thought to behave in negative ways, and non-prejudiced people are thought to behave in positive ways. Quite to the contrary of this pervasive lay theory, however, behavior during intergroup interactions depends on the interactants' motivations, previous intergroup contact experiences, and facets of the immediate social context. Thus, there is not a one-to-one mapping of prejudiced attitudes and the display of negative behavior during intergroup interactions. Rather, if, when, and how bias is expressed during intergroup interactions depends upon a number of psychological and socio-cultural factors.

The purpose of the present chapter is to review the literature exploring how prejudice and concerns about prejudice influence intergroup interactions. First, we offer a brief history of the research on intergroup interactions. We then provide a review of research regarding behavior during interactions between stigmatized and non-stigmatized individuals. In this section, we first investigate how cognitive processes, affect and arousal, motivations and goals, and socio-cultural norms influence the behavior that non-stigmatized individuals display during intergroup interactions. Next, we consider how the motivations and expectations that stigmatized individuals hold influence the bias expressed by their non-stigmatized interaction partners, and behavioral dynamics of intergroup interactions more generally. After our review of the factors that promote bias expression, we consider interaction dynamics other than behavior, such as individuals' cognitive and affective experiences during and after the interaction, focusing primarily on the possibility that the interaction participants' outcomes and experiences will diverge. We close the chapter by identifying directions for future research.

The reciprocal effect that contact has on intergroup prejudice is reviewed by Tausch and Hewstone (Chapter 33 of this volume), and, therefore, will not be included in the present review. Furthermore, because a preponderance of social psychological research on intergroup interaction, in particular, and prejudice and stereotyping, more generally, has examined relations between racial groups in North America, our review will draw heavily, albeit not exclusively, upon interracial contact dynamics. In addition, we focus primarily on research involving adults.

HISTORY OF RESEARCH ON INTERGROUP INTERACTIONS

Social psychology has a long history of research demonstrating differential behavior

during intergroup compared with intragroup interactions. Over 35 years ago, researchers illustrated that both verbal and non-verbal aspects of behavior often differ during intergroup in comparison with during intragroup interactions. For instance, early research revealed that Whites use colder voice tones (Weitz, 1972), maintain less eye contact and shorter glances (Fugita, Wexley, & Hillery, 1974), and create greater social distance (Word, Zanna, & Cooper, 1974) during interactions with Blacks than with other Whites. Similar patterns of negative non-verbal behavior have been documented during interactions between individuals with and without physical disabilities (Hebl & Kleck, 2000), presumed heterosexual and gay individuals, and thin/average weight and overweight individuals (Hebl, Chapter 21 of this volume), to name a few.

Despite the aforementioned early research, the study of intergroup interaction dynamics waned during the 1980s and 1990s. Indeed, both the authors of the 'Stereotyping and Prejudice' chapter and those of the 'Social Stigma' chapter in the *Handbook of Social Psychology* (Fiske, 1998 & Crocker, Major, & Steele, 1998; respectively) called for greater attention to dynamics of interactions between members of stigmatized and non-stigmatized social groups. Perhaps in partial response, there currently is a resurgence of interest in the dynamics of intergroup dyadic interactions. Over the past decade, researchers have focused on physiological (e.g., Page-Gould, Mendoza-Denton, & Tropp, 2008), behavioral (e.g., Dovidio, Kawakami, & Gaertner, 2002; Trawalter & Richeson, 2008), cognitive (e.g., Richeson & Trawalter, 2005), and affective (e.g., Pearson, West, Dovidio, et al., 2008) dynamics of intergroup interactions.

This newer wave of research deviates from earlier work in two important ways. First, there has been a notable shift from a near exclusive focus on members of socially valued groups to a greater inclusion of stigmatized individuals' experiences during intergroup interactions. Shelton (2000) noted the dearth of research in the prejudice domain that considered Blacks' experiences during the interaction. For example, a study of interracial interactions would often involve an examination of the extent to which Whites' racial beliefs influence their behavior toward Black individuals. Although the assumption is that these racial beliefs and behaviors have implications for Blacks' experiences during the interaction, Blacks' actual experiences would not actually be examined. However, research is increasingly examining minorities' reactions to, and impressions of, members of majority groups during intergroup interactions (e.g., Conley, Devine, Rabow, et al., 2002; Page-Gould, Mendoza-Denton, & Tropp, 2008; Pearson, West, Dovidio, et al., 2008; Vorauer & Kumhyr, 2001).

Moreover, Shelton (2000) noted that the exclusion of Blacks (and other stigmatized individuals) from intergroup interaction research stemmed from the larger problem of research paradigms that relegated Blacks to the position of passive objects that are 'reacted to' by Whites, rather than as active agents who may influence the interaction themselves. In other words, the attitudes, concerns, and cognitions of members of stigmatized groups were rarely examined as factors that shape their cross-group interaction experiences. Recent research, however, is also beginning to buck this trend; recent studies have focused on how low-status group members' attitudes (e.g., Ashburn-Nardo, Knowles, & Monteith, 2003) and concerns about prejudice (e.g., Miller & Myers, 1998) affect intergroup interactions.

The second trend in the literature on intergroup interactions represents a return to social psychology's roots. Perhaps in part due to the cognitive revolution in psychology in general and social psychology in particular, studies of intergroup contact not only waned in the 1980s and 1990s, but those studies that were conducted turned to decidedly non-social paradigms that focused on intrapersonal processes. Consider, once again, the typical study in which the effects of one participant's attitudes on their own behavior vis-à-vis a real, or imagined, outgroup interaction partner was assessed. Although this paradigm allowed for the examination of the attitude–behavior

relation and became particularly important in documenting the predictive validity of implicit attitudes, it obscured the truly interactive nature of an interaction. Recently, we (Richeson & Shelton, 2007; Shelton & Richeson, 2006a) and others (Hebl & Dovidio, 2005; Vorauer, 2006) have pushed for the field to employ paradigms that respect the interpersonal reality of intergroup interactions. Specifically, research on intergroup contact, we argue, has often missed part of the psychological reality of actual interactions.

Taken together, one of the most striking revelations from this new wave of research is that although many of the behaviors that emerge during intergroup encounters are often considered to be evidence of bias, they could also stem from factors other than prejudice that are often correlated with the intergroup context of an interaction. For instance, intergroup interactions are often less familiar and, thus, present greater uncertainty for individuals. Furthermore, some of the same 'negative' non-verbal behavior could also reflect anxiety stemming from any number of individual difference and situational factors. In other words, research suggests that it is no longer reasonable to infer negative attitudes from what is often perceived to be negative behavior. Instead, the behavior that individuals display during intergroup interactions seems to be shaped at least in part by their conscious motivations, concerns about the potential influence of prejudice during the interaction, and important facets of the social context. In addition, research on implicit cognition has found that individuals' unconscious attitudes and associations about different groups can also shape their behavior in ways that are dissociable from the attitudes that they hold explicitly (Dovidio, Kawakami, & Gaertner, 2002). In other words, on some occasions, behavior displayed during intergroup interactions is likely to reflect individuals' implicit, but not their explicit, attitudes, whereas on other occasions, behavior is likely to reflect individuals' explicit, but not their implicit, attitudes.

Indeed, understanding when, and under what conditions, which individuals will display negative behavior during intergroup interactions is far from simple. In the next section, we review research regarding the individual difference and situational factors that serve either to promote or, rather, to attenuate non-stigmatized individuals' expression of bias during intergroup interactions.

BIAS EXPRESSION DURING INTERGROUP ENCOUNTERS

Unlike almost any other social context, direct interpersonal contact between members of non-stigmatized groups and members of stigmatized groups sets the stage for the expression of bias. Bias expression during intergroup interactions, however, is also determined by a number of factors, both psychological and socio-cultural. In this section, we consider the influences of attitudes and motivations, as well as features of the social and societal contexts on the behavioral dynamics of intergroup interactions. We first consider the influence of these factors on bias expression by non-stigmatized individuals. After, we turn to an examination of the roles that members of stigmatized, devalued groups play in shaping the behavioral dynamics of intergroup interactions.

Non-stigmatized individuals' role in bias expression

Several models of attitude expression, prejudice, and discrimination have been forwarded to shed light on the circumstances under which members of non-stigmatized groups will behave in biased ways toward members of devalued, stigmatized groups. Although the models differ somewhat in content and focus, they all suggest that individuals' attitudes and cognitions play a significant role in the behavioral expression of bias, but that the influences of attitudes and cognitions are moderated by conscious motivations, as well as by social and contextual norms. For instance, in his MODE model of attitude expression, Fazio (1990) argues that bias expression is a function of individuals' underlying attitudes *and* the

extent to which they have the motivation and opportunity to modulate the influence of those attitudes. Similarly, Dovidio and Gaertner's Aversive Racism Theory (2004) suggests that for most individuals, overtly biased behavior will be rare, consistent with those individuals' non-prejudiced self-concepts. More subtle expressions of bias, however, will be relatively common during intergroup interactions, as will discriminatory behavior that is attributionally ambiguous – that is, behavior that could be caused either by prejudice or by some other factor.

Considered in tandem, the prevailing models of bias expression and behavior during intergroup interactions posit that such expression is shaped by attitudes in concert with motivations and aspects of the social context (see Figure 17.1). Next, we present the evidence for the direct and indirect influences of attitudes, motivation, and social context on the behavior displayed by non-stigmatized individuals during intergroup interactions.

Attitudes and cognitions

Members of non-stigmatized groups enter intergroup interactions with stereotypes and cognitions, based on cultural expectations and/or personal experiences. Stereotypes and evaluative attitudes are often spontaneously activated upon recognition of the group membership of an interaction partner. Throughout the history of the United States, for instance, one's racial group membership has been a defining dimension of social status and group dominance and, as a result, of group categorization and identity. Although many Whites report that they are non-prejudiced on self-report measures, and presumably believe that they are not prejudiced at a conscious level, they commonly harbor negative feelings and beliefs at an unconscious, implicit level (Nosek, Banaji, & Greenwald, 2002). For instance, Whites' perceptions of other Whites are generally favorable and involve the activation of traits such as intelligence, success, and education; Whites' perceptions of Blacks (men in particular) are less favorable, and include activation of traits such as aggression,

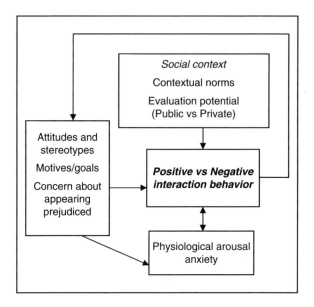

Figure 17.1   Role of non-stigmatized individuals in the expression of bias.

violence, and laziness (Wittenbrink, Judd, & Park, 1997).

Stereotypes typically influence intergroup interactions in predictable ways. Specifically, individuals often behave in ways that reflect their stereotypical expectations for interaction partners. For instance, young adults tend to believe that older adults are mentally slow and relatively incompetent (Hummert, Garstka, Shaner, et al., 1994). During interactions with older adults, consequently, younger adults have been found to speak with diminutive language and in an altered tone of speech similar to that used with children and pets (Ryan, Bourhis, & Knops, 1991). Similar effects have been found during interactions between individuals with and without physical disabilities (Hebl & Kleck, 2000). Sadly, stereotypical beliefs can often create reality through self-fulfilling prophecy effects (Word, Zanna, & Cooper, 1974), such that stereotyped targets end up behaving in stereotype-consistent ways in response to the treatment they receive during intergroup interactions.

As with stereotypes, attitudes can influence behavior during intergroup interactions. Indeed, there is a substantial body of work finding that individuals with more negative

attitudes about the group membership of an interaction partner behave in more negative ways, especially when non-verbal aspects of behavior are considered (see Crosby, Bromley, & Saxe, 1980, for a review). The impact of individuals' attitudes on behavior, however, becomes more complex when both verbal and non-verbal behaviors are considered, and when the distinction between explicit and implicit attitudes is made. Hebl and Dovidio (2005) argued that individuals' non-verbal behaviors are frequently at odds with their verbal behaviors. Even when non-stigmatized individuals' verbal communication with stigmatized individuals is fairly positive, non-verbal aspects of their behavior can be quite negative (e.g., McConnell & Leibold, 2001).

According to contemporary thinking, this dissociation between verbal and non-verbal behavior is due to the differential influences of explicit and implicit attitudes. Explicit and implicit attitudes are thought to influence behavior in different ways and under different conditions. Specifically, explicit attitudes shape behavior when people have the motivation, opportunity, and sufficient psychosocial resources to consider various courses of action. Consequently, explicit attitudes tend to be reflected in behaviors that are relatively controllable, such as how favorably a Black job candidate is evaluated by a White interaction partner (Dovidio, Kawakami, Johnson, et al., 1997). Implicit attitudes by contrast, influence behavior that is relatively difficult to monitor and control, or in situations that make behavioral control difficult. Implicit attitudes are likely to predict the *manner* or *quality* with which an individual interacts with a Black job candidate. More implicitly biased individuals may not rate Black and White job candidates differently, but they are likely to behave more negatively toward Black candidates as assessed by non-verbal measures of interest (e.g., eye contact), anxiety (rate of blinking), and friendliness (e.g., smiling and nodding; Dovidio, Kawakami, & Johnson, et al., 1997, 2002; McConnell & Liebold, 2001).Taken together, this research suggests that when explicit and implicit attitudes are not well correlated, their influences on behavior are likely to be quite distinct.

Affect and arousal

There is considerable evidence that emotions, such as feelings of threat and anxiety, are significant factors in the dynamics of intergroup interactions (Smith & Mackie, Chapter 7 of this volume). Negative affect may be particularly likely to translate into the display of negative, non-verbal behavior during intergroup interactions. As mentioned previously, people may be able to monitor and conceal their thoughts and cognitions (e.g., explicit beliefs), but they may be less skilled at monitoring and controlling their affective reactions. Hence, similar to implicit attitudes, affective reactions, such as anxiety, are particularly likely to 'leak out' through non-verbal and paraverbal channels. Consistent with this reasoning, non-stigmatized individuals often display non-verbal signs of anxiety and discomfort (e.g., excessive blinking) more during intergroup, compared with intragroup, interactions (Dovidio et al, 1997; Trawalter & Richeson, 2008).

Furthermore, the display of fewer affiliative behaviors (e.g., nodding, direct eye gaze) during intergroup relative to intra-group

interactions may be due to increased negative arousal, but not necessarily negative attitudes. Indeed, interracial interactions often evoke a state of physiological arousal that stems from an appraisal of the situation as a psychological threat. This malignant pattern of cardiovascular reactivity disallows the types of fluid behaviors that promote positive interpersonal interactions (Mendes, Blascovich, Hunter, et al., 2007) such that members of dominant groups sometimes respond to intergroup interactions by simply freezing – that is, they display reduced motoric behavior of any kind, including gesturing (Richeson & Shelton, 2003). This type of freezing behavior is likely to result in negative interaction experiences, and may be perceived as evidence of bias.

Motivations and goals

Although the effects of negative stereotypes, attitudes, and affect on behavior may seem insurmountable, individuals' motivations can both attenuate, as well as completely alter, their influence. Motivations can reflect chronic egalitarian values for behavior during intergroup interaction or, rather, they can stem from the social context (Plant & Devine, 1998). For example, many Whites express concerns that they will be viewed as prejudiced (Vorauer, Main, & O'Connell, 1998) and are motivated to behave in egalitarian ways during interactions with racial minorities (Plant & Devine, 1998). The motivation to appear non-prejudiced influences behavior during intergroup interactions. For instance, Shelton (2003) found that although Whites who were instructed to avoid prejudice reported feeling more anxious during an interaction with a Black partner than Whites who were not given this instruction, analyses of their non-verbal behavior revealed that they behaved less anxiously (they fidgeted less) than Whites who were not so instructed. Thus, although Whites were anxious during the interaction, their motivation not to be prejudiced was seemingly able to shunt the behavioral expression of anxiety. If Whites' anxiety had leaked during the interaction, perhaps their Black partner would have interpreted it as the expression of racial bias. Instead, the Black partners liked Whites who were instructed to avoid appearing prejudiced more than they liked Whites who were not attempting to avoid appearing prejudiced.

In addition to these direct influences on behavior, conscious motivation to behave in non-prejudiced ways can moderate the influence of implicit evaluations. With awareness and the time and opportunity to exert control, people who are motivated to respond without prejudice may be able to inhibit the effects of spontaneous stereotype activation on their behavior, at least for those behaviors that can be monitored and controlled. Dasgupta and Rivera (2006), for example, found that heterosexuals with high levels of implicit anti-gay bias behaved no differently during an interaction with a gay person than heterosexuals with lower anti-gay bias, if they held non-traditional, egalitarian beliefs about gender roles. In other words, individuals' desire to behave in egalitarian ways overrode the typical consequences of negative implicit attitudes.

Motivation to respond without prejudice can result in paradoxical behavioral outcomes. The effort required to control the expression of bias during intergroup interactions is cognitively demanding (Richeson & Trawalter, 2005), and, as a consequence, can lead individuals to behave in ways that are the opposite of their desired responses (Apfelbaum, Sommers, & Norton, 2008). Moreover, the arousal associated with the potential to reveal bias during intergroup interactions can lead members of dominant groups simply to avoid them when possible (Snyder, Kleck, Strenta, et al., 1979).

When non-stigmatized individuals cannot avoid intergroup interactions, they become focused on not acting inappropriately, particularly in ways that can be attributed to prejudice. Preoccupation with behaving in a non-prejudiced manner can further contribute to inconsistencies between non-stigmatized group members' verbal and non-verbal behaviors in intergroup interactions. As mentioned previously, members of non-stigmatized groups generally report feeling positively toward targets, while their non-verbal behaviors indicate more negative reactions (Hebl & Dovidio, 2005). This discrepancy may stem, in part, from concerns about appearing prejudiced. For instance, when Whites are concerned about acting in prejudiced ways during interracial interactions, they may focus their attention on managing their verbal behaviors (i.e., what they say), which are easier to monitor and control than many non-verbal aspects of behavior (e.g., blinking). Given that monitoring and controlling behavior is so cognitively demanding, however, these activities may actually facilitate the expression of individuals' more spontaneous, unconscious attitudes. In other words, concerns about appearing prejudiced could, unwittingly, serve to increase the display of both anxious behaviors, as well as behavior that reveals whatever unconscious cognitive and affective biases individuals have. Needless to say, neither type of behavior is likely to reflect individuals' largely egalitarian explicit attitudes.

In a series of studies, Vorauer and Turpie (2004) found that concerns about appearing prejudiced led low-prejudiced Whites to choke and display fewer intimacy building behaviors than they normally would during interracial interactions. Similarly, Shelton, Richeson, & Salvatore, (2005) found that during an interaction that involved discussing race-related topics with a Black partner and, thus, activating Whites' concerns about appearing prejudiced, Whites with higher levels of implicit racial bias were more engaged (as judged by their interaction partners) than Whites with lower levels of implicit racial bias. Taken together, this research suggests that triggering concerns about appearing prejudiced can result in behavior that is far from consistent with individuals' intergroup attitudes. Consequently, this work reveals the profound effects that individuals' motivations can have on the expression of biased behavior during intergroup interactions.

Social context

One explanation for the prevalence of subtle, rather than more overt, forms of bias during intergroup interactions stems from the role that the social context often plays in constraining behavior. When overt discrimination is discouraged, inhibited, or prohibited by social norms and/or the law, individuals are unlikely to respond in an overtly prejudicial fashion. For instance, there is no evidence of bias in formal actions made by potential employers toward gay and lesbians, but, rather, considerable bias in these employers' more spontaneous behaviors (Hebl, Chapter 21 of this volume). That is, employers did not discriminate against confederates portrayed as gay or lesbian on formal employment behaviors, such as permission to complete a job application and callbacks for further consideration. However, bias was expressed more subtly in employers' interaction behaviors. That is, employers spent less time, used fewer words, and smiled less when interacting with the gay applicants than with presumed heterosexual applicants. The pressure to behave in non-prejudiced ways because of contextual pressure, however, can also backfire. Individuals who are motivated to behave in non-prejudiced ways because of external pressures (such as the fear of social disapproval) are especially likely to feel anxious both in anticipation of (Plant, 2004), as well as during (Trawalter, Adam, Chase-Lansdale, et al., 2009), interracial interactions. Such individuals have also been found to display race-based patterns of selective attention to photographs of Blacks that are thought to reflect anxious reactions to Black individuals (Richeson & Trawalter, 2008) and, they are most susceptible to reactance in the form of increased negativity toward members of stigmatized groups (Plant & Devine, 2001). Specifically, Plant and Devine (2001) found that those who are primarily externally motivated to respond without prejudice, feel constrained and bothered by pressure to be politically correct and respond with angry/threatened affect when pressured to comply with such norms. In some cases, heightened arousal stemming from concerns about conforming to public pressure can result in the facilitation of individuals' dominant responses to members

of devalued groups (Lambert, Payne, Jacoby, et al., 2003). That is, public pressure to behave in non-prejudiced ways can actually increase prejudicial responding. In sum, this research suggests that the social context can both increase, as well as, attenuate biased responding, but the restriction of overt bias may actually serve to increase the likelihood that individuals will respond in subtly biased ways.

Summary

Bias can be expressed in intergroup interactions in blatant and subtle ways. The extent to which non-stigmatized individuals express both types of bias is shaped in part by the attitudes and motivations they bring to the interaction, the affect they experience during the interaction, and the norms that are salient in the social context in which the interaction occurs. These factors often have a straightforward impact on bias expression – for example, negative racial attitudes result in biased behaviors during interactions. Perhaps more interestingly, however, these factors sometimes result in counterintuitive effects – for example, norms prohibiting bias can lead non-stigmatized individuals to behave in biased ways during the interaction. These counterintuitive effects make it quite difficult for stigmatized individuals to know whether they are interacting with friend or foe. In the next section we turn to how stigmatized individuals' concerns about prejudice may complicate the situation even further.

Stigmatized individuals' roles in bias expression

In this section, we review literature on how stigmatized individuals' attitudes and motivations may sometimes lead non-stigmatized individuals to behave in relatively negative ways during intergroup interactions, whereas at other times these same factors can lead non-stigmatized individuals to feel more comfortable during intergroup interactions that ultimately results in positive interaction dynamics. It is important to note that we are not implying that stigmatized individuals' attitudes, motivations, and behaviors *cause* non-stigmatized individuals to be more or less biased. Instead, we review literature suggesting that the interpersonal, evaluative concerns with which members of stigmatized groups enter intergroup interactions contribute to the conditions that either give rise to or undermine the expression of behavior that is more or less negative during intergroup, compared with intragroup, interactions.

One clear theme that has emerged from the existing research on stigmatized individuals is the profound role of the potential for individuals to become a target of prejudice during intergroup encounters. Many stigmatized individuals' cognitions about, reactions to, and motivations during, interactions with non-stigmatized individuals seem to stem from their expectations and concerns regarding their interaction partners' prejudice levels. Indeed, stigmatized individuals often hold the stereotype that non-stigmatized individuals are prejudiced against the stigmatized group to which they belong. For example, Blacks' stereotypes of Whites largely concern images of Whites as prejudiced (Monteith & Spicer, 2000), and the more Blacks perceive that Whites are prejudiced against Blacks, the more negatively they feel about Whites (Livingston, 2002).

Given that stigmatized individuals often experience heightened arousal during intergroup interactions because of concern about the potential for prejudice and discrimination (Page-Gould, Mendoza-Denton, & Tropp, 2008; Shelton, 2003; Tropp, 2003), they are motivated to avoid being the target of prejudice during intergroup interactions. That is, they typically do *not* want to be evaluated according to group stereotypes, and/or be devalued or rejected during the interaction. In the next section, we review research regarding the effects of such interpersonal, evaluative prejudice concerns on behavioral dynamics during intergroup interactions, focusing on their effects for the expression of biased behaviors (see Figure 17.2).

Expecting prejudice

When stigmatized individuals anticipate interacting, or actually engage in interactions, with non-stigmatized interaction partners who are expected to be prejudiced, they respond quite negatively (Butz & Plant, 2006). For instance, Pinel (2002) led women who were dispositionally high in concern about being the target of sexism (i.e., high stigma conscious women) to believe that a male interaction partner was sexist. In response to this information, these high stigma conscious women acted critically toward their male interaction partners, which, in turn, resulted in unfavorable responses from their male partners in return. In other words, these high stigma conscious women's negative expectations created the conditions that led to negative behavior. Furthermore, it is highly likely that the male partner's behavior would not only be interpreted as gender biased, but would actually be more negative than the behavior he displays during interactions with other men. Consequently, Pinel's work suggests that stigma consciousness can create the disparate treatment that is often observed between intergroup and intragroup interactions.

In addition, when stigmatized groups expect to be the target of prejudice, they become vigilant for signs of prejudice (Kaiser, Vick, & Major, 2006; Major, Chapter 25 of this volume). For example, Richeson, Trawalter, and Shelton (2008) found that Blacks who were most concerned about being the target of racial prejudice tended to direct their gaze selectively toward white targets, suggesting an attentional vigilance for Whites, presumably because they are more likely to be a source of racial bias compared with Blacks.

Heightened vigilance out of concern about being the target of prejudice also consumes more of stigmatized individuals' cognitive resources, which, in turn, disrupts their ability to engage in positive interaction behaviors that may be more effortful. Consistent with this possibility, stigmatized individuals are particularly mindful during interactions with non-stigmatized individuals – carefully monitoring both their verbal and non-verbal behavior (Frable, Blackstone, & Scherbaum, 1990). Much like monitoring one's own thoughts and behaviors, monitoring those displayed by one's interaction partner also requires and consumes cognitive resources. Hence, the

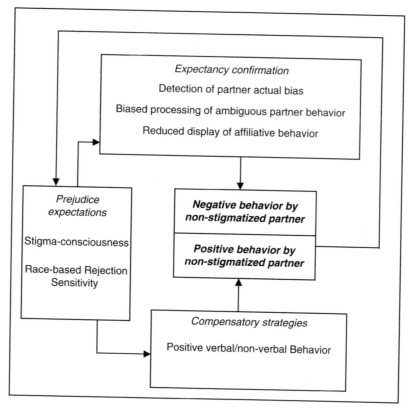

Figure 17.2   Role of Stigmatized individuals in the expression of bias by members of non-stigmatized groups.

increased mindfulness with which stigmatized individuals engage in intergroup interactions may consume resources that would otherwise be devoted to efforts to engage in positive behavior. Indeed, the stigmatized participants in the Frable, Blackstone, & Scherbaum (1990) study behaved in ways that suggest they were less engaged – as measured by how much they participated and were encouraging during the interaction – compared to their non-stigmatized partners during the interaction. Similarly, Ickes (1984) found that Blacks were less expressive than Whites during interracial interactions, suggesting that they may have been monitoring their partners' behaviors rather than focusing on their own.

Taken together, this research suggests that concerns about being the target of prejudice can contribute to negative interaction dynamics because stigmatized individuals' increased vigilance to their non-stigmatized interaction partners 1) increases the detection of their

partners' actual biased behaviors, 2) increases the extent to which their partners' ambiguous behaviors will be attributed to prejudice, and 3) reduces the extent to which they can behave in positive, affiliative ways during the interaction – a clear recipe for negative intergroup interactions.

Despite this impressive body of research, there is also work suggesting that just the opposite can result when stigmatized individuals are concerned about being the target of prejudice. That is, research suggests that at least under some conditions, stigmatized individuals who expect to be the target of prejudice behave in strategic ways that are designed to manage interactions with non-stigmatized individuals, perhaps even decreasing non-stigmatized individuals' tendency to display behaviors that could be interpreted as bias. Specifically, this work finds that stigmatized individuals employ compensatory strategies, such as smiling more and being more engaged in the interaction, to cope with or even ward off actual or anticipated discrimination during the interaction (Miller & Myers, 1998; Shelton, Richeson, & Salvatore, 2005). For example, in a study of gay and heterosexual male interaction dynamics, individual differences in stigma consciousness among gay men predicted the extent to which they were judged by their straight interaction partners to be interested and engaged in the interaction, as well as comfortable during the exchange (Miller & Malloy, 2003).

This research suggests, therefore, that concern about being the target of prejudice can sometimes facilitate smooth intergroup interactions. Indeed, Shelton, Richerson, Salvatore, et al. (2005) found that Whites who interacted with ethnic minorities who were primed to expect prejudice enjoyed the interaction more, liked their partners more, and experienced less negative affect during the interaction than did White partners of ethnic minority individuals who were not primed to expect prejudice. In Miller and Malloy's (2003) work on gay–straight interactions, moreover, the gay men who were most concerned with being stigmatized by heterosexual interaction partners were also liked more by their straight interaction partners. In other words, concern about being the target of prejudice in these studies seemed to result in positive evaluations by non-stigmatized interaction partners.

Summary

Perhaps for self-protective reasons, stigmatized individuals often enter intergroup interactions with the concern that they may be evaluated and treated negatively because of their low-status group membership. Such concerns can result both in behavior that facilitates, and in behavior that pre-empts, non-stigmatized individuals' expression of bias during intergroup interactions. In the next section we consider how these factors, as well as those associated with members of non-stigmatized groups, influence participants' affective and cognitive reactions to intergroup interactions.

BEYOND BEHAVIOR: HOW INTERGROUP INTERACTIONS ENGENDER DIVERGENT OUTCOMES

In the previous section of this chapter we focused on how individuals' attitudes, motivations, and prejudice concerns influence the expression of bias, in particular, and behavioral dynamics, more generally, during intergroup interactions. A focus on behavior alone is likely to obscure other important outcomes that contribute to individuals' assessments of whether an intergroup interaction is 'positive' or 'negative'. In this section, therefore, we review work examining how non-stigmatized and stigmatized individuals' intergroup attitudes, motivations, and prejudice concerns influence affective and cognitive outcomes of intergroup interactions.

We adopt a relational framework (Shelton & Richeson, 2006a) as we examine the ways in which affect and cognition are shaped during intergroup interactions. A schematic of the relational approach and its implications for the affective and cognitive outcomes of intergroup interactions for both interaction participants is presented in Figure 17.3.

Affective outcomes

Much like the behavioral outcomes reviewed previously, individuals' affective experiences during intergroup interactions are also shaped, at least in part, by their intergroup attitudes and prejudice concerns. What is intriguing, however, is that both intergroup attitudes and prejudice concerns can result in positive behavioral outcomes, but negative affective outcomes. Below, we review the evidence regarding these processes.

Attitudes The research that has been conducted on actual interracial interactions suggests that stigmatized and non-stigmatized individuals sometimes experience similar affective reactions during their encounters with one another, but on some occasions (and for some types of affective reactions) their affective experiences diverge. For example, Vorauer and Kumhyr (2001) found that

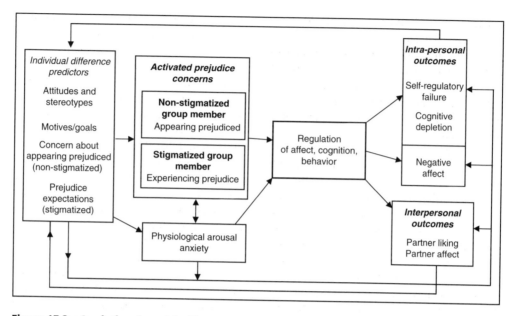

Figure 17.3 A relational model of intra-personal versus interpersonal interaction outcomes.

low-, but not high-, prejudiced Whites experienced more positive affect (e.g., friendly, happy, satisfied) after interacting with a First Nations compared to with a White partner. Interestingly, First Nations participants, but not White participants, experienced more discomfort (e.g., tense, frustrated, anxious) after interacting with high-prejudiced compared to with low-prejudiced White partners. Furthermore, whereas both low- and high-prejudiced Whites experienced more negative feelings toward the self (e.g., self-critical, angry at myself) after interacting with a First Nations compared to a White partner, only First Nations partners who had interactions with the high-prejudiced Whites experienced negative self-directed affect.

Stigmatized individuals' intergroup attitudes can also influence their affective experiences during intergroup interactions. Shelton and Richeson (2006b: Study 2) found, for instance, that among ethnic minority freshmen who were randomly assigned to have a White roommate, those with more negative attitudes toward Whites experienced less positive affect and more negative affect during interactions with their roommate. However, among ethnic minority freshmen

with ethnic minority roommates, their racial attitudes were not related to the amount of positive and negative affect they experienced during roommate interactions.

Unfortunately, there has been very little research on how stigmatized individuals' attitudes influence their partner's affective experiences during intergroup interactions. In one of the few studies to address this issue, however, there was no relation between ethnic minorities' racial attitudes and the affective experiences had by their White interaction partners (Shelton & Richeson, 2006b: Study 3).

Prejudice concerns As noted previously, individuals often enter intergroup interactions with a considerable amount of apprehension about how they will be perceived by the outgroup, and are motivated to make sure that they are perceived and treated in a positive manner. The evidence seems to be unequivocal, for instance, that the more stigmatized individuals are concerned about being the target of prejudice during intergroup interactions, the more negative their emotional reactions (e.g., Page-Gould, Mendoza-Denton, & Tropp, 2008; Shelton, Richerson,

Salvatore, et al., 2005). For example, Shelton, Richerson, Salvatore, et al. (2005) found that ethnic minorities who were primed to expect racial prejudice prior to an interracial interaction experienced more negative affect during the interaction than ethnic minorities who were not primed to expect prejudice toward them.

Similarly, a growing body of work now supports the notion that Whites' concerns with appearing prejudiced yield negative affective reactions during interracial encounters (Plant and Devine, 1998). For example, Vorauer, Main, & O'Connell (1998: Study 2) found that the more Whites expected a First Nations interaction partner to think that they were prejudiced, the more they expected to have negative feelings during the interaction, and the lower their self-esteem was after the interaction (Vorauer, Main, & O' Connell, 1998: Study 3). Taken together, these findings provide compelling evidence that both stigmatized and non-stigmatized individuals' relevant prejudice concerns can have deleterious consequences for their affective experiences in anticipation of, during, as well as after, interracial interactions.

Cognitive outcomes

In addition to eliciting various negative affective reactions, intergroup interactions may be cognitively demanding for individuals. Interacting with outgroup individuals is often a stressful experience (Blascovich, Mendes, Hunter, et al., 2001). Because contending with acute stressors is cognitively demanding, at least some types of intergroup interactions have been found to impair cognitive functioning. Furthermore, both intergroup attitudes and, somewhat ironically, concerns about being either the target or perpetrator of prejudice, have been found to affect the extent to which intergroup contact is cognitively demanding and, consequently, its effect on subsequent cognitive functioning as well (Richeson & Shelton, 2007).

Attitudes Research suggests that some of the cognitive demands of intergroup interactions seem to stem from efforts to modulate affective experiences (Richeson & Trawalter, 2005: Experiment 3). As reviewed previously, individuals' attitudes facilitate both the experience as well as expression of anxiety during intergroup interactions. Hence, intergroup attitudes are likely also to predict the cognitive outcomes of contact. Consistent with this prediction, Richeson and Shelton (2003) found that Whites' attitudes predicted the extent to which they were impaired on the Stroop task (a measure of cognitive functioning) after interracial, but not after same-race, interactions. Specifically, the more negative their attitudes toward Blacks, relative to Whites, the worse they performed. Similarly, the more negative Blacks' racial bias toward Whites, the worse they performed on the Stroop task after interacting with a White confederate, but not after interacting with a Black confederate (Richeson, Trawalter, & Shelton, 2005).

Not only can individuals' own attitudes affect their cognitive functioning after intergroup interactions, but there also is evidence to suggest that the attitudes harbored by one's interaction partner can wield considerable influence on individuals' cognitive functioning. For instance, encountering prejudiced individuals can be cognitively demanding for stigmatized individuals, especially when the prejudice displayed is relatively subtle (Murphy, Richeson, Shelton, et al., 2009; Salvatore & Shelton, 2007). Specifically, Salvatore and Shelton (2007) found that ethnic minorities preformed worse on a Stroop task after exposure to more subtle racial bias, compared to more blatant racial prejudice and no prejudice, which did not differ in their extent of cognitive disruption. The authors reasoned that the conflicting messages that often accompany subtle forms of bias (i.e., positive verbal messages but negative nonverbal messages) make Whites' behavior less predictable, which may require heightened attention and effort on the part of ethnic minorities to diagnose. Consequently, when subjected to more subtle negative behaviors, individuals may be uncertain of the cause of the behavior making it difficult to know how to cope, compared with the negative behavior that communicates blatant racial animus. Consistent with this hypothesis, Murphy, Richerson, Shelton, et al. (2009) found that interactions with blatantly prejudiced White individuals can be less cognitive depleting for Blacks than interactions with Whites whose bias is of a more subtle form.

Prejudice concerns   With respect to the cognitive consequences of motivation and prejudice concerns, research suggests that intergroup interactions prompt non-stigmatized individuals to engage in self-regulatory strategies in response to the apprehension associated with appearing or behaving in a prejudiced manner (Richeson & Trawalter, 2005; Trawalter & Richeson, 2006). Specifically, individuals carefully monitor their thoughts, feelings, and behaviors in order to avoid being perceived as prejudiced. Such regulation and monitoring of thoughts, feelings, and behavior is cognitively demanding, resulting in the temporary depletion of important cognitive resources. As an illustration of this idea, Richeson and Trawalter (2005: Experiment 1) activated the prejudice concerns of Whites prior to an interethnic interaction. Specifically, after completing an implicit measure of prejudice, Whites were told either that most people are more prejudiced than they think they are (prejudice feedback condition) or told that most people perform worse than they think they did (control condition). Then they made comments on a number of somewhat controversial topics, including campus diversity, with either a same-race or cross-race experimenter, and then completed the Stroop color-naming task to measure of cognitive functioning. Results revealed that after an interracial interaction, participants who received the prejudice feedback performed significantly worse on the Stroop task than participants who received the general performance feedback. The feedback did not influence participants' performance on the Stroop task after a same-race interaction, however. In other words, White participants' concerns about appearing prejudiced during the inter-ethnic interaction left them cognitively exhausted.

Prejudice concerns are also a cognitive burden for stigmatized individuals during intergroup encounters. Indeed, research on stereotype threat suggests that concerns about confirming group stereotypes can consume cognitive resources that would be better allocated to the performance task at hand (Steele, Spencer, & Aronson, 2002). Consistent with this logic, Inzlicht, McKay, and Aronson (2006) found that Blacks, especially those who were sensitive to race-based rejection, were cognitively depleted after being in an intergroup situation in which relevant group stereotypes were made salient. Taken together, this research suggests that concerns about behaving in prejudiced and/or stereotypical ways during intergroup interactions can tax individuals' cognitive resources, leaving them less able to manage the challenging tasks that they may face subsequently.

Summary

In sum, research reveals important affective and cognitive outcomes, costs, and consequences of intergroup interactions that may accompany the behavioral dynamics. On some occasions, these affective and cognitive consequences seem to come in the service of fostering positive behavioral dynamics during intergroup interactions. For instance, even when concerns about appearing prejudiced result in relatively positive behavioral dynamics (e.g., Shelton, 2003), the self-regulatory effort required to behave in such a positive manner may result in cognitive depletion (e.g., Richeson & Trawalter, 2005). Hence, it is important to consider multiple outcomes of intergroup interactions, from the perspectives of both interaction participants, in order to capture the many, and often divergent, outcomes that contribute to individuals' assessments of whether such interactions are 'positive' or 'negative.'

FUTURE DIRECTIONS

The research reviewed thus far suggests several directions that are ripe for future inquiry. Most notably, additional research is needed that investigates how the motivations, concerns, and attitudes that stigmatized individuals hold shape their non-stigmatized interaction partners' experiences. In other words, research is needed that considers not only how intergroup interactions affect stigmatized individuals, but also, how stigmatized individuals affect intergroup interactions. For instance, how exactly do stigmatized individuals make non-stigmatized individuals feel 'at ease' in the service of facilitating positive and/or simply effective interactions, especially non-stigmatized individuals who are concerned about appearing prejudiced? What cues do members of these groups use *in vivo* to discern that such compensatory efforts are necessary and likely to be effective, rather than simply responding in kind to any discomfort or negativity expressed by their interaction partners? Furthermore, what person, situational, or even cultural factors promote the deployment of compensatory responses to potential bias? Much like conventional models of attitude expression, it seems reasonable to assume that stigmatized individuals must be both willing and able to enact such behaviors in the face of the threat of being the target of prejudice. What factors predict which stigmatized individuals are willing to engage in these behaviors and what factors predict who will be able to do so, even if they are willing? In other words, how do stigmatized individuals come to develop an arsenal of compensatory strategies and how do they learn to employ them? Such questions are especially relevant for individuals with newly acquired stigmatizing conditions and characteristics (e.g., mental illnesses, older age), but they also speak to larger issues regarding the potential cumulative experiences of managing a stigmatized identity.

Future research should also begin to consider how to foster more positive intergroup interactions, for both interaction participants. The available evidence suggests that intergoup interactions can be stressful for both stigmatized and non-stigmatized individuals, and that positive interaction experiences for one participant often come with negative intra-individual costs (e.g., cognitive depletion and negative affect) for the other. So, what then can shape positive interaction outcomes for both? It is also incredibly important to begin to address the time-courses of some of the effects reviewed in this chapter, as well as the extent to which they predict other relevant intergroup outcomes. For instance, how long do individuals experience cognitive depletion after interracial interactions, and, perhaps more importantly, what (if anything) does the depletion experience predict regarding future interest in interracial interactions? For instance, does the effort to engage in interracial contact that results in depletion leave some individuals *more* likely to avoid interracial contact all together? Are 'depleted' individuals also more likely to express racial bias, because their inhibitory resources have largely been stripped? Effects such as these are likely to be relevant to intergroup interactions that last for longer time periods than the largely experimental work reviewed here, as well as to the dynamics of repeated interaction experiences between the same individuals that continue to be a black box of sorts regarding how interpersonal contact affects intergroup attitudes (see Page-Gould, Mendoza-Denton, & Tropp, 2008; Trail, Shelton, & West, 2009).

CONCLUSION

The research reviewed herein highlights the many nuances associated with behavioral, affective, and cognitive dynamics of intergroup interactions. This research attests to the growing body of work making the case that intergroup interactions can be stressful and demanding for both non-stigmatized and stigmatized individuals. Although much of the work on intergroup interactions was motivated by the desire to understand manifestations of prejudice, the extant research suggests that understanding all of the factors that make interactions difficult, including concerns about appearing prejudiced must also be considered. Furthermore, the concerns, motivations, and attitudes that stigmatized individuals bring to interactions must also be investigated in order to understand behavioral, as well as affective and cognitive, dynamics of intergroup interactions. Together, the two perspectives will provide a richer understanding of the conditions under which intergroup interactions are likely to reveal, contribute to, and even increase misunderstandings if not animus across group boundaries, or, rather, when they will promote positive intergroup attitudes and relations more broadly.

ACKNOWLEDGEMENTS

The production of this chapter was supported by a MacArthur Foundation fellowship to Jennifer Richeson, a National Science Foundation grant awarded to Nicole Shelton (BSC-0742390), and a grant from the National Institute of Mental Health of the NIH Office of Behavioral and Science Research (1R01MH078992) awarded to both authors.

REFERENCES

Allport, G. (1954). *The nature of prejudice*. New York: Doubleday.

Apfelbaum, E. P., Sommers, S. R., & Norton, M. I. (2008). Seeing race and seeming racist? Evaluating strategic colorblindness in social interaction. *Journal of Personality and Social Psychology, 95*, 918–932.

Ashburn-Nardo, L., Knowles, M. L, & Monteith, M. J (2003). Black Americans' implicit racial associations and their implications for intergroup judgment. *Social Cognition, 21*, 61–87.

Blascovich, J., Mendes, W. B., Hunter, S. B., Lickel, B., & Kowai-Bell, N. (2001). Perceiver threat in social interactions with stigmatized individuals. *Journal of Personality and Social Psychology, 80*, 253–267.

Butz, D. A., & Plant, E. A. (2006). Perceiving outgroup members as unresponsive: Implications for approach-related emotions, intentions, and behaviors. *Journal of Personality and Social Psychology, 91*, 1066–1079.

Conley, T., Devine, P. G., Rabow, J., & Evett, S. R. (2002). Gay men and lesbians' experiences in and expectations for interactions with heterosexuals. *Journal of Homosexuality, 44*, 83–109.

Crosby, F., Bromley, S., & Saxe, L. (1980). Recent unobtrusive studies of Black and White discrimination and prejudice: A literature review. *Psychological Bulletin, 87*, 546–563.

Dasgupta, N., & Rivera, L. M. (2006). From automatic anti-gay prejudice to behavior: The moderating role of conscious beliefs about gender and behavioral control. *Journal of Personality and Social Psychology.*

Dovidio, J. F. & Gaertner, S. L. (2004). Aversive racism. In M. P Zanna (Ed.), *Advances in experimental social psychology* (vol. 36, pp.1–52). San Diego, CA: Elsevier Academic Press.

Dovidio, J. F., Kawakami, K., & Gaertner, S. L. (2002). Implicit and explicit prejudice and interracial interaction. *Journal of Personality and Social Psychology, 82*, 62–68.

Dovidio, J. F., Kawakami, K., Johnson, C., Johnson, B., & Howard, A. (1997). On the nature of prejudice: Automatic and controlled processes. *Journal of Experimental Social Psychology, 33*, 510–540.

Fazio, R. H. (1990). Multiple processes by which attitudes guide behavior: The MODE model as an integrative framework. In M. P. Zanna (Ed.), *Advances in experimental social psychology* (Vol. 23, pp. 75–109). New York: Academic Press.

Frable, D. E., Blackstone, T., & Scherbaum, C. (1990). Marginal and mindful: Deviants in social interactions. *Journal of Personality and Social Psychology, 59*, 140–149.

Fugita, S. S., Wexley, K. N., & Hillery, J. M. (1974). Black-White differences in nonverbal behavior in an interview setting. *Journal of Applied Social Psychology, 4*, 343–350.

Hebl, M. R., & Dovidio, J. F. (2005). Promoting the "social" in the examination of social stigmas. *Personality and Social Psychology Review, 9*, 156–182.

Hebl, M. R., & Kleck, R. E. (2000). The social consequences of physical disability. In T. F Heatherton, R. E Kleck, M. R Hebl, and J. G Hull (Ed.), *The social psychology of stigma* (pp. 419–439), New York, NY: Guilford Press.

Hummert, M. L., Garstka, T. A., Shaner, J. L., & Strahm, S. (1994). Stereotypes of the elderly held by young, middle-aged, and elderly adults. *Journal of Gerontology: Psychological Sciences, 49*, 240–249.

Ickes, W. (1984). Compositions in Black and White: Determinants of interaction in interracial dyads. *Journal of Personality and Social Psychology, 47*, 330–341.

Inzlicht, M., McKay, L., & Aronson, J. (2006). Stigma as ego depletion: How being the target of prejudice affects self-control. *Psychological Science, 17*, 262–269.

Kaiser, C. R., Vick, S. B., & Major, B. (2006). Prejudice expectations moderate preconscious attention to cues that are threatening to social identity. *Psychological Science, 17*, 332–338.

Lambert, A. J., Payne, B. K., Jacoby, L. L., Shaffer, L. M., Chasteen, A. L., & Khan, S. R. (2003). Stereotypes as dominant responses: On the "social facilitation" of prejudice in anticipated public contexts. *Journal of Personality and Social Psychology, 84*, 277–295.

Livingston, R. W. (2002). The role of perceived negativity in the moderation of African Americans' implicit and explicit racial attitudes. *Journal of Experimental Social Psychology, 38*, 405–413.

McConnell, A. R., & Leibold, J. M. (2001). Relations between the Implicit Association Test, explicit racial attitudes, and discriminatory behavior. *Journal of Experimental Social Psychology, 37*, 435–442

Mendes, W. B., Blascovich, J., Hunter, S., Lickel, B., & Jost, J. T. (2007). Threatened by the unexpected: Challenge and threat during inter-ethnic interactions. *Journal of Personality and Social Psychology, 92*, 698–716.

Miller, S. & Malloy, T. E. (2003). Interpersonal behavior, perception, and affect in status-discrepant dyads: Social interaction of gay and heterosexual men. *Psychology of Men and Masculinity, 4*, 121–135.

Miller, C. T. & Myers, A. (1998). Compensating for prejudice: How heavyweight people (and others) control outcomes despite prejudice. In J. K Swim & C. Stangor (Eds.), *Prejudice: The Target's Perspective*, (pp. 191–218). San Diego, CA: Academic Press.

Monteith, M. J., & Spicer, C. V. (2000). Contents and correlates of Whites' and Blacks' racial attitudes. *Journal of Experimental Social Psychology, 36*, 125–154.

Murphy, M. C., Richeson, J. A., Shelton, J. A., Rheinschmidt, M., & Bergsieker, H. (2009). [Cognitive costs of subtle v. blatant prejudice during interracial interaction.] Unpublished raw data, Northwestern University, Evanston, IL.

Nosek, B. A., Banaji, M., & Greenwald, A. G (2002). Harvesting implicit group attitudes and beliefs from a demonstration web site. *Group Dynamics: Theory, Research, and Practice, 6*, 101–115.

Page-Gould, E., Mendoza-Denton, R., & Tropp, L. R (2008). With a little help from my cross-group friend: Reducing anxiety in intergroup contexts through cross-group friendship. *Journal of Personality and Social Psychology, 95*, 1080–1094.

Pearson, A. R, West, T. V, Dovidio, J. F, Powers, S. R., Buck R., & Henning, R. (2008). The fragility of intergroup relations: Divergent effects of delayed audiovisual feedback in intergroup and intragroup interaction. *Psychological Science, 19*, 1272–1279.

Pinel, E. C (2002). Stigma consciousness in intergroup contexts: The power of conviction. *Journal of Experimental Social Psychology, 38*, 178–185.

Plant, E. A (2004). Responses to interracial interactions over time. *Personality and Social Psychology Bulletin, 30*, 1458–1471.

Plant, E. A, & Devine, P. G (2001). Responses to other-imposed pro-Black pressure: Acceptance or backlash? *Journal of Experimental Social Psychology, 37*, 486–501.

Plant, E. A & Devine, P. (1998). Internal and external motivation to respond without prejudice. *Journal of Personality and Social Psychology, 75*, 811–832.

Richeson, J. A, & Shelton, J. N (2003). When prejudice does not pay: Effects of interracial contact on executive function. *Psychological Science, 14*, 287–290.

Richeson, J. A, & Shelton, J. N (2007). Negotiating interracial interactions: Costs, consequences, and possibilities. *Current Directions in Psychological Science.*

Richeson, J. A, & Trawalter, S. (2008). The threat of appearing prejudiced and race-based attentional biases. *Psychological Science, 19*, 98–102.

Richeson, J. A, & Trawalter, S. (2005). Why do interracial interactions impair executive function? A resource depletion account. *Journal of Personality and Social Psychology, 88, 934–947.*

Richeson, J. A, Trawalter, S., & Shelton, J. N (2005). African American's implicit racial attitudes and the depletion of executive function after interracial interactions. *Social Cognition, 23*, 336–352.

Richeson, J. A, Trawalter, S., & Shelton, J. N (2008). Effects of prejudice expectancies on visual attention. Unpublished Raw Data, Northwestern University, Evanston, ILs.

Ryan, E. B, Bourhis, R. Y, & Knops, U. (1991). Evaluative perceptions of patronizing speech addressed to elders. *Psychology and Aging, 6*, 442–450.

Salvatore, J., & Shelton, J. N (2007). Cognitive costs to exposure to racial prejudice. *Psychological Science, 18*, 810–815.

Shelton, J. N (2000). A re-conceptualization of how we study issues of racial prejudice. *Personality and Social Psychology Review, 4*, 374–390.

Shelton, J. N (2003). Interpersonal concerns in social encounters between majority and minority group members. *Group Processes and Intergroup Relations, 6*, 171–185.

Shelton, J. N., & Richeson, J. A. (2006a). Interracial interactions: A relational approach. *Advances in Experimental Social Psychology, 38*, 121–181.

Shelton, J. N, & Richeson, J. A (2006b). Ethnic minorities' racial attitudes and contact experiences with White people. *Cultural Diversity and Ethnic Minority Psychology, 12*, 149–164.

Shelton, J. N, Richeson, J. A, & Salvatore, J. (2005). Expecting to be the target of prejudice. Implications for interethnic interactions. *Personality and Social Psychology Bulletin, 31,* 1189–1202.

Shelton, J. N, Richeson, J. A, Salvatore, J., & Trawalter, S. (2005). Ironic effects of racial bias during interracial interactions. *Psychological Science, 16,* 397–402.

Sidanius, J., & Pratto, F. (1999). *Social dominance: An intergroup theory of social hierarchy and oppression.* New York, NY: Cambridge University Press.

Snyder, M. L, Kleck, R. E, Strenta, A., & Mentzer, S. J (1979). Avoidance of the handicapped: An attributional ambiguity analysis. *Journal of Personality and Social Psychology, 37,* 2297–2306.

Steele, C. M, Spencer, S. J, & Aronson, J. (2002). Contending with bias: The psychology of stereotype and social identity threat. In M. P. Zanna (Ed.) *Advances in experimental social psychology* (vol. 34, pp. 277–341). San Diego, CA: Academic Press.

Trail, T. E, Shelton, J. N, & West, T. V (2009). Interracial roommate relationships: Negotiating daily interactions. *Personality and Social Psychology Bulletin.*

Trawalter, S., Adam, E. K, Chase-Lansdale, P. L, & Richeson, J. A (2009). *Prejudice concerns get under the skin: External motivation to respond without prejudice shapes behavioral and physiological responses to interracial contact.* Manuscript under review.

Trawalter, S., & Richeson, J. A (2006). Regulatory focus and executive function after interracial interactions. *Journal of Experimental Social Psychology, 42,* 406–412.

Trawalter, S., & Richeson, J. A (2008). Let's talk about race, baby! When whites' and blacks' interracial contact experiences diverge. *Journal of Experimental Social Psychology, 44,* 1214–1217.

Tropp, L. R (2003). The psychological impact of prejudice: Implications for intergroup contact.

Group Processes and Intergroup Relations, 6, 131–149.

Turner, J. C, Hogg, M. A, Oakes, P. J, Reicher, S. D, & Wetherell, M. S (1987). *Rediscovering the social group: A self-categorization theory.* Oxford, England: Basil Blackwell.

Vorauer, J. D (2006). An information search model of evaluative concerns in intergroup interaction. *Psychological Review, 113,* 862–886.

Vorauer, J. D, & Kumhyr, S. M (2001) Is this about you or me? Self- versus other-directed judgments and feelings in response to intergroup interaction. *Personality and Social Psychology Bulletin, 27,* 706–719.

Vorauer, J., Main, K., & O'Connell, G. (1998). How do individuals expect to be viewed by members of lower status groups?: Content and implications of meta-stereotypes. *Journal of Personality and Social Psychology, 75,* 917–937.

Vorauer, J. D, & Turpie, C. (2004). Disruptive effects of vigilance on dominant group members' treatment of outgroup members: Choking versus shining under pressure. *Journal of Personality and Social Psychology, 27,* 706–709.

Weitz, S. (1972). Attitude, voice, and behavior: A repressed affect model of interracial interaction. *Journal of Personality and Social Psychology, 24,* 14–21.

Wittenbrink, B., Judd, C. M, & Park, B. (1997). Evidence for racial prejudice at the implicit level and its relationship with questionnaire measures. *Journal of Personality and Social Psychology, 72,* 262–274.

Word, C. O, Zanna, M. P, & Cooper, J. (1974). The nonverbal mediation of self-fulfilling prophecies in interracial interaction. *Journal of Experimental Social Psychology, 10,* 109–120.

18

Hate Crime

Rafaela M. Dancygier and Donald P. Green

ABSTRACT

The systematic study of hate crime presents an array of conceptual and methodological challenges. This chapter reviews the extant literature, identifies gaps, and proposes potential avenues for future empirical and theoretical extensions. We begin by discussing the concept of hate crime, explicating its definition and measurement. We next review the literature's attempts to establish bias motivation by examining perpetrators' psychological traits or by analyzing offenders' behaviors during the commission of hate crimes. We then consider contextual accounts that draw attention to offenders' social environment as well as to such macro-causal factors as political, historical-cultural, sociological, and economic circumstances that have been put forth in the explanation of hate crime. We conclude by suggesting theoretical and empirical syntheses of these diverse research programs.

HATE CRIME

A recent research review on the subject of hate crime, that is, criminal activity motivated by bigotry, concluded that 'the lack of theory with the demonstrated ability to explain or predict hate crime, coupled with the lack of evaluation research, makes it difficult to determine the realized or potential impact of criminal justice programs and policies aimed at preventing and effectively responding to hate crime' (Shively, 2005, p. v).

These lacunae are particularly troubling in light of the enduring importance of bigoted violence in the United States and beyond. Each year, US law enforcement agencies classify several thousand criminal incidents as hate crimes, the majority of which are motivated by racial bias (FBI, 2004). In many European countries, harassment and violence directed against the continent's ethnically distinct immigrant populations has also been a common occurrence (EUMC, 2005; McClintock, 2005; Witte, 1995).

What causes hate crime? Scholarly efforts to answer this question fall into three broad categories. A growing body of literature addresses the psychological characteristics that may predispose an individual to commit bigoted crime. Another branch of scholarship distinguishes between varying types of bias motivation to construct typologies of perpetrators. Finally, a third strand of research, existing largely in isolation from these individual-level accounts, examines how variation in contextual variables, such as unemployment rates, social structures, or political institutions, affects the incidence of hate crime. Although the three literatures are growing rapidly, explanations of hate crime that are both theoretically cogent and empirically supported remain elusive.

In this chapter, we review the extant literature, identify gaps, and propose potential avenues for future empirical and theoretical extensions. The chapter begins by discussing the concept of hate crime, explicating its definition and measurement. We next review the literature's attempts to establish bias motivation by examining perpetrators' psychological traits or by analyzing offenders' behaviors during the commission of hate crimes. We then consider contextual accounts that draw attention to offenders' social environment as well as to such macro-causal factors as political, historical-cultural, sociological, and economic circumstances that have been put forth in the explanation of hate crime. We conclude by suggesting theoretical and methodological syntheses of these diverse research programs and by summarizing the empirical generalizations that emerge from the literature.

BRIEF OVERVIEW OF THE TOPIC

The term 'hate crime' (or 'bias crime') first emerged in the United States in the early 1980s. Policy advocates, criminal justice practitioners, and journalists used the new terminology to describe the apparently rising incidence of bias-motivated attacks directed against homosexuals and racial, ethnic, and religious minorities (Jenness & Grattet, 2001). Despite its widespread use, the term is still shrouded in conceptual ambiguity, and scholars, as well as jurisdictions, have adopted varying definitions as a result (Petrosino, 2003). Within the United States alone, hate crime definitions and statutes differ considerably across states (Shively, 2005); outside of the United States, official definitions of bigoted violence also vary widely.

Historical experiences and legal traditions often inform these differences. In the United States, for example, laws prohibiting cross-burning and the desecration of religious sites preceded the hate crime legislation of the 1980s. While the First Amendment protects

hate speech in the United States, Canada, in line with many other Western nations, criminalizes the promotion of genocide and the incitement of hatred on the basis of 'color, race, religion, or ethnic origin where such incitement is likely to lead to a breach of the peace' (Levin, 2002, p. 242). In Germany and Austria, experiences with Nazism have led to the banning of extreme right-wing, anti-Semitic and anti-foreign propaganda, speech, and behavior. Establishing or joining fascist or neo-Nazi political parties, displaying neo-Nazi symbols, and denying the Holocaust are thus prohibited by law. In France, where Republican ideals have long rejected the differentiation of the citizenry into distinct categories based on ethnic or racial identities, bias crime legislation has been slow to develop. Until recently, most convictions related to racist crime referred to violations of laws that placed limits on freedom of expression, dating back to 1881. In 2003 and 2004, following a wave of racist and anti-gay violence, new legislation was introduced that allows for aggravated penalties for a range of offenses, provided racist or homophobic expressions accompany these crimes. The most broad-based definition of racist violence within the European Union (EU) is found in Great Britain, where grassroots and government initiatives to combat racist attacks date back to the early 1980s (Bleich, 2007; EUMC, 2005; McClintock, 2005). Here, all statutory and voluntary agencies that record and report racist incidents adopt the following definition: 'A racist incident is any incident, which is perceived to be racist by the victim or any other person' (Macpherson, 1999, p. 328).

In addition to discrepancies in legal frameworks, differences in data collection mechanisms complicate comparative analyses. In the United States, many law enforcement jurisdictions do not comply with the mandate to collect and report hate crime data (Shively, 2005); in France, government agencies are prohibited by law from recording statistics on the ethnic or racial origin of victims; and in Germany, data collection is skewed towards events that are linked to organized or political forms of racism (EUMC, 2005; Witte, 1995).

Moreover, regardless of variation in the nature of collection, cross-national differences in the commitment to the recording of hate crime data can significantly distort comparative investigations. In its comprehensive study on racist violence in Europe, the European Monitoring Centre on Racism and Xenophobia (EUMC, 2005) concluded that countries with the best-developed recording procedures (i.e., Finland, Great Britain, Sweden, and Germany) also exhibit the highest levels of racist violence. In light of these differences, the Center advises researchers to study the incidence of hate crime within countries over time, rather than cross-nationally.

Another area of disagreement concerns the scope of protected groups. Within the United States and Europe there is no consensus, for example, about whether hate crime laws should specify sexual orientation as a protected category, although the number of US states that do so has risen steadily.[1] While state statutes vary, the FBI's data collection efforts follow a definition that lists specific target groups and considers any 'criminal offense committed against a person or property which is motivated, in whole or in part, by the offender's bias against a race, religion, disability, sexual orientation, or ethnicity/national origin' a bias crime (FBI, 1999, p. 2). Craig and Waldo (1996, p.113) have provided a more expansive definition that encompasses 'words or actions intended to harm or intimidate an individual because of his or her perceived membership in or association with a particular group.' According to this definition, all individuals, even those belonging to numerically dominant groups, can be considered members of protected groups. This understanding of bias crime also informs the approach to such offenses in Britain, where the authorities have tended to view the incidence of racist crime as an indicator of the state of intergroup relations more generally (Witte, 1995). By contrast, Petrosino (2003, p. 10) has maintained that the conceptualization of hate crime should take into account empirical regularities, such as attacks against economically and politically disadvantaged groups by a more powerful

majority and thus classifies 'the victimization of minorities due to their racial or ethnic identity by members of the majority' as hate crimes. To complicate matters further, crime victims themselves sometimes wrongly attribute a bias motive to a non-bias offense.[2]

There is, then, a great deal of disagreement over which acts may count as hate crimes and which individuals may count as victims. From the standpoint of empirical social science, an expansive and general understanding of both crimes and victims would be welcome, as it would allow researchers to test relationships between acts, victims, and perpetrators, which in turn might shed light on the causes of the general phenomenon. Tests could reveal, for example, whether the incidence of verbal abuse or racist graffiti is explained by the same set of variables as physical attacks against ethnic minorities (see Dancygier, forthcoming). An inclusive conception of victim groups could also elucidate how varying local contexts might affect the occurrence of hate crime. Groups that constitute ethnic minorities in national censuses often represent the dominant majority in particular neighborhoods, and empirical investigations could uncover whether the dynamics that are said to produce perpetrators among the national majority population also generate perpetrators among these local majorities. As a practical matter, it remains unlikely that countries with widely varying historical and legal traditions will adopt similarly expansive definitions of hate crime and we would not suggest that social scientific concerns should be the only, or even the main, guiding principle in the adoption of such laws. Nevertheless, policymakers who are interested in combating hate crime and its causes should have an understanding of the potential empirical implications of different legal definitions of such crime.

While definitions may vary, a feature that is common to all prosecutions of hate crime is the challenge of producing convincing evidence. For an ordinary crime to be classified as a hate crime, evidence must indicate the perpetrator's animus toward the victim's putative group. Establishing motivation presents a range of conceptual and epistemological problems (Berk, 1990). Most hate crime statutes require that bigoted animus provide at least part of the offender's motivation, for otherwise crimes such as robbery or sexual assault that carry additional motivations would have to be excluded. While sensible as a practical matter, such a definition also creates ambiguity. Should the harassment of a gay individual that is followed by robbery count as a hate crime, even if economic gain is the apparent proximate motive of the robbery (Berk, Boyd, & Hammer, 2003)? Can perpetrators who exhibited bigoted beliefs towards a social group in the past be convicted of a hate crime if they commit criminal offenses against victims who belong to this group? One proposed assessment of bias motivation takes a perpetrator's history of membership in hate groups into account (Dunbar, 2003).

Alternatively, law enforcement and prosecutors could disregard a perpetrator's bias profile and simply focus on the bigoted character of the attack itself, for example, hate speech articulated during the commission of the crime. However, if bias motivation is crucial in hate crime, what motivations count? Some have suggested that the distinction between reactive and instrumental aggression can be usefully applied to the study of hate crime (Sullaway, 2004). In reactive hate crime, perpetrators are seen to act defensively and without much pre-meditation; they tend to be motivated by a desire to protect their social group from encroachment of an out-group in the form of in-migration (see Green, Strolovitch, & Wong, 1998a) or gang conflict (Levin & McDevitt, 1993). In contrast, those who commit instrumental hate crimes act with greater planning and seek to demonstrate their group's 'social dominance and … ideological resolve' (Dunbar, 2003, p. 204). Even if we accept both types of motivation as part of our definition of hate crime, data analysts still face the empirical challenge of identifying and measuring these motivations.

As is already apparent, the study of hate crime faces a range of conceptual and empirical challenges that researchers encounter at multiple levels of analysis. Taking stock of existing research, this chapter proposes an integrated multi-level framework that takes these complexities into account. As we will discuss shortly, much research has been dedicated to identifying the psychological characteristics that distinguish perpetrators of hate crime from the population at large. Although this work is intriguing, it remains difficult to connect slow-moving changes in such psychological profiles to the often quite rapidly erupting waves of hate crime. In order to understand how individuals who might be psychologically predisposed to committing hate crimes actually turn into perpetrators, we maintain that scholars also need to take these potential offenders' immediate social environment into account. Families, friends, and neighbors might provide the necessary rewards and incentives that make the commission of hate crime seem attractive.

Moreover, these social groups are in turn embedded in specific institutional settings that affect their support for bigoted violence. For example, if racist attacks are believed to deter victims from acquiring scarce jobs or housing, if law enforcement tends to turn a blind eye towards such offenses, or if media coverage appears to lend legitimacy to these crimes, an examination of economic conditions, policing practices and media content should accompany an analysis of hate crime. Finally, the behavior of victims also feeds back into the proliferation of bigoted offenses. If the fear of hate attacks leads individuals to seek relative safety in coethnic enclaves, hate crime might be seen to 'work' and perpetrators will continue to use this type of violence as an effective weapon to keep outsiders from settling in 'their' neighborhoods. In the aggregate, such dynamics can contribute to spatial segregation and in fact reinforce the cohesiveness and distinctiveness of the conflicting communities.

We recognize that no single study can incorporate all of the levels and feedback mechanisms that might be at work in the production of hate crime. However, if research on the causes of hate crime is to make progress, scholars should be cognizant of the interactions between potential perpetrators and the social and wider institutional environments in which they operate. Before moving to a discussion of these macro-level factors, we begin by reviewing the existing scholarship on individual perpetrator characteristics.

INDIVIDUAL-LEVEL ACCOUNTS

Psychological and behavioral traits

Since one ingredient common to all hate crime definitions is the bigoted motive of the offender, most theoretical accounts of hate crime start with the premise that perpetrators share certain psychological attributes that lead to the expression of prejudice. Individual-level accounts of hate crime tend to assume that certain cognitive and affective processes (e.g., stereotyping, displacement of frustration, feelings of social distance, perceptions that groups are arranged hierarchically) lead hate crime perpetrators to identify targets and to take action against them. Building on Adorno and colleagues (1950), Altemeyer (1981, 1996) developed a Right-Wing Authoritarianism (RWA) scale to show that individuals who fit the RWA profile – submissive to authority, aggressive when aggression is believed to be sanctioned by authority and conventional in their outlook – were most likely to be prejudiced. Others (Heitmeyer, Buhse, & Liebe-Freund, 1992; Hopf, Rieker, Sanden-Marcus, et al., 1995; Maaz, 1991) have also argued that the authoritarian personality comprises a set of character traits that are conducive to bigoted violence. Among authoritarians, we can also distinguish between leaders and followers. While most who score highly on the RWA scale tend to readily submit to authority, a small share of these prejudiced individuals fits the profile of those with a Social Dominance Orientation (SDO) (Sidanius & Pratto, 1999). Dominating authoritarians reject notions of equality and prefer hierarchical systems in which they dominate those who surround them (Altemeyer, 1998, 2004). According to Altemeyer, it is these 'double-highs' who appear to be 'the people most likely

to mobilize and lead extremist right-wing movements' (2004, p. 443).

Altemeyer concedes that 'One cannot easily administer personality tests to [members of] extremist groups' (ibid); but even if such tests were possible, a focus on prejudiced attitudes and personality profiles alone is insufficient if the goal is to predict the incidence of hate crime. In their study of alleged perpetrators of hate crime in North Carolina, Green, Abelson, and Garnett (1999) successfully distinguished hate crime perpetrators from ordinary citizens based on the formers' attitudes on interracial marriage, rap music, and immigration. But they also found that only a small subset of respondents whose attitudinal profile fits that of hate crime perpetrators do in fact commit crimes of hate, leading them to conclude that 'no psychological explanation can make sense of hate crime without considering the mechanisms by which individuals are spurred to action' (p. 452).

An alternative, but also indirect, way to assess bias motive is to investigate the observed behaviors and backgrounds of offenders. A quantitative analysis of perpetrators of xenophobic crime and violence in Germany involving 148 suspects concluded that the majority of offenders were teenage boys with low educational attainment who were more likely to be unemployed than their non-violent counterparts, did not come from broken families or from disadvantaged social milieus, and had no particular political or ideological convictions (Willems, Eckert, Würtz, et al., 1993). In their examination of perpetrators of extreme right-wing, anti-Semitic, and anti-foreigner violence using evidence based on court cases, police records and perpetrator biographies, Wahl and colleagues (2003) observed that the majority of hate crime offenders were not unemployed, but that hate crime offenders in general are more likely to be jobless than non-offenders (and note that unemployment may not be a predisposing factor but often a *consequence* of generally deviant behavior), and concluded that a history of aggressive behavior starting in early childhood, socially disadvantaged and violent parents, and low educational achievement are some of the distinctive features of the perpetrator population. While Wahl noted that most perpetrators have a history of delinquency, Levin and McDevitt (2002) found that most hate crime offenders in the United States are young males without a previous criminal record.

Ethnographic work that traces the biographies of individual hate criminals and xenophobic groups suggests the weakness of relying on socio-demographic predictors alone. In his study of skinhead subculture in the United States, Hamm (1993, 1994) interviewed 36 violent skinheads. Similar studies exist for Germany, which witnessed a rise of violent neo-Nazi activity in the early 1990s. A common finding of these studies is the accidental nature of involvement in racist groupings, the importance of family dynamics and youth rebellion, the lack of political or ideological commitment, and a resistance to formal organization (Bitzan, 1997; Hopf, Rieker, Sanden-Marcus, et al., 1995; Müller, 1997; Ross, 1996; Sichrovsky, 1993).

Attempts have also been made to link variation in perpetrator characteristics to observed differences in the manifestation of hate crime. Dunbar (2003) developed a multidimensional Bias Motivation Profile (BMP) that measures offenders' history of bigoted aggression, their membership in groups or gangs that advocate a hate-based ideology, their display of iconography that conveys this worldview (e.g., neo-Nazi garb, tattoos, literature), and the occurrence of hate speech during the attack. His analysis of the records of 58 convicted hate criminals in Los Angeles County, California, suggested that offenders who rank high on the BMP index are more likely to attack their victims in a pre-meditated, goal-oriented way, seeking to establish social dominance through racist crimes.[3] Interestingly, none of these highly biased motivated offenders committed hate crimes based on the sexual orientation of their victims. In their statistical analysis of hate crimes and other forms of assault in 11 US states, Messner, McHugh and Felson (2004) also found a difference between these two types of crimes; whereas alcohol and illicit drug use tended to be common among offenders who commit racially-motivated crimes, such intoxication was absent among perpetrators of non-racial bias crime.

In sum, scholars have demonstrated that hate crime perpetrators have statistically distinct attitudinal and behavioral profiles that set them apart from ordinary citizens, but these characteristics alone would greatly over predict the number of hate criminals. Moreover, scholars have observed variability among offender profiles that may be associated with variation in the type and quality of hate crimes. One of the most interesting findings is the fact that hate crime perpetrators, while often hostile to minority groups, seldom have a broad ideological outlook that calls for the suppression of these groups. Research has sought to illuminate these more nuanced bias motivations by investigating the modus operandi of hate crimes and categorizing offenders into different motivational classes.

Typology of hate crime motives

Typologies are common in research that attempts to gain an understanding of bias motivation (Franklin, 2000; Levin & McDevitt, 1993; McDevitt, Levin, & Bennett, 2002; Willems, 1995). These typologies attempt to account for the interplay between psychological and environmental conditions. Based on their analysis of 169 case files recorded by the Community Disorders Unit of the Boston Police Department over an 18-month period, McDevitt and colleagues (2002) classified offenders into four types. The most common type (66 percent of cases) was thrill-seekers who often left their neighborhood to attack victims that they perceived to be 'different' in acts that were 'triggered by an immature desire to display power and to experience a rush at the expense of someone else' (p. 308). Defensive hate crimes, in which perpetrators attack to protect their turf and resources from the intrusion of unwelcome outsiders constituted the second most common type of offense (25 percent).[4] The least common types of attacks identified by McDevitt, Levin, & Bennett, were retaliatory crimes (8 percent) that were part of a cycle of intergroup violence, and mission crimes (less than one percent) which were solely inspired by racial animus and the desire to purge the hated out-group. Franklin's (2000) typology of antigay behavior among young adults produces some analytical overlap; the author identified four factors – peer dynamics, antigay ideology, thrill-seeking, and self-defense – that accounted for two-thirds of the variance in motivations for hate crimes based on sexual orientation. Finally, Willems' (1995) typology of German perpetrators consisted of right-wing activists, ethnocentric youth, criminal youth, and fellow travelers; these offender types varied in their socioeconomic backgrounds, in their general propensity to commit violence and in their desire to express racial superiority through the commission of hate crimes. For example, while the typical right-wing activist tended to be rather successful in school and later employment and committed racially-motivated crimes if such acts were inspired and legitimized by racist ideologies, the average criminal youth generally needed no legitimatization to resort to such violence, did not always share racial animus, and featured education and job records that were marked by failure.

These typologies suggest that in addition to psychological predispositions, contextual factors provide important triggers in the commission of hate crimes. We next turn to a discussion of accounts that focus on environmental conditions to explain the incidence of bias-motivated crime.

CONTEXTUAL ACCOUNTS

A growing body of social scientific literature has addressed the importance of contextual variables in determining the occurrence of hate crime. A set of accounts points to the importance of would-be perpetrators' immediate surroundings, focusing, for example, on the importance of peer-group dynamics in turning adolescents into hate criminals. While these analyses still take the individual as the level of analysis, macro-causal accounts correlate broad, societal forces with the incidence of bias-motivated violent crimes. These macrosociological theories highlight amorphous and expansive phenomena such as modernization, integration, or economic recessions as essential building blocks in the production of hate crime in modern societies. Many of these accounts offer multi-causal narratives that draw on a variety of social forces, but we can nevertheless distinguish four types of macro-level accounts of hate crime: political, historical-cultural, sociological, and economic.

Small group and information environment

The above discussion of the psychological and behavioral profiles of hate crime offenders and the investigation of the various motives that underlie their acts suggests the potential significance of perpetrators' immediate social surroundings. Scholars have identified a variety of social mechanisms (e.g., contagion, conformism, extremification of attitudes, disinhibition, and yearning for group acceptance) that can be present in small-group dynamics and that may in turn induce individuals to commit crimes of hate (Rieker, 1997; Wahl, 1997; Watts, 1996; Willems, Eckert, Würtz, et al., 1993). Peer pressure and strong group norms tend to be common elements in hate crimes committed by members of white supremacist groups (Hamm, 1994; Kleg, 1993). Ethnographers have also found community norms, and the failure of a community to condemn acts of bigoted violence, to be important in legitimizing or even encouraging bias crime (Rieder, 1985; Sibbitt, 1997; Suttles, 1972). The reciprocal relationship between perpetrators and the communities that produce them thus suggests that efforts to prevent hate crimes need to adopt a multi-pronged approach (Bowling, 1993; Sibbitt, 1997).

European researchers have argued that the media may provide additional legitimization for the commission of hate crimes and point to two causal paths. First, media coverage of hate crime, especially if conveyed in a sensationalist manner, can have a demonstration effect that may lead to contagion. Several quantitative time-series analyses based on the German case, where a wave of spectacular xenophobic attacks received extensive media coverage in the early 1990s, showed not only that reported incidents of racially-motivated violence soared after these key events but that the types of violence were also replicated (Esser & Brosius, 1995, 1996; Karapin, 1996; Leenen, 1995; Quinkert & Jäger, 1991). Second, linguistic, semiotic, and communications experts have stressed how media coverage of these events may also identify target groups and propagate stereotypes about these groups that lend meaning and motivation to attacks directed against them (Jäger & Kretschmer, 1998; Scheffer, 1997). These effects can be quite localized. Ray and Smith (2004) argued, for example, that the local media's disproportionate coverage of Asian-on-White hate crime provided fertile ground for anti-Asian right-wing mobilization in Oldham, a town in northern England that witnessed inter-ethnic rioting in 2001. Politicians and political organizations may also appropriate the media for their own electoral ends by relying on the media's dissemination of hate-mongering political discourse to stoke existing xenophobic sentiments (Karapin, 1996; Koopmans, 1996; Koopmans & Olzak, 2004; Leenen, 1995; Thränhardt, 1995; von Trotha, 1995).

Despite their intuitive appeal, the main empirical limitation of studies that attempt to causally relate media coverage to waves of racist violence is the missing link between the dissemination of media messages and changes in the attitudes and behaviors of those who receive them. It is still unclear, for example, whether media coverage of interethnic violence or anti-immigrant rhetoric leads to an overall increase of prejudice in the general population, thereby expanding the pool of potential offenders, or whether such coverage provides the necessary trigger to turn already prejudiced individuals into perpetrators of bigoted violence. Based on the diverse perpetrator profiles reviewed earlier, both mechanisms might be at work.

The political setting

The media's decision to cover hate crime might in turn be tied to political trends. While politicians may use the media to promote their xenophobic message, what conditions allow political actors to promote hate in the first place? Most political accounts assume the existence of grievances, whether they are rooted in frustration, fear, or disdain, and seek to identify the circumstances under which these grievances are mobilized as social movements. Koopmans (1996) argued that the varying incidence of racist violence in Western Europe is partly a result of cross-national variation in opportunity structures. Assuming that violence is a relatively costly behavior, its incidence will be reduced 'where less costly alternatives are available, that is where extreme right and racist parties play a significant role within the political system' (p. 207). As a result, countries where strong, well-organized right-wing parties have established themselves (e.g., the National Front in France) are said to effectively substitute anti-minority political organization for anti-minority violence. Similarly, in a comparison of three Eastern German towns that saw comparable levels of skinhead organization but varied in their incidence of anti-foreigner rioting, Karapin (2002) attributed the occurrence of such attacks to the failures of the local political process to provide non-violent channels for the expression of immigration-related grievances. While political neglect of the majority's grievances is seen to contribute to anti-minority violence, a rise in minority political power produces similar effects. Examining anti-Semitic attacks targeting persons and property in pre-World War II Germany, King and Brustein (2006) showed that the increasing electoral strength of leftist parties (which were frequently perceived to be run by Jewish leaders) predicted this type of violence.

State actors have also been more directly complicit in the production of hate crime. Some scholars have argued that the ability and willingness of politicians to make inflammatory, anti-immigrant statements, rather than the influx of immigrants as such, heightens the salience of the 'immigration problem' and legitimizes racist violence (Karapin, 1996; Koopmans, 1996). In a similar vein, Koopmans and Olzak (2004) claimed that the legitimacy and resonance of racist violence as communicated by political parties and other public actors contribute to the spread of these attacks in Germany, but their results varied across victim groups (long-established immigrants versus asylum seekers) and location (eastern versus western states). Finally, political accounts have also stressed the timidity, incompetence, organizational bias or even ideological complicity of the police and the courts in failing to comply with hate crime legislation and to prevent racist violence (Hess, 1997; Ireland, 1997; Karapin, 2002; King, 2007; Weitekamp, Kerner, & Herberger, 1996). In short, both elite manipulation and political opportunity structures are said to independently influence the incidence of hate crime, although it is less often specified what opportunity structures are conducive to elite encouragement of racist violence.

Historical and cultural accounts

The centrality of political discourse in the production of hate crime is also a common theme in historical-cultural explanations. These accounts focus less on the short-term manipulation of xenophobic sentiments by elites, but contend that slow-moving, long-term cultural traditions and behavioral patterns are causally related to both hateful discourse and to hateful crimes. A central problem of this line of research is that the political-cultural variables that are said to produce variation in the occurrence of hate crimes are also correlated with the ways that these crimes are recorded, presented and interpreted. Koopmans' (1996) finding that France produces fewer perpetrators of racist violence than Germany or Britain may thus simply be an artifact of France's republican tradition referred to earlier which discourages any racially or ethnically-based data collection efforts.

More generally, it remains unclear how broad structural forces influence individual-level behavior. Perpetrators of hate crime may borrow from available cultural repertoires, but there is no consensus as to what extent a country's racist past may influence its citizens' propensity for committing hate crimes in the future. The anti-immigrant violence that swept through Germany in the early 1990s (especially the former East) and the concomitant resurgence of right-wing parties has thus been linked to the country's Nazi past by media pundits as well as by some academics (McFalls, 1997; Tuttle, 1994; von Trotha, 1995), while other scholarship has dismissed the claim that the outbreak of racist violence should be understood as a revival of Nazism (Merkl & Weinberg, 1997; Prowe, 1997).

Sociological explanations

Another slow-moving dynamic that is said to underlie modern societies' allegedly increased propensity for violent hate crime can be found in modernization theory, originally inspired by Durkheim. From this perspective, bias-motivated crime is seen as a variant of youth violence and delinquency more generally, behavioral reactions to the dislocations inherent in rapid social, economic and cultural change. The forces unleashed by globalization, for example, and the insecurities it engenders among a citizenry that is asked to adapt to economic and technological change, cause threatened individuals to search for convenient scapegoats among their country's minority populations. Those who perceive themselves to be losers as a result of these transformations are said to be likely to turn to hate crime, but two causal paths may connect modernization to the eruption of such violence: (1) anomie and social disintegration experienced by individuals or (2) solidaristic banding together of communities in response to perceived outside threats. These processes were deemed to be at work in the hate crime wave experienced in post-unification Germany, as the transition from communism and national unification ushered in large-scale economic dislocation, the collapse of social norms and authority, and the potential for social and spatial mobility (Boers, Ewald, Kerner, et al., 1994; Hagan, Merkens, & Boehnke, 1995; Heitmeyer, Buhse, & Liebe-Freund 1992; Watts, 1996).

Modernization, in the guise of more egal-itarian gender roles, is thought to play a role in antigay violence. Alden and Parker (2005) merged US census data and opinion data from the General Social Survey with records from the Uniform Crime Report (UCR) to investigate whether gender stratification, attitudes towards homosexuals, and views on gender roles at the city level affect the occurrence of hate crimes based on sexual orientation. Their analysis found that as a city's level of gender inequality decreases (measured as the ratios of male to female median incomes and unemployment rates), the likelihood of hate crimes based on sexual orientation increases, a result which the authors attributed to men's enhanced need to assert their masculinity as the economic gender gap narrowed. Interpretation of Alden and Parker's results, however, is ambiguous because social structure was predictive while attitudes were not. Measures of city-wide attitudes towards homosexuals did not predict antigay crime in a consistent manner, and gender role ideology had no effect.

While Alden and Parker's approach goes beyond many other accounts that stress broader sociological trends by actually mea-suring variation in collective opinions about gender roles and homosexuality, this lack of correspondence between aggregate attitudes and acts points to the general difficulty of empirically connecting social phenomena with individual-level actions in a cross-sectional setting. It also highlights the need for an improved understanding of how the behavior of the victim community affects the production of hate crime. Variation in the attitudinal variables that Alden and Parker use to explain antigay attacks (i.e., measures of homophobia and support for gay civil liberties) are also likely to produce variation in the extent to which homosexuals disguise or reveal their sexual orientation. As an empirical matter, widespread anti-gay attitudes might increase the fear of anti-gay attacks, reduce the visibility of homosexuals and in turn lower the incidence of homophobic crime, leading to anti-gay attitude estimates that are biased downwards.[5] As a policy matter, areas that feature lower victimization rates might only appear to be more tolerant of homosexuals.

Economic conditions and competition over resources

Economic accounts often do address victim behavior by directing attention to the real or perceived competition for material goods between perpetrators and their targets. Similar to sociological accounts, economic explana-tions of hate crime also consider economic dislocation and unemployment to be crucial variables. They tend to understand bigoted violence as a weapon in the competition over scarce resources, but also as a behavioral outcome of displaced frustration. Hovland and Sears (1940) thus understood the inverse correlation between anti-black lynchings and cotton prices, originally identified by Raper (1933), to mean that economically displaced Southern Whites released their frustrations through violent attacks against a vulnerable minority. Tolnay and Beck's (1995) research also reported a statistical link between lynching and cotton prices, but the authors posited that competition over resources, rather than economic frustration, was the root cause of these heinous crimes. These divergent interpretations reflect the fact that neither study had access to micro-level data that would provide insights into the perpetra-tors' economic or psychological outlook. Not only are the mechanisms that connect economic downturns to lynchings in dispute, but scholars have begun to question also the aggregate relationship between economic conditions and bigoted violence. Green, Glaser, and Rich (1998b) showed that when the famous lynching data set compiled by Raper (1933) was extended into the early years of the Depression, the correlation between lynchings and economic downturns largely vanished. Green et al. also pointed out that over-time fluctuations in macroeconomic conditions were poor predictors of anti-gay hate crimes in the contemporary period. These results, together with a fresh look at the laboratory experiments that originally gave rise to frustration–aggression theories, led the authors to speculate that the frustration–aggression nexus may decay over time. These experiments using animals found initial aggressive responses that disappeared in a matter of seconds (Azrin, Hutchinson, & Sallery, 1964; Miller, 1948; Roediger & Stevens, 1970). The authors speculate that *sustained* racist violence may be due to political campaigns that blame minorities for economic misfortunes.

In the German context, scholars also disagree about the extent to which economic forces contributed to the occurrence of right-wing violence. Krueger and Pischke (1997) assembled a data set recording different types among 1,056 anti-foreigner crimes at the county level, based on reports by 15 (Western) regional newspapers covered from 1991 to 1993. They found that the relationship between unemployment and these crimes disappeared once differences between East and West Germany are controlled for. Falk and Zweimüller's (2005) study, however, produced different results. According to their analysis of over 40,000 officially recorded crimes that occurred in Germany between 1996 and 1999, there was a robust relationship between unemployment and extremist crimes, even when economic and demographic covariates (e.g., the rate of youth unemployment, the level of schooling and the percentage of foreigners) were included. Moreover, the observed differences in the occurrence of right-wing violence between Eastern and Western states were due to nonlinear effects. At modest levels of unemployment, levels of right-wing crime were low, and the authors only found a weak statistical link between unemployment and such crime; but beyond a critical threshold of unemployment, additional increases in the

share of jobless were strongly associated with an increase in right-wing criminal acts. The inconsistencies between these studies are striking but may simply be due to methodological differences. To name but a few, the two studies covered different time periods, operated at different levels of aggregation (county versus state), and used different data sources (newspaper reports versus official data from the Federal Criminal Police Office, the *Bundeskriminalamt*).

In the study of ethnic conflict more generally, realistic group conflict theory posits that power differentials among groups, which in turn lead to differential outcomes in the distribution of material resources, drive intergroup hostility and violence (LeVine & Campbell, 1972). But the primacy of these real differences nevertheless leaves a number of variables and mechanisms unspecified. There may, for example, be many dimensions of competition (e.g., employment, housing, or political office). Does competition have to be zero-sum in nature and thus only affect goods that are subject to relatively fixed supply, such as housing? It is also unclear whether the dominant group uses violence preemptively in the face of a small, but growing, in-migrating group, or whether attacks are more common when intergroup power differentials are small (see discussion in Green, Glaser, & Rich, 1998a, p. 373–378). Finally, whether individuals perceive themselves to be in competition with another group may reflect not only the 'real' competition between them but the imagery of competition that political entrepreneurs generate when seeking to make such differences salient (Green, Glaser, & Rich, 1998b; Olzak, 1989). These interdependencies suggest that accounts focusing on competition over resources should incorporate variables relating to the small-group and information environment as well as to the wider political setting referred to earlier.

TOWARD A RESEARCH SYNTHESIS

While psychological and social-psychological explanations are useful in highlighting the internal processes and small-group dynamics that may push individuals (with or without previously-held bigoted beliefs) to commit crimes of hate, they generally fail to place these violent acts into the larger social context in which they occur. Conversely, macro-causal accounts stress the political, cultural, sociological and economic conditions that may or may not be empirically related to broader patterns of racist and homophobic violence but neglect to investigate how these structural forces turn ordinary citizens into hate criminals. If we want to gain a deeper understanding of the routine, unorganized occurrence of hate crimes, syntheses of theoretical perspectives and empirical methods at different levels of analysis will be crucial.

An integrated analysis of hate crime that takes into account macro-structural, contextual and individual-level dynamics will not only have to be sufficiently rich theoretically to encompass broad dynamics as well as micro-processes, but will also have to employ a variety of methodologies. Survey research and quantitative ecological studies should be supplemented with interviews with perpetrators and victims, as well as local ethnographies that capture the 'relationships between victim, offender, and statutory agents' and help situate hate crime incidents 'in the context of family, 'community' and neighbourhood, race, class, and age divisions' (Bowling, 1993, p. 244).

Some existing accounts of hate crime propose such integrated theoretical frameworks but fall short of employing multiple levels of data collection. Using hate crime data from New York City, Green and colleagues' (1998a) 'Defended Neighborhood' model demonstrated that in-migration into previously ethnically homogenous areas by an ethnically distinct group triggered a reaction by members of the dominant group against the perceived invasion. Here, hate crime was a tactic by which the old guard defended its collective identity, way of life, and status. Dancygier (forthcoming) extended this model by taking into account differences between groups. In her analysis of racist crime in

Greater London, Dancygier showed that this defensive logic only held in areas where the in-migrating group commanded the political and social resources to threaten the status of the once dominant group.

These studies are solely ecological in nature, but they suggest empirical implications that can be tested at various levels of analysis. For example, statistical data could be complemented with information on perpetrators to establish whether hate crimes that occur in homogeneous areas experiencing rapid demographic change are more likely to be committed by what McDevitt, Levin, & Bennett (2002) would classify as 'defensive' perpetrators. Ethnographic work could also illuminate whether perpetrators who allegedly act in their groups' collective interest do indeed enjoy community support and side-payments, as Pinderhughes' (1993) work suggested. Sibbitt's (1997) detailed case studies of two London boroughs with histories of racial harassment has found, for example, that there often exist reciprocal relationships between local communities and the hate crime offenders that arise in their midst, suggesting that 'the views of the 'perpetrator community' also need to be addressed in efforts to reduce racial harassment' (pp. vii–viii).

Another way to broaden these ecological studies would be to incorporate insights gleaned from the ethnic conflict literature. A variety of studies have drawn attention to the importance of group structures and elite behaviors in guiding their members' relations with an out-group (e.g., Brass, 1997; Fearon & Laitin, 1996; Varshney, 2002). For example, ethnic groups with strong social networks may exhibit a greater capacity and willingness to monitor and sanction violent attacks perpetrated by their own against an ethnic out-group, thus reducing the incidence of inter-group violence as would-be offenders expect punishment; but these self-monitoring networks may also be more easily captured by entrepreneurs intent on fomenting ethnic tensions (Fearon & Laitin, 1996). Hate crime scholars have also observed differences in retaliatory behavior that might be due to group-level processes.

Using an experimental method in which African-American and White males were exposed to videotaped assaults that varied the race of victims and perpetrators, Craig (1999) observed that African-American respondents were more likely to indicate a desire for revenge, noting that they would return to the scene of the crime with friends if caught in a similar situation.[6] Garofalo (1991) also provided evidence of retaliatory behavior between African-American and White offenders and victims in his study of hate crime in New York City, but noted that such reciprocity does not exist between Hispanics and Whites.

In sum, the study of hate crime has generated many promising leads but remains disjointed, due in large part to a paucity of reliable data. Rarely are incident reports gathered in ways that make them comparable across jurisdictions; even over time comparability is jeopardized by changing reporting standards and practices. The lack of reliable incident reports could in principle be overcome by surveys that measure both the incidence of hate crime and target groups' perceived risk of victimization, but these surveys remain rare. If the study of hate crime is to move forward, scholars in a wide range of disciplines must collaborate to generate the necessary individual and contextual data. This initiative requires more active involvement with interest groups and government agencies that collect hate crime data and interview crime victims.

Data collection efforts would also benefit from greater attentiveness to issues of sampling. Researchers, understandably, are drawn to areas where hate crimes occur with sufficient frequency to allow for meaningful description. The drawback of this approach is that the sample is drawn based on outcome variable rather than on the independent variable, such as economic or political competition. A more defensible research design would involve sampling locations in which a natural experiment has occurred, that is, where the independent variables have changed for exogenous reasons. Thus, when a moderate group leader retires and is replaced by someone who articulates xenophobic positions, does hate crime increase, as predicted by a theory of leader-generated norms, or does it decrease, as predicted by theories suggesting that open expression of xenophobic sentiments obviates the need for more xenophobic criminal behavior?

An ideal design would be one that looks not only at ecological outcomes, such as the number of hate crimes in different locations, but also tracks individual-level sentiment. Scholars remain uncertain whether hate crime constitutes a barometer of opinion in a given group or whether, instead, hate crime represents the behavior of a small number of rogue actors whose behavior is out of step with opinion within the same putative group. Hate crime perpetrators are often characterized as apolitical, but the question is whether the number of would-be hate crime perpetrators declines as public opinion becomes more tolerant. One reason that hate crime grabbed so much scholarly attention during the 1980s is that the apparent surge in hate crime ran counter to long-term trends of increasing tolerance as registered in public opinion polls. Even to this day, it remains unclear whether the trends in hate crime exposed the flawed manner in which opinion polls gauge prejudice; it could be argued, on the contrary, that the climate of tolerance set the stage for a backlash among hate criminals.[7]

SUMMARY AND CONCLUSION

In conclusion, the hate crime literature has only begun to make headway toward the overarching objective of formulating and testing explanations. Most research tends to be descriptive. Only a handful of studies have attempted to analyze quasi-experiments in which some structural factor, such as demographic change or economic dislocation, alters the rate of hate crime. Little or no research has attempted to evaluate the impact of policy interventions designed to reduce the quantity or severity of hate crime. We do not know, for example, whether attempts to publicize hate crime laws and the social norms that they embody have any effect on behavior. Ironically, hate crime research emerged with the advent of hate crime laws, yet this research area has yet to gauge the psychological or systemic impact of these laws.

Despite these important gaps, research has furnished a number of empirical findings that must inform any theory about the nature and origins of hate crime. First, it appears that relatively few hate crime perpetrators have a coherent political or racist ideology. Hate crimes seem to emanate from conditions that mobilize outgroup bias rather than propagate a coherent bigoted worldview. Second, these conditions seem to involve the perpetrator's local or small group environment. Broader macroeconomic conditions do not play a simple and direct role in mobilizing action; instead, the articulation of grievances and selection of targets seem to reflect the political environment and behavior of group leaders. Where community leaders cannot pursue a bigoted agenda through legitimate political channels, as is often the case when they attempt to maintain residential or workplace segregation, they may advocate or tacitly condone illegal tactics, such as violence and harassment. Third, it appears that hate crimes tend to occur when one group's hegemony over a given domain is threatened by the perceived encroachment of another group. Although turf defense is by no means the sole source of hate crime, this type of hate crime allows perpetrators to, in their own minds, stand up for their community and its core values, which in turn helps explain why hate crime perpetrators frequently lack a criminal background and fail to express remorse when apprehended. Finally, serious hate crimes occur relatively infrequently, even if one assumes a severe underreporting problem. But the incidence of hate crime may in turn severely understate its systemic consequences, for potential victims alter their behavior in ways that reduce the risk of attack. It appears that hate crime 'pays,' in the sense that the specter of hate crime does alter the way in the vast numbers of people live their daily lives.

NOTES

1 As US legislators have often been reluctant to be seen as sympathetic to homosexuals' interests or as legitimizing the gay 'lifestyle' (Berrill and Herek, 1992: 291–93; Haider-Markel & Meier, 1996; Jenness & Broad, 1997, p. 42), by the early 1990s, fewer than half of all states with hate crime statutes included sexual orientation as an applicable target category (Wang, 1994). Today, this number has increased to 30 (Shively, 2005), but public opinion is still divided. Surveying 630 Indiana voters, Johnson and Byers (2003) report that those respondents who oppose the inclusion of homosexuality as a target category also tend to oppose penalty-enhanced hate crime laws.

2 These ambiguities have important consequences for survey research, for respondents may use different standards for evaluating whether or not they have been the victim of a hate crime. As Herek, Cogan, & Gillis (2002) point out, 'directly asking respondents if they were the victim of a hate crime or bias crime is problematic because those terms may have different meanings for different respondents' (p. 337). In their sample of 450 lesbian, gay, and bisexual adults, the authors found that a small share of incidents that were thought to be motivated by the victim's sexual orientation were in fact not hate crimes.

3 It is noteworthy, however, that Dunbar's sample may differ from the typical perpetrator profile proposed by others. Perpetrators in his sample were also more likely than ordinary citizens to have a history of psychiatric treatment and educational problems; only a small minority of offenders was in full-time employment (almost half were unemployed); 87 percent had been previously convicted when the crime was committed; the majority had a history of substance abuse; and the mean age was 24.5.

4 Note that this type of individual-level behavior is consistent with Green, Strolvitch, & Wong's (1998a) 'Defended Neighborhood' model, in which previously homogeneous white areas that experience an influx of nonwhite minorities were found to be most likely to witness a high incidence of hate crimes.

5 Another severe limitation of Alden and Parker's study, which is acknowledged by the authors (2005, p. 337), is that there is no attempt to control for the size of a city's gay population. The fact that San Francisco observed more than 200 times as many anti-gay crimes than Knoxville, Tennessee, obviously cannot be explained solely by variations in these cities' levels of homophobia or views on gender equality.

6 While Craig's (1999) study is innovative, Sullaway (2004) points out that it suffers from methodological problems; e.g., the videotaped assault would not in fact be considered a hate crime according to statutes in California, the state where the study was conducted.

7 Hewitt's (2005) study of racism in South London illustrates how multiculturalist policies are seen by

some whites to be benefiting ethnic minorities at their expense, fostering racist resentment and violence.

REFERENCES

Adorno, T. W., Frenkel-Brunswik, E., Levinson, D. J., & Sanford, R. N. (1950). *The authoritarian personality.* New York: Harper and Row.

Alden, H. L., & Parker, K. (2005). Gender role ideology, homophobia and hate crime: linking attitudes to macro-level anti-gay and lesbian hate crimes. *Deviant Behavior, 26,* 321–343.

Altemeyer, R. (1981). *Right-wing authoritarianism.* Winnipeg: University of Manitoba Press.

Altemeyer, R. (1996). *The authoritarian specter.* Cambridge: Harvard University Press.

Altemeyer, R. (1998). The other "authoritarian person-ality." In M. P. Zanna (Ed.), *Advances in experimental social psychology* (Vol. 30, pp. 47–92). San Diego, CA: Academic Press.

Altemeyer, R. (2004). Highly dominating, highly author-itarian personalities. *Journal of Social Psychology, 144,* 421–447.

Azrin, N. H., Hutchinson, R. R., & Sallery, R. D. (1964). Pain-aggression toward inanimate objects. *Journal of Experimental Analysis of Behavior, 7,* 223–228.

Berk, R. A. (1990). Thinking about hate-motivated crimes. *Journal of Interpersonal Violence, 5,* 334–349.

Berk, R. A., Boyd, E. A., & Hammer, K. A. (2003). Thinking more clearly about hate-motivated crimes. In B. Perry (Ed.), *Hate and bias crime* (pp. 50–60). New York: Routledge.

Berrill, K. T., & Herek, G. M. (1992). Primary and secondary victimization in anti-gay hate crimes: Official response and public policy. In G. M. Herek & K. T. Berrill (Eds.), *Confronting violence against lesbians and gay men* (pp. 289–305). Newbury Park, CA: Sage Publications.

Bitzan, R. (Ed.) (1997). *Rechte Frauen, Skingirls, Walküren und feine Damen.* Berlin: Elefanten Press.

Bleich, Erik. (2007). Hate crime policy in Western Europe. *American Behavioral Scientist, 51,* 149–165.

Boers, K., Ewald, U., Kerner, H. J., Lautsch, E., & Sessar, K. (Eds.), (1994). *Sozialer Umbruch und Kriminalität.* Bonn: Forum Verlag Godesberg.

Bowling, B. (1993). Racial harassment and the process of victimization: conceptual and methodological implications for the local crime survey. *British Journal of Criminology, 33,* 231–250.

Brass, P. R. (1997). *Theft of an idol: Text and context in the representation of collective violence.* Princeton, NJ: Princeton University Press.

Craig, K. M., & Waldo, C. R. (1996). 'So, what's a hate crime anyway?' Young adults' perceptions of hate crimes, victims, and perpetrators. *Law and Human Behavior, 20,* 113–129.

Craig, K. M. (1999). Retaliation, fear, or rage: An investigation of African American and White reactions to racist hate crimes. *Journal of Interpersonal Violence, 14,* 138–151.

Dancygier, R. M. (forthcoming). *Immigration and Conflict in Europe.* New York: Cambridge University Press.

Dunbar, E. (2003). Symbolic, relational, and ideological signifiers of bias-motivated offenders: Toward a strategy of assessment.   *American Journal of Orthopsychiatry, 73,* 203–211.

Esser, F., & Brosius, H. B. (1995). *Eskalation durch Berichterstattung? Massenmedien und fremden-feindliche Gewalt.* Wiesbaden: Westdeutscher Verlag.

Esser, F., & Brosius, H. B. (1996). Television as arsonist? The spread of right-wing violence in Germany. *European Journal of Communication, 11,* 235–260.

European Monitoring Centre on Racism and Xenophobia (EUMC). (2005). *Racist violence in 15 EU member states.* Retrieved May 24, 2006, from http://eumc. eu.int/eumc/material/pub/comparativestudy/CS-RV-main.pdf

Falk, A., & Zweimüller, J. (2005). Unemployment and right-wing extremist crime. CEPR Discussion Paper No. 4997. Retrieved May 24, 2006, from www.cepr.org/pubs/dps/DP4997.asp

Fearon, J. D., & Laitin, D. D. (1996). Explaining interethnic cooperation. *The American Political Science Review, 90,* 715–735.

Federal Bureau of Investigation. (2004). *Hate crime statistics 2004.* Retrieved May 24, 2006, from http://www.fbi.gov/ucr/hc2004/tables/HateCrime2004.pdf

Federal Bureau of Investigation. (1999). *Hate crime data collection guidelines.* Retrieved May 14, 2006, from http://www.fbi.gov/ucr/hatecrime.pdf

Franklin, K. (2000). Antigay behaviors among young adults: Prevalence, patterns, and motivators in a noncriminal population. *Journal of Interpersonal Violence, 15,* 339–362.

Garofalo, J. (1991). Racially motivated crimes in New York City. In M. J. Lynch & E. B. Patterson (Eds.), *Race and criminal justice* (pp. 161–173). New York: Harrow & Heston.

Green, D. P., Abelson, R. P., & Garnett, M. (1999). The distinctive political views of hate-crime perpetrators and white supremacists. In D. A. Prentice & D. T. Miller (Eds.), *Cultural divides: Understanding and overcoming group conflict* (pp. 429–464). New York: Russell Sage Foundation.

Green, D. P., Strolovitch, D. Z., & Wong, J. S. (1998a). Defended neighborhoods, integration, and racially motivated crime. *American Journal of Sociology, 104*, 372–403.

Green, D. P., Glaser, J., & Rich, A. (1998b). From lynching to gay bashing: The elusive connection between economic conditions and hate crime. *Journal of Personality and Social Psychology, 75*, 82–92.

Hagan, J., Merkens, H., & Boehnke, K. (1995). Delinquency and disdain: social capital and the control of right-wing extremism among East and West Berlin youth. *American Journal of Sociology, 100*, 1028–1052.

Haider-Markel, D. P., & Meier, K. J. (1996). The politics of gay and lesbian rights: Expanding the scope of the conflict. *Journal of Politics, 58*, 332–349.

Hamm, M. S. (1994). A modified social control theory of terrorism: An empirical and ethnographic assessment of the American neo-Nazi skinheads. In M. S. Hamm (Ed.), *Hate crime: International perspectives on causes and control* (pp. 105–140). Cincinnati, OH: Anderson.

Hamm, M. S. (1993). *American skinheads: The criminology and control of hate crime.* Westport, CT: Praeger.

Heitmeyer, W., Buhse, H., & Liebe-Freund, J. (1992). *Die Bielefelder Rechtsextremismus-Studie: Erste Langzeituntersuchung zur politischen Sozialisation männlicher Jugendlicher.* Weinheim: Juventa.

Herek, G. M., Cogan, J. C., & Gillis, J. R. (2002). Victim experiences in hate crimes based on sexual orientation. *Journal of Social Issues, 58*, 319–339.

Hess, H. (1997). Skins, Stigmata und Strafrecht. *Kriminologisches Journal, 29*, 38–51.

Hewitt, R. (2005). *White backlash and the politics of multiculturalism.* Cambridge: Cambridge University Press.

Hopf, C., Rieker, P., Sanden-Marcus, M., & Schmidt, C. (1995). *Familie und Rechtsextremismus: familiale Sozialisation und rechtsextreme Orientierungen junger Männer.* Weinheim: Juventa.

Hovland, C. I., & Sears, R. R. (1940). Minor studies of aggression: VI. Correlation of lynchings with economic indices. *Journal of Psychology, 9*, 301–310.

Ireland, P. R. (1997). Socialism, unification policy and the rise of racism in eastern Germany. *International Migration Review, 31*, 541–568.

Jäger, S., & Kretschmer, D. (1998). Die Medien als Anstifter der Brandstifter? Völkischer Nationalismus in den Medien. In S. Jäger (Ed.), *Der Spuk ist nicht vorbei: Völkisch-nationalistische Ideologeme im öffentlichen Diskurs der Gegenwart* (pp. 120–213). Duisburg, Ger.: Duisburger Institut für Sprach- und Sozialforschung.

Jenness, V., & Broad, K. (1997). *Hate crimes: New social movements and the politics of violence.* New York: Aldine de Gruyter.

Jenness, V., & Grattet, R. (2001). *Making hate a crime: From social movement to law enforcement.* New York: The Russell Sage Foundation.

Johnson, S. D., & Byers, B. D. (2003). Attitudes toward hate crime laws. *Journal of Criminal Justice, 31*, 227–235.

Karapin, R. (1996). Explaining the surge in right-wing violence by German youth. Manuscript. New York: Hunter College. Unpubl. Ms.

Karapin, R. (2002). Antiminority riots in unified Germany: Cultural conflicts and mischanneled political participation. *Comparative Politics, 34*, 147–167.

King, R. D. (2007). The context of minority group threat: Race, institutions, and complying with hate crime law. *Law and Society Review, 41*, 189–224.

King, R. D., & Brustein, W. I. (2006). A political threat model of intergroup violence: Jews in pre-World War II Germany. *Criminology, 44*, 867–891.

Kleg, M. (1993). *Hate, prejudice, and racism.* Albany, NY: State University of New York.

Koopmans, R. (1996). Explaining the rise of racist and extreme right violence in Western Europe: Grievances or opportunities? *European Journal of Political Research, 30*, 185–216.

Koopmans, R., & Olzak, S. (2004). Discursive opportunities and the evolution of right-wing violence in Germany. *American Journal of Sociology, 110*, 198–230.

Krueger, A. B., & Pischke, J-S. (1997). A statistical analysis of crime against foreigners in unified Germany. *The Journal of Human Resources, 32*, 182–209.

Leenen, W. R. (1995). Ausländerfeindlichkeit und politische Öffentlichkeit. *Deutschland Archiv, 28*, 603–624.

Levin, B. (2002). From slavery to hate crime laws: The emergence of race and status-based protection in American criminal law. *Journal of Social Issues, 58*, 227–245.

Levin, J., & McDevitt, J. (2002). *Hate crimes revisited: America's war on those who are different.* Cambridge, MA: Westview Press.

Levin, J., & McDevitt, J. (1993). *Hate crimes: The rising tide of bigotry and bloodshed.* New York: Plenum Press.

LeVine, R. A., & Campbell, D. T. (1972). *Ethnocentrism: Theories of conflict, ethnic attitudes, and group behavior.* New York: Wiley.

Maaz, H-J. (1991). *Der Gefühlsstau: Ein Psychogramm der DDR.* Berlin: Argon.

Macpherson, Sir W. (1999) *The Stephen Lawrence inquiry. Report of an inquiry by Sir William Macpherson of Cluny.* Presented to Parliament by the Secretary of State for the Home Department by Command of Her Majesty. London: The Stationery Office.

McClintock, M. (2005). *Everyday fears: A survey of violent hate crimes in Europe and North America.* New York: Human Rights First.

McDevitt, J., Levin, J., & Bennett, S. (2002). Hate crime offenders: An expanded typology. *Journal of Social Issues, 58,* 303–317.

McFalls, L. H. (1997). Living with which past? Postwall, postwar German national identity. In S. Denham, I. Kacandes, & J. Petropoulos (Eds.), *A user's guide to German cultural studies* (pp. 297–308). Ann Arbor: University of Michigan Press.

Merkl, P., & Weinberg, L. (Eds.), (1997). *The revival of right-wing extremism in the 1990s.* London: Cass.

Messner, S. F., McHugh, S., & Felson, R. B. (2004). Distinctive characteristics of assaults motivated by bias. *Criminology, 42,* 585–618.

Miller, N.E. (1948). Theory and experiment relating to psychoanalytic displacement to stimulus-response generalization. *Journal of Abnormal and Social Psychology, 43,* 155–178.

Müller, J. (1997). *Täterprofile. Hintergründe rechtsextremistisch motivierter Gewalt.* Wiesbaden: Deutscher Universitäts-Verlag.

Olzak, S. (1989). Labor unrest, immigration, and ethnic conflict in urban America, 1880–1914. *American Journal Sociology 94,* 1303–1333.

Petrosino, C. (2003). Connecting the past to the future: Hate crime in America. In B. Perry (Ed.), *Hate and bias Crime* (pp. 9–26). New York: Routledge.

Pinderhughes, H. L. (1993). The anatomy of racially motivated violence in New York City: A case study of youth in southern Brooklyn. *Social Problems, 40,* 478–492.

Prowe, D. (1997). National identity and racial nationalism in the new Germany: Nazism versus the contemporary radical right. *German Politics and Society, 15,* 1–21.

Quinkert, A., & Jäger, S. (1991). Warum dieser Hass in Hoyerswerda? Die rassistische Hetze von BILD gegen Flüchtlinge im Herbst '91. DISS-Skript, No. 4. Duisburg: Duisburger Institut für Sprach- und Sozialforschung.

Raper, A. F. (1933). *The tragedy of lynching.* Chapel Hill: University of North Carolina Press.

Ray, L., & Smith, D. (2004). Racist offending, policing and community conflict. *Sociology, 38,* 681–699.

Rieder, J. (1985). *Canarsie: The Jews and Italians of Brooklyn against liberalism.* Cambridge, MA: Harvard University Press.

Rieker, P. (1997). *Ethnozentrismus bei jungen Männern: Fremdenfeindlichkeit und Nationalismus und die Bedingungen ihrer Sozialisation.* Weinheim: Juventa.

Roediger, H. L., & Stevens, M. C. (1970). The effects of delayed presentation of the object of aggression on pain-induced fighting. *Psychonomic Science, 21,* 55–56.

Ross, C. (1996). *Mordskameradschaft: Tim, unter Skinheads geraten.* Munich: Bertelsmann.

Scheffer, B., ed. (1997). *Medien und Fremdenfeindlichkeit: alltägliche Paradoxien, Dilemmata, Absurditäten und Zynismen.* Opladen: Leske und Budrich.

Shively, M. (2005). Study of literature and legislation on hate crime in America. United States Department of Justice. Retrieved May 24, 2006, from http://www.ncjrs.gov/pdffiles1/nij/grants/210300.pdf

Sibbitt, R. (1997). The perpetrators of racial harassment and violence. Home Office Research Study 176. London: Home Office.

Sichrovsky, P. (1993). *Unheilbar Deutsch: rechte Schicksale und Lebensläufe.* Köln: Kiepenheuer & Witsch.

Sidanius, J. & F. Pratto. (1999). *Social dominance: An intergroup theory of social hierarchy and oppression.* Cambridge: Cambridge University Press.

Sullaway, M. (2004). Psychological perspectives on hate crime laws. *Psychology, Public Policy, and Law, 10,* 250–292.

Suttles, G. D. (1972). *The social construction of communities.* Chicago, IL: University of Chicago Press.

Thränhardt, D. (1995). The political uses of xenophobia in England, France and Germany. *Party Politics, 1,* 323–345.

Tolnay, S. E., & Beck, E. M. (1995). *A festival of violence: An analysis of Southern lynchings, 1882–1930.* Urbana: University of Illinois Press.

Tuttle, D. (1994). The assimilation of East Germany and the rise of identity-based violence against foreigners in the unified German state. *German Politics and Society, 31,* 63–83.

Varshney, A. (2002). *Ethnic conflict and civic life: Hindus and Muslims in India.* New Haven, CT: Yale University Press.

von Trotha, T. (1995). Political culture, xenophobia and the development of the violence of the radical right in the Federal Republic of Germany. *Crime, Law, and Social Change, 24,* 37–47.

Wahl, K. (Ed.) (2003). *Skinheads, Neonazis, Mitläufer: Täterstudien und Prävention.* Opladen: Leske und Budrich.

Wahl, P. (1997). 'Wenn die Jungs mal loslegen': Anmerkungen zur Cliquen-Dynamik. In J. Kersten & H. Steinert (Eds.), *Jahrbuch für Rechts- und*

Kriminalsoziologie '96 (pp. 77–84). Baden-Baden: Nomos.

Wang, L. (1994). *Hate crime laws.* New York: Clark, Boardman, Callaghan.

Watts, M. W. (1996). Political xenophobia in the transition from socialism: Threat, racism and ideology among East German youth. *Political Psychology, 17,* 97–126.

Weitekamp, E., Kerner, H-J., & Herberger, S. (1996). Right-wing violence, xenophobia, and attitudes towards violence in Germany. Presented at the International. Study Group on Youth Violence and Control Conference, Minerva Center for Youth Policy, Haifa, Israel.

Willems, H. (1995). Development, patterns and causes of violence against foreigners in Germany. *Terrorism and Political Violence 7,* 162–181.

Willems, H., Eckert, R., Würtz, S., & Steinmetz, L. (1993). *Fremdenfeindliche Gewalt: Einstellungen, Täter, Konflikteskalation.* Opladen: Leske und Budrich.

Witte, R. (1995). Racist violence in Western Europe. *New Community, 21,* 489–500.

19

Racism

John F. Dovidio, Samuel L. Gaertner, and
Kerry Kawakami

ABSTRACT

Racism is a form of intergroup reaction (including thoughts, feelings, and behaviors) that systematically advantages one's own group and/or disadvantages another group defined by racial difference. Racism occurs at different social levels – culturally, institutionally, and individually. Individual racism, which is the focus of this chapter, involves the actions of individuals who act unfairly to restrict the opportunities of racialized groups. Although blatant racism continues to exist, it has substantially declined and new, more subtle forms of individual racism have emerged. In this chapter, we examine the psychological foundation of racism – social categorization. We then focus our review on four contemporary approaches to individual racism: symbolic, modern, aversive, and implicit racism. We conclude by summarizing dynamic similarities and differences among these perspectives and identifying the implications for strategies and interventions to combat racism.

RACISM

Racism represents an organized system of privilege and bias that systematically disadvantages a group of people perceived to belong to a specific race. When social categories are *racialized*, based most typically on their physical appearance, ethnicity, or religion, people attribute the observed characteristics of the group to genetically heritable qualities. There are three defining elements of racism. First, it reflects a culturally-shared belief that groups have distinguishing race-based characteristics that are common to their members. Second, the perceived inherent racial characteristics of another group make it inferior to one's own group. Third, racism involves not only negative attitudes and beliefs but also the

social power that enables these to translate into disparate outcomes that disadvantage other groups or offer unique advantages to one's own at the expense of others.

Racism is related to concepts such as discrimination, prejudice, and stereotyping but is more encompassing. Because racism is a culturally shared system of beliefs, it may be supported by 'evidence' of group difference and inferiority and may be sanctioned by social norms, policies, and laws. Although racism typically involves negative attitudes, it can also reflect a paternalistic orientation that fosters the dependency of a group or a set of beliefs that may ostensibly be favorable in some ways but that systematically limits the opportunities for group members and undermines their dignity.

In this chapter, we briefly review the history of the concepts of race and racism and discuss how racism can occur at cultural, institutional, and individual levels. Next, we examine the psychological foundation of racism – social categorization. We then focus our review on four contemporary approaches to individual racism. We conclude by summarizing dynamic similarities and differences among these perspectives and identifying the implications for strategies and interventions to combat racism.

BRIEF HISTORY OF RESEARCH ON RACE AND RACISM

The concept of race has played a central role in intergroup relations for centuries across a range of different societies (e.g., Ancient Egyptian and classic Greek, Roman, and Chinese civilizations). The concept of race acquired more formal status in science from the seventeenth through nineteenth centuries as a consequence of European imperialism and colonialism. The concept of race and associated beliefs about a hierarchy of races supported the exploitation of other groups and justified the subordination of certain groups as slaves during this period. Emerging sciences in the eighteenth and nineteenth centuries reinforced the concept of race, as well as racial hierarchies in characteristics such as intelligence. In the early 1900s in the United States, psychologists contributed to the social and intellectual climate that emphasized essential group differences and a 'natural' hierarchy of racial and ethnic groups by attributing immigrant group IQ differences to genetic qualities (Goddard, 1917).

By the mid-twentieth century, however, psychologists began to question the validity of broad inferences about fundamental differences in human capacities based on race. Racial prejudice and bias came to be recognized more generally in US society as unfair and irrational. In the late-1930s through the 1950s, stimulated politically by the Nazis' rise to power in Germany, historically by the Holocaust, and intellectually by the

classic work on the authoritarian personality (Adorno, Frenkel-Brunswik, Levinson, et al., 1950), racial biases were seen not simply as disruptions in rational processes but also as dangerous aberrations from normal thinking. As McConahay (1986) remarked, 'Hitler gave racism a bad name' (p. 121).

The term racism, as a bias distinct from personal prejudice, stereotyping, and discrimination was popularized by its use in the *Report of the National Advisory Commission on Civil Disorders* (1968). Whereas psychological work on prejudice, stereotyping, and discrimination traditionally focused on intrapsychic (e.g., cognitive, motivational, or psychodynamic) processes and interactions between individuals, racism operates significantly at broader social levels, as well. Although the specific form that racism takes evolves over time, adapting to social and cultural changes, it consistently functions to establish or reinforce the advantage of one group over others. In addition to operating through personal prejudice, stereotyping, and discrimination, racism is reflected in social codes (e.g., laws and standards) and institutions (Feagin, 2006).

The unique power of racism resides in how it can shape members of different groups to think and behave in ways that contribute to the perpetuation of group disparities, without necessarily involving their intention, awareness, or active support. Jones (1997) identified three applications of the term racism: cultural racism, institutional racism, and individual racism. Cultural racism involves beliefs about the superiority of one's racial cultural heritage over those of other races. Cultural racism occurs when one group exerts power to define cultural values for the society. It involves not only the preference for the culture, heritage, and values of one's own group (ethnocentrism) but also the imposition of this culture on other groups. As a consequence, the essence of racism is communicated to, and by, members of all racial groups in everyday activities and is passed on across generations.

Racism that becomes embedded in culture can also affect the personal identities and ideologies of minority group members in fundamental ways. In particular, racial identities develop as a function of one's experiences as a group member and how one interprets, internalizes, and adjusts to those experiences. The racial identity and culture of Black Americans, for example, have been hypothesized to reflect an evolutionary component, which developed from the cultural foundation of an African past, and a reactionary component, which is an adaptation to the historical and contemporary challenges of minority status in the United States. Because of the pervasiveness of racism, Black Americans may activate in their own minds racial stereotypes about their group, even without endorsement, that can adversely influence their performance in significant ways (i.e., 'stereotype threat' see Chapter 23 by Quinn, Kallen, & Spencer).

Under some circumstances, members of the target racial group may adopt and endorse system-justifying ideologies of the dominant cultural group that distract attention away from group-based disparities and inequity (Jost & Hunyady, 2005). Thus, members of a disadvantaged group may develop a 'false consciousness' in which they comply with and endorse cultural values that systematically disadvantage them. For example, an exclusive emphasis on individually-oriented meritocracy may obscure cultural forces in racism and lead to an over-reliance on individual rather than the collective action needed to address racism.

Institutional racism refers to the manipulation or toleration of institutional practices, policies (e.g., admissions criteria), and laws (e.g., poll taxes) that unfairly restrict the opportunities of particular groups of people (see also Feagin, 2006). Institutional racism can develop from intentional biases (e.g., limiting immigration on the basis of assumptions about the inferiority of other groups) or motivations to provide resources to one's own group (e.g., attempts to limit another group's voting power). However, it does not require individuals' intention to discriminate, the active support of individuals, or even the awareness of discrimination.

Institutional racism becomes 'ritualized' in ways that minimize the effort and energy individuals and groups need to expend to support it. In addition, it can also occur as a by-product of policies with one explicit goal but with unintended systematic race-based effects (e.g., harsher penalties for trafficking crack cocaine, which is more common among Blacks, than for powder cocaine, which is more common among Whites).

Institutional racism is typically not widely recognized as being racist or unfair because it is embedded in laws (which define what is right and moral) and accompanied by racial ideologies that justify it. The media and public discourse often direct attention away from potential institutional biases and instead focus on common connections or shared identities that can promote more harmonious group relations while preserving group-based disparities, privilege, and disadvantage in the *status quo* (Dovidio, Gaertner, & Saguy, 2009). Once social norms, laws, and policies are established, awareness of unfair treatment and consequences is needed to stimulate individual or collective action for social change toward equality.

Individual racism is closely affiliated with racial prejudice, stereotyping, and discrimination. Although prejudice has generally been conceptualized as an attitude, prejudice scales often include items concerning the defining elements of racism – specifically, endorsement of statements about innate group differences, the relative inferiority of the other group, and policies that reinforce or exacerbate group differences in fundamental resources (e.g., employment opportunities, health). Stereotypes often develop to justify group disparities that are actually rooted in cultural, institutional, or individual biases. Personal discrimination operates systematically not only to promote one's own advantage but also the advantaged position of one's group (Bobo, 1999). Because other chapters in this volume (for example, Henry's Chapter 26) emphasize the dynamics related to racism at broader levels, the remainder of this chapter focuses on processes involved in individual racism.

LITERATURE REVIEW: SOCIAL CATEGORIZATION AND RACISM

Whereas psychologists earlier considered racism to be a form of abnormal human functioning, researchers currently recognize that, at the individual level, racism is rooted in normal psychological processes. One fundamental process involves humans' propensity to categorize objects and people. Categorization forms an essential basis for human perception, cognition, and functioning; it is a critical process in the way that people actively derive meaning from complex environments. Categorization enables decisions to be made quickly about incoming information because the instant an object is categorized, it is assigned the properties shared by other category members. In this respect, people compromise total accuracy for efficiency when confronted with the often overwhelming complexity of their social world (see Fiske & Russell's Chapter 7).

Social categorization – the psychological classification of people into discrete groups – often occurs automatically on the basis of physical similarity, proximity, or shared fate (Campbell, 1958). Social categorization has immediate and profound effects on the perceptions of groups and their members. When people (or objects) are categorized into groups, actual differences between members of the same category tend to be perceptually minimized while differences between groups tend to become exaggerated and overgeneralized (Tajfel, 1969). Moreover, social categorization typically involves the identification of the individual with one of the groups, the ingroup, often to the exclusion of other groups (outgroups).

Perceiving a distinction between ingroup and outgroup members as a consequence of social categorization significantly shapes social perception, affect, cognition, and behavior (Tajfel & Turner, 1979; Turner, Hogg, Oakes, et al., 1987; see also Abrams & Hogg's Chapter 11). Emotionally, people spontaneously experience more positive affect toward other members of the ingroup than toward members of the outgroup (Otten & Moskowitz, 2000). Cognitively, people process information more deeply for ingroup than outgroup members (Van Bavel, Packer, & Cunningham, 2008), tend to discount negative behaviors of ingroup members (Hewstone, 1990), and encode negative actions of outgroup members in abstract ways (e.g., dishonest) that make these attributions more difficult to disconfirm in the future when encountering specific inconsistent instances (Maass, Salvi, Arcuri, et al., 1989). Behaviorally, people are more trusting of ingroup rather than outgroup members (Foddy, Platow, & Yamagishi, 2009), more helpful and cooperative with ingroup members (Dovidio, Gaertner, Validzic, et al., 1997), and they tend to behave in a more greedy and less trustworthy way toward members of other groups than if they were reacting to each other as individuals (Insko, Schopler, Gaertner, et al., 2001).

Traditionally, intergroup biases have been measured in explicit ways, which allow people to control their responses to appear in socially desirable ways. However, considerable recent attention has been devoted to implicit biases. In contrast to explicit processes, which are conscious and deliberative, implicit processes involve a lack of awareness and intention. The mere presence of the attitude object is often sufficient to activate the associated stereotype and attitude automatically. Implicit biases arise through overlearned associations (Kawakami, Dovidio, Moll, et al., 2000), which may be rooted in repeated personal experience, widespread media exposure, or cultural representations of different groups. In the United States, people automatically categorize others based on race, gender, and age, and these categories immediately elicit implicit evaluations and beliefs about members of the group (Blair, 2001) that systematically influence their thoughts and actions in biased ways (Greenwald, Poehlman, Uhlmann, et al., 2009).

Importantly, there are two aspects of social categorization that promote racism, beyond simply interpersonal prejudice, stereotyping, and discrimination. First, people often perceive a social category as a particular form of a *natural category*, in which members are defined by a shared genetic structure. As a consequence, people perceive the members of the group as possessing a common essence. Jost and Hamilton (2005: 213) further observed, 'Once a group is perceived as a natural kind – as having some unalterable essence – then it affords greater confidence in drawing inferences … about its members. As a result, perceivers make sweeping generalizations … about all group members, who are seen as being very similar to one another, especially on attributes related to the 'essential' basis for category membership.' Second, because individuals derive self-esteem (Tajfel & Turner, 1979) and a fundamental sense of the self (Turner, Hogg, Oakes, et al., 1987) from their group membership and social identity, social categorizations that produce ingroup–outgroup distinctions also arouse motivations to see one's group in relatively positive ways. The 'positive distinctiveness' of one's group can be achieved by identifying and/or emphasizing dimensions on which one's group is superior compared to other groups or by actively engaging in various forms of derogation and discrimination that create or reinforce the superior status of one's group (see also the Chapter 11 by Abrams & Hogg). Differential treatment of ingroup versus outgroup members, whether rooted in favoritism for one's own group or biases against the other group, contribute to the advantaged position of one's own group (Sidanius & Pratto, 1999). Thus social categorization produces perceptions and motivations that play central roles in racism.

FRAMEWORK FOR UNDERSTANDING CONTEMPORARY RACISM

Personal prejudices often translate into individual racism when they are manifested in actions that have the power to unfairly restrict the opportunities of racialized groups.

Notably, approaches to individual racism have emphasized both blatant and subtle influences (Kovel, 1970; Pettigrew & Meertens, 1995). Some of these approaches focus on how racism functions to fulfill personal needs and desires. Much of the traditional work on personality and prejudice, such as work on the authoritarian personality (Adorno, Frenkel-Brunswik, Levinson, et al., 1950; see the Chapter 10 by Son Hing & Zanna) was based on a Freudian psychoanalytic model that assumes that prejudice is an indicator of an underlying intrapsychic conflict. According to theorizing about the authoritarian personality, individual racism originates from socialization experiences with punitive parents who supported hierarchical relations (Adorno, Frenkel-Brunswik, Levinson, et al., 1950). Repressed anger towards punitive parental authority, identification with this authority, and displacement of this hostility onto other groups were hypothesized to account for the biases of authoritarians toward a range of different groups (see Duckitt, 2005).

Alternatively, nonpsychodynamic models have proposed that individual racism is the result of motivations to restore feelings of self-esteem (Fein & Spencer, 1997) or support a social hierarchy that favors one's group (Bobo, 1999). For example, social dominance theory (Sidanius & Pratto, 1999) assumes that people who endorse hierarchical relations between groups and who see intergroup relations in terms of group competition will be especially biased toward outgroups (see Son Hing & Zanna's Chapter 10). Indeed, functional relations between groups exert a substantial influence on intergroup bias generally, as well as racism in particular. Theories based on functional relations often point to competition and consequent perceived threat as a fundamental cause of intergroup prejudice and conflict. Realistic group conflict theory (Campbell, 1965; Sherif, 1966), for example, posits that perceived group competition for resources produces intergroup bias and conflict. In addition, Esses and her colleagues have found that individuals in Canada and the United States who perceive greater threat from immigrants are more biased against them (e.g., Esses, Dovidio, Jackson, et al., 2001; see also Esses, Jackson, and Bennett-AbuAyyash's Chapter 14 in this volume). In contrast, cooperatively interdependent relations between members of different groups that have positive outcomes reduce bias and promote intergroup harmony.

Functional relations do not have to involve explicit competition with members of other groups to generate biases. In the absence of any direct evidence, people typically presume that members of other groups are competitive. Moreover, discrimination can serve less tangible collective functions, such as achieving status and prestige, as well as concrete instrumental objectives. Perceived competition for both material resources (e.g., water, agricultural land) and less tangible resources (e.g., status and ethnic identity of the country) have been identified as critical elements of violent intergroup conflicts in the Sudan (Esses & Jackson, 2008), Rwanda (Adelman, 2008), and former Yugoslavia (Staub, 1996).

Contemporary approaches to individual racism acknowledge the persistence of blatant, intentional forms of racism resulting from individual personality, ideological differences, or perceived competition. However, these approaches also generally posit the existence of new forms of racism that may be based more in unconscious (implicit) biases, reflect ambivalence between these negative feelings and personal standards or norms against bias (see also Crandall & Eshleman, 2003), and operate more subtly and indirectly to produce individual racism. In the remainder of this section we review research on symbolic, modern, aversive, and implicit racism. The symbolic and modern racism frameworks, which emphasize political behavior, are closely tied to the US context. However, the general principles underlying aversive racism and implicit racism have been applied more generally cross-culturally. One common theme that these approaches share is that racism persists despite significant decreases in overt expressions of bias over time.

Symbolic racism

Symbolic racism theory (Sears & Henry, 2005) developed in response to a practical problem: the failure of traditional, 'old-fashioned' racism items to predict people's actual positions on racially-targeted policies and Black political candidates. Sears, Henry, and Kosterman (2000) observed, 'Few Whites now support the core notions of old-fashioned racism ... Our own view is that the acceptance of formal equality is genuine but that racial animus has not gone away; it has just changed its principal manifestations' (p. 77). Symbolic racism reflects the unique synthesis of politically conservative, individualistic values, and early-acquired negative racial affect, and it usually develops in adolescence, earlier than many other socio-political beliefs. It involves four basic belief components: (a) discrimination against Blacks is 'a thing of the past,'(b) Blacks' failure to progress is attributable to their unwillingness to work hard enough, (c) Blacks make excessive demands, and (d) Blacks have gotten more than they deserve. It is measured using self-reported responses to items such as, 'If Blacks would only try harder, they could be as well off as Whites,' and 'Blacks are getting too demanding for equal rights' (see Henry & Sears, 2002).

Symbolic racism predicts people's political attitudes and behavior better than do measures of old-fashioned racism, realistic threats, perceived intergroup competition, nonracial attitudes and values (e.g., individualism, egalitarianism), and political party affiliation and political ideology (see Sears & Henry, 2005). Specifically, symbolic racism uniquely predicts White Americans' attitudes toward a range of racially-relevant policies, including busing for school integration and affirmative action, as well as less explicitly race-targeted policies that disproportionately affect Blacks, such as policies relating to crime and welfare. Symbolic racism also predicts opposition to Black candidates, such as Jesse Jackson or Barack Obama, as well as support for ethnocentric White candidates, such as the former Ku Klux Klan leader David Duke.

Modern racism

Although modern racism theory was derived from symbolic racism theory, the two positions diverge on the hypothesized origins of bias. Whereas symbolic racism proposes that Whites' negative attitudes relate directly to the threat Blacks pose to Whites' worldview by violating core principles of individualism, modern racism theory hypothesizes that a variety of types of negative affect (e.g., fear, disgust) that are acquired through early socialization persist into adulthood. Both theories, though, assume that these feelings are expressed indirectly and symbolically, in terms of more abstract social and political issues (McConahay, 1986).

Modern racism is assessed using the Modern Racism Scale, a self-report measure similar to that used to assess symbolic racism. The scale was originally designed to be an indirect measure of racism relative to old-fashioned racism and thus less susceptible to biasing by social desirability concerns (McConahay, 1986). Like symbolic racism, modern racism predicts voting against political candidates who are Black or sympathetic toward Blacks, and voting on policies designed to assist Blacks such as affirmative action and school integration programs. It also predicts these political attitudes better than conservatism, identification as a Democrat or Republican, education, and most importantly personal interests in the outcomes of a vote (Henry, 2010).

Modern racism and symbolic racism approaches have been challenged on similar conceptual grounds. Because the scales are not pure, direct measures of stereotypes or prejudice against Blacks, critics have argued that both modern racism and symbolic racism scales primarily tap core non-racial principles underlying conservatism (such as opposition to excessive government intervention) rather than a form of racism, and there is evidence that a subset of high modern racism scorers are, indeed, principled conservatives rather than racists (Son Hing, Chung-Yan, Hamilton, et al., 2008). However, the consistent relationship between direct measures of negative racial attitudes and modern racism attitudes suggests that anti-Black affect is a significant component of some modern and symbolic racists. Alternatively, recent criticisms of the Modern Racism Scale have contended that this measure should no longer be classified as an indirect measure but as a blatant measure of racism. Indeed, responses on the Modern Racism Scale appear to be more susceptible to social desirability influences and self-presentational concerns than in the past (Fazio, Jackson, Dunton, et al., 1995). As McConahay (1986) noted over 20 years ago, 'It is expected that new items will have to be generated for the Modern Racism Scale as new issues emerge in American race relations and some of the current items become more reactive while the ambivalence lingers' (p. 123). Nevertheless, scores on the Modern Racism Scale still predict responses to political issues in ways independent of measures of blatant prejudice toward Blacks.

Aversive racism

Aversive racism represents yet another form of contemporary of racism (Kovel, 1970). Aversive racists sympathize with victims of past injustice, support principles of racial equality, and genuinely regard themselves as nonprejudiced, but at the same time possess conflicting, often nonconsious, negative feelings and beliefs about Blacks that are rooted in basic psychological processes (e.g., social categorization) that promote racial bias (Gaertner & Dovidio, 1986). Like symbolic and modern racism, and in contrast to the traditional form of racism, aversive racism is hypothesized to operate in subtle and indirect ways. However, unlike symbolic and modern racism approaches that focus on self-report scales to measure these concepts and their relationship to political behavior, work on aversive racism has traditionally examined a broader array of behaviors and differences in responses to Blacks and Whites. In addition, whereas modern and symbolic racism characterize the attitudes of political conservatives, aversive racism characterizes the biases of those who are politically liberal (Nail, Harton, & Decker, 2003) and believe that they are not prejudiced, but whose unconscious negative feelings and beliefs get expressed in subtle, indirect, and often rationalizable ways (see Dovidio & Gaertner, 2004; Gaertner & Dovidio, 1986; Pearson, Dovidio, & Gaertner, 2009). Because the basic premises of aversive racism are not tied to specific scale items concerning the US political context, the principles of aversive racism are applicable to intergroup behaviors of dominant groups toward minorities in other nations that have strong traditional egalitarian values, such as Canada (Son Hing, Chung-Yan, Hamilton, et al., 2008), England (Hodson, Hooper, Dovidio, et al., 2005), and the Netherlands (Kleinpenning & Hagendoorn, 1993).

In contrast to traditional approaches that emphasize the psychopathology of prejudice, the feelings and beliefs that underlie aversive racism are rooted in normal, often adaptive, psychological processes, such as social categorization and sociocultural influences, that are difficult even for people with strong egalitarian values to escape (see Gaertner & Dovidio, 1986). In addition, the negative feelings that aversive racists have toward Blacks do not reflect open hostility or hatred. Instead, aversive racists' reactions may involve discomfort, anxiety, or fear. That is, while they find Blacks 'aversive,' at the same time they also find any suggestion that they might be prejudiced 'aversive' as well.

The aversive racism framework also helps to identify when discrimination against Blacks and other minority groups will occur. Whereas old-fashioned racists exhibit a direct and overt pattern of discrimination, aversive racists' actions may appear more variable and inconsistent. Although at times they discriminate (manifesting their negative feelings) and at other times they do not (reflecting their egalitarian beliefs), their discriminatory behavior is predictable.

Because aversive racists consciously recognize and endorse egalitarian values and because they truly aspire to be nonprejudiced, they will *not* act inappropriately in situations with strong social norms when discrimination would be obvious to others and, just as importantly, to themselves. Specifically, when they are presented with a situation in which the normatively appropriate response is clear, aversive racists will not discriminate against Blacks. In these contexts, aversive racists will be especially motivated to avoid feelings, beliefs, and behaviors that could be associated with racist intent. Wrongdoing of this type would directly threaten their nonprejudiced self-image. However, aversive racists' unconscious negative feelings and beliefs, will be expressed but usually in subtle, indirect, and rationalizable ways. For instance, discrimination will occur in situations in which normative structure is weak, when the guidelines for appropriate behavior are vague, or when the basis for social judgment is ambiguous. In addition, discrimination will occur when an aversive racist can justify or rationalize a negative response on the basis of some factor other than race. Under these circumstances, aversive racists may engage in behaviors that ultimately harm Blacks but in ways that allow aversive racists to maintain their self-image as nonprejudiced and that insulate them from recognizing that their behavior is not egalitarian. Also, because it is typically less recognizable as bias, aversive racists often discriminate by exhibiting overly favorable responses to ingroup members (e.g., discounting negative aspects of their record when making personnel decisions) rather then overly negative responses to outgroup members.

Support for the aversive racism framework has been obtained across a broad range of experimental paradigms and participant populations, including helping behavior inside and outside of the laboratory, selection decisions in employment and college admission, interpersonal judgments, and policy and legal decisions (see Dovidio & Gaertner, 2004). Early tests of the aversive racism framework focused on prosocial behavior for both theoretical and practical reasons. Theoretically, because aversive racists are hypothesized to be particularly effective at censoring negative behavior toward Blacks, the biases associated with aversive racism may often manifest as differential *prosocial* responses toward Blacks and Whites in need. From a practical perspective, the Kerner Commission (*Report of the National Advisory Commission on Civil Disorders*, 1968), charged with investigating the causes of the 1967 race riots in the United States, cited White America's failure to assist Blacks in need, rather than actively trying to harm Blacks, as a primary cause of racial disparities and, ultimately, civil unrest. Indeed, it was research on the differential behavior of Whites toward Black and White motorists who were stranded on a highway that represented the first empirical work on aversive racism (Gaertner, 1973). The results of a meta-analysis of 31 experiments on Whites' interracial helping behavior conducted over the past 40 years evidence a stable pattern of discrimination reflective of aversive racism that has not subsided over time (Saucier, Miller, & Doucet, 2005). Based on these findings, the authors concluded that racism and discrimination against Blacks 'can and will exist as long as individuals harbor negativity toward Blacks at the implicit level' (p. 14).

Another domain in which aversive racism was hypothesized to emerge was in Whites' education and employment selection and evaluation decisions. In particular, the aversive racism framework suggests that biases against Black job applicants and employees, such as in hiring and promotion decisions, would likely not surface when candidates have impeccably strong qualifications but rather would occur when a candidate's qualifications are more marginal and could be argued either way on grounds that are ostensibly unrelated to race. Dovidio and Gaertner (2000), who examined White college students' hiring recommendations for Black and White applicants for a selective campus position in 1989 and 1999 found results consistent with this hypothesis. In addition, when the responses of participants in these two years were compared, whereas overt expressions of prejudice (measured by items on a self-report scale) declined over this 10-year period, the pattern of subtle discrimination in selection decisions remained essentially unchanged. More recent evidence reveals that people systematically shift the weight they place on different criteria to justify their less favorable evaluations and decisions about minority candidates (Hodson, Dovidio, & Gaertner, 2002).

Additional evidence for the persistence and prevalence of aversive racism comes from experiments on simulated juror decision making. In one such study, Johnson, Whitestone, Jackson, et al., (1995) examined the impact of introducing inadmissable (and nonrace-related) evidence that was damaging to a Black or White defendant's case on Whites' judgments of the defendant's guilt. Although there was no evidence of bias as a function of defendant race when participants were exposed to only admissible evidence, consistent with theorizing related to aversive racism, exposure to potentially incriminating evidence deemed inadmissible by the court increased perceptions that the Black, but not White, defendant was guilty of the crime. Furthermore, when probed about their decisions, participants' reported that they believed that the inadmissible evidence had *less* effect on their decisions when the defendant was Black than when the defendant was White, suggesting the unconscious and unintentional nature of their bias. Hodson, Hooper, & Dovidio, et al. (2005) replicated these findings in the United Kingdom using a similar paradigm, demonstrating the cross-national pervasiveness of this phenomenon.

Overall, these studies show that, in contrast to the dramatic decline in overt expressions of prejudice, subtle forms of discrimination continue to exist. Despite its subtle expression, the consequences of aversive racism are as significant and pernicious (e.g., the restriction of economic opportunity) as those of the traditional, overt form. One limitation of much of this earlier work on aversive racism, however, was that unlike symbolic and modern racism there was no assessment of individual differences in people's hypothesized unconscious negative racial feelings and beliefs. Therefore, respondents who reported that they were low in prejudice were presumed generally to be aversive racists.

Recent developments in assessing implicit biases, however, provide a solution to this problem. Because aversive racists are characterized as having explicit egalitarian attitudes but negative implicit racial attitudes (Dovidio & Gaertner, 2004), measures of prejudice at both a more conscious *and* nonconscious level are necessary. Whereas self-report methods are often used to assess explicit attitudes, implicit attitudes are typically gauged with response latency procedures, memory tasks, physiological measures (e.g., heart rate and galvanic skin response), and indirect self-report measures (e.g., biases in behavioral and trait attributions). The Implicit Association Test (IAT; see Greenwald, Poehlman, Uhlmann, et al. 2009), for example, relies on the basic assumption that when categorizing groups of stimuli people are faster when these groups are similar in valence and share a response key than when the groups of stimuli are dissimilar in valence. So, for example, if people associate negativity with Blacks, they would be faster at responding when pictures of Blacks and unpleasant concepts shared a response key than when pictures of Blacks and pleasant concepts shared a response key (see https://implicit.harvard.edu/). Importantly, responses on these types of measure are difficult to control and are often unintended.

New methodologies for assessing implicit attitudes have become increasingly useful in differentiating aversive racists (those who endorse egalitarian values but harbor implicit racial biases) from individuals who are truly nonprejudiced (those who endorse egalitarian ideals but do not harbor negative implicit biases) (Son Hing, Chung-Yan, & Hamilton, et al., 2008). Consistent with the aversive racism framework, whereas the majority of Whites in the United States appear nonprejudiced on self-report (explicit) measures of prejudice, a similar percentage of Whites typically show evidence of racial biases on implicit measures that are largely dissociated from their explicit views (e.g., Greenwald, Poehlman, Uhlmann, et al., 2009). Thus, a substantial proportion of Whites in the United States can be characterized as exhibiting reactions toward Blacks consistent with aversive racism.

Implicit racism

Initially, research on implicit attitudes focused on developing and refining measurement techniques, distinguishing implicit from explicit measures, and clarifying the origins and meaning of implicit measures of attitudes (cf. Karpinski & Hilton, 2001). More recent work has examined the predictive validity of implicit measures. A meta-analysis by Greenwald, Poehlman, & Uhlmann, (2009) of 122 research reports, for example, found that both implicit measures of attitudes such as the IAT and explicit measures predicted a range of behaviors to attitude objects (explicit attitudes average $r = .36$ and implicit attitudes average $r = .27$). However, the predictive validity of explicit measures for socially sensitive issues was much weaker. With respect to racial issues in particular, implicit attitudes (average $r = .24$) were a better predictor overall than explicit attitudes (average $r = .12$).

Notably, different theoretical perspectives suggest that a key factor in the relative validity of implicit and explicit measures for predicting behavior is the context in which the behavior occurs and the type of behavior being examined (Dovidio et al., 2001; Dovidio, Kawakami, Smoak, et al., 2009). For example, Fazio's (1990) MODE model indicates that whereas implicit measures will better predict spontaneous behaviors, explicit measures will better predict deliberative behaviors, including those in situations in which social desirability factors are salient (Fazio & Olson, 2003). Wilson, Lindsey, and Schooler (2000) also proposed that 'when dual attitudes exist, the implicit attitude is activated automatically, whereas the explicit one requires more capacity and motivation to retrieve from memory' (p. 104). Accordingly, the relative influence of explicit and implicit attitudes depends upon the type of response that is made. Explicit attitudes shape deliberative, well-considered responses in which the costs and benefits of various courses of action are weighed.

Implicit attitudes influence 'uncontrollable responses (e.g., some nonverbal behaviors) or responses that people do not view as an expression of their attitude and thus do not attempt to control' (p. 104). Thus, as in the MODE model, Wilson, Lindsey, and Schooler's position indicates that implicit measures of prejudice will better predict spontaneous interracial behavior, whereas explicit measures will better predict deliberative, controllable responses. Results related to racial attitudes and behaviors, in particular, and social attitudes and behaviors, in general, are largely consistent with this theorizing (for a review, see Dovidio, Kawakami, Smoak, et al., 2009).

These findings of different expressions of favorability of Whites in their spontaneous and deliberative behaviors can produce fundamental miscommunication between Blacks and Whites in interracial interaction. For instance from the perspective of aversive racism, Whites' explicit egalitarian attitudes may motivate favorable deliberative action (such as positive verbal expressions), but negative implicit attitudes may simultaneously produce undermining negative nonverbal behaviors. To the extent that most Whites harbor implicit racial biases but report being nonprejudiced, they will likely display conflicting signals about their feelings and beliefs toward Blacks in interracial interactions, which interferes with developing positive and cooperative intergroup relations (Dovidio, Kawakami, & Gaertner, 2002).

Son Hing and colleagues (2008) investigated another form of racial bias, discrimination against Asian job applicants in Canada, using a paradigm borrowed from research on aversive racism on candidate qualifications and selection decisions (Dovidio & Gaertner, 2000). Paralleling the findings of subtle bias against Blacks in the United States, these researchers found that when assessing candidates with more moderate qualifications, evaluators recommended White candidates more strongly for the position than Asian candidates with identical credentials. However, when evaluating candidates with exceptionally strong qualifications, no such selection

bias emerged. Moreover, Son Hing, Chung-Yan, Hamilton, et al. found that implicit bias against Asians (as measured by an IAT), but not explicit prejudice, predicted weaker support for hiring Asian candidates who had moderate qualifications. However, when the Asian candidate had distinctively strong qualifications (and a failure to hire the applicant could not be justified on the basis of factors other than race) neither implicit nor explicit prejudice predicted the hiring decision, which generally supported the hiring of the Asian applicant.

Taken together, current research reveals that implicit biases contribute in significant ways to racism. They contribute to disparate treatment of minorities in ways independent of explicit (self-reported) personal biases, and implicit biases play a particularly strong role in discrimination when people's cognitive resources are taxed, and in subtle forms of discrimination, which people find difficult to recognize, monitor, or control.

FUTURE DIRECTIONS

In summary, racism occurs at different social levels – culturally, institutionally, and individually. Blatant forms of individual racism continue to exist with negative consequences for Blacks and other racialized groups both inside and outside the United States. However, while expressions of overt prejudice and racism have substantially declined (see Dovidio & Gaertner, 2004), new more subtle forms of individual racism have emerged. Symbolic, modern, and aversive racism represent three such types of contemporary racism. Both symbolic and modern racism theories posit that the negative feelings toward Blacks which Whites acquire early in life blend with conservative, individualistic values to produce indirect biases toward Blacks. These biases commonly manifest themselves in positions on race-relevant social and political issues. Modern racists, like aversive racists, are relatively unaware of their racist feelings. Nevertheless, like aversive racism, the negative effects of modern and symbolic racism are observed primarily when discrimination can be justified on the basis of factors other than race. Thus, although the aversive racism framework often makes predictions similar to those of symbolic and modern racism theories, such as resistance to policies designed to benefit Blacks, it hypothesizes different underlying processes. Consistent with the assumed role of unconscious biases hypothesized in aversive racism, a rapidly growing literature documents the significant influence of implicit biases, both alone and in combination with explicit prejudice, on individual's discriminatory behavior.

The different processes hypothesized to be integral to contemporary forms of racism, particularly implicit and explicit responses, suggest potentially fruitful directions for research on the neurological underpinnings of individual racism. For example, the functional distinction between implicit and explicit biases and their potentially different influences have received converging support from work in cognitive neuroscience (see Chapter 4 by Quadflieg, Mason, & Macrae). Subliminal or brief exposure to Black faces elicits amygdala activation among Whites (which is related to an initial threat response) that is correlated with implicit racial attitudes (Cunningham, Johnson, & Raye, et al., 2004) but not to explicit attitudes (Phelps, O'Connor, Cunningham, et al., 2000). However, when conditions allow Whites to consciously control their responses, frontal activation (which is related to higher order executive function) also occurs. Thus, implicit and explicit attitudes appear to involve different neural circuits.

Another conceptual and practical challenge for future theorizing and research resides in developing strategies and interventions for combating these forms of contemporary racism. Traditional prejudice-reduction techniques have been concerned with changing conscious attitudes – old-fashioned racism – and direct explicit expressions of bias. Attempts to reduce these traditional forms of racial prejudice have typically involved educational strategies to enhance knowledge and appreciation of other groups (e.g.,

multicultural education programs), emphasize norms that prejudice is wrong, and involve straightforward messages (e.g., mass media appeals) (see Stephan & Stephan, 2001). However, because of its pervasiveness, subtlety, and complexity, the traditional techniques for eliminating bias that focus on the immorality of prejudice and illegality of discrimination are less likely to be effective for combating contemporary racism. Contemporary racists generally recognize that prejudice is bad, but they do not recognize that *they* are prejudiced.

Nevertheless, contemporary racism can be addressed with techniques aimed at its roots at both individual and collective levels. To the extent that negative implicit attitudes are related not only to aversive racism but are a component of the lingering negative affect assumed by symbolic and modern racism theories, interventions might productively focus on limiting the impact of, or changing, implicit bias. With respect to restricting the impact of implicit bias on behavior, it is possible for people with sufficient motivation and cognitive resources to control even relatively spontaneously expressed behavior (Dasgupta & Rivera, 2006; Olson & Fazio, 2004).

Other work suggests that implicit biases may not only be controllable under some conditions but that these biases can be reduced directly. To the extent that implicit attitudes and stereotypes are learned through socialization (Fazio & Olson, 2003; Karpinski & Hilton, 2001), they can also be unlearned or inhibited by well-learned countervailing influences. For example, extended practice in associating counter-stereotypic characteristics with racial and ethnic minority groups has been shown to inhibit the automatic activation of cultural stereotypes (Kawakami, Dovidio, Moll, et al., 2000). Likewise, consistently approaching a specific social category has been proven to be effective in increasing immediacy behavior and other actions related to creating social bonds with outgroup category members (Kawakami, Phills, Steele, et al., 2007). Implicit motivations to control prejudice can similarly inhibit the activation of spontaneous racial biases even when cognitive resources are depleted (Park, Glaser, & Knowles, 2008).

It may also be possible to capitalize on contemporary racists' conscious nonprejudiced intentions and induce self-motivated efforts to reduce the impact of unconscious biases by making them aware of these biases. Work by Monteith and colleagues (see Chapter 30 by Monteith, Arthur, & Flynn this volume) indicates that when low prejudiced people recognize discrepancies between their behavior toward minorities and their personal standards, they feel guilt and compunction, which subsequently produce motivations to respond without prejudice in the future. For example, Son Hing, Li, and Zanna (2002) exposed people identified as aversive racists (low in explicit prejudice but high in implicit prejudice) and nonprejudiced (low in both explicit and implicit prejudice) to a manipulation that made salient discrepancies between their behavior toward Asians and their nonprejudiced self-image. As the authors predicted, when these discrepancies were salient, aversive racists, who have underlying negative implicit attitudes, experienced uniquely high levels of guilt and exhibited a particularly strong motivation to engage in compensatory behavior.

In addition, when extended over time, this process of self-regulation can produce sustained changes in even automatic negative responses (Dovidio, Kawakami, & Gaertner, 2000). Moskowitz and colleagues (see Moskowitz & Ignarri, 2010, for a review) have found that interventions that enhance motivations to be egalitarian (e.g., having participants describe a personal incident in which they failed to be egalitarian) can not only attenuate but also actively *inhibit* nonconscious stereotyping. Repeated practice in inhibiting one's implicit bias may be one reason why people with more experience interacting with members of another group exhibit lower levels on implicit prejudice toward that group as a whole (see Tausch & Hewstone's Chapter 33).

To the extent that social categorization forms the foundation for intergroup bias generally and racism in particular, intervention can be targeted at the ways people categorize members of other racial groups. Social categorization is malleable; people can recategorize others in ways that fundamentally alter their responses. The interventions related to the common ingroup identity model (Gaertner & Dovidio, 2000; see Chapter 32 by Gaertner, Dovidio, & Houlette in this volume), for example, harness social categorization as a means to *reduce* intergroup bias. Specifically, if members of different groups are induced to think of themselves as a single superordinate in-group rather than as two separate groups, attitudes toward former out-group members will become more positive by reaping the benefits of in-group status. Enhancing the salience of a common ingroup identity has been shown to inhibit the activation of both implicit (Van Bavel & Cunningham, 2009) and explicit (Gaertner & Dovidio, 2000) biases.

SUMMARY AND CONCLUSION

In summary, racism permeates culture, institutions, and individual orientations toward minority group members. Its influence at each of these levels is often difficult to recognize and thus to combat. At the individual level, which was the focus of this chapter, overt and consciously endorsed racism have declined substantially over time in many countries. Nevertheless, subtle forms of racism continue to exist, driven in part by implicit biases, with consequences as severe as those related to old-fashioned racism. Thus, to contribute to the elimination of racism, future research needs not only to illuminate the dynamics of new forms of racism but also to develop new techniques to address the unique nature of contemporary racism.

ACKNOWLEDGEMENT

Preparation of this chapter was facilitated by a grant from the National Science Foundation #0613218 to Samuel L. Gaertner and John F.

Dovidio. Correspondence should be directed to: John F. Dovidio, Department of Psychology, Yale University, 2 Hillhouse Ave., P.O. Box 208205, New Haven, CT 06520. E-mail: john.dovidio@yale.edu

REFERENCES

Adelman, H. (2008). Theories of genocide: The case of Rwanda. In V. M. Esses & R. A. Vernon (Eds.), *Explaining the breakdown of ethnic relations: Why neighbors kill* (pp. 195–222). Malden, MA: Blackwell.

Adorno, T. W., Frenkel-Brunswik, E., Levinson, D. J., & Sanford, R. N. (1950). *The authoritarian personality.* New York: Harper.

Blair, I. V. (2001). Implicit stereotypes and prejudice. In G. B. Moskowitz (Ed.), *Cognitive social psychology: The Princeton symposium on the legacy and future of social cognition* (pp. 359–374). Mahwah, NJ: Erlbaum.

Bobo, L. D. (1999). Prejudice as group position: Microfoundations of a sociological approach to racism and race relations. *Journal of Social Issues, 55,* 445–472.

Campbell, D. T. (1958). Common fate, similarity and other indices of the status of aggregates of persons as social entities. *Behavioral Science, 3,* 14–25.

Campbell, D. T. (1965). Ethnocentric and other altruistic motives. In D. Levine (Ed.), *Nebraska symposium on motivation* (Vol. 13, ed., pp. 283–311). Lincoln, NE: University of Nebraska Press.

Crandall, C. S., & Eshleman, A. (2003). A justification-suppression model of the expression and experience of prejudice. *Psychological Bulletin, 129,* 414–446.

Cunningham, W. A., Johnson, M. K., Raye, C. L., Getenby, J. C., Gore, J. J., & Banaji, M. R. (2004). Separable neural components in the processing of Black and White faces. *Psychological Science, 15,* 806–813.

Dasgupta, N., & Rivera, L. M. (2006). From automatic anti-gay prejudice to behavior: The moderating role of conscious beliefs about gender and behavioral control. *Journal of Personality and Social Psychology, 91,* 268–280.

Dovidio, J. F., & Gaertner, S. L. (2000). Aversive racism and selection decisions: 1989 and 1999. *Psychological Science, 11,* 319–323.

Dovidio, J. F., & Gaertner, S. L. (2004). Aversive racism. In M. P. Zanna (Ed.), *Advances in experimental social psychology* (Vol. 36, pp. 1–51). San Diego, CA: Academic Press.

Dovidio, J. F., Gaertner, S. L., & Saguy, T. (2009). Commonality and the complexity of "we": Social attitudes and social change. *Personality and Social Psychology Review, 13,* 3–20.

Dovidio, J. F., Gaertner, S. L., Validzic, A., Matoka, K., Johnson, B., & Frazier, S. (1997). Extending the benefits of re-categorization: Evaluations, self-disclosure and helping. *Journal of Experimental Social Psychology, 33,* 401–420.

Dovidio, J. F., Kawakami, K., & Gaertner, S. L. (2000). Reducing contemporary prejudice: Combating explicit and implicit bias at the individual and intergroup level. In S. Oskamp (Ed.), *Reducing prejudice and discrimination* (pp. 137–163). Hillsdale, NJ: Erlbaum.

Dovidio, J. F., Kawakami, K., & Gaertner, S. L. (2002). Implicit and explicit prejudice and interracial interaction. *Journal of Personality and Social Psychology, 82,* 62–68.

Dovidio, J. F., Kawakami, K., Smoak, N., & Gaertner, S. L. (2009). The roles of implicit and explicit processes in contemporary prejudice. In R. E. Petty, R. H. Fazio, & P. Brinol (Eds.), *Attitudes: Insights from the new implicit measures* (pp. 165–192). New York: Psychology Press.

Duckitt, J. (2005). Personality and prejudice. In J. F. Dovidio, P. Glick, & L. A. Rudman (Eds.), *On the nature of prejudice: Fifty years after Allport* (pp. 395–412). Malden, MA: Blackwell.

Esses, V. M., & Jackson, L. M. (2008). Applying the Unified Instrumental Model of Group Conflict to understanding ethnic conflict and violence: The case of Sudan. In V. M. Esses & R. A. Vernon (Eds.), *Explaining the breakdown of ethnic relations: Why neighbors kill* (pp. 223–244). Malden, MA: Blackwell.

Esses, V. M., Dovidio, J. F., Jackson, L. M., & Armstrong, T. M. (2001). The immigration dilemma: The role of perceived group competition, ethnic prejudice, and national identity. *Journal of Social Issue, 57,* 389–412.

Fazio, R. H. (1990). Multiple processes by which attitudes guide behavior: The MODE Model as an integrative framework. In M. P. Zanna (Ed.), *Advances in experimental social psychology* (Vol. 23, pp. 75–109). Orlando, FL: Academic Press.

Fazio, R. H., & Olson, M. A. (2003). Implicit measures in social cognition research: Their meaning and uses. *Annual Review of Psychology, 54,* 297–327.

Fazio, R. H., Jackson, J. R., Dunton, B. C., & Williams, C. J. (1995). Variability in automatic activation as an unobtrusive measure of racial attitudes: A *bona fide* pipeline? *Journal of Personality and Social Psychology, 69,* 1013–1027.

Feagin, J. R. (2006). *Systemic racism: A theory of oppression.* New York: Routledge.

Fein, S., & Spencer, S. J. (1997). Prejudice as self-image maintenance: Affirming the self through derogating others. *Journal of Personality and Social Psychology, 73,* 31–44.

Foddy, M., Platow, M. J., & Yamagishi, T. (2009). Group-based trust in strangers: The role of stereotypes and expectations. *Psychological Science, 20,* 419–422.

Gaertner, S. L. (1973). Helping behavior and racial discrimination among liberals and conservatives. *Journal of Personality and Social Psychology, 25,* 335–341.

Gaertner, S. L., & Dovidio, J. F. (1986). The aversive form of racism. In J. F. Dovidio & S. L. Gaertner (Eds.), *Prejudice, discrimination, and racism* (pp. 61–89). Orlando, FL: Academic Press.

Gaertner, S. L., & Dovidio, J. F. (2000). *Reducing intergroup bias: The Common Ingroup Identity Model.* Philadelphia, PA: The Psychology Press.

Goddard, H. H. (1917). Mental tests and the immigrant. *Journal of Delinquency, 2,* 243–277.

Greenwald, A. G., Poehlman, T. A., Uhlmann, E. L., & Banaji, M. R. (2009). Understanding and using the Implicit Association Test: III. Meta-analysis of predictive validity. *Journal of Personality and Social Psychology, 97,* 17–41.

Henry, P. J. (2010). Modern racism. In J. M. Levine & M. A. Hogg, (Eds.), *Encyclopedia of group processes and intergroup relations* (Vol. 2, pp. 575–577). Thousand Oaks, CA: Sage.

Henry, P. J., & Sears, D. O. (2002). The Symbolic Racism 2000 Scale. *Political Psychology, 23,* 253–283.

Hewstone, M. (1990). The "ultimate attribution error"? A review of the literature on intergroup attributions. *European Journal of Social Psychology, 20,* 311–335.

Hodson, G., Hooper, H., Dovidio, J. F., & Gaertner, S. L. (2005). Aversive racism in Britain: Legal decisions and the use of inadmissible evidence. *European Journal of Social Psychology, 35,* 437–448.

Hodson, G., Dovidio, J. F., & Gaertner, S. L. (2002). Processes in racial discrimination: Differential weighting of conflicting information. *Personality and Social Psychology Bulletin, 28,* 460–471.

Insko, C. A., Schopler, J., Gaertner, L., Wildschut, T., Kozar, R., & Pinter, B., et al. (2001). Interindividual-intergroup discontinuity reduction through the anticipation of future interaction. *Journal of Personality and Social Psychology, 80,* 95–111.

Johnson, J. D., Whitestone, E., Jackson, L. A., & Gatto, L. (1995). Justice is still not colorblind: Differential racial effects of exposure to inadmissible evidence. *Personality and Social Psychology Bulletin, 21,* 893–898.

Jones, J. M. (1997). *Prejudice and racism* (2nd ed.). New York: McGraw-Hill.

Jost, J. T., & Hamilton, D. L. (2005). Stereotypes in our culture. In J. F. Dovidio, P. Glick, & L. A. Rudman (Eds.), *On the nature of prejudice: Fifty years after Allport* (pp. 208–224). Malden, MA: Blackwell.

Jost, J. T. & Hunyady, O. (2005). Antecedents and consequences of system justification ideologies. *Current Directions in Psychological Science, 14,* 260–264.

Karpinski, A., & Hilton, J. L. (2001). Attitudes and the Implicit Association Test. *Journal of Personality and Social Psychology, 81,* 774–788.

Kawakami, K, Dovidio, J. F., Moll, J., Hermsen, S., & Russin, A. (2000). Just say no (to stereotyping): Effects of training in trait negation on stereotype activation. *Journal of Personality and Social Psychology, 78,* 871–888.

Kawakami, K., Phills, C. E., Steele, J. R., & Dovidio, J. F. (2007). (Close) Distance makes the heart grow fonder: Improving implicit racial attitudes and interracial interactions through approach behaviors. *Journal of Personality and Social Psychology, 92,* 957–971.

Kleinpenning, G., & Hagendoorn, L. (1993). Forms of racism and the cumulative dimension. *Social Psychology Quarterly, 56,* 21–36.

Kovel, J. (1970). *White racism: A psychohistory.* New York: Pantheon.

Maass, A., Salvi, D., Arcuri, L., & Semin, G. R. (1989). Language use in intergroup contexts: The linguistic intergroup bias. *Journal of Personality and Social Psychology, 57,* 981–993.

McConahay, J. B. (1986). Modern racism, ambivalence, and the modern racism scale. In J. F. Dovidio & S. L. Gaertner (Eds.), *Prejudice, discrimination, and racism* (pp. 91–125). Orlando, FL: Academic Press.

Moskowitz, G. B., & Ignarri, C. (2010). Implicit goals and a proactive strategy of stereotype control. *Personality and Social Psychology Compass.* (in press).

Nail, P. R., Harton, H. C. & Decker, B. P. (2003) Political orientation and modern versus aversive racism: Tests of Dovidio and Gaertner's (1998) Integrated Model. *Journal of Personality and Social Psychology, 84,* 754–770.

Olson, M. A., & Fazio, R. H. (2004). Trait inferences as a function of automatically activated racial attitudes and motivation to control prejudiced reactions. *Basic and Applied Social Psychology, 26,* 1–11.

Otten, S., & Moskowitz, G. B. (2000). Evidence for implicit evaluative in-group bias: Affect-based spontaneous trait inference in a minimal group paradigm. *Journal of Experimental Social Psychology, 36,* 77–89.

Park, S. H., Glaser, J., & Knowles, E. D. (2008). Implicit motivation to control prejudice moderates the effect of cognitive depletion on unintended discrimination. *Social Cognition, 26*, 401–419.

Pearson, A. R., Dovidio, J. F., & Gaertner, S. L. (2009). The nature of contemporary prejudice: Insights from aversive racism. *Social and Personality Psychology Compass, 3*, 314–338.

Pettigrew, T. F., & Meertens, R. W. (1995). Subtle and blatant prejudice in Western Europe. *European Journal of Social Psychology, 25*, 57–76.

Phelps, E. A., O'Conner, K. J., Cunningham, W. A., Funayama, E. S., Gatenby, J. C., Gore, J. C., et al. (2000). Performance on indirect measures of race evaluation predicts amygdale activation. *Journal of Cognitive Neuroscience, 12*, 729–738.

Report of the National Advisory Commission on Civil Disorders (1968). New York: Bantam Books.

Saucier, D. A., Miller, C. T., & Doucet, N. (2005). Differences in helping Whites and Blacks: A meta-analysis. *Personality and Social Psychology Review, 9*, 2–16.

Sears, D. O., & Henry, P. J. (2005). Over thirty years later: A contemporary look at symbolic racism. In M. P. Zanna (Ed.), *Advances in experimental social psychology* (Vol. 37, pp. 95–150). San Diego, CA: Academic Press.

Sears, D. O., Henry, P. J., & Kosterman, R. (2000). Egalitarian values and contemporary racial politics. In D. O. Sears, J. Sidanius, & L. Bobo (Eds.), *Racialized politics: The debate about racism in America* (pp. 75–117). Chicago, IL: University of Chicago Press.

Sherif, M. (1966). *Group conflict and cooperation: Their social psychology.* London: Routledge and Kegan Paul.

Sidanius, J., & Pratto, F. (1999). *Social dominance: An intergroup theory of social hierarchy and oppression.* New York: Cambridge University Press.

Son Hing, L. S., Chung-Yan, G. A., Hamilton, L. K., & Zanna, M. P. (2008). A two-dimensional madel that employs explicit and implicit attitudes to characterize prejudice. *Journal of Personality and Social Psychology, 94*, 971–987.

Son Hing, L. S., Li, W., & Zanna, M. P. (2002). Inducing hypocrisy to reduce prejudicial responses among aversive racists. *Journal of Experimental Social Psychology, 38*, 71–78.

Staub, E. (1996). Cultural-societal roots of violence: The examples of genocidal violence and of contemporary youth violence in the United States. *American Psychologist, 51*, 117–132.

Stephan, W. G., & Stephan, C. W. (2001). *Improving intergroup relations.* Thousand Oaks, CA: Sage.

Tajfel, H. (1969). Cognitive aspects of prejudice. *Journal of Social Issues, 25*(4), 79–97.

Tajfel, H., & Turner, J. C. (1979). An integrative theory of intergroup conflict. In W. G. Austin & S. Worchel (Eds.), *The social psychology of intergroup relations* (pp. 33–48). Monterey, CA: Brooks/Cole.

Turner, J. C., Hogg, M. A., Oakes, P. J., Reicher, S. D., & Wetherell, M. S. (1987). *Rediscovering the social group: A self-categorization theory.* Oxford, England: Basil Blackwell.

Van Bavel, J. J. & Cunningham, W. A. (2009). Self-categorization with a novel mixed-race group moderates automatic social and racial biases. *Personality and Social Psychology Bulletin, 35*, 321–335.

Van Bavel, J. J., Packer, D. J., & Cunningham, W. A. (2008). The neural substrates of in-group bias. *Psychological Science, 19*, 1131–1139.

Wilson, T. D., Lindsey, S., & Schooler, T. Y. (2000). A model of dual attitudes. *Psychological Review, 107*, 101–126.

20

Sexism

Peter Glick and Laurie A. Rudman

ABSTRACT

Informed by the dominant model of 'prejudice as antipathy,' researchers initially defined sexism as 'hostility toward women.' Decades of research challenged this assumption, leading theorists to define sexism as subjectively favorable and unfavorable attitudes (toward both sexes) that reinforce gender inequality. This new framework focuses on how sexist attitudes, both explicit and implicit, reconcile male dominance with intimate heterosexual interdependence. Sexist beliefs not only influence expectations about each sex, but prescribe how men and women 'should' behave. Favorable emotional and behavioral reactions reward members of each sex when they conform to gender-traditional traits, while gender 'deviants' are punished. Thus, although ambivalent and context dependent, sexist attitudes serve a common goal: to reinforce traditional gender role and power distinctions.

SEXISM

In contrast to the often troubled and segregated relations between ethnic and 'racial' groups, men and women have frequent daily contact, often consider a partner from the other group to be their most intimate confidante, and believe that the group with, psychologically-speaking, 'minority' or lower status (i.e., women) are 'wonderful' (Eagly and Mladinic, 1989). It seems impossible to imagine, for example, that heterosexual men would ever initiate a genocide against women. And despite a long history of discriminatory treatment, undeniable progress has occurred in women's status (e.g., the influx of women into previously all-male occupations). As a result, many people simply do not view sexism as a social problem, and certainly not on a par with racism or ethnic hatreds (Czopp & Monteith 2003; Jackson, 1998).

So what's the problem? In two words, continued inequality. Given the subjectively positive tone that infuses gender relations, sexism cannot be defined using the standard definition of prejudice as 'an antipathy' (Allport, 1954, p. 9). However, if sexism is defined by attitudes that reinforce a gender hierarchy that disadvantages women, then sexism remains the most pervasive of all prejudices. All societies make social distinctions between men and women and, to a greater or lesser extent, women throughout the world have lower status, fewer resources, and less power than men (United Nations Development Programme, 2005). Gender inequality remains especially stark when one examines women's representation at the highest levels of power. Even in relatively egalitarian countries such as the United States, powerful female leaders – though increasingly present – remain quite rare. For example, only 14 percent of US Senators and 2.6 percent of CEOs of Fortune 500 companies are female (Mero, 2007; White House Project, 2006).

Thus, sexism is hardly a 'thing of the past' but remains an important force that profoundly shapes both men and womens' lives today. However, its dynamics differ so much from (and present a challenge to) prior conceptions of prejudice that sexism seems like the paradoxical prejudice. This chapter elucidates how and why sexism so uniquely combines dominance with generally affectionate (although also contingently hostile) intergroup relations.

HISTORY OF RESEARCH ON SEXISM

It was not until the 1970s, when women started to enter social psychology in significant numbers and a Women's Movement had burst onto the societal stage, that sexism became a serious object of research attention, a prejudice deemed worthy of systematic study. The first two decades of sexism research (roughly the 1970s through the 1980s) were guided by the presumption that because prejudice is an antipathy, sexism must therefore reflect hostility toward women. Thus, sexism research focused on negative stereotypes of women as less competent than men (Spence & Helmreich, 1972a) and on hostile discrimination, such as less positive evaluations of work produced by women (Goldberg, 1968; Swim, Borgida, Maruyama, et al., 1989), discrimination in hiring and promotion (Glick, Zion, & Nelson, 1988; Heilman, 1983), and sexual harassment (Fitzgerald, Gelfand, & Drasgow, 1995; Gutek, 1985; Pryor, Giedd, & Williams, 1995).

Sexism research remained a growth industry through the 1990s and into the current century. The last two decades, however, have marked a significant shift in how sexism is conceived, resulting in a more complex and nuanced view that reveals the limitations of conceiving of prejudice as an unalloyed antipathy. Instead of an exclusive focus on hostile discrimination, researchers began to consider the many subtle and even subjectively 'benevolent' ways sexism functions to maintain gender hierarchy, often with women's cooperation rather than resistance.

In sum, the history of sexism research is one of early neglect, followed by steadily increasing interest. It is also a history of a significant paradigm shift, with more recent research (from the 1990s onward) challenging not just the assumptions that guided early forays into sexism research, but the general model of prejudice as antipathy that has dominated the field for 50 years.

REVIEW OF SEXISM RESEARCH

Prejudices, like other attitudes, can be broken down into cognitive (beliefs and stereotype), affective (intergroup emotions), and behavioral (discriminatory actions) components. This tripartite division has been evident in sexism research, with an initial assumption, now demonstrated to be incorrect, that all three components were infused with negativity toward women.

Cognitive and affective components of sexism

The earliest sexism research tackled the cognitive aspects of sexism – beliefs about gender roles and gender differences in personality. Pioneers such as Janet Spence developed methodological tools, including the Attitudes toward Women Scale (AWS; Spence & Helmreich, 1972b) to measure such constructs as sexist attitudes and gender stereotypes. The AWS, which quickly became the most frequently used measure of prejudice against women, assesses overtly gender-traditional beliefs and the scale was subtitled as assessing 'the rights and roles of women in contemporary society' (Spence & Helmreich, 1972b: 66).

More specifically, the AWS tapped whether respondents thought that women ought to remain in traditional gender roles (e.g., raising children rather than working outside the home), abide by norms of lady-like behavior (e.g., that it is more 'repulsive' for women than for men to swear), and defer to men (e.g., whether the 'obey clause' ought to be part of marriage ceremonies and whether only men ought to be community leaders). AWS scores predict stronger endorsement of gender stereotypes and a greater likelihood of sexist discrimination (see Beere, 1990, for a review). Consistent with the argument that sexism reflects antipathy toward women, high AWS scores predict greater male aggression toward women (Scott & Tetreault, 1987) and more tolerance of men who commit aggression, such as rapists (Weidner & Griffitt, 1983) and domestic abusers (Hillier & Foddy, 1993).

Simultaneously, researchers examined another crucial cognitive aspect of sexism – gender stereotypes (i.e., beliefs about differences in the psychological attributes of women and men). This work initially focused on perceptions of stereotypically masculine and feminine personality traits (e.g., Broverman, Broverman, Clarkson, et al., 1972). Early research on gender stereotypes established that (relative to the other sex) men are generally perceived to be more competent, instrumental, and independent (or *agentic*) and women to be more warm, expressive, and supportive (or *communal*). Bem's Sex-Role Inventory (BSRI, Bem, 1974) and Spence, Helmreich, & Stapp (1974) Personal Attributes Questionnaire (PAQ) provided lists of stereotypically masculine (agentic/instrumental) and feminine (communal/expressive) traits that researchers used to measure both gender stereotyping and the gendered self-concept (Spence & Buckner, 2000).

Based on data collected in the 1970s, Williams and colleagues showed that these general stereotypes of men and women exhibit an impressive degree of cross-cultural consistency (see Williams & Best, 1990, for a comprehensive review). With the help of collaborators from more than two dozen nations, they confirmed that men are viewed as more agentic and women

as more communal the world over. This research also revealed early indications of potential problems with conceiving of sexism as antipathy. Although gender stereotyping was strongly evident in all nations, there was little consistency in whether the traits assigned to women or to men were, overall, considered to be more positive. That is, valence ratings of sex-stereotypical traits suggested that in some nations men were perceived more positively (as the antipathy model predicts the dominant group would be), but in other nations there was no difference or, in a seeming reversal of sexism, 'feminine' traits were rated more positively than 'masculine' ones.

Consistent with the latter finding, Eagly and Mladinic (1989) noted the startling fact that, as a group, women are evaluated more positively than men. What they termed the *women are wonderful effect* holds true for overall measures of attitude (such as 'feeling thermometers') as well as valence ratings of gender-stereotypical traits (i.e., how positively or negatively people view traits traditionally assigned to women versus men). These results were replicated not just in the United States, but also in other nations (Glick, Lameiras, Fiske, et al., 2004).

Are people merely being 'politically correct' in their attitudes toward women (i.e., claiming to have positive attitudes to avoid being labeled 'prejudiced')? Researchers have devised response latency techniques that bypass the ability to easily control prejudiced responses. Collectively known as *implicit measures*, these techniques do not ask people how they feel but instead, infer implicit attitudes and beliefs on the basis of task performance. For example, an implicit measure of gender attitudes might ask people to rapidly categorize male and female names with either positive words (e.g., joy, rainbow, vacation) or negative words (e.g., grief, poison, vomit). Pro-female implicit attitudes would be observed if people perform the female + good task faster (and with fewer errors) than the male + good task. This is precisely what research has found (Rudman & Goodwin, 2004), suggesting that women are automatically evaluated more positively than men.

The strong and consistent findings that women are generally liked better than men (by both men and women) led Eagly and Mladinic (1989) to ask, 'Are people prejudiced against women?' Their answer remained 'yes,' for reasons discussed below. Clearly, however, evidence for widespread antipathy toward women was not supported by research on gender stereotypes and attitudes. The cognitive and affective components of attitudes toward women instead suggest generally more positive views of women than of men.

Behavioral component of sexism: Sex discrimination

Research into sex discrimination (see also Chapter 27 by Smith, Brief, & Colella, this volume), the behavioral component of sexism, underwent a similar crisis to research on sexism's cognitive and affective aspects. Cumulative findings did not support the idea that people generally treat men more favorably than women. Researchers initially assumed, based on the antipathy model of prejudice, that evaluations of women and their products would typically be more negative. In what came to be known as the 'Goldberg paradigm,' the same product (e.g., an essay) was said to be produced either by a woman or a man, simply by altering the name of the author (Goldberg, 1968). This paradigm generated a host of studies on whether women face discrimination relative to men. A comprehensive meta-analysis, however, revealed that, on the whole, sex discrimination using the Goldberg paradigm was rather negligible, except under specific conditions where effects are sizable – when the product fits a 'masculine' domain (e.g., an essay about war or football), people devalue women's work relative to men's (Swim, Borgida, Maruyama, et al., 1989).

Empirical support for the selective devaluation of women in masculine domains has also consistently shown up in studies of workplace discrimination. For instance, the same résumé is evaluated more favorably if the applicant is

male as opposed to female when applicants seek male-dominated jobs (e.g., manager, police officer), but 'reverse discrimination' occurs for female-dominated jobs (e.g., secretary, nurse) (Glick, Zion, & Nelson,1988; Uhlmann & Cohen, 2007). Similarly, a meta-analysis of studies on the evaluation of male and female leaders showed that female leaders are not always rejected relative to men, but are selectively discriminated against when they enact a 'masculine' (e.g., directive, authoritarian) leadership style (Eagly, Makhijani, & Klonsky, 1992). Although context-dependent, such discrimination strongly reinforces men's power and diminishes women's because the most high status roles and occupations are stereotypically masculine.

In sum, research on the cognitive, affective, and behavioral components of sexism has long confirmed that men and women are believed to differ, elicit different affective reactions, and garner different treatment. However, stereotypical conceptions of the two sexes do not suggest a wholesale favoritism toward men: direct measures of affect suggest that women are actually liked more than men, and discrimination against women is highly context-dependent. In fact, in some ways (and in some contexts), women are favored over men. All of these facts run counter to the view of sexism as a generalized antipathy toward women. But even though women are, as a group, better liked than men, men are selectively preferred for powerful social roles, suggesting that sexism is driven more by an underlying motive to preserve gender hierarchy rather than by feelings of antipathy toward women.

INTEGRATIVE FRAMEWORK

We have already suggested what sexism is not – a general antipathy toward women. A better definition of sexism is *bias based on gender categorization*. This definition has the advantage of accommodating the fact that both men and women can be (and are) targets of sexism. We have already noted that men can be discriminated against when they pursue female-dominated jobs, but they can also be discriminated against when they enact stereotypically feminine traits, for example when they act 'too nice' or 'too weak' (e.g., Berdahl, 2007; Rudman, 1998). However, sexism (even when it targets individual men for derision because they fail to embody gendered ideals) primarily functions to reinforce and justify traditional gender roles and gender hierarchy (i.e., male dominance or patriarchy). This functional view of sexism helps to solve a variety of otherwise vexing puzzles about gender-related attitudes and behavior, such as why overall attitudes toward women are more positive than those toward men while, simultaneously, women are discriminated against (relative to men) for high status roles. In the past two decades, sexism research and theory has produced new conceptualizations of sexism as a complex, ambivalent, and context-dependent, yet still a highly predictable and understandable phenomenon.

Dominance and intimate interdependence

From a theoretical perspective, the structure of male–female relations is key to understanding sexism. Gender relations revolve around two basic structural facts (a) male dominance (or gender hierarchy) and (b) intimate interdependence between the sexes (due to traditional gender roles and heterosexual attraction). These twin facts shape the deep ambivalence of sexist attitudes.

Male dominance is ubiquitous across cultures (see Eagly & Wood, 1999). Around the world, men have more access to power and resources than women. Evolutionary psychologists argue that this reflects sexual selection; specifically that women's mate preferences for high status partners (who can provide for their offspring) acted to select greater dominance in men. In other words, evolutionary theorists suggest that because women have always pitted men against men in a competition for sexual access, men evolved to more competitive and aggressive dispositions (see Buss, 2003).

By contrast, social structural theorists argue that male dominance reflects cultural conditions that have changed during the course of societal evolution (Eagly & Wood, 1999). Specifically, while hunter-gatherer cultures were relatively more egalitarian, with men and women equally responsible for providing food on a day-to-day basis, agricultural and industrial societies produced surpluses that created competition for status and resources, resulting in social stratification. Because of women's greater ties to home and family life due to their reproductive role, men in agricultural and industrial societies could better compete for these surplus resources and monopolize positions of authority. It is during this period of cultural development that the social structural approach suggests patriarchy became entrenched.

However, as societies continued to develop, the nature of work has changed (e.g., with more sophisticated manufacturing machinery, strength differences favoring men over women become irrelevant). Further, women have gained greater control over reproduction with the introduction of birth control, allowing them more effectively to compete for jobs outside the home. These changes have profound implications for increasing gender equality (Jackson, 1998), which are evident in the dramatically increased proportion of women in the paid workforce in recent decades. Thus, social evolution continues, currently acting to increase women's status and opportunities. Nevertheless, men remain dominant when it comes to the top positions in government, business, and other social institutions, such as organized religions (Catalyst, 2006; United Nations Development Programme, 2005; The White House Project, 2006).

Whichever approach – evolutionary, social structural, or a combination of the two – one uses to explain the ubiquity of patriarchy, the fact of male dominance is central to understanding sexism. Sexist ideologies (including gender stereotypes) function to justify and reinforce patriarchy. For example, gender stereotypes assign men traits associated with status, power, and competence, suggesting that men have been 'designed' to dominate.

Across the globe, stereotypically masculine traits are associated with potency and activity (Williams & Best, 1990) and with status and power (Glick, Lameiras, Fiske, et al., 2004). Even stereotypical masculine traits, such as arrogance and egotism, that are rated as 'negative' or unfavorable (Eagly & Miladinic, 1989) serve to reinforce male dominance by assigning men traits associated with striving for or having power (Glick, Lameiras, Fiske, et al., 2004).

Intimate interdependence between men and women also represents a cross-cultural constant. Sexual reproduction directly ensures this in several ways. Men may dominate, but cannot reproduce without women. Further, heterosexual men are attracted to women as romantic objects, leading to intimate bonds (institutionalized in virtually all cultures through marriage). Men also rely on women in family life, where heterosexual reproduction facilitates traditional role divisions tying women to child-rearing and domestic tasks while men work outside the home (Eagly & Wood, 1999). These intimate interdependencies make it impossible to maintain male dominance through complete physical separation between the sexes (e.g., segregated neighborhoods). Rather, role distinctions reinforce gender hierarchy while maintaining intimacy and affection between the sexes. Thus, it is psychologically consistent for a man simultaneously to be reluctant to work with a woman (i.e., to resist women's influx into nontraditional, powerful, roles), but eager to marry one (i.e., to lavish affection on women who fulfill traditional roles and serve men's needs).

Gender roles and gender hierarchy

Sociologists and psychologist agree that dominant groups generally strive to reinforce their power and status through systems of stratification (e.g., see Jackman, 1994). Sidanius and Pratto (1999) note that high, as compared to low, status group members more strongly endorse ideologies that defend social stratification, such as social dominance orientation, which asserts that groups in society *should* have unequal outcomes. Consistent with the ubiquity of patriarchy, across cultures men score higher than women on social dominance orientation.

Social stratification can be maintained through *group-specific social roles* (with higher status roles reserved for members of the higher status group) instead of physical separation (van den Berge, 1960). Jackman (1994, 2005) contends that dominant groups find significant advantage to enforcing stratification through roles rather than spatial distancing because it allows them to infiltrate and control the daily life of subordinates, using paternalistic ideologies to avoid overt hostility. In contrast, physical separation makes it more likely that subordinate group members will influence each other to reject ideological justifications for the other group's dominance, stiffening their resistance.

Given that physical separation is neither desired nor easily achieved in the case of gender relations, role segregation is a primary means of maintaining gender hierarchy. This system helps to avoid overt intergroup hostility between the sexes, which would be costly for men given their high degree of dependence on women in so much of their daily lives. Importantly, sex differences in reproduction create an obvious way to accomplish a gendered division of labor in which men and women have differing roles.

Social role theory

Gender roles and gender hierarchy are, therefore, intimately connected. It is largely through gender roles and the different status and resources they confer that male dominance is maintained. The most prominent social structural theory of sexism, Eagly's (1987) social role theory (see also Eagly, Wood, & Diekman, 2000), proposes that gender stereotypes and sex differences in behavior stem from a gendered division of labor and gender hierarchy. Groups are stereotyped as possessing traits associated with the roles they perform, as well as traits related to the level of social status accorded to the group. In the case of gender, both role and status differences promote stereotypes of men as agentic and women as communal.

For example, when fictional groups are characterized as 'city workers' versus 'child raisers,' people construct gender-like stereotypes about them as (respectively) agentic and communal, even if information about individual group members contradicts these stereotypes (Hoffman & Hurst, 1990). Similarly, manipulations of status (independent of roles) result in perceptions of low status groups as communal and high status groups as agentic (Conway, Pizzamiglio, & Mount, 1996). Communal traits – such as warmth and expressiveness – are also low status traits because they are associated with ingratiation and are generally 'other profitable' (Peeters, 1983) in that they stress caring for and bonding with others rather than individual assertion. By contrast, agentic traits (such as competence, ambition, and competitiveness) reflect 'self-profitable' (Peeters, 1983) or self-assertive characteristics associated with gaining and exercising power and status (Galinsky, Gruenfeld, & Magee, 2003). Thus, gender stereotypes both reflect and reinforce gender roles and gender hierarchy.

Social role theory helps to explain why gender stereotypes are not merely descriptive beliefs about 'how men and women are' but prescriptive norms about 'how men and women ought to be.' To preserve traditional gender roles and hierarchy, individual men and women must embody the traits appropriate to their respective roles and status (Eagly, Wood, & Diekman, 2000). The fact that men are so strongly dependent on women to fulfill specific roles undoubtedly intensifies the prescriptiveness of female stereotypes.

Researchers have noted that gender stereotypes are strongly prescriptive (Fiske & Stevens, 1993). Further, the content of prescriptions for women and men is consistent with social role theory. Prentice and Carranza (2002) examined students' perceptions of the strongest gender prescriptions (i.e., the traits they believe society values most for each sex). For women, these include being warm, kind, interested in children, loyal,

and sensitive – traits that most directly suit them to their prescribed role as doting mothers and loyal wives. Men, in contrast, are prescribed business sense, athleticism, leadership ability, and self-reliance – traits that fit their traditional role as protectors (physical prowess) and providers (abilities related to occupational success).

Additionally, gender stereotypes are organized into subgroups – more specific subcategories of women and men (e.g., career women, macho men) – that elaborate upon the variety of more specific roles men and women play (Green, Ashmore, & Manzi, 2005). Women in particular tend to play multiple roles, with the most prominent traditional roles being wife and sex object – subgroups that repeatedly emerge in research where people are asked to generate 'types of women and men' (e.g., Eckes, 2002). These traditional subgroups of women are characterized as having stereotypically feminine traits, although the 'homemaker' is characterized mainly by feminine personality traits and the sex object type by feminine physical attributes. In societies in which it has become common (and accepted) for women to have careers in the paid workforce, a 'career woman' subgroup is also prominent, but – consistent with social role theory predictions – is characterized as having the masculine, agentic traits that work outside the home typically requires. Subgroups of men (e.g., business man, jock, family man) are also readily generated by research participants and are similarly associated with various male roles.

People also commonly use subcategories that serve to 'isolate' or 'encapsulate' people who 'deviate' from gender prescriptions (Green, Ashmore, & Manzi, 2005). Even the labels commonly used for men and women who do not fit the traditional mold tend to be openly derisive. Women who violate prescriptions for feminine niceness are grouped together under terms such as bitch, ice queen, or iron maiden. Men who violate prescriptions of masculine strength, assertion, and independence are labeled as wimps, wusses, and pussies.

Ambivalent sexism

Male dominance and intimate interdependence have another important consequence for sexist attitudes – they create ambivalence on the part of each sex toward the other. Glick and Fiske (1996, 1999, 2001) argue that male dominance leads to hostility between the sexes, expressed in traditional gender ideologies. Men demean assertive women in order to maintain and justify greater status, and women resent men for their power and privileges. At the same time, intimate interdependence between the sexes tempers hostility with subjectively benevolent (but still traditional) gender ideologies. Men idealize women who serve their needs (e.g., as wives, mothers, romantic objects), viewing them affectionately and offering them provision and protection. In kind, women idealize men who serve as their protectors and providers, particularly in societies where women are highly dependent on men to provide resources and security (Glick, Lameiras, & Fiske, et al., 2004). The co-occurrence of hostile and benevolent attitudes toward each sex indicates that gender attitudes are ambivalent.

The Ambivalent Sexism Inventory (Glick & Fiske, 1996) assesses hostile and benevolent sexism toward women, and the Ambivalence toward Men Inventory (Glick & Fiske, 1999) assesses hostility and benevolence toward men. Cross-national studies involving over two dozen nations across the world (Glick et al., 2000, Glick, Lameiras, Fiske, et al., 2004) have shown that these four ideologies are: (a) recognizable and coherent belief systems across a wide variety of nations, (b) moderately positively correlated at the individual level (i.e., are psychologically consistent, related ideologies), (c) strongly positively correlated when national averages are examined (i.e., are socially shared and endorsed as a coordinated set), and (d) predict national indices of actual structural gender inequality.

Although psychologists generally define ambivalence as a state of mental tension and conflict, Glick and Fiske (2001) have argued that ambivalent gender ideologies are psychologically coherent because they target different subtypes and collectively function to support male dominance and traditional gender roles. That is, the attitudes each gender has toward the other may encompass opposing valences, but their effect on gender relations is consistent. In particular, benevolent sexism is the 'carrot' women are offered as incentive to accept conventional gender relations, by promising men's affection, protection, and provision if women serve as faithful wives, mothers, and romantic objects. By contrast, hostile sexism is the 'stick' that intimidates women who fail to conform to gender prescriptions, seek power, or threaten to compete directly with men. Thus, even though benevolent sexism predicts more positive and hostile sexism more negative stereotypes of women (Glick, Lameiras, Fiske, et al., 2004), benevolence and hostility tend to be directed toward different types of women (e.g., affection toward homemakers and hostility toward career women; Glick, Diebold, Bailey-Werner, et al., 1997).

Ambivalent sexism theory directly challenges the validity of the antipathy model of prejudice, which would suggest that 'benevolent sexism' toward women is an oxymoron. But even though it represents subjectively positive attitudes toward women (e.g., that a 'good woman' ought to be cherished and 'put on a pedestal'), benevolent sexism is paternalistic because it characterizes women as the 'weaker sex' in need of men's protection. Ironically, benevolently sexist men generally protect women from threats posed by other men. In patriarchal societies, where women have few resources, men's hostile sexism sets up the threat that drives women into a male protector's arms for protection. In fact, Glick et al. (2000, 2004) have found that women consistently outscore men on benevolent sexism in those nations in which men most strongly endorse hostile sexism (nations in which women, not coincidentally, have the least power). In such cultures, faced with hostility if they seek their own independence, many women instead are forced into depending on men.

Benevolent sexism is particularly pernicious because it disarms women's resistance to gender inequality. Whereas women, on average, score lower than men on hostile sexism toward women, they often score as high as men on benevolent sexism. Further, women's benevolent sexism scores (as compared to men's) are more strongly correlated with their acceptance of other traditional gender beliefs. It seems that if women accept benevolent sexism, they tend to buy the rest of the 'deal' – that protection and provision is exchanged for staying 'in their place' (Glick, Lameiras, Fiske, et al., 2004). Lured by the promise of affection and protection, as well as benevolent sexism's subjectively positive tone, women are enticed to trade power for protection. In fact, women evaluate benevolently sexist men relatively favorably (Kilianski & Rudman, 1998), and merely exposing women to statements from the benevolent sexism scale leads them to view a hierarchical society as fair and just (Jost & Kay, 2005).

In sum, consistent with Jackman's (1994) view of paternalism as akin to governing with an iron fist in a velvet glove, ambivalent gender ideologies neatly reconcile the basic structural facts of male dominance and intimate interdependence between the sexes. These ideologies reinforce male dominance by providing not only hostile, but benevolent justifications that give women incentive to abide by traditional gender prescriptions and stick to traditional roles.

Descriptive and prescriptive discrimination

Even people who do not explicitly endorse sexist ideologies may discriminate on the basis of gender because gender stereotypes, learned early in life, become habitual and automatic. Both the descriptive and prescriptive aspects of gender stereotypes result in sex discrimination. Descriptive stereotypes do so by setting up expectations about what men and women are like that, in turn, color perceptions of individual men and women through stereotype-confirming cognitive biases that

shape cross-gender interactions. Specifically, gender stereotypes influence what information about others perceivers pay attention to, how they interpret ambiguous behaviors, and what they remember about others (for reviews, see Fiske, 1998, and Deaux & LaFrance, 1998).

Stereotypical expectations also set up 'shifting standards' by which women and men are judged (Biernat, 2003). Thus, a female ball-player's 'great hit' may be assumed to be less impressive than a male player's hit described using the same superlative. As a result, stereotypes still influence more 'objective' scales or measures (e.g., how many feet do you think she hit the ball?). Therefore, even when subjective ratings of women's and men's performance are similar in a masculine domain (e.g., 'She's a terrific manager'), women receive fewer tangible rewards (such as pay and promotion) than men (Vescio, Gervais, Snyder, et al., 2005). In essence, lowered expectations for female competence create evaluations whereby women's performance is judged as 'terrific' – *for a woman* (Biernat & Fuegan, 2001).

Finally, descriptive gender stereotypes can create self-fulfilling prophecies by influencing interaction (for a review, see Geis, 1993). For example, stereotypes of women as warm lead people to confide in women, a behavior likely to elicit empathetic responses. Behavioral confirmation also occurs because people shunt men and women into roles that demand different kinds of behavior. For instance, Skrypnek and Snyder (1982) gave male perceivers the task of negotiating a labor division for a project with an unseen partner. When they believed that this partner was female they assigned more 'feminine' sex-typed tasks to the partner, whereas if they believed the partner was male, they were more likely to assign 'masculine' tasks. These task assignments elicited either more feminine or masculine behavior that 'confirmed' the partner's alleged gender (even though all of the partners were actually women).

Descriptive stereotyping effects can be counteracted when an individual acts in a manner that unambiguously disconfirms the stereotype. As a result, early research on how individuating information affects the application of gender stereotypes seemed to suggest that individuals can easily avoid being stereotyped. For instance, although in the absence of other information Ann is assumed to be less assertive than Tom, if similar clear evidence of assertiveness is provided about each of them, Ann may be viewed as just as assertive as Tom (Locksley, Borgida, Brekke, et al., 1980). But what are the consequences when an individual is viewed as an exception to the stereotype? When stereotypes are merely descriptive, perceivers may be surprised that an individual does not fit their expectations, but accept the individual's behavior. Recall, however, that gender stereotypes are highly prescriptive as well. When *prescriptions* are violated, the reaction is not simply surprise, but anger, hostility, and social rejection (Rudman & Fairchild, 2004).

The different effects produced by descriptive and prescriptive stereotyping are charted in Figure 20.1. The bottom half of the figure summarizes the descriptive stereotyping effects reviewed above, which

occur because gender stereotypes affect the perceived *likelihood* or probability that men and women will act in specific ways. These likelihood expectations lead to stereotype-confirming biases when the target's behavior is stereotype-consistent or ambiguous enough to be interpreted as confirming the stereotype, but to surprise and adjustments in impressions of targets whose behavior obviously contradicts stereotypic expectations.

By contrast, prescriptive stereotypes not only set up likelihood expectations about how men and women typically behave, but also act as moral 'oughts' or expectations about how men and women 'should' behave, leading to anger toward people who violate these gendered rules (see the top of Figure 20.1). For example, prescriptions for men stress that they ought not to show personal weakness or emotionality (e.g., 'boys don't cry'), yield too much to others, lack ambition, or be overly dependent. These behaviors are not just unexpected of men, but tend to be viewed as distasteful or downright repulsive for men to exhibit (Prentice & Carranza, 2002). In other words, men are likely to be excoriated for acting in ways that indicate a

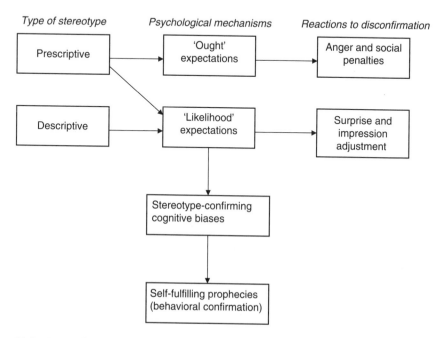

Figure 20.1 **Dynamics of descriptive and prescriptive stereotype.**

lack of status and power. These prescriptions are strongly enforced from early in life, where boys who are deemed to be weak are labeled as 'sissies' and risk not only social rejection by peers, but also are much more likely than girls who 'act masculine' (e.g., 'tomboys') to be deemed by adults to require clinical assistance (e.g., as having a gender-identity disorder; Zucker, Bradley, & Sanikhani, 1997). Similarly, heterosexual men tend to have strongly negative attitudes toward male homosexuality, leading to social rejection and sometimes violence toward peers who are labeled as 'gay' (Franklin & Herek, 2003; Herek, 1989).

Interestingly, girls and women are, in some ways, allowed greater latitude. On the one hand, because agentic traits confer status, girls and women may often be rewarded for exhibiting them (e.g., the athletic tomboy is likely to be accepted and respected by male peers as 'one of the guys'). On the other hand, prescriptions for feminine warmth and expressiveness remain strong and these traits are often perceived as incompatible with aspects of agency that are most directly related to achieving power and status. For example, although women who act in a self-promoting manner (e.g., by highlighting their prior successes and skills in a job interview) are perceived to be competent, they are downgraded on social dimensions (i.e., viewed as less socially skilled and less warm) in comparison to self-promoting men (Rudman, 1998). Self-promotion, which implicitly suggests 'I am better than others,' violates prescriptions that women ought to be modest and nice. Interestingly, even though men generally endorse sexist ideologies more than women, both female and male perceivers reject women who are perceived as violating prescriptions for feminine niceness (Rudman & Glick, 1999, 2001). Because the warmth prescription assigns favorable traits to women, women as well as men endorse it.

In sum, the prescriptive aspect of gender stereotypes creates problems for individuals who do not 'fit' the stereotype of their sex. People who demonstrate that they are exceptions to the stereotypic rule may escape being pigeon-holed as a typical man or typical woman, but this exceptionality puts them at serious risk of social rejection. For example, the mere fact of being successful in a cross-sexed domain can result in social rejection. People assume that a woman described as being at the top of her medical school class or a man described as being at the top of his nursing school class will be ostracized by peers (Cherry & Deaux, 1978; Yoder & Schleicher, 1996).

Both descriptive and prescriptive stereotyping can feed into workplace discrimination against women in high powered roles, such as management. Women who 'fit' traditional stereotypes risk being seen as 'too nice' and not agentic enough (Heilman, 1983). But if women attempt to fit the role by behaving more assertively, they risk being viewed as 'too aggressive' and 'not nice enough,' for a woman (e.g., Rudman & Glick, 1999). While some women manage to show just the right amounts of both warmth and assertiveness to be successful without incurring strong social penalties, women in high powered roles experience a conflict between gender roles and work roles that men do not.

Rudman and Fairchild (2004) have confirmed that gender 'deviants' of both sexes face hostility and social rejection from peers when they perform well on cross-sexed tasks. Women who succeeded at a 'masculine' knowledge test (e.g., on football, military equipment, and cars) and men who succeed at a 'feminine' test (e.g., on fashion, child-rearing, and romance) were more likely to be sabotaged (by both male and female peers) than their normative counterparts.

Punishment for women viewed as gender 'deviants' may often be sexualized. For instance, sexually harassing behavior is more likely to be encountered by women who pursue careers within traditionally masculine organizations, such as the military, Wall Street, or other male-dominated jobs (Gutek, 1985). Further, when a man's masculinity is threatened, he is more likely to sexually harass women who challenge male supremacy (Maass, Cadinu, Guarnieri, et al., 2003). In these cases, sexual harassment reflects a desire to tell women that they ought not to intrude in men's domains or take on masculine roles.

Although men who deviate from masculine prescriptions by behaving communally may be viewed as likable, they are also downgraded on their competence (e.g. Rudman, 1998; Rudman & Glick, 1999, 2001), suggesting that masculine prescriptions work to reinforce men's status and power. Thus, men are more likely to be rewarded for self-promotion, for acting as decisive leaders, and for seeking personal power and resources. But women are often handcuffed when it comes to the pursuit of status and power by prescriptions to maintain feminine niceness. For instance, women tend to frown and men to smile derisively at self-promoting women (Carranza, 2004). Similarly, female leaders (compared to men trained to act in the same manner) elicit more negative nonverbal reactions (Butler & Geis, 1990; Koch, 2005). These social punishments are likely to hinder women's ability to lead and to advocate for themselves.

Additionally, female leaders may elicit negative implicit attitudes (Carpenter & Banaji, 1998; Richeson & Ambady, 2001). Using response latency techniques (described above), people show more negative implicit attitudes toward female as compared to male authority figures, such as doctors and professors (Rudman & Kilianski, 2000). This is especially true for respondents who automatically associate male gender with high status roles (e.g., leader, boss) and female gender with low status roles (e.g., subordinate, helper). These results suggest that deeply ingrained beliefs about status hierarchies can elicit spontaneously negative reactions to female leaders.

The distinction between the descriptive and prescriptive functions of stereotypes has important implications for how sexism operates and how discrimination may most effectively be addressed. Earlier research focused on expectancy effects due to the descriptive aspect of stereotypes, which suggested that discrimination against women resulted primarily from a 'lack of fit' in masculine domains (Heilman, 1983), a

phenomenon that has been well documented in workplace discrimination (e.g., Glick, Zion, & Nelson, 1988). Eagly and Karau's (2002) role-congruity model of prejudice builds on this work, suggesting that discrimination occurs (in part) when perceivers expect that individual group members do not have the traits necessary for successful performance of a role. This explains why discrimination is context-dependent and why men sometimes face 'reverse discrimination' when they seek 'feminine' roles.

Although descriptive stereotypes remain an important reason for discrimination, remedies must not presume that this is the *only* reason for sex discrimination. Thus, early suggestions that stereotypes could be easily punctured by individuating information that the target is atypical failed to anticipate that stereotype-inconsistent behavior, in turn, violates prescriptive stereotypes. As a result, actors who thwart sex stereotypes by vigorously disconfirming them may face prejudice for violating gender prescriptions. For example, women who seek leadership roles face a difficult situation in which they must carefully toe the line between demonstrating sufficient agency while not disconfirming female stereotypes of warmth (Eagly & Karau, 2002; Gill, 2004; Rudman, 1998; Rudman & Glick, 2001).

Similarly, if descriptive stereotyping were the only source of discrimination, then changing the requirements of roles would offer an ideal solution, but this fails to take account of prescriptive stereotype effects. For instance, researchers had hoped that the trend toward 'feminization' of management roles in organizations, by emphasizing participatory leadership skills, would reduce 'lack of fit' between women and leadership. In other words, recognizing the importance of communal-expressive traits (e.g., ability to listen and relate to subordinates) for effective leadership was assumed to be a boon for women. However, Rudman and Glick (1999) showed that the 'feminization' of a managerial job description actually *increased* discrimination against agentic women. Because women are held to a higher standard of niceness, agentic women (who were seen as less warm or socially skilled than similarly agentic men) were deemed less hireable when the job was said to require both communal and agentic traits.

Thus, social punishments for violating feminine prescriptions (not just expectancy effects) must be taken into account when considering why and when sex discrimination occurs. Because women's (but not men's) work and gender roles are more likely to be odds (with the former demanding agency and the latter demanding nurturance), women face a double-bind. Exhibiting agency may be necessary for work success, but women who display agency too vigorously risk social rejection (and, therefore, negative work outcomes).

Punishments for gender deviance create powerful social pressures for individuals to conform to gendered expectations, influencing a wide range of choices, from leisure activities to occupational aspirations (Eagly, Wood, & Diekman, 2000). People seem to be well aware – and afraid – of the consequences of appearing to violate gender norms. For instance, individuals who were told that they were highly successful at a cross-sexed knowledge test were more likely to try to hide this success from others, lie about which test they succeeded at, and claimed a stronger interest in 'gender appropriate' activities than participants who succeeded at 'sex-appropriate' tasks (Rudman & Fairchild, 2004). In other words, people attempt to conceal their own deviation from gender norms and to compensate by emphasizing the ways in which they fit those norms. All of this creates and reinforces a gendered social reality that lends accuracy to gender stereotypes (e.g., Swim, 1994).

NEW DIRECTIONS

Clarifying how descriptive and prescriptive processes jointly affect reactions to stereo-type disconfirmation remains an important task for future research. Efforts to increase gender equality must address both aspects of stereotyping, but descriptive beliefs appear to be more dynamic than prescriptive rules. The former have changed as women have moved into the labor force (e.g., women are no longer expected to be incompetent), whereas prescriptions for feminine niceness remain intact (Diekman & Eagly, 2000; Prentice & Carranza, 2004). Finally, the two types of beliefs conceptually lead to different types of discrimination (based on 'lack of fit' versus punishment for rule violation) (Eagly & Karau, 2002; Gill, 2004). More systematic research is needed to untangle when there are common versus different antecedents and consequences of descriptive and prescriptive stereotyping.

How paternalistic or benevolent discrimination co-opts women into supporting male dominance is another important area for future research. Because benevolent sexism plays a role in heterosexual intimacy (e.g., with traditional women being cherished and adored), one possibility is that romance seduces women into relying on men for financial support and prestige rather than seeking power directly for themselves (Rudman & Heppen, 2003). For example, women may be reluctant to change the relationship dynamic from benevolence (men protecting women) to hostility (competing with men for economic resources) for fear that it will curb their love life, including their ability to marry. Because men are even more vested in gender hegemony, they might also be resistant to changing this dynamic. Investigations of how love, romance, and sexism interconnect to support gender hegemony remain in their infancy (e.g., Rudman & Fairchild, 2007; Rudman & Phelan, 2007), leaving open many possible avenues for future research to disentangle how heterosexual romance relates to gender inequality.

Finally, researchers are just beginning to study how gender prejudice operates 'below the radar' much of the time, in ways that perpetuate its invisibility. Research on implicit gender beliefs and attitudes has contributed much to this unveiling. For example, Rudman and Glick (2001) found that people who automatically associated women with communality and men with agency (based on reaction-time tests) rated female job applicants more negatively. However, the extent to which implicit associations reflect gender rules (as opposed to expectancies) is not clear. The effects of implicit gender beliefs and attitudes on discrimination have only begun to be tested.

SUMMARY AND CONCLUSIONS

Sexism theory and research has grown exponentially since the 1970s. Initially guided by the dominant model of prejudice as an antipathy, early sexism research focused on overtly hostile attitudes toward and discrimination against women. Exploration of how gender roles, descriptive and prescriptive stereotypes, and automatic gender biases sustain gender inequality has led to a new conceptualization of sexism. The new framework focuses on the close (and surprisingly complementary) relationship between male dominance and intimate interdependence between the sexes, rooted in men and womens' traditional social roles. Most importantly, sexism is now recognized to include both subjectively positive as well as hostile beliefs about both women and men, which function together to reinforce gender inequality. These beliefs not only influence expectations about how men and women are likely to behave, but create prescriptive attitudes about how men and women 'should' act. As a result, gender 'deviants' of both sexes face rejection and sabotage from peers. The new framework has also been informed by methodological advances in assessing implicit attitudes. Implicit stereotyping research has revealed that automatic gender stereotypes, operating without perceivers' awareness, affect evaluations of men and women and reinforce traditional gender roles. Promising research directions include how paternalistic or 'benevolent' sexism and heterosexual romance subtly contribute to the maintenance of gender inequality.

REFERENCES

Allport, G. W. (1954/1979). *The nature of prejudice.* Cambridge, MA: Perseus Books.

Bem, S. L. (1974). The measurement of psychological androgyny. *Journal of Consulting and Clinical Psychology, 42,* 155–162.

Beere, C. A. (1990). *Gender roles: A handbook of tests and measures.* New York: Greenwood Press.

Berdahl, J. L. (2007). Harassment based on sex: Protecting social status in the context of gender hierarchy. *Academy of Management Review, 32,* 641–658.

Biernat, M. (2003). Toward a broader view of social stereotyping. *American Psychologist, 58,* 1019–1027.

Biernat, M., & Fuegen, K. (2001). Shifting standards and the evaluation of competence: Complexity in gender-based judgment and decision making. *Journal of Social Issues, 57,* 707–724.

Bogardus, E. S. (1927). Race, friendliness, and social distance. *Journal of Applied Sociology, 11,* 272–287.

Broverman, I. K., Broverman, D. M., Clarkson, F. E., Rosenkrantz, P. S., & Vogel, S. R. (1972). Sex stereotypes. A current appraisal. *Journal of Social Issues, 28,* 59–78.

Buss, D. M. (2003). *Evolutionary psychology: The new science of the mind* (2nd ed.). Boston: Allyn and Bacon

Butler, D., & Geis, F. L. (1990). Nonverbal affect responses to male and female leaders. Implications for leadership evaluations. *Journal of Personality and Social Psychology, 58,* 48–59.

Carpenter, S., & Banaji, M. R. (1998, April). *Implicit attitudes and behavior toward female leaders.* Paper presented at the annual meeting of the Midwestern Psychological Association, Chicago, IL.

Carranza, E. (2004). *Is what's good for the goose derogated in the gander? Reactions to masculine women and feminine men.* Unpublished doctoral dissertation. Princeton University.

Catalyst (2006). *2005 Catalyst census of women corporate officers and top earners of the Fortune 500.* New York: Catalyst.

Cherry, F., & Deaux, K. (1978). Fear of success versus fear of gender-inappropriate behavior. *Sex Roles, 4,* 97–101.

Conway, M., Pizzamiglio, M. T., & Mount, L. (1996). Status, communality, and agency: Implications for stereotypes of gender and other groups. *Journal of Personality and Social Psychology, 71,* 25–38.

Czopp, A. M., & Monteith, M. J. (2003). Confronting prejudice (literally): Reactions to confrontations of racial and gender bias. *Personality and Social Psychology Bulletin, 29,* 532–544.

Deaux, K., & LaFrance, M. (1998). Gender. In D. T. Gilbert, S. T. Fiske, & G. Lindzey (Eds.), *The handbook of social psychology* (4th ed., pp. 788–827). New York: McGraw-Hill.

Diekman, A. B., & Eagly, A. H. (2000). Stereotypes as dynamic constructs: Women and men of the past, present, and future. *Personality and Social Psychology Bulletin, 26*, 1171–1188.

Eagly, A. H. (1987). *Sex differences in social behavior: A social role interpretation.* Hillsdale, NJ: Lawrence Erlbaum & Associates.

Eagly, A. H., & Karau, S. J. (2002). Role congruity theory of prejudice toward female leaders. *Psychological Review, 109*, 573–598.

Eagly, A. H., Makhijani, M. G., & Klonsky, B. G. (1992). Gender and the evaluation of leaders: A meta-analysis. *Psychological Bulletin, 111*, 3–22.

Eagly, A. H., & Mladinic, A. (1989). Gender stereotypes and attitudes toward women and men. *Personality and Social Psychology Bulletin, 15*, 543–558.

Eagly, A. H., & Wood, W. (1999). The origins of sex differences in human behavior: Evolved dispositions versus social roles. *American Psychologist, 54*, 408–423.

Eagly, A. H., Wood, W., & Diekman, A. (2000). Social role theory of sex differences and similarities: A current appraisal. In T. Eckes & H. M. Trautner (Eds.), *The developmental social psychology of gender* (pp. 123–174). Mahwah, NJ: Erlbaum.

Eckes, T. (2002). Paternalistic and envious gender stereotypes: Testing predictions from the Stereotype Content Model. *Sex Roles, 47*, 99–114.

Fiske, S. T. (1998). Stereotyping, prejudice and discrimination. In D. T. Gilbert, S. T. Fiske, & G. Lindzey (Eds.), *The handbook of social psychology* (4th ed., pp. 357–414). New York: McGraw-Hill.

Fiske, S. T. & Stevens, L. E. (1993). What's so special about sex? Gender stereotyping and discrimination. In S. Oskamp & M. Costanzo (Eds.), *Gender issues in contemporary society: Applied social psychology annual* (pp. 173–196). Newbury Park, CA: Sage.

Fitzgerald, L. F., Gelfand, M. J., & Drasgow, F. (1995). Measuring sexual harassment: theoretical and psychometric advances. *Basic and Applied Social Psychology, 17*, 425–445.

Franklin, K., & Herek, G. (2003). Violence toward homosexuals. In S. Plous (Ed.), *Understanding prejudice and discrimination* (pp. 384–401). New York: McGraw Hill.

Galinsky, A. D., Gruenfeld, D. H., & Magee, J. C. (2003). From power to action. *Journal of Personality and Social Psychology, 85*, 453–466.

Geis, F. L. (1993). Self-fulfilling prophecies: A social-psychological view of gender. In A. E. Beall & R. J. Sternberg (Eds.), *The psychology of gender* (pp. 5–54). New York: The Guilford Press.

Gill, M. J. (2004). When information does not deter stereotyping: Prescriptive stereotyping can foster bias under conditions that deter descriptive stereotyping. *Journal of Experimental Social Psychology, 40*, 619–632.

Glick, P., Diebold, J., Bailey-Werner, B., & Zhu, L. (1997). The two faces of Adam: Ambivalent sexism and polarized attitudes toward women. *Personality and Social Psychology Bulletin, 23*, 1323–1334.

Glick, P., & Fiske, S. T. (1996). The Ambivalent Sexism Inventory: Differentiating hostile and benevolent sexism. *Journal of Personality and Social Psychology, 70*, 491–512.

Glick, P. & Fiske, S. T. (1999). The Ambivalence toward Men Inventory: Differentiating hostile and benevolent beliefs about men. *Psychology of Women Quarterly, 23*, 519–536.

Glick, P., & Fiske, S. T. (2001). Ambivalent sexism. In M. P. Zanna (Ed.), *Advances in experimental social Psychology* (vol. 33, pp. 115–188). Thousand Oaks, CA: Academic Press.

Glick, P., et al. (2000). Beyond prejudice as simple antipathy: Hostile and benevolent sexism across cultures. *Journal of Personality and Social Psychology, 79*, 763–775.

Glick, P., Lameiras, M., Fiske, S. T., Eckes, T., Masser, B., Volpato, C., et al., (2004). Bad but bold: Ambivalent attitudes toward men predict gender inequality in 16 nations. *Journal of Personality and Social Psychology, 86*, 713–728.

Glick, P., Zion, C., & Nelson, C. (1988). What mediates sex discrimination in hiring decisions? *Journal of Personality and Social Psychology, 55*, 178–186.

Goldberg, P. (1968). Are women prejudiced against women? *Transaction, 5*, 316–322.

Green, R. J., Ashmore, R. D., & Manzi, R., Jr. (2005). The structure of gender type perception: Testing the elaboration, encapsulation, and evaluation framework. *Social Cognition, 23*, 429–464.

Gutek, B. A. (1985). *Sex and the workplace.* San Francisco: Jossey Bass.

Heilman, M. E. (1983). Sex bias in work settings: The lack of fit model. *Research in Organizational Behavior, 5*, 269–298.

Herek, G. M. (1989). Hate crimes against lesbians and gay men: Issues for research and policy. *American Psychologist, 44*, 948–955.

Hillier, L., & Foddy, M. (1993). The role observer attitudes in judgments of blame in cases of wife assault. *Sex Roles, 29*, 629–644.

Hoffman, C., & Hurst, N. (1990). Gender stereotypes: Perception or rationalization? *Journal of Personality and Social Psychology, 58*, 197–208.

Jackman, M. R. (1994). *The velvet glove: Paternalism and conflict in gender, class, and race relations.* Berkeley, CA: University of California Press.

Jackman, M. R. (2005). Rejection or inclusion of outgroups? In Dovidio, J. F., Glick, P., & Rudman, L. A. (Eds.), *On the nature of prejudice: 50 years after Allport* (pp. 89–105). Malden, MA: Blackwell Publishing.

Jackson, R. M. (1998). *Destined for equality: The inevitable rise of women's status.* Cambridge, MA: Harvard University Press.

Jost, J. T., & Kay, A. C. (2005). Exposure to benevolent sexism and complementary gender stereotypes: Consequences for specific and diffuse forms of system justification. *Journal of Personality and Social Psychology, 88*, 498–509.

Kilianski, S. E., & Rudman, L. A. (1998). Wanting it both ways: Do women approve of benevolent sexism? *Sex Roles, 39*, 333–352.

Koch, S. C. (2005). Evaluative affect display toward male and female leaders of task-oriented groups. *Small Group Research, 36*, 678–703.

Locksley, A., Borgida, E., Brekke, N., & Hepburn, C. (1980). Sex stereotypes and social judgment. *Journal of Personality and Social Psychology, 39*, 821–831.

Maass, A., Cadinu, M., Guarnieri, G., & Grasselli, A. (2003). Sexual harassment under social identity threat: The computer harassment paradigm. *Journal of Personality and Social Psychology, 85*, 853–870.

Mero, J. (2007, August). Fortune 500 Women CEOs. [Online archive]. *Fortune.*

Peeters, G. (1983). Relational and informational patterns in social cognition. In W. Doise, & S. Moscovici (Eds.), *Current issues in European social psychology* (pp. 201–237). UK: Maison des Sciences de l'Homme and Cambridge University Press.

Prentice, D. A., & Carranza, E. (2002). What women and men should be, shouldn't be, are allowed to be, and don't have to be: The contents of prescriptive gender stereotypes. *Psychology of Women Quarterly, 26*, 269–281.

Pryor, J. B., Giedd, J. L., & Williams, K. B. (1995). A social psychological model for predicting sexual harassment. *Journal of Social Issues, 51*, 69–84.

Richeson, J. A., & Ambady, N. (2001). Who's in charge? Effects of situational roles on automatic gender bias. *Sex Roles, 44*, 493–512.

Rudman, L. A. (1998). Self-promotion as a risk factor for women: The costs and benefits of counterstereotypical impression management. *Journal of Personality and Social Psychology, 74*, 629–645.

Rudman, L. A., & Fairchild, K. (2004). Reactions to counterstereotypic behavior: The role of backlash in cultural stereotype maintenance. *Journal of Personality and Social Psychology, 87*, 157–176.

Rudman, L. A., & Fairchild, K. (2007). The *F* word: Is feminism incompatible with beauty and romance? *Psychology of Women Quarterly, 31*, 125–136.

Rudman, L. A., & Glick, P. (2001). Prescriptive gender stereotypes and backlash toward agentic women. *Journal of Social Issues, 57*, 743–762.

Rudman, L. A., & Glick, P. (1999). Feminized management and backlash toward agentic women: The hidden costs to women of a kinder, gentler image of middle-managers. *Journal of Personality and Social Psychology, 77*, 1004–1010.

Rudman, L. A., & Goodwin, S. A. (2004). Gender differences in automatic ingroup bias: Why do women like women more than men like men? *Journal of Personality and Social Psychology, 87*, 494–509.

Rudman, L. A., & Heppen, J. (2003). Implicit romantic fantasies and women's interest in personal power: A glass slipper effect*? Personality and Social Psychology Bulletin, 29*, 1357–1370.

Rudman, L. A., & Kilianski, S. E. (2000). Implicit and explicit attitudes toward female authority. *Personality and Social Psychology Bulletin, 26*, 1315–1328.

Rudman, L. A., & Phelan, J. E. (2007). The interpersonal power of feminism: Is feminism good for relationships? *Sex Roles, 57*, 787–799.

Scott, R., & Tetreault, L. A. (1987). Attitudes of rapists and other violent offenders toward women. *Journal of Social Psychology, 127*, 375–380.

Sidanius, J., & Pratto, F. (1999). *Social dominance: An intergroup theory of social hierarchy and oppression.* Cambridge: Cambridge University Press.

Skrypnek, B. J., & Snyder, M. (1982). On the self-perpetuating nature of stereotypes about women and men. *Journal of Experimental Social Psychology, 18*, 277–291.

Spence, J. T., & Buckner, C. E. (2000). Instrumental and expressive traits, trait stereotypes, and sexist attitudes. *Psychology of Women Quarterly, 24*, 44–62.

Spence, J. T., & Helmreich, R. (1972a). Who likes competent women? Competence, sex-role congruence of interest, and subjects' attitudes toward women as determinants of interpersonal attraction. *Journal of Applied Social Psychology, 2*, 197–213.

Spence, J. T., & Helmreich, R. (1972b). The Attitudes Toward Women Scale: An objective instrument to measure attitudes toward the rights and roles of women in contemporary society. *JSAS Catalog of Selected Documents in Psychology, 2*, 66–67 (Ms. 153).

Spence, J. T., Helmreich, R. L., & Stapp, J. (1974). The Personal Attributes Questionnaire: A measure of sex-role stereotypes and masculinity and femininity. *JSAS: Catalog of Selected Documents in Psychology, 4*, 43–44.

Swim, J. K. (1994). Perceived versus meta-analytic effect sizes: An assessment of the accuracy of gender stereotypes. *Journal of Personality and Social Psychology, 66*, 21–36.

Swim, J. K., Borgida, E., Maruyama, G., & Myers, D. G. (1989). Joan McKay versus John McKay: Do gender stereotypes bias evaluations? *Psychological Bulletin, 105*, 409–429.

Swim, J. K., Aiken, K. J., Hall, W. S., & Hunter, B. A. (1995). Sexism and racism: Old–fashioned and modern prejudice. *Journal of Personality and Social Psychology, 68*, 199–214.

Tougas, F., Brown, R., Beaton, A. M., & Joly, S. (1995) Neosexism: Plus ça change, plus c'est pareil. *Personality and Social Psychology Bulletin, 21*, 842–849.

Uhlmann, E. L., & Cohen, G. L. (2007). Constructed criteria: Redefining merit to justify discrimination. *Psychological Science, 16*, 474–480.

United Nations Development Programme (2005). *Human development report 2005*. New York: Oxford University Press.

van den Berghe, P. L. (1960). Distance mechanisms of stratification. *Sociology and Social Research, 44*, 155–164.

Vescio, T. K., Gervais, S. J., Snyder, M., & Hoover, A. (2005). Power and the creation of patronizing environments: The stereotype-based behaviors of the powerful and their effects on female performance in masculine domains. *Journal of Personality and Social Psychology, 88*, 658–672.

Weidner, G., & Griffitt, W. (1983). Rape: A sexual stigma? *Journal of Personality, 51*, 152–166.

White House Project (2006). *Snapshots of current political leadership*. Retrieved May 04, 2006 from http://www.thewhitehouseproject.org/v2/researchandreports/snapshots.html.

Williams, J. E., & Best, D. L. (1990). *Measuring sex stereotypes: A multination study* (revised edition). Newbury Park, CA: Sage.

Yoder, J. D., & Schleicher, T. L. (1996). Undergraduates regard deviation from occupational gender stereotypes as costly for women. *Sex Roles, 34*, 171–188.

Zucker, K. J., Bradley, S. J., & Sanikhani, M. (1997). Sex differences in referral rates of children with gender identity disorder. *Journal of Abnormal Child Psychology, 25*, 217–227.

21

Heterosexism

Michelle R. Hebl, Charlie L. Law, and Eden King

ABSTRACT

In this chapter, we provide readers with an overview of much of the psychological research that has been conducted on heterosexism. We begin by discussing the history of heterosexism research and describe ways in which heterosexism differs from other 'isms (i.e., sexism, racism). We then consider characteristics associated with (a) exhibiting heterosexism, and (b) being the target of heterosexism. We situate our review within the context of social interactions and describe the misunderstandings, prejudice and discrimination, disclosure behaviors that often occur. Finally, we consider the interaction consequences of heterosexism and potential remediation strategies.

HETEROSEXISM

Heterosexism is an ideological system that reinforces the denigration of nonheterosexual identity, behavior, relationship, or community (see Herek, 2004). By 'nonheterosexual,' we refer to any identity, behavior, relationship, or community in which physical and/or emotional attraction to same-gender individuals exists. Heterosexism encompasses components of

- homophobia (e.g., fearing of feeling negativity toward gay men and lesbians),
- stereotyping (e.g., believing that most gay men are effeminate and/or most lesbians are masculine),
- prejudice (e.g., believing that gay men and lesbians should not be school teachers),
- discrimination (e.g., avoiding a lesbian coworker or refusing to rent an apartment to an openly gay man).

HISTORY OF HETEROSEXISM RESEARCH

Research on heterosexism is still in its infancy although the rate of such research has increased substantially over the past twenty years. The majority of such research is situated within the tradition of stigma research (see also the Chapter 25 by Major and Townsend in this volume), so it is here where we begin our brief review of its history.

The ancient Greeks first introduced the concept of 'stigma' by referring to it as a mark burned on or cut into the bearer, which indicated that the bearer was a criminal, sick, or should otherwise be avoided. In 1963, Goffman ignited research on the topic of stigmas by writing a poignant book that described stigmas and gave examples of how they are socially limiting and spoil one's identity (Goffman, 1963). He defined a stigma as an attribute that is discrediting and prevents full social acceptance for the stigmatized individual. Crocker, Major, and Steele, (1998) articulated four common features of stigma, including the fact that stigmatized individuals are: economically disadvantaged (e.g., Blacks earn less than Whites, obese women earn less than nonobese women), targets of negative stereotypes (e.g., obese individuals are viewed as lazy, slothful, and undisciplined), rejected interpersonally (e.g., physically disabled individuals are avoided and sought after as romantic partners less often than nonstigmatized individuals), and targets of social discrimination (e.g., Black applicants are hired less often than White applicants). All four of these criteria are relevant for nonheterosexuals. That is, they are: economically disadvantaged (e.g., Clain & Leppel, 2001), the target of negative stereotypes (e.g., Herek, 2002), rejected interpersonally (e.g., Herek, 2002), and the target of social discrimination (e.g., Hebl, Foster, Mannix, et al., 2002).

Heterosexism versus other 'isms'

Although heterosexism shares some common-alities with other stigmas, it differs from the other 'isms' (e.g., sexism, racism) in meaningful ways. First, heterosexism often involves an affective component in which individuals fear being gay, becoming gay, or being perceived as gay (Herek, 1984; Ragins, Cornwell, & Miller, 2003), and there is no parallel comparison for sexism or racism. Second, heterosexism involves a characteristic that can be concealed, which is not usually an option with gender or race. Thus, gay men and lesbians often spend a great deal of time managing their identities and deciding if, who, when, and how to disclose their identities to others (i.e., Goffman, 1963; Herek & Capitanio, 1996, King, Reilly, & Hebl, 2008b).

Third, heterosexism involves a character-istic that is perceived by most others to be controllable (see Jones, Farina, Hastorf, et al., 1984) and it is controllable stigmas that are reacted to with the greatest amount of negativity (Weiner, 1995). Based on the

belief that homosexuality is a lifestyle choice many people simply believe that individuals can and should change their nonheterosexual orientations. Fourth, heterosexism involves the all too often erroneous belief that non-heterosexual individuals have, or will soon contract, HIV/AIDS (Herek, Widaman, & Capitanio, 2005). This link between AIDS and heterosexism, which is not present with other 'isms,' further enhances the negativity directed toward nonheterosexual individuals.

Fifth, targets of heterosexism include individuals who do not comprise a federally protected class. While Title VII of the Civil Rights Act in the United States makes it illegal to discriminate on the basis of sex, religion, ethnicity, national origin, and race, it is often legal to discriminate against sexual minorities; the absence of overarching federal legal protection leaves nonheterosexual indi-viduals particularly vulnerable to the ill effects of stigma. Sixth, research on heterosexism was, by and large, absent because up until the 1970s, deviations from heterosexuality were considered psychological disorders. Thus, it makes sense that heterosexism research has a short history, and one that is much briefer than that of the other 'isms.'

In the last two decades, however, there has been a burgeoning of empirical research being conducted on heterosexism. Perhaps central to these efforts is the work of Herek, who – similarly to us – situates heterosexism within a stigma framework and recently introduced the construct of 'sexual stigma,' which he referred to as 'shared knowledge of society's negative regard for any non-heterosexual behavior, identity, relationship, or community' (2004: 14). We will review much of the other heterosexism research that has been done in the following sections.

OVERVIEW OF HETEROSEXISM RESEARCH: ANTECEDENTS TO HETEROSEXIST PREJUDICE AND BEHAVIOR

We review perceiver and target features that serve as antecedents and/or correlates to heterosexist prejudice and behaviors. While our review of these features is not exhaustive, we review characteristics that are consistently linked with heterosexism.

Perceiver characteristics

Who is most likely to stigmatize others on the basis of sexuality? Past research shows that a number of individual differences are associated with heightened heterosexism, including demographic and social variables and previous experience interacting with nonheterosexual individuals. We describe these constructs in more detail.

Gender

Research consistently shows that women tend to have less heterosexist attitudes, beliefs, and behaviors than men (Hoover & Fishbein, 1999; Johnson, brems, & Alford-Keating, 1997). A survey conducted by Herek (2002) revealed that women were more likely to support equal rights for gay men (92.2 percent) and lesbians (95.1 percent) than were men (gay men = 82.7 percent and lesbians = 86.6 percent), and women were more likely to support passing laws that protect gay men (82.7 percent) and lesbians (81.1 percent) than were men (gay men = 64.2 percent and lesbians = 65.2 percent). Meta-analyses consistently reveal that men are more heterosexist than women (Whitely, 2001; Whitely & Kite, 1995) with heterosexual men being particularly negative toward gay men (Herek, 2002).

Age and educational level

For age, research suggests that very young and very old individuals stigmatize nonheterosexual individuals more than middle-aged individuals do (e.g., Johnson, Brems, & Alford-Keating, 1997). For education, the relationship is linear –more education is associated with less heterosexism (Hoover & Fishbein, 1999; Lambert, Ventura, Hall, et al., 2006).

Religion

Many religions, particularly orthodox and/or conservative ones, denounce nonheterosexual lifestyles as unhealthy, immoral, and evil (see Jung & Smith, 1993; Linneman, 2004); thus, it is not surprising that religiosity is related to heterosexism. In fact, overall religiosity, specific religious beliefs, and religion-consistent behavior were all related to higher levels of homophobia, increased discomfort around gay men and lesbians, and less endorsement of human rights for gay men and lesbians (Bierly, 1985; Johnson, Brems, & Alford-Keating, 1997; Kunkel & Temple, 1992).

Political ideology and gender-related beliefs

Those who tend to be politically conservative, against feminist ideals, and are anti-abortion also express more heterosexism than politically liberal individuals (Hicks & Lee, 1997). Similarly, those who engage in sex-role stereotyping, have traditional gender-role beliefs, endorse male-role norms, and score high on ambivalent and modern sexism scales express more heterosexism than those who are lower on these constructs (Hoover & Fishbein, 1999; Whitley, 2001). These measures may be tapping constructs that overlap with heterosexist ideologies, which involve traditional beliefs about the order of society (i.e., unions should involve a man and a woman, man is the head of a household). In support of this, both social dominance orientation and right-wing authoritarianism are associated with heterosexism (Whitely, 1999).

Geographical location

Heterosexism is more prevalent in rural than urban areas (Eldridge, Mack, & Swank, 2006). In the United States those living in the Midwest and South have the most negative attitudes toward gay men and lesbians, while those living on the West coast have relatively positive attitudes (Dejowski, 1992; Irwin & Thompson, 1977). Differences based on geographical location may be partially explained by religion (fundamentalism is more prevalent in the South than in the West), increased likelihood of contact (gay men and lesbians may be more likely to be 'out' in urban versus rural areas), or different regional norms (larger concentrations of 'out' gay men and lesbians influence heterosexual behaviors).

Empathic concern

Lower levels of empathy are related to increased levels of prejudice, increased levels of homophobia, and decreased concern for the human rights of nonheterosexual individuals (Batson, Polycarpou, Harmon-Jones, et al., 1997b; Johnson, Brems, & Alford-Keating, 1997). A construct that is similar to empathy is perspective taking, or the ability to imagine what it must be like to live a day in the life of another person (Batson, Polycarpou, Harmon-Jones, et al., 1997b), and this is also negatively related to heterosexism (Johnson, Brems, & Alford-Keating, 1997).

Previous social contact

Perceivers who have had contact with nonheterosexual individuals, even limited amounts, tend to engage in less sexual stigmatization of this target group than those who have no such contact (Eldridge, Mack, & Swank, 2006; Grack & Richman, 1996). In a meta-analytic review of the contact hypothesis, Pettigrew & Tropp (2006) found some of the strongest evidence (relative to all stigmas that they examined) that prejudice reduction occurs when heterosexual individuals engage in intergroup contact with gay men and lesbians (see also Herek & Capitanio, 1996).

Target characteristics

Who is most likely to be the target of sexual stigma? Several target characteristics consistently emerge, some of which are static (e.g., gender) while others involve beliefs and behaviors that may be dynamic (e.g., degree of 'outness'; identity centrality and group identification; stereotypicality; perceptions of stigma). We discuss each in turn.

Gender

More negative attitudes are directed toward gay men than toward lesbians (Kerns & Fine, 1994). For instance, heterosexual participants view as mentally ill, have negative reactions to, and oppose adoption rights for gay men more than lesbians (Herek, 2002). Recall that these gender differences may be driven, in large part, from the responses of heterosexual men, who view gay men much more severely than they view lesbians (Herek, 2000).

Degree of 'outness'

At one extreme, nonheterosexual individuals may conceal their orientation to everyone, often experiencing a 'private hell' because they are constantly preoccupied with concealment (Smart & Wegner, 2000: 229). At the other extreme, nonheterosexual individuals may disclose to everyone, maximizing their psychological coherence (see Ragins, 2008) and be less vulnerable to psychological problems (see Waldo, 1999). But because these latter individuals are out to more people, they are statistically more likely to encounter discrimination. Alternatively, nonheterosexual individuals might avoid either extreme and 'come out' to a select number of individuals. This situation can also be challenging, however, because of what Ragins (2008: 194) refers to as 'disclosure disconnects,' in which being 'out' to some but not other individuals leads to role conflict, stress, and disharmony in trying to maintain psychological coherence.

Identity centrality and group identification

Identity centrality involves the extent to which individuals view their sexual orientation – it may be one of the most centrally defining features of themselves or it may be just one of many aspects that is important but not centrally defining. Group identification involves the extent to which individuals identify with other ingroup members. Those individuals who have central identities and/or strong identifications with their ingroups are likely to accrue both benefits and losses from such associations (Turner, 1991). For instance, nonheterosexual individuals may be more likely to compare the stress they experience to that which other nonheterosexual individuals report, thereby minimizing perceived discrimination because others are sure to have experienced worse treatment. However, strong identification with an ingroup can sometimes make individuals more, and not less, vulnerable (for a review, see Settles, 2004). When a negative event happens (e.g., a hate crime), individuals who strongly identify with their nonheterosexual orientation may personalize the event and it may exacerbate their vulnerability. As a result, such individuals may more acutely perceive and experience discrimination in social interactions.

Stereotypicality

The extent to which individuals show stereotypicality, or have traits that are stereotypic of their group, influences others' perceptions about them (Eberhardt, Davies, Purdie-Vaughns, et al., 2006). Nonheterosexual individuals may choose to engage in behaviors that increase the salience of their non-heterosexual orientation (e.g., wearing a pink triangle, participating in a gay pride march, wearing a particular hairstyle, enacting stereotypical mannerisms). As a result of acting stereotypically, then, targets might increase the associations that perceivers have between stereotypes and prejudice, which in turn might enhance perceivers' homophobic, prejudicial, and discriminatory responses to targets.

Chronic stigmatization, stigma consciousness, and rejection sensitivity

These three closely related concepts capture nonheterosexual individuals' anticipation of discrimination. First, nonheterosexual targets may possess varying levels of *chronic stigmatization*. Although this construct has not been examined specifically with respect to gay men and lesbians, it has been identified to influence the interactions of ethnic minorities (see Shelton, Richeson, & Salvatore, 2005; Vorauer, Main, & O'Connell, 1998). Non-heterosexual individuals may have a greater propensity to expect negative outcomes from interactants or engage in compensatory and/or negative behaviors themselves (see Vorauer, Main, & O'Connell, 1998). Second, nonheterosexual targets may also possess differing levels of *stigma consciousness* (see Pinel, 1999), or varying levels of perceptions about being the target of stereotypes and discrimination. Such targets may not necessarily internalize the stereotypes others hold but they may misperceive or overattribute

behaviors directed toward them to prejudice and discrimination (see Kleck & Strenta, 1980 for relevant research conducted with respect to physical disability). Third, nonheterosexual targets may vary in the extent to which they possess *rejection sensitivity*, or expectancies that they will be rejected because of their membership status (see Mendoza-Denton, Downey, Purdie, et al., 2002 for relevant research conducted with respect to race). Again, such sensitivity may make individuals vigilant and even hypervigilant about the behaviors and intentions of their interaction partners.

A FRAMEWORK FOR CONSIDERING HETEROSEXISM WITHIN MIXED INTERACTIONS

More recent research has gone beyond identifying antecedent conditions of heterosexism to understanding heterosexism within the context of *mixed interactions*, or interactions involving a perceiver (e.g., heterosexual interactant) and a target (e.g., nonheterosexual interactant). Figure 21.1 depicts an abbreviated version of a mixed interaction framework proposed by Hebl and Dovidio (2005), in which the dynamic interplay between perceiver and target becomes visible. Central to this framework is the belief that there are three characteristics that are commonly manifested in such interactions: misunderstandings, prejudice and discrimination, and disclosure behavior.

Misunderstandings

Mixed interactions often produce mismatches and misinterpretations between interaction partners (Dovidio, Hebl, Richeson, et al., 2006; see Chapter 17 by Richeson & Shelton in this volume). For instance, perceivers' limited past experience interacting with non-heterosexual individuals may result in anxiety and concerns with appearing egalitarian. Although the perceiver may not actually be prejudiced, the constellation of nonverbal behaviors associated with anxiety may be

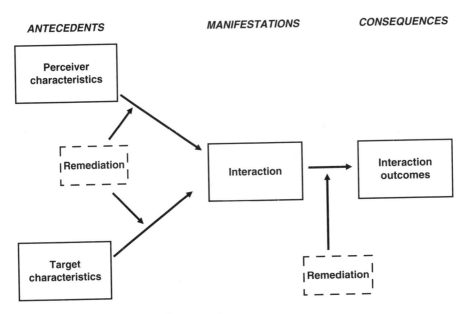

Figure 21.1   A mixed interaction framework.

interpreted, from the target's perspective, as discriminatory.

Additional misunderstandings in social interactions can be created by a disconnect in interactants' implicit and explicit attitudes. Explicit attitudes tend to be controllable and susceptible to social desirability concerns whereas implicit attitudes tend to be uncontrollable and reflect unintended, automatic attitudes. Perceivers tend to hold positive, explicit attitudes but negative, implicit attitudes toward stigmatized targets (see Dovidio, kawakami, & Gaertner, 2002; Shelton, Richeson, & Salvatore, 2005). These different sets of attitudes tend to influence different sets of behaviors – explicit attitudes tend to influence verbal behaviors while implicit attitudes tend to influence nonverbal behaviors (see Chapter 16 by Maio, Haddock, Antony, et al. in this volume). Hence, there is often a verbal/nonverbal mismatch in that perceivers may verbally communicate positive regard (i.e., give complements); but simultaneously nonverbally communicate negativity (i.e., less smiling and contact).

Further misunderstandings arise from erroneous cognitions that targets and perceivers hold about each other. For instance, targets often inaccurately believe that perceivers are

not as interested in interacting with them as the targets are with the perceivers, and perceivers hold these same erroneous beliefs about targets (Shelton, Richeson, & Salvatore, 2005). Both interactants avoid interactions because they fear they will be rejected by their interaction partners, but they interpret avoidance from others as a lack of others' interest. Clearly, these inaccurate and imbalanced assumptions may lead to increased stereotyping, prejudice, and discrimination.

Prejudice and discrimination in mixed interactions

Mixed interaction research involving heterosexual and nonheterosexual interactants reveals that prejudice and discrimination are alive and well. Clearly, overt types of prejudice and discrimination (e.g., hate crimes, failure to rent apartments to gay couples) continue to exist but there is also encouraging evidence suggesting that overt expressions are much less frequent today than in the past (Loftus, 2001). Unfortunately, more subtle expressions of heterosexism are abundant. To examine such expressions, Hebl and colleagues (e.g., Hebl, Foster, Mannix, et al., 2002; Hebl, King, Glick, et al.,

2007; King, Shapiro, Hebl, et al., 2006) introduced a distinction between 'formal' and 'interpersonal' forms of discrimination.

Formal discrimination consists of behaviors directed toward stigmatized group members that are typically prohibited by law (e.g., unfair selection and promotions). Interpersonal discrimination, however, consists of behaviors that are not legally sanctioned (e.g., nonverbal behaviors, socially isolating behaviors) but that can accumulate over time to create profound differences in advantage (Martell, Lane, & Emrich, 1996; Valian, 1998). Hebl, Foster, Mannix, et al. (2002) had confederate 'applicants' (blind to their condition) wear hats labeled with either 'Gay and Proud' (pretested as stigmatizing) or 'Texan and proud' (pretested as neutral) and apply for retail jobs. Researchers coded tape-recorded conversations between managers and 'applicants,' examined questionnaires indicating managerial reactions that were completed by applicants, and counted the job callbacks for three months following the initial interactions. The results revealed that gay and lesbian applicants did *not* experience formal discrimination (i.e., no differences in being told there were jobs available, being able to fill out applications, or in receiving job callbacks) relative to assumed heterosexual applicants. However, gay and lesbian applicants consistently faced more interpersonal discrimination (e.g., terminated interactions, less warmth, increased interaction distance, more rudeness) than did assumed heterosexual applicants. These results were replicated by Singletary & Hebl (2009) and reveal the importance of examining prejudice and discrimination in various forms. Many factors may restrain perceivers from formally discriminating against nonheterosexual targets (i.e., organizational policies, pressures of political correctness, increases in egalitarian attitudes), necessitating the examination of more covert, interpersonal discrimination.

Identity disclosure

Disclosures often happen within the context of social interactions and can alter social interactions profoundly in both positive and negative ways. Additionally, through a variety of ways (i.e., suspicions, information from second-hand sources, prior acknowledgments on the part of targets), perceivers may come to learn or suspect sexual orientation of nonheterosexual targets. In Figure 21.2, we present an illustration of the various ways in which these disclosures (from the target), information known/suspected (by the perceiver), and information disclosed (from the target) interact to influence mixed interactions. In the interests of clarity, this represents a simplification of the broader range of identity management strategies that nonheterosexual individuals might use.

Nonheterosexual targets may disclose their orientation to perceivers who already know or suspect the target's orientation (see cell A). Such disclosures, or 'acknowledgments,' can greatly benefit both interactants. Targets benefit from verifying their true identity to others (see Swann, Polzer, Seyle, et al., 2004; see also Ragins, 2008), and prevent the negative effects on mental health that are associated with keeping secrets (Fassinger, 1996; Smart & Wegner, 2000). Perceivers benefit because acknowledgments can reduce anxiety and self-regulatory efforts that occur when they must suppress a topic that is on their minds but is taboo for them to introduce. Perceivers may also appreciate acknowledgments to the extent that the disclosure makes them feel special, trusted, or otherwise important (see Jones & Archer, 1976; Taylor, Gould, & Brounstein, 1981). Acknowledgments may also hinder interactions if the content reveals poor adjustment (see Hebl & Skorinko, 2006) or is delivered too soon in an interaction (King, Reilly, & Hebl, 2008b).

Nonheterosexual targets may disclose to heterosexual perceivers who do not know or suspect the targets' sexual orientation (see cell B). Such targets may experience benefits but also become vulnerable to enhanced discrimination (Croteau, 1996). For perceivers, the more surprised and prejudiced they are, the more likely they will experience the disclosure as an awkward and negative event.

	Nonheterosexual target discloses	Nonheterosexual target does not disclose
Heterosexual perceiver suspects/knows	Target: self-verification, potential discrimination **A** Perceiver: relief from thought suppression, potential benefits of self-disclosure (feel special, trusted, important), motivation to appear nonprejudiced	Target: problems associated with concealment, potential identity disconnects, potentially avoid discrimination **C** Perceiver: thought suppression, motivation to appear nonprejudiced
Heterosexual perceiver does not suspect/know	Target: self-verification, potential discrimination **B** Perceiver: potential benefits of self-disclosure (feel special, trusted, important), surprise element, potentially awkward	Target: problems associated with concealment, potential identity disconnects, passing, potentially avoid discrimination **D** Perceiver: no detection

Figure 21.2   The ways disclosures interact to influence mixed interactions.

Benefits accrued in this scenario may also depend on disclosure characteristics (e.g., directness, timing; King, Reilly, & Hebl, 2008b).

Nonheterosexual targets may not disclose but perceivers may know and/or suspect targets' orientation (see cell C). This predicament presents challenges for perceivers because norms prevent them from initiating conversations about targets' stigmas. Thus, they may exert great efforts to suppress stigma-related thoughts. For prejudiced perceivers, this scenario may evoke rampant discrimination and the target (who has not disclosed) may not even recognize its origin.

Finally, the nonheterosexual targets may not disclose and heterosexual perceivers may not suspect or know targets' sexual orientation (see cell D). In this situation, the target is doing what Goffman (1963: 73) refers to as 'passing.' Such targets seemingly accrue the same interaction benefits given to nonstigmatized interactants because perceivers are unaware and cannot discriminate; yet, targets

must simultaneously manage potential stress and anxiety associated with being 'closeted' and concealing (e.g., Frable, Platt, & Hoey, 1998; Major & Gramzow, 1999).

CONSEQUENCES OF MIXED INTERACTIONS

Both the target and perceiver experience positive and negative consequences from mixed interactions. From the target's perspective, interactions that have gone well and are devoid of perceptions of discrimination, particularly when targets are able to successfully self-disclose, can be affirming and relieving (see Woods, 1993). Targets may feel reduced amounts of stress, experience congruency across life domains, increased social support, and increased voice (see Ragins, 2008). However, interactions that go badly for the target may create extensive problems.

Perceptions and experiences of discrimination are related to increased stress and poor physical health for targets (Waldo, 1999) and job-related outcomes such as lower organizational commitment, career commitment, organizational self-esteem and job satisfaction (Ragins and Cornwell, 2001). Perceivers also experience consequences. On the positive side, by denigrating others, perceivers may actually experience a stereotype 'lift' (Davies, Spencer, Quinn, et al., 2002), in which they bolster their own sense of self-esteem through denigrating others. Engaging in discrimination may also relieve perceivers' anxiety associated with an ambivalent state (see Crocker, Major, & Steele, 1998) and may be a desirable end state for those who are actually prejudiced (see Crandall and Eshleman, 2003). On the negative side, prejudiced perceivers may inhibit their own development processes, miss out on developing friendships, and suffer consequences in the workplace (e.g., reduced likelihood of being helped prosocially; King, Hebl, Matusik, et al., in press).

REMEDIATION STRATEGIES

Remediation strategies can do much to improve perceivers' and targets' experiences in mixed interactions. Such strategies can be categorized into those adopted by the target; those adopted by the perceiver and third-party individuals in the interaction; and those enacted at a larger institutional, organizational, or national levels.

What can nonheterosexual targets do?

We discuss four strategies that targets can adopt to remediate negative interactions and outcomes:

- optimal self-disclosures,
- concealment and counterfeiting,
- compensation,
- individuation.

Optimal self-disclosures
Research conducted on disclosures reveals a positive link between disclosing and both

healthy personal identity development, as well as professional related outcomes for nonheterosexual individuals (Button, 2001; Day & Schoenrade, 1997; Griffith & Hebl, 2002; Hebl & Kleck, 2002). As indicated in Figure 21.2, however, disclosures may result in both advantages and disadvantages; hence, we review characteristics associated with successful disclosure experiences: (a) reasons for disclosing ('if'), (b) timing of disclosures ('when'), (c) methods of disclosing ('how'), and (d) recipients of self disclosure ('to whom') may all greatly impact the success of such a remediation strategy.

First, deciding to disclose may be most strategic for targets whose nonheterosexual orientation is very central to their identities. Specifically, for individuals who experience 'personal hell' (i.e., Smart & Wegner, 2000) by remaining closeted and/or who otherwise strongly identify with their nonheterosexual identity, the potential discrimination that they face is greatly outweighed by the personal benefits that they derive from not having to hide their orientation from others. Second, the timing of the disclosure impacts the success, but in ways that may be optimally different for the heterosexual perceiver versus the nonheterosexual target. That is, targets prefer disclosing immediately in interactions and perceivers prefer receiving disclosures after the passage of some time (King et al., 2008b).

Third, targets vary in *how* they disclose with some doing it openly and directly (e.g., stating upfront 'I'm gay') while others do it indirectly (e.g., display a pink triangle; Crouteau, 1996). King, Reilly, & Hebl, (2008b) found that targets preferred to disclose in explicit ways and that perceivers showed no preference in the disclosures they received. Fourth, disclosures are most strategic when the recipients are supportive. Such disclosures can result in a win-win situation – nonheterosexual individuals feel confirmation of their identities and experience social support while heterosexual recipients are accepting, do not show or feel prejudice and discrimination, and even derive benefits from the disclosure (i.e., Jones and Archer, 1976; Taylor, Gould,

& Brounstein, 1981). Many of the positive outcomes that nonheterosexual individuals experience as a result of 'coming out' (i.e., job satisfaction, organizational commitment) are fully mediated by disclosure recipients' favorable reactions (Button, 2001; Griffith & Hebl, 2002). Thus, if there is some way that targets can learn how heterosexist their interactants are, they might use this information to decide whether disclosing would be strategic.

Concealment and counterfeiting

Some targets decide to conceal, or actively hide their nonheterosexual orientation, in an attempt to avoid discrimination (Woods, 1993). However, for many individuals, concealment is not a desirable or healthy goal (Cain, 1991; Coleman, 1982). Other targets decide to counterfeit, or engage in active deception such as changing pronouns of significant others or engaging in conversation that makes references to their having a heterosexual partner (Chrobot-Mason, Button, & DiClementi, 2001; Woods, 1993). Unfortunately, such a strategy can have psychological and physiological costs such as increased stress, decreased self-esteem, and obsessive thinking (Corrigan & Matthews, 2003; Lane & Wegner, 1995).

Compensation

Nonheterosexual individuals who suspect they might be the target of discrimination may compensate, or engage in verbal and nonverbal behaviors designed to circumvent others' negative reactions. For instance, targets might accentuate their friendliness or behave in ways that indicate interest, positivity, and/or kindness. Singletary & Hebl (in press) examined the potential effectiveness of the compensation strategy for nonheterosexual individuals by having 'Gay and Proud' applicants (see Hebl, Foster, Mannix, et al., 2002) make enthusiastic statements and smile more and use more eye contact with managers. Relative to a control condition in which they were not instructed to engage in compensation, targets who compensated experienced less interpersonal discrimination.

Individuation

Prejudicial and discriminatory reactions are heightened toward individuals when perceivers know only the stigmatized status and little else about the target (Fiske and Neuberg, 1990). For this reason, it is advantageous for targets to present perceivers with information beyond their stigmatizing status. Singletary and Hebl (in press) also examined this strategy and found that 'Gay and Proud' job applicants who individuated themselves experienced less interpersonal discrimination than those in a 'Gay and Proud' control condition.

What can the perceiver and/or others do?

Perceivers can also engage in remediation strategies although it may be fairly unlikely that perceivers who are heterosexist want to change their attitudes and behaviors. For perceivers who want to reduce their negative assumptions and/or for less prejudicial perceivers who nonetheless may display anxieties that can be interpreted as prejudice and discrimination, the most effective strategy might be to simply engage in increased intergroup contact. This has repeatedly been shown to be an effective means of reducing prejudice and discrimination and has been shown to be particularly effective in heterosexual/nonheterosexual mixed interactions.

Another strategy that may be effective is for perceivers to witness nonprejudiced attitudes and nondiscriminatory intentions being modeled by others. That is, in a study conducted by Zitek and Hebl (2007), individuals who heard others condemn discrimination against stigmatized individuals (including 'gays') showed significant increases in favorable attitudes and reduced behavioral intentions to discriminate than those who heard others condone or say nothing about such discrimination. Although such interactions lasted fewer than five minutes, the reductions in discrimination were both immediate and also showed longer-term effects still evident one month later. Thus, even seemingly small actions on the part of third-party individuals can have enormous consequences.

What can be done at the organizational and national level?

Initiatives that can be adopted by organizations are particularly advantageous to the target because they remove the burden of remediation from the victim of discrimination and also because the effects or these institutional strategies may impact more than a single interaction or relationship. We discuss two initiatives – protective legislation and other organizational policies.

Protective legislation

There may be nothing more remediative with regard to discrimination against nonheterosexual individuals than laws that prevent discrimination and make such behaviors illegal. Not surprisingly, Ragins and Cornwell (2001) identified that one of the most important factors influencing nonheterosexual individuals' perceptions of discrimination in the workplace was the presence of protective legislation. Unfortunately, such legal protection is limited. Title VII of the Civil Rights Act of 1964 did not include nonheterosexual individuals as a protected class. This lack of federal protection prompted a barrage of efforts to enact legislation, and in 1973, the Civil Services Commission issued a bulletin stating that federal agencies could not discriminate against an individual based on sexual orientation (Lewis, 1997). In this same year, the Board of Trustees at the American Psychiatric Association removed homosexuality as a mental disease from the *Diagnostic and Statistical Manual of Psychiatric Disorders*. Two years later, the Civil Service Reform Act made it illegal to discriminate against a federal employee 'on the basis of conduct which does not adversely affect the performance of the employee or applicant or the performance of others' (Human Rights Campaign [HRC], 2002). Furthermore, in 1998, President Clinton amended Executive Order 11478 and added 'sexual orientation' to the list of protected groups (Executive Order 13087, 1998), making it illegal for the federal government to discriminate against *civilian* employees based on sexual orientation.

Although nonheterosexual federal employees are protected from discrimination, millions of Americans across the country are not protected, and discrimination in the armed forces remains legal.

In 1994, the Employment Nondiscrimination Act (ENDA) was introduced to members of Congress, which would prohibit employers from using sexual orientation as the sole basis for making employment decisions. If passed, ENDA would not cover the following:

1) small businesses with fewer than fifteen employees,
2) religious organizations (including educational institutions substantially controlled or supported by religious organizations),
3) members of the armed forces,
4) the use of quotas or preferential treatment based on sexual orientation of the individual,
5) preferential treatment for any individual or group based on sexual orientation.

Despite these exceptions, this piece of legislation may pave the way for decreased heterosexism (cf. Badgett, 1995). Yet, because of heterosexism itself, ENDA has not yet been passed and continues to meet with resistance. Partly in response to this resistance, battles are being fought at the state-level. For instance, since 2004, 14 states and the District of Columbia have prohibited sexual orientation discrimination. Additional legislation is also underway that would further reduce discrimination such as The Tax Equity for Health Plan Beneficiaries Act (House of Representatives Version) and the Domestic Partner Health Benefits Equity Act (The Senate Version), both of which seek to alleviate the tax burden on gay men and lesbians, who must pay taxes on health insurance benefits for domestic partners, and the Family and Medical Leave Inclusion Act, which would allow employees leave to care for a seriously ill domestic partner, same-sex married partner, adult child, sibling or grandparent. The counter-offensive legislation (i.e., The Federal Marriage Amendment (FMA), The Don't Ask, Don't Tell Policy) that has been and is being introduced reveals that there are many institutionalized obstacles to extinguishing heterosexism and that there is still a long way to go.

Organizational policies

Many organizations are not waiting for legislation to pass and are simply taking matters in their own hands by mandating policies that forbid discrimination against gay employees, offer same-sex partner benefits, and welcome same-sex partners at company events. This, in turn, leads nonheterosexual employees to experience an organizational culture of support and inclusion (Friskopp & Silverstein, 1995; Mickens, 1994; Ragins & Cornwell, 2001). More specifically, Day and Schoenrade (2000) found that the inclusion of sexual orientation in an anti-discrimination statement was positively related to both job satisfaction and affective organizational commitment. Griffith and Hebl (2002) also found that those who worked for companies perceived to be gay-supportive reported more favorable job-related attitudes. Ragins and Cornwell (2001) found that nonheterosexual employees perceived less discrimination when they had gay supervisors and when they had larger percentages of gay coworkers in their group. In essence, these findings suggest that the organizational climate is a fundamental predictor of the extent to which heterosexism will be predicted and actually occurs (see also Welle & Button, 2004).

FUTURE DIRECTIONS FOR RESEARCH ON HETEROSEXISM

Research on heterosexism is still in its infancy; hence, there are many promising directions for future research. We particularly encourage researchers to examine heterosexism within the context of ongoing social interactions and to better identify the attitudes and behaviors of both heterosexual perceivers and nonheterosexual targets in mixed interactions. Figure 21.1 provides only a rudimentary model of such mixed interactions but we encourage researchers to develop more sophisticated models in which affect, cognitions, and behaviors involved

in heterosexist attitudes and behaviors, the 'coming out' experience, and effective personal strategies for combating heterosexism are better understood.

We also encourage researchers to examine more organizational-level strategies that can be adopted to reduce heterosexism. One such strategy may involve the use of diversity training programs. An ongoing program of research conducted by King and Hebl (2009) designed and compared three strategies of diversity training with regard to sexual orientation diversity: 1) goal-setting, or making goals about ways in which individuals can decrease heterosexism, 2) perspective-taking, or considering what it must be like to spend a day in the life of a nonheterosexual individual, and 3) stereotype discrediting, or actively debunking some of the most common myths that comprise heterosexism. The preliminary results of this longitudinal study suggest that such interventions can help to reduce heterosexism. Thus, carefully designed training programs might serve as a method by which to reduce heterosexism in organizations. Other research supports the notion that diversity training might reduce discrimination and/or perceptions of discrimination (King, Dawson, Kravitz, et al., 2008a) but more research is needed.

SUMMARY AND CONCLUSIONS

In this chapter, we reviewed the research that has been conducted on heterosexism by focusing both on who is most likely to stigmatize others ('perceiver characteristics') and on who is most likely to be stigmatized ('target characteristics'). The research reveals that perceivers who are male, very young or very old, less educated, more fundamental in their religiosity, more conservative in their political ideology, living in rural areas, low in empathy, and have not had much previous contact with gay men and lesbian are most likely to be heterosexist. The research also reveals that targets who are male, more 'out,' have more central gay identities, are higher in stereotypicality, and are more sensitive to reactions from others are more likely to experience heterosexism.

In this chapter, we also examined the impact of heterosexism by considering 'mixed interactions,' which are social interactions that occur between heterosexual and gay/lesbian individuals. The research has shown that such interactions (a) are plagued with many forms of misunderstandings, (b) involve prejudice and discrimination emanating from both sides of the interaction, and (c) can be altered dramatically via simple behaviors (i.e., disclosure behaviors) in both positive and negative ways. There are a number of elements that gay men and lesbians might adopt if and when they disclose, if they want to maximize the positive effect that the disclosure will have on its recipients. We described these elements as well as other strategies that gay men and lesbians might adopt to remediate negative interactions and outcomes. Perceivers can also act in ways that enhance such mixed interactions, and most of these behaviors involve increasing exposure to and interactions with gay men and lesbians. Finally, we described in this chapter the history of and important future role that protective legislation and organizational policies can play in improving the rights and welfare of gay men and lesbians.

We conclude by reminding readers that only a little more than 30 years ago gay men and lesbians were viewed by the American Psychiatric Association as having a mental disorder. In the last several decades, strides have been made in granting equality toward and increasing the tolerance and acceptance of gay men and lesbians. Indeed, attitudes toward those who are gay and lesbian are generally becoming more favorable, incidences of overt forms of discrimination have decreased, and many local laws and organizations now offer protection. Yet, this chapter reveals that more strides are needed as there is still a great deal of subtle, interpersonal discrimination, which may be just as pernicious as the more blatant forms. We hope future policies and protective laws will be passed and that more research will continue to focus on the stigma of heterosexism. Indeed, we look forward to a future in which individuals can reach their personal, social, and professional potentials, regardless of their sexual orientations.

REFERENCES

Badgett, M. V. L. (1995). The wage effects of sexual orientation discrimination. *Industrial and Labor Relations Review, 48*, 726–739.

Batson, C. D., Early, S., & Salvarani, G. (1997a). Perspective taking: Imagining how another feels versus imagining how you would feel. *Personality & Social Psychology Bulletin, 23*, 751–758.

Batson, C. D., Polycarpou, M. P., Harmon-Jones, E., Imhoff, H. J., Mitchener, E. C., Bednar, L. L., et al., (1997b). Empathy and attitudes: Can feeling for a member of a stigmatized group improve the feelings toward the group? *Journal of Personality and Social Psychology, 72*, 105–118.

Bierly, M. M. (1985). Prejudice toward contemporary outgroups as a generalized attitude. *Journal of Applied Social Psychology, 15*, 189–199.

Button, S. B. (2001). Organizational efforts to affirm sexual diversity: A cross-level examination. *Journal of Applied Psychology, 86*, 17–28.

Cain, R. (1991). Stigma management and gay identity development. *Social Work, 36*, 67–73.

Chrobot-Mason, D., Button, S. B., & DiClementi, J. D. (2001). Sexual identity management strategies: An exploration of antecedents and consequences. *Sex Roles, 45*, 321–336.

Clain, S. H., & Leppel, K. (2001). An investigation into sexual orientation discrimination as an explanation for wage differences. *Applied Economics, 33*, 37–47.

Coleman, E. (1982). Developmental stages of the coming out process. *Journal of Homosexuality, 8*, 31–43.

Corrigan, P. W., & Matthews, A. K. (2003). Stigma and disclosure: Implications for coming out of the closet. *Journal of Mental Health, 12*, 235–248.

Crandall, C. S., & Eshleman, A. (2003). A justification-suppression model of the expression and experience of prejudice. *Psychological Bulletin, 129*, 414–446.

Crocker, J., Major, B., & Steele, C. (1998). Social stigma. In S. Fiske, D. Gilbert, and G. Lindzey (Eds.), *Handbook of social psychology*, (Vol. 2, pp. 504–553). Boston, MA: McGraw Hill.

Croteau, J. M. (1996). Research on the work experiences of lesbian, gay, and bisexual people: An integrative review of methodology and findings. *Journal of Vocational Behavior, 48*, 195–209.

Davies, P. G., Spencer, S. J., Quinn, D. M., & Gerhardstein, R. (2002). Consuming images: How television commercials that elicit stereotype threat can restrain women academically and professionally. *Personality and Social Psychology Bulletin, 12,* 1615–1628.

Day, N. E., & Schoenrade, P. (1997). Staying in the closet versus coming out: Relationships between communication about sexual orientation and work attitudes. *Personnel Psychology, 50,* 147–163.

Day, N. E., & Schoenrade, P. (2000). The relationship among reported disclosure of sexual orientation, anti-discrimination policies, top management support and work attitudes of gay and lesbian employees. *Personnel Review, 29,* 346–363.

Dejowski, E. F. (1992). Public endorsement of restrictions on three aspects of free expression by homosexuals: Socio-demographic and trend analysis 1973–1088. *Journal of Homosexuality, 23,* 1–18.

Dovidio, J. F., Hebl, M. R., Richeson, J., & Shelton, N. (2006). Nonverbal behavior in intergroup context. In V. Manusov & M. L. Patterson (Eds.), *Handbook of nonverbal communication* (pp. 481–500). Thousand Oaks, CA: Sage.

Dovidio, J. F., Kawakami, K., & Gaertner, S.L. (2002). Implicit and explicit prejudice and interracial interaction. *Journal of Personality and Social Psychology, 82,* 62–68.

Eberhardt, J. L., Davies, P. G., Purdie-Vaughns, V. J., & Johnson, S. L. (2006). Looking deathworthy: Perceived stereotypicality of Black defendants predicts capital-sentencing outcomes. *Psychological Science, 17,* 383–386.

Eldridge, V. L., Mack, L., & Swank, E. (2006). Explaining comfort with homosexuality in rural America. *Journal of Homosexuality, 51,* 39–56.

Fassinger, R. E. (1996). Notes from the margins: Integrating lesbian experience into the vocational psychology of women. *Journal of Vocational Behavior, 48,* 160–175.

Fiske, S. T., & Neuberg, S. L. (1990). A continuum of impression formation, from category-based to individuating processes: Influences of information and motivation of attention and interpretation. In M. P. Zanna (Ed.), *Advances in experimental social psychology,* (Vol. 23, 1–68). San Diego, CA: Academic Press.

Frable, D. E. S., Platt, L., & Hoey, S. (1998). Concealable stigmas and positive self-perceptions: Feeling better around similar others. *Journal of Personality and Social Psychology, 74,* 909–922.

Friskopp, A., & Silverstein, S. (1995). *Straight jobs, gay lives; Gay and lesbian professionals, the Harvard Business School and the American workplace.* New York: Scribner.

Goffman, E. (1963). *Stigma: The management of spoiled identity.* New York, NY: Simon & Schuster.

Grack, C., & Richman, C. L. (1996). Reducing general and specific heterosexism through cooperative contact. *Journal of Psychology and Human Sexuality, 8,* 59–68.

Griffith, K. H., & Hebl, M. R. (2002). The disclosure dilemma for gay men and lesbians: "Coming out" at work. *Journal of Applied Psychology, 87,* 1191–1199.

Hebl, M. R., & Dovidio, J. F. (2005). Putting the social back in the examination of social stigmas. *Personality and Social Psychological Review, 9,* 156–182.

Hebl, M. R., Foster, J. M., Mannix, L. M., & Dovidio, J. F. (2002). Formal and interpersonal discrimination: A field study of bias toward homosexual applicants. *Personality and Social Psychology Bulletin, 28,* 815–825.

Hebl, M. R., King, E. B., Glick, P., Singletary, S., & Kazama, S. (2007). Hostile and benevolent behaviors toward pregnant women: Complementary interpersonal punishments and rewards that maintain traditional roles. *Journal of Applied Psychology, 92,* 1499–1511.

Hebl, M. R., & Kleck, R. E. (2002). Acknowledging one's stigma in the interview setting: Effective strategy or liability? *Journal of Applied Social Psychology, 32,* 223–249.

Hebl, M. R., & Skorinko, J. L. (2006). Acknowledging one's physical disability in the interview: Does "when" make a difference? *Journal of Applied Social Psychology, 35,* 2477–2492.

Herek, G. M. (2000). Sexual prejudice and gender: Do heterosexuals' attitudes toward lesbians and gay men differ? *Public Opinion Quarterly, 66,* 40–66.

Herek, G. M. (2002). Gender gaps in public opinion about lesbians and gay men. *Public Opinion Quarterly, 66,* 40–66.

Herek, G. M. (1984). Beyond "homophobia": A social psychological perspective on attitudes toward lesbians and gay men. *Journal of Homosexuality, 10,* 1–21.

Herek, G. M. (2004). Beyond "homophobia": Thinking about sexual stigma and prejudice in the twenty-first century. *Sexuality Research and Social Policy, 1,* 6–24.

Herek, G. M., & Capitanio, J.P. (1996). "Some of my best friends": Intergroup contact, concealable stigma, and heterosexuals' attitudes toward gay men and lesbians. *Personality and Social Psychology Bulletin, 22,* 412–424.

Herek, G. M., Widaman, K. F., & Capitanio, J. P. (2005). When sex equals AIDS: Symbolic stigma and heterosexual adults' inaccurate beliefs about sexual transmission of AIDS. *Social Problems, 52,* 15–37.

Hicks, G. R., & Lee, T. (1997). Public attitudes toward gays and lesbians: Trends and predictors. *Journal of Homosexuality, 51*, 57–77.

Hoover, R., & Fishbein, H. D. (1999). The development of prejudice and sex role stereotyping in white adolescents and white young adults. *Journal of Applied Developmental Psychology, 20*, 431–448.

Human Rights Campaign (2002). The state of the workplace: For lesbian, gay, and transgender American. Accessed May 23, 2006 from http://www.hrc.org/ Template.cfm?Section=Employment_Non-Discrimination_Act&Template=/ ContentManagement/ContentDisplay.cfm&ContentID=15245.

Irwin, P., & Thompson, N. L. (1977). Acceptance of the rights of homosexuals: A social profile. *Journal of Homosexuality, 3*, 107–121.

Johnson, M. E., Brems, C., & Alford-Keating, P. (1997). Personality correlates of homophobia. *Journal of Homosexuality, 34*, 57–69.

Jones, E. E., & Archer, R. L. (1976). Are there special effects of personalistic self-disclosure? *Journal of Experimental Social Psychology, 12*, 180–193.

Jones, E. E., Farina, A., Hastorf, A. H., Markus, H., Miller, D. T., & Scott, R. A. (1984). *Social stigma: The psychology of marked relationships.* New York: Freeman.

Jung, P. B., & Smith, R.F. (1993). *Heterosexism: An ethical challenge.* Albany: State University of New York Press.

Kerns, J. G., & Fine, M. A. (1994). The relation between gender and negative attitudes toward gay men and lesbians: Do gender role attitudes mediate this relation? *Sex Roles, 31*, 297–307.

King, E. B., Dawson, J. F., Kravitz, D. A., & Gulick, L. M. V. (2008). A longitudinal study of the relationships between diversity training, ethnic discrimination, and satisfaction in organizations. Unpublished manuscript. George Mason University.

King, E. B., Reilly, C., & Hebl, M. R. (2008). The best and worst of times: Dual perspectives of coming out in the workplace. *Group and Organization Management, 33*, 566–601.

King, E. B., & Hebl, M. R. (2009). Diversity training: Three strategies that attempt to reduce discrimination on the basis of sexual orientation. Unpublished manuscript. Rice University.

King, E. B., Hebl, M. R., Matusik, S., & George, J. (in press). Understanding tokenism: Antecedents and consequences of psychological climate for gender inequity. *Journal of Management.*

King, E. B., Shapiro, J., Hebl, M. R., Singletary, S., & Turner, S. (2006). The stigma of obesity in customer service: A mechanism of remediation and bottom-line consequences of interpersonal discrimination. *Journal of Applied Psychology, 91*, 579–593.

Kleck, R. E., & Strenta, A. (1980). Perceptions of the impact of negatively valued physical characteristics on social interaction. *Journal of Personality and Social Psychology, 39*, 861–873.

Kunkel, L. E., & Temple, L. L. (1992). Attitudes toward AIDS and homosexuals: Gender, marital status, and religion. *Journal of Applied Social Psychology, 22*, 1030–1040.

Lambert, E. G., Ventura, L. A., Hall, D. E., & Cluse-Tolar, T. (2006). College students' views on gay and lesbian issues: Does education make a difference? *Journal of Homosexuality, 50*, 1–30.

Lane, J. D., & Wegner, D. M. (1995). The cognitive consequences of secrecy. *Journal of Personality and Social Psychology, 69*, 1–17.

Lewis, G. B. (1997). Lifting the ban on gays in the civil service: Federal policy toward gay and lesbian employees since the Cold War. *Public Administration Review, 57*, 387–395.

Linneman, T. J. (2004). Homophobia and hostility: Christian conservative reactions to the political and cultural progress of lesbians and gay men. *Sexuality Research & Social Policy, 1*, 56–76.

Loftus, J. (2001). America's liberalization in attitudes toward homosexuality, 1973–1998. *American Sociological Review, 66*, 762–782.

Major, B., & Gramzow, R. H. (1999). Abortion as stigma: Cognitive and emotional implications of concealment. *Journal of Personality and Social Psychology, 77*, 735–745.

Martell, R. F., Lane, D. M., and Emrich, C. (1996). Male-female differences: A computer simulation. *American Psychologist, 51*, 157–158.

Mendoza-Denton, R., Downey, G., Purdie, V. J., Davis, A., & Pietrzak, J. (2002). Sensitivity to status-based rejection: Implications for African-American students' college experiences. *Journal of Personality and Social Psychology, 83*, 896–918.

Mickens, E. (1994). Including sexual orientation in diversity programs and policies. *Employment Relations Today, 12*, 263–75.

Pettigrew, T. F., & Tropp, L. R. (2006). A meta-analytic test of intergroup contact theory. *Journal of Personality and Social Psychology, 90*, 751–783.

Pinel, E. C. (1999). Stigma consciousness: The psychological legacy of social stereotypes. *Journal of Personality and Social Psychology, 76*, 114–128.

Ragins, B. R. (2008). Disclosure disconnects: Antecedents and consequences of disclosing invisible stigmas across life domains. *Academy of Management Review, 33*, 194–215.

Ragins, B. R., & Cornwell, J. M. (2001). Pint triangles: Antecedents and consequences of perceived workplace discrimination against gay and lesbian employees. *Journal of Applied Psychology, 86*, 1244–1261.

Ragins, B. R., Cornwell, J. M., & Miller, J. S. (2003). Heterosexism in the workplace. *Group & Organization Management, 28*, 45–74.

Settles, I. H. (2004). When multiple identities interfere: The role of identity centrality. *Personality and Social Psychology Bulletin, 30*, 487–500.

Shelton, J. N., Richeson, J. A., & Salvatore, J. (2005). Expecting to be the target of prejudice: Implications for interethnic interactions. *Personality and Social Psychology Bulletin, 31*, 1189–1202.

Singletary, S. L. B., & Hebl, M. R. (in press). Targeting the subtleties: Strategies for remediating interpersonal discrimination. *Journal of Applied Psychology.*

Smart, L., & Wegner, D.M. (2000). The hidden costs of stigma. In T. F. Heatherton, R. E. Kleck, M. R. Hebl & J. G. Hull (Eds.) *The social psychology of stigma* (pp. 220–242). New York: Guilford Press.

Swann, W. B., Jr., Polzer, J. T., Seyle, D. C., & Ko, S. J. (2004). Finding value in diversity: Verification of personal and social self-views in diverse groups. *Academy of Management Review, 29*, 9–27.

Taylor, D. A., Gould, R. J., & Brounstein, P. J. (1981). Effects of personalistic self-disclosure. *Personality and Social Psychology Bulletin, 7*, 487–492.

Turner, J. C. (1991). *Social influence.* Milton Keynes, UK: Open University Press.

Valian, V. (1998). *Why so slow? The advancement of women.* Cambridge, MA: MIT Press.

Vorauer, J. D., Main, K. J., & O'Connell, G. B. (1998). How do individuals expect to be viewed by members of lower status groups? Content and implications of meta-stereotypes. *Journal of Personality and Social Psychology, 4*, 917–937.

Waldo, C.R. (1999). Working in a majority context: A structural model of heterosexism as minority stress in the workplace. *Journal of Counseling Psychology, 46*, 218–232.

Welle, B., & Button, S. B. (2004). Workplace experiences of lesbian and gay employees: A review of current research. *International Review of Industrial and Organizational Psychology, 19*, 139–170.

Weiner, B. (1995). *Judgments of responsibility: A theory of social conduct.* New York, NY: Guilford.

Whitley, B. E. Jr. (2001). Gender-role variables and attitudes toward homosexuality. *Sex Roles, 45*, 691–721.

Whitely, B. E., & Kite, M. E. (1995). Sex difference in attitudes toward homosexuality: A comment on Oliver and Hyde (1993). *Psychological Bulletin, 117*, 146–154.

Woods, J. D. (with Lucas, J. H.). (1993). *The corporate closet: The professional lives of gay men in America.* New York: The Free Press.

Zitek, E. M., & Hebl, M. R. (2007). The role of social norm clarity in the influenced expression of prejudice over time. *Journal of Experimental Social Psychology, 43*, 867–876.

22

Anti-Immigration Bias

Ulrich Wagner, Oliver Christ, and
Wilhelm Heitmeyer

ABSTRACT

Migrants, especially those who cross national state boarders, become targets of political debates, often involving derogation of immigrants, and both discrimination and violence against them. This chapter starts with a brief look at the history of bias against immigrants and the history of the accompanying social psychological research. We then present the currently most prominent explanatory concepts for anti-immigrant bias, such as intergroup competition, threat, and emotions as well as national identification. Social psychological processes are embedded in and moderated by societal variables. A multilevel model of social context and psychological influences describes how societal variables affect the influence of social psychological processes on bias against immigrants. The chapter ends with a description of means to prevent and reduce bias against immigrants, followed by some recommendations for expanding future research by taking the needs of both the receiving society and migrants into account.

ANTI-IMMIGRATION BIAS

Migration is a central characteristic of the modern world (Adler & Gielen, 2003). Many countries, particularly in Western Europe as well as in traditional immigration countries such as the United States and Canada, are facing an increasing inflow of different immigrant groups (Pettigrew, 1998a). The integration of immigrants into society is a challenge for both immigrants and host societies. This is one of the reasons why the issues of immigration and multiculturalism are major topics in political and public debate.

Cross-culturally, immigrants face negative attitudes (e.g., Dovidio & Esses, 2001; Duckitt, 1993; Heitmeyer, 2002; Pettigrew, Jackson, Ben Brika, et al., 1998; Scheepers, Gijsberts, & Coenders, 2002) and negative stereotypes (Lee & Fiske, 2006) in host countries. These forms of bias against immigrants represent a serious social issue because they are often accompanied by discriminatory behavior and violence against immigrants (Wagner, Christ, & Pettigrew, 2008; Wagner and Christ, 2007) and they pave the way for right-wing extremism (Dovidio, Brigham, Johnson, et al., 1996; Schütz & Six, 1996; Talaska, Fiske, & Chaiken, 2008).

The chapter begins with a brief look at the history of bias against immigrants, which is closely connected to the history of racism. This is followed by an overview of current social psychological concepts explaining the emergence of prejudice against immigrants, especially intergroup competition, feelings of threat and emotions as well as national identification. In the third part we will present a more in-depth discussion of the simultaneous influence of social psychological and societal factors on bias against immigrants. The final section addresses ways of reducing bias against immigrants with a special focus on contact theory. We will summarize by placing emphasis on the fact that immigration is a challenge *and* an opportunity for both sides – immigrants and receiving societies.

RESEARCH HISTORY

Bias against immigrants is strongly connected to the concept of racism. The history of racism can be traced back to the mid fifteenth century when Portuguese navigators captured people living in the African sub-Saharan region and forced them to work as slaves in Europe and the colonies. Racism was grounded in the ideology of the inherent inferiority of non-natives (Fredrickson, 2002). Racist ideologies were accomplished and supported by scientific statements that tried to substantiate the emerging hierarchies between races according to phenotypic, genetic, and psychological differences. Early modern examples of racist biases against immigrants are the rejection of Irish immigrants in England in the nineteenth century and campaigns against South and East European immigrants in the United States in the early twentieth century (Miles, 1989). Thus, current prejudice against immigrants is based on a long history of negative stereotypes about immigrant groups (Mullen & Rice, 2003).

Social sciences and psychology began to focus on racist devaluations of ethnic groups as a reaction to the rise of Hitler in Germany and to the pseudo-scientific proofs of psychological race differences in Great Britain and the United States in the early 1920s (Miles, 1989; see also Chapter 2 by Duckitt, this volume). The analysis of bias against immigrants became an issue in *empirical* social science after World War

II, which focused especially on immigration to industrial countries in North America and Europe. Many of these early empirical analyses of bias toward immigrants were primarily descriptive (Katz & Braly, 1933; Sodhi & Bergius, 1953). In those days, social scientists also developed the necessary methodological tools as, for example, in conducting surveys. Up until the 1970s, the focus was mainly on migrant workers and their presence in the receiving countries. Only later did attitudes toward refugees who had fled war and civil war receive scientific attention.

Social psychology can look back on a tradition of more than 40 years of experimental laboratory research on intergroup relations (e.g., Blake & Mouton, 1961). This tradition has grown in importance due to the so-called minimal group experiments (Tajfel, Billig, Bundy, et al., 1971) which brought researchers' attention to the central role of social categorization and group identification in understanding intergroup relations. One consequence of this powerful experimental approach was that some scholars started to consider intergroup relations to be interchangeable. Thus it was assumed that they could all be traced back to the same basic psychological processes which are almost independent of context or the specific groups involved. However, the truth of this assumption can easily be challenged if one considers, for example, the relations between majority and minority groups in North America (with a White majority and a Black minority) and in South Africa (with a reversed population composition).

Sociologically-oriented research traditions started with the analysis of intergroup relations in real life or 'in the field' (e.g., Schuman, Steeh, Bobo, et al., 1997). Many of these studies were based on large surveys. However, even in this kind of research the possible problem of bias existed, since it focused primarily on the North American situation of Black and White relations (Dovidio & Esses, 2001). Again, the question is whether the results from this important US field of research, in which immigrant groups and ethnic minorities are clearly distinguished, can be extrapolated to the relation between new immigrants to Europe and its autochthonous population where people often do not differentiate between immigrants and ethnic minorities (Pettigrew, Jackson, Ben Brika, et al., 1998; Pettigrew, Wagner, & Christ, 2007).

SOCIAL PSYCHOLOGICAL EXPLANATIONS OF BIAS AGAINST IMMIGRANTS

In this section we will consider the explanatory power of classical social psychological predictors for understanding bias against immigrants. We will discuss the role of resource and identity conflicts and accomplishing emotions and then consider the effects of mere national ingroup identification (for discussion of other relevant variables, including social dominance orientation and authoritarianis, see Chapter 2 by Duckitt and Chapter 10 by Son Hing & Zanna, this volume).

Scarce resources, threat, and negative emotions

One of the most influential contributions to the understanding of intergroup conflict goes back to Muzafer Sherif (1966) field studies. In a series of field experiments in the United States involving boys aged 11–13 years, the authors showed that the struggle between groups for limited resources – in the Sherif studies a prize for a series of sports competitions – produces mutual prejudice and discrimination. This is also the central assumption in Sherif's realistic group conflict theory. The theory belongs to a group of similar theoretical developments within psychology and sociology like Allport's (1954) assumptions about instrumental relations between groups, Blumer's (1958) group position theory, relative deprivation theory (Stouffer, Suchman, DeVinney, et al., 1949) as well as group relative deprivation theory (Runciman, 1966). All of these theories

share the assumption that if group members perceive themselves as competing for material resources with the outgroup devaluation of the outgroup emerges.

Tajfel (1978; Tajfel & Turner, 1979) extended the perspective by proposing that not only restricted material resources are an important cause of intergroup conflict, but also group status and social identities which are derived from group memberships. According to social identity theory group members seek to improve the status of their ingroup in comparison to relevant outgroups in order to maintain or achieve a positive social identity. Thus, immigrants can become the target of prejudice when there is an indication of threat to the national ingroup's non-material status, such as, for example, important cultural values.

Threat and the perception of threat play an important role in many contemporary theories explaining prejudice toward immigrants. Immigration implies, by definition, moving and intrusion into a geographical area. Many scholars in the field assume that the perception of immigrants as a threat (e.g., Cottrell & Neuberg, 2005; Stephan & Renfro, 2002) is the relevant mediator between (the perception of) conflict over material or symbolic resources on the one hand and intergroup attitudes and behavior on the other. In this sense, Esses, Dovidio, Jackson, and Armstrong (2001; see also Esses, Jackson, & Abu-Ayyash, in press) argue in their instrumental model of group conflict that resource stress such as limited access to economic resources within a society, and the perception of a potential competing outgroup such as immigrants, lead to the perception of competition and anxiety. As a consequence, prejudice toward immigrants emerges (see also Esses, Jackson, & Armstrong, 1998).

A number of scholars have extended and further differentiated the concept of threat. Branscombe, Ellemers, Spears, et al., (1999) assume that another relevant predictor of bias against immigrants can be identity threat stemming from undermining the ingroup's distinctiveness from an outgroup. In addition, Guimond and Dambrun (2002) observed that there are more factors than relative deprivation that contribute to outgroup discrimination: Groups who are in an unjustified superior position show bias against outgroups. This can be explained by the assumption that relative gratification is a threat to societal justice norms (see also Jost, Banaji, & Nosek, 2004) and that prejudice emerges in order to justify the privileged ingroup position. Survey data from South Africa on prejudice against immigrants support this hypothesis (Dambrun, Taylor, McDonald, et al., 2006).

The effect of threat on outgroup rejection (for a meta-analytic summary see Riek, Mania, & Gaertner, 2006) and attitudes toward immigrants (e.g., Esses, Jackson, & Armstrong, 1998; Florack, Piontkowski, Rohrmann, Balzer, & Perzig, 2003; Stephan, Ybarra, Schwarzwald , et al., 1998; Ward & Masgoret, 2006; Wilson, 2001) is pervasive. Dovidio and Esses (2001) point out that there is a high likelihood that immigrants will be perceived as a threat, independent of their immigration success: If they are not viewed as successful, it is likely that they will be perceived as a threat to the country's economic prosperity. By contrast, if immigrants succeed, they are perceived as competing with the host society over jobs and other resources.

In a very recent theoretical development, Cuddy, Fiske, and Glick (2008; see also Cottrell & Neuberg, 2005) have connected perceived intergroup competition with outgroup stereotypes, emotions, and behavioral tendencies. In addition to traditional theories, they assume that the influence of intergroup competition is moderated by the status or power that is attributed to the outgroup. Competition is associated with a reduced perception of the outgroup as warm, whereas status varies positively with the degree to which the outgroup is perceived as competent. The *stereotype content model* (Cuddy, Fiske, & Glick, 2008) describes four kinds of stereotypes that derive from crossing high/low levels of the two orthogonal dimensions of competition (warmth) and status (competence): Outgroups perceived to be low in competition and high in status are admired, whereas outgroups high in competition and low in status are viewed with anger. The two remaining combinations are ambivalent: Envy is felt for those outgroups that are high on both competition and status, whereas pity is felt for outgroups that are low on both competition and competence. Thus, this perspective extends previous work by positing that negative stereotypes, emotions, and behaviors can also be observed in situations of low competition, namely when the outgroup is perceived to be of low status. Lee and Fiske (2006) demonstrated how this model can be applied to different immigrant groups to the United States. They showed that Asian immigrants are considered as highly competitive and of high status, with the consequence that this immigrant group was perceived as low in warmth and high in competence. In contrast to Asian immigrants, Latino and Irish immigrants were classified as less competitive and of lower status, which produced a stereotype of comparably lower competence but higher warmth.

Ingroup identification is a concept that has proved to be relevant in the tradition of the minimal group experiments. Simultaneously, sociologists and political scientists discussed national ingroup identification as predictor of national outgroup devaluation. In the following section we will connect these two lines of research and consider the influence of national ingroup identification on anti-immigrant bias.

National ingroup identification

Bias against immigrants is strongly connected with *ethnocentrism*, a term introduced by the sociologist William Graham Sumner in 1906. He defined ethnocentrism as 'the technical name for this view of things in which one's own group is the centre of everything, and all others are scaled and valued with reference to it' (1906, p. 13). Thus, ethnocentrism contrasts the ingroup to the outgroup and their (respective) evaluation with each other (see also Allport, 1954; Brewer, 2001). Immigrants constitute a salient outgroup.

Therefore, attitudes toward immigrants can only be understood by considering national group membership, which defines group boundaries and schemata for understanding and assessing outgroup behavior. Hence, variations in the importance of the national ingroup are a relevant predictor of attitudes toward immigrants.

Social identity theory (Tajfel, 1978; Tajfel & Turner, 1979; see also Brown, 2000, and see Chapter 11 by Abrams & Hogg, this volume) assumes that the differentiation between the ingroup and outgroups, as demonstrated in the minimal group experiments (Tajfel, Billing, Bundy, et al., 1971), is motivated by the members' desire to improve the evaluation of the ingroup and of their social identity. Scholars have argued about whether the motive for a positive social identity is primarily fulfilled by favoring the ingroup or derogating the outgroup (Hinkle & Brown, 1990). Recent summaries (Brewer, 1999; Brown & Zagefka, 2005) come to the conclusion that ingroup identification covaries with outgroup derogation, especially in contexts where, among others, the groups are interwoven in a conflict of interests and supported by ideologies of moral superiority and exclusion. Thus, according to social identity theory, national identification should be positively related to the rejection of immigrants.

Research has shown that identification with one's own country does indeed relate to derogation of immigrant groups. This has been demonstrated for the United States (Adorno, Frenkel-Brunswick, Levinson, et al., 1950; De Figueiredo & Elkins, 2003), Austria, Hungary, Poland, and Slovakia (Weiss, 2003), in the Flanders region of Belgium (Billiet, Maddens, & Beerten, 2003), and for Germany (Blank & Schmidt, 2003). However, researchers also argue that not all kinds of national attachment lead to the derogation of immigrant outgroups. For example, Kosterman and Feshbach (1989; see also Bar-Tal, 1997; Schatz & Staub, 1997; Staub, 1997) distinguish between nationalism and patriotism. According to Kosterman and Feshbach, nationalism 'refers

to a belief in national superiority and dominance' (p. 175), 'feelings of nationalism are inherently comparative – and almost exclusively, downward comparative' (p. 178). Accordingly, nationalism is measured with reference to other countries using items such as, 'In view of America's moral and material superiority, it is only right that we should have the biggest say in deciding United Nations policy.' In contrast to nationalism, patriotism describes a feeling of attachment to the nation that is critical and 'self referential' (De Figueiredo & Elkins, 2003, p. 178). Typical items for measuring patriotism ask about the approval of the respondents's own nation's democratic development and the progress it has made in the social security system. Research has shown that patriotism, in fact, often correlates negatively (De Figueiredo & Elkins, 2003; Heyder & Schmidt, 2002) or not at all with outgroup prejudice (Blank & Schmidt, 2003; Karasawa, 2002). Applying cross-lagged analyses to longitudinal data from Germany, Wagner, Becker, Christ, et al., (2010; see also Becker, Wagner, & Christ, 2007), showed that the path from national ingroup identification to the devaluation of immigrants was significantly positive, whereas the path from patriotism to devaluation of immigrants was significantly negative. Thus, nationalism heightens negative sentiments toward immigrants while patriotism at first glance seems to reduce such sentiments.

Taking a social identity theory perspective, Mummendey, Klink, and Brown (2001; see also Mummendey & Simon, 1997; Nigbur & Cinniralla, 2006) explain the different relations of nationalism and patriotism to outgroup derogation by different types of comparisons: National attachment leads to outgroup derogation when the nation is compared with relevant outgroups such as immigrants. If, however, a historical comparison *within* one's own group is made, such as a comparison of development of ingroup attributes in the past, no correlation of ingroup attachment and outgroup derogation should emerge. Using an experimental priming procedure, Mummendey and colleagues

(2001) found support for their hypothesis (for another moderator of ingroup perception, see Bastian & Haslam, 2008).

The distinction between nationalism and patriotism and their predicted differential effects on attitudes toward immigrants have not been without criticism. According to Cohrs, Dimitrova, Kalchevska, et al., (2004), the 'good kind' of ingroup identification, patriotism, consists of two components: National identification and general esteem for democratic values and norms. Cohrs, Dimitrova, Kalchevska, et al. (2004) argue that the two components of patriotism have opposing effects: Identification increases outgroup devaluation and adherence to democratic norms reduces it. Cohrs, Dimitrova, Kalchevska, et al. (2004), Becker, Wagner, and Christ (2007) as well as Wagner, Becker, Christ, et al. (2010) report evidence supporting this perspective. In addition, one has to keep in mind that any kind of national ingroup identification can be misused and turned into a cause of outgroup devaluation (see also Brewer, 2001). The patriotism demanded by politics in the 'war against terrorism' is a prominent example (see also Bar-Tal, 1997).

Threat is not only a mediator of national ingroup identification and rejection of immigrants, but also a moderator of the relation between identification and derogation. From the perspective of social identity theory especially those native-born citizens who are highly identified with their national ingroup and who perceive immigrants as threatening to their national ingroup's resources or values should be biased against immigrants (Ellemers, Spears, & Doosje, 1999). Accordingly, Bizman and Yinon (2001) demonstrated in a survey of Israeli nationals that group threat was positively related to prejudice against Russian immigrants, especially for those respondents who were highly identified with their country.

As we have shown above, attitudes toward immigration depend on psychological variables, such as perception of conflict, threat and emotions as well as national identification. The processes involved are also dependent on and embedded in specific economic, political and social conditions (Berry, 2001; Deaux, 2006), which function as moderators of the above described psychological processes.

SOCIETAL INFLUENCES

Immigrants are not welcomed in many societies. National states and their politicians often engage in political activities to limit immigration, especially under economic stress and against immigration that is economically motivated. Palmer (1996), for instance, demonstrated that Canadians' opinions on the acceptable number of immigrants in their country closely depend on the country's unemployment rate. In addition, countries also differ in their general political position toward immigration (Neumayer, 2005), which is rooted in different histories (Mullen & Rice, 2003). For example, Vala, Lopes, and Lima (2008) argue that Portugal has developed a strong anti-racism norm due to the country's self-perception and self-presentation of having had a unique history of colonialism. This ideological background of *Luso–Tropicalism* would lower the degree of rejection of immigrants. In fact, the authors found that the widely observed positive co-variation of national identitification and anti-immigrant prejudice did not hold true for Portugal.

The effects of different immigration policies can also be documented by comparing Germany and Canada. Both countries have received large numbers of immigrants in the last decades (see Dovidio & Esses, 2001). However, Canada has historically considered immigration as an integral part of its development as a nation, whereas German officials have denied this for Germany for a long time (Zick, Wagner, van Dick, et al., 2001). Esses, Wagner, Wolf, et al., (2006) proposed that this historical difference may also be reflected in citizens' acceptance of immigrants (see also Esses, Dovidio, Semenya, et al., 2005). In an experimental study, the authors showed that Canadian respondents high in social dominance orientation (Sidanius & Pratto, 1999), who endorse hierarchical status between groups, expressed less negative attitudes toward immigrants when immigrant and non-immigrants were presented as belonging to a common ingroup. In contrast, in the same experimental condition German respondents high in social dominance orientation showed a stronger degree of immigrant rejection.

Nationalism tends to be associated with outgroup rejection, especially if ingroup norms imply moral superiority, devaluation, and exclusion of immigrants (Brewer, 1999; Brown & Zagefka, 2005). This kind of ideology can be expected, particularly when ingroup membership is based on attributes that are inborn or difficult to change. Accordingly, in a series of survey and longitudinal studies with British respondents, Pehrson, Brown, and Zagefka (2009) showed that the positive co-variation of national ingroup identification and bias against immigrants holds especially true for native individuals who consider national group membership to be based on ethnic, i.e., essentialist and unchangeable attributes (see also Pehrson, Vignoles, & Brown, 2009).

There are a number of other societal factors that affect the relations between nationals and immigrants. One is described in Berry's (e.g., 2004) theory of acculturation expectations. Berry distinguished four acculturation strategies, depending on the intention of immigrants to have contact with members of their origin and host societies: Integration (intention to have contact with both origin and host societies), assimilation (no contact with origin, contact with host society), segregation (contact with origin, no contact with host society), and marginalization/separation (no contact with either). Host societies that expect their immigrants to integrate are probably the most harmonious concerning biases toward immigrants, not least because many immigrants also prefer integration as acculturation strategy, as surveys have demonstrated (e.g., Arends-Tóth & van de Vijver, 2002). This is also in line with Bourhis, Moïse, Perreault, et al., (1997) interactive acculturation model, according to which host society and immigrant community interact harmoniously, if both sides prefer either

integration or assimilation of immigrants (see also Rohmann, Piontkowski, & van Randenborgh, 2008). All other combinations of host societies' and migrants' acculturation expectations are predicted to develop in a problematic or even conflictual manner.

Bourhis, Moïse, Perreault, et al. (1997) considered similarity in acculturation attitudes. Similarity of host population and immigrants on other dimensions also influences bias against immigrants. In this context the native population's perceived difference with respect to immigrants in terms of language and cultural backgrounds is of great importance (Fiske, Kitayama, Markus, et al., 1998). Differences may also become relevant when members of an individualistic society meet those of a collectivist cultural background (Hofstede, 1980). Similarities in language and value orientation ostensibly help to avoid misunderstandings in everyday life (Wagner & Küpper, 2007). However, too much similarity can also produce identity threat and thus lead to bias against immigrants (see above, Branscombe, Ellemers, Spears, et al., 1999, Esses, Jackson, & Armstrong, 1998).

Societies' and individuals' attitudes toward immigrants are also strongly influenced by daily developments and discourses. Hitlan, Carrillo, Aikman, et al., (2007) demonstrated how US respondents' feelings of threat associated with immigrants and prejudice against immigrants increased as a consequence of the September 11th terrorist attacks (see also Esses, Dovidio, & Hodson, 2002). On the basis of cross-sectional survey data for 2001 to 2003, Verkuyten and Zaremba (2005) showed how attitudes toward immigrants in the Netherlands were affected by the rise and murder of the right-wing populist politician, Pim Fortuyn. Brosius, and Esser (1995) presented supportive evidence for the assumption that the increase in the number of hate crimes against immigrants in Germany in the early 1990s was the result of a political and media debate about immigrants in the context of an initiative to restrict the right of asylum.

Immigrants and immigration and their perception as a threat are often due less to direct interaction with immigrants, and more to indirect influence (Blumer, 1958). If, as described above, struggle for scarce material resources and identities are important predictors of bias against immigrants, one has to take into account that those struggles for scarce resources are rarely the consequence of direct experience with an immigrant person or a group of immigrants, but rather are the result of social narratives. Wagner, Zick, and van Dick (2002) used an experimental approach to analyse the effect of peer group attitudes on an individual's perception of immigrants. Following the experimental paradigm of social influence, they showed that participants expressed a higher or lower degree of prejudice on the blatant-subtle prejudice scale (Pettigrew & Meertens, 1995) depending on whether they witnessed more or less prejudiced responses of two confederates on the same attitude measurement.

From a politician's point of view, focusing on the topic of immigration is one of the most effective ways to turn political debates in a specific direction. A psychological reason for this is the fact that emphasizing salience of and differentiation from a non-national ingroup increases national ingroup cohesion and feelings of belongingness (Brewer, 2001; Turner, Hogg, Oakes, et al., 1987). In addition, due to their status of not belonging to the ingroup and their political powerlessness, immigrants can easily be used as scapegoats for nearly any undeserved development within societies, be it unemployment, deficits in the health system, problems in education, and so on, which, in turn, leads to bias against immigrants. Further psychological processes might accelerate immigrant derogation. The false consensus effect describes the phenomenon whereby people who strongly reject a certain outgroup also assume that a high percentage of their reference group members share their attitude position. Such a misperception can then be used to rationalize becoming more extreme and thus increase the level of bias against immigrants.

One of the strongest social factors influencing the evaluation of immigrants is the mass media (see also Chapter 15 by Mutz &

Goldman, this volume). Media discourse often relates economic and political threats to immigrants (Galliker, Herman, Imminger, et al., 1998). Such public debate is then reflected in individually perceived threat and attitudes toward immigrants as well as behaviour toward immigrant groups (e.g., Maio, Esses, & Bell, 1994; Wagner, Zick, & van Dick, 2002). Brosius and Esser (1995) analysed time lagged co-variation of media presentations of immigrants in Germany in the 1990s and hate crimes one week later. The two co-varied significantly, supporting the assumption that media presentation has a causal effect on violence against immigrants (see also Koopmans & Olzack, 2004).

THEORETICAL INTEGRATION

We have described national ingroup identification and threat as major psychological determinants of native populations' bias against immigrants. In addition we have presented evidence that the influence of these factors is moderated by societal attributes such as whether a society defines itself as a country of immigration, native populations' understanding of important features of national group membership, the nation's economic, democratic and social development as well as the political misuse of debates about immigration to hide political mistakes. Thus societal and political conditions set the stage for psychological effects: They influence the degree of perceived threat and ingroup identification. In addition, they modify the effects of threat and ingroup identification on bias against immigrants. Figure 22.1 describes this heuristic multilevel model of societal context and social psychological influences on individuals' rejection of immigrants.

Up to now, social psychology in general and research on the explanation of bias against immigrants in particular have widely ignored theoretical approaches that take a multilevel perspective, which considers the mutual moderation of psychological and societal processes (Pettigrew, 2006). One of the very few exceptions is Heitmeyer's social

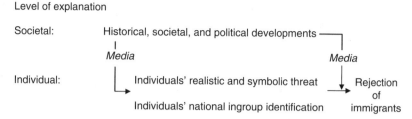

Figure 22.1   A multilevel model of societal context and social psychological influences on individuals' rejection of immigrants.

disintegration theory (Anhut & Heitmeyer, 2000). This framework posits that disintegration of majority society and its members is a central cause of their rejection of weak groups. Integration vs. disintegration can be described both as a societal variable and in terms of its effects on the individual. On the subjective individual level the degree of integration vs. disintegration is composed of three subcomponents, namely (1) the feeling of belonging to the community and having access to work, housing, education, and consumer goods, (2) of gaining moral recognition in terms of having institutional and political influence, and (3) emotional recognition reflected in receiving considerable degrees of attention and interpersonal support. The more structural elements of a country or some of its segments contribute to disintegration, the more disintegrated individuals are, and the higher the sensitivity for outgroup-rejecting ideologies and practices.

Multilevel theories emphasize the mutual influence of context and psychological processes. This does not automatically imply that the structure of psychological models varies between cultures and countries. Pettigrew and colleagues (Pettigrew, Jackson, Ben Brika, et al., 1998; Pettigrew, Wagner, & Christ, 2007) have shown that intergroup threat and emotions, as well as ingroup identification, play a role in understanding prejudice against immigrants in many European countries and North America. A multilevel perspective should, however, make clear that the *relative contribution* of these psychological factors to bias may vary as a function of the historical and societal context.

IMPROVING NATIVE–IMMIGRANT INTERGROUP RELATIONS

Attempts to improve intergroup relations should primarily focus on factors that directly worsen native–immigrant intergroup relations (Wagner & Farhan, 2008). Thus, the message is to reduce intergroup threat and to change group representations (see Esses, Dovidio, Jackson, et al., 2001) and identifications. The role and responsibility of politics and the media in reaching such a goal is self-evident. In addition, there is plenty of literature that shows that intervention programs, for example those implemented in schools, are helpful in overcoming mutual prejudice and segregation of different groups (Stephan, 1999). Initiatives of Israeli social psychologists provide an impressive example of how interventions can improve the acceptance of new immigrants (Amir, 1997).

Besides interventions that focus directly on factors that affect prejudice, bias, and violence, interventions can also be based on factors that are known to improve intergroup relations. One of the most prominent is intergroup contact (Allport, 1954; Pettigrew, 1998b, Pettigrew & Tropp, 2006). Allport (1954) proclaimed that intergroup contact will reduce prejudice if – at least in the contact situation itself – the involved group members have the same status position, interact cooperatively while pursuing the same goal, and if the intergroup encounter is supported by acknowledged authorities. Pettigrew (1998b) added that one of the features of intergroup contact that has the strongest prejudice-reducing effect is participants becoming friends. Recent research shows that the bias-reducing effect of intergroup contact is due, in part, to a reduction in intergroup threat in the contact situation (Pettigrew, 1998b; Pettigrew & Tropp, 2008). In addition, intergroup contact has a direct effect on group representations. Research on the common ingroup identity model (Dovidio, Gaertner, Saguy, et al., 2008; Gaertner & Dovidio, 2000; see also Chapter 32 by Gaertner, Dovidio, & Houlette, this volume) makes clear that positive intergroup contact can reduce prejudice by increasing the salience of a common ingroup identity (see also Brewer, 2008).

Intergroup contact offers an excellent opportunity for improving native-population– immigrant relationships (see Wagner, Christ, Wolf, et al., 2008a). Positive intergroup contact is used as a means for improving intergroup relations in cooperative education programs in schools (Slavin & Cooper, 1999). An example is Aronson and Patnoe's (1997) *The Jigsaw Classroom* (see also Johnson & Johnson, 2005, for a similar program of a slightly different theoretical background). Students of a class are divided into subgroups of four to six that are composed heterogeneously: some participants are of immigrant- and some of native background. These small groups have to solve a mutual problem. The information and knowledge that is needed for the task is selectively distributed among the group members. For example, if the group task is to prepare the biography of a famous person, one group member receives information about early childhood, the next group member about youth, etc. Thus, the group task can be successfully completed only if all group members make their contribution to it. In this way, Allport's conditions for positive intergroup contact are met. Cooperative training in schools has been implemented especially in the United States and Israel (Lemmer & Wagner, 2008; Stephan, 1999). In Israel, the training focuses on the relations between Eastern and Western European immigrants (Shachar, 1997), but of course they profit from a common ingroup identity (all are Jewish) and from a sense of

shared fate, given the opposition to the state of Israel.

The realization of intergroup contact depends on the availability of outgroup members: Face-to-face contact with immigrants can take place only if there are at least some immigrants present in indigenous citizens' life space. For those places where this is not the case interventions based on indirect contact effects could be an alternative. As Wright, Aron, McLaughlin-Volpe, et al., (1997) have convincingly demonstrated, the information that another ingroup member has contact with someone in the outgroup can improve the attitudes of those who are not personally participating in the intergroup contact situation. Some intervention programs have tested such a strategy and shown that it can be effective in improving attitudes to various outgroups, including immigrants (for a review see Turner, Hewstone, Voci, et al., 2007).

FUTURE DIRECTIONS

In a globalizing world migration and immigration will be central topics for the future. The social sciences have a key role to play in this development (see Heitmeyer, 2002). The integration of immigrants will be a challenge, but it also offers opportunities. Multiculturalism and intercultural competence are skills that will significantly affect individual sophistication and qualification, opportunities in the job market, access to resources, and participation in a civilized world community. Thus, immigration is also an opportunity. Contrary to many current discussions, it is possible that, in the long run, those who do not have the opportunity to participate in migration and the accompanying intercultural exchange, will be those who suffer from being excluded from an important development that is both personally and socially enriching.

The focus of this chapter was prejudice and bias against immigrants. We approached this issue primarily by focusing on the receiving society and its members. However, migration does not only affect the autochthonous population, but migration itself and the situation in the receiving countries has a strong effect on immigrants as well, for example on their well-being (e.g., Jasinskaja-Lahti, Liebkind, & Perhoniemi, 2006). Moreover, immigrants respond actively against perceived discrimination, sometimes by political engagement (Barreto & Munoz, 2003) and even extremism; more often, however, they respond by separating from the majority and focusing on their traditional values. Members of the receiving society might see this self-segregation as support for their own prejudice, thus blaming immigrants themselves for the discrimination they face (Zick & Küpper, 2005). Up to now, a conflict theory that takes into account both the perspective of the receiving society and that of the immigrating group is widely ignored in current research (for exceptions see Bourhis, Moïse, Perreault, et al., 1997; Deaux, 2006).

National state boundaries and even their blockade will not prevent migration. Extreme differences in access to resources will press people to leave their home countries. Others will be motivated to learn from foreign cultures. As this chapter has sought to show, social psychology can help to understand causes of anti-immigration bias in receiving societies and how to prevent it. However, real conflict resolution implies taking account of the needs of all parties involved in the conflict. Thus, our recommendation for future research is to extend its scope by explicitly analyzing the interaction of immigrants and the autochthonous population, their mutual influences on each other, and their societal and cultural context-dependence.

SUMMARY AND CONCLUSIONS

Over recent decades, social psychological researchers have responded when societies demanded social scientific contributions toward understanding and reducing conflicts between immigrants and receiving societies. Social psychology contributes to our understanding of the causes of bias against

immigrants and immigration, such as conflicts over resources and identities as well as relevant intergroup emotions and feelings of threat. In addition, social psychologists and colleagues from neighboring disciplines have used their knowledge about causes of bias against immigrants to develop appropriate bias prevention and reduction programs, based, for example, on intergroup contact theory.

Given the described state of knowledge, the time is now ripe to extend this perspective. This includes a better theoretical and empirical understanding of societal and ideological influences on bias against immigrants, with a special focus on the role of the press, to improve understanding of cultural variations in immigration processes, and to simultaneously consider immigrant and receiving society as well as their interaction. In addition, we would like to see more research of the kind that not only focuses on the ugly sides of intergroup bias and struggle, but that also takes account of the advantages and opportunities associated with migration.

ACKNOWLEDGEMENTS

We are grateful to Thomas F. Pettigrew and Johannes Ullrich as well as the editors of this volume for their comments on previous versions of this chapter. Correspondence should be directed to: Ulrich Wagner, Department of Social Psychology, University of Marburg, Marburg, 35032, Germany. E-mail: wagner1@staff.uni-marburg.de

REFERENCES

Adler, L. L., & Gielen, U. P. (2003). *Migration: Immigration and emigration in international perspective.* Westport, CT: Praeger.

Adorno, T. W., Frenkel-Brunswik, E., Levinson, D. J., & Sanford, R. N. (1950). *The authoritarian personality.* New York: Harper.

Allport, G. W. (1954). *The nature of prejudice.* Reading, MA: Addison Wesley.

Amir, Y. (1997). Diversity in society and cultural options in educational settings. In R. Ben-Ari, & Y. Rich

(Eds.), *Enhancing education in heterogeneous schools* (pp. 183–190). Ramat-Gan: Bar-Ilan University Press.

Anhut, R., & Heitmeyer, W. (2000). Desintegration, Konflikt und Ethnisierung. Eine Problemanalyse und theoretische Rahmenkonzeption [Disintegration, conflict and ethnicisation: A problem analysis and theoretical frame]. In W. Heitmeyer & R. Anhut (Eds.), *Bedrohte Stadtgesellschaft* (17–76). Weiheim: Juwenta.

Arends-Tóth, J., & van de Vijver, F. J. R. (2002). Multiculturalism and acculturation: views of Dutch and Turkish-Dutch. European Journal of Social Psychology, 33, 249–266.

Aronson, E., & Patnoe, S. (1997). *The jigsaw classroom* (2nd ed.). New York: Longman.

Barreto, M. A., & Munoz, J. A. (2003). Reexamining the "Politics of in-between": Political participation among Mexican immigrants in the United States. *Hispanic Journal of Behavioral Sciences, 25*, 427–447.

Bar-Tal, D. (1997). The monopolization of patriotism. In D. Bar-Tal, & E. Staub (Eds.), *Patriotism in the lives of individuals and nations* (pp. 246–270). Chicago: Nelson-Hall.

Bastian, B., & Haslam, N. (2008). Immigrants from the perspective of host and immigrants: Roles of psychological essentialism and social identity. *Asian Journal of Social Psychology, 11*, 127–140.

Becker, J., Wagner, U., & Christ, O. (2007). Nationalismus und Patriotismus als Ursache von Fremdenfeindlichkeit [Nationalism and patriotism as a cause of hostility against foreigners]. In W. Heitmeyer (Ed.), *Deutsche Zustände. Folge 5* (pp. 139–158). Frankfurt: Suhrkamp.

Berry, J. W. (2001). A psychology of immigration. *Journal of Social Issues, 57*, 615–631.

Berry, J. W. (2004). Fundamental psychological processes in intercultural relations. In D. Landis, J. M. Bennett, & M. L. Bennett (Eds.), *Handbook of intercultural training* (pp. 166–184). Thousand Oaks, CA: Sage.

Billiet, J., Maddens, B., & Beerten, R. (2003). National identity and attitude towards foreigners in a multinational state: A replication. *Political Psychology, 24*, 241–257.

Bizman, A., & Yinon, Y. (2001). Intergroup and interpersonal threats as determinants of prejudice: The moderating role of in-group identification. *Basic and Applied Social Psychology, 23*, 191–196.

Blake, R. R., & Mouton, J. S. (1961). Comprehension of own and of outgroup positions under intergroup competition. *Journal of Conflict Resolution, 5*, 304–310.

Blank, T., & Schmidt, P. (2003). National identity in a united Germany: Nationalism or patriotism? An empirical test with representative data. *Political Psychology, 24*, 259–288.

Blumer, H. (1958). Racial prejudice as a sense of group position. *Pacific Sociological Review, 23*, 3–7.

Bourhis, R. Y., Moïse, C. L., Perreault, S., & Senécal, S. (1997). Towards an interactive acculturation model: A social psychological approach. *International Journal of Psychology, 32*, 369–386.

Branscombe, N. R., Ellemers, N., Spears, R., & Doosje, B. (1999). The context and content of social identity threat. In N. Ellemers, R. Spears, & B. Doosje (Eds.), *Social identity: Context, commitment, content* (pp. 35–58). Oxford: Blackwell Science.

Brewer, M. B. (1999). The psychology of prejudice. Ingroup love or outgroup hate. *Journal of Social Issues, 55*, 429–444.

Brewer, M. B. (2001). Ingroup identification and intergroup conflict. In R. D. Ahmore, L. Jussim, & D. Wilder (Eds.), *Social identity, intergroup conflict, and conflict resolution* (pp. 17–41). Oxford: Oxford University Press.

Brewer, M. B. (2008). Deprovicialization. Social Identity Complexity and outgroup acceptance. In U. Wagner, L. Tropp, G. Finchilescu, & C. Tredoux (eds.), *Improving intergroup relations: Building on the legacy of Thomas F. Pettigrew* (pp. 160–176). Oxford: Blackwell.

Brosius, H. B., & Esser, F. (1995). *Eskalation durch Berichterstattung* [Escalation by media reports]. Opladen: Westdeutscher Verlag.

Brown, R. (2000). Social identity theory: Past achievements, current problems and future challenges. *European Journal of Social Psychology, 30*, 745–778.

Brown, R., & Zagefka, H. (2005). Ingroup affiliation and prejudice. In J. F. Dovidio, P. Glick, & L. A. Rudman (eds.), *On the nature of prejudice. Fifty years after Allport*. Malden, MA: Blackwell.

Cohrs, J. C., Dimitrova, D., Kalchevska, T., Kleinke, S., Tomova, I., Vasileva, M., et al. (2004). Ist patriotischer Nationalstolz wünschenswert? Eine differenzierte Analyse seiner psychologischen Bedeutung [Is patriotic national proud desirable? A differentiated analysis of its psychological meaning]. *Zeitschrift für Sozialpsychologie, 35*, 201–215.

Cottrell, C. A., & Neuberg, S. L. (2005). Different emotional reactions to different groups: A sociofunctional threat-based approach to „prejudice". *Journal of Personality and Social Psychology, 88*, 770–789.

Cuddy, A. J., Fiske, S. T., & Glick, P. (2008). Warmth and competence as universal dimensions of social perception: The stereotype content model and the BIAS map. *Advances in Experimental Social Psychology, 40*, 61–150.

Dambrun, M., Taylor, D. M., McDonald, D. A., Crush, J., & Meot, A. (2006). The relative deprivation-gratification continuum and the attitudes of South Africans towards immigrants: A test of the V-curve hypothesis. *Journal of Personality and Social Psychology, 91*, 1032–1044.

Deaux, K. (2006). *To be an immigrant.* New York: Russell Sage.

De Figueiredo, Jr., R. J. P., & Elkins, Z. (2003). Are patriots bigots? An inquiry into the vices of in-group pride. *American Journal of Political Science, 47*, 171–188.

Dovidio, J. F., Brigham, J. C., Johnson, B. T., & Gaertner, S. L. (1996). Stereotyping, prejudice, and discrimination: Another look. In C. N. Macrae, C. Stangor, & M. Hewstone (Eds.), *Stereotypes and stereotyping* (pp. 276–319). New York: Guilford.

Dovidio, J. F., & Esses, V. M. (2001). Immigrants and immigration: Advancing the psychological perspective. *Journal of Social Issues, 57*, 375–387.

Dovidio, J. F., Gaertner, S. L., Saguy, T., & Halabi, S. (2008). Fraom when to why: Understanding how contact reduces bias. In U. Wagner, L. Tropp, G. Finchilescu, & C. Tredoux (Eds.), *Improving intergroup relations. Building on the legacy of Thomas F. Pettigrew* (pp. 75–90). Oxford: Blackwell.

Duckitt, J. (1993). Prejudice and behavior: A review. *Current Psychology: Research and Reviews, 11*, 291–307.

Ellemers, N., Spears, R., & Doosje, B. (1999). *Social identity.* Oxford: Blackwell.

Esses, V. M., Dovidio, J. F., & Hodson, G. (2002). Public attitudes toward immigration in the United States ad Canada in response to the September 11, 2001 "Attack on America". *Analyses of Social Issues and Public Policy, 2*, 69–85.

Esses, V. M., Dovidio, J. F., Jackson, L. M., & Amstrong, T. L. (2001). The immigrant dilemma: The role of perceived group competition, ethnic prejudice, and national identity. *Journal of Social Issues, 57*, 389–412.

Esses, V. M., Dovidio, J. F., Semenya, A. H., & Jackson, L. M. (2005). Attitudes towards immigrants and immigration: The role of national and international identity. In D. Abrams, M. Hogg & J. M. Marques (Eds.), *The social psychology of inclusion and exclusion* (pp. 317–337). New York: Psychology Press.

Esses, V. M., Jackson, L. M., & Abu-Ayyash, C. (in press). Intergroup competition. In J. F. Dovidio, M. Hewstone, P. Glick, & V. M. Esses (Eds.), *Handbook of prejudice,* stereotyping, and discrimination. London, England: Sage.

Esses, V. M., Jackson, L. M., & Armstrong, T. L. (1998). Intergroup competition and attitudes towards immigrants and immigration: An instrumental model of group conflict. *Journal of Social Issues, 54*, 699–724.

Esses, V. M., Wagner, U., Wolf, C., Preiser, M., & Wilbur, C. (2006). Perceptions of national identity and attitudes toward immigrants and immigration in Canada and Germany. *International Journal of Intercultural Relations, 30*, 653–669.

Fiske, A. P., Kitayama, S., Markus, H. R., & Nisbett, R. E. (1998). The cultural matrix of social psychology. In D. T. Gilbert, S. T. Fiske, & G. Lindzey (Eds.), *The handbook of social psychology* (4th ed., Vol. 2, pp. 915–981). New York: McGraw Hill.

Florack, A., Piontkowski, U., Rohrmann, A., Balzer, T., & Perzig, S. (2003). Perceived intergroup threat and attitudes of host community members toward immigrant acculturation. *Journal of Social Psychology, 143*, 633–648.

Fredrickson, G. M. (2002). *Racism. A short history.* Princeton, NJ: Princeton University Press.

Galliker, M., Herman, J., Imminger, K., & Weimer, D. (1998). The investigation of contiguity: Co-occurrence analysis of print media using CD-ROMs as a new data source, illustrated by a discussion on migrant delinquency in a daily newspaper. *Journal of Language and Social Psychology, 17*, 200–219.

Guimond, S., & Dambrun, M. (2002). When prosperity breeds intergroup hostility: The effects of relative deprivation and relative gratification on prejudice. *Personality and Social Psychology Bulletin, 28*, 900–912.

Heitmeyer, W. (2002). *Deutsche Zustände. Folge 1* [German conditions. Sequel 1]. Frankfurt: Suhrkamp.

Heyder, A., & Schmidt, P. (2002). Deutscher Stolz. Patriotismus wäre besser [German pride. Patriotism would be better]. In W. Heitmeyer (Ed.), *Deutsche Zustände. Folge 1* (pp. 71–82). Frankfurt: Suhrkamp.

Hinkle, S., & Brown, R. (1990). Intergroup comparisons and social identity: Some links and lacunae. In D. Abrams & M. A. Hogg (Eds.), *Social identity theory: Constructive and critical advances* (pp. 48–70). New York: Harvester/Wheatsheaf.

Hitlan, R. T., Carrillo, K., Aikman, S. N., & Zarate, M. A. (2007). Attitudes toward immigrant groups and the September 11th Terrorist Attacks. *Peace and Conflict: Journal of Peace Psychology, 13*, 1–18.

Hofstede, G. (1980). *Culture's consequences: International differences in work-related values.* Beverly Hills, CA: Sage.

Jasinskaja-Lahti, I., Liebkind, K., & Perhoniemi, R. (2006). Perceived discrimination and well-being: A victim study of different immigrant groups. *Journal of Community and Applied Social Psychology, 16,* 267–284.

Johnson, D. W., & Johnson, R. T. (2005). New developments in Social Interdependence Theory. *Genetic, Social and General Psychology Monographs,131,* 285–358.

Jost, J. T., Banaji, M. R., & Nosek, B. A. (2004). A decade of system justification theory: Accumulated evidence of conscious and unconscious bolstering of the status quo. *Political Psychology, 25,* 881–920.

Karasawa, M. (2002). Patriotism, nationalism, and internationalism among Japanese citizens: An etic-emic approach. *Political Psychology, 23,* 645–666.

Katz, D. & Braly, K. (1933). Racial stereotypes of one hundred college students. *Journal of Abnormal and Social Psychology, 28,* 280–290.

Koopmans, R., & Olzak, S. (2004). Discursive opportunities and the evolution of Right-Wing violence in Germany. *American Journal of Sociology, 110,* 198–230.

Kosterman, R., & Feshbach, S. (1989). Toward a measure of patriotic and nationalistic attitudes. *Political Psychology, 10,* 257–273.

Lee, T. L., & Fiske, S. T. (2006). Not an outgroup, but not yet an ingroup: Immigrants in the stereotype content model. *International Journal of Intercultural Relations, 30,* 751–768.

Lemmer, G., & Wagner, U. (2008, August). *Improving ethnic intergroup relations – how effective are contact programs?* Paper presented at the EAESP-SPSSI Small Group Meeting on "Intergroup Contact: Recent advancements in basic and applied research", Marburg, Germany.

Maio, G. R., Esses, V. M., & Bell, D. W. (1994). The formation of attitudes toward new immigrant groups. *Journal of Applied Social Psychology, 24,* 1762–1776.

Miles, R. (1989). *Racism.* London: Routledge.

Mullen, B., & Rice, D. R. (2003). Ethnophaulisms and exclusion: The behavior consequences of cognitive representation of ethnic immigrant groups. *Personality and Social Psychology Bulletin, 29,* 1056–1067.

Mummendey, A., Klink, A., & Brown, R. (2001). Nationalism and patriotism: National identification and out-group rejection. *British Journal of Social Psychology, 40,* 159–172.

Mummendey, A., & Simon, B. (1997). Nationale Identifikation und die Abwertung von Fremdgruppen [National identification and the devaluation of outgroups]. In A. Mummendey & B. Simon (Eds.), *Identität und Verschiedenheit* (pp. 175–193). Bern: Huber.

Neumayer, E. (2005). Asylum recognition rates in Western Europe. *Journal of Conflict Resolution, 49,* 43–66.

Nigbur, D., & Cinnirella, M. (2006). National identification, type and specificity of comparison and their effects on descriptions of national character. *European Journal of Social Psychology, 37,* 672–691.

Palmer, D. (1996). Determinants of Canadian attitudes toward immigration: More than just racism? *Canadian Journal of Behavioural Sciences, 28,* 180–192.

Pehrson, S., Brown, R., & Zagefka, H. (in press). When does national identification lead to the rejection of immigrants? Cross-sectional and longitudinal evidence for the role of essentialist in-group definitions. *British Journal of Social Psychology.*

Pehrson, S., Vignoles, V. L., & Brown, R. (2009). National identification and anti-immigrant prejudice. Individual and contextual effects of national definitions. *Social Psychology Quarterly, 72,* 24–38.

Pettigrew, T. F. (1998a). Reactions towards the new minorities of Western Europe. *Annual Review of Sociology, 24,* 77–103.

Pettigrew, T. F. (1998b). Intergroup contact theory. *Annual Review of Psychology, 49,* 65–85.

Pettigrew, T. F. (2006). The advantages of multilevel approaches. *Journal of Social Issues, 62,* 615–620

Pettigrew, T. F., Jackson, J. S., Ben Brika, J., Lemaine, G., Meertens, R., Wagner, U., et al., (1998). Outgroup prejudice in Western Europe. In W. Stroebe & M. Hewstone (Eds.), *European Review of Social Psychology, Volume 8* (pp. 241–273). Chichester: Wiley.

Pettigrew, T. F., & Meertens, R. (1995). Subtle and blatant prejudice in Western Europe. *European Journal of Social Psychology, 25,* 57–75.

Pettigrew, T. F., & Tropp, L. R. (2006). A meta-analytic test of intergroup contact theory. *Journal of Personality and Social Psychology, 90,* 751–783.

Pettigrew, T. F., & Tropp, L. R. (2008). How does intergroup contact reduce prejudice? Meta-analytic tests of three mediators. *European Journal of Social Psychology, 38,* 922–934.

Pettigrew, T. F., Wagner, U., & Christ, O. (2007). Who opposes immigration? Comparing German with North American findings. *Du Bois Review: Social Science Research on Race, 4,* 19–39.

Riek, B. M., Mania, E. W., & Gaertner, S. L. (2006). Intergroup threat and outgroup attitudes: A meta-analytic review. *Personality and Social Psychology Review, 10,* 336–353.

Rohmann, A., Piontkowski, U. &, van Randenborgh, A. (2008). When attitudes do not fit: Discordance of acculturation attitudes as an antecedent of intergroup threat. *Personality and Social Psychology Bulletin, 34* 337–352

Runciman, W. G. (1966). *Relative deprivation and social justice.* Berkeley, CA: University of California Press.

Schatz, R. T., & Staub, E. (1997). Manifestations of blind and constructive patriotism: Personality correlates and individual-group relations. In D. Bar-Tal & E. Staub (Eds.), *Patriotism in the lives of individuals and nations* (pp. 229–245). Chicago, Il: Nelson-Hall.

Scheepers, P., Gijsberts, M., & Coenders, M. (2002). Ethnic exclusionism in European countries: Public opposition to civil rights for legal migrants as a response to perceived ethnic threat. *European Sociological Review, 18,* 17–34.

Schuman, H., Steeh, C. Bobo, L., & Krysan, M. (1997). *Racial attitudes in America.* Cambridge, MA: Harvard University Press.

Schütz, H., & Six, B. (1996). How strong is the relationship between prejudice and discrimination? A meta-analytic review. *International Journal of Intercultural Relations, 20,* 441–462.

Shachar, H. (1997). Effects of cooperative learning on intergroup interaction in the heterogeneous classroom. *Megamont, 38,* 367–382.

Sherif, M. (1966). *In common predicament: Social psychology of intergroup conflict and cooperation.* Boston, MA: Houghton Mifflin.

Sidanius, J., & Pratto, F. (1999). *Social Dominance: An intergroup theory of social hierarchy and oppression.* New York: Cambridge University Press.

Slavin, R. E., & Cooper, R. (1999). Improving inter-group relations: Lessons learned from cooperative learning programs. *Journal of Social Issues, 55,* 647–663.

Sodhi, K. S., & Bergius, R. (1953). *Nationale vorurteile* [National prejudice]. Berlin: Duncker und Humblot.

Staub, E. (1997). Blind versus constructive patriotism: Moving from embeddedness in the group to critical loyalty and action. In D. Bar-Tal & E. Staub (Eds.), *Patriotism in the lives of individuals and nations* (pp. 213–228). Chicago, Il: Nelson-Hall.

Stephan, W. G. (1999). *Reducing prejudice and stereotyping in schools.* New York: Teachers College Press.

Stephan, W. G., & Stephan, C. W. (2000). An integrated threat theory on prejudice. In S. Oskamp (Ed.), *Reducing prejudice and discrimination* (pp. 23–45). Mahwah, NJ: Lawrence Erlbaum.

Stephan, W. G., & Renfro, C. L. (2002). The role of threat in intergroup relations. In: D. M. Mackie & E. R. Smith (Eds.), *From prejudice to intergroup emotions.*

Differential reactions to social groups (p. 191–207). New York: Psychology Press.

Stephan, W. G., Ybarra, O., Martinez, C. M., Schwarzwald, J., & Tur-Kaspa, M. (1998). Prejudice toward immigrants in Spain and Israel: An integrated threat theory analysis. *Journal of Cross-Cultural Psychology, 29,* 559–576.

Stouffer, S. A., Suchman, E. A., DeVinney, L. C., Star, S. A., & Williams, R. A. Jr. (1949). *The American soldier: Adjustment during army life.* Princeton, NJ: Princeton University Press.

Sumner, W. G. (1906 / 1959). *Folkways.* New York: Dover.

Tajfel, H. (1978) (Ed.). *Differentiation between social groups.* London: Academic Press.

Tajfel, H., Billig, M. G., Bundy, R. P., & Flament, C. (1971). Social categorization and intergroup behav-ior. *European Journal of Social Psychology, 1,* 149–178.

Tajfel, H., & Turner, J. C. (1979). An integrative theory of intergroup conflict. In W. G. Austin & S. Worchel (Eds.), *The social psychology of intergroup relations* (pp. 33–47). Monterey, CA: Brooks/Cole.

Talaska, C. A., Fiske, S. T., & Chaiken, S. (2008). Legitimating racial discrimination: Emotions, not beliefs, best predict discrimination in a meta-analysis. *Social Justice Research, 21,* 263–296.

Turner, J. C. (1999). Some current issues in research on social identity and self-categorization theory. In N. Ellemers, R. Spears & B. Doosje (Eds.), *Social Identity* (pp. 6–34). Malden, MA: Blackwell.

Turner, J. C., Hogg, M. A., Oakes, P. J., Reicher, S. D., & Wetherell, M. S. (1987). *Rediscovering the social group.* Oxford GB: Blackwell.

Turner, R. N., Hewstone, M., Voci, A., Paolini, S., & Christ, O. (2007). Reducing prejudice via direct and extended cross-group friendship. In W. Stroebe & M. Hewstone (Eds.), *European review of social psychology* (Vol. 18, pp. 212–255). Hove, U.K.: Psychology Press.

Vala, J., Lopes, D., & Lima, M. (2008). Black immigrants in Portugal: Luso-Tropicalism and prejudice. *Journal of Social Issues, 64,* 287–302.

Verkuyten, M., & Zaremba, K. (2005). Interethnic relations in a changing political context. *Social Psychology Quarterly, 68,* 375–386.

Wagner, U., Becker, J. C., Christ, O., Pettigrew, T. F., & Schmidt, P. (2009). *A longitudinal test of the relation between nationalism, patriotism and outgroup derogation.* Manuscript submitted for publication.

Wagner, U. & Christ, O. (2007). Intergroup aggres-sion and emotions: A framework and first data. *M. Gollwitzer & G. Steffgen (Hrsg.), Emotions and aggressive behavior* (pp. 133–148). Göttingen: Hogrefe & Huber.

Wagner, U., Christ, O., & Pettigrew, T. F. (2008). Prejudice and group related behaviour in Germany. *Journal of Social Issues, 64,* 403–416.

Wagner, U., Christ, O., Wolf, C., van Dick, R., Stellmacher, J., Schlüter, E., et al., (2008). Social and political context effects on intergroup contact and intergroup attitudes. In U. Wagner, L. Tropp, G. Finchilescu, & C. Tredoux (Hrsg.), *Improving intergroup relations: Building on the legacy of Thomas F. Pettigrew* (pp. 195–209). Oxford: Blackwell.

Wagner, U., & Farhan, T. (2008). Programme zur Prävention und Veränderung von Vorurteilen gegenüber Minderheiten [Programs for the prevention and change of prejudice against minorities]. In L. E. Petersen & B. Six (Eds.), *Stereotype, Vorurteile und soziale Diskriminierung Theorien, Befunde und Interventionen* (pp. 223–282). Weinheim: Beltz.

Wagner, U., & Küpper, B. (2007). Kulturbegegnungen und -konflikte [Cultural encounters and conflicts]. In G. Trommsdorff & H. J. Kornadt (Eds.), *Enzyklopädie der Psychologie, C/VII, Band 3* (pp. 87–133) Göttingen: Hogrefe.

Wagner, U., Zick, A., & van Dick, R. (2002). Die Möglichkeit interpersonaler und massenmedialer Beeinflussung von Vorurteilen. [The possibility of interpersonal and mass-media influences on prejudice]. In K. Boehnke, D. Fuss & J. Hagan (Eds.), *Jugendgewalt und Rechtsextremismus.* (pp. 225–237). Weinheim: Juventa.

Ward, C., & Masgoret, A. M. (2006). An integrative model of attitudes toward immigrants. *International Journal of Intercultural Relations, 30,* 671–682.

Ward, C., & Masgoret, A. M. (2007). Immigrant entry into the workforce: A research note from New Zealand. *International Journal of Intercultural Relations, 31,* 525–530.

Wilson, T. C. (2001). Americans' views on immigration policy: Testing the role of threatened group interests. *Sociological Perspectives, 44,* 485–501.

Wright, S. C., Aron, A., McLaughlin-Volpe, T., & Ropp, S. A. (1997). The extended contact effect: Knowledge of cross-group friendships and prejudice. *Journal of Personality and Social Psychology, 73,* 73–90.

Zick, A., & Küpper, B. (2005). "Die sind doch selbst schuld, wenn man was gegen sie hat". Oder Wie man sich seiner Vorurteile entledigt. [They have themselves to blame, if one dislikes them. Or how to get rid of one's prejudices]. In W. Heitmeyer (Ed.), *Deutsche Zustände, Folge 3* (pp. 129–143). Frankfurt: Suhrkamp.

Zick, A., Wagner, U., van Dick, R., & Petzel, T. (2001). Acculturation and prejudice in Germany: Perspectives of majority and minority. *Journal of Social Issues, 57,* 541–557.

PART IV

Social Impact of Prejudice, Stereotyping and Discrimination

23

Stereotype Threat

Diane M. Quinn, Rachel W. Kallen,
and Steven J. Spencer

ABSTRACT

Stereotype threat occurs when people are in a situation where a negative identity-based stereotype can be applied to their performance. Concern about the stereotype can lead to decreased performance on a stereotype-relevant task. Initial research examined stereotype threat for African-Americans in intellectual testing situations and for women in math testing situations. In the current chapter, we review the following: (1) The generalizability of stereotype threat effects. (2) Research examining whether stereotypes are activated in stereotype-threat situations. (3) The mediating processes between a situation of threat and an inferior performance outcome. (4) The role of varying group identities in stereotype threat outcomes. (5) The effect of 'stereotype lift,' whereby positively stereotyped group members seem to gain a boost in performance in stereotype threat situations.

STEREOTYPE THREAT

Stereotype threat, originally defined by Steele and Aronson (1995) as 'being at risk of confirming, as self-characteristic, a negative stereotype about one's group' (p. 797) gave people a new way to think about how stereotypes affect their targets. Before Steele's work on stereotype threat, most research examining the effect of prejudice on stereotyped targets focused on one of two theoretical processes: The effects of overt words or actions of prejudiced individuals on targets (Goffman, 1963) or the internalization of stereotypical beliefs about the self by the targets (Allport, 1954). The theory of stereotype threat, however, offered a third perspective, suggesting that stereotype-relevant situations place targets of stereotypes in an uncomfortable predicament that can lead to poorer performance outcomes. It was proposed that simply being in a situation where negative group stereotypes could be applied to the self could have a significant effect on the target. Thus, according to the theory it was no longer necessary for there to be a specific, bigoted other or for the stereotyped target to endorse or internalize the stereotypes. Rather, it was enough that the stereotype was 'in the air' (Steele, 1997).

In the current chapter, we will first give a brief overview of the initial stereotype threat studies on race and gender. We will then turn to the major advancements and questions within stereotype threat research, with an emphasis on understanding the experience and outcomes of stereotype threat for people living with a stereotyped identity. We will end the chapter with suggestions for future research on stereotype threat that could help to extend theory and gain a better understanding of the long-term consequences of stereotype threat.

HISTORY OF STEREOTYPE THREAT

Research on the experiences of people with stereotyped identities, also called *stigma*, was relatively sparse within social psychology until the late 1980s and early 1990s. At that point and continuing since, a great deal of research has focused on how targets perceive, cope with, and are affected by prejudice and discrimination (for reviews see Crocker, Major, & Steele, 1998; Major & O'Brien, 2005). One question within research on stigma is why group differences occur in academic outcomes. For example, African-Americans have significantly lower scores than European-Americans on high stakes admissions tests such as the SAT (Camara & Schmidt, 1999). At the point in time when stereotype threat research was beginning, the explanations for these group differences varied from socialization differences (e.g., Eccles, Jacobs, & Harold, 1990) to socioeconomic obstacles (e.g., White, 1982) to genetic differences in intelligence (e.g., Herrnstein & Murray, 1994). Although there is not space in the current chapter to review these different explanations, the main difference between them and stereotype threat is that stereotype threat focuses on a *situational threat*. That is, performance decrements arise in particular situations due to the potential applicability of a stereotype.

Initial investigations into stereotype threat focused on stereotypes relating race and gender to academic achievement. In Steele and Aronson's (1995) seminal paper, African-American and European-American students were given a difficult test. Half of the students were told they were taking a test that was diagnostic of their verbal abilities, whereas the other half were simply told that the test measured problem solving strategies.

African-American students completing the 'diagnostic' test were assumed to be in a situation of stereotype threat because a negative group-based stereotype (African-Americans are not as intelligent as European-Americans) could be applied to them on the basis of their performance. Steele and Aronson hypothesized that being in such a situation would undermine performance, and indeed it did. Across several studies (and controlling for standardized aptitude test scores), African-American participants in the diagnostic condition performed worse than European-Americans in that condition. However, when participants were in the non-diagnostic condition, where no stereotypes could be applied, African-American and European-American students performed equally. The same pattern of stereotype threat was demonstrated for women in the domain of math (Spencer, Steele, & Quinn, 1999). Women consistently underperformed in comparison to men on a difficult math test when they were told that the test had shown gender differences in the past. However, when the stereotype was removed from the test-taking situation by telling participants that the same test was 'gender-fair,' women and men performed equally well. Thus, these initial studies demonstrated that race and gender differences could be erased by simple changes in the situational context.

REVIEW AND ANALYSIS OF CURRENT RESEARCH

From these early studies, several important theoretical and practical questions arose to which we will turn our attention in the following sections. First, who experiences stereotype threat? Are these gender and race effects generalizable to other groups and outcomes? Is a history of stigmatization necessary? Second, where is the stereotype in stereotype threat? Is there evidence that a stereotype is activated? Third, the initial research left open the question of mediation and much of the ensuing research has searched, often in vain, for the psychological mediators of stereotype threat. What are the mediating processes between stereotype threat and decreased performance? Fourth, how can stereotype threat effects be moderated and ameliorated? We will particularly focus on the role of identification with the stereotyped group here. Finally, a burgeoning literature on the phenomenon of 'stereotype lift' will be reviewed. Stereotype lift occurs when stereotype threat conditions result in increased performance for the non-stereotyped group (e.g., men taking a math test).

Who experiences stereotype threat?

Researchers have now replicated the race effects of stereotype threat for African-Americans, as well as Latinos, in intellectual testing situations (e.g., Aronson, Fried, & Good, 2002; Blascovich, Spencer, Quinn, et al., 2001; González, Blanton, & Williams, 2002; McKown & Weinstein, 2003; Schmader & Johns, 2003). Similarly, the research has continued to demonstrate consistent effects for women on both mathematical and spatial relations tasks (e.g., Inzlicht and Ben-Zeev, 2000; Johns, Schmader, & Martens, 2005; Martens, Johns, Greenberg, et al., 2006; Quinn & Spencer, 2001; Schmader & Johns, 2003). Stereotype threat has been generalized across age groups, demonstrating both race and gender effects in young children (e.g., McKown & Weinstein, 2003; Neuville & Croizet, 2007) and adolescents (Keller, 2002). Mirroring the race and gender effects, Croizet and Claire (1998) demonstrated that the stigma of low socioeconomic status (SES) presents a potential vulnerability for stereotype threat in French students. When a task was presented as diagnostic of intellectual ability, students of low SES performed worse than high SES students on the test, but performed equally when the test was described as non-diagnostic. These effects have recently been replicated with American students (Spencer & Castano, 2007). Stereotype threat effects have been found with the elderly when examining memorization performance (Levy, 1996). Finally, research has shown that people

with a history of mental illness can experience stereotype threat when their history is made public before taking a 'reasoning' test (Quinn, Kahng, & Crocker, 2004). Thus, stereotype threat not only affects intellectual outcomes for individuals as a function of race and gender, but may also arise in situations where age, social status, or other stereotyped identities are made salient.

Although the above studies show that performance outcomes can be swayed by the applicability of a stereotype, they do not rule out the possibility that stereotype threat is due to the internalization of negative stereotypes about one's own group. In order to show that stereotype threat is truly a situational threat, it is necessary to show that anyone (not just people from stigmatized groups) can experience the effects of threat. Aronson and colleagues (1999) highlighted this point by showing that even European-American men with strong math backgrounds can experience performance decrements. In two experiments, the male participants were informed that the test they were about to take was one in which Asian-American students typically outperformed European-Americans (or not). Results showed students who believed that they were taking a test on which their group (white men) typically did worse, underperformed in comparison to students who were not told this information. Thus, it does not seem that one needs to come from a group with a history of stigmatization, nor does an internalized sense of inferiority need to be present.

Lending further support, several other studies have created conditions of stereotype threat for members of dominant, normally non-stigmatized groups. Interestingly, such experimentally induced threat usually relies on an established stereotype. One such domain, for instance, relates to the processing of affective and non-verbal information, two characteristics that tend to be positively associated with women rather than men. In a series of studies, Leyens and colleagues (Leyens, Desert, Croizet, et al., 2000) demonstrated that when the stereotype about men's affective performance was made salient, they significantly underperformed on measures of affective processing. Similarly, Koenig and Eagly (2003) found that when men were presented with a task as diagnostic of 'social sensitivity,' rather than 'information processing,' men's ability to decode non-verbal behaviors was significantly decreased. Finally, taking the work into the realm of negotiating, Kray, Galinsky, and Thompson (2002) showed that they could reverse the stereotypical pattern of men outperforming women in negotiating tasks if they made it known before negotiation that more female-stereotypical skills were predictive of negotiation success.

The preceding work highlights that stereotype threat occurs when an identity is linked to a negative stereotype, and the identity *and* stereotype are relevant in a particular situation. Showing that the salience of identities affects performance outcomes, Shih, Pittinsky, and Ambady (1999) found that performance could be changed as a function of whether participants' Asian-American identities versus gender identities were made salient in a testing situation. When women were primed to think about themselves in terms of their Asian identity they performed better on a math test than when their gender identity was activated before the test. Similarly, when student-athletes were primed to think of their athlete identity they performed worse on a math test compared to when they were primed to think of themselves as students or were not identity-primed (Yopyk & Prentice, 2005). Finally, rather than examining 'mixed status' individuals (those with both positive and negative stereotyped identities), Gonzales and colleagues (2002) investigated individuals with two negatively stereotyped identities when they tested Latino women under situations of stereotype threat. As expected, it was shown that both identities had a negative influence on performance. Interestingly, the effect of gender on spatial performance was qualified by the effect of ethnicity, suggesting that perhaps global stereotypes relating to intellectual ability outweigh the more domain specific gender stereotypes about math competency. Thus, in order to understand who experiences stereotype threat, it is crucial to

know how a particular identity is related via stereotypes to a specific outcome.

Academic performance is certainly not the only outcome to which stereotyped identities are linked. Stereotypes should disrupt other types of performance, goals, and behaviors that are stereotype relevant, and as such, research on stereotype threat has extended beyond academic domains. For example, Stone and colleagues examined the effects of stereotype threat on athletic performance (Stone, 2002; Stone, Lynch, Sjomeling, et al., 1999). The researchers relied on the stereotypes that 'African-Americans are not athletically intelligent' and 'European-Americans are not naturally athletic.' When a golf putting task was described as diagnostic of natural athletic ability, European-American participants performed worse than participants in a control condition where the putting task was described simply as general measure of psychological factors in sports performance, and when the same task was described as diagnostic of sports intelligence, African-American participants underperformed compared to the participants in the control condition. Similar findings have been shown for women playing soccer (Chalabaev, Sarrazin, Stone, et al., 2008). Examining the effects of gender stereotypes in business negotiation contexts, Kray and colleagues (Kray, Galinsky, & Thompson, 2002; Kray, Thompson, & Galinsky, 2001) have found that when stereotypes about women's negotiating skills are salient, women perform worse than men in negotiation tasks. Research has even extended to examining stereotype threat and driving. Yeung and von Hippel (2008) found that when reminded of the stereotype that men are better drivers than women, women were more likely to hit jaywalkers in a driving simulator. In sum, stereotype threat research has now gone beyond the academic domain.

In addition to performance effects, stereotype threat has the potential to change the way people think and feel about stereotyped domains. For example, research indicates that while under stereotype threat, women are more likely to value non-quantitative domains and careers, and show increased negative thoughts and attitudes toward math (e.g., Cadinu, Maass, Frigerio, et al., 2003; Davies, Spencer, Quinn, et al., 2002). Moreover, when primed with gender stereotypes, women are more likely to select the role of problem solver (requiring cooperative interpersonal skills) rather than leader (more masculine), however, women not primed with such stereotypes are more inclined, like the men, to select leadership roles (Davies, Spencer, & Steele, 2005). Thus, not only does stereotype threat negatively affect performance in evaluative contexts, but it also can influence important decisions and experiences surrounding those stereotyped domains.

Where is the stereotype in stereotype threat?

At the core of stereotype threat is the stereotype itself. Stereotype threat is assumed to occur because situational features activate the relevant stereotype for the target. In order to show that it is the stereotype that is influencing outcomes, most of the research has focused on two ways of manipulating the relevant stereotypes. One method has been to manipulate the applicability of the stereotype to the target within the situation. For example, Shih, Pittinsky, & Ambady, (1999) made the stereotypes about women's math abilities directly self-relevant to women by describing the test as either 'gender-fair' or as producing 'gender-differences.' However, many studies both within and outside of the academic domain have also made the stereotypes applicable by describing a task simply as diagnostic of some ability or not (e.g., Croizet & Claire, 1998; Smith & White, 2002; Steele & Aronson, 1995; Stone, Lynch, Sjomeling, et al., 1999).

Are these manipulations affecting stereotype activation? Steele and Aronson's (1995) initial studies showed that under the diagnostic test instructions, not only were African-American participants more likely to complete word fragments with race and self-doubt related words, but they were also more likely to distance themselves from items

connected to African-American culture on a preferences checklist. Activation of more general gender stereotypes (e.g., women as ditzy) leads to decreased performance on a math test in situations that would otherwise be considered low in stereotype threat (Davies, Spencer, Quinn, et al., 2002). Moreover, recent work that has directly examined stereotype activation in women taking a difficult math test has provided evidence that women first activate and then actively try to suppress gender stereotypes while completing a math test (Logel, Iserman, Davies, et al., 2009).

A different way to consider how identity and stereotype collide to form situations of stereotype threat is to consider whether particular groups are aware of the negative stereotypes about them. In a particularly elegant design, McKown and Weinstein (2003) reasoned that if knowledge of stereotypes is necessary for stereotype threat to occur, effects should only be seen as children become aware of negative societal stereotypes about their groups. That is, only known stereotypes can be activated. Testing an ethnically diverse sample of children from ages 6 through 10 years old, McKown and Weinstein showed that as children got older they became more aware of racial stereotypes, and it was only students who were aware of these negative stereotypes about their group that showed performance decrements in the threat condition of a task (in this case, the diagnosticity of a verbal task was manipulated). In an examination of acculturation and stereotype threat, Deaux and colleagues (2007) found that second-generation Afro-Caribbean college students underperformed in a stereotype threat situation, whereas first generation Afro-Caribbeans did not. In a separate sample, results showed that whereas both first and second generation students were aware of negative stereotypes about African-Americans, only the second generation students were beginning to incorporate an African-American identity with their Afro-Caribbean identity. Thus, taking the results of the above studies together illustrate that in order for stereotype threat to occur, both knowledge of the stereotypes and a belief that the stereotypes are applicable to one's own identity are necessary.

What are the mediating processes between stereotype activation and behavior?

Thus far, we have reviewed research showing that performance can be affected by simple changes in the situation that make a negative stereotype more or less applicable to the members of stereotyped groups. We have also shown that, indeed, stereotype threat situations do activate negative stereotypes for people who identify with the specific stereotyped group that is relevant to the situation. What is not clear, however, is *how* stereotype threat leads to performance decrements. What psychological processes occur between the activation of the stereotype and the performance? Because this is a crucial question in understanding stereotype threat, numerous studies have been aimed at uncovering the psychological mediators. We will review both those constructs that have gained and failed to gain support. We will then end this section with two recent theoretical models that serve to integrate and advance our understanding of the mediating processes of stereotype threat.

Studies that have tested possible mechanisms for threat have yielded relatively few strong mediators, and often with mixed results. To begin, there have been a number of potential mediators that have failed to gain support: distraction, academic competence, personal worth (Steele & Aronson, 1995), stereotype endorsement (Leyens, Desert, Croizet, et al., 2000), evaluation apprehension, self-efficacy (O'Brien & Crandall, 2003; Spencer, Steele, & Quinn, 1999), self-esteem (Levy & Langer, 1994; Oswald & Harvey, 2001), perceived effort, and perceived difficulty of the task (Keller & Dauenheimer, 2003). Research on anxiety as a mediator has yielded mixed results. Some studies have failed to find any evidence for anxiety as a mediator (Gonzales, Blanton, & Williams, 2002; Keller & Dauenheimer, 2003;

Schmader & Johns, 2003). Others have offered evidence that anxiety may act to partially mediate stereotype threat effects for women's math performance (Spencer, Steele, & Quinn et al., 1999), and the relationship between ethnicity and performance on achievement tests (combined vocabulary, reading, and math) for African-Americans, Latinos, and European-Americans (Osborne, 2001).

Stronger evidence has been found for the role of anxiety when it is examined in less explicit ways (i.e., when self-report is not used). In a novel test of stereotype threat, Bosson, Haymovitz, and Pinel (2004) showed that when sexual orientation was primed, gay and bisexual men were less adept around pre-school children. Whereas this effect was mediated by non-verbal anxiety (as coded from videotapes of the interactions between the participants and the children), it was not mediated by self-reported anxiety. Research examining whether anxiety can be measured via physiological changes has found strong support. Blascovich and colleagues (2001) found that for African-Americans in a stereotype threat situation, blood pressure rose throughout the performance task and continued to stay higher than for African-Americans not under threat conditions (or for European-Americans regardless of threat conditions). Osborne (2007) showed that women taking a math test with stereotype threat instructions experienced increased skin conductance and diastolic blood pressure and decreased skin temperature – all physiological signs of anxiety. Taken together, these studies suggest that either lack of internal awareness (Nisbett & Wilson, 1977) or the desire to make a good impression may influence self-report measures of anxiety during and after stereotype threat situations, such that they fail to capture the actual anxiety being experienced. Thus, more covert ways of measuring anxiety may be necessary to gain further understanding of its role in stereotype threat.

In other studies of mediating mechanisms, researchers have tried to capture the more general concept of 'arousal' by examining how performance changes under circumstances in which arousal is known to vary.

Based on the well supported social facilitation effects of Zajonc (1965), O'Brien and Crandall (2003) reasoned that if stereotype threat causes arousal, the arousal should lead to better performance on an easy test and poorer performance on a difficult test. This is exactly the pattern they found with women completing difficult and easy math tests. Ben-Zeev, Fein, and Inzlicht (2005) further reasoned that in order to gain better evidence for arousal's role in stereotype threat, it would be necessary to show that participants under threat or no threat (using the 'gender differences' versus 'gender-fair' manipulation) showed the expected social facilitation effects on an unrelated tasks. Results of the study indicated that women under threat conditions performed better on an easy task (writing their names) and worse on a complex task (writing their names backward), and the opposite pattern was found when women were not under threat. Taking the anxiety and arousal findings together points toward an affective or emotional mediational path for stereotype threat. We will return to this point shortly.

Following a more cognitive approach, Schmader and Johns (2003) proposed that experiences of stereotype threat reduce working memory capacity which in turn leads to decreased performance. In a series of studies, Schmader and Johns found support for reduced working memory capacity as a mediator. Specifically, women under stereotype threat conditions related to math and Latinos under stereotype threat related to intelligence exhibited lower scores on measures of working memory capacity. In a third study, working memory decrements mediated the effect of stereotype threat on math performance for women. Also in support of the idea that stereotype threat results in momentary cognitive deficits, Quinn and Spencer (2001) examined the types of strategies men and women used when solving mathematical word problems. They found that women under stereotype threat more often found themselves unable to generate any strategy when solving the word problems compared to women not under stereotype threat and men in either condition.

The search for the mediating mechanisms of stereotype threat has moved from conscious self-reports, to more implicit measures of anxiety and arousal, to non-conscious measures of working memory decrements. Digging even deeper, researchers have begun to use neuroscience techniques to examine the neural pathways affected by stereotype threat (for a review see Derks, Inzlicht, & Kang 2008). Using fMRI technology to examine the parts of the brain that are most active during stereotype threat tasks, research has shown that when under non-stereotype threat – or even positive stereotype – conditions, participants utilize the most effective parts of their brains for the task. For example, in research by Krendl and colleagues (Krendl, Richeson, Kelley, et al., 2008), women who were not under stereotype threat while completing a difficult math task were primarily using the sections of the brain devoted to math processing. Likewise, Wraga and colleagues found that when women were doing spatial rotation under control or positive stereotype conditions, women were using brain segments associated with visual processing (Wraga, Helt, Jacobs, et al., 2007). In contrast, when women were under stereotype threat, the results of both studies showed more activity in the parts of the brain associated with emotional processing. That is, instead of efficiently focusing on the task, women under stereotype threat were also likely contending with negative emotions. Although it is not possible to know which specific emotions were sparked, given previous research on anxiety and arousal, it is likely women were feeling more anxious and concerned under stereotype threat.

Given the many different potential pathways and mechanisms reviewed above, it seems likely that stereotype threat either operates through multiple pathways or that there are multiple types of threat – each with their own mediating mechanisms. Two recent review papers outline these distinct possibilities. Schmader, Johns, and Forbes (2008) present a model of stereotype threat processes that brings together the mediating mechanisms proposed by stereotype threat research to specifically affect performance. In their model, they propose that when a person is in a situation of stereotype threat, it cues an imbalance between the person's (positive) sense of self and the negative stereotypes. This in turn leads to a physiological stress response, a cognitive monitoring process, and an appraisal process that spurs negative emotions. Any combination of these differing mechanisms can lead to a decrease in working memory efficiency, which in turn is theorized to decrease performance on any task that requires controlled processing, such as the type of difficult academic tasks often used in stereotype threat research. In addition, Schmader and colleagues assert that the cognitive monitoring process – such as when people are consciously monitoring their own performance for failures – can directly undermine performance on more automated tasks, such as a sports performance. In summary, Schmader and colleagues present a parsimonious model to account for how stereotype threat can lead to both a variety of mediating mechanisms and outcomes.

Taking a different, but not incompatible, stance, Shapiro and Neuberg (2007) propose that what has been studied as a single 'stereotype threat,' could instead be considered as multiple distinct threats. Shapiro and Neuberg note that there are two basic dimensions to take into account. First, who or what is the target of the threat? Is it primarily directed at the self or one's group? Second, what is the source of the threat? Is the threat emanating from the self, from in-group members, or from out-group members? The combination of these two dimensions results in six theoretically distinct threats: Threats to the self-concept that derive from the self, ingroup others, or outgroup others; and threats to one's group that derive from the self, ingroup others, or outgroup others. Each one of these threats may occur under different types of circumstances, engender different types of mediating mechanisms, and have effects on different types of outcomes. Recent empirical work by Wout, Danso, Jackson, et al., (2008) demonstrates that there are at least two distinct threats that affect women's math performance: self-threat and

group-threats. Women taking a diagnostic math test who believed they would be the only people to see their test scores still significantly underperformed compared to a non-diagnostic condition. That is, the threat seemed to stem from concern about their own competency. However, women taking a diagnostic math test who believed the test would reflect on their group instead of themselves – they believed their scores would be averaged with other women's and compared to men's scores – only showed a performance decrement if they were highly identified with their gender group. Thus, not only can self-threat and group-threats be separated, but only group-threats are tied to level of identification with one's group. Future research into the different types of stereotype threat has the potential to clarify the experience of stereotype threat.

In summary, research on the mediating processes of stereotype threat has uncovered a complex web of physiological and psychological mechanisms. Not every situation of stereotype threat may be 'threatening' in the same way, thus different situations can result in different mediators. In addition, studies using physiological and neuroscience measures show that often the body and brain are reacting in ways that people are either unable or unwilling to report. What can be concluded at this point is that there is not one, simple, mediator that accounts for the effects of stereotype threat. Mediators are likely situation, domain, and identity specific.

How can stereotype threat be moderated and ameliorated?

If stereotype threat partially explains how being a member of a stigmatized group translates into poorer outcomes, then it is crucial to understand how to ameliorate stereotype threat. Researchers have identified several types of individual differences, such as internal locus of control, negative thinking, and lowered expectancies that moderate stereotype threat effects (Cadinu, Maass, Frigerio, et al., 2003; Cadinu, Maass, Lombardo, et al., 2006; Cadinu, Maass,

Rosabianca, et al., 2005). These show promise in understanding who is more or less likely to experience stereotype threat. The bulk of the work to date, however, has been on understanding the relationship between identity and performance.

Identity is at the core of stereotype threat. Stereotypes are attached to specific social identities. Thus, stereotype threat arises when situations link identities with relevant stereotypes. Stated differently, stereotype threat occurs because of the knowledge that one possesses a stereotyped identity. Thus, in considering who might be the most vulnerable to stereotype threat, the first place to look is with those who are the most identified with a stereotyped group. Research on both racial group and gender identity has shown a connection between those who are the most 'stigma conscious,' defined by Pinel (1999) as those who are most self-conscious and aware of their stigma status, and performance in the stereotyped domain (Brown & Pinel, 2003). Indeed, Brown and Lee (2005) showed that level of stigma consciousness was related to lower GPA's for students with academically stigmatized identities (African-Americans and Latinos) but not for students without such identities (European-Americans and Asians). Examination of identification with one's gender group has shown that the more identified women are with their gender, the worse they perform on a math test when the performance is described as examining the link between gender and performance (Schmader, 2002; Wout, Danso, Jackson, et al., 2008). This has been shown not only in academic domains, but also with relevance to professional domains. Begeron, Block, and Echtenkamp (2006), found that gender role identity moderated stereotype threat effects for women on a sex-typed managerial task. Similarly, identifying with a stigmatized age group may act to moderate stereotype threat effects. O'Brien and Hummert (2006) found that memory performance was impaired for middle aged adults who identified with an older, but not a younger age group. In summary, to the extent that people are more aware of stereotypes about their groups and/or

are identified with the stereotype-relevant group, the stronger the effects of stereotype threat are.

Given what is known about stereotype threat and identity thus far, what can be done to eliminate the effects amongst stereotyped group members? One possibility is to distance the self from the stereotyped identity. Ambady and colleagues (Ambady, Paik, Steele, Owen-Smith, & Mitchell, 2004) found that women who were non-consciously primed with gender performed worse on a math test than those not primed, however, when those primed were able to individuate they performed better on the test. Likewise, self-affirmation tends to reduce stereotype threat. Martens and colleagues (2006) showed that when women (but not men) were able to self-affirm on a personally valued trait, the effects of stereotype threat on a math or spatial rotation task were eliminated. It is possible these effects occur because women are thinking of themselves in terms of a different – non-gender-related – identity. McGlone and Aronson (2007) found that reminding women of a positive, high achieving identity (private college student) improved math performance. Finally, Rosenthal and Crisp (2006) showed that blurring the intergroup boundaries by having women think about the similarities between men and women before a math task moderated the typical stereotype threat effect, such that women who thought about similarities (versus differences or control) did better. Thus, moving away from the stereotyped group identity toward thinking of the self as an individual, or reclassifying the group boundaries can reduce the effect of stereotype threat.

Of course group memberships are psychologically important in a variety of ways, and thus advising people to distance themselves from an identity may be ill-advised. A different strategy is to change the meaning of the stereotyped identity in order to make positive aspects more salient and/or negative (and stereotyped) aspects less salient. For example, a series of studies by Inzlicht and Ben-Zeev (2000) found that women in groups with only other women performed better on a math test compared to when they were in groups that included men (see also Sekaquaptewa & Thompson, 2003). Work by Marx and colleagues (Marx & Roman, 2002; Marx, Stapel, & Muller, 2005), however, demonstrates that even when a situation is high in stereotype threat and negative stereotypes are salient, identity can be used to *reduce* the threat and improve performance. In a series of studies, Marx and colleagues showed that in conditions of high math stereotype threat (i.e., test described as diagnostic of math ability) women's gender identity was more salient, which in turn made them more receptive to assimilating positive female math role models. When these positive, highly math competent female role models were available, the women in the studies overcame stereotype threat and performed well. Supporting the positive effects of role-models, research has shown that women who read about high achieving women perform better (McIntyre, Paulson, & Lord, 2003) and have a greater sense of their own math competency (Marx & Roman, 2002). Thus, there is clear evidence that having positive female role models reduces the effect of stereotype threat.

Bringing both the gender composition work and positive role model work together, Huguet and Regner (2007) examined stereotype threat in girls (ages 11–13) in their ordinary classrooms. They found that when a task was described as a geometry task versus a drawing task, the girls underperformed in comparison to the boys – but only in mixed-sex classrooms. When the same task was done is a classroom of all girls, the stereotype threat effect did not occur. Moreover, when asked to nominate high math achieving peers, girls in the mixed-sex groups tended to nominate boys, whereas girls in the same-sex group nominated girls. Thus, in both laboratory studies and field studies, the effects of stereotype threat can be ameliorated through changing what is salient about one's gender identity – when positive role models or peers are salient, stereotype threat disappears.

In summary, the situational salience and meaning of social identities seem quite malleable. To the extent that stereotyped identities can be made less salient, or, more positive aspects can be made more salient, performance decrements in stereotype threat situations can be overcome. This gives hope in helping members of stereotyped groups to surmount stereotype threat and perform at their full potential. In an unexpected twist however, it may be that the very situations that have been harming the performance of members of stereotyped groups have, at the same time, been boosting the performance of their non-stereotyped peers. We turn to this phenomenon of 'stereotype lift' next.

Stereotype lift

Although the focus of stereotype threat research is on the effects of negative stereotypes on members of stigmatized groups, stereotypes are always relative. For every group that is considered 'worse than,' there must be a group that is considered 'better than.' If women are 'bad at math' then men must be better. How are these groups on the positive side of the stereotype affected by stereotype threat situations? A weak but interesting pattern often appears when the results of stereotype threat studies are examined: The positively-stereotyped group seems to get a boost in the stereotype threat conditions compared to conditions designed to reduce stereotype threat (e.g., tests described as 'non-diagnostic' of an ability; or those explicitly described as 'gender-fair'). Although this 'stereotype lift' effect may not be statistically significant in a single study, Walton and Cohen (2003) found a small but highly significant effect ($d = .24$) in a meta-analysis of 28 studies. Thus, not only do negatively stereotyped group members underperform in conditions of stereotype threat, but the positively-stereotyped group members perform even better under these same conditions!

Like stereotype threat, stereotype lift is likely to be driven by multiple psychological processes. One such process is downward social comparison. As noted by Walton and Cohen (2003), perceived (or assumed) superiority under stereotype threat conditions is likely to lead to a greater sense of confidence and competence on the task.

Research on stereotype lift has generally supported this speculation. For example, Mendoza-Denton, Kahn, and Chan (2008) found that the stereotype lift effects on a math test were stronger when men were told that there were clear gender differences *and* that math ability is a fixed skill. The lift effect was weakened when men were told that math gender differences were due to effort. In essence, when the positively-stereotyped group can be assured that the negative stereotypes about the outgroup are 'true' they show a lift effect. Another way that a member of the valued group can feel more certain they are superior is when they strongly endorse group differences. In a test of this idea, Chatard, Selimbegovic, Konan, et al., (2008) found that French high school students performed better on a test described as an intelligence test when (a) the negative stereotypes about African immigrants' abilities were made salient (through describing the test as examining group differences) combined with either (b) greater individual endorsement of group differences or (c) more prejudiced beliefs toward the immigrant group.

In both of the above studies, the study design called explicit attention to group differences in order to show the stereotype lift effect. This brings up the issue of why some studies show a lift effect without directly mentioning group differences whereas others do not. Marx and Stapel (2006) hypothesized that group identity may not be as salient for people with the more positive stereotyped identities, and thus they will not be affected by identity without some cue to its relevance. In support of this hypothesis, Marx and Stapel (2006) showed that stereotype lift effects increased to the extent that men were reminded of their gender identity. Taking a different approach but also showing the necessity of an explicit identity cue, Chalabaev, Stone, Sarrazin, et al., (2008) asked men and women to complete a balancing task that was either described as one in which men were inferior, women were inferior, or no mention of gender differences. Thus, this was a novel task in which participants did not have preconceived stereotypes. Results showed a stereotype lift for both men and women (i.e., women did

better when the task was described as one on which men were inferior to women; men did better when the task was described as one on which women were inferior), but no corresponding stereotype threat occurred. In addition, for men only, increased self-confidence and engagement with the task (as measured by pre-task heart rate) mediated the stereotype lift effect.

FUTURE DIRECTIONS

Given that the basic stereotype threat effects have now been replicated and generalized, it may be time for researchers to broaden their temporal understanding of stereotype threat. To date, stereotype threat has been almost exclusively studied in short term (less than 1 hour) laboratory contexts. How do multiple instances of stereotype threat over months and years affect self and group level beliefs? The research has demonstrated that knowledge of stereotypes and stereotype threat can occur as young as elementary school, yet the research also shows that stereotype threat can be easily manipulated in young adults. What can be concluded from this combination of results? Are stereotype threat effects not additive over time? Is there only a momentary effect on performance and mood, but no lasting changes? Do students in school experience stereotype threat every day or every week there is a test? Or, do students get comfortable in a school or classroom and not experience stereotype threat for months or years at a time? Answering these questions will help to answer a larger theoretical question that has been posed about stereotype threat: How big are the effects in terms of real life outcomes? This question is already being debated (cf. Danaher & Crandall, 2008; Stricker & Ward, 2004), but the scope of stereotype threat effects is as yet unknown.

In addition, thinking about stereotype threat over time may bring to light how differences that seem small across laboratory studies – differences between gender and race for example – have quite different long term effects on life choices and outcomes. Part of the appeal of stereotype threat is that it can generalize across situations and groups, but it cannot be assumed that the experience of women in math, for example, is identical to African-Americans in intellectual testing situations, or to people with a concealed history of mental illness interviewing for a job. Even more challenging is understanding stereotype threat for people with multiple stigmatized identities. Although research under controlled laboratory conditions has shown that different identities can be made salient, there is still much work to do in understanding the ramifications of multiple identities – especially multiple stigmatized identities (e.g., Gonzales, Blanton, & Williams, 2002) in daily life.

Finally, how do experiences of stereotype threat compare with other experiences of prejudice and discrimination in terms of health? One useful model for understanding the relationship between living with a stigmatized identity and health outcomes is a stress and coping framework (e.g., Meyer, 1995; Miller, 2006; Miller & Kaiser, 2001; Williams, Neighbors, & Jackson, 2003). Should stereotype threat be regarded as a similar type of stressor as instances of perceived discrimination? If so, then examining cognitive appraisals and primary and secondary coping strategies may be a useful path. There is an evidence that examining appraisals within the stereotype threat situation is a productive avenue of understanding (e.g., Ford, Ferguson, Brooks, et al., 2004; Sawyer & Hollis-Sawyer, 2005; Schmader, Johns, & Forbes, 2008). Thus, future research needs to be directed at examining not only acute performance outcomes, but potential long-term health outcomes. Perhaps frequent small instances of stereotype threat take their toll by slowly accumulating a health burden as people deal with extra stress and negative emotions.

CONCLUSION

Stereotype threat research highlights an essential predicament of living with a stereotyped identity. By definition, stereotypes are known to all within a community, and such knowledge has effects on both the perceivers and targets. Research on stereotype threat shows that targets are affected by many subtle, environmental cues such as task domain, task instructions, and the constitution of identities within the immediate group. It is likely that these cues activate identity related stereotypes that then interfere with performance outcomes through the extra affective and cognitive mental work they require. Reactions to stereotype relevant cues are moderated by individual differences in group and domain identity strength as well as sensitivity to stereotyping concerns. Taken holistically, stereotype threat reveals a picture of how societal stereotypes and inequities can propagate without explicit words or actions of bigotry.

Research on stereotype threat is not only crucial to understanding the daily experiences of people living with stigmatized identities (for a review of broader identity threat issues see Steele et al., 2002), but also to highlighting the insidious nature of how group differences are maintained. In a stereotype threat situation, the majority group member may not believe the stereotype, but he or she reaps the subtle benefits of stereotype lift. The minority, or stereotyped, group member may not believe the stereotype, but he or she must contend with it – often with negative performance outcomes – all the same. Thus, without a single overt act of discrimination, without an explicit prejudiced thought, without internalized inferiority, the unequal *status quo* is maintained. With this realization, the nature of what it means to 'reduce prejudice' or present 'equal opportunities' changes. The challenges are greater.

REFERENCES

Allport, G. W. (1954). *The nature of prejudice*. Cambridge, Mass.: Addison-Wesley Publishing Company.

Ambady, N., Paik, S. K., Steele, J., Owen-Smith, A., & Mitchell, J. P. (2004). Deflecting negative self-relevant stereotype activation: The effects of individuation. *Journal of Experimental Social Psychology, 40*, 401–408.

Aronson, J., Fried, C. B., & Good, C. (2002). Reducing the effects of stereotype threat on African American college students by shaping theories of intelligence. *Journal of Experimental Social Psychology*, *38*, 113–125.

Aronson, J., Lustina, M. J., Good, C., Keough, K., Steele, C. M., & Brown, J. (1999). When White men can't do math: Necessary and sufficient factors in stereotype threat. *Journal of Experimental Social Psychology*, *35*, 29–46.

Ben-Zeev, T., Fein, S., & Inzlicht, M. (2005). Arousal and stereotype threat. *Journal of Experimental Social Psychology*, *41*, 174–181.

Bergeron, D. M., Block, C. J., & Echtenkamp, B. A. (2006). Disabling the able: Stereotype threat and women's work performance. *Human Performance*, *19*, 133–158.

Blascovich, J., Spencer, S. J., Quinn, D., & Steele, C. (2001). African Americans and high blood pressure: The role of stereotype threat. *Psychological Science*, *12*, 225–229.

Bosson, J. K., Haymovitz, E. L., & Pinel, E. C. (2004). When saying and doing diverge: The effects of stereotype threat on self-reported versus non-verbal anxiety. *Journal of Experimental Social Psychology*, *40*, 247–255.

Brown, R. P., & Lee, M. N. (2005). Stigma consciousness and the race gap in college academic achievement. *Self and Identity*, *4*, 149–157.

Brown, R. P., & Pinel, E. C. (2003). Stigma on my mind: Individual differences in the experience of stereotype threat. *Journal of Experimental Social Psychology*, *39*, 626–633.

Cadinu, M., Maass, A., Frigerio, S., Impagliazzo, L., & Latinotti, S. (2003). Stereotype threat: The effect of expectancy on performance. *European Journal of Social Psychology*, *33*, 267–285.

Cadinu, M., Maass, A., Lombardo, M., & Frigerio, S. (2006). Stereotype threat: The moderating role of locus of control beliefs. *European Journal of Social Psychology*, *36*, 183–197.

Cadinu, M., Maass, A., Rosabianca, A., & Kiesner, J. (2005). Why do women underperform under stereotype threat? Evidence for the role of negative thinking. *Psychological Science*, *16*, 572–578.

Camara, W. J., & Schmidt, A. E. (1999). *Group differences in standardized testing and social stratification.* New York: College Entrance Examination Board. (College Board Report, 99–5

Chalabaev, A. N., Sarrazin, P., Stone, J., & Cury, F. O. (2008). Do achievement goals mediate stereotype threat?: An investigation on females' soccer performance. *Journal of Sport & Exercise Psychology*, *30*, 143–158.

Chalabaev, A. N., Stone, J., Sarrazin, P., & Croizet, J.-C. (2008). Investigating physiological and self-reported mediators of stereotype lift effects on a motor task. *Basic and Applied Social Psychology, 30,* 18–26.

Chatard, A., Selimbegovic, L., Konan, P., & Mugny, G. (2008). Performance boosts in the classroom: Stereotype endorsement and prejudice moderate stereotype lift. *Journal of Experimental Social Psychology, 44,* 1421–1424.

Crocker, J., Major, B., & Steele, C. (1998). Social stigma. In D. T. Gilbert, S. T. Fiske, and G. Lindzey (Eds.) *The handbook of social psychology, Vols. 1 and 2 (4th ed.).* (pp. 504–553). New York, NY US: McGraw-Hill.

Croizet, J.-C., & Claire, T. (1998). Extending the concept of stereotype and threat to social class: The intellectual underperformance of students from low socioeconomic backgrounds. *Personality and Social Psychology Bulletin, 24,* 588–594.

Danaher, K., & Crandall, C. S. (2008). Stereotype threat in applied settings re-examined. *Journal of Applied Social Psychology, 38,* 1639–1655.

Davies, P. G., Spencer, S. J., Quinn, D. M., & Gerhardstein, R. (2002). Consuming images: How television commercials that elicit stereotype threat can restrain women academically and professionally. *Personality and Social Psychology Bulletin, 28,* 1615–1628.

Davies, P. G., Spencer, S. J., & Steele, C. M. (2005). Clearing the air: Identity safety moderates the effects of stereotype threat on women's leadership aspirations. *Journal of Personality and Social Psychology, 88,* 276–287.

Deaux, K., Bikmen, N., Gilkes, A., Ventuneac, A., Joseph, Y., Payne, Y. A., et al., (2007). Becoming American: Stereotype threat effects in Afro-Caribbean immigrant groups. *Social Psychology Quarterly, 70,* 384–404.

Derks, B., Inzlicht, M., & Kang, S. (2008). The neuroscience of stigma and stereotype threat. *Group Processes & Intergroup Relations, 11,* 163–181.

Eccles, J. S., Jacobs, J. E., & Harold, R. E. (1990). Gender role stereotypes, expectancy effects, and parents' socialization of gender differences. *Journal of Social Issues, 46,* 183–201.

Ford, T. E., Ferguson, M. A., Brooks, J. L., & Hagadone, K. M. (2004). Coping sense of humor reduces effects of stereotype threat on women's math performance. *Personality and Social Psychology Bulletin, 30,* 643–653.

Goffman, E. (1963). *Stigma: Notes on the management of spoiled identity.* Englewood Cliffs, N.J.: Prentice-Hall.

Gonzales, P. M., Blanton, H., & Williams, K. J. (2002). The effects of stereotype threat and double-minority status on the test performance of Latino women.

Personality and Social Psychology Bulletin, 28, 659–670.

Herrnstein, R. J., & Murray, C. (1994). *The bell curve: Intelligence and class structure in American life.* New York: Free Press.

Huguet, P., & Regner, I. (2007). Stereotype threat among schoolgirls in quasi-ordinary classroom circumstances. *Journal of Educational Psychology, 99,* 545–560.

Inzlicht, M., & Ben-Zeev, T. (2000). A threatening intellectual environment: Why females are susceptible to experiencing problem-solving deficits in the presence of males. *Psychological Science, 11,* 365–371.

Johns, M., Schmader, T., & Martens, A. (2005). Knowing is half the battle: Teaching stereotype threat as a means of improving women's math performance. *Psychological Science, 16,* 175–179.

Keller, J. (2002). Blatant stereotype threat and women's math performance: Self-handicapping as a strategic means to cope with obtrusive negative performance expectations. *Sex Roles, 47,* 193–198.

Keller, J., & Dauenheimer, D. (2003). Stereotype threat in the classroom: Dejection mediates the disrupting threat effect on women's math performance. *Personality and Social Psychology Bulletin, 29,* 371–381.

Koenig, A. M., & Eagly, A. H. (2005). Stereotype threat in men on a test of social sensitivity. *Sex Roles, 52,* 489–496.

Kray, L. J., Galinsky, A. D., & Thompson, L. (2002). Reversing the gender gap in negotiations: An exploration of stereotype regeneration. *Organizational Behavior and Human Decision Processes, 87,* 386–409.

Kray, L. J., Thompson, L., & Galinsky, A. (2001). Battle of the sexes: Gender stereotype confirmation and reactance in negotiations. *Journal of Personality and Social Psychology, 80,* 942–958.

Krendl, A. C., Richeson, J. A., Kelley, W. M., & Heatherton, T. F. (2008). The negative consequences of threat: A functional magnetic resonance imaging investigation of the neural mechanisms underlying women's underperformance in math. *Psychological Science, 19,* 168–175.

Leyens, J.-P., Desert, M., Croizet, J.-C., & Darcis, C. (2000). Stereotype threat: Are lower status and history of stigmatization preconditions of stereotype threat? *Personality and Social Psychology Bulletin, 26,* 1189–1199.

Levy, B. (1996). Improving memory in old age through implicit self-stereotyping. *Journal of Personality and Social Psychology, 71,* 1092–1107.

Levy, B., & Langer, E. (1994). Aging free from negative stereotypes: Successful memory in China among the American deaf. *Journal of Personality and Social Psychology, 66,* 989–997.

Logel, C., Iserman, E. C., Davies, P. G., Quinn, D. M., & Spencer, S. J. (2009). The perils of double consciousness: The role of thought suppression in stereotype threat. *Journal of Experimental Social Psychology.*

Major, B., & O'Brien, L. T. (2005). The social psychology of stigma. *Annual Review of Psychology, 56,* 393–421.

Martens, A., Johns, M., Greenberg, J., & Schimel, J. (2006). Combating stereotype threat: The effect of self-affirmation on women's intellectual performance. *Journal of Experimental Social Psychology, 42,* 236–243.

Marx, D. M., & Roman, J. S. (2002). Female role models: Protecting women's math test performance. *Personality and Social Psychology Bulletin, 28,* 1183–1193.

Marx, D. M., & Stapel, D. A. (2006). Understanding stereotype lift: On the role of the social self. *Social Cognition, 24,* 776–791.

Marx, D. M., Stapel, D. A., & Muller, D. (2005). We can do it: The interplay of construal orientation and social comparisons under threat. *Journal of Personality and Social Psychology, 88,* 432–446.

McGlone, M. S., & Aronson, J. (2007). Forewarning and forearming stereotype-threatened students. *Communication Education, 56,* 119–133.

McIntyre, R. B., Paulson, R. M., & Lord, C. G. (2003). Alleviating women's mathematics stereotype threat through salience of group achievements. *Journal of Experimental Social Psychology, 39,* 83–90.

McKown, C., & Weinstein, R. S. (2003). The development and consequences of stereotype consciousness in middle childhood. *Child Development, 74,* 498–515.

Mendoza-Denton, R., Kahn, K., & Chan, W. (2008). Can fixed views of ability boost performance in the context of favorable stereotypes? *Journal of Experimental Social Psychology, 44,* 1187–1193.

Meyer, I. H. (1995). Minority stress and mental health in gay men. *Journal of Health and Social Behavior, 36,* 38–56.

Miller, C. T. (2006). Social psychological perspectives on coping with stressors related to stigma. In S. Levin & C. van Laar (Eds.), *Stigma and group inequality: Social psychological perspectives* (pp. 21–44). Mahwah, NJ US: Lawrence Erlbaum Associates Publishers.

Miller, C. T., & Kaiser, C. R. (2001). A theoretical perspective on coping with stigma. *Journal of Social Issues, 57,* 73–92.

Neuville, E., & Croizet, J.-C. (2007). Can salience of gender identity impair math performance among 7–8 year old girls? The moderating role of task difficulty. *European Journal of Psychology of Education, 22,* 307–316.

Nisbett, R. E., & Wilson, T. D. (1977). Telling more than we can know: Verbal reports on mental processes. *Psychological Review, 84,* 231–259.

O'Brien, L. T., & Crandall, C. S. (2003). Stereotype threat and arousal: Effects on women's math performance. *Personality and Social Psychology Bulletin, 29,* 782–789.

O'Brien, L. T., & Hummert, M. L. (2006). Memory performance of late middle-aged adults: Contrasting self-stereotyping and stereotype threat accounts of assimilation to age stereotypes. *Social Cognition, 24,* 338–358.

Osborne, J. W. (2001). Testing stereotype threat: Does anxiety explain race and sex differences in achievement? *Contemporary Educational Psychology, 26,* 291–310.

Osborne, J. W. (2007). Linking stereotype threat and anxiety. *Educational Psychology, 27,* 135–154.

Oswald, D. L., & Harvey, R. D. (2000). Hostile environments, stereotype threat, and math performance among undergraduate women. *Current Psychology: Developmental, Learning, Personality, Social, 19,* 338–356.

Pinel, E. C. (1999). Stigma consciousness: The psychological legacy of social stereotypes. *Journal of Personality and Social Psychology, 76,* 114–128.

Quinn, D. M., Kahng, S. K., & Crocker, J. (2004). Discreditable: Stigma effects of revealing a mental illness history on test performance. *Personality and Social Psychology Bulletin, 30,* 803–815.

Quinn, D. M., & Spencer, S. J. (2001). The interference of stereotype threat with women's generation of mathematical problem-solving strategies. *Journal of Social Issues, 57,* 55–71.

Rosenthal, H. E. S., & Crisp, R. J. (2006). Reducing stereotype threat by blurring intergroup boundaries. *Personality and Social Psychology Bulletin, 32,* 501–511.

Sawyer, T. P., Jr., & Hollis-Sawyer, L. A. (2005). Predicting stereotype threat, test anxiety, and cognitive ability test performance: An examination of three models. *International Journal of Testing, 5,* 225–246.

Schmader, T. (2002). Gender identification moderates stereotype threat effects on women's math performance. *Journal of Experimental Social Psychology, 38,* 194–201.

Schmader, T., & Johns, M. (2003). Converging evidence that stereotype threat reduces working memory capacity. *Journal of Personality and Social Psychology, 85,* 440–452.

Schmader, T., Johns, M., & Forbes, C. (2008). An integrated process model of stereotype threat effects on performance. *Psychological Review, 115,* 336–356.

Sekaquaptewa, D., & Thompson, M. (2003). Solo status, stereotype threat, and performance expectancies: Their effects on women's performance. *Journal of Experimental Social Psychology, 39,* 68–74.

Shapiro, J. R., & Neuberg, S. L. (2007). From stereotype threat to stereotype threats: Implications of a multi-threat framework for causes, moderators, mediators, consequences, and interventions. *Personality and Social Psychology Review, 11,* 107–130.

Shih, M., Pittinsky, T. L., & Ambady, N. (1999). Stereotype susceptibility: Identity salience and shifts in quantitative performance. *Psychological Science, 10,* 80–83.

Smith, J. L., & White, P. H. (2002). An examination of implicitly activated, explicitly activated, and nullified stereotypes on mathematical performance: It's not just a woman's issue. *Sex Roles, 47,* 179–191.

Spencer, B., & Castano, E. (2007). Social class is dead. Long live social class! Stereotype threat among low socioeconomic status individuals. *Social Justice Research, 20,* 418–432.

Spencer, S. J., Steele, C. M., & Quinn, D. M. (1999). Stereotype threat and women's math performance. *Journal of Experimental Social Psychology, 35,* 4–28.

Steele, C. M. (1997). A threat in the air: How stereotypes shape intellectual identity and performance. *American Psychologist, 52,* 613–629.

Steele, C. M., & Aronson, J. (1995). Stereotype threat and the intellectual test performance of African Americans. *Journal of Personality and Social Psychology, 69,* 797–811.

Steele, C. M., Spencer, S. J., & Aronson, J. (2002). Contending with group image: The psychology of stereotype and social identity threat. In M. P. Zanna (Ed.), *Advances in experimental social psychology,* Vol. 34. (pp. 379–440): Academic Press, Inc.

Stricker, L. J., & Ward, W. C. (2004). Stereotype threat, inquiring about test takers' ethnicity and gender, and standardized test performance. *Journal of Applied Social Psychology, 34*(4), 665–693.

Stone, J. (2002). Battling doubt by avoiding practice: The effects of stereotype threat on self-handicapping in white athletes. *Personality and Social Psychology Bulletin, 28,* 1667–1678.

Stone, J., Lynch, C. I., Sjomeling, M., & Darley, J. M. (1999). Stereotype threat effects on Black and White athletic performance. *Journal of Personality and Social Psychology, 77,* 1213–1227.

Walton, G. M., & Cohen, G. L. (2003). Stereotype lift. *Journal of Experimental Social Psychology, 39,* 456–467.

White, K. R. (1982). The relation between socioeconomic status and academic achievement. *Psychological Bulletin, 91*, 461–481.

Williams, D. R., Neighbors, H. W., & Jackson, J. S. (2003). Racial/Ethnic discrimination and health: Findings from community studies. *American Journal of Public Health, 93*, 200–208.

Wout, D., Danso, H., Jackson, J., & Spencer, S. (2008). The many faces of stereotype threat: Group- and self-threat. *Journal of Experimental Social Psychology, 44*, 792–799.

Wraga, M., Helt, M., Jacobs, E., & Sullivan, K. (2007). Neural basis of stereotype-induced shifts in women's mental rotation performance. *Social Cognitive and Affective Neuroscience, 2*, 12–19.

Yeung, N. C. J., & von Hippel, C. (2008). Stereotype threat increases the likelihood that female drivers in a simulator run over jaywalkers. *Accident Analysis & Prevention, 40*, 667–674.

Yopyk, D. J. A., & Prentice, D. A. (2005). Am I an athlete or a student? Identity salience and stereotype threat in student-athletes. *Basic and Applied Social Psychology, 27*, 329–336.

Zajonc, R. B. (1965). Social facilitation. *Science*, 149, 269–274.

24

Internalized Devaluation and Situational Threat

Jennifer Crocker and Julie A. Garcia

ABSTRACT

In this chapter, we consider research and theory on the idea that prejudice and discrimination lower the self-esteem of people with stigmatized identities. We describe how studies of the effects of stigma on self-esteem progressively evolved to (a) examine moderators of the effects of social stigma on self-esteem; (b) examine how situational variables shape the meaning of prejudice, stereotypes, and stigma; (c) frame social stigma as a situational predicament with which targets of stigma actively cope; and (d) view the stigmatized as caught between protecting self-esteem at the cost of learning, relationships, and/or motivation versus sustaining learning, motivation, and relationships at the cost of self-esteem. We argue that situational cues, personal beliefs, and collective representations trigger a self-focused motivational orientation, which has undesirable consequences. Initial evidence shows that shifting from self-image goals to compassionate goals can protect the self-esteem of targets of stigma, and help create positive relationships between people with stigmatized and nonstigmatized identities.

INTERNALIZED DEVALUATION AND SITUATIONAL THREAT

Fifty years ago, social scientists generally assumed that targets of stigma and negative stereotypes internalized negative images and that this internalization could alter or even damage the personality of the stigmatized person (Scott, 1997). Allport for example, began his analysis of the psychological consequences of prejudice by asking, 'What would happen to your personality if you heard it said over and over again that you are lazy and had inferior blood?' (Allport, 1954, p. 42).

In this chapter, we consider the theoretical rationale for assuming that prejudice and stereotypes are internalized by their targets, and review the large body of research testing this assumption. We then describe how studies of the effects of stigma on self-esteem progressively evolved to (a) examine moderators of the effects of social stigma on self-esteem; (b) examine how situational variables and widely shared beliefs shape the meaning of prejudice, stereotypes, and stigma; (c) frame social stigma as a situational predicament with which targets of stigma actively cope; and (d) view the stigmatized as caught between a rock and a hard place – the rock involves protecting self-esteem at the cost of learning, relationships, and/or motivation; the hard place involves sustaining learning, motivation, and relationships at the cost of self-esteem. We conclude with suggestions for the next phase in the evolution of this research, arguing that situational cues, personal beliefs, and collective representations trigger a self-focused motivational orientation, which has a number of predicable and undesirable consequences. We suggest that shifting from goals focused on constructing, protecting, and enhancing desired self-images to goals focused on learning, contributing, and supporting others empower targets of stereotypes and prejudice.

HISTORY OF RESEARCH ON STIGMA AND SELF-WORTH

Internalization of devaluation, prejudice, and discrimination shapes beliefs about the self and the world. Stigmatized people sometimes decide that negative stereotypes of their group are valid, and stereotype themselves (e.g., Biernat, Vescio, & Green, 1996; Hogg & Turner, 1987; Lewin, 1948). For example, on average overweight people believe that overweight people lack self-discipline and dislike other overweight people just as much as thin people do (Crandall, 1994; Quinn & Crocker, 1999). Stigmatized people sometimes accept that they deserve their devalued status, and legitimize and defend the system that devalues them (Jost and Banaji, 1994; Sidanius, 1993).

Most research and theory on the internalization hypothesis, however, focuses on self-esteem. Self-esteem refers to personal and global feelings of self-worth, self-regard, or self-acceptance (Rosenberg, 1979). Both pragmatic and theoretical concerns contribute to the wide interest in self-esteem. Pragmatically, several measures of self-esteem with excellent psychometric properties have been available since the 1960s, and researchers include these measures in many studies, resulting in a large number of data sets on which to test hypotheses about self-esteem. Theoretically, psychologists widely regard self-esteem as a central indicator of mental health or psychological well-being (Taylor & Brown, 1988); self-esteem influences life satisfaction (Diener, 1984), the emotional experience of daily life (Pelham & Swann, 1989), and represents a broad psychological consequence of stereotyping, prejudice, and stigma. Social stigma spoils not only one's social identity in the eyes of others, but also one's experience of the self.

Most social psychological theory suggests that stigmatized people should have low self-esteem. Symbolic interactionists articulated this idea in the looking-glass self hypothesis. Sociologists such as Mead (1934) and Cooley (1956) argued that the self is a social construction; people develop their sense of who and what they are by observing and interpreting the responses they receive from others. Other people provide the looking-glass in which people see themselves reflected. People then incorporate that reflection into their own self-views. This analysis implies that social stigma and devaluation of one's identity distorts personality, creating internalized, stable, low trait self-esteem.

By the 1950s, social psychologists widely accepted this view as fact. In 1950, Dorwin Cartwright argued that, "the groups to which a person belongs serve as primary determinants of his self-esteem. To a considerable extent, personal feelings of worth depend on the social evaluation of the group with which a person is identified. Self-hatred and feelings of worthlessness tend to arise from membership in underprivileged or outcast groups." (p. 440) Erik Erikson claimed in 1956 that 'There is ample evidence of inferiority feelings and of morbid self-hate in all minority groups' (p. 155). And in his classic book, *The Nature of Prejudice*, Allport (1954) recognized that responses to oppression vary widely, but suggested that a common consequence was low self-esteem: 'Group oppression may destroy the integrity of the ego entirely, and reverse its normal pride, and create a groveling self-image' (p. 152).

Evidence for this proposition is mixed at best. The studies the Supreme Court cited in the Brown v Board of Education decision banning school segregation showed that Black children prefer white over black dolls (Clark & Clark, 1947) as evidence of low self-esteem. Yet, doll preference may not indicate low self-esteem (Porter & Washington, 1979). Using psychometrically sound and validated measures of self-esteem, researchers discovered that Black children did not widely suffer from low self-esteem (Rosenberg, 1965). A review of the literature in the late 1970s confirmed the absence of low self-esteem among Black Americans (Porter & Washington, 1979). Recent meta-analyses of hundreds of studies involving hundreds of thousands of research participants show that Black Americans actually have higher self-esteem than Whites, on average (Gray-Little & Hafdahl, 2000; Twenge & Crocker, 2002).

Crocker and Major (1989) speculated that resilient self-esteem was not unique to Blacks, but might also characterize many other stigmatized groups. They reviewed studies showing that stigmatized groups as varied as people with facial disfigurements, learning disabilities, mental retardation, physical handicaps, or who are obese do not have low self-esteem. Subsequent quantitative reviews generally support this conclusion. For example, meta-analyses of gender differences in self-esteem typically find small differences favoring males (Kling, Hyde, & Showers, 1999; Major, Barr, Zubek, et al., 1999). Studies comparing self-esteem in obese and nonobese populations also typically find no differences or very small differences (Friedman & Brownell, 1995; Miller & Downey, 1999). One recent study examined implicit self-esteem and found no differences between underweight, normal weight, overweight, and obese participants (Karpinski, Griffin, & Clabaugh, 2007).

REVIEW OF LITERATURE ON THE LINK BETWEEN STIGMA AND SELF-ESTEEM

In light of theory suggesting that the stigmatized incorporate others' negative views of them into their self-concepts, the failure to find low self-esteem among many stigmatized groups begs for explanation. Researchers suggest four explanations, positing that the effects of social stigma on self-esteem depend on: (1) moderator variables, (2) how targets of stigma construe the situation, (3) how targets of stigma cope with threats to their self-esteem, and (4) the goals or motivations of the stigmatized person.

The moderator solution

Perhaps the hypothesis that stigma causes low self-esteem applies only to some people. In other words, characteristics of the stigmatized could moderate the effect of stigma on self-esteem. Meta-analytic investigations support this view. For example, race differences in self-esteem depend on the gender, age, and education of the sample (Gray-Little & Hafdahl, 2000; Twenge & Crocker, 2002); gender differences depend on the age, race, and other characteristics of the sample (Kling, Hyde, & Showers, 1999; Major, Barr, Zubek, et al., 1999), and body weight differences depend on gender and ethnicity (Miller & Downey, 1999).

Unfortunately, meta-analytic investigations tend to focus on demographic moderator variables of the effects of stigma on self-esteem, because these are most consistently included in the published studies summarized in meta-analyses. Psychologists, however, care more about the psychological variables that might explain these effects. Researchers have proposed and studied several psychological moderators. The impact of a stigmatized identity on self-esteem depends, for example, on the importance or centrality of the identity to a person's self-concept (McCoy & Major, 2003), how contingent on others' approval the person's self-esteem is (Quinn & Crocker, 1998), and how much the person endorses system-justifying ideologies such as the Protestant Ethic (Quinn & Crocker, 1999) or belief in a just world (Major et al., 2002a). This research is reviewed in detail elsewhere (see Major & O'Brien, 2005; Major, Quinton, & McCoy, 2002b, for reviews)

These psychological moderators suggest that the effect of prejudice or stigma on self-esteem depends on the meaning people make of their devalued status. In other words, rather than passively accepting and incorporating negative views that others may hold of them, people may interpret and attempt to make sense of prejudice in the context of central beliefs, values, and self-concepts (Crocker, 1999).

The situational construction of self-esteem

In the past two decades, conceptualizations of self-esteem have shifted from viewing self-esteem as a stable trait to viewing it as a state. We briefly consider the evidence for this conclusion in research on self-esteem and constructing meaning from prejudice, discrimination, and stereotypes and the implications for self-esteem among targets of prejudice and discrimination. Psychologists typically construe self-esteem as a trait – a characteristic that is relatively stable over time and across situations (Rosenberg, 1979). But self-esteem varies from day to day or even moment to moment, depending on events such as success and failure, or acceptance and rejection (Heatherton & Polivy, 1991; Leary, Tambor, Terdal, et al., 1995); in other words, self-esteem is a state as well as a trait. Studies assessing self-esteem repeatedly (daily or several times a day) in the same people indicate that about two-thirds of the variance in self-esteem is between-person variance (i.e., reflects a trait), and about one third is within-person variance, reflecting situational constraints or even random fluctuations (Crocker, Karpinski, Quinn, et al., 2003). In other words, although people have an average or characteristic level of self-esteem, situations, events, and information available at the moment cause fluctuations in self-esteem around that typical level (Crocker & Wolfe, 2001).

Whether a particular social identity or characteristic is stigmatized depends on meanings derived from cues in that context (Crocker, Major, & Steele, 1998; Steele, Spencer, & Aronson, 2002). Consequently, the effects of stigma on self-esteem depend on the meaning given to that situation (Crocker, 1999). Meaning is partly shaped by personal experiences and beliefs, collective representations, and features of the situation itself –

often very subtle features (Crocker, 1999). Crocker and Major (1989) proposed that the effect of prejudice and discrimination on self-esteem depends on whether stigmatized people (a) attribute negative outcomes to prejudice and discrimination, rather than to their own difficulties; (b) compare their outcomes with those of ingroup members, who are similarly disadvantaged, rather than to the outcomes of advantaged outgroup members; and (c) place less importance or value on domains in which their group is disadvantaged. The impact of events on self-esteem, then, depends on both the beliefs that stigmatized people bring them (for example, whether they believe that prejudice against their group is widespread or rare, and whether they believe prejudice is justified or not), and features of the situation (for example, whether others are aware of their stigmatized identity, availability of ingroup and outgroup comparison information) that shape their attributions, social comparisons, and valuing of domains.

Since Crocker and Major's review, a great deal of research has examined these hypotheses. We do not review these findings here as extensive reviews are available elsewhere (see Crocker, Major, & Steele, 1998; Major & O'Brien, 2005; Major, Quinton, & McCoy, 2002b, for reviews). Rather, we aim to underscore the meta-perspective underlying this research and theory. Specifically, in this research both attributions to prejudice and self-esteem constitute social judgments constructed in the situation from available information. In this research, stigmatized people do not have damaged psyches; rather, like everyone else, they attempt to make sense of their world, their experiences, and themselves, and they use the information at hand to do so. In some situations, this results in lower self-esteem; in many situations, it does not.

Coping with the predicament of stigma

Whereas the social judgment perspective on stigma and self-esteem views stigmatized people as more or less passive processors of the beliefs and information available to them, who arrive at a situation-specific judgment of self-worth, the coping perspective views stereotypes and prejudice as a situational threat with which stigmatized people actively cope (Kaiser & Miller, 2004; Major & O'Brien, 2005; Miller & Kaiser, 2001). Goffman (1963) first proposed that stigmatized people actively cope, by managing or negotiating their identity, in his seminal monograph. The evidence Goffman cited was largely anecdotal, and although a few researchers pursued the implications of Goffman's analysis (e.g., Kleck & Strenta, 1980), only recently have social psychologists enthusiastically taken up Goffman's ideas in research.

Prejudice, discrimination, and stigma potentially threaten many important goals of stigmatized people (Swim & Thomas, 2006). For example, prejudice and discrimination might threaten (a) the ability to obtain important resources (such as housing or jobs); (b) the sense of control over events; and (c) the need to belong and be included in social groups (Swim & Thomas, 2006). At its core, social stigma threatens the goal to maintain, protect, and enhance self-esteem (Crocker, Major, & Steele, 1998). In this framework, stigmatized people face a situation-specific predicament – devaluation of their personal and collective identity – toward which they may direct a variety of coping resources.

The stress and coping approach to stigma emphasizes the primary and secondary coping strategies that stigmatized people use to protect themselves from these threats, or disengaging from the threat (Major & O'Brien, 2005). Primary coping strategies involve efforts to influence events or conditions to reduce the harm. Secondary coping strategies involve efforts to adapt, perhaps by changing how one thinks or feels about the event. Disengagement involves avoiding the threat.

Coping with self-esteem threats could involve actively proving or demonstrating that one does not fit the stereotype (Steele & Aronson, 1995), such as acting in a charming manner to avoid social rejection (Miller, Rothblum, Felicio, et al., 1995), passively

disengaging from the situation or domain (Schmader, Major, Eccleston, et al., 2001; Steele, 1997), or attributing the problem to others, such as the racism of an evaluator (Major & Crocker, 1993). In fact, almost any active, motivated response (even a cognitive response) to a self-esteem threat fits under the umbrella of 'coping.'

For self-esteem, the active coping framework views cognitive processes such as attributions to prejudice, ingroup versus outgroup comparisons, and domain devaluation as motivated. From a social judgment perspective, one arrives at a conclusion that an evaluator is prejudiced or not via an unmotivated (albeit imperfect) consideration of relevant information, such as beliefs about the prevalence of prejudice against one's group, inferences about evaluator biases, and beliefs about evaluation procedures. The desired conclusion is not determined in advance. In a coping process, on the other hand, people have a goal they want to achieve, a conclusion they want to reach, or a belief they want to defend. Consequently, their evaluation of the available information changes to support the desired conclusion (Kunda, 1990).

The coping perspective on stigma and self-esteem suggests that people could be motivated to perceive prejudice as a strategy to maintain or protect self-esteem. Attributing setbacks to negative stereotypes, prejudice, and discrimination can protect self-esteem when it frames the negative outcomes as unfair and undeserved, and caused by others' prejudice rather than mistakes or inadequacies of the self (Major et al., 2002b). If stigmatized people are motivated to maintain, protect, and enhance their self-esteem, they may prefer attributing negative outcomes to others' prejudice rather than to themselves. On the other hand, if stigmatized people are motivated to maintain and protect their beliefs that the world is just and people get what they deserve, they may prefer attributing negative outcomes to their own lack of deserving rather than to unfair prejudice (Kaiser & Major, 2004). The coping perspective emphasizes that stigmatized people actively cope with threats; the specific coping response depends, in part, on what goals have been threatened (Swim & Thomas, 2006).

ANALYSIS OF THE CURRENT STATE OF KNOWLEDGE

Research on stigma and self-esteem has changed a great deal in the last 50 years; targets of stigma are no longer viewed as passive victims who inevitably internalize their devaluation and suffer from low self-esteem. Instead, they are viewed as active agents who perceive, interpret, and make meaning of their experiences of stigmatization, and cope with those experiences. Recently, researchers have focused on the trade-offs involved in coping with the situational self-threat of stigma. Some coping responses protect self-esteem but create other problems. As Miller (2006) notes, 'coping with stigma often involves hard choices between imperfect options' (p. 38).

For example, efforts to protect self-esteem by attributing negative outcomes to prejudice and discrimination may have side-effects that can be either costly or beneficial. Pointing out prejudice can help to reduce it (Shelton & Stewart, 2004), yet people dislike those who claim to be victims of discrimination (Kaiser & Miller, 2001), and smooth social interaction often requires that people accept other's definitions of reality, including their views of the self (Sinclair, Hardin, & Lowery, 2006). Not confronting prejudiced people can cause targets of prejudice, especially those who think they should directly confront prejudice, to feel angry and disappointed in themselves (Shelton, Richeson, Salvatore, et al., 2006).

Disidentification provides another example of the costly trade-offs involved in protecting self-esteem for the stigmatized. Stigmatized people may protect self-esteem by devaluing the domains in which they or their group fares poorly (Schmader , Major, Eccleston, et al., 2001). Specifically, they may decide that success is impossible (for example, because tests are biased against them) or they may disengage their self-worth from achievement in the domain. Disidentification involves a trade-off between persistence and self-esteem protection; people who decide a task or a domain is unimportant or biased against them may withdraw effort, or simply quit (Shapiro & Neuberg, 2007). Giving up and withholding effort increase the likelihood of failure, which may create a downward spiral of self-threat, disengagement, and failure, which creates further self-threat, disengagement, and failure.

The idea that targets of prejudice are caught between a rock and a hard place, forced to choose between alternatives both with undesirable consequences, runs through a number of contemporary accounts of the experience of stigmatized people (Kaiser, 2006; Miller, 2006; Shelton, Richeson, & Salvatore, 2006; Sinclair, Hardin, & Lowery, 2006; Steele, 1997; Steele & Aronson, 1995). This perspective paints a less depressing picture of the experience of the stigmatized than the view held by most social scientists half a century ago. However, the current view still conveys a sense of being stuck with no discernable way forward. In the current zeitgeist, the stigmatized remain at the mercy of the stereotypes, prejudice, and discrimination that surround them, with no satisfying alternatives. Pursuing one goal, such as self-esteem, may require sacrificing another, such as persistence, interpersonal relationships, or confidence that justice will prevail. We think this view is grim – perhaps unnecessarily so.

Goals and motivations of the stigmatized person

As we have seen, the coping perspective raises the question of what the targets of stigma want – what goals do they pursue? We have proposed that the effects of stigma on self-esteem depend on the interpersonal goals and motivations of the stigmatized person (Crocker & Garcia, 2006; Crocker, Garcia, & Nuer, 2008). Research has only recently begun to examine this hypothesis; initial findings suggest it is a promising direction for future research.

Egosystem motivation and self-image goals

Stigmatized and nonstigmatized people alike often want to maintain, enhance, and protect self-esteem and specific desired self-images (Baumeister, 1998). Self-esteem and self-image are inextricably linked to beliefs about how others see the self (Cooley, 1956; Mead, 1934). Constructing desired images therefore requires doing things to ensure that other people *see and acknowledge* those qualities in the self (Leary & Kowalski, 1990). Attributing negative feedback to prejudice and disidentifying with domains in which one's group is negatively stereotyped, may sometimes reflect motivated pursuit of self-esteem and efforts to protect desired self-images, both in one's own eyes and in the eyes of others (Crocker, Garcia, & Nuer, 2008).

We propose that the effects of stigma on self-esteem depend on how much people are driven by egosystem motivation and self-image goals. Egosystem motivation has negative consequences for relationships, achievement, and mental health (Crocker, 2008). This motivation may be particularly problematic for members of stigmatized groups, because the negative images of their group can threaten self-image goals. Thus, in our view, egosystem motivation creates or contributes to many predicaments experienced by the stigmatized. For example, both stereotype threat (see Chapter 23 by Quinn, Kallen, & Spencer, this volume, for a review) and identity threat involve concerns about threats to desired images of the self and/or the groups. Stereotype threat (Steele, 1997) and identity threat should be problematic precisely when, and because, targets of stigma are driven by egosystem motivation. People with relatively low levels of egosystem motivation should be less vulnerable to the negative effects of stigma on self-esteem.

Ecosystem motivation and compassionate goals

Fortunately, egosystem motivation is not the only possible motivational framework for the self. Drawing on the biological notion of an ecosystem, we use the term 'ecosystem motivation' to refer to a motivational perspective in which people see themselves as part of a larger whole, a system of individuals whose needs are equally important, and whose actions have consequences for others, with repercussions for the entire system, that ultimately affect the ability of the individual to satisfy his or her own fundamental needs (Crocker, 2008). From an ecosystem perspective, people focus on how they can contribute or support others as they pursue their important goals; they have what we call compassionate goals. Ecosystem motivation is not altruistic in the sense that people act at the expense of the self; it is nonzero sum – good for the self and others (Crocker & Canevello, 2008b). Ecosystem motivation has considerable benefits for relationships, mental health, and achievement (Crocker, 2008; Crocker & Canevello, 2008b).

We propose that ecosystem motivation can protect and even increase the self-esteem and well-being of stigmatized people without the trade-offs noted by stigma researchers. For the stigmatized, ecosystem motivation involves shifting from concerns about the images or stereotypes others hold of them or their group, to concerns about how they can act constructively to create the relationships they want, or contribute to something that transcends the self. Shifting to ecosystem goals does not mean sacrificing one's own well-being for the sake of others. Rather, it involves searching for goals that are good for the self as well as others. Sometimes this might involve challenging others' prejudice, not as a judgment or criticism, but to create a mutually supportive relationship. In an ecosystem framework, people raise their concerns about possible prejudice and discrimination in a constructive, learning-oriented way, rather than accusing others or withdrawing (Crocker et al., 2008a).

In our view, people who are stigmatized have a lot to gain from shifting their motivational framework from egosystem to ecosystem goals. Such a shift not only benefits others, it also ultimately benefits the self by creating social support, fostering learning, and improving well-being. Shifting from egosystem to ecosystem goals could reverse the downward spiral of intergroup relations, and potentially create an upward spiral in its place (Crocker et al., 2008a).

Three studies provide initial evidence of the costs of egosystem motivation and the benefits of ecosystem motivation for targets of stigma.

Motivations for disclosing stigma

A daily report study of the effects of egosystem and ecosystem motivations for disclosing or concealing a concealable stigma supports the idea that ecosystem motivations have benefits for stigmatized people (Garcia & Crocker, 2008). Forty-eight depressed college students completed a measure of motivations to disclose or conceal their identity to others. For the next two weeks, at the end of each day participants were asked if they had an opportunity to disclose their depression that day. If they did have an opportunity to disclose, they were asked to report their reasons for or against disclosure and how they felt when they disclosed. After two weeks, they completed measures of how much they disclosed, and well-being. Although the well-being measure did not specifically include self-esteem, it was a composite of measures that correlate strongly with self-esteem, including low levels of depression, anxiety, and negative affect, and high levels of life satisfaction.

We measured motivation to disclose or conceal a concealable stigma with a modified version of a scale developed by Derlega, Winstead, and Folk-Barron (2000), originally designed to assess disclosing one's HIV-status to an intimate partner. In addition, participants completed measures of how much approval validation goals, identity validation goals (i.e., desire to be seen as depressed for depressed participants or a sexual minority for those who were nonheterosexual), and growth goals influenced their disclosure decisions. Factor analyses indicated that disclosure goals loaded on two uncorrelated factors, consistent with our theoretical conceptualization of egosystem and ecosystem motivations. The egosystem factor included reasons both for

disclosure and against disclosure: communication difficulty, conflict avoidance, fear of rejection, desire for others' approval, test other's reactions, catharsis, and duty to inform. The ecosystem factor only included reasons to disclose: personal growth, educating the other, similarity with the other, and being authentic.

We examined the effects of egosystem goals and ecosystem goals on disclosure and psychological well-being both in daily disclosure decisions and at the end of two weeks. In line with predictions, we found that participants from both groups disclosed more in daily disclosure decisions when they disclosed with ecosystem goals compared to egosystem goals. Egosytem goals predicted greater concealment in daily disclosure decisions. Counter to predictions, over two weeks, disclosure increased most when participants had both high egosystem and ecosystem goals. Consistent with predictions, participants in both groups experienced greater positive affect in daily disclosure decisions when they disclosed with ecosystem goals compared to egosystem goals. Counter to predictions, over two weeks, having both high egosystem and ecosystem goals predicted greater well-being exclusively for depressed participants. Taken together, these findings suggest that it is also important to consider the reactions of others' and the ramifications of disclosure for the self (i.e., have egosystem motivations), particularly for depressed people. This may be due, in part, to depression symptoms. People who are depressed have a heightened self-focused state (Pyszczynski, Greenberg, Hamilton, et al., 1991; Pyszczynski, Holt, & Greenberg, 1987) and tend to perceive, themselves, others, and the world negatively (Beck, 1967). Thus, it may be difficult for people with depression to both have and implement ecosystem goals because they may seem particularly risky. As depressive symptoms wane, and ecosystem motivations increase, the influence of egosystem goals on well-being might decrease.

It is also important to note that perceptions of stigma affected goal endorsement. Perceptions of stigma were uncorrelated with ecosystem goals, but positively correlated with egosystem goals. Although the direction of effects are unclear, these findings could suggest that when a person has ecosystem goals such as supporting others and being authentic, perceptions of stigma do not derail those objectives and are therefore uncorrelated. However, when a person has egosystem goals such as fearing rejection, they may be more vigilant for signs of rejection and may perceive stigma even when it may not be there.

Perceptions of stigma also affected disclosure rates. Reports of disclosure were lowest among participants who perceived stigma (i.e., they expected to be rejected if they disclosed their stigma), but only if they lacked ecosystem goals; perceived stigma did not predict lower disclosure for participants who had ecosystem goals. These findings support previous research indicating that perceived stigma is a barrier to revealing depression, yet suggests that regardless of perceived stigma, ecosystem goals can lead to increased disclosure.

Egosystem and ecosystem goals in African-American college students

A study of first-semester African-American students provides additional support for the costs of egosystem motivation and the benefits of ecosystem motivation for targets of stigma (Crocker, Canevello, & Webb, 2008). Because racial and ethnic minority students on predominantly white campuses are often devalued and stereotyped, we suspected that self-image goals may be particularly problematic for them, and compassionate goals particularly helpful. Forty-eight African-American students completed 22 surveys over their first semester of college. On days these students had high self-image goals, they felt significantly more anxious and stressed, and marginally more depressed. On days they had higher compassionate goals they were significantly more likely to feel that they belonged at the University of Michigan, and were less anxious, depressed, and stressed; they also self-regulated better (e.g., procrastinated less, got their work done on time).

Although only 42 African-American students completed both the pre- and post-test surveys, we found several significant effects of chronic self-image goals (averaged across the 20 reports) on changes from the start to the end of the first semester. Students with chronic self-image goals marginally decreased in self-esteem, and significantly increased in anxiety, depression, and stress. They also became significantly less learning-oriented and more ego-involved in academics, that is, more motivated to prove their ability. Although not significant, chronic compassionate goals predicted increased learning orientations, decreased ego-involvement in academics, decreased anxiety, and decreased imposter feelings. These results suggest that self-image goals negatively affect African-American students' well-being, including their self-esteem, whereas compassionate goals have benefits (although the effects on self-esteem did not reach significance).

We also received students' permission to obtain their first- and second-semester grades from the registrar. Chronic compassionate goals in the Fall semester predicted higher grades at the end of both Fall and Winter semesters of the freshman year, controlling for high school GPA (although these effects were only marginally significant, the effects were as strong as the effect for high school grades). At the same time, chronic self-image goals predicted lower grades at the end of both semesters of the freshman year, again controlling for high school GPA, and this effect was significant for second-semester grades. The predicted value of GPA for African-American students with the optimal combination of goals – low self-image and high compassionate goals – was 3.6, whereas the predicted value of GPA for students with the most detrimental combination of goals – high self-image and low compassionate goals – was 2.4, again controlling for high school GPA (SAT/ACT scores did not predict freshman year grades for this sample, so we did not control for them).

These two studies suggest that the effects of stigma on well-being in general, and self-esteem in particular, depend on the motivational orientations of targets of stigma. We think this approach has value for the study of stigma beyond its implications for self-esteem. Recent research in our laboratories suggests that ecosystem motivation creates positive cross-race relationships.

Egosystem and ecosystem goals in same- and cross-race roommate relationships

Interactions between people from different racial or ethnic groups are notoriously problematic, characterized by intergroup anxiety and tension (Blascovich, Mendes, Hunter, et al., 2001; Mendes, Blascovich, Major, et al., 2001; Stephan & Stephan, 1985). People sometimes cope with these tensions by avoiding intergroup contact (Plant & Devine, 2003). In some situations, however, people cannot avoid contact, and tension escalates into seemingly intractable conflict, with potentially destructive personal, interpersonal, and societal consequences (Prentice & Miller, 1999).

Although the fundamental problem of cross-group relationships is *relational,* researchers rarely study the dynamics of cross-group relationships as they unfold over time (but see Shelton, Trail, & West, in press; West, Shelton, & Trial, in press). We assume that the fundamental problem in many cross-race interactions is not racial antipathy, but perceived threats to desired self-images (Crocker & Garcia, 2006; Crocker et al., 2008a; Shelton & Richeson, 2006). People want to believe they are valuable and worthy (Pyszczynski, Greenberg, Solomon, et al., 2004; Steele, 1988). Sustaining this belief is difficult in cross-race interactions, in which people have different backgrounds, beliefs, and experiences, and different ideas about what makes people valuable and worthy. People in cross-race interactions have desired images relevant to their identities as members of valued or devalued groups (e.g., fair, unprejudiced, deserving of respect, intelligent). For disadvantaged group members, cross-race interactions raise concerns about devaluation and negative stereotypes, which threaten desired images (Steele, Spencer, & Aronson, 2002), and concerns about the image consequences of confronting prejudice (Shelton & Richeson, 2006). Likewise, for advantaged group members, cross-race interactions raise concerns about being seen as unfair and prejudiced, or unfairly benefitting from privileged status (Richeson & Shelton, 2007). Thus, for both people, cross-race interactions can threaten desired images.

Self-image goals may be particularly detrimental in cross-race relationships because they create anxiety. Our previous research has repeatedly shown that self-image goals elicit anxiety (Crocker, Canevello, Breines, et al., in press). Anxiety is particularly problematic in intergroup interactions because the nonverbal behaviors associated with anxiety overlap with those associated with dislike, and are interpreted as dislike in cross-race but not same-race interactions (Dovidio, Kawakami, & Gaertner, 2002). Consequently, compared to students in same-race interactions, students in cross-race interactions have more self-image goals, which create anxiety, which their relationship partners interpret as dislike.

Whereas self-image goals predict negative relationship dynamics and outcomes, *compassionate goals* predict positive dynamics and outcomes. Compassionate goals focus on supporting others, not to obtain something for the self, but out of caring and consideration for the well-being of others (Crocker & Canevello, 2008b). When people have compassionate goals they want to be a constructive force in their interactions with others, and avoid harming others.

Compassionate goals may be particularly helpful in cross-race relationships. Compassionate goals elicit calm, positive, other-directed affect, and reduce anxiety (Crocker & Canevello, 2008b; Crocker et al., in press). When students have compassionate goals, they report that their most important academic and relationship goals make them feel clear, peaceful, connected, loving, and empathic. These feelings, in turn, predict increased trust, empathic concern, support given, responsiveness, disclosure, understanding responses to conflict, constructive communication, and esteem for roommates. Furthermore, compassionate goals attenuate the effects of self-image goals on feeling afraid, confused, ambivalent, and pressured (Crocker & Canevello, 2008b). When compassionate goals increase, state anxiety decreases, and students with chronic compassionate goals decrease in trait anxiety in the first semester of college (Crocker et al., in press). Because cross-race relationships are fraught with anxiety, which is easily misinterpreted, compassionate goals should particularly help these relationships.

Roommate relationships are an ideal laboratory to investigate these processes. Students are randomly assigned to same- or cross-race roommates, creating a natural experiment. Given the importance of roommate relationships to many students' college experience, and the potential for roommate relationships to be a source of support or a source of stress, the poor quality of different-race roommate relationships may significantly affect not only relationship experiences, but also academic success and distress.

Crocker and Canevello (2008a) conducted a study of 65 roommate dyads (33 same-race dyads and 32 cross-race dyads). Roommate pairs were unacquainted prior to college, and were recruited early in the first semester of college, when their relationship was new. Each member of the dyads completed pretest measures of their relationship quality (satisfaction, commitment, and closeness), then completed online measures of their compassionate and self-image goals for their roommate relationship each day for 21 days. At the conclusion of the daily reports, they completed posttest measures of relationship quality. Analyses of change in relationship quality from pre- to post-test as a function of students' chronic goals (averaged across the 21 reports) and the racial match or mismatch of the dyad found self-image goals had stronger negative effects in different-race than same-race roommate pairs on change in relationship satisfaction, commitment, and

closeness. In contrast, compassionate goals had significantly stronger positive effects in cross-race than in same-race dyads. Because supportive relationships can increase self-esteem (Crocker & Canevello, in preparation), these findings suggest that compassionate goals may improve self-esteem for both participants in cross-race dyads.

AVENUES FOR FUTURE RESEARCH

Research on egosystem and ecosystem motivation, and self-image and compassionate goals, is very new. Few studies have examined the effects of these goals in the context of stigma, prejudice, and intergroup relationships. In the context of this chapter, one intriguing issue for future research is the effects of these goals on the self-esteem of people with different stigmatized identities. Compassionate goals might provide an alternate means of maintaining and even increasing self-esteem for members of stigmatized groups, who may be less inclined to attribute negative outcomes to prejudice and use other problematic methods of maintaining their self-worth. Initial research is promising, but whether self-image goals are problematic and compassionate goals helpful for members of all stigmatized or devalued groups in all contexts is unknown at present. Furthermore, research has not attempted to intervene by manipulating compassionate and self-image goals; strong conclusions about the causal effects of self-image and compassionate goals for people with stigmatized identities must await experimental evidence.

CONCLUSION

Social science research and theory have evolved over the past 50 years from the view that stigma is internalized by its targets, creating low self-esteem, to the view that stigma is a situational predicament, posing threats to self-esteem with which the stigmatized actively cope. Despite this evolution, psychologists continue to focus on the obstacles and barriers that stigma poses. The current zeitgeist views the stigmatized as caught between a rock and a hard place, in which protecting self-esteem has costs for motivation, achievement, and relationships.

This focus on problems and trade-offs leaves members of racial and ethnic minority groups with few tools to manage their self-esteem along with their relationships in these contexts. Without denying or diminishing the evidence that stereotyping, prejudice, and discrimination are hurtful to members of racial and ethnic minority groups, we believe it is useful to ask what individual members of these groups can do to minimize the negative consequences of stigma, including consequences for their self-esteem, and create close supportive relationships with people both within and outside their own identity group. We think it is also useful to ask what individual members of majority or nonstigmatized groups can do to create close, supportive relationships with people outside their own identity group, which can foster self-esteem, a sense of belonging, and ultimately the achievement of targets of stigma (Walton & Cohen, 2007).

We envision a future in which researchers study how targets of stigma can shift from being at the mercy of their stigma, reacting to or defending the self from devaluation and making hard choices between competing goals, to being the source of what they want to experience, proactively creating situations in which they are valued and feel valuable. In this imagined future, researchers would investigate the leverage that both stigmatized and nonstigmatized people have to create positive interactions that challenge negative assumptions others have of them, create meaningful connections with ingroup and outgroup members, and build self-esteem while satisfying their and others' fundamental need to belong.

The cynical reader may dismiss this vision as hopelessly Pollyanna-ish, naïvely ignoring the hard realities of deeply engrained attitudes toward stigmatized groups that help maintain the privileged position of a few. However, we believe such cynicism is unwarranted and unhelpful. In our view, this envisioned future is the next exciting challenge for research on stigma more generally, and stigma and self-esteem in particular.

REFERENCES

Allport, G. (1954). *The nature of prejudice*. New York: Doubleday/Anchor (original work published 1954).

Baumeister, R. F. (1998). The self. In D. T. Gilbert, S. T. Fiske & G. Lindzey (Eds.), *The handbook of social psychology* (4 ed., Vol. 2, pp. 680–740). New York: McGraw-Hill.

Beck, A. T. (1967). *Depression: Causes and treatment*. Philadelphia: Univeristy of Pennsylvania Press.

Biernat, M., Vescio, T. K., & Green, M. L. (1996). Selective self-stereotyping. *Journal of Personality and Social Psychology, 71*, 1194–1209.

Blascovich, J., Mendes, W. B., Hunter, S. B., Lickel, B., & Kowai-Bell, N. (2001). Perceiver threat in social interactions with stigmatized others. *Journal of Personality and Social Psychology, 80*, 253–267.

Cartwright, D. (1950). Emotional dimensions of group life. In M. L. Raymert (Ed.), Feelings and emotions (pp. 439–447). New York: McGraw Hill.

Clark, K. B., & Clark, M. P. (1947). Racial identification and racial preference in Negro children. In T. M. Newcomb & E. L. Hartley (Eds.), *Readings in Social Psychology* (pp. 239–252). New York: Holt, Rinehart, & Winston.

Cooley, C. H. (1956). *Human nature and the social order*. New York: Schocken: (Original work published 1902).

Crandall, C. S. (1994). Prejudice against fat people: Ideology and self-interest. *Journal of Personality and Social Psychology, 66*, 882–894.

Crocker, J. (1999). Social stigma and self-esteem: Situational construction of self-worth. *Journal of Experimental Social Psychology, 35*, 89–107.

Crocker, J. (2008). From egosystem to ecosystem: Implications for learning, relationships, and well-being. In H. A. Wayment & J. J. Brauer (Eds.), *Transcending self-interest: Psychological explorations of the quiet ego* (pp. 63–72). Washington, DC: APA.

Crocker, J., & Canevello, A. (2008a). Change in relationship quality in first-semester college roommates: Effects of interpersonal goals among same- and different race dyads. Unpublished raw data, University of Michigan, Ann Arbor.

Crocker, J., & Canevello, A. (2008b). Creating and undermining social support in communal relationships: The role of compassionate and self-image goals. *Journal of Personality and Social Psychology, 95*, 555–575.

Crocker, J., Canevello, A., Breines, J. G., & Flynn, H. (in press). Interpersonal goals and change in anxiety and dysphoria: Effects of compassionate and self-image goals. *Journal of Personality and Social Psychology*.

Crocker, J., Canevello, A., & Webb, F. R. (2008). Interpersonal goals and African-American students' adjustment to college. Unpublished raw data, University of Michigan, Ann Arbor.

Crocker, J., & Garcia, J. A. (2006). Stigma and the social basis of the self: A synthesis. In S. Levin & C. van Laar (Eds.), *Stigma and group inequality: Social psychological perspectives* (pp. 287–308). Mahwah, NJ: Erlbaum.

Crocker, J., Garcia, J. A., & Nuer, N. (2008). From egosystem to ecosystem in intergroup interactions: implications for intergroup reconciliation In A. Nadler, T. Molloy & J. D. Fisher (Eds.), *The social psychology of intergroup reconciliation* (pp. 171–194). Oxford: Oxford University Press.

Crocker, J., Karpinski, A., Quinn, D. M., & Chase, S. (2003). When grades determine self-worth: Consequences of contingent self-worth for male and female engineering and psychology majors. *Journal of Personality and Social Psychology, 85*, 507–516.

Crocker, J., Major, B., & Steele, C. M. (1998). Social stigma. In D. Gilbert, S. T. Fiske & G. Lindzey (Eds.), *Handbook of social psychology, 4th ed.* (4th ed., Vol. 2, pp. 504–553). New York: McGraw-Hill.

Crocker, J., & Major, B. M. (1989). Social stigma and self-esteem: The self-protective properties of stigma. *Psychological Review, 96*, 608–630.

Crocker, J., & Wolfe, C. T. (2001). Contingencies of self-worth. *Psychological Review, 108*, 593–623.

Derlega, V., Winstead, B., & Folk-Barron, L. (2000). Reasons for and against disclosing HIV-seropositive test results to an intimate partner: A functional perspective. In S. Petronio (Ed.), *Balancing the secrets of private disclosures* (pp. 53–69). Mahwah, NJ: Erlbaum.

Diener, E. (1984). Subjective well-being. *Psychological Bulletin, 95*, 542–575.

Dovidio, J. F., Kawakami, K., & Gaertner, S. L. (2002). Implicit and explicit prejudice and interracial interaction. *Journal of Personality and Social Psychology, 82*, 62–68.

Friedman, M. A., & Brownell, K. D. (1995). Psychological correlates of obesity: Moving to the next research generation. *Psychological Bulletin, 117*, 3–20.

Garcia, J. A., & Crocker, J. (2008). Coping with the stigma of depression: Egosystem and ecosystem goals. *Social Science and Medicine, 67*, 453–462.

Goffman, E. (1963). *Stigma: Notes on the management of spoiled identity*. Englewood Cliffs, NJ: Prentice-Hall.

Gray-Little, B., & Hafdahl, A. R. (2000). Factors influencing racial comparisons of self-esteem: A quantitative review. *Psychological Bulletin, 126*, 26–54.

Heatherton, T. F., & Polivy, J. (1991). Development and validation of a scale for measuring state self-esteem. *Journal of Personality and Social Psychology, 60*, 895–910.

Hogg, M. A., & Turner, J. C. (1987). Intergroup behaviour, self-stereotyping and the salience of social categories. *British Journal of Social Psychology, 26*, 325–340.

Jost, J. T., & Banaji, M. R. (1994). The role of stereotyping in system-justification and the production of false consciousness. *British Journal of Social Psychology, 33*, 1–27.

Kaiser, C. R. (2006). Dominant ideology threat and the interpersonal consequences of attributions to discrimination. In S. Levin & C. van Laar (Eds.), *Stigma and group inequality: Social psychological perspectives* (pp. 45–64). Mahwah, NJ: Erlbaum.

Kaiser, C. R., & Major, B. (2004). Judgments of deserving and the emotional consequences of stigmatization. In L. Z. Tiedens & C. W. Leach (Eds.), *The social life of emotions* (pp. 270–291). New York Cambridge University Press.

Kaiser, C. R., & Miller, C. T. (2001). Stop complaining! The social costs of making attributions to discrimination. *Personality and Social Psychology Bulletin, 27*, 254–263.

Kaiser, C. R., & Miller, C. T. (2004). A Stress and Coping Perspective on Confronting Abstract Sexism. *Psychology of Women Quarterly, 28*, 168–178.

Karpinski, A., Griffin, K. E., & Clabaugh, A. A. (2007). Implicit and explicit body image and self-esteem. Unpublished raw data, Temple University.

Kleck, R. E., & Strenta, A. (1980). Perceptions of the impact of negatively valued physical characteristics on social interactions. *Journal of Personality and Social Psychology, 39*, 861–873.

Kling, K. C., Hyde, J. S., & Showers, C. J. (1999). Gender differences in self-esteem: A meta-analysis. *Psychological Bulletin, 125*, 470–500.

Kunda, Z. (1990). The case for motivated reasoning. *Psychological Bulletin, 108*, 480–498.

Leary, M. R., & Kowalski, R. M. (1990). Impression management: A literature review and two-component model. *Psychological Bulletin, 197*, 34–47.

Leary, M. R., Tambor, E. S., Terdal, S. K., & Downs, D. L. (1995). Self-esteem as an interpersonal monitor: The sociometer hypothesis. *Journal of Personality and Social Psychology, 68*, 518–530.

Lewin, K. (1948). *Resolving social conflicts: Selected papers on group dynamics*. New York: Harper.

Major, B., Barr, L., Zubek, J., & Babey, S. H. (1999). Gender and self-esteem: A meta analysis. In J. W. B. Swann, J. H. Langlois & L. A. Gilbert (Eds.), *Sexism and stereotypes in modern society: The gender science of Janet Taylor Spence* (pp. 223–254). Washington DC: American Psychological Association.

Major, B., & Crocker, J. (1993). Social stigma: The consequences of attributional ambiguity. In D. M. Mackie & D. L. Hamilton (Eds.), *Affect, cognition, and stereotyping: Interactive processes in group perception* (pp. 345–370). New York: Academic Press.

Major, B., Gramzow, R., McCoy, S., Levin, S., Schmader, T., & Sidanius, J. (2002a). Attributions to discrimination: The role of group status and legitimizing ideology. *Journal of Personality and Social Psychology, 82*, 269–282.

Major, B., & O'Brien, L. T. (2005). The social psychology of stigma. *Annual Review of Psychology, 56*, 393–421.

Major, B., Quinton, W. J., & McCoy, S. K. (2002b). Antecedents and consequences of attributions to discrimination: Theoretical and empirical advances. In M. P. Zanna (Ed.), *Advances in experimental social psychology* (Vol. 34, pp. 251–330). San Diego: Academic Press.

McCoy, S. K., & Major, B. (2003). Group identification moderates emotional responses to perceived prejudice. *Personality and Social Psychology Bulletin, 29*, 1005–1017.

Mead, G. H. (1934). *Mind, self, and society.* Chicago: University of Chicago Press.

Mendes, W. B., Blascovich, J., Major, B., & Seery, M. (2001). Challenge and threat responses during downward and upward social comparisons. *European Journal of Social Psychology, 31*, 477–497.

Miller, C. T. (2006). Social psychological perspectives on coping with stressors related to stigma. In S. Levin & C. van Laar (Eds.), *Stigma and group inequality* (pp. 21–44). Mahwah, NJ Erlbaum.

Miller, C. T., & Downey, K. T. (1999). A meta-analysis of heavyweight and self-esteem. *Personality and Social Psychology Review, 3*, 68–84.

Miller, C. T., & Kaiser, C. R. (2001). A theoretical perspective on coping with stigma. *Journal of Social Issues, 57*, 73–92.

Miller, C. T., Rothblum, E. D., Felicio, D., & Brand, P. (1995). Compensating for stigma: Obese and nonobese women's reactions to being visible. *Personality and Social Psychology Bulletin, 21*, 1093–1106.

Pelham, B. W., & Swann, W. B., Jr. (1989). From self-conceptions to self-worth: On the sources and structure of global self-esteem. *Journal of Personality and Social Psychology, 57*, 672–680.

Plant, E. A., & Devine, P. G. (2003). The antecedents and implications of interracial anxiety. *Personality and Social Psychology Bulletin, 29*, 790–801.

Porter, J. R., & Washington, R. E. (1979). Black identity and self-esteem: A few studies of black self-concept, 1968–1978. *Annual Review of Sociology, 5*, 53–74.

Prentice, D. A., & Miller, D. T. (Eds.). (1999). *Cultural divides: Understanding and overcoming group conflict.* New York, NY: Russell Sage Foundation.

Pyszczynski, T., Greenberg, J., Hamilton, J., & Nix, G. (1991). On the relationship between self-focused attention and psychological disorder: A critical reappraisal. *Psychological Bulletin, 110*, 538–543.

Pyszczynski, T., Greenberg, J., Solomon, S., Arndt, J., & Schimel, J. (2004). Why do people need self-esteem? A theoretical and empirical review. *Psychological Bulletin, 130*, 435–468.

Pyszczynski, T., Holt, K., & Greenberg, J. (1987). Depression, self-focused attention, and expectancies for positive and negative future life events for self and others. *Journal of Personality and Social Psychology, 52*, 994–1001.

Quinn, D. M., & Crocker, J. (1998). Vulnerability to the affective consequences of the stigma of overweight. In J. S. C. Stangor (Ed.), *Prejudice: The Target's Perspective* (pp. 125–143). San Diego, CA: Academic Press.

Quinn, D. M., & Crocker, J. (1999). When ideology hurts: Effects of feeling fat and the Protestant ethic on the psychological well-being of women. *Journal of Personality and Social Psychology, 77*, 402–414.

Richeson, J. A., & Shelton, J. N. (2007). Negotiating interracial interactions: Costs, consequences, and possibilities. *Current Directions in Psychological Science, 16*, 316–320.

Rosenberg, M. (1965). *Society and the adolescent self-image.* Princeton, NJ: Princeton University Press.

Rosenberg, M. (1979). *Conceiving the self.* New York: Basic Books.

Schmader, T., Major, B., Eccleston, C., & McCoy, S. (2001). Devaluing domains in response to threatening intergroup comparisons: Perceiving legitimacy and the status-value asymmetry. *Journal of Personality and Social Psychology, 80*, 736–753.

Scott, D. M. (1997). *Contempt and pity: Social policy and the image of the damaged Black psyche 1880–1996.* Chapel Hill: University of North Carolina Press.

Shapiro, J. R., & Neuberg, S. L. (in press). From stereotype threat to stereotype threats: Implications of a multi-threat framework for causes, moderators, mediators, consequences, and interventions. *Personality and Social Psychology Review.*

Shelton, J. N., & Richeson, J. A. (2006). Interracial interactions: A relational approach. In M. P. Zanna (Ed.), *Advances in Experimental Social Psychology, Vol 38.* (pp. 121–181). San Diego, CA US: Elsevier Academic Press.

Shelton, J. N., Richeson, J. A., Salvatore, J., & Hill, D. M. (2006). Silence is not golden: The intrapersonal consequences of not confronting prejudice. In S. Levin & C. van Laar (Eds.), *Stigma and group inequality: Social psychological perspectives* (pp. 65–81). Mahwah, NJ: Erlbaum.

Shelton, J. N., & Stewart, R. E. (2004). Confronting perpetrators of prejudice: The inhibitory effects of social costs. *Psychology of Women Quarterly, 28,* 215–223.

Shelton, J. N., Trail, T. E., & West, T. V. (in press). Daily interracial interactions and interpersonal behaviors. *Personality and Social Psychology Bulletin.*

Sidanius, J. (1993). The psychology of group conflict and the dynamics of oppression: A social dominance perspective. In W. McGuire & S. Iyengar (Eds.), *Current approaches to political psychology* (pp. 183–219). Durham, NC: Duke University Press.

Sinclair, S., Hardin, C. D., & Lowery, B. S. (2006). Self-stereotyping in the context of multiple social identities. *Journal of Personality and Social Psychology, 90,* 529–542.

Steele, C. M. (1988). The psychology of self-affirmation: Sustaining the integrity of the self. In L. Berkowitz (Ed.), *Advances in experimental social psychology* (Vol. 21, pp. 261–302). New York: Academic Press.

Steele, C. M. (1997). A threat in the air: How stereotypes shape intellectual identity and performance. *American Psychologist, 52,* 613–629.

Steele, C. M., & Aronson, J. (1995). Stereotype threat and the intellectual test performance of African Americans. *Journal of Personality and Social Psychology, 69,* 797–811.

Steele, C. M., Spencer, S. J., & Aronson, J. (2002). Contending with group image: The psychology of stereotype and social identity threat. In M. P. Zanna (Ed.), *Advances in experimental social psychology* (Vol. 34, pp. 379–440). San Diego: Academic Press.

Stephan, W. G., & Stephan, C. W. (1985). Intergroup anxiety. *Journal of Social Issues, 41,* 157–175.

Swim, J. K., & Thomas, M. A. (2006). Responding to everyday discrimination: A synthesis of research on goal-directed, self-regulatory coping behaviors. In S. Levin & C. van Laar (Eds.), *Stigma and group inequality: Social psychological perspectives* (pp. 105–126). Mahwah, NJ: Erlbaum.

Taylor, S. E., & Brown, J. D. (1988). Illusion and well-being: A social-psychological perspective on mental health. *Psychological Bulletin, 103,* 193–210.

Twenge, J. M., & Crocker, J. (2002). Race, ethnicity, and self-esteem: Meta-analyses comparing Whites, Blacks, Hispanics, Asians, and Native Americans, including a commentary on Gray-Little and Hafdahl (2000). *Psychological Bulletin, 128,* 371–408.

Walton, G. M., & Cohen, G. L. (2007). A question of belonging: Race, social fit, and achievement. *Journal of Personality and Social Psychology, 92,* 82–96.

West, T. V., Shelton, J. N., & Trial, T. E. (in press). Relational anxiety in interracial interactions. *Psychological Science.*

25

Coping with Bias

Brenda Major and Sarah S. M. Townsend

ABSTRACT

This chapter reviews theory and research on how people cope with stigma-related threats to their identity. It adopts a coping perspective, in which targets of prejudice, discrimination, and negative stereotypes are viewed as active agents who negotiate their social interactions so as to achieve desired goals. Prior theoretical perspectives on how people negotiate devalued social identities are reviewed and common coping dimensions identified. Moderators of ways of coping with stigma-related identity threats are discussed. The chapter closes with a discussion of whether individual coping efforts can be effective at overcoming the effects of stigmatization. It is suggested that understanding the effectiveness of efforts to cope with stigma requires looking at multiple outcome variables and multiple types of coping simultaneously, and adopting a more complex understanding of what is meant by 'effective coping.'

COPING WITH BIAS

This chapter considers how people who are stigmatized cope with being a target of negative stereotypes, prejudice, and discrimination. People who are stigmatized have (or are believed to have) an attribute that marks them as different and leads them to be devalued in the eyes of others in particular contexts (Crocker, Major, & Steele, 1998; Goffman, 1963). In stigmatization, these attributes or 'marks' become associated with discrediting dispositions, or negative evaluations and stereotypes (Jones, Farina, Hastorf, et al., 1984). These stereotypes are generally widely shared and well known among members of a culture and become a basis for prejudice and discrimination against members of the negatively stereotyped

category (Crocker, Major, & Steele, 1998; Steele, 1997). Thus, negative stereotypes, prejudice, and discrimination are defining features of the predicament of stigmatization (Link & Phelan, 2001). Here, we consider how the stigmatized cope with this predicament. By focusing on coping, we seek to strike a balance between acknowledging the negative impact of prejudice, stereotyping, and discrimination on the lives of the stigmatized and recognizing the multiple strengths and resilience that stigmatized individuals and groups also display.

HISTORY

The traditional or classic view of prejudice, stereotyping, and discrimination regards the effects of stigma as being so negative and pervasive that few, if any, are able to escape them. From this perspective, although individuals may engage in cognitive, emotional, and behavioral strategies in an effort to overcome the negative effects of stigmatization they are likely to fail (Link, Mirotznik, & Cullin, 1991). This view is reflected in Gordon Allport's (1954) famous comment, 'One's reputation, whether false or true, cannot be hammered, hammered, hammered into one's head without doing something to one's character' (p. 142).

Despite this pessimistic outlook, early scholars described various ways in which people who are stigmatized may respond to their situation (see Tables 25.1 and 25.2). For example, in a chapter titled 'Traits Due to Victimization,' Allport (1954) posed the question 'Ask yourself what would happen to your own personality if you heard it said over and over again that you were lazy, a simple child of nature, expected to steal and had inferior blood?' And he answered that 'A child who finds himself rejected and attacked on all sides … develops defenses' (p. 142). Allport went on to describe 13 different persecution-produced traits, or 'ego defenses' that individuals employ in response to being the target of prejudice and discrimination, including, for example: denial

of membership, withdrawal and passivity, strengthening in-group ties, identification with the dominant group, aggression against own group, fighting back (militancy), and enhanced striving.

Allport (1954) proposed that the ego-defenses used by targets of prejudice typically fall into one of two types: 'extropunitive' or 'intropunitive.' Victims who adopt the former type of ego-defenses, according to Allport, blame outside causes for their handicaps, whereas victims who adopt the latter take the responsibility upon themselves for adjusting to the situation. Ego-defenses Allport classified as extropunitive included strengthening of in-group ties, prejudice against other groups, aggression and revolt, and enhanced striving. Defenses he classified as intropunitive included denial of membership in own group, withdrawal and passivity, and in-group aggression.

In his classic treatise on the pervasive negative effects of stigma, Irving Goffman (1963) also described a number of ways in which people who are stigmatized attempt to 'manage' their spoiled identities. He suggested, for example, that targets of prejudice and discrimination may respond to their predicament by hiding their stigma, trying to correct their stigma, working harder to overcome negative stereotypes associated with their stigma, withdrawing from interactions with the nonstigmatized, and associating only with others who share their stigma.

REVIEW OF RESEARCH

Evidence that stigmatization can have devastating effects on those who are its targets is plentiful. Prejudice and discrimination lead to these negative effects through multiple pathways (see Major & O'Brien, 2005). They limit individuals' and groups' access to, and bias the treatment they receive within, important life domains, such as the housing market, workplace, educational settings, health care system, and the criminal justice system (see Chapter 29 by Penner, Albrecht, Orom, et al., Chapter 28 by Schmukler,

Table 25.1 Classification schemes for coping responses

Author	Classification categories
Allport (1954)	1. Extropunitive 2. Intropunitive
Tajfel and Turner (1986)	1. Individual mobility 2. Social creativity 3. Social competition

Miller and Major (2000)	1. Problem-focused
	   a. Targeted at self
	   b. Targeted at others/social context
	   c. Targeted at immediate situation
	2. Emotion-focused

Miller and Kaiser (2001)	1. Disengagement coping
	2. Engagement coping
	   a) Secondary-control
	   b) Primary-control

Table 25.2   Possible coping responses as categorized within each classification system

Response to stigma	Allport (1954)	Tajfel and Turner (1986)	Miller and Major (2000)	Miller and Kaiser (2001)
Ingroup aggression	Intropunitive			
Outgroup prejudice, slyness	Extropunitive			
Sympathy with all victims	Intropunitive			
Change comparison dimensions (Symbolic status striving)	Intropunitive	Social creativity	Emotion-focused	
Change value assigned to group attributes		Social creativity	Emotion-focused	Engagement (secondary)
Selective comparisons with low status outgroups		Social creativity	Emotion-focused	Disengagement
Devalue stigmatized domains (disidentification; withdrawal)	Intropunitive		Emotion-focused	Engagement (secondary)
Self-protective attributions; vigilance for prejudice	Extropunitive		Emotion-focused	Engagement (secondary)
Deny/minimize existence of prejudice, meritocratic worldview	Intropunitive		Emotion-focused	Disengagement
Increased ingroup identification	Extropunitive		Emotion-focused	
Distraction (away from stressor)				Engagement (secondary)
Acceptance of predicament				Engagement (secondary)
Emotion regulation and emotional expression			Emotion-focused	Engagement (primary)
Eliminate stigmatizing condition; leave group		Individual mobility	Problem-focused (self)	
Reduce applicability of stigma to self; conceal/disguise stigma; decreased ingroup identification	Intropunitive	Individual mobility	Problem-focused (self)	
Compensate, enhanced striving	Extropunitive		Problem-focused (self)	Engagement (primary)
Confirm group stereotype (clowning)	Intropunitive		Problem-focused (self)	
Avoid situations or particular others			Problem-focused (situations)	Disengagement
Affiliate with ingroup			Problem-focused (situations)	Disengagement
Change other's attitudes; prevent prejudice actions			Problem-focused (others/ context)	
Compete with outgroup		Social competition		
Collective action (aggression, revolt)	Extropunitive	Social competition	Problem-focused (others/ context)	Engagement (primary)

Note: Blank spaces indicate that the authors did not make explicit mention of this response or coping strategy in their classification system.

Rasquiza, Dimmitt, et al., and Chapter 27 by Smith, Brief, & Collela et al., this volume). Stigma exposes individuals to being ignored, excluded, patronized, and ridiculed as well as targeted by physical violence (Herek, 2000). Others' negative stereotypes of, and expectations for, the stigmatized can create self-fulfilling prophecies, whereby perceivers' expectancy-driven behaviors lead the target to behave in expectancy-confirming ways, and even to develop expectancy-consistent self-perceptions (e.g., Harris, Milich, Corbitt, et al., 1992; Jussim, Palumbo, Chatman, et al., 2000). Stigmatized individuals' awareness of the negative stereotypes that are applied to individuals like themselves can lead them to experience 'stereotype threat,' with accompanying increases in anxiety, decreases in working memory, and impairments in performance in negatively stereotyped domains (Steele & Aronson, 1995; see Chapter 23 by Quinn, Kallen, & Spencer, this volume).

In short, there is ample evidence that being the target of prejudice and discrimination poses a significant threat on multiple levels.

Comparisons of the stigmatized to the nonstigmatized document the destructive effects of stigmatization. Studies reveal disparities between members of stigmatized and nonstigmatized groups in a variety of domains, including educational outcomes (Steele, 1997), health outcomes (Jackson, Brown, Williams, et al., 1996) and psychological outcomes (e.g., Twenge & Crocker, 2002). These comparisons, however, also reveal surprising paradoxes. Members of many chronically stigmatized groups often fail to exhibit the signs of psychological maladjustment that many theories would predict. For example, the vast majority of individuals with disabilities, such as those who are blind, quadriplegic, or developmentally disabled, report positive levels of well-being (see Diener & Diener, 1996, for a review). Members of stigmatized groups often have levels of self-esteem as high if not higher than members of nonstigmatized groups (Crocker & Major, 1989). Furthermore, members of chronically disadvantaged groups often do not report discontent with their situations (Major, 1994). For example, even though women are typically paid less than men for comparable work and contribute a greater share of family work than do their husbands, they typically report no less satisfaction with their lives, jobs, or marriages than do men (see Crosby, 1982; Major, 1994, for reviews). In addition, substantial variability in responses exists among the stigmatized. Although some stigmatized groups on average have higher self-esteem than the nonstigmatized, others do not (e.g., Miller & Downey, 1999; Twenge & Crocker, 2002). Within the same stigmatized group, some individuals show signs of psychological maladjustment, whereas others do not (Friedman & Brownell, 1995). Variability is evident even within the same individual as the situation changes. For example, research on ability-stigmatized groups reveals that test performance is highly sensitive to situational factors, such that the stigmatized sometimes perform more poorly on intellectual tasks than those not so stigmatized, but at other times they perform just as well (see Chapter 23 by Quinn, Kallen, & Spencer, this volume).

These accumulating findings make it clear that within any given domain, stigmatization has neither uniform nor invariably negative effects on its victims. Further, they point to the need for a different theoretical perspective on reactions to stigmatization that goes beyond viewing the stigmatized solely as helpless victims of others' negative beliefs, attitudes, and behaviors. New perspectives on stigma view targets of prejudice and discrimination as active agents who negotiate their social interactions so as to maintain their self-esteem and achieve specific goals. (e.g., Crocker & Major, 1989; Major & O'Brien, 2005; Steele, 1997; Steele, Spencer, & Aronson, 2002). Here, we review theory and research examining ways in which people who are targets of negative stereotypes, prejudice, and discrimination cope with this predicament.

NEW FRAMEWORK: STRESS AND COPING

Contemporary efforts to understand targets' psychological and physical responses to prejudice and discrimination give a prominent role to transactional models of stress and coping (notably Lazarus & Folkman's, 1984 model; see, e.g., Allison, 1998; Clark, Anderson, Clark, et al., 1999; Miller & Kaiser, 2001; Major & O'Brien, 2005; Major, Quinton, McCoy, et al., 2000; Miller, 2006; Miller & Major, 2000; Miller & Myers, 1998; Swim, Cohen, & Hyers, 1998; Swim & Thomas, 2006). A core premise of transactional models of stress and coping is that there is not a one-to-one relationship between exposure to a stressor and stress response. Rather, individuals vary widely in their response to stressful events, depending on how they appraise the event and how they cope with it. As applied to stigma, it is assumed that bearing (or being perceived to bear) a stigma is a stressful predicament – it puts a person at risk of experiencing a variety of acute and/or chronic negative life events and circumstances that are stressful, i.e., that have the potential to tax or exceed the adaptive resources of the individual.

The stigmatized experience stress as a byproduct of their low social status and poor access to resources, environmental factors which subject them to chronic strain and daily hassles (Allison, 1998). They also experience stress as a result of the poorer treatment they receive from others. Importantly, stigmatized individuals' understanding of how their stigma is viewed in the larger society also can be a significant source of stress (Link, Mirotznik, & Cullin, 1991). Most stigmatized individuals are aware of the dominant cultural stereotypes and evaluations of their stigma (Goffman, 1963; Steele, 1997). Based on their prior experiences (direct or vicarious) with being the target of negative stereotypes, prejudice, and discrimination, and/or on their exposure to representations of their stigma in the larger culture, members of stigmatized groups are thought to develop feelings, beliefs, and expectations about their stigma and its potential effects (Crocker, Major, & Steele, 1998; Link & Phelan, 2001; Major & O'Brien, 2005; Steele, 1997). These 'collective representations' or 'states of mind' include awareness that they are devalued by others because of their stigma, knowledge of the negative stereotypes that are applied to their stigma within the dominant culture, uncertainty about how others will react to them, and anxiety about being a target of prejudice and/or discrimination (Crocker, Major, & Steele, 1998). These representations have the potential to create stress even in the absence of obvious forms of discriminatory behavior on the part of others and even when no other person is present in the immediate situation.

According to stress and coping perspectives, how individuals respond and adapt to these various stigma-induced stressors differs depending on their cognitive appraisals (e.g., how threatening they perceive an event or situation to be) and the coping strategies they employ in response to events appraised as stressful. Cues in the immediate situation that make stigma relevant and signal to an individual that he or she is at risk of being devalued, negatively stereotyped, or discriminated against in that situation because of his or her social identity can lead it to be appraised (consciously or nonconsciously) as containing threats to the self (Crocker, Major, & Steele, 1998; Major & O'Brien, 2005; Steele, Spencer, & Aronson, 2002). Individual factors also shape appraisals. For example, individuals who are high in chronic expectations or apprehension of being negatively stereotyped and discriminated against because of their social identity are more likely to appraise ambiguous events or situations as threatening to their social identity (Mendoza-Denton, Purdie, Downey, et al., 2002; Pinel, 1999).

Responses to threat appraisals include involuntary stress responses as well as coping responses (Compas, Connor-Smith, Saltzman, et al., 2001). Involuntary stress responses in reaction to social identity threat include increased anxiety (Spencer, Steele & Quinn, 1999), arousal (Ben-Zeev, Fein, & Inzlicht, 2005) and blood pressure (Blascovich, Spencer, Quinn, et al., 2001), as well as decreased working memory capacity (Schmader & Johns, 2003) and impaired performance on intellectually demanding tasks (Steele & Aronson, 1995). Situational cues that heighten social identity threat also increase automatic vigilance to subliminally presented social identity threat-related stimuli, as does being high in prejudice apprehension (Kaiser, Vick, & Major, 2006). This research is reviewed elsewhere in this handbook (see Chapter 23 by Quinn, Kallen, & Spencer, this volume) so we will not review it here. Rather, in the remainder of this chapter we focus on the second key process posited to shape how people respond to stigma-related threats: coping.

Coping with stigmatization

Coping refers to efforts to regulate emotion, cognition, behavior, physiology and the environment in response to events or circumstances appraised as stressful (Lazarus & Folkman, 1984). Some scholars further restrict use of the word coping to efforts that are conscious and volitional (Compas, Connor-Smith, Saltzman, et al., 2001). Coping efforts are process oriented and context-specific, and are distinct from more stable dispositions that can serve as coping resources (e.g., high self-esteem, optimism). Importantly, coping is also distinct from its outcomes. That is, just because people engage in efforts to cope with a stressor does not mean that their efforts are successful.

Several scholars have attempted to identify fundamental dimensions that distinguish among different ways in which people cope in response to threatened social identities (see Tables 25.1 and 25.2 for a list of the classification systems and categorization of the various coping responses within each system, respectively). As mentioned earlier, Allport (1954), working within the classic view of stigmatization, proposed one scheme for categorizing coping responses to stigmatization. In addition, Tajfel and Turner's (1986) Social Identity Theory, although not framed in terms of a stress and coping model, is another influential theory of how people attempt to maintain a positive social identity in the face of threat. Tajfel and Turner classified ways that people respond to a negative social identity into three categories: individual mobility, social creativity, or social competition. Individual mobility efforts are those in which individuals try to leave or dissociate themselves from their (negatively valued) group. Social creativity efforts are those in which people seek to positively distinguish their own group by redefining or altering the elements of the comparison situation so as to make their own group seem more positive. Examples include socially comparing one's own group with other groups on some new dimension on which one's ingroup fares better, and changing the value assigned to group attributes so that comparisons which were previously negative are now perceived as positive. Social competition efforts are attempts to improve the value or status of one's own group, for example, by competing directly with other groups.

Applying transactional models of stress and coping to stigmatization provides new methods of conceptualizing the efforts of individuals who are chronic targets of prejudice to regulate their emotions, behavior, or environments in an effort to deal with their predicament. Miller and Major (2000) used the distinction between problem-focused and emotion-focused coping developed by Folkman, Lazarus, Gruen, et al., (1986) as a framework for conceptualizing coping with stigma. *Problem-focused* (or active) coping efforts are geared toward changing the nature of the relationship between the person and the environment, and hence eliminating the source of stress. *Emotion-focused* coping is geared toward regulating stressful emotions. Within the domain of coping with stigma, Folkman et al. argued that problem-focused efforts can be further distinguished as targeted toward the *self*, toward *others*, or toward the *situation* in which the self and others interact.

Coping efforts that target the self involve changing some aspect of the self to reduce the likelihood that one will experience the negative effects of stigmatization. These strategies are similar to the individual mobility strategies described by Tajfel and Turner (1986) and would be classified as intropunative by Allport (1954). To the extent that they perceive it is possible to do so, stigmatized individuals often try to eliminate the stigmatizing condition, for example, by going on a diet, undergoing plastic surgery or seeking therapy. Alternatively, they may try to reduce the applicability of the stigmatizing condition to the self, for example, by concealing or disguising it if possible (Goffman, 1963; Major & Gramzow, 1999). They may also try to compensate for their stigma, for example, by working harder, preparing more, or persisting longer in domains in which they are negatively stereotyped, so as to achieve desired goals. For example, heavyweight women who were interacting with a partner who they believed could see them (and who hence believed that their stigma could have a negative effect on their interaction) amplified their social skills during the interaction, compared to heavyweight women who thought their partner could not see them (Miller, Rothbaum, Felicio, et al., 1995).

Problem-focused coping efforts can also be targeted toward structuring situations so as to avoid the problems associated with prejudice. One way to do this would be to avoid situations that expose one to the prejudice of others. Heavyweight people, for example, may avoid places such as the beach or health club which are especially likely to expose them to censure. If a situation cannot be avoided, people selectively avoid others within that situation who they expect to be especially prejudiced (e.g., Swim, Cohen & Hyers, 1998). Stigmatized individuals also structure their situation by selectively affiliating with members of their own stigmatized group, thereby gaining social support as well as a respite from prejudice (Goffman, 1963; Schmitt & Branscombe, 2002). Finally, problem-focused coping efforts can also be targeted at others or the larger social context, for example, by seeking to change others' attitudes toward one's stigma through confrontation, by preventing others from acting on their prejudice, or by engaging in collective action to combat discrimination. These strategies are similar to social competition within Tajfel and Turner's (1986) classification scheme, and extropunitive defenses within Allport's (1954) framework.

In contrast to problem-focused coping, emotion-focused coping is aimed at minimizing negative affect and protecting self-esteem (both individual and collective) from stigma-related stressors such as prejudice. These strategies are most similar to those Tajfel and Turner (1986) called 'social creativity' strategies. The majority of social psychological research conducted on coping with stigma over the last 20 years has examined emotion-focused coping efforts. A number of different types of emotion-focused coping responses to stigmatization have been identified, and several reviews of this empirical literature exist (e.g., Crocker & Major, 1989; Crocker, Major, & Steele, 1998; Major & O'Brien, 2005; see Chapter 24 by

Crocker and Garcia, this volume). Thus, the following review is meant to be illustrative rather than exhaustive.

One way in which the stigmatized regulate emotion and protect self-esteem in the face of threats to their identity is by withdrawing their efforts from and/or disengaging their self-esteem from domains in which they are negatively stereotyped or fear being a target of discrimination (e.g., Major, Spencer, Schmader, et al., 1998b; Steele, 1997). For example, women taking a difficult math test who were exposed to negative gender stereotypes chose to answer fewer math questions and focused instead on answering verbal questions (Davies, Spencer, Quinn, et al., 2002). Individuals may also regulate their emotions through selective social comparisons. For example, stigmatized individuals may selectively compare themselves or their outcomes with members of their own stigmatized group (who are likely to share poor outcomes), rather than with members of more advantaged groups (Major, 1994). They may also selectively construe available comparison information, dismissing the nonstigmatized as too dissimilar from the self, thereby making upward comparisons with them irrelevant (e.g., Major, Schiacchitano, & Crocker, 1993). By doing so, the stigmatized can protect themselves from the potentially painful emotional consequences of upward social comparisons.

Attributions can also be used to regulate emotion and protect self-esteem in the face of identity threat (see Major, Quinton, & McCoy, 2002a, for a review). One strategy to reduce negative emotions and protect self-esteem is to deny or minimize that one is a target of prejudice (Crosby, 1982). This strategy may allow the individual to maintain a worldview in which outcomes are believed to be fairly determined and based on individual merit. This, in turn may enable the individual to feel less personally vulnerable to prejudice and to appraise his or her situation as less threatening (Major, Kaiser, O'Brien, et al., 2007). An alternative emotion regulation strategy is to attribute rejection or poor outcomes to the prejudice of others, rather than to internal, stable characteristics of oneself (Crocker & Major, 1989; Major et al., 2002a). People who have repeatedly been targets of discrimination or witnessed it against others like themselves may adopt a worldview in which social outcomes are explained in terms of bias, discrimination, and favoritism (Crocker, Luhtanen, Broadnax, et al., 1994; Sellers & Shelton, 2003). Although this worldview may heighten their perceived vulnerability to prejudice, it may nonetheless have protective qualities when they are faced with blatant evidence of prejudice and discrimination (Major, Kaiser, O'Brien, et al., 2007; Sellers & Shelton, 2003)

Increasing identification with others who share one's stigma (one's ingroup) can also serve as an emotion-regulation coping strategy (Allport, 1954; Schmitt & Branscombe, 2002). So too can decreasing identification with others who share one's stigma. Some research has shown that experiencing a threat to social identity (such as learning that pervasive prejudice exists against one's group) increases group identification (Jetten, Branscombe, Schmitt, 2001), whereas other research has shown that identity threat leads individuals to distance themselves from their group (Kaiser & Miller, 2001; McCoy & Major, 2003; Steele & Aronson, 1995).

Miller and Kaiser (2001) proposed that coping responses to stigma-related threat can also be distinguished by whether they reflect *disengagement from the stressor* (avoidance) or *engagement with the stressor* (approach). Forms of disengagement coping include avoiding or withdrawing from situations or persons in which stigma may pose a problem, avoiding social comparisons with the nonstigmatized, disguising or concealing a stigma, and denying and/or minimizing prejudice. Examples of engagement coping, in which the individual attempts to control either the stressful situation or themselves, include compensating, attempting to shed a stigma, and engaging in collective action. Miller and Kaiser (2001) classified self-protective attributions and devaluing domains in which the group fares poorly as examples of engagement coping as well, in which the goal

of the individual is to adapt to the stressful event.

In summary, people who are targets of negative stereotypes, prejudice and discrimination engage in a variety of cognitive and behavioral efforts to cope with this predicament. Although scholars use different labels, several core dimensions along which coping with stigma differs have been identified. In response to stigma-related threats, the stigmatized may cope by regulating their emotion or self-esteem (social creativity) or by attempting to eliminate the stress, for example by changing themselves (individual mobility), aspects of the situation that is generating the stress, or by attempting to change others or the social context (social competition). Some strategies engage (approach) the stressor, whereas others are attempts to disengage from (avoid) the stressor. It is important to note, however, that there is considerable overlap among categories, and a single coping strategy may serve multiple functions. In addition, people typically use multiple coping strategies rather than a single strategy. Allport (1954), for example, noted that the same person may employ both intropunitive and extropunitive defenses.

Moderators of coping

The recognition that individuals vary widely in their responses to stigmatization spurred efforts to identify factors that differentiate these responses. What determines, for example, whether an individual denies that he or she is a target of prejudice vs. blames negative outcomes on prejudice? What leads an individual to withdraw vs. confront when faced with predudice? Or to identify more closely with vs. disidentify from others who share his or her stigma? Allport (1954) believed that coping responses (ego-defenses) used in response to prejudice are largely an individual matter, determined by an individual's life circumstances, personality, and attitudes. More recent theory and research addressing this question indicate that coping responses to stigmatization are multiply determined, shaped by characteristics of the person, situation, stressor, stigma, and socio-cultural context (see Crocker & Major, 1989; Crocker, Major, & Steele, 1998; Major & O'Brien, 2005; Major et al., 2002a for reviews).

Several individual level factors influence how an individual copes with prejudice or discrimination in a particular situation. One is the individual's primary goal. Most research on coping with stigmatization or a negative social identity has implicitly or explicitly assumed that the primary goal of the individual is to maintain or protect personal or collective self-esteem. This assumption can be seen in Allport's (1954) emphasis on ego-defenses, Tajfel and Turner's (1986) emphasis on strategies to achieve positive group identity, and Crocker and Major's (1989) focus on self-esteem protective strategies. Other goals, however, such as ensuring a smooth and positive interaction, or attaining desired resources, can take precedence in some situations and influence how people cope with threats in those situations (see Miller, 2006; Swim & Thomas, 2006). A coping strategy used to protect self-esteem (e.g., blaming rejection on another's prejudice) might interfere with ensuring a smooth interaction or making a good impression (e.g., Kaiser & Miller, 2001). When another person controls important resources that an individual desires, making a good impression may take precedence over maintaining self-esteem.

Another important individual determinant of coping responses is the extent to which the target is aware of his or her devaluation by others and expects to be a potential target of discrimination (e.g., Link & Phelan, 2001; Mendoza-Denton, Purdie, Downey, et al., 2002). For example, among individuals with nonvisible stigmas, greater perceived devaluation is associated with increased concealment of the stigma from others (Link, Mirotznik, & Cullin, 1991; Major & Gramzow, 1999). Among individuals with group-based stigmas, greater perceived devaluation is associated with increased attributions to discrimination (Pinel, 1999). The stigmatized person's level of identification with his or her stigmatized group also influences coping responses (e.g., Major, Quinton &

Schmader, 2003). For example, reading about pervasive prejudice and discrimination against Latinos led Latino Americans who were initially highly identified with their group to become even more identified with their group, but it led Latino Americans initially low in group identification group identification to become even less group identified (McCoy and Major, 2003).

Tajfel and Turner (1986) proposed that individual's beliefs about the nature and structure of the relations between groups in society, namely, the extent to which they regard group boundaries as permeable and group status differences as stable and legitimate, influence how members of low status groups cope with a threatened social identity. For example, they proposed that individuals who regard group boundaries as permeable are more likely to engage in individual mobility strategies (e.g., attempt to pass or shed their stigma), whereas those who regard group boundaries as impermeable and stable are more likely to employ social creativity strategies (e.g., reduce social comparisons with the nonstigmatized). Those who perceive that group boundaries are impermeable and group status differences are unstable and illegitimate are more likely to employ strategies of social competition (social change). Considerable support exists for these predictions (e.g., Ellemers, Wilke, & van Knippenberg, 1993).

Legitimacy appraisals play a particularly important role in how targets cope with devaluation and disadvantage (Allport, 1954; Major, 1994; Major & Schmader, 2001). Targets of prejudice may regard their devaluation as legitimate for several reasons. Those who acquire a stigma later in life, such as those who develop a mental illness, or who become unemployed, may have internalized society's negative view of those with their stigmatizing attribute long before it became applied to the self (Link, Mirotznik, & Cullin, 1991). Targets may appraise their devaluation as legitimate because they feel they have control over whether or not they bear the stigma (e.g., overweight), and hence feel responsible for it (Crocker, Cornwell, & Major, 1993). Targets may also appraise their devaluation as legitimate because they endorse attitudes, beliefs, and values that justify status differences in society (Allport, 1954; Jost & Hunyady, 2002; Major & Schmader, 2001). In western, capitalistic societies, a dominant worldview is the belief in meritocracy (Kleugel & Smith, 1986). This worldview is status-justifying because it locates the cause of people's outcomes within their own efforts, merit, or deservingness, and hence holds them responsible for their station in life. The more members of stigmatized groups (women, Latinos, Blacks) endorse meritocratic beliefs, the less likely they are to attribute poor personal outcomes to discrimination (Major et al., 2002b), the less likely they are to say that their group is a victim of discrimination (Major et al., 2002b) and the more likely they are to hold their own group responsible when informed that their group is a target of pervasive prejudice (Major, Kaiser, O'Brien, et al., 2007).

Situational factors also influence how people cope with threats to social identity, such as whether negative stereotypes and prejudice are blatant or subtle (e.g., Major, McCoy, Kaiser, et al., 2003), and whether ingroup or outgroup others are present. Sechrist, Swim, and Stangor (2004), for example, found that women and ethnic minorities blamed negative outcomes on discrimination when they were alone or with members of their own group, but not when they were with members of the dominant outgroup. Situational cues that prime meritocratic beliefs reduce the likelihood that stigmatized groups will attribute personal rejection to discrimination and increase the extent to which they hold their own group responsible for disadvantage (McCoy & Major, 2007). The nature of the stigma-related threats that individuals confront, such as whether the threats are daily hassles (being ignored in a store), personal insults, attacks against the group, or major life events (being denied a job, education, or critical health care), is also likely to influence how people will cope (Allison, 1998; Clark, Anderson, Clark, et al., 1999).

Although insufficient attention has been devoted to this issue, how an individual copes with stigma-related threats is also influenced by the type of stigmatizing attribute they bear (or are perceived to bear). Stigmas vary along a number of dimensions, such as whether or not they are readily visible to others, perceived as controllable at onset or offset, thought to be contagious or dangerous, associated with a recognizable group identity, and originate at birth or later in life (Goffman, 1963; Jones, Farina, Hastorf, et al., 1984). Differences among stigmatizing attributes affect not only how stigmatized individuals and groups are treated by others, but also how they cope with stigmatization (Crocker & Major, 1989; Crocker, Major, & Steele, 1998). For individuals whose stigma is readily visible to others, for example, concealment is rarely a coping option. Among those whose stigma is not readily visible to others, in contrast, concealment is a frequent coping response (Link, Mirotznik, & Cullin, 1991; Major & Gramzow, 2002). Individuals with less visible stigmas have more difficulty finding similar others with whom they can affiliate, socially compare and interact with than those with visible stigmas (Frable, Platt, & Hoey, 1998).

The perceived controllability or changeability of a stigma also shapes coping. People who perceive they have some control over or can change their stigma, e.g., the overweight, mentally ill, or facially disfigured, are more likely to cope with prejudice through self-focused efforts, for example, by attempting to shed their stigmatized status, than those who perceive no control over their stigma. For example, compared to members of ethnic minority groups, overweight women are less likely to blame rejection on discrimination, less likely to identify with their ingroup (others who are overweight), and more likely to display prejudice against their ingroup on both explicit and implicit measures (Crandall, 1994; Crocker, Cornwell, & Major, 1993). In Tajfel and Turner's (1986) terminology, group boundaries are perceived as permeable when a stigma is perceived to be controllable or changeable, thus leading to individual mobility efforts rather than social change efforts. The extent to which a stigmatizing attribute is entitative, or seen as a recognizable group, also shapes coping responses. Some stigmas, such as the tribal stigmas of race, ethnicity, or religion, are more entitative than others (e.g., a hairlip, heavyweight). People whose stigma is entitative are more likely to identify with others who share their stigma than are those whose stigma is character or appearance based (Crump & Major, 2008), and may be more likely to attribute negative outcomes to prejudice, seek out similar others for affiliation, and engage in collective efforts on behalf of their group.

FUTURE DIRECTIONS: IS COPING EFFECTIVE?

As the above review indicates, people who face negative stereotypes, prejudice and discrimination engage in varied efforts to regulate their emotion, cognition, behavior, and the environment. These coping efforts are influenced by characteristics of the person, the situation, the stigma, and the social context. Research on coping has contributed to an emerging picture of the target of prejudice as an active, motivated agent rather than a passive victim, and has enriched our understanding of the phenomenology of stigma. A key question, however, remains relatively unexamined: How effective are individual coping efforts in overcoming the effects of stigmatization? As noted above, just because people engage in efforts to cope with a stressor does not mean that their efforts are successful.

Stigma, and the negative stereotypes, prejudice, and discrimination that result from it, are sociocultural problems. They originate outside of the individual. The beliefs that the stigmatized hold about their potential for being devalued, discriminated against, and negatively stereotyped are also products of the larger social context. Coping, in contrast, is typically conceptualized as an individual endeavor. In the classic or traditional view, the effects of stigma are so negative and pervasive that few are able to escape its deleterious effects (e.g., Allport, 1954; Link, Mirotznik, & Cullin, 1991). Research that emphasizes

targets' resilience (e.g., Crocker & Major, 1989) poses a challenge to this view. If individuals are able to take steps that are effective at managing some of the negative effects of stigmatization, does it imply that being the target of pervasive negative stereotypes, prejudice, and discrimination is not as negative or pervasive as thought? Does it imply that individuals could easily overcome the effects of stigmatization, if only they 'coped' in the right way?

In our view, evidence that targets' coping efforts are effective at ameliorating the negative effects of stigmatization in some domains does not imply that the effects of stigmatization are not pervasive and severe. Gaining a complete picture of the effects of stigmatization and of the effectiveness of efforts to cope with it requires looking at multiple outcome variables simultaneously, as well as multiple types of coping. It also requires a more complex understanding of what is meant by 'effective coping.' Is it feeling good about the self? Doing well in school? Feeling identified with one's ingroup? Getting along well with members of outgroups? Engaging in efforts to combat prejudice? Maintaining a sense of control over one's outcomes? All of these have been discussed as valid measures of good outcomes (see Swim & Thomas, 2006). For those who are stigmatized, obtaining any one of these outcomes may be achievable, but achieving all may be difficult.

Research examining the effectiveness of efforts to cope with prejudice focuses on a relatively few outcome variables, primarily self-esteem, intellectual performance, and intergroup attitudes. Further, research tends to examine only one of these outcome variables at a time. This research strategy reveals that a particular coping strategy can be successful with respect to a particular outcome variable in a particular situation. For example, in response to a personal threat, blaming negative outcomes on the prejudice of another person, rather than on internal, stable aspects of the self, can protect self-esteem, especially when prejudice cues are blatant (Major, Gramzow, McCoy, et al., 2002). Behaving in an especially sociable way can lead others to view an overweight woman in a more positive light (Miller, Rothblum, Felicio, et al., 1995).

But coping strategies that are engaged in to achieve one goal may inhibit attainment of other goals. A coping strategy that is successful in achieving one desired outcome (e.g., decreasing negative affect) may lead to other undesired outcomes (e.g., social isolation). Within sociology, labeling theorists refer to this concept as 'secondary deviance,' noting that labeled persons' attempts at 'defense, attack, or adaptation' may themselves produce labeling effects that exacerbate the problem (see Link, Mirotznik, & Cullin, 1991). An example would be when a person isolates him or herself because of a fear of others' negative evaluations, and becomes even more withdrawn and socially excluded as a result.

Consider the coping strategy of concealment, a frequent coping response of the nonvisibly stigmatized (Goffman, 1963; Jones, Farina, Hastorf, et al., 1984). A person may cope with a nonvisible stigma by concealing it from others, thereby allowing her to avoid social disapproval and preserve important social relationships, both of which may be considered signs of effective coping. However, concealment also has costs. Goffman (1963) noted that people who conceal or disguise a stigma may suffer from fear that their stigma will be discovered, leading to anxiety in interactions with the nonstigmatized, feelings of inauthenticity, and preoccupation with discovery. Consistent with this view, Major and Gramzow (1999) found that the more women who had an abortion felt they would be stigmatized by others if they were to know of their abortion, the more they concealed it from others. Concealment, however, was in turn associated with increased intrusive thoughts of the abortion which in turn were associated with increases in psychological distress over a two year period post abortion.

A study examining the effectiveness of different coping orientations among people with mental illness stigma provides further evidence that some forms of coping

may backfire. Link and colleagues (1991) examined whether the coping orientations of secrecy, avoidance-withdrawal, and education (preventive telling) were effective at reducing the deleterious effects of being diagnosed (and labeled) as a mental patient. They found that mental patients were significantly more demoralized (a measure of psychological distress) and likely to be unemployed than a sample of community residents. This gap widened the more mental patients (but not community residents) reported that they expected mental patients to be devalued and discriminated against. That is, *the belief that mental patients are stigmatized* was a significant predictor of distress and unemployment among mental patients.

None of the three coping orientations was effective in reducing the negative impact of expectations of devaluation and discrimination on either employment status or feelings of demoralization; in fact, they were positively associated with negative outcomes. That is, the more patients endorsed secrecy (e.g., 'If you have a serious mental illness, the best thing to do is keep it a secret'), avoidance-withdrawal (e.g., 'If I thought someone I knew held negative opinions about psychiatric patients, I would try to avoid him or her') and education (e.g., 'I've found that it's best to help the people close to me to understand what psychiatric treatment is like') as methods of coping with the stigma of being diagnosed with mental illness, the more demoralized they were and the more likely they were to be unemployed (controlling for employment status prior to diagnosis). Link and colleagues (1991) suggest that part of the reason expecting to be stigmatized was associated with demoralization and unemployment was that it led patients to adopt harmful coping orientations. They concluded that stigma cannot be addressed effectively by individual coping efforts because the problem is not an individual problem – it resides in the sociocultural context.

We believe that this assessment of coping is too pessimistic. Both secrecy and avoidance-withdrawal are examples of disengagement coping (Miller & Kaiser, 2001). Research on the adaptiveness of different types of coping in the general stress and coping literature reveals that disengagement coping is a particularly ineffective form of coping, often exacerbating rather than ameliorating psychological distress (e.g., Major, Richards, Cooper, et al., 1998). Research examining the effectiveness of other forms of coping with prejudice, such as turning to others for social support, devaluing domains in which one is negatively stereotyped, or confronting perpetrators of prejudice, is needed. Some research, for example, suggests that identifying more closely with the ingroup is associated with enhanced well-being, at least among those who have group-based stigmas (Schmitt & Branscombe, 2002). It is also important to examine the match between coping strategy and stressor. Attempting repeatedly to change a stigma, for example, may be adaptive if the stigma is changeable, but maladaptive if it is not.

Research focusing on multiple outcome variables is also needed to yield a more complete understanding of the consequences of coping. Research investigating the consequences of attributing threatening events to prejudice illustrates the importance of this. This strategy has been shown to be effective in buffering self-esteem in the face of personal set-backs, especially when prejudice is blatant. Thus, if the criterion of success is maintaining self-esteem, attributing negative events to discrimination is an effective coping strategy. However, those who claim prejudice may be labeled as complainers and ostracized by individuals who control important outcomes (Kaiser & Miller, 2001). If this coping strategy is used chronically, it may eventually result in group-related rejection sensitivity, which is associated with poorer, rather than better, outcomes. People who chronically perceive themselves as targets of prejudice may avoid situations in which they suspect prejudice may occur (Pinel, 1999), experience anxiety in interactions with outgroup members (Stephan & Stephan, 1996), disengage their self-esteem from domains important for academic or economic success (Major et al., 1998b; Schmader,

Major, & Gramzow, 2001), and be uncertain of their academic abilities (Inzlicht, McKay, & Aronson, 2006). These outcomes, in turn, may lead to poorer academic performance (Mendoza-Denton et al., 2002).

Because prejudice and discrimination are social problems, the most effective long-term strategies for coping are likely to be those which are directed toward changing the sociocultural context which fosters stereotyping, prejudice, and discrimination. To the extent that the stigmatized join together to reject what the culture assigns to them, they may be able to develop socially reinforced coping efforts that will allow for a more successful outcome than individual efforts alone (Link, Mirotznik, & Cullin, 1991). These strategies are more likely to be observed among those who bear stigmas that are unchangeable and entitative, such as the group-based stigmas of race or gender, than among those who those who bear changeable or more uniquely defining stigmas. Even if they do not join with others to combat stigmatization, however, we do not believe that the stigmatized are imprisoned by stigma, powerless to take action that will improve their lives. As conveyed in the poem *Still I Rise* by Maya Angelou, despite facing prejudice and discrimination, people are often resilient, managing to maintain a sense of pride, dignity, hopefulness, and well-being:

> You may write me down in history
> With your bitter, twisted lies,
> You may trod me in the very dirt
> But still, like dust, I'll rise …
> You may shoot me with your words,
> You may cut me with your eyes,
> You may kill me with your hatefulness,
> But still, like air, I'll rise …
> (selected verses from *Still I Rise* by Maya Angelou, 1994)

REFERENCES

Allison, K. W. (1998). Stress and oppressed category membership. In J. K. Swim & C. Stangor (Eds.), *Prejudice: The target's perspective* (pp. 145–170). San Diego, CA: Academic Press.

Allport, G. W. (1954/1979). *The nature of prejudice.* Cambridge, MA: Perseus Books.

Angelou, M. (1994). *The complete collected poems of Maya Angelou.* New York: Random House.

Ben-Zeev, T., Fein, S., & Inzlicht, M. (2005). Arousal and stereotype threat. *Journal of Experimental Social Psychology, 41,* 174–181.

Blascovich, J., Spencer, S. J., Quinn, D. M., & Steele, C. M. (2001). Stereotype threat and the cardiovascular reactivity of African-Americans. *Psychological Science, 12,* 225–229.

Compas, B. E., Connor-Smith, J. K., Saltzman, H., Thomsen, A. H., & Wadsworth, M. E. (2001). Coping with stress during childhood and adolescence: Problems, progress and potential in theory and research. *Psychological Bulletin, 127,* 87–127.

Clark, R., Anderson, N. B., Clark, V. R., & Williams, D. R. (1999). Racism as a stressor for African Americans: A biopsychosocial model. *American Psychologist, 54,* 805–16.

Crandall, C. S. (1994). Prejudice against fat people: Ideology and self-interest. *Journal of Personality and Social Psychology, 66,* 882–894.

Crocker, J., Cornwell, B., & Major, B. (1993). The stigma of overweight: The affective consequences of attributional ambiguity. *Journal of Personality and Social Psychology, 64,* 60–70.

Crocker, J., Luhtanen, R., Blaine, B., & Broadnax, S. (1994). Collective self-esteem and psychological well-being among White, Black, and Asian college students. *Personality and Social Psychology Bulletin, 20,* 502–513.

Crocker, J., & Major, B. (1989). Social stigma and self-esteem: The self-protective properties of stigma. *Psychological Review, 96,* 608–630.

Crocker, J., Major, B., & Steele, C. (1998). Social stigma. In D. Gilbert, S. T. Fiske, & G. Lindzey (Eds.), *Handbook of social psychology* (4th ed., pp. 504–553). Boston: McGraw Hill.

Crosby, F. (1982). *Relative deprivation and working women.* New York: Oxford University Press.

Crump, S., & Major, B. (2008). [Stigma and entitativity]. Unpublished raw data.

Davies, P. G., Spencer, S. J., Quinn, D. M., & Gerhardstein, R. (2002). Consuming images: How television commercials that elicit stereotype threat can restrain women academically and professionally. *Personality and Social Psychology Bulletin, 28,* 1615–1628.

Diener, E., & Diener, M. (1996). Most people are happy. *Psychological Science, 7,* 181–185.

Ellemers, N., Wilke, H., & van Knippenberg, A. (1993). Effects of the legitimacy of low group or individual status on individual and collective status-enhancement strategies. *Journal of Personality and Social Psychology, 64,* 766–778.

Folkman, S., Lazarus, R. S., Gruen, R. J., & DeLongis, A. (1986). Appraisal, coping, health status, and psychological symptoms. *Journal of Personality and Social Psychology, 50,* 571–579.

Frable, D. E. S., Platt, L., & Hoey, S. (1998). Concealable stigmas and positive self-perceptions: Feeling better around similar others. *Journal of Personality and Social Psychology, 74,* 909–922.

Friedman, M. A., & Brownell, K. D. (1995). Psychological correlates of obesity: Moving to the next research generation. *Psychological Bulletin, 117,* 3–20.

Goffman, E. (1963). *Stigma: Notes on the management of spoiled identity.* Englewood Cliffs, NJ: Prentice-Hall.

Harris, M. J., Milich, R., Corbitt, E. M., Hoover, D. W., & Brady, (1992). Self-fulfilling effects of stigmatizing information on children's social interactions. *Journal of Personality and Social Psychology, 63,* 41–50.

Herek, G. M. (2000). The psychology of sexual prejudice. *Current Directions in Psychological Science, 9,* 19–22.

Inzlicht, M., McKay, L., & Aronson, J. (2006). Stigma as ego depletion: How being the target of prejudice affects self-control. *Psychological Science, 17,* 262–269.

Jackson, J. S., Brown, T. N., Williams, D. R., Torres, M., Sellers, S. L., and Brown, K. (1996). Racism and the physical and mental health status of African Americans: A thirteen year national panel study. *Ethnicity and Disease, 6,* 132–147.

Jetten, J., Branscombe, N. R., Schmitt, M. T., & Spears, R. (2001). Rebels with a cause: Group identification as a response to perceived discrimination from the mainstream. *Personality and Social Psychology Bulletin, 27,* 1204–1213.

Jones, E. E., Farina, A., Hastorf, A. H., Markus, H., Miller, D., & Scott, R. A. (1984). *Social stigma: The psychology of marked relationships.* New York: Freeman.

Jost, J. T., & Hunyady, O. (2002). The psychology of system justification and the palliative function of ideology. In W. Stroebe & M. Hewstone (Eds.), *European review of social psychology* (Vol. 13, pp. 111–153). London: Psychology Press.

Jussim, L., Palumbo, P., Chatman, C., Madon, S., & Smith, A. (2000). Stigma and self-fulfilling prophecies. In T. F. Heatherton, R. E. Kleck, M. R. Hebl, & J. G. Hull (Eds.), *The social psychology of stigma* (pp. 374–418). New York: Guilford.

Kaiser, C. R., & Miller, C. T. (2001). Reacting to impending discrimination: Compensation for prejudice and attributions to discrimination. *Personality and Social Psychology Bulletin, 27,* 1357–1367.

Kaiser, C. R., Vick, S. B., & Major, B. (2006) Prejudice expectations moderate preconscious attention to social identity threatening cues. *Psychological Science, 17,* 332–338.

Kleugel, J. R., & Smith, E. R. (1986). *Beliefs about inequality: Americans' view of what is and what ought to be.* Hawthorne, NJ: Aldine de Gruyer.

Lazarus, R. S., & Folkman, S. (1984). *Stress, appraisal, and coping.* New York: Springer.

Link, B. G., & Phelan, J. C. (2001). Conceptualizing stigma. *Annual Review of Sociology, 27,* 363–385.

Link, B. G., Mirotznik, J. & Cullin, F. T. (1991). The effectiveness of stigma coping orientations: Can negative consequences of mental illness labeling be avoided? *Journal of Health and Social Behavior, 32,* 302–320.

Major, B. (1994). From social inequality to personal entitlement: The role of social comparisons, legitimacy appraisals, and group membership. In M. P. Zanna (Ed.), *Advances in experimental social psychology* (Vol. 26, pp. 293–355). San Diego, CA: Academic Press.

Major, B. & Gramzow, R. (1999). Abortion as stigma: Cognitive and emotional implications of concealment. *Journal of Personality and Social Psychology, 77,* 735–746.

Major, B., Gramzow, R., McCoy, S. K., Levin, S., Schmader, T., & Sidanius, J. (2002). Perceiving personal discrimination: The role of group status and status legitimizing ideology. *Journal of Personality and Social Psychology, 80,* 782–796.

Major, B., Kaiser, C. R., O'Brien, L., & McCoy, S. K. (2007). Perceived discrimination as worldview threat or worldview confirmation: Implications for self-esteem. *Journal of Personality and Social Psychology, 92,* 1068–1086.

Major, B., McCoy, S. K., Kaiser, C. R., & Quinton, W. J. (2003). Prejudice and self-esteem: A transactional model. In W. Stroebe & M. Hewstone (Eds.), *European review of social psychology* (Vol. 14, pp. 77–104).

Major, B., & O'Brien, L. T. (2005). The social psychology of stigma. *Annual Review of Psychology, 56,* 393–421.

Major, B., Richards, M. C., Cooper, M. L., Cozzarelli, C. & Zubek, J. (1998). Personal resilience, cognitive appraisals, and coping: An integrative model of adjustment to abortion. *Journal of Personality and Social Psychology, 74,* 735–752.

Major, B., Quinton, W. J., & McCoy, S. K. (2002). Antecedents and consequences of attributions to discrimination: Theoretical and empirical advances. In M. P. Zanna (Ed.), *Advances in experimental social psychology* (Vol. 34, pp. 251–330). New York: Academic Press.

Major, B., Quinton, W. J., McCoy, S. K., & Schmader, T. (2000). Reducing prejudice: The target's perspective. In S. Oskamp (Ed.), *Reducing prejudice* (pp. 211–237). New York: Sage.

Major, B., Quinton, W. J., & Schmader, T. (2003). Attributions to discrimination and self-esteem: Impact of group identification and situational ambiguity. *Journal of Experimental Social Psychology, 39,* 220–231.

Major, B., Schiacchitano, A. M., & Crocker, J. (1993) Ingroup/outgroup comparisons and self-esteem. *Personality and Social Psychology Bulletin, 19,* 711–721.

Major, B., & Schmader, T. (2001). Legitimacy and the construal of social disadvantage. In J. Jost & B. Major (Eds.), *The psychology of legitimacy: Emerging perspectives on ideology, justice, and intergroup relationships* (pp. 176–204). New York, NY: Cambridge University Press.

Major, B., Spencer, S., Schmader, T., Wolfe, C., & Crocker, J. (1998). Coping with negative stereotypes about intellectual performance: The role of psychological disengagement. *Personality and Social Psychology Bulletin, 24,* 34–50.

McCoy, S. K., & Major, B. (2003). Group identification moderates emotional responses to perceived prejudice. *Personality and Social Psychology Bulletin. 29,* 1005–1017.

McCoy, S. K., & Major, B. (2007). Priming meritocracy and the psychological justification of inequality. *Journal of Experimental Social Psychology, 43,* 341–351.

Mendoza-Denton, R., Purdie, V. J., Downey, G., Davis, A., & Pietrzak, J. (2002). Sensitivity to status-based rejection: Implications for African American students' college experience. *Journal of Personality and Social Psychology, 83,* 896–918.

Miller, C. T. (2006). Social psychological perspectives on coping with stressors related to stigma. In S. Levin & C. van Laar (Eds.) *Stigma and group inequality: Social psychological perspectives. The Claremont symposium on Applied Social Psychology* (pp. 21–44). Mahwah, NJ: Lawrence Erlbaum Associates, Inc.

Miller, C. T., & Downey, K. T. (1999). A meta-analysis of heavyweight and self-esteem. *Personality and Social Psychology Review, 3,* 68–84.

Miller, C. T., & Kaiser, C. R. (2001). A theoretical perspective on coping with stigma. *Journal of Social Issues, 57,* 73–92.

Miller, C. T., & Major, B. (2000). Coping with stigma and prejudice. In T. F. Heatherton, R. E. Kleck,

M. R. Hebl, & J. G. Hull (Eds.), *The social psychology of stigma* (pp. 243–272). New York: Guilford.

Miller, C. T., & Myers, A. M. (1998). Compensating for prejudice: How obese people (and others) control outcomes despite prejudice. In J. K. Swim & C. Stangor (Eds.), *Prejudice: The target's perspective* (pp. 191–218). San Diego, CA: Academic Press.

Miller, C. T., Rothblum, E., Felicio, D., & Brand, P. (1995). Compensating for stigma: Obese and nonobese women's reaction to being visible. *Personality and Social Psychology Bulletin, 21,* 1093–1106.

Pinel, E. C. (1999). Stigma consciousness: The psychological legacy of social stereotypes. *Journal of Personality and Social Psychology, 76,* 114–128.

Schmader, T., & Johns, M. (2003). Converging evidence that stereotype threat reduces working memory capacity. *Journal of Personality & Social Psychology, 84,* 440–452.

Schmader, T., Major, B., & Gramzow, R. H. (2001). Coping with ethnic stereotypes in the academic domain: Perceived injustice and psychological disengagement. *Journal of Social Issues, 57,* 93–111.

Schmitt, M. T., & Branscombe, N. R. (2002). The meaning and consequences of perceived discrimination in disadvantaged and privileged social groups. In W. Stroebe & M. Hewstone (Eds.), *European review of social psychology* (Vol. 12, pp. 167–200). Chichester, United Kingdom: Wiley.

Sechrist, G. B., Swim, J. K., & Stangor, C. (2004). When do the stigmatize make attributions to discrimination occurring to the self and others? The roles of self-presentation and need for control. *Journal of Personality and Social Psychology, 87,* 111–122.

Sellers, R. M., & Shelton, J. N. (2003). The role of racial identity in perceived racial discrimination. *Journal of Personality and Social Psychology, 84,* 1079–1092.

Spencer, S. J., Steele, C. M., & Quinn, D. M. (1999). Stereotype threat and women's math performance. *Journal of Experimental Social Psychology, 35,* 4–28.

Steele, C. M. (1997). A threat in the air: How stereotypes shape intellectual identity and performance. *American Psychologist, 52,* 613–629.

Steele, C. M., & Aronson, J. (1995). Stereotype threat and the intellectual test performance of African Americans. *Journal of Personality and Social Psychology, 69,* 797–811.

Steele, C. M., Spencer, S. J., & Aronson, J. (2002). Contending with group image: The psychology of stereotype threat and social identity threat. In M. P. Zanna (Ed.), *Advances in experimental social psychology* (Vol. 34, pp. 379–440), San Diego, CA: Academic Press.

Stephan, W. G., & Stephan, C. W. (1996). *Intergroup relations.* Madison, WI: Brown & Benchmark Publishers.

Swim, J. K., Cohen, L. L., & Hyers, L. L. (1998). Experiencing everyday prejudice and discrimination. In J. Swim & C. Stangor (Eds.), *Prejudice: The target's perspective* (pp. 37–61). San Diego, CA: Academic Press.

Swim, J. K., & Thomas, M. A. (2006). Responses to stigma: A synthesis of research on goal–directed, self–regulatory coping behaviors. In S. Levin & C. van Laar (Eds.) *Stigma and group inequality: Social psychological perspectives. The Claremont symposium on Applied Social Psychology* (pp. 105–126). Mahwah, NJ: Lawrence Erlbaum Associates, Inc.

Twenge, J., & Crocker, J. (2002). Race, ethnicity, and self-esteem: Meta-analyses comparing Whites, Blacks, Hispanics, Asians, and Native Americans, including a commentary on Gray-Little and Hafdahl (2000). *Psychological Bulletin, 128,* 371–408.

Tajfel, H., & Turner, J. C. (1979). An integrative theory of intergroup conflict. In W. G. Austin & S. Worchel (Eds.) *The psychology of intergroup relations* (pp. 33–48). Monterey, CA: Brooks/Cole.

Tajfel, H. & Turner, J. C. (1986). The social identity theory of intergroup behaviour. In S. Worchel, & W. Austin (Eds.) *Psychology of Intergroup Relations* (pp. 7–24). Chicago: Nelson Hall.

26

Institutional Bias

P.J. Henry*

ABSTRACT

This chapter focuses on conceptual and theoretical issues surrounding the study of institutional bias, those institutionally ingrained prejudices and discriminatory practices that lead to inequality across social groups. The first section of the chapter looks at the history and background of the conceptualization of institutional bias, from its relatively recent inception as a construct for scientific analysis. The next section covers a select representation of research domains and theoretical perspectives relevant to the causes and perpetuation of institutional bias. The chapter continues with a proposed two-dimensional model for conceptualizing institutional bias, and concludes by suggesting how such a model may be useful for future theory and practice in the service of ameliorating this poorly understood social problem.

INSTITUTIONAL BIAS

Institutional bias involves discriminatory practices that occur at the institutional level of analysis, operating on mechanisms that go beyond individual-level prejudice and discrimination. It would be easy to conclude erroneously that negative discrimination toward an outgroup could be eliminated if individuals' negative associations, stereotypes, and prejudices toward that outgroup were eliminated. Even in ideal settings where individuals hold no stereotypes or prejudices toward a group, discrimination may still occur. That scenario describes institutional bias at its most insidious, where blame for unequal treatment can be found in no individual, at least not very easily. Of the types of intergroup processes that exist, institutional bias is one of the least understood by

social scientists (Bonilla-Silva, 1997; Feagin, 2006) and remains relatively untouched by theoretical approaches, particularly in social psychology (Berard, 2008).

Examples of institutional bias are practically boundless, as the domains where it is found and the groups it affects are considerably varied. Name just about any social institution and likely there will be institutional bias, in some form against some social group. Historically, it has been around for thousands of years, with slavery being arguably its oldest manifestation. Domains of institutional bias include those covered in this section of the text, 'Social Impact of Prejudice, Stereotyping, and Discrimination,' which includes analyses of discrimination in the labor market, education, law, health care, and politics, but institutional discrimination has been documented also in the criminal justice system (Walker, Spohn, & DeLone, 1996), environmental management (Cable, Hastings, and Mix, 2002), the retail and housing markets (Sidanius and Pratto, 1999), and (for gays and lesbians) the military (Shawver, 1995), among others. Groups negatively affected by institutional bias include virtually any group that experiences prejudice and discrimination at the individual level, such as groups based on race and ethnicity, nationality, sex, religion, sexual orientation, age, disability, body size, etc.

The goal of this chapter is not to focus on the consequences of institutional bias, because this type of research is reviewed elsewhere in this volume. Instead, the goal here is to focus on abstract, generalizable conceptual issues surrounding institutional bias, and theoretical issues concerning its cause and perpetuation, areas that have received much less research focus. The hope is that by having a clear idea of what institutional bias is, what causes it, and what perpetuates it, the scientific community will be better equipped to find solutions for it.

HISTORY AND BACKGROUND OF THE CONCEPTUALIZATION OF INSTITUTIONAL BIAS

Although institutional bias has probably existed as long as there have been groups to oppress, the history of the scientific study of institutional bias has been relatively short. An important milestone in the study of institutional bias probably was not the recognition that institutional bias or discrimination exists as a social problem. The fact that institutions can be biased, discriminatory, or racist is not especially surprising or enlightening (Jones, 1972).

Rather, I speculate that the important milestone for the social sciences came in recognizing that institutional bias could operate from mechanisms separate from individual bias, and that institutional bias is not merely based on the sum of discriminatory actions of prejudiced individuals. Credit for the term 'institutional racism' (an early variant

of the term institutional bias used here) that incorporates this distinction has been given to the civil rights activists Stokely Carmichael (a.k.a. Kwame Ture) and Charles Hamilton, particularly for its use as a concept distinguishable from individual racism, in their 1967 book 'Black Power' (see Berard, 2008; Bowser. 1995; Jones, 1972).[1] However, earlier scientific research recognized that discrimination at an institutional level can be examined separately from individual prejudices. For example, a report in 1964, with the informative title 'Discrimination Without Prejudice' published by the Institute for Social Research (ISR) at the University of Michigan, discusses at length a study of 'organizational discrimination' against the hiring and promotion of racial and religious minorities in the American workplace (Kahn, Gurin, Quinn, et al., 1964). Nevertheless, Camichael and Hamilton helped trigger the scientific treatment of the problem of institutional bias (Jones, 1972; Knowles and Prewitt, 1969). Early conceptualizations of the construct have had considerable longevity, even with the passage of time and the fact that work on institutional bias has become a highly interdisciplinary endeavor, including work done in sociology, economics, law, political science, social work, and social psychology. The conceptualization of institutional bias presented here builds directly off this early legacy.

Conceptualizing institutional bias

The definition of institutional bias I provide here is borrowed directly from the definition of institutional racism used by Jones (1972: 131), modified to include a broader range of social groups: Those established laws, customs, and practices which systematically reflect and produce group-based inequities in any society. An institution may be biased whether or not the individuals maintaining those practices have biased intentions.

The distinction between institutional and individual bias can be seen in this definition, and helps to explain differences between changes in expressions of prejudice among individuals in a culture that are not met by commensurate changes in group-based disparities. This distinction is related to (and compounded by) the fact that individual-level prejudices are not strongly related to individual-level discriminatory behaviors anyway (Dovidio, Brigham, Johnson, et al., 1996), but goes even further by illustrating the discrepancies that exist across individual and institutional levels of analysis. For example, there has been documented an important decline in individually expressed prejudice and endorsement of negative stereotypes against Blacks in the United States (Devine and Elliot, 1995; Schuman, Steeh, Bobo, et al., 1998), but this decline has occurred despite the fact that discrimination against Blacks is still widespread, and in some domains unchanged or even worse decades after the civil rights era (Sidanius and Pratto, 1999; Walker, Spohn, & DeLone, 1996). For example, there were over nine times as many Blacks incarcerated in the United States in 2003 ($N = 884,500$) compared to 50 years earlier, 1954 ($N = 98,000$; Mauer and King, 2004), and by 2007, Blacks were incarcerated at a rate over four times that of Whites.[2] In other words, negative outcomes for Blacks in domains like the criminal justice system in the United States may have *worsened* since the civil rights movement. Although there are many plausible explanations for these kinds of disparities, they nevertheless point to the fact that changes in individual-level bias may not be met by the same changes in institutional group-based differences.[3]

Identifying institutional bias from its outcomes

From the very beginning, institutional bias has been defined by its outcomes, by noting domains along which some groups have advantages over others, and speculating that the source of the disparity is in group-based bias (like racism; Carmichael and Hamilton, 1967). Conceptualizing institutional bias in this way may be necessary due to its invisibility, particularly to dominant groups who are not victimized by it or who do not experience it

first-hand (Bonilla-Silva, 1997). Institutional bias reveals itself when studies document group-based disparities in society; or during disasters like Hurricane Katrina, when ethnic minorities were disproportionately harmed by their general location in low-lying (and flood prone), less expensive parts of New Orleans without a means of escape (Henkel, Dovidio, & Gaertner 2006); or the war between African ethnic groups in Rwanda, when international attention that could have prevented the massacre of hundreds of thousands failed to do so (Barnett, 2002). In other words, institutional bias may be revealed perhaps only through its negative consequences. This legacy of early definitions of institutional racism continues with the definition of institutional bias presented above ('practices which systematically reflect and produce group-based inequities'), and is consistent with current approaches to the problem (e.g., Jones, 1997; Sidanius and Pratto, 1999; Walker, Spohn, & DeLone, 1996).

But following this initial conceptualization of institutional bias as based on outcomes came contentious reactions, especially during the more conservative era of individual responsibility during the Reagan–Thatcher 1980s (e.g., Block and Walker, 1982). Defining institutional bias by its outcomes makes the definition circular: Group-based differences are a sign of institutional bias, which is defined by group-based differences. Scientists began wondering if a distinction should be made between bias and inequality. As put by one British law professor,

> To what extent should we distinguish between discrimination and 'inequality'? Confusion may arise between process and product . . . Inequality may be used as one index by which the presence of discrimination is assessed, but is an act to be regarded as discriminatory simply when minority group members are disproportionately adversely affected? (McCrudden, 1982: 304)

The alternative is that group-based disparities in outcomes may be caused by other factors, such as features of the disadvantaged group itself (Block and Walker, 1982; Scott, 1979), including the group members' attitudes, choices, and motivation (Hoffman and Reed, 1982). For example, one study showed that the personalities and tastes of underrepresented minorities (e.g., women, ethnic minorities) explain much of the variability in differences in wages between the groups (Filer, 1986). These kinds of findings shift the responsibility for group-based differences to the group itself rather than to institutions.

These different perceptions of the causes of group-based disparities, whether caused by the victimized group versus a victimizing society, are reflected in social attitudes. In the United States, Blacks and Whites differ greatly in these attributions of the source of group-based disparities, with Whites putting far more responsibility on Blacks than on society for their disadvantaged status (Kluegel and Smith, 1986). Conservative opposition to programs like affirmative action is mediated most strongly by beliefs that Blacks as a group are responsible for group-based disparities that harm them (Reyna, Henry, Korfmacher, et al., 2006).

This thorny issue concerning responsibility for inequality goes beyond the analysis provided here. A softer stance for the identification of institutional bias would note that group-based differences in outcomes may be a sign of institutional bias at least in part, although they cannot be viewed as a perfect indicator.

Power and legitimacy

A conceptualization of institutional bias would not be complete without some discussion of two further constructs: power and legitimacy. Both play an important role in the identification of institutional bias and who is affected by it.

Issues of power existed in the first conceptualization of institutional racism (Carmichael and Hamilton, 1967) and researchers since then have agreed that power probably plays just as important a role in institutional bias as it does in individual bias (Henry and Pratto, 2010; Jones, 1997). Institutional bias is much more likely to occur at the hands of groups in society who hold power, because those groups

will be the ones who control the institutions and therefore determine and carry out the policies that are part of those institutions (Pincus, 1999). Perceptions of power may also play an important role in determining what is and what is not institutional bias. For example, policies that favor some minority groups, such as the pre-boarding of airplane passengers with disabilities, are not seen as biased against those without disabilities because fully physically able people are relatively more powerful than the disabled. Similarly (borrowed from Block and Walker, 1982), left-handed Westerners (like myself) have to write in languages that move from left-to-right (which is awkward and occasionally messy) and otherwise have to navigate through a world built for right-handed people. But this example, too, is not considered institutional bias because left-handed people are not relatively powerless compared to right-handed people. An important condition for institutional bias seems to be the relatively lower power of the disadvantaged group.

Legitimacy, too, has been studied extensively as an intergroup construct (Jost and Major, 2001), and may have special utility for understanding institutional discrimination. The legitimacy of institutional bias involves perceptions that a particular institutional policy is fair, deserved, or justifiable in some manner. Some institutional policies that harm groups with less power go uncontested because of perceptions of legitimacy (Walker, Spohn, & DeLone, 1996). For example, drinking laws in the United States prohibit alcohol consumption by people under the age of 21, which is arguably a form of age-based institutional bias against a relatively powerless group. However, this bias goes almost entirely uncontested because Americans generally believe the legally enforced drinking age is legitimate, given the shared cultural belief that teenagers are especially vulnerable to negative consequences of drinking (see, e.g., the website Why 21?, summarizing research on the special effects of alcohol on teenagers, www.why21.org/teen/).

Issues of legitimacy become much more controversial concerning other policies like racial profiling, which many also perceive as legitimate (Glaser, 2005). If Blacks are statistically disproportionately more likely to commit crime, why not have the police disproportionately target them? If terrorists are statistically disproportionately more likely to be of Muslim or Arab descent, why not disproportionately search or question them at airports? Because perceptions of legitimacy, responsibility, and deservingness can be directed toward groups as a whole (e.g., Reyna, Henry, Korfmacher, et al., 2006; Weiner et al., 1988), they provide an explanation for the interpretation of some institutional policies as biased and others as not. Issues of legitimacy play a critical role in determining what forms of institutional bias are worth fighting against, and which are not (cf. issues of fairness and justifiability, McCrudden, 1982).

REVIEW OF THEORIES CONCERNING THE CAUSES AND PERPETUATION OF INSTITUTIONAL BIAS

As suggested throughout this text, not all institutional bias is the sum of individual-level prejudice and consequently processes underlying individual-level theories concerning prejudice and discrimination may be different from processes at broader social levels of analysis (see also Henry and Pratto, 2010). Theories designed to ameliorate individual-level prejudice, including contact theory, recategorization theory, education and socialization, motivations to control prejudice, confronting individual acts of prejudice, among many of the theories and methods proposed in Part V of this handbook, may be ill-equipped for reducing some forms of institutional bias.

Consequently, the theories presented here concerning the causes and maintenance of institutional biases focus on societal-level influences. Theories at this level are limited in number and empirically thin. Where theorizing does exist, it comes largely from perspectives in sociology, economics, and law. The following approaches were selected as being particularly relevant to the context of societal-level discrimination patterns. Space limitations prevent a more exhaustive inclusion of approaches and allow for only a superficial treatment of those included. Each approach described here could easily compose its own chapter.

Constructed groups and constructed memories

Sociologists have made several claims that the establishment and perpetuation of institutional bias would not be possible without collective social constructions. Although there is little empirical evidence to support the claims, the sheer logic alone is persuasive. First, social groups must be socially constructed and consensually perceived for institutional bias to exist (Bonilla-Silva, 1997). This idea goes beyond individual tendencies to categorize individuals as suggested by social cognition theories (Fiske and Taylor, 1991) to involve socially shared categories and labels (e.g., social identity theory, Tajfel, 1981). For example, the well-known phenomenon of participants expressing bias toward invented groups labeled as 'Wallonian,' 'Pirenean,' and 'Danirean' (Hartley, 1946; cited in Allport, 1954) is important for understanding individual-level prejudice processes, but does not capture the qualities of socially shared constructions. Social constructions will not always cause institutional bias, but they are a necessary condition. There would be no institutional bias without socially shared constructions of groups.

Adding to this point is the notion of social construction of memories, especially the idea of 'collective memory' and, especially, 'collective forgetting' that may contribute to institutional bias (Feagin, 2006). Members of powerful groups collectively leave out of their cultural memory the extent and intensity of historical discrimination and bias against less powerful groups in society, and as a consequence such forgetting assumes that all social groups currently are operating on an equal playing field. Collective forgetting can happen, for example, by leaving the history of discrimination and oppression out of the education system, or through rewriting texts to gloss over or ignore past mistreatment of disadvantaged groups. Again, there is little empirical evidence that directly connects collective forgetting to institutional bias, but the idea mirrors the important role that constructs such as denial of discrimination play as a key component of individual-level modern and symbolic racism (Henry and Sears, 2002; McConahay, 1986).

Cultural bias

Social constructions such as shared social categorizations and collective forgetting may be part of a larger syndrome of cultural bias that bestows greater social value and worth to people and products of one culture over others. Cultural discrimination has been distinguished from institutional discrimination (e.g., Jones, 1997). It has been defined as a biased cultural worldview that benefits the dominant group through its suffusion 'throughout culture via institutional structures, ideological beliefs, and personal everyday actions of people in the culture,' and is 'passed on from generation to generation' (Jones, 1997: 472). By this definition, cultural bias works its way into institutional bias. For example, in locations where the dominant culture is individualistic, rules and procedures will be built around individualistic values. In a culture with more collectivistic values, there would likely exist different policies, laws, and procedures. A collectivistic person living in an individualistic culture might struggle, then, with an instinctive pull toward following collectivistic traditions (e.g., priority on the family) within procedures that are individualistically based.

There are a variety of dimensions on which cultural bias may emerge to benefit groups in power. Jones (1986) identifies several along which Black culture may differ from White, including ideas about the use of time, the pacing and patterning of behavior, and approaches to problem solving and creativity. Many cultures worldwide value a White conception of these dimensions and when

those values work their way into institutions, policies, laws, and procedures they can disadvantage people from different cultural backgrounds.

Some of the clearest evidence for the entrenchment of cultural bias comes from social psychological research on the Implicit Association Test (IAT; Greenwald, McGhee, & Schwartz, 1998), the tool used to determine how quickly a person pairs positive or negative words with names or faces of people from a particular social group. The ability to pair positive words more quickly with names or faces from one group compared to another group suggests an implicit positive bias toward that group. Although there is a great deal of controversy surrounding the interpretation of these effects (e.g., Blanton and Jaccard, 2006) at the least these effects show cultural biases favoring groups in power over other social groups (Karpinski and Hilton, 2001; Uhlmann, Brescoll, & Paluck, 2006).

Cultural bias is an international phenomenon as well, to be found in international agencies like the United Nations, which appears to have a European bent. One may compare, for example, the number of cultural heritage sites the United Nations (through UNESCO) deems worthy of protection as a World Heritage Site across different regions of the globe. These sites of outstanding universal value are located mostly in major Western European countries like Italy, Spain, France, and Germany, compared to other regions of the world whose cultures are valued less, like Southeast Asia, South America, or sub-Saharan Africa. For example, an examination of the list up to the year 2008 shows that Italy alone has nearly as many sites as the combined countries of sub-Saharan Africa, despite the fact Italy has less than 2 percent of the land mass of sub-Saharan Africa. Surely many factors contribute to these discrepancies, including the historical global influence of the sites in Europe, their superior state of preservation, the infrastructure supporting their maintenance, etc. Nevertheless, the discrepancy is vast. It is worth raising the question of the possible influence of bias on such discrepancies even if non-biased policies contribute in part to the discrepancy.

As suggested by the definition, cultural bias is rooted in historical patterns of intergroup relations that result in beliefs and ideologies favoring the higher power group, and which are passed from one generation to the next (Jones, 1997). This cultural bias creates a circle of self-fulfilling prophecies of failures for people who do not benefit from the cultural bias, in which failure to meet criteria or requirements based on cultural biases (e.g., standardized academic admissions tests; Jensen, 1980) often perpetuates further failures (Feagin, 2006). For example, immigrants who do not meet requirements for higher level employment positions may be placed in lower positions that may lead to greater rates of turnover, decreased morale, and decreased ambition. These kinds of patterns help to explain one way cultural biases may transform into the kinds of outcomes that reveal institutional biases.

Economics

The idea of the rational and economically driven actor has been criticized in social psychology, based on the array of evidence suggesting that humans do not operate on purely economic principles, such as the rational weighing of costs and benefits (see, for example, Mansbridge, 1990; Strack and Deutsch, 2007). Although the frame of the rational and self-interested actor may have limitations for understanding individuals and the decisions people make, it may describe general market forces much better, including those involved in institutional bias.

Perhaps the most logical argument of an economics approach is that institutional biases have an economic advantage for business, especially if these biases are based on objectively fair, non-group based policies. For example, businesses have a financial incentive to hire people who are more likely to stay in the job, who are geographically mobile, and who are generally more productive, who in turn tend to be members of more powerful groups in society (Larwood, Gutek, &

Gattiker, 1984). In the banking industry, it is financially safer for banks to give loans with lower interest rates only to people with higher incomes and who provide larger downpayments, which rules out multitudes from disadvantaged groups.

Additionally, institutional agents need to placate others, especially clients who may be operating off biases (Larwood, Gutek, & Gattiker, 1984). For example, an unbiased manager in a consulting firm, in order to increase profits, may hire only White men if he knows that clients will react poorly toward female or ethnic minority representatives. Profit-driven decisions may therefore elicit bias even from otherwise unbiased individuals. This argument was the defense taken by the CEO of Shoney's Incorporated, Ray Danner, who, when confronted with an employment discrimination lawsuit, claimed that market forces dictated that White customers do not want to see Black restaurant employees (Watkins, 1993, cited in Whitely and Kite, 2006).[4]

This point of the economic advantages of institutional bias has been challenged by Nobel Prize-winning economist Gary Becker in his classic *The Economics of Discrimination* (1971), particularly in the labor and retail markets. His basic argument is that institutional bias is generally disadvantageous for both the perpetrators of discrimination and the victims. An employer may lose out on productive or skilled workers by discriminating against them, and consequently lose out on profits. Institutional bias continues, then, only when the costs associated with discrimination match the 'tastes' or prejudices that the perpetrator has. If the costs of discrimination do not outweigh the preferences for discrimination, there will be no change and bias will continue.

By extending this argument, economic factors alone may help reduce institutional bias, and there appears to be evidence for this proposition. For example, the integration of the armed forces was partly due to the inefficiencies and costs of maintaining a segregated military (Mershon and Schlossman, 1998). Use of Spanish in advertising in the United States is probably not so much due to cultural sensitivity and inclusion as it is to the massive collective purchasing power of Latino Americans (Korzenny and Korzenny, 2005). Furthermore, many companies are offering domestic partner benefits as a strategic means of hiring and retaining competitive skilled gay and lesbian employees (Gunther, 2006).

Perhaps driven by the influence of economic factors, much research on diversity seems to have the goal of revealing its benefits to productivity, creativity, and problem solving (Antonio, Chang, Hakuta, et al., 2004; Christian, Porter, & Moffitt 2006; Cox, Lobel, & McLeod, 1991; Leung, Maddux, Galinsky, et al., 2008). Persuading a business to make more fair policy changes may require appeals not so much to justice and morality as to profits and the bottom line.

Group-based interests and legitimizing ideologies

In a related vein, one major movement in the social sciences has considered the influence of rational interests based on groups. This argument suggests that bias and (especially) racism is a function of different social groups competing over resources (e.g., competition for jobs, for government resources like good schools), in what have been called theories of realistic group conflict (Bobo and Hutchings, 1996; LeVine and Campbell, 1972). Institutional biases fulfill the function of depleting resources from another group and adding those resources to one's own. If you are an agent of an institution, or otherwise are in a position to make and change policy, you may be likely to develop procedures that favor your group especially when faced with perceived threats from another group (e.g., Huddy, Feldman, Taber, et al., 2005).

Extending this idea further is the theory of social dominance (Sidanius and Pratto, 1999), which assumes that groups in power have a vested interest in maintaining that power and will rely on a range of strategies for doing so. One strategy is the use of legitimizing ideologies, or beliefs that help

to justify discriminatory and biased policies in a society (Pratto, Sidanius, Stallworth, et al., 1994; Jost and Hunyady, 2005). Legitimizing ideologies draw from a range of moral, biological, religious, and group-based beliefs and attitudes to help explain and justify group-based differences in society. For example, stereotypes represent one broad category of legitimizing ideologies, as in the belief that women are not skilled in math, which helps justify keeping women out of the sciences (and therefore reserving those positions for men). As another example, the belief in a just world (Lerner, 1980) suggests that people get what they deserve in life, putting the responsibility for social disparities on members of low-status groups. These legitimizing ideologies are so pervasive that even members of society who are harmed by them often will endorse them (Jost, Banaji, & Nosek, 2004).

Regardless of the form the legitimizing ideology takes, they all serve the same function of ensuring the group-based hierarchy maintains itself. Legitimizing ideologies can work their way into institutions by justifying policies and procedures that allow for differential treatment of minority groups, influencing the perceptions of legitimacy that can determine if a policy even can be called biased at all, as described earlier.

Social capital

The concept of social capital, more commonly used in sociology and political science, refers to the breadth and effectiveness of a community's social networks and organizational capacity, which can allow members of that community to efficiently accomplish goals and gain resources in a variety of domains (Coleman, 1988). Importantly for the study of institutional bias, social capital is associated with social control, providing its beneficiaries with greater access to jobs and promotions, family support, academic achievement, and status more generally (Portes, 1998).

Members of disadvantaged groups may face institutional biases in part because they lack social capital. That is, members of disadvantaged groups simply may not have the connections, the mutually beneficial interpersonal relationships, and the trust of others as those groups with power in a society (Feagin, 2006; Kao, 2004), particularly the kind of 'bridging' social capital that crosses social groups (Putnam, 2000) and which would provide important advantages especially for people of disadvantaged social groups like ethnic minorities (Braddock and McPartland, 1987). Furthermore, whatever social capital disadvantaged groups have may not translate into the same kinds of benefits as the social capital of those who have power (Dunham and Wilson, 2007). Conversely, members of more powerful groups in society have the capacity to continue the transmission of their privileged status through such networks of their families, friends, and professional colleagues, a capacity that embeds itself into institutions and perpetuates itself across generations. Group-based disparities in these forms of social capital contribute to inequalities between groups.

A FRAMEWORK FOR CONTEXTUALIZING RESEARCH AND THEORY ON INSTITUTIONAL BIAS

One important challenge faced by theoretical approaches to institutional bias is that it is not a uniform construct and can take different forms. A key goal here is to integrate conceptualizations of the different forms of institutional bias into a useful model for contextualizing theory and research. This model focuses on different dimensions of institutional bias that have been raised in the literature.

Two dimensions of institutional bias

Social scientists have identified different dimensions of institutional bias, including how deeply embedded the bias is within larger organizations (Feagin and Feagin, 1978; Sidanius and Pratto, 1999), how intentional the bias is (Feagin and Feagin, 1978; Jones, 1997; Pincus, 1999), and how overt or covert the prejudice is (also identified as, respectively, 'de jure' and 'de facto' discriminatory practices; Jones, 1997).

The model in Table 26.1 provides an integration of these approaches, identifying two dimensions involved in institutional bias and the different qualities of bias that emerge from them. The goal is not simply to enumerate descriptive differences, but to provide dimensions with scientific and theoretical utility through revealing types of bias that may have different causes and mechanisms, yet which nevertheless result in the same consequences of differential group outcomes. The model includes two dimensions, labeled (1) sum-of-individuals versus standards-of-practice forms of bias, and (2) intentional versus unintentional bias. These dimensions create four quadrants that reveal four manifestations of institutional bias. Each leads to group-based disparities, but may require different approaches for resolving or mitigating their effects on intergroup inequality.

Table 26.1   Dimensions of institutional bias

	Intentional (explicitly group-based)	Unintentional (not explicitly group-based)
Sum-of-individuals	Examples: • Hiring choices based on candidate's sex • Police harassing African Americans based on race	Examples: • Hiring choices based on networking • Police pulling over drivers who appear suspicious
Standards-of-practice	Examples: • Slavery • Apartheid • Military policy and marriage laws that exclude gays and lesbians	Examples: • Insurance policies • Bank lending policies • University enrollment • Economically justified business practices

Note: Adapted from Feagin and Feagin (1978); Jones (1997); Sidanius and Pratto (1999)

Dimension #1: Sum-of-individuals versus standards-of-practice

Institutional bias may be created by the sum of discriminatory actions by individuals, or may be created by standards of practice in use by the institution (see Sidanius and Pratto, 1999). Institutional bias that is created by the sum of individuals would lead to major group-based inequalities through the discriminating actions of a critical mass of individuals who are agents of public or private institutions, across time and geographical space in a society.

Institutional bias created by standards-of-practice involves the written or unwritten rules, laws, or procedures that lead to differential outcomes for members of different groups. For example, apartheid laws in South Africa that required Blacks to use separate restrooms, restaurants, and other public facilities were forms of standards-of-practice bias. This type of institutional discrimination is particularly problematic because even entirely unprejudiced or unbiased agents could still produce inequalities simply by following company or institutional protocol. For example, a personnel director responsible for hiring prison guards or fire fighters could be completely free of individual bias, but could perpetuate institutional discrimination against women and some ethnic minorities simply by adhering to the company's minimum height requirements.[5]

Many uses of the term institutional bias (or institutional discrimination/racism) are restricted to describe only bias that is involved in standards of practice (Knowles and Prewitt, 1969; Mayhew, 1968), such that individuals need not be prejudiced or discriminatory for institutional bias to have its insidious effects. However, if institutional bias is defined by outcomes reflecting group-based inequalities, then institutional bias needs to include both standards-of-practice and sum-of-individuals forms of bias.

Dimension #2: Intentional versus unintentional institutional bias

The distinction between intentional and unintentional institutional bias mirrors similar distinctions made for individual bias, namely explicit versus implicit expressions of prejudice (e.g., Dovidio, Kawakami, & Gaertner, 2002). Intentional institutional bias is conducted for the purpose of excluding a particular group from receiving a certain form of benefit or positive outcome, and may be written into policies (e.g., slavery, anti-gay marriage legislation) or part of the unwritten rules of an institution (e.g., hiring practices that keep immigrants in the kitchen instead of the front of a restaurant). Unintentional biases also may be written into policies (e.g., university enrollment based on performance on culturally biased standardized tests) or may be part of the unwritten rules of an institution (e.g., promotions based on networking ability).

The most dangerous quadrant?

As shown in Table 26.1, these two dimensions produce four quadrants or types of institutional bias: (a) sum-of-individual bias that is intentional, (b) sum-of-individual bias that is unintentional, (c) standards-of-practice bias that is intentional, and (d) standards-of-practice bias that is unintentional. One quadrant stands out as being especially dangerous, and controversial: standards-of-practice bias that is unintentional. In a vacuum these standards of practice are based on entirely rational and superficially unbiased policies and procedures that do not target specific groups directly. However, within certain contexts, especially contexts where historically a group has faced discrimination, they promote continuing bias. For example, medical school admissions are based typically on academic preparation, a completely rational policy to ensure success in a rigorous training program. However, if some social groups (e.g., ethnic minorities) have a history of being disproportionately underrepresented in education, especially the kind of education needed to prepare one for medical school, then such objective admissions policies will necessarily lead to less representation of those groups in the field of medicine. Similarly, insurance companies use actuary tables based on objective, economically driven standards for determining their policy premiums. But if some social groups are more likely to fall under a 'risk' category (e.g., have homes in lower-income locations with little access to services, as is disproportionately the case for ethnic minorities; Squires, 2003), then the members of that group are more likely to pay higher premiums despite the rational and objective nature of the policy. These policies are dangerous for the perpetuation of inequalities precisely because of the lack of direct evidence of bias.

THE FUTURE OF THEORY AND APPLICATION CONCERNING INSTITUTIONAL BIAS

There seems to be a great deal of room for the development of theories concerning the causes and mechanisms of institutional bias. Notably missing from the social-scientific picture are data concerning these mechanisms, especially how the mechanisms are linked to the disparate outcomes observed in societies across the globe and affecting a wide variety of social groups. Indeed, forecasting the future of institutional bias in social psychology research is challenging because there are not strong foundations concerning its mechanisms. Because of this need for a clearer, empirically driven understanding of these mechanisms, the study of institutional bias is wide open for directing research energy.

An additional challenge arises in forecasting how existing theory on institutional bias can be applied to providing solutions to the problem of institutional bias. The theoretical approaches summarized earlier provide some clues for understanding the mechanisms and conditions necessary for the creation and persistence of institutional bias, but they do not easily point to readily available solutions to the problem. For example, how does one counter the socially shared construction of groups, or cultural biases that have roots in centuries-old intergroup relations? Nevertheless, as suggested throughout this chapter, it seems clear that the solution to institutional biases will require different

approaches compared to those used to solve individual bias.

Theoretical and practical solutions to institutional bias

The strategy for changing institutional bias will depend on the type of institutional bias that is at work. As Table 26.1 shows, institutional bias can take many different forms, and the form it takes will determine how best to manage it. Solutions need to be sensitive to these different manifestations.

The one form of institutional discrimination that would seem most amenable to bias-reduction strategies based on individual-level theories would be that found in the sum-of-individuals/unintentional quadrant in Table 26.1. If group-based disparities are caused in part by the sum of the actions and decisions of individual agents who do not intend to act in a biased fashion, then education, prejudice awareness programs, diversity training, the employment of minorities in decision-making roles, etc., would all be plausible ways of reducing, even if piecemeal, this form of institutional bias. If these individual agents of bias do not intend to be biased, then strategies that collectively reveal their biases and increase their awareness may be effective.

Not all individual agents of institutions, however, are so interested in equality between groups. For example, research indicates that people with group-based dominance motives may be especially attracted to powerful social roles (Sidanius, Pratto, Martin, et al., 1991). The forms of institutional bias found in the sum-of-individuals/intentional quadrant of Table 26.1 might be resistant to individual-level efforts to reduce bias. Rather, such acts of bias might need to be dealt with in a legal fashion, resorting to discrimination lawsuits or formal reprimands by superiors. Of course, resorting to discrimination lawsuits will be effective only to the extent that a social group is protected by law. Many groups are not so protected, including gays and lesbians, the obese, or many individuals with concealable stigmas like mental illness or depression.

Not all forms of institutional bias can be easily traced to individual actions, however, as suggested by the standard-of-practice forms of institutional bias. These institutional biases will require bias-reduction strategies that are not rooted in individual-level theory. Considering the quadrant of standards-of-practice/intentional bias shown in Table 26.1, strategies could involve civil rights legislation, or change through popular protest, or minority agitation (see, e.g., Feagin and Feagin, 1978; Feagin, 2006).

Finally, there is the Table 26.1 quadrant of standards-of-practice/unintentional bias. Strategies for reducing institutional bias in this quadrant may need to be directed at the institutional level, through reparations policies such as affirmative action, welfare policies, minority recruitment programs, as well as through involvement of minority input in decisions about policies and procedures (Feagin, 2006; Jones, 1997). Repairing this form of institutional bias is especially tricky because it involves repairing the consequences of policies that do not have clear group-based implications. As suggested earlier, at the root of the controversy are perceptions of who is responsible for such repair: society, or the groups themselves.

Fighting institutional bias through reforming institutions

There are other institutional-based approaches that could help reduce all forms of institutional bias. One solution may be to target leaders of institutions. Because leaders of organizations or institutions have power in determining the policies and procedures that may be biased, as well as help set the corporate norms and culture, they present an important source of change (Crain, Mahard, & Narot, 1982; Reskin, 1998). For example, in one major corporation, after a simple discussion by a CEO with the supervisors concerning minority recruitment, the hiring of women and ethnic minorities in the corporation increased substantially (reported in Dovidio, 1993). This idea is consistent with the important role that authority figures can play in ensuring the effectiveness of reducing

intergroup prejudices through intergroup contact (Pettigrew and Tropp, 2006).

Organizations also can be formed to help monitor institutional bias and enforce its change, and in the United States various public and private organizations have emerged. The federal government established the Commission on Civil Rights and the Equal Employment Opportunity Commission (EEOC) to help monitor employment discrimination, and private organizations such as the American Civil Liberties Union (ACLU) help prosecute illegal cases of institutional bias.

Civil rights legislation and the passage of laws establishing the illegality of institutional discrimination is another means through which institutional bias may be fought (see Henry, 2010), and at the very least sends the message from an overarching institution (i.e., the government) that group-based bias is unacceptable. Because many laws in the United States are based upon a constitution that was written during an inherently racist historical period, sociologist Joe Feagin has even proposed rewriting the US Constitution with the input of disadvantaged groups as a necessary beginning for the legislative battle of institutional biases (Feagin, 2000, 2006).

In sum, it seems clear that if institutional bias is to be reduced, it needs to be approached as a system that operates independently from individual biases. Solutions that target prejudice and bias reduction strategies in individuals may not be very effective for reducing the biases in institutions that result in large group-based disparities. Important steps for social scientists will be having a better understanding of the different forms that institutional biases can take, recognizing that different types of institutional bias may have different mechanisms driving them, and understanding that those different mechanisms may require different solutions.

NOTES

*Correspondence should be directed to: PJ Henry, New York University – Abu Dhabi, 19 Washington Square North, New York, NY 10011. E-mail: pj.henry@nyu.ed

1 The word 'bias' is used in this chapter because social psychological conceptions of discrimination focus mostly on behaviors. Bias is a broader term meant to capture any attitude, belief, or behavior that might contribute to the problem of differential, group-based outcomes.

2 Data from 2007 were made available from the US Department of Justice, Bureau of Statistics, available on the internet at http://www.ojp.usdoj.gov/bjs.

3 The reverse also may be true, that improvements in institutions may not be met by improvements in individual attitudes. For example, policies like school integration programs designed to improve individual-level intergroup attitudes have sometimes had no effect or have worsened individual-level intergroup attitudes (Amir, 1969). Although contact theory has since developed enough for us to understand why (e.g., Pettigrew and Tropp, 2006), these kinds of institutional-policy versus individual-attitude discrepancies further illustrate the complexities of the mechanisms of bias operating at both levels.

4 Notably, Danner lost the case.

5 The issue of responsibility for bias on the part of individuals following biased institutional protocol is murky. For example, Adolf Eichmann, as part of his defense at the Nazi war crimes tribunal in Jerusalem, insisted that he was merely following the protocol of his job of transporting Jews to death camps, and could not be held individually responsible for animosity toward Jews (indeed, not following through on his job could have had lethal consequences for him in the Nazi regime). The jury held him responsible anyway, and he was hanged (Arendt, 1963/1994).

ACKNOWLEDGEMENT

This chapter was written with the support of a research fellowship from the Alexander von Humboldt Foundation at the Institut für interdisziplinäre Konflikt und Gewaltforschung (IKG), the University of Bielefeld, Germany.

REFERENCES

Allport, G. W. (1954). *The nature of prejudice*. Reading, MA: Addison-Wesley.

Amir, Y. (1969). Contact hypothesis in ethnic relations. *Psychological Bulletin, 71*, 319–342.

Antonio, A. L., Chang, M. J., Hakuta, K., Kenny, D. A., Levin, S., and Milem, J. F. (2004). Effects of racial diversity on complex thinking in college students. *Psychological Science, 15*, 507–510.

Arendt, H. (1994). *Eichmann in Jerusalem: A report on the banality of evil*. New York: Penguin Books. (Original work published in 1963).

Barnett, M. (2002). *Eyewitness to a genocide: The United Nations and Rwanda*. Ithaca, NY: Cornell University Press.

Becker, G. S. (1971). *The economics of discrimination*. Chicago: University of Chicago Press.

Berard, T. J. (2008). The neglected social psychology of institutional racism. *Sociology Compass, 2*, 637–764.

Blanton, H., and Jaccard, J. (2006). Arbitrary metrics in psychology. *American Psychologist, 61*, 27–41.

Block, W. E., and Walker, M. A. (Eds.). (1982). *Discrimination, affirmative action, and equal opportunity: An economic and social perspective*. Vancouver, BC: The Fraser Institute.

Bobo, L. D., and Hutchings, V. L. (1996). Perceptions of racial group competition: Extending Blumer's theory of group position to a multiracial social context. *American Sociological Review, 61*, 951–972.

Bonilla–Silva, E. (1997). Rethinking racism: Toward a structural interpretation. *American Sociological Review, 62*, 465–480.

Bowser, B. P. (2005). *Racism and anti-racism in world perspective*. Thousand Oaks, CA: Sage.

Braddock, J. H., and McPartland, J. M. (1987). How minorities continue to be excluded from equal employment opportunities: Research on labor market and institutional barriers. *Journal of Social Issues, 43*, 5–39.

Cable, S., Hastings, D. W., and Mix, T. L. (2002). Different voices, different venues: Environmental racism claims by activists, researchers, and lawyers. *Human Ecology Review, 9*, 26–42.

Carmichael, S., and Hamilton, C. V. (1967). *Black power: The politics of liberation in America*. New York: Vintage Books.

Christian, J., Porter, L. W., and Moffitt, G. (2006). Workplace diversity and group relations: An overview. *Group Processes and Intergroup Relations, 9*, 459–466.

Coleman, J. S. (1988). Social capital in the creation of human capital. *American Sociological Review, 94*, S95–S120.

Cox, T. H., Lobel, S. A., and McLeod, P. L. (1991). Effects of ethnic group cultural differences on cooperative and competitive behavior on a group task. *Academy of Management Journal, 34*, 827–847.

Crain, R. L., Mahard, R. E., and Narot, R. E. (1982). *Making desegregation work: How schools create social climates*. Cambridge, MA: Ballinger.

Devine, P. G., and Elliot, A. J. (1995). Are racial stereotypes really fading? The Princeton trilogy revisited. *Personality and Social Psychology Bulletin, 21*, 1139–1150.

Dovidio, J. F. (1993). The subtlety of racism. *Training and development, 47*, 51–57.

Dovidio, J. F., Brigham, J. C., Johnson, B. T., and Gaertner, S. L. (1996). Stereotyping, prejudice, and discrimination: Another look. In C. N. Macrae, C. Stangor, and M. Hewstone (Eds.), *Stereotypes and stereotyping* (pp. 276–319). New York: Guilford.

Dovidio, J. F., Kawakami, K., and Gaertner, S. L. (2002). Implicit and explicit prejudice and interracial interaction. *Journal of Personality and Social Psychology, 82*, 62–68.

Dunham, R., and Wilson, G. (2007). Race, within–family social capital, and school dropout: An analysis of Whites, Blacks, Hispanics, and Asians. *Sociological Spectrum, 27*, 207–221.

Feagin, J. R. (2000). *Racist America: Roots, current realities and future reparations.* New York: Routledge.

Feagin, J. R. (2006). *Systemic racism: A theory of oppression.* New York: Routledge.

Feagin, J. R., and Feagin, C. B. (1978). *Discrimination American style: Institutional racism and sexism.* Englewood Cliffs, NJ: Prentice-Hall.

Filer, R. K. (1986). The role of personality and tastes in determining occupational structure. *Industrial and Labor Relations Review, 39*, 412–424.

Fiske, S. T., and Taylor, S. E. (1991). *Social cognition* (2nd ed.). New York: McGraw-Hill.

Glaser, J. (2005). Intergroup bias and inequity: Legitimizing beliefs and policy attitudes. *Social Justice Research, 18*, 257–282.

Greenwald, A. G., McGhee, D. E., and Schwartz, J. L. K. (1998). Measuring individual differences in implicit cognition: The implicit association test. *Journal of Personality and Social Psychology, 74*, 1464–1480.

Gunther, M. (2006). Queer Inc. *Fortune, 154*, 94–110.

Hartley, E. L. (1946). *Problems in prejudice.* New York: King's Crown Press.

Henkel, K. E., Dovidio, J. F., and Gaertner, S. L. (2006). Institutional discrimination, individual racism, and Hurricane Katrina. *Analyses of Social Issues and Public Policy, 6*, 99–124.

Henry, P. J. (2010). Civil rights legislation. To appear in J. Levine and M. Hogg (Eds.), *The Encyclopedia of Group Processes and Intergroup Relations* (pp. 83–86). Thousand Oaks, CA: Sage Publications.

Henry, P. J., and Pratto, F. (2010). Power and racism. In A. Guinote and T. Vescio (Eds.), *The social psychology of power* (pp. 341–362). New York: Guilford.

Henry, P. J., and Sears, D. O. (2002). The Symbolic Racism 2000 Scale. *Political Psychology, 23*, 253–283.

Hoffman, C., and Reed, J. (1982). When is imbalance not discrimination? In W. E. Block and M. A. Walker (Eds.), *Discrimination, affirmative action, and equal opportunity: An economic and social perspective* (pp. 187–216). Vancouver, BC: The Fraser Institute.

Huddy, L., Feldman, S., Taber, C., and Lahav, G. (2005). Threat, anxiety, and support of antiterrorism policies. *American Journal of Political Science, 49*, 593–608.

Jensen, A. R. (1980). *Bias in mental testing.* New York: Free Press.

Jones, J. M. (1986). Racism: A cultural analysis of the problem. In J. F. Dovidio and S. L. Gaertner (Eds.), *Prejudice, discrimination, and racism* (pp. 279–314). Orlando, FL: Academic Press.

Jones, J. M. (1972). *Prejudice and racism.* Reading, MA: Addison-Wesley.

Jones, J. M. (1997). *Prejudice and racism (2nd ed.).* New York: McGraw-Hill.

Jost, J. T., Banaji, M. R., and Nosek, B. A. (2004). A decade of system justification theory: Accumulated evidence of conscious and unconscious bolstering of the status quo. *Political Psychology, 25*, 881–920.

Jost, J. T., and Hunyady, O. (2005). Antecendents and consequences of system-justifying ideologies. *Current Directions in Psychological Science, 14*, 260–265.

Jost, J. T., and Major, B. (Eds.) (2001). *The psychology of legitimacy: Emerging perspectives on ideology, justice, and intergroup relations.* New York: Cambridge University Press.

Kahn, R. L., Gurin, G., Quinn, R. P., Baar, E., and Kraut, A. I. (1964). *Discrimination without prejudice: A study of promotion practices in industry* (Organizational Studies Series 2, Report 1). Ann Arbor, MI: University of Michigan Institute for Social Research.

Kao, G. (2004). Social capital and its relevance to minority and immigrant populations. *Sociology of Education, 77*, 172–183.

Karpinski, A., and Hilton, J. L. (2001). Attitudes and the Implicit Association Test. *Journal of Personality and Social Psychology, 81*, 774–788.

Kluegel, J. R., and Smith, E. R. (1986). *Beliefs about inequality: Americans' view of what is and what ought to be.* New York: Aldine de Gruyteer.

Knowles, L. L., and Prewitt, K. (1969). *Institutional racism in America.* Englewood Cliffs, NJ: Prentice-Hall.

Korzenny, F., and Korzenny, B. A. (2005). *Hispanic marketing: A cultural perspective.* Oxford, England: Elsevier.

Larwood, L., Gutek, B., and Gattiker, U. E. (1984). Perspectives on institutional discrimination and resistance to change. *Group and Organization Studies, 9*, 333–352.

Lerner, M. (1980). *The belief in a just world.* New York: Plenum Press.

LeVine, R. A., and Campbell, D. T. (1972). *Ethnocentrism: Theories of conflict, ethnic attitudes, and group behavior.* New York: Wiley.

Leung, A. K., Maddux, W. W., Galinsky, A. D., and Chiu, C. (2008). Multicultural experience enhances creativity: The when and how. *American Psychologist, 63*, 169–181.

Mansbridge, J. J. (Ed.) (1990). *Beyond self-interest.* Chicago: University of Chicago Press.

Mauer, M., and King, R. S. (2004). *Schools and prisons: 50 years after Brown versus Board of Education* [briefing paper]. Washington, DC: The Sentencing Project. Retrieved from the Internet at on August 5, 2008.

Mayhew, L. H. (1968). *Law and equal opportunity.* Cambridge, MA: Harvard University Press.

McConahay, J. B. (1986). Modern racism, ambivalence, and the Modern Racism Scale. In J. F. Dovidio and S. L. Gaertner (Eds.), *Prejudice, discrimination, and racism* (pp. 91–125). Orlando, FL: Academic Press.

McCrudden, C. (1982). Institutional discrimination. *Oxford Journal of Legal Studies, 2*, 303–367.

Mershon, S., and Schlossman, S. (1998). *Foxholes and color lines: Desegregating the U.S. Armed Forces.* Baltimore, MD: Johns Hopkins University Press.

Pettigrew, T., and Tropp, L. (2006). A meta-analytic test of intergroup contact theory. *Journal of Personality and Social Psychology, 90*, 751–783.

Pincus, F. L. (1999). From individual to structural discrimination. In F. L. Pincus and H. J. Ehrlich (Eds.), *Race and ethnic conflict: Contending views on prejudice, discrimination, and ethnoviolence* (pp. 120–124). Boulder, CO: Westview.

Portes, A. (1998). Social capital: Its origins and applications in modern sociology. *Annual Review of Sociology, 24*, 1–24.

Pratto, F., Sidanius, J., Stallworth, L., and Malle, B. F. (1994). Social dominance orientation: A personality variable predicting social and political attitudes. *Journal of Personality and Social Psychology, 67*, 741–763.

Putnam, R. D. (2000). *Bowling alone: The collapse and revival of American community.* New York: Simon and Schuster.

Reskin, B. F. (1998). *The realities of affirmative action in employment.* Washington, DC: American Sociological Association.

Reyna, C., Henry, P. J., Korfmacher, W., and Tucker, A. (2006). Examining the principles in principled conservatism: The role of responsibility stereotypes as cues for deservingness in racial policy decisions.

Journal of Personality and Social Psychology, 90, 109–128.

Schuman, H., Steeh, C., Bobo, L. D., and Krysan, M. (1998). *Racial attitudes in America: Trends and interpretations.* Cambridge, MA: Harvard University Press.

Scott, R. R. (1979). Review of Discrimination American style: Institutional racism and sexism by J. R. Feagin and C. B. Feagin. *Contemporary Sociology, 8*, 759.

Shawver, L. (1995). *And the flag was still there: Straight people, gay people, and sexuality in the U.S. military.* Binghamton, NY: Haworth Press.

Sidanius, J., and Pratto, F. (1999). *Social dominance: An intergroup theory of social hierarchy and oppression.* New York: Cambridge University Press.

Sidanius, J., Pratto, F., Martin, M., and Stallworth, L. (1991). Consensual racism and career track: Some implications of social dominance theory. *Political Psychology, 12*, 691–721.

Squires, G. D. (2003). Racial profiling, insurance style: Insurance redlining and the uneven development of metropolitan areas. *Journal of Urban Affairs, 25*, 391–410.

Strack, F., and Deutsch, R. (2007). The role of impulse in social behavior. In A. W. Kruglanski and E. T. Higgins (Eds.), *Social psychology: Handbook of basic principles, 2nd ed.* (pp. 408–431).New York: Guilford Press.

Sumner, W. G. (1906). *Folkways: A study of the sociological importance of usages, manners, customs, mores, and morals.* Boston: Ginn and Co.

Tajfel, H. (1981). *Human groups and social categories.* New York: Cambridge University Press.

Uhlmann, E. L., Brescoll, V. L., and Paluck, E. L. (2006). Are members of low status groups perceived as bad, or badly off? Egalitarian negative associations and automatic prejudice. *Journal of Experimental Social Psychology, 42*, 491–499.

Walker, S., Spohn, C., and DeLone, M. (1996). *The color of justice: Race, ethnicity, and crime in America.* Belmont, CA: Wadsworth.

Watkins, S. (1993, October 18). Racism du jour at Shoney's. *The Nation*, pp. 424–428.

Weiner, B., Perry, R. P., and Magnusson, J. (1988). An attributional analysis of reactions to stigmas. *Journal of Personality and Social Psychology, 55*, 738–748.

Whitely, B. E., and Kite, M. E. (2006). *The psychology of prejudice and discrimination.* Belmont, CA: Wadsworth.

27

Bias in Organizations

Alexis N. Smith, Arthur P. Brief, and
Adrienne Colella

ABSTRACT

This chapter examines bias in an organizational context. The workplace, it is argued, is a strong situation that enables subtle prejudice and stereotypes to manifest unfair discrimination and systematized bias. We focus on the experiences of African-Americans to examine the social and psychological processes that occur to influence relationships, work behaviors, and career advancement of under-represented and stigmatized individuals at work. In addition, several organizational tales are presented to illustrate how organizations, as strong situations, can have a hand in intensifying or reducing unfair discrimination and inequality. We close the chapter with a discussion of how theory and research on bias can be improved by building bridges between social psychological and organizational perspectives. It is argued that we would do more to reduce bias by building theories and conducting research where the action is: in organizations.

BIAS IN ORGANIZATIONS

Racial equality in America remains more of a dream than a reality (e.g., Brief & Hayes, 1997). Work organizations, in all sectors of the economy, are central to such between group inequalities (e.g., Baron & Bielby, 1980). Organizations hire, train, compensate, promote, and dismiss individuals; and as such, are the vehicles through which economic mobility is acquired. The aim of this chapter is to entice social psychologists concerned with inequalities produced by unfair discrimination to think organizationally, to recognize (a) organizations' contribution to unfair discrimination, (b) the pragmatic importance of organizations for reducing between group

economic differences, and (c) their uniqueness as psychological settings. By doing so, we hope the questions social psychologists pose will be altered, the methods chosen to seek answers to those questions broadened, and the boundaries around the answers obtained made clearer.

The remainder of our chapter unfolds as follows. First, snap-shots of organizations as inequality producers will be presented to emphasize they are at the heart of the problem and must be where solutions are applied. Next, the idea that organizations are particularly 'strong situations' (e.g., Mischel, 1973) that guide behaviors, including ones that entail unfair discrimination, will be advanced and defended. Third, ways in which prejudices and negative stereotypes arise in and influence organizational behavior are explored. Fourth, strategies for reducing unfair discrimination in organizations are examined. The chapter closes with discussions of why unfair discrimination in organizations and its causes have not been attended to adequately by psychologists and of what a future interdisciplinary research agenda to remedy this situation might look like.

ORGANIZATIONS AND INEQUALITY

As the overwhelming majority of Americans earn their livelihoods in an organization (Pfeffer, 1998), it should be obvious that organizations are where the action is in regards to both studying the causes of unfair group economic differences and reducing them. 'Because of their ubiquity, however, [organizations] fade into the background and we need to be reminded of their impact' (Scott, 1992: 3). The intent of this section is to be that reminder by examining briefly the impact of work organizations on Black Americans.

In our examination of bias in organizations we focus on the experiences of Blacks in the workplace. We choose anti-Black racism as the illustrative theme of this chapter because this particular form of prejudice is a stark demonstration of how historical biases can infect attitudes and behaviors even in the highly regulated and supposedly meritocratic context of the modern workplace. While much of the research presented in this chapter is specifically about racism, some of it focuses on and can be applied to other forms of bias (e.g., sexism, heterosexism, and ageism). While racism is in many ways similar to other forms of group-based bias (see Chapter 20 by Glick & Rudman and Chapter 21 by Hebl, Law, & King, this volume), it is qualitatively different in other ways (e.g., for example the historic ties of anti-Black racism to slavery and de jure segregation; see DiTomaso, Post & Parks-Yancey, 2007). Thus, the reader should note that the dynamics of bias may vary depending upon the target. Nevertheless, our intention is to use the experience of American

Blacks as an illustration of the impact of bias in organizations

The impact of racial bias against blacks appears to be especially adverse compared to other demographic groups. Examining unemployment statistics for example, the unemployment rate among adult White workers is 4.1 percent, among Hispanic workers it is 5.4 percent, while 9.4 percent of Black workers are unemployed (US Bureau of Labor Statistics, 2006a). Recall, it is organizations that do the hiring and firing. Moreover, in a study of urban inequality in Los Angeles, almost 60 percent of Black respondents reported experiencing some form of work-related discrimination (only 25 percent of Whites reported similar discrimination) (Bobo & Suh, 2000). Taking these numbers to the national level, it is not surprising that in fiscal year 2005 almost 30,000 racial discrimination charges were filed with the EEOC against private sector employers (US Equal Employment Opportunity Commission, 2006).

Despite progress stemming from changing social norms and legislation like the Civil Rights Act of 1964, there is still widespread evidence that racial disparities persist in workplaces (Reskin, 1998). For instance, America's Black workers are still grossly underpaid relative to their White counterparts, with Blacks earning an average of $0.79 on every dollar earned by White employees (Neumark, 1999; US Bureau of Labor Statistics, 2005). In 2005, among full-time wage and salary workers, the median weekly earnings of Blacks ($520) was much lower than those of Whites ($672); and despite reports that the earnings gap is decreasing (e.g., Alexis, 1998; Couch & Daly, 2002), the gap has actually widened in recent years with Whites making more and Blacks making less (US Bureau of Labor Statistics, 2006d). A growing earnings gap may explain recent Urban Institute studies that report that the number of Black families entering the middle class has stagnated (The Urban Institute, 2003).

Although differences in education, human capital, and job experience partially explain such advancement differentials, a significant portion of gap remains unexplained, leaving discrimination as a possible a cause (Cohen, 2001; Couch & Daly, 2002; Gill, 1989). For instance, Cawley, Heckman, and Vytlacil (1999) examined wages and ability and found that cognitive ability and human capital measures combined explained less than one third of the variance in Black-White wage differentials. These authors concluded that the wage return to ability is not uniform across races – what one earns on the job does depend on race. Moreover, there is evidence that race can also be implicated in persistent disparities in treatment and opportunity at every step of the employment process.

Black and White applicants encounter different treatment and work opportunities even before approaching the organization's door. Interviews with employers indicate that they commonly recruit applicants by word-of-mouth referrals or by targeting job advertisements to particular neighborhoods, often avoiding inner city, predominately Black neighborhoods (Kirschenman & Neckerman, 1991). Word-of-mouth referrals generally travel through employees' social networks, which tend to be racially segregated (Elliott, 2001); such informal recruitment strategies tend to produce applicants similar to those employees already in place (Reskin & McBrier, 2000). Thus, from the outset, Blacks and Whites have different levels of knowledge about job openings.

Moreover, studies show that equally qualified Black and White applicants have different experiences during the selection process. Using a technique, called the audit study, researchers carefully match Black and White job applicants in terms of qualifications, backgrounds, and/or relevant skills. Thus, the researcher may attribute any differences in their treatment to race (for a critique of the audit study method, see Heckman, 1998). Studies of this sort have reported that despite espoused color-blind selection policies employers routinely granted interviews to significantly more White applicants (Pager & Quillian, 2005); Black males were three times as likely to be turned down for a job as were White males (Mincy,

1993; see also Mincy, Lewis, & Han, 2006); White applicants were almost 10 percent more likely to receive interviews than were Black applicants (Bendick, Jackson, & Reinoso, 1994); and over 20 percent of employers generally treated Black applicants less favorably than White applicants. A final study that manipulated names (Black-sounding versus White-sounding) of job applicants on matched resumes found that applicants with White-sounding names were 50 percent more likely to be called for interviews than were those with Black-sounding names (Bertrand & Mullainathan, 2004).

Unfortunately, computer simulations of the impact of these types of decisions have shown that even miniscule differences at the lower levels of an organization's hierarchy can produce wide disparity at the top levels (Martell, Parcel, & Kazuko, 1996). This suggests that even if Blacks are hired by firms in relatively large numbers (for example, in response to pressure to comply with affirmative action), Black–White disparities often emerge in other areas such as pay, placement, and opportunities to advance (Mitra, 1999).

Indeed, certain intra-organizational practices instigate differentials in Blacks' advancement rates. In a review of the audit studies mentioned above, Bendick, Jackson, & Reinoso (1994) found that Whites were steered into jobs that were below their qualifications 37 percent less often than were their Black counterparts. Further, research indicates that when Black employees are promoted, they are often promoted into jobs with less power and responsibility than Whites and are relegated to stereotypical jobs – for example, those dealing with 'minority issues' (Collins, 1989, 1997; Mueller, Parcel, & Kazuko, 1989). Also, studies have shown that shortly after entry into an organization Blacks are more likely to be assigned to a Black supervisor than are their White counterparts (Lefkowitz, 1994), and subsequently have significantly less opportunity to proceed to higher status positions of authority than do employees who are matched with White mentors (Smith & Elliott, 2002).

The trend of demographically matching professionally immobile supervisors with new minority employees, over time results in disproportionate numbers of minority employees locked in dead-end positions. The authors concluded that minority employees have a 'sticky floor' that effectively bars them from positions of authority.

Finally, there is some evidence of Black–White differences in informal day-to-day interaction in the workplace. Research has indicated that compared to Whites, Black employees often face a less welcoming workplace, which may include fewer mentors to sponsor and guide them, greater social isolation from important informal networks (Reskin, 1998), greater supervisory control of their work (Sidanius & Pratto, 1999), and more everyday incidents of devaluation and exclusion (Deitch, Barsky, Butz, et al., 2003; Essed, 1991).

In essence, although organizations have increased the absolute numbers of minority employees, the above discussion suggests that racial integration at all levels of organizations has not been achieved. This lack of integration has detriments for both Black and White workers. Compared to White employees, Blacks in the workplace more often hold what Kanter (1977) has called 'token' status, where they are treated like symbols or representatives of a category rather than as individuals. Having token status can result in being held to a different or higher standard (Cox & Nkomo, 1986) and reductions in self-esteem and well being (Forman, 2003). Furthermore, Brief and his colleagues (2005) observed that much of the literature on racial diversity indicates that as demographic heterogeneity within organizations increases, majority group members (e.g., Whites) experience reduced organizational commitment and job satisfaction (Mannix & Neale, 2005; Mueller, Finley, Iverson, et al., 1999; Reskin, McBrier, & Kmec, 1999; Riordan, 2000; Tsui, Egan, & O'Reilly, 1992; Tsui & Gutek, 1999; Williams and O'Reilly, 1998). Further, as minority representation in workgroups increased, Whites reported feeling less trust in and attraction to peers

(Chattopadhyay, 1999; Riordan and Shore, 1997).

In sum, evidence indicates Black workers are treated differently by organizations at every step of the employment process and that White workers appear to respond negatively to an increasing Black presence in the workplace. Such negative reaction is especially problematic as Whites occupy many more positions of power in organizations than minorities; they are over ten times more likely to be executives, managers, or other professionals than Blacks (US Bureau of Labor Statistics, 2006c). This power places Whites in positions to discriminate against members of other groups (also see Blumer, 1960; Deprét & Fiske, 1993; Feagin, 2000). If the sorts of inequalities we have reviewed are to be alleviated, it seems one cannot avoid addressing unfair (e.g., race-based) discrimination in organizations.

ORGANIZATIONS AS STRONG SITUATIONS

Given that organizations are producers of racial inequalities, what is it about them that social psychologists should know? This is a difficult question to answer, for the literature that could be drawn upon is extraordinarily broad and encompasses contributions from psychology, sociology, economics and the humanities (Zald, 1993) as well as from management scholars. While elsewhere in the chapter we will allude to salient procedural features of organizations, in this section we will emphasize that organizations psychologically constitute 'strong situations' (e.g., Mischel, 1973) and, in doing so, explain why this is the case.

The organizations people work for can be thought of as providing them with 'scripts' (e.g., Goffman, 1967, Schank & Abelson, 1977), specifying how they ought to act. These scripts serve to reduce the variance in employee behaviors, assuming employees have the ability and motivation to perform them. One form these scripts come in is prescribed roles that must be dependably performed for organizations to survive (Katz, 1964). These roles are communicated to employees, for example, through job descriptions, training programs, performance appraisal and reward systems, and orders from their bosses. Employees also learn what is expected of them through more informal means, for instance, by observing and interacting with organizational peers and superiors (Ashforth & Mael, 1989).

So, dependable role performance, doing what the organization expects of you, largely becomes a question of motivation (Katz, 1964). For some scholars, the motivation to follow organizational scripts comes from obedience or adherence to bureaucracy. For example, Stanley Milgram (1974) wrote that obedience is, 'embedded in a larger atmosphere where social relationships, career aspirations, and technical routines set the dominant tone. Typically, [the obedient person is] a functionary who has been given a job to do and who survives to create an impression of competence in his work' (p. 187). Similarly, observing Eichmann's trial, Hannah Arendt (1963) wrote: '[it is] the nature of every bureaucracy ... to make functionaries and mere cogs in the administrative machinery out of men ... He acted in accordance with the rule' (pp. 289, 293).

Social psychology scholars have attributed subordinates' motivation to fulfill organizational scripts as tendencies to view their superiors as legitimate authority figures (French & Raven, 1959), and therefore deserving of deference or obedience. Organizations, by their very nature, are characterized by hierarchical authority structures. Higher levels have authority over those occupying lower levels. Herbert Simon (1945) defined authority as 'the power to make decisions which guide the actions of another' (p. 125; also, see Simon, 1951). Simon further differentiated authority from other kinds of influence by noting that subordinates hold in abeyance their own critical facilities for choosing between alternatives and use the formal criterion of the receipt of a command or signal as their basis for choice. Moreover, he recognized that employees need not receive a priori commands, but instead yield to both implicit and explicit instruction from above.

Of course, normative obedience to authority has its limits, even when that authority is viewed as legitimate. For example, some orders may be so blatantly pernicious that a subordinate may be unable to accept them. To use the language of Chester I. Barnard's (1938) classic *Functions of the Executive*, such orders would fall outside a subordinate's 'zone of indifference.' Which orders will a subordinate find acceptable and which not? Barnard asserted that the greater the inducements offered to the subordinate, the wider the range of directive that subordinate will find acceptable. In line with this, Hornstein (1986) found that even among corporate officials, acceptance of one's boss's authority is both the norm and also a product of financial pressures. Thus, a given employee's likelihood of behaving in accordance with organizational scripts may be quite high indeed, reducing only when normative behavior or personal finances permit.

Importantly, in organizations obedience to authority is seen as a good, in that it enables predictable role performance and continued organizational thriving. The dark side of authority is evident in the following organizational tale told by Brief (1998), which demonstrates how an organization's hierarchy can produce discrimination without explicitly invoking employee prejudice.

In late 1992, Shoney's agreed to pay $132.5 million in response to allegations that the restaurant company discriminated against its Black employees. Only 1.8 percent of Shoney's restaurant managers were Black, and 75 percent of its Black restaurant employees held jobs in three low-paying, non-customer-contact positions (e.g., dishwasher). A former vice president of the company stated that the firm's discriminatory practices were the result of the Chief Executive Officer's (CEO's) unwritten policy that 'Blacks should not be employed in any position where they would be seen by [white] customers' (Watkins, 1993: 424). At lower levels of the organization, such analyses by the CEO translated into some managers feeling they needed to 'lighten-up: their restaurants – a company euphemism for reducing the number of Black employees – and to hire 'attractive White girls' instead (p. 424). Shoney's CEO reasoned that a restaurant's performance was affected positively if the racial makeup of the unit's customer contact personnel *matched* the customer population served. In other words, the CEO implicitly instructed units serving White customer populations to employ White customer contact personnel. This reasoning, prioritizing an ostensibly bottom-line objective, may appear plausible and even non-prejudicial.

It is probably naïve to believe that if an organization uses a matching rule to exclude Blacks, the use of the same sort of rule to include Blacks is precluded. For example, using the same business logic as Shoney's CEO, the former president of Avon Corporation concluded that his company's inner-city markets became significantly more profitable when additional Black and Hispanic personnel were placed in them (Cox & Blake, 1991). According to the president, this was because newly placed personnel were uniquely qualified to understand certain aspects of the world-view of the minority populations in the inner city. Although the staffing consequences of the two forms of the rule are different, they both rest on the same business logic – racial matching enhances organizational effectiveness.

The idea of a business justification to discriminate, at first glance, may seem farfetched. It is not. Prior to the civil rights movement, these justifications were explicitly part of management education. Take, for instance, the lessons taught by Barnard (1938). He stated that some employees cannot be advanced and may be terminated because '... they "do not fit" where there is no question of formal competence. This question of "fitness" involves such matters as education, experience, age, sex, personal distinctions, prestige, race' (p. 224). More than three decades after the publication of Barnard's advice to executives, a Black manager wrote, 'I believe that many of the problems I

encountered were of fit ... I was out of the "place" normally filled by Black people in the company' (Jones, 1973: 114).

Taken together, business justifications to discriminate occur when one advocates racially matching customers and employees (as was done by Shoney's CEO) and when one advocates person-organization fit regarding race (as was done by Barnard). The latter matching rule warrants further discussion because of their potential prevalence in practice. This stems from the increasing attention person-organization fit ideas are getting in the practice literature (e.g. Bowen, Ledford, & Nathan, 1991; Kristof-Brown, Zimmerman, & Johnson, 2005) and from research findings indicating that organizations do select people like those already in place (e.g., Schneider, 1987). Obviously, fit is not inevitably connected to race, but too often race serves as a proxy for other characteristics such as attitudes, personality and/or values. Thus, concerns about fit could too easily translate into a concern for race – one that constitutes a plausible, non-prejudicial business justification to discriminate.

The potential for unfair discrimination is demonstrated empirically in a series of experiments that replicated the strong situation of Shoney's (Brief, Dietz, Cohen, et al., 2000). Participants were randomly informed or not that their boss thought it was important to hire a White candidate for an open position because 'the vast majority of the workforce is White' and 'the fine relationship we have with our people' should not be jeopardized. Participants receiving a business justification to discriminate against Black job candidates tended to do so, independent of their attitudes toward Blacks. Again, even in the absence of individual bias, organizations (as strong situations) elicit discrimination through the authoritative power of discriminatory scripts.

In sum, the organizations in which people earn their livelihoods are, by their very nature and by necessity, powerful shapers of behavior. They are contexts in which free will is operating but under very constrained circumstances (Solomon, 2003).

STEREOTYPES AND PREJUDICES IN AND AROUND ORGANIZATIONS

While the organization is a strong situation and therefore a powerful determinant of behavior, individual attitudes and beliefs drive behavior as well. Referring back to the Brief et al. (2000) experiments, an interactive effect of a business justification to discriminate and participants' modern racism was detected consistently. In line with theory (McConahay, 1986) no main effect for modern racism was expected or observed because modern racists behave consistently with their negative racial attitudes only if they are embedded in 'a context in which there is a plausible, non-prejudiced explanation available for what might be considered prejudiced behavior ...' (McConahay, 1986: 100). The beast of modern racism was released in the experiments by a business justification supplied by a boss (see Brief, Buttram, Elliot, et al., 1995; Petersen & Deitz, 2002). In the current section, we explore how individual stereotypes and prejudices arise and play out in organizational contexts.

Stereotypes are particularly troublesome in those organizations where human resource management (HRM) policies, procedures, and practices allow individual managers a great deal of discretion, providing little in the way of written guidelines or effective oversight (American Psychological Association, 1991; Bielby, 2000; Mittman, 1992; also, see Brown, 1982; Edelman & Petterson, 1999; Glasser, 1988; Holzer, 1998; Konrad & Linnehan, 1995; Leonard, 1984). Such a loose HRM system (i.e., one that permits much personal discretion in personal decision making roles) can result in personnel decisions driven by personal beliefs and biases (e.g., Braddock & McPartland, 1987; Reskin, 1998). Managers who make such ascriptions tend to disregard inconsistent information and lower their expectations for members of the negatively stereotyped group (e.g., Foschi, Lai, & Sigerson,1994; Heilman, 1984; Nieva and Gutek, 1980), resulting in racial differentials in performance evaluations (e.g., Greenhaus, Parasuraman, & Wormley,

1990; Kraiger & Ford, 1985; Roberson & Block, 2001). Additionally, it is known that bias in perceptions can result in self-fulfilling prophecies where, for example, managers unknowingly elicit confirmatory behaviors from members of the stigmatized group (Operario & Fiske, 2001; Word, Zanna, & Cooper, 1974).

Assuming our previous emphasis on organizations as strong situations has merit, then we must examine some of the ways negative beliefs about, and attitudes toward, out-groups may be driven and justified by organizations. Eagly and her colleagues have shown that stereotypes emerge as explanations (or justifications) for existing divisions of labor (e.g., Eagly, 1995; Eagly & Steffen, 1986; also see Bayton, McAlister, & Hamer, 1956; Hoffman & Hurst, 1990; Jost & Banaji, 1994; Skrypnek & Snyder, 1982). Highly skewed race or sex composition in labor markets is likely to activate stereotypes automatically (e.g., Heilman, 1995) and without the observers awareness (e.g., Fiske, 1998). Thus, personnel decision-makers and others observing a paucity of Blacks in an occupation may evoke a stereotype that justifies the extant representation, and further, acting on that stereotype may lead to decisions that perpetuate this under-representation.

Regrettably, that structure in the United States is problematic for Blacks. Too often Blacks are under-represented in occupations characterized by high skill and wage levels and over-represented in less demanding and lucrative ones. For example, while Blacks comprise 10.8 percent of the total civilian labor force in the United States, they make up only 5.1 percent of engineers and architects, 4.7 percent of lawyers, and 5.3 percent of physicians; alternatively, Blacks comprise 32.5 percent of nursing aids, orderlies, and attendants; 20.1 percent of maids and housekeepers; and, 26.3 percent of mail clerks (except postal service) (US Bureau of Labor Statistics, 2006b). Thus, a vicious cycle may exist: Social structure, in the form of occupational roles, could elicit negative stereotypes about Blacks, which if acted upon by personnel decision-makers (consciously or unconsciously), would serve to maintain the existing social structure.

Thus, negative stereotypes may surface in work organizations as businesses justifications and as explanations for observed occupational structures. These and other accounts illustrate forms of prejudice analogous to a virus that has mutated (Dovidio & Gaertner, 1986). Old-fashioned or blatant racism is dying in the United States and being replaced by a subtle, indirect, and rationalizable type of bigotry (e.g., Gaertner & Dovidio, 1986; Katz & Haas, 1988: Kinder & Sears, 1981; McConahay, 1986). Moreover, those infected with such a virus may not know they are ill (e.g., Banaji, Nosek & Greenwald, 2004; Gaertner & Dovidio, 1986; Greenwald & Banaji, 1995; Wilson , Lindsey & Schooler, 2000; but see Arkes & Tetlock, 2004). Using the implicit association test (IAT; Greenwald, McGhee & Schwartz, 1998), researchers have shown that individuals can be unconsciously prejudiced against certain groups and that these silent biases outside of one's awareness may drive their beliefs and behaviors. Although this perspective is contested (for a review, see Tetlock & Mitchell, forthcoming; but also see Jost, Rudman, Blair, Carney, Dasgupta, Glaser & Hardin, forthcoming), it has been applied to workplace fairness and equal opportunity policy conversations where it is argued that due to individuals' unconscious (and presumably, uncontrolled) biases, organizations should rely upon administrative controls to check otherwise unmitigated individual bias (e.g., Kang & Banaji, 2006; see also Mitchell & Tetlock, 2006 for a review). This notion of implicit biases may appear to undermine the social constructionist paradigm advanced here (i.e., the influence of strong situations on individual behavior). However, while we believe implicit associations are at play in the minds of some organizational decision makers, we recognize other potentially important contextual factors (e.g., accountability to EEO policies, individuating bias-reducing information present in face-to-face intergroup interactions, and personal and social imperatives to reduce the bias – behavior relationship) should also play

a role. Thus our position is best construed as one characterized by a person-by-situation interaction (e.g., Elgar & Magnuss, 1976).

We shall return to this issue in a later section. For now, the role of implicit attitudes and their potential effects are acknowledged as one of the host of influences on biased behavior. Moving forward, organizations, because of their hierarchical nature, can be thought of as psychologically strong situations capable of releasing the beast of modern forms of prejudice and enabling unfair discrimination (Brief, Dietz, Cohen, et al., 2000; also see Ziegert & Hanges, 2005). In the next section, we examine the potential for these strong situations to inhibit discrimination.

REDUCING UNFAIR DISCRIMINATION IN ORGANIZATIONS

Given that organizations are strong situations which can serve to perpetuate racial discrimination due to obedience to authority and individual's 'excess baggage' of racial stereotypes and prejudice, is it inevitable that White majority organizations discriminate against their Black members or potential members? The answer is 'no.' While the picture appears bleak, organizations can, and have, combated racism within their ranks. Given our discussion of organizations as hierarchical structures where obedience to authority and shared culture provide a strong situation to determine behavior, it is unlikely that grassroots efforts to diminish racism can prevail in organizations. The impetus for change must come from the top. Thus, the leadership must view the amelioration of racism as an organizational imperative.

From leadership's perspective there can be many reasons for doing so including, but not limited to, avoiding costly and embarrassing litigation stemming from reported discrimination, maintaining a positive reputation for recruitment and business interests, and some leaders may attempt to attack racism because they feel it is a moral imperative. Once a top-down strategic decision has been made to get rid of racism, there are several tactics that organizations use to do so. The two most comprehensive strategies for changing an organization's racism script, affirmative action and diversity management programs, are discussed briefly below.

Affirmative action programs

A great deal has been written about the effectiveness of affirmative action (AA) programs in terms of combating discrimination (for an extensive reviews see Harper & Reskin, 2005; Kravitz, Harrison, Turner, et al., 1997). Empowered by Title VII of the CRA, AA applies to all employers with 50 or more employees and $50,000 or more in contracts and specifies that they must engage in 'affirmative action' to actively prevent discrimination through the use of targeted recruitment, selection and advancement programs (for detailed reviews of affirmative action program guidelines, see Kravitz, Harrison, Turner, et al., 1997). Importantly, AA programs can only go as far as considering demographics as a qualification in addition to merit, a practice referred to as 'weak preferential treatment.' Any 'strong preferential treatment,' entailing little or no merit consideration, is illegal. Unfortunately, popular opinion often misses this important detail. Instead, the common assumption is that AA means race or gender over merit considerations resulting in the en masse hiring of unqualified minorities and women. This inaccurate perception of AA leads to a host of unintended consequences, some of which we discuss below.

A consistent result in research on affirmative action is that those who do not benefit from it find it unfair (Crosby, Iyer, Clayton, et al., 2003). Much of this research supports the notion that affirmative action leads to negative attitudes about those who benefit, fostering a 'stigma of incompetence' (Heilman & Haynes, 2005). A stigma of incompetence refers to non-beneficiaries' prejudiced beliefs that those who benefit from affirmative action are not worthy on their own merit. (For a full review, see Heilman &

Haynes, 2005.) This stigma also directly diminishes beneficiaries' self-appraisals, lowering self-efficacy and performance (Carter, 1991; Heilman, Battle, Keller et al., 1998, 1991; Heilman & Alcott, 2001). This is most likely to occur when beneficiaries believe they were selected based on group membership rather than merit (see Crosby, Iyer, Clayton, et al., 2003 for a review).

While it is widely acknowledged that women and minorities are generally better off in today's labor market than they were prior to 1965 (Leonard, 1984; Reskin, 1998), there is still a great deal of debate about the extent to which affirmative action programs combat employment discrimination (cf. Crosby & VanDeVeer, 2000). This ambiguity is due to the fact that AA programs are aimed at getting traditionally under-represented group members into positions, but are not concerned with their development and success. Affirmative action fails to address more subtle, ongoing forms of discrimination that occur once someone joins an organization (Cleveland, Vescio, & Barnes-Farrell, 2005). Such neglect may be one reason why organizations and organizational scholars have switched their focus from affirmative action to diversity management programs.

Diversity management programs

Beginning in the late 1980s, 'diversity' became a watchword in many organizations. For example, it was reported that 79 percent of organizations had some form of diversity program in place (Esen, 2005). Conceptually, diversity programs differ from affirmative action programs along several dimensions (Thomas, 1992). First, diversity programs tend to consider diversity in broader terms than race and sex, addressing differences in age, nationality, functional area, union status, etc. (Thomas, 1992). Second, diversity programs go beyond concern with numbers, to focus on ensuring that (a) everyone can achieve their potential, (b) diverse points of view are heard and used, and (c) working toward common ends is the norm. Third, diversity programs typically address the causes of discrimination. Effective programs would begin by honestly evaluating the current and historical scripts for dealing with diversity issues, and then use this information to develop diversity program efforts (Jackson & Associates, 1992). Finally, while AA programs are meant to be temporary measures until there is appropriate numerical representation of protected groups, diversity management is considered an ongoing process (Thomas, 1992).

The extent to which organizations actually develop and use programs with all of the above features is unclear. What is clear is that this new diversity management focus in both the corporate and academic worlds is primarily interested in diversity's effects on organizational performance variables. With this spotlight on harnessing the productive capacity of diversity, something has been gained and something has been lost. What has been gained is that there is now concern for what happens inside the organization with respect to the treatment of people who have been traditionally under-represented. What has been lost is the focus on discrimination. Managing diversity is not the same as eliminating discrimination. Diversity initiatives, of the best kind, focus on creating a healthy, inclusive, and well performing organizational workforce (Cox, 1993; Thomas, 1992). It might be assumed that in order to achieve the intended goals of an 'ideal' diversity management program, discrimination must be eliminated. However, there are several reasons why discrimination, per se, may not be addressed by diversity programs.

First, most organizations cite business reasons as the impetus for having diversity programs (Kulik & Roberson, 2008) which makes business outcomes the bottom line for supporting and retaining diversity initiatives. If an organization does find that having racially diverse work groups leads to more conflict, poorer morale, and more turnover (as indicated in some studies; e.g., Kochan, Bezrukova, Ely, et al., 2003) – the business case for promoting diversity flies out the window (Hansen, 2003), which could then lead organizations to become increasingly less

concerned with diversity. A second reason why diversity programs may not address discrimination is that they often take the form of retooled affirmative action programs: focusing on increasing representation, but ignoring issues of organization culture and interpersonal treatment. Therefore, we are back to the same problem of relying solely on AA programs to eliminate discrimination. In fact, the situation may even be worse: Ely and Thomas (2001) demonstrated that when diversity programs were implemented solely to address discrimination, rather than to aid in organizational learning and development, more discrimination seemed to result.

Taken together, the above evidence indicates that diversity management programs that focus on the bottom line value of diversity to an organization are evaluated in those terms. Thus, the value of a given diversity initiative is no longer based upon how well it protects rights, but is based instead on immediate organizational benefits. Some have taken notice of this trend and have begun to enact diversity management programs that attempt to change the work environment through organizational development and learning. For example, Ely and Meyerson (2000) presented research on a diversity program based on gradual change through an iterative process of developing organizational scripts that establish equality, rather than the status quo, as a norm. Meyerson and Fletcher (2000) reported that implementations of this framework have yielded 'small wins,' or incremental successes, that have slowly changed organizational cultures to more inclusive and rewarding environments for all.

CONCLUDING THOUGHTS

In the pursuit of the causes of unfair discrimination, social psychologists have investigated the phenomenon largely in the confines of the laboratory, while organizational scholars have focused on documenting its existence in organizations. Perhaps these different orientations might be explained by differences in interest between theory building and solving real world problems. We hope not. Social psychologists and organizational scholars should both be interested in the construction and application of theories aimed at solving social problems in the contexts in which they occur.

In addressing this united research agenda, a number of methodological alternatives surface. For example, theoretically salient features of organizations can be brought into the laboratory (Weick, 1965). Regrettably, we too infrequently have observed this strategy in either the social psychological or organizational literatures. Similarly, in the field we have too heavily focused on correlational studies, to the exclusion of true or quasi-experiments, longitudinal investigations, or qualitative studies. Such myopic methodology restricts our potential contribution to merely documenting the existence of bias, rather than the causes or solutions.

Clearly, if context is taken seriously, there is a need to broaden the ways in which unfair workplace discrimination is studied, however, doing so will not be easy. For instance, we lack experience in meaningfully bringing organizational features into the laboratory and in gauging implicit attitudes in organizational settings. The literature on organizational social psychology would be significantly broadened if organizational and psychological scientists took an interdisciplinary perspective on studying the individual as well as contextual antecedents, processes, and consequences of discrimination.

Our current biases in pursuing the causes of unfair discrimination lead us to want to focus on implicit attitudes and the automaticity of behaviors in organizational context characterized as strong situations. In those contexts, we would not want to see neglected the roles of other organizationally salient psychological variables such as stereotypes construed in emotional terms (e.g., Fiske et al., 2002) and system justifications (Jost et al., 2004). It is important to note that many of these psychological and social variables actually suggest different and sometimes opposing realities and outcomes. For example, the implicit association and social constructionist perspectives

come from very different paradigms and as such make different assertions about how bias unfolds in the real world (Tetlock & Mitchell, forthcoming; but also see Jost et al., forthcoming). Recall, however, we advocate an interactionist perspective recognizing that biases and situations work together to produce discrimination.

Implicit in recognizing the potential methodological difficulties that lie in synthesizing organizational and social psychological approaches, is the question of the content or foci of our scholarship. Here, our overwhelming interest has been in pursuing the causes of unfair discrimination. However, attention must focus on *both* the causes of and solutions to unfair discrimination *in organizations*. Successfully enacting this problem-solving focus likely will entail serious consideration of the material needs of organizations and the restraints of the environments in which they are embedded. Those environments contain legal pressures, competitive demands, consumer preferences, labor supplies, and the desires of special interest groups. Without attention to these organizational pressures, theoretical and experimental approaches to solving the problems of unfair discrimination will not wash in realistic contexts. In the spaces between social psychology and organizational studies there is a lot to be learned; but is that not what scholarship is all about?

REFERENCES

Alexis, M. (1998). Assessing 50 years of African-American economic status, 1940–1990. *The American Economic Review, 88*, 368–375. American Psychological Association. (1991). In the Supreme Court of the United States: Price Waterhouse v. Ann B. Hopkins. Amicus Curiae Brief for the American Psychological Association. *American Psychologist, 46*, 1061–1070.

Arendt, H. (1963). *Eichmann in Jerusalem: A report on the banality of evil.* New York: Viking.

Arendt, H. (1978). *The Jew as pariah.* New York: Grove Press.

Arkes, H. R., & Tetlock, P. E. (2004). Attributions of implicit prejudice, or 'Would Jesse Jackson 'fail' the

Implicit Association Test?' *Psychological Inquiry, 15,* 257–278.

Ashforth, B. E., and Mael, F. (1989). Social identity theory and the organization. *Academy of Management Review, 14,* 20–39.

Banaji, M. R., Nosek, B. A., & Greenwald, A. G. (2004). No place for nostalgia in science: A response to Arkes and Tetlock. *Psychological Inquiry, 15,* 279–310.

Barnard, C. I. (1938). *The functions of the executive.* Cambridge, MA: Harvard University Press.

Baron, J. N., & Bielby, W. T. (1980). Bringing the firm back in: Stratification, segmentation, and the organization of work. *American Sociological Review, 45,* 737–765.

Bayton, J. A., McAlister, L. B., & Hamer, J. (1956). Race-class stereotypes. *Journal of Negro Education, 25,* 75–78.

Bendick, M., Jr., Jackson, C. W., & Reinoso, V. A. (1994). Measuring employment discrimination through controlled experiments. *Review of Black Political Economy, 23,* 25–48.

Bertrand, M., & Mullainathan, S. (2004). Are Emily and Brendan more employable than Lakisha and Jamal? A field experiment on labor market discrimination. *The American Economic Review, 94,* 991–1014.

Bielby, W. T. (2000).Minimizing workplace gender and racial bias. *Contemporary Sociology, 29,* 120–129.

Blumer, H. (1960). Race prejudice as group position. *Pacific Sociological Review, 1,* 3–5.

Bobo, L. D., & Suh, S. A. (2000). Surveying racial discrimination: Analyses from a multiethnic labor market (pp. 335–374). In L. D. Bobo, M. L. Oliver, J. H. Johnson, Jr., A. Valnezuela, Jr. (Eds.), *Prismatic metropolis: Inequality in Los Angeles.* New York: Russell Sage Foundation.

Bowen, D. E., Ledford, G. E., & Nathan, B. N. (1991). Hiring for the organization, not the job. *Academy of Management Executive, 5,* 35–51.

Braddock, J. H., III, & McPartland, J. M. (1987). How minorities continue to be excluded from equal employment opportunities: Research on labor market and institutional barriers. *Journal of Social Issues, 43,* 5–39.

Brief, A. P. (1998). *Attitudes in and around organizations.* Thousand Oaks, CA: Sage.

Brief, A. P., Buttram, R. T., Elliott, J. D., Reizenstein, R. M., & McCline, R. L. (1995). Releasing the beast: A study of compliance with orders to use race as a selection criterion. *Journal of Social Issues, 51,* 177–193.

Brief, A. P., Dietz, J., Cohen, R. R., Pugh, S. D., & Vaslow, J. B. (2000). Just doing business: Modern racism and obedience to authority as explanations for employment discrimination. *Organizational Behavior and Human Decision Processes, 81,* 72–97.

Brief, A. P., & Hayes, E. L. (1997).The continuing "American dilemma": Studying racism in organizations. In C. L. Cooper & D. M. Rousseau (Eds.), *Trends in organizational behavior* (Vol. 4, pp. 89–105). New York: John Wiley.

Brief, A. P., Umphress, E. E., Dietz, J., Burrows, J., Butz, R., and Scholten, L. (2005). Community maters: Realistic group conflict theory and the impact of diversity. *Academy of Management Journal, 48,* 830–844.

Brown, C. (1982). The Federal attack on labor market discrimination: The mouse that roared? In R. Ehrenberg (Ed.), *Research in labor economics* (Vol. 5, pp. 33–68). Greenwich, CT: JAI.

Carter, S. L. (1991). *Reflections of an affirmative action baby.* New York: Basic Books.

Cawley, J., Heckman, J., & Vytlacil, E. (1999). Meritocracy in America: Wages within and across occupations. *Industrial Relations, 38,* 250–296.

Chattopadhyay, P. (1999). Beyond direct and symmetrical effects: The influence of demographic composition and organizational culture on processes and outcomes. *Administrative Science Quarterly, 43,* 749–780.

Cleveland, J. N., Vescio, T. K., & Barnes-Farrell, J. L. (2005). Gender discrimination in organizations. In R. L. Dipboye, & A. Colella (Eds.), *Discrimination at work: The psychological and organizational bases* (pp. 149–176). Mahwah, NJ: Lawrence Erlbaum Associates.

Cohen, P. N. (2001). Race, class, and labor markets: The White working class and racial composition of U.S. metropolitan areas. *Social Forces, 77,* 207–229.

Collins, S. M. (1989). The marginalization of Black executives. *Social Problems, 36,* 369–381.

Collins, S. M. (1997). Black mobility in White corporations: Up the corporate ladder but out on a limb. *Social Problems, 44,* 55–67.

Couch, K., & Daly, M. C. (2002). Black – White wage inequality in the 1990's: A decade of progress. *Economic Inquiry, 40,* 31–41.

Cox, T., Jr. (1993). *Cultural diversity in organizations. Theory, research, and practice.* San Francisco: Berret-Koehler.

Cox, T., Jr., & Blake, S. (1991). Managing cultural diversity: Implications for organizational competitiveness. *The Executive, 5,* 45–56.

Cox, T., Jr., & Nkomo, S. M. (1986). Differential appraisal criteria based on race of the rate. *Group and Organization Studies, 11,* 101–119.

Crosby, F. J., Iyer, A., Clayton, S., & Downing, R. A. (2003). Affirmative action: Psychological data and the policy debates. *American Psychologist, 58,* 93–115.

Crosby, F. J., & VanDeVeer, C. (Eds.). (2000). *Sex, race, and merit: Debating affirmative action in education and employment.* Ann Arbor: University of Michigan Press.

Deitch, E. A., Barsky, A., Butz, R. M., Brief, A. P., Chan, S. S. Y., & Bradley, J. C. (2003). Subtle yet significant: The existence and impact of everyday racial discrimination in the workplace. *Human Relations, 56,* 1299–1324.

Depret, E., and Fiske, S. T. (1993). Perceiving the powerful: Intriguing individuals versus threatening groups. *Journal of Experimental Social Psychology, 35,* 461–480.

Dovidio, J. F., & Gaertner, S. L. (1986). Prejudice, discrimination, and racism: Historical trends and contemporary approaches. In J. F. Dovidio & S. L. Gaertner (Eds.), *Prejudice, discrimination, and racism* (pp.1–34). Orlando, FL: Academic Press.

DiTomaso, N., Post, C., & Parks-Yancey, R. (2007). Workforce diversity and inequality: Power, status, and numbers. *Annual Review of Sociology, 33,* 473–501.

Dubin, R. (1987). *The world of work.* New York: Garland Publishing Inc. (Original work published 1958).

Eagly, A. H. (1995). The Science and politics of comparing women and men. *American Psyhologist, 50,* 145–158.

Eagly, A. H., & Steffen, V. J. (1986). Gender stereotypes, occupational roles, and beliefs about part-time employees. *Psychology of Women Quarterly, 10,* 252–262.

Edelman, L. B., & Petterson, S. M. (1999). Symbols and substance in organizational response to civil rights law. *Research in Social Stratification and Mobility, 17,* 107–135.

Elliott, J. R. (2001). Referral hiring and ethnically homogeneous jobs: How prevalent is the connection and for whom? *Social Science Research, 30,* 401–425.

Ely, R. J., & Meyerson, D. (2000). Theories of gender in organizations: A new approach to organizational analysis and change. *Research in Organizational Behavior, 22,* 103–151.

Ely, R. J., & Thomas, D. A. (2001). Cultural diversity at work: The effects of diversity perspectives on work group process and outcomes. *Administrative Science Quarterly, 46,* 229–273.

Esen, E. (2005). *2005 workplace diversity practices survey report.* Alexandria, VA: Society for Human Resource Management.

Essed, P. (1991). *Understanding everyday racism.* Newbury Park, CA: Sage.

Feagin, J. (2000). *Racist America: Roots, current realities, future reparations.* New York: Routledge.

Fiske, S. T. (1998). Stereotyping, prejudice, and discrimination. In D. T. Gilbert, S. T. Fiske, & G. Lindzey (Eds.), *The handbook of social psychology* (Vol. 2, pp. 357–411). New York: McGraw-Hill.

Fiske, S. T., Cuddy, A. J. C., Glick, P., and Xu, J. (2002). A model of (often mixed) stereotype content: Competence and warmth respectively followed from perceived status and competition. *Journal of Personality and Social Psychology, 82,* 878–902.

Forman, T. A. (2003). The social psychological costs of racial segmentation in the workplace: A study of African Americans' well-being. *Journal of Health and Social Behavior, 44,* 332–352.

Foschi, M., Lai, L., & Sigerson, K. (1994). Gender and double standards in the assessment of job applicants. *Social Psychology Quarterly, 57,* 326–339.

Fossett, M. A., & Kiecolt, K. J. (1989). The relative size of minority populations and White racial attitudes. *Social Science Quarterly, 70,* 820–835.

French Jr., J. R. P., and Raven, B. (1959). The bases of social power. In D. Cartwright (Ed.) *Studies in Social Power* (pp. 150–167). Oxford: University of Michigan.

Gaertner, S. L., & Dovidio, J. F. (1986). The aversive form of racism. In J. F. Dovidio & S. L. Gaertner (Eds.), *Prejudice, discrimination, and racism* (pp. 61–89). San Diego: Academic Press.

Gill, A. (1989). The role of discrimination in determining occupational structure. *Industrial and labor Relations Review, 42,* 610–623.

Glasser, I. (1988). Affirmative action and the legacy of racial injustice. In P. A. Katz & D. A. Taylor (Eds.), *Eliminating racism: Profiles in controversy* (pp. 341–357). New York: Plenum.

Goffman, E. (1967). *Interaction ritual: Essays on face-to-face interaction.* Oxford: Aldine.

Greenhaus, J. H., Parasuraman, S., & Wormley, W. M. (1990). Effects of race on organizational experiences, job performance evaluations, and career outcomes. *Academy of Management Journal, 33,* 64–86.

Greenwald, A. G., & Banaji, M. R. (1995). Implicit social cognition: Attitudes, self-esteem, and stereotypes. *Psychological Review, 102,* 4–27.

Greenwald, A. G., McGhee, D. E., & Schwartz, J. L. K. (1998). Measuring individual differences in implicit cognition: The implicit association test. *Journal of Personality and Social Psychology, 74,* 1464–1480.

Hansen, F. (2003, April). Diversity's business case: Doesn't add up. *Workforce, 82,* 28–33.

Harper, S., & Reskin, B. (2005). Affirmative action at school and on the job. *Annual Review of Sociology, 31,* 357–380.

Heckman, J. J. (1998).Detecting discrimination. *Journal of Economic Perspectives, 12,* 101–116.

Heilman, M. E. (1984). Information as a deterrent against sex discrimination: the effects of applicant sex and information type on preliminary employment decisions. *Organizational Behavior and Human Decision Processes, 33*, 174–186.

Heilman, M. E. (1995). Sex stereotypes and their effects in the workplace: What we know and what we don't know. *Journal of Social Behavior and Personality, 10*, 3–26.

Heilman, M. E., & Alcott, V. B. (2001). What I think you think of me: Women's reactions to being viewed as beneficiaries of preferential selection. *Journal of Applied Psychology, 86*, 574–582.

Heilman, M. E., Battle, W. S., Keller, C. E., & Lee, R. A. (1998). Type of affirmative action policy: A determinant of reactions to sex-based preferential selection? *Journal of Applied Psychology, 83*, 190–205.

Heilman, M. E., & Haynes, M. C. (2005).Combating organizational discrimination: Some unintended consequences. In R. L. Dipboye & A. Colella (Eds.), *Discrimination at work: The psychological and organizational bases* (pp. 353–377). Mahwah, NJ: Lawrence Erlbaum Associates.

Heilman, M. E., Rivero, J., & Brett, J. (1991). Skirting the competence issue: Effects of sex-based preferential selection on task choices of women and men. *Journal of Applied Psychology, 76*, 99–105.

Hoffman, C., & Hurst, N. (1990). Gender stereotypes: Perception or rationalization? *Journal of Personality and Social Psychology, 58*, 197–208.

Holzer, H. J. (1998). Employer skill demands and labor market outcomes of Blacks and women. *Industrial and labor Relations Review, 52*, 82–98.

Hornstein, H. A. (1986). When corporate courage counts. *Psychology Today, 20*, 56–60.

Jackson, S. E. & Associates. (1992). *Diversity in the workplace*. New York: Guilford Press.

Jones, E. W. (1973). What it's like to be a Black manager. *Harvard Business Review, 51*, 114.

Jost, J. T., & Banaji, M. R. (1994). The role of stereotyping in system-justification and the production of false consciousness. *British Journal of Social Psychology, 33*, 1–27.

Jost, J. T., Banaji, M. R., & Nosek, B. A. (2004). A decade of system justification theory: Accumulated evidence of conscious and unconscious bolstering of the status quo. *Political Psychology, 25*, 881–920.

Jost, J. T., Rudman, L. A., Blair, I. V., Carney, D. R., Dasgupta, N., Glaser, J., & Hardin, C. D. (2009). The existence of implicit bias is beyond reasonable doubt: A refutation of ideological and methodological objections and executive summary of ten studies that no manager should ignore. *Research in Organizational Behavior, 29,* 39–69.

Kang, J., & Banaji, M. R. (2006). Fair measures: A behavioral realist revision of 'Affirmative Action'. *California Law Review, 94*, 1063–1118.

Kanter, R. M. (1977). *Men and women of the corporation*. New York: Basic Books.

Katz, D. (1964). The motivational basis of organizational behavior. *Behavioral Science, 9*, 131–146.

Katz, I., & Haas, R. G. (1988). Racial ambivalence and American value conflict: Correlational and priming studies of dual cognitive structures. *Journal of Personality and Social Psychology, 55*, 893–905.

Kinder, D. R., & Sears, D. O. (1981). Prejudice and politics: Symbolic racism versus racial threats to the good life. *Journal of Personality and Social Psychology, 40*, 414–431.

Kirschenman, J., & Neckerman, K. M. (1991). We'd love to hire them, but ..." The meaning of race for employers. In C. Jencks & P. E. Peterson (Eds.), *The Urban Underclass* (pp. 103–134). Washington, DC: Brooking Institutions Press.

Kochan, T., Bezrukova, K., Ely, R., Jackson, S., Aparna, J., Jehn, K., et al. (2003). The effects of diversity on business performance: Report of the diversity research network. *Human Resource Management, 42*, 3–21.

Konrad, A. M., & Linnehan, F. (1995). Formalized HRM structures: Coordinating equal employment opportunity or concealing organizational practices? *Academy of Management Journal, 38*, 787–820.

Kraiger, K., & Ford, J. K. (1985). A meta-analysis of rate race effects in performance ratings. *Journal of Applied Psychology, 70*, 56–65.

Kravitz, D. A., Harrison, D. A., Turner, M. E., Levine, E. L., Chaves, W., Brannick, M. T., et al. (1997). Affirmative action: A review of psychological and behavioral research. *Bowling Green, OH: Society for Industrial and Organizational Psychology.*

Kristof-Brown, A. L., Zimmerman, R. D., & Johnson, E. C. (2005). Consequences of individuals' fit at work: A meta-analysis of person-job, person-organization, person-group, and person-supervisor fit. *Personnel Psychology, 58*, 281–343.

Kulik, C. T., & Roberson, L. (2008). Diversity initiative effectiveness: What organizations can (and cannot) expect from diversity recruitment, diversity training, and formal mentoring programs. In A. P. Brief (Ed.), *Diversity at work*. Cambridge: Cambridge University Press.

Lefkowitz, J. (1994). Race as a factor in job placement: Serendipitous findings of "ethnic drift." *Personnel Psychology, 47*, 497–513.

Leonard, J. S. (1984). Employment and occupations advance under affirmative action. *Review of Economics and Statistics, 66*, 377–385.

Mannix, E., & Neale, M. A. (2005). What differences make a difference? The promise and reality of diverse teams in organizations. *Psychological Science in the Public Interest, 6*, 31–55.

Martell, R. F., Lane, D. M., & Emrich, C. (1996). Male-female differences: A computer simulation. *American Psychologist, 51*, 157–158.

McConahay, J. B. (1986). Modern racism, ambivalence, and the modern racism scale. In J. F. Dovidio & S. L. Gaertner (Eds.), *Prejudice, discrimination, and racism* (pp. 91–125). Orlando, FL: Academic Press.

Meyerson, D. E., & Fletcher, J. K., (2000). A modest manifesto for shattering the glass ceiling. *Harvard Business Review, Jan.-Feb.*, 126–136.

Milgram, S. (1974). *Obedience to authority: An experimental view.* New York: Harper & Row.

Mincy, R. B. (1993). The Urban Institute audit studies: their research and policy context. In M. Fix., & R. J. Struyk. (Eds.), *Clear and convincing evidence: Measurement of discrimination in America* (pp. 165–186). Washington, DC: The Urban Institute Press.

Mincy, R. B., Lewis, C. E., Jr., & Han, W. (2006). Left behind: Less-educated young Black men in the economic boom of the 1990's. In R. B. Mincy (Ed.), *Black males left behind.* Washington DC: The Urban Institute Press.

Mischel, W. (1973). Toward a cognitive social learning reconceptualization of personality. *Psychological Review, 80*, 252–283.

Mitchell, G., & Tetlock, P. E. (2006). Antidiscrimination law and the perils of mindreading. *Ohio State Law Journal, 67*, 1023–1121.

Mitra, A. (1999). The allocation of Blacks in large firms and establishments and Black – White wage inequality in the U.S. economy. *Sociological Inquiry, 69*, 382–403.

Mittman, B. S. (1992). Theoretical and methodological issues in the study of organizational demography and demographic change. *Research in the Sociology of Organizations, 10*, 3–53.

Mueller, C. W., Finley, A., Iverson, R. D., & Price, J. L. (1999). The effects of group racial composition on job satisfaction, organizational commitment, and career commitment: The case of teachers. *Work and Occupations, 26*, 187–219.

Mueller, C. W., Parcel, T. L., & Kazuko, T. (1989). Particularism in authority outcomes of Black and White supervisors. *Social Science Research, 18*, 1–20.

Neumark, D. (1999).Wage differentials by race and sex: The roles of taste discrimination and labor market information. *Industrial Relations, 38*, 414–445.

Nieva, V. F., & Gutek, B. A. (1980). Sex effects on evaluation. *Academy of Management Review, 5*, 267–276.

Operario, D. & Fiske, S. T. (2001). Causes and consequences of stereotypes in organizations. In M. London (Ed.), *How people evaluate others in organizations: Applied Research in Psychology.*

Office of Federal Contract Compliance Programs Guidelines – Revised Order No. 4 (pp. 45–62). Mahwah, NJ: Lawrence Erlbaum Associates.

Pager, D., & Quillian, L. (2005). Walking the talk? What employers say versus what they do. *American Sociological Review, 70*, 355–380.

Petersen, L. E., & Dietz, J. (2002). Social discrimination in a personnel selection context: The effects of an authority's instruction to discriminate and followers' authoritarianism. *Journal of Applied Social Psychology, 30*, 206–220.

Pfeffer, J. (1998). Understanding organizations: Concepts and controversies. In D. T. Gilbert, S. T. Fiske, & G. Lindzey (Eds.). *The handbook of social psychology*, Vol. 2 (4th ed., pp. 733–777). New York: McGraw-Hill.

Reskin, B. F. (1998). *The realities of affirmative action in employment.* Washington, DC: American Sociological Association.

Reskin, B. F., & McBrier, D. B. (2000). Why not ascription? Organizations' employment of male and female managers. *American Sociological Review, 65*, 210–233.

Reskin, B., McBrier, D. B., & Kmec, J. A. (1999). The determinants and consequences of workplace sex and race composition. *Annual Review of Sociology, 25*, 335–361.

Riordan, C. M. (2000). Relational demography within groups: Past developments, contradictions, and new directions. In G. R. Ferris (Ed.), *Research in personnel and human resources management* (Vol. 19, pp. 131–173). Amsterdam: Elsevier Science.

Riordan, C. M., & Shore, L. M. (1997). Demographic diversity and employee attitudes: An empirical examination of relational demography within work units. *Journal of Applied Psychology, 82*, 342–358.

Roberson, L., & Block, C. J. (2001). Racioethnicity and job performance: A review and critique of theoretical perspectives on the causes of group differences. *Research in Organizational Behavior, 23*, 247–326.

Schank, R. C., & Abelson, R. P. (1977). *Scripts, plans, goals, and understanding: An inquiry into human knowledge structures.* Oxford: Lawrence Erlbaum.

Schneider, B. (1987). The people make the place. *Personnel Psychology, 40*, 437–453.

Scott, W. R. (1992). *Organizations: Rational, natural, and open systems.* Upper Saddle River, NJ: Prentice-Hall.

Sidanius, J., & Pratto, F., (1999). *Social dominance: An intergroup theory of social hierarchy and oppression.* Cambridge, MA: Cambridge University Press.

Simon, H. A. (1945). *Administrative behavior.* New York: The Free Press.

Simon, H. (1951). A formal theory of the employment relationship. *Econometrica, 19*, 293–305.

Skrypnek, B. J., & Snyder, M. (1982). On the self-perpetuating nature of stereotypes about women and men. *Journal of Experimental Social Psychology, 18*, 277–291.

Smith, R. A., & Elliott, J. R. (2002). Does ethnic concentration influence access to authority? An examination of contemporary urban labor markets. *Social Forces, 81*, 255–279.

Solomon, R. C. (2003). *Not passion's slave: Emotions and choice.* New York: Oxford University Press.

Tetlock, P. E., & Mitchell, G. (2008). Calibrating prejudice in milliseconds. *Social Psychological Quarterly, 71*, 12–16.

Tetlock, P. E., & Mitchell, G. (2009). Unconscious prejudice and accountability systems: What must organizations do to prevent discrimination? *Research in Organizational Behavior, 29*, 3–38.

The Urban Institute (2003, April 29). *Affirmative action: Is it still needed?* Retrieved May 15, 2006, from http://www.urban.org/url.cfm?ID=900617

Thomas, R. R. (1992). Managing diversity: A conceptual framework. In S. E. Jackson and Associates (Eds.), *Diversity in the workplace* (pp. 306–318). New York: Guilford Press.

Tsui, A. S., Egan, T. D., & O'Reilly, C. A., III. (1992). Being different: Relational demography and organizational attachment. *Administrative Science Quarterly, 37*, 549–579.

Tsui, A. S., & Gutek, B. A., (1999). *Demographic differences in organizations: Current research and future directions.* New York: Lexington Books.

U.S. Bureau of Labor Statistics. (2000). *Working in the 21st century.* Retrieved June 1, 2006 from http://www.bls.gov/opub/home.htm.

U.S. Bureau of Labor Statistics. (2005). *Current Population Survey: Median weekly earnings of full-time wage and salary workers, by sex, race, and Hispanic origin, annual averages, 1986–2000.* Washington, DC: U.S. Government Printing Office.

U.S. Bureau of Labor Statistics. (2006a). *Characteristics of the unemployed: Unemployed persons by marital status, race, Hispanic, or Latino ethnicity, age, and sex.* Retrieved May 15, 2006 from ftp://ftp.bls.gov/pub/special.requests/lf/aat24.txt

U.S. Bureau of Labor Statistics. (2006b). *Employed persons by detailed occupation, sex, race, and Hispanic or Latino ethnicity.* Retrieved May 15, 2006 from ftp://ftp.bls.gov/pub/special.requests/lf/aat11.txt

U.S. Bureau of Labor Statistics. (2006c). *Employed persons by occupation, race, Hispanic, or Latino ethnicity, and sex.* Retrieved May 15, 2006 from http://ftp.bls.gov/pub/special.requests/lf/aat10.txt

U.S. Bureau of Labor Statistics. (2006d). *Median weekly earnings of full-time wage and salary workers by selected characteristics.* Retrieved May 15, 2006 from http://ftp.bls.gov/pub/special.requests/lf/aat37. txt

U.S. Equal Employment Opportunity Commission, Office of Research, Information, and Planning. (2006, April 25). *Special report: Diversity in the finance industry.* Retrieved May 15, 2006 from http://www.eeoc.gov/stats/reports/finance/index.html

Watkins, S. (1993). Racism du jour at Shoney's. *The Nation*, pp. 424–428.

Weick, K. E. (1965). Laboratory experimentation with organizations. In J. G. March (Ed.), *Handbook of organizations* (pp. 194–260). Chicago: Rand, McNally & Company.

Williams, K. Y., & O'Reilly, C. A. (1998). Demography and diversity in organizations: A review of 40 years of research . In B. M. Staw & L. L. Cummings (Eds.), *Research in organizational behavior* (Vol. 20, pp. 77–140). Greenwich, CT: JAI Press.

Wilson, T. D., Lindsey, S., & Schooler, T. Y. (2000). A model of dual attitudes. *Psychological Review, 107*, 101–126.

Word, C. O., Zanna, M. P., & Cooper, J. (1974). The nonverbal mediation of self- fulfilling prophecies in interracial interaction. *Journal of Experimental Social Psychology, 10*, 109–120.

Zald, M. N. (1993). Organization studies as a scientific and humanistic enterprise: Toward a reconceptualization of the foundations of the field. *Organization Science, 4*, 513–528.

Ziegert, J. C., & Hanges, P. J. (2005). Employment discrimination: The role of implicit attitudes, motivation, and a climate for racial bias. *Journal of Applied Psychology, 90*, 553–562.

28

Public Policy

Kristina R. Schmukler, Ana Rasquiza,
Julie Dimmit, and Faye J. Crosby

ABSTRACT

In this chapter we review the social psychological study of bias in relation to public policies related to race, class, and in-group benefit, namely affirmative action, immigration, welfare, and taxation. We start with a brief historical review of the fundamental research in this area. Then we turn to contemporary research, first summarizing the major findings and outlining the primary explanations of the findings. Our review finds that most research examines how bias may affect attitudes toward public policy. We suggest that future research might profit from reversing the causal arrow, in other words, concentrate less on how bias influences people's perceptions of given policies and might look at how given policies influence the formation and expression of bias.

PUBLIC POLICY

In the present chapter, we review the literature on bias and public policy. We start with a brief look at the work of social psychologists who were active in the late 1940s and throughout the 1950s, and mention work undertaken in the 1960s and 1970s concerning intergroup relations and desegregation. After the historical survey, we turn to contemporary research, first summarizing the major findings and then outlining the primary explanations of the findings. In our treatment of the contemporary studies, we privilege the policy of affirmative action because, more than any other contemporary policy, affirmative action has generated a voluminous research literature (for review see: Crosby, Iyer, & Sincharoen, 2006). We also reference the literature on

other public policies, namely immigration, welfare, and taxation policy, to show that the dynamics of affirmative action are not unique. The final section of the chapter suggests that future research might profit from reversing the causal arrow. We look at how new research might concentrate less on how bias influences people's perceptions of given policies and look more at how given policies influence the formation and expression of bias.

HISTORICAL BACKGROUND

Observers of social science history have noted that the social psychological study of bias that is covered in this chapter originated in the United States and dates from the end of World War II (Smith, 1984,

2003). The War prompted scholars to address with new vigor questions of prejudice and inter-group hostility (Allport, 1954). How, scholars wondered, had anti-Semitism flared up so ferociously that, by 1945, six million Jews had been killed in Europe? Hitler's ascendance also provoked the relocation of numerous scholars like Lewin and Adorno to the United States. The transplantation of European sensibilities within the 'can-do' atmosphere of the United States resulted in a flowering of theory and research previously unseen.

One group of researchers, led by Adorno, answered the questions about virulent anti-Semitic bias by proposing that individuals with a certain personality type, namely the authoritarian personality, are both particularly prone to follow the commands of leaders and to be especially suspicious of people who belong to different ethnic or racial groups than themselves (Adorno, Frenkel, Brunswick, et al., 1950). In turn, Adorno's team developed an instrument, known as the F-scale or the Fascism scale (Christie, 1991). Those with high scores on the F-scale were classified as authoritarian and were considered 'pre-fascists.' Some research on the authoritarian personality documented conditions that foster the development of authoritarianism, such as teaching a child to be blindly obedient (Schooler, 1976). Meanwhile, researchers debated the strength of the hypothesized link between authoritarianism, on the one hand, and prejudice and out-group bias, on the other (Lipset & Raab, 1970; see Chapter 2 by Duckitt, this volume).

Implicit in some of the early research on the authoritarian personality was the assumption of national differences (Christie, 1991). The research was comforting to those who were able to believe that their own childhoods had differed from the childhoods of the Nazis. They could imagine that their own backgrounds had spared them from becoming biased and hate-filled. Milgram's (1974) work on obedience put an end to the comfort. Milgram dramatically demonstrated that present circumstances could elicit anti-social behavior even from people with perfectly acceptable

childhoods. Milgram was active in the 1960s, as were a number of other psychologists like Zimbardo, Darley, and Latané who made compelling cases for the importance of situational factors as determinants of behavior (Crosby & Bearman, 2006).

World War II brought about cultural exchanges both within the borders of the United States as well as across international borders. Some units of the armed forces were integrated during the war, and the federal government increased its efforts to bring about greater racial integration in American society than had been present prior to the war (Stouffer, Suchman, DeVinney, et al., 1949). Even as ethnic discrimination continued, Americans increasingly embraced the ideal of racial equity (Myrdal, 1944), and social psychologists began to study in earnest what happened when individuals from different groups were brought together. Deutsch and Collins (1951) found that propinquity increased liking, even across ethnic lines. Allport (1954) enumerated the conditions – such as voluntary rather than forced contact, equal status, and non-competition over resources likely to amplify the positive effects of inter-group contact.

Meanwhile, the Clarks and their colleagues examined the effects of segregation on the self-images of Black children (Pettigrew, 2004). In their famous doll studies, the Clarks demonstrated that Black children identified the white doll as the one they wished to play with and as the one valued in society, even as they recognized that they themselves resembled the black doll. Research by the Clarks and other psychologists associated with the Society for the Psychological Study of Social Issues (SPSSI) was cited in footnote 11 of the unanimous 1954 decision of the Supreme Court in the case of *Brown v The Board of Education of Topeka, Kansas*, which decided that segregated schools violated the equal protection clause of the fourteenth amendment of the constitution (Smith & Crosby, 2008). The reference to social scientific findings in footnote 11 constituted the first time that the Court ever referenced research in the social sciences within a decision.

Any joy the Clarks and colleagues felt about having exerted a positive influence on desegregation policy was short-lived however, for, in the 1955 decision known as *Brown II*, the Court decided to ignore Kenneth Clark's fervent plea that the Court set expectations about the dates by which school systems should achieve various benchmarks of desegregation (Smith & Crosby, 2008). Instead of providing guidelines (let alone mandates) for change, the Court in *Brown II* emphasized states' rights over federal rights and merely suggested that schools proceed with deliberate speed, devising whatever individual systems they thought best. Not surprisingly, desegregation proceeded extremely unevenly (Orfield & Eaton, 1996; Pettigrew, 2004; Pettigrew & Green, 1976).

During the 1960s and 1970s, many American social scientists continued to study race relations. The Civil Rights Movement was in full swing during the 1960s, although as the famous Kerner Report noted, the United States was hardly living up to its ideology of equal treatment for all citizens (National Advisory Commission on Civil Disorders, 1968). Two topics were of particular interest to social psychologists: (a) White resistance to integration (Braddock & McPartland, 1989; Cook, 1979); and (b) the effects of desegregation, primarily on Black educational and employment attainments (Crain, 1971; Crain & Mahard, 1978; Schofield, 1995; Wells, 1995). The time had not yet come for social scientists to notice the positive effects of desegregation on the outlooks and achievements of Whites (Gurin, 2004). Nor was there much concern with the racially biased attitudes (Ellison, & Powers, 1994) or racially discriminatory behavior of ethnic minorities (Crosby, Bromley, & Saxe, 1980) given the realities of the time.

Looking back over the social psychological research of the decades since World War II, Crosby and Bearman (2006) reflected on the effectiveness of academic research in improving race relations. One of the observations of Crosby and Bearman is that psychologists have become increasingly sophisticated about the influences of social systems, systems that are in turn affected by policy policies. Crosby and Bearman also commented on the continuum of attitudes, ranging from those that actively oppose equality among various sub-groups in any population to those that favor pro-active dismantling of the current systems of inequality.

American social psychologists were not alone; during the 1960s and 1970s, social psychology began to gain a foothold in Europe. Some European scholars, like Moscovici, Zavalloni, and Weinberger (1972) concentrated their attention on the dynamics of small group interactions, looking especially at how groups might come to make riskier decisions than individuals and at how minorities might influence majorities in small group settings (Turner, Brown, & Tajfel , 1979).

Occasionally, European researchers empirically investigated the real-world consequences of the phenomena that they produced in the laboratory, as for example when Middleton, Tajfel, & Johnson(1970) studied the nationalistic attitudes of children, but rarely did they make explicit the policy implications of their laboratory work. It is nonetheless abundantly clear that the human tendency to assort into groups and to seek advantage for one's own group relative to out-groups has a lot to tell scholars about how bias may affect people's attitudes toward various public policies as well as about the need for public policies to manage the potentially pernicious effects of people's biases.

REVIEW OF THE LITERATURE ON ATTITUDES TOWARD PUBLIC POLICIES

Psychologists have researched attitudes toward a variety of public policies in an attempt to understand the ways in which these policies are received by the general public. Researchers have been particularly interested in looking at the connections between attitudes toward public policies, and various aspects of the attitude holders, such as their position in society and their other attitudes and feelings. Some researchers have looked at the interactions among aspects of policies and aspects of the people reacting to policies.

One policy that has been intensively studied is affirmative action (Crosby, 2004; Kravitz, Harrison, Turner, et al., 1997). Affirmative action occurs whenever an institution pro-actively goes out of its way to assure fair treatment of members of all ethnic groups and of both genders. Perhaps more than any other single policy, affirmative action tacitly acknowledges the inequities of the status quo and explicitly works to decrease inequities.

In this section we summarize the literature on several public policies, but we devote most of our attention to attitudes toward affirmative action because, among the policies we examine, that policy has been most intensively studied and because affirmative action can be understood as a policy that specifically seeks to counteract directly racial and gender imbalances. Although a number of studies have examined affirmative action in countries other than the United States (Combs & Nadkarni, 2005; Feather & Boeckmann, 2007; Konrad & Hartmann, 2001; Krings, Tschan, & Bettex, 2007), the bulk of the research has looked at the attitudes of American citizens. For expository coherence, our focus is on the dynamics of attitudes toward affirmative action in the United States.

Affirmative action

Attitudes toward affirmative action have been studied for nearly forty years. As noted by Crosby (2004) the general public is volatile in its attitudes toward the policy. Given the general lack of knowledge about what affirmative action is and how it operates, it is unsurprising to find variation in attitudes (Crosby & Cordova, 1996; Golden, Hinkle, & Crosby, 2001). Nonetheless, reviews of the research literature have revealed that the variations in attitudes are not random (Crosby, Iyer, & Sincharoen, 2006; Harrison, Kravitz, Mayer, et al., 2006; Schmukler, Thompson, & Crosby, 2008). Attitudes are influenced by aspects of the attitude holders, perceptions of the policy, and interactions between the two (Crosby, Iyer, & Sincharoen, 2006).

Attitudes toward affirmative action as a function of the attitude holder

Attitudes toward affirmative action vary as a function of the attitude holder (Harrison, Kravitz, Mayer, et al., 2006). Studies have shown that those who might benefit from affirmative action are more likely to support the policy than those who think they will be negatively affected by the policy (Bobo & Kluegel, 1993). Harrison and his associates (2006) performed extensive meta-analyses, which confirmed the two following trends in attitudes toward affirmative action. Women tend to support affirmative action more than men and people of color tend to support affirmative action more than Whites do. There is also a reliable positive association between education and support for affirmative action (Sidanius, Pratto, & Bobo, 1996). Those who report high levels of social dominance orientation (SDO) dislike affirmative action (Sidanius, Pratto, & Bobo, 1996). Numerous studies have linked negative attitudes toward affirmative action with sexist and racist biases (for full reviews, see Crosby, Iyer, Sincharoen 2006; Harrison, Kravitz, Mayer, 2006.)

Researchers have also examined how beliefs about merit are interlaced with opinions about affirmative action: Those who support affirmative action often cite its merit-upholding values, but those with negative attitudes toward affirmative action say with equal frequency that the policy violates meritocratic values (Bobocel, Son Hing, et al., 2002). Similarly, researchers have found that the dedication to meritocracy has a complicated relationship with affirmative action attitudes. People who believe that dis-crimination remains a problem and who value fairness tend to be supportive of affirmative action. Conversely, those who think that all are treated equally and who value fairness tend to dislike affirmative action (Aberson & Haag, 2003; Kluegel & Smith, 1986; Reyna, Tucker, Korfmacher et al., 2005).

Attitudes toward affirmative action as a function of policy

Numerous studies have shown that attitudes toward affirmative action vary according to how the policy is framed as well as perceived (for a full review, see Crosby, Iyer, & Sincharoen 2006). Americans tend to give higher approval ratings to 'soft' policies such as outreach programs for underrepresented groups but dislike 'hard' policies such as quotas (Harrison, Kravitz, Mayer, et al., 2006; Kravitz & Klineberg, 2000, Kravitz & Platania, 1993). The effect of policy type on attitudes is seen in many research settings whether attitude holders are provided with a definition of the policy by the researchers or asked to produce one themselves (Golden, Hinkle, & Crosby, 2001; Quinn, Ross, & Esses, 2001).

Researchers have also found that the target of affirmative action affects approval rates. People are more apt to approve of affirmative action for the disabled than for minorities (Kravitz & Platania, 1993). In one study, three times as many participants approved of governmental aid for women as for Blacks, with aid to Blacks being approved by only 20 percent of participants (Sniderman & Piazza, 1993). Whether or not a justification is given for affirmative action also affects approval; generally approval increases when a justification is given (Aberson & Haag, 2003; Knight & Hebl, 2005; Reyna, Tucker, Korfmacher, et al., 2005).

Synthesizing the findings

As will be discussed later, social psychologists have interpreted the findings on attitudes toward affirmative action in light of various theories (Crosby, 2004). Prejudiced people and those who approve of social hierarchies tend to dislike affirmative action and to see affirmative action as going against the interests of their own groups. Some people see the policy, or aspects of the policy, as violating principles that they hold dear.

Attitudes toward other policies

Given that attitudes toward affirmative action vary as a function of two specific variables (aspects of the attitude holder and aspects of the policy), the question arises: Are the attitude fluctuations unique to affirmative action, or do studies from other public policies show similar tendencies? Do the theories used to explain variations in attitudes toward affirmative action also apply to variations in attitudes toward other policies?

For an informed answer, we take a look into three public policies: immigration, welfare, and taxation. Like affirmative action, immigration and welfare have long been seen as policies with ethnic or racial overtones. Like affirmative action, taxation can be seen either as government intrusion or as governmental assurance of the rights of all.

Immigration

Research shows that attitudes toward immigration policies (as well as toward immigrant populations) reliably vary as a function of some aspects of the attitude holder (Deaux, 2006). Level of education plays a role in attitudes toward immigration policy. Higher levels of education have been associated with pro-immigration attitudes both in the United States (Alba, Rumbaut, & Marotz, 2005; Chandler & Tsai, 2001; Espenshade & Hempstead, 1996) and in different European nations (Jackson, Brown, Brown, et al., 2001; Pettigrew, 1998).

Those with conservative political orientations and those with high social dominance orientation (SDO) tend to hold negative attitudes toward immigration (Chandler & Tsai, 2001; Pratto & Lemieux, 2001). Esses, Dovidio, Jackson, et al., (2001) found a positive association between social dominance orientation and anti-immigration views in both the United States and Canada. They also found the relationship to be mediated by zero-sum beliefs, that is, beliefs that more for immigrants means less for non-immigrants. Researchers have also found strong associations between high SDO, right wing authoritarianism, and ethnic prejudice in a number of different cultures (Bart, Van Klel, & Kossowka, 2005; Duckitt & Sibley, 2007; Khan & Liu, 2008; Villano & Zani, 2007).

Some characteristics of attitude-holders do not reliably relate to attitudes toward immigration policy. Chandler and Tsai (2001) report inconsistent findings regarding gender: A 1993 Gallup poll showed that women were more in favor of immigrants than men; yet, in the 1994 General Social Survey, women were less supportive of legal immigration than were men. There also appears to be some instability in the attitudes of different ethnic minorities within the United States toward immigrants (Espenshade & Hempstead, 1996).

Attitudes toward immigration are associated with perceptions of social groups. Stephan, Ybarra, and Bachman (1999) found that Americans who perceived immigrants as a credible threat to their in-group members were more likely to be prejudiced against immigrants. Other studies also note the association between in-group threat and negative attitudes toward immigration policy (Alba, Rumbaut, & Marotz, 2005; Esses, Dovidio, Jackson, et al., 2001; Pratto & Lemieux, 2001). Alba, Rambaut, & Marotz, (2005) report that Whites who overestimate the number of non-Whites in the United States have more negative attitudes toward immigrants, and the more the distortion, the more the negativity.

Recent research shows that attitudes toward immigration, like attitudes toward affirmative action, also vary as a function of the policy (Deaux, 2006). Studies indicate that attitudes toward immigration policy tend to vary according to how the policy is framed (Fujiwara, 2005). Sometimes individual-level variables interact with framing. For example, Pratto and Lemieux (2001) found that framing immigration policy as a form of social dominance over immigrants was supported by people who were high on social dominance orientation (SDO) and felt threatened by immigrants. Framing immigration policy as a plan that promoted equality among immigrants and current US citizens, in contrast, gained support from citizens who were low on SDO.

Welfare policy

Attitudes toward welfare and welfare policies have also been shown to vary as a function of characteristics of the attitude holder. Concerning ethnicity, Black Americans show warmer feelings toward welfare, more support for welfare spending, less support for family

caps, then do White Americans (Soss, Schram, Vartanian, et al., 2003). The amount of income an individual receives is also associated with attitudes toward welfare. Using data from the General Social Surveys (1972–1998), Epstein (2004) found that when the top and bottom income quintiles were calculated, both Black and White top income groups showed less support for welfare spending than the lowest income groups.

Attitudes toward welfare also vary as a function of the ways in which the policy has been presented or framed (Bullock, Wyche, & Williams, 2001; Fujiwara, 2005; Gilens, 1996). Typical is an experimental study that documented the effects of reading a newspaper article that stressed either the need for aid among the poor or the importance of strict work requirements. The former elicited more support for welfare than the latter (Shen & Edwards, 2005).

Tax policy

Attitudes toward tax policy also vary as a function of the attitude holder. Attitudes are affected by one's level of education about tax policy (Eriksen & Fallan, 1996). Self interest also appears to have an effect on attitudes toward taxation when there is a proposed tax increase (Chong, Citrin, & Conley, 2001; Tedin, Matland, & Weiher, 2001). Green and Gerken (1989) studied attitudes of smokers and non-smokers toward cigarette taxation. A significant difference was found between smoker and non-smoker attitudes toward cigarette-tax, with non-smokers supporting the tax far more than smokers. Along the same lines, White Americans are not likely to support tax increases where there is no apparent payoff for their group, such as a bond for building a new school in a predominantly Black neighborhood (Bobo & Kluegel, 1993; Tedin, Matland, & Weiher, 2001).

Studies show that, like affirmative action, attitudes toward welfare, immigration, and taxation vary as a function of the policy. Respondents in various studies on taxation show different attitudes toward the same information depending upon how the information about the tax policy is framed

(Hasseldine & Hite, 2003; McCaffery & Baron, 2004). Perceptions of fairness also play into attitudes toward taxation policy, and self-interest plays a diminished role when policies are seen to be fair (Cuccia & Carnes, 2001).

CURRENT STATE OF THEORIZING

Unlike economists, virtually no social psychologists take as a given that people's reactions to various public policies are simply the consequence of how a 'rational man' (or 'rational woman') moves through his (or her) social and economic environment (Crosby & Stockdale, 2007). Thus, in her inquiry into immigration, when Deaux (2006) pauses to consider the evidence about whether immigrants do, in fact, grab jobs away from natives or do, in fact, pose a disproportionate burden on health-care systems, she steps away from the usual mind-set of the social psychologist. Similarly, Crosby (2004) breaks out of disciplinary constraints when, in her book-length treatise, she questions the policy and practice of affirmative action, synthesizing the evidence of the effectiveness and fairness of the policy as implemented as well as evidence of how bias colors people's reactions.

Underlying the great bulk of the psychological studies is the assumption that people's reactions are of critical interest for what they tell us about the dynamics of social interactions. The social psychological literature on bias and attitudes toward public policies seeks not only to document variations in attitudes but also to conceptualize the reasons for variations.

Four explanations

Four different reasons for variations in attitudes toward public policies seem especially important. First, people differ in the extent to which they are biased or prejudiced. Second, people differ in the extent to which they orient toward social dominance. Third, people differ in how much they perceive various policies to threaten their own group's interests. Finally,

people differ in the principles or values that they hold to be important and also in how much emphasis they place on their principles and values. When social psychologists explain opposition to policies in terms of bias, dominance orientation, or perceived threat to self-interest, there is often an underlying presumption that the policies are good and opposition to them is bad; but no such presumption is present when opposition is framed in terms of principles (Clayton & Crosby, 1986; Crosby, 2004). When reactions to policies are explained in terms of bias, social dominance orientation, and principles, social scientists point out that people often act in ways that do not promote their own material self-interest; obviously, perceived threats (which may or may not be realistic) provide a different approach.

Prejudice

The first explanation for variations in people's reactions to public policies suggests that negative attitudes toward equalizing policies result from racism and sexism. Over the last 70 years, discrimination has reduced much less dramatically than the avowed changes in people's attitudes, leading some to suggest that racism and sexism have not gone away but have, rather, just gone underground. Theorists have stressed different varieties of modern racism.

In an attempt to understand racial hostilities in the United States, Sears developed the concept of *symbolic politics* (Sears & Henry, 2003). According to the concept of symbolic politics, racist attitudes, combined with a strong adherence to traditional American values of self-reliance and individualism, explain White opposition to a number of policies such as school integration, affirmative action, and progressive reforms to the systems of welfare, immigration, and taxation.

Symbolic politics scholars propose that Whites' racist attitudes do not derive directly from the personal circumstances of White people but rather result from abstract, over-arching ideas about society (Henry & Sears, 2003). Symbolic racism, furthermore, is not expressed as a direct dislike of Blacks, but rather as a lack of support for certain policies that would mitigate inequalities among ethnic groups. Defining their theory as 'a blend of anti-Black affect and the kind of traditional American values embodied in the Protestant Ethnic' (Kinder & Sears, 1981: 416) symbolic racism theorists see that dominant group members are motivated less by their individual material self-interests than by the psychological or symbolic values of different policies.

In a series of empirical studies, researchers were able to show that Whites' attitudes toward policies like busing and welfare were less connected to their personal situations than to the general feeling among Whites about whether or not Blacks deserved to be treated in certain ways (Kinder, 1986; Kinder & Sears, 1981; Sears & Henry, 2003). Whites who felt Blacks were given unfair advantages or special treatment disliked the equalizing policies, whether or not the policies posed a threat to their own status or well-being.

Related to the theory of symbolic racism is the theory of *aversive racism* (Dovidio, Kawakami, & Gaertner, 2000). The aversive racist is one who maintains a negative view of people of color but would be dismayed to become aware of the extent of his or her own prejudice. The aversive racist does not treat people of color poorly when the action could be linked directly to skin color. Yet given the opportunity to justify differentiating behavior, the aversive racist will show a pro-White bias. The aversive racist might, for example, justify his or her opposition to progressive immigration policy on economic grounds ('our people need those jobs') and never give conscious recognition to how stereotypes influence his or her reasoning. Researchers have posited that aversive sexism functions in much the same way as aversive racism (Crosby & Dovidio, 2008). Affirmative action research can be used to illustrate the actions of both aversive racists and sexists; aversive sexists would attribute their dislike for affirmative action to the perception of unfair advantage it would give women, whereas the aversive

racist would use a similar argument to justify their dislike of affirmative action for people of color.

Modern racism has been found to play a role in people's attitudes toward other public policies in a fashion similar to the role it plays in attitudes toward affirmative action. Both in the United States (Mullen, 2001) and in Europe (Pettigrew & Meertens, 1995; Zick, Pettigrew, & Wagner, 2008), members of the dominant groups hold negative opinions about minority members and these negative opinions go hand-in-hand with suspicion of progressive immigration policies. Aversive racism is also evident in some people's attitudes toward welfare policies. Work by Gilens (1996) has traced a steady increase in media representation of the poor as Black and undeserving. He and other scholars (Neubeck & Cazenave, 2001) argue that the media has influenced the public's negative attitudes and beliefs about Blacks and welfare policy. In a large-scale survey in 1990, 59 percent of Whites reported that Blacks would rather use welfare than get a job, 46 percent of Whites reported the same attitude toward Latino/as, while only 3 percent of Whites felt the same about Whites (Davis & Smith, 2000).

Social dominance orientation

The second theory that has been used by researchers to explain attitudes toward affirmative action and other public policies is social dominance theory. According to social dominance theory, some people like society to be hierarchically arranged, and some favor flattened hierarchies. Thus, inter-group bias may be due to the need to maintain the current stratification among groups (Sidanius, Pratto, van Laar, et al., 2004).

Social dominance theory maintains that attitudes toward affirmative action are determined not only by how people feel about out-groups but also by how people feel about social hierarchy. Researchers have found that those who score high on SDO are unsupportive of affirmative action (Sidanius, Pratto, & Bobo, 1996), and are also likely to support punitive immigration policies (Esses,

Dovidio, Jackson, et al., 2001; Pratto & Lemieux, 2001).

Self-interest

A third explanation for people's reactions to public policies differs from the first two theories in that it proposes that decisions about public policy are not due to ideas (either principled or prejudiced or both) but are rather due to material self-interest which, in turn, is thought, to a greater or lesser degree (Frey & Tropp, 2006; Otten & Epstude, 2006; Tropp & Wright, 2001), to include the interest of one's membership group (Bobo, 2000). To the extent that a policy is seen to threaten the interest of one's membership group, the policy is disliked.

Bobo (2000) has posited that people view affirmative action poorly when it is not seen as beneficial to one's own group. According to Bobo, White people would be less likely to support affirmative action due to a worry that other groups will be given privileges that would put Whites at a disadvantage. A survey of working-class Whites linked their concern about competition with Blacks to their lack of support for affirmative action (Bobo & Kluegel, 1993) Similarly, immigration may be most feared and disliked by those who have (or who assume that they have) the most to lose (Esses, Jackson & Armstong, 1998).

Looking at attitudes toward welfare policy, researchers have also found indirect support for the theory of inter-group threat. Soss et al. (2003) found larger percentages of minorities in states that have enacted punitive welfare reform measures. Presumably minorities did not flock to states where it would be hard to live; rather, it seems that the regressive measures came in response to the threat that minorities were felt to pose to state budgets.

Principle and value-based attitudes

The final theory we will discuss was developed to explain people's attitudes toward public policies and posits that values and principles drive negative attitudes toward affirmative action and other equalizing policies (Sniderman, Piazza, Tetlock, et al., 1991; Sniderman & Tetlock, 1986). A research study conducted by Sniderman, Piazza, Tetlock, et al., (1991) illustrates the theory that dedication to the principles of hard work and individualism, not racism, drives reactions to public policy. The researchers asked conservatives and liberals to allot governmental assistance to Blacks and found that as long as the recipients in question adhered to 'traditional' American values, the conservatives actually allotted more assistance to Blacks than did liberals. Sniderman and his collaborators argue that this finding supports their view that Americans make their decisions regarding government policies, like affirmative action, dependent on values like merit, work ethic and individualism.

Of course, not all societies are as individualistic as American society. Contrasting the collective orientation of Japan with the individualistic orientation of the United States, Ozawa, Crosby, and Crosby (1996) conducted a test of the proposal that people's reactions to affirmative action derive at least in part from their (often unstated) principles. Ozawa et al. gave packets of information to American and Japanese students describing a company that had engaged in sex discriminatory practices. The American students, especially the women, were more upset than the Japanese students about the practices. The packet then asked students their reactions to four possible remedies to the discrimination, one of which was a classic form of group-based affirmative action. The collectivistic Japanese students endorsed the affirmative action solution significantly more than the individualistic American students did. In this study the Japanese students who traditional hold more collectivist ideals supported group-based affirmative action despite the fact that they the sexist practices upset them less then the American students. This lends support to the idea that group-based remedies posed a threat to the individualistic values of the Americans.

Compatibility among perspectives

It is important to note that all four explanations of the variation in people's attitudes are feasible given different situations. What motivates one individual's attitudes toward any public policy might not be important to others (Crosby, 2004). Thus, racism may be at the base of some people's opposition to affirmative action, inclusive immigration policies, and progressive welfare and taxation reforms, while other people may oppose the policies because of their genuinely held values or worries about the material well-being of their membership groups.

Even in any one individual, various motives may combine. Those high in social dominance orientation may also be, and indeed typically are, quite prejudiced. Those who are prejudiced may overestimate the threats posed to them by various groups and various policies; such a relationship has been found among different nationalities in Europe (see Pettigrew, Christ, Wagner, et al., 2008; Semyonov. Raijman, Tov, et al., 2004; Stephan, Ybarra, & Bachman, 1999). Finally, people are capable of being both principled, in the sense of adhering to 'traditional' American values, and, simultaneously, racist and/or sexist (Crosby & Smith, 2007; Schmukler, Thompson, & Crosby, 2008). One can, for example, hold the biased opinion that women are unable to work as hard as men and therefore show negative attitudes toward affirmative action for women, based on the 'principled' idea that women, with their inability to work as hard as men, do not deserve to advance at work.

PROMISING AVENUES FOR FUTURE RESEARCH

We suggest that much could be learned by looking at bias in public policy from a new angle. Rather than just studying the ways that bias affects attitudes toward public policy, researchers could examine the ways in which public policy may be able to decrease bias or at least to interrupt the behavioral and societal consequences of prejudicial attitudes. By examining how policies influence the behavioral expression of bias, researchers may deepen our understanding of the basic processes by which the attitudes of individuals

result in patterns of behavior among social groups.

A program of research aimed at understanding the connections between bias, public policy, and discriminatory treatment might start with two fundamental observations, both amply supported by laboratory and field research. First, people are poor information-processors. Second, people easily form in-group biases.

Years of social psychological research tell us that human beings are cognitive misers, taking any available shortcut to decision making. People often fall prey to the fundamental attribution error, mistakenly over emphasizing the power of disposition and underestimating the sway of the situation over human behavior. Thus, for example, people often attend to gender and race and use these variables to explain behaviors by others. In addition, we know that people harbor implicit biases, that are linked to decisions made automatically rather than though a deliberative thought process (DeCoster, Banner, Smith, et al., 2006; Smith-McLallen, Johnson, Dovidio, et al., 2006).

We also know that people tend to gravitate toward group membership (Leonardelli & Brewer, 2001). Minimal group studies, in which group membership is experimentally engineered and transient, show us that given even the smallest reason to affiliate, people will do so. Once affiliated with a group, people tend to overvalue their own group and undervalue out-group (Hewstone, Rubin, & Willis, 2002).

If two fundamental observations form the start of a research program on the connections among bias, policy, and discrimination, additional findings from both lab and field studies permit us to take some additional steps. In terms of basic processes, it is important to note that the affiliative urge does not always result in out-group derogation and dislike. Dovidio, Gaertner, and Validzic (1998), for example, were able to demonstrate some conditions that prevented participants in a minimal group experiment from disliking each other. Specifically, groups that were told that their performance on the task was either equal to that of other groups and that they had worked on a different task than the other group did not show bias.

Building on fundamental observations and additional data, researchers have begun to look at how policies can influence the relationship between individual bias and societal discrimination (Crosby, 2004). One policy that has been extensively studied, especially within the United States, is affirmative action. The need to keep strict records, mandated by Executive Order 11246 for all businesses that hold federal contracts, has helped organizations overcome the problems of poor decision-making. The use of objective measures of people's qualifications has diminished the importance of stereotypes. In a study of employment-based affirmative action, Thomas (2003) found that managers who had worked for companies with active affirmative action polices, showed reduced bias in their hiring practices. By removing the managers' need to rely on heuristics and assumptions, not only did affirmative action reduce discrimination in hiring decisions, it also reduced bias in the minds of the managers. Therefore the affirmative action hiring policy worked in two ways, it reduced the discrimination in hiring and decreased the prejudice attitudes of the managers.

Similarly, by keeping track of ethnicity in higher education, administrators have been able to find the hidden impediments to minority success and to reduce or eliminate barriers (Crosby & Clayton, 2001). Instructive in this regard is the University of California. The University of California is mandated by law to accept the 'top 12.5 percent' of high school students. Determination of who is at the top depends in part on grades earned in high school classes. In a policy known as 'the AP bump,' grades in advanced placement (AP) courses count for one point more than grades earned in regular classes. Thus, for example, an A in Biology earns students four points, while an A in AP Biology earns students five points. Eventually the administration noticed that this rule was partially responsible for blocking admission to Black and Latino/a because under-represented

students disproportionately attend schools that offer only a few AP courses, while Whites disproportionately attend schools that offer many. In order to compensate for the unfairness of the system, administrators created changes to admission policy. For example, they developed a means for students to attend community college and then transfer to the university if their grades in community college were high enough (Crosby, 2004).

SUMMARY AND CONCLUSIONS

Understanding how to motivate people to replace familiar and comfortable systems with newer systems is a challenge for psychologists. The challenge becomes greater when the old systems appear to be fair while the new systems appear to give preference to a distinct group (Crosby & Bearman, 2006). Researchers have begun to map how the proponents of affirmative action have worked for change and how the opponents have worked against it. What is needed now is more strenuous observation, not only in terms of affirmative action but also in terms of many other social policies.

Although explicit reports of prejudice have been on the decline for decades, many researchers have suggested that prejudices are still at work in hidden and unconscious ways. People may be unaware of their own biases, especially when they can frame their decisions in ways consistent with the traditional values of their societies. We know that bias operates at the detriment of intergroup equality. Public policies that help diminish the social harm occasioned by persistent bias deserve study as do policies that help diminish the bias itself.

ACKNOWLEDGEMENTS

We would like to thank Valentina Rubinstein and Yelizaveta Cherkasova for their help with editing the chapter. Correspondence should be directed to: Faye J Crosby, Psychology Department, University of California, Santa

Cruz, Santa Cruz, CA 95064. E-mail: fjcrosby@ucsc.edu

REFERENCES

Aberson, C. L., & Haag, S. C. (2003). Beliefs about affirmative action and diversity and their relationship to support for hiring policies. *Analysis of Social Issues and Policy, 3,* 121–138.

Adorno, T. W., Frenkel-Brunswick, E., Levinson, D. J., & Sanford, R. N. (1950). *The authoritarian personality.* New York: Harper.

Alba, R., Rumbaut, R. G., & Marotz, K. (2005). A distorted nation: Perceptions of racial/ethnic group sizes and attitudes toward immigrants and other minorities. *Social Forces, 84,* 901–919.

Allport, G. W. (1954). *The nature of prejudice.* Cambridge, MA: Addison-Wesley.

Bart, D., Van Klel, A., & Kossowka, M. (2005) Authoritarian and social dominance in Western and Eastern Europe: The importance of sociopolitical context and pf political interest and involvement. *Political Psychology, 26,* 299–320.

Bobo, L. (2000). Race and beliefs about affirmative action: Addressing the effects of interests, group threat, ideology, and racism. In D. O. Sears, J. Sidanius, & L. Bobo (Eds.), *Racialized politics: The debate about racism in America* (pp. 137–164). Chicago: University of Chicago Press.

Bobo, L., & Kluegel, J. R. (1993). Opposition to race-targeting: Self-interest, stratification ideology, or racial attitudes? *American Sociological Review, 58,* 443–464.

Bobocel, D. R., Son Hing, L. A., Holmvall, C. M., & Zanna, M. P. (2002). Policies to redress social injustice: Is the concern for justice a cause both of support and of opposition. In M. Ross & D. Miller (Eds.), *The justice motive in everyday life* (pp. 204–225). New York: Cambridge University Press.

Braddock, J. H., II, & McPartland, J. M. (1989). Social psychological processes that perpetuate racial segregation: The relationship between school and employment desegregation. *Journal of Black Studies, 19,* 267–289.

Bullock, H. E., Wyche, K. F., & Williams, W. R. (2001). Media images of the poor. *Journal of Social Issues, 57,* 229–249.

Chandler, C. R., & Tsai, Y. (2001). Social factors influencing immigration attitudes: An analysis of data from the general social survey. *The Social Science Journal, 38,* 177–188.

Christie, R. (1991). Authoritarianism and related constructs. In J. P. Robinson, P. R. Shaver, & L.

Wrightsman (Eds.), *Measures of personality and social psychological attitudes* (pp. 551–571). San Diego: Academic Press.

Chong, D., Citrin, J., & Conley, P. (2001). When self-interest matters. *Political Psychology, 22,* 541–570.

Clayton, S., & Crosby, F. (1986). Postscript: The nature of connections. *Journal of Social Issues, 42,* 189–194.

Combs, G. M., & Nadkarni, S. (2005). The tale of two cultures: Attitudes towards affirmative action in the United States and India. *Journal of World Business, 40,* 158–171.

Cook, S. (1979). Social science and school desegregation: Did we mislead the Supreme Court? *Personality and Social Psychology Bulletin, 5,* 420–437.

Crain, R. L. (1971). School integration and the academic achievement of Negroes. *Sociology of Education, 44,* 1–26.

Crain, R. L., & Mahard, R. E. (1978). School racial composition and Black college attendance and achievement test performance. *Sociology of Education, 51,* 81–101.

Crosby, F. J. (2004). *Affirmative action is dead; long live affirmative action.* New Haven, CT: Yale University Press.

Crosby, F. J., & Bearman, S. (2006). The uses of a good theory. *Journal of Social Issues, 62,* 415–438.

Crosby, F., Bromley, S., & Saxe, L. (1980). Recent unobtrusive studies of black and white discrimination and prejudice: A literature review. *Psychological Bulletin, 87,* 546–563.

Crosby, F. J., & Clayton, S. (2001). Affirmative action: Psychological contributions to policy. *Analyses of Social Issues and Public Policy, 1,* 71–87.

Crosby, F. J., & Cordova, D. I. (1996). Words worth of wisdom: Toward an understanding of affirmative action. *Journal of Social Issues, 52,* 33–49.

Crosby, F. J., & Dovidio, J. F. (2008). Discrimination in America and legal strategies for reducing it. In E. Borgida & S. Fiske (Eds), *Psychological science in court: Beyond common knowledge* (pp. 23–43). Boston: Blackwell.

Crosby, F. J., Iyer, A., Clayton, S., & Downing, R. (2003). Affirmative action: Psychological data and the policy debates. *American Psychologist, 58,* 93–115.

Crosby, F. J., Iyer, A., & Sincharoen, S. (2006). Understanding affirmative action. *Annual Review of Psychology, 57,* 586–611.

Crosby, F. J., & Smith, A. E. (2007). The University of Michigan cases: Social scientific studies of diversity and fairness. In R. L. Weiner, B. Bornstein, R. Schopp, & S. Willborn (Eds.), *Legal decision making in everyday life: Controversies in social consciousness* (pp. 121–142). New York: Springer.

Crosby, F. J., & Stockdale, M. S. (2007). Understanding sex discrimination. In F. J. Crosby, M. S. Stockdale, &

A. S. Ropp (Eds.), *Sex discrimination in the workplace: An interdisciplinary approach* (pp. 3–5). Boston: Blackwell.

Cuccia, A. D., & Carnes, G. A. (2001). A closer look at the relation between tax complexity and tax equity perceptions. *Journal of Economic Psychology, 22*, 113–140.

Davis, J. A., & Smith, T. W. (2000). *General Social Surveys, 1972–1990*. Chicago: National Opinion Research Center.

Deaux, K. (2006). *To be an immigrant*. New York: Russell Sage Foundation.

DeCoster, J., Banner, M. J., Smith, E. R., & Semin, G. R. (2006). On the inexplicability of the implicit: Differences in the information provided by implicit and explicit tests. *Social Cognition, 24*, 5–21.

Deutsch, M., & Collins, M. (1951). *Interracial housing*. Minneapolis: University of Minnesota Press.

Dovidio, J. F., Gaertner, S. L., & Validzic, A. (1998). Intergroup bias: Status, differentiation, and a common in-group identity. *Journal of Personality and Social Psychology, 75*, 109–120.

Dovidio, J. F., Kawakami, K., & Gaertner, S. L. (2000). Reducing contemporary prejudice: Combating explicit and implicit bias at the individual and intergroup level. In S. Oskamp (Ed.), *Reducing prejudice and discrimination* (pp. 137–163). Mahwah, New Jersey: Lawrence Erlbaum Associates, Publishers.

Duckitt, J., & Sibley, C., G. (2007). Right wing authoritarianism, social dominance orientation and the dimensions of generalized prejudice. *European Journal of Personality, 21*, 113–130.

Ellison, C. G., & Powers, D. A. (1994). The contact hypothesis and racial attitudes among Black Americans. *Social Science Quarterly, 75*, 385–400.

Epstein, W. M. (2004). Cleavage in American attitudes toward social welfare. *Journal of Sociology and Social Welfare, 31*, 177–201.

Eriksen, K., & Fallan, L. (1996). Tax knowledge and attitudes towards taxation: A report on a quasi-experiment. *Journal of Economic Psychology, 17*, 387–402.

Espenshade, T. J., & Hempstead, K. (1996). Contemporary American attitudes toward U. S. immigration. *International Migration Review, 30*, 535–570.

Esses, V. M., Dovidio, J. F., Jackson, L. M., & Armstrong, T. L. (2001). The immigration dilemma: The role of perceived group competition, ethnic prejudice, and national identity. *Journal of Social Issues, 57*, 389–412.

Esses, V. M., Jackson, L. M., & Armstrong, T. L. (1998). Intergroup competition and attitudes toward immigrants and immigration: An instrumental model of group conflict. *Journal of Social Issues, 54*, 699–724.

Falomir-Pichastor, J. M., Munoz-Rojas, D., Invernizzi, F., & Mugny, G. (2004). Perceived in-group threat as a factor moderating the influence of in-group norms on discrimination against foreigners. *European Journal of Social Psychology, 34*, 135–153.

Feather, N. T., & Boeckmann, R. J. (2007). Gender, discrimination beliefs, group-based guilt, and response to affirmative action for Australian women. *Psychology of Women Quarterly*, 31, 290–304.

Frey, F., & Tropp, L. (2006). Being seen as individuals versus as group members: Extending research on metaperception to intergroup contexts. *Personality and Social Psychology Review, 10*, 265–280.

Fujiwara, L. H. (2005). Immigrant rights are human rights: The reframing of immigrant entitlement and welfare. *Social Problems, 52*, 79–101.

Gilens, M. (1996). Race and poverty in America: Public misperceptions and the American news media. *Public Opinion Quarterly, 60*, 515–541.

Golden H., Hinkle S., & Crosby F. J. (2001). Reactions to affirmative action: Substance and semantics. *Journal of Applied Social Psychology, 31*, 73–88.

Green, D. P., & Gerken, A. E. (1989). Self-interest and public opinion toward smoking and restrictions and cigarette taxes. *Public Opinion Quarterly, 53*, 1–16.

Green, D. P., Kahneman, D., & Kunreuther, H. (1994). How the scope and method of public funding affect willingness to pay for public goods. *Public Opinion Quarterly, 58*, 49–67.

Gurin, P. (2004). The educational value of diversity. In P. Gurin, J. S. Lehman, & E. Lewis (Eds.), *Defending diversity: Affirmative action at the University of Michigan* (pp. 97–188). Ann Arbor, MI: University of Michigan Press.

Harrison, D. A., Kravitz, D. A., Mayer, D. M., Leslie, L. M., & Lev-Arey, D. (2006). Understanding attitudes toward affirmative action programs in employment: Addressing reactions to redressing discrimination. *Journal of Applied Psychology. 91*, 1013–1036.

Hasseldine, J., & Hite, P. A. (2003). Framing, gender and tax compliance. *Journal of Economic Psychology, 24*, 517–533.

Henry, P., & Sears, D. (2003). The origins of symbolic racism. *Journal of Personality and Social Psychology, 85*, 259–275.

Hewstone, M., Rubin, M., & Willis, H. (2002). Intergroup bias. *Annual Review of Psychology, 53*, 575–604.

Jackson, J. S., Brown, K. T., Brown, T. N., & Marks, B. (2001). Contemporary immigration policy orientation among dominant-group members in Western Europe. *Journal of Social Issues, 57*, 431–456.

Khan, S., S., & Liu, J., H. (2008). Intergroup attributions and ethnocentrism in the Indian subcontinent: The ultimate attribution error. *Journal of Cross-Cultural Psychology*, 39, 16–36.

Kinder, D. (1986). The continuing American dilemma: White resistance to racial change 40 years after Myrdal. *Journal of Social Issues*, 42, 151–169.

Kinder, D., & Sears, D. (1981). Prejudice and politics: Symbolic racism versus racial threats to the good life. *Journal of Personality and Social Psychology*, 40, 414–431.

Kluegel, J. R., & Smith, E. R. (1986). *Beliefs about inequality: Americans' views of what is and what ought to be, social institutions and social change.* New York: A. de Gruyter.

Knight, J. L., & Hebl, M. R. (2005). Affirmative reaction: The influence of type of justification on non-beneficiary attitudes toward affirmative action plans in higher education. *Journal of Social Issues, 61*, 547–568.

Konrad, A. M., & Hartmann, L. (2001). Gender differences in attitudes towards affirmative action programs in Australia: Effects of beliefs, interests and attitudes toward women. *Sex Roles*, 45, 415–432.

Kravitz, D. A. (1995). Attitudes toward affirmative action plans directed at Blacks: Effects of plan and individual differences. *Journal of Applied Social Psychology, 25*, 2192–2220.

Kravitz, D. A., Harrison, D. A., Turner, M. E., Levine, E. L., Chaves W., Brannick, M., et al. (1997). *Affirmative action: A review of psychological and behavioral research.* Bowling Green, OH: Society for Industrial and Organizational Psychology.

Kravitz, D. A., & Klineberg, S. L. (2000). Reactions to two versions of affirmative action among Whites, Blacks and Hispanics. *Journal of Applied Psychology, 85*, 597–611.

Kravitz, D. A., & Platania, J. (1993). Attitudes and beliefs about affirmative action: Effects of target and of respondent sex and ethnicity. *Journal of Applied Psychology, 78*, 928–938.

Krings, F., Tschan, F., & Bettex, S. (2007). Determinants of attitudes towards affirmative action in a Swiss sample. *Journal of Business and Psychology*, 21, 585–611.

Leonardelli, G. J., & Brewer, M. B. (2001). Minority and majority discrimination: When and why. *Journal of Experimental Social Psychology, 37*, 468–485.

Lipset, S. M., & Raab, S. M. (1970). *The politics of unreason.* New York: Harper and Row.

McCaffery, E. J., & Baron, J. (2004). Framing and taxation: Evaluation of tax policies involving household composition. *Journal of Economic Psychology, 25*, 679–705.

Middleton, M. R., Tajfel, H., & Johnson, N. B. (1970). Cognitive and affective aspects of children's national attitudes. British Journal of Social & Clinical Psychology, 9, 122–134. Milgram, S. (1974). Obedience to authority: An experimental view. New York: Harper and Row.

Moscovici, S., Zavalloni, M., & Weinberger, M. (1972). Studies on polarization of judgments: II. person perception, ego involvement and group interaction. *European Journal of Social Psychology, 2*, 92–94.

Mullen, B. (2001). Ethnophaulisms for ethnic immigrant groups. *Journal of Social Issues, 57*, 457–475.

Myrdal, G. (1944). *An American dilemma.* New York: Harper. National Advisory Commission on Civil Disorders (1968). *Report.* Washington, D.C.: U. S. Government Printing Office.

Neubeck, K. J., & Cazenave, N. A. (2001) *Welfare racism: Playing the race card against America's poor.* New York: Routledge.

Orfield, G., & Eaton, S. E. (1996). *Dismantling desegregation: The quiet reversal of Brown v. Board of Education.* New York: The New Press.

Otten, S., & Epstude, K. (2006). Overlapping mental representations of self, ingroup, and outgroup: Unraveling self-stereotyping and self-anchoring. *Personality and Social Psychology Bulletin, 32*, 957–969.

Ozawa, K., Crosby, M., & Crosby, F. (1996). Individualism and resistance to affirmative action: A comparison of Japanese and American samples. *Journal of Applied Social Psychology, 26*, 1138–1152.

Pettigrew, T. F. (1998). Reactions toward the new minorities in Western Europe. *Annual Review of Sociology, 24*, 77–103.

Pettigrew, T. F. (2004). A half century after Brown v Board of Education. *American Psychologist, 59*, 521–529.

Pettigrew, T. F., Christ, O., Wagner, U., Meertens, R. W., van Dick, R., & Zick, A. (2008). Relative deprivation and intergroup prejudice. *Journal of Social Issues, 64*, 385–401.

Pettigrew, T. F., & Green, R. L. (1976) School desegregation in large cities: A critique of the Coleman "white flight" thesis. *Harvard Educational Review, 46*, 1–53.

Pettigrew, T. F., & Meertens, R. W. (1995). Subtle and blatant prejudice in Western Europe. *European Journal of Social Psychology, 25*, 57–75.

Pratto, F., & Lemieux, A. F. (2001). The psychological ambiguity of immigration and its implications for promoting immigration policy. *Journal of Social Issues, 57*, 413–430.

Quinn, K. A., Ross, E. M., & Esses, V. M. (2001). Attribution of responsibility and reactions to affirmative action: Affirmative action as help. *Personality and Social Psychology Bulletin, 27*, 321–331.

Reyna, C., Tucker, A., Korfmacher, W., & Henry, P. J. (2005). Searching for common ground between supporters and opponents of affirmative action. *Political Psychology, 26,* 667–682.

Sears, D. O., & Henry, P. J. (2003). The origins of symbolic racism. *Journal of Personality and Social Psychology, 85,* 259–275.

Schmukler, K. R., Thompson, E. M., & Crosby, F. J. (2008). Affirmative action: Images and realities. In G.S. Parks, S. E. Jones, & W. J. Cardi (Eds.), *Critical race realism: Intersections of psychology, race, and law* (pp. 155–164). New York: The New Press.

Schofield, J. W. (1995). Review of research on school desegregation's impact on elementary and secondary school students. In J. A. Banks & C. A. Banks (Eds.), *Handbook of research on multicultural education* (pp. 597–616). New York: Macmillan.

Schooler, C. (1976). Serfdom's legacy. *American Journal of Sociology, 81,* 1265–1286.

Semyonov, M., Raijman, R., Tov, A. Y., & Schmidt, P. (2004). Population size, perceived threat and exclusion: A multiple indicators analysis of attitudes toward foreigners in Germany. *Social Science Research, 44,* 681–701.

Shen, F., & Edwards, H. H. (2005). Economic individualism, humanitarianism, and welfare reform: A value-based account of framing effects. *Journal of Communication, 55,* 795–809.

Sidanius, J., Pratto, F., & Bobo, L. (1996). Racism, conservatism, affirmative action, and intellectual sophistication: A matter of principled conservatism or group dominance? *Journal of Personality and Social Psychology, 70,* 476–490.

Sidanius, J., Pratto, F., van Laar, C., & Levin, S. (2004). Social dominance theory: Its agenda and method. *Political Psychology, 25,* 845–880.

Smith, A. E., & Crosby, F. J. (2008). From Kansas to Michigan: The path from desegregation to diversity. In G. Adams, M. Biernat, N. Branscombe, C. Crandall, & L. S. Wrightsman (Eds.), *Commemorating Brown: The social psychology of racism and discrimination* (pp. 99–113). Washington, DC: APA Books.

Smith, M. B. (1984). The American soldier and its critics: What survives the attack on positivism? *Social Psychology Quarterly, 47,* 192–198.

Smith, M. B. (2003). *For a significant social psychology: The collected writings of M. Brewster Smith.* New York: New York University Press.

Smith-McLallen, A., Johnson, B. T., Dovidio, J. F., & Pearson, A. M. (2006). Black and White: The role of color bias in implicit race bias. *Social Cognition, 24,* 46–73.

Sniderman, P. M., & Piazza, T. (1993). *The scar of race.* Cambridge, MA: Harvard University Press.

Sniderman, P. M., Piazza, T., Tetlock, P. E., & Kendrick, A. (1991). The new racism. *American Journal of Political Science, 35,* 423–447.

Sniderman, P., & Tetlock, P. (1986). Symbolic racism: Problems of motive attribution in political analysis. *Journal of Social Issues, 42,* 129–149.

Soss, J., Schram, S. F., Vartanian, T. P., & O'Brien, E. (2003). The hard line and the color line: Race, welfare, and the roots of get-tough reform. In S. F. Schram, J. Soss, & R. C. Fording (Eds.). *Race and the politics of welfare reform* (pp. 225–252). Ann Arbor : University of Michigan Press.

Stephan, W. G., Ybarra, O., & Bachman, G. (1999). Prejudice toward immigrants. *Journal of Applied Social Psychology, 29,* 2221–2237.

Stouffer, S. A., Suchman, E. A., DeVinney, L. C., Star, S. A., & Williams, R. M. (1949) *The American soldier. Adjustment During Army Life* (Vol 1). Princeton: Princeton University Press.

Tedin, K. L., Matland, R. E., & Weiher, G. R. (2001). Age, race, self-interest, and financing public schools through referenda. *Journal of Politics, 63,* 270–294.

Thomas, W. F. (2003). The meaning of race to employers: A dynamic qualitative perspective. *Sociological Quarterly, 44,* 227–242.

Tropp, L. R., & Wright, S. C. (2001). The inclusion of ingroup in the self. *Personality and Social Psychology Bulletin, 27,* 585–600.

Turner, J. C. (1975). Social comparison and social identity: Some prospects for intergroup behaviour. *European Journal of Social Psychology, 5,* 5–34.

Turner, J. C., Brown, R. J., & Tajfel, H. (1979). Social comparison and group interest in ingroup favouritism. *European Journal of Social Psychology, 9,* 187–204. \Villano, P., & Zani, B. (2007). Social dominance orientation and prejudice in an Italian sample. *Psychological Reports, 101,* 614–616.

Wells, A. S. (1995). Reexamining research on school desegregation: Long- versus short-term effects. *Teachers College Record, 96,* 691–706.

Zick, A., Pettigrew, T. F., & Wagner, U. (2008). Ethnic prejudice and discrimination in Europe. *Journal of Social Issues, 64,* 233–251.

AUTHORS' NOTES

Correspondence should be directed to Faye J Crosby, Department of Psychology, University of California Santa Cruz, Santa Cruz, CA 95064. 831 459 3568. fjcrosby@ucsc.edu We would like to thank YeliVali Rubinstein for their help with editing the chapter.

29

Health and Health Care Disparities

Louis A. Penner*, Terrance L. Albrecht,
Heather Orom, Donyell K. Coleman,
and Willie Underwood III

ABSTRACT

The chapter focuses on causes of health disparities between Blacks and Whites. Health disparities are differences in health status that are not biological in origin and thus, at least theoretically, can be prevented from occurring or eliminated once identified. Biological and largely racist explanations of differences in health status were dominant until the mid-twentieth century when socioeconomic, political, and psychological causes received increased attention. In this context, the chapter gives special attention to how stereotyping, prejudice, and discrimination affect disparities in health care. We first discuss how prejudice and discrimination might affect patient health and health-related attitudes and behavior. Then we discuss how provider bias might affect the quality of care received by Black patients. We conclude that stereotyping, prejudice, and discrimination play important roles in health disparities. Finally we relate health disparities research to more basic research on racial bias and discrimination and suggest potential avenues of future research.

HEALTH AND HEALTH CARE DISPARITIES

> Of all the forms of inequality, injustice in health care is the most shocking and inhumane.
> Martin Luther King Jr.

This chapter concerns the roles of stereotypes, prejudice and discrimination in health disparities. The term, health disparities, is somewhat ambiguous, and has been defined in a number of different ways. In this chapter we use the definition proposed by Braveman (2006):

> Health disparities do not refer to all differences in health. A health disparity is a particular type of difference in health; it is a difference in which disadvantaged social groups—such as the poor, racial/ethnic minorities, women, or other groups who have persistently experienced social disadvantage or discrimination—systematically experience worse health or greater health risks than more advantaged social groups. (p. 167)

A critical aspect of Braveman's definition is that health disparities result from social, political, and economic processes and thus, at least theoretically, can be prevented from occurring or can be eliminated once identified.

Although almost any social group may experience health disparities, we will focus on disparities in health status and health care between people in the United States who self-identify as White or non-Hispanic European American and people who self-identify as Black or African-American (or Afro-Caribbean).[1] America is not the only country where health disparities among people of different ethnicities exist. Even in countries where the government provides health care to all citizens or at least subsidizes health care to a much greater extent than in the United States (for example, Canada and the United Kingdom), health disparities among people of different ethnicities still occur (Banks, Marmot, Oldfield, et al., 2006; Lasser, Himmelstein, & Woolhandler, 2006; Millett, Gray, Saxena, et al., 2007). Racial/ethnic health disparities in the United States have, however, been better documented and more thoroughly studied than health disparities in other places in the world. This is the reason why we focus on health disparities in the United States; we assume the processes we discuss are also related to health disparities elsewhere in the world. We begin by briefly presenting some data on Black–White health disparities in the United States.

In the United States, Whites are physically and mentally healthier than Blacks, Hispanics, or Native-Americans; and the largest differences in health status are between Whites and Blacks (IOM, 2003; National Center for Health Statistics, 2003, 2006; Agency for Healthcare Research and Quality (2005). The average life expectancy for Blacks (73.1 years) is less than Whites (78.3 years) (National Center for Health Statistics, 2006). Annual mortality rates among Black infants are almost three times as great as among White infants and this difference between Blacks and Whites persists more or less across the life span (National Center for Health Statistics, 2003). These mortality statistics become more disturbing when placed in a historical context. Not surprisingly, mortality rates among both Blacks and Whites have declined dramatically over the last half century. However, the disparity in Black-White mortality rates has actually increased (National Center for Health Statistics, 2006). In 1950, the age-adjusted death rate per 100,000 people among Blacks was 1.22 times greater than the death rate among Whites; in 2004, the death rate among Blacks was *1.31* times greater than the death rate among Whites.

The incidence rates for almost all diseases and illnesses are higher among Blacks than Whites (National Health Statistics, 2006). For example, the incidence rate of tuberculosis infections among Blacks is approximately eight to nine times the rate among Whites; the incidence rate of asthma is four to six times as high, and the incidence of diabetes is about twice as high (Howard University National Human Genome Center, 2006). In national surveys, Blacks are more likely than Whites to report that they are in poor health and have physical limitations on their daily activities (National Center for Health Statistics, 2006). Also, birth weights of neonates are lower, preterm births are more common, maternal mortality is higher, and prenatal care is less frequent among Blacks than among Whites (National Health Statistics, 2006). For ten of the most common kinds of cancer, Blacks have lower five-year survival rates and higher mortality rates than Whites (SEER, 2005). These cancer survival/mortality differences remain even when Blacks and Whites are equated on incidence rates and the stage at which the cancer was diagnosed. Socioeconomic status (SES) certainly plays some role in these differences, but there are still substantial Black–White differences in health status and mortality rates after SES and related factors (e.g. insurance coverage) are controlled (Chu, Miller, & Springfield, 2007; Williams and Collins, 1995).

In this chapter we discuss how prejudice, stereotyping, and discrimination may contribute to these health disparities. The chapter has four sections. In the first, we present a brief history of early research on the causes of health disparities between Blacks and Whites. This is followed by a discussion of contemporary research. Then we summarize the current state of knowledge about how prejudice, stereotyping, and discrimination may contribute to health disparities, and we propose a framework for integrating theory and research on this topic. Finally, we briefly discuss future research on health care disparities that might inform both contemporary theories of prejudice and stereotyping and practical efforts to reduce racial/ethnic health disparities.

A BRIEF HISTORY OF RESEARCH ON BLACK-WHITE HEALTH DISPARITIES

Almost from its beginnings, Western medicine embraced the assumption that innate genetic differences existed between the races and that some races are biologically superior to others (Byrd and Clayton, 2000, 2002). Over the years, the belief that differences in the character, abilities, and physiology of people were linked to their racial identity/color became widely accepted among medical scientists (Byrd and Clayton, 2000). The emergence of the slave trade in the fourteenth and fifteenth centuries further exacerbated such beliefs, as did conflicts between European Christians and darker-skinned North African Muslims. The notion of large racial differences became part of scientific doctrine during the so-called 'age of enlightenment.' For example, Carl Linnaeus, known as the 'Father of Biological Classification,' believed that Blacks and Whites were separate species and assigned degrading psychological and behavioral attributes to Blacks (Byrd and Clayton, 2000).

In the United States polygenism – the theory that human races were separate biological species – dominated scientific theory from the early-seventeenth century until perhaps as recently as the early-twentieth century (Byrd and Clayton, 2000). Polygenism may provide a rationale for the infamous Tuskegee syphilis experiments. Started in the 1930s, these studies were originally based on the premise that the long-term effects of syphilis would be different among Black men than among White men. To study the progression of the disease, United States Public Health Service denied treatment to large numbers of Black men afflicted with syphilis long after effective treatments for syphilis became available (Jones, 1993).

The Black sociologist and social activist, W. E. B. Du Bois edited the first scholarly monograph that seriously challenged widely-accepted biological explanations of poorer health among Blacks relative to Whites in the United States. In *The Health and Physique of the Negro American*, Du Bois (1906) used census data and insurance company records to make the case that with improved sanitary conditions, education, economic opportunities, and better medical care, the health of Blacks would steadily improve until it was equal to that of Whites.

Although Du Bois' ideas were widely accepted among Black civic and health organizations, they had relatively little impact on medical science or practice of the time. The problem of Black–White health disparities was largely ignored by the federal government until the late 1990s. In 1999, the US Commission on Civil Rights issued a report arguing that the federal government's failure to enforce anti-discrimination laws was a major source of health disparities in the United States (*The Health Care Challenge: Acknowledging Disparity, Confronting Discrimination and Ensuring Equality*). Four years later, the Institute of Medicine (IOM) issued its report on health disparities, *Unequal Treatment: Confronting Racial and Ethnic Disparities in Health Care* (IOM, 2003), which concluded that the major cause of disparities in the health status of Blacks and Whites was large and widespread disparities in the quantity and quality of the health care received by Blacks and by Whites. Further, the IOM believed that processes related to prejudice, stereotyping, and discrimination played a direct, proximal role in health care disparities.

More recently research has shifted its emphasis from explanations of health *differences* based on the biological inferiority of Blacks to explanations of health *disparities* based on contemporary understanding of genetics and economic, sociological, and psychological factors. This relatively dramatic shift is due to work by: public health and medical researchers, who demonstrated that differences in health care were as powerful as genetic factors in predicting survival rates from diseases (e.g., Bach, Schrag, Brawley, et al., 2002) and that the health care Blacks receive was almost invariably poorer than that received by Whites (Lee, Gehlbach, Hosmer, et al., 1997); sociologists, who found that socioeconomic variables and environmental differences were typically more powerful predictors of people's health status than their phenotypic race or ethnicity (e.g., Williams and Collins, 1995); psychologists, who identified the health consequences of being the target of prejudice and/or discrimination (e.g., Clark, Anderson, Clark, et al., 1999); and communication researchers, who found that Black and White patients were treated differently by their

health providers (e.g., Cooper-Patrick, Gallo, Gonzales, et al., 1999).

CONTEMPORARY RESEARCH ON BLACK–WHITE HEALTH DISPARITIES

Any overview of research on the causes of Black–White health disparities must acknowledge the fact that there is no single cause. Multiple interdependent causes operate simultaneously at societal, interpersonal, and intrapersonal levels to explain Black–White disparities. Although our focus will be on the roles of stereotyping, prejudice, and discrimination in health disparities, there are other important causes as well. In Figure 29.1, we present a model (adapted from Penner, Albrecht, Coleman, et al., 2007) of the possible causes of Black–White disparities in health status in the United States. This model provides an organizational framework for this section of the chapter. However,

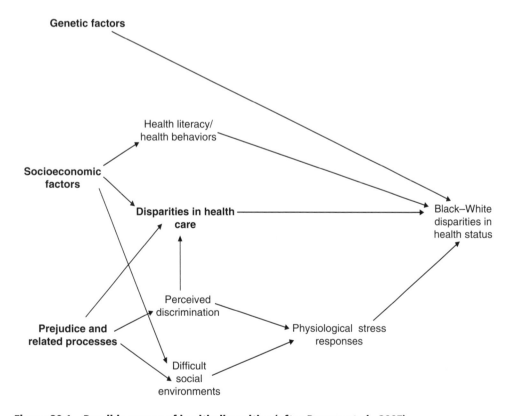

Figure 29.1   Possible causes of health disparities (after Penner et al., 2007).

we acknowledge that this model is still preliminary because even a multi-element model with several mediated paths may not contain all the possible causes of health disparities.

The model identifies three *exogenous* causes of Black–White health disparities: Genetic Factors, Socioeconomic Factors, and Prejudice and Related Processes. The effects of the latter two variables are primarily mediated through Disparities in Healthcare.

Genetic factors

Contemporary genetic explanations of differences in the health status of Blacks and Whites should not be confused with racist theories of the innate biological inferiority of Blacks discussed in the previous section. Many diseases have a genetic component; and people inherit some degree of genetic susceptibility to various diseases. Blacks and Whites come from different genetic populations and have different genetic admixtures (i.e., the percentage of genes that come from various populations, such as African or Northern European). Therefore, the argument is that some significant portion of Black–White differences in health status originates from genetics (Frank, 2007).

Genetic explanations of *some* Black–White differences in health status are valid. For example, Huntington's disease is most prevalent among people of European ancestry; and sickle cell anemia most commonly affects people of African and Mediterranean ancestry. Thus, as indicated in Figure 29.1, genetic factors are a plausible direct source of some disparities (or perhaps *differences*) in the health status of Blacks and Whites. However, the influence of these genetic factors must be placed in context. Health status, like almost any human characteristic, reflects the complex interplay between genes and environment. To identify either one of them as the unitary or even dominant cause may be a dangerous oversimplification of how genes express themselves in a complex environment.

Further, placing too much emphasis on genetic explanations of Black–White differences in health status can have some negative consequences. One consequence of over-emphasizing the role of genetics in Black–White differences in health is that it may lead some people to grossly misuse the colloquial concept of race (Frank, 2007) and resort to racial/ethnic stereotypes. A racial phenotype (e.g., the color of a person's skin) or a social construction of a person's race (what race others believe the person to be) is, at best, a rather imperfect proxy for the person's actual genetic population admixture (Gower, Fernandez, Beasley, et al., 2003). Further, the genetic differences among people from the five major population groups (African, Asian, Caucasian [White], Native American, and Oceanic [Pacific Islander]) are quite small in the United States, where there has been extensive admixing of populations. Race has a great deal of meaning to social psychologists who study stereotyping, prejudice, and discrimination, but it has little biological meaning.

Socioeconomic factors

The second exogenous variable in the model is socioeconomic factors. No matter how they measure socioeconomic status (SES) (i.e., education, income, occupational prestige, or some combination of the three), researchers find that the lower the individual's SES, the poorer their mental and physical health (LaVeist, 2005). Further, SES predicts health status, rather than the reverse (Williams and Collins, 1995). In the United States, Blacks, as a group, have lower incomes, and less education than Whites (LaVeist, 2005). Thus, many researchers view SES as a major cause of Black–White health disparities.

As shown in the model, SES is associated with disparities in health literacy/health behaviors, which concerns: (1) knowledge of, and attitudes about, appropriate health care activities, and/or (2) engaging in these activities (Sentell and Halpin, 2006). SES also directly affects people's access to health care and the quality of health care they receive (IOM, 2003). Finally, SES is associated with difficult social environments, which includes things such as chronic exposure to difficult living conditions, environmental hazards and other acute and chronic stressors that may negatively affect people's health (Mays, Cochran, & Barnes, 2007).

Socioeconomic factors are clearly an important source of Black–White health status disparities, but their influence on disparities must be placed in context. As noted earlier, when differences in SES are statistically controlled, large Black–White disparities in health status still remain. For example, in a study of mortality rates, it was found that after equating Blacks and Whites in the United States on education and income, there was still an excess of 38,000 deaths per year among Blacks (Franks, Muennig, Lubetkin, et al., 2006). Thus, SES provides only a partial explanation of health status disparities.

Prejudice, stereotyping, and discrimination

The final exogenous variable in the model, prejudice and related pocesses, is the major focus of this chapter. This variable contributes to disparities in health status through multiple paths. For example, prejudice and discrimination may force people to live in difficult social environments (e.g., isolated and/or segregated housing) that create feelings of social exclusion and other stressors that, as noted above, have serious negative health consequences (e.g., Everson-Rose and Lewis, 2005).

The model also posits that people who report that they have been the target of discrimination (perceived discrimination) experience poorer mental and physical health (e.g., Borrell, Kiefe, Williams, et al., 2006; Williams, Neighbors, & Jackson, 2003). Mays, Cochran, & Barnes, (2007) and others (e.g., Clark, Anderson, Clark, et al., 1999; Pascoe and Richman, 2009) propose that prejudice and discrimination increase allostatic load on the body, which makes people more susceptible to disease. This explanation is intuitively appealing, but it has been difficult to establish a definitive causal link between perceived prejudice/discrimination and physiological stress responses (see, for

example, Brown, Matthews, Bromberger, et al., 2006). Further examination of the relevant physiological and psychological stress responses is outside the scope of this chapter. Thus, we now turn to the primary question of interest: How are stereotyping, prejudice, and discrimination related to health care disparities?

STEREOTYPING, PREJUDICE, DISCRIMINATION AND HEALTH CARE DISPARITIES

As previously discussed, the IOM committee (2003) found large and persistent disparities between Blacks and Whites in the health care received by Blacks and by Whites. These disparities were present even when variables such as SES, geographic location, and insurance status were controlled. The IOM committee argued that stereotyping and prejudice were major contributors to health care disparities. We now consider how they may be manifested among both patients and providers.

The patient perspective

When Blacks interact with health care providers, the social context is likely to be quite different from when Whites interact with providers. About 75 percent of Black patients' medical interactions are racially discordant (i.e., the interaction is with a provider of a different race/ethnicity); compared to about 20 percent for Whites (Chen, Fryer, Phillips, et al., 2005). Thus, if feelings and thoughts related to ethnicity and racial relations are activated in medical interactions, this is much more likely to occur in interactions involving Black patients.

Clear differences have been found between how Blacks and Whites feel about their medical care. National surveys find that, relative to Whites, Blacks are significantly more likely to believe their race negatively affects their health care (Johnson, Saha, Arbelaez, et al., 2004a) and that discrimination occurs in their interactions with White physicians

(Malat and Hamilton, 2006). Blacks also trust their physicians less (Boulware, Cooper, Ratner, et al., 2004; Halbert, Armstrong, Gandy, et al., 2006). However, Black patients tend to be more satisfied with their medical encounter (LaVeist and Nuru-Jeter, 2002) and their medical care (LaVeist and Carroll, 2002) when their physician is Black than when their physician is White. LaVeist and colleagues (2003) reported that Black patients were more likely to schedule appointments with their physicians and were less likely to postpone or delay these appointments when they had a Black physician rather than a White physician.

Several explanations have been posited to explain Black patients' negative reactions to medical interactions, especially racially discordant ones. The first is that Black patients' knowledge of the past history of racism in medical science (see above) might create mistrust of medical care. This proposal, while reasonable, is a matter of some dispute. Brandon and colleagues (2005) found that Blacks were no more aware of the Tuskegee experiment than Whites; and when Blacks were told about Tuskegee this did not significantly increase their distrust of their medical care (however, cf. White, 2005).

A second explanation is that Blacks' feelings of mistrust in the health care system are due to their perceptions of the general level of racism in society. The more racism Blacks perceive in the world around them, the less trust they report in the health care system (Benkert et al., 2006). Preliminary results from our own work (Penner, Dovidio, Edmondson, et al., 2009) are consistent with this explanation. We found that among very low SES Black patients, reports of perceived past discrimination were negatively correlated with satisfaction with their own medical care, and evaluation of the specific physician who treated them.

A third explanation of why Blacks may respond negatively to racially discordant medical interactions comes from the work of Dovidio and colleagues (e.g., Dovidio, Penner, Albrecht, et al., 2008). They propose that Blacks may mistrust White health care providers because of the mixed cues Blacks receive in interracial interactions. This proposal builds on Dovidio and Gaertner's (2004) theory of aversive racism, which posits that many Whites simultaneously hold both positive, explicit or conscious racial attitudes and stereotypes, and negative, implicit or nonconscious racial attitudes and stereotypes. These people are labeled 'aversive racists' because such individuals would actually find their implicit racial feelings and thoughts aversive if they became aware of them.

These conflicting thoughts and feelings may affect Whites' behaviors in interracial interactions. Easily controllable verbal behaviors (e.g., greetings, how polite they are) reflect Whites' conscious attitudes toward Blacks, and communicate positive regard. However, Whites' more subtle and less controllable nonverbal behaviors (or verbal behaviors that are not carefully monitored) reflect their automatic or implicit attitudes and communicate negative regard (see Dovidio, Kawakami, Johnson, et al., 1997). Thus, Whites can give mixed signals to Black partners in an interaction.

Research further suggests that when Blacks and Whites interact, they are differentially sensitive to different kinds of behaviors and channels of communication. Whites tend to focus on conscious intentions and controllable behaviors, and not recognize when their actions are racially biased (Swim, Scott, Sechrist, et al., 2003). Conversely, Blacks tend to show heightened attentiveness and sensitivity to nonverbal cues of prejudice (Richeson and Shelton, 2005). If Blacks attend to Whites' nonverbal behaviors, which may signal more negativity than Whites' verbal behaviors, Blacks are likely to form more negative impressions of the encounter, be more distrustful of their White partner, and be less satisfied with the interaction than Whites (Dovidio, Gaertner, Kawakami, et al., 2002).

Trust and related kinds of affect have direct health care consequences. If Black patients mistrust their provider and/or perceive discrimination, they are less likely to obtain further health care, obtain needed screening tests (e.g., mammogram, blood pressure tests) and adhere to prescribed drug regimens (Bird, Bogart, & Delahanty, 2004; Thompson, Valdimarsdottir, Winkel, et al., 2004). Recently, Penner et al. (2009a) found that that perceived past discrimination was negatively associated with Black patients' adherence to their physicians' recommendations, which in turn, affected their health.

The provider perspective

It seems unlikely that provider-based disparities in contemporary health care are primarily due to the blatantly racist stereotypes and attitudes that were more common in United States 50 or 60 years ago, or to the racist medical theories discussed in the history section. We suspect an overwhelming majority of health care providers sincerely reject explicit forms of racial prejudice in both their personal and professional lives. However, as noted above, contemporary ethnic bias takes more subtle and indirect forms and this kind of bias likely contributes to disparities in health care. There are two separate, but related ways in which subtle prejudice and stereotyping might produce health care disparities: (1) through their impact on diagnosis and treatment recommendations; (2) through their impact on the quality of interactions between patients and providers.

Diagnoses and treatment recommendations

The theory of aversive racism proposes that aversive racists' negative feelings and implicit attitudes affect their behavior toward Blacks in subtle and indirect ways that would not immediately identify them as racially biased. For instance, Hodson, Dovidio, & Gaertner, (2002) found that aversive racists discriminated against Black job applicants only when there was ambiguity about the applicants' qualifications for the job. Given such findings, Penner, Albrecht, Coleman, et al. (2007a) proposed that there would be greater differences in how physicians treat Black and White patients when physicians are in high-discretion situations (such as making a

referral for a procedure) than in low-discretion situations, such as administering standard treatments for clearly diagnosed diseases. In fact, this is what is generally found (Geiger, 2003). LaVeist and colleagues (2003), for example, found that Blacks were significantly less likely than Whites to be *referred* for diagnostic testing for heart disease, but among Blacks and Whites who received these tests there were no subsequent differences in the receipt of *treatment* (a lower discretion situation).

A similar pattern emerges for prostate cancer treatment, a disease for which there is no universally agreed upon standard of care (Underwood, De Monner, Ubel, et al., 2004). Blacks diagnosed with prostate cancer are significantly more likely than Whites to receive no immediate treatment ('watchful waiting') (Shavers, Brown, Klabunde, et al., 2004a). Further, among patients who receive watchful waiting, Blacks wait longer before their first medical monitoring visit and are monitored less frequently than Whites (Shavers, Brown, Potosky, et al., 2004b). Griggs and her associates report a similar kind of finding. They studied breast cancer patients who are given adjuvant or prophylactic chemotherapy to increase the probability of successful surgery and/or reduce the probability of recurrence of the disease. They found that in these cases Black women were less likely than White women to receive the recommended doses of chemotherapy (Griggs, Sorbero, Stark, et al., 2003; Griggs, Culakova, Sorbero, et al., 2007).

These data are, of course, correlational but there is experimental work on health care disparities as well. Schulman, Berlin, Harless, et al. (1999) asked primary care physicians to view video tapes of patients complaining about chest pain (in actuality, the patients were actors). The gender and ethnicity of the patients (Black or White) were systematically manipulated. Schulman, Berlin, Harless, et al. found that Blacks were significantly less likely than Whites to be referred for further testing. These results are consistent with findings from archival studies of differences in the treatment of Black and White cardiology patients (see, for example, Vaccarino, Rathore, Wenger, et al., 2005; cf. Arber, McKinlay, Adams, et al., 2006).

Contemporary theories of prejudice also predict that physicians' implicit racial attitudes and stereotypes are better predictors of their treatment decisions than are their explicit attitudes and stereotypes. A recent study by Green, Carney, Pallin, et al. (2007) supports this prediction. Green, Carney, Pallin, et al., (2007) first assessed physicians' explicit and implicit attitudes toward Blacks and Whites. Next, physicians read vignettes about hypothetical emergency room patients with symptoms of serious heart problems, in which race of the patients in the vignettes was systematically varied. The physicians showed no explicit biases against Blacks; however, on the implicit measure (the Implicit Association Test, Greenwald, McGhee, & Schwartz, et al., 1998), physicians' attitudes were more negative toward Blacks than Whites and they were more likely to associate uncooperativeness with Blacks than Whites. More importantly, Green, Carney, Pallin, et al., (2007) found that physicians' implicit biases were strongly associated with their recommendations to give patients blood-thinning drugs (the appropriate treatment given the symptoms); physicians who were more biased were less likely to recommend these drugs for Black patients. (Sabin, Rivera, & Greenwald, 2008, replicated the bias findings, but the implicit biases were not related to treatment recommendations.)

van Ryn and associates (van Ryn, 2002: van Ryn and Burke, 2000; van Ryn, Burgess, Malat, et al., 2006) proposed a social-cognitive model of how patient ethnicity influences physicians' treatment decisions. Specifically, they posited that patient ethnicity constitutes a potent means whereby physicians place patients in social categories, which activate implicit and explicit stereotypes about individuals who belong to these categories. These stereotypes influence physicians' interpretations of patient's symptoms, which then affect physicians' decisions about diagnosis and treatment. Consistent with this model, van Ryn, Burgess, Malat, et al., (2006)

found that physicians do stereotype Black patients (e.g., as less educated and less likely to comply with medical recommendations than Whites) and that these stereotypes mediated physicians' decisions about the suitability of Black patients for coronary bypass surgery.

Similarly, Bogart, Catz, Kelly, et al., (2001) found that physicians rated hypothetical Black HIV patients as significantly more likely to be nonadherent than White HIV patients. The medical significance of this finding is that adherence to treatment is one of the major predictors of whether physicians will even provide antiretroviral therapies (see also Delahanty, Ram, Postrado, et al., 2001; Martin, 1993). Finally, Abreu (1999) found that implicit priming of stereotypic attributes of Blacks caused therapists to rate patients as more hostile. Collectively, these studies support van Ryn and Williams' (2003) argument that, 'patient sex, age, social economic status … and race/ethnicity can influence providers' beliefs about and expectations of patients independent of other factors' (p. 497).

Health care interactions

The second way in which prejudice and stereotypes might affect health care is via their impact on face-to-face health care interactions. Relative to racially concordant medical interactions (i.e., patient and physician share the same race/ethnicity), racially discordant medical interactions (most commonly White physician-Black patient) are shorter in length (Cooper, Roter, Johnson, et al., 2003), less patient-centered (Johnson, Roter, Powe, et al., 2004b), and characterized by less positive affect (Johnson, et al., 2004). They involve fewer attempts at relationship building (Siminoff, Graham, & Gordon, 2006) and less patient participation in decision making (Cooper-Patrick, Gallo, Gonzales, 1999; Kaplan, Gandek, Greenfield, et al., 1995; Koerber, Gajendra, Fulford, et al., 2004). Further, racially discordant medical interactions are more likely to be verbally dominated by the physician, (Johnson, et al.,

2004), and contain less information for the patients (Gordon, Street, Sharf, et al., 2006; Penner, Eggly, Harper, et al., 2007b). Finally, Oliver, Goodwin, Gotler, et al. (2001) found that White physicians spent significantly less time planning treatment, providing health education, assessing health knowledge, engaging in informal conversation, and answering questions with Black as compared to White patients. Physicians spent more time discussing what they hoped to accomplish and assessing substance abuse with Black than White patients.

As we close this section, it must be noted that while these disparities in medical interactions, are consistent and pervasive, there are no published studies that have assessed pre-interaction thoughts and/or feelings of providers and correlated these with behaviors in medical interactions. However, Penner et al. (2010) report data that suggest physicians' implicit and explicit racial attitudes do, in fact, affect their interactions with Black patients. Briefly, our participants were physicians at a primary care facility that served an exclusively Black patient population. We measured physicians' explicit and implicit attitudes (using the IAT) toward Blacks. After each interaction between a physician and a Black patient, we assessed the physician's commonality with the patient and willingness to share the decision-making with the patient and the patient's commonality with the physician, satisfaction with the interaction, and perceptions of physician warmth. Physicians' implicit and explicit attitudes predicted physician reports of commonality and shared decision-making and patient reports of commonality and satisfaction with the interaction; physicians' implicit attitudes also predicted patient perceptions of physician warmth. In all relationships more anti-black physician bias was associated with less positive reactions to the interaction. These findings demonstrate a relationship between racial attitudes and physician and patient reactions to a medical interaction. They are consistent with social psychological theories of how racial bias can affect social interactions between Blacks and Whites (e.g.,

Dovidio, Penner, Albrecht, et al., 2008). We discuss these theories more in the next section.

ANALYSIS OF THE CURRENT STATE OF KNOWLEDGE

The following statements would seem to summarize the current state of knowledge about Black-White health care disparities. First, there are instances where Blacks respond as favorably to White health care providers as to Black providers. However, when given a choice, there is a clear preference among Black patients for providers who are also Black. Second, when there is a Black-White disparity in diagnoses and treatments, almost invariably it is Black patients who receive the less valid diagnoses and the less effective or appropriate treatments. Third, there are instances where racially concordant and racially discordant medical interactions are similar in content, tone, and outcomes, but it is much more common for there to be disparities. If there is a disparity, racially discordant medical interactions are almost invariably less positive and productive than racially concordant interactions. How can we best understand these findings?

We believe that one very useful approach is to view health care disparities through the lens of social psychological theories of intergroup bias: 'the systematic tendency to evaluate one's own group ... or its members more favorably than a nonmembership group or its members' (Hewstone, Rubin, & Willis, 2002: 576). Intergroup bias is associated with a social categorization process that is more or less automatic and spontaneously activates positive feelings and beliefs about ingroup members and less positive or even negative feelings about outgroup members (Gaertner and Dovidio, 2000). The activation of such thoughts and feelings can take place outside of conscious awareness and control (Blair, 2001; Wittenbrink, Judd, & Park, 1997) and is often played out in the interactions between members of an ingroup and members of an outgroup (Wilder and Simon, 1998).

The activation of an in-group-out-group distinction is most likely to occur when the physician and patient come from different racial or ethnic groups, but an ethnic difference is not the only cue that would activate these processes. Social class is likely an important cue as well. Substantial differences between the education and income of the provider and the patient are more likely in racially discordant than racially concordant medical interactions. In addition to these demographic and socio-economic cues to group differences, Stewart and her colleagues (Stewart, Brown, Donner, et al, 2000, Stewart, 1995) have argued that most physicians view themselves as members of one group (health care providers), who, as part of their job, interact with members of another group (patients). This difference in roles would probably on its own lead to intergroup bias and social categorization processes. The role differences may also reinforce and make more salient the other social class differences that exist between physicians and many minority patients. This would make intergroup bias and social categorization still more likely.

There are other factors that may also contribute to the perception of strong ingroup-outgroup differences in interactions involving Black patients. In the United States, patients who are poor and members of ethnic minorities are less likely than wealthier majority patients to have continuity in their medical care. That is, they are less likely to see the same physician on different visits and, thus, less likely to have an ongoing provider-patient relationship with one physician (Doescher, Saver, Fiscella, et al., 2001). Intergroup bias is typically more probable among strangers than familiars (Pettigrew and Tropp, 2006).

Further, poor and minority patients are substantially more likely than wealthy, majority patients to see physicians trained outside the United States (most commonly from India or Pakistan) (IOM, 2003). For example, Bellochs and Carter (1990) found that, in the poorest neighborhoods in New York City, over 70 percent of the health care providers were graduates of foreign medical schools. The social and cultural differences between Black patients and foreign-trained providers may be even greater than the differences between Blacks and White American providers. This would make the probability of intergroup bias still higher.

Intergroup bias may heighten explicit thoughts and feelings, such as Black patients' distrust of White providers discussed earlier. It is also quite likely that these explicit processes are accompanied by implicit stereotypes and attitudes about members of another ethnic group among both providers and patients. As suggested above, these implicit biases will almost certainly affect the perceptions and behaviors of both patients and providers.

This does *not* mean that racially discordant medical interactions will automatically and invariably be more difficult and less productive than racially concordant ones. However, the conditions we have discussed do make such negative outcomes more likely to occur. Further, they may occur despite the best intentions of both parties to the interaction.

DIRECTIONS FOR FUTURE RESEARCH

We must begin this section by repeating the caveat offered earlier. The premise that stereotyping, prejudice, and discrimination are major causes of health care disparities is intuitively appealing, widely accepted by most professional medical organizations, and was at the core of the IOM report. However, the evidence in support of it is still largely circumstantial. Thus, one major task for future research is to further investigate these relationships and confirm or disconfirm the importance of stereotyping, prejudice, and discrimination in health care disparities. As reported above, Penner et al. (2010) obtained results that show this relationship, but clearly much more empirical work is needed. The remainder of this section is based on the assumption that this future research will confirm the importance of these phenomena as causes of health care disparities.

First, we consider more 'basic' social psychological research. Racially discordant medical interactions provide an excellent natural laboratory in which to study how subtle forms of stereotyping and prejudice might affect both affective and cognitive processes. For example, van Ryn and her colleagues (Burgess, van Ryn, Crowley-Matoka, et al., 2006), have laid out a detailed set of hypotheses about when racial stereotyping would affect health providers' diagnostic and treatment decisions. These hypotheses provide some rigorous and precise tests of Kunda and Spencer's (2003) theories about when people will and will not rely on stereotypes when interacting with minority group members. Specifically, Burgess, van Ryn, Crowley-Matoka, et al. (2006) propose that stereotypic judgments about minority group patients are most likely to occur, '(w)hen providers must make complicated judgments quickly, with insufficient and imperfect information' (p. 123). Testing this idea in a health care setting would add to the body of knowledge about when and why stereotyping occurs. It might also be useful to study how stereotypes affect communication between physicians and patients. That is, it seems unlikely that stereotypes only affect the physicians' treatment decisions. Rather, it seems quite probable that they also affect the physicians' behaviors toward and communication with their patients. For example, van Ryn and Burke (2000) found that physicians are likely to believe that Black patients are less intelligent, less well educated, and less pleasant and rational than White patients who were actually equivalent to the Blacks on these attributes. If a physician who is having a conversation with a Black patient about some treatment decision implicitly holds these stereotypes, this may well affect the physician's behavior toward the patient. For example, the physician may do less to elicit questions or opinions from the patient and as a result the patient will probably actually ask fewer questions. The patient's behavior will thus reinforce the stereotype and influence the physician's treatment decision. Further, the physician's communication will almost certainly affect how the patient responds to recommendations for treatment. (See Albrecht, Eggly, Gleason, et al., 2008.)

As another example of research possibilities, Amodio and Devine (2006) have argued that implicit cognitive and affective processes are independent and have unique explicit correlates. Specifically, their theory predicts that cognition predicts judgments and impressions, while affect predicts interpersonal preferences and social distance. If so, then diagnoses and treatment decisions involving Black patients should be better predicted by implicit stereotypes (i.e., cognitions) than by implicit attitudes (i.e., affect), while behavior toward Blacks during medical interactions would be better predicted by implicit attitudes.

Finally, racially discordant medical interactions might provide a context in which to further test Dovidio et al.'s (2002, 2008) proposals about the causes and consequences of mistrust in Black-White interactions. Some of our own work can be used to illustrate this. As noted earlier, we have examined how Black patients' feelings of being the target of past discrimination, in general, affect their reactions to specific medical interactions and physicians. As expected, the more perceived discrimination (i.e., the less racial trust), the less satisfied the Black patients were with the interaction and the less connection or commonality they felt with their physician (Penner, Dovidio, Edmondson, et al., 2009a).

Turning to applied or 'action' research, social psychological theories of stereotyping, prejudice, and discrimination may be of considerable practical value in developing interventions aimed at reducing health care disparities. For example, Gaertner and Dovidio (2000) proposed that replacing individuals' separate social or group identities with a *common group identity* will reduce intergroup bias. Penner, Dailey, Markova, et al. (2009b) posited that increasing a common group identity would improve the quality of interactions between low income Black patients and foreign-born and trained physicians. They developed an intervention designed to create a common identity between the patients and the physicians. Specifically, prior to interactions between the patients and physicians, Penner et al. gave each of them instructions and materials (e.g., buttons and pens with same the team name on them) intended to increase their sense of being members of the same team working on a common problem – improving the patients' health. The intervention resulted in significantly more trust of physicians among experimental group patients relative to control group patients for as long as four months after the intervention.

Burgess and colleagues (2007) made several recommendations for ways to reduce 'unintentional bias' among health care providers. The recommendations came almost entirely from social psychological theory and research. For example, Burgess, van Ryn, Dovidio, et al. (2007) suggested some interventions that would make physicians view minority group patients as individuals rather than as members of an outgroup. The specific rationale for these interventions came from research on how and when it is possible to change stereotypes (e.g., Blair, 2001). In another example, they used the contact hypothesis (Pettigrew and Tropp, 2006) as the basis of suggestions on how to reduce providers' anxiety and unease when interacting with members of ethnic minorities. Specifically, Burgess, van Ryn, Dovidio, et al. suggested physicians be provided with opportunities to engage in, 'interactive, facilitated discussions (with) colleagues of different race and ethnicity … to enhance providers' confidence in interracial interactions' (p. 884). Other suggestions included exposing providers to information about their own unconscious negative racial stereotypes and attitudes. This proposal was based on findings from Rokeach (1973) and others (e.g., Leippe and Eisenstadt, 1994) that indicate such self-confrontation procedures may cause negative emotional states that motivate people to counteract the effects of these prejudiced thoughts and feelings.

In summary, future research on health disparities offers a unique opportunity for a symbiotic relationship between basic and applied research. That is, this research may simultaneously help social psychologists better understand the processes responsible for stereotyping, prejudice, and discrimination

and help public health researchers develop effective ways to address the important and pervasive social problem of health disparities.

SUMMARY AND CONCLUSIONS

Overall the health of both Blacks and Whites in the United States has improved over the last 50 years; however, Black–White disparities in health status and health care are pervasive and show no sign of diminishing in the near future. Early research on health disparities offered overly simplistic and often racist biological explanations of why Whites were generally healthier than Blacks. Such explanations have largely been abandoned in favor of more sophisticated ones that consider genetic, economic, sociological, and psychological factors as causes of health disparities. Contemporary research strongly suggests that prejudice, stereotyping, and discrimination play critical roles in Black-White health disparities. For example, prejudice and discrimination are environmental stressors that take a physiological toll on their targets. Prejudice, stereotyping, and discrimination also affect the quality of the health care patients receive in several different ways. Being part of a group that has been the target of prejudice and discrimination creates mistrust, which negatively affects patient health-related behaviors and their reactions to health care. On the provider side, there is remarkably consistent evidence that Blacks receive poorer health care than Whites and there is reason to believe that implicit and explicit prejudice and stereotyping among health care providers play important roles in treatment disparities. There is much less current evidence demonstrating a link between implicit and/or explicit bias and disparities in medical interactions, but social psychological theory and research on the effects of racial bias in social interactions makes it very likely that such a relationship exists. This creates substantial research opportunities for both basic and applied researchers. That is, medical interactions in which the provider and patient are from different racial/ethnic groups provide a unique opportunity to test current theories of how explicit and implicit racial thoughts and feelings are manifested in social interactions in the real world. And at the same time, these theories may provide a valuable means to develop interventions to reduce health care disparities.

NOTES

*Correspondence should be directed to: Louise A. Penner c/o Karmanos Cancer Institute 4100 John R. Detroit Michigan 48201. E-mail: pennerl@karmanos.org.

1 Following the conventional usage in the research literature in this area, we use the term 'Black' to describe people who self-identify as Black African-American and Afro-Caribbean; and the term 'White' to describe people who self-identify as non-Hispanic European-American and Caucasian. Also, as used here, 'race' refers to a social construction, not a description of a group's genetic characteristics.

ACKNOWLEDGEMENTS

Preparation of the chapter was partially supported by a grant from the National Institute of Child Health and Development (1R21HD050450) to the first author and by a grant from the National Cancer Institute (U01CA114583) to Terrance L. Albrecht and Peter Lichtenberg. Heather Orom was supported by an AHRQ training grant (HS013819).

REFERENCES

Abreu, J. M. (1999). Conscious and nonconscious African American stereotypes: Impact on first impression and diagnostic ratings by therapists. *Journal of Consulting and Clinical Psychology, 67*, 387–393.

Agency for Healthcare Research and Quality (2005). 2005 National healthcare disparities report. Washington, DC: DHSS

Albrecht, T. L., Eggly, S., Gleason, M., Harper, F., Foster, T., Peterson, A., et al., (2008) The influence of clinical communication on patients decision making about clinical trials, *Journal of Clinical Oncology, 26*, 2666–2273.

Amodio, D. M., and Devine, P. G. (2006). Stereotyping and evaluation in implicit race bias: Evidence for independent constructs and unique effects on behavior. *Journal of Personality and Social Psychology, 91*, 652–661.

Arber, S., McKinlay, J., Adams, A., Marceau, L., Link, C., and O'Donnell, A. (2006). Patient characteristics and inequalities in doctors' diagnostic and management strategies relating to CHD: A video–simulation experiment. *Social Science and Medicine, 62*, 103–115.

Bach, P. B., Schrag, D., Brawley, O. W., Galaznik, A., Yakren, S., and Begg, C. B. (2002). Survival of blacks and whites after a cancer diagnosis. *Journal of the American Medical Association, 287*, 2106–2113.

Banks, J., Marmot M., Oldfield Z., and Smith J. P. (2006). Disease and disadvantage in the United States and in England. *Journal of the American Medical Association, 295*, 2037–2045.

Bellochs, C., and Carter, A. B. (1990). *Building primary health care in New York City's low income communities*. New York: Community Health Service Society of New York.

Benkert, R., Peters, R. M., Clark, R., and Keves-Foster, K. (1998). Effects of perceived racism, cultural mistrust, and trust in providers on satisfaction with care. *Journal of the National Medical Association, 98*, 1532–1540.

Bird, S. T., Bogart, L. M., and Delahanty, D. L. (2004). Health–related correlates of perceived discrimination in HIV care. *AIDS Patient Care and STDs, 18*, 19–26.

Blair, I. V. (2001). Implicit stereotypes and prejudice. In G. B. Moskowitz (Ed.), *Cognitive social psychology: The Princeton symposium on the legacy and future of social cognition* (pp. 359–374). Mahwah, NJ: Erlbaum.

Bogart, L. M., Catz, S. L., Kelly, J. A., and Benotsch, E. G. (2001). Factors influencing physicians' judgments of adherence and treatment decisions for patients with HIV disease. *Medical Decision Making, 21*, 28–36.

Borrell, L. N., Kiefe, C. I., Williams, D. R., Diez–Roux, A.V., and Gordon-Larsen, P. (2006). Self-reported health, perceived racial discrimination, and skin color in African Americans in the CARDIA study. *Social Science and Medicine, 63*, 1425–1427.

Boulware, L. E., Cooper, L. A., Ratner, L. E., LaVeist, T. A., and Powe, N. R. (2003). Race and trust in the health care . *Public Health Reports, 118*, 358–365.

Brandon D. T., Isaac, L. A., and LaVeist, T. A. (2005). The legacy of Tuskegee and trust in medical care: Is Tuskegee responsible for race differences in mistrust of medical care? *Journal of the National Medical Association, 97*, 951–956.

Braveman, P. (2006). Health disparities and health equity: Concepts and measurement. *Annual Review of Public Health, 27*, 167–194.

Brown C., Matthews, K. A., Bromberger, J., and Yuefang, C. (2006). The relation between perceived unfair treatment and blood pressure in a racially/ethnically diverse sample of women. *American Journal of Epidemiology, 164*, 257–262.

Burgess, D., van Ryn, M., Dovidio, J., and Saha, S. (2007). Reducing racial bias among health care providers: Lessons from social–cognitive psychology. *Journal of General Internal Medicine, 8*, 882–887.

Burgess, D. J., van Ryn, M., Crowley-Matoka, M., and Malat, J. (2006). Understanding the provider contribution to race/ethnicity disparities in pain treatment: Insights from dual process models of stereotyping. *Pain Medicine, 7*, 119–134.

Byrd, W. M., and Clayton, L. A. (2000). *An American health dilemma: Race, medicine, and healthcare in the United States 1900–2000.* New York: Routledge.

Byrd, W. M., and Clayton, L. A. (2002). *An American health dilemma: A medical history of African Americans and the problem of race.* New York: Routledge.

Chen, F. M., Fryer, G. E., Phillips, R. L., Wilson, E., and Pathman, D. E. (2005). Patients' beliefs about racism, preferences for physician race, and satisfaction with care. *Annals of Family Medicine, 3*, 139–143.

Chu, K. C., Miller, B. A., and Springfield, S. A. (2007). Measures of racial/ethnic health disparities in cancer mortality rates and the influence of socioeconomic status. *Journal of the National Medical Association, 99*, 1092–1100, 1102–1104.

Crisp, R., and Hewstone, M. (2007). Multiple social categorization. In M. Zanna (Ed.) *Advances in experimental social psychology* (Vol. 39, pp. 164–254). San Diego, CA: Academic Press.

Clark, R., Anderson, N., Clark, V. R., and Williams, D. R. (1999). Racism as a stressor for African Americans: A biopsychosocial model. *American Psychologist, 54*, 805–816.

Cooper, L. A., Roter, D. L., Johnson, R. L., Ford, D. E., Steinwachs, D. M, and Powe, N. R. (2003). Patient-centered communication, ratings of care, and concordance of patient and physician race. *Annals of Internal Medicine, 139*, 907–915.

Cooper–Patrick, L., Gallo, J. J., Gonzales, J. J., Vu, H. T., Powe, N. R., Nelson, C., et al., (1999). Race, gender, and partnership in the patient–physician relationship. *The Journal of the American Medical Association, 282*, 583–589.

Delahanty, J., Ram, R., Postrado, L., Balis, T., Green-Paden, L., et al., (2001). Differences in rates of depression in schizophrenia by race. *Schizophrenia Bulletin, 27*, 29–38.

Doescher, M. P., Saver, B. G., Fiscella, K., and Franks, P. (2001). Racial/ethnic inequities in continuity and site of care: Location, location, location. *Health Services Research, 36*, 78–89.

Dovidio, J. F., and Gaertner, S. L. (2004). Aversive racism. In M. P. Zanna (Ed.), *Advances in experimental social psychology* (Vol. 36, pp. 1–51). San Diego, CA: Academic Press.

Dovidio, J. F., Gaertner, S. L., Kawakami, K., and Hodson, G. (2002). Why can't we just get along? Interpersonal biases and interracial distrust. *Cultural Diversity and Ethnic Minority Psychology, 8*, 88–102.

Dovidio, J. F., Kawakami, K., Johnson, C., Johnson, B., and Howard, A. (1997). On the nature of prejudice: Automatic and controlled processes. *Journal of Experimental Social Psychology, 33*, 510–540.

Dovidio, J., Penner, L., Albrecht, T., Norton, W. E., Gaertner, S., and Shelton, N. (2008). Disparities and distrust: The implications of psychological processes for understanding disparities in health and health care. *Social Science and Medicine, 67*, 478–486.

DuBois, W. E. B. (Ed.) (1906). *The health and physique of the negro american. report of a social study made under the direction of Atlanta University; Together with the proceedings of the eleventh conference for the study of the negro problems.* Atlanta, Ga: Atlanta University Press.

Everson–Rose, S. A., and Lewis, T. T. (2005). Psychosocial factors and cardiovascular disease. *Annual Review of Public Health, 26*, 469–500.

Frank, R. (2007). What to make of it? The (Re)emergence of a biological conceptualization of race in health disparities research. *Social Science and Medicine, 64*, 1977–1983.

Franks, P., Muennig P., Lubetkin E., and Jia H. (2006). The burden of disease associated with being African-American in the United States and the contribution of socio-economic status. *Social Science and Medicine, 62*, 2469–2478.

Gaertner, S. L., and Dovidio, J. F. (2000). *Reducing intergroup bias: The common ingroup identity model.* Philadelphia, PA: The Psychology Press.

Geiger, H. J. (2003). Racial and ethnic disparities in diagnosis and treatment: A review of the evidence and a consideration of causes. In B. Smedley, A. Stith, and A. Nelson (Eds.), *Unequal Treatment: Confronting racial and ethnic disparities in health care* (pp. 417–454). Washington, DC: The National Academies Press.

Gordon, H. S., Street, R. L., Sharf, B. F., Kelly, P. A., and Souchek, J. (2006). Racial differences in trust and lung cancer patients' perceptions of physician communication. *Journal of Clinical Oncology, 24*, 904–909.

Gower, J. R., Fernandez, T., Beasley, M., Shriver, M. D., and Goran, M. I. (2003). Using genetic admixture to explain racial differences in insulin–related phenotypes. *Diabetes, 52,* 1047–1051.

Green, A. R., Carney, D. R., Pallin, D. J., Ngo, L. H., Raymond, K. L., Iezzoni, L. I., et al., (2007). The presence of implicit bias in physicians and its predictions of thrombolysis decisions for Black and White patients. *Journal of General Internal Medicine, 22,* 1231–1238.

Greenwald, A. G., McGhee, D. E., and Schwartz, J. L. (1998). Measuring individual differences in implicit social cognition: the implicit association test. *Journal of Personality and Social Psychology, 74,* 1464–1480.

Griggs, J. J., Culakova, E., Sorbero, M. E., Poniewierski, M. S., Wolff, D. A., Crawford, J., et al., (2007). Social and racial differences in selection of breast cancer adjuvant chemotherapy regimens. *Journal of Clinical Oncology, 25,* 2522–2527.

Griggs, J. J., Sorbero, M. E., Stark, A. T., Heininger, S. E., and Dick, A. W. (2003). Racial disparity in the dose and dose intensity of breast cancer adjuvant chemotherapy. *Breast Cancer Research and Treatment, 81,* 21–31.

Hall, J.A., Roter, D.L., and Katz, N.R. (1988). Meta-analysis of correlates of provider behavior in medical encounters. *Medical Care, 26,* 657–675.

Halbert, C. H., Armstrong, K., Gandy, O. H., and Shaker, L. (2006). Racial differences in trust in health care providers. *Archives of Internal Medicine, 166,* 896–901.

Hewstone, M., Rubin, M., and Willis, H. (2002). Intergroup bias. *Annual Review of Psychology, 53,* 575–604.

Hodson, G., Dovidio, J. F., and Gaertner, S. L. (2002). Processes in racial discrimination: Differential weighting of conflicting information. *Personality and Social Psychology Bulletin, 28,* 460–471.

Howard University National Human Genome Center (2006). Gene-environment studies of asthma among African–Americans. Retrieved September 10, 2006 http://www.genomecenter.howard.edu/researchprograms.htm

Institute of Medicine. (IOM) (2003). *Unequal treatment: Confronting racial and ethnic disparities in health care.* B.D. Smedley, A.Y. Stith, and A.R. Nelson, (Eds.), Washington, DC: National Academies Press.

Johnson, R. L., Saha, S., Arbelaez, J. J., Beach, M. C., and Cooper, L. A. (2004a). Racial and ethnic differences in patient perceptions of bias and cultural competence in health care. *Journal of General Internal Medicine, 19,* 101–110.

Johnson, R. L., Roter, D., Powe, N. R., and Cooper, L. A. (2004b). Patient race/ethnicity and quality of patient-physician communication during medical visits. *American Journal of Public Health, 94,* 2084–2090.

Jones, J. H. (1993) *Bad Blood: The Tuskegee syphilis experiment, Revised edition.* New York: Free Press.

Kaplan, S. H., Gandek, B., Greenfield, S., Rogers, W., and Ware, J. E. (1995). Patient and visit characteristics related to physicians' participatory decision-making style. Results from the Medical Outcomes Study. *Medical Care, 33,* 1176–1187.

Koerber, A., Gajendra, S., Fulford, R. L., BeGole, E., and Evans, C. A. (2004). An exploratory study of orthodontic resident communication by patient race and ethnicity. *Journal of Dental Education, 68,* 553–562.

Kunda, Z., and Spencer, S. J. (2003). When do stereotypes come to mind and when do they color judgment? A goal-based theoretical framework for stereotype activation and application. *Psychological Bulletin, 129,* 522–544.

Lasser, K. E., Himmelstein, D. U., and Woolhandler, S. (2006). Access to care, health status, and health disparities in the United States and Canada: Results of a cross-national population-based survey. *American Journal of Public Health, 96,* 1300–1307.

LaVeist, T. A. (2005). Disentangling race and socioeconomic status: A key to understanding health inequalities. *Journal of Urban Health, 82* (Suppl. 3), iii26–34.

LaVeist, T. A., and Carroll, T. (2002). Race of physician and satisfaction with care among African-American patients. *Journal of the National Medical Association, 94,* 937–943.

LaVeist, T. A., and Nuru-Jeter, A. (2002). Is doctor-patient race concordance associated with greater satisfaction with care? *Journal of Health and Social Behavior, 43,* 296–306.

LaVeist, T. A., Nuru-Jeter, A., and Jones, K. E. (2003). The association of doctor-patient race concordance with health services utilization. *Journal of Public Health Policy, 24,* 312–323.

Lee, A. J., Gehlbach, S., Hosmer, R. M., and Baker, C. S. (1997). Medicare treatment differences for blacks and whites. *Medical Care, 35,* 1173–1189.

Leippe, M. R. and Eisenstadt, D. (1994). Generalization of dissonance reduction: Decreasing prejudice through induced compliance. *Journal of Personality and Social Psychology, 67,* 395–413.

Malat, J., and Hamilton, M. A. (2006). Preference for same-race health care providers and perceptions of interpersonal discrimination in health care. *Journal of Health and Social Behavior, 47,* 173–187.

Martin, T. W. (1993). White therapists' differing perceptions of black and white adolescents. *Adolescence, 28,* 281–289.

Mays, V. M., Cochran, S. D., and Barnes, N. (2007). Race, racism and the health outcomes among African Americans. *Annual Review of Psychology, 58*, 565–592.

Millett, C., Gray, J., Saxena, S., Netuveli, G., Khunti K., and Majeed A. (2007). Ethnic disparities in diabetes management and pay-for-performance in the UK: The Wandsworth prospective diabetes study. PLoS Medicine, 4, 1087–1092.

National Center for Health Statistics (2003). *Health United States 2003 with chartbook on trends in the health of Americans*. Hyattsville, MD: U.S. Government Printing Office.

National Center for Health Statistics (2006). *Health United States 2006 with chartbook on trends in the health of Americans*. Hyattsville, MD: U.S. Government Printing Office.

Oliver, M. N., Goodwin, M. A., Gotler, R. S., Gregory, P. M., and Strange, K. C. (2001). Time use in clinical encounters: Are African-American patients treated differently? *Journal of the National Medical Association, 93*, 380–385.

Pascoe, E. A., and Richman, L. S. (2009). Perceived discrimination and health: A meta–analytic review. *Psychological Bulletin, 135*, 531–554

Penner, L. A., Albrecht, T. L., Coleman, D. K., and Norton, W. (2007a). Interpersonal perspectives on Black-White health disparities: Social policy implications. *Social Issues and Policy Review, 1*, 63–98.

Penner, L. A., Dovidio, J. F., Edmondson, D., Albrecht, T. L., Markova, T., Gaertner, S. L., et al., (2009a). Subtle racism, experience of discrimination, and black-white health disparities *Journal of Black Psychology, 35*, 180–203.

Penner, L. A., Dovidio, J. F., West, T. V., Gaertner, S. L., Albrecht, T. L., Daily, R. K., and Markova, T., (2010). Aversive Racism and Medical Interactions with Black Patients: A Field Study. *Journal of Experimental Social Psychology, 46*, 436–440.

Penner, L. A., Eggly, S., Harper, F. W. K., Albrecht, T. L., and Ruckdeschel, J. C. (2007b). Patient attributes and information provided about clinical trials. *Proceedings of the American Association for Cancer Research Science of Cancer Health Disparities in Racial/Ethnic Minorities and the Medically Underserved*, 95.

Penner, L. A., Dailey, R. Markova, T., Porcerelli, J., Dovidio, J., and Gaertner, S. (February, 2009b). Using the common group identity model to increase trust and commonality in racially discordant medical interactions. Annual Meeting of Society of Personality and Social Psychology, Tampa, Florida.

Pettigrew, T., and Tropp, L. (2006). A meta-analytic test of intergroup contact theory. *Journal of Personality and Social Psychology, 90*, 751–783.

Richeson, J. A., and Shelton, J. N. (2005). Thin slices of racial bias. *Journal of Nonverbal Behavior, 29*, 75–86.

Rokeach, M. (1973). *The nature of human values*. New York: Free Press

Roter, D. L., Stewart, M., Putnam, S. M., Lipkin, M. Jr., Stiles, W., and Inui, T. S. (1997). Communication patterns of primary care physicians. *Journal of American Medical Association, 277*, 350–356.

Sabin, J. A., Rivera, F. P., and Greenwald, A. G., (2008). Physician implicit attitudes and stereotypes about race and quality of medical care. *Medical Care, 46*, 678–685.

Schulman, K. A., Berlin, J. A., Harless, W., Kerner, J. F., Sistrunk, S., et al. (1999). The effect of race and sex on physicians' recommendations for cardiac catheterization. *The New England Journal of Medicine, 340*, 618–626.

Sentell, T. L., and Halpin, H. A. (2006). Importance of adult literacy in understanding health disparities. *Journal of General Internal Medicine, 21*, 862–866.

Shavers, V. L., Brown, M., Klabunde, C. N., Potosky, A. L., Davis, W., Moul, J. W., et al., (2004a). Race/Ethnicity and the intensity of medical monitoring under 'watchful waiting' for prostate cancer. *Medical Care, 42*, 239–250.

Shavers, V. L., Brown, M. L., Potosky, A. L., Klabunde, C. N., Davis, W. W., Moul, J. W., et al., (2004b). Race/ethnicity and the receipt of watchful waiting for the initial management of prostrate cancer. *Journal of General Internal Medicine, 19*, 146–155.

Siminoff, L. A., Graham, G. C., and Gordon, N. H. (2006). Cancer communication patterns and the influence of patient characteristics: Disparities in information-giving and affective behaviours. *Patient Education and Counselling, 62*, 355–360.

Stewart, M. A. (1995). Effective physician-patient communication and health outcomes: A review. *Canadian Medical Association Journal, 152*, 1423–1433.

Stewart, M. A., Brown, J. B., Donner, A., Mcwhinney, I., Oates, J., Weston, W., et al., (2000). The impact of patient–centered care on outcomes. *Journal of Family Practice, 49*, 796–804.

Surveillance, Epidemiology, and End Results (SEER) Program (2005). *SEER*Stat Database: Incidence – SEER 9 Regs Public-Use, Nov 2004 Sub (1973–2003)*, National Cancer Institute, DCCPS, Surveillance Research Program, Cancer Statistics Branch, released April 2006, based on the November 2005 submission. Web site: http://www.seer.cancer.gov

Swim, J. K., Scott, E. D., Sechrist, G. B., Campbell, B., Stangor, C. (2003). The role of intent and harm in judgments of prejudice and discrimination. *Journal of Personality and Social Psychology, 84*, 944–959.

Thompson, H. S., Valdimarsdottir, H. B., Winkel, G., Jandorf, L., and Redd, W. (2004). The group-based Medical Mistrust Scale: Psychometric properties and association with breast cancer screening. *Preventive Medicine, 38*, 209–218.

Underwood, W., De Monner, S., Ubel, P., Fagerlin, A., Sanda, M. G., and Wei, J. T. (2004). Racial/ethnic disparities in the treatment of localized/regional prostate cancer. *The Journal of Urology, 171*, 1504–1507.

van Ryn, M. (2002). Research on the provider contribution to race/ethnicity disparities in medical care. *Medical Care, 40*, 1140–1151.

van Ryn, M., Burgess, D., Malat, J., and Griffin, J. (2006). Physicians' perception of patients' social and behavioral characteristics and race disparities in treatment recommendations for men with coronary artery disease. *American Journal of Public Health, 96*, 351–357.

van Ryn, M., and Burke, J. (2000). The effect of patient race and socio-economic status on physicians' perceptions of patients. *Social Science and Medicine, 50*, 813–828.

van Ryn, M., and Williams, D. (2003). Commentary on racial disparities in health care. *Medical Care Research and Review, 60*, 496–508.

Vaccarino, V., Rathore, S. S., Wenger, N. K., Frederick, P. D., Abramson, J. L., Barron, H. V.,

Manhapra, A., Mallik, S., and Krumholz, H. M. (2005). Sex and racial differences in the management of acute myocardial infarction, 1994 through 2002. *New England Journal of Medicine, 353*, 671–682.

White R. M. (2005). Misinformation and misbeliefs in the Tuskegee Study of untreated syphilis fuel mistrust in the healthcare system. *Journal of the National Medical Association, 97*, 1566–1573.

Wilder, D., and Simon, A. F. (1998). Categorical and dynamic groups: Implications for social perception and intergroup behavior. In C. Sedikides, and J. Schopler (Eds), *Intergroup cognition and intergroup behavior.* (pp. 27–44). Mahwah, NJ, Lawrence Erlbaum Associates.

Williams, D. R., and Collins, C. (1995). US Socioeconomic differences and racial differences in health: Patterns and explanations. *Annual Review of Sociology, 21*, 349–386.

Williams, D. R., Neighbors, H. W., and Jackson, J. S. (2003). Racial/ethnic discrimination and health: Findings from community studies. *American Journal of Public Health, 93*, 200–208.

Wittenbrink, B., Judd, C., and Park, B. (1997). Evidence for racial prejudice at the implicit level and its relationship with questionnaire measures. *Journal of Personality and Social Psychology, 72*, 262–274.

PART V

Combating Prejudice, Stereotyping and Discrimination

30

Self-Regulation and Bias

Margo J. Monteith*, Steven A. Arthur,
and Sarah McQueary Flynn

ABSTRACT

Self-regulation has been extensively investigated as a means for changing implicit as well as explicit prejudicial biases. We first discuss motivational factors influencing regulatory inclinations, and then turn to two regulatory strategies. The first strategy involves the suppression of prejudicial biases – a strategy that often backfires. The second strategy involves conflict monitoring and the exertion of regulatory control through processes described in the Self-Regulation of Prejudice (SRP) model. Empirical findings are reviewed related to the central features of the SRP model, with attention to recent advances made possible by social neuroscientific investigations. Individual difference and situational factors that can facilitate or interfere with the self-regulation of prejudice are then discussed. We conclude by highlighting critical directions for future research.

SELF-REGULATION AND BIAS

All in all, we are forced to conclude that prejudice in a life is more likely than not to arouse some compunction, at least some of the time. It is almost impossible to integrate it consistently with affiliative needs and human values.

(Allport, 1954: 329)

This quote from Gordon Allport underscores one of the fundamental aspects of the individual experience of prejudice in modern society. Namely, as a people we place value on the notions of equality and justice as rights inherent to all individuals. However, many psychological processes leave us prone to negative feelings toward outgroups. Indeed, most contemporary theoretical conceptualizations of prejudice echo this sense of conflict or competing motivations (e.g., Devine, 1989; Dovidio and Gaertner, 1998; Sears and Henry, 2003).

Various psychological processes contribute to this conflict, or more specifically to a reluctance to whole-heartedly embrace non-prejudice in all aspects of one's being and life. In this chapter, we begin with an overview of past perspectives on the nature of this conflict. We then discuss exactly what is being regulated when someone attempts to control intergroup bias, and what determines when such attempts will be made. In the following section we compare potential strategies for the self-regulation of bias, discussing the pros and cons of each method, and we outline a working model of the self-regulation process, discussing each step involved in regulating bias. Finally, we conclude with a discussion of potential future directions for self-regulation research.

BRIEF HISTORY

Decades of research have been devoted to understanding factors that encourage prejudice. For example, research using minimal groups has demonstrated how easily one can develop a preference for one's ingroup – even ingroups based on arbitrary distinctions – at the expense of outgroups (Tajfel and Turner, 1986). This bias is the result of natural cognitive processes (e.g., categorization) and can be observed not only at an overt level, but also at the implicit level of evaluation (Ashburn-Nardo, Voils, & Monteith, 2001). Other factors that encourage a leaning toward prejudice despite general adherence to principles of equality and justice include socialization processes (e.g., Katz, 2003), pervasive value orientations (e.g., individualism; Katz and Hass, 1988), and personality (e.g. Altemeyer, 1996). To be sure, changing social norms increasingly condemn prejudice and discrimination towards minority and other stigmatized groups (Crandall, Eshleman, & O'Brien, 2002), but a multitude of individual- and society-level factors continue to reinforce stereotypes and negative evaluative biases. Thus is born the conflict characteristic of modern prejudices, where people regard prejudice as unjust, offensive, or perhaps even abominable, but it remains deeply rooted in their psyche and aspects of their world view.

There are several ways to deal with this conflict. Some people choose to maintain their prejudices, but attempt to justify them to others and often even to themselves. Examples of this process are seen in symbolic and modern racism theories (Sears and Henry, 2003) and aversive racism theory (Dovidio and Gaertner, 1998). Other psychological variables, such as a belief in personal responsibility and individualism (e.g., Biernat, Vescio, Theno, et al., 1996; Katz and Hass, 1988) or social hierarchies (Sidanius and Pratto, 1999), can assist in justifying and rationalizing intergroup biases.

However, it is also possible that a person may choose to confront their biases and take steps to overcome prejudiced responding. This process involves the use of self-regulatory resources to alter one's experienced or expressed biases.

LITERATURE REVIEW AND FRAMEWORK

The process of self-regulation involves exerting conscious control over behavior to achieve a desired outcome (Mischel, 1996). This ability has long been recognized as one of the more important aspects of human psychology, allowing people to achieve long-term goals by altering present behavior (Carver and Scheier, 1990; James, 1890). The following two sections discuss what constructs are regulated when attempting to control prejudice and identify certain motivational and individual difference variables that influence the likelihood that one will regulate prejudiced responses.

What needs to be regulated? Automatic activation and controlled processes

One of the most influential methodological breakthroughs made in the social psychological literature on stereotyping and prejudice during the past two decades has been the application of cognitive psychology's distinction between automatic (oftentimes referred to as implicit) and controlled (oftentimes referred to as explicit) processes (e.g., Roediger, 1990; Shiffrin and Schneider, 1977). A full discussion of this distinction is beyond the scope of this chapter (but see Devine and Sharp, 2009), although several points should be made regarding their difference. As applied in social psychology and the study of stereotyping and prejudice in particular, controlled processes involve relatively high levels of intention, attention, and conscious awareness of biased intergroup responding or lack thereof. Individuals are aware of the contents of their explicit attitudes and can use deliberative processes to evaluate and/or regulate such attitudes or their expression. Rather than responding in biased ways, a conscious decision may be made to inhibit prejudiced responses and to respond in less prejudiced ways instead.

However, this represents only part of the challenge for self-regulating prejudiced responses. Automatic or implicit processes are typically described as those that are activated and used without conscious intent and conscious awareness (Greenwald and Banaji, 1995). The last two decades of social psychological research has uncovered a variety of methods for assessing such implicit biases (see Fazio and Olson, 2003), with the most commonly used methods involving priming (e.g., Fazio, Jackson, Dunton, et al., 1995) and the Implicit Association Test (IAT; Greenwald, McGhee, Schwartz, et al., 1998). There is much evidence that, without conscious bidding or the intent to have biased thoughts, feelings, or actions, stereotypes and evaluative biases can be activated and applied when responding to outgroups (see Bargh, 1999; Dasgupta, 2004). Moreover, this automatic activation may occur for individuals whose consciously held attitudes are low as well as high in prejudice (Devine, 1989).

Once implicit biases are formed, they can be difficult to unlearn via the traditional methods by which social psychologists induce explicit attitude change (e.g., providing strong counter-attitudinal information or arguments, Gregg, Seibt, & Banaji, 2006). Several theorists have recently postulated and provided evidence suggesting that explicit and implicit attitudes are learned and altered through different mental reasoning systems (Gawronski and Bodenhausen, 2006; Rydell and McConnell, 2006). Specifically, explicit attitudes are formed and changed through propositional reasoning that allows for more rapid change in the evaluation of objects. Implicit attitudes, in contrast, appear to be changed via a relatively slow-learning associative system that relies on simple associative evaluations.

Nonetheless, recent findings suggest that implicit biases are malleable, in that situational factors can influence the likelihood of their activation and application (for a review, see Dasgupta, 2009). For example, exposure to counter stereotypic exemplars of a social group (e.g., women in high status positions) has been shown to decrease implicit bias on the IAT in both the short term and over longer periods of time (Dasgupta and Rivera, 2008). Similarly, asking participants to visualize a counter stereotypical woman led to decreased stereotypical bias on the IAT (Blair, Ma, & Lenton, 2001). Other strategies involve requiring participants to engage in counter stereotypic training (i.e., associating females with stereotypically male characteristics and vice versa (Kawakami, Dovidio, & van Kamp, 2005).

It is important to note that while these various techniques have demonstrated the malleability of implicit biases, they do not constitute the type of self-regulation of interest in this chapter. For example, in none of this research did individuals have the goal of exerting regulatory resources so as to minimize the activation or impact of automatically activated constructs.

Who regulates their prejudiced responding?

For someone to regulate behavior to achieve a goal, they obviously must have some degree of motivation for achieving the goal. This motivation can take many forms, such as receiving a reward or avoiding punishment, or a desire to maintain a positive image of the self. Researchers have identified and devoted much time to studying several types of motivations for regulating prejudice.

One critical factor is people's personal attitudes and standards. People who hold low-prejudice attitudes or standards for responding to members of stereotyped groups are personally motivated to try to respond in egalitarian ways (e.g., Devine, 1989). These individuals are often identified according to their explicit reports of non-prejudiced attitudes on self-report measures such as the Attitudes Towards Blacks Scale (ATB; Brigham, 1993).

Motivation to control prejudice can also be measured more directly by asking people to report on the reasons *why* (if any) they attempt to regulate their bias (Dunton and Fazio, 1997;

Plant and Devine, 1998). For example, Plant and Devine have successfully identified two general motivations for avoiding prejudiced responses. One is an internal motivation driven by a desire to act in accord with personal standards of egalitarianism. The other is a motivation that is driven by external reasons, such as the desire to avoid negative reactions from others for behaving in prejudiced ways. These two motivations are not opposite ends of one continuum, but instead are relatively independent constructs on which individuals can vary.

Research examining internal and external motivations to control prejudice has supported their critical role in the self-regulation of intergroup biases at both the explicit and implicit levels (Plant and Devine, 1998; Plant, Devine, & Brazy, 2003). Specifically, findings indicate that explicit bias is regulated consistently by highly internally motivated individuals, but people low in internal motivation regulate bias only in public and only if they are externally motivated to do so. For implicit bias, findings suggest that people with high-internal/low-external motivation scores exhibit lower levels of implicit bias than other people, presumably because their motivations to be nonprejudiced are both highly internalized and autonomous (i.e., not based on external contingencies or mandates) (Devine, Plant, Amodio, et al., 2002). These individuals appear to have less implicit bias that requires regulation.

When people are sufficiently motivated to engage in the self-regulation of prejudice, precisely how do they pursue this goal? The extant literature has focused on two main strategies. The first involves the suppression of stereotypic thoughts and biases. The second strategy involves the regulation of prejudice through processes of monitoring, inhibition, and the exertion of control. We turn now to a discussion of these strategies.

Self-regulation via thought suppression

When one wants to avoid biased thinking or responses, an obvious strategy would be to attempt to banish stereotypic thoughts from the mind. People can try to focus on other thoughts, perhaps trying to ignore group membership of others or focusing on non-stereotypic individuating information. This suppression strategy was first investigated by Macrae and colleagues (1994). Participants first spent five minutes writing about a 'day in the life' of a person shown in a photograph who had characteristics suggesting that he was a skinhead. Half of the participants were told to avoid stereotypic thoughts as they wrote their passages. Participants in a control condition were given no special instructions. Not surprisingly, passages written in the control condition showed greater evidence of stereotyping than passages written in the suppression condition. However, this research also revealed a less desirable consequence of suppression. Specifically, when participants were asked to write another passage about a skinhead (this time with no suppression instructions), those who had suppressed stereotypes during the first passage-writing task showed evidence of even greater stereotyping than participants who had never suppressed stereotypes in the first place. This paradoxical effect of stereotype suppression was also revealed in the form of heightened stereotype accessibility following suppression (Study 3) and behavioral distancing from a stereotypic target (Study 2).

Why are attempts to avoid biased thoughts associated with these types of rebound effects? According to Wegner's (1994) model of mental control, two processes are activated when people attempt to avoid unwanted thoughts. First, a conscious, controlled operating process searches for appropriate distracter thoughts and, second, an automatic, ironic monitoring process continually searches consciousness for evidence of the unwanted thoughts. The controlled operating process will successfully keep the unwanted thoughts at bay as long as it is not taxed by other cognitive demands and the need for suppression remains salient. However, the simultaneous activity of the ironic monitoring process is thought to have the unfortunate effect of priming the unwanted thoughts

(Macrae, Bodenhausen, Milne, et al., 1994) and building associations between these thoughts and the distracter thoughts (Wegner, 1994). Thus, when the conscious monitoring process is taxed or relaxed, the suppressed thoughts will rebound and flood the mind even more than if one had not attempted suppression in the first place.

In addition to the rebound effect, stereotype suppression can have a number of other negative consequences (for a review, see Monteith, Sherman, & Devine, 1998). For instance, suppression can result in impaired memory for nonstereotypic individuating information and superior memory for stereotypic behaviors. It also takes a toll on regulatory resources, which can result in increased stereotyping of groups that were not even the initial targets of one's suppression attempts (Gordijn, Hindriks, Koomen, et al., 2004).

Despite the pessimistic implications of much stereotype suppression research, there are some people for whom this regulatory strategy appears to meet with greater success (see Monteith, Sherman, & Devine, 1998). People who have a strong personal desire to avoid stereotypic thoughts (e.g., low-prejudice individuals) show less evidence of stereotype hyperaccessibility and use following suppression than people who lack such internal motivation to control prejudice (Monteith, Spicer, & Tooman, 1998; Gordijn, Hindriks, Koomen, et al., 2004). In addition, low-prejudice individuals do not experience a depletion of regulatory resources following stereotype suppression (Gordijn, Hindriks, Koomen, et al., 2004), perhaps because egalitarian thoughts provide ready replacements.

There are conditions under which even high-prejudice people do not show the stereotype rebound effect. If social norms call for continual avoidance of the use of stereotypes after the initial suppression period and cognitive resources are sufficient for continued suppression, rebound has not been observed (Monteith, Spicer, & Tooman, 1998; Wyer, Sherman, & Stroessner, 2000). Gailliot and colleagues (2007) also found that strengthening self-control resources among high-prejudice individuals helps to reduce stereotype rebound and the depletion of regulatory resources during suppression. The more optimistic implications of these findings for the strategic use of stereotype suppression among high-prejudice individuals should be tempered with the cautionary note that backlash may eventually occur. That is, because high-prejudice individuals' personal preference is to put their stereotypes to use in their everyday thinking, they may become angry over pressures to respond in egalitarian ways and later lash out with biased responses (Plant and Devine, 2001).

In sum, regulating intergroup bias by essentially trying to ignore it and banishing stereotypic thoughts from the mind can be successful in the short-term. However, stereotype suppression is often associated with the paradoxical effects of stereotype rebound and hyperaccessability. Furthermore, we have doubts about whether suppression can alter the basic cognitive and affective structures of the mind in which semantic and evaluative associations are rooted. That is, there is no reason to believe that suppression can produce long-term changes to the underlying, biased associations that feed into the activation and application of bias in intergroup contexts. We turn now to another method of self-regulation that may have greater promise for enduring change.

Self-regulation: Monitoring, inhibiting, and exerting control

As we have noted, the foremost difficulties associated with stereotypic and prejudicial biases are that they are often activated without awareness or intent and then influence responses before inhibition can occur. Do these circumstances surrounding the operation of intergroup bias mean that it is inevitable at worst and more than likely to occur at best (see Bargh, 1999)? Casual consideration of human response patterns would seem to suggest that we do have the capacity for deautomatization. When sufficiently motivated, people may draw upon self-regulatory processes to achieve desired change. Two theoretical frameworks are particularly informative for understanding how people can learn to control and change unwanted response patterns.

First, according to Gray's neuropsychological model of motivation and learning (Gray and McNaughton, 1996), the seat of self-regulation is the behavioral inhibition system (BIS). This system becomes active when a discrepancy is detected between expected and actual events. This activation results in enhanced attention to the event, increased arousal, and a momentary and automatic interruption of ongoing responding. During this interruption, exploratory-investigative behavior is initiated to identify stimuli and responses that predict the occurrence of the unwanted, or discrepant, response. Associations between various cues surrounding the discrepant response, the aversive consequences of it, and the discrepant response itself are then created. In the future, the presence of these response-contingent punishment cues is thought to trigger the BIS, providing a warning for the need to engage self-regulatory processes.

A second, more recent perspective on control can be found in the cognitive neuroscience literature. Much of this research makes use of technologies such as fMRI and PET to identify neural substrates associated with aspects of self-regulation (see Amodio and Lieberman, 2009). Guided by previous theoretical conceptions of control, researchers have identified a *conflict monitoring* system that is sensitive to events that can produce conflict between potential responses, and a *regulatory* system that allows for the inhibition of unintended responses and execution of the desired responses. The conflict monitoring system is associated with brain activity localized in the anterior cingulate cortex (ACC) (specifically, when measured most precisely, with activity in the dorsal ACC). In contrast, the regulatory system appears to be associated with activity in the lateral prefrontal cortex.

Research reported by Cunningham and colleagues (2004) illustrates the operation of these systems. Consistent with a growing body of findings, this research implicated the amygdala (a brain structure associated

learning and emotional stimuli) as involved in implicit prejudice. Specifically, Cunningham et al. (2004) found greater amygdala activity to Black versus White faces when they were presented subliminally. However, when the faces could be consciously perceived, greater activity was observed in the dACC and lPFC for Black than for White faces. These findings imply greater control activity among participants as they viewed Black faces.

These perspectives on control have provided researchers with frameworks needed for formulating and testing hypotheses about how people may learn to control their prejudiced responses through self-regulation. We turn now to a summary of this work, integrating affective, cognitive, and behavioral evidence for the self-regulation of prejudice with recent advances made possible with the social neuroscientific level of analysis. We first describe a model for understanding how change may be achieved through self-regulation, and then turn to relevant empirical investigations.

The self-regulation of prejudice model

Monteith and colleagues (Monteith, 1993; Monteith, Ashburn-Nardo, Voils, et al., 2002; for reviews, see Monteith and Voils, 2001; Monteith and Mark, 2005) have developed and tested the Self-Regulation of Prejudice Model (SRP Model) for understanding how self-regulation may enable individuals to deautomatize their prejudiced patterns of responding (see Figure 30.1). The model starts with the now well-documented fact that stereotypes and implicit evaluative biases can be automatically activated and used as a basis for responding (e.g., Devine, 1989). For people who hold low-prejudice attitudes, such a response constitutes a discrepancy from one's personal standards, (e.g., Monteith and Voils, 1998). Prejudiced responses may also be experienced as discrepancies from standards among high-prejudice individuals, although in their case the discrepancies are not from personal standards that are linked with strong feelings of moral obligation but

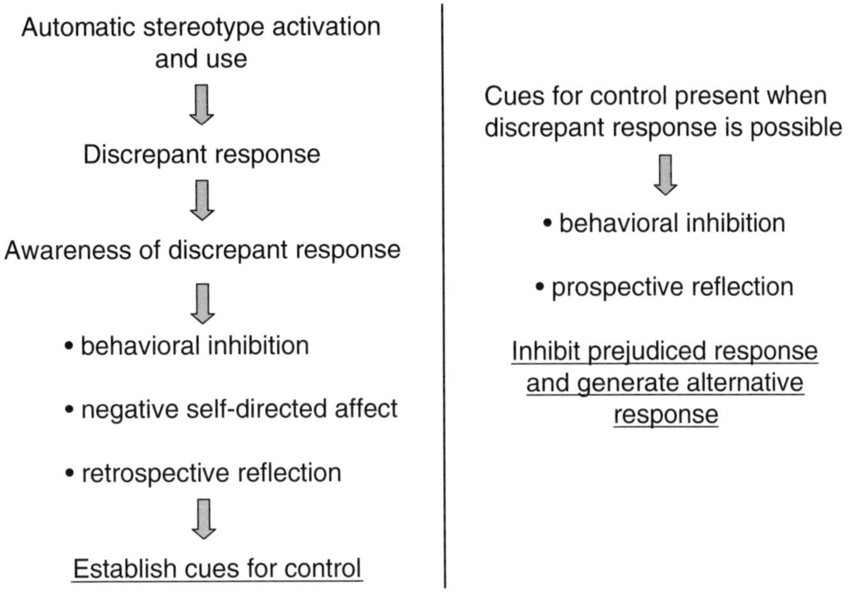

Automatic stereotype activation
and use

⇩

Discrepant response

⇩

Awareness of discrepant response

⇩

• behavioral inhibition

• negative self-directed affect

• retrospective reflection

⇩

Establish cues for control

Cues for control present when
discrepant response is possible

⇩

• behavioral inhibition

• prospective reflection

Inhibit prejudiced response
and generate alternative
response

Figure 30.1   The self-regulation of prejudice model.

rather from standards based more on societal pressures to respond in non-prejudiced ways (Monteith, Devine, & Zuwerink, 1993; Monteith and Walters, 1998).

According to the SRP model, awareness that one has engaged in a prejudiced response that is discrepant from non-prejudiced standards leads to a variety of consequences that are critical to subsequent self-regulatory efforts. First, arousal should be momentarily increased and accompanied by *behavioral inhibition* (a brief interruption of ongoing responding), Second, awareness of the discrepancy should elicit negative affect. This affect should take the form of guilt and self-disappointment among low-prejudice individuals (Higgins, 1987). In contrast, high-prejudice individuals' discrepancies should elicit general discomfort, threat, and potentially other-directed negative affect because their discrepancies involve violating pressure from others to respond in less prejudiced ways (Higgins, 1987).

The SRP model then posits that a brief period of *retrospective reflection* will ensue in which attentional resources are directed toward noting indicators of the discrepant response, such as features of the situation and

environment in which the discrepant response occurred. The natural consequence of becoming aware of a prejudice-related discrepant response, experiencing negative affect, and attending to features of the situation present when the discrepant response occurred is the establishment of *cues for control*. In other words, associations are built between stimuli that predict the occurrence of a discrepant response, the discrepant response itself, and the negative self-directed affect resulting from awareness of one's discrepancy.

For example, consider the types of incidents that White participants have reported to us in interviews designed to tap into people's detection of their prejudice-related discrepancies (Monteith et al., in preparation). Reports include events such as catching themselves locking their car doors at a traffic light upon seeing a Black man; assuming a group of Black students were not as smart as Whites; and supposing that Black children at a daycare would bully more than the White children. A low-prejudice individual who becomes aware of such biased reactions should experience negative self-directed affect. A momentary pausing should occur, and stimuli present or in some way related to the discrepant response should be noted (e.g., the intersection the person is at, features of the Black person at the traffic light. etc.). These consequences should result in the establishment of cues for control, or the building of associations between the prejudiced response (in this case, locking the car doors), the negative affect, and related stimuli (e.g., the man's race). Theoretically, this process should take only milliseconds.

Such initial discrepancy experiences are critical for the self-regulation of prejudiced responses in the future. The presence of cues for control in subsequent situations when a prejudiced response is possible should trigger behavioral inhibition, enabling the person to engage in *prospective reflection*. Responses based on automatically activated stereotypes and prejudice thus can be inhibited and nonbiased responses can be generated instead. Theoretically, this process of self-regulation should, with practice, result in the deautomatization of prejudiced responses, and the consistent generation of less biased responses. We turn now to research illustrating how the various processes described in the SRP have been tested.

Prejudice-related discrepancies and affect

The SRP model suggests that, with time and practice, regulatory control over prejudiced responses may be routinized and initiated spontaneously in the presence of cues for control (see Monteith, Ashburn-Nardo, Voils, et al., 2002). However, this can happen only if people are first aware that they are prone to biases that require control. People's awareness that they are prone to prejudice-related discrepancies has been assessed in a number of studies with the Should-Would Discrepancy Questionnaire (see Monteith and Mark, 2005, for a review). In one section of the questionnaire, participants report the extent to which they *would* have a biased response for various situations that are described (e.g., feeling uncomfortable when shaking the hand of a Black person). In another section, they report the extent to which they *should* have a biased response in each situation based on their personal

standards for responding. Discrepancy scores are then generated by subtracting each *should* rating from the corresponding *would* rating and summing the resulting difference scores. This research has revealed that the vast majority of participants (approximately 80%) report positive discrepancies, indicating an awareness that they are prone to responding in ways that are more prejudiced than their personal standards suggest are appropriate.

According to the SRP model, awareness of one's discrepant responses must give rise to feelings of negative affect to be useful for learning to change one's prejudiced patterns of responding. One strategy for investigating the affective consequences of discrepancy awareness has involved having participants report their current feelings after they complete the Should-Would Discrepancy Questionnaire (see Monteith and Mark, 2005). To the extent that participants report prejudice-related discrepancies, these inconsistencies should have affective consequences. Results consistently reveal that larger discrepancy scores are associated with greater general discomfort among participants at all levels of explicit prejudice and with self-directed negative affect (e.g., guilt) among participants who hold low-prejudice attitudes.

Experimental investigations in which discrepant responses are manipulated (Monteith, 1993; Monteith, Ashburn-Nardo, Voils, et al., 2002) have also tested discrepancy-associated affective consequences. For example, Monteith (1993) created discrepancies by leading heterosexual participants to believe that their negative evaluations of a supposed law school applicant stemmed from his being gay. These experiments have consistently shown that discrepancy experiences create discomfort and, among low-prejudice individuals, feelings of guilt and disappointment with the self.

Amodio et al. (2007) recently tested a dynamic conceptualization of discrepancy-associated guilt. Consistent with the SRP, they hypothesized that guilt initially functions as a negative reinforcement cue and reduces approach motivation, interrupting ongoing behavior and enhancing processing of the transgression to learn from mistakes. Then guilt transforms into approach-motivated behavior to facilitate more personally acceptable responding in the future. The low-prejudice White participants in this research viewed faces of Whites, Asians, and Blacks while EEG recordings were made. Participants were given bogus feedback that they had negative reactions when viewing faces of Blacks to induce feelings of guilt. Then participants reported their interest in reading various magazine articles, several of which were relevant to prejudice reduction ('e.g., 10 ways to reduce prejudice in everyday life'). Results showed that elevated guilt was associated with decreased approach motivation (i.e., reduced left-frontal cortical asymmetry). In contrast, when the opportunity for pursuing a prejudice-reducing activity was introduced, guilt was associated with increased approach motivation (i.e., increased left-frontal cortical asymmetry). These results support the functional significance of guilt in the prejudice reduction process, an issue that we explore further below.

Behavioral inhibition and retrospective reflection

According to the SRP model, a brief interruption of ongoing behavior, following detection of prejudice-related discrepancies, and retrospective reflection are essential to the development and subsequent operation of cues for control. Behavioral inhibition has been indexed in a variety of experiments with reaction time measures. For example, Monteith et al. (2002) found that participants who received physiological feedback suggesting that they were having negative reactions to pictures of Blacks took longer (in *ms*) to press a spacebar to continue with the picture-viewing task (indicating conflict detection), compared to participants who received feedback suggesting that they were having negative reactions to race-unrelated pictures. Research by Amodio and colleagues (2004) provides more direct evidence of conflict detection among low-prejudice individuals. Here electroencephalographic activity was monitored while White participants completed the weapons identification task

(Payne, 2001). Errors on the task (i.e., mistakenly shooting unarmed black targets) were associated with activity in the ACC that occurs when conflicts that result from failures to implement control are detected (e.g., Gehring and Fencsik, 2001).

The retrospective reflection thought to occur following discrepancy detection has been assessed in a variety of experiments with thought-listing tasks. For example, Monteith et al. (2002) found that participants given feedback suggesting that they were having prejudiced reactions in relation to pictures of Blacks were uniquely preoccupied with their reactions to their pictures compared to participants who believed that they had negative reactions to non race-related pictures.

Prospective reflection and prejudice regulation in the presence of cues for control

The discrepancy consequences discussed thus far should ultimately be helpful to the self-regulation of prejudiced responses by establishing cues or signals of the possibility of responding with bias. These cues should trigger prospective reflection and a more careful generation of responses in the future. In one study relevant to these hypotheses (Monteith, 1993), low-prejudice heterosexual participants were led to believe that they displayed either a subtle bias in relation to gays, or a subtle bias that was unrelated to prejudice. The critical tests of prospective reflection and inhibition of prejudiced responses occurred in a supposedly separate second study about humor, which included two jokes that played on stereotypes of gays. The results indicated that participants who believed they had previously responded with subtle anti-gay bias took longer (in *ms*) to evaluate these anti-gay jokes and evaluated them less favorably than participants in the prejudice-unrelated control condition.

In another test of these processes reported by Monteith et al. (2002), low-prejudice White participants took a racial IAT and were given a summary of their performance indicating an anti-Black bias. Participants then reported their current feelings. Later, as part of a supposedly unrelated task, participants viewed words on a computer screen and indicated their first reaction to each word. Some of the words were the traditionally Black names from the IAT. Monteith et al. reasoned that these words should function as discrepancy-relevant cues for participants who felt guilty about their earlier IAT performance. Results indicated that participants who experienced more negative self-directed affect took longer (in *ms*) to respond to these names in the like/dislike task, and were more likely to provide positive evaluations of traditionally Black names.

In sum, a good deal of research suggests that people can successfully monitor, inhibit, and exert control over their prejudiced responses. Nonetheless, many important issues require additional investigation. For instance, perhaps the initial heightened attention to prejudice-relevant cues increases sensitivity to stereotype-consistent information and instigates conscious regulatory processes, but regulation becomes more automatic with practice. On a related vein, can previously developed cues for control pre-consciously signal the need for the recruitment of executive control and regulation? And might the pre-conscious signaling of the need for control interrupt the automatic activation of biases? Recent advances in neuroscientific methods for studying self-regulation may provide the answers to such questions. For example, Cunningham et al. (2004) found that ACC activity in response to the presentation of Black versus White faces (albeit at conscious levels of presentation) is associated with the modulation of amygdala activity.

Factors affecting the difficulty of self-regulating prejudiced responses

Regardless of the particular strategy used for self-regulating prejudiced responses, certain factors are likely to affect the ease of executing regulation. One such factor is self-control strength. Muraven and Baumeister (2000) argued that self-control is a limited resource resembling a muscle. Like an overworked muscle, self-control resources can be weakened and depleted by having multiple regulatory demands or stressors (Muraven, Baumeister, & Tice, 1999). Likewise, self-control strength can be increased by exercising the 'self-control muscle' through regulatory activity that is not too taxing on the system (Gailliot, Plant, Butz, et al., 2007). Thus, the ease of self-regulating prejudiced responses may depend on other regulatory demands and experiences with regulation.

Certain psychological states and situations can affect the likelihood of bias activation, which obviously has implications for how much regulatory effort needs to be exerted to control prejudiced responses. For example, angry affect increases the activation of implicit intergroup biases, relative to neutral and sad mood states (DeSteno, Dasgupta, Bartlett, et al., 2004). Also, shared reality theory (Hardin and Conley, 2001) suggests that bias activation will vary according to the presumed attitudes of people one is around. In a series of studies, Lowery and colleagues (2001) had White participants complete several types of implicit measures assessing anti-Black bias under the guidance of either a White or a Black experimenter. Because racial prejudice presumably is less acceptable to Blacks than to Whites, participants were expected to show less automatic bias in the presence of a Black experimenter. Indeed, this was the case on both a Black–White IAT (Experiments 1–3) and on a subliminal priming measure using Black and White faces (Experiment 4).

These results suggest that people will tune their attitudes to match those of people with whom they interact, and that this process may occur in a relatively automatic fashion, without explicit instructions. Furthermore, fMRI evidence was recently obtained suggesting that conflict monitoring and self-regulation occur at an early stage (as indexed by increased ACC activity) when norms to respond without prejudice are made salient (Amodio, Kubota, Harmon-Jones, et al., 2006).

Self-control strength can also be conceptualized as an individual difference variable, with some people possessing more of this resource than others. Payne and his colleagues (Govorun and Payne; 2006; Payne, 2005) examined the role of this individual difference variable in the regulation of automatic racial biases on the weapons identification task and the IAT. These researchers employed the Process Dissociation Procedure (PDP; see Jacoby, 1991) to statistically determine the extent to which an individual's performance on these tasks is driven by automatic activation of stereotypes and the exertion of executive control. Results indicated that participants with poor executive control (measured with an antisaccade task, which is a measure of voluntary attentional control that involves controlling the automatic orienting response) showed less evidence of controlled processing on the implicit bias tasks and committed more race-based errors. In other words, people with greater executive cognitive control had more ability to counteract automatic bias.

Personal costs of self-regulating prejudiced responses

Although self-regulation may effectively curb intergroup biases, one should keep in mind that exerting executive control is cognitively taxing. Bias regulation thus comes with some costs to the regulator. These costs have been investigated in numerous studies examining self-regulation during interracial interactions. Because this line of research is summarized elsewhere in this volume (see Chapter 17 by Richeson and Shelton, this volume), we mention it only briefly here. For instance, Richeson and Shelton (2003) found that White participants prone to implicit prejudices showed decreased performance on a Stroop task (a measure of executive functioning) following an interracial interaction. Presumably the effort exerted to regulate responses during the interracial interaction took a toll on executive processing resources. Note, however, that the regulatory effort exerted by Whites during interracial interactions can ultimately have positive effects on Blacks' perceptions. Whites who regulate are perceived as engaged interaction partners and are evaluated favorably (Shelton,

Richeson, Salvatore, et al., 2005). Thus, self-regulation does appear to pay off in important respects, despite the fact that it is decidedly taxing at times. Future research is needed to determine whether the cognitive costs associated with the regulation of prejudice are reduced with practice. Theoretically, this should be the case.

CONCLUSIONS AND FUTURE DIRECTIONS

We have reviewed research concerning two methods of self-regulation that people appear to use when they are appropriately motivated to attempt to inhibit, control, and possibly to change their intergroup biases. Relying solely on suppression provides, at best, a short-term solution; at worst, suppression produces rebound effects that paradoxically increase the need for subsequent self-regulatory efforts. Practicing self-regulation through the processes described in the SRP model appears to enable people to identify situations that call for heightened control efforts (i.e., through the establishment of cues for control), and involves learning to become more efficient and effective at engaging one's regulatory system so as to avoid biases. In the absence of counterprevailing forces, this process should result in the deautomatization of bias and the generation of non-biased responses as the default. However, in a world that continues to reinforce stereotypes and with human minds and motivational systems that incline people toward bias, some level of regulation (even if the regulation is itself automated) may be a perpetual necessity.

Currently, little is known about the effects of self-regulation relative to other possible means to modifying implicit biases. For example, precisely what changes with counterstereotypic imagery (Blair, Ma, & Lenton, 2001), stereotype negation training (Kawakami et al., 2005) or the formation of common ingroup representations (see Dovidio et al., 2003) in comparison to self-regulation? Recent advances that allow responses to be decomposed into relatively automatic versus controlled components (Conrey, Sherman, Gawronski, et al., 2005; Payne, 2005), as well as social neuroscientific advances such as those reviewed herein, should be useful for comparing exactly what changes (or fails to change) with different change strategies. Such research will have implications for whether self-regulation should be coupled with other strategies to provide the most promising path for changing implicit biases. Several recent lines of research have identified select groups of people who do not appear to hold implicit intergroup biases (Devine, Plant, Amodio, et al., 2002; Livingston and Drwecki, 2007; Moskowitz, Gollwitzer, Wasel, et al., 1999). However, we currently know little about precisely how this comes to be the case.

As researchers continue to study the self-regulation of intergroup bias, an important focus will be on how to increase people's awareness of biases resulting from implicit processes and an appreciation of their detrimental effects. For example, widespread availability of the IAT and publicity surrounding it has provided a grassroots opportunity for heightening awareness (but see Blanton and Jaccard, 2006). However, there remains a strong tendency to attribute bias to factors that are irrelevant to intergroup evaluations or to dismiss the possibility that intergroup responses are indeed affected by the bias (Monteith, Voils, & Ashburn-Nardo, 2001). Confronting people in their everyday lives when bias is observed seems essential for heightening awareness of subtle biases. A thorough understanding is needed of how confrontation can increase awareness most effectively (Czopp and Monteith, 2003; Czopp, Montheith, & Mark, 2006), without creating backlash (Plant and Devine, 2001).

Since the first social psychological studies of prejudice, there have been several distinct waves of research resulting from the union of historical forces shaping the form of prejudice and the research methods available for studying it (e.g., see Dovidio, 2001). Currently, the emphasis on understanding implicit biases reflects the general movement away from explicitly endorsing prejudiced attitudes and methodological advances for investigating implicit processes. These processes, although manifested in subtle ways, may well reflect the operation of the most deeply rooted causes of intergroup bias, those that are intrinsic to the human psyche (e.g., the tendency to categorize people into ingroups and outgroups; preference for the familiar and similar). Returning to Allport's quote at the beginning of this chapter, there is evidence that awareness of these subtle biases and recognition of their inconsistency with affiliative needs and human values arouses compunction and instigates self-regulatory efforts. However, we believe that there is still much to learn about how to encourage such self-regulation, factors that enhance or impede regulatory efforts, and ultimately how effective self-regulation can be in the eradication of intergroup biases.

ACKNOWLEDGEMENT

Preparation of this chapter was supported in part by Grant MH56536 from the National Institute of Mental Health to Margo Monteith.

NOTE

*Correspondence should be directed to: Margo J. Monteith, Purdue University, Department of Psychological Sciences, 703 Third Street, Rm PSYC 2172, West Lafayette, IN 47907-2081.

REFERENCES

Allport, G.W. (1954). *The nature of prejudice*. Reading, MA: Addison-Wesley.

Altemeyer, B. (1996). *The authoritarian specter*. Cambridge, MA: Harvard University Press.

Amodio, D.M., Devine, P.G., and Harmon-Jones, E. (2007). A dynamic model of guilt: Implications for motivation and self–regulation in the context of prejudice. *Psychological Science, 18*, 524–530.

Amodio, D.M., Harmon-Jones, E., Devine, P.G., Curtin, J.J., Hartley, S.L., and Covert, A.E. (2004). Neural signals for the detection of unintentional race bias. *Psychological Science, 15*, 88–93.

Amodio, D.M., Kubota, J.T., Harmon-Jones, E., and Devine, P.G. (2006). Alternative mechanisms for regulating racial responses according to internal vs external cues. *Social Cognitive and Affective Neuroscience, 1*, 26–36.

Amodio, D.M., and Lieberman, M.D (2009). Pictures in our heads: Contributions of fMRI to the study of prejudice and stereotyping. In T. Nelson (Ed), *Handbook of prejudice, discrimination, and stereotyping* (pp. 347–366). New York: Psychology Press.

Ashburn-Nardo, L., Voils, C.I., and Monteith, M.J. (2001). Implicit associations as the seeds of intergroup bias: How easily do they take root? *Journal of Personality and Social Psychology, 81*, 789–799.

Bargh, J. A. (1999). The cognitive monster: The case against the controllability of automatic stereotype effects. In S. Chaiken and Y. Trope (Eds.), *Dual process theories in social psychology* (pp. 361–382). New York: Guilford.

Biernat, M., Vescio, T.K., Theno, S.A., and Crandall, C.S. (1996). Values and prejudice: Understanding the impact of American values on outgroup attitudes. In C. Seligman, J.M. Olson, and M.P. Zanna (Eds.), *The psychology of values* (pp. 153–189). Mahwah, NJ: Erlbaum.

Blair, I.V., Ma, J.E., and Lenton, A.P. (2001). Imagining stereotypes away: The moderation of implicit stereotypes through mental imagery. *Journal of Personality and Social Psychology, 81*, 828–841.

Blanton, H., and Jaccard, J. (2006). Arbitrary metrics redux. *American Psychologist, 61*, 62–71.

Brigham, J.C. (1993). College students' racial attitudes. *Journal of Applied Social Psychology, 23*, 1933–1967.

Carver, C.S., and Scheier, M.F. (1990). Origins and functions of positive and negative affect: A control-process view. *Psychological Review, 97*, 19–35.

Conrey, F.R., Sherman, J.W., Gawronski, B., Hugenberg, K., and Groom, C.J. (2005). Separating multiple processes in implicit social cognition: The Quad Model of implicit task performance. *Journal of Personality and Social Psychology, 89*, 469–487.

Crandall, C.S., Eshleman, A., and O'Brien, L.T. (2002). Social norms and the expression and suppression of prejudice: The struggle for internalization. *Journal of Personality and Social Psychology, 82*, 359–378.

Cunningham, W.A., Johnson, M.K., Raye, C.L., Catenby, J.C., Gore, J.C., and Banaji, M.R. (2004). Separable neural components in the processing of Black and White faces. *Psychological Science, 15*, 806–813.

Czopp, A.M., and Monteith, M.J. (2003). Confronting prejudice (literally): Reactions to confrontations of racial and gender bias. *Personality and Social Psychology Bulletin, 29*, 532–545.

Czopp, A.M., Monteith, M.J., and Mark, A.Y. (2006). Standing up for a change: Reducing bias through interpersonal confrontation. *Journal of Personality and Social Psychology, 90*, 784–803.

Dasgupta, N. (2004). Implicit ingroup favouritism, outgroup favouritism, and their behavioural manifestations. *Social Justice Research, 17*, 143–169.

Dasgupta, N. (2009). Mechanisms underlying the malleability of implicit prejudice and stereotypes: The role of automaticity and cognitive control. In T. Nelson (Ed), *Handbook of prejudice, stereotyping, and discrimination* (pp. 267–284). New York: Psychology Press.

Dasgupta, N., and Rivera, L.M. (2008). When social context matters: The influence of long-term contact and short-term exposure to admired outgroup members on implicit attitudes and behavioral intentions. *Social Cognition, 26*, 112–123.

DeSteno, D., Dasgupta, N., Bartlett, M.Y., and Aida, C. (2004). Prejudice from thin air: The effect of emotion on automatic intergroup attitudes. *Psychological Science, 15*, 319–324.

Devine, P.G. (1989). Stereotypes and prejudice: Their automatic and controlled components. *Journal of Personality and Social Psychology, 56*, 5–18.

Devine, P.G., Plant, E.A., Amodio, D.M., Harmon-Jones, E., and Vance, S.L. (2002). The regulation of explicit and implicit race bias: The role of motivations to respond without prejudice. *Journal of Personality and Social Psychology, 82*, 835–848.

Devine, P.G., and Sharp, L.B. (2009). Automaticity and control in stereotyping and prejudice. In T. Nelson (Ed.), *Handbook of prejudice, stereotyping, and discrimination* (pp. 61–88). New York: Psychology Press.

Dovidio, J.F. (2001). On the nature of contemporary prejudice: The third wave. *Journal of Social Issues, 57*, 826–849.

Dovidio, J.F., and Gaertner, S.L. (1998). On the nature of contemporary prejudice: The causes, consequences, and challenges of aversive racism. In J.L. Eberhardt and S.T. Dovidio, J.F., Gaertner, S.L., and Kawakami, K. (2003). Intergroup contact: The past, present, and future. *Group Processes and Intergroup Relations, 6*, 5–21.

Dunton, B. C., and Fazio, R. H. (1997). An individual difference measure of motivation to control prejudiced reactions. *Personality and Social Psychology Bulletin, 23*, 316–326.

Fazio, R.H., Jackson, J.R., Dunton, B.C., and Williams, C.J. (1995). Variability in automatic activation as an unobtrusive measure of racial attitudes: A bona fide pipeline? *Journal of Personality and Social Psychology, 69*, 1013–1027.

Fazio, R.H., and Olson, M.A. (2003). Implicit measures in social cognition research: Their meaning and use. *Annual Review of Psychology, 54*, 297–327.

Gailliot, M.T., Plant, E.A., Butz, D.A., and Baumeister, R.F. (2007). Increasing self-regulatory strength can reduce the depleting effect of suppressing stereotypes. *Personality and So* Gailliot, M.T *cial Psychology Bulletin, 33*, 281–294.

Gawronski, B., and Bodenhausen, G.V. (2006). Associative and propositional processes in evaluation: An integrative review of implicit and explicit attitude change. *Psychological Bulletin, 132*, 692–731.

Gehring, W.J., and Fencsik, D.E. (2001). Functions of the medial frontal cortex in the processing of conflict and errors. *Journal of Neuroscience, 21*, 9430–9437.

Gordijn, E.H., Hindriks, I., Koomen, W., Dijksterhuis, A., and Knippenberg, A.V. (2004). Consequences of stereotype suppression and internal suppression motivation: A self-regulation approach. *Personality and Social Psychology Bulletin, 30*, 212–224.

Govorun, O., and Payne, B.K. (2006). Ego depletion and prejudice: Separating automatic and controlled components. *Social Cognition, 24*, 111–136.

Gray, J.A., and McNaughton, N. (1996). The neuropsychology of anxiety: Reprise. In Hope, D.A. (Ed.), *Nebraska Symposium on Motivation, 1995: Perspectives on anxiety, panic, and fear. Current theory and research in motivation* (Vol. 43., pp. 61–134). Lincoln, NE: University of Nebraska Press.

Greenwald, A.G., and Banaji, M.R. (1995). Implicit social cognition: Attitudes, stereotypes, self-esteem, and self-concept. *Psychological Review, 109*, 3–25.

Greenwald, A.G., McGhee, D.E., and Schwartz, J.L.K. (1998). Measuring individual differences in implicit cognition: The implicit association test. *Journal of Personality and Social Psychology, 74*, 1464–1480.

Gregg, A.P., Seibt, B., and Banaji, M.R. (2006). Easier done than undone: Asymmetry in the malleability of implicit preferences. *Journal of Personality and Social Psychology, 90*, 1–20.

Hardin, C.D., and Conley, T.D. (2001). A relational approach to cognition: Shared experience and relationship affirmation in social cognition. In G. B. Moskowitz (Ed.), *Future directions in social cognition* (pp. 3–17). Hillsdale, NJ: Erlbaum.

Higgins, E.T. (1987). Self-discrepancy theory: A theory relating self and affect. *Psychological Review, 94*, 319–340.

James, W. (1890). *The principles of psychology.* New York: Henry Holt and Company.

Jacoby, L.L. (1991). A process dissocation framework: Separating automatic from intentional uses of memory. *Journal of Memory and Language, 30*, 513–541.

Katz, P.A. (2003). Racists or intolerant multiculturalists? How do they begin? *American Psychologist, 58*, 897–909.

Katz, I., and Hass, R.G. (1988). Racial ambivalence and American value conflict: Correlational and priming studies of dual cognitive structures. *Journal of Personality and Social Psychology, 55*, 593–905.

Kawakami, K., Dovidio, J.F., and van Kamp, S. (2005). Kicking the habit: Effects of nonstereotypic association training and correction processes on hiring decisions. *Journal of Experimental Social Psychology, 41*, 68–75.

Livingston, R.W., and Drwecki, B.B. (2007). Why are some individuals not racially biased? Susceptibility to affective conditioning predicts nonprejudice toward Blacks. *Psychological Science, 18*, 816–823.

Lowery, B.S., Hardin, C. D., and Sinclair, S. (2001). Social influence on automatic racial prejudice. *Journal of Personality and Social Psychology, 81*, 842–855.

Macrae, C.N., Bodenhausen, G.V., Milne, A.B., and Jetten, J. (1994). Out of mind but back in sight: Stereotypes on the rebound. *Journal of Personality and Social Psychology, 67*, 808–817.

Mischel, W. (1996). From good intentions to willpower. In P.M. Gollwitzer and J.A. Bargh (Eds.), *The psychology of action: Linking cognition and motivation to behavior* (pp. 197–218). New York: Guilford Press.

Monteith, M.J. (1993). Self-regulation of prejudiced responses: Implications for progress in prejudice reduction efforts. *Journal of Personality and Social Psychology, 65*, 469–485.

Monteith, M.J., Ashburn–Nardo, L., Voils, C.I., and Czopp, A. M. (2002). Putting the brakes on prejudice: On the development and operation of cues for control. *Journal of Personality and Social Psychology, 83*, 1029–1050.

Monteith, M.J., Devine, P.G., and Zuwerink, J.R. (1993). Self-directed versus other-directed affect as a consequence of prejudice-related discrepancies. *Journal of Personality and Social Psychology, 64*, 198–210.

Monteith, M.J., and Mark, A.Y. (2005). Changing one's prejudiced ways: Awareness, affect, and self-regulation. In W. Stroebe and M. Hewstone (Eds.), *European review of social psychology* (Vol. 16, pp. 113–154). Hove, E. Sussex: Psychology Press.

Monteith, Mark, and Ashburn-Nardo (in press).

Monteith, M.J., Sherman, J., and Devine, P.G. (1998a). Suppression as a stereotype control strategy. *Personality and Social Psychology Review, 2*, 63–82.

Monteith, M.J., and Spicer, C.V., and Tooman, G. (1998b). Consequences of stereotype suppression: Stereotypes on AND not on the rebound. *Journal of Experimental Social Psychology, 34*, 355–377.

Monteith, M.J., and Voils, C.I. (1998). Proneness to prejudiced responses: Toward understanding the authenticity of self-reported discrepancies. *Journal of Personality and Social Psychology, 75*, 901–916.

Monteith, M.J., and Voils, C.I. (2001). Exerting control over prejudiced responses. InG. Moskowitz (Ed.), *Cognitive social psychology: The Princeton Symposium on the legacy and future of social cognition* (pp. 375–388). Mahwah, NJ: Erlbaum.

Monteith, M.J., Voils, C.I., and Ashburn–Nardo, L. (2001). Taking a look underground: Detecting, interpreting, and reacting to implicit racial biases. *Social Cognition, 19*, 395–417.

Monteith, M.J., and Walters, G.L. (1998). Egalitarianism, moral obligation, and prejudice-related personal standards. *Personality and Social Psychology Bulletin, 24*, 186–199.

Moskowitz, G.B., Gollwitzer, P.M., Wasel, W., and Schaal, B (1999). Preconscious control of stereotype activation through chronic egalitarian goals. *Journal of Personality and Social Psychology, 77*, 167–184.

Muraven, M., and Baumeister, R.F. (2000). Self–regulation and depletion of limited resources: Does self-control resemble a muscle? *Psychological Bulletin, 126*, 247–259.

Muraven, M., Baumeister, R.F., and Tice, D.M. (1999). Longitudinal improvement of self-regulation through practice: Building self-control strength through repeated exercise. *Journal of Social Psychology, 139*, 446–457.

Payne, B.K. (2001). Prejudice and perception: The role of automatic and controlled processes in misperceiving a weapon. *Journal of Personality and Social Psychology, 81*, 181–192.

Payne, B.K. (2005). Conceptualizing control in social cognition: How executive control modulates the expression of automatic stereotyping. *Journal of Personality and Social Psychology, 89*, 488–503.

Plant, E.A., and Devine, P.G. (1998). Internal and external motivation to respond without prejudice. *Journal of Personality and Social Psychology, 75*, 811–832.

Plant, E.A., and Devine, P.G. (2001). Responses to other-imposed pro-Black pressure: Acceptance or backlash? *Journal of Experimental Social Psychology, 37*, 486–501.

Plant, E.A., Devine, P.G., and Brazy, P.C. (2003). The bogus pipeline and motivations to reduce prejudice: Revisiting the fading and faking of racial prejudice. *Group Processes and Intergroup Relations, 6*, 187–200.

Richeson, J.A., and Shelton, J.N. (2003). When prejudice does not pay: Effects of interracial contact on executive function. *Psychological Science, 14*, 287–290.

Roediger, H.L. (1990). Implicit memory: retention without remembering. *American Psychologist, 45*, 1043–1056.

Rydell, R.J., and McConnell, A.R. (2006). Understanding implicit and explicit attitude change: A systems of reasoning analysis. *Journal of Personality and Social Psychology, 91*, 995–1008.

Sears, D.O., and Henry, P.J. (2003). The origins of symbolic racism. *Journal of Personality and Social Psychology, 85*, 259–275.

Shelton, J.N., Richeson, J.A., Salvatore, J., and Trawalter, S. (2005). Ironic effects of racial bias during interracial interactions. *Psychological Science, 16*, 397–402.

Shiffrin, R.M., and Schneider, W. (1977). Controlled and automatic human information processing: II. Perceptual learning, automatic attending, and a general theory. *Psychological Review, 84*, 127–190.

Sidanius, J., and Pratto, F. (1999). *Social dominance: An intergroup theory of social hierarchy and oppression.* New York: Cambridge University Press.

Tajfel, H., and Turner, J.C. (1986). The social identity theory of intergroup behavior. In W.G. Austin and S. Worchel (Eds.), *Psychology of intergroup relations* (2nd ed., pp. 7–27). Chicago: Nelson-Hall.

Wegner, D.M. (1994). Ironic processes of mental control. *Psychological Review, 101*, 34–52.

Wyer, N.A., Sherman, J.W., and Stroessner, S.J. (2000). The roles of motivation and ability in controlling the consequences of stereotype suppression. *Personality and Social Psychology Bulletin, 26*, 13–25.

31

Prejudice and Perceiving Multiple Identities

Richard J. Crisp

ABSTRACT

This chapter provides a review and integration of research into how the recognition and use of multiple identities in person perception can encourage reductions in prejudice, stereotyping, and intergroup discrimination. The chapter considers levels of increasing categorical complexity while weaving together these previously distinct strands into a coherent overall framework. Taking the common ingroup identity model as a starting point, it considers how dual identity and crossed categorization formulations developed as both viable characterizations of the complexity of real intergroup relations, as well as the means to counter cognitive and motivational pressures towards ingroup favoritism. It then charts the emergence of more recent conceptualizations of category complexity and associated implications for social identity, ingroup projection and cognitive flexibility in impression formation. Finally, possible directions for future research are discussed with a focus on developing policy and practice to promote, encourage and enhance harmonious intergroup relations.

PREJUDICE AND PERCEIVING MULTIPLE IDENTITIES

Think for a moment of all the different ways in which you could classify yourself. I am, for example, a psychologist, male, young(ish), British, and liberal. This is quite an array of identities and, of course, there are many more. We know that which of these identities is used to define ourselves – or others – depends on a variety of factors, including context and motivation – but also that identities are not mutually exclusive. We can, and often are, identified and identify others according to combinations of group memberships. Examples of this are easy to bring to mind: a disabled athlete, a young Briton, a female engineer. We now know that the nature of these multiple identifications can have significant implications for understanding, and attenuating, prejudice and intergroup discrimination. This chapter is all about these multiple identities and what they mean for intergroup relations. I review the current state of research, discussing when and how a recognition of multiple identities leads to specifiable effects on intergroup attitudes. Finally, possible directions for future research are discussed with a focus on developing policy and practice to promote, encourage and enhance harmonious intergroup relations.

Research on multiple identities has sometimes used the term 'identity' and 'categorization' interchangeably. In what follows I will use the term *categorization* when referring to the structure of relations between ingroups and outgroups (e.g., a context defined by multiple categorizations), but *identity* when referring specifically to self-defining categories (e.g., when one possesses multiple identities). Of course all multiple categorization contexts involve individuals who, by definition, potentially possess multiple identities. As we will see, however, to fully understand the relationship between prejudice and perceiving multiple identities one must take the wider context (involving relationships between ingroup and outgroup categories) into account.

BACKGROUND AND HISTORY

Anthropologists, sociologists, and political scientists were amongst the first to observe some unique consequences associated with societies characterized by multiple categorizations. For instance, Evans-Pritchard (1940) and Murphy (1957) both documented cases of reduced conflict in cultures with cross-cutting bases for affiliation. LeVine and Campbell (1972) argued that group members actively make use of cross-cutting affiliations because they ensure security and stability (it is more difficult, for instance, to have conflicting relations with a group, based on territory, that is simultaneously an ally according to common ancestry). Later research has confirmed that cross-cutting ties can be important at a societal level (Cairns & Mercer, 1984) and this has emerged as an important concept for political scientists (Carter, 2006).

Social psychological research is grounded in these observations, but developed a focus on the mental processes involved in the perception and use of multiple categorizations. The earliest investigations focused on the implications for person perception of cross-cutting bases for group membership. Based on an understanding of categorization processes in judgments of physical and social stimuli (e.g., Doise, 1978; Wilder, 1986), and work using the minimal group paradigm (Tajfel, Flament, Billig, et al., 1971), Deschamps and Doise (1978) proposed that when two category dimensions were salient in any given intergroup context (e.g., gender *and* race), and they provided the basis for characterizing others as *both* ingroup and outgroup members at the same time, then bias would be reduced. In two studies they investigated the effects of crossing an existing social category (female/male) with an experimentally induced category (red/blue; from distributing red or blue pens). They found that for performance estimations (number of successfully completed games) there was significant ingroup favoring bias between categories in the simple condition (categorization in terms of gender) but no bias when the simple categorization criterion was crossed with the experimental categorization.

Subsequent work continued to use the minimal group paradigm, and provided further evidence for the potential bias-reducing qualities of cross-cutting categorization. Notably, Vanbeselaere's (1987) minimal group study revealed reliable discrimination in the simple categorization condition but not in the cross-cutting categorization condition. Further studies revealed similar, although more complex, findings with real groups. Brewer, Ho, Lee, et al., (1987) outlined four patterns of evaluation that can result from cross-cutting categorization that took account of varied historical and cultural factors (e.g. status, numerosity, power) (see also Hewstone, Islam, & Judd, 1993).

From this early work, research has flourished to provide a detailed account of the antecedents, processes and outcomes associated with multiple categorization. In what follows I will document how people use multiple criteria for categorization in both social and non-social judgment, and how attention to these complex criteria predicts changes in how we evaluate people in different groups as well as how we define our own multiple identities. I will outline cognitive processes that vary as a function of the number of categories attended to as well as motivational and affective factors that play an important role. We now know that thinking about multiple criteria can impact on social judgment and behavior in a number of specific ways, from 'decategorizing' judgments, to promoting 'recategorization'. In this chapter I will review current knowledge about prejudice and perceiving multiple identities, I will integrate past theorizing, and present a new integrative theoretical framework for understanding why, when and how multiple identities play a critical role in shaping our social worlds.

LITERATURE REVIEW

In this section I review research that has tested whether making multiple categorizations salient has the potential to reduce prejudice and intergroup discrimination. This review will highlight the unique cognitive and motivational processes associated with different forms of multiple categorization, and will form the basis for the integrative framework discussed later in the chapter.

Social categorization is inherently hierarchical, reflecting human classification systems more generally. For example, an 'alsatian' is a 'dog' which is an 'animal'. People typically categorize at the 'basic level' (Rosch, Mervis, Gray, et al., 1976) which is in the middle of a conceptual hierarchy. For example, 'female/male' or ' black/white' are basic level categories, 'all humans' is the most inclusive category; 'an individual' is the least inclusive category. The common ingroup identity model specifies the effects on intergroup evaluations when people are encouraged to change the way they categorize from this basic level to a more inclusive level. This model is discussed elsewhere in this volume (see Chapter 32 by Gaertner, Dovidio, Houlette, this volume), so the brief summary

that follows will focus specifically on research that will be important for integrating this model into the multiple identities framework developed in this chapter.

Common ingroup identities

The original conceptualization of the common ingroup identity model (Gaertner, Dovidio, Anastasio, et al., 1993; for recent reviews see Dovidio, Gaertner, Hodson, et al., 2006; Chapter 32 by Gaertner, Dovidio, Houlette, this volume) rests upon the idea that by changing the nature of categorical representation from 'us' and 'them' to a more inclusive 'we' it is possible to reduce intergroup bias. This recategorization reduces bias by increasing the attractiveness of former outgroup members, once they are included within a superordinate ingroup.

For the purposes of this chapter the important thing to note is that recategorization has been found to be highly successful at reducing prejudice, but this is not the case in every intergroup situation. Under some conditions encouraging categorization at a superordinate level can *increase* intergroup bias. Recategorization involves a blurring of the boundaries between former ingroupers and outgroupers; they become more similar, they lose their distinctiveness within a new common ingroup. Maintaining such distinctiveness, however, represents a basic drive associated with social identification. Distinctive social categorizations clarify and define social situations, providing a means for predicting how ingroupers and outgroupers will behave (Tajfel & Turner, 1979), reducing uncertainty, and providing a set of prescriptive ingroup norms to guide perceivers' behavior (Hogg, 2000). It is therefore not just a desire for positivity that drives group members, but also a desire for *distinctiveness* (Brewer, 1991) – a drive that can manifest itself in the form of increased *evaluative* differentiation (ingroup favoritism). When distinctiveness is compromised, being more ingroup favoring is a clear way of re-establishing *us* as different from *them* (and re-establishing that 'we are *better* than they are' Hogg & Abrams, 1988).

Blurring boundaries via recategorization may, therefore, constitute a threat to social identity and provide the motivation for ingroup bias as a means of re-establishing subgroup distinctiveness (Brown & Abrams, 1986). Empirical evidence has supported this hypothesis. For instance, Hornsey and Hogg (2000) found greater inter-subgroup bias when participants were recategorized exclusively as university students than when their faculty area subgroups were made salient (see also Dovidio, Gaertner, & Validzic, 1998; González & Brown, 1998).

When does recategorization reduce bias, and when does it increase bias? Identification with groups, the extent to which they are important to perceivers, appears to the key determinant of motivated bias as a reaction to distinctiveness threat (Jetten, Spears, & Postmes, 2004). Studies have shown that recategorization that emphasizes a salient superordinate identity and de-emphasizes subgroup identities can increase or decrease bias as a function of subgroup identification. Crisp, Stone, and Hall (2006) compared baseline subgroup evaluations (British participants evaluating the British and the French) with a recategorization condition in which a superordinate 'European' categorization was made salient (i.e., by virtue of a supposed newspaper article discussing closer integration between European member states). This recategorization led to higher intergroup bias (British versus French) – but only for higher ingroup subgroup identifiers. In other words, recategorization increased bias only for people who regarded the original subgroup (British) as being of central importance to their sense of self-definition. Similarly, van Leeuwen, van Knippenberg, and Ellemers (2003) found that identification predicted bias *after* the merging of two minimal groups, but not before. These studies support the idea that while recategorization can reduce bias for lower identifiers, when identification with groups is high (which is, of course, a characteristic of pervasive intergroup conflicts), it can represent a threat to ingroup distinctiveness, and motivate increased intergroup bias (for a review see Crisp, 2006).

Dual identification

Recategorization, as specified by the common ingroup identity model, involves shifting from a less inclusive to a more inclusive identity. As the research reviewed above illustrates, however, this shift in self-definition may not improve intergroup relations, and when identification with the original subgroups is high, may even make things worse. To counter this desire for distinctiveness in common ingroup contexts, Dovidio, Gaertner, & Validzic (1998) developed the idea of simultaneous subordinate/superordinate categorization. By maintaining recognition of subgroup distinctiveness, while simultaneously bringing groups together within a common ingroup, they argued that reactive tendencies associated with identification can be curtailed. Importantly, this development of the common ingroup identity model moved from conceptualizing identities as mutually exclusive, to arguing that perceivers can categorize themselves and others along multiple dimensions of categorization *simultaneously*.

The dual identity idea is appealing as a solution to the problem of high identification and distinctiveness threat. In contrast to the category selection process outlined in the first part of this review, here perceivers are encouraged to focus not on one category or another, but instead to focus simultaneously on two criteria (one which subsumes the other: for example, it is possible to be British *and* European at the same time). Do people have the cognitive capacity to integrate multiple categorizations in this way? Recent work suggests they do. Halford, Baker, McCredden, et al., (2005) found, in fact, that people were able to process information that can be decomposed along up to four cross-cutting subtask dimensions. Social psychological research has confirmed people's ability (and tendency) to use (at least) two dimensions of categorization in social judgment (e.g., Stangor, Lynch, Duan, et al., 1992). Thus, while context and motivation can lead to selectivity in category use (as discussed in the earlier section), there is no cognitive limit on perceiving (at least) dual identities, and people typically do so in the absence of salient cues for the dominance of a single category dimension.

In the context of students' university department identities, the dual identity approach has been found to be effective at reducing bias (Dovidio, Gaertner, & Validzic, 1998; see also Hornsey & Hogg, 2000). Furthermore, Crisp, Stone, & Hall (2006) found that a dual identity reduced bias specifically for higher identifiers – precisely those group members who should view reduced distinctiveness as a threat to identity. Importantly, this approach preserves social identity at the subordinate level, while simultaneously promoting improved intergroup attitudes at the superordinate level, apparently reducing any threat experienced by higher ingroup identifiers, and avoiding reactive increases in bias.

The dual identity reformulation of the common ingroup identity model represents an important conceptual development of the research discussed so far. Research into the common ingroup identity model has examined what happens when people shift from a subgroup to a superordinate level of self-categorization (e.g., *British* to *European*). This involves forsaking an original identity to adopt a new one. Explicit in the dual identity approach is the idea that people can *simultaneously* define themselves according to more than just one single identity and that they can identify as members of two different groups at the same time. In the following section another multiple categorization approach is discussed that also focuses on what happens when two dimensions of categorization are simultaneously salient. Importantly, this approach incorporates and extends the idea that simultaneous categorization along multiple criteria has significant implications for prejudice and intergroup discrimination.

Crossed categorization

In the crossed categorization paradigm, two dimensions are made simultaneously salient for participants making group-relevant social judgments. Take, for example, gender and age; instead of considering only females versus males or young versus old, in crossed-categorization contexts perceivers attend to both of these dimensions. Then females and males can be seen to *share* a common category; both females and males can be young, or both females and males can be old. For young females then, the cross-cutting membership 'young' becomes salient, so a shared membership can be realized with *young* males. On the other hand, young females will also be even more different from old males, who can contrast two *non-shared* memberships with young females (see Table 31.1).

Work on crossed categorization clearly overlaps with that described in the previous section on the common ingroup/dual identity model. It examines the effects on intergroup evaluations when a simultaneously salient common identity cross-cuts an initial intergroup distinction (see Crisp & Hewstone, 2007; Dovidio, Gaertner, Hodson, et al., 2006). In Table 31.1, for instance, the first three columns of the crossed categorization design (young females versus old females or young males) can be taken as illustrative of designs used in common ingroup identity research. With respect to young females versus old females, 'female' here is a common ingroup identity shared between young and old people. With respect to young females versus young males, 'young' is a common ingroup identity shared between

Table 31.1 Four composite subgroups formed by crossing two dimensions of social categorization, gender, and age

Female (ingroup)		Male (outgroup)	
Young (ingroup)	Old (outgroup)	Young (ingroup)	Old (outgroup)
Young female (ingroup/ingroup)	Old female (outgroup/ingroup)	Young male (ingroup/outgroup)	Old male (outgroup/outgroup)

females and males. Put another way, the mixed membership groups in columns 2 and 3 map on to the dual identity outgroups discussed in the previous section. Research that has compared evaluations amongst these cells in crossed categorization designs has provided strong support that the shared identity does elicit reduced intergroup bias (Crisp & Hewstone, 1999; Mullen, Migdal, & Hewstone, 2001; Urban & Miller, 1998), both at the explicit level (e.g., Deschamps & Doise, 1978; Crisp, Hewstone, & Rubin, 2001; Vanbeselaere, 1987) and the implicit level (Crisp & Hewstone, 2000) and even on measures of stereotype threat (Rosenthal & Crisp, 2006). This research supports the idea that simultaneous categorization/dual identity combinations of group membership can encourage reductions in intergroup bias, and can do so while taking care of needs for differentiation (Brewer, 1991; Crisp, 2006).

The crossed categorization and dual identity models share a focus on simultaneously salient ingroup and outgroup identities, but they also differ in some important ways as well. One clear difference is that crossed categorization research has focused not only on shared common ingroup categories (columns 1 to 3 in Table 31.1) but also on simultaneously salient *non*-shared memberships (column 4 in Table 31.1). Categorization can create *convergent* as well as divergent bases for group affiliation and work on crossed categorization has also examined what happens when categories *reinforce* existing boundaries. For instance, a white female may feel not quite so different from a black *female*, but may feel considerably more different from a *black male* when gender is salient alongside race (creating a 'double outgroup'). Here the salience of an additional categorization has reinforced the distinctiveness of the initial dichotomy. This is so for many instances of ethnopolitical conflict. For example, in Belfast, Northern Ireland, Catholics and Protestants tend to live in different places (e.g., Ardoyne versus Shankhill Road), espouse different politics (Nationalist-Republican versus Unionist-Loyalist) and even support different football teams (e.g., Cliftonville versus Linfield);

part of the problem is precisely that there are few social categories cross-cutting the religious dimension (Boal, 1969; cited in Hewstone, Cairns, Voci, et al., 2005).

Empirically it is clear that double outgroup targets are discriminated against more than either dual identity groups or simple outgroups (against dual identity groups, see Diehl, 1990; against both dual identity and single outgroups, see Crisp, Hewstone, & Rubin, 2001). Where conflict is characterized by converging categories, building cross-cutting ties that create dual identity groups ('mixed membership groups', the groups featured in columns 2 and 3 of Table 31.1) may be an important way to foster more harmonious intergroup relations. The research that is reviewed in the next section has focused on the conditions under which making dual identities salient will help reduce bias against groups defined by converging (double) outgroup memberships.

Enhancing the effectiveness of dual identities

Research into crossed categorization has identified different patterns of evaluation across the four composite groups (see Table 31.1) formed from crossing two dimensions of categorization. The patterns can be represented by notation referring to the relative composition of ingroup and outgroup identities (i.e., 'i' and 'o' respectively). For instance, the baseline additive pattern specifies that double ingroups (ii) are evaluated more positively than double outgroups (oo) with mixed groups (io and oi) evaluated in-between these two extremes (ii > io = oi > oo). There are six main patterns that have been observed (Brewer, Ho, Lee, et al., 1987; Hewstone, Islam, & Judd, 1993) and several moderators have been identified that predict when each of the varied patterns of evaluation will be observed. Detailed reviews of these patterns and the conditions under which they are observed can be found elsewhere (see Crisp, Ensari, Hewstone, et al., 2002; Crisp & Hewstone, 1999, 2007; Crisp, Stone, & Hall, 2006; Urban & Miller, 1998).

Here, I will focus on why these patterns are important for understanding when creating dual identities will be more or less effective. They are important because the patterns model, in situations where multiple dimensions of categorization are salient, the impact of shifting attention away from converging categorizations that reinforce social divides (e.g., Republican/Catholic versus Loyalist/ Protestant) to dual identity categorizations that emphasize a common ingroup identity (e.g., *Young*/Catholic and *Young*/Protestant). Put another way, in contexts defined by convergent categorization (such as religion and politics in Northern Ireland) encouraging perceivers to focus on shared, common ingroup identities ('mixed' category groups), instead of converging differences (double outgroups) should improve intergroup attitudes.

It is well established that creating mixed category groups (i.e., dual identity groups) is an effective way to reduce bias compared to when targets are defined totally by outgroups. This is represented by the additive pattern (ii > io = oi > oo), where the mixed groups that share a common ingroup identity (io or oi) with the perceiver (ii) are evaluated more positively than are total outgroups (oo). This is the most frequently observed pattern in this research (Crisp & Hewstone, 1999; Urban & Miller, 1998). Other research has identified conditions under which deviations from this baseline additive pattern will be observed. Compared to the additive pattern, induction of a positive mood or priming participants to focus on ingroup constituents of targets leads to a social inclusion pattern, ii = io = oi > oo (Crisp, Walsh, & Hewstone, 2006b); whereas negative affect or outgroup priming leads to a social exclusion pattern, ii > io = oi = oo (Crisp, Hewstone, Paolini, et al., 2003; Kenworthy, Canales, Weaver, et al., 2003). More complex patterns have been observed depending on an interaction between positive affect and differential importance (see Miller, Kenworthy, Carnales, et al., 2006, for a detailed review).

If we regard these patterns as describing the extent to which mixed (dual identity) groups reduce bias *relative* to double outgroups,

we can think about them as specifying the conditions under which application of the dual identity model will be more or less *effective* at improving intergroup relations. For example, the social inclusion pattern represents a highly successful application of the dual identity model, because evaluations of dual identity (mixed) groups become as positive as they are for total ingroup members (ii = io = oi > oo). In contrast, the social exclusion pattern represents a highly unsuccessful application of the dual identity model, because evaluations remain as negative as for people defined as double outgroupers (ii > io = oi = oo).

The basic rule here is that anything that increases the *relative* salience of common ingroup identities will reduce differentiation, anything that increases the relative salience of targets' outgroup identities will enhance differentiation. Recategorization (Gaertner & Dovidio, 2000) works because it makes the common ingroup more *salient* as a basis for evaluating others than former outgroup categorization. Convergent categorization promotes more negative evaluations because the converging memberships make outgroup categorizations more *salient*. Relatedly, positive affect primes the common ingroup identity, making it more salient; negative affect primes outgroup categories, making differences more salient (reducing, in relative terms, the effectiveness of common ingroups).

The research on dual identities shows that it is possible to reduce bias by keeping distinctiveness concerns satisfied. Research on crossed categorization, where two dimensions of categorization are simultaneously salient, offers further empirical support for the idea that dual identities can reduce bias without risk of violating needs for differentiation. Does creating dual identities therefore offer the best all round solution for reducing intergroup bias? The answer to this is a qualified yes; that is, dual identities are generally effective at reducing bias, but under some conditions even though motivations to retain positive distinctiveness may be satisfied by simultaneous category salience, bias may *still* remain, and even increase, due to a process called *ingroup projection*. When ingroup projection occurs, and when it can be avoided, is discussed in the next section.

Ingroup projection and category correlation

Earlier I discussed how the dual identity and crossed-categorization models can be aligned in their specification of simultaneously salient common ingroup identities. One difference between the models is the additional focus on convergent identities (double outgroups) in crossed categorization research. There is, however, a further significant difference. The two models have typically focused on simultaneous categorizations that differ in the extent of their relatedness; that is, the extent to which the two categories are *correlated*. This distinction is representative of an important characteristic of different dual identities that has implications for how effective they will be at reducing intergroup bias.

To elaborate, research on crossed categorization has involved category dimensions that bear no relation to each other (e.g., Asian and female), while research on the common ingroup identity/dual identity model involves subcategories that are nested within a superordinate inclusive group (e.g., British and European). For example, British women can be a subgroup of British and a subgroup of women, but this does not imply that either Asian or woman categories subsume the other. In contrast, British and French are subgroups of European, but European *cannot* be seen as a subgroup of British or French. Put another way, ethnicity and gender are uncorrelated, orthogonal. Being Asian does not make it more likely that you are either male or female; but with nested groups, being British indicates, by definition, that you are also European.

The degree of overlap between the subgroup and superordinate identities makes no difference with respect to distinctiveness concerns (Brewer, 1991; Jetten, Spears, & Postmes, 2004); irrespective of relatedness, a simultaneously salient cross-cutting or common ingroup that is shared between an ingroup and outgroup reduces differentiation while retaining the distinctiveness of the original identity. However, the extent to which simultaneously salient categories are correlated does have important implications for another psychological process related to intergroup evaluations.

An early indication of the importance of category relatedness was provided by Eurich-Fulcher and Schofield (1995) who that found no decrease in biased evaluations when *correlated* categories were crossed. A more specific model of why correlated dual identities may not reduce bias (and may increase bias) is provided by Mummendey and colleagues in the form of the ingroup projection model (Mummendey & Wenzel, 1999; for a review see Mummendey, this volume). The ingroup projection model states that in intergroup contexts where a superordinate group is salient, the ingroup prototype will be projected *on to* the superordinate group. That is, ingroup subgroup members will see the prototype of their subgroup as being also the defining characteristic of the superordinate group. If both the ingroup and outgroup are conceptualized as part of a superordinate category (a relevant comparison context), and the ingroup prototype has been projected onto the superordinate category, then the outgroup will be seen, by definition, as deviating from the subgroup-defined norm (Wenzel, Mummendey, Weber, et al., 2003).

Projection involves both cognitive and motivational processes. On the one hand, the perception of subgroup characteristics as prototypical of superordinate groups can be seen as an example of broader heuristic processes evident from research on the false consensus effect (see Marks & Miller, 1987). On the other hand, rejection of former outgroupers due to their atypicality in relation to the ingroup-defined superordinate prototype can be linked to processes outlined by the subjective group dynamics model (Marques, Abrams, Paez, et al., 1998). This model argues that deviant ingroup members (in this case common ingroup members) are discriminated against in an effort to protect the positive ingroup stereotype (discrimination against deviants prevents them from having a detrimental impact on the positive ingroup norm). Consistent with this idea that discrimination of former outgroupers is motivated by the desire to preserve the positive ingroup stereotype, ingroup projection is only expected when there is high identification at both the subgroup and superordinate levels of categorization (i.e., when the groups *matter* to people; Mummendey & Wenzel, 1999). In sum, the result of a high correlation between dual identities can be ingroup projection and corresponding motivated bias to preserve the positive superordinate stereotype.

According to the ingroup projection model dual identities will therefore increase bias, but, of course, there is also much evidence, discussed earlier in this chapter, that dual identities often decrease bias. Given what we know about the crossed categorization and dual identity models, the relationship between categories that make up the dual identity appears to be one factor that can reduce the likelihood of ingroup projection. When they are highly correlated, simultaneously salient dual identities can allow ingroup projection. For example, a female engineer might experience discrimination because males project their gender stereotypic attributes to the (contextually) superordinate occupation category. Females are therefore perceived as ingroup (engineer) deviants, and so are discriminated against to protect the subjective validity of male engineers' ingroup norm. In contexts where a dual identity is defined, however, by *uncorrelated* categories, there is no route by which ingroup projection can occur. Because there is no relationship between the two categories that comprise the dual identity, there is no way that one can be seen as normative of the other and no way that someone could perceive one of their groups as representative of the other. For example, white women cannot project their white identity onto their female identity because there is no overlap or correlation between race and gender (white women should therefore feel more positive towards black women relative to when just race is salient). Consistent with this, Waldzus,

Mummendey, Wenzel et al. (2003) found that projection does not occur when the superordinate category is perceived as having a complex representation. This is consistent with the idea that low correlation between dual identities can inhibit projection. High superordinate complexity means there cannot be a high correlation between the subgroup and superordinate category dimensions.

It is important to note that dual identities are not always either *completely* correlated or uncorrelated. It is not that nested identities (e.g., British/European) will always lead to projection while unrelated identities (British/women) will not. These are simply extreme end points of the relatedness continuum. As Waldzus et al.'s research illustrates, the extent to which projection occurs varies, depending upon the inter-related characteristics of the multiple identities involved. Thus, apparently nested subgroup-superordinate dual identities will be effective at reducing intergroup bias *to the extent* that they do not share overlapping characteristics (that is, the extent to which they are uncorrelated).

To summarize, we can further qualify the conditions under which dual identities will be successful in reducing intergroup bias from an integration of work on crossed categorization and ingroup projection. Dual identities, irrespective of whether they are formed from nested or unrelated dimensions, prevent motivated bias associated with compromised distinctiveness. However, while both types of dual identity satisfy distinctiveness-based motivations, they differ in the extent to which they satisfy subjective norm motivations. When nested dual identities are defined by a high degree of overlap this increases the likelihood of ingroup projection, creating a context of comparability within which former outgroups are seen as non-normative and therefore evaluated negatively. However, motivations to exclude non-normative outgroupers from superordinate groups will only occur when identification with both the subgroup and superordinate group is high. In contrast, irrespective of identification, unrelated dual identities (e.g., black and women)

Table 31.2 **Bias associated with dual identities as a function of identification and category correlation**

	Relationship between constituent categories	
Identification with both constituent categories	Uncorrelated	Correlated
Low	LOW BIAS No distinctiveness threat No normative threat	LOW BIAS No distinctiveness threat No normative threat
High	LOW BIAS No distinctiveness threat No normative threat	HIGH BIAS No distinctiveness threat Normative threat (ingroup projection)

present no opportunity for ingroup projection, and no means by which former outgroupers can be considered non-normative. Correspondingly, when dual identities are not seen to be highly correlated, this will offer both maximal protection from distinctiveness threat (Brewer, 1991) and ingroup projection (Mummendey & Wenzel, 1999). These outcomes are illustrated in Table 31.2.

So far I have discussed how perceivers can shift identities to a higher level of inclusiveness, and how simultaneous categorization, dual identity and crossed categorization, can satisfy needs for differentiation; and how low overlap between dual identities is necessary to avoid ingroup projection. I now review one final perspective on the study of multiple identities, a perspective that focuses on multiple identity complexity.

Identity complexity

Roccas and Brewer (2002) proposed that individuals' representation of their multiple group memberships can vary along a *complexity* dimension. This dimension describes an individual's subjective representation of the interrelationships among his or her multiple group identities. It refers to the degree of overlap perceived to exist between groups of which a person is simultaneously a member. When one's representation is low in complexity, it is an indication that one perceives a high overlap between both the typical characteristics of one's various social category memberships, as well as an overlap between the actual members

of those same categories. High complexity, by contrast, implies that the representation of each ingroup category is distinct from the others. Brewer and Pierce (2005) have shown that higher levels of social identity complexity are associated with greater outgroup tolerance, including greater support for affirmative action and multiculturalism. Greater complexity was also related to higher education levels, liberal political ideology, and age. This work illustrates how awareness of multiple identities can have a positive impact not only at an inter-group level, but also at an intra-group level.

In contrast to the focus on intra-category complexity described above, we can also think about *inter*-category complexity, that is, complexity inherent to particular intergroup relations. Research has shown that by increasing the number of categories that participants need to process in forming an impression (Crisp, Hewstone, & Rubin, 2001), or by making the nature of the relationship between those categories more complex (Hall & Crisp, 2005), bias can be reduced, apparently due to an abandoning of categorization as guide to forming impressions of others, in favor of a more individuated strategy. For instance Hall and Crisp asked participants to simply think about alternative ways that they could classify a target group member, other than the way that had been described (i.e., a student from a local rival university), ensuring that the categories generated were unrelated to each other. On an evaluative measure of group product (a drawing of a boat) they observed a reduction in bias when participants generated multiple alternative categories that could be used to define the outgroup member (notably, this did not occur when the categories generated were related, consistent with Brewer's specification of low identity complexity). Further support for this idea was recently obtained from work on stereotype threat; Gresky, Eyck, Lord and McIntyre (2005) showed that womens' math performance improved, following a threat, when multiple ingroup identities were salient.

We have argued that having to consider multiple criteria for social categorization could reduce bias in some conditions because of extreme structural complexity (Crisp & Hewstone, 2006; Crisp, Hewstone, & Rubin, 2001; Hall & Crisp, 2005). Since categorization is psychologically *functional* (Allport, 1954; Turner, Hogg, Oakes, et al., 1987), beyond some complexity threshold (where the number and/or relatedness of category dimensions defines complexity), categories may simply no longer usefully predict evaluative judgments. Supporting this idea is recent research that has shown humans to be no longer accurate when processing information cross-classified according to more than four dimensions (Halford, Baker, McCredden, et al., 2005). The findings of Crisp et al. and Hall and Crisp support the idea that beyond such a threshold, the salience of any single categorical basis for evaluative judgment is diminished. Importantly, the reduced bias observed in these studies is associated not with recategorization at a higher level of inclusiveness, but a more personalized and individuated way of viewing others (see Brewer & Miller, 1984; from a self-categorization perceptive, above the complexity threshold, an individuated conceptualization of others could be considered the best fit for defining the social context). In sum, when simultaneously salient multiple identities requiring attention cross the complexity threshold, bias is reduced, but this is via a process distinct from that discussed earlier in this chapter. Rather than shifting to a more inclusive level of categorization, or the formation of a dual identity composite subgroup, high complexity leads to a shift to

the lowest level of abstraction, an individuated impression of the target person. Decategorization, in isolation, may be a limited strategy because shifting focus to perceive people as individuals rather than group members may evoke *subtyping* without generalization of positive attitudes to the group as a whole (that is, the cognitive isolation of the target person from the overall group representation; Hewstone, 1994; Weber & Crocker, 1983). Theoretically, however, repeated exposure to multiple identities may eventually develop a processing style that avoids automatic categorization and stereotyping (see Crisp & Hewstone, 2007 for an extended discussion).

A NEW FRAMEWORK

In this section I outline when each of the types of multiple categorization discussed above will occur and what implications encouraging categorization at each of four levels (see Figure 31.1) has for prejudice and intergroup discrimination. The common thread used to link the research reviewed is the idea that people can shift between single or combined representations of social identity at levels of abstraction defined by differential inclusiveness.

Superordinate categorization

All other things being equal, people appear to typically categorize at the basic level, here level 2, the middle of any conceptual hierarchy. Shifting to define intergroup relations in terms of a more inclusive superordinate category (level 1) represents the common ingroup identity model. Consistent with the research reviewed earlier we would expect recategorization to reduce intergroup bias most successfully in contexts where there is lower identification with original subgroups (Crisp, 2006; Crisp, Stone, & Hall, 2006), and so no implied threat to distinctiveness (Brewer, 1991; Hornsey and Hogg, 2000). Higher identifiers, however, will likely react to recategorization with increased ingroup favoritism, and in such contexts, probably

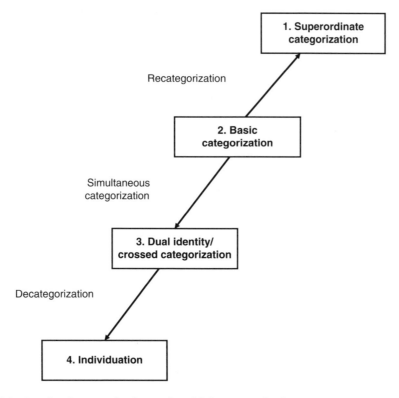

Figure 31.1   Levels of categorization and multiple categorization.

where intergroup conflict is prolonged and systemic, a dual identity approach may be more successful (level 3).

Simultaneous categorization

Level 3 represents contexts in which both subgroup and superordinate group identities are simultaneously salient; category combinations here represent a more specific level of abstraction than basic or superordinate categorization. This level encompasses the dual identity reformulation of the common ingroup identity model and the crossed categorization approach. Composite groups defined by a shared identity (e.g., *white* females and *white* males; white *females* and black *females*) should yield reductions in bias, even for higher identifiers, consistent with findings from the dual identity and crossed categorization literatures. These composite (ingroup / outgroup) groups are perceived as similar to the self (there is a shared ingroup identity), but at the same time do not compromise distinctiveness because the target remains an outgrouper on a second dimension of group membership. Compared to double outgroups, emphasizing the possibility of new composites that share a common ingroup identity can reduce bias, especially when positive mood is engendered, or those shared identities are emphasized (Crisp & Hewstone, 2007). Importantly, however, even when superordinate and subgroup levels are simultaneously salient, so that social identity motivations to retain positive distinctiveness are satisfied, bias may remain and even increase due to *ingroup projection*. To avoid this, categories that comprise dual identities should not be highly correlated (that is, share too many overlapping characteristics).

Individuation

At level 4, the lowest level of abstraction, individuation follows decategorization resulting from a high level of multiple identity complexity. When the number and/or complexity of the categories that require attention reaches a critical threshold there is a shift from categorical to individuated perception. No one basis for categorization is then used to guide impression formation. This shift leads to reduced category use (Crisp, Hewstone, & Rubin, 2001), an increase in the perception of individuating attributes (Hutter & Crisp, 2005), and less intergroup bias (Crisp, Hewstone, & Rubin, 2001; Hall & Crisp, 2005).

Moving between levels

Categorization at each of these levels may be defined by context and perceiver processing tendencies. The natural level is the basic level, yet context will determine whether superordinate identities replace existing subgroups (level 2; e.g., following a corporate merger) or composite subgroup identities are salient (level 3, e.g., a female engineer may be acutely aware of her minority status in a male-dominated field, uniquely attributable to a focus on dual identities). In some contexts, of course, collective identities will not be salient and personal identities will dominate (level 4). As well as context, perceiver characteristics may exert a pull towards particular levels. For instance, under conditions of limited resources there will be a tendency to process at less complex and higher levels of inclusiveness (Brewer, 1988; Fiske & Neuberg, 1990). For instance, Hutter and Crisp (2006) showed that cognitive load can prevent the formation of composite subgroups formed from dual identities. The need for assimilation and differentiation will also motivate perceivers to strive towards classification at more inclusive or less inclusive levels (Brewer, 1991). Importantly, apart from these context and perceiver focused determinants of categorization level, we can also *encourage* perceivers to define themselves at different levels, and this is the aim of the intervention models discussed earlier in this chapter.

A note on continua

Figure 31.1 illustrates the four categorization levels that have been identified in this review. It is important to note, however, that this conceptualization does not imply rigidity, nor does it imply exclusivity. The different levels map on to well-established continua used as frameworks to understand impression formation such as Tajfel's (1978) interpersonal-intergroup continuum, or Turner's (1982) conceptualization of depersonalization as a cognitive redefinition of the self; a shift along an intra-group – inter-group behaviour continuum representing a more salient personal or social identity. Similarly, it is consistent with Brewer (1988) and Fiske and Neuberg's (1990) dual process models (the latter model is distinguished from the former by the assumption that group-level categorization is the default). The model as presented here maps onto these models in terms of process, but draws out and specifically focuses on the implications at different levels of this continuum for multiple identities. Turner (1985) has argued that such continua are not meant to be rigid conceptualizations with opposite poles but rather levels of psychological abstraction related by class inclusion that can be simultaneously salient. This framework should be interpreted as such; it maps onto existing continua to (a) focus specifically on the multiple identities that can exists within such continua and (b) explicitly allow a conceptualization of dual identities, representing simultaneous salience at different level of abstraction.

DIRECTIONS FOR FUTURE RESEARCH

Which multiple categorization strategy is most likely to achieve improved intergroup relations? As Gaertner, Dovidio, Banker et al. (2000) have noted, a unique combination of different strategies, implemented simultaneously or sequentially, will probably be required depending upon the unique characteristics of the particular intergroup relations at hand. Gaertner et al. suggested, for instance, that while for more implicit forms of bias recategorization (level 1) may be a good starting point, decategorization (level 4) will be the best place to start when intergroup relations are characterized by high levels of overt hostility (to enable personalized interactions to set the basis for developing cross-group divides without inhibition associated with intergroup conflict; see the earlier discussion of how negative affect reduces the effectiveness of dual identity strategies). When identification with subgroups is high, however, dual identification (level 3) may be the best way to initially avoid distinctiveness threat (Brewer, 1991).

Such discussions highlight the importance of recognizing the perils and pitfalls, as well as the advantages, of different multiple categorization strategies. Recategorization (level 1) works when identification is low, but not when subgroup identification is high; but high identification is one characteristic that defines pervasive intergroup conflict. Decategorization (level 4) works for individuals but does not easily generalize to overall group stereotypes. Dual identity (level 3) satisfies distinctiveness motivations, but when the two identities are highly correlated this may lead to ingroup projection and rejection of (what become) deviant outgroupers. This is only when identification is high, but this, along with status differences, is often characteristic of real and pervasive intergroup conflicts. The apparent robustness of promoting dual identities that are not highly correlated makes this type of multiple categorization a compelling contender for a catch-all strategy. Whether this will turn out to be the case, and the contexts where different strategies operate best, will be important questions for future research.

SUMMARY AND CONCLUSIONS

In this chapter I have reviewed the current state of research on multiple social identities, and what implications they have for the study of prejudice, stereotyping, and discrimination. People can shift from one identity to another, either due to context and accessibility, or strategically to avoid being tarnished by a threat to one of their identities. People can also be encouraged to shift to more inclusive identities, which can then lead to a reduction in bias as specified by the common ingroup identity model. However, recategorization can threaten distinctiveness, especially for higher identifiers, so preserving the subgroup identity within a superordinate category can be necessary to avoid contravening needs for distinctiveness. This simultaneous category salience implied by the dual identity model maps directly onto research on crossed categorization where two dimensions of categorization are made simultaneously salient. This research confirms findings from dual identity research that a simultaneously salient common ingroup identity can reduce intergroup bias, but crossed categorization research also describes contexts in which categories converge to define double outgroups and high levels of bias. Research has shown that orientation towards ingroup or outgroup constituents of multiple category targets (most notably by positive or negative mood) can determine the extent to which a dual identity (mixed identity) will be successful in deceasing bias relative to double outgroups. While dual identities formed from either highly related or unrelated categories can satisfy distinctiveness needs, only dual identities that are not highly correlated can prevent ingroup projection and the danger of further derogation of outgroups. Finally, when intergroup relations are perceived to be high in category complexity, this can also reduce bias via a shift from an exclusively categorical to an individuated approach to impression formation. These different outcomes associated with different types of multiple categorization are summarized in Table 31.3.

The research reviewed in this chapter can be conceptualized within a hierarchy that maps onto existing continua of impression formation, but which emphasizes specifically the implications of multiple identities at each level. Context and motivation combine to determine how categorizations are used to define intergroup relations; but where a

Table 31.3   Outcomes associated with different combinations of multiple identity salience

	Superordinate category salience			
	Low		High	
	Subgroup salience: Low	Subgroup salience: High	Subgroup salience: Low	Subgroup salience: High
Level of categorization	Individuation (4)	Basic categorization (2)	Superordinate categorization (1)	Dual identity/ Crossed categorization (3)
Associated process	Decategorization	Categorization	Recategorization	Simultaneous categorization
Bias	Low Bias	High Bias	Low id: Low Bias High id: High Bias	Uncorrelated: Low Bias Correlated: High Bias

Note: Level 3 bias shown for contexts involving high identification at both subgroup and superordinate levels. Low identification at both levels leads to low bias irrespective of the correlation between the two salient categorizations that comprise the dual identity.

history of intergroup discrimination has made stigmatized identities chronically accessible, policy, practice and educational intervention can encourage people to recognize alternative ways of perceiving others. Research on multiple identities has provided an extensive array of alternative strategies for changing the way that people think about social groups. Continued research into when and how such strategies are most effective will help bring us closer to realizing goals of greater egalitarianism and improved intergroup relations.

ACKNOWLEDGEMENTS

The writing of this chapter was supported by a British Academy Research Development Award (BARDA 47819) to R. J. Crisp, a Leverhulme Trust (F/00236/M) grant to R. J. Crisp and M. A. Hogg and an Economic and Social Research Council grant (RES-00022-2033) to R. J. Crisp and N. R. Hall. Correspondence should be directed to: R. J. Crisp at the Centre for the Study of Group Processes, Department of Psychology, Keynes College, University of Kent, Canterbury, Kent CT2 7NP, UK. E-mail: r.crisp@kent.ac.uk.

REFERENCES

Allport, G. W. (1954). *The nature of prejudice.* Garden City, NY: Doubleday.

Boal, F. W. (1969). Territoriality on the Shankhill-Falls divide, Belfast. *Irish Geography, 6*, 30–50.

Brewer, M. B. (1988). A dual process model of impression formation. In R. Wyer & T. Srull (Eds.), *Advances in social cognition* (Vol. 1, pp. 1–36). Hillsdale, NJ: Lawrence Erlbaum Associates, Inc..

Brewer, M. B. (1991). The social self: On being the same and different at the same time. *Personality and Social Psychology Bulletin, 17*, 475–482.

Brewer, M. B., Ho, H., Lee, J., & Miller, N. (1987). Social identity and social distance among Hong Kong school children. *Personality and Social Psychology Bulletin, 13*, 156–65.

Brewer, M. B., & Miller, N. (1984). Beyond the contact hypothesis: Theoretical perspectives on desegregation. In N. Miller & M. B. Brewer (Eds.), *Groups in contact: The psychology of desegregation* (pp. 281–302). San Diego, CA: Academic Press.

Brewer, M. B., & Pierce, K. P. (2005). Social identity complexity and outgroup tolerance. *Personality and Social Psychology Bulletin, 31*, 428–437.

Brown, R. J., & Abrams, D. (1986). The effects of intergroup similarity and goal interdependence on intergroup attitudes and task performance. *Journal of Experimental Social Psychology, 22*, 78–92.

Cairns, E., & Mercer, G. W. (1984). Social identity in Northern Ireland. *Human Relations, 37*, 1095–1102.

Carter, N. A. (2006). Political institutions and multiple social identities. In R. J. Crisp & M. Hewstone (Eds.). *Multiple social categorization: Processes, models and applications* (pp. 239–268). Hove, E. Sussex: Psychology Press (Taylor & Francis).

Crisp, R. J. (2006). Commitment and categorization in common ingroup contexts. In R. J. Crisp & M. Hewstone (Eds.). *Multiple social categorization: Processes, models and applications*(pp. 90–111). Hove, E. Sussex: Psychology Press (Taylor & Francis).

Crisp, R. J., Ensari, N., Hewstone, M., & Miller, N. (2002). A dual-route model of crossed categorization effects. In W. Stroebe & M. Hewstone (Eds.). *European review of social psychology* (Vol. 13, pp. 35–74). Hove, E. Sussex: Psychology Press (Taylor & Francis).

Crisp, R. J., & Hewstone, M. (1999). Differential evaluation of crossed category groups: Patterns, processes, and reducing intergroup bias. *Group Processes and Intergroup Relations, 2,* 303–333.

Crisp, R. J., & Hewstone, M. (2000). Multiple categorization and social identity. In D. Capozza & R. Brown (Eds.). *Social identity processes: Trends in theory and research.* (pp. 149–166). Beverly Hills: Sage.

Crisp, R. J., & Hewstone, M. (2007). Multiple social categorization. In M. P. Zanna (Ed.). *Advances in experimental social psychology* (vol. 39, pp. 163–254). Orlando, FL: Academic Press

Crisp, R. J., Hewstone, M, Richards, Z., & Paolini, S. (2003). Inclusiveness and crossed categorization: Effects on co-joined category evaluations of in-group and out-group primes. *British Journal of Social Psychology, 42,* 25–38.

Crisp, R. J., Hewstone, M., & Rubin, M. (2001). Does multiple categorization reduce intergroup bias? *Personality & Social Psychology Bulletin, 27,* 76–89.

Crisp, R. J., Stone, C. H., & Hall, N. R. (2006). Recategorization and subgroup identification: Predicting and preventing threats from common ingroups. *Personality and Social Psychology Bulletin, 32,* 230–243.

Crisp, R. J., Walsh, J., & Hewstone, M. (2006b). Crossed categorization in common ingroup contexts. *Personality and Social Psychology Bulletin, 32,* 1204–1218.

Deschamps, J.-C., & Doise, W. (1978). Crossed category memberships in intergroup relations. In H. Tajfel (Ed.), *Differentiation between social groups* (pp. 141–158). Cambridge: Cambridge University Press.

Diehl, M. (1990). The minimal group paradigm: Theoretical explanations and empirical findings. In W. Stroebe & M. Hewstone (Eds.), *European review of social psychology* (Vol. 1, pp. 263–292). Chichester: Wiley.

Doise, W. (1978). *Groups and individuals. Explanations in social psychology,* Cambridge: Cambridge University Press.

Dovidio, J. F., Gaertner, S. L., Hodson, G., Riek, M. B., Johnson, K. M., & Houlette, M. (2006). Recategorization and crossed categorization: The implications of group salience and representations for reducing bias. In R. J. Crisp & M. Hewstone (Eds.). *Multiple social categorization: Processes, models and applications* (pp. 65–89). Hove, E. Sussex: Psychology Press (Taylor & Francis).

Dovidio, J. F., Gaertner, S. L., & Validzic, A. (1998) Intergroup bias: Status, differentiation and a common in-group identity. *Journal of Personality and Social Psychology, 75,* 1, 109–120.

Eurich-Fulcher, R., & Schofield, J. W. (1995). Correlated versus uncorrelated social categorizations: The effect on intergroup bias. *Personality and Social Psychology Bulletin, 21,* 149–159.

Evans-Pritchard, E. E. (1940). *The Nuer.* London: Oxford University Press.

Fiske, S. T., & Neuberg, S. L. (1990). A continuum of impression formation from category based to individuating process: Influences of information and motivation on attention an interpretation. *Advances in experimental social psychology, 23,* 1–74. .

Gaertner, S. L., & Dovidio, J. F. (2000). *Reducing intergroup bias: The Common Ingroup Identity Model.* Philadelphia, PA: The Psychology Press/Taylor & Francis.

Gaertner, S. L., Dovidio, J. F., Anastasio, P. A., Bachman, B. A., & Rust, M. C. (1993). The common ingroup identity model: Recategorization and the reduction of intergroup bias. In W. Stroebe and M. Hewstone (Eds.), *European review of social psychology* (Vol. 2, pp. 247–278). Chichester: J. Wiley.

Gaertner, S. L., Dovidio, J. F., Banker, B. S., Houlette, M., Johnson, K. M., & McGlynn, E. A. (2000). Reducing intergroup conflict: From superordinate goals to decategorization, recategorization, and mutual differentiation. *Group dynamics: Theory, Research, and Practice, 4,* 98–114.

González, R., & Brown, R. J. (2003). Generalization of positive attitude as a function of subgroup and superordinate group identifications in intergroup contact. *European Journal of Social Psychology, 33,* 195–214.

Gresky, D. M., Eyck, L. L. T., Lord, C. G., & McIntyre, R. B. (2005). Effects of salient multiple identities on women's performance under mathematics stereotype threat. *Sex Roles, 53,* 703–716.

Halford, G. S., Baker, R. McCredden, J. E., & Bain, J. D. (2005). How many variables can humans process? *Psychological Science, 16,* 70–76.

Hall, N. R., & Crisp, R. J. (2005). Considering multiple criteria for social categorization can reduce intergroup bias. *Personality and Social Psychology Bulletin, 31,* 1435–1444.

Hewstone, M. (1994). Revision and change of stereotypic beliefs: In search of the elusive subtyping model. In W. Stroebe & M. Hewstone (Eds.), *European review of social psychology* (Vol. 5, pp. 69–109). Chichester: J. Wiley.

Hewstone, M., Cairns, Voci, A., Paolini, S., McLernon, F., Crisp, R. J., & Niens, U. (2005). Intergroup contact in a divided society: Challenging segregation in Northern Ireland. In D. Abrams, J. M. Marques, & M. A. Hogg (Eds.), *The social psychology of inclusion and exclusion* (pp. 265–292). Philadelphia, PA: Psychology Press.

Hewstone, M., Islam, M. R., & Judd, C. M. (1993). Models of crossed categorization and intergroup relations. *Journal of Personality and Social Psychology, 64,* 779–793.

Hogg, M. A. (2000). Subjective uncertainty reduction through self-categorization: A motivational theory of social identity processes. *European Review of Social Psychology, 11,* 223–255.

Hogg, M. A., & Abrams, D. (1988). *Social identifications: A social psychology of intergroup relations and group processes.* London: Routledge.

Hornsey, M. J., & Hogg, M. A. (2000). Subgroup relations: a comparison of mutual intergroup differentiation and common ingroup identity models of prejudice reduction. *Personality and Social Psychology Bulletin, 26,* 242–256.

Hutter, R. R. H., & Crisp, R. J. (2005). The composition of category conjunctions. *Personality and Social Psychology Bulletin, 31,* 647–657.

Hutter, R. R. H., & Crisp, R. J. (2006). Implications of cognitive busyness for the perception of category conjunctions. *Journal of Social Psychology, 146,* 253–256.

Jetten, J., Spears, R., & Postmes, T. (2004). Intergroup distinctiveness and differentiation: A meta-analytic integration. *Journal of Personality and Social Psychology, 86,* 862–879.

Kenworthy, J. B., Canales, C. J., Weaver, K. D., & Miller, N. (2003). Negative incidental affect and mood congruency in crossed categorization. *Journal of Experimental Social Psychology, 39,* 195–219.

Kruglanski, A. W. (1996). Motivated social cognition: Principles of the interface. In E. T. Higgins & A. W. Kruglanski,(Eds.), *Social psychology: Handbook of basic principles* (pp. 493–520). New York: Guilford.

Levine, R. A., & Campbell, D. T. (1972). *Ethnocentrism: Theories of conflict, ethnic attitudes and group behaviour.* New York: Wiley.

Marks, G., & Miller, N. (1987). Ten years of research on the false-consensus effect: An empirical and theoretical review. Psychological Bulletin, 102, 72–90.

Marques, J. M., Abrams, D., Paez, D., & Martinez-Taboada, C. (1998). The role of categorization and ingroup norms in judgement of groups and their members. *Journal of Personality and Social Psychology, 75,* 976–988.

Miller, N., Kenworthy, J., Carnales, C. J., & Stenstrom, D. M. (2006). Explaining the effects of crossed categorization on ethnocentric bias. In Crisp, R. J. & Hewstone, M. (Eds.) *Multiple social categorization: Processes, models and applications* (pp. 160–188). Hove, E. Sussex: Psychology Press (Taylor & Francis).

Mullen, B., Migdal, M. J., & Hewstone, M. (2001). Crossed categorization versus simple categorization and intergroup evaluations: a meta-analysis. *European Journal of Social Psychology, 31,* 721–736.

Mummendey, A., & Wenzel, M. (1999). Social discrimination and tolerance in intergroup relations: Reactions to intergroup difference. *Personality and Social Psychology Review, 3,* 158–174.

Murphy, R. F. (1957). Intergroup hostility and social cohesion. *American Anthropologist, 59,* 1018–1035.

Roccas, S., & Brewer, M. B. (2002). Social identity complexity. *Personality and Social Psychology Review, 6,* 88–106.

Rosch, E., Mervis, C.B., Gray, W., Johnson, D., & Boyes-Braem, P. (1976). Basic objects in natural categories. *Cognitive Psychology, 8,* 382–439.

Rosenthal, H. E. S., & Crisp, R. J. (2006). Reducing stereotype threat by blurring intergroup boundaries. *Personality and Social Psychology Bulletin, 32,* 501–511.

Stangor, C., Lynch, L., Duan, C., & Glass, B. (1992). Categorization of individuals on the basis of multiple social features. *Journal of Personality and Social Psychology, 62,* 207–218.Tajfel, H. (1978). Social categorization, social identity and social comparison. In Tajfel, H. (Ed.), *Differentiation between social groups: Studies in the social psychology of intergroup relations* (pp. 61–76). London: Academic Press.

Tajfel, H., Flament, C., Billig, M., & Bundy, R. P. (1971). Social categorization and intergroup behaviour. *European Journal of Social Psychology, 1,* 149–178.

Tajfel, H., & Turner, J. C. (1979). An integrative theory of intergroup conflict. In W. G. Austin & S. Worchel (Eds.), *The Social Psychology of Intergroup Relations* (pp. 33–47). California: Brooks/Cole.

Turner, J. C. (1982). Towards a cognitive redefinition of the social group. In H. Tajfel (Eds.), *Social identity and intergroup relations,* (pp.15–40). Cambridge: Cambridge University Press.

Turner, J. C., Hogg, M. A., Oakes, P. J., Reicher, S. D. & Wetherell, M. S. (1987). *Rediscovering the social group: A self-categorization theory.* Oxford, England: Basil Blackwell.

Urban, L. M., & Miller, N. M. (1998). A theoretical analysis of crossed categorization effects: A meta-analysis. *Journal of Personality and Social Psychology, 74,* 894–908.

van Leeuwen, E., van Knippenberg, D., & Ellemers, N. (2003). Continuing and changing group identities: The effects of merging on social identification and ingroup bias. *Personality and Social Psychology Bulletin, 29,* 697–690.

Vanbeselaere, N. (1987). The effect of dichotomous and crossed social categorizations upon intergroup discrimination. *European Journal of Social Psychology, 17,* 143–156.

Waldzus, S., Mummendey, A., Wenzel, M., & Weber, U. (2003). Towards tolerance: Representations of superordinate categories and perceived ingroup prototypicality. *Journal of Experimental Social Psychology, 39,* 31–47.

Weber, R., & Crocker, J. (1983). Cognitive processes in the revision of stereotypic beliefs. *Journal of Personality and Social Psychology, 45,* 961–977.

Wenzel, M., Mummendey, A., Weber, U., & Waldzus, S. (2003). The ingroup as pars pro toto: projection from the ingroup onto the inclusive category as a precursor to social discrimination. *Personality and Social Psychology Bulletin, 29,* 461–473.

Wilder, D. A. (1986). Social Categorization: Implications for creation and reduction of intergroup bias. In L. Berkowitz (Ed.), *Advances in experimental social psychology* (Vol. 19, pp. 293–355). New York: Academic Press.

32

Social Categorization

Samuel L. Gaertner, John F. Dovidio, and
Melissa A. Houlette

ABSTRACT

This chapter examines the fundamental influences of social categorization and identity in intergroup relations, both in terms of creating intergroup conflict and in promoting more positive intergroup relations. First we review the influence that social categorization has on the ways that people think about, feel about, and act towards members of their own group (the ingroup) and other groups (outgroups). Then we discuss three influential category-based approaches for reducing intergroup biases: Decategorization, Mutual Intergroup Differentiation, and Recategorization. Each of these approaches has considerable empirical support. Finally, we consider the challenges and opportunities that these approaches present for future research and practical interventions.

SOCIAL CATEGORIZATION

Human activity is rooted in interdependence. Group systems involving greater mutual cooperation have substantial survival advantages for individual group members over those systems without reciprocally positive social relations (Schino, 2007; Trivers, 1971). However, the decision to cooperate with non-relatives (i.e., to expend resources for another's benefit) is a dilemma of trust because the ultimate benefit for the provider depends on others' willingness to reciprocate. Indiscriminate trust and altruism that are not reciprocated are not effective survival strategies.

Social categorization and group boundaries provide the bases for achieving the benefits of cooperative interdependence without the risk of excessive costs. Ingroup membership is a form of contingent cooperation. By limiting aid to mutually acknowledged ingroup members, total costs and risks of nonreciprocation can be contained. Thus, ingroups are bounded communities of mutual trust and obligation that facilitate interdependence, coordination, and cooperation. The ways in which people perceive social categories and understand their group membership thus play a critical role in both prejudice toward members of other groups and social harmony within one's group.

The present chapter examines the fundamental influences of social categorization and identity in intergroup relations, both in terms of creating intergroup conflict and in ameliorating intergroup tensions. In the next section, we describe the shift historically in the study of prejudice from a focus primarily on individual-level processes to one that recognizes the importance of group-level processes, as well. After that, we review the critical influence that social categorization has on the ways that people think about, feel about, and act towards members of their own group (the ingroup) and other groups (outgroups). Because of the importance of social categorization in intergroup bias, recent approaches have targeted this process for reducing prejudice, stereotyping, and discrimination. We review three influential category-based approaches for reducing intergroup biases, and then we consider related challenges and opportunities for future research and practical interventions.

BRIEF HISTORICAL BACKGROUND

Prejudice and discrimination are nearly universal, across time and culture, and a variety of different frameworks have been developed to understand these phenomena. Traditional approaches focused largely on the biases of individuals, examining the role of personality and individual needs and goals. For example, classic work on the authoritarian personality (Adorno, Frenkel-Brunswik, Levinson, et al., 1950) identified a number of personal experiences (e.g., childhood experiences and parental discipline) and social orientations (e.g., conventionalism and support for traditional family structure) associated with high levels of prejudice. Moreover, these prejudiced people – high authoritarians – tended to view the world in terms of rigid, well-demarcated, and unambiguous social categories.

Whereas the research on the authoritarian personality tended to portray social categorization as an abnormal representation of the social world, other approaches recognized social categorization more as a functional and normal process. For instance, Sherif, Harvey, White, et al., (1961), in their classic Robbers Cave studies, emphasized the foundational role of social categorization in demarcating ingroup and outgroup

membership and proposed that the functional relations between ingroups and outgroups are critical in determining intergroup attitudes. According to this position, competition between groups produces prejudice and discrimination, whereas intergroup interdependence and cooperative interaction that result in successful outcomes reduce intergroup bias (see also Campbell, 1965).

Other work further emphasized that social categorization was a normal social-cognitive process but also recognized the role of social categorization *per se*, independent of negative functional intergroup relations, as a basis for developing prejudice. Gordon Allport (1954/1979) in his seminal work, *The Nature of Prejudice*, wrote about the normality and inevitability of social categorization: 'The human mind must think with the aid of categories … Categories are the basis for normal prejudgment. We cannot possibly avoid this process' (p. 20). Moreover, Allport proposed that the differentiation between members of the ingroup and those of the outgroup represented the foundation for the development of prejudice. He noted that 'in-groups are psychologically primary. We live in them, and sometimes, for them. Hostility toward out-groups helps strengthen our sense of belonging, but it is not required' (p. 42).

In his highly influential article, 'Cognitive Aspects of Prejudice,' Tajfel (1969) further emphasized that the cognitive bases of prejudice were not primarily irrational or psychopathological but rather directly related to social categorization and the search for social meaning. Moreover, his subsequent research leading to the formulation of Social Identity Theory (SIT; Tajfel & Turner, 1979) further revealed how the mere categorization of people into ingroups and outgroups devoid of normal meaning and immediate functional relations – 'minimal groups' – was sufficient to initiate intergroup bias and prejudice.

Tajfel and Turner's (1979) SIT and Turner, Hogg, Oakes, Reicher, et al., (1987) Self-Categorization Theory (SCT) also emphasized the motivational and functional aspects of social categorization. Tajfel and Turner proposed that a person's need for positive self-identity may be satisfied by membership in valued social groups. This need motivates social comparisons and actions (e.g., discrimination) that favorably differentiate ingroup from outgroup members, thereby providing a basis for maintained, restored or enhanced feelings of status and esteem.

Currently, social psychologists widely acknowledge the central roles of social categorization and social identity in intergroup relations (see Brewer, 2001). In the next section we review the literature on one of the most basic features associated with these processes – the categorization of people into ingroups and outgroups – which forms the psychological foundation for prejudice, stereotyping, and discrimination.

SOCIAL CATEGORIZATION AND BIAS

One universal facet of human thinking essential for efficient functioning is the ability to quickly and effectively sort the many different objects, events and people encountered into meaningful categories (Hamilton & Sherman, 1994). Categorization enables decisions about incoming information to be made quickly because the instant an object is categorized, it is assigned the properties shared by other category members. Thus, time-consuming consideration of the meaning of every experience is eliminated because it is inefficient. Categorization often occurs automatically on the basis of physical similarity, proximity, or shared fate (Campbell, 1958). In this respect, people seem willing to compromise total accuracy for efficiency when confronted with the often overwhelming complexity of their social world (Fiske & Taylor, 1991; see also the Chapter 7 by Fiske & Russell, this volume).

When people or objects are categorized into groups, real differences between members of the same category tend to be perceptually minimized in making decisions or forming impressions. Members of the same category are regarded as more similar than they actually are, and more similar than they were before

they were categorized together (Tajfel, 1969). In addition, distinctions between members of different categories become exaggerated. Thus, categorization enhances perceptions of similarities within and differences between groups. For *social* categorization, this process is more ominous than for nonhuman objects, because these within- and between-group distortions have a tendency to generalize to additional dimensions (e.g., character traits) beyond those that differentiated the categories originally (Allport, 1954/1979).

Moreover, in the process of social categorization, people typically classify themselves *into* one of the social categories (and *out of* the others). The identification with one's ingroup has a profound influence on people's conceptions of the self and others. Individuals gain not only material support from the ingroup, but also they experience substantial psychological benefit in terms of a sense of belonging and security from the ingroup (Correll & Park, 2005). People derive positive esteem from the status and distinctiveness of their group (Tajfel & Turner, 1979) and construe themselves in fundamental ways in terms of this collective identity, seeing themselves as embodying group values and characteristics (Hogg & Reid, 2006). In addition, the mere recognition that another person shares ingroup membership brings the person closer to the self psychologically (Brewer, 1979). While attempts to positively differentiate the ingroup from outgroups sometimes stem from a pro-ingroup orientation (i.e., a preference for ingroup members) rather than an anti-outgroup orientation, the disadvantaged status of outgroup members due to preferential treatment of one group over another can be as pernicious as discrimination based on anti-outgroup orientations

Categorization of individuals into groups is potentially alterable. An individual can categorize the self along a continuum that ranges from the self as a separate individual with personal motives, goals, and achievements represented as 'I' at one extreme to the self as the embodiment of a social collective or group represented by 'We' at the other. At the individual level, one's personal welfare and goals are most salient and important. At the group level, the goals and achievements of the group are merged with one's own (see Brown & Turner, 1981), and the group's welfare is paramount. Intergroup relations begin when people think about themselves as a group member ('we') rather than as a distinct individual ('I').

Upon social categorization of people as members of the ingroup or outgroups, people favor ingroup members. People favor ingroup members in reward allocations (Tajfel, Billig, Bundy, et al., 1971), esteem (Rabbie, 1982), and in the evaluation of the products of their labor (Ferguson & Kelley, 1964). They are spontaneously more positive in their evaluations of ingroup than outgroup members (Otten & Moskowitz, 2000). Cognitively, people process information more deeply for ingroup than for outgroup members (Van Bavel, Packer, & Cunningham, 2008), perceive ingroup members as more heterogeneous than outgroup members (Boldry, Gaertner, & Quinn, 2007). Individuals also retain information in a more detailed fashion for ingroup than outgroup members (Park & Rothbart, 1982), have better memory for information about ways ingroup members are similar and outgroup members are dissimilar to the self (Wilder, 1981), and remember less positive information about outgroup members (Howard & Rothbart, 1980).

Because of the greater self-other overlap in representations for people defined as ingroup members (Smith & Henry, 1996), people process information about and make attributions to ingroup members more on the basis of self-congruency than they do for outgroup members. People see greater connection between other members of the ingroup and the self (Aron, McLaughlin-Volpe, Mashek, et al., 2005) and expect ingroup members to share one's attitudes and values more than do outgroup members (Robbins & Krueger, 2005). In part as a consequence, people are more generous and forgiving in their attributions about the behaviors of ingroup relative to outgroup members. Positive behaviors and successful outcomes are more likely to be attributed to internal, stable characteristics of ingroup than outgroup members, whereas negative outcomes are more likely to be ascribed to the personal characteristics of outgroup than ingroup members (Hewstone, 1990). Furthermore, observed positive (negative) behaviors of ingroup members are encoded in memory at higher (lower) levels of abstraction, whereas the reverse is true for behaviors of outgroup members (Maass, Salvi, Arcuri, et al., 1989). Undesirable actions of outgroup members are encoded at more abstract levels that presume intentionality and dispositional origin (e.g., 'she is hostile') than identical behaviors of ingroup members (e.g., 'she slapped the girl'). Desirable actions of outgroup members, however, are encoded at more concrete levels (e.g., 'she walked across the street holding the old man's hand') relative to the same behaviors of ingroup members (e.g., 'she is helpful').

These cognitive biases help to perpetuate social biases and stereotypes even in the face of countervailing evidence. For example, because positive behaviors of outgroup members are encoded at relatively concrete levels, it becomes less likely that counter-stereotypic positive behaviors would generalize across situations or to other outgroup members (see also Karpinski & von Hippel, 1996). People do not remember that an outgroup member was 'helpful,' but only the very concrete descriptive actions. Thus, outgroup stereotypes tend to be generally resistant to change by simply observing counterstereotypic outgroup behaviors.

Language plays another role in intergroup bias because collective pronouns such as 'we' or 'they' that are used to define people's ingroup or outgroup status are frequently paired with stimuli having strong affective connotations. Thus, these pronouns may acquire important evaluative properties of their own. These words (we, they) can potentially increase the availability of positive or negative associations and thus influence beliefs about, evaluations of and behaviors toward other people, often spontaneously and without awareness (Perdue, Dovidio, Gurtman, et al., 1990).

Also, shared group membership decreases psychological distance from and facilitates arousal of promotive tension or empathy toward ingroup members (Hornstein, 1976). Moreover, empathy for a person in need of assistance is more strongly predictive of helping behavior when that target is an ingroup member than an outgroup member (Stürmer, Snyder, & Omoto, 2005). Relatedly, prosocial behavior is offered more readily to ingroup than to outgroup members (Piliavin, Dovidio, Gaertner, et al., 1981). People are also more likely to be cooperative, trustful, and exercise more personal restraint when using endangered resources shared with ingroup members than with others (Kramer & Brewer, 1984).

Because categorization plays such an important role in the etiology of intergroup bias, it is the focus of recent approaches to combating intergroup bias. In particular, the ways people categorize others can be modified, and the effects of categorization can vary as a function of the relationships between groups. In the next section, we review three category-based approaches for reducing intergroup bias.

CATEGORIZATION-BASED MODELS FOR REDUCING INTERGROUP BIAS

The process of social categorization is fluid, and people belong to many groups that are hierarchically organized in terms of their inclusiveness. The level of category inclusiveness that will be dominant within a particular context can be modified by altering a perceiver's goals, motives, and expectations, as well as factors within the situational context. This flexibility of social categorization, and consequently social identity, is important because of its implications for altering the way people think about members of other groups and, accordingly, how positively they feel about them. In terms of the most effective way to structure the social world to promote harmonious intergroup relations, several empirically-supported category-based alternatives have been proposed. Although

various models share common theoretical assumptions about the importance of social categorization and identity in intergroup relations, they suggest different strategies for reducing bias and conflict.

Decategorization/personalization

Based on the assumption that the categorization of people into different groups, specifically the ingroup and an outgroup, forms the foundation for bias, the goal of *decategorization* (see Wilder, 1981) is to weaken the salience of group boundaries. Specifically, decategorization interventions encourage people from different groups to regard one another primarily as distinct individuals and interact in interpersonal (i.e., 'me and you') in contrast to approaches that emphasize group-based (i.e., 'we versus they') modes of relating to one another (e.g., see Brewer, 1988; Fiske, Lin, & Neuberg, 1999; Miller & Brewer, 1984; Tajfel & Turner, 1979). In addition, if decategorization occurs through personalized interactions in which information about each other's unique qualities is exchanged, intergroup bias will be further reduced by undermining the validity of the outgroup stereotypes (Brewer & Miller, 1984; Miller, 2002; Miller, Brewer, & Edwards, 1985).

Although there are similarities between perceiving ingroup and outgroup members in a decategorized way (as 'separate individuals') and having 'personalized interactions' with outgroup members, decategorization and personalization are theoretically distinct concepts. Decategorization involves viewing either outgroup members (see Wilder, 1986) or members of both groups as 'separate individuals' and can promote individuated responses even in the absence of interaction or information exchange. For example, receiving information demonstrating variability in the opinions of outgroup members or seeing outgroup members respond as individuals rather than as a group renders each member more distinctive, potentially blurring the prior categorization scheme (Wilder, 1978). Decategorization reduces intergroup bias in part by improving attitudes toward others previously seen primarily in terms of their outgroup membership, but also by producing less favorable responses to people formerly perceived mainly in terms of their membership in the ingroup (Gaertner, Mann, Murrell, et al., 1989).

In contrast, personalization involves receiving self-relevant, more intimate information about members of the outgroup. Thus, personalization involves perceiving outgroup members in a more individuated and differentiated way but also includes a focus on information about an outgroup member that is relevant to the self. Repeated personalized interactions with a variety of outgroup members should over time undermine the value of the category stereotype as a source of information about members of that group. Thus, the effects of personalization would be expected to generalize to new situations as well as to heretofore unfamiliar outgroup members. For the benefits of personalization to generalize, however, it is necessary for outgroup members' group identities to be salient to some degree, although not primary, during the interaction to enable the group stereotype to be weakened (see Brewer & Miller, 1984; Miller, 2002). Miller (2002) observed that 'if personalized information processing means that information concerning social category membership lacks any salience during the interaction, whatever information and/or affect was acquired cannot generalize to other members of the category ... A key point, however, is that in most contact situations ... cues providing information about the category identity of the interacting persons are constantly present' (p. 399; see also Brown & Hewstone, 2005).

A number of experimental studies provide evidence supporting this theoretical perspective. In Miller, Brewer, and Edwards (1985), for example, intergroup contact that permitted more personalized interactions (e.g., when interaction was person-focused rather than task focused) resulted not only in more positive attitudes toward those outgroup members present, but to other outgroup members

viewed on video. Thus, these conditions of intergroup contact reduced bias in both an immediate and generalizable fashion.

Whereas decategorization is designed to degrade group boundaries entirely and personalization attempts to make group membership secondary to personal connections between individuals, another approach acknowledges the difficulty of eliminating perceptions of group identities and instead focuses on changing perceptions of the relationship between the groups while emphasizing the positive distinctiveness of each group.

Mutual intergroup differentiation

One of the fundamental premises of SIT is that people are motivated to maintain the positive distinctiveness of their social identity. Interventions that threaten the integrity of collective identity, such as attempts to degrade group boundaries, can sometimes arouse resistance and exacerbate bias (Jetten, Spears, & Postmes, 2004). Recognizing the potential of identity threat to arouse intergroup bias, Brown and Hewstone (2005; see also Hewstone & Brown, 1986) introduced a different categorization-based framework for reducing intergroup bias. In their Mutual Intergroup Differentiation Model, Brown, and Hewstone posit that intergroup relations will be harmonious when group identities remain *mutually differentiated* rather than blurred, but maintained in the context of cooperative intergroup interaction. Thus, relative to the decategorization strategies, this perspective proposes that maintaining group distinctiveness within a cooperative intergroup relationship would be associated with low levels of intergroup threat and, consequently, with lower levels of intergroup bias. In addition, the salience of intergroup boundaries provides an associative mechanism through which changes in outgroup attitudes that occur during intergroup contact can generalize to the outgroup as a whole.

Supportive of the Mutual Intergroup Differentiation Model (see also Chapter 33 by Tausch & Hewstone, this volume), several studies have demonstrated that the effects of positive contact produce more generalized reductions in bias toward the outgroup when people are aware of the intergroup, rather than interpersonal, nature of the interaction (see Kenworthy, Turner, Hewstone, et al., 2005; Pettigrew, 1998). Evidence in support of this approach (see also Brown & Hewstone, 2005) comes from the results of an experiment by Brown and Wade (1987) in which work teams composed of students from two different faculties engaged in a cooperative effort to produce a two-page magazine article. When the representatives of the two groups were assigned separate roles in the team task (one group working on figures and layout, the other working on text), the contact experience had a more positive effect on intergroup attitudes than when the two groups were not provided with distinctive roles (see also Deschamps & Brown, 1983; Dovidio, Gaertner, & Validzic, 1998).

The Mutual Intergroup Differentiation Model further proposes that beyond the salience of social categories, the perceived typicality of outgroup members is a critical moderator of the extent to which positive intergroup contact can reduce bias toward the outgroup as a whole. Rothbart and John (1985) suggested, and subsequent research has demonstrated, that the more representative (prototypical) of his or her group a person is perceived to be, the greater the likelihood that impressions about that person will generalize to change perceptions of the group overall (e.g., Wilder, Simon, & Faith, 1996).

Consistent with this basic proposition of the model, the relationship between exposure to counterstereotypic group members and amount of stereotype change for the social group is moderated by the degree of perceived typicality of the group members (Hewstone, Hassebrauck, Wirth, et al., 2000). More change occurs when people are presented with counterstereotypic information about representative than nonrepresentative group members (Weber & Crocker, 1983). In addition, cooperative intergroup contact is more effective for improving attitudes toward the outgroup when the outgroup members

involved are perceived as more typical of their group (Brown, Eller, Leeds, et al., 2007). The moderating effect of typicality, however, occurs primarily when the outgroup is perceived as homogeneous rather than heterogeneous (Brown, Vivian, & Hewstone, 1999). Perceptions of typicality reduce the likelihood that group members who demonstrate counterstereotypic qualities will be seen as exceptions, which can be discounted, or as representing a subtype of the group, leaving the overall group stereotype intact and outgroup evaluation largely unaffected.

Whereas decategorization focuses on degrading social categorization and Mutual Intergroup Differentiation emphasizes the importance of maintaining distinctive social identities, a third approach, the Common Ingroup Identity Model (Gaertner & Dovidio, 2000; Gaertner, Dovidio, Anastasio, et al., 1993) posits the value of creating an overriding shared identity – *recategorization* – for members of different groups.

Common ingroup identity

The key idea of the Common Ingroup Identity Model is that factors that induce members of different groups to recategorize themselves as members of the same more inclusive group can reduce intergroup bias through cognitive and motivational processes involving ingroup favoritism (Gaertner & Dovidio, 2000; Gaertner, Dovidio, Anastasio, et al., 1993). Thus, more positive beliefs, feelings, and behaviors, usually reserved for ingroup members, are extended or redirected to former outgroup members because of their recategorized ingroup status. Consequently, recategorization dynamically changes the conceptual representations of the different groups from an 'Us' versus 'Them' orientation to a more inclusive, superordinate connection: 'We.'

Figure 32.1 presents the general framework and specifies the causes and consequences of a common ingroup identity. Specifically, it is hypothesized that the different types of intergroup interdependence and cognitive, perceptual, linguistic, affective, and environmental factors (listed on the left)

Causes ⟶ Mediators ⟶ Consequences

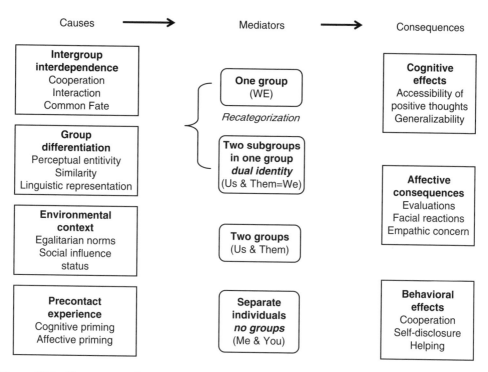

Figure 32.1 The common ingroup identity model.

can either independently or in concert alter individuals' cognitive representations of the aggregate (listed in the center). Included among the different factors that can increase the perception of a common ingroup identity are the features specified by Allport's (1954; see also Williams, 1947) Contact Hypothesis: cooperative intergroup interaction, equal status, and egalitarian norms. In addition, common ingroup identity may be achieved by increasing the salience of existing common superordinate memberships (e.g., a school, a company, a nation) or categories (e.g., students; Gómez, Dovidio, Huici, et al., 2008) or by introducing factors (e.g., common goals or fate; see Gaertner, Dovidio, Rust, et al. 1999) that are perceived to be shared by the memberships. These resulting cognitive representations (i.e., one group, two subgroups within one group [a dual identity], two groups, or separate individuals) are then proposed to result in the specific cognitive, affective and overt behavioral consequences (listed on the right). For instance, cooperative intergroup interaction improves outgroup attitudes and

reduces bias between members of different groups through its effect on creating a more inclusive, common identity.

Once former outgroup members are regarded as ingroup members, it is proposed that they would be accorded the benefits of ingroup status heuristically. There would likely be more positive thoughts, feelings, and behaviors (listed on the right) toward these former outgroup members by virtue of categorizing them now as ingroup members. Consistent with this hypothesis, studies across a range of naturalistic groups reveal that stronger perceptions of a common ingroup identity mediate positive intergroup relations. This research includes students attending a multi-ethnic high school (Gaertner, Rust, Dovidio, et al., 1996), banking executives who had experienced a corporate merger (Bachman, 1993), and members of stepfamilies (Banker & Gaertner, 1998). Other field research demonstrates that more salient common identity relates to more favorable intergroup attitudes for members of majority (Smith & Tyler, 1996) and minority (Pfeifer, Ruble, Bachman, et al., 2007) racial and ethnic groups and across national groups (Klandermans, Sabucedo, & Rodriguez, 2004). Experimental evidence of intergroup attitudes in support of the Common Ingroup Identity Model comes from research using both ad hoc and real groups, with children as well as adults, and in the US (e.g., Nier, Gaertner, Dovidio, et al., 2001; see Gaertner & Dovidio, 2000) and in other countries (e.g., Guerra, Rebelo, & Monteiro, 2004; Montiero, Guerra & Rebelo, 2009; Rebelo, Guerra, & Monteiro, 2004).

In addition, recategorization in terms of a common ingroup identity can promote intergroup forgiveness and trust. For instance, Wohl and Branscombe (2005) showed that increasing the salience of Jewish students' 'human identity,' in contrast to their 'Jewish identity,' increased their perceptions of similarity between Jews and Germans, as well as their willingness to forgive Germans for the Holocaust and their willingness to associate with contemporary German students. A shared superordinate identity has also been shown to affect responsiveness to others. Kane, Argote, and Levine (2005) found that group members were more accepting of a newcomer's innovation when the newcomer shared a superordinate identity with them than when the newcomer did not, and that the strength of superordinate group identification was positively related to the extent to which group members accepted the innovative solution. Also, people are more responsive to the needs of former outgroup members perceived within a common ingroup identity (Dovidio, Gaertner, Validzic, et al., 1997) across a range of situations, including emergency situations (Levine, Prosser, Evans, et al., 2005).

For example, Houlette, Gaertner, Johnson, et al. (2004) evaluated hypotheses derived from the Common Ingroup Identity Model in a quasi field experiment in the context of the Green Circle school-based anti-bias intervention program, which is designed to combat a range of biases (based on weight and sex, as well as race and ethnicity) among first- and second-grade children. The guiding assumption of the Green Circle Program,

which is practically and theoretically compatible with the Common Ingroup Identity Model, is that helping children bring people from different groups conceptually into their own circle of caring and sharing fosters appreciation of their common humanity, as well as respect for their differences. In particular, facilitators engage children in a variety of exercises designed to expand the circle, for instance, emphasizing, 'All of us belong to one family – the human family.' In terms of outcomes, the Green Circle intervention motivated the children to be more inclusive in selecting their most preferred playmate. Specifically, compared to children in the control condition who did not participate in Green Circle activities, those who were part of Green Circle showed significantly greater change in willingness to select other children who were different than themselves in race and in sex as a child that they 'would most want to play with.' These changes in the most preferred playmate involve a child's greater willingness to cross group boundaries in making friends – a factor that is one of the most potent influences in producing more positive attitudes toward the outgroup as a whole (Pettigrew, 1998).

The development of a common ingroup identity does not necessarily require each group to forsake its less inclusive group identity completely (Gaertner, Mann, Murrell, et al., 1989). As depicted by the 'subgroups within one group' (i.e., a dual identity) representation, it is possible for members to conceive of two groups (for example, science and art majors) as distinct units (thereby establishing 'mutual group differentiation') within the context of a superordinate (i.e., University identity) social entity. Establishing a common superordinate identity while simultaneously maintaining the salience of subgroup identities (i.e., developing a dual identity as two subgroups within one group) may be particularly effective because it permits the benefits of a common ingroup identity to operate without arousing countervailing motivations to achieve positive distinctiveness.

In summary, the evidence reviewed reveals quite consistent support for the key principle of the Common Ingroup Identity Model: Successfully inducing ingroup and outgroup members to adopt a more inclusive, one-group representation inclusive of both groups reduces intergroup bias toward one another. Furthermore, this key principle has been supported across studies using a variety of methodological approaches with participants of different ages, races and nationalities.

SOCIAL CATEGORIZATION AND THE REDUCTION OF BIAS: CHALLENGES AND OPPORTUNITIES

Although social categorization is generally recognized as a foundational process in the development and maintenance of prejudice and discrimination, each of the social categorization models discussed in the previous section suggests different ways for reducing intergroup bias. In this section, we review conceptual and pragmatic challenges for categorization-based models for reducing bias that may apply generally or to specific key elements of particular frameworks. The three issues of primary focus are (a) threats to valued identities; (b) relations among subgroup identity, intergroup relations, and superordinate identity; and (c) generalization beyond the contact situation.

Threats to valued identities

Earlier we discussed how altering social categorization in the form of decategorization of ingroup and outgroup members can be threatening if it requires people to abandon central and valued social identities. Feelings of identity threat, however, typically motivate people to re-establish a sense of positive intergroup distinctiveness, which can readily be achieved by re-emphasizing intergroup boundaries and the superiority of the ingroup over an outgroup on important dimensions (Hornsey & Hogg, 2001).

Moreover, to the extent that decategorization requires people to deviate from customary

ways of organizing and orienting to the world, it can create feelings of uncertainty. Feelings of uncertainty are hypothesized to motivate identification with a discrete and socially valued group (Hogg, 2001), which in turn can elicit further intergroup bias. These processes related to needs for positive social identity and uncertainty reduction thus undermine the stability, and thus viability, of decategorization for reducing prejudice and discrimination.

Recategorization that aims to replace subgroup identities with a common ingroup identity may not only arouse uncertainty but also directly threaten the integrity of a central social identity. For instance, Hornsey and Hogg (2000) found that attempts to de-emphasize humanities and math-science majors' group identities while emphasizing their inclusive university student identity increased bias toward one another relative to conditions that emphasized their separate major identities (Humanities and Science-Math). Extending these findings, Crisp, Stone and Hall (2006) found a very similar pattern of results but only among those who identified highly with their college major for whom attempts to de-emphasize these identities should be most threatening. Thus, when recategorization attempts threaten group identity, intergroup bias will very likely increase.

However, in these studies, it would be imprecise to conclude that there was an increase in bias *following* recategorization because the studies (e.g., Hornsey & Hogg, 2000) that explicitly measured participants' group representations also indicate that participants did not actually accept the recategorized group identity as their primary impression of the memberships. Rather, we conclude that bias may sometimes increase upon the threat of recategorization – a threat of loss of previous group distinctiveness. Nevertheless, the findings of these studies also suggest that there are circumstances in which maintaining the salience of the subgroup identities, particularly within the context of a cooperative intergroup relations or a superordinate identity (i.e., a dual identity) can be beneficial.

Relations among subgroup identity, superordinate, identity, and intergroup relations

The Mutual Intergroup Differentiation Model (Brown & Hewstone, 2005; Hewstone & Brown, 1986) proposes that maintaining distinctive group identities, which limits identity threat, within the context of positive functional relationships between groups is critical for reducing intergroup biases. In addition, the Common Ingroup Identuty Model recognizes that when group identities are central to people's self-definition, attempting to induce recategorization in ways that ignore the importance of these subgroup identities can be very threatening and result in increased intergroup bias. The dual identity representation within the Common Ingroup Identity Model, which does not necessarily require members to forsake their subgroup identities while accepting a common superordinate identity (Gaertner & Dovidio, 2000; Gaertner, Mann, Murrell, et al., 1989), apparently overcomes this problem and, at least in multi-ethnic settings, increases positive attitudes toward outgroup members more generally (Gaertner, Rust, Dovidio, et al., 1996). Yet, as evidenced by the inconsistent effects obtained in our survey studies involving corporate mergers and stepfamilies, a dual identity is not universally beneficial in terms of reducing intergroup bias. Across our three survey studies, although a one-group representation was consistently associated with lower bias, a dual identity was associated with increased bias, except within the multi-ethnic high-school context. Thus, a challenge for future research is to identify the factors that moderate the utility of the one-group and dual identity forms of recategorization.

One likely candidate is the nature of the relations between the subgroups, not just functionally (e.g., in terms of context of cooperation, as suggested by the Mutual Intergroup Differentiation Model) but also in terms of their group identities. A dual identity is more effective for reducing bias when subgroups have distinctive, complementary identities than when they have similar identities, which can arouse identity threat (Jetten, Spears, & Postmes, 2004).

A study by Dovidio, Gaertner, & Validzic (1998) that varied equality of group status (equal or unequal) and whether the groups had the same or different perspectives toward their task supported these ideas about group distinctiveness. When groups were of equal status but held different perspectives toward a common problem, members of the two subgroups had a stronger sense of common identity and lower intergroup bias relative to the other three conditions. In addition, the one-group representation mediated the relation between the experimental manipulations of status and task perspective on intergroup bias. These findings are consistent with the proposed value of equal status, primarily, as Hewstone and Brown (1986) proposed, when the distinctiveness between groups is maintained by emphasizing their different but complementary skills or resources during intergroup cooperation that could be instrumental for the achievement of their mutual goals (Lamoreaux, 2008).

In addition, domains of group life may vary in relatedness in at least two overlapping but separable ways. First, they may vary in terms of the relatedness of the primary function they serve for their members. There are several domains of group life, such as family, school, business, nation, religion, and ethnicity. Within each domain there are usually many different groups (e.g., the Jones family, the Smith family) that serve the same primary function for their members. For example, because a second marriage can represent the formation of a new family composed of formerly separate families, the new stepfamily and its component families both serve the same primary function and are therefore within the same domain of group life – the family (Banker & Gaertner, 1998). In some instances, however, a superordinate group entity represents a different domain than its component subgroups. For example, a high school is an educational institution that represents a different domain of group life than the ethnic identity groups of the students who comprise its student body (Gaertner,

Rust, Dovidio, et al., 1996; see also Hall & Crisp, 2005). Second, groups may vary in the relatedness of their subgroup identities and the activity (or goals) of the superordinate group. For example, students from different religious groups may work together as a superordinate group to design a multidenominational chapel or a college dormitory. In this example, designing a multidemoninational chapel is *related* to the subgroups' religious identities whereas designing a college dormitory is *unrelated* to those identities.

Previous research by Deschamps and Brown (1983; Brown & Wade, 1987) explored the effects of assigning the same or different tasks to groups working together for a common purpose. Indeed, the Mutual Intergroup Differentiation Model (Brown & Hewstone, 2005; Hewstone & Brown, 1986) posits that groups will experience greater identity threat and higher intergroup bias when they work toward a common goal and perform the same task as one another than when they perform different tasks. Whereas the work supporting the Mutual Intergroup Differentiation Model focuses on differences and similarities between the subgroups and the resulting threats to the group identities, we suggest that it may also be enlightening to focus on the structural similarities and differences between the superordinate group and its component subgroups.

Specifically, we propose that when subgroups and their superordinate group identities are in more highly related domains of group life, or when subgroup identities relate more strongly to the activity or goals of the superordinate group, these subgroup identities will be perceived more competitively. In this circumstance, threat to subgroup identity is likely to occur and, because they are on the same dimension, members of subgroups may be particularly likely to project their group's values and standards onto the superordinate group. Mummendey and Wenzel (1999) have proposed that when a common identity is made salient for members of different groups, members of one group or both groups may begin to regard their subgroup's characteristics (such as norms, values, and

goals) as more prototypical of the common, inclusive category compared to those of the other subgroup. As a consequence, they may assume that their group is more representative of the inclusive category and therefore is superior to the other subgroup. Members of the other subgroup may be seen not only as inferior exemplars but also as deviants who justly deserve unequal and possibly harsh treatment.

Also, subgroup members may be apprehensive that members of the other subgroup will unfairly impose their values and standards upon the superordinate group, a concern that would also threaten subgroup identity. When subgroup and superordinate groups are in different domains of group life, such as with ethnic and school identity in our multiethnic high school study, subgroup distinctiveness is apparent and, because the domains are different, projection of group standards onto the superordinate group is likely to be weaker.

Understanding the different potential relationships between subgroup and superordinate group identities represents one potential interpretation of the inconsistent relationship between a dual identity and intergroup bias across settings. When subgroup and superordinate group identities are in different domains, stronger dual identity representations typically relate to less bias. For example, among students attending a multi-ethnic high school, the more strongly they endorsed the belief that the student body felt like different groups playing on the same team the lower their bias toward each of the groups represented at the school (Gaertner, Rust, Dovidio, et al., 1996). Also, minority students at the school who described themselves using both an ethnic group identity as well as an American superordinate identity had lower bias toward other groups in the school than those who described themselves only in terms of their ethnic identity. Additional survey studies further suggest that the benefits of a strong superordinate identity remain relatively stable even when the strength of the subordinate identity becomes equivalently high (Huo, Smith, Tyler, et al., 1996; Smith & Tyler, 1996) and, rather than representing competing identities, there seems to be a positive correlation between minority students' American and ethnic identities (Huo, 2003). However, when subgroup and superordinate group identities are in comparable domains, the experience of a dual identity often relates to greater intergroup bias (Waldzus, Mummendey, Wenzel, et al., 2004). For instance, in the context of bank mergers and blended families, in which subgroup and superordinate identities may be viewed as mutually exclusive, the strength of dual identity was related to *less* favorable intergroup attitudes (see Gaertner & Dovidio, 2000). Thus, beyond previous research that focused on understanding the impact of the relationship between subgroup identities, the effectiveness of a dual identity for reducing intergroup bias is also critically moderated by the compatibility of subgroup identities with the overarching superordinate identity.

Generalization beyond the contact situation

Although theoretically the benefits of recategorization as *one group* may have limited generalizability when meaningful group differences are involved, it is likely that even when this superordinate categorization is the dominant perception, some degree of original group memberships still remain (Miller, 2002), particularly when the groups are visually distinctive. These vestiges of previous group memberships are likely to be sufficient to permit generalization of the benefits of recategorization even under conditions that primarily promote a one-group representation. Supportive of this possibility, González and Brown (2003, 2006) showed that both recategorization as one group and a dual identity among laboratory groups supposedly differing in size and status were related to reduced levels of intergroup bias toward those who were present during intergroup contact and this reduced bias generalized to additional ingroup and outgroup members observed on video. Similarly, some results from Guerra, Rebelo, and Monteiro et al. (*in press*) and Rebelo, Guerra, and

Monteiro, et al. (2004) with European and African Portuguese children revealed that recategorization involving one group and a dual identity effectively generalized its positive effects to the outgroup as a whole as well as across different contexts of interaction (i.e., the school and the neighborhood). Thus, compared to conditions that maintained only the separate group identities, circumstances that foster recategorization as primarily one group or as a dual identity produce not only lower levels of bias toward outgroup members present during contact but also generalize to the outgroup as a whole and over time.

CONCLUSION

We have reviewed some ideas about the role of social categorization in creating and reducing intergroup bias, and we focused on three different category-based approaches for reducing intergroup bias: decategorization, mutual intergroup differentiation, and recategorization. Conceptually, each of these approaches recognizes the potent and pervasive influence of social categorization in the ways people perceive, think about, feel about, and act toward others. These different approaches, which have received empirical support over the years, not only consider the core role of social categorization but also illuminate different facets of the complexity of intergroup relations.

Rather than viewing decategorization, mutual intergroup differentiation, and recategorization approaches as competing perspectives, it is more productive to recognize their convergent and complementary themes. For instance, Personalization, Mutual Intergroup Differentiation, and Common Identity approaches all recognize, but with somewhat different perspectives, the value of maintaining some vestige of original subgroup identities for generalization to occur beyond members present in the contact situation. Also, the Mutual Intergroup Differentiation Model considers the value of maintaining separate group identities within positive functional relations between groups, whereas work on a dual identity within the framework of Common Ingroup Identity Model focuses of the nature and compatibility of the different subgroup identities, not only in relationship to each other but also in relation to a superordinate identity. These approaches thus recognize the potential dangers of arousing identity threat but address this issue differently, conceptually and pragmatically.

In addition, future work might productively consider how the processes described in these models may operate in a complementary fashion, perhaps sequentially, to reduce intergroup bias in a more general and sustained way (Gaertner & Dovidio, 2000; Hewstone, 1996; Pettigrew, 1998). For instance, while recategorization as one group may itself often be fleeting and unstable, it seems to be capable of initiating behaviors, such as self-disclosure and helping, that call forth reciprocity and can thus have more permanent intergroup consequences. Mutual self-disclosure and helping, in turn, can initiate decategorization processes that can reduce bias through additional, independent, interpersonal pathways.

Which sequence of processes is most effective may depend upon the initial nature of the intergroup relationships. In situations of intense conflict, decategorization may provide the most constructive starting point because of the threat aroused by recognition of different group identities. When groups have compatible identities, mutual intergroup differentiation can offer a productive first step, because it limits identity threat between the groups while reinforcing cooperative relations that can produce personalization and the development of a new superordinate identity. Understanding the developmental nature of intergroup relations can therefore inform both intergroup theory and practical interventions in valuable ways.

ACKNOWLEDGEMENT

Preparation of this chapter was facilitated by a grant from the National Science Foundation # 0613218 to Samuel L. Gaertner and John F. Dovidio. Correspondence should be directed to: Samuel L. Gaertner, Department of Psychology, University of Delaware, Newark, DE 19716. E-mail: gaertner@udel.edu

REFERENCES

Adorno, T. W., Frenkel-Brunswik, E., Levinson, D. J., & Sanford, R. N. (1950). *The authoritarian personality.* New York: Harper.

Allport, G. W. (1954/1979). *The nature of prejudice.* New York: Addison-Wesley.

Aron, A., McLaughlin-Volpe, T., Mashek, D., Lewandowski, G., Wright, S. C., & Aron, E. N. (2005). Including others in the self. In W. Stroebe & M. Hewstone (Eds.), *European review of social psychology* (Vol. 15, pp. 101–132). Hove, E. Sussex, U.K.: Psychology Press.

Bachman, B. A. (1993). *An intergroup model of organizational mergers.* Unpublished Ph.D. Dissertation, Department of Psychology, University of Delaware, Newark.

Banker, B. S., & Gaertner, S. L. (1998). Achieving stepfamily harmony: An intergroup relations approach. *Journal of Family Psychology, 12,* 310–325.

Boldry, J. G., Gaertner, L., & Quinn, J. (2007). Measuring the measures: A meta-analytic investigation of the measures of outgroup homogeneity. *Group Processes and Intergroup Relations, 10,* 147–178.

Brewer, M. B. (1979). Ingroup bias in the minimal intergroup situation: A cognitive-motivational analysis. *Psychological Bulletin, 86,* 307–324.

Brewer, M. B. (1988). A dual process model of impression formation. In T. Srull & R. Wyer (Eds.). *Advances in social cognition* (Vol. 1, pp. 1–36). Hillsdale, NJ: Erlbaum.

Brewer, M. B. (2001). The many faces of social identity: Implications for political psychology. *Political Psychology, 22,* 115–125.

Brewer, M. B., & Miller, N. (1984). Beyond the contact hypothesis: Theoretical perspectives on desegregation. In N. Miller & M. B. Brewer (Eds.), *Groups in contact: The psychology of desegregation* (pp. 281–302). Orlando, FL: Academic Press.

Brown, R, Eller, A., Leeds, S., & Stace, K. (2007). Intergroup contact and intergroup attitudes: A longitudinal study. *European Journal of Social Psychology, 37,* 692–703.

Brown, R., & Hewstone, M. (2005). An integrative theory of intergroup contact. In M. P. Zanna (Ed.), *Advances in experimental social psychology* (Vol. 37, pp. 255–343). San Diego, CA: Academic Press.

Brown, R. J., & Turner, J. C. (1979). The criss-cross categorization effect in intergroup discrimination. *British Journal of Social and Clinical Psychology, 18,* 371–383.

Brown, R. J., & Turner, J. C. (1981). Interpersonal and intergroup behavior. In J. C. Turner & H. Giles (Eds.), *Intergroup behavior* (pp. 33–64). Chicago, IL: The University of Chicago Press.

Brown, R. J., Vivian, J., & Hewstone, M. (1999). Changing attitudes through intergroup contact: The effects of group membership salience. *European Journal of Social Psychology, 29,* 741–764.

Brown, R. J., & Wade, G. (1987). Superordinate goals and intergroup behavior: The effect of role ambiguity and status on intergroup attitudes and task performance. *European Journal of Social Psychology, 17,* 131–142.

Campbell, D. T. (1958). Common fate, similarity and other indices of the status of aggregates of persons as social entities. *Behavioral Science, 3,* 14–25.

Campbell, D. T. (1965). Ethnocentric and other altruistic motives. In D. Levine (Eds.), *Nebraska symposium on motivation* (Vol. 13, pp. 283–311). Lincoln, NE: University of Nebraska Press.

Crisp, R. J., Stone, C. H., & Hall, N. R. (2006). Recategorization and subgroup identification: Predicting and preventing threats from common ingroups. *Personality and Social Psychology Bulletin 32,* 230–243.

Correll, J., & Park, B. (2005). A model of the ingroup as a social resource. *Personality and Social Psychology Review, 9,* 341–359.

Deschamps, J. C., & Brown, R. (1983). Superordinate goals and intergroup conflict. *British Journal of Social Psychology, 22,* 189–195.

Dovidio, J. F., Gaertner, S. L., & Validzic, A. (1998). Intergroup bias: Status, differentiation, and a common ingroup identity. *Journal of Personality and Social Psychology, 75,* 109–120.

Dovidio, J. F., Gaertner, S. L., Validzic, A., Matoka, K., Johnson, B., & Frazier, S. (1997). Extending the benefits of re-categorization: Evaluations, self-disclosure and helping. *Journal of Experimental Social Psychology, 33,* 401–420.

Ferguson, C. K., & Kelley, H. H. (1964). Significant factors in over-evaluation of own groups' products. *Journal of Abnormal and Social Psychology, 69,* 223–228.

Fiske, S. T., Lin, M., & Neuberg, S. L. (1999). The continuum model: Ten years later. In S. Chaiken & Y. Trope (Eds.), *Dual process theories in social psychology* (pp. 211–254). New York: Guilford.

Fiske, S. T., & Taylor, S. E. (1991). *Social cognition* (2nd ed). New York: McGraw-Hill.

Gaertner, S. L., Dovidio, J. F., Rust, M. C., Nier, J., Mottola, G. R. Banker, B., Nier, J., Ward, C. M. & Houlette, M. (1999). Reducing intergroup Bias: Elements of Cooperation. *Journal of Personality and Social Psychology. 76,* 388–402.

Gaertner, S. L., & Dovidio, J. F. (2000). *Reducing intergroup bias: The Common Ingroup Identity Model.* Philadelphia, PA: Psychology Press.

Gaertner, S. L., Dovidio, J. F., Anastasio, P. A., Bachman, B. A., & Rust, M. C. (1993). The common ingroup identity model: Recategorization and the reduction of intergroup bias. In W. Stroebe & M. Hewstone (Eds.), *European review of social psychology* (Vol. 4. pp. 1–26). New York: John Wiley & Sons.

Gaertner, S. L., Dovidio, J. F., Banker, B., Rust, M., Nier, J., Mottola, G., & Ward, C. (1997). Does racism necessarily mean anti-Blackness? Aversive racism and pro-Whiteness. In M. Fine, L. Powell, L. Weis, & M. Wong (Eds.), *Off white* (pp. 167–178). London: Routledge.

Gaertner, S. L., Mann, J., Murrell, A., & Dovidio, J. F. (1989). Reducing intergroup bias: The benefits of recategorization. *Journal of Personality and Social Psychology, 57,* 239–249.

Gaertner, S. L., Rust, M. C., Dovidio, J. F., Bachman, B. A., & Anastasio, P. A. (1996). The Contact Hypothesis: The role of a common ingroup identity on reducing intergroup bias among majority and minority group members. In J. L. Nye & A. M. Brower (Eds.), *What's social about social cognition?* (pp. 230–360). Newbury Park, CA: Sage.

Gómez, A., Dovidio, J. F., Huici, C., Gaertner, S. L. & Cuardrado, I. (2008). The other side of We: When outgroup members express common identity. *Personality and Social Psychology Bulletin, 34,* 1613–1626.

González, R., & Brown, R. (2003). Generalization of positive attitude as a function of subgroup and superordinate group identification in intergroup contact. *European Journal of Social Psychology, 33,* 195–214.

González, R., & Brown, R. (2006). Dual identities and intergroup contact: Group status and size moderate the generalization of positive attitude change. *Journal of Experimental Social Psychology, 42,* 753–767.

Guerra, R., Rebelo, M., & Monteiro, M. B. (2004, June). *Changing intergroup relations: Effects of recategorization, decategorization and dual identity in the reduction of intergroup discrimination.* Paper presented at Change in Intergroup Relations: 7th Jena Workshop on Intergroup Processes, Friedricht Schiller University, Jena.

Guerra, R., Rebelo, M. M. B., Riek, B. M., Mania, E. W., Gaertner, S. L. & Dovidio, J. F. (in press). How should intergroup contact be structured to reduce bias among majority and minority group children? *Group Processes and Intergroup Behavior.*

Hall, N. R., & Crisp, R. J. (2005). Considering multiple criteria for social categorization can reduce intergroup bias. *Personality and Social Psychology Bulletin, 31,* 1435–1444.

Hamilton, D. L., & Sherman, J. W. (1994). Stereotypes. In R. S. Wyer & T. K. Srull (Eds.), *Handbook of social cognition* (Vol. 2, pp. 1–68). Hillsdale, NJ: Erlbaum.

Hewstone, M. (1990). The 'ultimate attribution error'? A review of the literature on intergroup causal attribution. *European Journal of Social Psychology, 20,* 311–335.

Hewstone, M., & Brown, R. J. (1986). Contact is not enough: An intergroup perspective on the "Contact Hypothesis." In M. Hewstone & R. Brown (Eds.), *Contact and conflict in intergroup encounters* (pp. 1–44). Oxford: Basil Blackwell.

Hewstone, M., Hassebrauck, M., Wirth, A., & Waenke, M. (2000). Pattern of disconfirming information and processing instructions as determinants of stereotype change. *British Journal of Social Psychology, 39,* 399–411.

Hogg, M. A. (2001). Self-category and subjective uncertainty resolution: Cognitive and motivational facets of social identity and group membership. In J. P. Forgas, K. D. Williams, & L. Wheeler (Eds.), *The social mind: Cognitive and motivational aspects of interpersonal behavior* (pp. 323–349). New York: Cambridge University Press.

Hogg, M. A., & Reid, S. A. (2006). Social identity, self-categorization, and the communication of group norms. *Communication Theory, 16,* 7–30.

Hornsey, M. J., & Hogg, M. A.. (2000). Subgroup relations: A comparison of mutual intergroup differentiation and common ingroup identity models of prejudice reduction. *Personality and Social Psychology Bulletin 26,* 242–256.

Hornstein, H. A. (1976). *Cruelty and kindness: A new look at aggression and altruism.* Englewood Cliffs, NJ: Prentice Hall.

Houlette, M., Gaertner, S. L., Johnson, K. M., Banker, B. S., Riek, B. M., & Dovidio, J. F. (2004). Developing a more inclusive social identity: An elementary school intervention. *Journal of Social Issues, 60,* 35–56.

Howard, J. M., & Rothbart, M. (1980). Social categorization for in-group and out-group behavior. *Journal of Personality and Social Psychology, 38,* 301–310.

Huo, Y. J. (2003). Procedural justice and social regulation across group boundaries: Does subgroup identity undermine relationship-based governance. *Personality and Social Psychology Bulletin, 29,* 336–348.

Huo, Y. J., Smith, H. H., Tyler, T. R., & Lind, A. E. (1996). Superordinate identification, subgroup identification, and justice concerns: Is separatism the problem. Is assimilation the answer? *Psychological Science, 7,* 40–45.

Jetten, J., Spears, R., & Postmes, T. (2004). Intergroup distinctiveness and differentiation: A meta-analytic integration. *Journal of Personality and Social Psychology, 86,* 862–879.

Kane, A. A., Argote, L., & Levine, J. M. (2005). Knowledge transfer between groups via personnel rotation: Effects of social identity and knowledge quality. *Organizational Behavior and Human Decision Processes, 96,* 56–71.

Kenworthy, J. B., Turner, R. N., Hewstone, M., & Voci, A. (2005). Intergroup contact: When does it work, and why? In J. F. Dovidio, P. Glick & L. A. Rudman (Eds.), *On the nature of prejudice: Fifty years after Allport* (pp. 278–292). Malden, MA: Blackwell.

Karpinski, A., & Von Hippel, W. (1996). The role of the linguistic intergroup bias in expectancy maintenance. *Social Cognition, 14,* 141–163.

Klandermans, B., Sabucedo, J. M., & Rodriguez, M. (2004). Inclusiveness of identification among farmers in the Netherlands and Galicia. *European Journal of Social Psychology, 34,* 279–295.

Kramer, R. M., & Brewer, M. B. (1984). Effects of group identity on resource utilization in a simulated commons dilemma. *Journal of Personality and Social Psychology, 46,* 1044–1057.

Lamoureaux, M. J. (2008). Reducing intergroup bias: When intergroup contact is instrumental for achieving group goals. Unpublished Ph.D. Dissertation, Department of Psychology, University of Delaware, Newark.

Levine, M., Prosser, A. Evans, D., & Reicher, S. (2005). Identity and emergency intervention: How social group membership and inclusiveness of group boundaries shape helping behavior. *Personality and Social Psychology Bulletin, 31,* 443–453.

Maass, A., Salvi, D., Arcuri, L., & Semin, G. R. (1989). Language use in intergroup contexts: The linguistic intergroup bias. *Journal of Personality and Social Psychology, 57,* 981–993.

Miller, N. (2002). Personalization and the promise of contact theory. *Journal of Social Issues, 58,* 29–44.

Miller, N., & Brewer, M. B. (1984). The social psychology of desegregation: An introduction. In N. Miller &

M. B. Brewer (Eds.), *Groups in contact: The psychology of desegregation* (pp. 1–10). Orlando, FL: Academic Press.

Miller, N., Brewer, M. B., & Edwards, K. (1985). Cooperative interaction in desegregated settings: A laboratory analog. *Journal of Social Issues, 41,* 63–79.

Monteiro, M. B., Guerra, R., & Rebelo, M. (2009). Reducing prejudice: Common Ingroup and Dual Identity in unequal status intergroup encounters. In S. Demoulin, J.-P. Leyens, & J. F. Dovidio (Eds.), *Intergroup misunderstandings: Impact of divergent social realities* (pp. 273–290). New York: Psychology Press.

Mummendey, A., & Wenzel, M. (1999). Social discrimination and tolerance in intergroup relations: Reactions to intergroup difference. *Personality and Social Psychology Review 3,* 158–174.

Nier, J. A., Gaertner, S. L., Dovidio, J. F., Banker, B. S., & Ward, C. M. (2001). Changing interracial evaluations and behavior: The effects of a common group identity. *Group Processes and Intergroup Relations, 4,* 299–316.

Otten, S., & Moskowitz, G. B. (2000). Evidence for implicit evaluative in-group bias: Affect-based spontaneous trait inference in a minimal group paradigm. *Journal of Experimental Social Psychology, 36,* 77–89.

Park, B., & Rothbart, M. (1982). Perception of out-group homogeneity and levels of social categorization: Memory for the subordinate attributes of in-group and out-group members. *Journal of Personality and Social Psychology, 42,* 1051–1068.

Perdue, C. W., Dovidio, J. F., Gurtman, M. B., & Tyler, R. B. (1990). "Us" and "Them": Social categorization and the process of intergroup bias. *Journal of Personality and Social Psychology, 59,* 475–486.

Pettigrew, T. F. (1998). Intergroup Contact Theory. *Annual Review of Psychology, 49,* 65–85.

Pfeifer, J. H., Ruble, D. N., Bachman, M. A., Alvarez, J. M., Cameron, J. A., & Fuligni, A. J. (2007). Social identities and intergroup bias om immigrant and non-immigrant children. *Developmental Psychology, 43,* 496–507.

Piliavin, J. A., Dovidio, J. F., Gaertner, S. L., & Clark, R. D., III. (1981). *Emergency intervention.* New York: Academic Press.

Rabbie, J. M. (1982). The effects of intergroup competition and cooperation on intragroup and intergroup relationships. In V. J. Derlega & J. Grzelak (Eds.), *Cooperation and helping behavior: Theories and research* (pp. 128–151). New York: Academic Press.

Rebelo, M., Guerra, R., & Monteiro, M. B. (2004, June). *Reducing prejudice: Comparative effects of three theoretical models.* Paper presented at the Fifth Biennial Convention of the Society for the Psychological Study of Social Issues, Washington, DC.

Robbins, J. M., & Krueger, J. I. (2005). Social projection to ingroups and outgroups: A review and meta-analysis. *Personality and Social Psychology Review, 9,* 32–47.

Rothbart, M., & John, O. P. (1985). Social categorization and behavioral episodes: A cognitive analysis of the effects of intergroup contact. *Journal of Social Issues, 41,* 81–104.

Schino, G. (2007). Grooming and agonistic support: A meta-analysis of primate reciprocal altruism. *Behavioral Ecology, 18,* 115–120.

Sherif, M., Harvey, O. J., White, B. J., Hood, W. R., & Sherif, C. W. (1961). *Intergroup conflict and cooperation: The Robbers Cave experiment.* Norman, OK: University of Oklahoma Book Exchange.

Smith, E. R., & Henry, S. (1996). An ingroup becomes part of the self: Response time evidence. *Personality and Social Psychology Bulletin, 22,* 635–642.

Stürmer, S., Snyder, M., & Omoto, A. M. (2005). Prosocial emotions and helping: The moderating role of group membership. *Journal of Personality and Social Psychology, 88,* 532–546.

Smith, H. J., & Tyler, T. R. (1996). Justice and power: When will justice concerns encourage the advantaged to support policies which redistribute economic resources and the disadvantaged to willingly obey the law? *European Journal of Social Psychology, 26,* 171–200.

Tajfel, H. (1969). Cognitive aspects of prejudice. *Journal of Social Issues, 25,* 79–97.

Tajfel, H., Billig, M. G., Bundy, R. P., & Flament, C. (1971). Social categorisation and intergroup behavior. *European Journal of Social Psychology, 1,* 149–177.

Tajfel, H., & Turner, J. C. (1979). An integrative theory of intergroup conflict. In W. G. Austin & S. Worchel (Eds.), *The social psychology of intergroup relations* (pp. 33–48). Monterey, CA: Brooks/Cole.

Trivers, R. L. (1971). The evolution of reciprocal altruism. *The Quarterly Review of Biology, 46,* 35–57.

Turner, J. C., Hogg, M. A., Oakes, P. J., Reicher, S. D., & Wetherell, M. S. (1987). *Rediscovering the social group: A self-categorization theory.* Oxford, England: Basil Blackwell.

Van Bavel, J. J., Packer, D. J., & Cunningham, W. A. (2008). The neural substrates of in-group bias. *Psychological Science, 19,* 1131–1139.

Waldzus, S., Mummendey, A., Wenzel, M., & Boettcher, F. (2004). Of bikers, teachers, and Germans: Groups' diverging views about their prototypicality. *British Journal of Social Psychology, 43*, 385–400.

Weber, R., & Crocker, J. (1983). Cognitive processes in the revision of stereotypic beliefs. *Journal of Personality and Social Psychology, 45*, 961–977.

Wilder, D. A. (1978). Reducing intergroup discrimination through individuation of the outgroup. *Journal of Personality and Social Psychology, 36*, 1361–1374.

Wilder, D. A. (1981). Perceiving persons as a group: Categorization and intergroup relations. In D. L. Hamilton (Ed.), *Cognitive processes in stereotyping and intergroup behavior* (pp. 213–257). Hillsdale, NJ: Erlbaum.

Wilder, D. A. (1986). Social categorization: Implications for creation and reduction of intergroup bias. In L. Berkowitz (Ed.), *Advances in experimental social psychology* (Vol. 19, pp. 291–355). Orlando, FL: Academic Press.

Wilder, D. A., Simon, A. F., & Faith, M. (1996). Enhancing the impact of counterstereotypic information. Dispositional attributions for deviance. *Journal of Personality and Social Psychology, 71*, 276–287.

Wohl, M. J. A., & Branscombe, N. (2005). Forgiveness and collective guilt assignment to historical perpetrator groups depend on level of social category inclusiveness. *Journal of Personality and Social Psychology, 88*, 288–303.

Williams, R. M. Jr. (1947). *The reduction of intergroup tensions.* New York: Social Science Research Council.

33

Intergroup Contact

Nicole Tausch* and Miles Hewstone

ABSTRACT

This chapter reviews the overwhelming evidence in support of the contact hypothesis, whereby positive contact between members of different groups is associated with reduced prejudice and improved intergroup relations. We address the generalization of contact effects, and summarize recent advancements in theory and research, reviewing the benefits of different types of contact, the person and group factors that can limit the effectiveness of contact, and the underlying psychological processes that mediate the effect of contact on prejudice. We then show that contact also affects non-conscious, automatic processes, the strength and meaningfulness of outgroup attitudes, and the willingness to trust and forgive outgroups. We conclude by identifying a number of challenging issues for future research, including behavioral, ideological, and collective consequences of contact.

The notion that contact between members of different groups can, under certain conditions, reduce prejudice is one of the most prominent ideas underlying approaches to improve intergroup relations. The aim of this chapter is to present an overview of the vast literature on intergroup contact and to highlight recent developments in the field. After giving a brief summary of the early research which provided the basis for Allport's (1954) formulation of the 'contact hypothesis,' we present an overview of the empirical evidence and address the issue of generalization of positive contact effects. Our main section focuses on recent advancements in contact theory and research. In this section we address the benefits of different types of contact, discuss the person and group factors that are likely to limit the effectiveness of contact, and examine the underlying psychological processes that mediate the effect of contact on prejudice. This section also covers recent developments in terms of the range of outcome variables assessed in contact research. We conclude this chapter by identifying a number of challenging issues for future research.

THE ORIGINS OF THE CONTACT HYPOTHESIS

The relationship between intergroup contact and prejudice was first studied in the context of race relations in the United States in the 1930s and 1940s (see Allport, 1954). Whereas some early researchers reported negative effects of contact (e.g., Sims and Patrick, 1936), studies that examined interracial contact under favorable conditions (e.g., Smith, 1943) generally demonstrated a negative association between contact and prejudice (see Dovidio, Gaertner, & Kawakami, 2003; Pettigrew, 2005, for historical overviews). An initial formulation of the contact hypothesis was put forward by Williams (1947), who suggested that contact would be maximally effective when the two groups shared similar status, interests, and tasks; when the contact situation promotes intimate interactions; when group stereotypes are disconfirmed; and when activities cut across group lines. Based on Williams' work, as well as on findings of a series of studies conducted on the effects of desegregated housing in the early 1950s (e.g., Deutsch and Collins, 1951; Wilner, Walkley, & Cook, 1952), Allport (1954) concluded that:

> Prejudice (unless deeply rooted in the character structure of the individual) may be reduced by equal status contact between minority and majority groups in the pursuit of common goals. The effect is greatly enhanced if this contact is sanctioned by institutional supports (i.e., by law, custom or local atmosphere), and if it is of a sort that leads to the perception of common interests and common humanity between members of the two groups. (p. 281)

By spelling out the critical conditions (equal status, cooperation towards a common goal, institutional support) necessary for prejudice reduction to occur, Allport's (1954) formulation was highly influential and has inspired hundreds of empirical studies (see Pettigrew and Tropp, 2006). We review this literature in the following sections, focusing in particular on evidence for Allport's hypothesis and on important extensions of his ideas.

EVIDENCE FOR THE CONTACT HYPOTHESIS

The prejudice-reducing effect of contact is now well established. A meta-analysis conducted by Pettigrew and Tropp (2006) with 515 studies and 713 independent samples

obtained a significant negative relationship between contact and prejudice (mean $r = -.22$), suggesting that contact is an effective tool for reducing prejudice. Empirical work investigating the effects of Allport's (1954) prerequisite conditions has also generally been supportive of his ideas. There is now extensive evidence that improved intergroup attitudes result under *equal status* conditions, both prior to (e.g., Brewer and Kramer, 1985) and during (Cohen and Lotan, 1995) the contact, and when contact receives institutional support (e.g., Landis, Hope, & Day, 1984). The notion that *cooperation towards a common goal* can reduce intergroup prejudice has also received substantial support from both field (e.g., Sherif, 1966) and laboratory (e.g., Brown and Abrams, 1986) experiments, and has been successfully applied in educational settings in the form of cooperative learning groups (e.g., Aronson and Patnoe, 1997). The effectiveness of this strategy does, however, depend on a positive outcome of that endeavor (e.g., Worchel, Andreoli, & Folger, 1977) and it is beneficial when members of the two groups work on different but equally valued task dimensions to circumvent potential threats to group distinctiveness (e.g., Brown and Wade, 1987). Moreover, research that has disentangled the importance of cooperation and common goals suggests that the latter may be of lesser importance (Gaertner, Dovidio, Rust, et al., 1999).

Although, overall, this work suggests that Allport's (1954) contact conditions are important, Pettigrew and Tropp's (2006) meta-analysis indicated that even unstructured contact reduces prejudice ($r = -.20$). The presence of Allport's conditions enhances this effect considerably ($r = -.29$), but given the basic effect, these factors should be seen as facilitating rather than as absolutely necessary conditions.

A number of early narrative reviews of the contact literature (e.g., Amir, 1976) questioned, however, whether the beneficial effects of intergroup contact would generalize beyond the immediate contact situation. Such generalization is crucial for the wider effectiveness of intergroup contact as an intervention. Pettigrew (1998) distinguished three important kinds of generalization of contact effects: across situations, from the encountered group member to the outgroup as a whole, and to other, uninvolved outgroups.

Generalization across situations is rarely investigated and evidence from the few available studies is mixed, with some studies reporting limited (e.g., Minard, 1952) and others substantial (Nesdale and Todd, 1998) generalization to different contexts. A meta-analytic examination of this type of generalization suggests, however, that cross-situational generalization generally occurs (Pettigrew and Tropp, 2006).

The evidence for generalization from encountered group members to the outgroup as a whole is particularly strong (see Brown and Hewstone, 2005; see also Pettigrew and Tropp, 2006). There is now copious evidence demonstrating that this type of generalization is most likely to happen when categories are salient during contact (Hewstone and Brown, 1986; see also below) and when the encountered group member is typical of the group in general (e.g., Wilder, 1984).

Finally, there is also evidence for the higher-order generalization from one outgroup to other, uninvolved outgroups (Tausch et al., in press). According to Pettigrew (1997) this might occur through a process of 'deprovincialization', that is, the increasing view that ingroup norms, customs, and lifestyles are not the only acceptable ways to manage the social world. Consistent with such generalized effects, Pettigrew (1997) showed that respondents who had an outgroup friend were also more accepting of many other outgroups, even groups that were not present in their country (see also Pettigrew and Tropp, 2006). Thus, overall, it seems that the beneficial effects of contact generalize substantially.

ADVANCES IN CONTACT THEORY AND RESEARCH

Since the initial work on the effectiveness of Allport's (1954) prerequisite conditions, research on intergroup contact has advanced both theoretically and empirically. It has extended Allport's ideas about *when* contact would be optimally effective in achieving generalized prejudice reduction, focusing in particular on the different ways in which the groups can be categorized during contact. Moreover, increasing awareness that the objective contact conditions can be perceived in different ways and greater attention to how members of disadvantaged groups react to intergroup contact has led researchers to identify important person and group factors that lessen the effectiveness of contact. Realizing the difficulty of bringing about direct face-to-face contact in some intergroup contexts, a number of recent approaches have also started to explore alternatives to direct contact. Innovations in statistical methodology (e.g., Baron and Kenny, 1986) have further led to a greater focus on the psychological mechanisms that mediate the effects of contact on prejudice, addressing the question of *why* contact reduces prejudice. Moreover, developments in attitude measurement (e.g., Greenwald, McGee, & Schwartz, 1998) have widened the spectrum of available outcome measures and have extended our knowledge of *what* contact can change. Below we will summarize the most important of these recent developments. Figure 33.1 integrates Allport's (1954) contact hypothesis and recent developments in the field into a theoretical framework of intergroup contact effects.

When does contact work? Varying levels of categorization during contact

Categorizing people into ingroup and outgroup members has profound effects on feelings towards, and treatment of, others (Tajfel and Turner, 1979). Three distinct lines of research that were developed in the 1980s thus examined the nature of cognitive group representations during contact (see Hewstone, 1996, for a review). Although each was based on the social identity/self-categorization

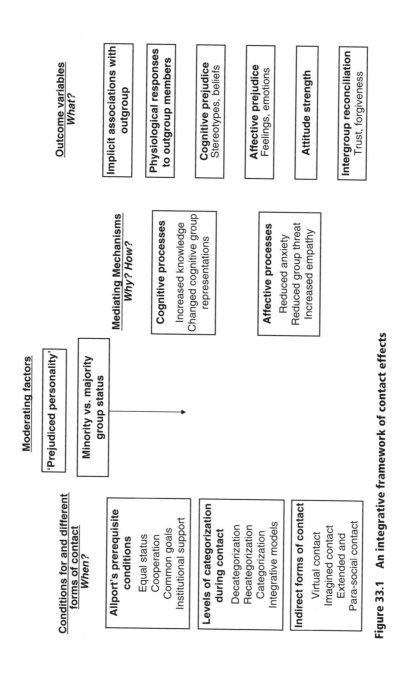

Figure 33.1 An integrative framework of contact effects

approach (Tajfel and Turner, 1979; Turner, Hogg, Oakes, et al., 1987), they drew different conclusions as to how contact should ideally be structured (see also Chapter 32 by Gaertner, Dovidio, & Houlette, this volume).

Decategorization

The decategorization approach recommends that group identities are de-emphasized so that group members conceive of themselves as separate individuals (Wilder, 1986). An influential version of this approach, Brewer and Miller's (1984) personalization perspective, suggests that contact should promote opportunities to get to know outgroup members and disclose intimate personal information. This attention to idiosyncratic information would be accompanied by less attention to category-based information, and the repeated utilization of individual information should then reduce the usefulness of the category and eliminate stereotypical outgroup perceptions. Evidence for this model comes from a number of experimental studies (e.g., Bettencourt, Brewer, Croak, et al., 1992) showing that cooperative contact in a person-oriented condition produces less ingroup bias in the allocation of rewards than contact in a task-oriented condition. There is also evidence that self-disclosure during contact is associated with more positive intergroup attitudes and more heterogeneous outgroup perceptions (Turner Hewstone, & Voci, 2007).

Also consistent with the importance of personalization are the prejudice-reducing effects of 'acquaintance potential' during contact (Cook, 1978) and, in particular, of intergroup friendship (Pettigrew, 1997). For example, Pettigrew (1997) demonstrated that people who had an outgroup friend expressed less prejudice towards the outgroup as a whole than did people who had an outgroup neighbor or co-worker, but not a friend (see also Pettigrew and Tropp, 2006). Levin and colleagues (2003) provided longitudinal evidence showing that college students who had more outgroup friends in their second and third years at college were less biased in favor of their ethnic group at the end of their fourth year. However, the finding that prejudice at the end of their first year was also associated with fewer outgroup friends in their second and third years suggests that the relation between intergroup friendship and prejudice is likely to be reciprocal.

Recategorization

Rather than aiming to eliminate the use of social categories altogether, the *recategorization* approach (also referred to as the Common Ingroup Identity Model; Gaertner, Mann, Murrell, et al., 1989; see also Chapter 32 by Gaertner, Dovidio, & Houlette, this volume) proposes that prejudice can be reduced by transforming cognitive group representations from two groups ('Us' and 'Them') to one inclusive social entity ('We'). This should redirect the cognitive and motivational processes that produce positive feelings towards ingroup members to former outgroup members who are now part of the more inclusive one-group representation. There is an impressive body of evidence supporting this model by, for example, showing that a superordinate categorization during contact significantly reduces prejudice, especially compared to situations in which two group memberships remain salient (for a review see Gaertner and Dovidio, 2000).

Categorization

The categorization model differs sharply from the decategorization and recategorization approaches. Hewstone and Brown (1986) argued that an individuation of encountered group members can distance the encountered group member from the outgroup and thereby inhibit generalization. They also suggested that it seems unlikely that the creation of a superordinate identity will overcome powerful ethnic and racial categorizations or be sustainable beyond the contact situation. Instead, they proposed that group affiliations should be salient during contact and that the encountered outgroup members should be sufficiently typical or representative of their group to ensure generalization of positive contact effects. Both experimental (van Oudenhoven, Groenewald, & Hewstone, 1996; Wilder,

1984) and correlational (e.g., Voci and Hewstone, 2003) evidence supports this idea (see Brown and Hewstone, 2005, for a review). Nonetheless, this approach is not without its problems as making category memberships salient may reinforce stereotypes and perceptions and lead to anxiety, which risks the generalization of negative information (Greenland and Brown, 1999; Islam and Hewstone, 1993; Stephan and Stephan, 1985). Recent work has therefore made efforts to integrate these different theoretical models, building on their respective advantages and disadvantages.

Integrative models

Miller (2002) argued that personalized contact does not preclude the salience of social categories; these different types of contact are, in fact, orthogonal and can act simultaneously. Consistent with these ideas, Ensari and Miller (2002) demonstrated that personalized contact led to generalized positive effects only when the encountered group member was typical or when group categories were made salient.

Gaertner and colleagues (1996) suggested that a dual identity approach, where members of groups maintain both the original ingroup–outgroup distinction *and* a superordinate identity might be optimal for contact to improve intergroup relations. Results suggest, however, that a dual identity is effective mainly for members of minority groups, while members of majority groups tend to prefer a common group representation (Gaertner, Rust, Dovidio, et al., 1996; González and Brown, 2006). A dual identity approach may also fall prey to 'ingroup projection' (e.g., Wenzel, Mummendey, Weber, et al., 2003) – the tendency to perceive one's own subgroup as more prototypical of the superordinate group than the outgroup, which is associated with negative outgroup attitudes.

Pettigrew (1998) proposed an, as yet untested, three-stage longitudinal model. He suggested that decategorization should optimally happen first to reduce anxiety and discomfort and increase interpersonal liking. The social categories should be made salient in the next step in order to achieve generalization of positive affect to the outgroup as a whole. Recategorization may then happen at a later stage to achieve maximal prejudice reduction. Brewer and Gaertner (2001) noted, however, that the order in which these processes unfold may depend upon the specific features of the contact situation. For example, categorization may emerge frequently during cooperative contact between groups to neutralize threats to the original identities.

Finally, Hewstone and Brown have argued that the bipolar opposition between interpersonal and intergroup contact (Hewstone, 1996; Hewstone and Brown, 1986; Brown and Hewstone, 2005) should now be abandoned in favor of a two-dimensional conception. While their earlier work had only implicitly acknowledged the importance of both interpersonal and intergroup contact, their later work was explicit in recognizing the importance of *both* interpersonal and intergroup dimensions. They proposed that Allport's (interpersonal) conditions should be paired with their own (intergroup) condition, to predict that contact that is 'high' on both interpersonal and intergroup dimensions (e.g., cross-group friends who maintain awareness of their respective group memberships) should be most effective, for which they report extensive evidence.

Participant factors as boundary conditions

Researchers are becoming increasingly aware that the same objective contact conditions can be perceived differently by different people, which may affect the success of contact interventions (see Tropp, 2006). Below we summarize person and group factors that are likely to shape subjective experiences of intergroup contact.

Individual levels of prejudice

A number of individual difference variables that can impact on the effectiveness of contact have been proposed (see Stephan, 1987, for a review). Participants' initial level of prejudice as they enter a contact situation has received particular attention and was recognized by Allport (1954) as a potential barrier to prejudice reduction. In fact, there is evidence that interacting with outgroup members is highly challenging and requires increased self-regulation among highly-prejudiced individuals, which can result in impaired executive function (Richeson and Shelton, 2003; Vorauer and Kumhyr, 2001). Moreover, interventions that exert pressure to suppress prejudice can have 'backlash' effects for more prejudiced, less internally motivated participants, who react with more negative attitudes (Plant and Devine, 2001).

Nonetheless, there is also evidence that contact may be particularly effective for prejudiced participants. For example, Maoz (2003) showed that, although Israeli 'hawks' were less motivated to interact with Palestinians and had more negative outgroup attitudes before an encounter programme than did 'doves', they showed greater positive attitude change in response to the intervention. Similarly, Pettigrew and Tropp's (2006) meta-analysis revealed that contact situations where participants were given no choice whether to participate yielded by far the largest effect sizes ($r = -.28$ versus $-.22$). They argued that this could be due to greater variability in initial prejudice levels, less constraint by ceiling effects, and greater cognitive dissonance for more prejudiced, less motivated, participants.

Minority group status

Recent work suggests that members of disadvantaged groups construe intergroup interactions in different ways than do members of advantaged groups (Tropp, 2006). Specifically, they are less likely to be convinced that they have equal status in the interaction and are more likely to anticipate prejudice and discrimination against them from members of the dominant group (Shelton, 2003; Tropp, 2006). This is, of course, likely to reduce the effectiveness of contact. Tropp and Pettigrew (2005a) found in a meta-analytic analysis that the relationship between contact and prejudice

was significantly weaker for members of disadvantaged groups ($r = -.18$), compared to members of dominant groups ($r = -.23$). They also demonstrated that Allport's (1954) optimal contact conditions did not contribute to predicting the strength of the contact–prejudice relationship among minority group members. Additional findings indicate that personalized contact is less effective for members of minority groups (Bettencourt, Charlton, & Kernahan, 1997) and that members of low status groups are less inclined to cooperate with the higher-status group during contact, and less likely to form a superordinate group representation (Seta, Seta, & Culver, 2000).

Indirect forms of contact

Most research so far has examined either actual face-to-face contact or retrospective reports of such contact. Bringing about direct intergroup interactions can, however, involve serious practical obstacles as it requires that there are contact opportunities (e.g., Wagner and Machleit, 1986). Several recent approaches have therefore investigated the effectiveness of more indirect forms of contact. These include contact that takes place remotely via the internet, mental imagery of contact experiences, and vicarious contact experienced via other ingroup members or the media.

Virtual contact

Amichai-Hamburger and McKenna (2006) argued that the internet might be uniquely suited to the implementation of optimal contact. It enables contact among individuals who otherwise would not have the opportunity to meet, creates a protected and controlled environment, and allows scheduling multiple contacts spanning extended time periods. The relative anonymity of the internet makes self-disclosure more likely and may also reduce the difficulty of creating equal-status conditions as many of the cues that people use to infer status are not available. It also allows manipulating category salience quite easily. Empirical studies on virtual contact are still sparse.

However, demonstrating that the internet has the potential to create effective intergroup contact, Yablon and Katz (2001) showed that internet-based group communication between Jewish and Bedouin Arab students in Israel improved outgroup attitudes among Jewish students, while Bedouin students' outgroup attitudes remained positive throughout the duration of the project.

Imagined contact

Turner and colleagues (2007) extended the idea that actual experiences may not be necessary to improve intergroup attitudes still further. Based on work on the effects of mental imagery on social perception, these authors investigated whether simply imagining contact with outgroup members could improve intergroup attitudes. Turner et al. demonstrated that participants who imagined talking to an outgroup member showed significantly lower levels of prejudice and viewed the outgroup as more variable than participants who were instructed to just think about an outgroup member. Thus, it seems that intergroup contact is a highly flexible means of improving intergroup attitudes, which may even have some effects when simply imagined.

Extended contact

The 'extended contact hypothesis' (Wright, Aron, McLaughlin-Volpe, et al., 1997) posits that the mere knowledge that an ingroup member has a close relationship with an outgroup member can improve outgroup attitudes. Wright et al. suggested that this form of contact could be particularly beneficial because it is less anxiety-provoking than face-to-face contact, can lead to changes in perceived ingroup and outgroup norms regarding intergroup interactions, and should involve highly salient social categories.

A series of experimental and correlational studies (e.g., Paolini, Hewstone, Cairns, et al., 2004; Turner, Hewstone, Voci, et al., 2008a; Wright, Aron, McLaughlin-Volpe, et al., 1997) have provided empirical evidence that people knowing about, or observing, intergroup friendships show less prejudice than those who do not, over and above a number of control variables such as direct contact experiences (see Turner, Hewstone, Voci, et al., 2008b, for a review). The extended contact hypothesis has also been successfully applied in prejudice-reduction programs in school settings (Cameron and Rutland, 2006; Liebkind and McAlister, 1999). Moreover, some work suggests that extended contact can also happen via the media ('parasocial' contact, see Schiappa, Gregg, & Hewes, 2005). Schiappa et al. (2005) provided evidence that watching television programmes that portrayed intergroup contact was associated with lower levels of prejudice. Recent research examining moderators of the effectiveness of extended contact suggested that extended contact is most predictive of attitudes when no direct experiences with outgroup members are available (Christ, Hewstone, Tausch, et al., 2009; Schiappa, Gregg, & Hewes, 2005); when prejudiced attitudes are based on cognition (thoughts and beliefs about the outgroup) rather than affect (feelings and emotions towards the outgroup); and for outgroups that generate cognitive as opposed to affective responding (Paolini, Hewstone, Cairns, et al., 2007).

Why does contact work? An analysis of mediating mechanisms

After identifying the conditions that facilitate successful contact, researchers investigating intergroup contact effects started to focus on the theoretical development of the contact hypothesis, examining the psychological mechanisms that mediate its well-established effect on prejudice reduction. Although the effects of contact may partly be due to mere exposure (i.e., the principle that familiarity fosters liking; see Bornstein, 1989), this research demonstrated that a variety of more sophisticated cognitive and affective mechanisms are at work.

Cognitive mechanisms

Allport (1954) suggested that unfavorable outgroup attitudes are due to a lack of information about that outgroup and that contact can thus reduce prejudice by providing opportunities to learn about the outgroup. *Increased knowledge* can reveal similarities and thus lead to liking (see Pettigrew, 1998), and can reduce uncertainty about how to interact with others (Stephan and Stephan, 1985). Providing information about the historical background of a group can lead to the recognition of injustice and thereby improve attitudes. For example, a number of early studies found a positive correlation between White Americans' knowledge about the history and demography of Black Americans and attitudes towards Black Americans (see Stephan and Stephan, 1984, for a review). Stephan and Stephan (1984) demonstrated that White Americans' amount of contact with Hispanics increased knowledge about Hispanic culture, which partially mediated the effects of contact on outgroup attitudes (see also Eller and Abrams, 2004).

Contact can not only increase factual knowledge, but can teach alternative behaviours towards outgroup members (Pettigrew, 1998). This, in turn, can change people's attitudes by (a) setting new norms for intergroup behavior, and (b) cognitive dissonance reduction (see also Leippe and Eisenstadt, 1994), which serves to justify attitude-inconsistent behavior. There is some empirical support that behavioral change does, in fact, partially mediate the relationship between contact and attitudes (Eller and Abrams, 2004).

Changing *how the two groups are cognitively represented* is an important goal of the approaches to categorization during contact discussed earlier. Evidence that cognitive representations of intergroup relations indeed mediate contact effects comes from a few correlational studies. For example, in a survey of students in a multi-ethnic high school, Gaertner et al. (1996) examined different representations of the ingroup and the outgroup (as one group, separate groups, separate individuals, or different groups on the same team) as potential mediators of the relationship between the quality of intergroup contact and prejudice reduction. They showed

that the relationship between contact and prejudice reduction was mediated by a common group identity for majority group members and by a dual identity ('two groups on one team') for minority group members (see also Eller and Abrams, 2004).

Another line of research has shown further that through repeated, intimate contact the outgroup becomes incorporated into the self-concept (Aron, Aron, Tudor, et al., 1991; see Pettigrew, 1998) and the inclusion of outgroup members in the self-concept then leads to more positive outgroup attitudes (Eller and Abrams, 2004). There is also evidence that extended contact works through this process (Turner, Hewstone, Voci, et al., 2008a). Work on extended contact further suggests that not just the structure, but also the content of group identities is malleable, showing that more positive perceived ingroup and outgroup norms regarding intergroup interactions partially mediate the relationship between extended contact and positive outgroup attitudes (Turner, Hewstone, Voci, et al., 2008a).

Affective mechanisms

Although there is evidence for the importance of cognitive mediating mechanisms, current work points to the pivotal role of affective processes in intergroup contact (Pettigrew and Tropp, 2008; Tropp and Pettigrew, 2005b). This work indicates that contact exerts its effect on prejudice reduction both by reducing negative affect (anxiety and threat), and by inducing positive affective processes such as empathy.

Intergroup anxiety is a negative affective state which is experienced when anticipating future, or expecting actual, contact with an outgroup member. It stems from the expectation of negative consequences for oneself during intergroup interactions, such as embarrassment or rejection, and may be augmented in the presence of negative outgroup stereotypes, a history of intergroup conflict, or a high ratio of outgroup to ingroup members (Stephan and Stephan, 1985). Anxiety is accompanied by a narrowed cognitive and perceptual focus and information-processing biases that can undermine positive effects of contact (e.g., Wilder and Shapiro, 1989). High levels of intergroup anxiety may lead to the avoidance of contact altogether (Plant and Devine, 2003; Shelton and Richeson, 2005) or, if contact does occur, render the interaction awkward and less enjoyable (e.g., Shelton, 2003). Because this negative affective state is linked to outgroup members, it is strongly associated with negative outgroup attitudes (e.g., Stephan and Stephan, 1985).

An extensive body of research has shown that successful intergroup contact helps to overcome these apprehensions, and that reduced anxiety is a key mediator in the negative relationship between contact and prejudice (e.g., Islam and Hewstone, 1993; Voci and Hewstone, 2003; see Pettigrew and Tropp, 2008, for a meta-analytic test). Observing or knowing about intergroup interactions or friendships, or imagining oneself successfully interacting with an outgroup member, similarly reduces anxiety, which mediates the effects of extended contact (Paolini, Hewstone, Cairns, et al., 2004; Turner, Hewstone, Voci, et al., 2008a) and imagined contact (Turner, Crisp, & Lambert 2007) on prejudice reduction.

Negative intergroup relations are often characterized by perceptions that the outgroup poses *a threat to the ingroup*. These threats can be realistic and involve conflicting interests, such as competition for scarce resources, territory, political or economic power, or they can be more symbolic, involving perceived discrepancies in beliefs and values (Stephan and Stephan, 2000). As we have described above, cooperative contact improves intergroup attitudes, suggesting that contact works partly by changing the perceived functional relations between groups (see Dovidio, Gaertner, Kawakami, 2003). Stephan and Stephan (2000) argued that both the amount and the nature of intergroup interactions (e.g., whether contact is cooperative or competitive, intimate or superficial) are likely to determine the extent to which the outgroup is seen as realistically or symbolically threatening. In line with

these ideas, Tausch and colleagues (2007) demonstrated that reductions in perceived group-level threats are significant mediators in the relationship between contact and prejudice, but only for people who identify strongly with their ingroup. For low identifiers, reduction in individual-level concerns (i.e., intergroup anxiety) mediated the relationship between contact and prejudice reduction. Thus, this work demonstrates a case of moderated mediation, showing that different mediators can operate for different subgroups.

Empathy has both emotional (empathic concern) and cognitive (perspective taking) facets and is associated with positive attitudes and prosocial behavior (Batson, Polycarpou, Harmon-Jones, et al., 1997; Finlay and Stephan, 2000). A handful of studies have now demonstrated that contact positively affects perspective taking and empathy and that these variables partially mediate contact effects on prejudice (Harwood, Hewstone, Paolini, et al., 2005; Tam, Hewstone, Cairns, et al., 2005; see Pettigrew and Tropp, 2008, for a meta-analytic test). Aberson and Haag (2007) further provided evidence consistent with a three-stage theoretical model in which contact was associated with increased perspective taking, which was associated with more positive views of the outgroups, partly by reducing intergroup anxiety.

What can contact change? Dependent variables in intergroup contact research

The aim of contact interventions is to reduce prejudice and to improve intergroup relations. Earlier work on intergroup contact focused primarily on cognitive (e.g., stereotypes and beliefs) and affective (feelings and emotions) aspects of prejudice, generally finding greater effects of contact on the affective than the cognitive components (see Tropp and Pettigrew, 2005b). More recent work has started to go beyond assessing prejudice per se, and has examined the effects of contact on the strength of attitudes, implicit associations with, and physiological reactions to, outgroup members, as well as indices of intergroup reconciliation in settings of conflict.

Attitude strength

Not just the valence of intergroup attitudes, but also their strength, can have important implications for intergroup relations. Research has shown that strong attitudes (e.g., attitudes that are held with greater certainty, are more important, more accessible in memory, and less ambivalent) are more stable over time, more resistant to change, more likely to influence information processing and judgements, and more likely to guide behavior (Krosnick and Petty, 1995). Vonofakou and colleagues (2007) presented a first test of the impact of contact on attitude strength. They demonstrated that contact with outgroup friends was not only associated with more positive attitudes towards the outgroup, but also with meta-attitudinally (i.e., based on participants' own assessment of the nature of their attitudes) stronger and more accessible outgroup attitudes. The authors also showed that the effects of contact on attitude strength were mediated by reduced intergroup anxiety, demonstrating the broad influence of intergroup anxiety in shaping outgroup attitudes.

However, Christ et al. (2009) only found evidence for an effect of indirect contact on attitude strength, like that of direct contact, when indirect contact had occurred over time.

Implicit associations

A few recent studies have explored the effects of contact on implicit bias. For example, Tam, Hewstone, Cairns et al. (2005) examined the effects of contact with grandparents on Implicit Association Test (IAT, Greenwald, McGee, & Schwartz, 1998) scores and found that the quantity (but not the quality) of contact was associated with less implicit bias towards the elderly. Similarly, Turner, Hewstone, & Voci, (2007) found that opportunities for contact with South Asians (e.g., living in mixed neighborhoods, going to mixed schools), but not the number of South Asian friends, predicted more positive implicit associations with the outgroup among White

British students. The fact that implicit bias was influenced by non-evaluative contact measures (opportunity and quantity of contact) rather than more evaluative measures (contact quality and friendship), bypassing relevant mediating variables (e.g., perspective taking, intergroup anxiety, which predicted explicit attitudes), suggests that the effect on implicit measures may be explained by greater familiarity with the outgroup (see Turner, Hewstone, & Voci, 2007). Moreover, Aberson and Haag (2007) found that the interaction between the quantity and quality of contact predicted implicit attitudes, indicating that the nature of the environmental associations, that is whether associations or experiences are mostly positive or negative, matters.

Physiological reactions to outgroup members

Recent research has started to explore the physiological responses, and even neural substrates, involved in evaluations of and responses to outgroups. This work demonstrated that contact is associated with reduced automatic physiological threat responses to outgroup members. For example, Blascovich and colleagues (2001) showed that participants who reported more contact with Black people exhibited reduced physiological threat reactions (i.e., responses of the autonomic system like sweating and increased heart rate) during interracial interactions. Recent findings also suggest that contact can moderate the neural processing of faces of other races. Measuring event-related potentials in response to faces, Walker et al. (2008) showed that differences in Whites' processing of own versus other-race faces were reduced with increased self-reported outgroup contact, demonstrating the malleability of internal neural responses through external social experiences such as intergroup contact.

Trust and forgiveness

Research with a focus on conflict resolution has stressed the importance of intergroup trust and forgiveness as markers of intergroup reconciliation. Trust facilitates the achievement of mutually beneficial outcomes during negotiations, making it a key concept for research on peace building (see Kramer and Carnevale, 2001). Forgiveness, on the other hand, is an emotional state that permits the relationship between the conflicting parties to move forward after a transgression (Cairns, Tam, Hewstone, et al., 2005). A few studies have now demonstrated that intergroup contact is associated with greater trust and forgiveness, even among respondents who have personally been affected by intergroup violence (Hewstone, Cairns, Voci, et al., 2006; see also Tam, Hewstone, Harwood, et al., 2007).

DIRECTIONS FOR FUTURE RESEARCH

Although recent studies have examined the effects of contact on a wide spectrum of variables, evidence showing that contact affects actual behavior towards outgroup members is still sparse (see Malhotra and Liyanage, 2005, for some limited evidence), or non-existent. Behaviors are constrained by habits, social norms, and given social structures (Ajzen, 1988). Thus, while contact may change someone's attitudes towards an outgroup, other pressures that determine behavior, such as ingroup norms that prescribe antagonistic behavior towards outgroup members, may have even stronger effects (see McCauley, 2003). Hence, a major challenge for future research is to examine the effects of contact on behavior, and to establish the conditions that need to be created to achieve more positive intergroup behavior that is sustained beyond the immediate intervention.

Moreover, changes in outgroup attitudes often do not go hand in hand with changes in the ideological beliefs that sustain group inequality. Jackman and Crane (1986), for example, demonstrated that friendly contact with Blacks improved Whites' affective reactions towards Blacks, but left their (generally negative) attitudes towards programs that combat inequality in housing, jobs, and education unchanged. Similarly, Dixon,

Durrheim, and Tredoux (2007) found that while White South Africans were generally in favor of equality in education, employment, and land ownership, they tended to oppose interventions such as school quotas, affirmative action, and land restitution. The beneficial effects of interracial contact on such resistance were weaker and less consistent than its effects on other forms of prejudice.

The uncertain effects of intergroup contact on ideological orientations also raise a broader issue concerning the potential consequences of positive contact for disadvantaged groups. Wright (2001) observed that, by reducing differentiation between groups, contact may weaken members of disadvantaged groups' motivation to engage in collective action to reduce inequalities. Consistent with this idea, Dixon, Durrheim, and Tredoux (2007) found that the more contact Black South Africans had with Whites, the *less* they supported policies aimed at promoting racial equality. Wright and Lubensky (2008) further demonstrated that the association between contact with Whites and reduced collective action tendencies among Black Americans was mediated by reduced ingroup identification and views that group boundaries were permeable. Saguy and colleagues (2009) examined the effects of contact that is focused on intergroup commonalities (as opposed to differences) among experimentally-created groups that differed in power. They found that commonality-focused contact led members of the disadvantaged group to be unrealistically optimistic about the amount of resources they would receive from the outgroup. Regardless of contact type, the advantaged group always distributed more resources to the ingroup than to the outgroup. This suggests that positive contact that emphasizes group commonalities may have the effect of misleading members of disadvantaged groups into believing that the inequality will be addressed.

Addressing the needs of members of disadvantaged groups is perhaps the greatest challenge for future research on intergroup contact (see also Dovidio, Gaertner, & Saguy, 2008). One approach underlines the importance of the *content* of contact interventions. Saguy, Dovidio, and Pratto (2008) demonstrated that while members of advantaged groups prefer to talk about group commonalities during contact, members of disadvantaged groups want to address inequalities. The effect of group position on desire to talk about inequalities was mediated by the motivation to change power relations. Future research could draw on this work to identify the conditions under which contact promotes positive intergroup attitudes without compromising the realization of group-based goals. Emphasizing commonalities, while at the same time addressing unjust group inequalities during contact, may result in greater prejudice reduction for members of disadvantaged groups (cf. Tropp and Pettigrew, 2005a), without diverting attention away from group inequality (Saguy and colleagues, 2009), and promote necessary changes in advantaged group members' ideological beliefs regarding group inequality (Dixon, Durrheim, and Tredoux, 2007; Jackman and Crane, 1986).

CONCLUSION

A half century of empirical work on intergroup contact has contributed enormously to our understanding of the effects of intergroup contact as a tool for reducing prejudice. In this chapter we have sought to summarize the overwhelming evidence for Allport's (1954) contact hypothesis and to provide an extensive overview of new developments in contact theory and research. We have demonstrated that we now know a great deal about the different types of contact that can reduce prejudice, the factors and conditions that facilitate or inhibit the effectiveness of contact, and the cognitive and affective processes that mediate contact effects. We have also shown that contact goes below the surface, affecting non-conscious, automatic processes, the strength and meaningfulness of outgroup attitudes, and the willingness to trust and forgive, even against the backdrop of violent intergroup conflict. Future research needs to supplement and complement this

detailed investigation of change at the level of individual cognitions and feelings with an examination of the behavioral, ideological, and collective consequences of contact.

NOTE

*Correspondence should be directed to: Nicole Tausch at the School of Psychology, Cardiff University, Tower Building, Park Place, Cardiff, CF10 3AT, UK. E-mail: TauschN@cf.ac.uk

REFERENCES

Aberson, C. L., and Haag, S. C. (2007). Contact, perspective taking, and anxiety as predictors of stereotype endorsement, explicit attitudes, and implicit attitudes. *Group Processes and Intergroup Relations, 10*, 179–201.

Allport, G. W. (1954). *The nature of prejudice.* Reading, MA: Addison-Wesley.

Ajzen, I. (1988). *Attitudes, personality and behavior.* Chicago: Dorsey.

Amichai-Hamburger, Y., and McKenna, K. Y. A. (2006). The contact hypothesis reconsidered: Interacting via the internet. *Journal of Computer-mediated Communication, 11*, 825–843.

Amir, Y. (1976). The role of intergroup contact in change of prejudice and intergroup relations. In P. A. Katz (Ed.), *Towards the elimination of racism* (pp. 245–280). New York: Pergamon.

Aron, A., Aron, E. N., Tudor, M., and Nelson, G. (1991). Close relationships as including the other in the self. *Journal of Personality and Social Psychology, 60*, 241–253.

Aronson, E., and Patnoe, S. (1997). *The jigsaw classroom.* New York: Longman.

Baron, R., and Kenny, D. A. (1986). The moderator-mediator variable distinction in social psychological research: Conceptual, strategic, and statistical considerations. *Journal of Personality and Social Psychology, 51*, 1173–1182.

Batson, C. D., Polycarpou, M. P., Harmon-Jones, E., and Imhoff, H. J. (1997). Empathy and attitudes: Can feeling for a member of a stigmatized group improve feelings toward the group? *Journal of Personality and Social Psychology, 72*, 105–118.

Bettencourt, B. A., Brewer, M. B., Croak, M. R., and Miller, N. (1992). Cooperation and reduction of intergroup bias: The role of reward structure and social interaction. *Journal of Experimental Social Psychology, 28*, 301–319.

Bettencourt, B. A., Charlton, K., and Kernahan, C. (1997). Numerical representation of groups in cooperative settings: Social orientation effects on ingroup bias. *Journal of Experimental Social Psychology, 33,* 630–659.

Blascovich, J., Mendes, W. B., Hunter, S. B., Lickel, B., and Kowai-Bell, N. (2001). Perceiver threat in social interactions with stigmatized others. *Journal of Personality and Social Psychology, 80,* 253–267.

Bornstein, R. F. (1989). Exposure and affect: Overview and meta-analysis of research, 1968–1987. *Psychological Bulletin, 106,* 265–289.

Brewer, M. B., and Gaertner, S. L. (2001). Toward reduction of prejudice: Intergroup contact and social categorization. In R. Brown and S. Gaertner (Eds.), *Blackwell handbook of social psychology: Intergroup processes* (pp. 451–474). Oxford: Blackwell.

Brewer, M. B., and Kramer, R. M. (1985). The psychology of intergroup attitudes and behaviour. *Annual Review of Social Psychology, 36,* 219–243.

Brewer, M. B., and Miller, N. (1984). Beyond the contact hypothesis: Theoretical perspectives on desegregation. In N. Miller and M. B. Brewer (Eds.), *Groups in contact: The psychology of desegregation* (pp. 281–302). Orlando, FL: Academic Press.

Brown, R., and Abrams, D. (1986). The effects of intergroup similarity and goal interdependence on intergroup attitudes and task performance. *Journal of Experimental Social Psychology, 22,* 78–92.

Brown, R. J., and Hewstone, M. (2005). An integrative theory of intergroup contact. In M. Zanna (Ed.), *Advances in Experimental Social Psychology* (Vol. *37,* pp. 255–331). San Diego, CA: Academic Press.

Brown, R. J., and Wade, G. S. (1987). Superordinate goals and intergroup behaviour: The effects of role ambiguity and status on intergroup attitudes and task performance. *European Journal of Social Psychology, 17,* 131–142.

Cairns, E., Tam, T., Hewstone, M., and Niens, U. (2005). Intergroup forgiveness and intergroup conflict: Northern Ireland, a case study. In E. L. Worthington (Ed.), *Handbook of Forgiveness* (pp. 461–476). New York: Brunner/Routledge.

Cameron, L., and Rutland, A. (2006). Extended contact through story reading in school: Reducing children's prejudice towards the disabled. *Journal of Social Issues, 62,* 469–488.

Christ, O., Hewstone, M., Tausch, N., Wagner, U., Voci, A., Hughes, J., and Cairns, E. (2009). Direct contact as a moderator of extended contact effects: Cross-sectional and longitudinal impact on attitudes and attitude strength. *Manuscript submitted for publication.*

Cohen, E. G., and Lothan, R. A. (1995). Producing equal status interaction in the heterogeneous classroom. *American Educational Research Journal, 32,* 99–120.

Cook, S. W. (1978). Interpersonal and attitudinal outcomes in cooperating interracial groups. *Journal of Research and Development in Education, 12,* 97–113.

Deutsch, M., and Collins, M. (1951). *Interracial housing: A psychological evaluation of a social experiment.* Minneapolis, MI: Univ. of Minnesota Press.

Dixon, J., Durrheim, K., and Tredoux, C. (2007). Intergroup contact and attitudes toward the principle and practice of racial equality. *Psychological Science, 18,* 867–872 .

Dovidio, J. F., Gaertner, S. L., and Kawakami, K. (2003). Intergroup contact: the past, present and future. *Group Processes and Intergroup Relations, 6,* 5–21.

Dovidio, J. F., Gaertner, S. L., and Saguy, T. (2008). Another view of 'we': Majority and minority group perspectives on a common ingroup identity. In W. Stroebe and M. Hewstone (Eds.), *European Review of Social Psychology* (Vol. 18, pp. z296–330). Hove, E. Sussex: Psychology Press.

Eller, A., and Abrams, D. (2004). Come together: longitudinal comparisons of Pettigrew's reformulated intergroup contact model and the common ingroup identity model in Anglo-French and Mexican-American contexts. *European Journal of Social Psychology, 34,* 1–28.

Ensari, N., and Miller, N. (2002). The outgroup must not be so bad after all: The effects of disclosure, typicality, and salience on intergroup bias. *Journal of Personality and Social Psychology, 83,* 313–329.

Finlay, K. A., and Stephan, W. G. (2000). Improving intergroup relations: The effects of empathy on racial attitudes. *Journal of Applied Social Psychology, 30,* 1720–1737.

Gaertner, S., and Dovidio, J. (2000). *Reducing intergroup bias: The common ingroup identity model.* Hove, E. Sussex: Psychology Press.

Gaertner, S. L., Dovidio, J. F., Rust, M. C., Nier, J., Banker, B., Ward, C. M. et al. (1999). Reducing intergroup bias: Elements of intergroup cooperation. *Journal of Personality and Social Psychology, 76,* 388–402.

Gaertner, S. L., Mann, J. A., Murrell, A. J., and Dovidio, J. F. (1989). Reducing intergroup bias: The benefits of recategorization. *Journal of Personality and Social Psychology, 57,* 239–249.

Gaertner, S. L., Rust, M. C., Dovidio, J. F., Bachman, B. A., and Anastasio, P. A. (1996). The Contact Hypothesis: The role of a common ingroup identity on reducing intergroup bias among majority and minority group members. In J. L. Nye and A. M. Brower (Eds.), *What's social about social cognition?* (pp. 230–260). Newbury Park, CA: Sage Publications.

Gonzalez, R., and Brown, R. (2006). Dual identities in intergroup contact: Group status and size moderate the generalization of positive attitude change. *Journal of Experimental Social Psychology, 42,* 753–767.

Greenland, K., and Brown, R. J. (1999). Categorization and intergroup anxiety in contact between British and Japanese nationals. *European Journal of Social Psychology, 29,* 503–521.

Greenwald, A. G., McGee, D. E., and Schwartz, J. L. K. (1998). Measuring individual differences in implicit cognition: The implicit association test. *Journal of Personality and Social Psychology, 74,* 1464–1480.

Harwood, J., Hewstone, M., Paolini, S., and Voci, A. (2005). Grandparent-grandchild contact and attitudes towards older adults: Moderator and mediator effects. *Personality and Social Psychology Bulletin, 31,* 393–406.

Hewstone, M. (1996). Contact and categorization: Social psychological interventions to change intergroup relations. In C. N. Macrae, C. Stangor, and M. Hewstone (Eds.), *Stereotypes and stereotyping* (pp. 323–368). New York: Guildford.

Hewstone, M., and Brown, R. (1986). Contact is not enough: An intergroup perspective on the 'contact hypothesis'. In M. Hewstone and R. Brown (Ed.), *Contact and conflict in intergroup encounters* (pp. 1–44). Oxford: Blackwell.

Hewstone, M., Cairns, E., Voci, A., Hamberger, J., and Niens, U. (2006). Intergroup contact, forgiveness, and experience of 'The Troubles' in Northern Ireland. *Journal of Social Issues, 62,* 99–120.

Islam, M. R., and Hewstone, M. (1993). Dimensions of contact as predictors of intergroup anxiety, perceived outgroup variability, and outgroup attitude: An integrative model. *Personality and Social Psychology Bulletin, 19,* 700–710.

Jackman, M. R., and Crane, M. (1986). 'Some of my best friends are black …': Interracial friendship and whites' racial attitudes. *Public Opinion Quarterly, 50,* 459–486.

Kramer, R. M., and Carnevale, P. J. (2001). Trust and intergroup negotiation. In R. Brown and S. Gaertner (Eds.), *Blackwell Handbook of Social Psychology: Intergroup processes* (pp. 431–450). Oxford, UK: Blackwell.

Krosnick, J. A., and Petty, R. E. (1995). Attitude strength: An overview. In R. E. Petty and J. A. Krosnick (Eds.), *Attitude strength: Antecedents and consequences* (pp.1–24). Hillsdale, NJ: Lawrence Erlbaum.

Landis, D., Hope, R. O., and Day, H. R. (1984). Training for desegregation in the military. In N. Miller

and M. B. Brewer (Eds.), *Groups in contact: The psychology of desegregation* (pp. 257–278). Orlando, FL: Academic Press.

Leippe, M. R., and Eisenstadt, D. (1994). Generalization of dissonance reduction: Decreasing prejudice through induced compliance. *Journal of Personality and Social Psychology, 67,* 395–413.

Levin, S., van Laar, C., and Sidanius, J. (2003). The effects of ingroup and outgroup friendships on ethnic attitudes in college: A longitudinal study. *Group Processes and Intergroup Relations, 6,* 76–92.

Liebkind, K., and McAlister, A. L. (1999). Extended contact through peer modelling to promote tolerance in Finland. *European Journal of Social Psychology, 29,* 765–780.

Malhotra, D., and Liyanage, S. (2005). Long-term effects of peace workshops in protracted conflicts. *Journal of Conflict Resolution, 49,* 908–924.

Maoz, I. (2003). Peace-building with the hawks: Attitude change of Jewish-Israeli hawks and doves following dialogue encounters with Palestinians. *International Journal of Intercultural Relations, 27,* 701–714.

McCauley, C. (2002). Head-first versus feet-first in peace education. In G. Salomon and B. Nevo (Eds.), *Peace education: The concept, principles, and practices around the world* (pp. 247–257). Mahwah, NJ: Lawrence Erlbaum.

Miller, N. (2002). Personalization and the promise of contact theory. *Journal of Social Issues, 58,* 387–410.

Minard, R. D. (1952). Race relationships in the Pocahontas coal field. *Journal of Social Issues, 8,* 29–44.

Nesdale, D., and Todd, P. (1998). Intergroup ratio and the contact hypothesis. *Journal of Applied Social Psychology, 28,* 1196–1217.

Paolini, S., Hewstone, M., and Cairns, E. (2007). Direct and indirect intergroup friendship effects: Testing the moderating role of the affective and cognitive bases of prejudice. *Personality and Social Psychology Bulletin, 33,* 1406–1420.

Paolini, S., Hewstone, M., Cairns, E., and Voci, A. (2004). Effects of direct and indirect cross-group friendships on judgments of Catholics and Protestants in Northern Ireland: The mediating role of an anxiety-reduction mechanism. *Personality and Social Psychology Bulletin, 30,* 770–786.

Pettigrew, T. F. (1997). Generalized intergroup contact effects on prejudice. *Personality and Social Psychology Bulletin, 23,* 173–185.

Pettigrew, T. F. (1998). Intergroup contact theory. *Annual Review of Psychology, 49,* 65–85.

Pettigrew, T. F. (2005). Intergroup contact: Theory, research and new perspectives. In J. A. Banks and C. A. Banks (Eds.), *Handbook of research on multicultural education* (pp. 770–781). New York: Jossey–Bass.

Pettigrew, T. F., and Tropp, L. R. (2006). A meta–analytic test of intergroup contact theory. *Journal of Personality and Social Psychology, 90*, 751–783.

Pettigrew, T. F., and Tropp, L. R. (2008). How does contact reduce prejudice? A meta-analytic test of three mediators. *European Journal of Social Psychology, 38*, 922–934.

Plant, E. A., and Devine, P. G. (2001). Responses to other-imposed pro-Black pressure: Acceptance or backlash? *Journal of Experimental Social Psychology, 37*, 486–501.

Plant, E. A., and Devine, P. G. (2003). The antecedents and implications of interracial anxiety. *Personality and Social Psychology Bulletin, 29*, 790–801.

Richeson, J. A., and Shelton, J. N. (2003). When prejudice does not pay: Effects of interracial contact on executive function. *Psychological Science, 14*, 287–290.

Saguy, T., Dovidio, J. F., and Pratto, F. (2008) Beyond contact: Intergroup contact in the context of power relations. *Personality and Social Psychology Bulletin, 34*, 432–445.

Saguy, T., Tausch, N., Dovidio, J. F., and Pratto, F. (2009). The irony of harmony: Positive intergroup contact produces false expectations for equality. *Psychological Science, 20*, 114–121

Schiappa, E., Gregg, P. B., and Hewes, D. E. (2005). The parasocial contact hypothesis. *Communication Monographs, 72*, 92–115.

Seta, C., Seta, J. J., and Culver, J. (2000). Recategorization as a method for promoting intergroup cooperation: Group status matters. *Social Cognition, 18*, 354–376.

Shelton, J. N. (2003). Interpersonal concerns in social encounters between majority and minority group members. *Group Processes and Intergroup Relations, 6*, 171–185.

Shelton, J.N., and Richeson, J.A. (2005). Intergroup contact and pluralistic ignorance. *Journal of Personality and Social Psychology, 88*, 91–107.

Sherif, M. (1966). *Group conflict and cooperation: Their social psychology.* London: Routledge and Kegan Paul.

Sims, V. M., and Patrick, J. R. (1936). Attitude toward the Negro of northern and southern college students. *Journal of Social Psychology, 7*, 192–204.

Smith, F. T. (1943). *An experiment in modifying attitudes towards the Negro.* New York: Columbia University.

Stephan, W. G. (1987). The contact hypothesis in intergroup relations. In C. Hendrick (Ed.), *Group processes and intergroup relations. Review of personality and social psychology, Vol. 9* (pp. 13–40). Thousand Oaks, CA, US: Sage Publications.

Stephan, W. G., and Stephan, C. W. (1984). The role of ignorance in intergroup relations. In N. Miller and M. B. Brewer (Eds.), *Groups in contact: The psychology of desegregation* (pp. 229–255). Orlando, FL: Academic Press.

Stephan, W. G., and Stephan, C. W. (1985). Intergroup anxiety. *Journal of Social Issues, 41*, 157–175.

Stephan, W. G., and Stephan, C. W. (2000). An integrated threat theory of prejudice. In S. Oskamp (Ed.), *Reducing prejudice and discrimination* (pp. 23–46). Hillsdale, NJ: Erlbaum.

Tajfel, H., and Turner, J. C. (1979). An integrative theory of intergroup conflict. In W. G. Austin and S. Worchel (Eds.), *The psychology of intergroup relations* (pp. 33–48). Monterey, CA: Brooks/Cole.

Tam, T., Hewstone, M., Cairns, E., Tausch, N., Maio, G., and Kenworthy, J.B. (2007). The impact of intergroup emotions on forgiveness in Northern Ireland. *Group Processes and Intergroup Relations, 10*, 119–135.

Tam, T., Hewstone, M., Harwood, J., Voci, A., and Kenworthy, J. (2005). Intergroup contact and grandparent–grandchild communication: The effects of self-disclosure on implicit and explicit biases against older people. *Group Processes and Intergroup Relations, 9*, 413–429.

Tausch, N., Hewstone, M., Kenworthy, J. B., Psaltis, C., Schmid, K., Popan, J. R., Cairns, E., & Hughes, J. (in press). 'Secondary transfer' effects of intergroup contact: Alternative accounts and underlying processes. *Journal of Personality and Social Psychology.*

Tausch, N., Tam, T., Hewstone, M., Kenworthy, J. B., and Cairns, E. (2007). Individual-level and group-level mediators of contact effects in Northern Ireland: The moderating role of social identification. *British Journal of Social Psychology, 46*, 541–556.

Tropp, L.R. (2006). Stigma and intergroup contact among members of minority and majority status groups. In S. Levin and C. van Laar (Eds.), *Stigma and group inequality: Social psychological perspectives* (pp. 171–191). Mahwah, NJ: Erlbaum.

Tropp, L. R., and Pettigrew, T. F. (2005a). Relationships between intergroup contact and prejudice among minority and majority status groups. *Psychological Science, 16*, 951–957.

Tropp, L. R., and Pettigrew, T. F. (2005b). Differential relationships between intergroup contact and affective and cognitive dimensions of prejudice. *Personality and Social Psychology Bulletin, 31*, 1145–1158.

Turner, J. C., Hogg, M. A., Oakes, P. J., Reicher, S. D., and Wetherell, M. S. (1987). *Rediscovering the social group: A self–categorization theory.* Cambridge, MA: Blackwell.

Turner, R. N., Crisp, R. J., and Lambert, E. (2007). Imagining intergroup contact can improve intergroup attitudes. *Group Processes and Intergroup Relations, 10,* 427–441.

Turner, R. N., Hewstone, M., and Voci, A. (2007). Reducing explicit and implicit outgroup prejudice via direct and extended contact: The mediating role of self–disclosure and intergroup anxiety. *Journal of Personality and Social Psychology, 93,* 369–388.

Turner, R. N., Hewstone, M., Voci, A., and Vonofakou, C. (2008a). A test of the extended intergroup contact hypothesis: The mediating role of perceived ingroup and outgroup norms, intergroup anxiety and inclusion of the outgroup in the self. *Journal of Personality and Social Psychology, 95,* 843–860.

Turner, R. N., Hewstone, M., Voci, A., Paolini, S., Christ, O. (2008b). Reducing prejudice via direct and extended cross-group friendship. In W. Stroebe and M. Hewstone (Eds.), *European Review of Social Psychology* (Vol. 18, pp. 212–255). Hove, E. Sussex: Psychology Press.

van Oudenhoven, J. P., Groenewald, J. T., and Hewstone, M. (1996). Cooperation, ethnic salience and generalization of inter ethnic attitudes. *European Journal of Social Psychology, 26,* 649–662.

Voci, A., and Hewstone, M. (2003). Intergroup contact and prejudice toward immigrants in Italy: The mediational role of anxiety and the moderational role of group salience. *Group Processes and Intergroup Relations, 6,* 37–54.

Vonofakou, C., Hewstone, M., and Voci, A. (2007). Contact with outgroup friends as a predictor of meta-attitudinal strength and accessibility of attitudes towards gay men. *Journal of Personality and Social Psychology, 92,* 804–820

Vorauer, J. D., and Kumhyr, S. M. (2001). Is this about you or me? Self-versus other-directed judgements and feelings in response to intergroup interaction. *Personality and Social Psychology Bulletin, 27,* 706–719.

Wagner, U., and Machleit, U. (1986). 'Gastarbeiter' in the Federal Republic of Germany: Contact between Germans and migrant populations. In M. Hewstone and R. Brown (Ed.), *Contact and conflict in intergroup encounters* (pp. 59–78). Oxford: Blackwell.

Walker, P. M., Silvert, L., Hewstone, M., and Nobre, A. C. (2008). Social contact and other–race face processing in the human brain. *Social Cognitive and Affective Neuroscience, 3,* 16–25.

Wenzel, M., Mummendey, A., Weber, U., and Waldzus, S. (2003). The ingroup as pars pro toto: Projection from the ingroup onto the inclusive category as a precursor to social discrimination. *Personality and Social Psychology Bulletin, 29,* 461–473.

Williams, R. M., Jr. (1947). *The reduction of intergroup tensions.* New York, NY: Social Science Research Council.

Wilder, D. A. (1984). Intergroup contact: The typical member and the exception to the rule. *Journal of Experimental Social Psychology, 20,* 177–194.

Wilder, D. A. (1986). Social categorization: Implications for creation and reduction of intergroup bias. In L. Berkowitz (Ed.), *Advances in experimental social psychology* (Vol. 19, pp. 291–355). Orlando, FL: Academic Press.

Wilder, D. A., and Shapiro, P. N. (1989). The role of competition-induced anxiety in limiting the beneficial impact of positive behaviour by an out-group member. *Journal of Personality and Social Psychology, 56,* 60–69.

Wilner, D. M., Walkley, R. P., and Cook, S. W. (1952). *Human relations in interracial housing: A study of the contact hypothesis.* Minneapolis, MN: University of Minnesota Press.

Worchel, S., Andreoli, V. A., and Folger, R. (1977). Intergroup cooperation and intergroup attraction: The effect of previous interaction and outcome of combined effort. *Journal of Experimental Social Psychology, 13,* 131–140.

Wright, S. C. (2001). Strategic collective action: Social psychology and social change. In R. Brown and S. Gaertner (Eds.), *Blackwell Handbook of Social Psychology: Intergroup processes* (pp. 409–430). Oxford, UK: Blackwell.

Wright, S. C., Aron, A., McLaughlin-Volpe, T., and Ropp, S. A. (1997). The extended contact effect: Knowledge of cross-group friendships and prejudice. *Journal of Personality and Social Psychology, 73,* 73–90.

Wright, S. C., and Lubensky, M. (2008). The struggle for social equality: Collective action vs. prejudice reduction. In S., Demoulin, J. P. Leyens, and J. F., Dovidio, (Eds.) *Intergroup misunderstandings: Impact of divergent social realities* (pp. 291–310), New York: Psychology Press.

Yablon, Y. B., and Katz, Y. J. (2001). Internet–based group relations: A high school peace education project in Israel. *Education Media International, 38,* 175–182.

34

Individual Mobility

Naomi Ellemers and Colette Van Laar

ABSTRACT

Theory and research on prejudice has often characterized individual mobility as an effective and attractive strategy for members of devalued social groups to combat stereotyping and discrimination. It has been assumed that individuals who have sufficient merit and invest enough effort should be able to prove their personal value and hence move up in the status structure, despite the prejudice and discrimination directed towards their group. This chapter focuses on the limits of the effectiveness of individual mobility as a strategy to address negative group-based expectations about the self. We argue that due to the mechanisms addressed here individual mobility beliefs and the behaviours thus elicited tend to reinforce rather than challenge group-based inequality.

INDIVIDUAL MOBILITY

A general conviction, commonly voiced by politicians, journalists, and business leaders is that social outcomes are determined by individual competence and effort, or by the priorities people set and the life choices they make. In this view, the limited participation of ethnic minority group members in the labour force can easily be attributed to factors such as lower observed levels of educational attainment, for instance. Likewise, the dearth of women in higher management is often explained by arguing that women tend to give priority to their family commitments over their professional careers. Thus, the primary responsibility for people's social standing (or lack of it) is placed in the individuals themselves, while less attention is paid to the possible role of characteristics of the social structure, negative group-based stereotypes, or lack of opportunities afforded to members of certain social groups. In contrast, this chapter focuses on the limits of the effectiveness of individual mobility as a strategy to address negative group-based expectations about the self. We argue that due to the mechanisms addressed here individual mobility beliefs and the behaviours thus elicited tend to reinforce rather than challenge group-based inequality.

HISTORY OF THE PROBLEM

Similar notions are also reflected in some social scientific approaches to these issues, and are sometimes voiced quite explicitly. In his classic work on the nature of prejudice for instance, Allport (1979) recommended that those who are faced with prejudice should simply work harder to overcome this social handicap, by stating that 'to redouble one's efforts is a healthy response to an obstacle' (p. 156). Other social scientists refer to similar notions in a more implicit way (e.g., Jost & Banaji, 1994; Taylor & McKirnan, 1984; Wright, Taylor, & Moghaddam, 1990), by arguing that people have a natural tendency to accept group-based disadvantage as relatively stable and legitimate, and hence are most likely to seek individual-level solutions when they try to address and improve their social standing.

In this chapter we will first review the relevant literature and research explaining how such individual mobility belief systems are sustained. We argue that just world beliefs and implicitness of modern discrimination contribute to the conviction that people's outcomes generally depend on their individual merit – not on their group memberships. Then we will present an alternative approach, in that we detail some of the psychological mechanisms that contribute to this illusion of meritocracy. We outline how this effectively legitimizes and stabilizes historically developed intergroup status differences, instead of contributing to equal opportunities or resulting in a more just distribution of social outcomes according to individual merit.

REVIEW OF RELEVANT RESEARCH

Belief in a just world

A well-established phenomenon in social psychology is that people want to believe that the world is a just place, in which every individual receives the outcomes they deserve (Hafer & Olson, 1989). These meritocracy beliefs are widespread and firmly held. In fact, past research shows that – regardless of whether their group is advantaged or disadvantaged – people do not like to think of the ways in which their outcomes may be determined by their group membership instead of their individual merit (Major, Gramzow, McCoy, et al. 2002).

For instance, when men are asked to think of the ways in which they are privileged due to their gender, they report lower well-being. Likewise, women feel worse when asked to consider the gender-based disadvantages they encounter (Branscombe, 1998; Schmitt & Branscombe, 2002).

It is obvious why members of advantaged groups should be motivated to believe that the more favourable outcomes they receive are just, since this suggests greater merit, effort, or achievement (Schmitt, Ellemers, & Branscombe, 2003). The denial of category-based discrimination legitimizes existing differences in social standing, preventing members of dominant groups from feeling guilty about their advantages, and making it less likely that they will act to change the rules of the system or have to give up their privileges (Ellemers, 2001; Wright, 2000).

What is surprising is that those who are *disadvantaged* due to their group membership are also quite reluctant to recognize that this is the case (Schmitt & Branscombe, 2002). Even though attributing poor outcomes to discrimination can preserve self-esteem to the extent that this is seen as an external cause (Major, 1994), members of disadvantaged groups feel worse when they are asked to think of the ways in which their social group membership makes it more difficult for them to obtain favourable individual outcomes (Branscombe, 1998).

In sum, there is a popular conviction that existing differences in societal outcomes (e.g., career success, access to financial resources) are legitimate and just, because they accurately reflect the differential merit of individuals. At the same time, however, labour statistics show that women and ethnic minorities still are less successful in work settings than might be expected on the basis of their level of education – arguably a proxy for individual merit (sources: 'Arbeidsmarkt-analyse, 2006' – statistics of the Dutch labour market; 'She Figures, 2006' – European Union report on academic careers of men and women in Europe; see also Riach & Rich, 2002). Thus, individual meritocracy beliefs are maintained despite concrete evidence for systematic differences in outcomes attained by members of different social groups.

Implicitness of discrimination sustains meritocracy beliefs

The shared belief (among members of advantaged and disadvantaged groups alike) in the meritocratic nature of differential social outcomes is further reinforced because biases are often subtle or covert in contemporary societies, in which blatant expressions of prejudice and discrimination are suppressed as socially undesirable behaviour (Dovidio, 2001; Glick & Fiske, 1996, 2001; Jackman, 1994; Swim, Aikin, Hall, et al. 1995). As a result, group-based discrimination has become less obvious as new opportunities seem to be offered to members of disadvantaged social groups (through legislation and affirmative action policies), and examples of individual successes seem to underline the meritocratic nature of modern society. Thus the subtlety of modern prejudices reinforces the notion that individual mobility is an effective strategy to address group-based disadvantage; if people have sufficient merit and try hard enough, they should be able to move up in the status structure.

Social psychological theory (Taylor & McKirnan, 1984) and research (Wright, Taylor, & Moghaddam, 1990) suggest that individual mobility is the method targets of discrimination prefer to use to address low status. In fact, this strategy is used even when there is reason to doubt the fairness of the system, because objective chances of success are small (Wright, 2000). This again reflects the individual meritocracy ideology, which conceptualizes people as separate individuals, who operate independently to optimize their individual outcomes and well-being. An exclusive focus on personal identities and individual merit, however, does not satisfactorily explain the systematic differences observed in successes and failures when members of different groups try to improve their social standing. Instead, attempts to avoid or escape negative group-based expectations through individual mobility imply that

people's *social identity* is at stake. We argue that this involves different and additional mechanisms that cannot be explained from a purely individualistic perspective.

NEW FRAMEWORK

To more fully understand why individual merit alone does not account for the differential success of individual mobility attempts, we consider the limits of individual mobility as a strategy to address group-based disadvantage. Social psychological theory and research not only reveal the conditions under which individual mobility is most likely to be pursued and the different forms it can take, but also identify its cognitive, motivational, and behavioural consequences. The theoretical perspective that sheds the most light on these issues is social identity theory (Tajfel & Turner, 1979), which illuminates the ways in which individuals cope with their membership in socially devalued groups.

Antecedents of individual mobility

Theory (Tajfel & Turner, 1979) and research (e.g., Ellemers, 1993; Wright Taylor, & Moghaddam, 1990) on individual mobility has emphasized how social structure determines whether and how the disadvantaged seek to improve their plight (see also: Bettencourt, Charlton, Dorr, et al. 2001). *Perceived permeability of group boundaries* is seen as the primary factor determining whether people are likely to pursue individual mobility. When people believe that personal merit alone determines outcomes and group boundaries are seen as permeable (as is the case in most contemporary Western societies), members of disadvantaged groups are hypothesized to pursue individual mobility. By contrast, when people generally believe group membership prevents the achievement of certain outcomes, and group boundaries are considered impermeable (e.g., as in the Indian social caste system), individual mobility is less likely to be pursued as a strategy to improve one's social outcomes.

The effects of perceived boundary permeability, however, are complex (Jackson, Sullivan, Harnish, et al. 1996). For instance, research shows that the degree to which group membership is subjectively important for an individual determines whether or not they respond to the perceived permeability of group boundaries (Ellemers, Spears, & Doosje, 1997). People who strongly identify with their (disadvantaged) group tend to remain loyal to it, even when it is possible for them to leave and gain access to a more favourably endowed group. By contrast, those who care little for their affiliation with the group will psychologically distance themselves from it, and seek out opportunities to demonstrate that they are worthy of individual status improvement, even if it is not objectively possible to realize a change of group membership (Ellemers, Spears, & Doosje, 1997).

Other characteristics of the intergroup status structure also matter. When status relations between groups are seen as legitimate and stable, this effectively rules out the possibility for larger scale social change (Bettencourt, Charlton, Dorr, et al. 2001; Ellemers, Wilke, & van Knippenberg, 1993). As a result, people might view individual mobility as the only way to improve their personal standing, even when it is unclear whether or not group boundaries are permeable. Thus, conditions that indicate that group-level change is unlikely, can move group members towards seeing individual mobility as the only way towards status improvement.

In sum, although the permeability of group boundaries is generally seen as the main factor determining whether people will pursue individual mobility to cope with group-based disadvantage, a number of other considerations also matter. Perceived permeability can be conceived more broadly as the subjective importance of the group for the self, and the extent to which group membership is seen to prevent achievement of higher social status. Indeed, it is for this reason that meritocracy belief systems are so powerful – regardless of the objective opportunities society offers, they sustain the conviction that group boundaries are permeable and communicate that individual mobility represents the royal road towards status improvement.

Forms of individual mobility

There are a number of different forms individual mobility attempts can take. The most obvious is when people physically distance the self from their group and formally gain access to another group (e.g., resigning employment in a low-status organization to accept a job at a more prestigious organization). This form of individual mobility not only applies when people change schools or employers, but can also refer to people who relocate to a more attractive housing area or join more prestigious leisure clubs, such as when ethnic minority students re-negotiate their identity after they enter schools dominated by white majority students (Ethier & Deaux, 1994; Levin, van Laar, & Foote, 2006, 2003).

However, people can also pursue individual mobility without actually leaving their group. This is more likely to occur when group membership is based on physical characteristics (e.g., gender or ethnic group memberships). Under these conditions, achieving individual mobility entails a psychological distancing of the self from the group, for instance, by claiming that negative group-based expectations (even if typical of other group members) do not apply to the self. For example, an ambitious management trainee might state that, unlike most women, she puts her career ahead of family and has no desire to have children. Unfortunately, such claims of exceptionality simultaneously reinforce stereotypical views of other members of the group in one individual's attempt to achieve mobility.

A further step would be to deny the validity of group-based differences by maintaining that individuals should not be evaluated in terms of their group memberships. In this way, individual mobility can be pursued by emphasizing the relevance of personal, rather than social, identity. This strategy advocates differences in individual merit as the only valid basis for judging and rewarding individuals, and characterizes evaluation based on group membership as unacceptable, even immoral. The aim of this kind of individual mobility is not to gain inclusion in a group with higher standing, but to achieve the individual outcomes that match one's own merit.

A final way to achieve individual mobility entails an opposite strategy, in which one embraces one's social identity, instead of denying its relevance. Instead of renouncing a group-based identity, people may try to employ it to achieve individual mobility by maintaining that by virtue of their group membership they embody valuable traits. For example, a female employee might argue that she can provide typically feminine qualities (e.g., social emotional sensitivity) that the current management team is lacking. Alternatively, she might appeal to legal requirements that necessitate promoting some women into management. It is important to note that the added value of group-based characteristics is predicated in this case on their current lack of representation among the higher status group. The unique and distinctive contribution of these characteristics will be lessened when some individuals have succeeded in their individual mobility attempts. Thus, although people can use their group membership to their individual advantage when they present prototypical group traits as a source of added value and diversity, this may nevertheless improve their own, but not other group members' outcomes.

In sum, individual mobility may be achieved in a variety of ways. In addition to actually leaving the group, people may acknowledge group-based differences but distance the self from the group, deny the relevance of group-memberships altogether, or use alleged group characteristics as a stepping stone towards better individual outcomes.

Consequences of individual mobility

What are the cognitive, affective, and behavioural consequences of individual mobility attempts? Cognitively, those who aim for individual mobility will try to decrease the association between the self and the devalued group, or with devalued group traits. They may try to achieve this by, for instance, emphasizing distinctions between different group members to communicate to others that group-based expectations do not necessarily apply to themselves (Doosje, Ellemers, & Spears, 1995). In addition to emphasizing intra-group hetereogeneity, members of devalued groups may also seek out commonalities between their own group and more highly valued groups, thus more generally undermining the validity of group membership as a cue to the ascription of traits to individual group members (Doosje, Spears, Ellemers, et al. 1999).

Behaviourally, in addition to demonstrating superior competence, upwardly mobile individuals are likely to present themselves as non-prototypical group members. Importantly, this may involve displaying characteristics that are only tangentially related to task competence, or are even completely irrelevant to individual achievement. For instance, women who aim for a successful career tend to describe themselves as having steretoypically masculine personality traits or life choices (Ellemers, Van den Heuvel, De Gilder, et al. 2004). In cases where group membership is not immediately visible, the pursuit of individual mobility may even involve the denial or concealment of one's group-based identity. For instance, people may be untruthful about their social background, deny their ethnic heritage, or hide their family, in order to pass as members of a group with higher social standing. While this may seem an effective method to cope with a devalued identity, it creates a cognitive and emotional burden that undermines self-confidence and future performance (Barreto, Ellemers, & Banal, 2006; Quinn, 2006; Quinn, Kahng, & Crocker, 2004).

Affectively, individual mobility alters the degree of involvement or identification with the devalued group. When individual group members work towards individual mobility, they are primarily concerned with their individual outcomes, not with the outcomes of their group. It is easy to imagine a gradual transition between individual mobility and social change with the accumulation of successful individuals eventually resulting in a more positive evaluation of the group. However, we argue that there is an inherent tension between individual and collective strategies because, rather than fostering a re-consideration of intergroup relations, individual mobility generally serves to legitimize and stabilize existing intergroup differences (Ellemers, 2001; Ellemers & Barreto, 2008).

Decreased identification with the devalued group accompanies most if not all of the other cognitive and behavioural consequences of individual mobility outlined above. In fact, group identification can be seen both as a cause and consequence of individual mobility, and may provide the key to understanding the significance and implications of specific cognitive and behavioural strategies. As we have seen above, individual mobility attempts can emerge in many different forms, and are not always easily recognized for what they are. However, when the level of identification with the devalued group is decreased, this implies a loosening of affective ties between the self and the group. When people disconnect the self from the group, they are less emotionally affected by the plight of other group members. This makes it more likely that they will search for individual mobility opportunities that set the self apart from the group. In turn, when group members cognitively emphasize intra-group differences, focus on traits that distinguish them from other ingroup members, or conceal their group identity, they further lower their level of identification with the group. Importantly, this also makes it less easy for themselves as well as for others around them to perceive that they may suffer from group-based disadvantage – not from some form of personal inadequacy.

Success and failure of individual mobility strategies

Although individual mobility may seem an attractive strategy, there are a number of mechanisms that can render it less successful

or attractive. The most obvious limitation is that – because of individual mobility attempts and its cognitive, behavioural, and affective consequences outlined above – individuals who are in key positions (teachers, selection officers, managers, evaluators) often continue to have societal stereotypes, prejudices, and low expectations of low status or stigmatized groups that lead to discrimination (for reviews see Crocker, Major, & Steele, 1998; Major & O'Brien, 2005; Schmitt & Branscombe, 2000; Steele, Spencer, & Aronson, 2002; Wheeler & Petty, 2001). Prejudice and discrimination reduce the likelihood that individuals will engage in upward mobility attempts and that these attempts will be successful, by creating attributional ambiguity, self-stereotyping, and disidentification effects.

Ambiguity of group-based discrimination
Substantial research has shown that negative intentions are not necessary for discrimination, which often results from automatic processes (Dovidio, Brigham, Johnson, et al., 1996; Macrae, Bodenhausen, Milne, et al., 1994). Thus discrimination can be subtle and indirect, and members of low-status groups may often be uncertain as to whether they have been discriminated against or whether their outcomes stem from individual inadequacy (Major & Crocker, 1993; Major, Quinton, & Schmader, 2003; Rutte, Diekmann, Polzer, et al., 1994). This uncertainty makes it more difficult for victims of prejudice and observers to recognize when unfair treatment occurs. Indeed, modern, subtle, and indirect forms of prejudice are often not identified by those who are exposed to it, and therefore are likely to remain unchallenged (Barreto & Ellemers, 2005a; 2005b). As a result, subtle (as compared to more traditional and blatant) prejudice can have more negative consequences for targets, in that they not only suffer lower well-being, but also show decreased self-confidence and impaired task performance (Sechrist, Swim, & Stangor, 2004; Shelton, Richeson, Salvatore, et al. 2006).

Even when upwardly mobile members of low-status groups recognize that they are treated unfairly, confronting subtle discrimination can have substantial social costs. Due to their meritocracy beliefs, others – especially high-status group members – have a vested interest in perceiving another's failure to indicate a lack of individual deservingness (Ellemers, 2001; Schmitt, Ellemers, & Branscombe 2003). As a result, individuals who attribute their unfavourable outcomes to discrimination are perceived as complainers and troublemakers, and as not taking responsibility for their own outcomes. Although this is especially true when discrimination is subtle, it occurs even when discrimination is blatant (Garcia, Reser, Amo, et al., 2005; Kaiser, 2006; Kaiser & Miller, 2001, 2003; Stangor, Swim, van Allen, et al. 2002).

Thus, with prejudice and discrimination currently being expressed implicitly and ambiguously, members of stigmatized groups are in a double bind. Failure to recognize that personal outcomes stem from group-based negative treatment leads to reduced well-being, motivation, and performance. However, identifying and confronting group-based discrimination leads to negative interpersonal and social consequences. In both cases, the widely-shared denial of group-based discrimination limits the likely success of individual mobility attempts.

Self-stereotyping and stereotype threat

Social stigmas can affect the outcomes of disadvantaged group members even in the absence of a discriminating party. Research on stereotype threat shows that the mere salience of negative stereotypes in a specific performance context can lead members of stigmatized groups to experience anxieties that divert their attention from the task at hand, leading them to underperform (Steele & Aronson, 1995; Steele, Spencer, & Aronson 2002). The research also shows that especially those who are most able, who care most about the domain, and who are most identified with their group, are most likely to suffer the negative consequences of stereotype threat (Schmader, 2002; van Laar, Levin, & Sinclair, 2008).

Alternatively, previous experiences with negative stereotypes, prejudice, and discrimination can undermine motivation for low-status group members by affecting expectancies and value, the two essential components of motivation. Prior experiences with negative stereotypes, prejudice, and discrimination can lead members of low-status groups to believe that it will be harder or impossible for them to obtain good outcomes (van Laar, 2000), and to anticipate that doing so will involve significant stress and difficulty (e.g., Cadinu, Maass, Frigerio, et al., 2003). Barreto and colleagues (2004) confirmed that previous experiences with discrimination lead members of stigmatized (as compared to nonstigmatized) groups to appraise the same opportunity less favourably. Specifically, they showed that while token (partially open) opportunity systems motivate better performance by non-stigmatized participants, stigmatized participants feel threatened by these same systems as a result of which they reported negative emotions, and displayed suboptimal performance.

Thus, lowered expectancies resulting from prejudice and discrimination may distract and discourage members of stigmatized groups, leading them to perform poorly. In sum, even when a specific performance context shows no concrete evidence of prejudice or is unlikely to involve direct discrimination, the application of negative group-based expectations to the self, and lowered expectations of success based on previous experiences with discriminatory treatment, make it less likely that members of stigmatized groups will display the competence needed to take advantage of individual mobility opportunities.

Domain disengagement

When members of stigmatized groups have to perform in domains that are typically associated with outgroup success, they may suffer from stereotype threat (Inzlicht & Ben Zeev, 2000), reduced cognitive capacity (Richeson & Shelton, 2003), and impaired self-regulation (Inzlicht, McKay, & Aronson, 2006). To the extent that they attune to the negative attitudes of outgroup members have towards them (Sinclair & Huntsinger, 2006), they experience interaction anxiety (Shelton, 2003; Tropp, 2006), and increased sensitivity to rejection (Mendoza Denton, Downey, Purdie, et al., 2002). As a result, members of stigmatized groups tend to lower the *value* they attach to succeeding in a domain, by psychologically withdrawing from the domain and focus their attention on domains in which they do not face negative stereotypes (Crocker & Major, 1989; Derks, van Laar, & Ellemers, 2006, 2007; van Laar & Derks, 2003). Such domain disidentification has been found in females with regard to math, and African Americans and other minorities with regard to general academic achievement (Major & Schmader, 1998; Osborne, 1995, Verkuyten & Thijs, 2004).

Self-segregation and domain disidentification protect individual well-being, as they allow members of stigmatized groups to seek social support with other ingroup members and to excel in alternative domains. At the same time, this reduces contact with the majority group, limiting disadvantaged group members' access to knowledge and resources that the dominant group possesses. Thus, when members of stigmatized groups cease to value educational and work performance, they may forfeit their ability to attain higher social status. Further, the concentration of members of stigmatized groups in alternative domains reinforces the stereotypes of the group, creating a downward spiral that impairs individual mobility.

Lack of positive role models

Although individual advancement may be objectively possible or even encouraged, the awareness that only a few – if any – of those who are 'like me' have succeeded in the past reduces the subjective expectancy of success (Barreto, Ellemers, & Palacios, 2004; Wright, Taylor, & Moghaddam, 1990). Even when members of the low-status group have been successful in the past, this does not necessarily facilitate the mobility of other members of their group. In fact, the conditions under which they were able to achieve this

success may deter other group members from attempting the same. If, to be successful, upwardly mobile members of stigmatized groups communicate that the group stereotype does not apply to them, their self-declared exceptionality reinforces the stereotypicality of other members of their group (Ellemers, Van den Heuvel, De Gilder, et al., 2004).

This has three important consequences. First, members of low-status groups who have been successful in this way are likely not motivated to aid other members of their group. Second, their negative views of the ingroup may be particularly powerful in influencing others, as the way they perceive other members of their group may be seen as reflecting the group's 'true nature,' instead of being exposed as prejudicial (Baron, Burgess, & Kao, 1991). Third, as they aim to convince others that the negative group stereotype does not apply to them, successful individuals take great pains to demonstrate that they are different from other members of their group and may even try to conceal their stigmatized identity. For instance, the need to conform to behavioural norms of the dominant outgroup easily leads these individuals to overcompensate, as when women who are successful in work contexts tend adopt extremely masculine styles (Eagly, Makhijani, & Klonsky, 1992; Ellemers, Van den Heuvel, De Gilder, et al., 2004), making it less likely that they are seen as relevant or attractive role models by other ingroup members.

Resistance to affirmative action policies

Various societal and organizational policies have been designed to proactively reduce or eliminate unfair group-based historical disadvantages. Affirmative action policies include targeted recruitment and training of underrepresented individuals and preferences for underrepresented candidates. These measures effectively raise the proportion of members of underrepresented groups in education and workplaces (see Crosby, 2004; and Konrad & Linnehan, 1999, for reviews).

Additionally, members of stigmatized groups can find the mere presence of such programs motivating, as they communicate that others acknowledge and aim to address their plight (Highhouse, Stierwalt, Bachiochi, et al., 1999; Taylor, 1994).

Nevertheless, there has been concern that such policies in fact make it more difficult for beneficiaries to prove that they deserve the opportunities they receive (Heilman & Blader, 2001; Maio & Esses, 1998; van Laar, Levin, & Sinclair 2008). If affirmative action policies are not well explained or others are not informed of the credentials of affirmative action candidates, people underestimate the competence of affirmative action employees, who may themselves start to doubt their own abilities (see Heilman & Alcott, 2001). Such doubts interfere with performance and the motivation to take on challenging tasks, making success less likely (for reviews see Crosby, 2004; Truax, Cordova, Wood, et al., 1998; Turner & Pratkanis, 1994). Thus, poor implementation or lack of explanation about the competence of individuals who benefit from such policies may easily backfire and cause resistance against these programs and their beneficiaries (Federico & Sidanius, 2002; James, Brief, Dietz, et al., 2001).

As a result of such lack of understanding, people have come to question the necessity of affirmative action measures, arguing that group-based disadvantage no longer exists (see Schmitt, Ellemers, & Branscombe 2003; Ellemers & Barreto, 2008, for a review). US legislation has even deemed some of these policies to be unconstitutional (source: NRC/Handelsblad, July 26, 2006), again contributing to the notion that differential outcomes reflect differences in individual merit, instead of relating to group-based discrimination and disadvantage.

FUTURE DIRECTIONS

While individual mobility tends to be seen as the strategy of choice to escape negative group-based expectations (in lay opinion as well as by some social scientists), we set out to highlight the limitations and disadvantages of this approach. We first demonstrated that just world beliefs and the implicitness of contemporary discrimination help sustain individual meritocracy beliefs, even if these do not paint a realistic picture of actual opportunities for position improvement. We then used a social identity perspective to explain that strong meritocracy beliefs lead people to distance the self from their disadvantaged groups in a variety of ways. Importantly, we argued that the resulting reluctance to see the self as representing one's disadvantaged group leads to lower ingroup identification, and further contributes to the denial of group-based disadvantage. This new framework allows us to understand the mechanisms through which – despite their strong meritocracy beliefs – members of disadvantaged groups are set up for individual failure. The negative expectations others have based on their group membership result in self-stereotyping and stereotype threat effects. Additionally, members of disadvantaged groups are at risk of disengaging from important performance domains and suffer from lack of positive role models. As a result, systematic discrimination and group-based disadvantage remain ambiguous and unchallenged, while individual members of such groups tend to become demotivated, disengage from important domains, and underperform. Thus they seemingly justify and confirm negative expectations held about their group, and contribute to resistance and distrust of affirmative action measures that might target their problems at a group level.

Our main aim in this chapter was to identify a number of problems and concerns that come into play when individuals try to disconfirm group-based stereotypes and expectations through individual mobility. Awareness of these issues is crucial for individuals who are exposed to group-based discrimination, as well as for managers, policy makers, and scientists. While the pessimistic view might be that individual mobility is more of an illusion than a reality, there may be reason for optimism once these difficulties are understood and appropriately taken into account. It is in this spirit that we end by pointing to some future directions for research.

Providing support and respect

A recurring issue is that a number of (self-) defeating mechanisms (e.g., self-stereotyping and stereotype threat) affect even successful members of stigmatized groups, who continue to feel devalued because of their group membership. Nevertheless, while it has been documented that members of stigmatized groups show low well-being, are focused on failure rather than success, and evidence low performance in contexts dominated by outgroup members, research has also demonstrated that these threats and negative performance effects can be alleviated when stigmatized groups' characteristics are explicitly valued (Derks, van Laar, and Ellemers, 2006, 2007; 2009). More generally, recent research confirms the importance of respect for one's social identity as a key component in the well-being, motivation, and performance of members of stigmatized groups (Barreto & Ellemers, 2002; Huo & Molina, 2006). This suggests that instead of denying or ignoring the devalued social identity of individual group members (as has been advocated, for instance, in 'color blind' policies), it is important to explicitly acknowledge, affirm, and value membership in disadvantaged groups.

Another reason why the social identity of stigmatized group members needs to be acknowledged is that those who pursue individual mobility are often highly visible and face the scrutiny of other ingroup members. As we have seen, attempts to demonstrate one's individual worth despite negative group-based expectations often imply a distancing of the self from the group. This may involve adopting behaviours typical of the dominant outgroup (e.g., speech habits and dress styles) that may be viewed as implying a devaluation or rejection of ingroup norms and traditions. As a result, instead of being admired as a role model, upwardly mobile group members tend

rather to be seen as 'sell-outs' or as betraying their true identity. Thus, upwardly mobile individuals risk losing the encouragement and support of other ingroup members (Branscombe & Ellemers, 1998). At the same time, however, research shows that the example of and support of other ingroup members may be particularly important to the motivation and performance of members of stigmatized groups, particularly in challenging settings (Branscombe, Schmitt, & Harvey, 1999; Levin, van Laar & Foote, 2006, 2003; Marx & Roman, 2002). Although ingroup support appears to be important, how such support can be assured while pursuing upward mobility, or how this affects motivation and performance, are as yet little understood and deserve more research attention.

Implicit and dynamic processes

Researchers have thus far focused either on the perspective of the dominant group (e.g., stereotyping and discrimination) or of the stigmatized group (e.g., self-defeating mechanisms). However, there is an increasing awareness that it is crucial to examine the *interactions* between members of stigmatized and nonstigmatized groups and assess how their mutual responses to each other develop over time (Hebl & Dovidio, 2005; Shelton, 2000). It is in these dynamic interaction processes that important mobility decisions are made, and studying these interactions will show how the mobility strategies of members of stigmatized groups are shaped through interactions with outgroup members.

Current methodological developments towards more implicit and (continuous) psycho-physiological methodologies promise to allow a better grasp of how automatic and unconscious processes prompt threats to members of stigmatized groups and how they can be alleviated (e.g., Scheepers & Ellemers, 2005). Threat is an essential variable that has been particularly difficult to assess. The typical self-report measures presume respondents' awareness of internal states and fail when denial of threat forms part of the coping strategy. Furthermore, recent research has pointed out the need to distinguish between threat and challenge, as the alleviation of threat is important for well-being, but the induction of challenge is crucial to foster motivation and enhance individual task performance (Derks, van Laar, & Ellemers, 2009). The current movement towards using more implicit and physiological measures will contribute to understanding these dynamics by providing the kinds of unobtrusive, covert, and continuous data missing in existing research.

Individual goal achievement and self-regulation

Another recent development that holds clear promise is the increasing connection between work on social stigma and the research on individual goal achievement and self-regulation (Derks, van Laar, & Ellemers, 2006; Keller & Dauenheimer, 2003; Sassenberg & Hansen, 2007; Swim, 2006). This line of theory and research specifies the different ways in which individuals can work towards the realization of specific goals, distinguishing between those who focus on the achievement of success (promotion focus), and those who focus on the avoidance of failure (prevention focus; Higgins, 1997). Importantly, recent research shows that group processes and intergroup relations can also elicit a focus on promotion or prevention (e.g., Levine, Higgins, & Choi, 2000; Sassenberg, Jonas, Shah, et al. 2007; Shah, Brazy, & Higgins, 2004), and that the collective focus that characterizes a particular group can affect the behavioural strategies adopted, as well as the emotions experienced after success and failure by individual group members (Faddegon, Scheepers, & Ellemers, 2006).

Research on regulatory focus and its consequences for people's affective responses and strategies for goal pursuit has the potential to provide important insights into how members of stigmatized groups are affected by stereotypes, discrimination, and stressful interactions with members of the dominant group, and how they might best cope with such impediments to individual goal achievement. Further knowledge about the possibilities for situational or group-based induction of a promotion or prevention orientation can inform the design of interventions or policies to support individually mobile members of stigmatized group in achieving their goals.

CONCLUSION

We have addressed individual mobility as a strategy individual group members can use to avoid the consequences of group-based discrimination, and examined the conditions under which this is most likely to be successful. In contrast to the view that individuals can act independently to optimize their own outcomes and well-being, we have emphasized that it is crucial to take into account that people's *group-based identity* is at stake, and this has important psychological and behavioural consequences. Indeed, although individual mobility may seem an attractive strategy for the individual, we have outlined a number of (self-fulfilling and self-defeating) mechanisms that can render it less successful or attractive. These mechanisms have to be taken into account when considering the potential effects of individual mobility as a strategy to combat prejudice and discrimination. Based on our review of the relevant literature, we advocate that future theory and research examines the broader implications of individual mobility for the perceptions and behaviours of those who are subjected to discrimination, as well as for those who hold prejudiced views of others. In doing so, care should be taken to consider that people's social identity, not just their personal identity, is at stake.

REFERENCES

Allport, G. W. (1979). *The Nature of Prejudice.* Reading, Massachusetts: Addison-Wesley.

Arbeidsmarktanalyse 2006, Raad voor Werk en Inkomen. ISBN 13: 9789059016781. Reed Business.

Baron, R. S., Burgess, M. L., & Kao, C. F. (1991). Detecting and labeling prejudice: Do female perpetrators go undetected? *Personality and Social Psychology Bulletin, 17*, 115–123.

Barreto, M., & Ellemers, N. (2002). The impact of respect versus neglect of self-identities on identification and group loyalty. *Personality and Social Psychology Bulletin, 28*, 629–639.

Barreto, M., & Ellemers, N. (2005a). The burden of benevolent sexism: How it contributes to the maintenance of gender inequalities. *European Journal of Social Psychology, 35*, 633–642.

Barreto, M., & Ellemers, N. (2005b). The perils of political correctness: Men's and women's responses to old-fashioned and modern sexist views. *Social Psychology Quarterly, 68*, 75–88.

Barreto, M., Ellemers, N., & Banal, S. (2006). Working under cover: Performance-related self-confidence among members of contextually devalued groups who try to pass. *European Journal of Social Psychology, 36*, 337–352.

Barreto, M., Ellemers, N., & Palacios, M. S. (2004). The backlash of token mobility: The impact of past group experiences on individual ambition and effort. *Personality and Social Psychology Bulletin, 30*, 1433–1445.

Bettencourt, B. A., Charlton, K., Dorr, N., & Hume, D.L. (2001). Status differences and in-group bias: A meta-analytic examination of the effects of status stability, status legitimacy, and group permeability. *Psychological Bulletin, 127*, 520–542.

Branscombe, N. R. (1998). Thinking about one's gender-group's privileges or disadvantages: Consequences for well-being in women and men. *British Journal of Social Psychology, 37*, 167–184.

Branscombe, B., & Ellemers, N. (1998). Use of individualistic and group strategies in response to perceived group-based discrimination. In J. Swim & C. Stangor (Eds.), *Prejudice: The Target's Perspective* (243–266). New York: Academic Press.

Branscombe, N. R., Schmitt, M. T., & Harvey, R. D. (1999). Perceiving pervasive discrimination among African Americans: Implications for group identification and well-being. *Journal of Personality and Social Psychology, 77*, 135–149.

Cadinu, M., Maass, A., Frigerio, S., Impagliazzo, L., & Latinotti, S. (2003). Stereotype threat: The effect of expectancy on performance. *European Journal of Social Psychology, 33*, 267–285.

Crocker, J., & Major, B. (1989). Social stigma and self-esteem: The self-protective properties of stigma. *Psychological Review, 96*, 608–630.

Crocker, J., Major, B., & Steele, C. (1998). Social stigma. In D. T. Gilbert, S. T. Fiske, & G. Lindzey (Eds.), *The Handbook of Social Psychology* (4th ed., Vol. 2, pp. 504–553). Boston, MA: Mcgraw-Hill.

Crosby, F. J. (2004). *Affirmative Action is Dead; Long Live Affirmative Action*. New Haven, CN: Yale University Press.

Derks, B., van Laar, C., & Ellemers, N. (2006). Striving for success in outgroup settings: Effects of contextually emphasizing ingroup dimensions on stigmatized group members? Social identity and performance styles. *Personality and Social Psychology Bulletin, 32*, 576–588.

Derks, B., van Laar, C., & Ellemers, N. (in press). Working for the self or working for the group: How self- vs. group-affirmation affect collective behavior in low status groups. *Journal of Personality and Social Psychology*.

Derks, B., van Laar, C., & Ellemers, N. (2007). Social creativity strikes back: Improving low status group members' motivation and performance by valuing ingroup dimensions. *European Journal of Social Psychology, 37*, 470–493.

Doosje, B., Ellemers, N., & Spears, R. (1995). Perceived intragroup variability as a function of group status and identification. *Journal of Experimental Social Psychology, 31*, 410–436.

Doosje, B., Spears, R., Ellemers, N., & Koomen, W. (1999). Group variability in intergroup relations: The distinctive role of social identity. In W. Stroebe & M. Hewstone (Eds.), *European Review of Social Psychology* (Vol. 10, pp. 41–74). Chichester: John Wiley.

Dovidio, J.F. (2001). On the nature of contemporary prejudice: The third wave. *Journal of Social Issues, 57*, 829–849.

Dovidio, J. F., Brigham, J. C., Johnson, B. T., & Gaertner, S. L. (1996). Stereotyping, prejudice, and discrimination: Another look. In C. N. Macrae, C. Stangor & M. Hewstone (Eds.), *Foundations of Stereotypes and Stereotyping* (pp. 276–319). New York: Guilford.

Eagly, A. H., Makhijani, M. G., & Klonsky, B. G. (1992). Gender and the evaluation of leaders: A meta-analysis. *Psychological Bulletin, 111*, 3–22.

Ellemers, N. (1993). The influence of socio-structural variables on identity enhancement strategies. *European Review of Social Psychology, 4*, 27–57.

Ellemers, N. (2001). Individual upward mobility and the perceived legitimacy of intergroup relations. In J. T. Jost, & B. Major (Eds.) *The Psychology of Legitimacy; Emerging Perspectives on Ideology, Justice, and Intergroup Relations* (pp. 205–222). Cambridge University Press.

Ellemers, N., & Barreto, M. (2008). Maintaining the illusion of meritocracy. In S. Demoulin, J.-P. Leyens, & J. F. Dovidio (Eds.). *Intergroup Misunderstandings:*

Impact of Divergent Social Realities (pp. 191–212). Hove, E. Sussex: Psychology Press.

Ellemers, N., Spears, R., & Doosje, B. (1997). Sticking together or falling apart: Group identification as a psychological determinant of group commitment versus individual mobility. *Journal of Personality and Social Psychology, 72*, 123–140.

Ellemers, N., Van den Heuvel, H., De Gilder, D., Maass, A., & Bonvini, A. (2004). The underrepresentation of women in science: Differential commitment or the queen bee syndrome? *British Journal of Social Psychology, 43*, 315–338.

Ellemers, N., Wilke, H., & van Knippenberg, A. (1993). Effects of the legitimacy of low group or individual status on individual and collective identity enhancement strategies. *Journal of Personality and Social Psychology, 64*, 766–778.

Ethier, K.A., & Deaux, K. (1994). Negotiating social identity when contexts change: Maintaining identification and responding to threat. *Journal of Personality and Social Psychology, 67*, 243–251.

Faddegon, K., Scheepers, D., & Ellemers, N. (2006). If we have the will, there will be a way: Regulatory focus as a group identity.

Federico, C. M., & Sidanius, J. (2002). Racism, ideology, and affirmative action revisited: The antecedents and consequences of "principled objections" to affirmative action. *Journal of Personality and Social Psychology, 82*, 488–502.

Garcia, D. M., Reser, A. H., Amo, R. B., Redersdorff, S., & Branscombe, N. R. (2005). Perceivers' responses to in-group and out-group members who blame a negative outcome on discrimination. *Personality and Social Psychology Bulletin, 31*, 769–780.

Glick, P., & Fiske, S. T. (1996). The ambivalent sexism inventory: Differentiating hostile and benevolent sexism. *Journal of Personality and Social Psychology, 70*, 491–512.

Glick, P., & Fiske, S. T. (2001). Ambivalent sexism. In M. P. Zanna (Ed.), *Advances in Experimental Social Psychology* (Vol. 33, pp. 115–188). San Diego, CA: Academic Press.

Hafer, C. L., & Olson, J. M. (1989). Beliefs in a just world and reactions to personal deprivation. *Journal of Personality, 57*, 799–823.

Hebl, M. R., & Dovidio, J. F. (2005). Promoting the "social" in the examination of social stigmas. *Personality and Social Psychology Review, 9*, 156–182.

Heilman, M. E., & Alcott, V. B. (2001). What I think you think of me: Women's reactions to being viewed as beneficiaries of preferential selection. *Journal of Applied Psychology, 86*, 574–582.

Heilman, M. E., & Blader, S. L. (2001). Assuming preferential selection when the admissions policy is unknown: The effects of gender rarity. *Journal of Applied Psychology, 86*, 188–193.

Higgins, E. T. (1997). Beyond pleasure and pain. *American Psychologist, 52*, 1280–1300.

Highhouse, S., Stierwalt, S. L., Bachiochi, P., Elder, A. E., & Fisher, G. (1999). Effects of advertised human resource management practices on attraction of African American applicants. *Personnel Psychology, 52*, 425–442.

Huo, Y. J., & Molina, L. E. (2006). Is pluralism a viable model of diversity? The benefits and limits of subgroup respect. *Group Processes and Intergroup Relations, 9*, 359–376.

Inzlicht, M., & Ben Zeev, T. (2000). A threatening intellectual environment: Why females are susceptible to experiencing problem-solving deficits in the presence of males. *Psychological Science, 11*, 365–371.

Inzlicht, M., McKay, L., & Aronson, J. (2006). Stigma as ego depletion: How being the target of prejudice affects self-control. *Psychological Science, 17*, 262–269.

Jackman, M. R. (1994). *The velvet glove: Paternalism and conflict in gender, class, and race relations.* Berkeley, CA: University of California Press.

Jackson, L. A., Sullivan, L. A., Harnish, R., & Hodge, C. N. (1996). Achieving positive social identity: Social mobility, social creativity, and permeability of group boundaries. *Journal of Personality and Social Psychology, 70*, 241–254.

James, E. H., Brief, A. P., Dietz, J., & Cohen, R. R. (2001). Prejudice matters: Understanding the reactions of Whites to affirmative action programs targeted to benefit Blacks. *Journal of Applied Psychology, 86*, 1120–1128.

Jost, J.T., & Banaji, M.R. (1994). The role of stereotyping in system-justification and the production of false consciousness. *British Journal of Social Psychology, 33*, 1–27.

Kaiser, C. R. (2006). Dominant ideology threat and the interpersonal consequences of attributions to discrimination. In S. Levin & C. van Laar (Eds.), *Stigma and Group Inequality: Social Psychological Approaches* (pp. 45–64). Mahwah, NJ: Erlbaum.

Kaiser, C. R., & Miller, C. T. (2001). Stop complaining! The social costs of making attributions to discrimination. *Personality and Social Psychology Bulletin, 27*, 254–263.

Kaiser, C. R., & Miller, C. T. (2003). Derogating the victim: The interpersonal consequences of blaming events on discrimination. *Group Processes and Intergroup Relations, 6*, 227–237.

Keller, J., & Dauenheimer, D. (2003). Stereotype threat in the classroom: Dejection mediates the disrupting threat effect on women's math performance.

Personality and Social Psychology Bulletin, 29, 371–381.

Konrad, A. M., & Linnehan, F. (1999). Affirmative action: History, effects and attitudes. In G. N. Powell (Ed.), *Handbook of Gender and Work* (pp. 429–452). Thousand Oaks, CA: Sage.

Levin, S., van Laar, C., & Foote, W. (2006). Ethnic segregation and perceived discrimination in college: Mutual influences and effects on social and academic life. *Journal of Applied Social Psychology, 36*, 1471–1501.

Levin, S., van Laar, C., & Sidanius, J. (2003). The effects of ingroup and outgroup friendships on ethnic attitudes in college: A longitudinal study. *Group Processes and Intergroup Relations, 6*, 76–92.

Levine, J. M., Higgins, E. T., & Choi, H. S. (2000). Development of strategic norms in groups. *Organizational Behavior and Human Decision Processes, 82*, 88–101.

Macrae, C. N., Bodenhausen, G. V., Milne, A. B., & Jetten, J. (1994). Out of mind but back in sight: Stereotypes on the rebound. *Journal of Personality and Social Psychology, 67*, 808–817.

Maio, G. R., & Esses, V. M. (1998). The social consequences of affirmative action: Deleterious effects on perceptions of groups. *Personality and Social Psychology Bulletin, 24*, 65–74.

Major, B. (1994). From social inequality to personal entitlement: The role of social comparisons, legitimacy appraisals, and group membership. In M. P. Zanna (Ed.). *Advances in Experimental Social Psychology* (Vol. 26, pp. 293–348.). San Diego, CA: Academic Press.

Major, B., & Crocker, J. (1993). Social stigma: The consequences of attributional ambiguity. In D. M. Mackie & D. L. Hamilton (Eds.), *Affect, Cognition, and Stereotyping: Interactive Processes in Group Perception* (pp. 345–370). San Diego, CA: Academic Press.

Major, B., Gramzow, R. H., McCoy, S. K., Levin, S., Schmader, T., & Sidanius, J. (2002). Perceiving personal discrimination: The role of group status and legitimizing ideology. *Journal of Personality and Social Psychology, 82*, 269–282.

Major, B., & O'Brien, L. T. (2005). The social psychology of stigma. *Annual Review of Psychology, 56*, 393–421.

Major, B., Quinton, W. J., & Schmader, T. (2003). Attributions to discrimination and self-esteem: Impact of group identification and situational ambiguity. *Journal of Experimental Social Psychology, 39*, 220–231.

Major, B., & Schmader, T. (1998). Coping with stigma through psychological disengagement. In J. K. Swim &

C. Stangor (Eds.), *Prejudice: The Target's Perspective* (pp. 219–241). San Diego, CA: Academic Press.

Marx, D. M., & Roman, J. S. (2002). Female role models: Protecting women's math test performance. *Personality and Social Psychology Bulletin, 28*, 1183–1193.

Mendoza Denton, R., Downey, G., Purdie, V. J., Davis, A., & Pietrzak, J. (2002). Sensitivity to status-based rejection: Implications for African American students' college experience. *Journal of Personality and Social Psychology, 83*, 896–918.

Osborne, J. W. (1995). Academics, self-esteem, and race: A look at the underlying assumptions of the disidentification hypothesis. *Personality and Social Psychology Bulletin, 21*, 449–455.

Quinn, D. M. (2006). Concealable versus conspicuous stigmatized identities. In S. Levin & C. van Laar (Eds.), *Stigma and Group Inequality: Social Psychological Approaches* (pp. 88–103). Mahwah, NJ: Erlbaum.

Quinn, D. M., Kahng, S. K., & Crocker, J. (2004). Discreditable: Stigma effects of revealing a mental illness history on test performance. *Personality and Social Psychology Bulletin, 30*, 803–815.

Riach, P., & Rich, J. (2002). Field experiments of discrimination in the market place. *The Economic Journal, 112*, 480–518.

Richeson, J. A., & Shelton, J. N. (2003). When prejudice does not pay: Effects of interracial contact on executive function. *Psychological Science, 14*, 287–290.

Rutte, C. G., Diekmann, K. A., Polzer, J. T., Crosby, F. J., & Messick, D. M. (1994). Organization of information and the detection of gender discrimination. *Psychological Science, 5*, 226–231.

Sassenberg, K., & Hansen, N. (2007). The impact of regulatory focus on affective responses to social discrimination. *European Journal of Social Psychology, 37*, 421–444.

Sassenberg, K., Jonas, K. J., & Shah, J. Y, & Brazy, P. C. (2007). Why some groups just feel better: The regulatory fit of group power. *Journal of Personality and Social Psychology, 92*, 249–267.

Scheepers, D., & Ellemers, N. (2005). When the pressure is up: The assessment of social identity threat in low and high status groups. *Journal of Experimental Social Psychology, 41*, 192–200.

Schmader, T. (2002). Gender identification moderates stereotype threat effects on women's math performance. *Journal of Experimental Social Psychology, 38*, 194–201.

Schmitt, M. T., & Branscombe, N. R. (2000). The meaning and consequences of perceived discrimination in disadvantaged and privileged social groups. In W. Stroebe & M. Hewstone (Eds.), *European Review of Social Psychology* (Vol. 12, pp. 166–199). Chichester: John Wiley.

Schmitt, M. T., & Branscombe, N. R. (2002). The internal and external causal loci of attributions to prejudice. *Personality and Social Psychology Bulletin, 28*, 484–492.

Schmitt, M. T., Ellemers, N., & Branscombe, N. R. (2003). Perceiving and responding to sex discrimination at work. In S. A. Haslam, D. van Knippenberg, M. J. Platow, & N. Ellemers (Eds.), *Social Identity at Work: Developing Theory for Organizational Practice* (pp. 277–292). New York: Psychology Press.

Sechrist, G. B., Swim, J. K., & Stangor, C. (2004). When do the stigmatized make attributions to discrimination occurring to the self and others? The roles of self-presentation and need for control. *Journal of Personality and Social Psychology, 87*, 111–122.

Shah, J. Y., Brazy, P. B., & Higgins, E. T. (2004). Promoting us or preventing them: Regulatory focus and the nature of in-group bias. *Personality and Social Psychology Bulletin, 30*, 433–446.

She figures 2006: Women and Science – Statistics and Indicators. European Commission – Community Research. ISSN 1018–5593.

Shelton, J. N. (2000). A reconceptualization of how we study issues of racial prejudice. *Personality and Social Psychology Review, 4*, 374–390.

Shelton, J. N. (2003). Interpersonal concerns in social encounters between majority and minority group members. *Group Processes and Intergroup Relations, 6*, 171–185.

Shelton, J. N., Richeson, J. A., Salvatore, J., & Hill, D. M. (2006). Silence is not golden: The intrapersonal consequences of not confronting prejudice. In S. Levin & C. van Laar (Eds.), *Stigma and Group Inequality: Social Psychological Approaches* (pp. 65–81). Mahwah, NJ: Erlbaum.

Sinclair, S., & Huntsinger, J. (2006). The interpersonal basis of self-stereotyping. In S. Levin & C. van Laar (Eds.), *Stigma and Group Inequality: Social Psychological Approaches.* Mahwah, NJ: Lawrence Erlbaum.

Spears, R., Doosje, B., & Ellemers, N. (1997). Self-stereotyping in the face of threats to group status and distinctiveness: The role of group identification. *Personality and Social Psychology Bulletin, 23*, 538–553.

Stangor, C., Swim, J. K., Van Allen, K. L., & Sechrist, G. (2002). Reporting discrimination in public and private contexts. *Journal of Personality and Social Psychology, 82*, 69–74.

Steele, C. M., & Aronson, J. (1995). Stereotype threat and the intellectual test performance of African Americans. *Journal of Personality and Social Psychology, 69*, 797–811.

Steele, C. M., Spencer, S. J., & Aronson, J. (2002). Contending with group image: The psychology of stereotype and social identity threat. In M. P. Zanna (Ed.), *Advances in Experimental Social Psychology* (Vol. 34, pp. 379–440). San Diego, CA: Academic Press.

Swim, J. K. (2006). Responding to everyday discrimination: A synthesis of research on goal directed, self-regulatory coping behaviors. In S. Levin & C. van Laar (Eds.), *Stigma and Group Inequality: Social Psychological Approaches* (pp. 105–126). Mahwah, NJ: Erlbaum.

Swim, J. K., Aikin, K. J., Hall, W. S., & Hunter, B. A. (1995). Sexism and racism: Old-fashioned and modern prejudices. *Journal of Personality and Social Psychology, 68*, 199–214.

Tajfel, H., & Turner, J. C. (1979). An integrative theory of intergroup conflict. In W. G. Austin & S. Worchel (Eds.), *The Social Psychology of Intergroup Relations* (pp. 33–47). Monterey, CA: Brooks/Cole.

Taylor, M. C. (1994). Impact of affirmative action on beneficiary groups: Evidence from the 1990 General Social Survey. Special issue: Social psychological perspectives on affirmative action. *Basic & Applied Social Psychology, 15*, 143–178.

Taylor, D.M., & McKirnan, D.J. (1984). A five stage model of intergroup relations. *British Journal of Social Psychology, 23*, 291–300.

Tropp, L. R. (2006). Stigma and intergroup contact among members of minority and majority status groups. In S. Levin & C. van Laar (Eds.), *Stigma and Group Inequality: Social Psychological Approaches* (pp. 171–191). Mahwah, NJ: Erlbaum.

Truax, K., Cordova, D. I., Wood, A., Wright, E., & Crosby, F. (1998). Undermined? Affirmative action from the target's point of view. In J. K. Swim & C. Stangor (Eds.), *Prejudice: The Target's Perspective* (pp. 171–188). San Diego, CA: Academic Press.

Turner, M. E., & Pratkanis, A. R. (1994). Affirmative action as help: A review of recipient reactions to preferential selection and affirmative action. *Basic & Applied Social Psychology, 15*, 43–69.

van Laar, C. (2000). The paradox of low academic achievement but high self-esteem in African American students: An attributional account. *Educational Psychology Review, 12*, 33–61.

van Laar, C., & Derks, B. (2003). Managing stigma: Disidentification from the academic domain. In F. Salili & R. Hoosain (Eds.), *Learning and Motivation in a Multicultural Setting* (pp. 345–393). Greenwich, CN: Information Age Publishing.

van Laar, C., Levin, S., and Sinclair, S. (2008). Social identity and personal identity concerns in stereotype threat: The case of affirmative action. *Basic and Applied Social Psychology.* 30, 295–310.

Verkuyten, M., & Thijs, J. (2004). Psychological disidentification with the academic domain among ethnic minority adolescents in The Netherlands. *British Journal of Educational Psychology, 74*, 109–125.

Wheeler, S. C., & Petty, R. E. (2001). The effects of stereotype activation on behavior: A review of possible mechanisms. *Psychological Bulletin, 127*, 797–826.

Wright, S. C. (2000). Strategic collective action: Social psychology and social change. In: R. Brown & S. Gaertner (Eds.). *Blackwell Handbook of Social Psychology: Intergroup Processses* (pp. 409–430). Oxford: Blackwell.

Wright, S. C., Taylor, D. M., & Moghaddam, F. M. (1990). Responding to membership in a disadvantaged group: From acceptance to collective protest. *Journal of Personality and Social Psychology, 58*, 994–1003.

35

Collective Action and Social Change

Stephen C. Wright

ABSTRACT

Social psychology's primary approach to improving intergroup relations has been prejudice reduction. However, this chapter reviews the discipline's contributions to an alternative approach – collective action and social protest. Informed by Relative Deprivation Theory and rooted in Social Identity Theory, the chapter describes four psychological processes that underpin collective action: collective identity, perceived boundary permeability, feelings of legitimacy/injustice, and collective control (instability/agency). These four emerge through a process of mutual influence to motivate collective action or to steer the individual towards inaction or individual efforts to improve one's personal position. In addition, brief discussions will highlight several recent important additions to the literature, and the chapter concludes by contrasting the psychology of collective action with that of prejudice reduction.

COLLECTIVE ACTION AND SOCIAL CHANGE

As the title of this section of the handbook – 'Combating bias' – reveals, one goal of research and theorizing on prejudice has been to uncover ways of reducing it. An underlying assumption of this work is that reducing individual prejudice will spur broader reductions in social injustice; that improving intergroup attitudes can lead to social change. However, reducing the negative thoughts (stereotypes), attitudes (prejudice), and actions (discrimination) of individuals represents only one potential route to increase social justice. This chapter reviews social psychology's contribution to an alternative approach focusing on collective action and social protest.

Although both approaches explore intergroup injustice and both are plainly implicated in major intergroup relations theories (e.g., Turner, Hogg, Oakes, et al., 1987), research in the two areas has developed quite independently (Wright & Lubensky, 2009). Also, collective action has received far less attention than has prejudice reduction from social psychologists (at least those working in the dominant tradition of 'psychological social psychology' rather than 'sociological social psychology'). Nonetheless, social psychology's focus on how the social context influences individual psychological processes has provided important insights on the processes that fuel and direct or undermine participation in collective action (see Simon & Klandermans, 2001; Reicher, 2004; Van Zomeren, Postmes, & Spears, 2008; Wright, 2001a, for reviews).

Social psychology has increasingly settled on a definition that locates collective action in the individual participant's intentions. Thus, a group member engages in *collective action* any time they are *acting as a representative of the group and the action is directed at improving the conditions of the entire group* (Wright, Taylor, & Moghaddam, 1990). This definition is consistent with the recognition that human action can be intergroup as well as interpersonal (Tajfel, 1982). Interpersonal behavior results when the self and the other are perceived in terms of their unique personal identities (characteristics that distinguish us as unique and separate from others). However, intergroup behavior occurs when the self and the others are perceived in terms of their collective identities (their memberships in different groups). Collective action is a specific case of intergroup behavior that is strategic in its intent to maintain or improve the ingroup's position, and can be contrasted with individual action, which involves efforts to improve one's personal position.

The issue of definition is not trivial. First, this definition differs from perspectives that describe collective action as necessarily involving people acting in concert and in a similar way. The current definition sees collective action as based on neither the number of participants nor the specific content or eventual outcome of the action. Thus, collective action can be engaged in by a single individual as long as the intent is to create change for the collective. Conversely, joint action by a large group where each individual is motivated by personal self-interest would not qualify as collective action.

This has important implications for several theories of collective action participation. For example, Stürmer and Simon's (2004) Dual-Pathway Model proposes that one pathway to participation results from three motives (Klandermans, 1997). One of these motives is

the possibility of positive change in ingroup status (the *collective motive*). However, the other two broad classes of motives focus on the personal concerns about admiration or ridicule by meaningful others, and direct personal costs or rewards, like loss of time or money, getting hurt, or having fun. Hornsey and colleagues (2006) add another personal concern that can motivate participation; the desire to publicly express one's personal values. Thus, one might participate in a group action to meet personal goals or improve one's personal situation. However, the more participation is motivated by these individualistic concerns, the less it is actually *collective* and the less it meets the current definition of collective action.

The current analysis also differs in important ways from the sociological perspectives which tie collective action to participation in *social movements*. A social movement represents a specific form of collective action, marked by sustained and organized action by a fairly large group of people (see McAdam, McGarthy, & Zald, 1996). Although an analysis of collective action, as defined here, is clearly relevant to understanding participation in social movements, the present analysis also considers episodic, normative, and spontaneous actions, and action engaged in by single individuals or small groups. At the same time, this analysis will not consider the additional specific conditions and resources necessary to build and sustain a social movement.

BRIEF HISTORICAL OVERVIEW

Group-based inequality is a near ubiquitous feature of social life. Some groups hold positions of power and advantage while others are stigmatized and disadvantaged. Although some members of dominant groups feel guilt and even outrage about their privilege and may support efforts to reduce inequality (see Leach, Iyer, & Pedersen, 2006), the dominant response of those with privilege is to defend it (see Morton, Postmes, Haslam, et al., 2009; Sidanius & Pratto, 1999; Tajfel, 1982).

Even advantaged group members who support social change are often inspired by appeals from the subordinated group. Thus, it is largely the province of the disadvantaged to initiate social change. Although illegitimate subordination is almost always met with some kind of resistance (Reicher, 2004; Reicher & Haslam, 2006), dramatic rapid social change often results from disruptive collective actions.

Most early discussions of collective action reflected sentiments made famous in LeBon's (1895/1947) analysis of crowd behavior. Group action was described as devolution into irrational, instinctive, antisocial behavior, with participants losing the self-control that constrained individuals acting alone. Although most social psychological analyses have abandoned this view (see Tajfel & Turner, 1979; Reicher, 2004), it remains common in popular representations of social protests and political demonstrations.

Research dating back to the classic study of Stouffer, Suchman, DeVinney, et al. (1949) demonstrates that rather than *objective* disadvantage, it is the *subjective* experience of disadvantage that best predicts dissatisfaction and subsequent action. This recognition lead to the development of Relative Deprivation Theory (see Walker & Smith, 2002) and a focus on social comparison as the engine driving collective action. That is, assertive action on behalf of our group results from the feelings of deprivation that accompany comparisons we make with better-off outgroups (e.g., Mummendey, Kessler, Klink, et al., 1999; Smith & Ortiz, 2002). Research on Relative Deprivation Theory also explored the cognition/emotion distinction, showing that collective action participation is more strongly influenced by emotions like anger, frustration, and resentment that emerge from feelings of injustice, than by the mere recognition of group deprivation and cold evaluations of injustice (e.g., Smith & Ortiz, 2002, see also Van Zomeren, Postmes, & Spears, 2008)

However, the most significant advance in the social psychology of collective action was provided by Tajfel and Turner's (1979) Social Identity Theory (SIT). Although the *Social Identity approach* and theories like Self-Categorization Theory (SCT; Turner, Hogg, Oakes, et al., 1987) that emerged from it have had a powerful impact on a range of topics, describing the psychological underpinnings of collective action was a primary theme of the original theory. SIT continues to provide a clear and coherent framework on the topic and has inspired numerous valuable elaborations over the last 30 years.

ANALYSIS OF THE CURRENT STATE OF KNOWLEDGE

While group-based inequality is nearly universal, direct collective action is relatively rare. The explanation for this can be found in the complexity of psychological mechanisms that must align to overcome the barriers to direct action.

The psychological determinants of collective action

This section of the chapter will describe an organizing framework that is based in SIT, and includes the key components of much of the theorizing and research that has followed (see Stürmer & Simon, 2004; Van Zomeren Postmes, & Spears 2008; Wright, 2001a). In this framework, collective action is seen to emerge from the dynamic interplay between four critical psychological processes. The first is *collective identity*. By definition, taking action on the ingroup's behalf requires that the actor have a sense that membership in the group represents a meaningful aspect of the self. However, in addition to this sense of collective identity, the decision to engage in collective action is also impacted by the individual's assessment and the individual's assessment of three *socio-structural variables*.

Since one response to membership in a disadvantaged group is to ignore group interests and attempt to improve one's personal position, collective action is much more likely when individuals are unable or unwilling to move across the boundaries between the groups. Thus, *perceived boundary impermeability* is a key predictor of collective action. Both Relative Deprivation Theory and SIT describe the *assessment of the legitimacy* of the ingroup's lower status and the resulting feelings of injustice when that position is thought to be illegitimate as a critical determinant of collective action. Finally, SIT proposes that collective action is most likely to emerge when the illegitimate status differences between the groups are perceived to be *unstable*. Others have expanded on the concept of instability utilizing the concepts of collective efficacy (see Van Zomeren, Postmes, & Spears 2008) or collective control (see Wright, 2001a), but it appears that endorsement of collective action is often associated with the belief that meaningful change is possible. This section reviews the literature on each of these four critical psychological processes, but it will also describe ways that they interact in a dynamic and complex relationship of mutual influence.

Collective identity

By definition, action on the ingroup's behalf requires recognition of one's group membership and some sense that membership represents a meaningful aspect of the self. That is, the group must provide a meaningful collective identity. When this collective identity becomes the primary self-representation, a process of depersonalization occurs such that *me* as independent individual is replaced with *me* as interchangeable exemplar. My thoughts and actions now reflect my understanding of the normative values, beliefs, and actions of the ingroup. This change should not be misunderstood as some kind of loss of self. Collective identities can be experienced as profoundly meaningful self-representations. What changes is not the degree to which the self is meaningful, but which meaningful self – the collective or the personal self – guides thought and action. Collective action, therefore, requires that the relevant collective identity eclipse personal identity as the current self-representation.

The process by which this happens is constrained not only by the strength of one's personal identity, but also by the strength of other competing collective identities that provide alternative self-representations. Not only are there numerous domains of collective self-representation (e.g., tribal, political, national, occupational), within each are numerous levels, including smaller *subcategories* and more inclusive *superordinate* categories (Turner, Hogg, Oakes, et al., 1987). At times, identification with subcategories can undermine interest in collective action, while at other times it enhances interest. For example, Condor (1986) found that women who identified with the subgroup 'traditional women' showed little interest in collective action on behalf of women. Conversely, Stürmer and Simon (2004) showed that identification with the subgroup 'gay activists' was a better predictor of action to advance gay rights than was identification with the broader gay community.

Self-representation as a member of a superordinate group that includes both the disadvantaged and advantaged groups can also influence collective action. Encouraging members of two groups to identify with a superordinate category can reduce intergroup prejudice (see Gaertner & Dovidio, 2000). For example, inter-ethnic prejudice can be reduced when members of different ethnic groups focus on their shared national identity. However, this can also reduce collective action by the disadvantaged group (Wright & Lubensky, 2009), as the superordinate national identity replaces identification with the disadvantaged ethnic group.

A collective identity alone, however, is not sufficient to inspire collective action. As defined here, collective action represents a specific form of group-based behavior. It is a response to perceived group disadvantage or threat – collective action involves efforts to improve the relative status of the ingroup or to ward off perceived threats to the status of the ingroup. Thus, collective action requires the recognition that the ingroup is threatened or disadvantaged in some way. This recognition often results from a process of group-based social comparison where the ingroup's current situation is compared to that of a higher status outgroup or to the ingroup at a time when the current threat did not exist. The discussion that follows considers first how it is that one specific ingroup can become one's primary self-representation, and second how social comparison processes can lead us to perceive that collective identity as threatened, or not.

Tajfel (1982) described two factors: the degree to which current environmental cues make that self-representation salient, and the chronic accessibility of the group membership for the particular individual. Self-Categorization Theory (SCT; e.g., Turner, Hogg, Oakes, et al., 1987) describes these factors in terms of category *fit* and *accessibility*.

Fit   Fit represents the degree to which a given categorization simplifies and organizes the social context. Thus, a given self-representation will become salient to the degree that the situation makes that collective identity *apparent* and *useful*. For example, many highly-publicized examples of disruptive collective action appear to follow 'trigger events.' These events are seldom the true *cause* of subsequent protest (see Klandermans, 1997). However, when group leaders or the media *frame* these events in intergroup terms, as a case of collective injustice, this heightens the salience of the relevant collective identity. Thus, *consciousness raising* (e.g., Taylor & McKirnan, 1984) or *identity framing* (Gamson, 1992) involves (through political rhetoric or social action) efforts to frame negative events as examples of collective injustice.

Accessibility   The relevance of a given collective identity is also influenced by its accessibility in the individual's mind. Accessibility can be *temporarily* increased by frequent use, or when that self-representation is relevant to current goals. However, *chronic* accessibility results when the individual strongly *identifies* with the group; when the group has enduring psychological significance for the individual. Chronically accessible ingroups can become the dominant

self-representation in a wide array of circumstances.

Ingroup identification has been shown to be critical prerequisite to collective action among a wide range of groups, including ethnic minorities in the United States (Deaux, Reid, Martin, et al., 2006; Wright & Tropp, 2002), the women's movement (Condor, 1986), the Gray Panthers, the fat acceptance and the gay rights movements (Stürmer & Simon, 2004), union members (e.g., Blader, 2007), citizen groups (Drury & Riecher, 2005), and laboratory created groups (Blair & Jost, 2003). As summarized nicely by Doosje and Ellemers (1997), "'die-hard" members are more predisposed to act in terms of the group, and make sacrifices for it, than are "fair-weather" members' (p. 358).

Fit and accessibility   Although the conceptual distinction has proven useful, fit and accessibility are intimately related. For example, enduring features of the intergroup structure influence a group's ability to attract strong identification. A group's relative numerical size, for example, influences its current salience and ability to attract identification. Minority status (e.g., being the lone women in a room full of men) can make group membership temporarily salient. Also, a group whose size allows it to simultaneously meet competing needs for differentiation from others (distinctiveness) and inclusion with others (belongingness) can attract strong identification (see Brewer, 2009).

A group's relative status also influences its capacity to attract identification. Generally, we seek to be part of groups that compare well with other groups in order to enhance our self-esteem. Thus, high-status groups can attract strong identification. This creates a dilemma. Groups most in need of disruptive collective actions – low-status groups – contribute less positively to self-esteem, making them less able to attract strong identification from members. However, it is clear that low status does not preclude the possibility of strong ingroup identification. Schmitt and Branscombe (2002) provide compelling evidence that perceiving pervasive discrimination against one's low-status ingroup can paradoxically lead to strong ingroup identification.

What is perhaps most interesting is the flexibility of the self-categorization processes. Our social world can be 'carved up' in many ways. Although we often experience the currently salient intergroup distinction as powerful and enduring, it is, in fact, often a highly flexible and fleeting self-representation. When situations change, those who were ingroup members become outgroup members, and *vice versa*. New categorizations bring new norms that legitimize subordination of others who were previously ingroup members. Similarly, those who were members of the dominant outgroup can become comrades with and defenders of those who were once subordinated (see Reicher, 2004).

However, when a psychologically meaningful social group provides the primary basis for self-definition and thus becomes the guide for action, collective action is but one of many possible group-based behaviors. Specifically, collective action emerges as a response to perceived group threat or disadvantage. Thus, we must consider how a relevant collective identity comes to be seen as threatened or disadvantaged.

Intergroup social comparisons A strong and salient collective identity provides the foundation for another essential element in the collective action process – intergroup social comparisons. When a collective self-representation is dominant, self-understanding and self-evaluation are now based on comparisons with other groups rather than individuals. If these intergroup comparisons reveal that the ingroup holds a chronic position of disadvantage, the resulting threat to collective identity brings the group member one step closer to action.

However, in some cases, increasing the salience of group membership does not increase collective action (e.g., Lalonde & Silverman, 1994; Wright, 2001b). This may result because a collective self-representation can also inspire *intragroup* rather than *intergroup* comparisons. Smith, Spears, and

Owen (1994) argue that making salient a disadvantaged ingroup can also heighten attention to one's personal position *within* the group as well as the ingroup's lower status relative to the outgroup. Which form of comparison is most likely depends on whether *the ingroup is made salient within the context of a clearly defined intergroup relationship* (Wright, 1997). Only when the ingroup stands in contrast (even opposition) to a relevant outgroup, will a salient collective identity produce intergroup comparisons.

Thus, a salient collective identity, while necessary, is not sufficient to ensure collective action. When will the disadvantaged group be seen as standing in contrast to a dominant outgroup? This brings us to the second key process in the emergence of collective action.

Assessment of sociostructural variables

For comparisons with the dominant outgroup to seem appropriate and for these comparisons to inspire a direct challenge to the *status quo*, disadvantaged group members' assessment of three aspects of the social structure are critical (Tajfel & Turner, 1979). Are individuals locked into their membership in the disadvantaged group (i.e., are the boundaries between groups *permeable*)? Is the unequal status of the two groups justified (i.e., are current intergroup relations *legitimate*)? Can the ingroup's position be improved (i.e., is the current state of affairs *stable*)? These assessments of boundary permeability, legitimacy, and stability determine whether comparisons with the advantaged outgroup make sense and whether a collective response is appropriate.

Boundary permeability: Mobility or change

One response to group-based inequality is to try to improve one's personal position by leaving the low-status ingroup. While the existing social psychological research and theorizing has focused on one form of upward mobility and has used the terms *social mobility* and *individual mobility* synonymously, I propose that there are two forms of mobility: the traditional conception of *individual mobility* involving efforts by the individual to move out of one group into another (see, Derks, van Laar, & Ellemers 2009; Ellemers, Spears, & Doosje, 1997; Jetten, Iyer, Tsivrikos, et al. 2008; Reicher & Haslam, 2006; Verkuyten & Reijerse, 2008; Wright, 2001a); and *social mobility* which involves focusing on a larger superordinate category and working to improve one's personal position within this larger social group.

When the boundaries dividing the two groups are perceived to be permeable, *individual mobility* seems possible, and disadvantaged group members may attempt to abandon their current ingroup in favor of a more secure and positively valued alternative group membership (see Wright, 2001b). Thus, individual mobility results from the belief that one can cross both the ingroup boundary ('I can leave') and the outgroup boundary ('I can join'). For example, a laborer dissatisfied with the working conditions on the shop floor can work hard, get additional education, and publicly endorse company rules in an effort to move up into management.

However, a second form of mobility – *social mobility* – involves attempting to deemphasize one's local collective identity, focusing instead on one's membership in a larger superordinate category, and working to improve one's personal status within this group. In this case, the assessment of boundary permeability involves only the ingroup. 'Can I leave (or deny) my collective identity?' To understand *social mobility* it is necessary to recognize that relations between groups at any given level of abstraction exist within a larger superordinate category that provides the frame of reference for the subgroups (Hornsey & Hogg, 2000; Mummendey & Wenzel, 1999; Turner, Hogg, Oakes, et al., 1987). For example, relations between ethnic groups are defined and understood within the values and rules of a larger social category – often a nation or collection of nations. Relations between Blacks and Whites are understood in terms of their shared membership in the American nation, just as First Nations/White relations are defined in terms of the Canadian nation. Social mobility involves attempting to ignore or deny the

relevance of group membership and focus exclusively on one's personal identity within the larger superordinate category. Thus, an African American or member of a First Nation attempts to ignore ethnic/racial categorization and focuses on personal success within the larger American or Canadian society.

Both *social* and *individual* mobility involve attempts to abandon or ignore one's current collective identity, making them psychologically incompatible with collective action (Derks, van Laar, & Ellemers, 2009; Ellemers, 2001). Thus, a collective action orientation is strengthened by the belief that, regardless of personal talent or effort, individual movement out of the disadvantaged ingroup is impossible (e.g., Reicher & Haslam, 2006; Wright, Taylor, & Moghaddam 1990). This perception of boundary impermeability results from two classes of perceived barriers: *external* and *internal*. External barriers involve physical characteristics that are difficult to ignore or change (e.g., gender or race), structural or legal impediments (e.g., national borders, institutional discrimination), or practical concerns (e.g., time or financial costs). Internal barriers are psychological. Moral obligation, personal commitments, and/or strong ingroup identification can make it impossible to imagine leaving or denying one's ingroup, even when external barriers are weak (e.g., Blair & Jost, 2003). The individual's relative status within the ingroup and their personal competence can also influence assessments of boundary permeability. High status and highly competent members may be more likely to see social or individual mobility as an option (Wright, Taylor, & Moghaddam, 1990).

The importance of psychological barriers makes clear the mutual relationship between boundary permeability and collective identity. A strong collective identity makes it difficult to consider alternative self-representations, be it membership in a higher status group (individual mobility) or focusing solely on personal identity (social mobility). Reciprocally, assessments of boundary permeability can influence ingroup identification. When abandoning the ingroup and/or joining the outgroup seems unlikely or impossible, commitment to the current ingroup is heightened as is motivation to improve its position. Conversely, believing that upward mobility is possible can lead to dissociation from the disadvantaged ingroup (Ellemers, 2001; Lalonde & Silverman, 1994). Thus, there is a reciprocal causal relationship between strength of collective identity and assessments of boundary permeability

Boundary permeability is often characterized as a dichotomy between *open* and *closed* groups (e.g, Van Zomeren, Postmes, & Spears2008). However, in contemporary North American society (and many other intergroup contexts) the system is neither entirely meritocratic, nor is upward mobility impossible. Instead, barriers and restrictions result in only a small percentage of the qualified members of the disadvantaged group being able to gain access to advantaged positions, creating a situation described as *tokenism* (Wright et al., 1990). A number of studies (e.g., Barreto, Ellemers, & Palacios, 2004; Reynolds, Oakes, Haslam, et al. 2000; Wright, 2001b) reveal that, while complete boundary impermeability produces strong interest in collective action, when as few as two percent of the qualified members of the disadvantaged group are allowed access to advantaged positions collective action is replaced with a preference for individual action. The slightest hint of permeability appears to undermine collective action. Tokenism may have this effect because it makes salient personal identities, encouraging interpersonal comparisons with the few successful tokens. Further, tokenism may obfuscate assessments of the legitimacy and stability of the ingroup's low-status position (Wright, 1997).

Cognitive alternatives

Although believing one cannot leave the ingroup makes individual or social mobility impossible, boundary impermeability does not invariably produce collective action. Collective action also requires that the individual be able to imagine a situation where the ingroup's status and treatment is improved. Tajfel and Turner (1979) describe this as perceiving *cognitive* *alternatives*. This belief that things can (and should) be better is primarily determined by perceptions of current intergroup relations in terms of *legitimacy* and *stability*.

Legitimacy: Politicized identity, emotions, and delegitimizing the status quo

Justice is a central theme in theories of intergroup relations (e.g., Jost & Major, 2001; Walker & Smith, 2002) and social movements (e.g., Gamson, 1992; Klandermans, 1997). Inequality is not always understood to be unfair, and as long as the current social hierarchy is perceived as legitimate, efforts to create social change are unlikely (e.g., Blader, 2007) and low-status groups may even justify and support the system that subjugates them (see Jost & Major, 2001). Only when the legitimacy of the status quo is questioned are the seeds of collective action sown.

Perceived illegitimacy can inspire collective action in two ways. First, illegitimacy is the catalyst for a collective identity to *politicize* – for identification with a broader societal ingroup to be transformed into identification with a smaller group defined by its struggle with the outgroup seen as responsible for the ingroup's subordination (Simon & Klandermans, 2001). Stürmer and Simon (2004) review evidence that identification with politicized groups like the Gay Rights movement, the Grey Panthers, or the Fat Acceptance movement is a much better predictor of collective action participation than is identification with the larger disadvantaged groups which these organizations represent (i.e., gay men, older people, fat people). Thus, like boundary permeability, legitimacy assessments share a mutual relationship with collective identification. Ingroup identification spurs assessments of legitimacy, and the resulting perceptions of group-based injustice can transform collective identification into a more potent politicized form.

Illegitimacy also spurs collective action by inciting strong negative emotions. Relative Deprivation Theory holds that emotions like resentment, frustration, and anger result from feelings of *entitlement*. When the ingroup is thought to deserve more, resulting feelings of resentment, frustration, and anger spur disruptive collective action (e.g., Mummendey, Kessler, Klink, et al., 1999; Wright, Taylor, & Moghaddam1990). Similarly, guided by the burgeoning literature on intergroup emotions, a new wave of research has shown that feelings of group-based anger can inspire confrontational action tendencies that underpin disruptive collective action (e.g., Smith, Cronin, & Kessler, 2008; Van Zomeren, Spears, Fischer et al. 2004).

Since collective action hinges on perceived illegitimacy, it is not surprising that most stable systems have elaborate ideologies that justify the existing social order, nor is it surprising that these ideologies are strongly endorsed by those benefiting from that social order (see Sidanius & Pratto, 1999). Religious doctrine, class and caste systems, individualism, and capitalism have all been used to legitimize the subordination of some groups, while defending the privilege of others. For example, the Western doctrine of *meritocracy*, establishes individual merit as the only justifiable basis for advancement. This ideology not only confers moral superiority to social mobility over collective action, it also explains and justifies the low status held by members of some groups – they simply lack the abilities or motivation to move up. Similarly, the doctrine of absolutism, which dominated in Europe from the seventeenth through nineteenth centuries, described the unrestrained power and wealth of a small nobility as ordained by god and, therefore, unquestionably justified. In addition, these belief structures can be seductive even to those they subjugate because they appeal to another strong motive, the desire to believe that the world we live in is stable and predictable (e.g., Kay, Gaucher, Napier, et al., 2008).

Thus, it is also not surprising that efforts to mobilize disadvantaged groups usually involve tactics and rhetoric explicitly designed to undermine the dominant legitimizing ideology. Consciousness raising efforts involve showing not only that the ingroup is disadvantaged, but that this disadvantage results from illegitimate oppression by an advantaged outgroup (see Martin,

Brickman, & Murray, 1984; Wright & Lubensky, 2009). The construction of negative stereotypes about the outgroup can be an important part of building a strong collective action orientation (Reynolds, Oakes, Haslam, et al., 2000). Stott and Drury (2004) describe negative outgroup stereotypes as the 'ideological justification … for collective conflict' (p. 20). Simon and Klandermans (2001) argue that making adversarial attributions towards an opponent 'from which "we" emerge as the innocent victims or good guys and "they" as the perpetrators or bad guys' (p. 325) is critical to forming the politicized identity that leads to collective action. Thus, social change efforts involve simultaneous attempts to delegitimize the ideologies supporting current inequalities and legitimization of an alternative narrative describing the outgroup as the oppressor.

Stability: Perceiving collective control If the ingroup's low status is thought to be immutable, collective action will seem unreasonable, even foolish. Thus, interest in collective action also requires that potential participants see change as possible. Tajfel and Turner (1979) describe this as *perceived instability*. Social movements theorists like Gamson (1992) have also described *agency frames* as the belief that change is possible. Similar to Bandura's (1997) notion of *collective efficacy*, agency refers to the extent to which group members feel capable of producing action that can reduce or remove the injustice they face (see also, Van Zomeren, Postmes, & Spears, 2008).

Although similar, *agency* (or *collective efficacy*) and *perceived instability* are not identical. Wright (2001a) described the distinction in terms of *perceived control*. In order to believe that one's group has control one must believe: (a) that social change is contingent upon behavior (i.e., that the situation is modifiable), and (b) that my group in particular can execute the behaviors necessary to produce that change (see also, Mummendey, Kessler, Klink, et al., 1999). The first judgment corresponds with *perceived stability*, and the second with *agency* (or *collective efficacy*). Thus, perceived *collective control* can be undermined by a belief that the system is unresponsive to actions (stability), or that the ingroup lacks the resources or abilities necessary to effect change (lack of efficacy).

This distinction has several implications. Clearly, perceiving the system as stable makes the question of agency irrelevant. Thus, efforts to build collective action must first undermine the perceived inevitability of the current social order. One interesting way this happens is observing successful collective action by other low-status groups (see Reicher, 2004). Successful liberation movements in Africa and India may have provided evidence that change is possible for those who organized the civil rights movement in the United States, and similarly the success of that movement may have influenced growth in the anti-apartheid movement in South Africa and the women's movement in North America. The success of others provides evidence of instability (Martin, Brickman, & Murray, 1984).

However, group members must also believe that their ingroup has the resources and capacities to influence a malleable system. Here, Resource Mobilization theories (e.g., McAdam, McGarthy, & Zald, 1996) seem highly relevant. This perspective describes the presence or absence of needed resources as the key determinant of collective action. While early theorizing focused exclusively on the objective presence of resources and had little interest in psychological variables, recent versions (e.g., Gamson, 1992; Klandermans, 1997) focus on both objective availability of resources and subjective expectation that the ingroup can effectively utilize them.

Boundary permeability, legitimacy, and collective control

Although perceptions of boundary permeability, illegitimacy, and control represent distinct assessments, in most situations they will strongly influence one another. For example, a system allowing no movement between groups will likely be seen as less just than one that allows even minimal individual mobility (Wright, 2001b). Similarly, individual mobility will be much less attractive if the advantaged group's position is felt to be entirely illegitimate. Thus, boundary impermeability can heighten perceived illegitimacy, and perceived illegitimacy can heighten psychological boundary impermeability. Similarly, when the ingroup's low status is illegitimate and mobility impossible, one can have confidence that other ingroup members will join the collective action, thus increasing collective efficacy (Wright, 2001b). Likewise, clear evidence that the current situation is about to change (high instability) can inspire psychological processes that make the new alternative appear increasingly legitimate (see Pettigrew, 1961).

Thus, a number of psychological processes (too numerous to fully examine here) facilitate a convergence of these three assessments to produce either a strong collective action orientation (i.e., strong collective identity, clear boundary impermeability, illegitimacy, and collective control), or a general acceptance (even defense) of the social hierarchy (i.e., perceived boundary permeability, legitimacy, and lack of control). Kessler and Mummendey (2002) provide evidence that judgments of permeability, legitimacy, and control, along with collective identification form a 'stable configuration of beliefs' emerging through parallel processes and mutual influence (see also, Verkuyten and Reijerse, 2008).

Nonetheless, it is also true that these three assessments need not always align. For example, the current status hierarchy can be considered illegitimate but uncontrollable. Smith, Cronin, & Kessler (2008) demonstrated that perceptions that the ingroup is unfairly disadvantaged and that things will likely get worse are associated with feelings of sadness (and perhaps fear), which do not lead to collective action participation, but rather to withdrawal and avoidance. Thus, feeling both unjustly treated and pessimistic undermines a collective action orientation, producing disgruntled acceptance.

Summary

Much of social psychology's contemporary theorizing on the determinants of collective action is rooted in Relative Deprivation Theory and SIT. A wide array of research has supported the importance of collective identity, boundary permeability, legitimacy/ justice, and collective control (stability/ efficacy) as the mechanisms that inspire and support collective action, and a number of theoretical accounts have unpacked, elaborated, and expanded on these ideas. For example, the concept of politicized collective identity (Simon & Klandermans, 2001) provides a clearer understanding of the form of collective identification most directly associated with collective action participation. Work on tokenism (e.g., Wright, 2001b) has broadened the discussion of boundary permeability. Recent integrations of intergroup emotion theory (e.g., Smith, Cronin, & Kessler, 2008; Leach Iyer & Pedersen 2006; Van Zomeren, Spears, Fischer, et al., 2004) have strengthened and deepened our understanding of the role of legitimacy. Finally, the complex relationships between these variables have been brought into sharper focus leading to the conclusion that these four key variables interact in a dynamic process of mutual influence either to motivate collective action or to steer individuals towards inaction or individual action aimed at improving one's personal position (see Figure 35.1).

Forms of collective action

So far, we have examined what leads group members to collective action, with no direct consideration of the form that action might take. Collective action can range from mass protest by larger social movements, to the actions by small ad hoc groups, to individuals acting alone. Behaviors can range from education and consciousness raising, to lobbying, negotiation and voting, to protest letters, petitions, and even riots and bombings. There is not sufficient space here to consider each of this broad array of actions individually. However, one distinction seems particularly relevant – the distinction between actions that disrupt and threaten the rules of the current system and those designed only to alter the position of groups within that system.

Normative versus nonnormative action

Wright, Taylor, & Moghaddam (1990) proposed a distinction between collective actions that conform to the rules of the larger social system and those that do not. This perspective is consistent with SCTs observation that relations between groups are defined within a shared superordinate group (Turner, Hogg, Oakes, et al., 1987). It is the norms of this superordinate group that define action by one of the constituent groups as normative

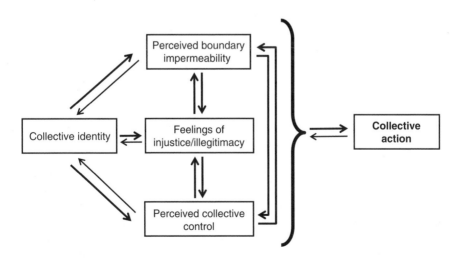

Figure 35.1   The psychological determinants of collective action.

or nonnormative. Thus, while actors may perceive their actions as appropriate, legitimate, or moral based on norms within their local subgroup, they will also know whether these actions are consistent (or not) with the norms of the more inclusive group. For example, although suicide bombings may be legitimate and normative within the subgroups engaged in this practice, they know that this action is outside the norms of larger societal community. Note, this normative/nonnormative distinction is not simply between violent and non violent action. Nonviolent civil disobedience, for example, can be nonnormative. Alternatively, some intergroup contexts (e.g., a hockey game) expect violence as normative intergroup behavior.

Nonnormative actions are, by definition, more disruptive than normative action as they challenge not only the current status of subgroups, but also the means by which group status is determined. These kinds of novel and disruptive actions will obviously draw greater attention from the advantaged outgroup and will demand a response. Normative collective action can also evoke resistance, as it too challenges the status of the advantaged group. However, it usually involves less risk than nonnormative action. Thus, when a normative avenue is available and perceived to be effective, this avenue is likely to be engaged first (Wright, 2001a). In addition, strong endorsement of normative collective action is likely when collective identity is strong, and the current group status arrangement is thought to be legitimate but changeable, because imbedded in this assessment is an acceptance of the rules by which group status is determined. However, if normative tactics prove ineffective or the advantaged group is seen to be engaging in nonnormative actions to maintain their power, the legitimacy of the system is compromised and normative may give way to nonnormative action.

Recently, Reicher, Stott, and Drury have refocused attention on the fluid and dynamic relationship between the form that collective actions will take and the content of collective identity (e.g., Drury & Reicher, 2005; Reicher, 2004). They describe how the militancy and disruptiveness of group actions depends on the norms and values associated with the collective identity that emerges within a group, and what specific collective identity will emerge is, in part, determined by the actions of the outgroup. For example, Stott and colleagues (2007) have shown that the violence of British football hooligans is, in part, a direct and systematic response to the actions of the police who seek to control these groups. When the actions of the police serve to define groups of young football fans as 'hooligans' and reinforce the perception that they are likely to act violently, these fans take on the proffered self-representation and respond to police 'provocation' with violence. However, when the police act in ways that provide an alternative self-definition, as just 'supporters of their football team,' these young fans are less likely to be violent. The actions and attitudes of the authority play a major role in shaping the self-representation (collective identity) of group members, thus strongly influencing whether collective action will be violent or not.

Drury and Reicher (2005) extend this argument, focusing on ways that collective actions change over time in response to a changing intergroup context. Current collective action results from a dynamic process involving not only the actions of the outgroup, but also the ingroup's own previous actions. A limited and normative protest can morph into disruptive nonnormative action as the group's collective identity becomes increasingly politicized and radicalized when the outgroup (or agents of the outgroup, such as the police) responds to their past actions with resistance and increasingly nonnormative tactics. This radicalization is often ironically the result of both growing feelings of empowerment, as group members effectively express their collective identity and values through their actions, and growing frustration and resentment at the escalation of the outgroup's efforts to subvert and suppress these expressions. Thus, normative action gives way to nonnormative action because a new collective identity emerges from changing perceptions of the intergroup context that itself results from the actions and reactions of both groups.

To date, Drury, Stott, Reicher, and colleagues' research on this dynamic approach has focused primarily on crowd behavior and actions opposed by the police. However, the value of this approach in describing not only when and why collective action occurs but how different forms of collective actions will emerge and evolve over time suggests that this approach should play an increasingly important role in our understanding of social change.

Promising innovative directions

In addition to the important elaborations and developments in the SIT and Relative Deprivation traditions already discussed, several other recent additions to the literature are likely to be important in the next wave of research and theorizing. The first group of ideas focuses on motivators of collective action that may supplement and complement those already considered. The second set of ideas broaden the focus of collective action by considering the possibility that some members of the advantaged group may act as allies, and that third party audiences may also play a crucial role in shaping social change efforts. The final idea considers directly the relationship between prejudice reduction and the generation of collective action and comes to a perhaps unexpected conclusion.

Broadening the array of motivations

A number of lines of recent work have explored several additional motives that may also guide collective action. For example, several research programs have uncovered contexts where the relationship between collective action participation and beliefs about its likely effectiveness are inconsistent or small (e.g., Hornsey, Blackwood, Louis, et al., 2006; Kessler and Mummendey, 2002), and several interesting explanations for this have been forwarded.

It's personal (not collective) action

Stürmer and Simon's (2004) Dual-Pathway Model provides two potential explanations. The first relates to the very definition of collective action. That is, what appears to be collective action may not be collective at all. Since collective action is often measured in terms of participation (or intention to participate) in joint action with other ingroup members, it is possible that these actions are not motivated by collective concerns at all. At times, individualistic concerns about approval from others or opportunities for personal rewards, like having fun with friends (Stürmer & Simon, 2004), or the desire to publicly express cherished personal values (Hornsey, Blackwood, Louis, et al., 2006), motivate participation in group action. In these cases, the effectiveness of this action in changing the ingroup's status is not relevant, as participation is motivated by individual not group concerns.

Affirming collective identity

Stürmer and Simon's (2004) second explanation focuses on the power of ingroup identification to overwhelm and make unimportant beliefs about the effectiveness of a given action. Collective action provides an opportunity to demonstrate and instantiate a valued collective identity 'as a living agent, a locus of possibility' (Drury & Reicher, 2005, p. 54). Collective action can affirm the existence, legitimacy, and distinctiveness of the relevant collective identity, and these affirmations can, in and of themselves, be enough to motivate action.

'Rallying the troops'

Hornsey and colleagues (2006) point out that collective action can also be motivated by *intragroup* concerns. Collective actors may realize they stand little chance of creating meaningful change, but nonetheless expect they will inspire other ingroup members to join or continue the fight. This point is reminiscent of descriptions of consciousness-raising, where the intended audience of collective action is the ingroup, and the intent is not to produce social change but rather to have ingroup members recognize existing boundary impermeability, illegitimacy, and collective control.

Moral conviction Skitka and colleagues have recently extended the concept of illegitimacy as a motivator of action by exploring the particular power of *moral conviction* – the 'strong and absolute belief that something is right or wrong, moral or immoral' (Skitka & Baumen, 2008: 31). Moral convictions compel action, more so than other strongly held beliefs, because they describe what one 'ought' to do. When something carries the mark of immorality, no other explanation is needed for opposing it, considering alternative perspectives will be strongly resisted, and failing to oppose it in favor of other considerations (e.g., personal preferences, normative conventions, potential costs) will evoke regret, shame, or guilt. Thus, if the current ingroup position can be framed as a moral violation or as resulting from immoral acts by the outgroup, taking action to rectify the situation becomes a moral mandate, making other concerns (e.g., stability, efficacy) less relevant.

Allies in the outgroup

Research has also begun to examine when advantaged group members might support disadvantaged groups engaged in collective action. Those who see the disadvantaged group's low status as a direct result of past discrimination by the ingroup (Leach, Iyer & Pedersen, 2006), and those who are most able to take the perspective of the disadvantaged outgroup (Mallet, Huntsinger, Sinclair, et al., 2008) appear most likely to become allies with the disadvantaged group's efforts. However, when there is ambiguity surrounding the legitimacy of group differences, such as under conditions of tokenism (when only a small percentage of qualified disadvantaged group members are given access to advantaged positions), support for social change may only emerge when there are clear messages focusing the attention on the plight of the disadvantaged group (Wright & Richard, 2010). Finally, advantaged group support is most likely when the recognition of ingroup culpability lead to feelings of collective shame or moral outrage. The power of feelings

of collective guilt to motivate meaningful support for the disadvantaged group remains an issue of disagreement among researchers (e.g., Iyer, Schmader, & Lickel, 2007; Mallet, Huntsinger, Sinclair, et al., 2008).

Influencing third, parties

Another exciting addition has been the recognition that social change often involves more than two groups. In addition to the focal ingroup and the relevant opponent, there are often third parties (e.g., the general public, the international community, etc.) who may be seen as potential impediments, or allies in social change efforts (see Simon & Klandermans, 2001). Thus, these third parties can also be important targets of influence (see also Hornsey, Blackwood, Louis, et al., 2006).

Collective action and prejudice reduction: Two solitudes

I began this chapter contrasting collective action and prejudice reduction as strategies for creating social change. I conclude by returning to this comparison. Prejudice reduction emphasizes changing 'hearts and minds' (improving attitudes) as the catalyst for social change, while collective action involves direct action designed to alter the group status hierarchy. Further, while most theories of prejudice recognize that members of all groups can (and do) feel negatively towards outgroups, prejudice reduction research has focused primarily on advantaged group members – those with the power to turn prejudice into discrimination. Work on collective action, by contrast, focuses primarily on disadvantaged groups.

At first glance, these strategies might appear complementary; one offering methods for improving the attitudes of the advantaged, the other informing efforts by the disadvantaged to build social movements. However, careful examination exposes fundamental contradictions. First, prejudice reduction approaches focus on creating harmony, while collective action has at its core intergroup conflict. Second, when we break from the traditional focus of the prejudice reduction literature on members of the dominant (advantaged) group and consider instead the psychology of the disadvantaged group, we find that many of the same psychological mechanisms are implicated in prejudice reduction and collective action, but in opposite ways. Prejudice reduction procedures usually call for perceptions of group boundaries as weak and unimportant and for the generation of positive regard for outgroup members. In direct contradiction of collective action theories, many models of prejudice reduction have emphasized reducing the focus on collective identity, focusing on group similarities, or identification with a larger superordinate category. Admittedly, several recent prejudice reduction models (e.g., the Brown & Hewstone, 2005, model of intergroup contact, and Wright and colleagues', 2005, inclusion of other in the self model) do not call for reducing the salience of group differences. However, even in these models, recognition of group differences and maintaining the salience of collective identity is primarily concerned with maintaining the salience of the other's (one's interaction partner's) collective identity in order that positive feelings about the individual interaction partner will be generalized to his or her group as a whole. The focus is not on maintaining the salience of one's own collective identity in an effort to strengthen connections and commitments to the ingroup and its interest. Rather, high salience of the other's collective identity is intended to strengthen one's connections with the outgroup.

Thus, for members of the disadvantaged groups the psychological requirements of prejudice reduction are, in many ways, directly contradictory to those required to initiate and sustain collective action. Members of disadvantaged groups cannot simultaneously have high and low identification with the ingroup. They cannot simultaneously be highly aware and largely unaware of their collective identity. They cannot be largely unaware of inequality between groups and at the same time recognize their group's relative disadvantage. They cannot see the boundaries between groups as both firm and impenetrable but also blurred and unimportant. They cannot simultaneously see the advantaged outgroup as a cooperative partner and also as a discriminating exploiter, nor can they see the intergroup relationship as both cooperative and adversarial. Therefore, it will be extremely difficult for disadvantaged group members to simultaneously be optimal participants in efforts to reduce prejudice, and also be assertive facilitators of collective action. Stated in more provocative manner: 'however well-intentioned they may be, many procedures used to reduce prejudice may also serve to undermine collective action by the disadvantaged group' (Wright & Lubensky, 2009: 303).

Finally, the focus on improving thoughts and feelings towards the outgroup that is the heart of prejudice reduction may be far too narrow. Members of the advantaged group may come to *like* members of the disadvantaged group while still failing to notice or question structural inequalities between the two groups (e.g., Saguy et al., 2009). In such cases, these advantaged group members may provide little support for efforts to reduce intergroup inequality (e.g., Dixon, Durrheim, & Tredoux, 2007), while at the same time their superficial demonstrations of positive attitudes towards the disadvantaged group may disarm social change efforts (Wright & Lubensky, 2009; see also Hopkins & Kahani-Hopkins, 2006).

Thus, in addition to the numerous innovative investigations of the causes, the forms, and the outcomes of collective action, what looms large on the horizon is a need to consider the competing psychologies of collective action and prejudice reduction. To date, these two areas of research have largely been considered quite separately and uniting these two solitudes in intergroup relations research seems essential, as it is likely that in the end prejudice reduction and collective action are both necessary if we are to build more just and egalitarian societies.

SUMMARY AND CONCLUSIONS

Often intergroup inequality goes unaddressed, even unnoticed. It can inspire individual efforts to move out of the ranks of the disadvantaged and seek access to a more advantaged personal position, leaving the systemic inequality between groups unchanged. However, at times group members recognize that their disadvantage is collective in nature and respond with action intended to improve the general state of affairs for the group as a whole. Social psychological research and theorizing has shown that this type of action – collective action – emerges when four key psychological processes align. Of central importance is collective identification. Those who define themselves most clearly in terms of their membership in the relevant disadvantaged group are most likely to make intergroup comparisons and thus experience threats as collective in nature. They are also more likely to see improving the conditions of the ingroup as the only appropriate solution. A strong collective identity is also likely to facilitate the three assessments of the intergroup context that combine to support collective action: (a) the belief that the boundaries between the ingroup and more advantaged outgroups are impermeable – that individual mobility is not possible; (b) the belief that the ingroup's current position is undeserved – that their disadvantage is illegitimate; and (c) and the conviction that current situation is unstable – that change is possible. Through a dynamic and complex pattern of mutual influence, these three assessments can inspire the emotions as well as the sense of collective efficacy that motivate direct action. Thus, inaction and individual self-interest are replaced by collective action. Whether this action will be normative or non normative, violent or non violent, incidental or sustained depends on the strength and specific qualities of the beliefs and emotions that emerge from these assessments, the success or failure of initial efforts, as well as from the response of the relevant outgroup and its agents. Recent additions to the literature have highlighted the complexity of the phenomenon, investigating additional motives and considering more fully the role of members of the advantaged group and third parties as both audience and allies to collective action.

Given the ubiquity of group-based inequality, the substantial costs that can accompany violent and non normative collective action, and the dramatic societal change that can result from successful collective actions, this remains a critical area of study. The presence or absence of collective action efforts is a key determinant of the stability of discriminatory social systems. Thus, clarifying the psychological underpinnings of this critical form of social behavior should remain a vital project for social psychologists interested in understanding and reducing group-based inequality and social injustice.

REFERENCES

Bandura, A. (1997). *Self-efficacy: The exercise of control.* New York: Freeman.

Barreto, M., Ellemers, N., & Palacios, M. S. (2004). The backlash of token mobility: The impact of past group experiences on individual ambition and effort. *Personality and Social Psychology Bulletin, 30,* 1433–1445.

Blader, S. (2007). What leads organizational members to collectivize? Injustice and identification as precursors of union certification. *Organization Science, 18,* 108–126.

Blair, I., & Jost, J. (2003). Exit, loyalty, and collective action among workers in a simulated business environment: Interactive effects of group identification and boundary permeability. *Social Justice Research, 16,* 95–108.

Brewer, M. (2009). Motivations underlying ingroup identification: Optimal distinctiveness and beyond. In S. Otten, T. Kessler, & K. Sassenberg (Eds.), *Intergroup relations: The role of motivation and emotion* (pp. 3–22). New York: Psychology Press.

Brown, R., & Hewstone, M. (2005). An integrative theory of intergroup contact. In M. P. Zanna (Ed.), *Advances in experimental social psychology,* (Vol. 37, pp. 255–343). San Diego, CA: Elsevier Academic Press.

Condor, S. (1986) Sex role beliefs and 'traditional women': Feminists and intergroup perspectives. In S. Wilkinson (Ed.), *Feminist social psychology:*

Developing theory and practice. Milton Keynes: Open University Press.

Deaux, K., Reid, A., Martin, D., & Bikmen, N. (2006). Ideologies of diversity and inequality: Predicting collective action in groups varying in ethnicity and immigrant status. *Political Psychology, 27*, 123–146.

Derks, B., van Laar, C., & Ellemers, N. (2009). Working for the self or working for the group: How self- versus group affirmation affects collective behavior in low-status groups. *Journal of Personality and Social Psychology, 96*, 183–202.

Dixon, J.A., Durrheim, K., & Tredoux, C. (2007). Intergroup contact and attitudes toward the principle and practice of racial equality. *Psychological Science, 18*, 867–872.

Doosje, B., & Ellemers, N. (1997). Stereotyping under threat: The role of group identification. In R. Spears & P. J. Oakes (Eds.), *The social psychology of stereotyping and group life* (pp. 257–272). Oxford: Blackwell.

Drury, J., & Reicher, S. D. (2005). Explaining enduring empowerment: A comparative study of collective action and psychological outcomes. *European Journal of Social Psychology, 35*, 35–38.

Ellemers, N. (2001). Individual upward mobility and the perceived legitimacy of intergroup relations. *The psychology of legitimacy: Emerging perspectives on ideology, justice, and intergroup relations* (pp. 205–222). New York, NY US: Cambridge University Press.

Ellemers, N., Spears, R., & Doosje, B. (1997). Sticking together of falling apart: In-group identification as a psychological determinant of group commitment versus individual mobility. *Journal of Personality and Social Psychology, 72*, 617–626.

Gaertner S. L., & Dovidio, J. F. (2000). *Reducing intergroup bias: The common ingroup identity model.* Philadelphia, PA: Psychology Press.

Gamson, W. A. (1992). The social psychology of collective action. In A. D. Morris & C. McClurg Mueller (Eds.), *Frontiers in social movement theory* (pp. 53–76). New Haven, CT: Yale University Press.

Hopkins, N., & Kahani-Hopkins, V. (2006). Minority group members' theories of intergroup contact: A case study of British Muslims' conceptualizations of 'Islamophobia' and social change. *British Journal of Social Psychology, 45*, 245–264.

Hornsey, M., Blackwood, L., Louis, W., Fielding, K., Favor, K., Morton, T., et al. (2006). Why do people engage in collective action? Revisiting the role of perceived effectiveness. *Journal of Applied Social Psychology, 36*, 1701–1722.

Hornsey, M., & Hogg, M. (2000). Intergroup similarity and subgroup relations: Some implications for assimilation. *Personality and Social Psychology Bulletin, 26*, 948–958.

Iyer, A., Schmader, T., & Lickel, B. (2007). Why individuals protest the perceived transgressions of their country: The role of anger, shame, and guilt. *Personality and Social Psychology Bulletin, 33*, 572–587.

Jetten, J., Iyer, A., Tsivrikos, D., & Young, B. (2008). When is individual mobility costly? The role of economic and social identity factors. *European Journal of Social Psychology, 38*, 866–879.

Jost, J., & Major, B. (Eds.) (2001). *The Psychology of Legitimacy: Emerging Perspectives on Ideology, Justice, and Intergroup Relations.* Cambridge University Press.

Kay, A., Gaucher, D., Napier, J., Callan, M., & Laurin, K. (2008). God and the government: Testing a compensatory control mechanism for the support of external systems. *Journal of Personality and Social Psychology, 95*, 18–35.

Kessler, T., & Mummendey, A. (2002). Sequential or parallel processes? A longitudinal field study concerning determinants of identity-management strategies. *Journal of Personality and Social Psychology, 82*, 75–88.

Klandermans, B. (1997). *The social psychology of protest.* Oxford, England: Blackwell.

Lalonde, R. N., & Silverman, R. A. (1994). Behavioral preferences in response to social injustice: The effects of group permeability and social identity salience. *Journal of Personality and Social Psychology, 66*, 78–85.

LeBon, G. (1895, translated 1947). *The crowd: A study of the popular mind.* London: Ernest Benn.

Leach, C., Iyer, A., & Pedersen, A. (2006). Anger and guilt about ingroup advantage explain the willingness for political action. *Personality and Social Psychology Bulletin, 32*, 1232–1245.

Mallett, R., Huntsinger, J., Sinclair, S., & Swim, J. (2008). Seeing through their eyes: When majority group members take collective action on behalf of an outgroup. *Group Processes & Intergroup Relations, 11*, 451–470.

Martin, J., Brickman, P., & Murray, A. (1984). Moral outrage and pragmatism: Explanations for collective action. *Journal of Experimental Social Psychology, 20*, 484–496.

McAdam, D., McGarthy J. D., & Zald, M. N. (Eds.), (1996). *Comparative perspectives on social movements: Political opportunities, mobilizing structures, and cultural framings.* New York: Cambridge University Press.

Morton, T., Postmes, T., Haslam, S., & Hornsey, M. (2009). Theorizing gender in the face of social change: Is there anything essential about essentialism?. *Journal of Personality and Social Psychology, 96*, 653–664.

Mummendey, A., Kessler, T., Klink, A., & Mielke, R. (1999). Strategies to cope with negative social identity: Predictions by social identity theory and relative deprivation theory. *Journal of Personality and Social Psychology, 76*, 229–245.

Mummendey, A., Wenzel, M. (1999). Social discrimination and tolerance in intergroup relations: Reactions to intergroup difference. *Personality & Social Psychology Review, 3*, 158–174

Pettigrew, T. F. (1961). Social psychology and desegregation research. *American Psychologist, 16*, 105–112.

Reicher, S. D. (2004). The context of social identity: Domination, resistance and change. *Political Psychology, 25*, 921–946.

Reicher, S., & Haslam, S. A. (2006). Rethinking the psychology of tyranny: The BBC prison study. *British Journal of Social Psychology, 45*, 1–40.

Reynolds, K., Oakes, P., Haslam, A., Nolan, M., & Dolnik, L. (2000). Responses to powerlessness: Stereotyping as an instrument of social conflict. *Group Dynamics: Theory, Research and Practice, 4*, 275–290.

Saguy, T., Tausch, N., Dovidio, J. F., Pratto, F. (in press). The irony of harmony: Intergroup contact can produce false expectations for equality. *Psychological Science.*

Schmitt, M. T., & Branscombe, N. R. (2002). The meaning and consequences of perceived discrimination in disadvantaged and privileged social groups. In W. Stroebe & M. Hewstone (Eds.), *European Review of Social Psychology* (Vol. 12, pp. 167–199). Chichester, England: Wiley.

Sidanius, J., & Pratto, F. (1999). *Social dominance: An intergroup theory of social hierarchy and oppression.* New York: Cambridge University Press.

Simon, B., & Klandermans B. (2001). Politicized collective identity: A social psychological analysis. *American Psychologist, 56*, 319–331.

Skitka, L. J., & Bauman, C. W. (2008). Moral conviction and political engagement. *Political Psychology, 29*, 29–54.

Smith, H., Cronin, T., & Kessler, T. (2008). Anger, fear, or sadness: Faculty members' emotional reactions to collective pay disadvantage. *Political Psychology, 29*, 221–246.

Smith, H. J., & Ortiz, D. J (2002). Is it just me?: The different consequences of personal and group relative deprivation. In I. Walker & H. J. Smith (Eds.), *Relative deprivation: Specification, development and integration* (pp. 91–118). Cambridge: Cambridge University Press.

Smith, H., Spears, R., & Owen, M. (1994). "People like us": The influence of personal deprivation and group membership salience on justice evaluations. *Journal of Experimental Social Psychology, 30*, 277–299.

Stott, C., Adang, O., Livingstone, A., & Schreiber, M. (2007). Variability in the collective behaviour of England fans at Euro2004: 'Hooliganism', public order policing and social change. *European Journal of Social Psychology, 37*, 75–100.

Stott, C., & Drury, J. (2004). The importance of social structure and social interaction in stereotype consensus and content: Is the whole greater than the sum of its parts?. *European Journal of Social Psychology, 34*, 11–23.

Stouffer, S. A., Suchman, E. A., DeVinney, L. C., Star, S. A., & Williams, R. M. (1949). *The American soldier: Adjustment during army life* (Vol. 1). Princeton, NJ: Princeton University Press.

Stürmer, S., & Simon, B. (2004). Collective action: Towards a dual-pathway model. In W. Stroebe & M. Hewstone (Eds.), *European review of social psychology* (Vol. 15, pp. 59–99). Chichester, England: Wiley.

Tajfel, H. (Ed.) (1982). *Social identity and intergroup relations.* Cambridge: Cambridge University Press.

Tajfel, H., & Turner, J. C. (1979). An integrative theory of intergroup conflict. In W. G. Austin, & S. Worchel (Eds.), *The social psychology of intergroup relations* (pp. 33–48). Monterey, CA: Brooks/Cole.

Taylor, D. M., & McKirnan, D. J. (1984). A five stage model of intergroup relations. *British Journal of Social Psychology, 23*, 291–300.

Turner, J. C., Hogg, M. A., Oakes, P. J., Reicher, S. D., & Wetherell, M. S. (1987). *Rediscovering the social group: A self-categorization theory.* New York: Blackwell.

Van Zomeren, M., Postmes, T., & Spears, R. (2008). Toward an integrative Social Identity Model of Collective Action: A quantitative research synthesis of three socio-psychological perspectives. *Psychological Bulletin, 134*, 504–535.

Van Zomeren, M., Spears, R., Fischer, A. H., & Leach, C. W. (2004). Put your money where your mouth is!: Explaining collective action tendencies through group-based anger and group efficacy. *Journal of Personality and Social Psychology, 87*, 649–664.

Verkuyten, M., & Reijerse, A. (2008). Intergroup structure and identity management among ethnic minority and majority groups: The interactive effects of perceived stability, legitimacy, and permeability. *European Journal of Social Psychology, 38*, 106–127.

Walker, I., & Smith, H. J. (Eds.) (2002). *Relative deprivation: Specification, development, and integration.* Cambridge, England: Cambridge University Press.

Wright, S. C. (1997). Ambiguity, shared consensus and collective action: Generating collective protest in response to tokenism. *Personality and Social Psychology Bulletin, 23,* 1277–1290

Wright, S. C. (2001a). Strategic collective action: Social psychology and social change. In R. Brown & S. L. Gaertner (Eds.), *Intergroup processes: Blackwell handbook of social psychology* (Vol. 4, pp. 409–430). Oxford, England: Blackwell.

Wright, S. C. (2001b). Restricted intergroup boundaries: Tokenism, ambiguity and the tolerance of injustice. In J. Jost & B. Major (Eds.), *The psychology of legitimacy: Emerging perspectives on ideology, justice, and intergroup relations* (pp. 223–254). New York: Cambridge University Press.

Wright, S.C., & Lubensky, M. (2009). The struggle for social equality: Collective action versus prejudice reduction. In S. Demoulin, J. P. Leyens, & J. F. Dovidio (Eds.), *Intergroup misunderstandings: Impact of divergent social realities* (pp. 291–310). Philadelphia, PA: Psychology Press.

Wright, S.C., & Richard, N. T (2010). Cross-group helping: Perspectives on why and why not. In S. Stürmer and M. Snyder (Eds.), *The psychology of prosocial behavior: Group processes, intergroup relations, and helping* (pp. 311–335). Wiley Blackwell.

Wright, S. C., Taylor, D. M., & Moghaddam, F. M. (1990). Responding to membership in a disadvantaged group: From acceptance to collective protest. *Journal of Personality and Social Psychology, 58,* 994–1003.

Wright, S. C, & Tropp, L. R. (2002). Collective action in response to disadvantage: Intergroup perceptions, social identification, and social change. In I. Walker & H. J. Smith, (Eds.), *Relative deprivation: Specification, development, and integration* (pp. 200–236). New York: Cambridge University Press.

PART VI

Commentary: Future Research on Prejudice, Stereotyping and Discrimination

36

Looking to the Future

Thomas F. Pettigrew

ABSTRACT

This handbook provides a broad sweep of what has been learned over the past century about intergroup prejudice, stereotyping, and discrimination. In looking ahead, this chapter discusses a series of pressing concerns for future work. First, issues such as causation and the time dimension, as well as the possible universalism of intergroup phenomena, require further consideration. Second, there is a need to place intergroup phenomena in a wider, multi-level context – both down to the biological level and up to the social structural level. Third, future work must integrate the many theories and findings detailed in this volume. Three examples are discussed: combining (a) cognitive with affective factors, (b) the perspectives of both disadvantaged and advantaged groups, and (c) prejudice reduction approaches with collective action concerns. Finally, the chapter reflects on policy implications. Hopefully, the future will witness more longitudinal, multi-level, interdisciplinary, and integrative research that directly addresses these concerns.

LOOKING TO THE FUTURE

The study of prejudice, stereotyping, and discrimination has been central to social psychology since the discipline's origins a century ago. As early as 1904, W. I. Thomas (2004) – author of the famous dictum, 'if men define situations as real, they are real in their consequences' (Thomas & Thomas, 1928: 572), challenged the prevailing dictum of 'racial antipathy as a fixed and irreducible element.' Freed of caste-feeling, he surmised, racial prejudice was perhaps no more stable than fashions. Thomas presaged Martin Luther King's famous words by predicting that the day will come when individual abilities will count for more than skin color.

The present chapter provides a brief overview of historical developments in the study of prejudice, stereotyping, and discrimination (see also Chapter 2 by Duckitt in this volume). It then identifies topics meriting more attention in the future, argues for the need for greater context for research, and fuller integration of theory and research in this area. Finally, policy implications of research on intergroup bias are considered.

LOOKING BACK

Early quantitative instruments in social psychology typically involved intergroup relations. Thus, Emory Bogardus (1928) introduced his social distance scale to measure attitudes toward immigrants. A notable advance and still in use today, this easily administered instrument offers an early example of a Guttman cumulative scale. To measure religious attitudes and beliefs, Louis Thurston (1928) published another scaling technique to measure attitudes. A few years later, Rensis Likert (1932) pioneered an even simpler and more effective scaling method – so-called 'Likert scales' that are still widely employed to measure prejudice and related constructs. These improvements in attitude scaling initiated quantitative research on individual prejudice.

This early work took place largely within sociological social psychology. The 1930s witnessed the entry of psychological social psychologists into the study of intergroup relations (Pettigrew, 2004). Two studies from this period remain classics. One is the famous study of ethnic stereotypes at Princeton University, conducted by Daniel Katz and Kenneth Braly (1933), which began the useful series of studies over the years of stereotypes at the same institution (Madon, Guyll, Aboufadel, et al., 2001). In the other, Otto Klineberg (1935a) conducted the first major social psychological study on race. He tested over 3,000 10–12-year old African-American children in Harlem with an array of intelligence measures. The results from repeated samples and different measures demonstrated clearly that the intelligence test score averages of southern-born Black children improved with each year in New York schools. The differences were not trivial; over the full range of grades, the mean gains approximated a full standard deviation. These dramatic results could not be accounted for by selection bias. Klineberg secured the Southern school grades of 562 Black youth who had gone North, and found them typical of the Black school populations from which they had migrated. Later these results were replicated in three other cities – Cleveland, Philadelphia, and Washington (Dombey, 1933; Lee, 1951; Long, 1934). In the same year, Klineberg published a general volume on the topic, *Race Differences* (1935b).

Inspired by insights from Germany's Frankfurt School, the 1940s witnessed the systematic study at the University of California at Berkeley of personality factors underlying prejudice (see Chapter 10 by Son Hing & Zanna in this volume). This work culminated in the publication of *The Authoritarian Personality* (Adorno, Frenkel-Brunswik, Levinson, et al., 1950). Comparable work was conducted elsewhere with similar results (e.g., Allport & Kramer, 1946).

In time, a distinctive model of human beings evolved in social psychology that shaped the discipline's approach to intergroup relations. This model holds humans as possessing bounded rationality and to be situationally malleable. They are also held to be guided by their subjective view of the world and to be highly reactive to their environment (Pettigrew, 1991c). With the development of such specialties as experimental economics that often retrace social psychology's earlier work, other social sciences have established similar models of humanity.

The theories and research on intergroup relations in the first half of the twentieth century were succinctly summarized and advanced by Gordon Allport (1954) in his influential volume, *The Nature of Prejudice*. This book shaped research on the topic for decades and, using as a structure the main topics it considered, a 50th-anniversary volume has recently been published (Dovidio, Glick, & Rudman, 2005). Now this handbook provides a sweeping view of where the field finds itself today. Moreover, each of the previous chapters ends with a section on what seems promising for future efforts in understanding prejudice, stereotypes, and discrimination. This final chapter builds on these sections with four interrelated discussions on:

- topics for future emphases,
- the need for greater context,
- future integration of theories and findings, and
- social policy considerations.

LOOKING FORWARD: TOPICS FOR FUTURE EMPHASES

Among the many promising topics for future attention, several warrant special mention – causation, the time dimension, the influence of social class, power and ideologies, and the universalism of intergroup processes.

The vexing problem of causation

The authors of the chapters in this handbook necessarily employ cautious language when describing the relationship between key variables – e.g., 'this suggests that ...'; 'it can be argued that ...'; 'it may be that ...' Asserting causation with confidence is one of the most difficult problems in social science (Pettigrew, 1996). But it is a crucial one to overcome if the study of intergroup phenomena is to advance and to be useful for social policy.

Experimental research, of course, surmounts this problem, but it can be challenged on grounds of insufficient external validity. And such validity is especially important for intergroup relations. Rigorous probability surveys and field research can overcome the external validity issue, but they routinely face the causation issue. Increasingly, longitudinal analyses have been used in the study of intergroup relations to attack the causation problem. Hopefully, this trend will continue to develop despite its cost and complexities. Here econometrics, with its considerable experience in analyzing overtime models, can be helpful; and recent advanced statistical computer packages also aid such efforts.

As in many areas of social psychology, bidirectional, non-recursive causation is likely to be a common finding. For example, we know that intergroup contact typically decreases prejudice (Pettigrew & Tropp, 2006; and see Chapter 33 by Tausch & Hewstone in this volume); but it is also widely found that prejudiced people tend to avoid such contact (Pettigrew, Wagner, Christ, et al., 2007). Likewise, Chapters 26 and 28 on institutional bias (by Henry) and public policy (by Schmukler, Rasquiza, Dimmitt, & Crosby)

respectively, in this volume cite pointed examples of such bidirectional causation.

The time dimension in intergroup processes

Longitudinal research also addresses another issue for future focus – the time dimension in intergroup phenomena. This understudied aspect of intergroup processes has been repeatedly mentioned throughout the previous chapters – especially in the chapters on developmental perspectives (Chapter 6 by Killen, Richardson, & Kelly); dyadic interactions (Chapter 17 by Richeson & Shelton); intergroup competition (Chapter 14 by Esses, Jackson, & Bennett-AbuAyyash); institutional bias (Chapter 26 by Henry); individual mobility (Chapter 34 by Ellemers & van Laar); public policy (Chapter 28 by Schmukler, Rasquiza, Dimmit, & Crosby); self-regulation (Chapter 30 by Monteith); social categorization (Chapter 32 by Gaertner, Dovidio, & Houlette); self-categorization (Chapter 11 by Abrams & Hogg); and stereotype threat (Chapter 23 by Quinn, Kallen, & Spencer). Each has considered continuous processes that evolve overtime. For instance, Quinn and her co-authors advocate future longitudinal research to uncover the effects of multiple instances of stereotype threat over long periods of time. Moreover, without repeated measures over extended periods of time, we will also overlook critical selection biases that occur in most social processes.

Yet, like most social psychological research, intergroup studies have focused largely on static, short-term effects; dependent variables are rarely measured more than once or twice (Pettigrew, 1991a). Yet it appears that the most vital intergroup processes involve *long-term, cumulative effects*. Muzafer Sherif's (1936, 1966) famous findings in both his autokinetic and Robbers' Cave studies highlight the significance of slowly evolving cumulative effects measured frequently. Had he stopped measuring his dependent variables after one or two trials, he would have completely missed the effects that appear in virtually every social psychologist's lectures.

Intergroup investigators, too, may well have been missing overtime change effects – especially those wrought by social norms and the 'strong situations' emphasized in the organizational chapter. Clearly, future work on cumulative effects is needed to elucidate further the many intergroup processes described in this volume.

The influences of social class, power, and ideologies

Social class, a core construct of sociology, is often overlooked in intergroup research in psychological social psychology. But, as discussed in the chapter on health discrimination, social class is tightly entwined with racial and group differentiations – typically enhancing the prejudice, stereotypes, and discrimination under study. Sociological social psychologists have long included social class in their work, and they offer numerous ways it can be entered into experimental as well as field research.

Power, a fundamental construct of political scientists, has also been too often overlooked in social psychology. Henry's chapter on institutional bias deals with the concept explicitly. And Susan Fiske is another striking exception to this trend, for she has repeatedly employed social power in her work. She stresses that power leads to 'vertical distance' which operates to shape and further group prejudice, stereotypes, and discrimination (e.g., Fiske & Berdahl, 2007; Harris & Fiske, 2008). In addition, sociological social psychologists have also studied power with a variety of experimental approaches (e.g., Molm, 1988; Ridgeway, 2001). Hopefully, such work will create greater interest in power and how it can be incorporated into social psychological theory and research.

Ideology, another central concept of political science, has also not received the attention it deserves in social psychology's study of prejudice, stereotypes, and discrimination. The discipline all too often concentrates on particular attitudes considered one at a time. Gregory Maio and his colleagues in their chapter on attitudes cite the striking exceptions to this trend

in the prejudice literature – multiculturalism, color-blindness, individualism, communalism, right-wing authoritarianism, and social dominance orientation. Nationalism is yet another ideology. The major contributions that these exceptions have made to the field speak to the usefulness of more explicitly utilizing ideology as a basic concept in the study of intergroup relations.

The universalism of intergroup processes

Future attention needs to be directed to the question of the universalism of intergroup processes – though the same can be said for social psychological findings in general. The massive preponderance of intergroup research has been conducted in North America and Western Europe. But do the results from this work generalize to intergroup relations in other parts of the world?

To date, the answer to this question is a tentative *yes* – as exemplified by the recent intensive social psychological research in South Africa (Finchilescu & Tredoux, 2010). A survey study of German attitudes toward immigrants found the correlates of these opinions to be remarkably similar to those found in Canada and the United States – despite strikingly different histories and laws regarding immigration (Pettigrew, Wagner, & Christ, 2007). And a meta-analysis of intergroup contact effects in 38 nations found remarkably similar mean reductions of prejudice. Across six major areas of the world, the correlational mean contact effect varied between −.196 and −.256 (Pettigrew & Tropp, 2006). Consider, too, the success around the globe of Aronson's jigsaw technique for children (Aronson & Patnoe, 1997) – Australia (Walker & Crogan, 1998), Germany (Eppler & Huber, 1990), Japan (Araragi, 1983), and the United States (Aronson & Gonzalez, 1988).

Given the enormous variety in intergroup histories and current situations around the globe, how could this be true? One theory contends that social psychological processes typically mediate the effects of macro-variables on individuals (Pettigrew, Jackson, Ben Brika, et al., 1998). It further holds that these meso-level processes operate in comparable ways across societies and cultures. But since structural and cultural macro-variables differ sharply around the world, macro-level effects on individuals vary widely even though the social psychological processes are similar. Thus, future work on a variety of 'isms' would profit from fuller consideration of the potential common processes as well as differential influences across cultures that underlie dehumanization (see Chapter 12 by Leyens & Demoulin), racism (see Chapter 19 by Dovidio, Gaertner, & Kawakami), racial disparities in health and health care (see Chapter 29 by Penner, Albrecht, Orom, Coleman, & Underwood), sexism (see Chapter 20 by Glick & Rudman), heterosexism (see Chapter 21 by Hebl, Law, & King), and anti-immigrant bias (see Chapter 22 by Wagner, Christ, & Heitmeyer).

THE NEED FOR GREATER CONTEXT

The wide-ranging previous chapters have demonstrated the importance of context for intergroup phenomena. To gain enhanced context, social psychological work centered on the individual and situational levels of analysis needs to become multilevel – both levels below (e.g., neuroscience) and above (e.g., organizational) the situational level. The micro-levels can clarify psychological processes – as shown in the neuroscience chapter (by Quadflieg, Mason, & Macrae). The macro-levels can connect these processes to the structural levels necessary to advance effective social policies. Such efforts will require the use of the many multi-level statistical computer packages now available as well as greater collaboration with the biological sciences and the other social sciences.

Note how often this contextual point has been made throughout this volume. Mark Schaller and his colleagues close their chapter on evolutionary processes with a call for more multi-level research. Similarly, Lex Smith and

her colleagues implore social psychologists 'to think organizationally' and to consider the power of the 'strong situations' established in organizations. P. J. Henry offers a framework specifically designed to contextualize bias within institutions. In the same vein, Amanda Dickman and her colleagues stress the importance of social structural changes altering social roles that in turn change attitudes and beliefs. Crocker and Garcia consider the joint effects of internalized devaluation and situational threat. Yzerbyt, in his chapter on motivation, points out that Tajfel's (1982) influential social identity theory held that 'structural features of the social system shape people's perceptions of the intergroup situation …' Finally, the two political science writers, Rafaela Dancygier and Donald Green, advance a context times personality interaction model for understanding hate crimes.

In short, there is widespread agreement that future intergroup research must give greater attention to the context of the processes under study. In turn, this point implies the future need to integrate what we know.

THE FUTURE INTEGRATION OF THEORIES AND FINDINGS

Integrating the many strands of intergroup theory and the supporting multitude of research results will be no easy task for social psychology – a discipline that has traditionally lacked bold theory (Pettigrew, 1991b). The rapidly expanding use of meta-analyses in the field is a major tool in this endeavor. The previous chapters suggest three areas in immediate need of integration: (a) balancing cognitive and affective processes; (b) balancing the perspectives and effects of both advantaged and disadvantaged groups; and (c) integrating prejudice reduction and collective action in a broader view of social change.

Balancing cognitive and affective processes

Starting with the 'information revolution' (Shannon & Weaver, 1949; Wiener, 1948), psychological social psychology together with other branches of psychology turned from an emphasis on motivation to a single-minded focus on cognition. Indeed, social cognition's emphasis on stereotypes virtually replaced the study of prejudice. This extensive work has greatly enhanced our understanding of stereotypes and their operation (see Chapters 9 and 7 by Yzerbyt and by Fiske & Russell, respectively). For instance, the rise of stereotypes for outgroup sub types highlights an important component of modern prejudice (Ashmore, Del Boca, & Wohlers, 1986; Deaux & LaFrance, 1998).

But this single-minded focus on stereotypes stifled other developments. In particular, 'cold' cognitive concerns ignored the 'hot' emotional core of prejudice. Allport (1954) maintained that stereotypes were typically rationalizations for negative affect. He noted that developmental research showed that negative feelings toward outgroups typically came first in children before they had acquired a clear understanding of just which people comprised the disliked outgroup. But this insight was largely ignored during these years.

Also ignored in psychology was the sociological insistence that group stereotypes are social products, advanced and validated continuously by the mass media and actual social conditions (see Chapters 15 and 3 on the mass media by Mutz and Goldman, and measurement by Correll, Judd, Park, & Wittenbrink, respectively). Consequently, their adoption by individuals does not necessarily signify deep-seated prejudice.

One might interpret these trends in the 1970s as meaning that social psychologists at this point were retreating from controversy and social policy just as society itself was retreating from conflict and reform. But this interpretation is too harsh. The focus on stereotypes may appear at first to involve less controversy and little policy significance compared to prejudice. But Fiske and her colleagues (Fiske, Bersoff, Borgida, et al., 1991) disprove such an impression. In the critical US Supreme Court case of *Price Waterhouse v. Hopkins* involving gender discrimination, gender stereotype research

proved as convincing to the High Court as social science evidence had in *Brown v. Board of Education* (1954).

European social psychologists returned a group emphasis to intergroup research. Though also largely cognitively focused, Henri Tajfel's (1982) social identity theory (SIT) did not receive immediate adoption in the United States. Save for a few researchers, such as Marilynn Brewer (1979) and David Wilder (1990; Wilder & Shapiro, 1984), American social psychology paid scant attention to SIT contentions during this period. But now SIT and self-categorization theory (SCT; Turner, Hogg, Oakes, et al., 1987) have gained a strong North American base.

During the last two decades of the twentieth century, social psychologists broadened their theory and research on prejudice and discrimination considerably. In particular, a turn away from limited stereotype work to more direct concern with prejudice and discrimination became evident. This trend coincided with a more general shift from purely cognitive concerns to increased attention to emotion and motivation. And this shift is evident throughout the preceding chapters.

Two seminal volumes on stereotypes, both edited by David Hamilton, highlight the overdue correction. In *Cognitive Processes in Stereotyping and Intergroup Behavior* (Hamilton, 1981), affect received brief mention and mood and emotion are not even in the index. A dozen years later, *Affect, Cognition and Stereotyping* (Mackie & Hamilton, 1993) centers on the role of affect (see Chapter 8 by Smith & Mackie on Affective Processes in this volume). In this second book, Eliot Smith (1993) even defines prejudice as 'a social emotion experienced with respect to one's social identity as a group member, with an outgroup as a target' (p. 304). And a spate of empirical work using a variety of methods supported the critical importance of affect for prejudice (Dijker, 1987; Edwards & von Hippel, 1995; Esses, Haddock, & Zanna, 1993; Pettigrew, 1997; Stangor, Sullivan, & Ford, 1991). Likewise, the primary mediators and effects of intergroup contact turned out to be largely affective (Pettigrew & Tropp, 2008,

2010; Tropp & Pettigrew, 2005b). Indeed, from a sociology of science perspective, one can surmise that the sudden rise in attention to emotion was fueled in large part by the introduction of new methods for more easily and adequately measuring emotion (see Chapter 3 by Correll, Judd, Park, & Wittenbrink).

Following this focus first on cognition, then on affect, the task now is to *integrate* what we have learned in both areas. And numerous chapters in this volume offer promising advances in this direction. In their chapter on cognitive processes, Susan Fiske and Ann Marie Russell set the tone when they state: 'Increasingly we are realizing that the brain does not divide along departmental boundaries; social, affective, cognitive, and behavioral processes all mingle. The challenge for next-generation research will be to incorporate these complexities while still distilling general principles.'

The neuroscience chapter by Quadflieg and colleagues suggests 'that thinking stereotypically may be an inherently evaluative rather than mere cognitive process.' Quadflieg and her co-authors base this idea on the neuroimaging result that stereotype activation is associated with enhanced responses in brain regions that link to both semantic knowledge and evaluative processing. Eliot Smith and Diane Mackie, in their affective processes chapter, provide further examples of how cognition and affective processes operate together in key intergroup phenomena. For instance, for the subtly prejudiced, underlying negative *feelings* toward an outgroup can lead to avoidance or outright discrimination against the outgroup, but only when these behaviors can be *rationalized* as due to some ostensibly non-group cause (Gaertner & Dovidio, 1986; Pettigrew & Meertens, 1995).

One can hopefully anticipate that future research in this area will routinely include both cognitive and affective measures, and advance models that combine both types of processes. But such integrated models may typically show affective factors to be dominant with cognitive factors often serving as moderators and mediators. This prediction flows from the many important advances neatly summarized in the affective processes chapter.

Balancing the perspectives and effects of both advantaged and disadvantaged groups

Not surprisingly, as Wright points out in his chapter, Collective Action and Social Change, early work on prejudice, stereotypes, and discrimination overwhelmingly focused on advantaged groups. They are more powerful and more responsible for the discriminatory norms and practices. Such groups were deemed 'the problem,' and hence received the most attention. But intergroup relations and interaction by definition entails two or more groups; consequently, a complete understanding requires equal attention to the disadvantaged – the targets of the prejudice, stereotypes, and discrimination.

Gaertner, Dovidio, and Houlette, in their chapter on social categorization, succinctly describe the differences that typically occur between ingroups and outgroups in general. For disadvantaged groups specifically, Major and Townsend point out a balance must be sought in understanding both the damage wrought by their constrained life chances and choices as well as their resilience. Here the authors are recasting a thorny historical issue in the study of intergroup relations (Adam, 1978; Pettigrew, 1978, 2004). In the 1920s and 1930s, environmentalism replaced Social Darwinism throughout American social science. This dramatic alteration in thinking triggered a *tradition of White culpability* in the study of American race relations that prevailed into the 1960s. This tradition strove to disprove racist claims of Black inferiority by demonstrating that racial segregation and discrimination created racial disparities in the litany of social indices from health and crime statistics to test scores. Kenneth Clark and Mamie Clark's (1947) celebrated doll studies were a central component of this tradition. But this view, in emphasizing the damage of racism, paid scant attention to African-American resilience. Reflecting the Civil Rights Movement of the 1960s a new *tradition of African-American proaction* emerged; it emphasized the minority's resilience almost to the point of denying damage from racism. In recent years, this needed balance between damage and resilience has been a hallmark of research as summarized in the chapter on coping.

The overdue correction to integrate the perspectives of both the disadvantaged and the advantaged is also now well underway and firmly embraced in the previous chapters. This effort has been led by Jennifer Richeson, Nicole Shelton, and their colleagues. The chapter by Richeson and Shelton summarizes the research on intergroup dyadic interactions – a direct effort to combine the dual perspectives. They demonstrate that 'it is important to consider multiple outcomes of intergroup interactions, from the perspectives of both interaction participants, in order to capture the many, and often divergent, outcomes that contribute to individuals' assessments of whether such interactions are "positive" or "negative."'

Integrating prejudice reduction and collective action in a broader view of social change

In his chapter, Stephen Wright closes with the challenge to future research to *unite* social psychology's emphases on prejudice reduction and collective action. Because of both its theoretical and policy importance, this call deserves enthusiastic endorsement. We can illustrate what it is needed by considering the effects of intergroup contact – the discipline's quintessential method of reducing prejudice – on the potential for collective action for social change (Pettigrew, 2010).

A growing literature supports an unintended, negative effect of contact on minority mobilization for collective action. Let's call it 'the Reicher effect' since Stephen Reicher (2007) was one of the first to note the phenomenon. He held that successful intergroup contact, in reducing the hostile attitudes and feelings of the disadvantaged toward the

advantaged, had the unintended effect of also decreasing the potential for the mobilization of the disadvantaged for social change.

Saguy, Tausch, Dovidio, et al., (2009) provide the most convincing results. In their first investigation, they randomly assigned college student subjects to groups who possessed either high or low power in the situation. Once together, the groups discussed either commonalities they shared or the differences between them. The commonalities groups represented more ideal contact, the differences groups more negative contact. Just as Reicher predicts, the commonalities groups led the low-power participants to develop heightened expectations for fair treatment by the high-power participants that proved somewhat unrealistic.

Turning to real life and the truly disadvantaged – a low-power group of Arab citizens of Israel – Saguy and her collaborators again replicated the Reicher effect. Arab Israelis who report the most positive contact with Jewish Israelis also evince less support for social change as well as increased perceptions of Jewish Israelis as fair. There is probably some verisimilitude involved here. Those Jewish Israelis who have genuinely positive contact with Arab Israelis are more likely in fact to be fairer and more open to equitable intergroup relations than other Jewish Israelis. Hence, contact effects on the disadvantaged minority result from interaction with a biased selection of the advantaged group.

Wright and Lubensky (2009) present two further studies. First, they surveyed African-American and Latino(a)-American students on a predominantly White campus of the University of California. For both minority groups, contact with White students related to lower ingroup identification and this effect in turn related to more positive racial attitudes together with less endorsement of collective action. Put differently, intergroup contact's positive relationship with racial attitudes and negative relationship with collective action were both mediated by a reduction in ingroup identification. But two revealing *non*-findings are important in these results. Intergroup contacts were not related to viewing Whites as 'oppressors,' nor were attitudes toward Whites significantly related with support for collective action. In short, the Reicher effect emerges via a two-step linkage between contact and support for collective action; but other, unmeasured processes are clearly also involved in these data.

In their second study, Wright and Lubensky (2009) conducted a survey of African-American students at a predominantly Black university. These results replicated the findings of their California study. But this time, boundary permeability – the minority perception that upward mobility is possible – was also measured. This new variable, like ingroup identification, mediated intergroup contact's effects. Contact related positively with this perception of mobility which in turn related with more favorable attitudes toward Whites and less endorsement of collective action. Once again, however, views about Whites and collective action were *not* significantly associated.

In a South African survey, the quality of intergroup contact was associated with less perception of collective discrimination (Dixon, Durrheim, Tredoux, et al., 2010). Both racial attitudes and personal experiences of racial discrimination mediated this effect. Thus, intergroup contact quality – measured by such ratings as how friendly, helpful, and equal status the contact was (basically tapping Allport's key facilitating dimensions) – related to more positive racial attitudes and fewer reports of personal discrimination. These mediators in turn were associated with a diminished sense of group discrimination. Of particular note, however, this survey did not find the *quantity* of intergroup contact to be significantly related to any of its measures save contact quality.

In another South African survey, Durrheim (2010) uncovered different contact effects for Blacks and Whites. Among White South Africans, extensive contact with Black South Africans related to both lessened racial stereotyping and enhanced support for major social policies that would be 'transformative.' However, among Black respondents, contact

with Whites had little overall effect on their views of Whites and related to decreased support for transformative policies – once more, the Reicher effect. But Durrheim also noted that those Black respondents who reported having contact with high-status Whites revealed a particular *lack* of sympathy for Whites. Again, this counter-Reicher effect suggests the operation of additional processes that further minority mobilization.

The relationship between the prejudice-reducing and social mobilization processes is more complex than just the Reicher effect. As with most social phenomena, the distinction between the two processes can easily be drawn too tightly. First, meta-analysis shows that the prejudice-reducing effects of cross-group interaction are considerably stronger for the advantaged who have the power than for the less-powerful disadvantaged (Tropp & Pettigrew, 2005a). Indeed, the South African surveys suggest interracial contact for Blacks can sometimes lead to *increased* prejudice against Whites when the status differences between the interactants are large. These majority-minority differences mitigate, though they do not resolve, Reicher's phenomenon.

Second, Reicher's analysis focuses exclusively on the need to mobilize the aggrieved less powerful group to achieve social change. This factor is critically important, but it is not the whole story (Simon & Klandermans, 2001; Walker & Smith, 2002). Successful social change also requires some waning in the power of the advantaged and in their determination to maintain the *status quo*, some recognition by the powerful of the unfairness and illegitimacy of the hierarchical situation. In American history, every major societal change – from the American Revolution and the abolition of slavery to the Civil Rights Movement of the 1960s – first witnessed this weakening in the dominant group. And the typical substantial and positive changes wrought by the intergroup contact of majority members contribute directly to this additionally important factor in social change.

This point gains support from the many studies that show intergroup contact typically relates to more favorable attitudes among majority participants toward specific structural changes (Pettigrew & Tropp, 2010). Recall that Durrheim found this phenomenon in his South African investigation. And another South African survey obtained the strongest evidence yet obtained of intergroup contact shaping policy preferences (Dixon, Durrheim, Tredoux, et al., 2010). A random digit dialing telephone survey of South Africans found that both the frequency and quality of interracial contact related positively to White support for both racial compensatory and racial preferential policies of redress. For example, agreement with 'spending more of your province's education budget on schools in largely black neighborhoods' correlated significantly with both contact quantity (+.13) and quality (+.33).

This process within the advantaged group is critical. Mallett, Huntsinger, Sinclair, et al. (2008) show that those among the advantaged who are most able to take the perspective of the disadvantaged outgroup appear most likely to become allies with the disadvantaged group's efforts. And the ability to adopt the outgroup's perspective is a proven result of intergroup contact (Pettigrew & Tropp, 2008).

Such weakening of the majority's tenacity to maintain discriminatory norms is at least as important as furthering the minority's direct actions for social change. Indeed, the two processes are inseparably intertwined. The weakening of majority resolve helps to heighten the minority's perceptions not only that the *status quo* is unjust but also that it is vulnerable and can be altered.

The Reicher effect alerts us to the need for intergroup contact theorists to cast a broader net in considering the implications of intergroup contact effects – especially those involving minorities. Social phenomena, and social change in particular, are complex processes with multiple and often conflicting effects. And contact between the advantaged and disadvantaged yields additional effects than the one Reicher emphasizes. Some of these other effects of contact can stimulate, rather than retard, minority mobilization and their desire for change.

Thus, it is too simple to hold that a strident ingroup identification and rejection of the majority group is always needed for political mobilization. Simon and Ruhe (2008), studying Turkish immigrants in Germany, found that *dual identification* – with firm identities as both a minority group member (Turkish) *and* as a member of the larger society (German) – maximizes politicization.

Moreover, the disadvantaged learn from encounters with the advantaged the full extent of the discrimination their group faces. They see what majority members possess, their life styles and opportunities – many of which are denied to them and their group. In short, cross-group contact can enhance frustration with the collective discrimination endured by their group and generate group-relative deprivation.

Indeed, there is an extensive research literature that shows how *group relative deprivation* adds to the potential for collective action (Smith & Pettigrew, 2010; Walker & Smith, 2001). In the United States in the 1960s, it was the better-educated young African-Americans with the *most* interracial contact who led the Civil Rights Movement (Mathews & Prothro, 1966; Pettigrew, 1964; Searles & Williams, 1962). They had the resources, and their interracial contact gave them the necessary knowledge of the White world and its weaknesses to lead the protest effort. They were also more likely to know White allies who joined their cause.

Similarly, Poore, Gagne, Barlow, et al. (2002) found that the more Inuits in Canada experienced contact outside of their isolated communities, the more they perceived the systematic discrimination their group faced. The several studies that clearly establish the Reicher effect did not test the potential effects of intergroup contact both to limit the resolve of majorities to maintain the *status quo* and to heighten minority awareness of discrimination.

Clearly, the effects of intergroup contact on social change are complex. At least three processes are involved in the link between intergroup contact and the protest mobilization of the disadvantaged. Indeed, there is supporting research for each of the three, but research has yet to study them concurrently.

- Intergroup contact improves the attitudes of members of the advantaged group toward the disadvantaged and intergroup policies. These effects can weaken their resolve to maintain the discriminatory status quo.
- Contact also improves the attitudes of the disadvantaged toward the advantaged, and this process can lessen their resolve to mobilize for social change (the Reicher effect).

But since intergroup contact has significantly greater effects on majorities than minorities (Tropp & Pettigrew, 2005a), this effect may typically be somewhat smaller than the previous process.

- Intergroup contact can also operate to heighten a disadvantaged group's sense of group-relative deprivation.

This occurs because contact provides the opportunity for minorities to learn what the majority possesses that is denied to them. Witness the contact experience of America's Civil Rights Movement leadership, the Poore study of Canada's Inuits, and Durrheim's finding that South African Blacks' contact with higher-status Whites relates to *less* sympathy for Whites. Intergroup contact also allows the disadvantaged to gauge the weaknesses of the advantaged that can be exploited through protest mobilization.

A fourth possible process is highly relevant to such multi-group societies as South Africa (Dixon, Durrheim, Tredoux, et al., 2010). Positive contact *between* disadvantaged groups can help unite them so that they can mount a stronger, more cohesive protest that offers an improved chance for success.

It is clear that the Reicher effect often occurs, but it is an incomplete description of the complex relationship between intergroup contact and the mobilization of the disadvantaged for social change. The pointed distinction made by Wright and Lubensky (2009) between collective action participation and such prejudice reduction approaches as intergroup contact is too sharply drawn. As with most social phenomena, the two approaches are intricately entwined. Some contact outcomes further mobilization, others counter it. And mobilization itself can in turn influence intergroup contact – increasing it with outgroup allies and decreasing it with outgroup opponents.

Research that simultaneously studies all these complex processes is a needed next step to answer Wright's call to unite the prejudice reducing and protest mobilization processes. But this is just one of many instances in the handbook when the integration of various theories and processes is indicated.

SOCIAL POLICY CONSIDERATIONS

Given the massive amount of research on the policy-sensitive realms reported in this handbook, what are the policy implications of all this work? Of course, as Smith and Mackie warn, there are 'no magic bullets.' Yet many of the preceding chapters suggest promising future interventions. For example, the health disparities chapter describes an ingenious use of the superordinate group model. Recall that Penner and his colleagues formed doctor-patient 'teams' that led to greater trust by patients of their physicians. Similarly, several chapters emphasize the power of social roles to diminish both prejudice and discriminatory behavior. Yzerbyt, following Kurt Lewin, suggests that altering situations so that people's core motives generate intergroup tolerance can be a general basis for successful interventions. Similarly, the organizational chapter (by Smith, Brief, & Collela) notes that positive change is far more likely when it is viewed as 'good for business.' Wagner, Christ, and Heitmeyer in their chapter, stress the need to devise interventions that lessen intergroup threat. They also mention the vital role that the mass media play in influencing the level of threat. This point joins with the intriguing observation of Mutz and Goldman that the mass media can set and enforce intergroup norms.

In these many ways social psychology has endeavored to diminish prejudice, modify stereotypes, and lessen discriminatory behavior. These efforts have often been successful – as with applications of intergroup contact theory; and these achievements have been helpful. They make later positive social change more possible. Yet it must be said that most of these efforts do not directly address the core problems of discriminated-against minorities. As a well-studied case in point, consider African-American distress today. The basic problems are structural – rampant housing segregation, poverty, job discrimination, poor education, massive imprisonment – the list goes on (Pettigrew, 2007). Most of these structural barriers are direct legacies of two centuries of slavery and another century of legal segregation. Thus, these problems are deeply embedded in American society and have proven extremely difficult to correct.

Two interrelated barriers restrain the policy usefulness of social psychological findings. First, the discipline's foci on the individual and situational levels of analysis lie below that of the structural level at which these discrepancies primarily reside. Consequently, to be useful, social psychological analyses must be embedded in the structures that obstruct intergroup equality. For example, we know the features of optimal intergroup contact, but how do we shape institutions so that they routinely provide such contact? The institutional and organizational chapters tackle this key query. And answers are most likely to emerge from future interdisciplinary work with other social sciences that primarily focus on the structural level of analysis – as Dancygier and Green make clear in their chapter on hate crime.

Second, there is a related problem with social psychology's concept of 'discrimination' – as the measurement chapter by Correll and his colleagues discuss at length. It would be more precise for the discipline to adopt such terms as 'micro-discrimination,' 'discriminatory behavior,' and 'individual discrimination' so as to delineate it sharply from structural discrimination. The latter can and does persist even when majority members no longer regard it as 'just.' Housing, employment, educational, and penal forms of racial discrimination in the United States have become seen in time as normative – 'as just the way things are done' – without their dire consequences being easily recognized. That micro-, meso-, and macro-discrimination forms can be effectively linked is demonstrated in the chapters by Diekman, Eagly, and Johnston and by Dancygier and Green as well as routinely by other social science disciplines. Hopefully, such links will become a future emphasis in psychological social psychology as well.

A FINAL WORD

As with all well-studied phenomena, the more we have learned about prejudice, stereotypes, and discrimination, the more we understand just how subtle and complex these phenomena are. And the suggestions made here for future work – more longitudinal, multi-level, interdisciplinary, and integrative research – will only further complicate the picture. But the world *is* complex. And the many advances described in this handbook point to the growing maturity of this area of study.

REFERENCES

Adam, B. D. (1978). Inferiorization and "self-esteem." *Social Psychology* (now *Social Psychology Quarterly*), *41*, 47–53.

Adorno, T. W., Frenkel-Brunswik, E., Levinson, D. J., & Sanford, R. N. (1950). *The authoritarian personality.* New York: Harper.

Allport, G. W. (1954). *The nature of prejudice.* Reading, MA: Addison-Wesley.

Allport, G. W., & Kramer, B. M. (1946). Some roots of prejudice. *Journal of Psychology, 22,* 9–39.

Araragi, C. (1983). The effect of the jigsaw learning method on children's academic performance and learning attitude. *Japanese Journal of Educational Psychology, 31,* 102–12.

Aronson, E., & Gonzalez, A. (1988). Desegregation, jigsaw, and the Mexican-American experience. In P. A. Katz & D. A. Taylor (Eds.), *Eliminating racism:*

Profiles in controversy (pp. 301–314). New York: Plenum Press.

Aronson, E., & Patnoe, S. (1997). *The jigsaw classroom: Building cooperation in the classroom* (2nd ed). New York: Addison Wesley Longman.

Ashmore, R. D., Del Boca, F. K., & Wohlers, A. J. (1986). Gender stereotypes. In R. D. Ashmore & F. K. Del Boca (Eds.), *The social psychology of female-male relations*. New York, NY: Academic Press.

Bogardus, E. S. (1928). *Immigration and race attitudes*. Boston, MA: Heath.

Brewer, M. B. (1979). In-group bias in the minimal intergroup situation: A cognitive-motivational analysis. *Psychological Bulletin, 86*, 307–324.

Brown v. Board of Education of Topeka, 347 U.S. 483 (1954).

Clark, K. B., & Clark, M.P. (1947). Racial identification and preference in Negro children. In T. M. Newcomb & E. L. Hartley (Eds.), *Readings in social psychology*. (pp. 169–178). New York, NY: Holt.

Deaux, K., & LaFrance, M. (1998). Gender. In D. T. Gilbert, S. T. Fiske, & G. Lindzey (Eds.), *Handbook of social psychology* (Vol. 2) (pp. 788–827). Boston, MA: McGraw-Hill.

Dijker, A. J. M. (1987). Emotional reactions to ethnic minorities. *European Journal of Social Psychology, 17*, 305–325.

Dixon, J., Durrheim, K., Tredoux, C., Tropp, L., Clack, B., & Eaton, L. (2010). A paradox of integration? Interracial contact, prejudice reduction and perceptions of racial discrimination. *Journal of Social Issues*, in press.

Dombey, E. H. (1933). *A comparison of the intelligence test scores of Southern and Northern born Negroes residing in Cleveland*. Unpublished Master's thesis, Western Reserve University.

Dovidio, J. F., Glick, P., & Rudman, L. A. (Eds.) (2005). *On the nature of prejudice: Fifty years after Allport*. Malden, MA: Blackwell, 2005.

Durrheim, K. (2010). Racial contact and change in South Africa. *Journal of Social Issues*, in press.

Edwards, K., & von Hippel, W. (1995). Hearts and minds: The priority of affective versus cognitive factors in person perception. *Personality and Social Psychology Bulletin, 21*, 996–1011.

Eppler, R., & Huber, G. L. (1990). Wissenserwerb im Team: Empirische Untersuchung von Effekten des Gruppen-Puzzles. [Knowledge acquisition in a team: Empirical investigation of the effects of group puzzles.] *Psychologie in Erziehung und Unterricht, 37*, 172–178.

Esses, V. M., Haddock, G., & Zanna, M. P. (1993). Values, stereotypes and emotions as determinants of intergroup attitudes. In D. M. Mackie & D. L. Hamilton (Eds.), *Affect, cognition, and stereotyping*. San Diego, CA: Academic Press.

Finchilescu, G., & Tredoux, C. (Eds.) (2010). The changing landscape of intergroup relations in South Africa. *Journal of Social Issues*, in press.

Fiske, S. T., & Berdahl, J. (2007). Social power. In A. W. Kruglanski & E. T. Higgins, *Social psychology: Handbook of basic principles* (2nd ed.) (pp. 678–692). New York: Guilford Press.

Fiske, S. T., Bersoff, D. N., Borgida, E., Deaux, K., & Heilman, M. E. (1991). Social science research on trial: Use of sex stereotyping research in *Price Waterhouse v. Hopkins*. *American Psychologist, 46*, 1049–1060.

Gaertner, S. L., & Dovidio, J. F. (1986). The aversive form of racism. In J. F. Dovidio & S. L. Gaertner (Eds.) *Prejudice, discrimination, and racism* (pp. 61–90). Orlando, FL: Academic Press.

Hamilton, D. L. (Ed.) (1981). *Cognitive processes in stereotyping and intergroup behavior*. Hillsdale, NJ: Erlbaum.

Harris, L. T., & Fiske, S. T. (2008). Diminishing vertical distance: Power and social status as barriers to intergroup reconciliation. A. Nadler, T. E. Malloy, & J. D. Fisher (Eds.). *The social psychology of intergroup reconciliation* (pp. 301–317). New York: Oxford University Press.

Katz, D., & Braly, K. W. (1933). Racial stereotypes of 100 college students. *Journal of Abnormal and Social Psychology, 28*, 280–290.

Klineberg, O. (1935a). *Negro intelligence and urban residence*. New York, NY: Columbia University Press.

Klineberg, O. (1935b). *Race differences*. New York, NY: Harper & Row.

Lee, E. S. (1951). Negro intelligence and selective migration: A Philadelphia test of the Kleinberg hypothesis. *American Sociological Review, 16*, 227–233.

Likert, R., (1932). A technique for the measurement of attitudes. *Archives of Psychology, 140*, 1–55.

Long, H. H. (1934). The intelligence of colored elementary pupils in Washington, D. C. *Journal of Negro Education, 3*, 205–222.

Mackie, D. M., & Hamilton, D. L. (1993). *Affect, cognition, and stereotyping*. San Diego, CA: Academic Press.

Madon, S., Guyll, M., Aboufadel, K., Montiel, E., Smith, A., Palumbo, P., et al., (2001). Ethnic and national stereotypes: The Princeton trilogy revisited and revised. *Personality and Social Psychology Bulletin, 27*(8), 996–1010.

Mallett, R., Huntsinger, J., Sinclair, S., & Swim, J. (2008). Seeing through their eyes: When majority group members take collective action on behalf of an outgroup. *Group Processes and Intergroup Relations, 11*, 451–470.

Mathews, D. R., & Prothro, J. W. (1966). *Negroes and the new southern politics.* New York: Harcourt, Brace & World.

Molm, L. D. (1988). The structure and use of power. *Social Psychology Quarterly, 52,* 108–122.

Pettigrew, T. F. (1964). *A profile of the Negro American.* New York: Van Nostrand.

Pettigrew, T. F. (1978). Placing Adam's argument in a broader perspective: Comment on the Adam paper. *Social Psychology* (now *Social Psychology Quarterly*), *41,* 58–61.

Pettigrew, T. F. (1991a). The importance of cumulative effects: A neglected emphasis of Sherif's work. In D. Granberg & G. Sarup (Eds.), *Social judgment and intergroup relations: Essays in honor of Muzafer Sherif* (pp. 89–103). New York, NY: Springer-Verlag.

Pettigrew, T. F. (1991b). Toward unity and bold theory: Popperian suggestions for two persistent problems of social psychology. In C. Stephan, W. Stephan, & T. F. Pettigrew, (Eds.), *The future of social psychology* (pp. 13–27). New York: Springer-Verlag.

Pettigrew, T. F. (1991c) Is unity possible? A summary. In C. Stephan, W. Stephan, & T. F. Pettigrew (Eds.), *The future of social psychology* (pp. 99–121.) New York: Springer-Verlag.

Pettigrew, T. F. (1996). *How to think like a social scientist.* New York: Harper Collins.

Pettigrew, T. F. (1997). The emotional component of prejudice: Results from Western Europe. In S. A. Tuch and J. K. Martin (Eds.), *Racial attitudes in the 1990s: Continuity and change* (pp. 76–90). Westport, CN: Praeger.

Pettigrew, T. F. (2004). The social science study of American race relations in the 20th century. In C. S. Crandall and M. Schaller (Eds.), *The social psychology of prejudice: Historical and contemporary issues* (pp. 1–32.) Seattle, WA: Lewinian Press, 2004.

Pettigrew, T. F. (2007). Still a long way to go: American Black-White relations today. In G. Adams, M. Biernat, N. R. Branscombe, C. S. Crandall, and L. S. Wrightsman (Eds.), *Commemorating brown: The social psychology of racism and discrimination* (pp. 45–61). Washington, DC: American Psychological Association Press.

Pettigrew, T. F. (2010). Commentary: South African contributions to the study of intergroup relations. *Journal of Social Issues,* in press.

Pettigrew, T. F., Jackson, J., Ben Brika, J., Lemain, G., Meertens, R., Wagner, U., et al., (1998). Outgroup prejudice in Western Europe. In W. Stroebe & M. Hewstone (Eds.), *European Review of Social Psychology* (Vol. 8) (pp. 241–273). Chichester, U.K.: Wiley.

Pettigrew, T. F., & Meertens, R. W. (1995). Subtle and blatant prejudice in Western Europe. *European Journal of Social Psychology, 57,* 57–75.

Pettigrew, T. F., & Tropp, L. R. (2006). A meta-analytic test of intergroup contact theory. *Journal of Personality and Social Psychology, 90* (5), 751–783.

Pettigrew, T. F., & Tropp, L. R. (2008). How does intergroup contact reduce prejudice? Meta-analytic tests of three mediators. *European Journal of Social Psychology, 38,* 922–934.

Pettigrew, T. F., & Tropp, L. R. (2010). *When groups meet: The dynamics of intergroup contact.* Philadelphia, PA: Psychology Press.

Pettigrew, T. F., Wagner, U., & Christ, O. (2007) Who opposes immigration? Comparing German results with those of North America. *DuBois Review, 4* (1), 19–39.

Pettigrew, T.F., Wagner, U., Christ, O., & Stellmacher, J. (2007). Direct and indirect intergroup contact effects on prejudice: A normative interpretation. *International Journal of Intercultural Relations, 31* (4), 41–425.

Poore, A. G., Gagne, F., Barlow, K. M., Taylor, J. E., & Wright, S. C. (2002). Contact and the person-group discrimination discrepancy in an Inuit community. *Journal of Psychology, 136,* 371–382.

Ridgeway, C. L. (2001). The emergence of status beliefs. In J. T. Jost & B. Major (Eds.), *The psychology of legitimacy* (pp. 257–277). New York: Cambridge University Press.

Reicher, S. (2007). Rethinking the paradigm of prejudice. *South African Journal of Psychology, 35,* 412–432.

Saguy, T., Tausch, N., Dovidio, J. F., & Pratto, F. (2009). The irony of harmony: Intergroup contact can produce false expectations for equality. *Psychological Science, 20,* 114–121.

Searles, R., & Williams, Jr., S. A. (1962). Negro college students' participation in sit-ins. *Social Forces, 40,* 215–220.

Shannon, C. E., & Weaver, W. (1949). *The mathematical theory of communication.* Urbana, Ill: University of Illinois Press.

Sherif, M. (1936). *The psychology of social norms.* New York: Harper & Brothers.

Sherif, M. (1966). *In common predicament.* Boston: Houghton Mifflin.

Simon, B., & Klandermans, B. (2001). Politicized collective identity: A social psychological analysis. *American Psychologist, 56,* 319–331.

Simon, B., & Ruhe, D. (2008). Identity and politicization among Turkish migrants in Germany: The role of dual identification. *Journal of Personality and Social Psychology, 95* (6), 1354–1366.

Smith, E. R. (1993). Social identity and social emotions: Toward new conceptions of prejudice. In D. M. Mackie & D. L. Hamilton (Eds.), *Affect, cognition, and stereotyping.* San Diego, CA: Academic Press.

Smith, H., & Pettigrew, T. F. (2010). Group relative deprivation as a predictor: Four meta-analytic tests. Unpublished paper, Dept. of Psychology, Sonoma State University.

Stangor, C. L., Sullivan, A., & Ford, T. E. (1991). Affective and cognitive determinants of prejudice. *Social Cognition, 9,* 359–380.

Tajfel, H. (Ed.) (1982). *Social identity and intergroup relations.* Cambridge, U.K.: Cambridge University Press.

Thomas, W. I. (1904). The psychology of race-prejudice. *American Journal of Sociology, 9,* 593–611. Reprinted in part in T. F. Pettigrew (Ed.), *The sociology of race relations: Reflection and reform* (pp. 7–9). New York: Free Press, 1980.

Thomas, W. I., & Thomas, D. S. (1928). *The child in America: Behavior problems and programs.* New York: Knopf.

Tropp, L. R., & Pettigrew, T. F. (2005a). Relationships between intergroup contact and prejudice among minority and majority status groups. *Psychological Science, 16,* 651–653.

Tropp, L. R., & Pettigrew, T. F. (2005b). Differential relationships between intergroup contact and affective and cognitive dimensions of prejudice. *Personality and Social Psychology Bulletin, 31* (8), 1145–1158.

Thurstone, L. L. (1928). Attitudes can be measured. *American Journal of Sociology, 33,* 529–54.

Turner, J. C., Hogg, M. A., Oakes, P. J., Reicher, S. D., & Wetherell, M. (1987). *Rediscovering the social group: Self-categorization theory.* Oxford, UK: Blackwell.

Walker, I., & Crogan, M. (1998). Academic performance, prejudice, and the jigsaw classroom: New pieces to the puzzle. *Journal of Community and Applied Social Psychology, 8,* 381–393.

Walker, I. & Smith, H. (2002). (Eds.), *Relative deprivation: Specification, development and integration.* New York: Cambridge University Press.

Wiener, N. (1948). *Cybernetics.* MIT Press: Cambridge, MA.

Wilder, D. A. (1990). Some determinants of the persuasive power of in-groups and out-groups: Organization of information and attribution of independence. *Journal of Personality and Social Psychology, 59* (6), 1202–1213.

Wilder, D. A., & Shapiro, P. N. (1984). Role of outgroup cues in determining social identity. *Journal of Personality and Social Psychology, 47* (2), 342–348.

Wright, S. C., & Lubensky, M. (2009). The struggle for social equality: Collective action vs. prejudice reduction. In S. Demoulin, J. P. Leyens, & J. F. Dovidio (Eds.), *Intergroup misunderstandings: Impact of divergent social realities* (pp. 291–310) Philadelphia: Psychology Press.

Subject Index

children and 101, 105
definition of 180, 183
depersonalization and 182
emotion theory and 134, 142
group-based 181, 183, 185–6, 231, 316
organizations and 186
person-based 183
prejudice and 16, 152, 189
regulation of 188
relational 183
respect and 570
SCT and 180, 183
self-esteem and 418
social categorization and 101, 528, 530, 546
social inclusion and 189
stereotyping and 122
stigma and 398
theory (*see* Social Identity Theory)
threat 186, 270, 414–15, 417, 419, 511, 535
Social Identity Theory (SIT) 14–15, 21, 36–8, 40, 101, 116, 133, 148, 179–84, 186, 188, 227, 235, 363, 365–6, 415, 430, 527, 531, 563, 579–80, 587, 589, 604.
See also
Self-Categorization Theory
social mobility 181, 188, 226, 227, 582–4
social movements 218, 301, 578, 584–5, 587, 590
social neuroscience 17, 66
social norms 12, 16, 133, 153, 171, 188, 251, 262, 283, 303, 307, 312, 314, 319, 442, 494, 497, 555, 602
Social Psychological Theory 103, 396, 484, 563, 602–3
social psychology
bias and 18, 371, 436
collective action and 578
group competition and 225
intergroup reactions and 278
organizational 451
prejudice and 108, 148 (*see also* prejudice)
Relative Deprivation Theory and 586–7, 586
sexism and 329
social categories and 75

Social Identity Theory and 579
theory (*see* Social Psychological Theory)
Social Role Theory 214, 334–4
state verbs (SV) 153
stereotype(s)
activation 70–2, 75, 150, 282, 383–4, 499, 605
belonging and 122–3
business justification for 448
characteristics of 7
children and **106**
content model (*see* Stereotype Content Model)
controlling and, 123
cultural 7, 89–91, 323, 414
definition of 7, 46, 265
descriptive **337**
development of, 117
group 7, 215–16
information and 122
lift 381, 388–9, 390, 496–7
measuring 51–5, 51
meta- 198–9
motivations and goals and 281–2
nationality and 210
object appraisal and 270
organizations and 447–8
peers and **107**
process (*see* stereotyping)
psychology of 81
racial 103, 314, 448, 484
suppression 496–7
threat (*see* stereotype threat)
trait communicability and 90
understanding 123
See also stereotyping
Stereotype Content Model (SCM) 7, 12, 39–40, 120–1, 140, 153, 201–3, 205, 214, 231, 364
stereotype threat
anxiety and 384
arousal and 385
characteristics of 383
control over 386–7, 386
history of research in 380
identity and 387, 390
mechanisms for 385–6
processes in 11
research 390
self-stereotyping and 567

as situational threat (*see also* situational threat), 381
stereotype activation and 384
stereotype lift and, 381
targets of 381–3, 381
See also stereotype(s); stereotyping
stereotypicality 52, 349
stereotyping
ambiguous 119
ambivalent 120
categorization and 105, 147
childhood 99, 103–5
cognition and 118–19, 135, 165, 228, 483
definition of 98, 182
descriptive 336, 339
discrimination and 103
emotion and, 134
enhancing self and 123
explicit 52
factors influencing 149, 180
feeling connected and 152–3, 153
gay 244 (*see also* gays; homosexuals; lesbians)
gender 72, 330, 340
group 102, 123, 217–18
history of 46
invalidity and 123
measures of 58
media influence on 241–2, 244–5, 252
motivation and 122, 147–8, 151, 152, 158
neural correlates of 66
nonconscious 324
outcome measures of 246
overdetermination of 152
prejudice and 148
prescriptive 337
racial 103, 314
reducing 252
research 4, **5**
role of media in 248
SCM and 202
self- 567, 569–70
social functions of 188
Social Identity Theory and 180
social system and 229
stealth 117–22
See also stereotype(s); stereotype threat

Author Index